GEOGRAPHY

The World and Its People

Special TENNESSEE Edition

NATIONAL GEOGRAPHIC

SENIOR AUTHOR
Richard G. Boehm, Ph.D.

David G. Armstrong, Ph.D.

Francis P. Hunkins, Ph.D.

Glencoe McGraw-Hill

New York, New York
Columbus, Ohio
Woodland Hills, California
Peoria, Illinois

ABOUT THE AUTHORS

NATIONAL GEOGRAPHIC

The National Geographic Society, founded in 1888 for the increase and diffusion of geographic knowledge, is the world's largest nonprofit scientific and educational organization. Since its earliest days, the Society has used sophisticated communication technologies, from color photography to holography, to convey geographic knowledge to a worldwide membership. The School Publishing Division supports the Society's mission by developing innovative educational programs—ranging from traditional print materials to multimedia programs including CD-ROMS, videos, and software.

SENIOR AUTHOR
Richard G. Boehm

Richard G. Boehm, Ph.D., was one of seven authors of *Geography for Life,* national standards in geography, prepared under Goals 2000: Educate America Act. He was also one of the authors of the *Guidelines for Geographic Education,* in which the five themes of geography were first articulated. In 1990 Dr. Boehm was designated "Distinguished Geography Educator" by the National Geographic Society. In 1991 he received the George J. Miller award from the National Council for Geographic Education (NCGE) for distinguished service to geographic education. He was President of the NCGE and has twice won the *Journal of Geography* award for best article. He has received the NCGE's "Distinguished Teaching Achievement" award and presently holds the Jesse H. Jones Distinguished Chair in Geographic Education at Southwest Texas State University in San Marcos, Texas.

David G. Armstrong

David G. Armstrong, Ph.D., is Dean of the School of Education at the University of North Carolina at Greensboro. A social studies education specialist with additional advanced training in geography, Dr. Armstrong was educated at Stanford University, University of Montana, and University of Washington. He taught at the secondary level in the state of Washington before beginning a career in higher education. Dr. Armstrong has written books for students at the secondary and university levels, as well as for teachers and university professors. He maintains an active interest in travel, teaching, and social studies education.

Francis P. Hunkins

Francis P. Hunkins, Ph.D., is Professor of Education at the University of Washington. He began his professional career as a teacher in Massachusetts. He received his masters degree in education from Boston University and his doctorate from Kent State University with a major in general curriculum and a minor in geography. Dr. Hunkins has written numerous books and articles dealing with general curriculum, social studies, and questioning and thinking for students and educators at elementary, middle school, high school, and university levels.

Focus on Tennessee

Author

Theodore H. Schmudde, Ph.D.
Professor of Geography
University of Tennessee

Reviewers

Donna Jett
Powell Middle School
Powell, Tennessee

Ida Haskew Smith
South Pittsburg Elementary
South Pittsburg, Tennessee

Glencoe/McGraw-Hill
A Division of The ***McGraw-Hill*** *Companies*

Printed in the United States of America.
Send all inquiries to:
Glencoe/McGraw-Hill
8787 Orion Place
Columbus, Ohio 43240-4027

ISBN 0-07-824131-6 (Student Edition) ISBN 0-07-824132-4 (Teacher Wraparound Edition)
2 3 4 5 6 7 8 9 027/043 05 04 03 02

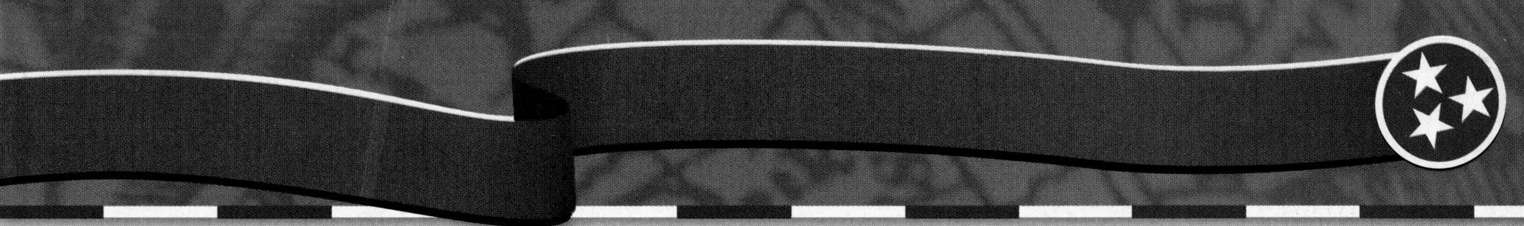

CONSULTANTS

General Content Consultants

Dr. Sari Bennett
Director, Center for Geographic Education
University of Maryland Baltimore County
Baltimore, Maryland

Shabbir Mansuri
Founding Director

Susan L. Douglass
Affiliated Scholar
Council on Islamic Education
Fountain Valley, California

United States and Canada

Dr. David A. Lanegran
John S. Holl Professor of Geography
Macalester College
St. Paul, Minnesota

Latin America

Dr. Jose F. Betancourt
Professor of Geography
State University of New York—Oneonta
Oneonta, New York

Europe

Dr. Charles F. Kovacik
Director, Center of Excellence for Geographic Education
University of South Carolina
Columbia, South Carolina

Russia

Dr. Charles R. Gildersleeve
Professor of Geography
University of Nebraska at Omaha
Omaha, Nebraska

North Africa, Southwest Asia, and Central Asia

Dr. Jeffrey A. Gritzner
Department of Geography
The University of Montana
Missoula, Montana

Africa South of the Sahara

Dr. Richard S. Palm
Professor of Geography
University of Wisconsin—Eau Claire
Eau Claire, Wisconsin

Asia

Dr. Kenji Oshiro
Professor of Geography
Wright State University
Dayton, Ohio

Australia, Oceania, and Antarctica

Dr. Brock Brown
Associate Professor of Geography and Planning
Southwest Texas State University
San Marcos, Texas

TEACHER REVIEWERS

Brent Adcox
Cornersville High School
Cornersville, Tennessee

Peter John Arroyo
Space Coast Middle School
Port St. John, Florida

Nora Austin
Chestnut Hill Community School
Belchertown, Massachusetts

William Ball
West Central Junior/Senior High School
Francesville, Indiana

Beverly A. Blamer
Fremont Middle School
Fremont, Michigan

Sue Brinkley
Hampshire Unit School
Hampshire, Tennessee

Lee Ann Burrow
Bob Courtway Middle School
Conway, Arkansas

Kim Cavanaugh
Congress Middle School
Boynton Beach, Florida

Janet S. D'Meo-Townley
Park Middle School
Scotch Plains, New Jersey

Connie Dunn
Mulberry High School
Mulberry, Arkansas

Kristine Louise Edwards
Dodge Intermediate School
Twinsburg, Ohio

Gale Olp Ekiss
Powell Junior High School
Mesa, Arizona

Dawn Forman
Hawthorne Junior/Senior High
Gainesville, Florida

Paula Gordon
Nettleton Intermediate Center
Jonesboro, Arkansas

Destin L. Haas
Benton Central Junior/Senior High
Oxford, Indiana

Daniel Hanczar
West Allegheny Middle School
Imperial, Pennsylvania

Phillip G. Hays
Conrad Weiser Middle School
Robesonia, Pennsylvania

Julie Hill
Bob Courtway Middle School
Conway, Arkansas

Donna Jett
Powell Middle School
Powell, Tennessee

Jacquelyn J. Jones
International Teacher and Administrator of American Schools in Costa Rica
San José, Costa Rica

Camille King-Thompson
Williston Middle School
Williston, Florida

Rick Lyndsey
Roosevelt Full Service
West Palm Beach, Florida

Sara Monschein
Oakridge Middle School
Naples, Florida

Wanda J. Petersen
Landrum Middle School
Ponte Vedra, Florida

Mary Ann Polve
Mesa High School
Mesa, Arizona

Nancy Pund
Deltona Middle School
Deltona, Florida

Jean Serafino
Chestnut Hill Community School
Belchertown, Massachusetts

William Sim
L.L. Wright Middle School
Ironwood, Michigan

Ida Haskew Smith
South Pittsburg Elementary
South Pittsburg, Tennessee

Janice Suddith
Paul Laurence Dunbar Middle School for Innovation
Lynchburg, Virginia

Joseph Turso
Wayne Hills High School
Wayne, New Jersey

Contents

Features

NATIONAL GEOGRAPHIC

EYE on the Environment

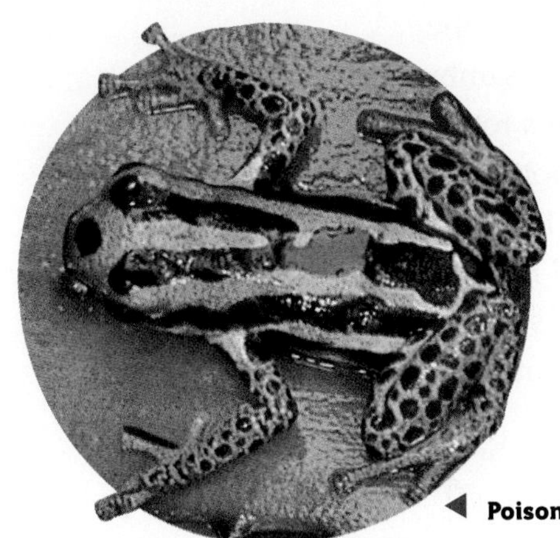
Poison arrow frog

Skills

Geography Skills

Technology Skills

Critical Thinking Skills

Study and Writing Skills

Making Connections

◀ Teen from Senegal

Who, What, Where in the World?

Cultural Close-Up

GeoLab Activity

Komodo dragon ▶

FOCUS ON TENNESSEE

Maps

NATIONAL GEOGRAPHIC Reference Atlas

NATIONAL GEOGRAPHIC Geography Handbook

Unit 1 Geography of the World

Unit 2 The United States and Canada

Unit 5 Russia

Unit 6 North Africa, Southwest Asia, and Central Asia

Unit 7 Africa South of the Sahara

Unit 8 Asia

Unit 9 Australia, Oceania, and Antarctica

▲ Road sign in Tennessee

Charts and Graphs

NATIONAL GEOGRAPHIC Geography Handbook

Unit 1 Geography of the World

Unit 2 The United States and Canada

Focus on Tennessee

Unit 3 Latin America

Unit 4 Europe

Unit 5 Russia

Unit 6 North Africa, Southwest Asia, and Central Asia

Unit 7 Africa South of the Sahara

Unit 8 Asia

Unit 9 Australia, Oceania, and Antarctica

Be an Active Reader!

How Should I Read My Textbook? Reading your social studies book is different than other reading you might do. Your textbook has a great amount of information in it. It is an example of nonfiction writing—it describes real-life events, people, ideas, and places.

Here are some reading strategies that will help you become an active textbook reader. Choose the strategies that work best for you. If you have trouble as you read your textbook, look back at these strategies for help.

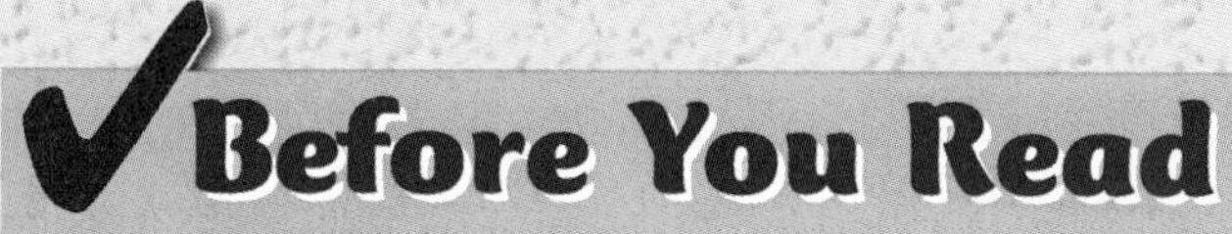

Before You Read

Set a Purpose

- Why are you reading the textbook?
- How might you be able to use what you learn in your own life?

Preview

- Read the chapter title to find out what the topic will be.
- Read the subtitles to see what you will learn about the topic.
- Skim the photos, charts, graphs, or maps.
- Look for vocabulary words that are boldfaced. How are they defined?

Draw From Your Own Background

- What do you already know about the topic?
- How is the new information different from what you already know?

If You Don't Know What A Word Means...

- think about the setting, or *context*, in which the word is used.
- check if prefixes such as *un*, *non*, or *pre* can help you break down the word.
- look up the word's definition in a dictionary or glossary.

Question

- What is the main idea?
- How well do the details support the main idea?
- How do the photos, charts, graphs, and maps support the main idea?

Connect

- Think about people, places, and events in your own life. Are there any similarities with those in your textbook?

Predict

- Predict events or outcomes by using clues and information that you already know.
- Change your predictions as you read and gather new information.

Visualize

- Use your imagination to picture the settings, actions, and people that are described.
- Create graphic organizers to help you see relationships found in the information.

Reading Do's

Do . . .

✔ establish a purpose for reading.

✔ think about how your own experiences relate to the topic.

✔ try different reading strategies.

Reading Don'ts

Don't . . .

⊘ ignore how the textbook is organized.

⊘ allow yourself to be easily distracted.

⊘ hurry to finish the material.

Summarize

- Describe the main idea and how the details support it.
- Use your own words to explain what you have read.

Assess

- What was the main idea?
- Did the text clearly support the main idea?
- Did you learn anything new from the material?
- Can you use this new information in other school subjects or at home?

Reference Atlas

ATLAS KEY

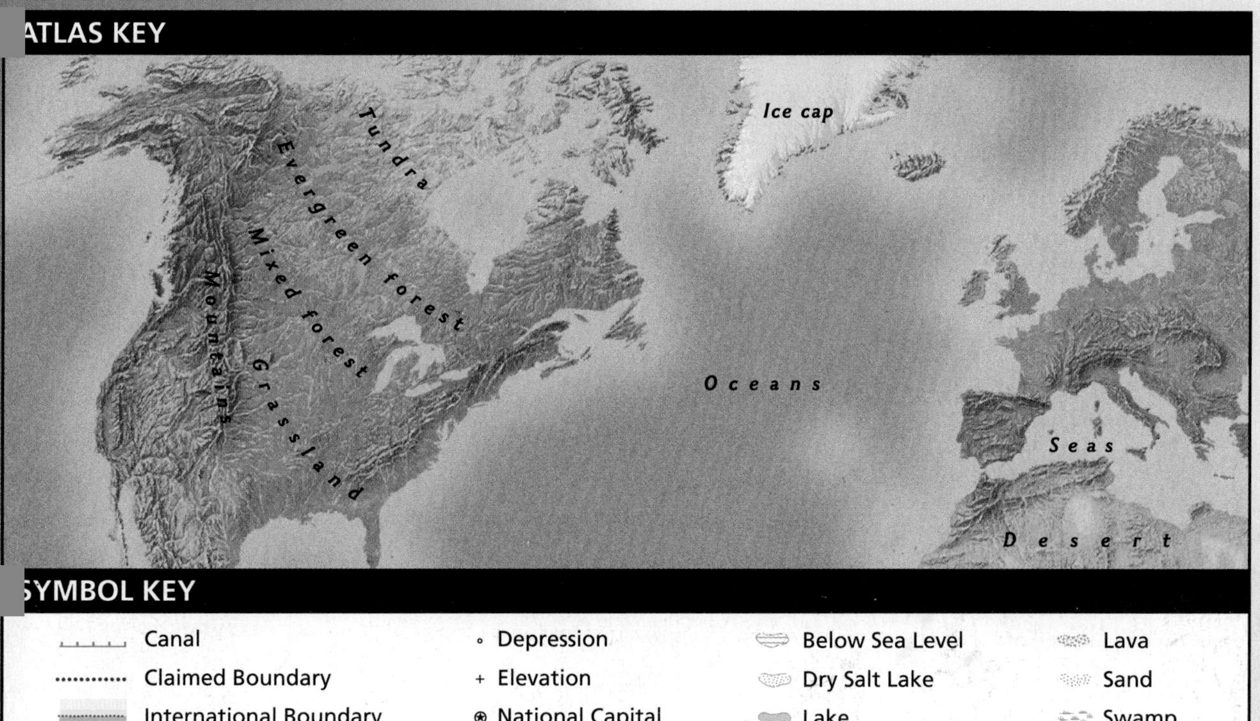

SYMBOL KEY

Canal
Claimed Boundary
International Boundary
Depression
Elevation
National Capital
Towns
Below Sea Level
Dry Salt Lake
Lake
Rivers
Lava
Sand
Swamp

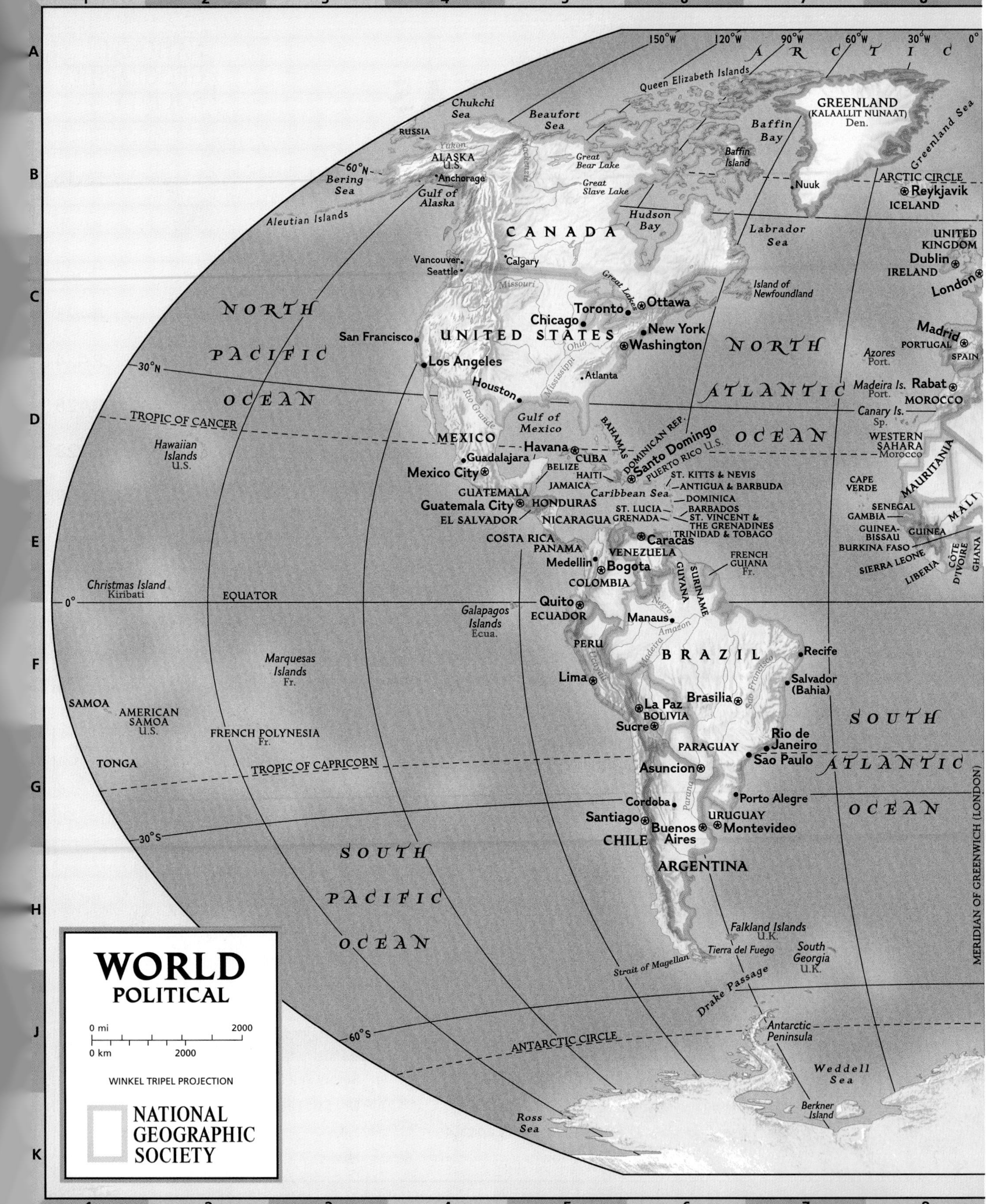

WORLD
POLITICAL
0 mi
2000
0 km
2000
WINKEL TRIPEL PROJECTION
NATIONAL GEOGRAPHIC SOCIETY
ARCTIC
GREENLAND (KALAALLIT NUNAAT) Den.
Greenland Sea
Queen Elizabeth Islands
Chukchi Sea
Beaufort Sea
Baffin Bay
Baffin Island
RUSSIA
ALASKA U.S.
Anchorage
Bering Sea
Gulf of Alaska
Aleutian Islands
Great Bear Lake
Great Slave Lake
Nuuk
ARCTIC CIRCLE
Reykjavik
ICELAND
Hudson Bay
Labrador Sea
CANADA
UNITED KINGDOM
Dublin
IRELAND
London
Vancouver
Seattle
Calgary
Island of Newfoundland
Great Lakes
Ottawa
Toronto
Chicago
New York
Washington
San Francisco
UNITED STATES
Los Angeles
Atlanta
Houston
NORTH PACIFIC OCEAN
NORTH ATLANTIC OCEAN
Madrid
PORTUGAL
SPAIN
Azores Port.
Madeira Is. Port.
Rabat
MOROCCO
Canary Is. Sp.
WESTERN SAHARA Morocco
TROPIC OF CANCER
Hawaiian Islands U.S.
Gulf of Mexico
MEXICO
BAHAMAS
DOMINICAN REP.
Santo Domingo
PUERTO RICO U.S.
Havana
CUBA
Guadalajara
Mexico City
BELIZE
HAITI
JAMAICA
ST. KITTS & NEVIS
ANTIGUA & BARBUDA
DOMINICA
Caribbean Sea
GUATEMALA
Guatemala City
HONDURAS
EL SALVADOR
NICARAGUA
ST. LUCIA
GRENADA
BARBADOS
ST. VINCENT & THE GRENADINES
TRINIDAD & TOBAGO
Caracas
COSTA RICA
PANAMA
VENEZUELA
Medellín
Bogota
COLOMBIA
GUYANA
SURINAME
FRENCH GUIANA Fr.
CAPE VERDE
MAURITANIA
SENEGAL
GAMBIA
GUINEA-BISSAU
GUINEA
MALI
BURKINA FASO
SIERRA LEONE
LIBERIA
CÔTE D'IVOIRE
GHANA
Christmas Island Kiribati
EQUATOR
Galapagos Islands Ecua.
Quito
ECUADOR
Manaus
PERU
BRAZIL
Recife
Salvador (Bahia)
Lima
Marquesas Islands Fr.
SAMOA
AMERICAN SAMOA U.S.
FRENCH POLYNESIA Fr.
La Paz
BOLIVIA
Sucre
Brasilia
PARAGUAY
Rio de Janeiro
Sao Paulo
TONGA
TROPIC OF CAPRICORN
Asuncion
SOUTH ATLANTIC OCEAN
Cordoba
Porto Alegre
Santiago
Buenos Aires
URUGUAY
Montevideo
CHILE
ARGENTINA
SOUTH PACIFIC OCEAN
Falkland Islands U.K.
Tierra del Fuego
South Georgia U.K.
Strait of Magellan
Drake Passage
Antarctic Peninsula
ANTARCTIC CIRCLE
Weddell Sea
Berkner Island
Ross Sea
MERIDIAN OF GREENWICH (LONDON)
150°W
120°W
90°W
60°W
30°W
0°
60°N
30°N
0°
30°S
60°S

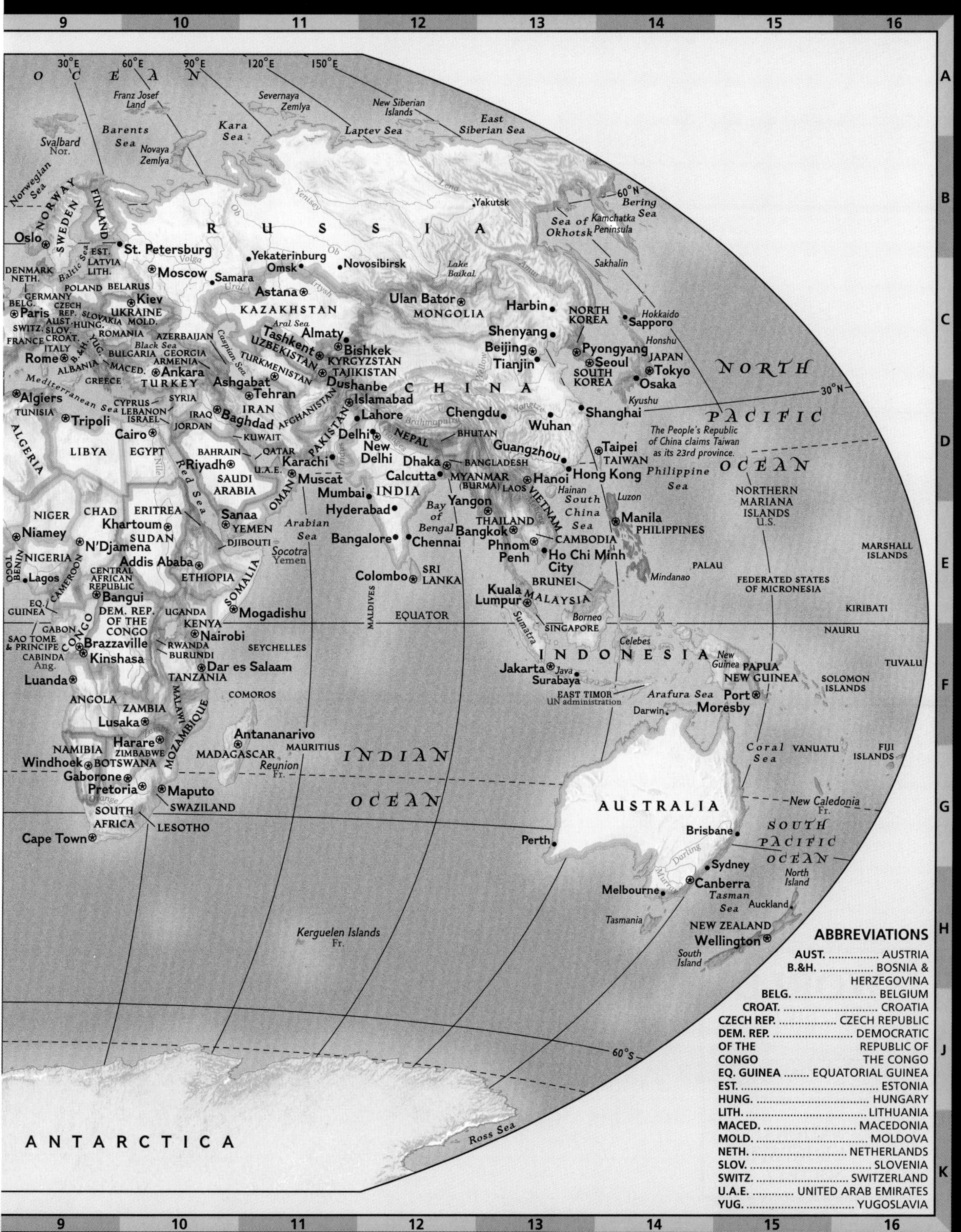
9
10
11
12
13
14
15
16
A
B
C
D
E
F
G
H
J
K
30°E
60°E
90°E
120°E
150°E
O C E A N
Franz Josef Land
Severnaya Zemlya
New Siberian Islands
East Siberian Sea
Laptev Sea
Kara Sea
Barents Sea
Novaya Zemlya
Svalbard
Nor.
Norwegian Sea
NORWAY
SWEDEN
FINLAND
Lena
Yenisey
Yakutsk
60°N
Bering Sea
Sea of Okhotsk
Kamchatka Peninsula
R U S S I A
Oslo
St. Petersburg
Volga
Ob
Baltic Sea
EST.
LATVIA
LITH.
DENMARK
NETH.
Moscow
Yekaterinburg
Omsk
Novosibirsk
Lake Baikal
Amur
Sakhalin
Samara
Ural
Irtysh
POLAND
BELARUS
GERMANY
BELG.
CZECH REP.
Kiev
UKRAINE
Astana
KAZAKHSTAN
Ulan Bator
MONGOLIA
Harbin
NORTH KOREA
Hokkaido
Sapporo
Paris
SWITZ.
AUST.
SLOVAKIA
HUNG.
MOLD.
ROMANIA
Aral Sea
Almaty
Shenyang
Honshu
FRANCE
SLOV.
CROAT.
YUG.
B.&H.
Black Sea
AZERBAIJAN
Caspian Sea
Tashkent
Bishkek
KYRGYZSTAN
Beijing
Pyongyang
JAPAN
Rome
ITALY
BULGARIA
GEORGIA
ARMENIA
UZBEKISTAN
TAJIKISTAN
Tianjin
Yellow
Seoul
SOUTH KOREA
Tokyo
NORTH
ALBANIA
MACED.
Ankara
TURKMENISTAN
Dushanbe
Osaka
GREECE
TURKEY
Ashgabat
C H I N A
Kyushu
30°N
Mediterranean Sea
Algiers
CYPRUS
SYRIA
Tehran
Islamabad
Shanghai
TUNISIA
LEBANON
ISRAEL
IRAQ
Baghdad
IRAN
AFGHANISTAN
Lahore
Chengdu
Yangtze
Wuhan
PACIFIC
Tripoli
JORDAN
KUWAIT
PAKISTAN
Brahmaputra
The People's Republic of China claims Taiwan as its 23rd province.
ALGERIA
Cairo
NEPAL
Delhi
BHUTAN
LIBYA
EGYPT
Nile
BAHRAIN
QATAR
New Delhi
Ganges
Indus
Guangzhou
Taipei
TAIWAN
OCEAN
Riyadh
Red Sea
U.A.E.
Karachi
Dhaka
BANGLADESH
SAUDI ARABIA
Muscat
OMAN
Calcutta
MYANMAR (BURMA)
LAOS
Hanoi
Hong Kong
Philippine Sea
NORTHERN MARIANA ISLANDS
U.S.
Mumbai
INDIA
Hainan
VIETNAM
Luzon
NIGER
CHAD
ERITREA
Sanaa
Hyderabad
Bay of Bengal
Yangon
South China Sea
Manila
Niamey
Khartoum
SUDAN
YEMEN
Arabian Sea
THAILAND
Bangkok
PHILIPPINES
N'Djamena
DJIBOUTI
Bangalore
Chennai
Phnom Penh
CAMBODIA
MARSHALL ISLANDS
NIGERIA
CAMEROON
BENIN
TOGO
Addis Ababa
Socotra
Yemen
Ho Chi Minh City
PALAU
CENTRAL AFRICAN REPUBLIC
ETHIOPIA
SOMALIA
SRI LANKA
Colombo
Mindanao
FEDERATED STATES OF MICRONESIA
Lagos
BRUNEI
EQ. GUINEA
Bangui
MALDIVES
Kuala Lumpur
MALAYSIA
DEM. REP. OF THE CONGO
UGANDA
Mogadishu
EQUATOR
Borneo
KIRIBATI
GABON
KENYA
Sumatra
SINGAPORE
NAURU
SAO TOME & PRINCIPE
CONGO
Nairobi
Celebes
Brazzaville
RWANDA
SEYCHELLES
CABINDA
Ang.
Kinshasa
BURUNDI
I N D O N E S I A
New Guinea
PAPUA NEW GUINEA
TUVALU
Luanda
Dar es Salaam
Jakarta
Java
Surabaya
TANZANIA
SOLOMON ISLANDS
COMOROS
EAST TIMOR
UN administration
Arafura Sea
Port Moresby
ANGOLA
ZAMBIA
MALAWI
Darwin
Lusaka
MOZAMBIQUE
Antananarivo
Coral Sea
VANUATU
FIJI ISLANDS
NAMIBIA
Harare
ZIMBABWE
MAURITIUS
MADAGASCAR
I N D I A N
Windhoek
BOTSWANA
Reunion
Fr.
Gaborone
Pretoria
Maputo
O C E A N
AUSTRALIA
New Caledonia
Fr.
SOUTH AFRICA
SWAZILAND
LESOTHO
Orange
SOUTH PACIFIC OCEAN
Cape Town
Perth
Brisbane
Darling
Sydney
Murray
North Island
Canberra
Melbourne
Tasman Sea
Auckland
Tasmania
Kerguelen Islands
Fr.
NEW ZEALAND
Wellington
South Island
60°S
Ross Sea
A N T A R C T I C A
ABBREVIATIONS
AUST. .... AUSTRIA
B.&H. .... BOSNIA & HERZEGOVINA
BELG. .... BELGIUM
CROAT. .... CROATIA
CZECH REP. .... CZECH REPUBLIC
DEM. REP. OF THE CONGO .... DEMOCRATIC REPUBLIC OF THE CONGO
EQ. GUINEA .... EQUATORIAL GUINEA
EST. .... ESTONIA
HUNG. .... HUNGARY
LITH. .... LITHUANIA
MACED. .... MACEDONIA
MOLD. .... MOLDOVA
NETH. .... NETHERLANDS
SLOV. .... SLOVENIA
SWITZ. .... SWITZERLAND
U.A.E. .... UNITED ARAB EMIRATES
YUG. .... YUGOSLAVIA

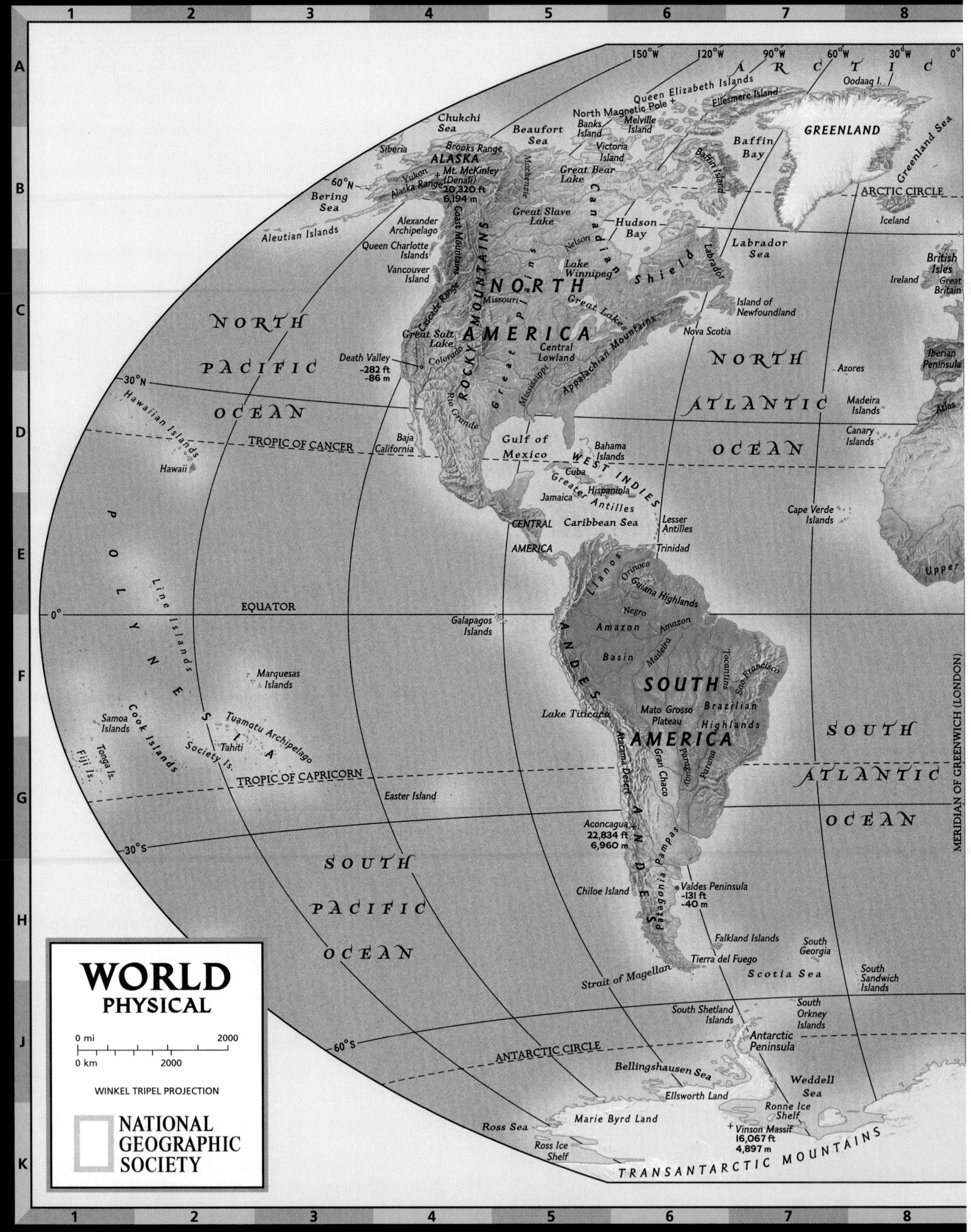

WORLD
PHYSICAL
WINKEL TRIPEL PROJECTION
NATIONAL GEOGRAPHIC SOCIETY
NORTH AMERICA
SOUTH AMERICA
NORTH PACIFIC OCEAN
SOUTH PACIFIC OCEAN
NORTH ATLANTIC OCEAN
SOUTH ATLANTIC OCEAN
ARCTIC
GREENLAND
ALASKA
ROCKY MOUNTAINS
ANDES
TROPIC OF CANCER
TROPIC OF CAPRICORN
EQUATOR
ARCTIC CIRCLE
ANTARCTIC CIRCLE
MERIDIAN OF GREENWICH (LONDON)
TRANSANTARCTIC MOUNTAINS

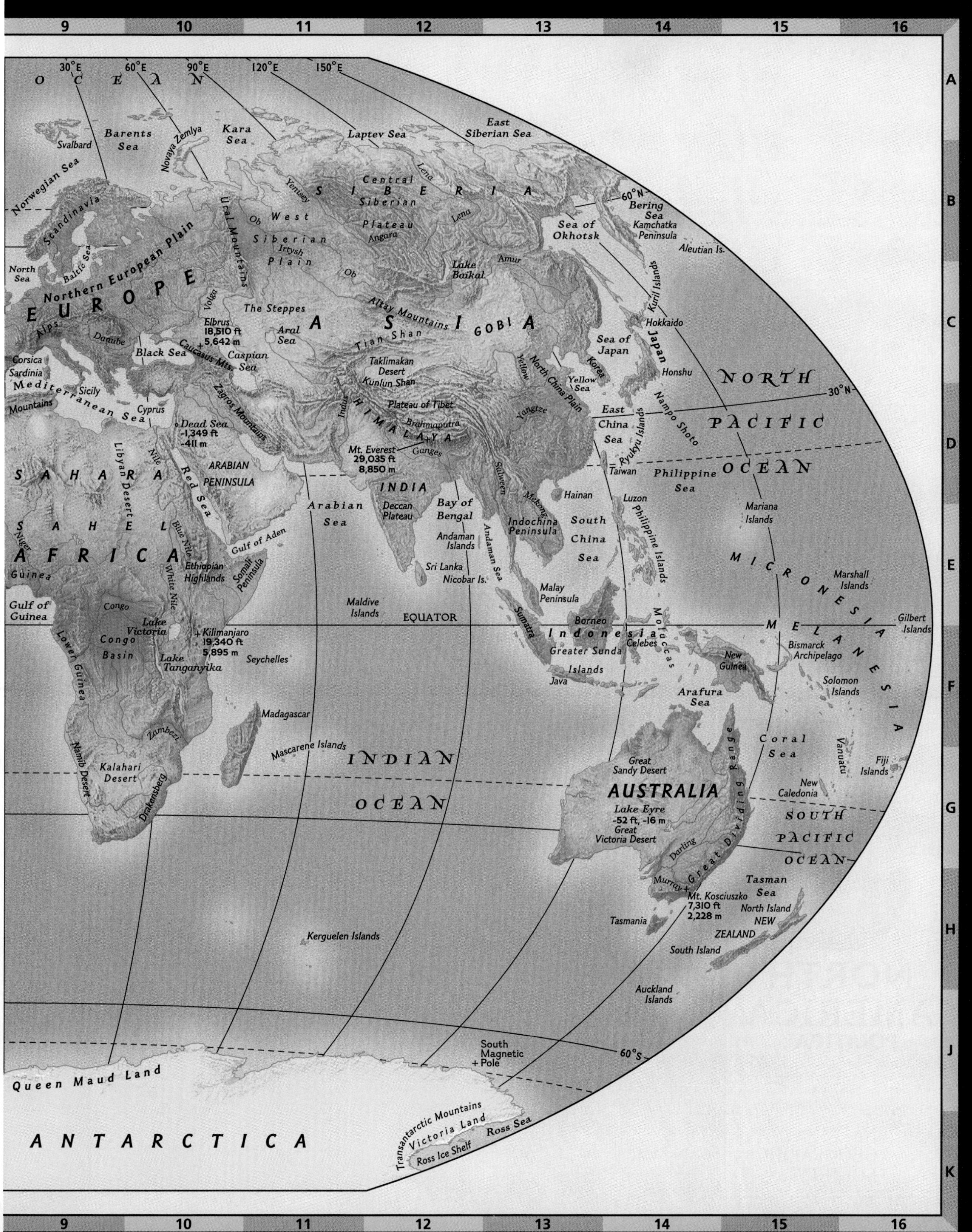

EUROPE
ASIA
AFRICA
AUSTRALIA
ANTARCTICA
INDIAN OCEAN
NORTH PACIFIC OCEAN
SOUTH PACIFIC OCEAN
SIBERIA
GOBI
SAHARA
SAHEL
HIMALAYA
INDIA
ARABIAN PENINSULA
MICRONESIA
MELANESIA
Indonesia
EQUATOR
Mt. Everest 29,035 ft 8,850 m
Elbrus 18,510 ft 5,642 m
Dead Sea -1,349 ft -411 m
Kilimanjaro 19,340 ft 5,895 m
Lake Eyre -52 ft, -16 m
Mt. Kosciuszko 7,310 ft 2,228 m
South Magnetic Pole
Queen Maud Land
Ross Sea
Ross Ice Shelf
Victoria Land
Transantarctic Mountains

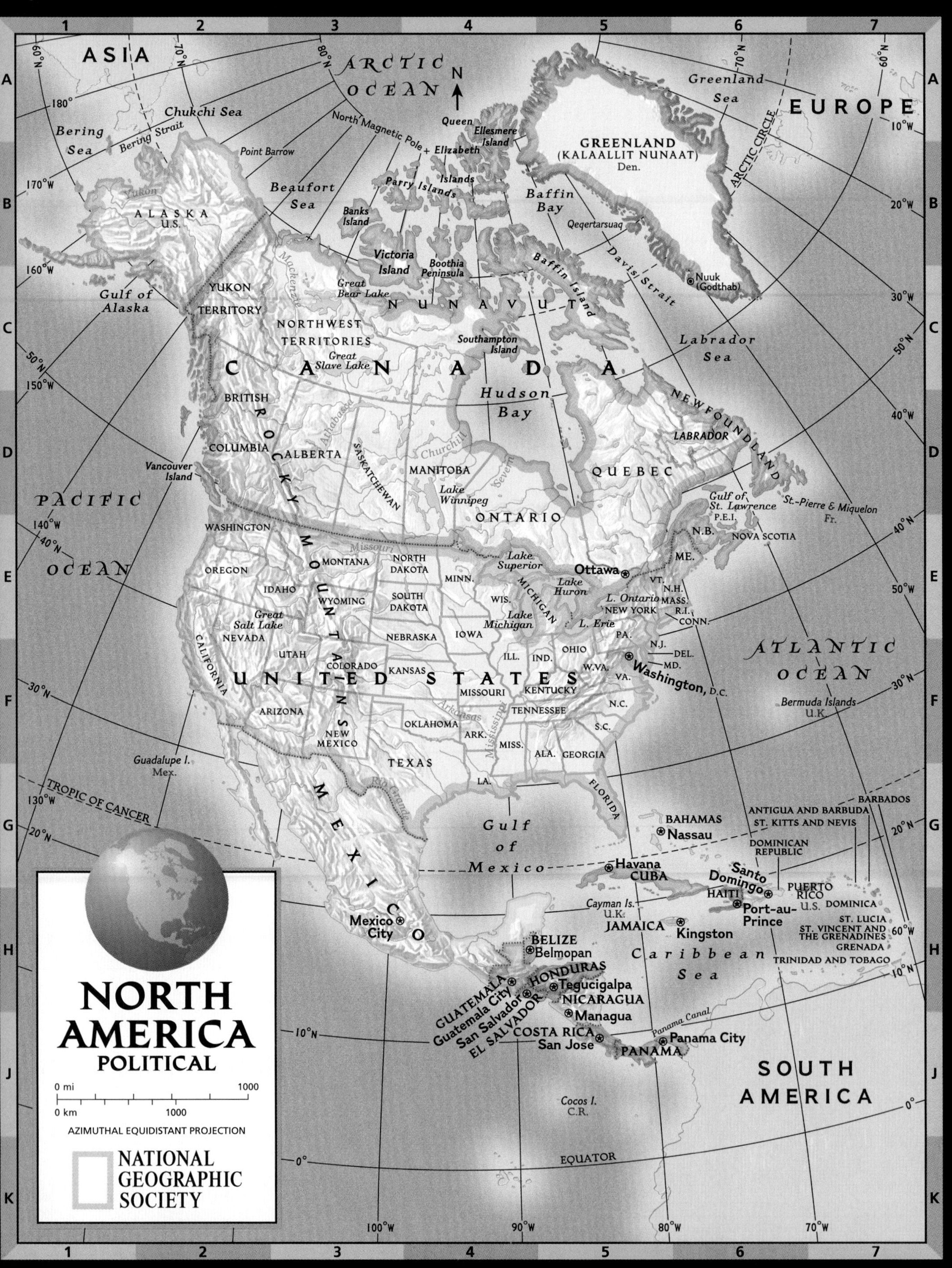
NORTH AMERICA
POLITICAL
AZIMUTHAL EQUIDISTANT PROJECTION
NATIONAL GEOGRAPHIC SOCIETY
ASIA
ARCTIC OCEAN
EUROPE
GREENLAND (KALAALLIT NUNAAT) Den.
CANADA
UNITED STATES
MEXICO
PACIFIC OCEAN
ATLANTIC OCEAN
SOUTH AMERICA
Hudson Bay
Gulf of Mexico
Caribbean Sea
Ottawa
Washington, D.C.
Mexico City
Havana
Nassau
Kingston
Port-au-Prince
Santo Domingo
Belmopan
Guatemala City
San Salvador
Tegucigalpa
Managua
San Jose
Panama City
Nuuk (Godthab)

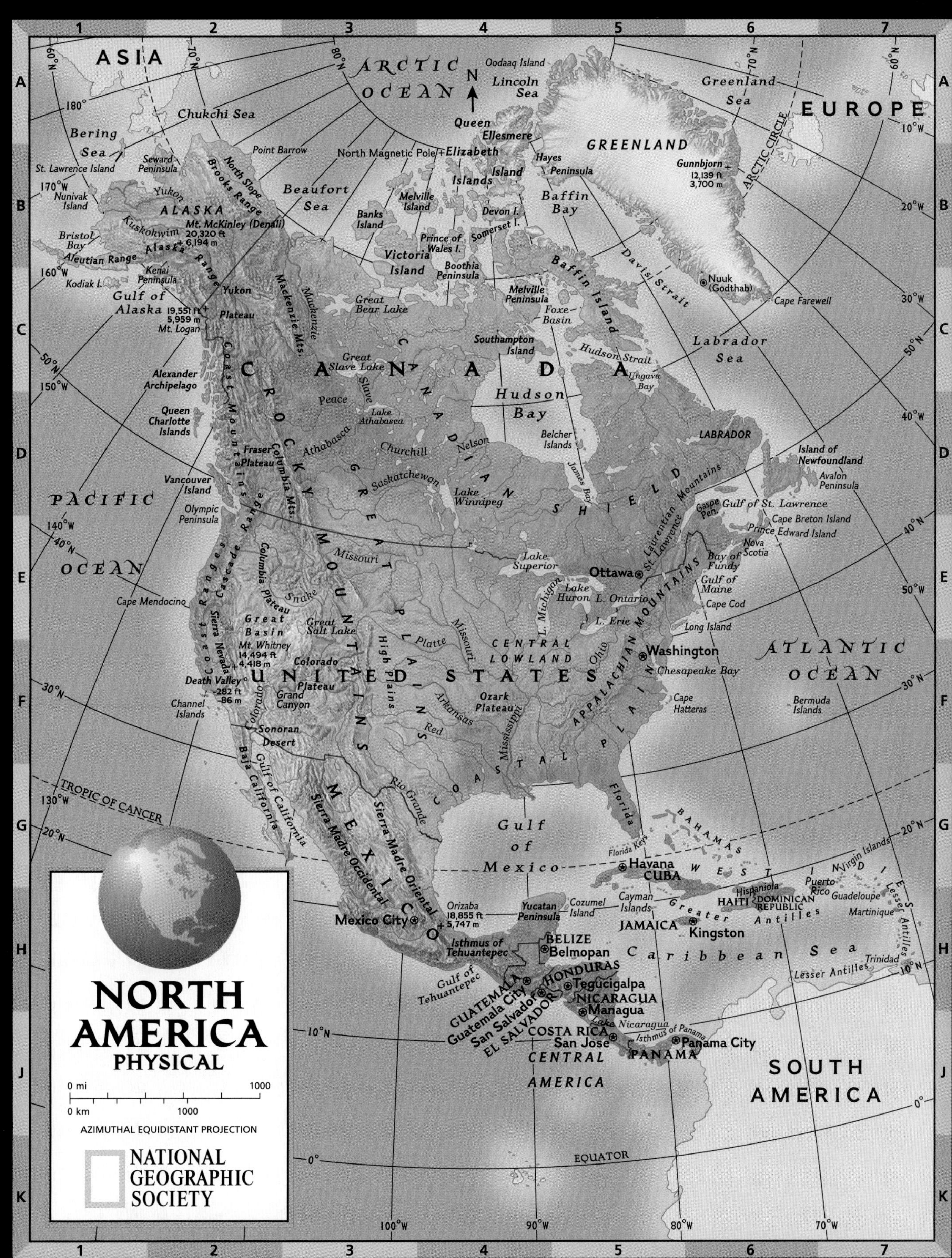
NORTH AMERICA
PHYSICAL
AZIMUTHAL EQUIDISTANT PROJECTION
NATIONAL GEOGRAPHIC SOCIETY
ARCTIC OCEAN
PACIFIC OCEAN
ATLANTIC OCEAN
ASIA
EUROPE
SOUTH AMERICA
GREENLAND
CANADA
UNITED STATES
MEXICO
ALASKA
CENTRAL AMERICA
ROCKY MOUNTAINS
CANADIAN SHIELD
GREAT PLAINS
CENTRAL LOWLAND
APPALACHIAN MOUNTAINS
COASTAL PLAIN
Hudson Bay
Gulf of Mexico
Caribbean Sea
Gulf of Alaska
Bering Sea
Chukchi Sea
Beaufort Sea
Baffin Bay
Labrador Sea
Greenland Sea
Lincoln Sea
Mt. McKinley (Denali) 20,320 ft 6,194 m
Mt. Whitney 14,494 ft 4,418 m
Death Valley -282 ft -86 m
Orizaba 18,855 ft 5,747 m
Gunnbjorn 12,139 ft 3,700 m
Ottawa
Washington
Mexico City
Havana
Kingston
Belmopan
Guatemala City
San Salvador
Tegucigalpa
Managua
San Jose
Panama City
Nuuk (Godthab)
TROPIC OF CANCER
ARCTIC CIRCLE
EQUATOR

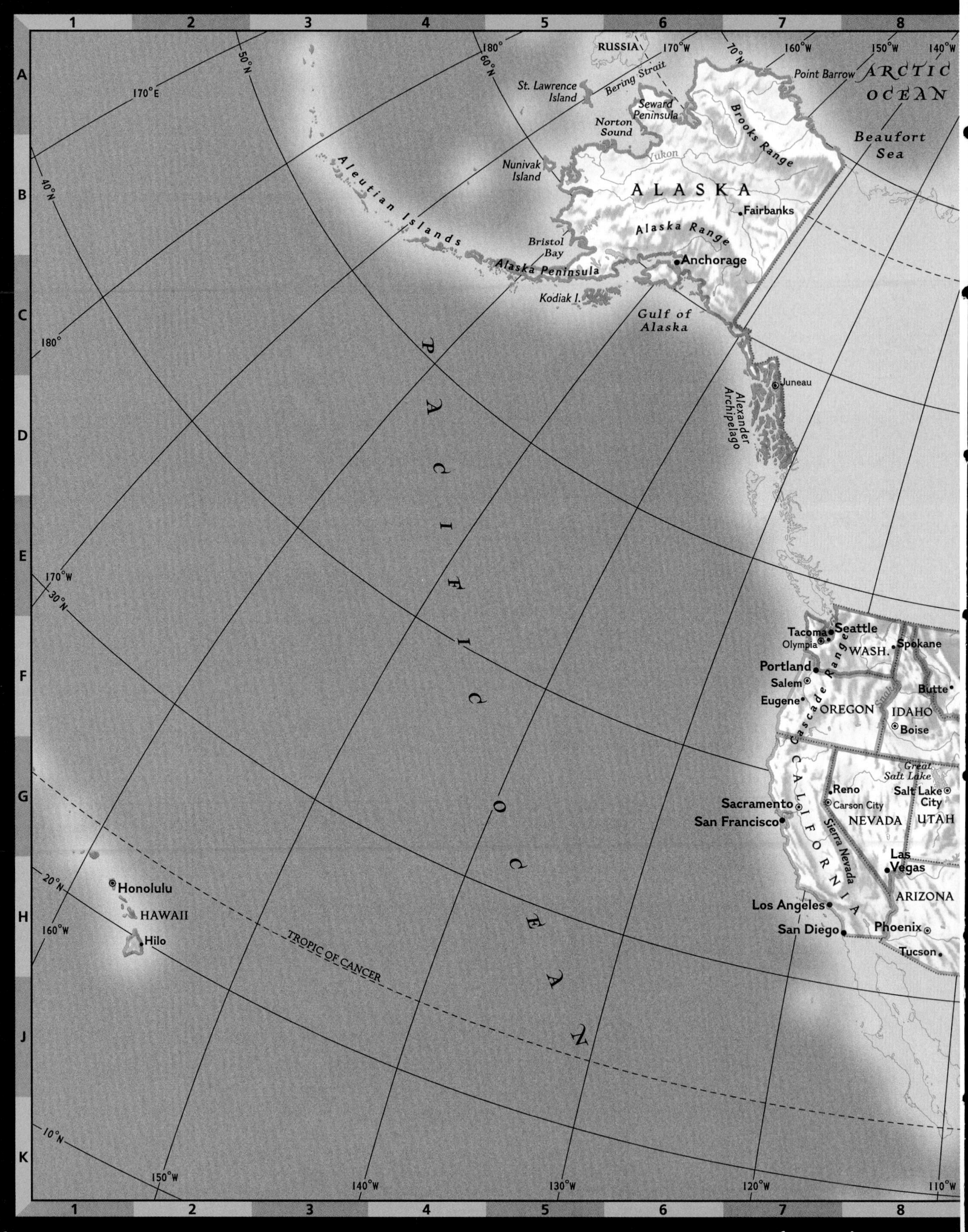

RUSSIA
St. Lawrence Island
Bering Strait
Seward Peninsula
Norton Sound
Point Barrow
ARCTIC OCEAN
Beaufort Sea
Brooks Range
Yukon
Nunivak Island
ALASKA
Fairbanks
Aleutian Islands
Alaska Range
Bristol Bay
Anchorage
Alaska Peninsula
Kodiak I.
Gulf of Alaska
Juneau
Alexander Archipelago
PACIFIC OCEAN
Seattle
Tacoma
Olympia
WASH.
Spokane
Portland
Salem
Cascade Range
Butte
Eugene
OREGON
IDAHO
Boise
Great Salt Lake
Reno
Salt Lake City
Sacramento
Carson City
San Francisco
NEVADA
UTAH
CALIFORNIA
Sierra Nevada
Las Vegas
Honolulu
HAWAII
Hilo
ARIZONA
Los Angeles
San Diego
Phoenix
Tucson
TROPIC OF CANCER
170°E
180°
170°W
160°W
150°W
140°W
130°W
120°W
110°W
70°N
60°N
50°N
40°N
30°N
20°N
10°N

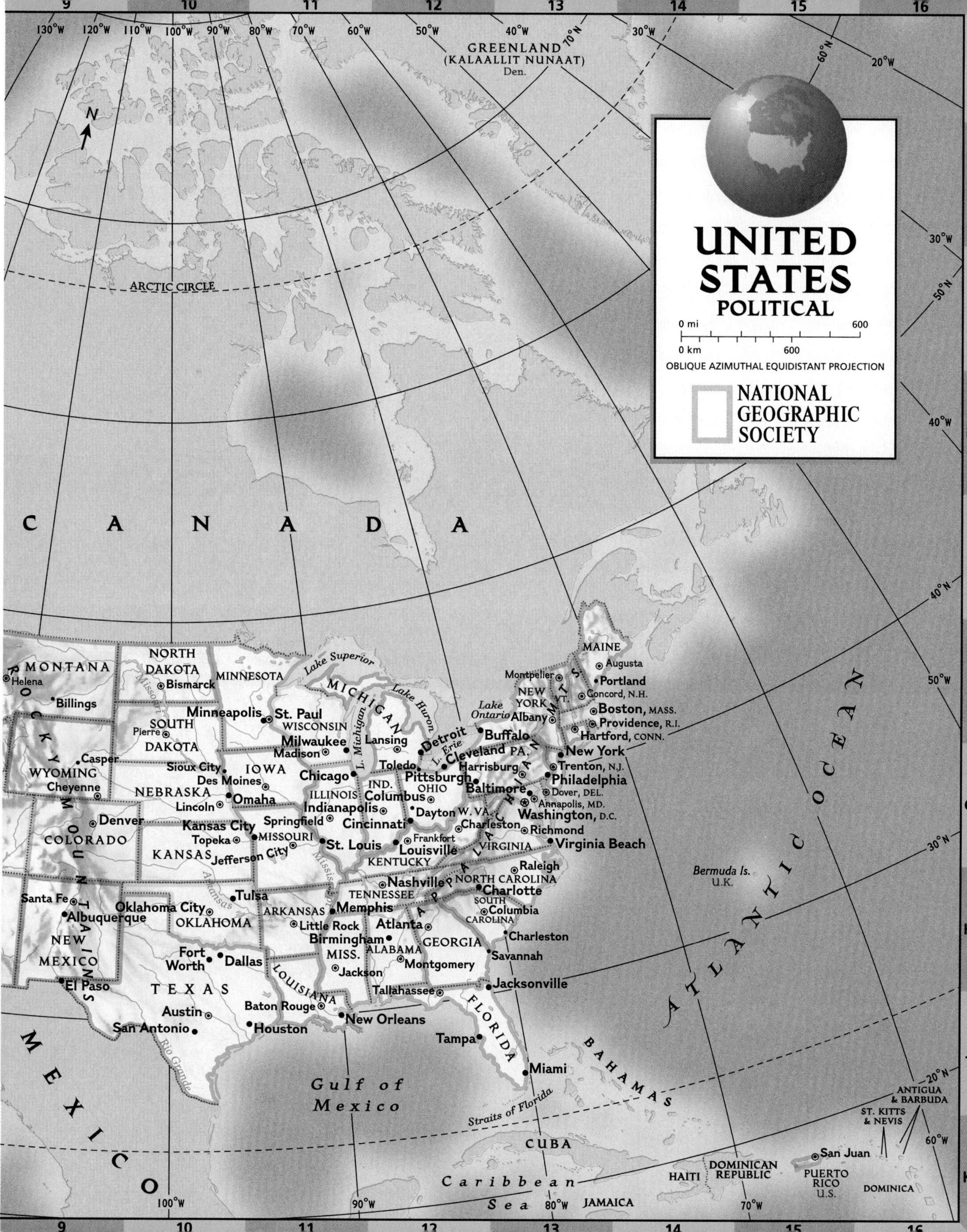

UNITED STATES
POLITICAL
0 mi 600
0 km 600
OBLIQUE AZIMUTHAL EQUIDISTANT PROJECTION
NATIONAL GEOGRAPHIC SOCIETY
GREENLAND (KALAALLIT NUNAAT) Den.
ARCTIC CIRCLE
CANADA
MONTANA
Helena
Billings
NORTH DAKOTA
Bismarck
MINNESOTA
SOUTH DAKOTA
Pierre
Minneapolis
St. Paul
WISCONSIN
MICHIGAN
Lake Superior
Lake Huron
L. Michigan
Milwaukee
Madison
Lansing
Detroit
L. Erie
Lake Ontario
Buffalo
Albany
NEW YORK
Montpelier
VT.
MAINE
Augusta
Portland
Concord, N.H.
Boston, MASS.
Providence, R.I.
Hartford, CONN.
New York
Trenton, N.J.
Philadelphia
Dover, DEL.
Annapolis, MD.
Washington, D.C.
Baltimore
Harrisburg
PA.
Pittsburgh
Cleveland
Toledo
OHIO
Columbus
Dayton
W. VA.
Charleston
Richmond
VIRGINIA
Virginia Beach
Raleigh
NORTH CAROLINA
Charlotte
SOUTH CAROLINA
Columbia
Charleston
Savannah
GEORGIA
Atlanta
Jacksonville
FLORIDA
Tallahassee
Tampa
Miami
APPALACHIAN MTS.
WYOMING
Casper
Cheyenne
ROCKY MOUNTAINS
Sioux City
IOWA
Des Moines
NEBRASKA
Omaha
Lincoln
Chicago
IND.
ILLINOIS
Indianapolis
Springfield
Cincinnati
Frankfort
Louisville
KENTUCKY
St. Louis
Denver
COLORADO
Kansas City
Topeka
KANSAS
MISSOURI
Jefferson City
Missouri
Mississippi
Arkansas
Nashville
TENNESSEE
Memphis
ARKANSAS
Little Rock
Tulsa
Oklahoma City
OKLAHOMA
Santa Fe
Albuquerque
NEW MEXICO
El Paso
Fort Worth
Dallas
TEXAS
Austin
San Antonio
Houston
Rio Grande
LOUISIANA
Baton Rouge
New Orleans
MISS.
Jackson
ALABAMA
Birmingham
Montgomery
MEXICO
Gulf of Mexico
Straits of Florida
BAHAMAS
CUBA
Caribbean Sea
JAMAICA
HAITI
DOMINICAN REPUBLIC
PUERTO RICO U.S.
San Juan
ANTIGUA & BARBUDA
ST. KITTS & NEVIS
DOMINICA
Bermuda Is. U.K.
ATLANTIC OCEAN

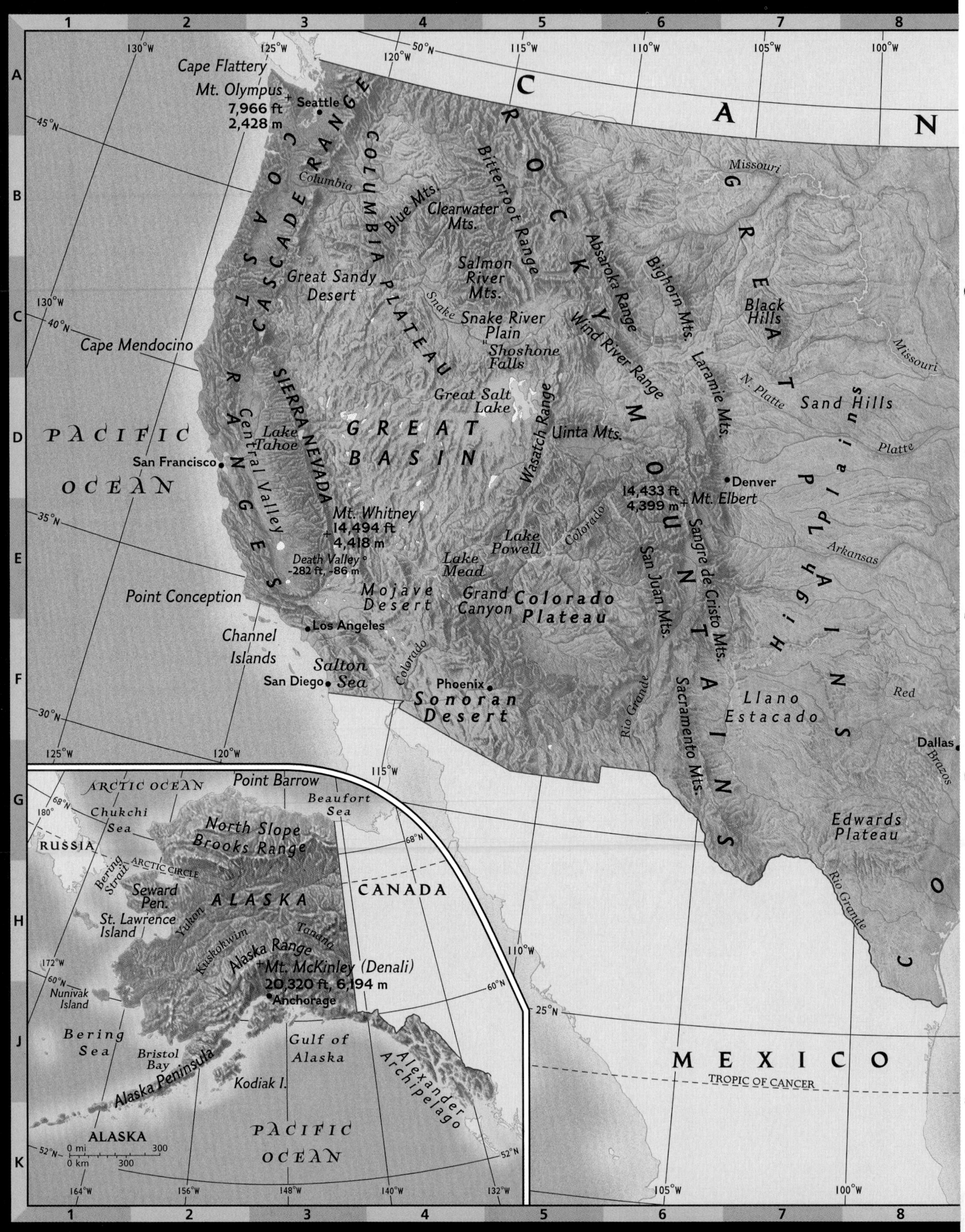

Cape Flattery
Mt. Olympus
7,966 ft
2,428 m
Seattle
CASCADE RANGE
COLUMBIA PLATEAU
ROCKY MOUNTAINS
GREAT PLAINS
CANADA
Columbia
Blue Mts.
Clearwater Mts.
Bitterroot Range
Absaroka Range
Bighorn Mts.
Missouri
Great Sandy Desert
Salmon River Mts.
Black Hills
Snake
Snake River Plain
Wind River Range
Cape Mendocino
Shoshone Falls
Laramie Mts.
SIERRA NEVADA
Great Salt Lake
N. Platte
Sand Hills
PACIFIC OCEAN
Lake Tahoe
GREAT BASIN
Wasatch Range
Uinta Mts.
Platte
San Francisco
Central Valley
COAST RANGES
Denver
14,433 ft
4,399 m
Mt. Elbert
Mt. Whitney
14,494 ft
4,418 m
Colorado
Lake Powell
Arkansas
Death Valley
-282 ft, -86 m
Lake Mead
San Juan Mts.
Sangre de Cristo Mts.
High Plains
Point Conception
Mojave Desert
Grand Canyon
Colorado Plateau
Los Angeles
Channel Islands
Salton Sea
San Diego
Phoenix
Sonoran Desert
Rio Grande
Sacramento Mts.
Llano Estacado
Red
Dallas
Brazos
Edwards Plateau
MEXICO
TROPIC OF CANCER
ARCTIC OCEAN
Point Barrow
Beaufort Sea
Chukchi Sea
RUSSIA
North Slope
Brooks Range
Bering Strait
ARCTIC CIRCLE
Seward Pen.
ALASKA
CANADA
St. Lawrence Island
Yukon
Tanana
Kuskokwim
Alaska Range
Mt. McKinley (Denali)
20,320 ft, 6,194 m
Anchorage
Nunivak Island
Bering Sea
Bristol Bay
Gulf of Alaska
Alexander Archipelago
Alaska Peninsula
Kodiak I.
PACIFIC OCEAN
0 mi 300
0 km 300

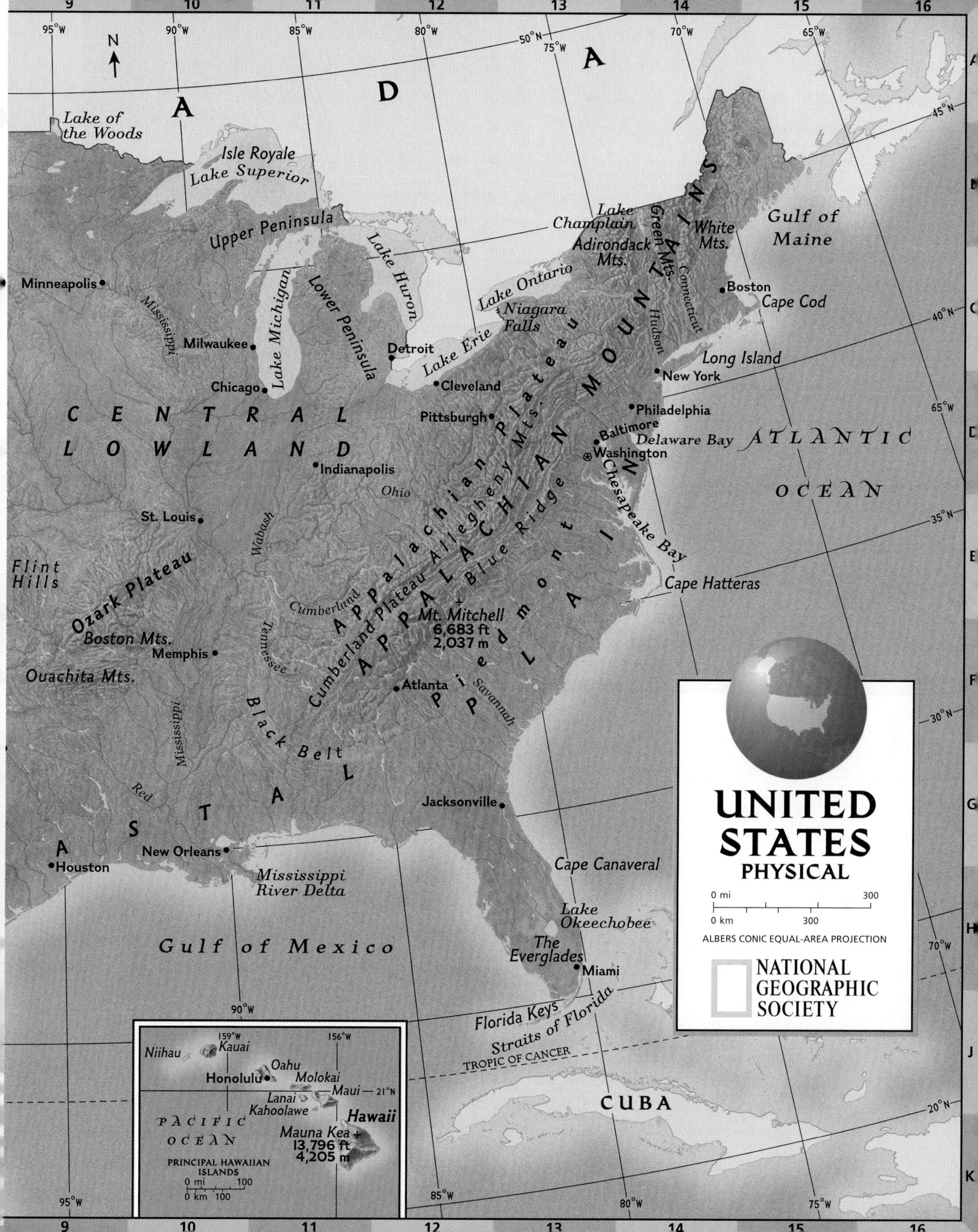

UNITED STATES
PHYSICAL
0 mi 300
0 km 300
ALBERS CONIC EQUAL-AREA PROJECTION
NATIONAL GEOGRAPHIC SOCIETY
C A N A D A
Lake of the Woods
Isle Royale
Lake Superior
Upper Peninsula
Lake Michigan
Lower Peninsula
Lake Huron
Lake Ontario
Lake Erie
Niagara Falls
Lake Champlain
Adirondack Mts.
Green Mts.
White Mts.
Gulf of Maine
Connecticut
Hudson
Boston
Cape Cod
Long Island
New York
Philadelphia
Baltimore
Delaware Bay
Washington
Chesapeake Bay
ATLANTIC OCEAN
Cape Hatteras
APPALACHIAN MOUNTAINS
Appalachian Plateau
Allegheny Mts.
Blue Ridge
Cumberland Plateau
Piedmont
Mt. Mitchell
6,683 ft
2,037 m
Minneapolis
Mississippi
Milwaukee
Chicago
Detroit
Cleveland
Pittsburgh
CENTRAL LOWLAND
Indianapolis
Ohio
St. Louis
Wabash
Flint Hills
Ozark Plateau
Boston Mts.
Ouachita Mts.
Cumberland
Tennessee
Memphis
Atlanta
Savannah
Black Belt
Red
COASTAL PLAIN
Jacksonville
New Orleans
Houston
Mississippi River Delta
Cape Canaveral
Lake Okeechobee
The Everglades
Miami
Gulf of Mexico
Florida Keys
Straits of Florida
TROPIC OF CANCER
CUBA
Niihau
Kauai
Oahu
Honolulu
Molokai
Maui
Lanai
Kahoolawe
Hawaii
Mauna Kea
13,796 ft
4,205 m
PACIFIC OCEAN
PRINCIPAL HAWAIIAN ISLANDS
0 mi 100
0 km 100
159°W
156°W
21°N
95°W
90°W
85°W
80°W
75°W
70°W
65°W
50°N
45°N
40°N
35°N
30°N
20°N

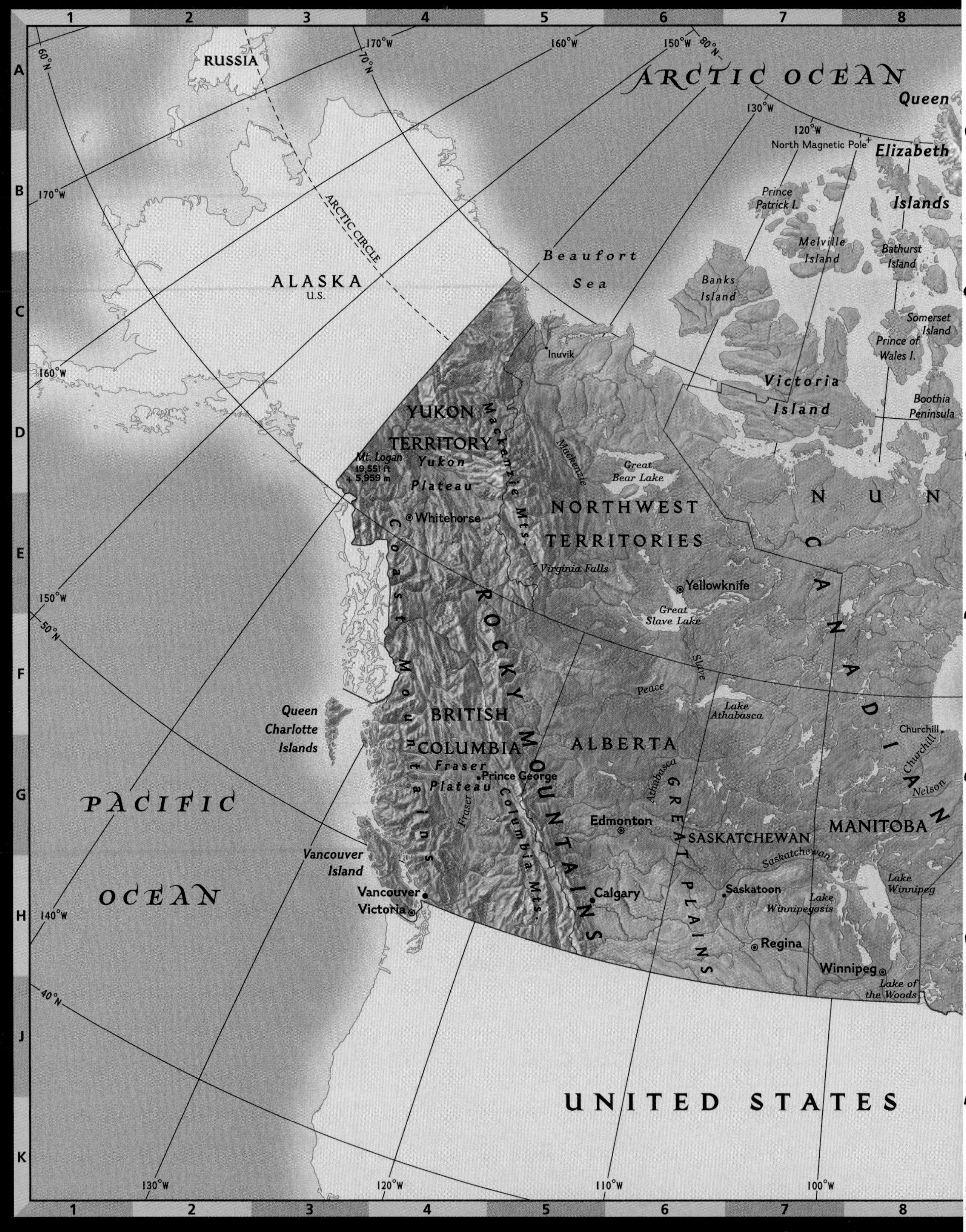

RUSSIA
ARCTIC OCEAN
Queen Elizabeth Islands
North Magnetic Pole
Prince Patrick I.
Melville Island
Bathurst Island
Banks Island
Somerset Island
Prince of Wales I.
Victoria Island
Boothia Peninsula
Beaufort Sea
ALASKA
U.S.
ARCTIC CIRCLE
Inuvik
YUKON TERRITORY
Yukon Plateau
Mt. Logan 19,551 ft 5,959 m
Whitehorse
Mackenzie Mts.
Mackenzie
Great Bear Lake
NORTHWEST TERRITORIES
NUNAVUT
Virginia Falls
Yellowknife
Great Slave Lake
Slave
Peace
Lake Athabasca
Coast Mountains
ROCKY MOUNTAINS
BRITISH COLUMBIA
ALBERTA
Athabasca
GREAT PLAINS
Fraser Plateau
Prince George
Fraser
Columbia Mts.
Queen Charlotte Islands
PACIFIC OCEAN
Vancouver Island
Vancouver
Victoria
Edmonton
Calgary
SASKATCHEWAN
Saskatchewan
Saskatoon
Regina
MANITOBA
CANADIAN
Churchill
Nelson
Lake Winnipeg
Lake Winnipegosis
Winnipeg
Lake of the Woods
UNITED STATES
170°W
160°W
150°W
140°W
130°W
120°W
110°W
100°W
80°N
70°N
60°N
50°N
40°N

CANADA
PHYSICAL/POLITICAL
0 mi 400
0 km 400
AZIMUTHAL EQUIDISTANT PROJECTION
NATIONAL GEOGRAPHIC SOCIETY
GREENLAND
(KALAALLIT NUNAAT)
Den.
ICELAND
Ellesmere Island
Devon Island
Baffin Bay
Baffin Island
Davis Strait
Melville Peninsula
Foxe Basin
Iqaluit
Southampton Island
Hudson Strait
Labrador Sea
Ungava Bay
Hudson Bay
Belcher Islands
NEWFOUNDLAND
LABRADOR
Cartwright
Schefferville
Happy Valley-Goose Bay
Smallwood Reservoir
Churchill Falls
Island of Newfoundland
St. John's
Avalon Peninsula
QUEBEC
James Bay
Manicouagan Reservoir
Sept-Iles
Anticosti I.
Gulf of St. Lawrence
St.-Pierre & Miquelon Fr.
Gaspe Pen.
PRINCE EDWARD ISLAND
Cape Breton I.
Charlottetown
NEW BRUNSWICK
NOVA SCOTIA
Halifax
Fredericton
Saint John
Bay of Fundy
ATLANTIC OCEAN
SHIELD
ONTARIO
Lake Nipigon
Thunder Bay
Lake Superior
Rouyn-Noranda
Chicoutimi
Quebec City
St. Lawrence
Montreal
Ottawa
Sudbury
Lake Huron
Lake Michigan
Toronto
L. Ontario
Niagara Falls
London
L. Erie
N
A V U T
80°N 70°N 60°N 50°N 40°N
40°W 30°W 20°W 10°W 50°W 60°W 70°W 80°W 90°W
9 10 11 12 13 14 15 16
A B C D E F G H J K

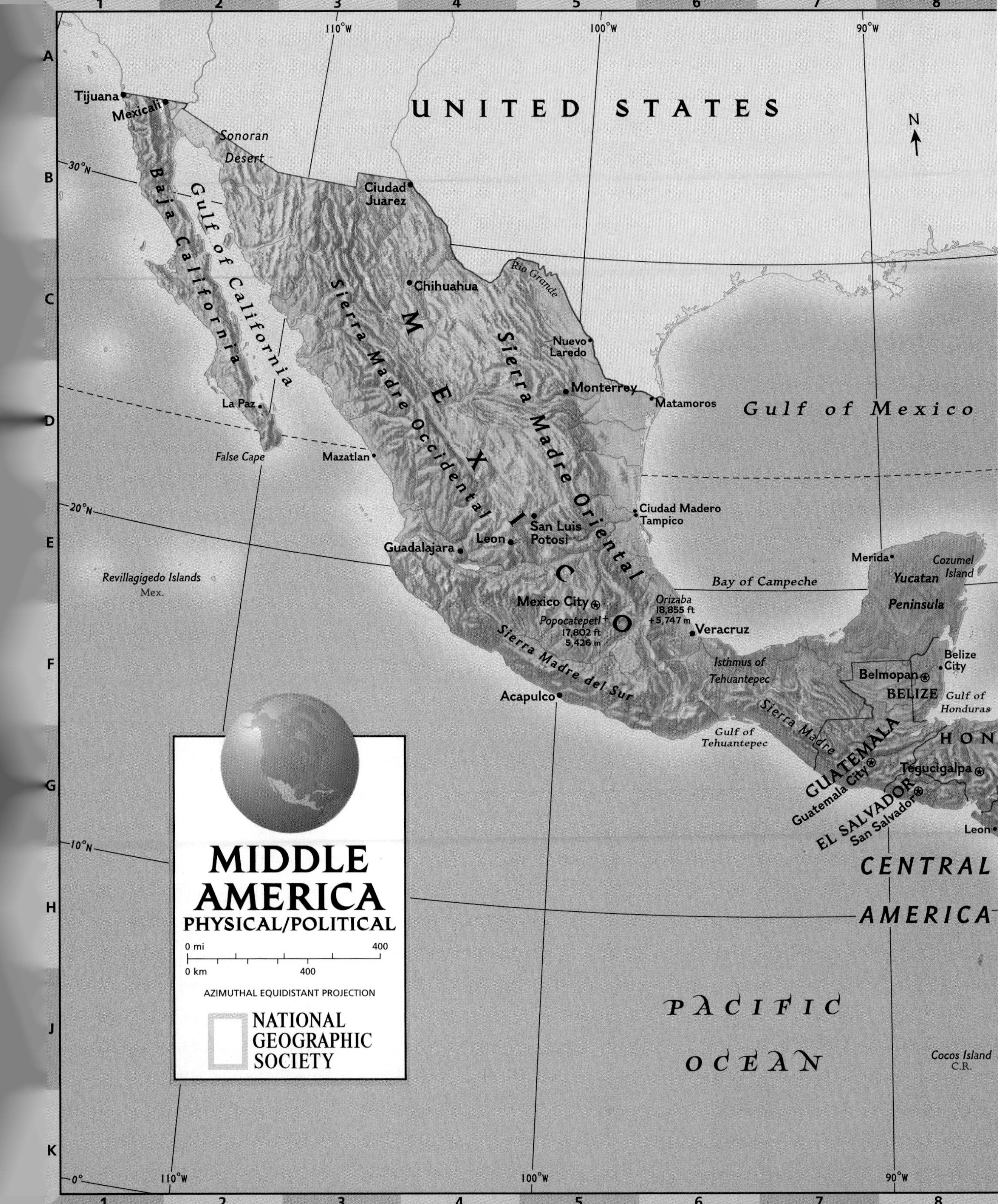
MIDDLE AMERICA
PHYSICAL/POLITICAL
0 mi
400
0 km
400
AZIMUTHAL EQUIDISTANT PROJECTION
NATIONAL GEOGRAPHIC SOCIETY
UNITED STATES
MEXICO
Gulf of Mexico
PACIFIC OCEAN
CENTRAL AMERICA
Tijuana
Mexicali
Sonoran Desert
Baja California
Gulf of California
Ciudad Juarez
Chihuahua
Rio Grande
Sierra Madre Occidental
Sierra Madre Oriental
Nuevo Laredo
Monterrey
Matamoros
La Paz
False Cape
Mazatlan
Ciudad Madero
Tampico
San Luis Potosi
Leon
Guadalajara
Revillagigedo Islands
Mex.
Bay of Campeche
Merida
Cozumel Island
Yucatan Peninsula
Mexico City
Orizaba
18,855 ft
5,747 m
Popocatepetl
17,802 ft
5,426 m
Veracruz
Sierra Madre del Sur
Isthmus of Tehuantepec
Acapulco
Belize City
Belmopan
BELIZE
Gulf of Honduras
Gulf of Tehuantepec
Sierra Madre
GUATEMALA
Guatemala City
HON
Tegucigalpa
EL SALVADOR
San Salvador
Leon
Cocos Island
C.R.
N
110°W
100°W
90°W
30°N
20°N
10°N
0°
1
2
3
4
5
6
7
8
A
B
C
D
E
F
G
H
J
K

ATLANTIC OCEAN
BAHAMAS
Freeport
Nassau
Andros Island
Straits of Florida
TROPIC OF CANCER
Turks & Caicos Islands U.K.
WEST INDIES
Havana
CUBA
Camaguey
Holguin
Santiago de Cuba
Isle of Youth
Cayman Islands U.K.
Hispaniola
Santiago
Santo Domingo
HAITI
Port-au-Prince
DOMINICAN REPUBLIC
San Juan
Puerto Rico U.S.
Virgin Islands U.S. U.K.
ST. KITTS & NEVIS
ANTIGUA & BARBUDA
Guadeloupe Fr.
DOMINICA
Martinique Fr.
ST. LUCIA
BARBADOS
ST. VINCENT & THE GRENADINES
GRENADA
TRINIDAD & TOBAGO
Tobago
Port of Spain
Trinidad
Bird I. Venez.
Greater Antilles
Lesser Antilles
Montego Bay
JAMAICA
Kingston
Caribbean Sea
Aruba Neth.
Curacao
Neth. Bonaire
DURAS
Coco
Mosquito Coast
NICARAGUA
Managua
Lake Nicaragua
COSTA RICA
San Jose
Puerto Limon
Gulf of Mosquitos
Isthmus of Panama
Panama City
PANAMA
David
Gulf of Panama
SOUTH AMERICA
EQUATOR
30°N
20°N
10°N
0°
80°W
70°W
60°W

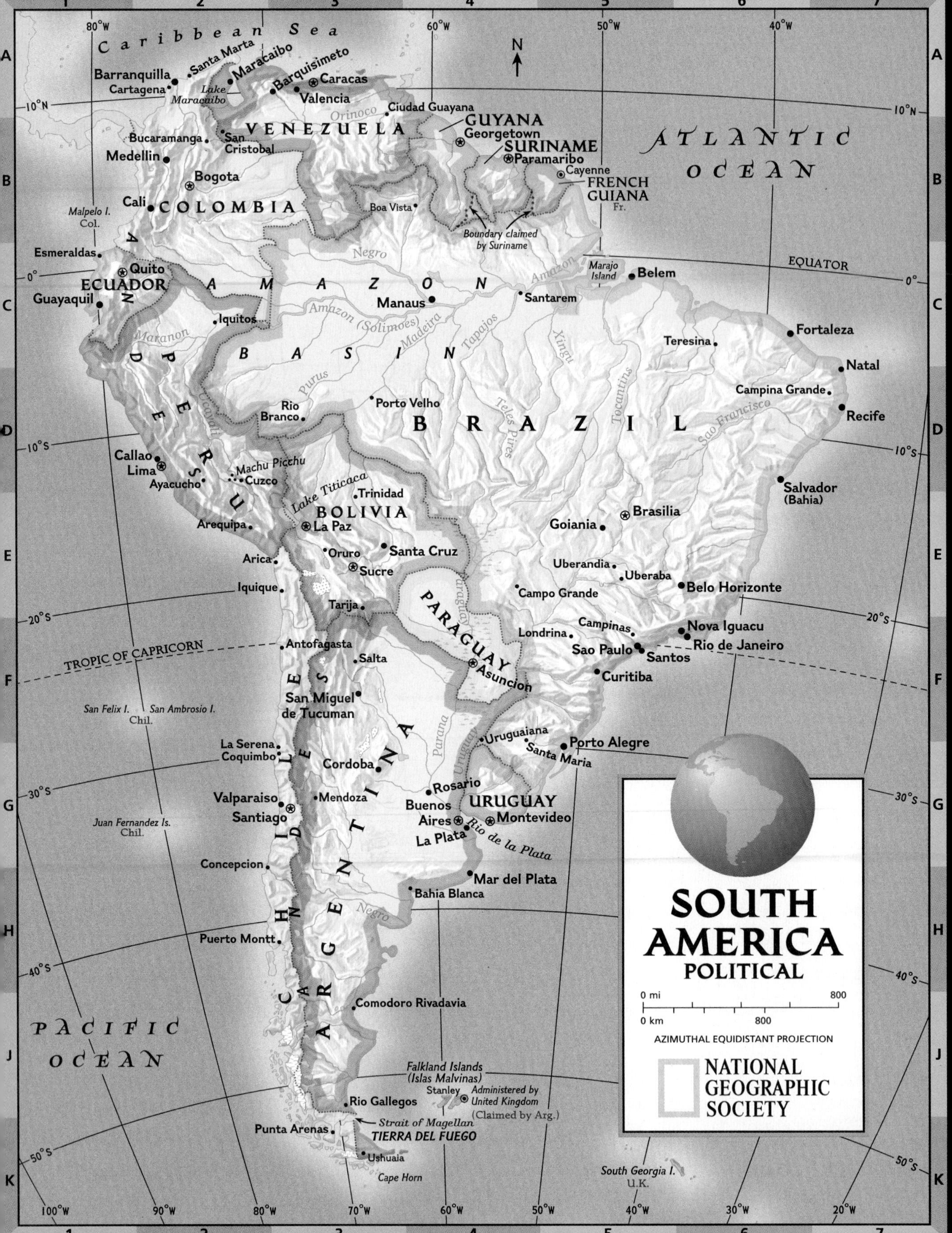
SOUTH AMERICA
POLITICAL
AZIMUTHAL EQUIDISTANT PROJECTION
NATIONAL GEOGRAPHIC SOCIETY
Caribbean Sea
ATLANTIC OCEAN
PACIFIC OCEAN
VENEZUELA
GUYANA
SURINAME
FRENCH GUIANA
Fr.
COLOMBIA
ECUADOR
PERU
BRAZIL
BOLIVIA
PARAGUAY
CHILE
ARGENTINA
URUGUAY
AMAZON BASIN
ANDES
Barranquilla
Cartagena
Santa Marta
Maracaibo
Lake Maracaibo
Barquisimeto
Caracas
Valencia
Orinoco
Ciudad Guayana
Georgetown
Paramaribo
Cayenne
Bucaramanga
San Cristobal
Medellin
Bogota
Cali
Malpelo I.
Col.
Boa Vista
Boundary claimed by Suriname
Esmeraldas
Quito
Guayaquil
Negro
Amazon
Marajo Island
Belem
EQUATOR
Manaus
Santarem
Iquitos
Maranon
Amazon (Solimoes)
Madeira
Tapajos
Xingu
Fortaleza
Teresina
Natal
Purus
Campina Grande
Recife
Rio Branco
Porto Velho
Ucayali
Teles Pires
Tocantins
Sao Francisco
Callao
Lima
Machu Picchu
Cuzco
Ayacucho
Lake Titicaca
Trinidad
Salvador (Bahia)
Brasilia
Goiania
Arequipa
La Paz
Santa Cruz
Oruro
Sucre
Arica
Uberlandia
Uberaba
Belo Horizonte
Iquique
Campo Grande
Tarija
Paraguay
Campinas
Nova Iguacu
Londrina
Rio de Janeiro
Sao Paulo
Santos
TROPIC OF CAPRICORN
Antofagasta
Salta
Asuncion
Curitiba
San Felix I.
San Ambrosio I.
Chil.
San Miguel de Tucuman
Parana
Uruguay
Uruguaiana
Porto Alegre
La Serena
Coquimbo
Santa Maria
Cordoba
Rosario
Valparaiso
Mendoza
Buenos Aires
Montevideo
Santiago
Juan Fernandez Is.
Chil.
La Plata
Rio de la Plata
Concepcion
Mar del Plata
Bahia Blanca
Negro
Puerto Montt
Comodoro Rivadavia
Falkland Islands (Islas Malvinas)
Stanley
Administered by United Kingdom
(Claimed by Arg.)
Rio Gallegos
Strait of Magellan
Punta Arenas
TIERRA DEL FUEGO
Ushuaia
Cape Horn
South Georgia I.
U.K.
0 mi 800
0 km 800
10°N
0°
10°S
20°S
30°S
40°S
50°S
100°W
90°W
80°W
70°W
60°W
50°W
40°W
30°W
20°W
N

SOUTH AMERICA
PHYSICAL
0 mi 800
0 km 800
AZIMUTHAL EQUIDISTANT PROJECTION
NATIONAL GEOGRAPHIC SOCIETY
Caribbean Sea
ATLANTIC OCEAN
PACIFIC OCEAN
Caracas
Lake Maracaibo
Orinoco
VENEZUELA
LLANOS
GUYANA
Georgetown
SURINAME
Paramaribo
Cayenne
FRENCH GUIANA
Angel Falls
Total drop=
3,212 ft 979 m
Bogota
COLOMBIA
GUIANA HIGHLANDS
Boundary claimed by Suriname
Malpelo I.
Quito
ECUADOR
Negro
Amazon
Marajo Island
EQUATOR
AMAZON
Selvas
BASIN
Madeira
Tapajos
Xingu
Purus
Ucayali
Teles Pires
Tocantins
BRAZIL
Sao Francisco
ANDES
Lima
Machu Picchu
Lake Titicaca
MATO GROSSO PLATEAU
BRAZILIAN HIGHLANDS
Brasilia
BOLIVIA
La Paz
Altiplano
Sucre
Salar de Uyuni
PARAGUAY
Paraguay
GRAN CHACO
TROPIC OF CAPRICORN
Iguazu Falls
Asuncion
San Felix I.
San Ambrosio I.
Parana
Uruguay
ARGENTINA
PAMPAS
Aconcagua
22,834 ft
6,960 m
Santiago
Buenos Aires
URUGUAY
Montevideo
Juan Fernandez Is.
Rio de la Plata
Negro
PATAGONIA
-131 ft
-40 m
Valdes Peninsula
Chiloe Island
Gulf of San Jorge
Taitao Peninsula
Wellington I.
Falkland Islands (Islas Malvinas)
Stanley
Strait of Magellan
Tierra del Fuego
Cape Horn
South Georgia I.

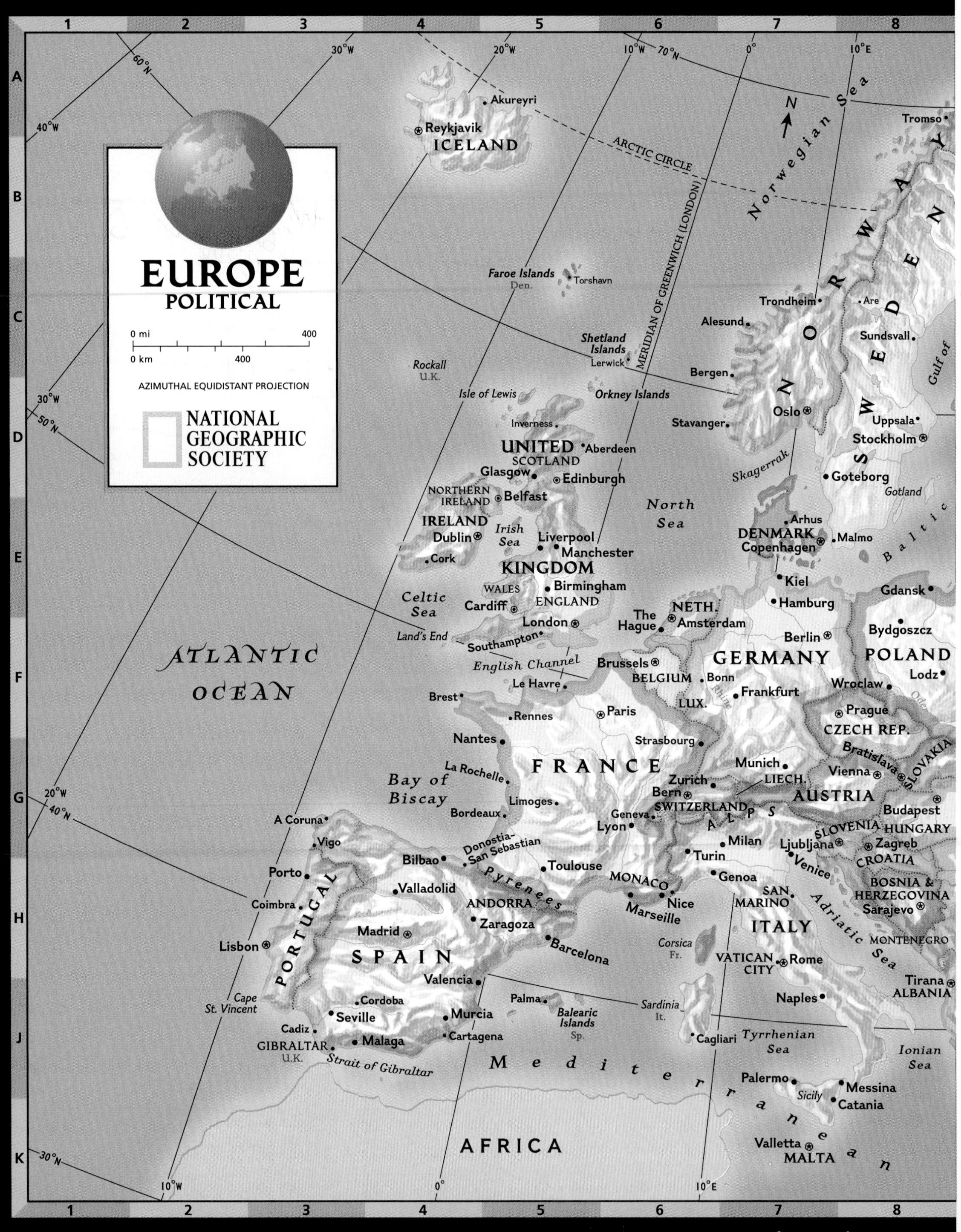

EUROPE
POLITICAL
0 mi 400
0 km 400
AZIMUTHAL EQUIDISTANT PROJECTION
NATIONAL GEOGRAPHIC SOCIETY
ATLANTIC OCEAN
ICELAND
Reykjavik
Akureyri
ARCTIC CIRCLE
Norwegian Sea
MERIDIAN OF GREENWICH (LONDON)
Faroe Islands
Den.
Torshavn
Shetland Islands
Lerwick
Orkney Islands
Rockall
U.K.
Isle of Lewis
Inverness
UNITED KINGDOM
SCOTLAND
Aberdeen
Glasgow
Edinburgh
NORTHERN IRELAND
Belfast
IRELAND
Dublin
Cork
Irish Sea
Liverpool
Manchester
WALES
Birmingham
ENGLAND
Cardiff
London
Celtic Sea
Land's End
Southampton
English Channel
North Sea
NORWAY
SWEDEN
Tromso
Trondheim
Are
Alesund
Sundsvall
Bergen
Oslo
Stavanger
Uppsala
Stockholm
Skagerrak
Goteborg
Gotland
Gulf of
DENMARK
Arhus
Copenhagen
Malmo
Baltic
Kiel
Hamburg
Gdansk
NETH.
The Hague
Amsterdam
Berlin
Bydgoszcz
GERMANY
POLAND
Brussels
BELGIUM
Bonn
Rhine
Frankfurt
Wroclaw
Lodz
Oder
LUX.
Prague
CZECH REP.
Le Havre
Brest
Rennes
Paris
Strasbourg
Nantes
FRANCE
Munich
Bratislava
SLOVAKIA
Vienna
La Rochelle
Zurich
LIECH.
Bay of Biscay
Bern
AUSTRIA
Limoges
SWITZERLAND
Budapest
Bordeaux
Geneva
Lyon
ALPS
SLOVENIA
HUNGARY
A Coruna
Milan
Ljubljana
Zagreb
Vigo
Donostia-San Sebastian
Bilbao
Turin
Venice
CROATIA
Toulouse
Porto
Pyrenees
MONACO
Genoa
BOSNIA & HERZEGOVINA
Valladolid
SAN MARINO
Sarajevo
Coimbra
ANDORRA
Nice
Marseille
Adriatic Sea
PORTUGAL
Zaragoza
ITALY
MONTENEGRO
Madrid
Lisbon
Corsica
Fr.
SPAIN
Barcelona
VATICAN CITY
Rome
Valencia
Tirana
ALBANIA
Cape St. Vincent
Cordoba
Palma
Balearic Islands
Sp.
Sardinia
It.
Naples
Seville
Murcia
Cadiz
Cartagena
Cagliari
Tyrrhenian Sea
Ionian Sea
GIBRALTAR
U.K.
Malaga
Strait of Gibraltar
Mediterranean
Palermo
Sicily
Messina
Catania
Valletta
MALTA
AFRICA

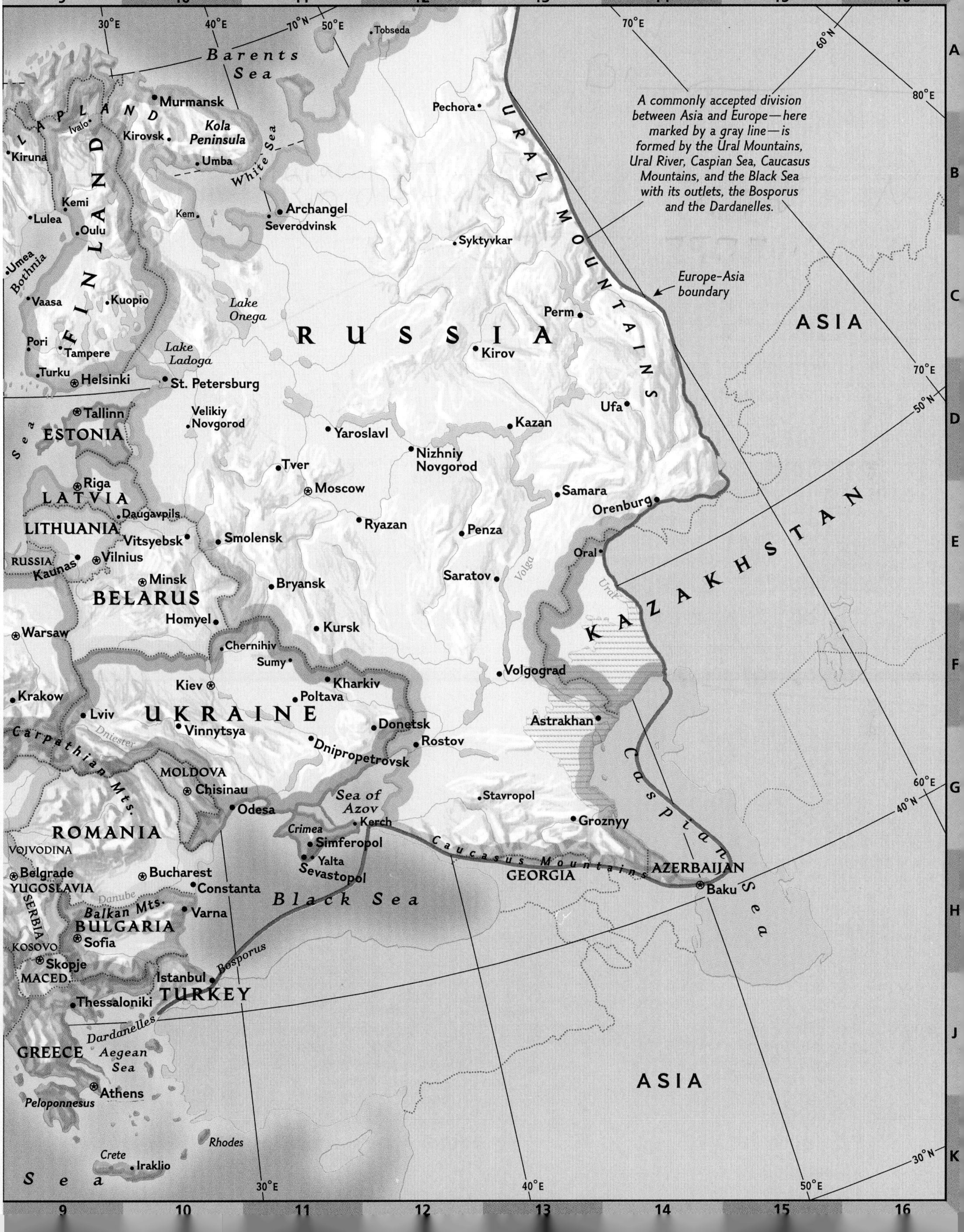
A commonly accepted division between Asia and Europe—here marked by a gray line—is formed by the Ural Mountains, Ural River, Caspian Sea, Caucasus Mountains, and the Black Sea with its outlets, the Bosporus and the Dardanelles.
Europe-Asia boundary
Barents Sea
White Sea
Kola Peninsula
LAPLAND
FINLAND
Gulf of Bothnia
RUSSIA
URAL MOUNTAINS
ASIA
KAZAKHSTAN
Caspian Sea
Caucasus Mountains
Black Sea
Sea of Azov
Crimea
Bosporus
Dardanelles
Aegean Sea
ESTONIA
LATVIA
LITHUANIA
BELARUS
UKRAINE
MOLDOVA
ROMANIA
BULGARIA
YUGOSLAVIA
SERBIA
VOJVODINA
KOSOVO
MACED.
GREECE
TURKEY
GEORGIA
AZERBAIJAN
Carpathian Mts.
Balkan Mts.
Lake Onega
Lake Ladoga
Peloponnesus
Murmansk
Kirovsk
Umba
Ivalo
Kiruna
Kemi
Lulea
Oulu
Umea
Vaasa
Kuopio
Pori
Tampere
Turku
Helsinki
St. Petersburg
Kem
Archangel
Severodvinsk
Tobseda
Pechora
Syktyvkar
Perm
Kirov
Ufa
Kazan
Yaroslavl
Nizhniy Novgorod
Tver
Moscow
Velikiy Novgorod
Tallinn
Riga
Daugavpils
Vitsyebsk
Smolensk
Kaunas
Vilnius
Minsk
Ryazan
Penza
Samara
Orenburg
Oral
Saratov
Volga
Ural
Bryansk
Homyel
Warsaw
Kursk
Chernihiv
Sumy
Kharkiv
Kiev
Poltava
Volgograd
Krakow
Lviv
Vinnytsya
Dniester
Donetsk
Astrakhan
Dnipropetrovsk
Rostov
Chisinau
Odesa
Stavropol
Kerch
Groznyy
Simferopol
Yalta
Sevastopol
Belgrade
Bucharest
Constanta
Danube
Varna
Baku
Sofia
Skopje
Istanbul
Thessaloniki
Athens
Rhodes
Crete
Iraklio
Sea
30°E
40°E
50°E
70°E
80°E
70°N
60°N
50°N
40°N
30°N
60°E
9 10 11 12 13 14 15 16
A B C D E F G H J K

EUROPE
PHYSICAL
0 mi 400
0 km 400
AZIMUTHAL EQUIDISTANT PROJECTION
NATIONAL GEOGRAPHIC SOCIETY
Reykjavik
ICELAND
ARCTIC CIRCLE
Norwegian Sea
Faroe Islands
Shetland Islands
Orkney Islands
Outer Hebrides
MERIDIAN OF GREENWICH (LONDON)
SCANDINAVIA
NORWAY
SWEDEN
Gulf of
Oslo
Stockholm
Highlands
British Isles
Edinburgh
Belfast
UNITED KINGDOM
IRELAND
Dublin
Irish Sea
Great Britain
Cardiff
London
North Sea
Jutland
DENMARK
Copenhagen
Zealand
Baltic
Amsterdam
NETH.
Berlin
NORTHE
POLAND
ATLANTIC OCEAN
English Channel
BELGIUM
Brussels
GERMANY
Rhine
Oder
Elbe
LUX.
Seine
Paris
Brittany
Prague
CZECH REP.
Loire
FRANCE
Danube
Bratislava
SLOVAKIA
Bay of Biscay
Mont Blanc 15,771 ft 4,807 m
Bern
SWITZ.
LIECH.
Vienna
AUSTRIA
Budapest
HUNGARY
ALPS
Massif Central
Rhone
SLOVENIA
Drava
Ljubljana
Zagreb
CROATIA
Sava
Cantabrian Mountains
Pyrenees
MONACO
Po
BOSNIA & HERZEGOVINA
Sarajevo
Douro
PORTUGAL
IBERIAN PENINSULA
SPAIN
Madrid
Tagus
Lisbon
Ebro
ANDORRA
Riviera
SAN MARINO
Apennines
Adriatic Sea
Corsica
ITALY
VATICAN CITY
Rome
Tirana
ALBANIA
Sardinia
Tyrrhenian Sea
Balearic Islands
Baetic Mountains
GIBRALTAR
Strait of Gibraltar
Mediterranean
Ionian Sea
Sicily
Etna 10,902 ft 3,323 m
Valletta
MALTA
AFRICA
60°N
50°N
40°N
30°N
40°W
30°W
20°W
10°W
0°
10°E
70°N

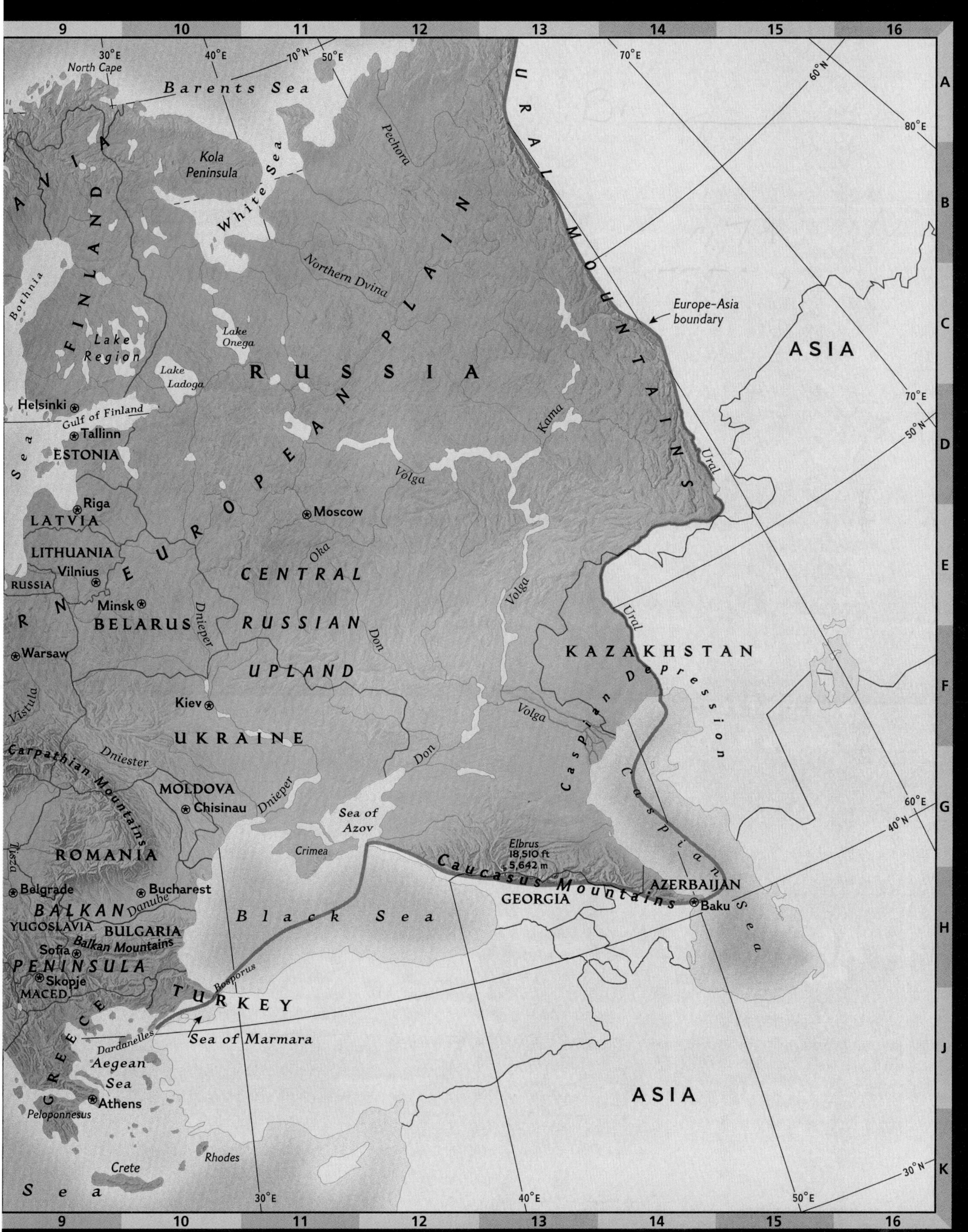

Barents Sea
North Cape
Kola Peninsula
White Sea
Pechora
URAL MOUNTAINS
Northern Dvina
Europe-Asia boundary
ASIA
FINLAND
Bothnia
Lake Region
Lake Onega
Lake Ladoga
RUSSIA
Helsinki
Gulf of Finland
Tallinn
ESTONIA
Kama
Volga
Ural
Riga
LATVIA
Moscow
LITHUANIA
Oka
Vilnius
RUSSIA
CENTRAL RUSSIAN UPLAND
Minsk
BELARUS
Dnieper
Don
Warsaw
NORTHERN EUROPEAN PLAIN
KAZAKHSTAN
Caspian Depression
Vistula
Kiev
UKRAINE
Carpathian Mountains
Dniester
MOLDOVA
Chisinau
Sea of Azov
Caspian Sea
Elbrus 18,510 ft 5,642 m
Crimea
ROMANIA
Caucasus Mountains
AZERBAIJAN
GEORGIA
Baku
Belgrade
Bucharest
BALKAN PENINSULA
Danube
Black Sea
YUGOSLAVIA
BULGARIA
Balkan Mountains
Sofia
Skopje
MACED.
Bosporus
TURKEY
GREECE
Dardanelles
Sea of Marmara
Aegean Sea
Athens
Peloponnesus
ASIA
Rhodes
Crete
Sea

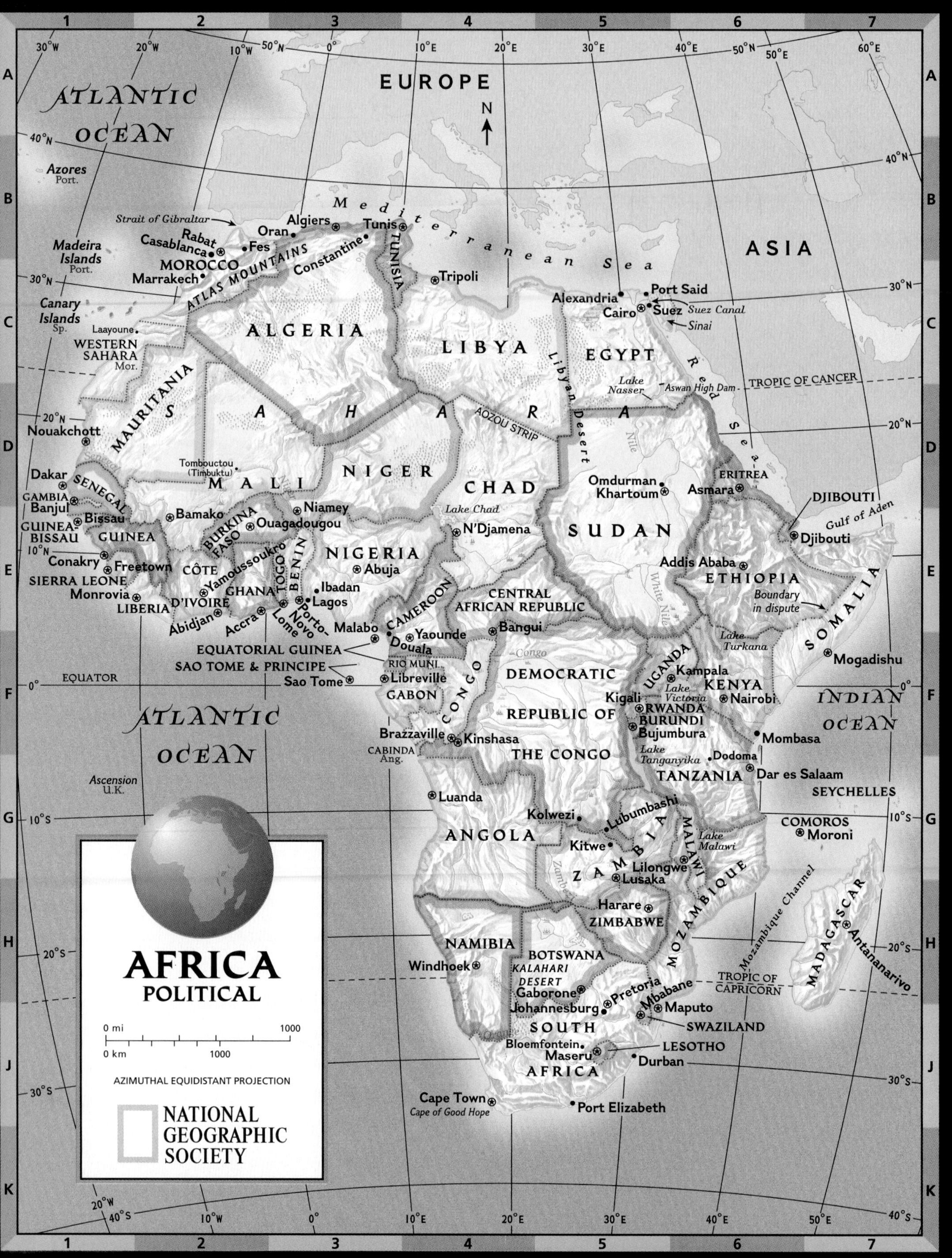
AFRICA
POLITICAL
EUROPE
ASIA
ATLANTIC OCEAN
INDIAN OCEAN
Mediterranean Sea
Red Sea
Gulf of Aden
Mozambique Channel
SAHARA
ATLAS MOUNTAINS
Libyan Desert
KALAHARI DESERT
TROPIC OF CANCER
TROPIC OF CAPRICORN
EQUATOR
Strait of Gibraltar
Suez Canal
Sinai
Lake Nasser
Aswan High Dam
AOZOU STRIP
Lake Chad
Lake Turkana
Lake Victoria
Lake Tanganyika
Lake Malawi
Nile
White Nile
Congo
Zambezi
Boundary in dispute
Azores Port.
Madeira Islands Port.
Canary Islands Sp.
Ascension U.K.
CABINDA Ang.
RIO MUNI
Cape of Good Hope
MOROCCO
ALGERIA
TUNISIA
LIBYA
EGYPT
WESTERN SAHARA Mor.
MAURITANIA
MALI
NIGER
CHAD
SUDAN
ERITREA
DJIBOUTI
ETHIOPIA
SOMALIA
SENEGAL
GAMBIA
GUINEA-BISSAU
GUINEA
SIERRA LEONE
LIBERIA
CÔTE D'IVOIRE
BURKINA FASO
GHANA
TOGO
BENIN
NIGERIA
CAMEROON
CENTRAL AFRICAN REPUBLIC
EQUATORIAL GUINEA
SAO TOME & PRINCIPE
GABON
CONGO
DEMOCRATIC REPUBLIC OF THE CONGO
UGANDA
KENYA
RWANDA
BURUNDI
TANZANIA
SEYCHELLES
COMOROS
ANGOLA
ZAMBIA
MALAWI
MOZAMBIQUE
ZIMBABWE
NAMIBIA
BOTSWANA
SOUTH AFRICA
SWAZILAND
LESOTHO
MADAGASCAR
Rabat
Casablanca
Fes
Marrakech
Oran
Algiers
Tunis
Constantine
Tripoli
Alexandria
Port Said
Cairo
Suez
Laayoune
Nouakchott
Tombouctou (Timbuktu)
Dakar
Banjul
Bissau
Conakry
Freetown
Monrovia
Bamako
Ouagadougou
Niamey
Yamoussoukro
Abidjan
Accra
Lome
Porto-Novo
Lagos
Ibadan
Abuja
N'Djamena
Omdurman
Khartoum
Asmara
Djibouti
Addis Ababa
Mogadishu
Malabo
Yaounde
Douala
Bangui
Libreville
Sao Tome
Brazzaville
Kinshasa
Kampala
Kigali
Bujumbura
Nairobi
Mombasa
Dodoma
Dar es Salaam
Moroni
Luanda
Kolwezi
Lubumbashi
Kitwe
Lilongwe
Lusaka
Harare
Windhoek
Gaborone
Pretoria
Johannesburg
Mbabane
Maputo
Bloemfontein
Maseru
Durban
Cape Town
Port Elizabeth
Antananarivo
N
0 mi 1000
0 km 1000
AZIMUTHAL EQUIDISTANT PROJECTION
NATIONAL GEOGRAPHIC SOCIETY

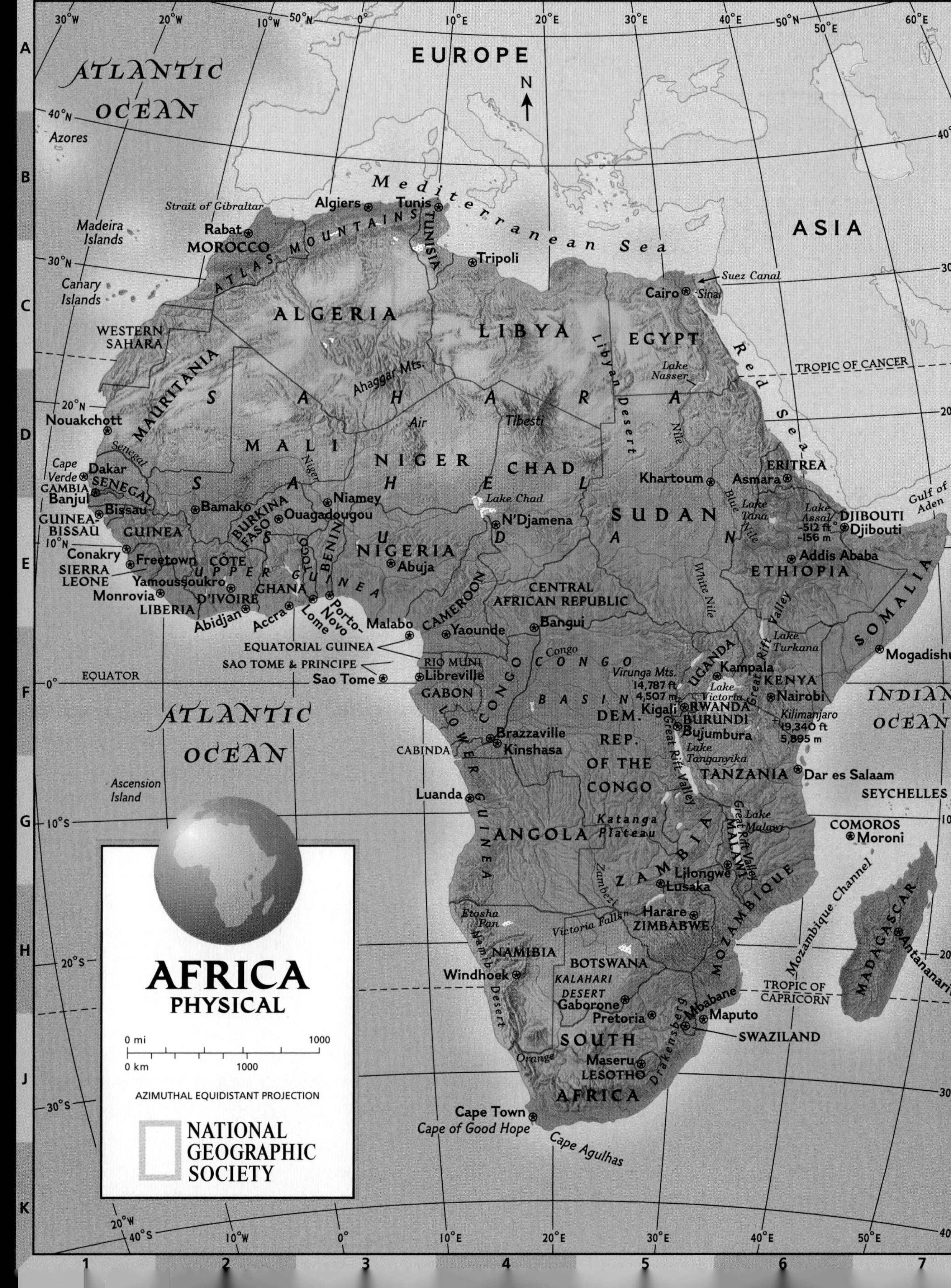

AFRICA
PHYSICAL
0 mi
1000
0 km
1000
AZIMUTHAL EQUIDISTANT PROJECTION
NATIONAL GEOGRAPHIC SOCIETY
EUROPE
ASIA
N
ATLANTIC OCEAN
ATLANTIC OCEAN
INDIAN OCEAN
Mediterranean Sea
Red Sea
Gulf of Aden
Mozambique Channel
Azores
Madeira Islands
Canary Islands
Strait of Gibraltar
Cape Verde
Ascension Island
SEYCHELLES
COMOROS
Moroni
Suez Canal
Sinai
TROPIC OF CANCER
EQUATOR
TROPIC OF CAPRICORN
Algiers
Tunis
TUNISIA
Rabat
MOROCCO
ATLAS MOUNTAINS
Tripoli
Cairo
ALGERIA
LIBYA
EGYPT
WESTERN SAHARA
MAURITANIA
Ahaggar Mts.
SAHARA
Libyan Desert
Lake Nasser
Nile
Nouakchott
Air
Tibesti
MALI
NIGER
CHAD
Senegal
Niger
Dakar
SENEGAL
GAMBIA
Banjul
Bissau
GUINEA-BISSAU
GUINEA
Bamako
BURKINA FASO
Ouagadougou
Niamey
SAHEL
Lake Chad
N'Djamena
Khartoum
Asmara
ERITREA
SUDAN
Blue Nile
Lake Tana
Lake Assal -512 ft -156 m
DJIBOUTI
Djibouti
Conakry
Freetown
SIERRA LEONE
Monrovia
LIBERIA
CÔTE D'IVOIRE
Yamoussoukro
Abidjan
GHANA
Accra
TOGO
Lome
BENIN
Porto-Novo
UPPER GUINEA
NIGERIA
Abuja
Addis Ababa
ETHIOPIA
SOMALIA
Mogadishu
White Nile
CENTRAL AFRICAN REPUBLIC
Bangui
CAMEROON
Yaounde
Malabo
EQUATORIAL GUINEA
SAO TOME & PRINCIPE
Sao Tome
RIO MUNI
Libreville
GABON
CONGO
Congo
CONGO BASIN
Virunga Mts. 14,787 ft 4,507 m
UGANDA
Kampala
Lake Turkana
Great Rift Valley
KENYA
Nairobi
Lake Victoria
Kigali
RWANDA
BURUNDI
Bujumbura
Kilimanjaro 19,340 ft 5,895 m
Brazzaville
Kinshasa
CABINDA
LOWER GUINEA
DEM. REP. OF THE CONGO
Lake Tanganyika
TANZANIA
Dar es Salaam
Luanda
ANGOLA
Katanga Plateau
ZAMBIA
Lake Malawi
MALAWI
Lilongwe
Lusaka
Zambezi
MOZAMBIQUE
MADAGASCAR
Antananarivo
Etosha Pan
Victoria Falls
Harare
ZIMBABWE
NAMIBIA
Namib Desert
Windhoek
BOTSWANA
KALAHARI DESERT
Gaborone
Pretoria
Mbabane
Maputo
SWAZILAND
Drakensberg
SOUTH AFRICA
Orange
Maseru
LESOTHO
Cape Town
Cape of Good Hope
Cape Agulhas

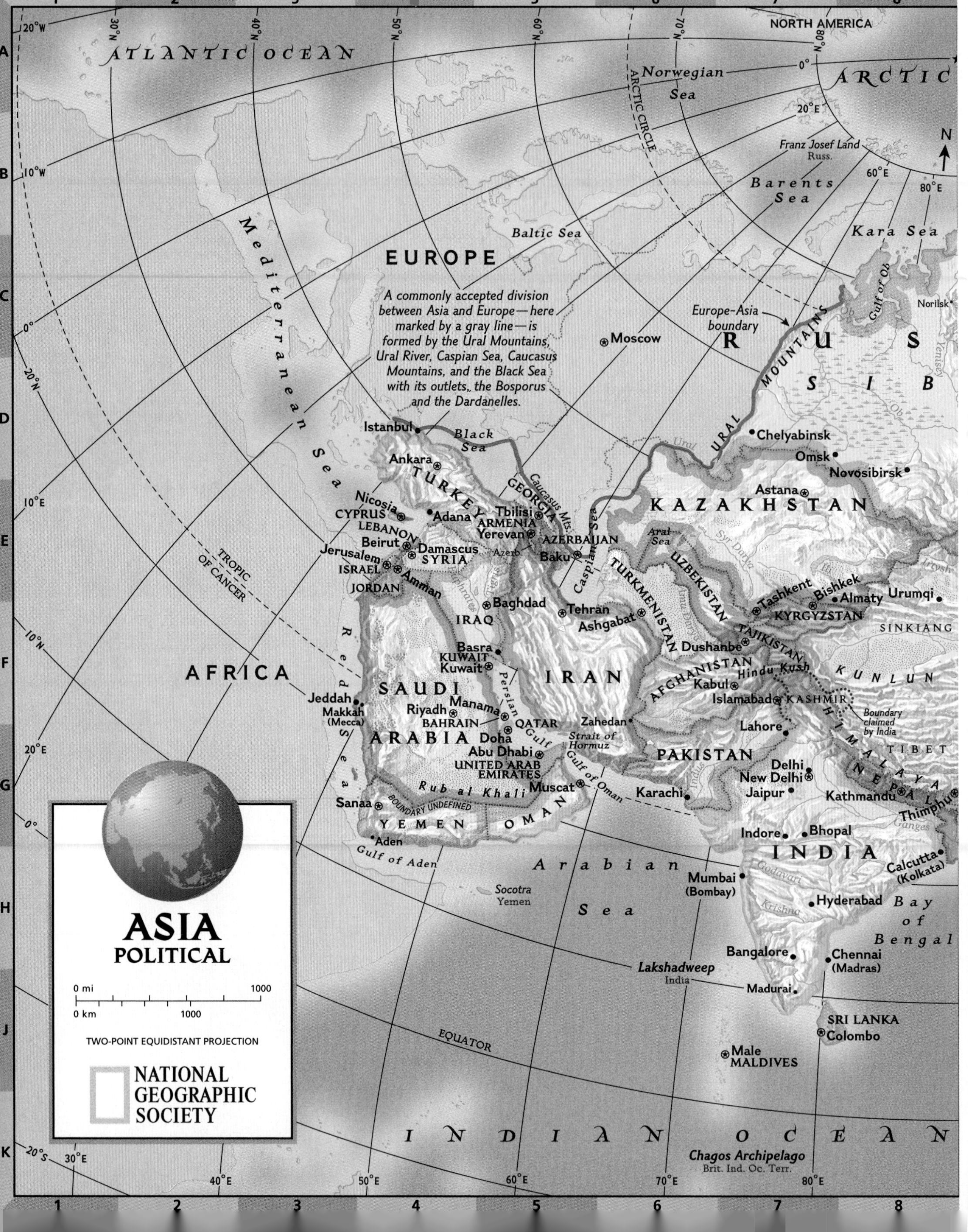

ASIA
POLITICAL
0 mi
1000
0 km
1000
TWO-POINT EQUIDISTANT PROJECTION
NATIONAL GEOGRAPHIC SOCIETY
NORTH AMERICA
ATLANTIC OCEAN
ARCTIC
Norwegian Sea
ARCTIC CIRCLE
Franz Josef Land
Russ.
Barents Sea
Kara Sea
Baltic Sea
EUROPE
A commonly accepted division between Asia and Europe—here marked by a gray line—is formed by the Ural Mountains, Ural River, Caspian Sea, Caucasus Mountains, and the Black Sea with its outlets, the Bosporus and the Dardanelles.
Europe-Asia boundary
URAL MOUNTAINS
Gulf of Ob
Norilsk
Moscow
RUS
SIB
Mediterranean Sea
Istanbul
Black Sea
Ankara
TURKEY
Chelyabinsk
Omsk
Novosibirsk
Astana
KAZAKHSTAN
Nicosia
CYPRUS
Adana
GEORGIA
Tbilisi
ARMENIA
Yerevan
Caucasus Mts.
AZERBAIJAN
Azerb.
Baku
Caspian Sea
LEBANON
Beirut
Damascus
SYRIA
Jerusalem
ISRAEL
Amman
JORDAN
Aral Sea
Syr Darya
UZBEKISTAN
TURKMENISTAN
Amu Darya
Tashkent
Bishkek
Almaty
Urumqi
KYRGYZSTAN
SINKIANG
TROPIC OF CANCER
Baghdad
IRAQ
Euphrates
Tigris
Tehran
Ashgabat
Dushanbe
TAJIKISTAN
Basra
KUWAIT
Kuwait
IRAN
AFGHANISTAN
Kabul
Hindu Kush
KUNLUN
AFRICA
Red Sea
Jeddah
Makkah (Mecca)
SAUDI ARABIA
Riyadh
Manama
BAHRAIN
QATAR
Doha
Persian Gulf
Zahedan
Islamabad
KASHMIR
Boundary claimed by India
Lahore
Strait of Hormuz
Abu Dhabi
UNITED ARAB EMIRATES
PAKISTAN
Indus
TIBET
Delhi
New Delhi
Jaipur
HIMALAYA
NEPAL
Kathmandu
Thimphu
Rub al Khali
Muscat
Gulf of Oman
Karachi
Sanaa
BOUNDARY UNDEFINED
YEMEN
OMAN
Aden
Gulf of Aden
Indore
Bhopal
Ganges
INDIA
Calcutta (Kolkata)
Arabian Sea
Mumbai (Bombay)
Godavari
Socotra
Yemen
Hyderabad
Krishna
Bay of Bengal
Bangalore
Chennai (Madras)
Lakshadweep
India
Madurai
SRI LANKA
Colombo
EQUATOR
Male
MALDIVES
INDIAN OCEAN
Chagos Archipelago
Brit. Ind. Oc. Terr.

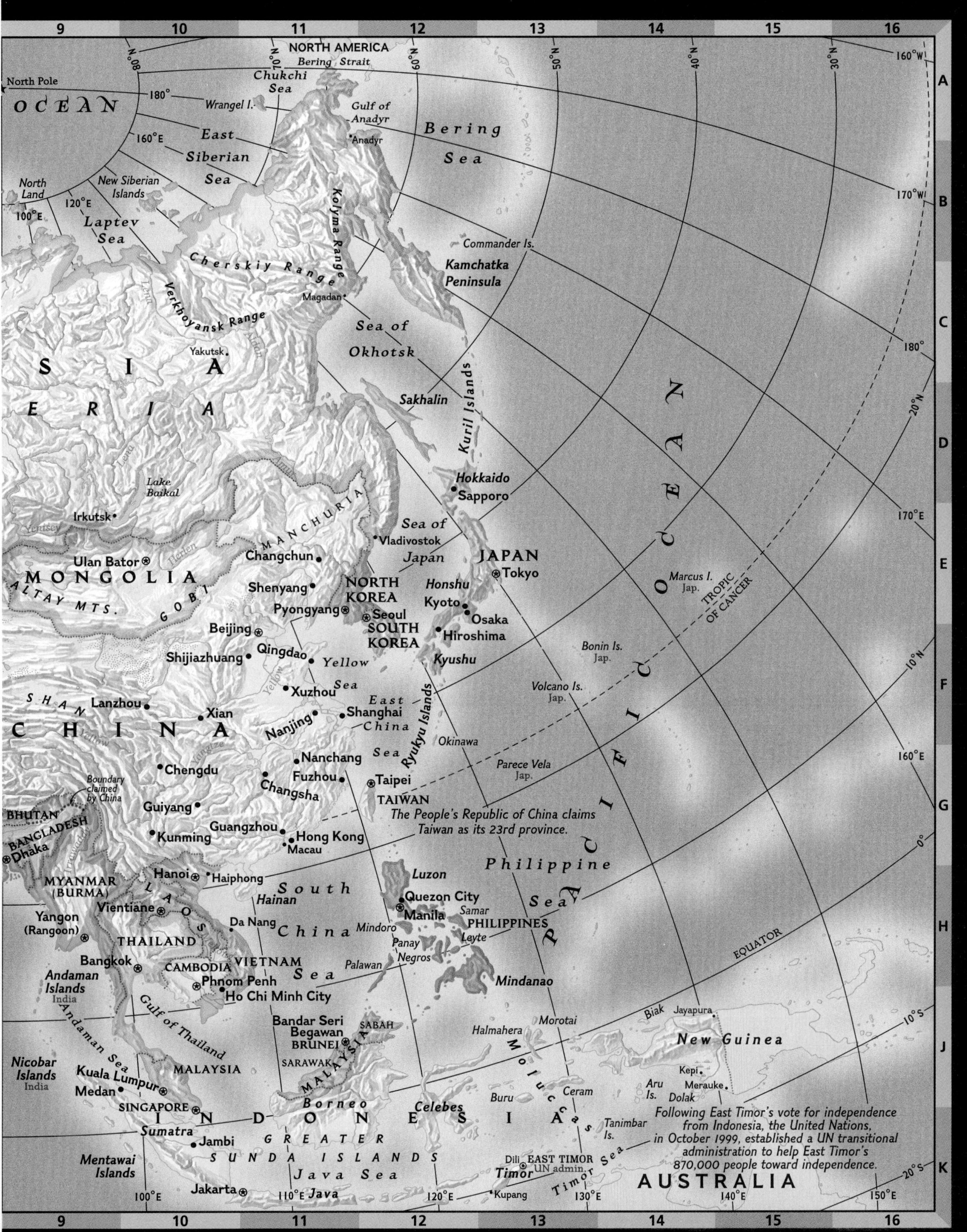
NORTH AMERICA
Bering Strait
Chukchi Sea
North Pole
OCEAN
Wrangel I.
Gulf of Anadyr
Anadyr
Bering Sea
East Siberian Sea
North Land
New Siberian Islands
Laptev Sea
Kolyma Range
Cherskiy Range
Verkhoyansk Range
Commander Is.
Kamchatka Peninsula
Magadan
Sea of Okhotsk
Yakutsk
Sakhalin
Kuril Islands
Lake Baikal
Irkutsk
Hokkaido
Sapporo
MANCHURIA
Sea of Japan
Vladivostok
JAPAN
Tokyo
Changchun
Ulan Bator
MONGOLIA
ALTAY MTS.
GOBI
Shenyang
NORTH KOREA
Honshu
Kyoto
Osaka
Pyongyang
Seoul
SOUTH KOREA
Hiroshima
Beijing
Qingdao
Shijiazhuang
Yellow Sea
Kyushu
Xuzhou
East China Sea
Ryukyu Islands
Lanzhou
Xian
Shanghai
Nanjing
CHINA
Okinawa
Nanchang
Chengdu
Fuzhou
Taipei
Changsha
TAIWAN
Boundary claimed by China
BHUTAN
BANGLADESH
Dhaka
Guiyang
Guangzhou
Kunming
Hong Kong
Macau
The People's Republic of China claims Taiwan as its 23rd province.
Marcus I. Jap.
TROPIC OF CANCER
Bonin Is. Jap.
Volcano Is. Jap.
Parece Vela Jap.
PACIFIC OCEAN
Philippine Sea
Luzon
MYANMAR (BURMA)
Hanoi
Haiphong
LAOS
South China Sea
Hainan
Quezon City
Manila
Samar
Vientiane
Yangon (Rangoon)
Da Nang
Mindoro
PHILIPPINES
Leyte
THAILAND
Panay
Negros
Bangkok
CAMBODIA
VIETNAM
Palawan
Mindanao
Andaman Islands India
Phnom Penh
Ho Chi Minh City
Andaman Sea
Gulf of Thailand
Bandar Seri Begawan
BRUNEI
SABAH
Halmahera
Morotai
Biak
Jayapura
New Guinea
Nicobar Islands India
MALAYSIA
SARAWAK
Moluccas
Kuala Lumpur
Medan
Borneo
Celebes
Buru
Ceram
Aru Is.
Kepi
Merauke
Dolak
SINGAPORE
INDONESIA
Sumatra
Jambi
GREATER SUNDA ISLANDS
Java Sea
Java
Jakarta
Mentawai Islands
Tanimbar Is.
Dili
EAST TIMOR
UN admin.
Timor
Timor Sea
Kupang
AUSTRALIA
EQUATOR
Following East Timor's vote for independence from Indonesia, the United Nations, in October 1999, established a UN transitional administration to help East Timor's 870,000 people toward independence.
180°
160°E
120°E
100°E
110°E
130°E
140°E
150°E
160°W
170°W
170°E
160°E
80°N
70°N
60°N
50°N
40°N
30°N
20°N
10°N
0°
10°S
20°S
9
10
11
12
13
14
15
16
A
B
C
D
E
F
G
H
I
J
K

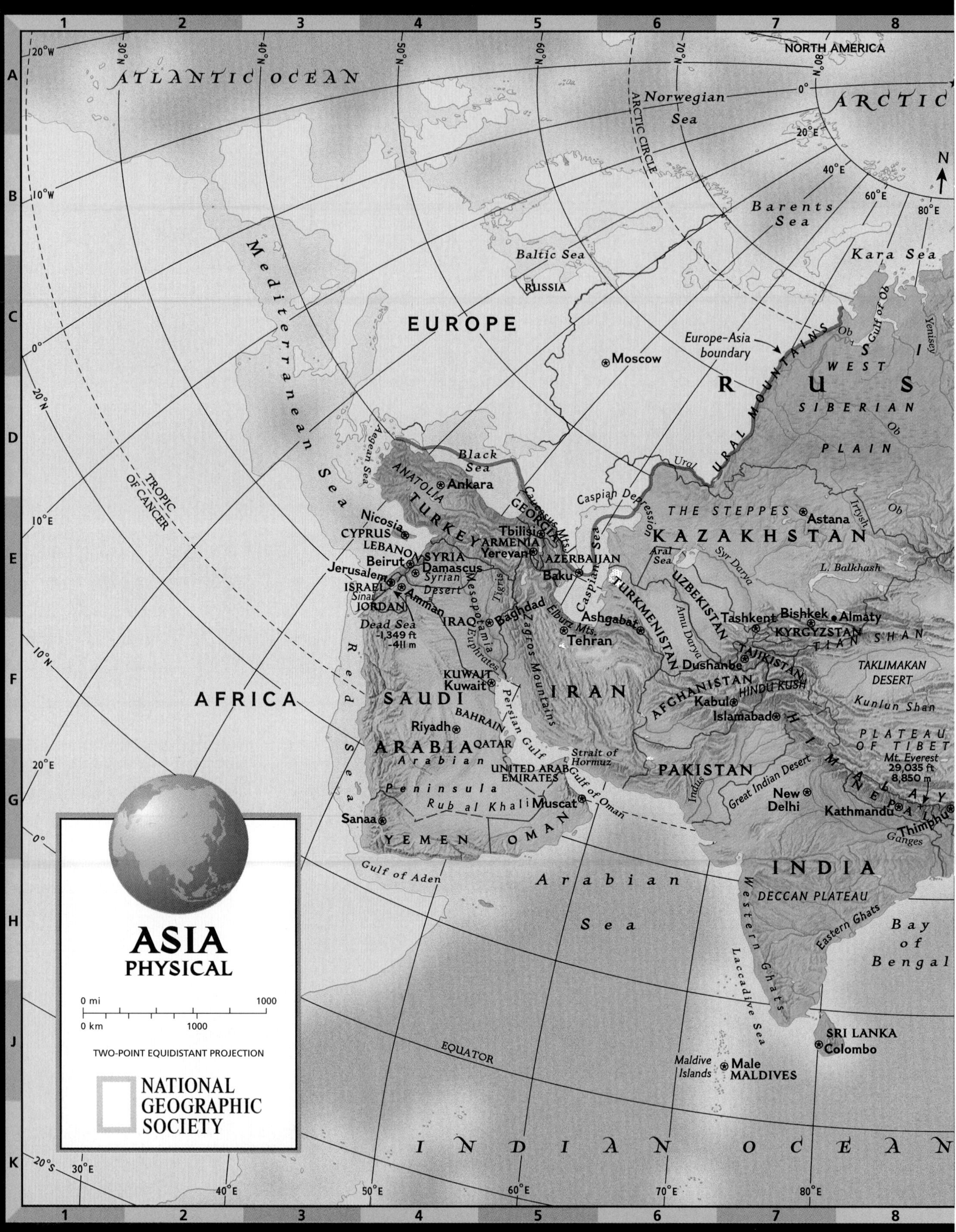
ASIA
PHYSICAL
TWO-POINT EQUIDISTANT PROJECTION
NATIONAL GEOGRAPHIC SOCIETY
ATLANTIC OCEAN
ARCTIC
NORTH AMERICA
Norwegian Sea
Barents Sea
Kara Sea
Baltic Sea
RUSSIA
EUROPE
Moscow
Mediterranean Sea
Europe-Asia boundary
URAL MOUNTAINS
WEST SIBERIAN PLAIN
Black Sea
Caspian Sea
Caspian Depression
Ankara
TURKEY
ANATOLIA
GEORGIA
Tbilisi
ARMENIA
Yerevan
AZERBAIJAN
Baku
Nicosia
CYPRUS
LEBANON
Beirut
SYRIA
Damascus
Syrian Desert
Jerusalem
ISRAEL
JORDAN
Amman
Dead Sea -1,349 ft -411 m
IRAQ
Baghdad
THE STEPPES
Astana
KAZAKHSTAN
Aral Sea
UZBEKISTAN
TURKMENISTAN
Ashgabat
Tehran
IRAN
Tashkent
Bishkek
Almaty
KYRGYZSTAN
TIAN SHAN
TAJIKISTAN
Dushanbe
AFGHANISTAN
Kabul
Islamabad
HINDU KUSH
TAKLIMAKAN DESERT
PLATEAU OF TIBET
Mt. Everest 29,035 ft 8,850 m
AFRICA
Red Sea
KUWAIT
Kuwait
SAUDI ARABIA
Riyadh
BAHRAIN
QATAR
UNITED ARAB EMIRATES
Persian Gulf
Strait of Hormuz
Gulf of Oman
Muscat
OMAN
YEMEN
Sanaa
Gulf of Aden
PAKISTAN
New Delhi
Kathmandu
Thimphu
INDIA
DECCAN PLATEAU
Arabian Sea
Bay of Bengal
SRI LANKA
Colombo
Male
MALDIVES
EQUATOR
INDIAN OCEAN
TROPIC OF CANCER
ARCTIC CIRCLE

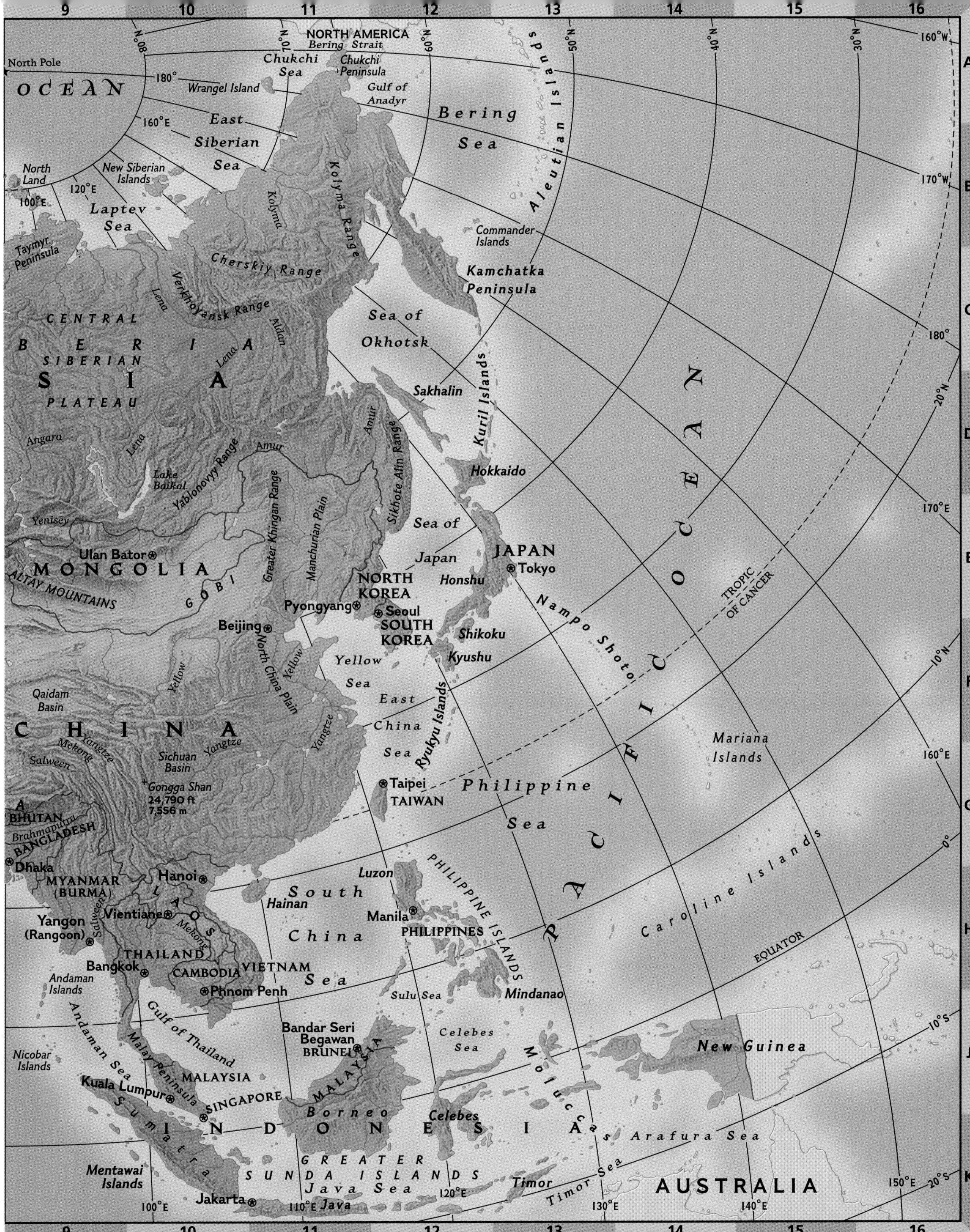

NORTH AMERICA
Bering Strait
Chukchi Sea
Chukchi Peninsula
Gulf of Anadyr
Wrangel Island
North Pole
OCEAN
East Siberian Sea
New Siberian Islands
North Land
Laptev Sea
Taymyr Peninsula
Bering Sea
Aleutian Islands
Commander Islands
Kamchatka Peninsula
Kolyma
Kolyma Range
Cherskiy Range
Verkhoyansk Range
Lena
Aldan
CENTRAL SIBERIAN PLATEAU
SIBERIA
ASIA
Sea of Okhotsk
Sakhalin
Kuril Islands
Hokkaido
Amur
Sikhote Alin Range
Angara
Lake Baikal
Yablonovyy Range
Yenisey
Greater Khingan Range
Manchurian Plain
Sea of Japan
JAPAN
Tokyo
Honshu
Shikoku
Kyushu
Ulan Bator
MONGOLIA
ALTAY MOUNTAINS
GOBI
NORTH KOREA
Pyongyang
Seoul
SOUTH KOREA
Beijing
North China Plain
Yellow
Yellow Sea
East China Sea
Ryukyu Islands
Nampo Shoto
PACIFIC OCEAN
TROPIC OF CANCER
Qaidam Basin
CHINA
Yangtze
Mekong
Salween
Sichuan Basin
Gongga Shan 24,790 ft 7,556 m
Taipei
TAIWAN
Philippine Sea
Mariana Islands
BHUTAN
Brahmaputra
BANGLADESH
Dhaka
MYANMAR (BURMA)
Hanoi
LAOS
Vientiane
Yangon (Rangoon)
Hainan
Luzon
South China Sea
Manila
PHILIPPINES
PHILIPPINE ISLANDS
Caroline Islands
EQUATOR
THAILAND
Bangkok
CAMBODIA
VIETNAM
Phnom Penh
Andaman Islands
Andaman Sea
Sulu Sea
Mindanao
Gulf of Thailand
Malay Peninsula
Nicobar Islands
Bandar Seri Begawan
BRUNEI
MALAYSIA
Celebes Sea
Moluccas
New Guinea
Kuala Lumpur
SINGAPORE
Sumatra
Borneo
Celebes
INDONESIA
Arafura Sea
GREATER SUNDA ISLANDS
Java Sea
Mentawai Islands
Jakarta
Java
Timor
Timor Sea
AUSTRALIA
80°N
70°N
60°N
50°N
40°N
30°N
20°N
10°N
0°
10°S
20°S
180°
160°E
120°E
100°E
110°E
130°E
140°E
150°E
170°E
160°W
170°W
9 10 11 12 13 14 15 16
A B C D E F G H J K

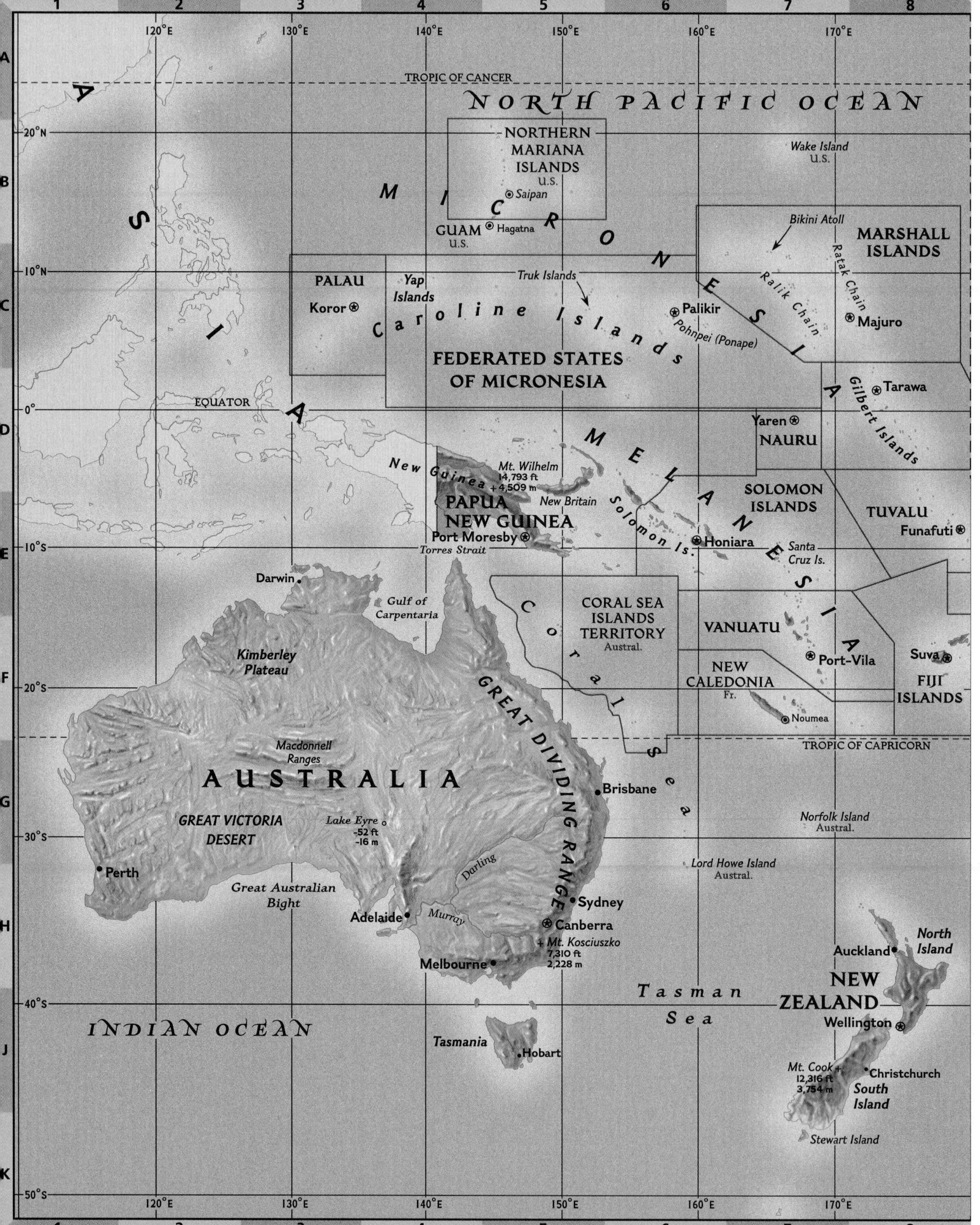
NORTH PACIFIC OCEAN
TROPIC OF CANCER
NORTHERN MARIANA ISLANDS
U.S.
Saipan
GUAM
U.S.
Hagatna
MICRONESIA
Wake Island
U.S.
Bikini Atoll
MARSHALL ISLANDS
Ralik Chain
Ratak Chain
Majuro
PALAU
Koror
Yap Islands
Truk Islands
Caroline Islands
Palikir
Pohnpei (Ponape)
FEDERATED STATES OF MICRONESIA
Tarawa
Gilbert Islands
EQUATOR
ASIA
Yaren
NAURU
MELANESIA
New Guinea
Mt. Wilhelm
14,793 ft
4,509 m
PAPUA NEW GUINEA
New Britain
Solomon Is.
SOLOMON ISLANDS
TUVALU
Funafuti
Port Moresby
Torres Strait
Honiara
Santa Cruz Is.
Darwin
Gulf of Carpentaria
CORAL SEA ISLANDS TERRITORY
Austral.
VANUATU
Port-Vila
Suva
FIJI ISLANDS
Kimberley Plateau
NEW CALEDONIA
Fr.
Noumea
Coral Sea
GREAT DIVIDING RANGE
TROPIC OF CAPRICORN
Macdonnell Ranges
AUSTRALIA
Brisbane
GREAT VICTORIA DESERT
Lake Eyre
-52 ft
-16 m
Norfolk Island
Austral.
Darling
Lord Howe Island
Austral.
Perth
Great Australian Bight
Sydney
Adelaide
Murray
Canberra
Mt. Kosciuszko
7,310 ft
2,228 m
Melbourne
Auckland
North Island
NEW ZEALAND
Tasman Sea
Wellington
INDIAN OCEAN
Tasmania
Hobart
Mt. Cook
12,316 ft
3,754 m
Christchurch
South Island
Stewart Island
120°E
130°E
140°E
150°E
160°E
170°E
20°N
10°N
0°
10°S
20°S
30°S
40°S
50°S
1 2 3 4 5 6 7 8
A B C D E F G H J K

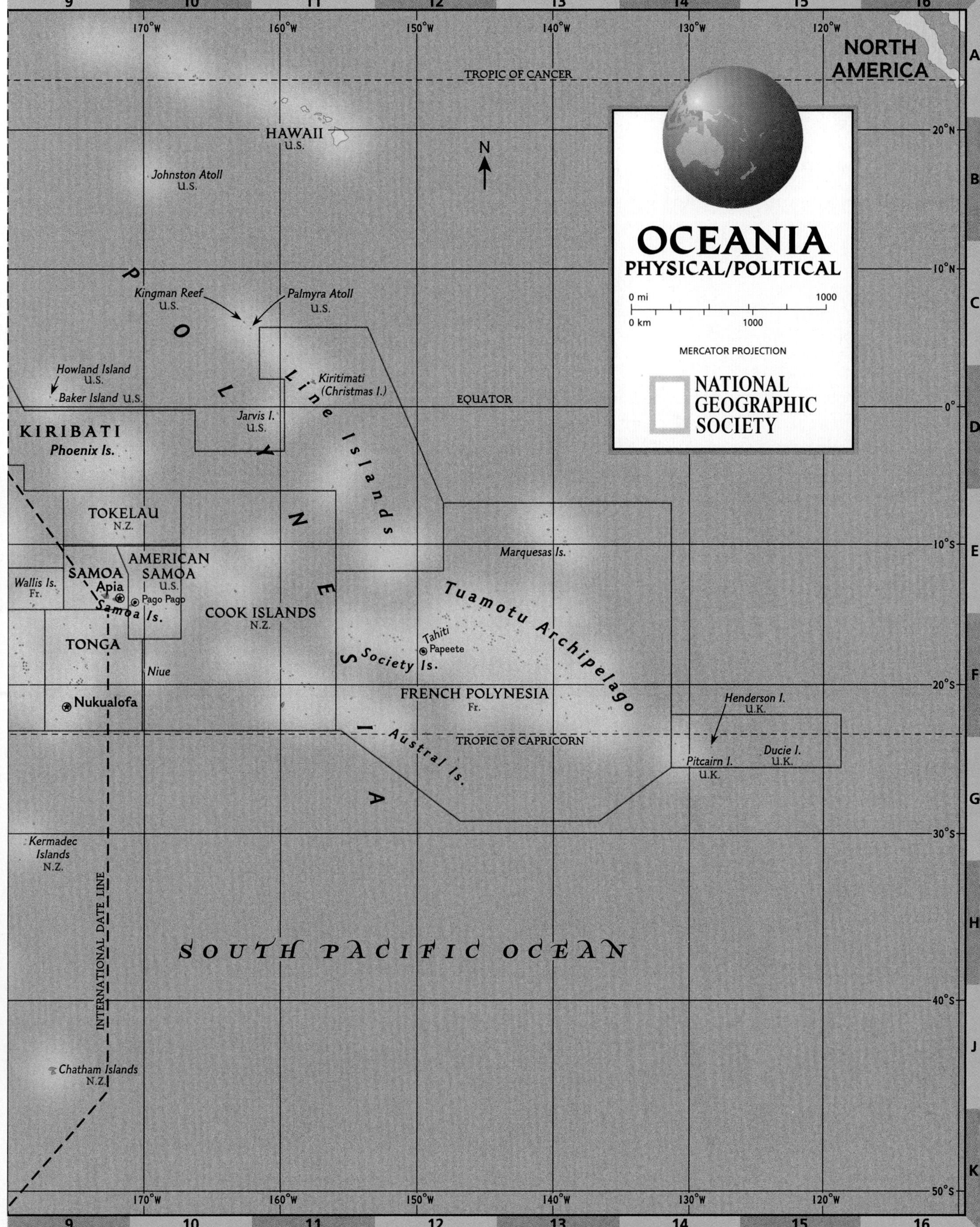

OCEANIA
PHYSICAL/POLITICAL
0 mi 1000
0 km 1000
MERCATOR PROJECTION
NATIONAL GEOGRAPHIC SOCIETY
NORTH AMERICA
TROPIC OF CANCER
HAWAII U.S.
Johnston Atoll U.S.
N
POLYNESIA
Kingman Reef U.S.
Palmyra Atoll U.S.
Howland Island U.S.
Baker Island U.S.
Kiritimati (Christmas I.)
Line Islands
Jarvis I. U.S.
EQUATOR
KIRIBATI
Phoenix Is.
TOKELAU N.Z.
SAMOA
Apia
AMERICAN SAMOA U.S.
Pago Pago
Samoa Is.
Wallis Is. Fr.
COOK ISLANDS N.Z.
TONGA
Niue
Nukualofa
Marquesas Is.
Tuamotu Archipelago
Tahiti
Papeete
Society Is.
FRENCH POLYNESIA Fr.
Austral Is.
TROPIC OF CAPRICORN
Henderson I. U.K.
Pitcairn I. U.K.
Ducie I. U.K.
Kermadec Islands N.Z.
INTERNATIONAL DATE LINE
SOUTH PACIFIC OCEAN
Chatham Islands N.Z.
170°W 160°W 150°W 140°W 130°W 120°W
20°N 10°N 0° 10°S 20°S 30°S 40°S 50°S
9 10 11 12 13 14 15 16
A B C D E F G H J K

RUSSIA
CHINA
MONGOLIA
Ulan Bator
Beijing
Pyongyang
NORTH KOREA
Seoul
SOUTH KOREA
JAPAN
Tokyo
INDIA
MYANMAR (BURMA)
Hanoi
Vientiane
LAOS
VIETNAM
THAILAND
Bangkok
Yangon (Rangoon)
CAMBODIA
Phnom Penh
Taipei
TAIWAN
Manila
PHILIPPINES
Bandar Seri Begawan
BRUNEI
Kuala Lumpur
MALAYSIA
SINGAPORE
INDONESIA
Jakarta
PALAU
Koror
FEDERATED STATES OF MICRONESIA
Palikir
MARSHALL ISLANDS
Majuro
Tarawa
KIRIBATI
Yaren
NAURU
PAPUA NEW GUINEA
Port Moresby
SOLOMON ISLANDS
Honiara
TUVALU
Funafuti
VANUATU
Port-Vila
FIJI ISLANDS
Suva
SAMOA
Apia
TONGA
Nuku'alofa
AUSTRALIA
Canberra
NEW ZEALAND
Wellington
NORTH PACIFIC
INDIAN OCEAN
Sea of Okhotsk
Bering Sea
Sea of Japan
Yellow Sea
East China Sea
South China Sea
Philippine Sea
Sulu Sea
Celebes Sea
Java Sea
Arafura Sea
Coral Sea
Tasman Sea
Andaman Sea
Great Australian Bight
MICRONESIA
MELANESIA
POLYNESIA
TROPIC OF CAPRICORN
105°E
120°E
135°E
150°E
165°E
180°

PACIFIC RIM
PHYSICAL/POLITICAL
0 mi
1500
0 km
1500
MILLER CYLINDRICAL PROJECTION
NATIONAL GEOGRAPHIC SOCIETY
Gulf of Alaska
Kodiak I.
Alexander Archipelago
Queen Charlotte Islands
Vancouver Island
Coast Mountains
ROCKY MOUNTAINS
Cascade Range
GREAT PLAINS
CANADIAN SHIELD
CANADA
Hudson Bay
Ottawa
Great Lakes
Missouri
CENTRAL LOWLAND
Washington
APPALACHIAN MTS.
UNITED STATES
Mississippi
COASTAL PLAIN
ATLANTIC OCEAN
PACIFIC OCEAN
Baja California
Gulf of California
Sierra Madre Occidental
Sierra Madre Oriental
MEXICO
Gulf of Mexico
TROPIC OF CANCER
Hawaiian Islands
HAWAII U.S.
Nassau
BAHAMAS
Havana
CUBA
JAMAICA
HAITI
DOMINICAN REPUBLIC
Santo Domingo
Mexico City
BELIZE
HONDURAS
GUATEMALA
Guatemala City
Tegucigalpa
San Salvador
EL SALVADOR
NICARAGUA
Managua
San Jose
COSTA RICA
PANAMA
Panama City
Caribbean Sea
Caracas
LLANOS
VENEZ.
Bogota
COLOMBIA
Kiritimati
Line Islands
EQUATOR
Galapagos Islands Ecua.
Quito
ECUADOR
AMAZON BASIN
BRAZIL
ANDES
PERU
Lima
Marquesas Is.
POLYNESIA
COOK ISLANDS N.Z.
Tuamotu Archipelago
Society Is.
FRENCH POLYNESIA Fr.
Austral Is.
Pitcairn Island U.K.
La Paz
BOLIVIA
SOUTH PACIFIC OCEAN
Santiago
CHILE
ARGENTINA
PATAGONIA
Chiloe Island
45°N
30°N
15°N
0°
15°S
30°S
45°S
165°W
150°W
135°W
120°W
105°W
90°W
75°W
9
10
11
12
13
14
15
16
A
B
C
D
E
F
G
H
J
K

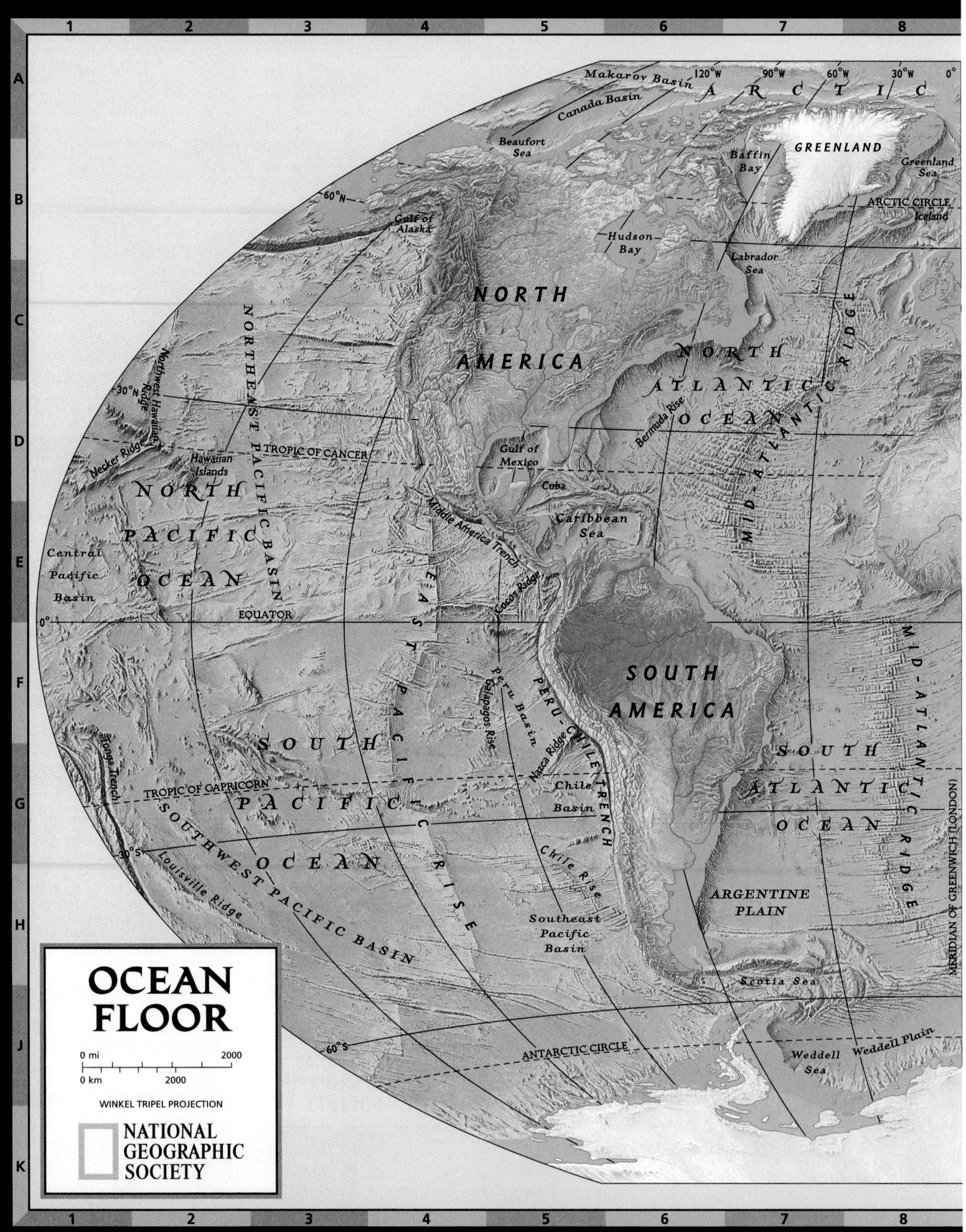
OCEAN
FLOOR
WINKEL TRIPEL PROJECTION
NATIONAL
GEOGRAPHIC
SOCIETY
NORTH
AMERICA
SOUTH
AMERICA
NORTH
PACIFIC
OCEAN
SOUTH
PACIFIC
OCEAN
NORTH
ATLANTIC
OCEAN
SOUTH
ATLANTIC
OCEAN
GREENLAND
Makarov Basin
Canada Basin
Beaufort Sea
Baffin Bay
Greenland Sea
Iceland
Hudson Bay
Labrador Sea
Gulf of Alaska
Gulf of Mexico
Cuba
Caribbean Sea
Bermuda Rise
MID-ATLANTIC RIDGE
NORTHEAST PACIFIC BASIN
Northwest Hawaiian Ridge
Necker Ridge
Hawaiian Islands
Central Pacific Basin
Middle America Trench
Cocos Ridge
EAST PACIFIC RISE
Peru Basin
Galapagos Rise
PERU-CHILE TRENCH
Nazca Ridge
Chile Basin
Chile Rise
Southeast Pacific Basin
Tonga Trench
SOUTHWEST PACIFIC BASIN
Louisville Ridge
ARGENTINE PLAIN
Scotia Sea
Weddell Sea
Weddell Plain
TROPIC OF CANCER
TROPIC OF CAPRICORN
EQUATOR
ARCTIC CIRCLE
ANTARCTIC CIRCLE
MERIDIAN OF GREENWICH (LONDON)
120°W
90°W
60°W
30°W
0°
60°N
30°N
0°
30°S
60°S
0 mi
2000
0 km
2000

30°E
60°E
90°E
150°E
POLE PLAIN
OCEAN
Nansen Basin
Laptev Sea
East Siberian Sea
Kara Sea
Barents Sea
Norwegian Sea
60°N
Bering Sea
Sea of Okhotsk
North Sea
EUROPE
Kuril Trench
Northwest Pacific Basin
ASIA
Sea of Japan
NORTH PACIFIC OCEAN
Black Sea
Mediterranean Sea
30°N
Ryukyu Trench
Kyushu-Palau Ridge
TROPIC OF CANCER
Red Sea
Philippine Sea
Arabian Sea
Bay of Bengal
South China Sea
Mariana Trench
AFRICA
Arabian Basin
Central Pacific Basin
Borneo
EQUATOR
0°
New Guinea
MID-INDIAN RIDGE
Mid-Indian Basin
Investigator Ridge
Java Trench
Madagascar
Coral Sea
Walvis Ridge
SOUTHWEST INDIAN RIDGE
INDIAN OCEAN
AUSTRALIA
TROPIC OF CAPRICORN
SOUTH PACIFIC OCEAN
Perth Basin
30°S
Crozet Basin
South Australian Basin
North Island
Tasman Sea
Tasmania
South Island
SOUTHEAST INDIAN RIDGE
Enderby Plain
South Indian Basin
60°S
ANTARCTIC CIRCLE
ANTARCTICA
9 10 11 12 13 14 15 16
A B C D E F G H J K

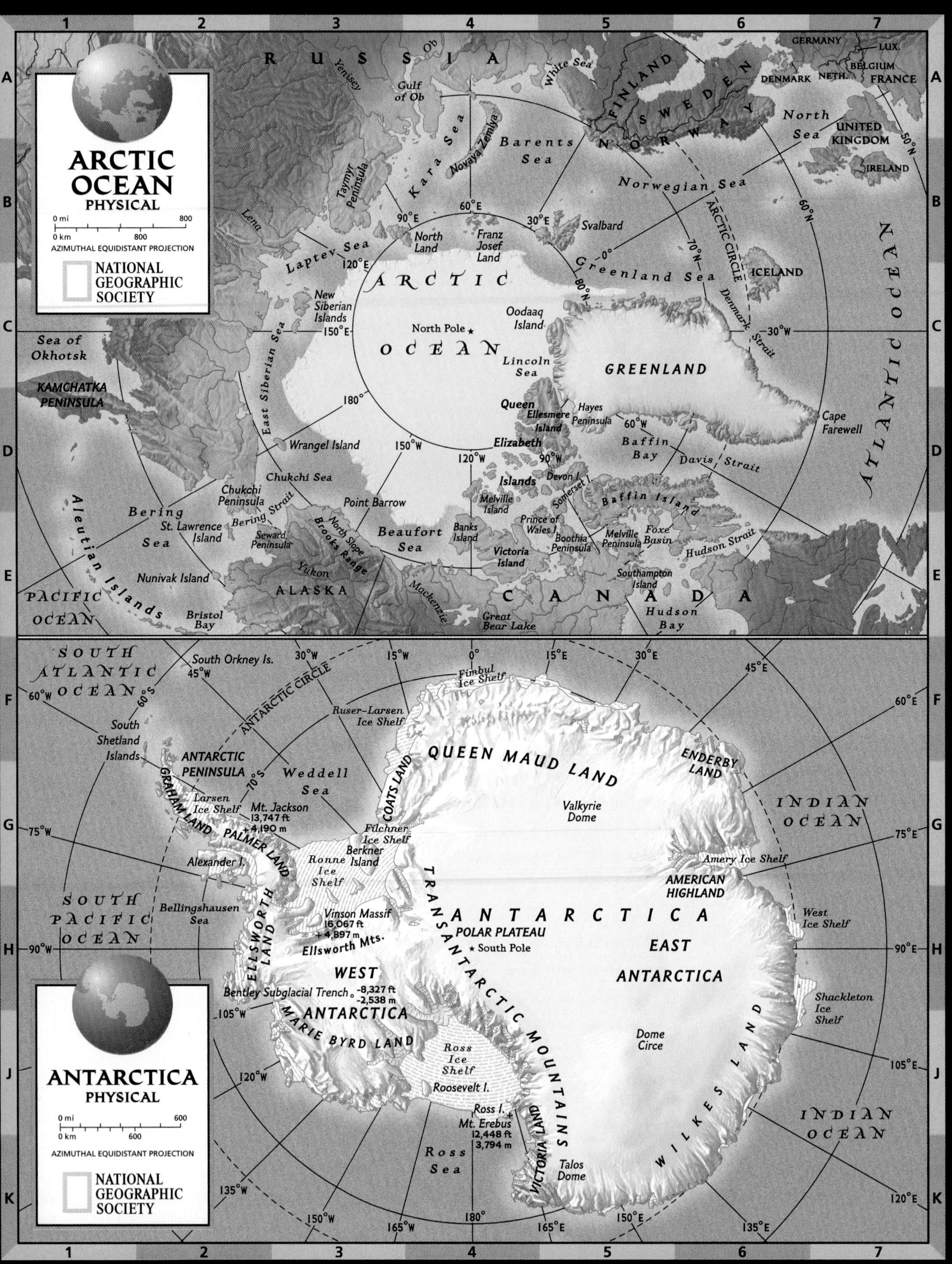
ARCTIC OCEAN
PHYSICAL
AZIMUTHAL EQUIDISTANT PROJECTION
NATIONAL GEOGRAPHIC SOCIETY
RUSSIA
ARCTIC OCEAN
North Pole
GREENLAND
ICELAND
FINLAND
SWEDEN
NORWAY
ALASKA
CANADA
Barents Sea
Kara Sea
Laptev Sea
Norwegian Sea
Greenland Sea
Baffin Bay
Beaufort Sea
Chukchi Sea
Bering Sea
East Siberian Sea
Sea of Okhotsk
ATLANTIC OCEAN
PACIFIC OCEAN
ANTARCTICA
PHYSICAL
AZIMUTHAL EQUIDISTANT PROJECTION
NATIONAL GEOGRAPHIC SOCIETY
SOUTH ATLANTIC OCEAN
SOUTH PACIFIC OCEAN
INDIAN OCEAN
QUEEN MAUD LAND
ENDERBY LAND
ANTARCTIC PENINSULA
Weddell Sea
Ross Sea
Ross Ice Shelf
Ronne Ice Shelf
Amery Ice Shelf
TRANSANTARCTIC MOUNTAINS
WEST ANTARCTICA
EAST ANTARCTICA
South Pole
Vinson Massif 16,067 ft 4,897 m
Mt. Erebus 12,448 ft 3,794 m
Mt. Jackson 13,747 ft 4,190 m
Bentley Subglacial Trench -8,327 ft -2,538 m
WILKES LAND
MARIE BYRD LAND

GEOGRAPHY HANDBOOK

A geographer is a person who studies the earth and its people. Have you ever wondered if you could be a geographer? One way to learn how is to use this **Geography Handbook.** It will show you that geography is more than studying facts and figures. It also means doing some of your own exploring of the earth. By learning how to use geographic tools, such as globes, maps, and graphs, you will get to know and appreciate the wonders of our planet.

Geologists studying a volcano ▲

Table of Contents

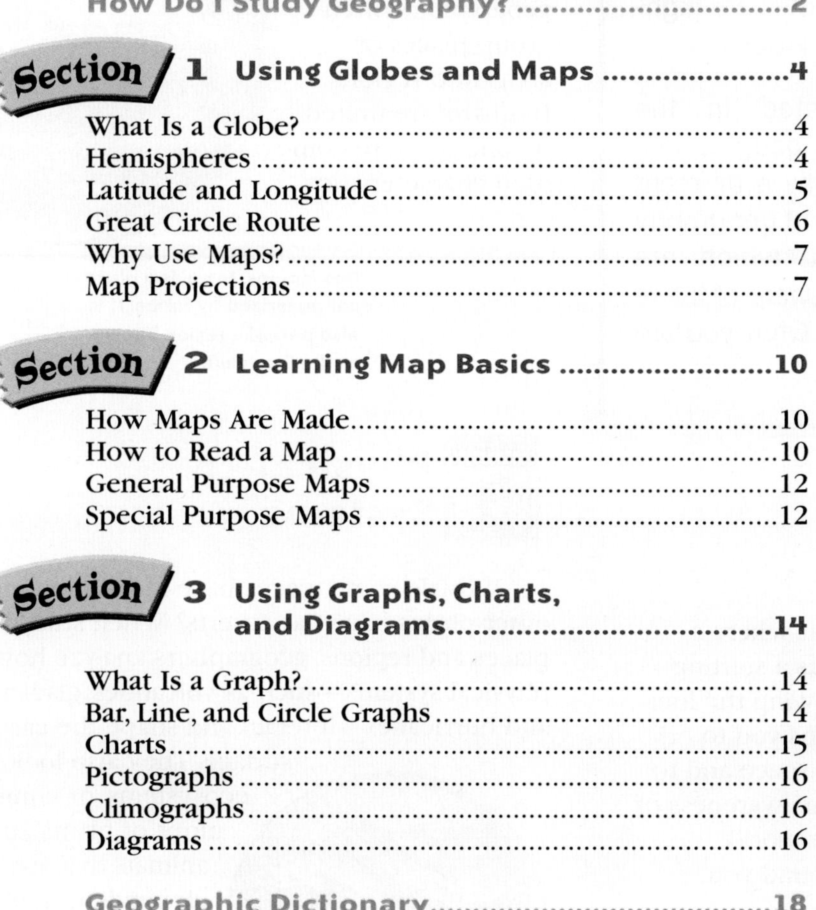

Polar ice cap ▼

◀ Lava flow

How Do I Study Geography?

Everything you see, touch, use, and even hear is related to geography—the study of the world's people, places, and environments. How can you possibly study such a huge amount of information in your geography class? Where do you start?

Geographers—people who study geography—ask themselves this question, too. To understand how our world is connected, some geographers have broken down the study of geography into five themes. The **Five Themes of Geography** are (1) location, (2) place, (3) human/environment interaction, (4) movement, and (5) regions. These themes are highlighted in blue throughout this textbook.

Most recently, as suggested in the ***Geography Standards for Life,*** geographers have begun to look at geography a different way. They break down the study of geography into **Six Essential Elements**, which are explained for you below. Being aware of these elements will help you sort out what you are learning about geography.

ELEMENT 1 The World in Spatial Terms

Geographers first take a look at where a place is located. **Location** serves as a starting point by asking "Where is it?" Knowing the location of places helps you to orient yourself in space and to develop an awareness of the world around you.

This street sign is located in Paris, France.

ELEMENT 2 Places and Regions

Geographers also look at places and regions. **Place** includes those features and characteristics that give an area its own identity or personality. These can be physical characteristics—such as landforms, climate, plants, and animals—or human characteristics—such as language, religion, architecture, music, politics, and way of life.

To make sense of all the complex things in the world, geographers often group places or areas into regions. **Regions** are united by one or more common characteristics.

Des Moines, Iowa, is a place characterized by farms. It is also part of a region known as the Corn Belt.

ELEMENT 3 Physical Systems

Why do some places have mountains and other places have flat deserts? When studying places and regions, geographers analyze how physical systems—such as volcanoes, glaciers, and hurricanes—interact and shape the earth's surface. They also look at ecosystems, or communities of plants and animals that are dependent upon one another and their particular surroundings for survival.

A glacier carved this deep valley in New Zealand.

Geography?

ELEMENT 4 Human Systems

Geographers also examine human systems, or how people have shaped our world. They look at how boundary lines are determined and analyze why people settle in certain places and not in others. An ongoing theme in geography is the continual **movement** of people, ideas, and goods.

People, vehicles, and goods move quickly through Asmara, the capital of Eritrea.

ELEMENT 5 Environment and Society

The study of geography includes looking at **human/environment interaction,** or how and why people change their surroundings. Throughout history, people have cut forests and dammed rivers to build farms and cities. Some activities have led to air and water pollution. The physical environment affects human activities as well. The type of soil and amount of water in a place determines if crops can be grown. Earthquakes and floods also affect human life.

Romanian farmers work in a field near a nuclear power plant.

ELEMENT 6 The Uses of Geography

Understanding geography, and knowing how to use the tools and technology available to study it, prepares you for life in our modern society. Individuals, businesses, and governments use geography and maps of all kinds on a daily basis. Computer programs, such as geographic information systems (GIS), allow us to make informed decisions about how to make the best use of our place and region.

A cartographer uses GIS to make a map.

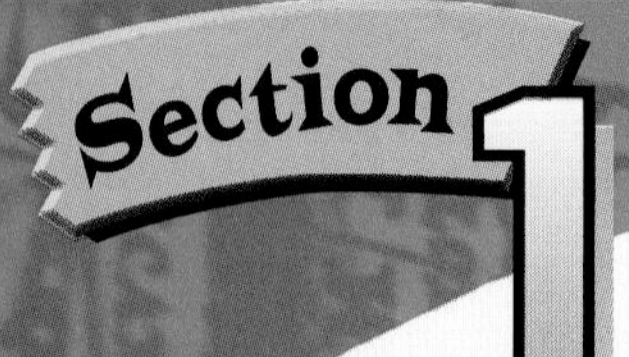

Using Globes and Maps

Guide To Reading

Main Idea

Globes and maps provide different ways of showing features of the earth.

Terms to Know

- globe
- hemisphere
- latitude
- longitude
- grid system
- absolute location
- great circle route
- projection

What Is a Globe?

A **globe** is a model of the earth that shows the earth's shape, lands, distances, and directions as they truly relate to one another. A world globe can help you find your way around the earth. By using one, you can locate places and determine distances.

Hemispheres

To locate places on the earth, geographers use a system of imaginary lines that crisscross the globe. One of these lines, the Equator, circles the middle of the earth like a belt. It

NATIONAL GEOGRAPHIC

Hemispheres

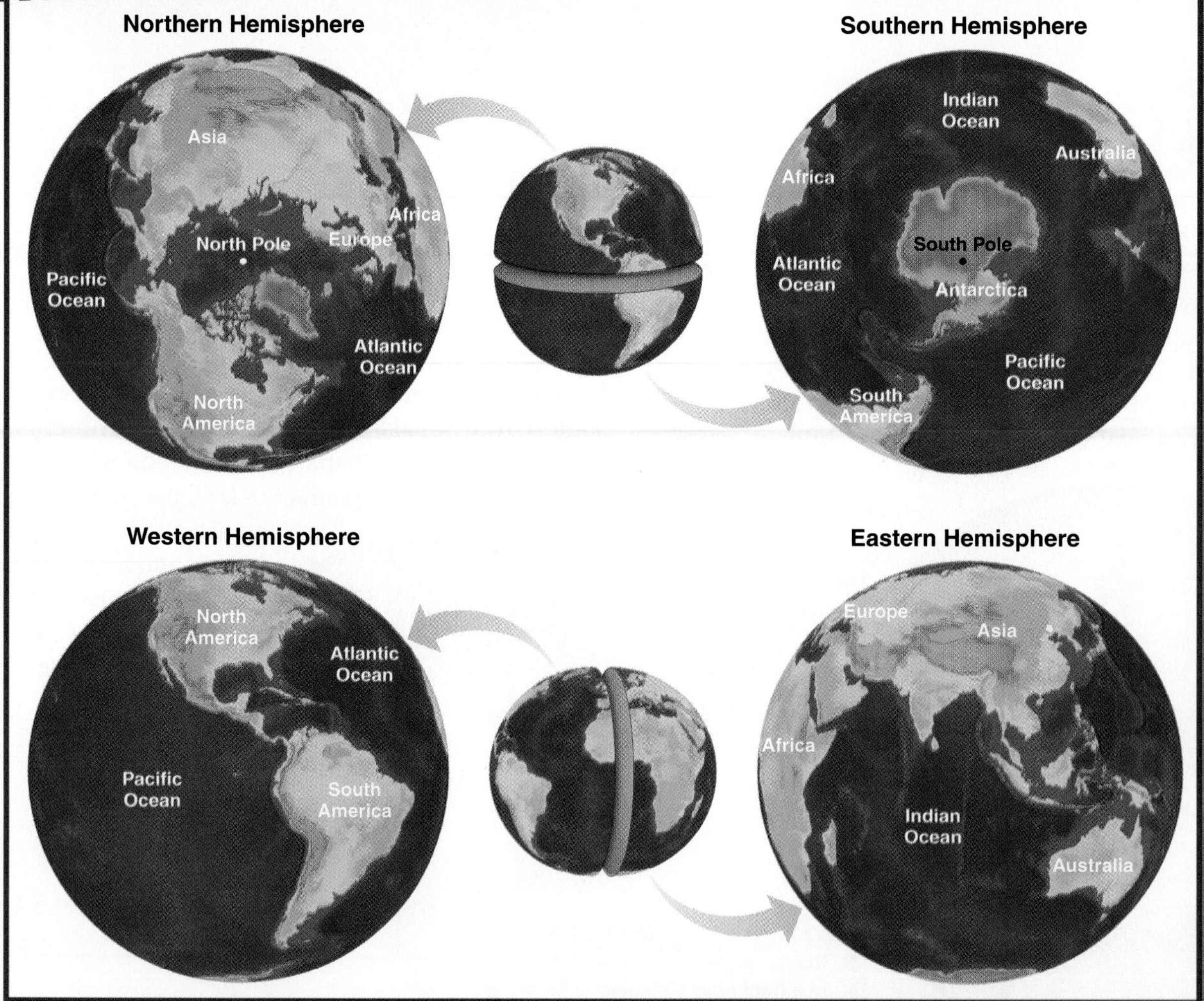

divides the earth into "half spheres," or **hemispheres.** Everything north of the Equator is in the Northern Hemisphere. Everything south of the Equator is in the Southern Hemisphere.

Another imaginary line runs from north to south and helps divide the earth into half spheres in the other direction. Find this line—called the Prime Meridian or the Meridian of Greenwich—on a globe. Everything east of the Prime Meridian for 180 degrees is in the Eastern Hemisphere. Everything west of the Prime Meridian for 180 degrees is in the Western Hemisphere. In which hemispheres is North America located? It is found in both the Northern Hemisphere and the Western Hemisphere.

Latitude and Longitude

The Equator and the Prime Meridian are the starting points for two sets of lines used to find any location. *Parallels* circle the earth like stacked rings and show **latitude,** or distance measured in degrees north and south of the Equator. The letter *N* or *S* following the degree symbol tells you if the location is north or south of the Equator. The North Pole, for example, is at 90°N (North) latitude, and the South Pole is at 90°S (South) latitude.

Two important parallels in between the poles are the Tropic of Cancer at 23½°N latitude and the Tropic of Capricorn at 23½°S latitude. You can also find the Arctic Circle at

NATIONAL GEOGRAPHIC

Latitude and Longitude

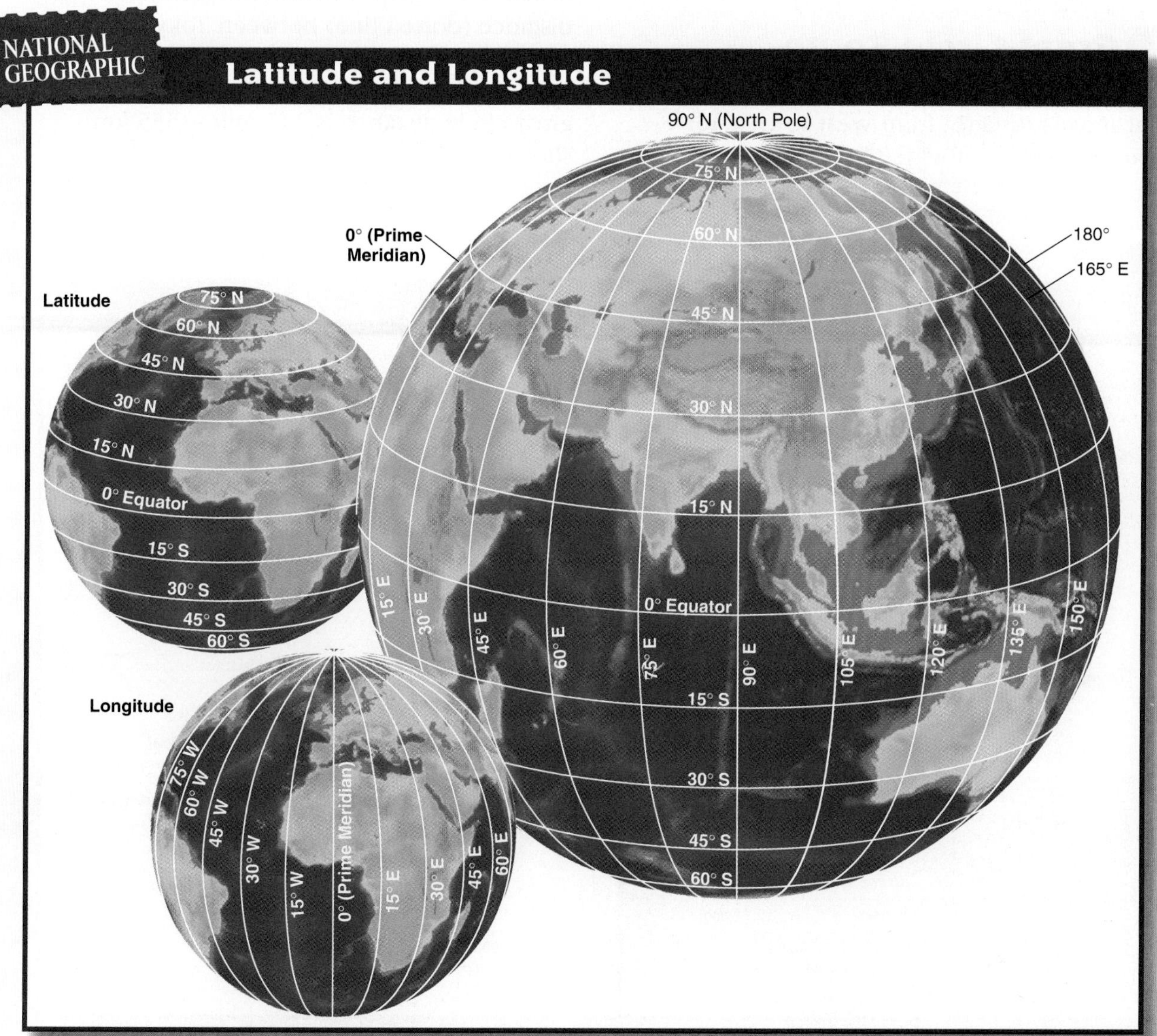

66½°N latitude and the Antarctic Circle at 66½°S latitude.

Meridians run from pole to pole and crisscross parallels. Meridians signify **longitude,** or distance measured in degrees east *(E)* or west *(W)* of the Prime Meridian. The Prime Meridian, or 0° longitude, runs through Greenwich, England. On the opposite side of the earth is the 180° meridian, also called the International Date Line.

Lines of latitude and longitude cross each other in the form of a **grid system.** You can find a place's **absolute location** by naming the latitude and longitude lines that cross exactly at that place. For example, the city of Tokyo, Japan, is located at 36°N latitude and 140°E longitude.

Great Circle Route

A straight line of true direction—one that moves directly from west to east, for example—is not always the shortest distance between two points on the earth. To find the shortest distance between any two places, take a piece of string and stretch it around a globe from one point to another. The string will form part of a *great circle,* or an imaginary line that follows the curve of the earth. A line drawn along the Equator is an example of a great circle. Traveling along a great circle is called following a **great circle route.** Airplane pilots use great circle routes to reduce travel time and to save fuel.

The idea of a great circle shows one important difference between using a globe and using a map. Because a globe is round, it accurately shows great circles. However, on a flat map the great circle route between two points may not appear to be the shortest distance. On map A below, the great circle distance (dotted line) between Tokyo and Los Angeles appears to be far longer than the true direction distance (solid line). In fact, the great circle distance is 345 miles (555 km) shorter, which is evident on map B.

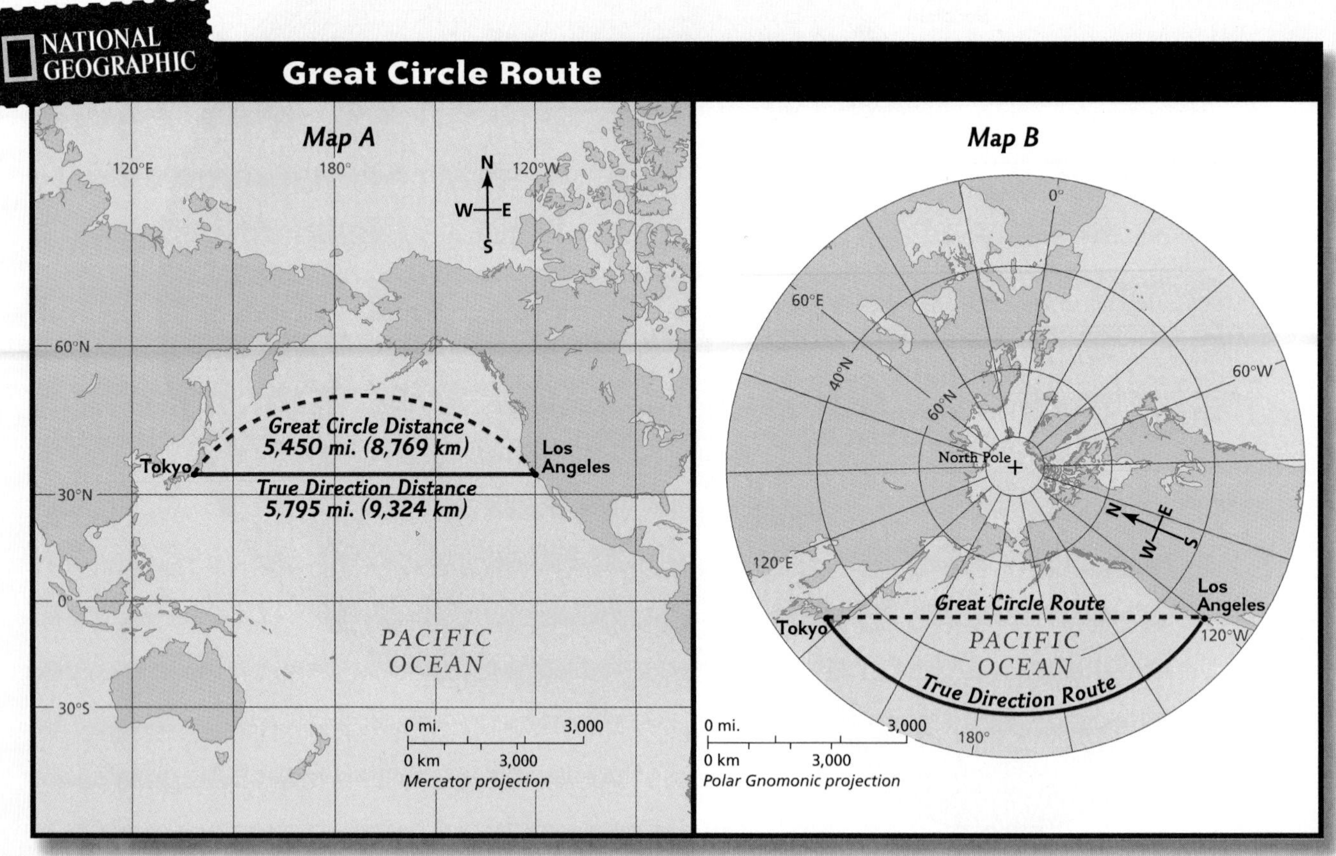

Why Use Maps?

Globes are the best, most accurate way to show the round earth. Using a globe has its difficulties, though. First, a globe is too big and awkward to carry around. Also, a globe cannot show you the whole world at one time. For these reasons, geographers use maps instead. A map is made by taking data from a round globe and placing it on a flat surface. It is important to remember that the earth's features, which are shown accurately on a globe, become distorted when the curves of a globe become straight lines on a flat map.

Map Projections

Imagine taking the whole peel from an orange and trying to flatten it on a table. You would either have to cut it or stretch parts of it. Mapmakers face a similar problem in showing the surface of the round earth on a flat map. When the earth's surface is flattened, big gaps open up. To fill in the gaps, mapmakers stretch parts of the earth. They choose to show either the correct shapes of places or their correct sizes. It is impossible to show both. As a result, mapmakers have developed different **projections**, or ways of showing the earth on a flat piece of paper. Each projection has its strengths and weaknesses. None is a completely accurate representation of the earth, but all prove useful in one way or another.

Mercator Projection The *Mercator projection* shows land shapes fairly accurately, but not size or distance. Areas that are located far from the Equator are quite distorted on this projection. Alaska, for example, appears much larger on a Mercator map than it does on a globe. The Mercator projection does show true directions, however. This makes it very useful for sea travel.

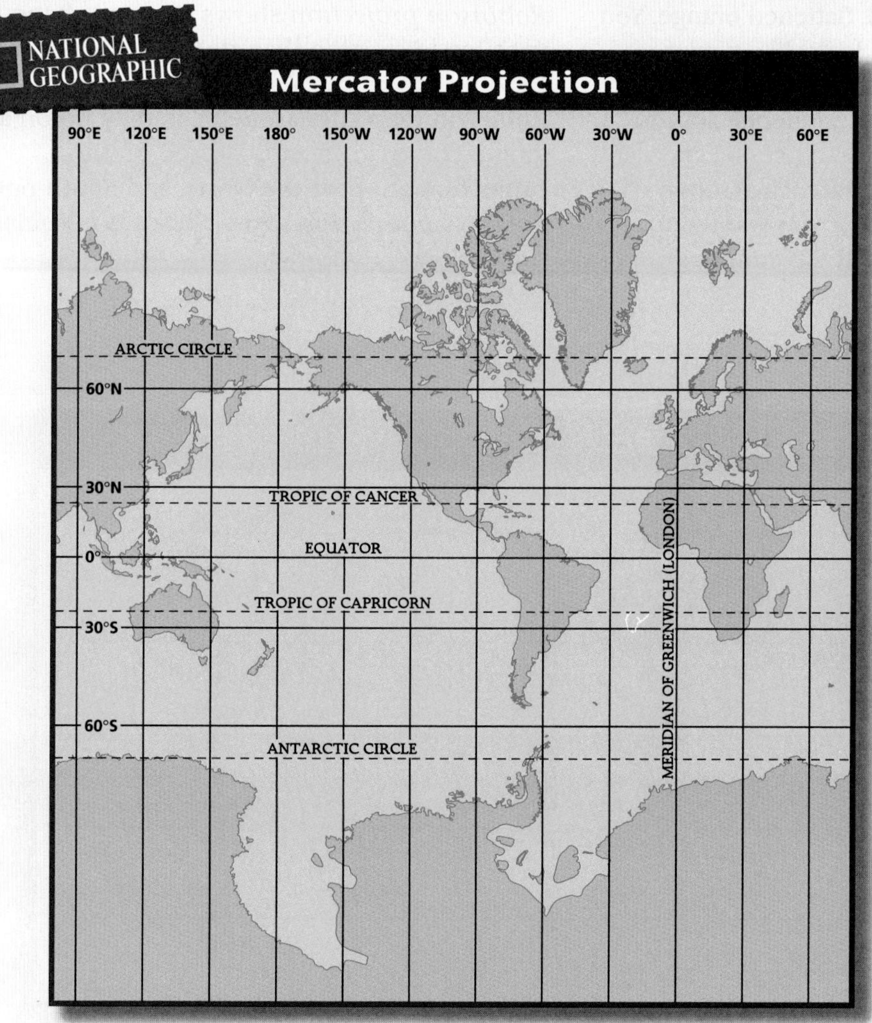

GEOGRAPHY HANDBOOK

NATIONAL GEOGRAPHIC

Goode's Interrupted Projection

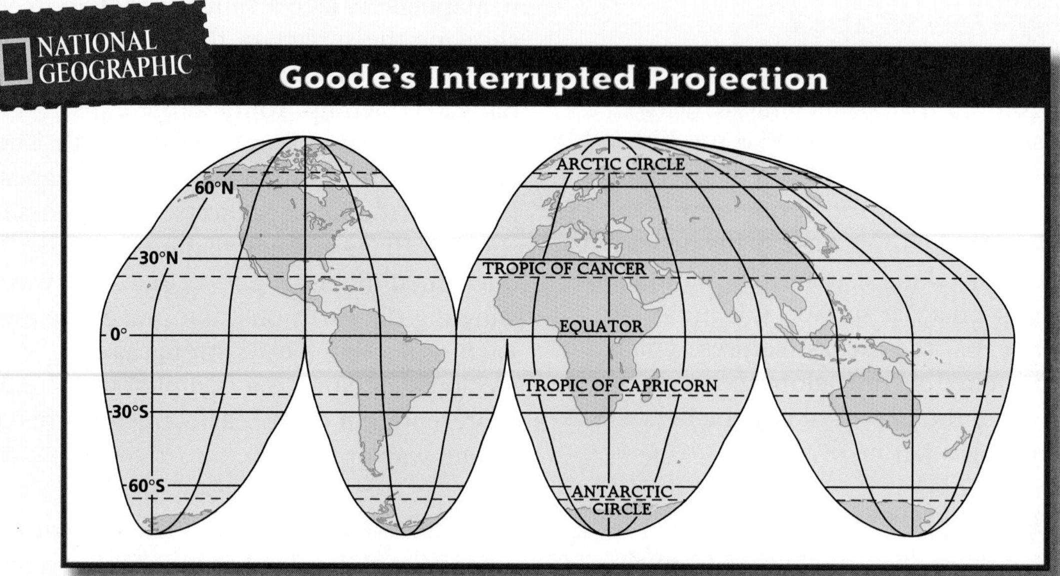

Goode's Interrupted Projection Take a second look at your peeled, flattened orange. You might have something that looks like a map based on *Goode's interrupted projection.* A map with this projection shows continents close to their true shapes and sizes. Distances—especially in the oceans—are less accurate. The Goode's projection would be helpful if you wanted to compare land area data about the continents.

Robinson Projection A map using the *Robinson projection* shows size and shape with less distortion than does a Mercator map. Land on the western and eastern sides of the Robinson map appear much as they do on a globe. The areas most distorted on this projection are near the North and South poles. You may notice that many atlases use Robinson projections.

NATIONAL GEOGRAPHIC

Robinson Projection

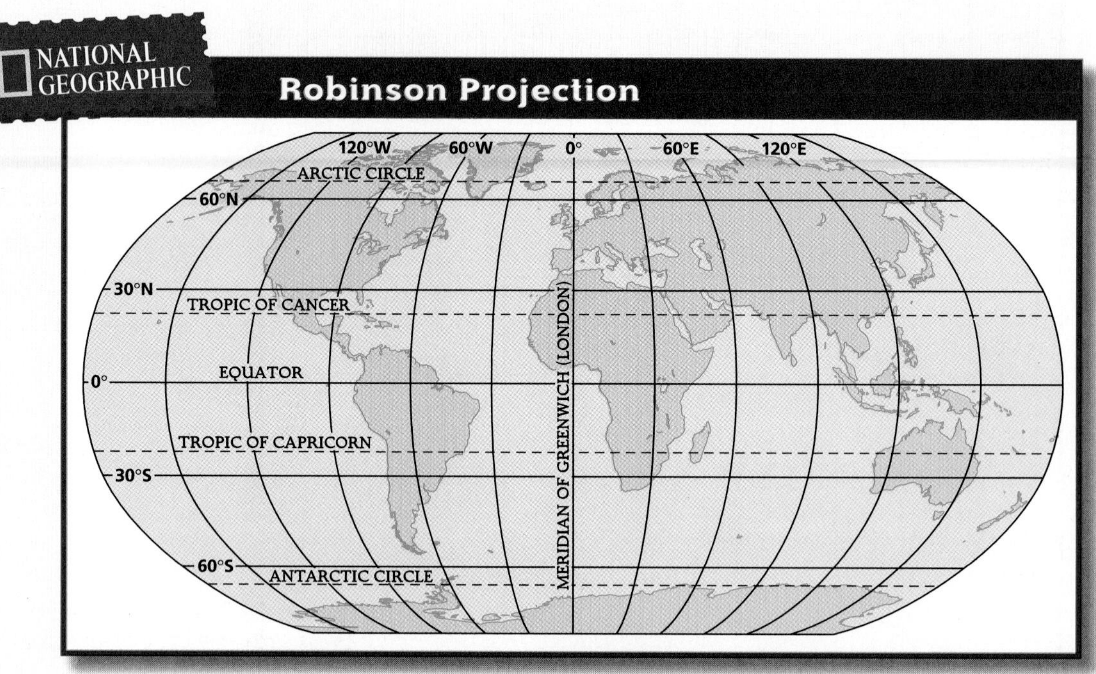

Winkel Tripel Projection

Mapmakers are always looking for a more accurate way to show the round earth on flat paper. The *Winkel Tripel projection* gives a good overall view of the continents' shapes and sizes. You may notice a close similarity between the Winkel Tripel and Robinson projections. Land areas in a Winkel Tripel projection are not as distorted near the poles as they are in the Robinson projection. In 1998 the National Geographic Society began using the Winkel Tripel projection for its reference maps of the world.

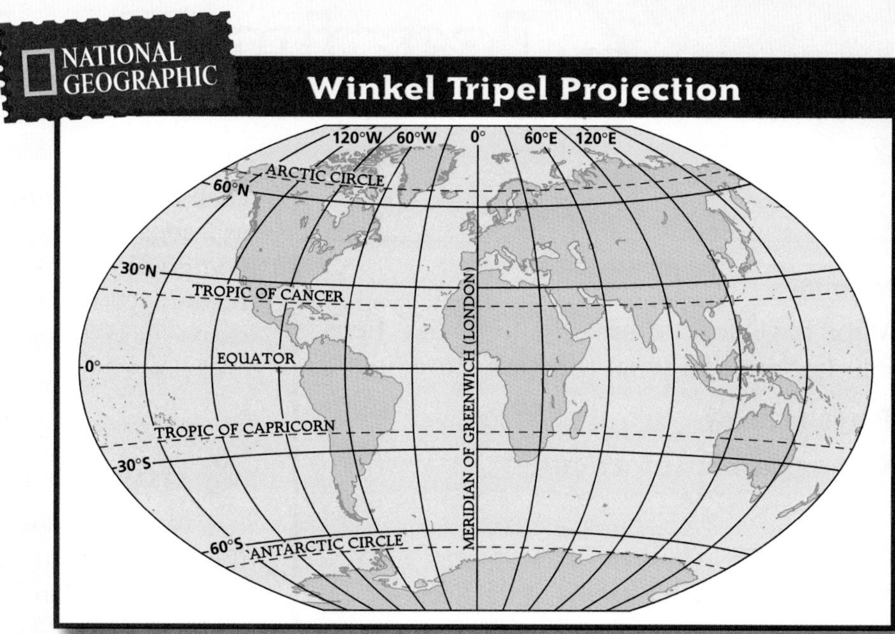

Section 1 Assessment

Defining Terms

1. **Define** globe, hemisphere, latitude, longitude, grid system, absolute location, great circle route, projection.

Recalling Facts

2. What imaginary line divides the earth into the Northern and the Southern Hemispheres?
3. What imaginary line divides the earth into the Eastern and the Western Hemispheres?
4. What is the best way to find the shortest distance between two places?

Critical Thinking

5. **Drawing Conclusions** Why do map projections distort some parts of the earth?
6. **Making Comparisons** What map projection has fairly accurate shapes in the center but increasing distortion toward the edges?

Graphic Organizer

7. **Organizing Information** Create a chart like this one. On the left, list three words or phrases that describe globes. On the right, do the same for maps.

Globes	Maps

Applying Geography Skills

8. **Analyzing Globes** Look at the globe showing latitude on page 5. Where on the globe do parallels, or lines of latitude, become shorter?

Learning Map Basics

Guide To Reading

Main Idea

Maps have several basic features that help you understand what they are showing.

Terms to Know

- geographic information systems (GIS)
- map key
- cardinal directions
- compass rose
- intermediate directions
- scale bar
- scale
- relief
- elevation
- contour line

How Maps Are Made

For more than 4,000 years, people have made maps to organize their knowledge of the world. The reason for producing maps has not changed over the centuries, but the tools of mapmaking have. Today satellites located thousands of miles in space gather data about the earth below. The data are then sent back to the earth, where computers change the data into images of the earth's surface. Mapmakers analyze and use these images to produce maps.

For modern mapmakers, computers have replaced pen and paper. Most mapmakers use computers with software programs called **geographic information systems (GIS)**. With GIS, each kind of information on a map is kept as a separate electronic "layer" in the map's computer files. Because of this modern technology, mapmakers are able to make maps—and change them—more quickly and easily.

How to Read a Map

Maps can direct you down the street, across the country, or around the world. An ordinary map holds all kinds of information. Learn the map's code, and you can read it like a book.

Map Key The **map key** explains the lines, symbols, and colors used on a map. Look at the map of Spain below. Its key shows that dots mark major cities. A circled star indicates the national capital—in Spain's case, the city of Madrid. Some keys tell which lines stand for national boundaries, roads, or railroads. Other

map symbols may represent human-made or natural features, such as canals, forests, or natural gas deposits.

Compass Rose An important step in reading any map is to find the direction marker. A map has a symbol that tells you where the **cardinal directions**—north, south, east, and west—are positioned. Sometimes all of these directions are shown with a **compass rose.** An **intermediate direction,** such as southeast, may also be on the compass rose. Intermediate directions fall between the cardinal directions.

Latitude and Longitude Lines

Like globes, maps have lines of latitude and longitude that form a grid. Every place on the earth has a unique position or "address" on this grid. Knowing this address makes it easier for you to locate cities and other places on a map. For example, what is the grid address of Madrid, Spain? The map on page 10 shows you that the address is 41°N latitude, 4°W longitude.

Scale A measuring line, often called a **scale bar,** helps you determine distance on a map. The map's **scale** tells you what distance on the earth is represented by the measurement on the scale bar. For example, 1 inch on the map may represent 200 miles on the earth. Knowing the scale allows you to see how large an area is. Map scale is usually given in both miles and kilometers.

Each map has its own scale. What scale a mapmaker uses depends on the size of the area shown on the map. If you were drawing a map of your backyard, you might use a scale of 1 inch equals 5 feet. In contrast, the scale bar on the map above of Austin, Texas, shows that about ¾ inch represents 8 miles. Scale is important when you are trying to compare the size of one area to another.

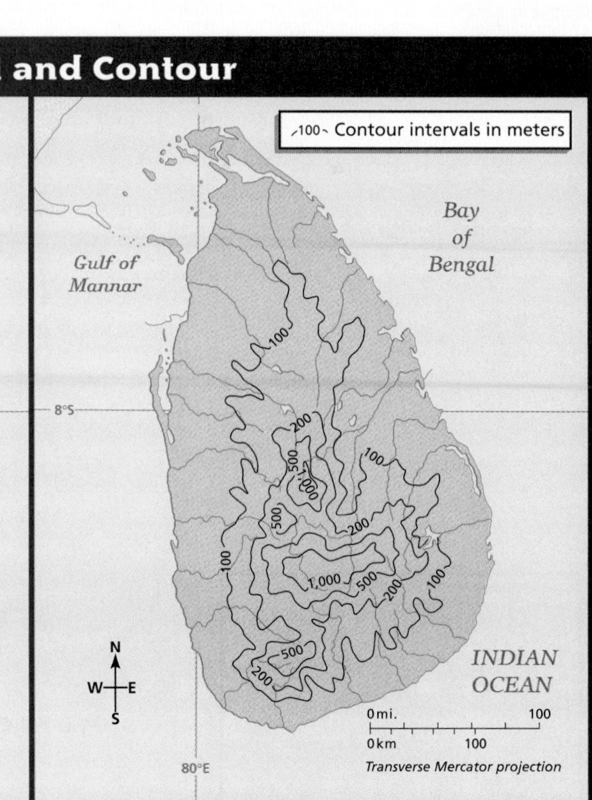

General Purpose Maps

Maps are amazingly useful tools. You can use them to preserve information, to display data, and to make connections between seemingly unrelated things. Geographers use many different types of maps. Maps that show a wide range of general information about an area are called *general purpose maps.* Two of the most common general purpose maps are political and physical maps.

Political Maps *Political maps* show the names and boundaries of countries and identify only major physical features. The political map of Spain on page 10, for example, shows the boundaries between Spain and other countries. It also shows cities and rivers within Spain and bodies of water surrounding Spain.

Physical Maps *Physical maps* call out landforms and water features. The physical map of Sri Lanka above shows rivers and mountains. The colors used on physical maps include brown or green for land, and blue for water. These colors and shadings may show **relief**—or how flat or rugged the land surface is. In addition, physical maps may use colors to show **elevation**—the height of an area above sea level. A key explains what each color and symbol stands for.

Contour Maps One kind of physical map, called a *contour map,* also shows elevation. A contour map has **contour lines**—one line for each major level of elevation. All the land at the same elevation is connected by a line. These lines usually form circles or ovals—one inside the other. If contour lines come very close together, the surface is steep. If the lines are spread apart, the land is flat or rises very gradually. Compare the contour map of Sri Lanka above to its physical map.

Special Purpose Maps

Some maps are made to present specific kinds of information. These are called *special purpose maps.* They usually show patterns, often emphasizing one subject or theme. Special purpose maps may present climate, natural resources, or population density. They may also display historical information, such as battles or territorial changes. The map's title tells what kind of special information it shows. Colors and symbols in the map key are especially important on these types of maps.

One type of special purpose map uses colors to show population density, or the average number of people living in a square mile or square kilometer. As with other maps, it is important to first read the title and the key. The population density map of Egypt to the right gives a striking picture of differences in population density. The Nile River valley and delta are very densely populated. In contrast, the desert areas east and west of the river are home to few people.

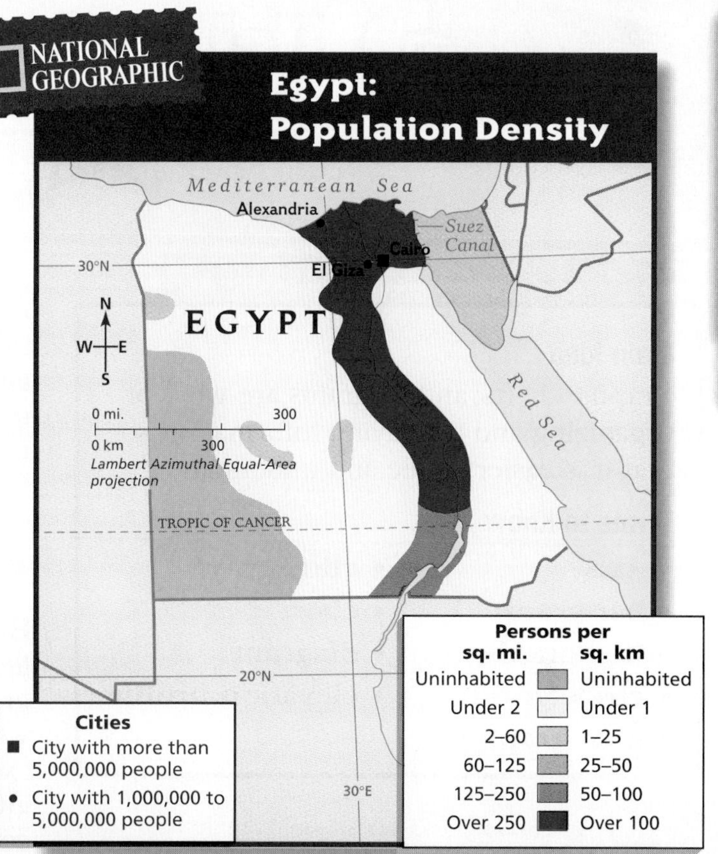

Assessment

Defining Terms

1. **Define** geographic information systems (GIS), map key, cardinal directions, compass rose, intermediate directions, scale bar, scale, relief, elevation, contour line.

Recalling Facts

2. Why do people make maps?
3. What are the four cardinal directions?
4. What are two of the most common types of general purpose maps?

Critical Thinking

5. **Drawing Conclusions** Would you use a large scale or a small scale to draw a map showing your route to school? Why?
6. **Synthesizing Information** Draw a compass rose that shows the cardinal and intermediate directions.

Graphic Organizer

7. **Organizing Information** Create a diagram like the one below. In each of the outer ovals, write an example of a feature that you would find on a typical physical map.

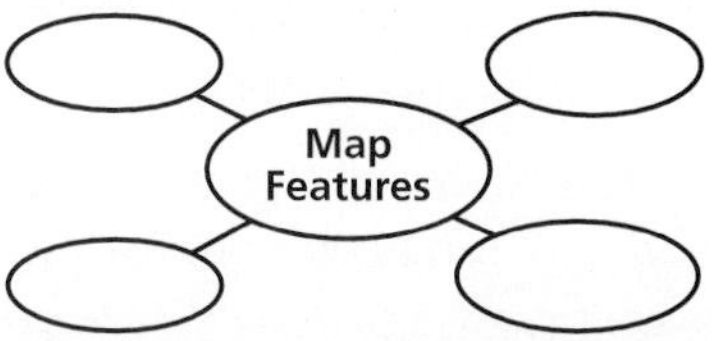

Applying Geography Skills

8. **Analyzing Maps** Look at the map of Egypt above. At what latitude and longitude is Alexandria located? Use the key to describe the population density of Alexandria and its surrounding area.

3 Using Graphs, Charts, and Diagrams

Guide To Reading

Main Idea

Graphs, charts, and diagrams are ways of organizing and displaying information so that it is easier to see and understand.

Terms to Know

- axis
- bar graph
- line graph
- circle graph
- pictograph
- climograph
- chart
- diagram
- elevation profile

What Is a Graph?

A graph is a way of summarizing and presenting information visually. Each part of a graph gives useful information. First read the graph's title to find out its subject. Then read the labels along the graph's axes—the vertical line along the left side of the graph and the horizontal line along the bottom of the graph. One axis will tell you what is being measured. The other axis tells what units of measurement are being used.

Bar, Line, and Circle Graphs

Bar Graphs Graphs that use bars or wide lines to compare data visually are called bar graphs. Look carefully at the bar graph below, which compares world languages. The vertical axis lists the languages. The horizontal axis gives speakers of the language, in millions. By comparing the lengths of the bars, you can quickly tell which language is spoken by the most people. Bar graphs are especially useful for comparing quantities, and they may show the bars rising up from the bottom of the graph or extending out from the vertical axis.

NATIONAL GEOGRAPHIC

Comparing World Languages

Languages	Numbers of Speakers (in millions)
Chinese (Mandarin)	885
English	322
Spanish	266
Bengali	189
Hindi	182
Portuguese	170
Russian	170
Japanese	125
German	98
Chinese (Wu)	77

Source: *National Geographic Atlas of the World*, 1997.

Line Graphs A line graph is a useful tool for showing changes over a period of time. The amounts being measured are plotted on the grid above each year, and then are connected by a line. Line graphs sometimes have two or more lines plotted on them. The line graph on page 15 shows that the number of farms in the United States has decreased since 1940. The vertical axis lists the number of farms in millions. The horizontal axis shows the passage of time in ten-year periods from 1940 to 1998.

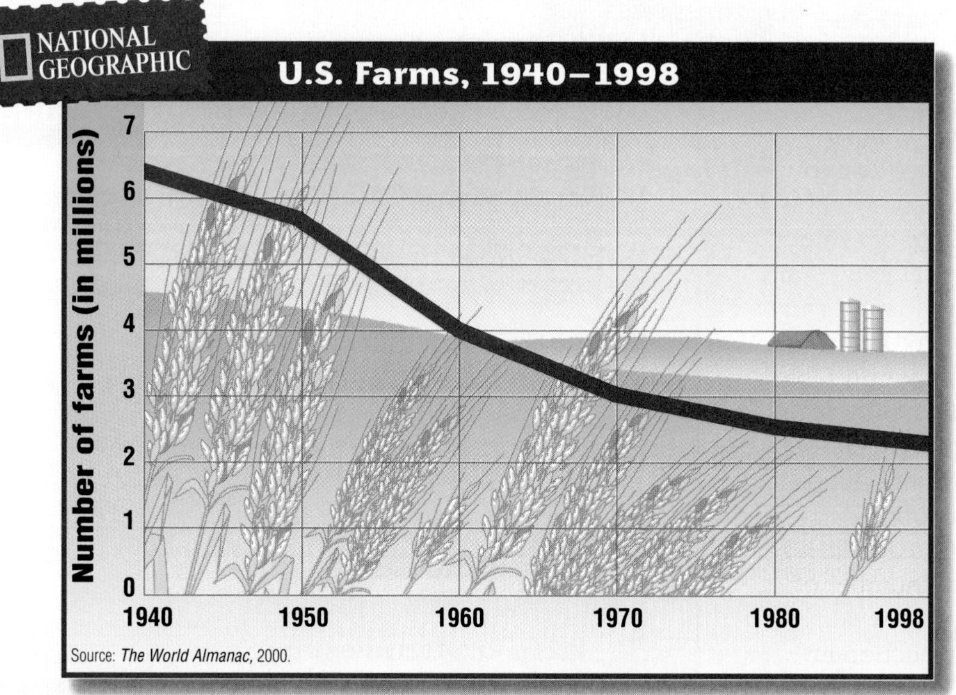

Circle Graphs You can use **circle graphs** when you want to show how the *whole* of something is divided into its *parts.* Because of their shape, circle graphs are often called pie graphs. Each "slice" represents a part or percentage of the whole "pie." On the circle graph below, the whole circle represents the world's population in 1999. The slices show how this population is divided among the world's five largest continents.

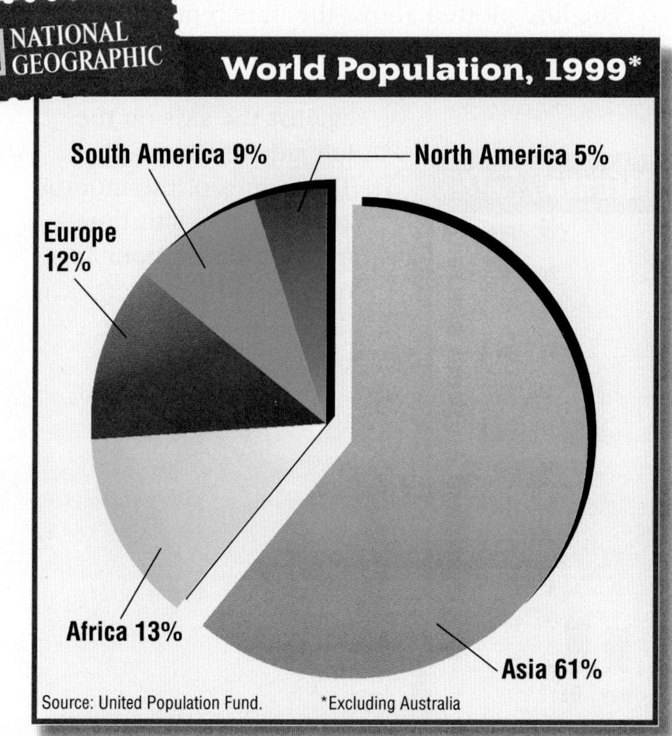

Charts

Charts present related facts and numbers in an organized way. They arrange data, especially numbers, in rows and columns for easy reference. Look at the chart on page 85. To interpret the chart, first read the title. It tells you what information the chart contains. Next, read the labels at the top of each column and on the left side of the chart. They explain what the numbers or data on the chart are measuring. One kind of chart, a *flowchart,* joins certain elements of a chart and a diagram. It can show the order of how things happen or how they are related to each other. The flowchart on page 132 presents the branches of the United States government. Notice how the chart shows the relationship among the tasks and the offices or bodies of each branch.

Pictographs

Like bar and circle graphs, pictographs are good for making comparisons. Pictographs use rows of small pictures or symbols, with each picture or symbol representing an amount. The pictograph on the right shows the number of automobiles produced in the world's five major automobile-producing countries. The key tells you that one car symbol stands for 1 million automobiles. Pictographs are read like a bar graph. The total number of car symbols in a row adds up to the auto production in each selected country.

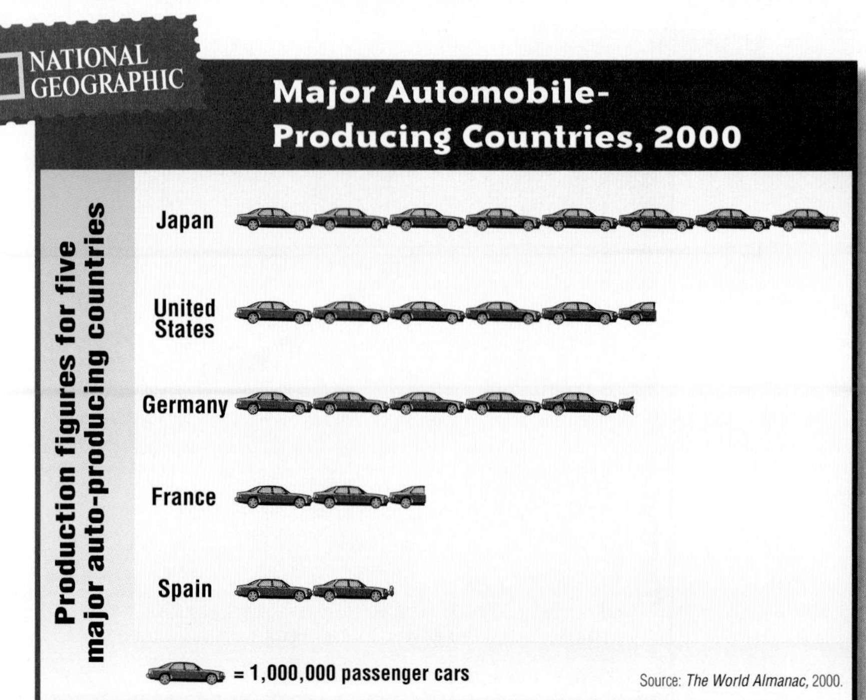

Climographs

A climograph, or climate graph, combines a line graph and a bar graph. It gives an overall picture of the climate—the long-term weather patterns—in a specific place. Because climographs include several kinds of information, you need to read them carefully.

Note that the vertical bars on the climograph below represent average amounts of precipitation (rain, snow, or sleet) in each month of the year. These bars are measured against the axis on the right side of the graph. The line plotted above the bars represents changes in the average monthly temperature. You measure this line against the axis on the left side of the graph. The names of the months are shown in shortened form on the bottom axis of the graph.

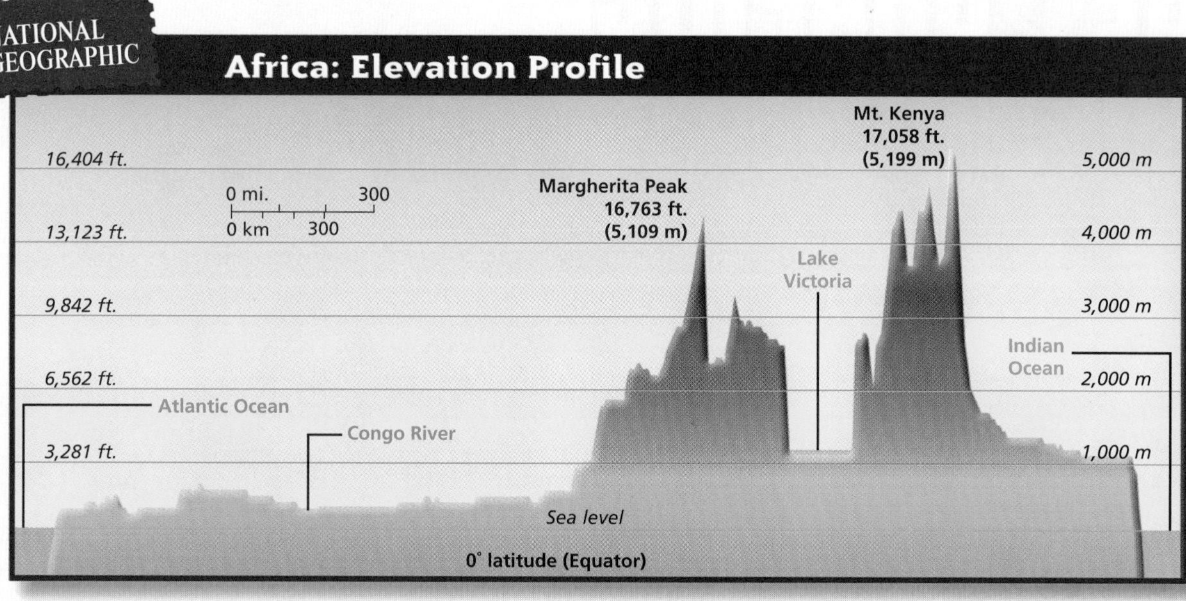

Diagrams

Diagrams are drawings that show steps in a process, point out the parts of an object, or explain how something works. You can use a diagram to assemble a stereo. The diagram on page 212 shows how locks enable ships to move through a canal. An **elevation profile** is a type of diagram that can be helpful when comparing the elevations of an area. It shows a profile, or side view, of the land as if it were sliced and you were viewing it from the side. (For reasons of scale, the profile is exaggerated.) The elevation profile of Africa above clearly shows low areas and mountains. The line of latitude at the bottom tells you where this profile was "sliced."

Section 3 Assessment

Defining Terms

1. **Define** axis, bar graph, line graph, circle graph, pictograph, climograph, chart, diagram, elevation profile.

Recalling Facts

2. How does a bar graph differ from a line graph?
3. What percentage does the whole circle in a circle graph always represent?
4. What two features does a climograph show?

Critical Thinking

5. **Synthesizing Information** Draw and label a flowchart showing the steps in some simple process—for example, making a sandwich or doing laundry.

Graphic Organizer

6. **Organizing Information** Create a chart like the one below. In the left column, list the types of graphs that are discussed in this section. In the right column, list what each type of graph is most useful for showing.

Types of Graphs	Useful for showing . . .

Applying Geography Skills

7. **Analyzing Graphs** Look at the bar graph on page 14. Which language is the most widely spoken? About how many people speak it?

NATIONAL GEOGRAPHIC

GEOGRAPHIC DICTIONARY

As you read about the world's geography, you will encounter the terms listed below. Many of the terms are pictured in the diagram.

absolute location exact location of a place on the earth described by global coordinates

basin area of land drained by a given river and its branches; area of land surrounded by lands of higher elevations

bay part of a large body of water that extends into a shoreline, generally smaller than a gulf

canyon deep and narrow valley with steep walls

cape point of land that extends into a river, lake, or ocean

channel wide strait or waterway between two landmasses that lie close to each other; deep part of a river or other waterway

cliff steep, high wall of rock, earth, or ice

continent one of the seven large landmasses on the earth

delta flat, low-lying land built up from soil carried downstream by a river and deposited at its mouth

divide stretch of high land that separates river systems

downstream direction in which a river or stream flows from its source to its mouth

elevation height of land above sea level

Equator imaginary line that runs around the earth halfway between the North and South Poles; used as the starting point to measure degrees of north and south latitude

glacier large, thick body of slowly moving ice

gulf part of a large body of water that extends into a shoreline, generally larger and more deeply indented than a bay

harbor a sheltered place along a shoreline where ships can anchor safely

highland elevated land area such as a hill, mountain, or plateau

hill elevated land with sloping sides and rounded summit; generally smaller than a mountain

island land area, smaller than a continent, completely surrounded by water

isthmus narrow stretch of land connecting two larger land areas

lake a sizable inland body of water

latitude distance north or south of the Equator, measured in degrees

longitude distance east or west of the Prime Meridian, measured in degrees

lowland land, usually level, at a low elevation

map drawing of the earth shown on a flat surface

meridian one of many lines on the global grid running from the North Pole to the South Pole; used to measure degrees of longitude

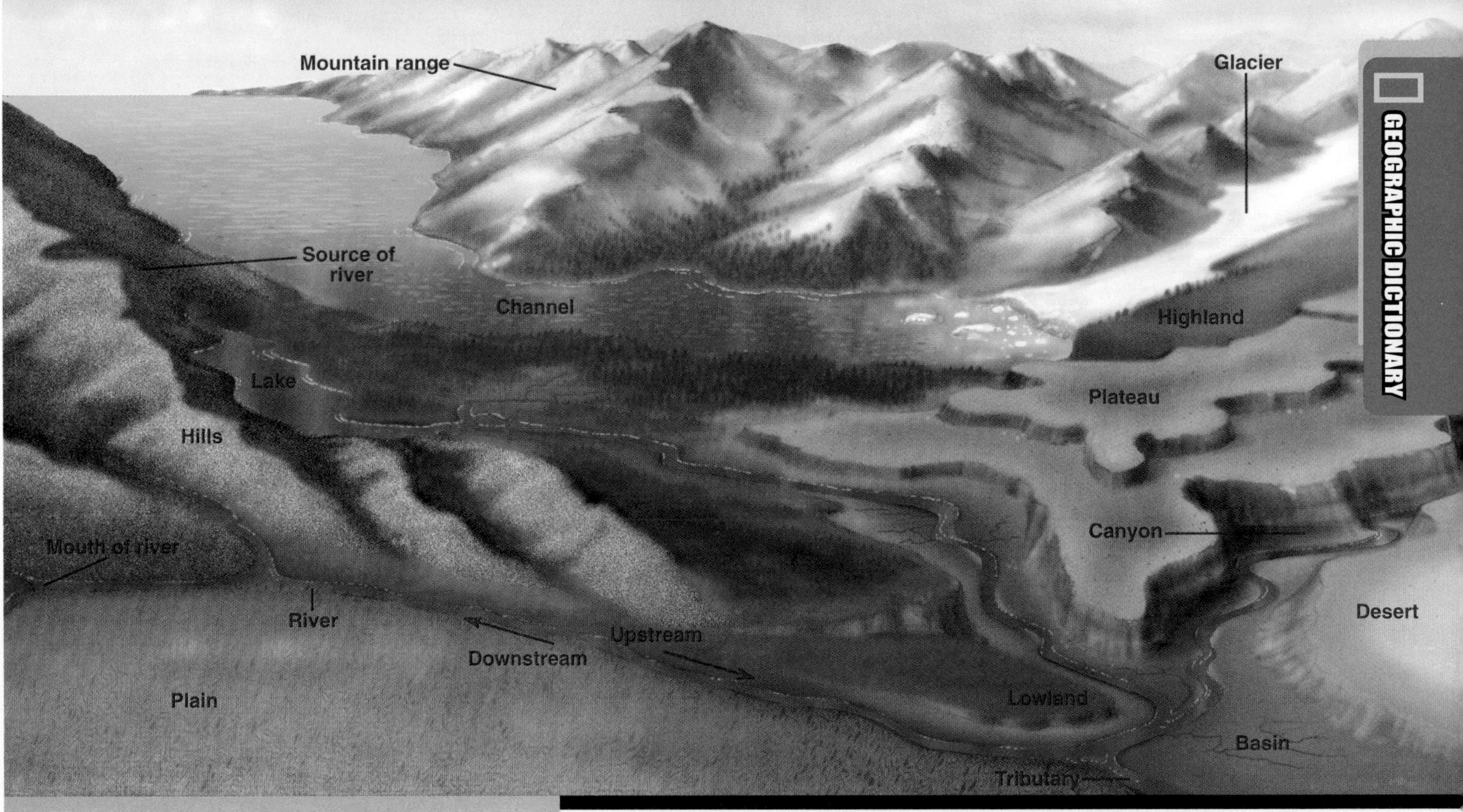

mesa broad, flat-topped landform with steep sides; smaller than a plateau

mountain land with steep sides that rises sharply (1,000 feet or more) from surrounding land; generally larger and more rugged than a hill

mountain peak pointed top of a mountain

mountain range a series of connected mountains

mouth (of a river) place where a stream or river flows into a larger body of water

ocean one of the four major bodies of salt water that surround the continents

ocean current stream of either cold or warm water that moves in a definite direction through an ocean

parallel one of many lines on the global grid that circles the earth north or south of the Equator; used to measure degrees of latitude

peninsula body of land jutting into a lake or ocean, surrounded on three sides by water

physical feature characteristic of a place occurring naturally, such as a landform, body of water, climate pattern, or resource

plain area of level land, usually at low elevation and often covered with grasses

plateau area of flat or rolling land at a high elevation, about 300–3,000 feet high

Prime Meridian line of the global grid running from the North Pole to the South Pole through Greenwich, England; starting point for measuring degrees of east and west longitude

relief changes in elevation over a given area of land

river large natural stream of water that runs through the land

sea large body of water completely or partly surrounded by land

seacoast land lying next to a sea or an ocean

sound broad inland body of water, often between a coastline and one or more islands off the coast

source (of a river) place where a river or stream begins, often in highlands

strait narrow stretch of water joining two larger bodies of water

tributary small river or stream that flows into a large river or stream; a branch of the river

upstream direction opposite the flow of a river; toward the source of a river or stream

valley area of low land between hills or mountains

volcano mountain created as liquid rock and ash erupt from inside the earth

Unit 1

Athlete at Olympic Games, Sydney, Australia

City of Hong Kong, China

The World

You are about to journey to dense rain forests, bleak deserts, bustling cities and marketplaces, and remote villages. You are entering the world of geography—the study of the earth and all its people. Imagine that you could visit any place in the world. Where would you want to go? What would you want to see?

Hot air balloon floating over cultivated fields, Egypt

NGS ONLINE
www.nationalgeographic.com/education

Chapter 1

Looking at the Earth

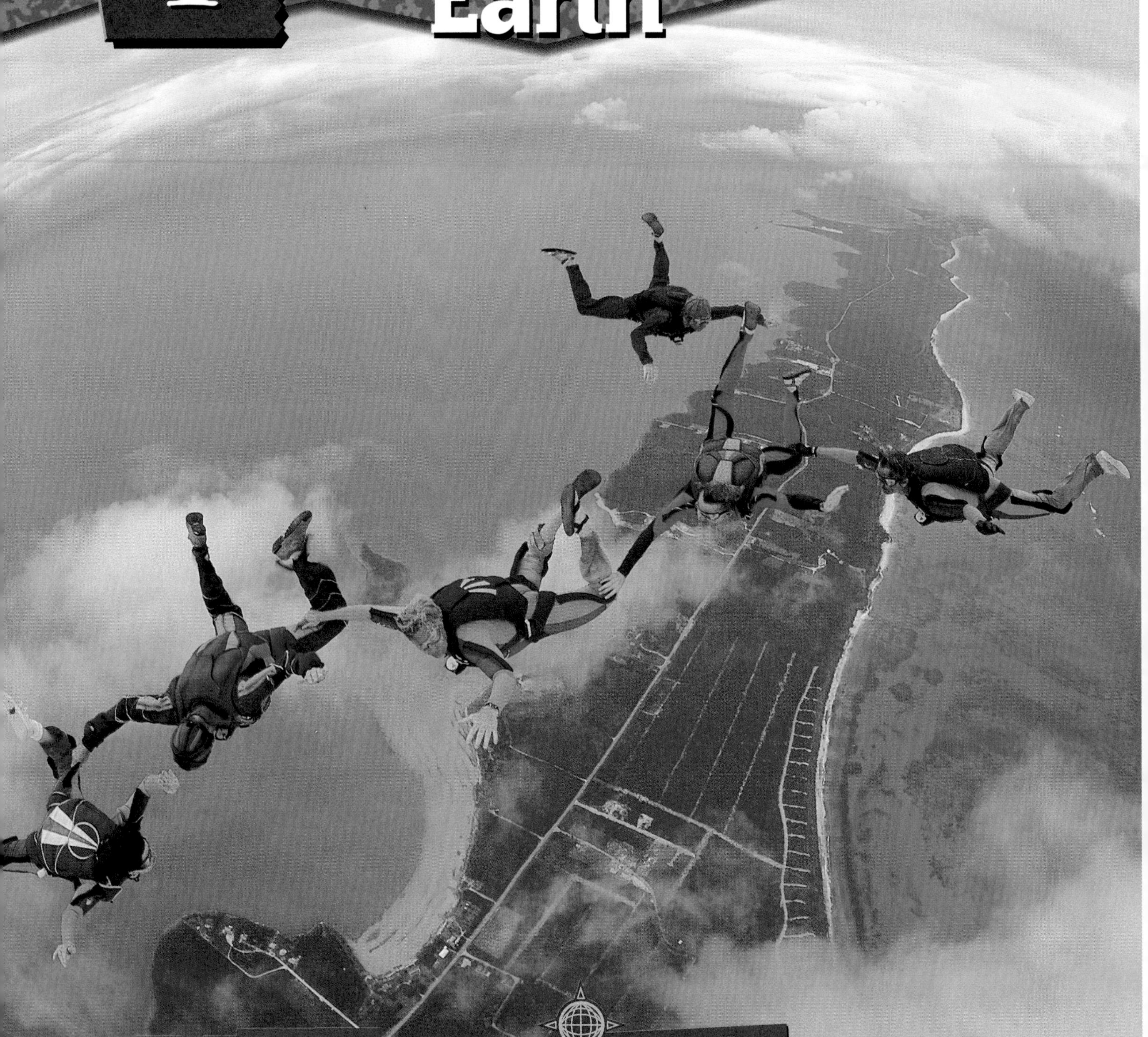

The World and Its People NATIONAL GEOGRAPHIC

To learn more about Earth's structure and landforms, view ***The World and Its People*** **Chapter 1** video.

Geography Online

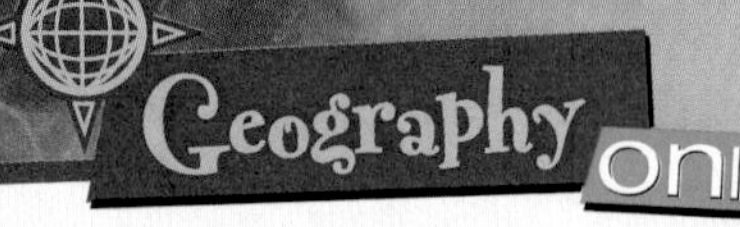

Chapter Overview Visit the ***Geography: The World and Its People*** Web site at gwip.glencoe.com and click on **Chapter 1—Chapter Overviews** to preview information about Earth.

Section 1 Thinking Like a Geographer

Guide to Reading

Main Idea

Geographers use various tools to understand the world.

Terms to Know

- geography
- landform
- environment
- region
- Global Positioning System (GPS)
- geographic information systems (GIS)

Places to Locate

- China
- Yangtze River
- United States
- Andes
- Antarctica
- California

Reading Strategy

Create a chart like this one and write three details or examples for each heading.

How Geographers View the World 1. 2. 3.
Tools of Geography 1. 2. 3.
Uses of Geography 1. 2. 3.

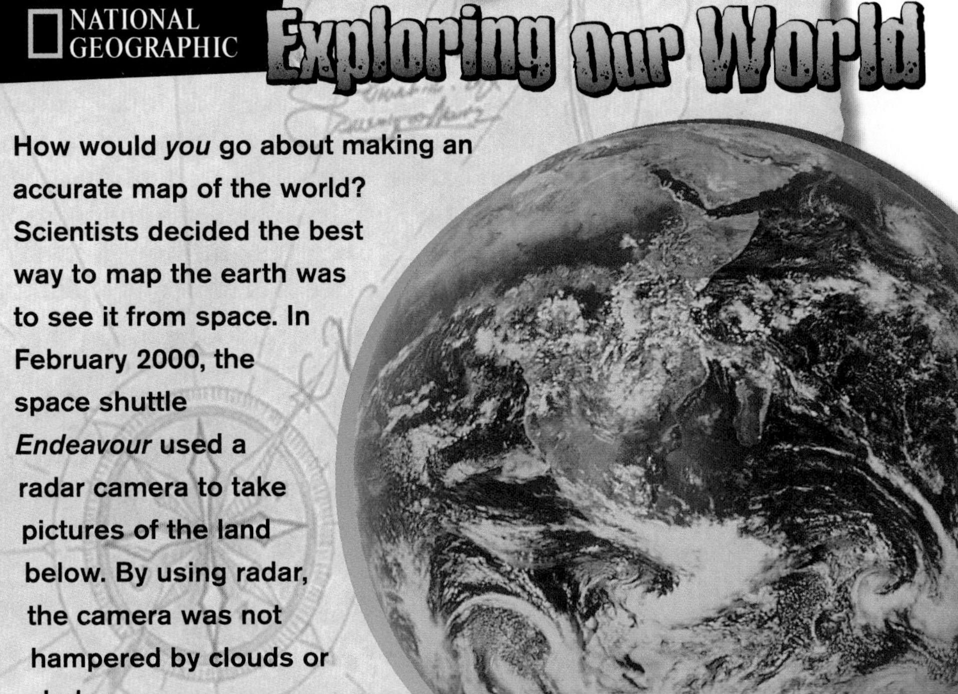

NATIONAL GEOGRAPHIC **Exploring Our World**

How would *you* go about making an accurate map of the world? Scientists decided the best way to map the earth was to see it from space. In February 2000, the space shuttle *Endeavour* used a radar camera to take pictures of the land below. By using radar, the camera was not hampered by clouds or darkness.

Why do geographers want to know exactly what the earth looks like? Think about the following: In **China,** the spring flooding of the **Yangtze** (YANG•SEE) **River** threatens people and crops every year. In 1998 the floods killed more than 4,000 people. After studying the land and the climate, officials in China's government sought solutions. They built dams to hold some of the floodwaters back. Recently, the number of people who died from the floods fell to 700.

This is just one example of how people around the world use geographic knowledge collected from various sources. **Geography** is the study of the earth in all its variety. When you study geography, you learn about the earth's land, water, plants, and animals. This is physical geography. You also study people—where they live, how they live, how they change and are influenced by their environment, and how different groups compare to one another. This is human geography.

◀ Skydiving over Key West, Florida

A Geographer's View of Place

Geographers look at major issues—like the flooding of the Yangtze, which affects millions of people. They also look at local issues—like where the best place is for a company to build a new store in town. Whether major or local, geographers try to understand both the physical and human characteristics, or features, of an issue.

Physical Characteristics Geographers study places. They look at *where* something is located on the earth. They also try to understand what the place is *like*. They ask: What features make a place similar to or different from other places?

To answer this question, geographers identify the landforms of a place. **Landforms** are individual features of the land, like mountains and valleys. Geographers also look at water. Is the place near the ocean or on a river? Does it have plentiful or very little freshwater? They consider whether the soil will produce crops. They see how much rain the place usually receives and how hot or cold the area is. They find out whether the place has minerals, metals, trees, or other resources.

Human Characteristics Geographers also look at the human characteristics of the people living in the place. Do many or only a few people live there? Do they live close together or far apart? Why? What kind of government do they have? What religion do they follow? What kinds of work do they do? What languages do they speak? From where did the people's ancestors come?

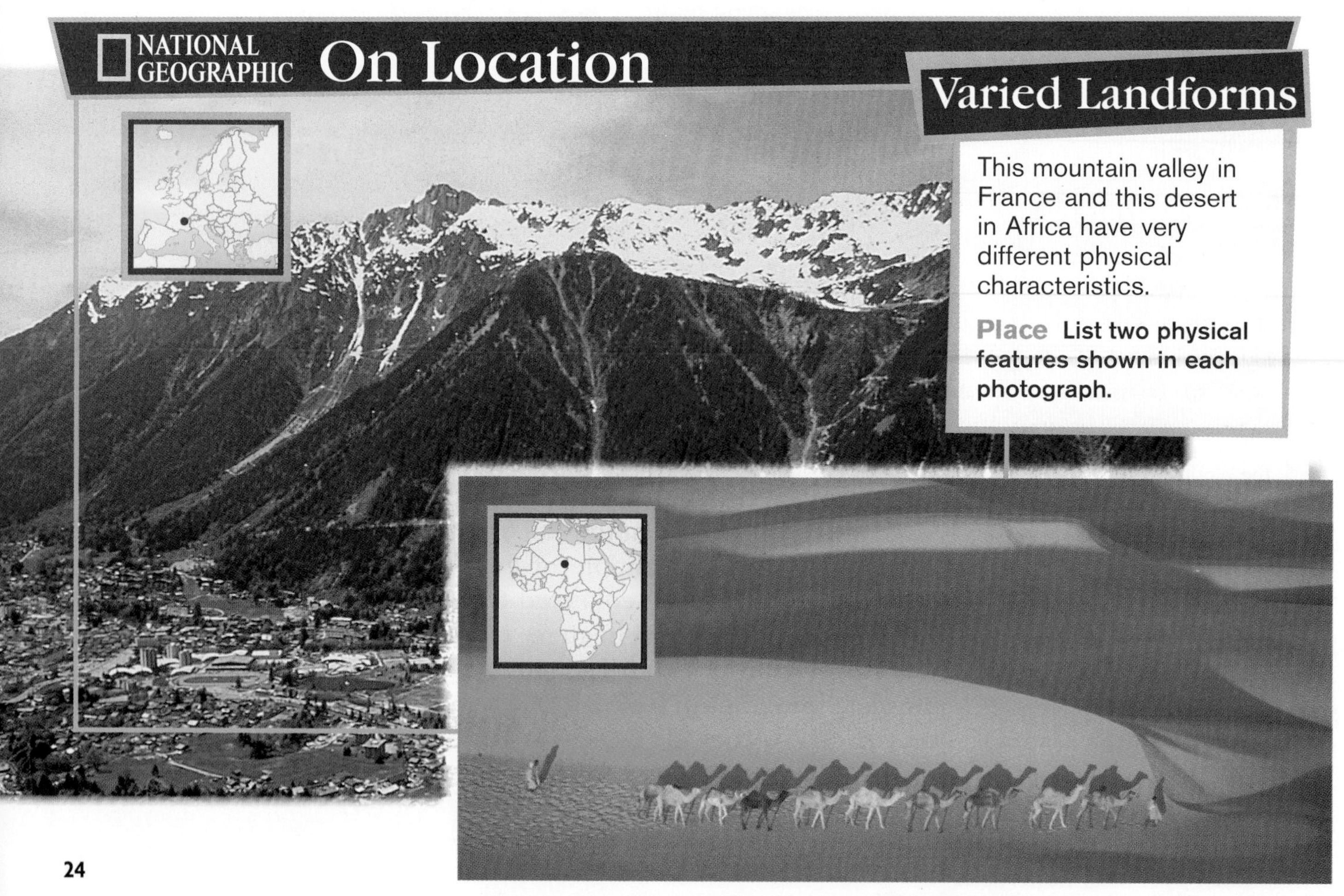

This mountain valley in France and this desert in Africa have very different physical characteristics.

Place List two physical features shown in each photograph.

People and Places Geographers are especially interested in how people interact with their environment, or natural surroundings. People can have a major impact on the environment. Remember how the Chinese built dams along the Yangtze? When they did so, they changed the way the river behaved in flood season.

Where people live often has a strong influence on *how* they live. People near the sea might catch fish and build ships for trade. Those living inland might farm or take up ranching. Of course, as the people of the world use more computers and other technology in their work, the surrounding environment may have less of an influence on what types of work they do.

Regions Geographers carefully study individual cities, rivers, and other landforms. They also look at the big picture, or how individual places relate to other places. In other words, geographers look at a region, or an area that shares common characteristics. Regions can be relatively small—like your state or town. They can also be huge—like all of the western **United States.** Some regions may even include several countries because these countries have similar environments, or because their people follow similar ways of life and speak the same language. The countries along the western side of South America are often discussed as a region—the Andean countries—because the **Andes,** a series of mountain ranges, run through all of them.

✓Reading Check **What do geographers study to determine the human characteristics of a place?**

The Tools of Geography

Geographers need tools to study people and places. Maps and globes are the main tools they use. As you read in the Geography Handbook on page 11, geographers use many different types of maps. Each type gives geographers a particular kind of information about a place.

Collecting Data for Mapping Earth How do geographers gather information so they can make accurate maps? One way is to take photographs from high above the earth. These are called LANDSAT photos and show details such as the shape of the land, what plants cover an area, and how land is being used. Special cameras can even reveal hidden information. Photos of **Antarctica** taken from radar cameras show rivers of ice 500 miles (805 km) long—all hidden by snow.

How do geographers accurately label the exact locations of places on a map? Believe it or not, the best way to find a location is from outer space. A group of satellites traveling around the earth make up the Global Positioning System (GPS). A GPS receiver is a special device that receives signals from these satellites. When the receiver is put at a location, the GPS satellite can tell the exact latitude and longitude of that place. As a result, a mapmaker can know where exactly on the earth the particular area is located. GPS devices are even installed in vehicles to help drivers find their way.

NATIONAL GEOGRAPHIC **On Location**

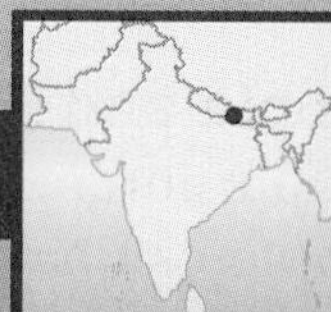

Mt. Everest

GPS satellites locate and *measure* places on the earth. A GPS receiver placed on top of Mt. Everest, the tallest mountain in the world, showed that it is 7 feet (2.1 m) higher than people had previously thought.

Location **Why is it important for geographers to know exactly where places are located on the earth?**

Geographic Information Systems Today geographers use another powerful tool in their work—computers. Special computer software called **geographic information systems (GIS)** helps geographers gather many different kinds of information about the same place. After typing in all the data they collect, geographers use the software to combine and overlap the information on special maps.

As a result, different kinds of information about the same place can be compared. People then use that information to make decisions. For example, in the 1990s, GIS technology was used to help settle an argument over how to use resources in northern **California.** A logging company wanted to cut down parts of a forest. Environmental groups said that doing so would destroy the nesting areas of some rare birds. Geographers created maps that showed both the forest and the nesting sites—and then overlapped these maps. People could then see which areas had to be protected and which could be cut.

Web Activity Visit the ***Geography: The World and Its People*** Web site at gwip.glencoe.com and click on **Chapter 1—Student Web Activities** to learn more about geographic information systems.

Reading Check **What is the difference between GPS and GIS?**

Uses of Geography

Have you ever gone on a long-distance trip in a car or taken a subway ride? If you used a road map or subway map to figure out where you were going, you were using geography. This is just one of the many uses of geographic information.

Geographic information is used in planning. Government leaders use geographic information to plan new services in their communities. They might plan how to handle disasters or how much new housing to allow in an area. Companies can see where people are moving in a region to make their plans for expanding.

In addition, the availability of geographic information helps people make sound decisions. Perhaps a question arises over whether a new building should be constructed. City leaders look at street use to see if the area can handle additional traffic. They make sure the area has the power, water, and sewage systems the building will need.

Businesses use geographic information for making decisions, too. Many businesses study population trends to see what areas need new products or services. Some businesses offer geographic information to their customers. Suppose you were looking for an apartment to rent. Some realtors have a computer program that can identify all the apartments of a certain size and price in an area. The program can create a map so you can see exactly where each apartment is located.

Finally, geographic information helps people manage resources. Many natural resources, such as oil or coal, are available only in limited supply. Geographic information can help people find more of those resources. Other resources, such as trees or water, can be replaced or renewed. People can use geographic information to show them how to manage these resources so they are not all used up.

Reading Check **Why do people have to manage resources carefully?**

Assessment

Defining Terms

1. **Define** geography, landform, environment, region, Global Positioning System (GPS), geographic information systems (GIS).

Recalling Facts

2. **Place** What two kinds of characteristics of a place do geographers study?
3. **Technology** What are the main tools of geography?
4. **Human/Environment Interaction** What are three uses for geography?

Critical Thinking

5. **Understanding Cause and Effect** How have the physical characteristics of your region affected the way people live there?
6. **Categorizing Information** Give five examples of regions. Begin with an area near you that shares common characteristics, then look for larger and larger regions.

Graphic Organizer

7. **Organizing Information** Draw a diagram like this one. In the center, write the name of a place you would like to visit. In the outer ovals, identify the types of geographic information you would like to learn about this place.

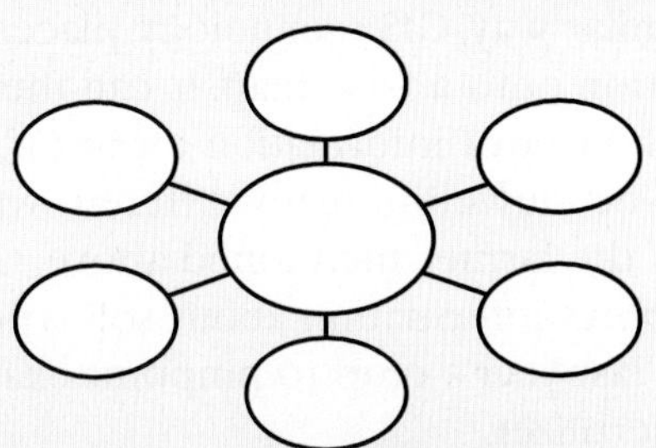

Applying Geography Skills

8. **Analyzing Maps** Find Egypt on the map on page RA23 of the **Reference Atlas.** Along what physical feature do you think most Egyptians live? Why? Turn to the population map of Egypt on page 13 of the **Geography Handbook** to see if you are correct.

Making Connections

ART | SCIENCE | LITERATURE | TECHNOLOGY

Geographic Information Systems

What if a farmer could save money by applying fertilizer only to the crops that needed it? Today, thanks to computer technology called geographic information systems (GIS), farmers can do just that.

The Technology

Geographic information systems (GIS) use computer software to combine and display a wide range of information about an area. GIS programs start with a map showing a specific location on the earth. This map is then linked with other information about that same place, such as satellite photos, amounts of rainfall, or where houses are located.

Think of geographic information systems as a stack of overhead transparencies. Each transparency shows the same general background but highlights different information. The first transparency may show a base map of an area. Only the borders may appear. The second transparency may show only rivers and highways. The third may highlight mountains and other physical features, buildings, or cities.

In a similar way, GIS technology places layers of information onto a base map. It can then switch each layer of information on or off, allowing data to be viewed in many different ways. In the case of the farmer mentioned above, GIS software combines information about soil type, plant needs, and last year's crop to pinpoint exact areas that need fertilizer.

How It Is Used

GIS technology allows users to quickly pull together data from many different sources and construct maps tailored to specific needs. This helps people analyze past events, predict future scenarios, and make sound decisions.

A person who is deciding where to build a new store can use GIS technology to help select the best location. The process might begin with a list of possible sites. The store owner gathers information about the areas surrounding each place. This could include shoppers' ages, incomes, and educations; where shoppers live; traffic patterns; and other stores in the area. The GIS software then builds a computerized map composed of these layers of information. The store owner can use the information to decide on a new store location.

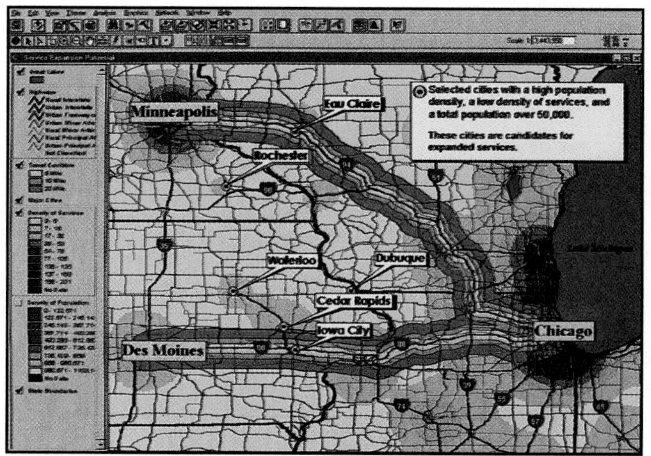

Graphic image created using ArcView® GIS software, and provided courtesy of Environmental Systems Research Institute, Inc.

Making the Connection

1. What is GIS technology?
2. How do GIS programs analyze data in a variety of ways?
3. **Drawing Conclusions** How could a school district use GIS technology to locate the best place to add a new school?

Section 2

The Earth in Space

Guide to Reading

Main Idea

The earth has life because of the sun. The earth has different seasons because of the way it tilts and revolves around the sun.

Terms to Know

- solar system
- orbit
- atmosphere
- axis
- revolution
- leap year
- summer solstice
- winter solstice
- equinox

Places to Locate

- Earth
- sun
- moon

Reading Strategy

Draw a diagram like this one and list three facts about the sun in the first column. In the second, write how these facts contribute to life on the earth.

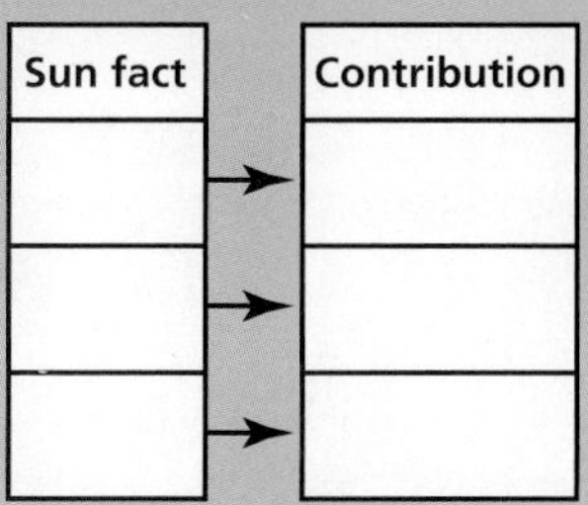

NATIONAL GEOGRAPHIC **Exploring Our World**

The sun warms the earth, but the sun's warmth barely reaches Antarctica at the southern tip of our planet. Even in summer, temperatures are often below 0°F (−18°C). Winter temperatures may fall to −100°F (−73°C). Every part of this scientist's body must be protected against the freezing cold as he moves through an enormous ice tunnel in Antarctica.

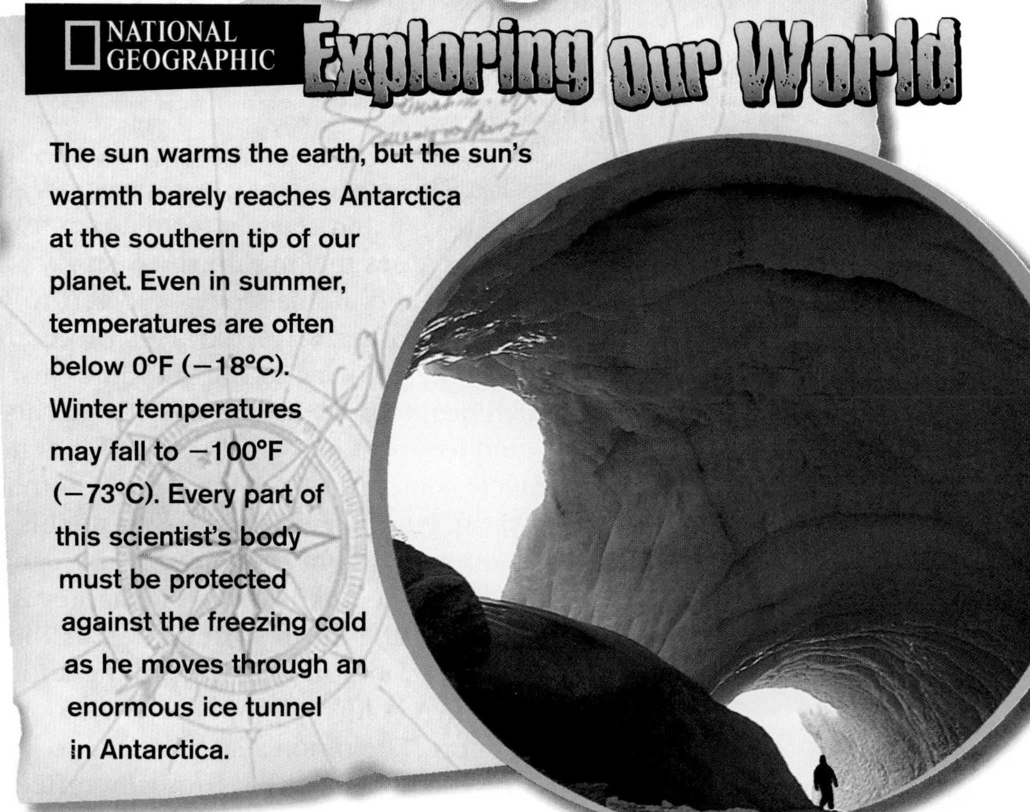

The sun's heat provides life on our planet. **Earth,** eight other planets, and thousands of smaller bodies all revolve around the **sun.** Together with the sun, these bodies form the solar system. Look at the diagram of the solar system on page 30. As you can see, Earth is the third planet from the sun.

The Solar System

Each planet travels along its own path, or orbit, around the sun. The paths they travel are ellipses, which are like stretched-out circles. Each planet takes a different amount of time to complete one full trip around the sun. Earth makes one trip in 365¼ days. Mercury orbits the sun in just 88 days. Far-off Pluto takes almost 250 years!

Planets can be classified into two types—those that are like Earth and those that are like Jupiter. Earthlike planets are Mercury, Venus, Mars, and Pluto. These planets are solid and small. They have few or no moons. They also rotate, or spin, fairly slowly.

The other four planets—Jupiter, Saturn, Neptune, and Uranus—are huge. Uranus, the smallest of the four, is 15 times the size of Earth.

Solar Eclipse

One of the most spectacular sights in the sky is a solar eclipse. This event takes place when the moon passes between Earth and the sun and covers some or all of the sun. The photograph here shows a total eclipse, when the moon completely blocks the sun. When the moon blocks the sun's light, a large shadow is cast on part of Earth.

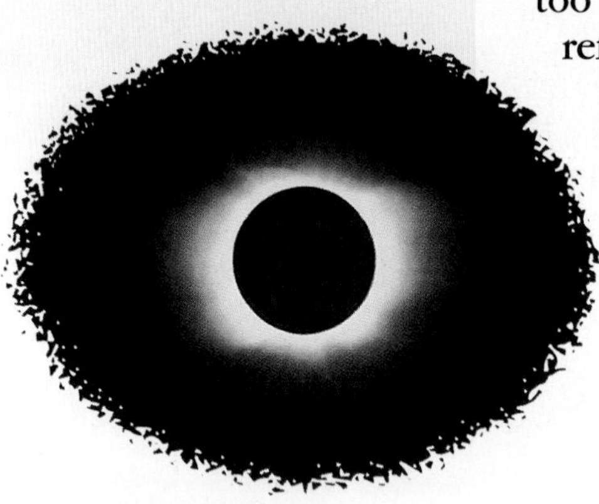

These planets are more like balls of gas than rockier Earthlike planets. They spin rapidly and have many moons. Surrounding each one is a series of rings made of bits of rock and dust.

Sun, Earth, and Moon The sun—about 93 million miles (150 million km) from Earth—is made mostly of intensely hot gases. Reactions that occur inside the sun make it as hot as 27 million degrees Fahrenheit (about 15 million degrees Celsius). As a result, the sun gives off light and warmth. Life on Earth could not exist without the sun.

The layer of air surrounding Earth—the atmosphere—also supports life. This cushion of gases measures about 1,000 miles (1,609 km) thick. Nitrogen and oxygen form about 99 percent of the atmosphere, with other gases making up the rest.

Humans and animals need oxygen to breathe. The atmosphere is important in other ways, too. This protective layer holds in enough of the sun's heat to make life possible, just as a greenhouse keeps in enough heat to protect plants. Without this protection, Earth would be too cold for most living things. At the same time, the atmosphere also reflects some heat back into space so that Earth will not become too warm. Finally, the atmosphere shields living things. It screens out some rays from the sun that are dangerous. You will learn more about the atmosphere in Chapter 2.

Earth's nearest neighbor in the solar system is its **moon.** The moon orbits Earth, taking about 30 days to complete each trip. A cold, rocky sphere, the moon has no water and no atmosphere. The moon also gives off no light of its own. When you see the moon shining, it is actually reflecting light from the sun.

The Solar System

Analyzing the Diagram

Earth and eight other planets in our solar system travel around the sun.

Movement Between what two planets' orbits is Earth's orbit?

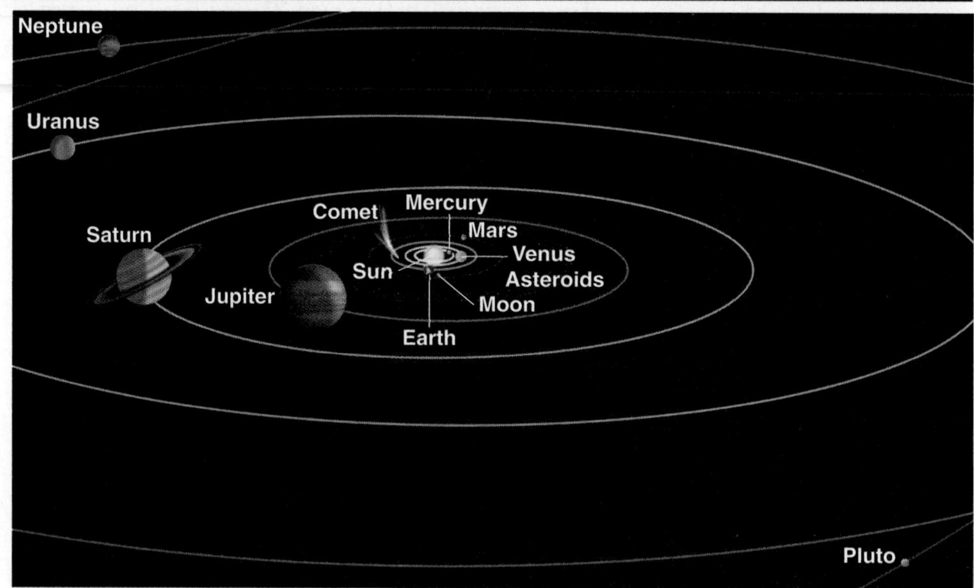

Seasons

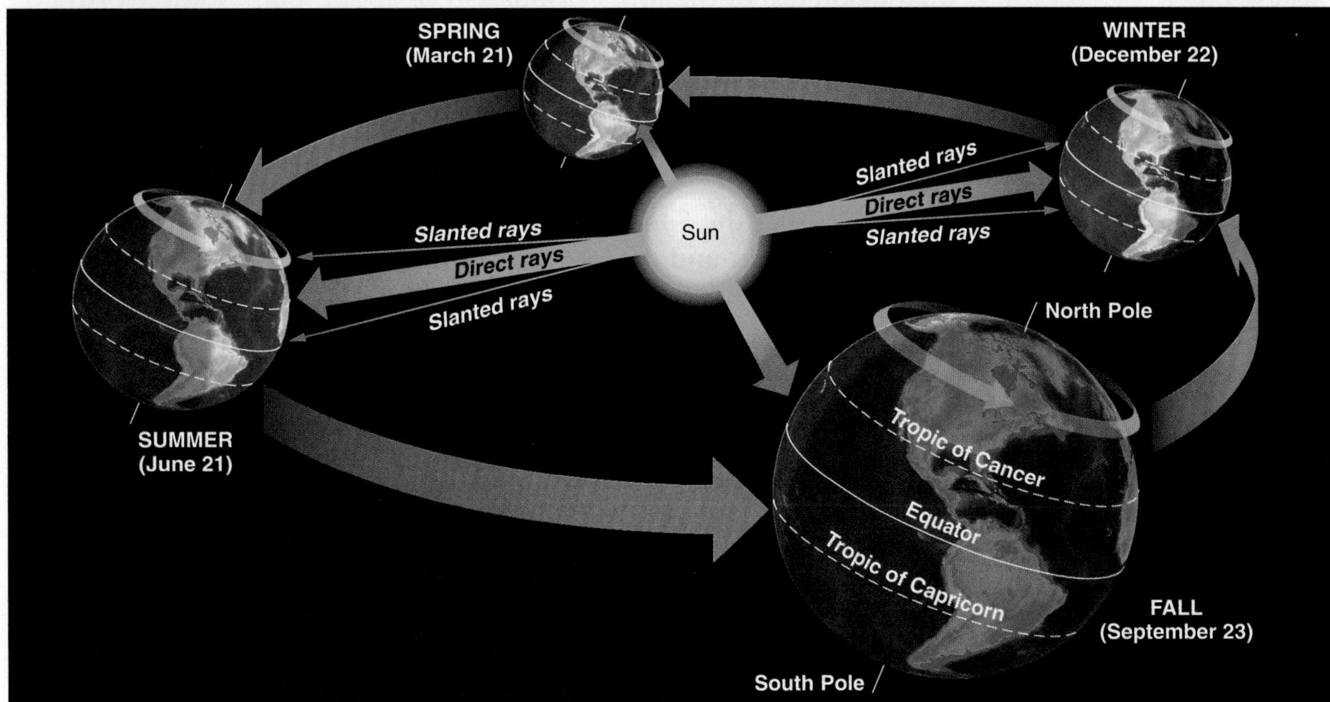

Analyzing the Diagram

Because Earth is tilted, different areas receive direct rays from the sun at different times of the year.

Movement **How does this fact cause changes in seasons?**

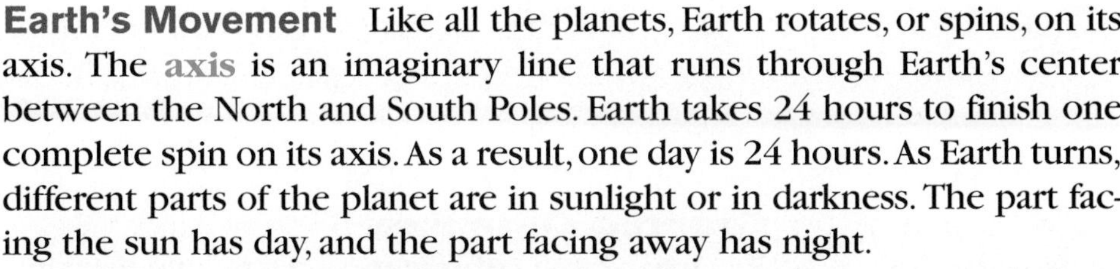

Earth's Movement Like all the planets, Earth rotates, or spins, on its axis. The **axis** is an imaginary line that runs through Earth's center between the North and South Poles. Earth takes 24 hours to finish one complete spin on its axis. As a result, one day is 24 hours. As Earth turns, different parts of the planet are in sunlight or in darkness. The part facing the sun has day, and the part facing away has night.

Earth has another motion, too. The planet makes one **revolution,** or complete orbit around the sun, in 365¼ days. This period is what we define as one year. Every four years, the extra one-fourths of a day are combined and added to the calendar as February 29. A year that contains one of these extra days is called a **leap year.**

✓Reading Check **How does Earth's orbit affect you?**

The Sun and the Seasons

Earth is tilted 23½ degrees on its axis. As a result, seasons change as Earth makes its year-long orbit around the sun. To see why this happens, look at the four globes in the diagram above. Notice how sunlight falls directly on the northern or southern halves of Earth at different times of the year. Direct rays from the sun bring more warmth than the slanted rays. When the people in a hemisphere receive those direct rays from the sun, they enjoy the warmth of summer. When they receive only indirect rays, they experience winter, which is colder.

Solstices and Equinoxes Four days in the year have special names because of the position of the sun in relation to Earth. These days mark the beginnings of the four seasons. On or about June 21, the North Pole is tilted toward the sun. On noon of this day, the sun appears directly overhead at the line of latitude called the Tropic of Cancer (23½°N latitude). This day is the **summer solstice,** the day in the Northern Hemisphere with the most hours of sunlight and the fewest hours of darkness. It is the beginning of summer—but only in the Northern Hemisphere. In the Southern Hemisphere, it is the day with the fewest hours of sunlight and marks the beginning of winter.

Six months later—on or about December 22—the North Pole is tilted away from the sun. At noon, the sun's direct rays strike the line of latitude known as the Tropic of Capricorn (23½°S latitude). In the Northern Hemisphere, this day is the **winter solstice**—the day with the fewest hours of sunlight. This same day, though, marks the beginning of summer in the Southern Hemisphere.

Spring and autumn begin midway between the two solstices. These are the **equinoxes,** when day and night are of equal length in both hemispheres. On or about March 21, the *vernal equinox* (spring) occurs. On or about September 23, the *autumnal equinox* occurs. On both of these days, the noon sun shines directly over the Equator.

✓Reading Check **Which seasons begin on the two equinoxes?**

Assessment

Defining Terms

1. Define solar system, orbit, atmosphere, axis, revolution, leap year, summer solstice, winter solstice, equinox.

Recalling Facts

2. Region What bodies make up the solar system?

3. Science List two gases that are found in the atmosphere.

4. Movement What two motions does Earth make in space?

Critical Thinking

5. Analyzing Information How does the position of Earth determine whether a day is one of the solstice or equinox days?

6. Summarizing Information In a paragraph, describe why you experience seasonal changes.

Graphic Organizer

7. Organizing Information Draw two diagrams like those below. In the first, list the effects of Earth's rotation on human, plant, and animal life. In the second, list effects if Earth were to stop rotating.

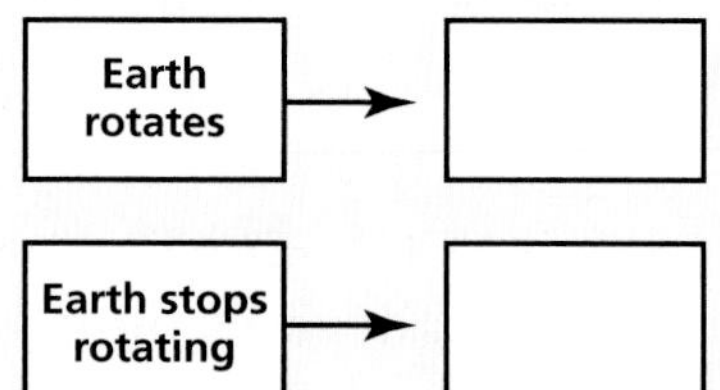

Applying Geography Skills

8. Analyzing Diagrams Look at the diagram on page 31. When the sun's direct rays hit the Tropic of Capricorn, what season is it in the Northern Hemisphere?

Geography Skill

Using a Map Key

To understand what a map is showing, you must read the **map key,** or legend. The map key explains the meaning of special colors, symbols, and lines on the map.

Learning the Skill

Colors in the map key may represent different elevations or heights of land, climate areas, or languages. Lines may stand for rivers, streets, or boundaries.

Maps also have a **compass rose** showing directions. The **cardinal directions** are north, south, east, and west. North and south are the directions of the North and South Poles. If you stand facing north, east is the direction to your right. West is the direction on your left. The compass rose might also show **intermediate directions,** or those that fall between the cardinal directions. For example, the intermediate direction *northeast* falls between north and east. To use a map key, follow these steps:

- Read the map title.
- Read the map key to find out what special information it gives.
- Find examples of each map key color, line, or symbol on the map.
- Use the compass rose to identify the four cardinal directions.

Practicing the Skill

Look at the map of Washington, D.C., below to answer the following questions.

1. What does the red square represent?
2. What does the blue square represent?
3. Does the Washington Monument lie east or west of the Lincoln Memorial?
4. From the White House, in what direction would you go to get to the Capitol?

Applying the Skill

Find a map in a newspaper or magazine. Use the map key to explain three things the map is showing.

GO TO

Practice key skills with **Glencoe Skillbuilder Interactive Workbook, Level 1.**

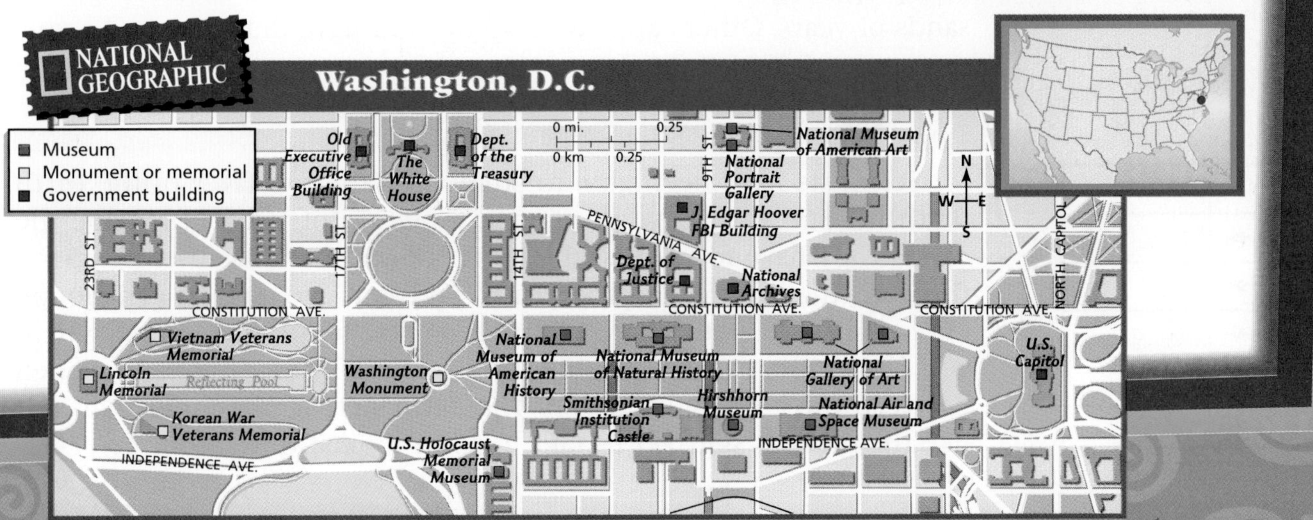

Section 3

The Earth's Structure

Guide to Reading

Main Idea

Forces both inside the earth and on its surface affect the shape of the land.

Terms to Know

- core
- mantle
- magma
- crust
- continent
- plate tectonics
- earthquake
- tsunami
- fault
- weathering
- erosion
- glacier

Places to Locate

- South America
- Africa
- Himalaya
- Asia

Reading Strategy

Create a chart like this one. Write five forces that change the shape of the land. Then write five effects these forces can have on the earth.

Forces	Effects
→	
→	
→	
→	
→	

NATIONAL GEOGRAPHIC **Exploring Our World**

Forces beneath the earth's surface shape the land and the lives of the people who live on it. Here in the Azores Islands, a volcano makes cooking easy. People wrap pots of meat and vegetables in a cloth and bury the bundle in a hole where heat from deep inside the earth rises to the surface. The temperature reaches 200°F (93°C), which is hot enough to steam the food.

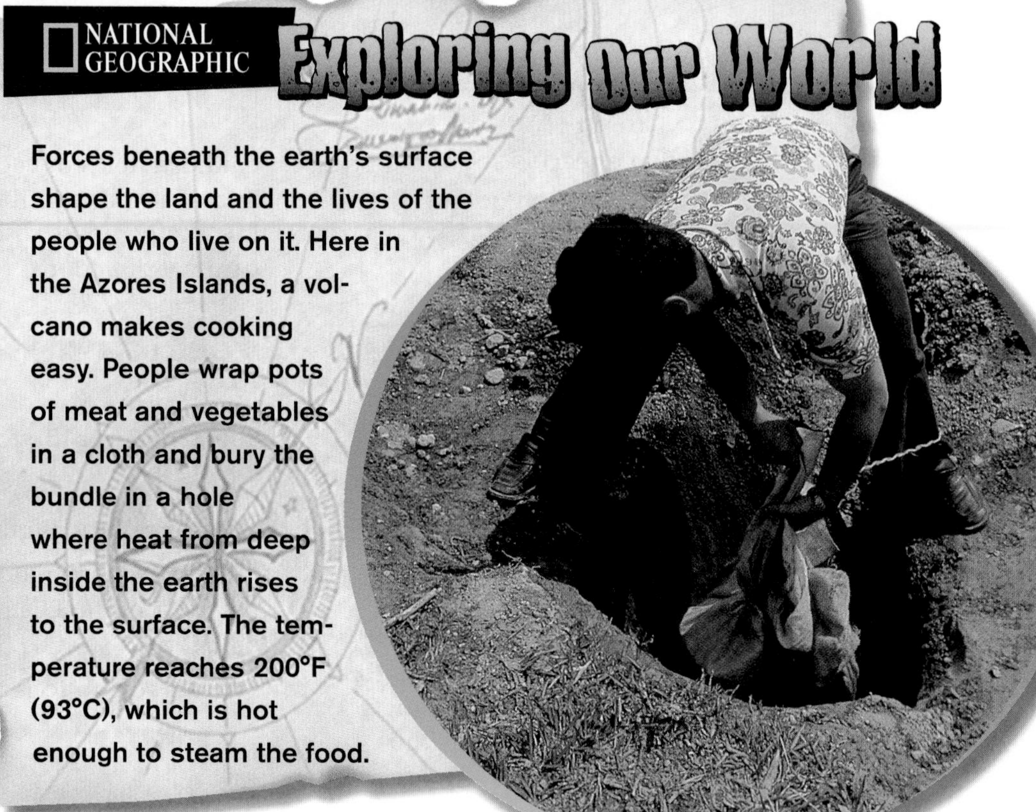

It is amazing to think that the earth thousands of miles beneath your feet is so hot that it has turned metal into liquid. Although you may not feel these forces, what lies inside the earth affects what lies on top. Mountains, deserts, and other landscapes were formed over millions of years by forces acting below the earth's surface—and they are still changing today. Some forces work slowly and show no results for thousands of years. Others appear suddenly and have dramatic, and sometimes very destructive, effects.

Inside the Earth

Scientists have been able to study only the top layer of the earth firsthand. Still, they have developed a picture of what lies inside the earth. They have found that the inside of the earth has three layers—the core, the mantle, and the crust. Have you ever seen a cantaloupe cut in half? The earth's core is like the center of the cantaloupe, where you find the seeds. The mantle is like the flesh of the fruit, sandwiched between the core and the skin. The earth's crust, or topmost layer, is like the melon's skin. Let us take a closer look at these three layers.

In the center of the earth is a dense **core** of hot iron mixed with other metals. The very center is solid, but the outer core is so hot that the metal has melted into liquid. Surrounding the core is the **mantle,** a layer of rock about 1,800 miles (2,897 km) thick. Like the core, the mantle also has two parts. The section nearest the core remains solid, but the rock in the outer mantle sometimes melts. If you have seen photographs of an active volcano, then you have seen this melted rock, called **magma,** when it flowed to the surface in a volcanic eruption.

The uppermost layer of the earth, the **crust,** is relatively thin. It reaches only 31 to 62 miles (50 to 100 km) deep. The crust includes the ocean floors. It also includes seven massive land areas known as **continents.** The crust is thinnest on the ocean floor. It is thicker below the continents. Turn to the map on page 41 to see where the earth's seven continents are located.

Reading Check What layer of the earth is thinnest?

NATIONAL GEOGRAPHIC

Earth's Layers

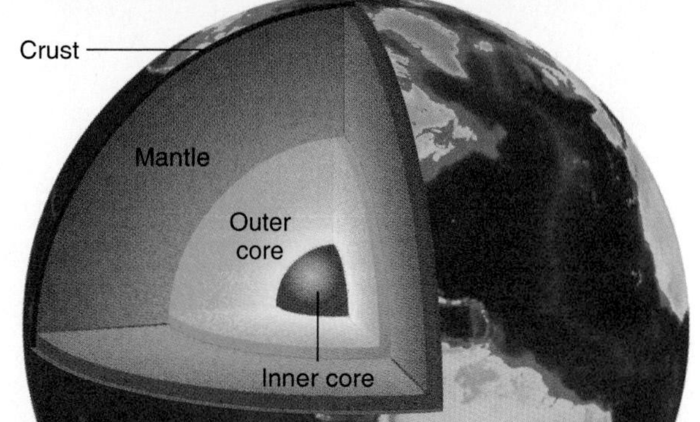

Analyzing the Diagram

Hot rock and metal—some of it liquid—fill the center of the earth.

Region What is the innermost layer inside the earth called? In what layer do you find the continents?

Forces Beneath the Earth's Crust

Most of you have probably watched science shows about earthquakes and volcanoes. You have probably also seen news on television discussing the destruction caused by earthquakes. These events result from forces at work inside the earth.

Plate Movements Scientists have developed a theory about the earth's structure called **plate tectonics.** This theory states that the crust is not an unbroken shell but consists of plates, or huge slabs of rock, that move. The plates float on top of the liquid rock in the upper part of the mantle. They move—but often in different directions. Oceans and continents sit on these gigantic plates, as the diagram on page 36 shows.

Have you ever noticed that the eastern part of **South America** seems to fit into the western side of **Africa?** That is because these two continents were once joined together in a landmass that scientists call Pangaea. Millions of years ago, however, the continents moved apart. Tectonic activity caused them to move. The plates are still moving today, but they move so slowly that you do not feel it. The plate under the Pacific Ocean moves to the west at the rate of about 4 inches (10 cm) a year. That is about the same rate that a man's beard grows. The plate along the western edge of South America moves east at the rate of about 1.8 inches (5 cm) a year. That is a little faster than your finger nails grow. Turn to page 45 to see what Pangaea looked like before and after it experienced this movement, known as *continental drift.*

Tectonic Plate Boundaries

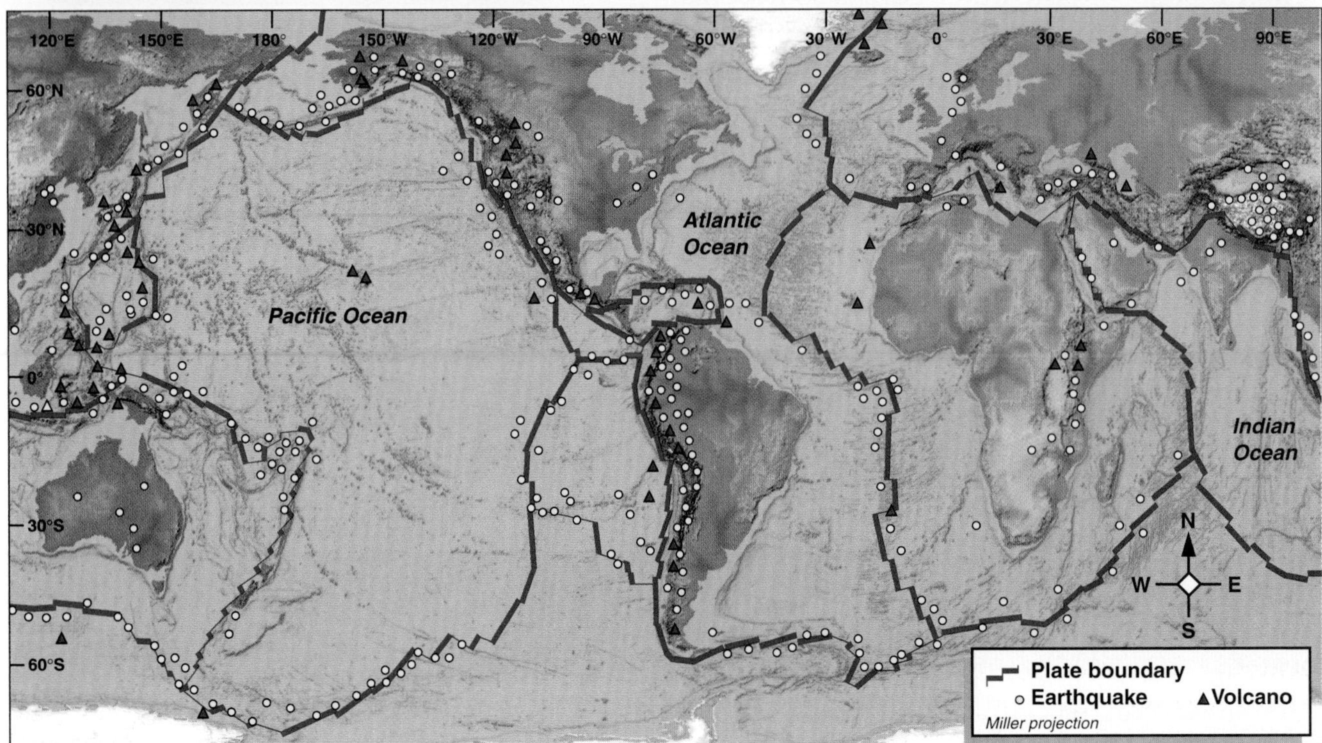

Analyzing the Diagram

Most of North America sits on one plate.

Region What pattern do you see among plate boundaries, earthquakes, and volcanoes?

When Plates Meet The movements of the earth's plates have actually shaped the surface of the earth. Sometimes the plates spread, or pull away from each other. That type of tectonic action separated South America and Africa millions of years ago. Sometimes, though, the plates push against each other. When this happens, one of three events occurs, depending on what kinds of plates are involved.

If two continental plates smash into each other, the collision produces high mountain ranges. This kind of collision produced the **Himalaya** in South **Asia.**

If a continental plate and an ocean plate move against each other, the thicker continental plate slides over the thinner ocean plate. The edge of the lower plate melts into the mantle, causing molten rock to build up and perhaps erupt in a volcano. Another result may occur from the pressure that builds up between the two sliding plates. This pressure may cause one plate to move suddenly. The result is called an **earthquake,** or a violent and sudden movement of the earth's crust.

Earthquakes can be very damaging to both physical structures and human lives. They can collapse buildings, destroy bridges, and break apart underground water or gas pipes. Undersea earthquakes can cause huge waves called **tsunamis** (tsu•NAH•mees). These waves may reach as high as 98 feet (30 m). Such waves can cause severe flooding of coastal towns.

Sometimes two plates do not meet head-on but move alongside each other. To picture this, put your hands together and then move them in opposite directions. When this action occurs in the earth, the two plates slide against each other. This movement creates **faults,** or cracks in the earth's crust. Violent earthquakes can happen near these faults. In 1988, for example, an earthquake struck the country of Armenia. About 25,000 people were killed, and another 500,000 lost their homes. One of the most famous faults in the United States is the San Andreas Fault in California. The earth's movement along this fault caused a severe earthquake in San Francisco in 1906 and another less serious quake in 1989.

Reading Check **What happens when two continental plates collide?**

Forces Shaping Landforms

The forces under the earth's crust that move tectonic plates cause volcanoes and earthquakes to change the earth's landforms. Once formed, however, these landforms will continue to change because of forces that work on the earth's surface.

Weathering **Weathering** is the process of breaking surface rock into boulders, gravel, sand, and soil. Water and frost, chemicals, and even plants cause weathering. Water seeps into cracks of rocks and then freezes. As it freezes, the ice expands and splits the rock. Sometimes entire sides of cliffs fall off because frost has wedged the rock apart. Chemicals, too, cause weathering when acids in air pollution mix with rain and fall back to the earth. The chemicals eat away the surfaces of stone structures and natural rocks. Even tiny seeds that fall into cracks can spread out roots, causing huge boulders to eventually break apart.

Architecture

In earthquake-prone parts of the world, engineers design new buildings to stand up to tremors, or shaking of the earth. Flexible structures allow buildings to sway rather than break apart. Placing a building on pads or rollers cushions the structure from the motion of the ground. Some so-called intelligent buildings automatically respond to tremors, shifting their weight or tightening and loosening joints.

Looking Closer How can studying earthquake-damaged buildings help designers improve future construction?

San Francisco, California, 1989 ▶

Erosion **Erosion** is the process of wearing away or moving weathered material. Water, wind, and ice are the greatest factors that erode, or wear away, surface material. Moving water in oceans, rivers, streams, and rain can erode even the hardest stone over time. Rainwater working its way to streams and rivers picks up and moves soil and sand. These particles make the river water similar to a giant scrub brush that grinds away at riverbanks and any other surface in the water's path.

Wind is also a major cause of erosion as it lifts weathered soil and sand. The areas that lose soil often become unable to grow crops and support life. The areas that receive the windblown soil often benefit from the additional nutrients to the land. When wind carries sand, however, it acts as sandpaper. Rock and other structures are carved into smooth shapes.

The third cause of erosion is ice. Giant, slow-moving sheets of ice are called **glaciers.** Forming high in mountains, glaciers change the land as they inch over it. Similar to windstorms, glaciers act like sandpaper as they pick up and carry rocks down the mountainside, grinding smooth everything beneath them. Some glaciers are thousands of feet thick. The weight and pressure of thousands of feet of ice also cut deep valleys at the mountain's base.

Reading Check **List three things that can cause weathering.**

Assessment

Defining Terms

1. **Define** core, mantle, magma, crust, continent, plate tectonics, earthquake, tsunami, fault, weathering, erosion, glacier.

Recalling Facts

2. **Region** What are the three layers inside the earth?
3. **Movement** In what three ways can tectonic plates move?
4. **Science** What are the three greatest factors that cause erosion?

Critical Thinking

5. **Making Comparisons** How does water play a role in both processes of weathering and erosion?
6. **Understanding Cause and Effect** How does erosion hurt some areas yet benefit others?

Graphic Organizer

7. **Organizing Information** Draw a diagram like this one, then label the inner arrows with inside forces that shape landforms. Label the outer arrows with surface forces that change the earth's landforms.

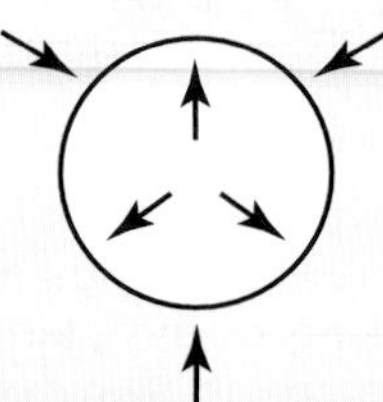

Applying Geography Skills

8. **Analyzing Diagrams** Look at the diagram of tectonic plate boundaries on page 36. Why might it be a problem that most of the world's population lives along the western edge of the Pacific Ocean?

Landforms

Guide to Reading

Main Idea

Landforms in all their variety affect how people live.

Terms to Know

- elevation
- plain
- plateau
- isthmus
- peninsula
- island
- continental shelf
- trench
- strait
- channel
- delta

Places to Locate

- Mt. Everest
- North European Plain
- Plateau of Tibet
- Grand Canyon
- Mariana Trench
- Strait of Magellan

Reading Strategy

Draw a diagram like this one. In each of the surrounding circles, write the name of a landform and a fact about it.

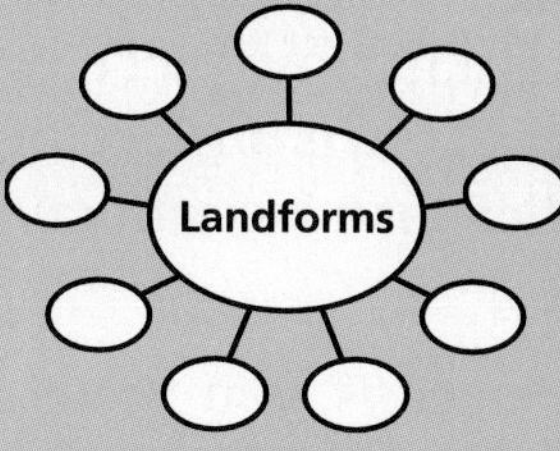

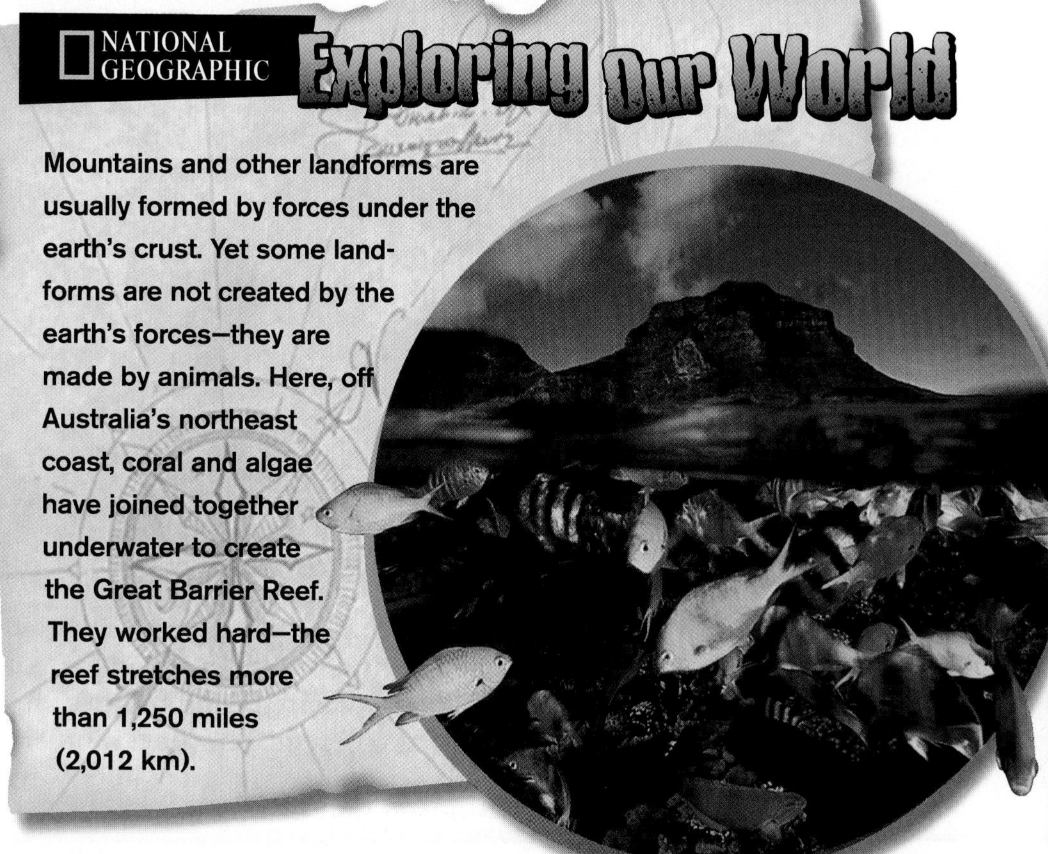

Mountains and other landforms are usually formed by forces under the earth's crust. Yet some landforms are not created by the earth's forces—they are made by animals. Here, off Australia's northeast coast, coral and algae have joined together underwater to create the Great Barrier Reef. They worked hard—the reef stretches more than 1,250 miles (2,012 km).

The earth's land surface consists of seven continents. These are North America, South America, Europe, Africa, Asia, Australia, and Antarctica. All have a variety of landforms, or individual features of the land—even icy Antarctica.

Types of Landforms

Look at the illustration on page 18 of the **Geography Handbook.** Notice the many different forms that the land may take. Which ones are familiar to you? Which ones are new to you?

On Land Mountains are huge towers of rock formed by the collision of the earth's tectonic plates or by volcanoes. Some mountains may be a few thousand feet high. Others can soar higher than 20,000 feet (6,096 m). The world's tallest mountain is **Mt. Everest,** located in South Asia's Himalaya mountain ranges. It towers at 29,035 feet (8,850 m)—nearly 5.5 miles (8.9 km) high.

Mountains have high peaks and steep, rugged slopes. Hills are lower and more rounded, though they are still higher than the land

The Great Rift Valley in Africa is surrounded by mountains (above). Canyons, like the Grand Canyon in Arizona (right), are carved from plateaus.

Place How are valleys and canyons similar?

around them. Some hills form at the foot, or base, of mountains. As a result, these hills are called foothills.

In contrast, plains and plateaus are mostly flat. What makes them different from one another is their **elevation,** or height above sea level. **Plains** are low-lying stretches of flat or gently rolling land. Many plains reach from the middle of a continent to the coast. The **North European Plain** is an example. **Plateaus** are also flat but have higher elevation. With some plateaus, a steep cliff forms on one side where the plateau rises above nearby lowlands. With others, such as the **Plateau of Tibet** in Asia, the plateau is surrounded by mountains.

Between mountains and hills lie valleys. A valley is a long stretch of land lower than the land on either side. You often find rivers at the bottom of valleys. Canyons are steep-sided lowlands that rivers have cut through a plateau. One of the most famous canyons is the **Grand Canyon** in Arizona. For millions of years, the Colorado River flowed over a plateau and carved through rock, forming the Grand Canyon.

Geographers describe some landforms by their relationship to larger land areas or to bodies of water. An **isthmus** is a narrow piece of land that connects two larger pieces of land. A **peninsula** is a piece of land with water on three sides. A body of land smaller than a continent and completely surrounded by water is an **island.**

Under the Oceans If you were to explore the oceans, you would see landforms under the water that are similar to those on land. The map on page RA32 of the **Reference Atlas** shows you what the ocean floors look like. Off each coast of a continent lies a plateau called a

continental shelf that stretches for several miles underwater. At the edge of the shelf, steep cliffs drop down to the ocean floor.

Tall mountains and very deep valleys line the ocean floor. Valleys here are called **trenches,** and they are the lowest spots in the earth's crust. The deepest one, in the western Pacific Ocean, is called the **Mariana Trench.** This trench plunges 35,840 feet (10,924 m) below sea level. How deep is that? If Mt. Everest were placed into this trench, the mountain would have to grow 1.3 miles (2 km) higher just to reach the ocean's surface.

Landforms and People Humans have settled on all types of landforms. Some people live at high elevations in the Andes mountain ranges of South America. The people of Bangladesh live on a low coastal plain. Farmers in Ethiopia work the land on a plateau called the Ethiopian Highlands.

Why do people decide to live in a particular area? Climate—the average temperature and rainfall of a region—is one reason. You will read more about climate in the next chapter. The availability of resources is another reason. People settle where they can get freshwater and where they can grow food, catch fish, or raise animals. They might settle in an area because it has good supplies of useful items such as trees for building, iron for manufacturing, or petroleum for making energy. You will read more about resources in Chapter 3.

✓Reading Check **How are plains and plateaus similar? How are they different?**

Applying Map Skills

1. What are the names of the seven large landmasses on the earth?
2. What are the earth's four major oceans?

Find NGS online map resources @ www.nationalgeographic.com/maps

NATIONAL GEOGRAPHIC

World Continents and Oceans

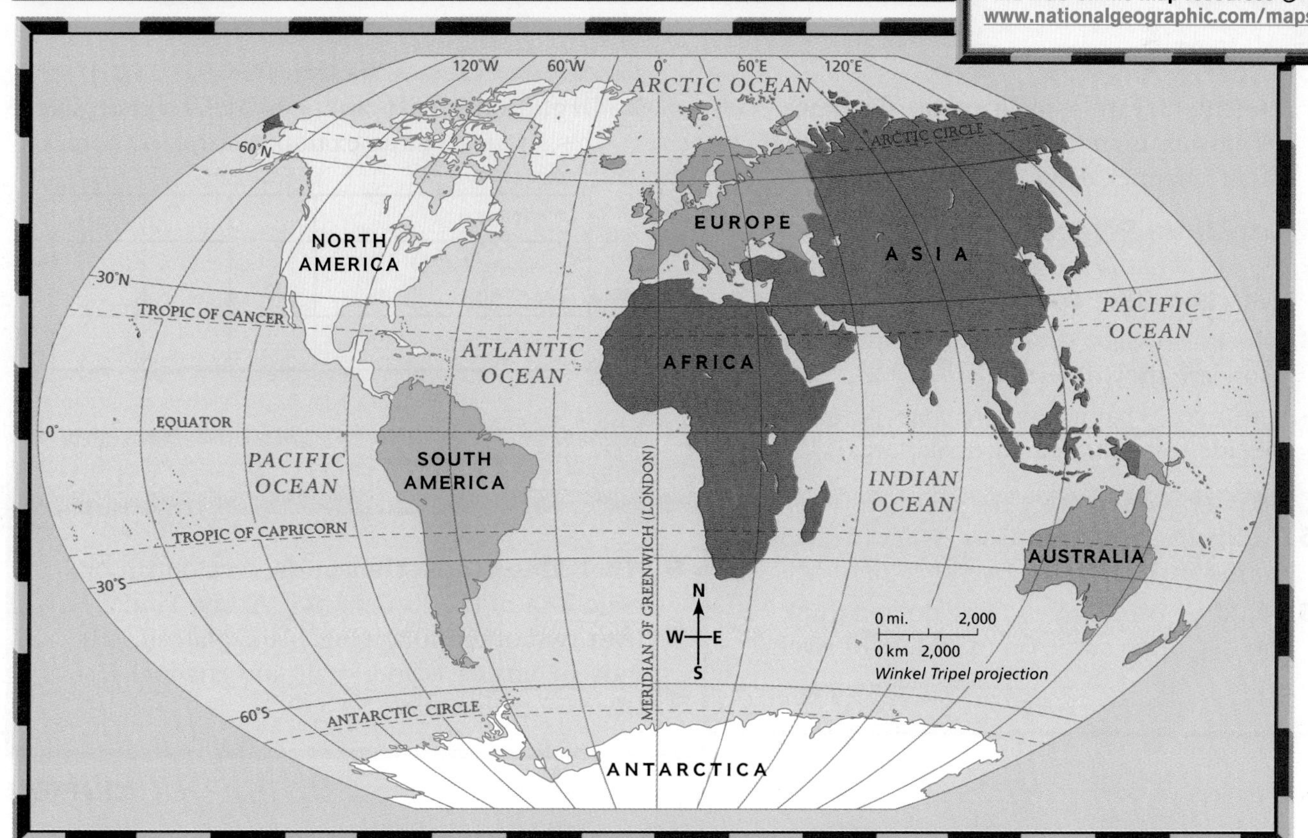

Bodies of Water

About 70 percent of the earth's surface is water. Most of that water is salt water, which people and animals cannot drink. Only a small percentage is freshwater, which is drinkable.

Oceans, made of salt water, are the earth's largest bodies of water. Smaller bodies of salt water are connected to oceans but are at least partly enclosed by land. These bodies include seas, gulfs, and bays.

Two other bodies of water form passages that connect two larger bodies of water. A **strait** is a narrow body of water between two pieces of land. The **Strait of Magellan** flows between the southern tip of South America and an island called Tierra del Fuego (tee•EHR•uh DEHL fyu•AY•goh). This strait connects the Atlantic and the Pacific Oceans. A wider passage is called a **channel.** The Mozambique Channel separates southeastern Africa from the island of Madagascar.

Bodies of freshwater appear on the world's continents and islands. They include larger bodies like lakes and rivers as well as smaller ones such as ponds and streams. The point at which a river originates—usually high in the mountains—is called its source. The mouth of a river is where it empties into another body of water. As you learned in Section 3, rivers carry soil and sand. They eventually deposit this soil at the mouth, which builds up over time to form a **delta.**

✓Reading Check **What is the difference between the source and the mouth of a river?**

Assessment

Defining Terms

1. **Define** elevation, plain, plateau, isthmus, peninsula, island, continental shelf, trench, strait, channel, delta.

Recalling Facts

2. **Place** What is the difference between mountains and hills?
3. **Place** How are straits and channels similar? How are they different?
4. **Culture** What are two reasons people decide to settle in a particular area?

Critical Thinking

5. **Analyzing Information** What two landforms are created by rivers?
6. **Making Inferences** Why do you think people often settle on the edges of rivers?

Graphic Organizer

7. **Organizing Information** Make a chart like this and give three examples for each item.

Landforms			
Landforms Under the Ocean			
Types of Bodies of Water			

Applying Geography Skills

8. **Analyzing Maps** Look at the world map on page RA4 of the **Reference Atlas.** Find at least two of the following: plain, plateau, isthmus, peninsula, island, strait, and channel. List their specific names.

Reading Review

Section 1 Thinking Like a Geographer

Terms to Know

geography
landform
environment
region
Global Positioning System (GPS)
geographic information systems (GIS)

Main Idea

Geographers use various tools to understand the world.

✓ Place Geographers study the physical and human characteristics of places.

✓ Culture Geographers are especially interested in how people interact with their environment.

✓ Technology To study the earth, geographers use maps, globes, photographs, the Global Positioning System, and geographic information systems.

✓ Economics People can use information from geography to plan, make decisions, and manage resources.

Section 2 The Earth in Space

Terms to Know

solar system
orbit
atmosphere
axis
revolution
leap year
summer solstice
winter solstice
equinox

Main Idea

The earth has life because of the sun. The earth has different seasons because of the way it tilts and revolves around the sun.

✓ Science The sun's light and warmth allow life to exist on Earth.

✓ Science The atmosphere is a cushion of gases that protects Earth and provides air to breathe.

✓ Movement Earth spins on its axis to make day and night.

✓ Movement The tilt of Earth and its revolution around the sun cause changes in seasons.

Section 3 The Earth's Structure

Terms to Know

core
mantle
magma
crust
continent
earthquake
plate tectonics
tsunami
fault
weathering
erosion
glacier

Main Idea

Forces both inside the earth and on its surface affect the shape of the land.

✓ Region Earth has an inner and outer core, a mantle, and a crust.

✓ Movement The continents are on large plates of rock that move.

✓ Movement Earthquakes and volcanoes can reshape the land.

✓ Movement Wind, water, and ice can change the look of the land.

Section 4 Landforms

Terms to Know

elevation
plain
plateau
isthmus
peninsula
island
continental shelf
trench
strait
channel
delta

Main Idea

Landforms in all their variety affect how people live.

✓ Location Mountains, plateaus, valleys, and other landforms are found on land and under the oceans.

✓ Science About 70 percent of the earth's surface is water.

✓ Culture People have adapted in order to live on various landforms.

Chapter 1

Assessment and Activities

Using Key Terms

Match the terms in Part A with their definitions in Part B.

A.

1. elevation
2. landform
3. summer solstice
4. plate tectonics
5. geographic information systems
6. Global Positioning System
7. erosion
8. equinox
9. fault
10. weathering

B.

a. height above sea level
b. wearing away of the earth's surface
c. theory that the earth's crust consists of huge slabs of rock that move
d. a group of satellites around the earth
e. special software that helps geographers gather and use information
f. when day and night are of equal length
g. a process that breaks surface rocks into gravel, sand, or soil
h. a crack in the earth's crust
i. the day with the most hours of sunlight
j. particular features of the land

Reviewing the Main Ideas

Section 1 Thinking Like a Geographer

11. **Place** Give three examples of the physical characteristics of a place.
12. **Region** How is a region different from a place?
13. **Human/Environment Interaction** Give an example of how people use geographic knowledge.

Section 2 The Earth in Space

14. **Region** How many planets are in the solar system?
15. **Movement** What movement of Earth causes day and night?
16. **Movement** How does Earth's revolution around the sun relate to the seasons?

Section 3 The Earth's Structure

17. **Movement** How do the plates in the earth's crust move?
18. **Movement** Give an example of erosion.

Section 4 Landforms

19. **Place** Which has a higher elevation—plains or plateaus?
20. **Movement** What two reasons lead people to settle in a particular region?

The World

Place Location Activity

On a separate sheet of paper, match the letters on the map with the numbered places listed below.

1. North America
2. Pacific Ocean
3. Africa
4. South America
5. Antarctica
6. Australia
7. Atlantic Ocean
8. Asia

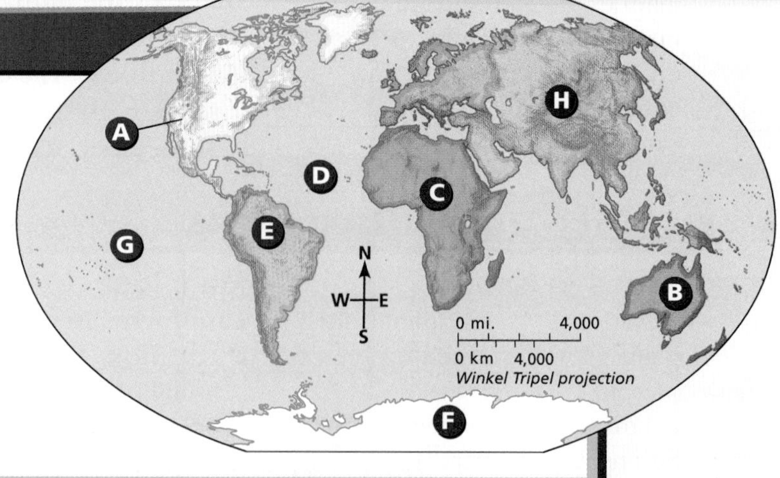

Self-Check Quiz Visit the ***Geography: The World and Its People*** Web site at gwip.glencoe.com and click on **Chapter 1—Self-Check Quizzes** to prepare for the Chapter Test.

Critical Thinking

21. **Making Comparisons** Why do people in Australia snow-ski during the Northern Hemisphere's summer months?
22. **Understanding Cause and Effect** Create a diagram like this one. In the left box, write "plate movements." In the right box, describe the effect that this force has on the earth. Draw five more pairs of boxes and do the same for the other forces that shape the earth: earthquakes, volcanoes, weathering, and erosion.

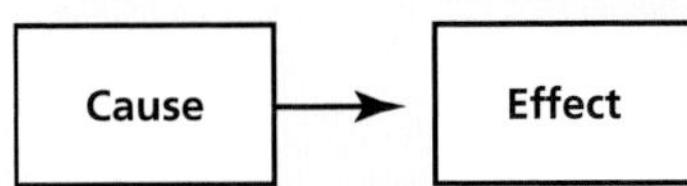

GeoJournal Activity

23. **Writing a Paragraph** Write a description of how the earth looks in your area. Then sketch a picture of your area showing all the landforms and bodies of water you described. Label each landform and body of water that you show.

Mental Mapping Activity

24. **Focusing on the Region** Draw a simple outline map of the earth, then label the following:
    - core
    - mantle
    - crust
    - atmosphere

Technology Skills Activity

25. **Building a Database** Use a word processing program to make a database like the following. In each row of the left column, list one of the following landforms: mountain, hill, plain, plateau, valley, canyon, isthmus, peninsula, and island. In the other columns, write a fact about each landform and give an example.

Landform	Facts	Example

Standardized Test Practice

Directions: Study the maps below, then answer the question that follows.

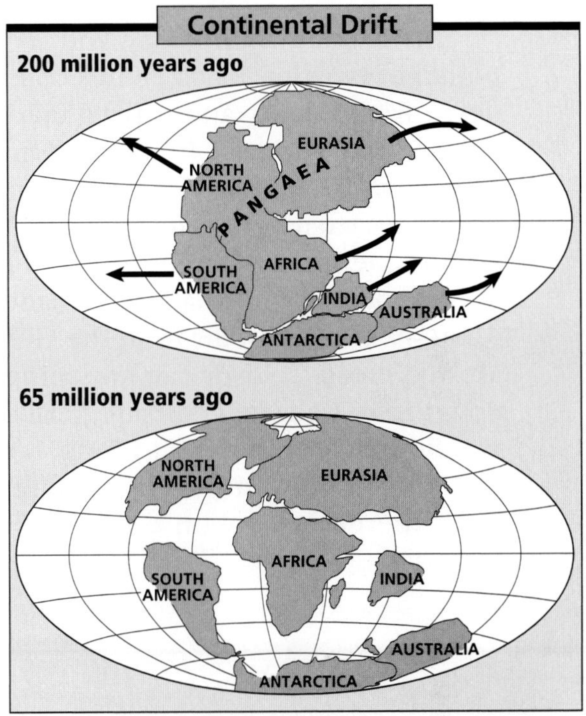

1. **What "supercontinent" do many scientists believe existed 200 million years ago?**
   - **A** Eurasia
   - **B** Pangaea
   - **C** Gondwana
   - **D** Antarctica

Test-Taking Tip: Use information *on the maps* to answer this question. Read the title above the maps and then the two subtitles. If you reread the question, you see it is asking about a certain time period. Make sure you use the correct map above to answer the question.

GeoLAB ACTIVITY

Tornadoes: Swirling Fury

1 Background

It is a stormy, humid day. You see a funnel of twisting, black clouds coming down from the sky and stirring up dust on the ground below. Tornado warning: Take cover! The United States has more tornadoes each year than anywhere else on the planet. Over the central part of our country—nicknamed Tornado Alley—warm, moist air from the Gulf of Mexico meets cold, dry air sweeping down from Canada. These are perfect conditions for tornadoes to form. Learn more about these storms by making and experimenting with a model of a tornado.

2 Materials

- **2 empty 2-liter clear soda bottles**
- **black marker**
- **1 rubber washer that is the same size as the bottle openings**
- **duct tape**
- **water**
- **paper towels**
- **glitter**

A Tornado Hits Oakfield, Wisconsin

Believe It or Not!

The United States has the most violent weather in the world. Our country experiences 1,000 tornadoes, 5,000 floods, and 10,000 strong thunderstorms in an average year.

What to Do

1. Use the marker to label one bottle "A" and the other "B."
2. Fill Bottle A three-fourths full of water. Dry the top and outside of the bottle completely. Add a small amount of glitter to the water.
3. Tape the rubber washer to the opening of Bottle A. Do not cover the washer hole with tape.
4. Put Bottle B upside down on Bottle A. Tape the mouths of both bottles together. Make sure the seal is tight and use several layers of tape.
5. Turn the bottles over so that Bottle A is on top. Then quickly swirl the bottles a couple of times, as you would stir something in a bowl.
6. Set the bottles on a table with Bottle A on top and observe the "tornado." The spinning funnel you see is called a *vortex.*
7. Repeat the experiment several times. Compare how water near the center and edges of the vortex moves each time. Observe what happens when you spin the bottles faster or slower.

4 LAB ACTIVITY REPORT

1. Describe what you saw when you swirled the bottles and set them down.
2. Does water near the center of the vortex move any differently than water at the edges of the vortex? Explain.
3. What did you observe when you swirled the bottles faster or slower?
4. **Drawing Conclusions** Did the vortex always spin in the same direction? What should you do to make it spin in the opposite direction?

▲ **Glitter added to the water allows you to see the vortex more clearly.**

Extending the Lab

Activity

Find out what you should do if a tornado warning is announced in your area. Discover what to do if you are outside, in a car, or inside a building. Use the information you gather to create a tornado safety poster. Present your poster to the class.

Chapter 2

Water, Climate, and Vegetation

The World and Its People NATIONAL GEOGRAPHIC

To learn more about water, climate, and vegetation, view ***The World and Its People*** **Chapter 2** video.

Geography Online

Chapter Overview Visit the ***Geography: The World and Its People*** Web site at gwip.glencoe.com and click on **Chapter 2—Chapter Overviews** to preview information about water, climate, and vegetation.

Section 1

The Water Planet

Guide to Reading

Main Idea

Water is one of the earth's most precious resources.

Terms to Know

- water vapor
- water cycle
- evaporation
- condensation
- precipitation
- collection
- glacier
- groundwater
- aquifer

Places to Locate

- Pacific Ocean
- Atlantic Ocean
- Indian Ocean
- Arctic Ocean

Reading Strategy

Make a diagram like this one. Starting at the top, write the steps of the water cycle—each in a separate square—in the correct sequence.

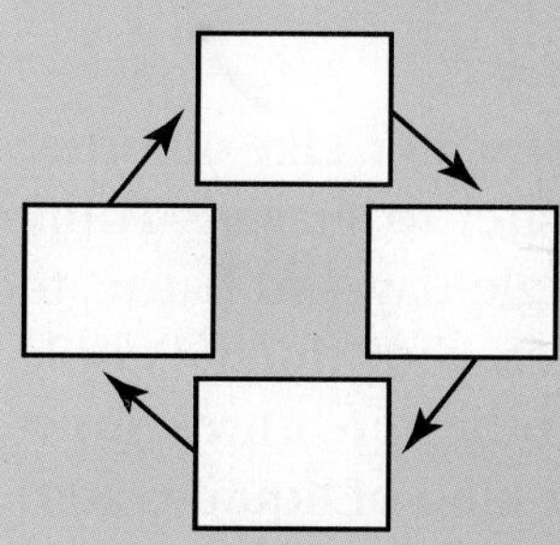

NATIONAL GEOGRAPHIC **Exploring Our World**

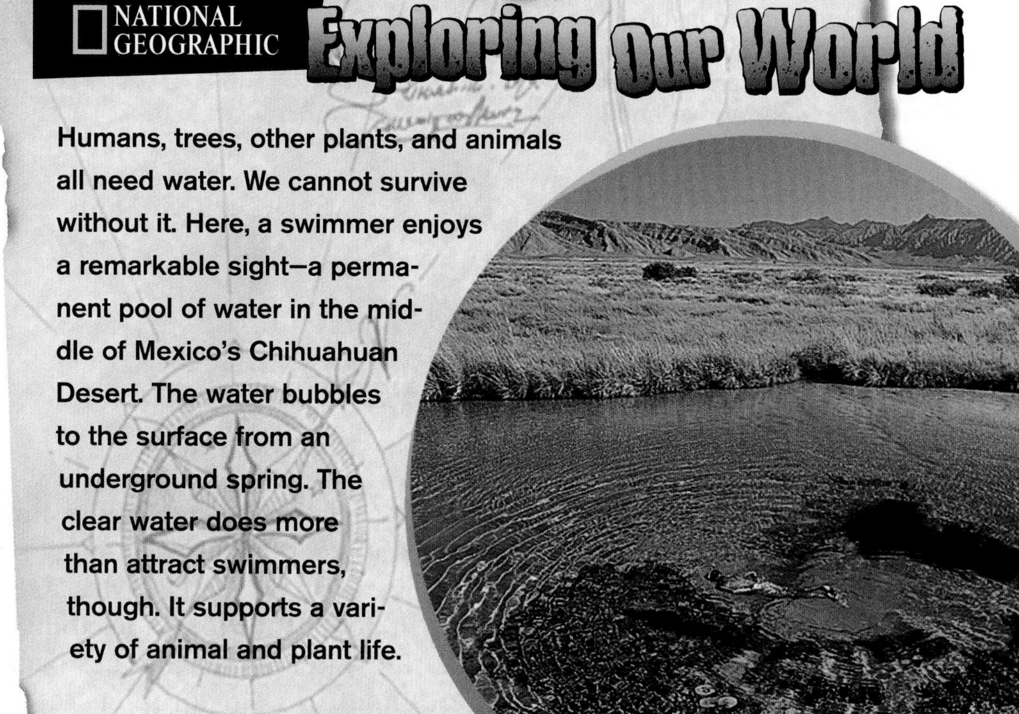

Humans, trees, other plants, and animals all need water. We cannot survive without it. Here, a swimmer enjoys a remarkable sight—a permanent pool of water in the middle of Mexico's Chihuahuan Desert. The water bubbles to the surface from an underground spring. The clear water does more than attract swimmers, though. It supports a variety of animal and plant life.

Some people call Earth "the water planet." Why? Water covers about 70 percent of the earth's surface. Water exists all around you in many different forms. Streams, rivers, lakes, seas, and oceans contain water in liquid form. The atmosphere holds **water vapor,** or water in the form of gas. Glaciers and ice sheets are masses of water that have been frozen solid. As a matter of fact, the human body itself is about 60 percent water.

The Water Cycle

The total amount of water on the earth does not change, but it does not stay in one place, either. Instead, the water moves constantly. In a process called the **water cycle,** the water goes from the oceans to the air to the ground and finally back to the oceans.

Look at the diagram on page 50 to see how the water cycle works. The sun drives the cycle by evaporating water mostly from the surface of oceans, but also from lakes and streams. In **evaporation,** the sun's heat turns liquid water into water vapor—also called *humidity.* The amount of water vapor that the air holds depends on the air

◀ The Yellowstone River in Paradise Valley, Montana

The Water Cycle

Analyzing the Diagram

The water cycle involves evaporation, condensation, precipitation, and the collection of water above and below the ground.

Movement How does water get from the ground to the oceans?

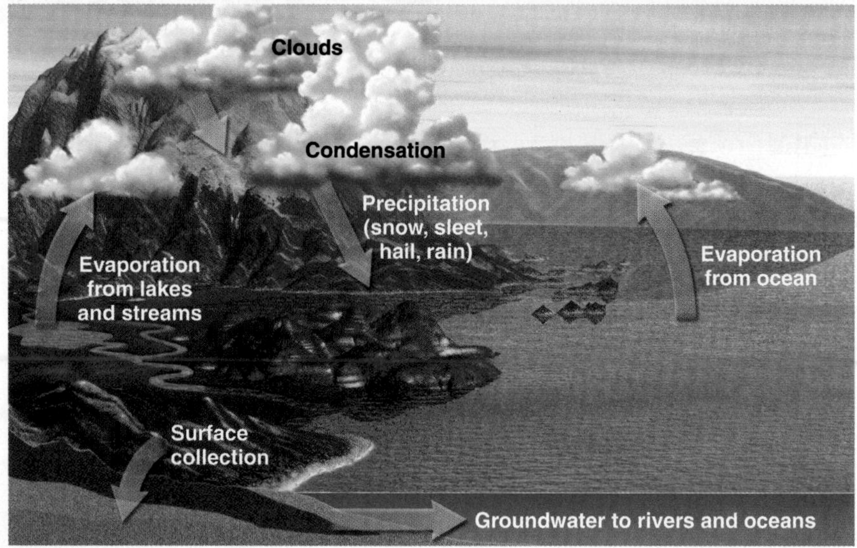

temperature. Warm air can hold more humidity than cool air, which you have probably felt on warm, muggy summer days.

In addition, warm air tends to rise. As warm air rises higher in the atmosphere, it cools, thus losing its ability to hold as much humidity. As a result, the water vapor changes back into a liquid in a process called **condensation.** Tiny droplets of water come together to form clouds. Eventually, the water falls back to the earth as some form of **precipitation**—rain, snow, sleet, or hail—depending on the temperature of the surrounding air.

When this precipitation reaches the earth's surface, it soaks into the ground and collects in streams and lakes. During **collection,** streams and rivers both above and below the ground carry the water back to the oceans, and the cycle begins again.

✓ Reading Check **What kind of air—warm or cold—holds the most water vapor?**

Water Resources

It is a hot day, and you rush home for a glass of water. Like all other people—and all plants and animals—you need water to survive. Think about the many ways you use water in just a single day—to bathe, to brush your teeth, to cook your food, and to quench your thirst. People and most animals need freshwater to live. Many other creatures, however, make their homes in the earth's much larger kind of liquid water: salt water.

Freshwater Only about 2 percent of the water on the earth is freshwater. Eighty percent of that freshwater is frozen in **glaciers,** or giant sheets of ice. Only a tiny fraction of the world's freshwater—not even four-hundredths of a percent—is found in lakes and rivers.

When you think of freshwater, you probably think of mighty rivers and huge lakes. People can get freshwater from another source, though. Groundwater is water that fills tiny cracks and holes in the rock layers below the surface of the earth. This is a vital source of water because there is 10 times more groundwater than there is water in rivers and lakes. Groundwater can be tapped by wells. Some areas have aquifers, or underground rock layers that water flows through. In regions with little rainfall, both farmers and city dwellers sometimes have to depend on aquifers and other groundwater for most of their water supply.

Salt Water All the oceans on the earth are part of a huge, continuous body of salt water—almost 98 percent of the planet's water. Look at the map on page 58. You will see that the four major oceans are the **Pacific Ocean,** the **Atlantic Ocean,** the **Indian Ocean,** and the **Arctic Ocean.**

The Pacific Ocean is the largest and deepest of these four oceans. It covers almost 64 million square miles (166 million sq. km)—more than all the land areas of the earth combined. As you learned in Chapter 1, bodies of salt water smaller than the oceans are called seas, gulfs, bays, or straits. Look back at the diagram on page 18 of the Geography Handbook to see these features again.

✓Reading Check **What is the difference between groundwater and aquifers?**

Assessment

Defining Terms

1. Define water vapor, water cycle, evaporation, condensation, precipitation, collection, glacier, groundwater, aquifer.

Recalling Facts

2. Region What percentage of the earth is covered by water?
3. Movement In which part of the water cycle does water return to the earth?
4. Region What are the world's four oceans?

Critical Thinking

5. Understanding Cause and Effect How does the temperature of the air affect the amount of humidity that you feel? How does the air's temperature also influence the form of precipitation that falls?
6. Drawing Conclusions Why do you think it is important to keep groundwater free of dangerous chemicals?

Graphic Organizer

7. Organizing Information Draw a diagram like this one. List at least four sources of freshwater and salt water on the lines under each heading.

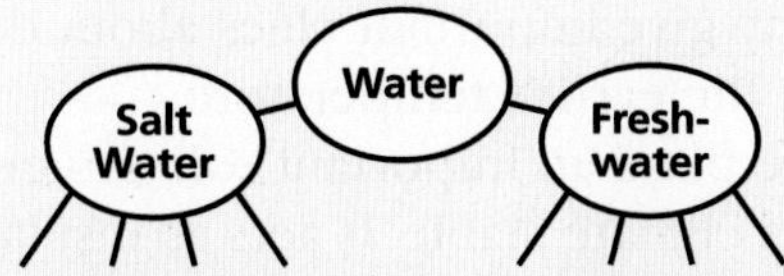

Applying Geography Skills

8. Analyzing Diagrams Look at the diagram of the water cycle on page 50. From where does water evaporate?

Making Connections

ART | SCIENCE | LITERATURE | TECHNOLOGY

Exploring Earth's Water

More than two-thirds of the earth's surface is covered with water, yet scientists know more about the surface of the moon than they do about the ocean floor. Using an AUV, or autonomous underwater vehicle, called *Autosub,* researchers hope to gain new understanding about the earth's watery surface.

What It Does

It looks like a giant torpedo, but *Autosub* is really a battery-powered robotic submarine that is 23 feet (7 m) long. Its mission is to explore parts of the ocean that are beyond the reach of other research vessels or are too dangerous for humans. Although it is still being tested, *Autosub* has already conducted hundreds of underwater missions.

Exploring Ice Shelves

One of the most promising areas of research for *Autosub* lies in seawater under the ice shelves near Greenland in the Arctic and near Antarctica at the southern extreme of the globe. Traditional submarines are unable to explore these places safely. Satellite photographs show that the area of the ice shelves is changing. Scientists want to use *Autosub*'s technology to measure changes in the thickness of sea ice. They believe that this information may give important clues about the possible rise in the earth's temperature.

Sea ice plays an important role in keeping the earth's climate stable. It acts as insulation—a kind of protection—between the ocean and the atmosphere. Sea ice reflects light, so it limits the amount of heat absorbed into the water and keeps the ocean from getting too warm. In winter, sea ice helps prevent heat from escaping the warmer oceans into the atmosphere.

What the Future Holds

So far, *Autosub*'s missions have been fairly short. Scientists hope to someday program *Autosub* to make long voyages, sampling seawater and collecting data from ocean floors. The information that *Autosub* provides will help scientists make better predictions about the earth's climate.

▲ ***Autosub* can be launched from shore, towed out to sea by a small boat, or lowered by a crane into the water.**

Making the Connection

1. What is *Autosub*?
2. Why do scientists want to use *Autosub* to explore under the ice shelves?
3. **Understanding Cause and Effect** How could a loss of sea ice affect the earth's climate?

Section 2 Climate

Guide to Reading

Main Idea

Wind and water carry rainfall and the sun's warmth around the world to create different climates.

Terms to Know

- weather
- climate
- tropics
- monsoon
- tornado
- hurricane
- typhoon
- drought
- El Niño
- La Niña
- current
- local wind
- rain shadow
- greenhouse effect
- rain forest

Places to Locate

- Equator
- Tropic of Cancer
- Tropic of Capricorn

Reading Strategy

Make a chart like this one. Write at least two details that explain how each force contributes to climate.

Sun	Wind	Water

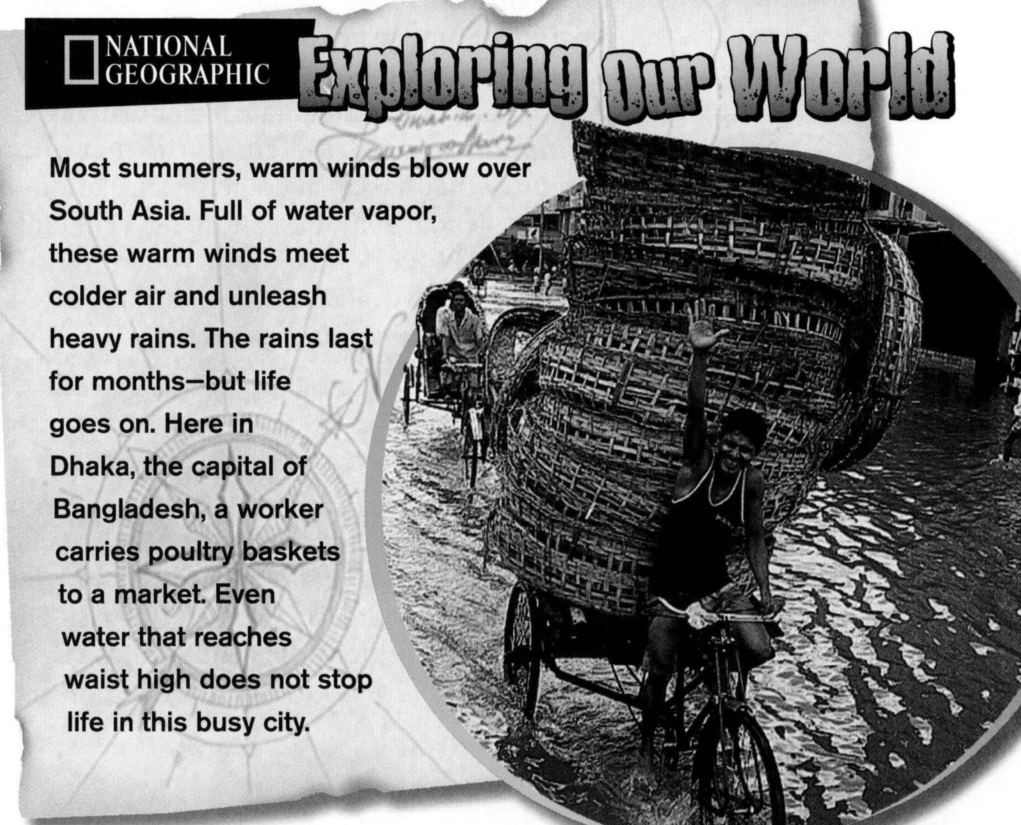

Most summers, warm winds blow over South Asia. Full of water vapor, these warm winds meet colder air and unleash heavy rains. The rains last for months—but life goes on. Here in Dhaka, the capital of Bangladesh, a worker carries poultry baskets to a market. Even water that reaches waist high does not stop life in this busy city.

Why are some areas of the world full of lush forests, while others are covered by bone-dry deserts? Why do some people struggle through chilling winters, while others enjoy a day at the beach? To understand these mysteries, you need to unlock the secrets of climate.

Weather and Climate

As you learned in Chapter 1, the earth is surrounded by the atmosphere, which holds a combination of gases we call air. The atmosphere's many layers protect life on the earth from harmful rays of the sun. The layer of atmosphere immediately surrounding the earth is also where you will find weather patterns. Suppose a friend calls you and asks what it is like outside. You might say, "It's a beautiful day—warm and sunny!" You are describing the weather. **Weather** refers to the unpredictable changes in air that take place over a short period of time.

Suppose that a cousin from another part of the country asks what summers and winters are like in your area. You might say, "Summers are usually hot and rainy, and winters are cool but dry." Your answer describes not the weather but your area's climate. **Climate** is the usual, predictable pattern of weather in an area over a long period of time. It is affected by the sun, the wind, the oceans and other bodies of water, landforms, and even people.

You might also say to your cousin, "Usually we get a little rain in the summer. Last year, though, we went two months without any rain!" You recognize that the weather does not always follow its *usual* climate pattern. Some years it rains more than others; some years the temperature is lower than others.

To understand climate, scientists have to look at the extremes of *temperature* and *precipitation* that an area can have. Consider a country that has an average precipitation of 38 inches (97 cm) a year. In any year, it may be as low as 13 inches (33 cm) or as high as 63 inches (160 cm). Imagine if you were a farmer trying to grow food there. How would your crops be affected if you received only one-third of the rain you expected?

✓Reading Check **What is the difference between weather and climate?**

The Sun and Climate

What causes climate? The original source of climate is the sun. It gives off energy and light that all plants and animals need to survive. The sun's rays warm the air, water, and land on our planet. Warm gases and liquids are lighter than cool gases and liquids. Because they are lighter, the warmer gases and liquids rise. Then wind and water carry this warmth around the globe, distributing the sun's heat.

NATIONAL GEOGRAPHIC **On Location**

Washington, D.C.

A cross-country skier braves a blizzard in our nation's capital.

Place **When scientists study climate, what two factors do they analyze?**

Prevailing Wind Patterns

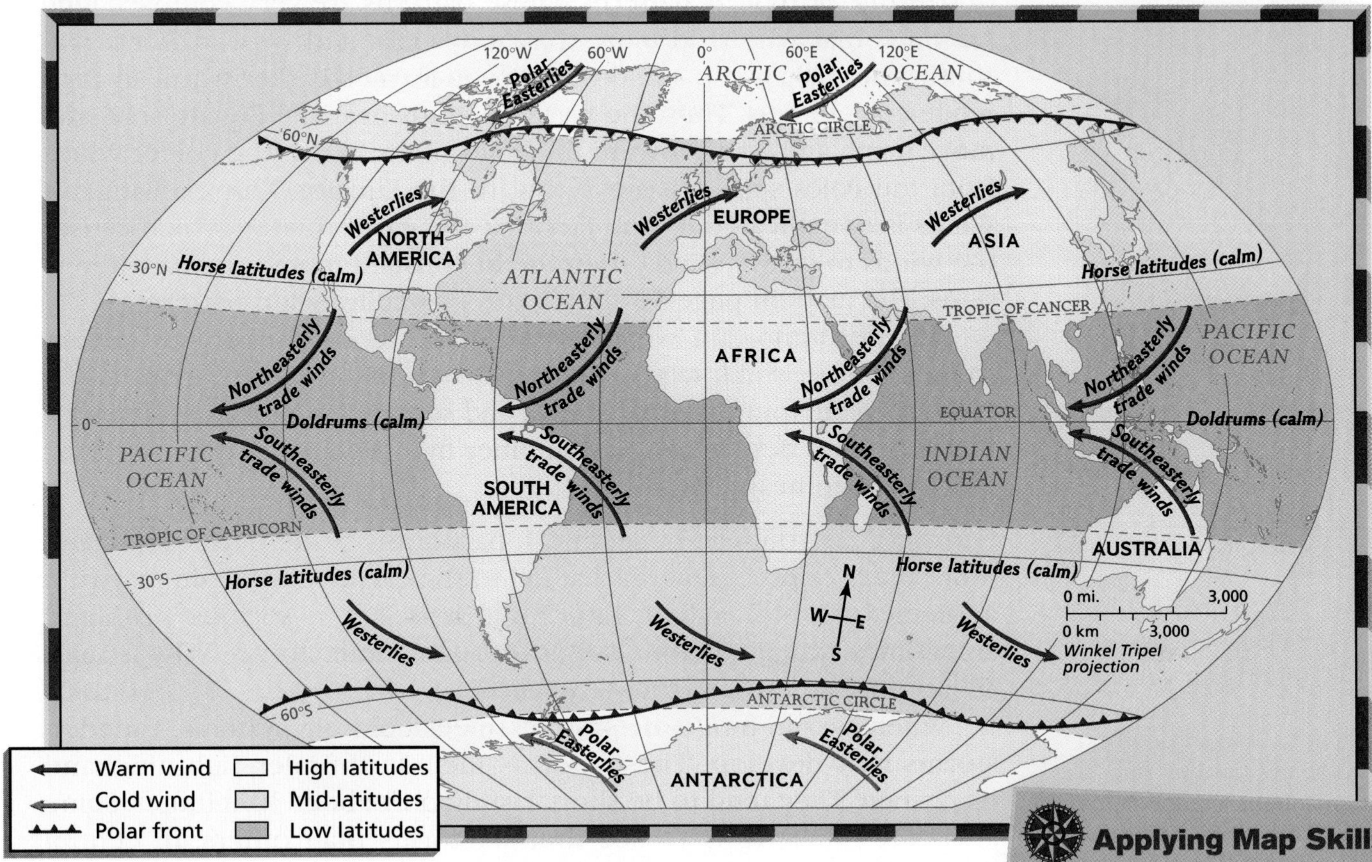

Warm wind
Cold wind
Polar front
High latitudes
Mid-latitudes
Low latitudes

Applying Map Skills

1. In which general direction does the wind blow over North America?
2. What winds did European sailors use to get to South America and the islands north of it?

Find NGS online map resources @ www.nationalgeographic.com/maps

Latitude and Climate Climate is also affected by the angle at which the sun's rays hit the earth. As you learned in Chapter 1, because of the earth's tilt and revolution around the sun, the sun's rays hit various places at different angles at different times of the year. The sun's rays hit places in low latitudes—regions near the **Equator**—more directly than places at higher latitudes. The areas near the Equator, known as the **tropics,** lie between the **Tropic of Cancer** (23½°N latitude) and the **Tropic of Capricorn** (23½°S latitude). If you lived in the tropics, you would almost always experience a hot climate, unless you lived high in the mountains where temperatures are cooler. Find the low-latitude tropics on the map above. (To learn how to use latitude and longitude, turn to page 62.)

Outside the tropics, the sun is never directly overhead. The mid-latitudes extend from the tropics to about 60° both north and south of the Equator. When the North Pole is tilted toward the sun, the sun's rays fall more directly on the Northern Hemisphere. This affects our climate by giving us warm summer days. Six months later, the South Pole is tilted toward the sun, and the seasons are reversed. At the high latitudes near the North and South Poles, the sun's rays hit *very* indirectly. Climates in these regions are always cool or cold.

✓Reading Check **How does the tilt of the earth affect climate?**

The Wind's Effect on Climate

Movements of air are called winds. From year to year, winds follow *prevailing,* or typical, patterns. These patterns are very complex. One reason is that winds do more than move east and west or north and south. They also go up and down. As you learned earlier, warm air rises while cold air falls. Thus, the warmer winds near the Equator rise and move north and south toward the Poles of the earth. The colder winds from the Poles sink and move toward the Equator. This exchange of winds is complicated by the fact that the earth rotates, which causes the winds to curve. Winds, then, are in constant motion in many directions. The map on page 55 shows you prevailing wind patterns.

Another important wind pattern is the monsoon. **Monsoons** are tremendous seasonal winds that blow over continents for months at a time. They are found mainly in Asia and some areas in Africa. Although they often are destructive, the summer monsoons in South Asia bring much-needed heavy rains.

Mt. Pinatubo

Mt. Pinatubo (PEE•nah•TOO•boh) is a volcanic mountain in the Philippine Islands. Its eruption in the early 1990s had a tremendous impact on the world's climate. The powerful explosion shot massive amounts of ash and sulfur dioxide into the earth's atmosphere. The ash and chemicals blocked some of the sun's rays from reaching the earth. As a result, the world's climate was cooler for two years after the volcano's blast.

Storms As you read in Section 1, part of the water cycle is rain and other types of precipitation that fall to the earth. A little rain may ruin a picnic or spoil a ball game, but it is not a serious problem. Sometimes, though, people suffer through fierce storms. Why is that? What causes these destructive events?

When warm, moist air systems meet cold air systems, thunderstorms may develop. These storms include thunder, lightning, and heavy rain. They tend to be short, lasting only about 30 minutes. Some areas are more likely to see thunderstorms than others. In central Florida, as many as 90 days a year may experience thunderstorms.

A thunderstorm may produce another danger—a tornado. **Tornadoes** are funnel-shaped windstorms that sometimes form during severe thunderstorms. They occur all over the world, but the United States has more tornadoes than any other area. Winds in tornadoes often reach 250 miles (402 km) per hour.

Hurricanes, or violent tropical storm systems, form over the warm Atlantic Ocean in late summer and fall. Hurricanes bring high winds that can reach more than 150 miles (241 km) per hour. They also produce rough seas and carry drenching rain. Hurricanes strike North America and the islands in the Caribbean Sea. They also rip through Asia, although in that region they are called **typhoons.** These storms can do tremendous damage. Their strong winds destroy buildings and snap power lines. Heavy rains can flood low-lying areas.

El Niño and La Niña In 1998 the world experienced unusual weather. Heavy rains brought floods to Peru, washing away whole villages. Europe, eastern Africa, and most of the southern United States also had severe flooding. In the western Pacific, normally heavy rains never came. Indonesia suffered a **drought,** a long period of extreme dryness. The land there became so dry that forest fires burned thousands of acres of trees. Thick smoke from the fires forced drivers to put their headlights on at noon!

Why did these disasters take place? They resulted from a combination of temperature, wind, and water effects in the Pacific Ocean called **El Niño** (ehl NEE•nyoh). The name "El Niño" was coined by early Spanish explorers in the Pacific. They use the phrase—which refers to the Christ child—because the effect hits South America around Christmas.

El Niños form when cold winds from the east are weak. Without these cold winds, the central Pacific Ocean grows warmer than usual. More water evaporates, and more clouds form. The thick band of clouds changes wind and rain patterns. Some areas receive heavier than normal rains and others have less than normal rainfall.

Does El Niño come every year? Scientists have found that El Niño occurs about every three years. They also found that in some years, the opposite kind of unusual weather takes place. This event is called **La Niña** (lah NEE•nyah), Spanish for "girl," because the effects are the opposite of those in El Niño. Winds from the east become very strong, cooling more of the Pacific. When this happens, heavy clouds form in the western Pacific.

✓Reading Check **Why do El Niños occur?**

Ocean Currents

Winds carry large masses of warm and cool air around the earth. At the same time, moving streams of water called **currents** carry warm or cool water through the world's oceans. Look at the map on page 58. As you can see, these currents follow certain patterns. Notice how the warm currents tend to move along the Equator or from the Equator to the Poles. The cold currents carry cold polar water toward the Equator.

These currents affect the climate of land areas. Look at the warm current called the Gulf Stream. It flows from the Gulf of Mexico along the east coast of North America. Then it crosses the Atlantic Ocean toward Europe, where it is called the North Atlantic Current. Winds that blow over these warm waters bring warm air to western Europe. Because these winds blow from west to east, areas in Europe enjoy warmer weather than areas lying west of the Gulf Stream in Canada.

✓Reading Check **What areas of the world would be affected by a change in the Gulf Stream?**

NORMAL CONDITIONS

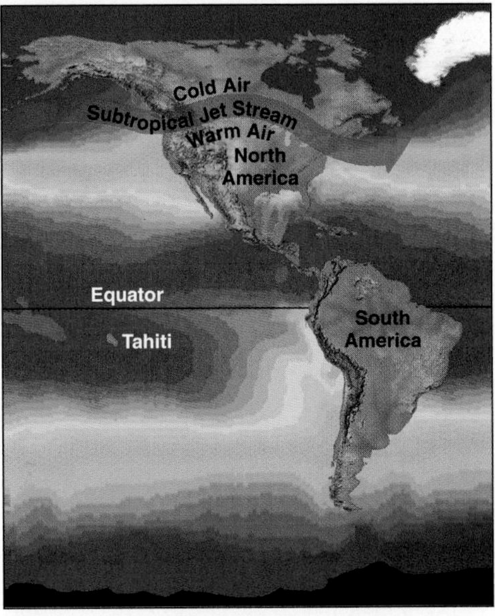

EL NIÑO CONDITIONS

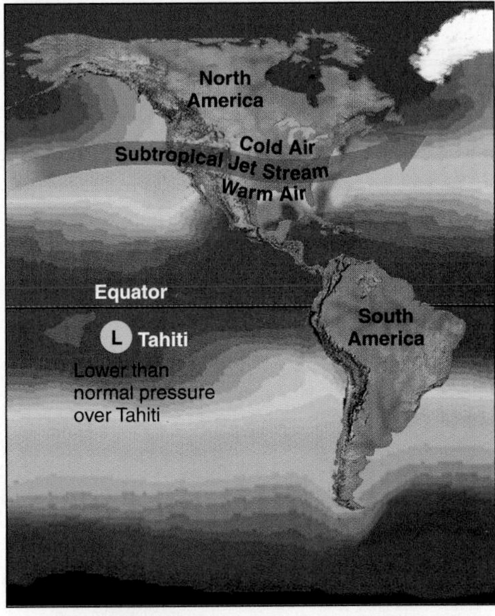

Analyzing the Diagram

The temperature of the oceans varies from warm (dark red) to very cold (dark purple).

Movement **What happens to the Jet Stream during El Niño conditions?**

NATIONAL GEOGRAPHIC

World Ocean Currents

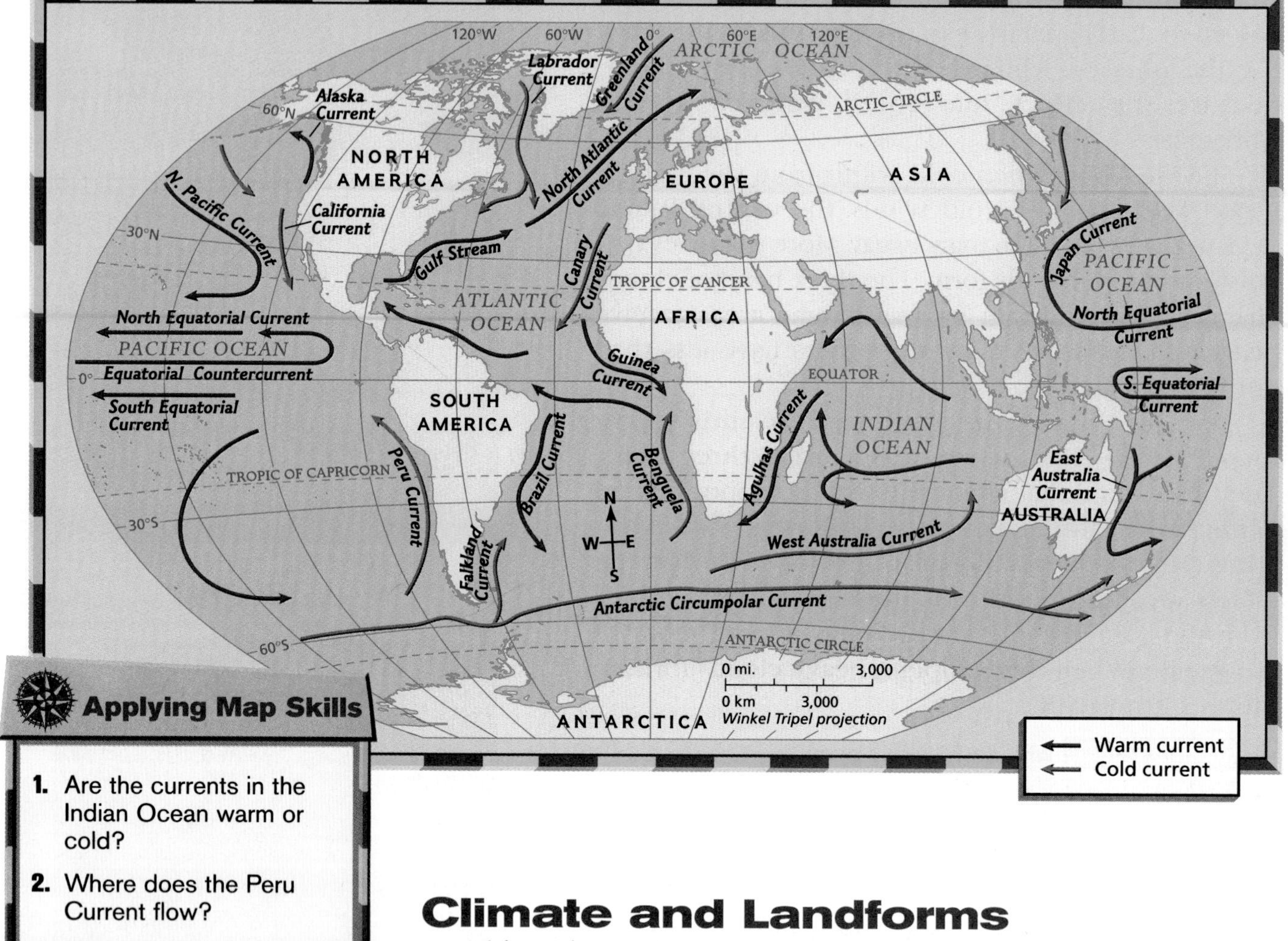

Applying Map Skills

1. Are the currents in the Indian Ocean warm or cold?
2. Where does the Peru Current flow?

Find NGS online map resources @ www.nationalgeographic.com/maps

Climate and Landforms

Although wind and water affect climate, the shape of the land has an effect on climate as well. *Where* landforms are in relation to one other and to water influences climate, too.

Landforms and Local Winds Geographers study major wind patterns that blow over the earth. When they study the climate of a given area, however, geographers also look at what they call local winds. **Local winds** are patterns of wind caused by landforms in a particular area.

Some local winds occur because land warms and cools more quickly than water does. As a result, cool sea breezes keep coastal areas cool during the day. After the sun sets, the opposite occurs. The air over the land cools more quickly than the air over water. At night, then, a land breeze blows from the land out to the sea.

A similar effect happens near mountains. Air warmed by the sun rises up mountain slopes during the day. At night, cooler air moves down the mountain into the valley below. Have you ever seen fog lying on a valley floor on a cool morning? That fog was caused by the cool air that came down the mountain during the night.

Mountains, Temperature, and Rainfall The higher the elevation of a particular place, the lower the temperature that place will have. In high mountains, the air becomes thinner and cannot hold as much heat from the sun. The temperature drops. Even near the Equator, where the sun's rays strike the earth directly, snow covers the peaks of high mountains.

The cooling effect of elevation is not as strong on high plateaus, however. Why is this so? As you learned in Chapter 1, plateaus are flat surfaces, so there are no rising air currents as there are along mountainsides. Some plateaus—as in the southwestern United States—can reach as much as a mile above sea level. Even these high plateaus can hold the sun's warmth.

Mountains also have an effect on rainfall. When warm moist winds blow inland from the ocean toward a coastal mountain range, the winds are forced upward over the mountains. As these warm winds rise, the air cools and loses its moisture. Rain or snow falls on the mountains. The climate on this *windward*—or wind-facing—side of mountain ranges is moist and often foggy. Trees and vegetation are thick and green.

By the time the air moves over the mountain peaks, it is cool and dry. This creates a **rain shadow,** a dry area on the side of the mountains facing away from the wind. Geographers call this side the *leeward* side. The dry air of a rain shadow warms up again as it moves down the leeward side, giving the region a dry or desert climate.

A rain shadow occurs along the western coast of the United States. Winds moving east from the Pacific Ocean lose their moisture as they move upward on the windward slopes of the coastal mountains. Great deserts and dry basins are located on the leeward side of these ranges.

✓Reading Check **Why are areas of higher elevation often cooler?**

Rain Shadow

Analyzing the Diagram

Rain shadows usually occur on the inland sides of mountain ranges near oceans.

Location What is the term for the side of a mountain where precipitation falls?

Shanghai, China

Shanghai, China (right), like other modern cities, is generally warmer than the rural areas around it (above).

Human/Environment Interaction **Why are cities warmer than surrounding areas?**

The Impact of People on Climate

People's actions can affect climate. You may have noticed that temperatures in large cities are generally higher than those in nearby rural areas. Why is that? The city's streets and buildings absorb more of the sun's rays than do the plants and trees of rural areas.

Cities are warmer even in winter. People burn fuels to warm houses, power industry, and move cars and buses along the streets. This burning raises the temperature in the city. The burning also releases a cloud of chemicals into the air. These chemicals blanket the city and hold in more of the sun's heat, creating a so-called *heat island.*

The Greenhouse Effect The burning of fuels may be creating a worldwide problem. In the past two hundred years, people have burned coal, oil, and natural gas as sources of energy. Burning these fuels releases certain gases into the air.

Some scientists warn that the buildup of these gases presents dangers. It creates a greenhouse effect—like a greenhouse, the gases prevent the warm air from rising and escaping into the atmosphere. As a result, the overall temperature of the earth will increase. Some scientists predict disastrous results from this global warming. The ice at the North and South Poles will melt, they say. Ocean levels will rise and flood coastal cities. In addition, global warming will make some areas that are now fertile unable to grow crops. It may become much harder to feed all the world's people.

Not all scientists agree about the greenhouse effect. Some argue that the world is not warming. Others say that even if it is, the predictions of disaster are extreme. Many scientists are studying world temperature trends closely. They hope to be able to discover whether the greenhouse effect is a real threat.

Clearing the Rain Forests Along the Equator, you can see dense forests called **rain forests** that receive high amounts of rain each year. In some countries, people are clearing large areas of these forests. They want to sell the lumber from the trees. They also want to use the land to grow crops or as pasture for cattle. Clearing the rain forests, though, can hurt the world's climate.

One reason is related to the greenhouse effect. People often clear the forests by burning down trees in an area. This burning releases more gases into the air, just like burning oil or natural gas does. The other danger of clearing the rain forests is related to rainfall. Remember the water cycle discussed in Section 1? Water on the earth's surface evaporates into the air and then falls as rain. In the rain forests, much of this water evaporates from the leaves of trees. If the trees are cut, less water will evaporate. As a result, less rain will fall. Scientists worry that, over time, the area that now holds rain forests will actually become dry and unable to grow anything.

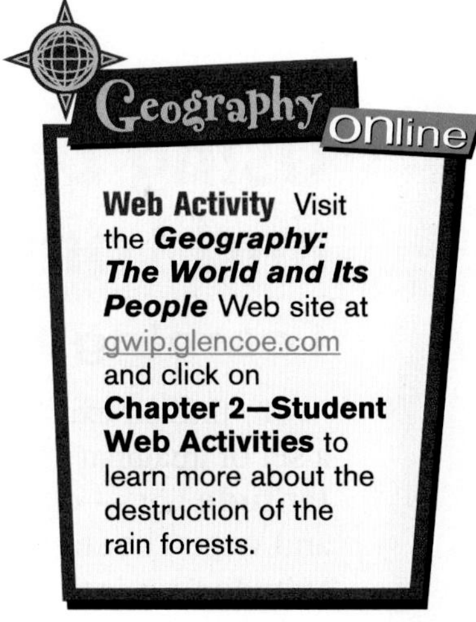

Web Activity Visit the ***Geography: The World and Its People*** Web site at gwip.glencoe.com and click on **Chapter 2—Student Web Activities** to learn more about the destruction of the rain forests.

Reading Check **What is the greenhouse effect?**

Assessment

Defining Terms

1. **Define** weather, climate, tropics, monsoon, tornado, hurricane, typhoon, drought, El Niño, La Niña, current, local wind, rain shadow, greenhouse effect, rain forest.

Recalling Facts

2. **Movement** What five elements affect climate?
3. **Location** Between what two lines of latitude are the tropics?
4. **Place** Provide an example of how landforms influence climate.

Critical Thinking

5. **Making Comparisons** How does the amount of rainfall on the windward side of a mountain differ from that on the leeward side?
6. **Summarizing Information** What general patterns do wind and currents follow?

Graphic Organizer

7. **Organizing Information** Draw a diagram like this one. In the first box, list three human actions that lead to the greenhouse effect. In the third box, list four possible results of the greenhouse effect.

Applying Geography Skills

8. **Analyzing Maps** Look at the world ocean currents map on page 58. Which two continents lie completely outside the tropics?

Geography Skill

Using Latitude and Longitude

Learning the Skill

To find an exact location, geographers use a set of imaginary lines. One set of lines—**latitude** lines—circles the earth's surface east and west. The starting point for numbering latitude lines is the Equator, which is 0° latitude. Every other line of latitude is numbered from 1° to 90° and is followed by an N or S to show whether it is north or south of the Equator. Latitude lines are also called parallels.

A second set of lines—**longitude** lines—runs vertically from the North Pole to the South Pole. Each of these lines is also called a meridian. The starting point—0° longitude—is called the Prime Meridian (or Meridian of Greenwich). Longitude lines are numbered from 1° to 180° followed by an E or W—to show whether they are east or west of the Prime Meridian.

To find latitude and longitude, choose a place on a map. Identify the nearest parallel, or line of latitude. Is it located north or south of the Equator? Now identify the nearest meridian, or line of longitude. Is it located east or west of the Prime Meridian?

Practicing the Skill

1. On the map below, what is the exact location of Washington, D.C.?
2. What cities on the map lie south of 0° latitude?
3. What city is located near 30°N, 30°E?

Applying the Skill

Turn to page RA2 of the **Reference Atlas.** List the latitude and longitude for one city. Ask a classmate to use the information to find and name the city.

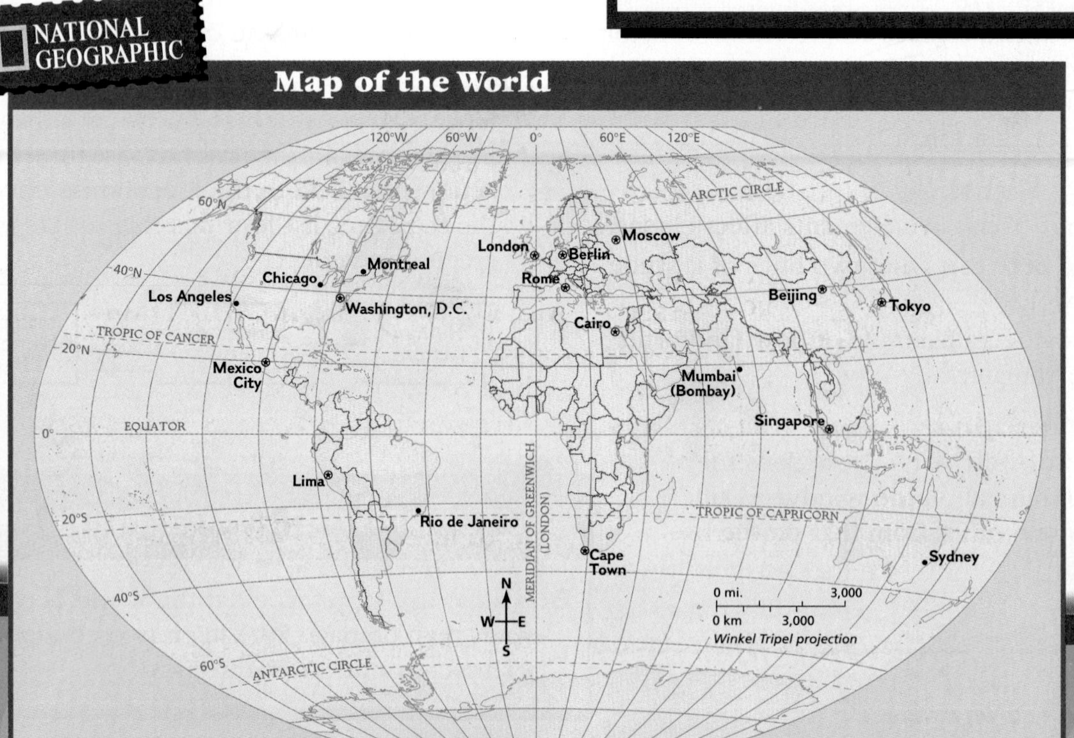

Section 3

Climate Zones and Vegetation

Guide to Reading

Main Idea

Geographers divide the world into different climate zones, each of which has special characteristics.

Terms to Know

- canopy
- savanna
- marine west coast climate
- Mediterranean climate
- humid continental climate
- humid subtropical climate
- subarctic
- tundra
- permafrost
- steppe
- timberline

Reading Strategy

Complete a chart like the one below by listing the categories of each type of climate next to the correct headings.

Climate Type	Categories
Tropical	
Mid-Latitude	
High Latitude	
Dry	
Highland	

NATIONAL GEOGRAPHIC **Exploring Our World**

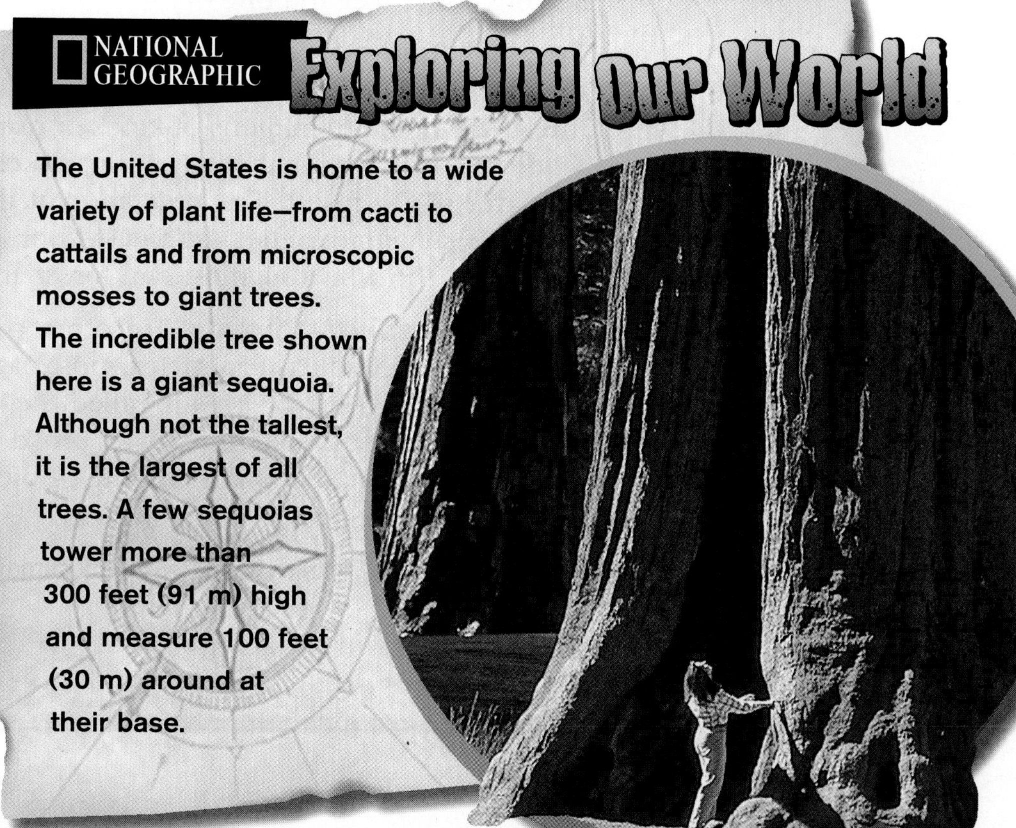

The United States is home to a wide variety of plant life—from cacti to cattails and from microscopic mosses to giant trees. The incredible tree shown here is a giant sequoia. Although not the tallest, it is the largest of all trees. A few sequoias tower more than 300 feet (91 m) high and measure 100 feet (30 m) around at their base.

Why do you think a photograph of a giant tree is in a chapter on climate? The reason is that climate and vegetation go together. Consider this: The state of Washington sits next to the state of Idaho. The plant life in western Washington, however, is much more similar to that of the United Kingdom, which is thousands of miles away, than it is to the plant life in eastern Washington and Idaho, which touch each other. Why? The patterns of temperature, wind, and precipitation in western Washington and the United Kingdom are similar.

Scientists use these patterns to group climates into many different types. They have put the world's climates into five major groups: tropical, mid-latitude, high latitude, dry, and highland. Three of these groups—tropical, mid-latitude, and high latitude—are based on an area's latitude, or distance from the Equator. Some of these major groups have subcategories of climate zones within them. In addition, each climate zone has particular kinds of plants that grow in it.

Tropical Climates

The tropical climate gets its name from the tropics—the areas along the Equator reaching from 23½°N to 23½°S. If you like warm weather all during the year, you would love a tropical climate. The tropical climate region can be separated into two types—tropical rain forest and tropical savanna. The tropical rain forest climate receives up to 100 inches (254 cm) of rain a year. As a result, the rain forest climate is wet in most months. The tropical savanna climate has two distinct seasons—one wet and one dry.

Tropical Rain Forest Climate Year-round rains in some parts of the tropics produce lush vegetation and thick rain forests. These forests are home to millions of kinds of plant and animal life. Tall hardwood trees such as mahogany, teak, and ebony form the **canopy,** or top layer of the forest. The vegetation at the canopy layer is so thick that little sunlight reaches the forest floor. The Amazon Basin in South America is the world's largest rain forest area.

Tropical Savanna Climate In other parts of the tropics, such as southern India and eastern Africa, most of the year's rain falls in just a few months of the year. This is called the wet season. The rest of the year is hot and dry. **Savannas,** or broad grasslands with few trees, occur in this climate region. Find the tropical savanna climate areas on the map on page 65.

Reading Check **Where are the tropical climate zones found?**

NATIONAL GEOGRAPHIC **On Location**

Tropical Vegetation

The **tropical rain forest** climate remains wet most of the year (far left), whereas the **tropical savanna** climate has a distinct wet and dry season (below).

Region **What is a savanna?**

World Climate Regions

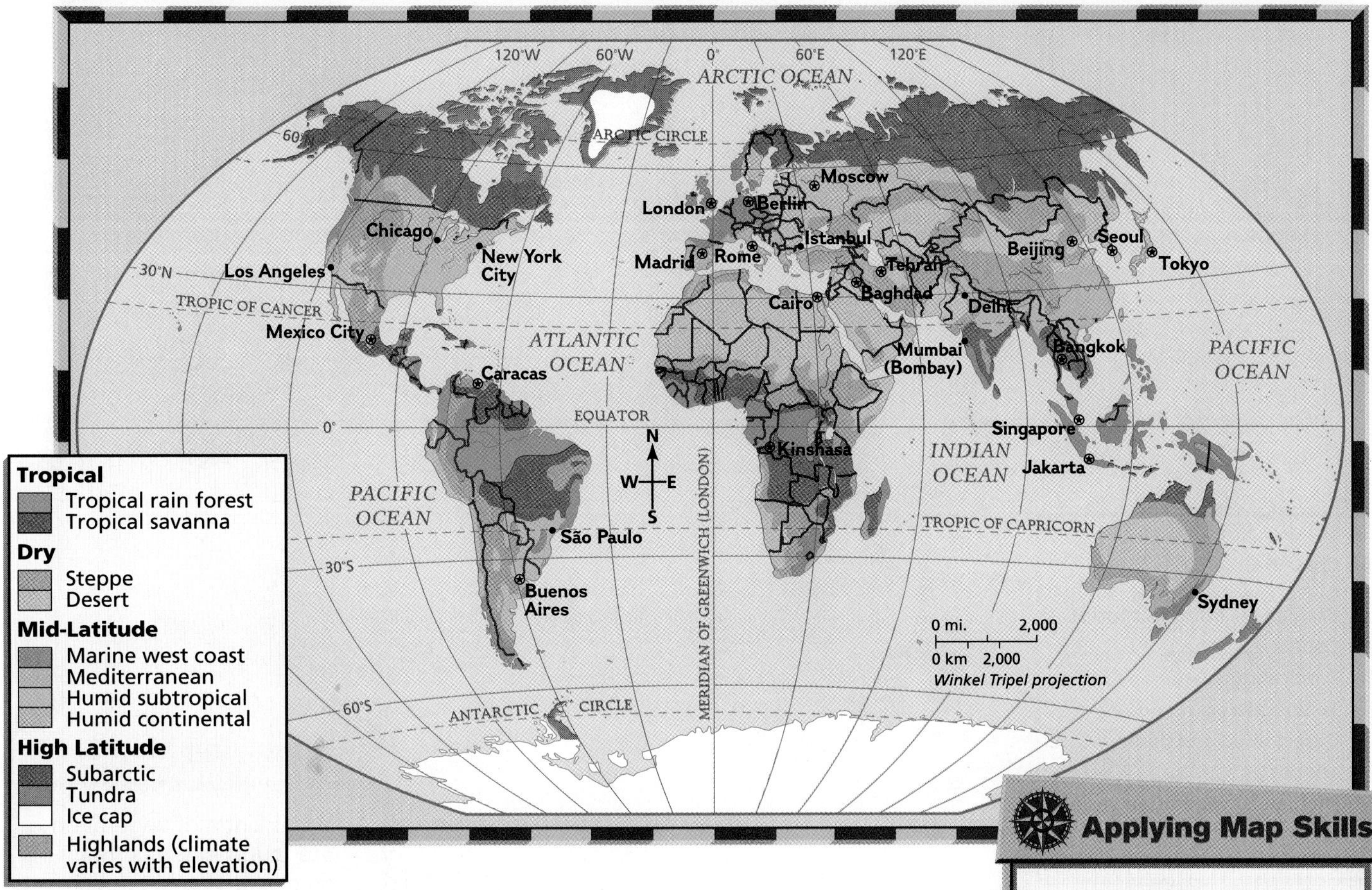

Tropical
- Tropical rain forest
- Tropical savanna

Dry
- Steppe
- Desert

Mid-Latitude
- Marine west coast
- Mediterranean
- Humid subtropical
- Humid continental

High Latitude
- Subarctic
- Tundra
- Ice cap
- Highlands (climate varies with elevation)

0 mi. 2,000
0 km 2,000
Winkel Tripel projection

Applying Map Skills

1. Which climate covers most of the southeastern United States?
2. Which climate is most common in countries directly on the Equator?

Find NGS online map resources @ www.nationalgeographic.com/maps

Mid-Latitude Climates

Mid-latitude, or moderate, climates are found in the middle latitudes of the Northern and Southern Hemispheres. They extend from about 23½° to 60° both north and south of the Equator. Most of the world's people—probably including you—live within these two bands around the earth. They are called mid-latitude because they are in the middle of both the Northern Hemisphere and the Southern Hemisphere. The mid-latitude climates are neither as close to the Equator as the tropics nor as close to the Poles as the high latitude climates.

The mid-latitude region includes more and different climate zones than other regions. This variety results from a mix of air masses. As you remember from Section 2, warm air comes from the tropics, and cool air comes from the polar regions. In most mid-latitude climates, the temperature changes with the seasons. Sometimes the climate zones in this region are called *temperate climates.*

Marine West Coast Climate Coastal areas that receive winds from the ocean usually have a mild **marine west coast climate.** If you lived in one of these areas, your winters would be rainy and mild, and your summers would be cool. These areas usually have strong growth

World Natural Vegetation Regions

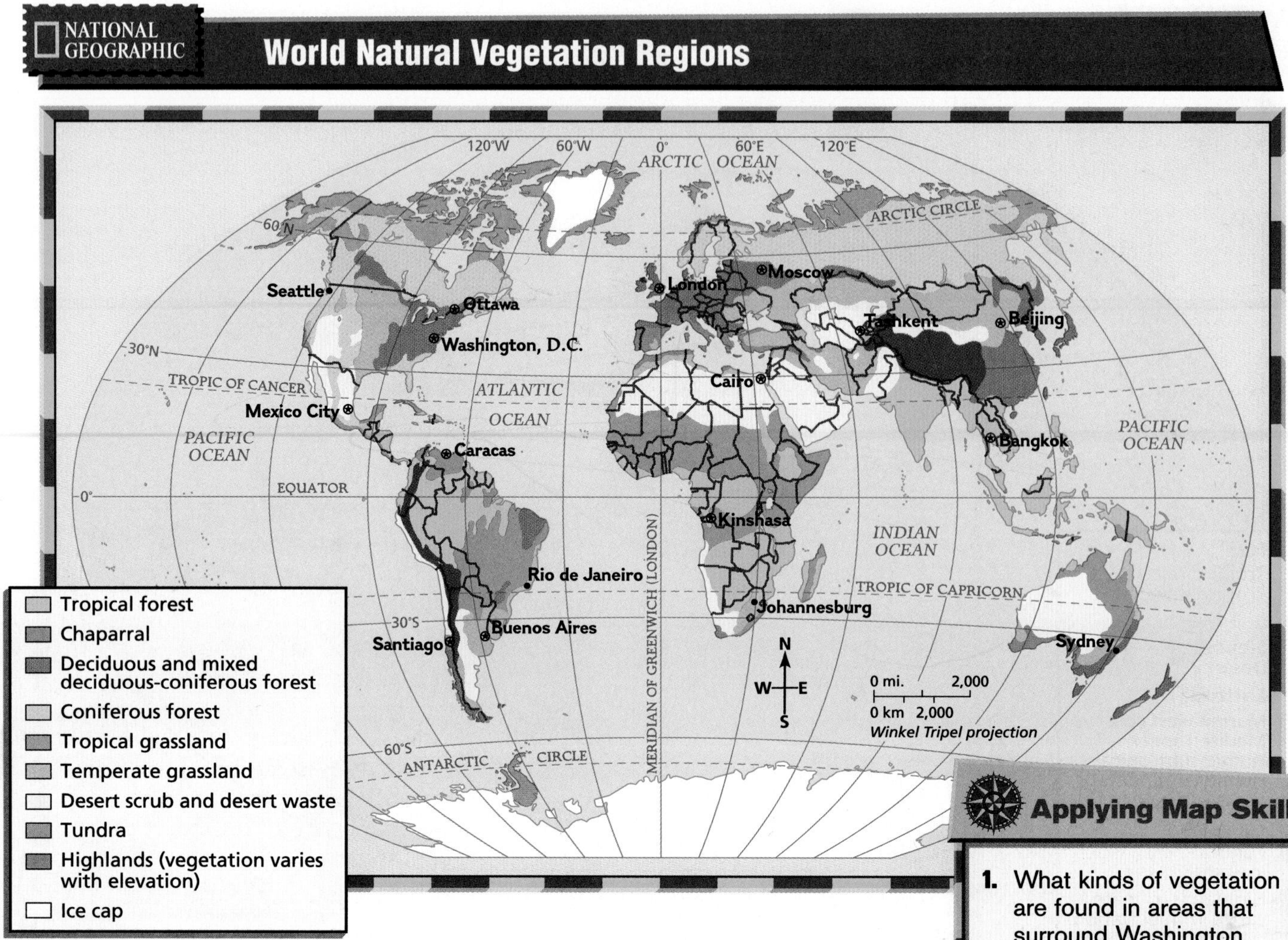

- Tropical forest
- Chaparral
- Deciduous and mixed deciduous-coniferous forest
- Coniferous forest
- Tropical grassland
- Temperate grassland
- Desert scrub and desert waste
- Tundra
- Highlands (vegetation varies with elevation)
- Ice cap

Applying Map Skills

1. What kinds of vegetation are found in areas that surround Washington, D.C., and Moscow?
2. What type of vegetation grows naturally around Bangkok?

Find NGS online map resources @ www.nationalgeographic.com/maps

of *deciduous* trees—those that lose their leaves in the fall. Some areas with this climate—like the northwestern United States—receive heavy rain. They can develop temperate rain forests, where evergreens like cedar, fir, and redwood grow.

Mediterranean Climate Another mid-latitude coastal climate is called a **Mediterranean climate** because it is similar to the climate found around the Mediterranean Sea. This climate has mild, rainy winters like the marine west coast climate. Instead of cool summers, however, people living in a Mediterranean climate experience hot, dry summers. The vegetation that grows in this climate includes shrubs and short trees. Some are evergreens, but others lose their leaves in the dry season.

Humid Continental Climate If you live in inland areas of North America, Europe, or Asia, you usually face a harsher **humid continental climate.** In these areas, winters can be long, cold, and snowy. Summers are short but may be very hot. Deciduous trees grow in forests, and vast grasslands flourish in some areas of this zone.

Humid Subtropical Climate Mid-latitude regions close to the tropics have a **humid subtropical climate.** Rain falls throughout the year but is heaviest during the hot and humid summer months. Humid subtropical winters are generally short and mild. Trees like oak, magnolia, and palms grow in this zone.

✓Reading Check **What causes the mid-latitude region to have more and different climate zones than other regions?**

High Latitude Climates

High latitude climate regions lie mostly in the high latitudes of each hemisphere, from 60°N to the North Pole and 60°S to the South Pole. These climates are generally cold, but some are more severely cold than others.

Subarctic Climate In the high latitudes nearest the mid-latitude zones, you will find the **subarctic** climate. The few people living here face severely cold and bitter winters, but temperatures do rise above freezing during summer

Mid-Latitude Vegetation

Fir trees (bottom left) thrive in a **marine west coast** climate. Shrubs and olive trees (top right) grow in a **Mediterranean** climate. Deciduous trees (bottom right) flourish in a **humid continental** climate. Palm trees are common in **humid subtropical** zones.

Place **Which type of vegetation is most common in your area?**

months. Huge evergreen forests called *taiga* (TY•guh) grow in the subarctic region, especially in northern Russia.

Tundra Climate Closer to the Poles than the subarctic zone lie the **tundra** areas. The tundra is a vast rolling plain without trees. The climate in this zone is harsh and dry. In parts of the tundra and subarctic regions, the lower layers of soil are called **permafrost** because they stay permanently frozen. Only the top few inches of the ground thaw during summer months. Because the surface is flat and the soil below is frozen, water tends to stay on the land when it melts. This provides the moisture that plants need to grow. You will find sturdy grasses and low-growing berry bushes in the tundra.

Ice Cap Climate On the polar ice caps and the great ice sheets of Antarctica and Greenland, the climate is bitterly cold. Monthly temperatures average below freezing. Temperatures in Antarctica have been measured at −128°F (−89°C)! Although no other vegetation grows here, *lichens*—or funguslike plants and mosses—can live on rocks.

✓Reading Check **What are the three types of high latitude climates?**

NATIONAL GEOGRAPHIC **On Location**

High Latitude Vegetation

Vegetation in high latitude climates includes **tundra** grasses and bushes (top left), **subarctic** evergreen forests (bottom left), and **ice cap** lichens (background).

Region **How does permafrost affect vegetation in the tundra and subarctic regions?**

Dry Climate Vegetation

The vegetation that survives **desert** and **steppe** climates includes cacti (above) and short grasses (left).

Region Are very dry climates always hot? Explain.

Dry Climates

Dry climate refers to dry or partially dry areas that receive little or no rainfall. Temperatures can be extremely hot during the day and very cold at night. Dry climates can also have severely cold winters. You can find dry climate regions at any latitude.

Desert Climate The driest climates have less than 10 inches (25 cm) of rainfall a year. Regions with such climates are called deserts. Only scattered plants such as cacti can survive a desert climate. With roots close to the surface, cacti can collect any rain that falls. Most cacti are found only in North America. In other countries, however, small areas of thick plant life dot the deserts. These arise along rivers or where underground springs reach the surface.

Steppe Climate Many deserts are surrounded by partly dry grasslands and prairies known as **steppes.** The word *steppe* comes from a Russian word meaning "treeless plain." The steppes get more rain than deserts, averaging 10 to 20 inches (25 to 51 cm) a year. Bushes and short grasses cover the steppe landscape. The Great Plains of the United States has a steppe climate.

✓ Reading Check **Where are steppe climate zones often located?**

Highland Vegetation

The wildflowers and shrubs that grow in meadows above the timberline are often called *alpine* vegetation. This name refers to the Alps mountain ranges in Europe.

Location **How does elevation affect climate?**

Highland Climate

As you read in Section 2, the elevation of a place changes its climate dramatically. Mountains tend to have cool climates—and the highest mountains have very cold climates. This is true even for mountains that are on the Equator. A highland, or mountain, climate has cool or cold temperatures year-round.

If you climb a mountain, you will reach an area called the timberline. The **timberline** is the elevation above which no trees grow. Once you reach the timberline, you will find only small shrubs and wildflowers growing in meadows.

Reading Check **What is the timberline?**

Section 3 Assessment

Defining Terms

1. **Define** canopy, savanna, marine west coast climate, Mediterranean climate, humid continental climate, humid subtropical climate, subarctic, tundra, permafrost, steppe, timberline.

Recalling Facts

2. **Region** What are the five types of climate regions?
3. **Region** How do the climate zones in the mid-latitude region differ?
4. **Region** What kind of vegetation grows in the tundra climate zone?

Critical Thinking

5. **Making Comparisons** What do the tropical savanna and humid continental climates have in common?
6. **Drawing Conclusions** How can snow exist in the tropics along the Equator?

Graphic Organizer

7. **Organizing Information** Draw a globe like this one. Label the three climate regions that are based on latitude, then identify the lines of latitude that separate the climate regions.

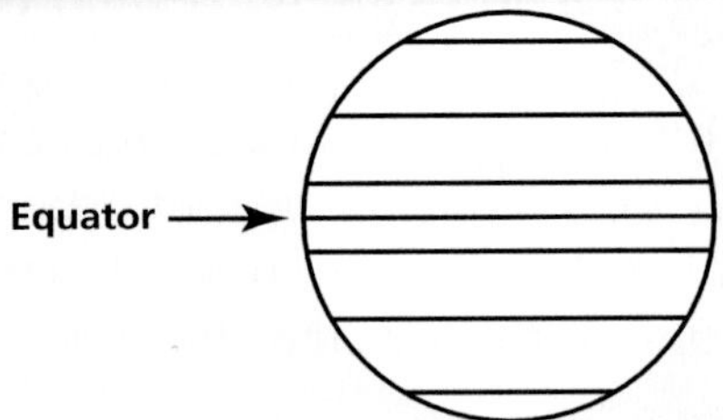

Applying Geography Skills

8. **Analyzing Maps** Look at the world natural vegetation regions map on page 66. What type of natural vegetation thrives around Cairo?

Chapter 2 Reading Review

Section 1 The Water Planet

Terms to Know

- water vapor
- water cycle
- evaporation
- condensation
- precipitation
- collection
- glacier
- groundwater
- aquifer

Main Idea

Water is one of the earth's most precious resources.

✓ Region Water covers about 70 percent of the earth's surface.

✓ Movement Water follows a cycle of evaporation, condensation, precipitation, and collection on and beneath the ground.

✓ Science Humans and most animals need freshwater to live. Only a small fraction of the world's water is found in rivers and lakes.

Section 2 Climate

Terms to Know

- weather
- climate
- tropics
- monsoon
- tornado
- hurricane
- typhoon
- drought
- El Niño
- La Niña
- current
- local wind
- rain shadow
- greenhouse effect
- rain forest

Main Idea

Wind and water carry rainfall and the sun's warmth around the world to create different climates.

✓ Region Climate is the usual pattern of weather over a long period of time. It includes extremes in temperature and rainfall.

✓ Region The tropics, near the Equator, receive more of the sun's warmth than other regions.

✓ Location Landforms and position near water affect climate in a local area.

✓ Culture Human actions like building cities, burning fuels, and clearing the rain forests can affect climate.

Section 3 Climate Zones and Vegetation

Terms to Know

- canopy
- savanna
- marine west coast climate
- Mediterranean climate
- humid continental climate
- humid subtropical climate
- subarctic
- tundra
- permafrost
- steppe
- timberline

Main Idea

Geographers divide the world into different climate zones, each of which has special characteristics.

✓ Region The world has five main climate regions that are based on latitude, amount of moisture, and/or elevation. These regions are tropical, mid-latitude, high latitude, dry, and highland.

✓ Region Each climate zone has particular kinds of vegetation.

Fishing on the Pacific Ocean ▶

Chapter 2 Assessment and Activities

Using Key Terms

Match the terms in Part A with their definitions in Part B.

A.

1. evaporation
2. savanna
3. monsoon
4. tundra
5. condensation
6. greenhouse effect
7. rain forest
8. El Niño
9. precipitation
10. current

B.

a. moving streams of water in the oceans
b. treeless plain in which only the top few inches of ground thaw in summer
c. weather pattern in the Pacific Ocean
d. seasonal wind that blows over a continent
e. buildup of certain gases in the atmosphere that hold the sun's warmth
f. water that falls back to the earth
g. dense forest that receives much rain
h. water vapor changes back into a liquid
i. sun's heat turns water into water vapor
j. broad grassland in the tropics

Reviewing the Main Ideas

Section 1 The Water Planet

11. **Movement** What are the four steps in the water cycle?
12. **Region** What percentage of the world's water is freshwater?
13. **Region** What has more freshwater—lakes and rivers or groundwater?

Section 2 Climate

14. **Movement** How do wind and water affect climate?
15. **Location** How do mountains affect rainfall?
16. **Human/Environment Interaction** Why are cities warmer than nearby rural areas?

Section 3 Climate Zones and Vegetation

17. **Region** Which climate region has the most climate zones? Why?
18. **Place** What kind of vegetation grows in Mediterranean climates?
19. **Place** In what climate zone would you find large grasslands?

World Oceans and Currents

Place Location Activity

On a separate sheet of paper, match the letters on the map with the numbered places listed below.

1. Arctic Ocean
2. Atlantic Ocean
3. California Current
4. Japan Current
5. Indian Ocean
6. Gulf Stream

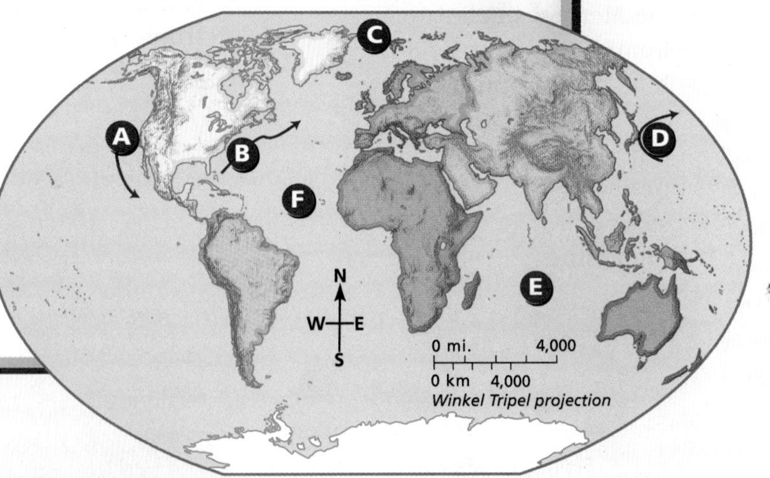

Self-Check Quiz Visit the ***Geography: The World and Its People*** Web site at gwip.glencoe.com and click on **Chapter 2—Self-Check Quizzes** to prepare for the Chapter Test.

Critical Thinking

20. **Analyzing Information** From where does the freshwater in your community come? How can you find out?
21. **Categorizing Information** Create five webs like the one shown here. In each large oval, write the name of a climate region. In the medium-sized ovals, write the name of each climate zone in that region. For each zone, fill in the three small ovals with the usual weather in summer, the usual weather in winter, and the kind of vegetation.

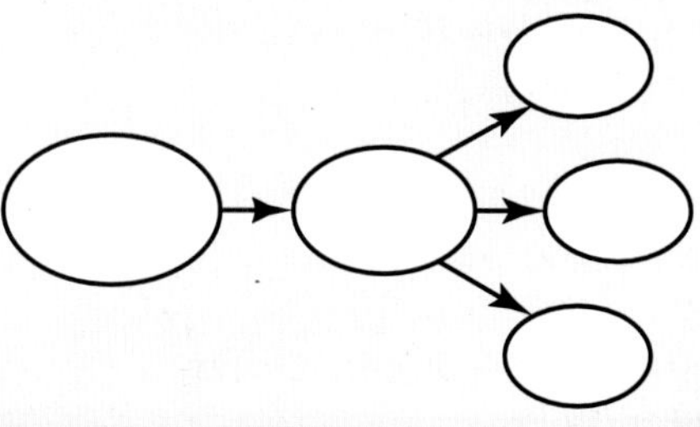

GeoJournal Activity

22. **Writing a Poem** Make a list of all the types of precipitation that you can think of. Write a poem about precipitation and climate using the words in your list.

Mental Mapping Activity

23. **Focusing on the Region** Draw a freehand map of the world's oceans and continents. Label the following items:
    - Equator
    - North America
    - Pacific Ocean
    - Africa
    - high latitude climate regions
    - tropical climate regions

Technology Activity

24. **Using the Internet** Research a recent hurricane or tornado. Find out when and where it happened, how much force the storm had, and what damage it caused.

Standardized Test Practice

Directions: Study the graph, then answer the following question.

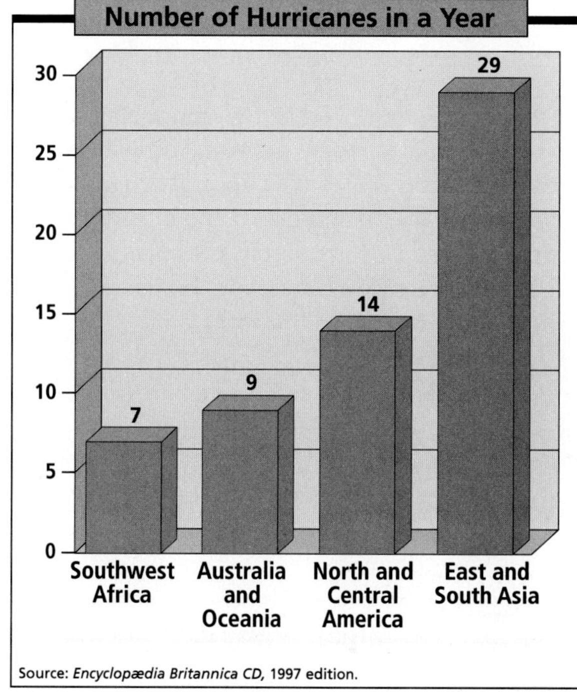

1. How many more hurricanes does East and South Asia experience in a year than North and Central America?

F 29

G 14

H 9

J 15

Test-Taking Tip: Make sure you read the question carefully. It is not asking for the total number of hurricanes in East and South Asia. Instead, the question asks how many *more* hurricanes one region has than another.

EYE on the Environment

THE OCEANS
Deep Trouble

Endangered Seas Next time you are in the grocery store, walk past the fresh seafood section. You will see fish, shrimp, and other seafood on ice. The abundance and variety of seafood available makes it seem as if the oceans can provide us with food forever. Unfortunately, that is not true. Oceans worldwide are in deep trouble because of human activities. There are several trouble spots around the world.

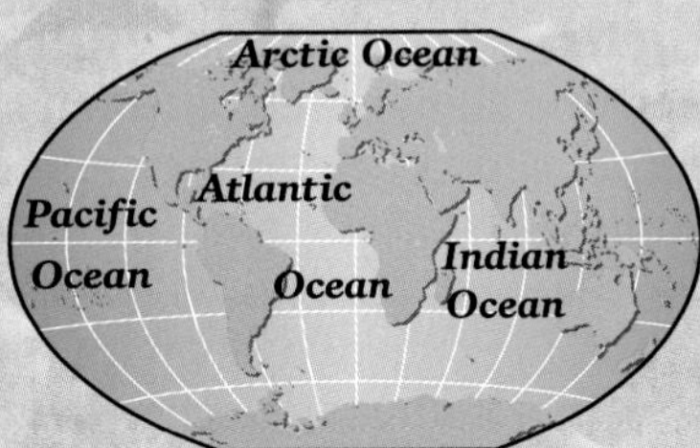

- Grand Banks — Overfishing in the northwest Atlantic Ocean has seriously harmed once-rich populations of cod, halibut, and other fish.
- Gulf of Mexico — Pollution from United States's rivers causes a "dead zone" in the Gulf each summer. Fish die due to a lack of oxygen in the water.
- Yellow Sea — China's industries have dumped poisons into these Pacific Ocean waters. This sea may have the world's highest levels of heavy metals.
- Kara Sea — The former Soviet Union dumped huge quantities of radioactive wastes into these Arctic waters.

Saving Oceans It is not too late to preserve the oceans. Some steps have been taken.

- More than 1,200 protected zones exist along coasts worldwide.
- Countries are assigning individual catch limits to fishing boats.
- Science organizations are collecting data on oceans and urging government leaders to pass laws to protect marine environments.

Starfish

Workers clean a beach after an oil spill.

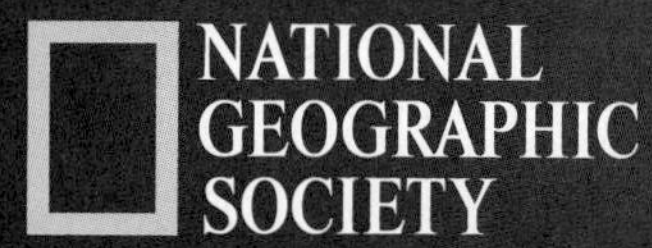

Bottlenose dolphin

Making a Difference

Underwater Explorer Imagine exploring where no one has ever been before. Dr. Sylvia Earle has! Earle explores deep in the oceans, discovering new kinds of animals, plants, and systems of life. Earle is a marine biologist and former chief scientist of the National Oceanic and Atmospheric Administration (NOAA). Now she is leading a research project called the Sustainable Seas Expeditions. Using a special, one-person submersible called *DeepWorker*, Earle and her team are studying deepwater habitats in the United States's National Marine Sanctuary system. This system includes 12 underwater parks that lie in coastal waters around the continental United States and in Hawaii and American Samoa.

DeepWorker has a clear acrylic dome that covers the pilot's head and shoulders. Mechanical arms allow the pilot to work underwater. The expedition team takes photographs and collects data on marine organisms and their habitats in the sanctuaries. Sylvia Earle and her team hope that their research will help people worldwide realize how important the oceans are and why we need to protect them.

Marine biologist Sylvia Earle

What Can You Do?

Get Involved

How can you help the oceans? Recycle and do not pollute! About 77 percent of all pollutants in the oceans originate on land. Plastic and other trash in ocean waters kill fish, sea birds, turtles, seals, and whales.

Find Out More

Learn more about the 12 national marine sanctuaries. Find out where the sanctuaries are located and the types of marine organisms found in each. Visit the Web site www.sanctuaries.nos.noaa.gov. Locate the sanctuaries on a world map.

Use the Internet

Follow the progress of the Sustainable Seas Expeditions. Check the project's "Sanctuary Log" at http://sustainableseas.noaa.gov/missions/missions.html. You can also see what it is like to pilot *DeepWorker*, by visiting www.nationalgeographic.com/monter...

Earle studying animals in Hawaiian waters

Chapter 3

The World's People

The World and Its People NATIONAL GEOGRAPHIC

To learn more about the world's culture regions, view ***The World and Its People*** **Chapter 3** video.

Geography Online

Chapter Overview Visit the ***Geography: The World and Its People*** Web site at gwip.glencoe.com and click on **Chapter 3–Chapter Overviews** to preview information about the world's people.

Section 1 Culture

Guide to Reading

Main Idea

People usually live with others who follow similar beliefs learned from the past.

Terms to Know

- culture
- ethnic group
- dialect
- monarchy
- dictator
- democracy
- economic system
- cultural diffusion
- civilization
- culture region

Places to Locate

- Iraq
- Egypt
- India
- China

Reading Strategy

Draw a diagram like this one. In each section, write one of the eight elements of culture and give an example of it from the United States today.

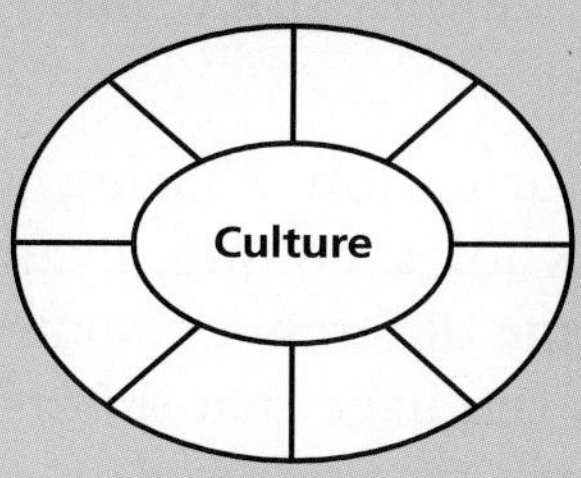

NATIONAL GEOGRAPHIC **Exploring Our World**

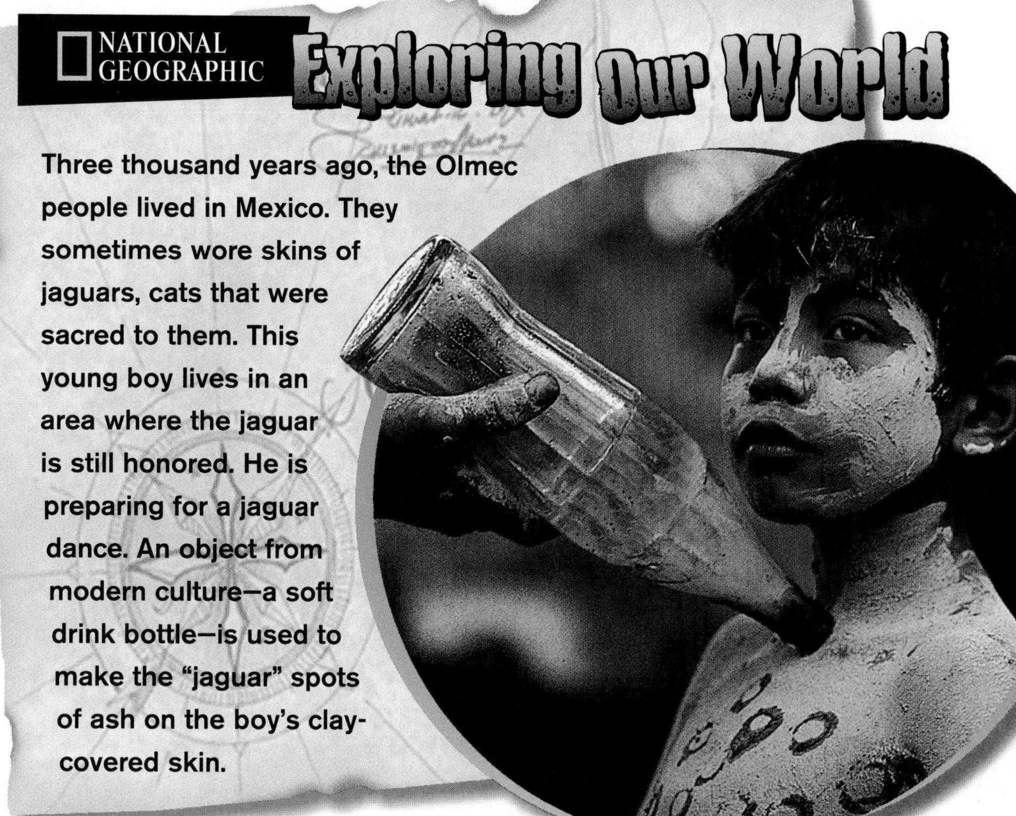

Three thousand years ago, the Olmec people lived in Mexico. They sometimes wore skins of jaguars, cats that were sacred to them. This young boy lives in an area where the jaguar is still honored. He is preparing for a jaguar dance. An object from modern culture—a soft drink bottle—is used to make the "jaguar" spots of ash on the boy's clay-covered skin.

If you wake up to rock music, put on denim jeans, speak English, and celebrate the Fourth of July, those things are part of your culture. If you eat flat bread for breakfast, speak Spanish, and take part in celebrations honoring the jaguar, those things are part of your culture.

What Is Culture?

As used in geography, **culture** is the way of life of a group of people who share similar beliefs and customs. In studying a society's culture, geographers look at eight elements called *traits.* They study what groups the society is divided into, what language the people speak, and what religion they follow. They examine people's daily lives. They consider what history the people share and what artworks they have created. They also look at how the society is governed and how the people make a living.

Social Groups One way of studying cultures is by looking at the different groups of people in the society. For instance, geographers study how many people are rich, poor, and in the middle class. They

◀ Thousands of Indians meet for an annual Hindu festival.

World Religions

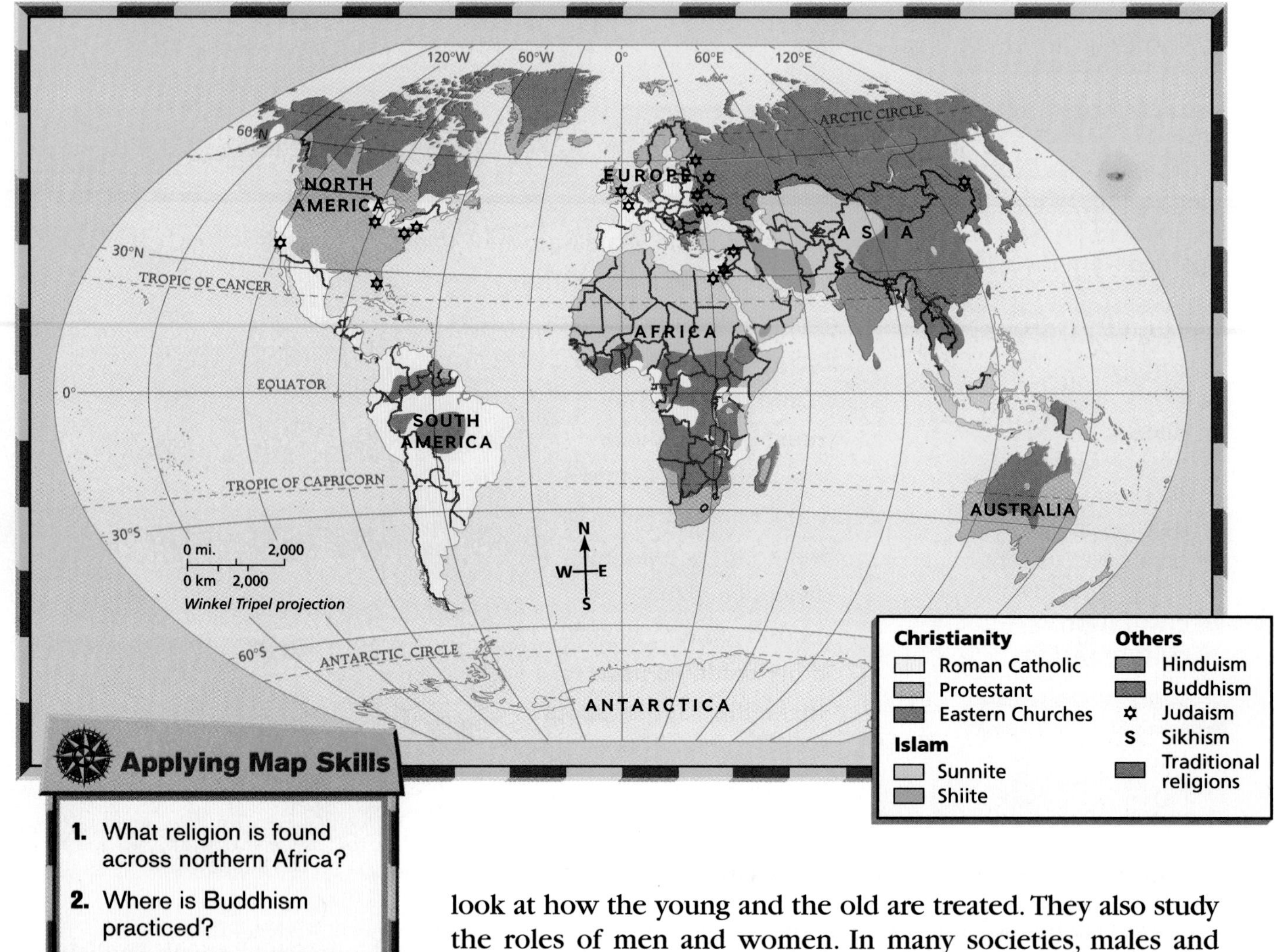

Applying Map Skills

1. What religion is found across northern Africa?
2. Where is Buddhism practiced?

Find NGS online map resources @ www.nationalgeographic.com/maps

look at how the young and the old are treated. They also study the roles of men and women. In many societies, males and females have different rights and responsibilities. Understanding those differences is a vital part of understanding a particular culture.

Geographers also examine how people in the culture treat others who are different from themselves. Most countries include people who belong to different ethnic groups. An **ethnic group** is a group of people who share a common culture, language, or history. Many societies have people who have moved there from another place. Many have people who practice different religions.

Language People use language to share information. Sharing a language is one of the strongest unifying forces for a culture. Even within a culture, though, geographers find language differences. Some people may speak a **dialect,** or a local form of a language that differs from the main language. The differences may include pronunciation and the meaning of words. For example, people in the northeastern United States say "soda," whereas people in the Midwest say "pop." Both groups are referring to soft drinks, however.

Religion Another important part of culture is religion. In many cultures, religion helps people answer basic questions about life's meaning. Religious beliefs vary significantly around the world. Struggles over religious differences are a problem in many countries. Some of the major world religions are Buddhism, Christianity, Hinduism, Islam, and Judaism. The map on page 78 shows you the main areas where these religions are practiced.

Daily Life Do you enjoy eating pizza, tacos, yogurt, and eggrolls? All of these foods came from different cultures. What people eat and *how* they eat it—whether with their fingers, silverware, chopsticks, and so on—reflect their culture. What people wear also reflects cultural differences. The same is true of how people build traditional homes in their societies.

History A culture group has a shared history, and that history shapes how they view the world. People remember the successes of the past and often celebrate holidays to honor the heroes and heroines who brought about those successes. Stories about these heroes reveal the personal characteristics that the people think are important. A group also remembers the dark periods of history, when they met with disaster or defeat. These experiences, too, influence how a group of people sees itself.

Arts People express their culture through the arts. Art is not just paintings and sculptures, but also architecture, dance, music, theater, and literature. By viewing the arts of a culture, you can gain insight into what the people of that culture think is beautiful and important.

Government The kind of government, or political system, a society has reflects its culture. Some countries are led by individuals. In a **monarchy,** kings and queens inherit the right to rule. In others, **dictators** take control of the government and rule the country as they wish.

In many countries today, power rests with the people of the nation. Citizens choose their leaders by voting for them. When the people of a country hold the power of government, we call that government a **democracy.** Some places have mixed forms of government. For example, the United Kingdom is both a monarchy and a democracy. The queen is the symbolic head of the country, but the power to rule is in the hands of elected leaders.

NATIONAL GEOGRAPHIC **On Location**

Celebrations

In most cultures, people often bring out their most beautiful clothes for events like weddings. This wedding guest is from Morocco (upper left), and this bride is from Mauritius.

Place What aspects of daily life besides clothing reflect culture?

The Economy People must make a living, whether in farming or in industry or by providing services such as designing a Web page or preparing food. Geographers look at how people in a culture earn a living. They also look at the culture's economic system.

An **economic system** sets rules for how people decide what goods and services to produce and how they are exchanged. In a *traditional economy,* things are done "the way they have always been done." Economic decisions are based on customs and beliefs—often religious—handed down from generation to generation. For example, if your grandparents and parents fished for a living, you will fish for a living.

In a *market economy,* individuals make decisions about what to produce. People who own businesses make what they think customers want. Customers have the freedom to choose what products they will buy. A market economy is based on *free enterprise.* This is the idea that you have the right to own property or businesses and make a profit without the government interfering. People are free to choose what jobs they will do and for whom they will work.

In a *command economy,* however, the government owns businesses and controls decisions about what goods and services will be produced. A command economy is often called *socialism* or *communism,* depending on how much the government is involved. In some command economies, the government even decides which people receive training for particular jobs.

✓Reading Check **What is culture?**

Sri Lanka

Some people in Sri Lanka harvest tea (left). Others work in factories making dolls to be sold around the world (below).

Place **On what is a market economy based?**

NATIONAL GEOGRAPHIC

World Culture Regions

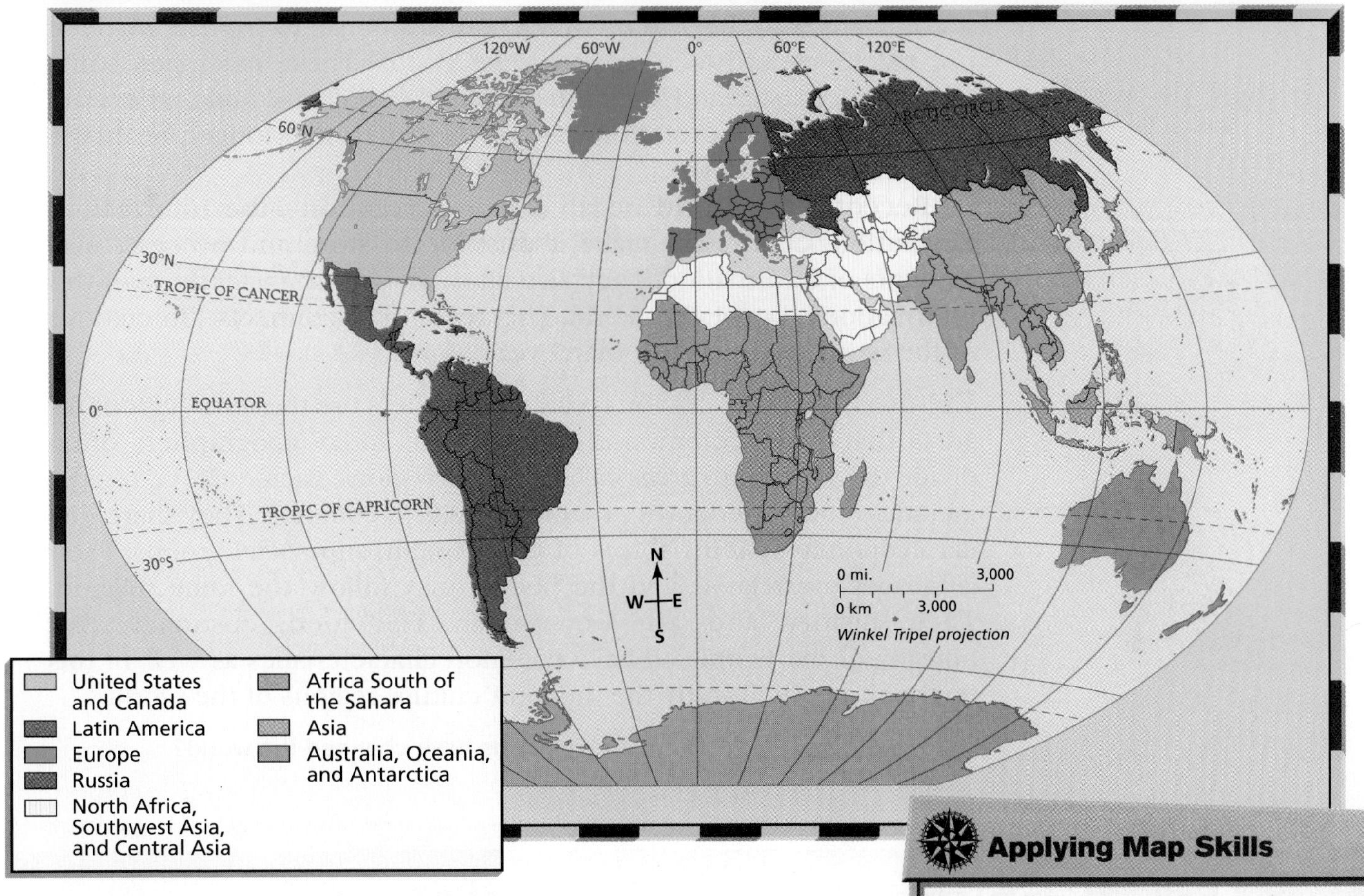

Applying Map Skills

1. Which culture region includes most nations of Africa?
2. What culture region is on the continents of both Africa and Asia?

Find NGS online map resources @ www.nationalgeographic.com/maps

Cultural Change

Cultures do not remain the same. Humans constantly invent new ideas and technologies and create new solutions to problems. Trade, the movement of people, and war can spread these changes to other cultures. The process of spreading new knowledge and skills to other cultures is called **cultural diffusion.** Today the Internet is making cultural diffusion take place more rapidly than ever before.

Culture Over Time Historians have traced the tremendous changes that humans have made in their cultures. In the first human societies, people lived by hunting animals and gathering fruits and vegetables. They were *nomadic,* or lived in small groups that moved from place to place to follow sources of food.

Starting about 10,000 years ago, people learned to grow food by planting seeds. This change brought about the Agricultural Revolution. Groups stayed in one place and built settlements. Their societies became more complex. As a result, four **civilizations,** or highly developed cultures, arose in river valleys in present-day **Iraq, Egypt, India,** and **China.** These civilizations included cities, complex governments and religions, and systems of writing. The map on page 83 shows you where these civilizations were located.

Thousands of years later—in the 1700s and 1800s—came a new set of changes in the world. Some countries began to *industrialize,* or use machines and factories to make goods. These machines could work harder, faster, and longer than people or animals could. As a result of the Industrial Revolution, people began to live longer, healthier, more comfortable lives.

Recently, the world began a new revolution—the Information Revolution. Computers make it possible to store and process huge amounts of information. They also allow people to instantly send this information all over the world. This revolution connects the cultures of the world more closely than ever before.

Culture Regions As you recall, geographers use the term *regions* for areas that share common characteristics. Today geographers often divide the world into areas called culture regions. Each **culture region** includes different countries that have traits in common. They share similar economic systems, forms of government, and social groups. Their languages are related, and the people may follow the same religion. Their history and art are similar. The food, costumes, and housing of the people all have common characteristics as well. In this textbook, you will study the different culture regions of the world.

Reading Check **What three revolutions have changed the world?**

Assessment

Defining Terms

1. **Define** culture, ethnic group, dialect, monarchy, dictator, democracy, economic system, cultural diffusion, civilization, culture region.

Recalling Facts

2. **Culture** What kinds of social groups do geographers study?
3. **Government** What are the different forms of government a society may have?
4. **Culture** In what ways does cultural diffusion occur?

Critical Thinking

5. **Understanding Cause and Effect** How does history shape a people's culture?
6. **Making Comparisons** Describe two kinds of economic systems.

Graphic Organizer

7. **Organizing Information** Create a diagram like this one that describes features of your culture. On the lines write the types of food, clothing, language, music, and so on.

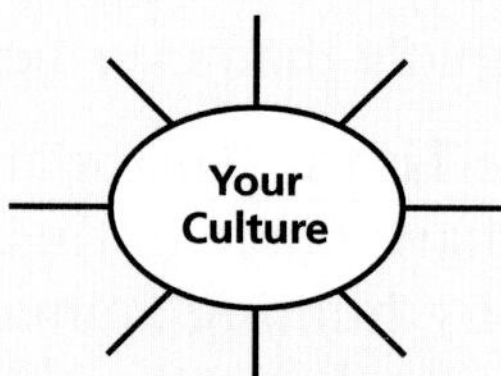

Applying Geography Skills

8. **Analyzing Maps** Look at the map on page 81. In which culture region do you live? In which culture region(s) did your ancestors live?

Geography Skill

Reading a Special Purpose Map

Special purpose maps concentrate on a single theme. This theme may be to show the battles of a particular war or endangered species, for example.

Learning the Skill

To read a special purpose map, follow these steps:

- Read the map title. It tells what kind of special information the map shows.
- Find the map's scale to determine the general size of the area.
- Read the key. Colors and symbols in the map key are especially important on this type of map.
- Analyze the areas on the map that are highlighted in the key. Look for patterns.

Practicing the Skill

Look at the map below to answer the following questions.

1. What is the title of the map?
2. Read the key. What four civilizations are shown on this map?
3. Which civilization was farthest west? East?
4. What do the locations of each of these civilizations have in common?

Applying the Skill

Find a special purpose map in a newspaper or magazine. Write three questions about the map's purpose, then have a classmate answer the questions.

GO TO Practice key skills with **Glencoe Skillbuilder Interactive Workbook, Level 1.**

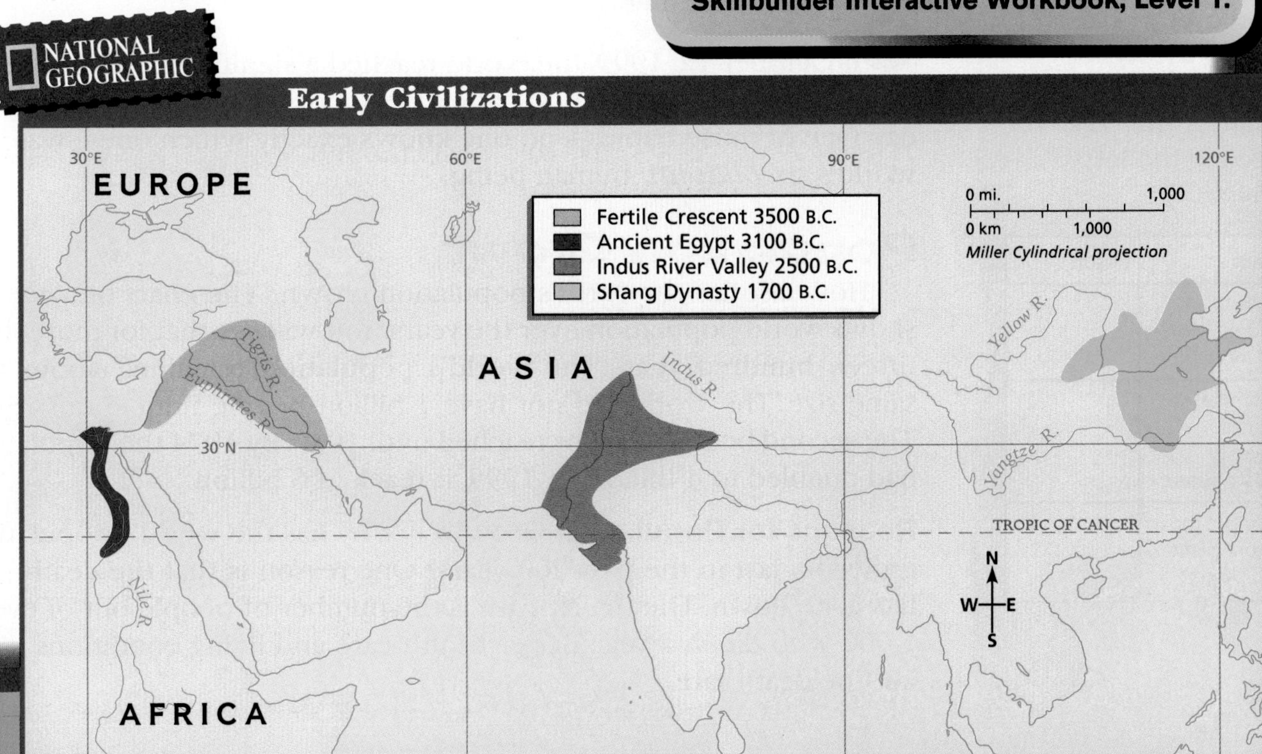

Section 2

Population

Guide to Reading

Main Idea

The world's population is growing rapidly, and how and where people live are changing, too.

Terms to Know

- death rate
- birthrate
- famine
- population density
- urbanization
- emigrate
- refugee

Places to Locate

- Afghanistan
- Nepal
- Mexico City
- Buenos Aires

Reading Strategy

Draw a chart like this one. In the right column, write a result of the fact listed in the left column.

Fact	Result
World population is increasing.	
Population is not evenly distributed.	
People move from place to place.	

Imagine that you and your friends are in Berlin, Germany. Can you hear the music? Every summer, hundreds of thousands of young people gather here for a music festival. Although most of these young people are here only to visit, many thousands of others come to find jobs and new lives. Germany faces challenges in finding room for its newcomers.

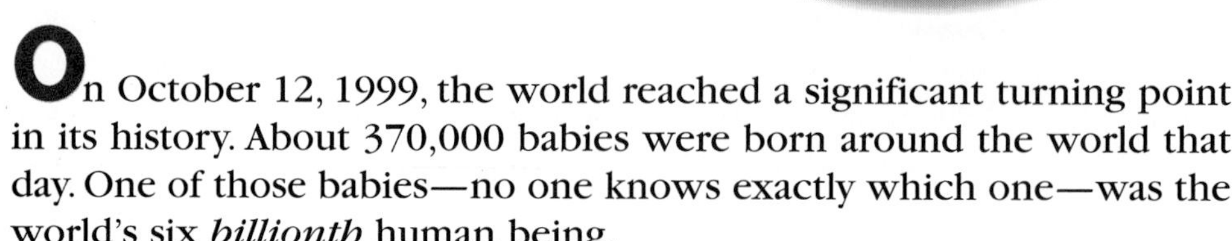

On October 12, 1999, the world reached a significant turning point in its history. About 370,000 babies were born around the world that day. One of those babies—no one knows exactly which one—was the world's six *billionth* human being.

Population Growth

How fast has the earth's population grown? The chart on page 85 shows world population over the years. You will see that for more than fifteen hundred years, the world's population remained about the same size. The world did not have 1 billion people until about 1800. The second billion was not reached until 1930. By 1974 the population had doubled to 4 billion. In 1999, it reached 6 billion.

Reasons for Population Growth Why has the world's population grown so fast in the past 200 years? One reason is that the death rate has gone down. The **death rate** is the number of people out of every 1,000 who die in a year. Better health care and living conditions have cut the death rate.

World Population

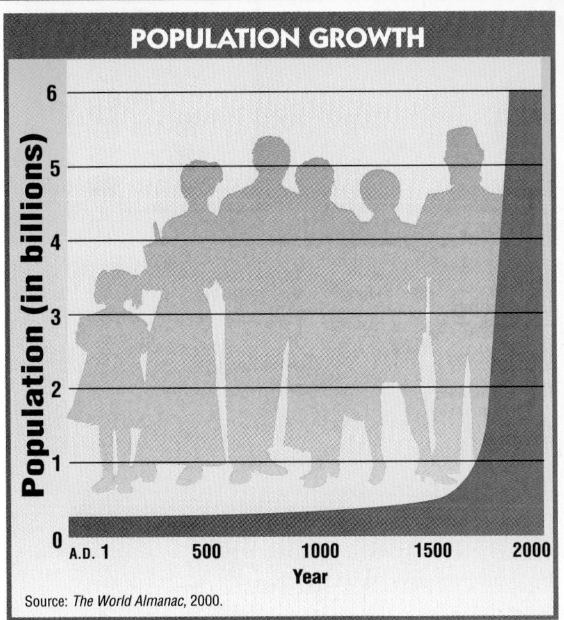

MOST POPULOUS COUNTRIES

Country	Millions of People
China	1,254.1
India	1,000.8
United States	281.0
Indonesia	211.8
Brazil	168.0
Pakistan	146.5
Russia	146.5

Source: *National Geographic Atlas of the World; The World Almanac*, 2000.

Analyzing the Graph and Chart

The world's population is expected to reach about 9 billion by 2050.

Place Which country has the second-largest number of people?

Visit gwip.glencoe.com and click on **Chapter 3—Textbook Updates.**

Another reason for the fast growth in the world's population is that in some regions of the world the birthrate is high. The **birthrate** is the number of children born each year for every 1,000 people. In Asia, Africa, and Latin America, families traditionally are large because children help with farming. High numbers of births have combined with low death rates to increase population growth in these areas. As a result, population in these continents has doubled every 25 years or so.

Challenges From Population Growth Rapid population growth presents many challenges. An increase in the number of people means that more food is needed. Fortunately, since 1950 world food production has increased faster than population on all continents except Africa. Because so many people there need food, bad weather or war can ruin crops and bring disaster. Millions may suffer from **famine,** or lack of food.

Also, populations that grow rapidly may use resources more quickly than populations that do not grow as fast. Some countries face shortages of water and housing. Population growth also puts a strain on a country's economy. If there are more people, they need more jobs. Some experts are optimistic about the future. They predict that as the number of humans rises, the levels of technology and creativity will also increase.

✓Reading Check **How do the definitions of death rate and birthrate differ?**

Where People Live

Where do all the people live? Actually, the world's people live on a surprisingly small part of the earth. As you learned in Chapter 2, land covers only about 30 percent of the earth's surface. Half of this land is

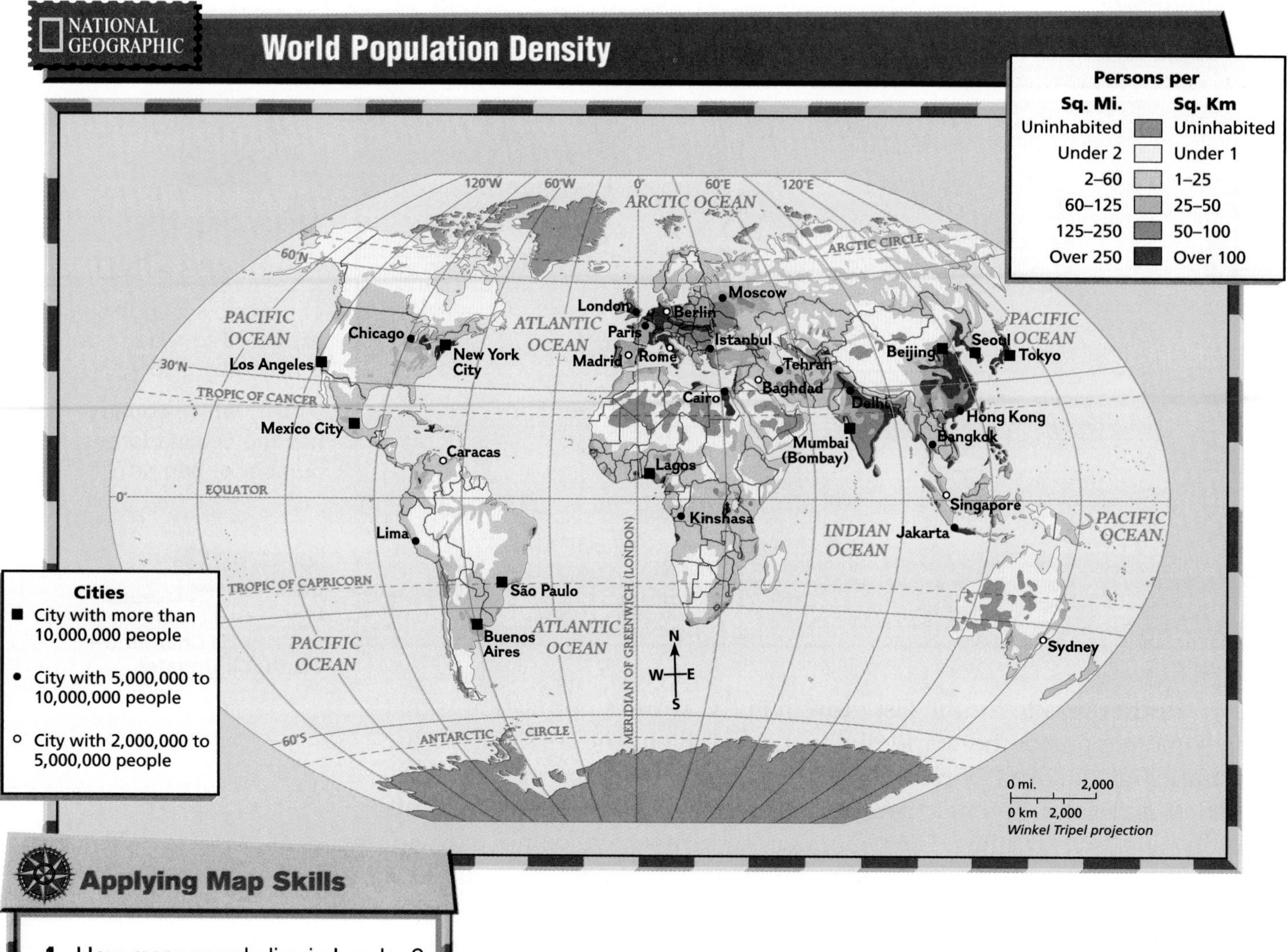

Applying Map Skills

1. How many people live in London?
2. What cities have more than 10 million people?

Find NGS online map resources @ www.nationalgeographic.com/maps

not usable by humans, however. Large numbers of people cannot survive on land covered with ice, deserts, or high mountains. The world's people, then, live on a small fraction of the earth's surface.

Population Distribution Even on the usable land, population is not distributed, or spread, evenly. People naturally prefer to live in places that have plentiful water, good land, and a favorable climate. During the industrial age, people moved to places that had important resources such as coal or iron ore to run or make machines. People gather in other areas because these places hold religious significance or because they are government and transportation centers. The table on page 85 shows you the most populous countries in the world. Four of these countries are located on the Asian continent.

Population Density Geographers have a way of determining how crowded a country or region is. They measure **population density**—the average number of people living in a square mile or square kilometer. To arrive at this figure, the total population is divided by the total land area. For example, the countries of **Afghanistan** and **Nepal**

have about the same number of people. They are very different in terms of population density, though. With a smaller land area, Nepal has 447 people per square mile (173 people per sq. km). Afghanistan has an average of only 103 people per square mile (40 people per sq. km). Nepal, then, is more crowded than Afghanistan.

Remember that population density is an *average.* It assumes that people are distributed evenly throughout a country. Of course, this seldom happens. A country may have several large cities where most of the people actually live. In Egypt, for example, overall population density is 173 people per square mile (67 people per sq. km). In reality, about 99 percent of Egypt's people live within 20 miles (32 km) of the Nile River. The rest of Egypt is desert. Thus, some geographers prefer to figure a country's population density in terms of farmable or usable land rather than total land area. When Egypt's population density is measured this way, it equals about *5,550 people* per square mile. The map on page 13 of the **Geography Handbook** shows how population density can vary within a country. The areas with high density in Egypt follow the path of the Nile River.

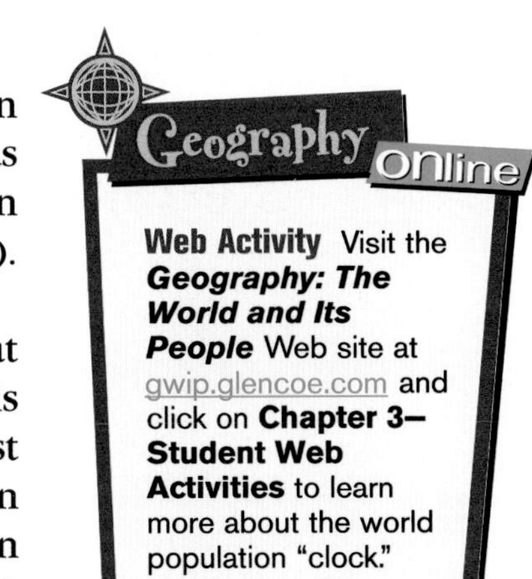

Web Activity Visit the ***Geography: The World and Its People*** Web site at gwip.glencoe.com and click on **Chapter 3–Student Web Activities** to learn more about the world population "clock."

Reading Check **What is population density?**

Population Movement

Throughout the world, people are moving in great numbers from place to place. Some people move from city to city, or suburb to suburb. More and more people are leaving villages and farms and moving to cities. This movement to cities is called **urbanization.**

NATIONAL GEOGRAPHIC **On Location**

Kosovo, Yugoslavia

In 1999 a civil war exploded in Kosovo, a province of Yugoslavia. Thousands of people were forced from their homes.

Movement **What causes people to become refugees?**

People move to cities for many reasons. The biggest one is to find jobs. Rural populations have grown, but the amount of land that can be farmed has not increased to meet the growing number of people who need to work and to eat. As a result, many people find city jobs in manufacturing or in services like tourism.

Nearly half the world's people live in cities—a far higher percentage than ever before. Between 1960 and 2000, the population of **Mexico City** more than tripled. Other cities in Latin America, as well as cities in Asia and Africa, have seen similar growth. Some of these cities hold a large part of a country's entire population. About one-third of Argentina's people, for instance, live in the city of **Buenos Aires.**

Some population movement is between countries. Some people **emigrate,** or leave the country where they were born and move to another. They are called *emigrants* in their homeland and referred to as *immigrants* in their new country. In the past 40 years, millions have left Africa, Asia, and Latin America to find jobs in the richer nations of Europe and North America. Some people were forced to flee their country because of wars, food shortages, or other problems. They are **refugees,** or people who flee to another country to escape persecution or disaster.

Reading Check **Why do so many people move from rural areas to cities?**

Section 2 Assessment

Defining Terms

1. **Define** death rate, birthrate, famine, population density, urbanization, emigrate, refugee.

Recalling Facts

2. **Culture** What are three problems caused by overpopulation?
3. **Human/Environment Interaction** Why do people live on only a small fraction of the earth?
4. **Economics** What is the main reason for growing urbanization?

Critical Thinking

5. **Making Comparisons** What is the difference between an emigrant and an immigrant?
6. **Understanding Cause and Effect** Why have populations in areas of Asia, Africa, and Latin America doubled every 25 years or so?

Graphic Organizer

7. **Organizing Information** Draw a diagram like this one, and list three causes of population growth.

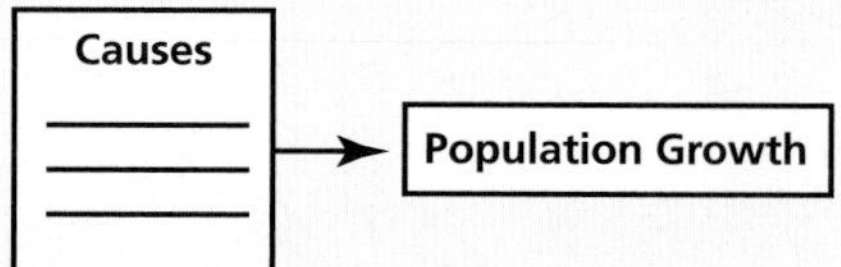

Applying Geography Skills

8. **Analyzing Maps** Look at the population density map on page 86. How would you describe the population density around Tokyo?

Making Connections

ART SCIENCE LITERATURE TECHNOLOGY

Counting Heads

How do we know there are more than 280 million people in the United States? Who counts the people? Every 10 years since 1790, the United States Census Bureau has counted heads in this country. Why and how do they do this?

The First Census

After the American colonies fought the Revolutionary War and won their independence, the new government ordered a census. By knowing how many people were in each state, the government could divide the war expenses fairly. The census would also determine the number of people that each state could send to Congress.

This census began in August 1790, about a year after George Washington became president. The law defined who would be counted and required that every household be visited by census takers. These workers walked or rode on horseback to gather their data. By the time it was completed, the census counted 3.9 million people.

The first census asked for little more than one's name and address. Over time, the census added questions to gather more than just population data. By 1820, there were questions about a person's job. Soon after, questions about crime, education, and wages appeared.

Changing Technology

As the country's population grew and the quantity of data increased, new technology helped census workers. In 1890 clerks began to use a keypunch device, invented by a Census Bureau worker, to add the numbers. The Tabulating Machine, as it was called, used an electric current to sense holes in punched cards and to keep a running total of the data. In 1950 the census used its first computer to process data. Now census data are released over the Internet.

Remarkably, one technology slow to change has been the way the government takes the census. Not until 1960 did the U.S. Postal Service become the major means of conducting the census. Even today, census takers go door-to-door to gather information from those who do not return their census forms in the mail.

▲ **The Electric Tabulating Machine processed the 1890 census in 2½ years, a job that would have taken nearly 10 years to complete by hand.**

Making the Connection

1. In what two ways were population data from the first census used?
2. How has technology changed the way census data are collected and processed?
3. **Drawing Conclusions** Why do you think the national and state governments want information about people's education and jobs?

Section 3

Resources and World Trade

Guide to Reading

Main Idea

Because many resources are limited and distributed unevenly, countries must trade for goods.

Terms to Know

- natural resource
- renewable resource
- nonrenewable resource
- export
- import
- tariff
- quota
- free trade
- developed country
- developing country

Places to Locate

- Brazil
- China

Reading Strategy

Draw a chart like the one below, then write in the names of different resources and how they are used.

Resource	Use

NATIONAL GEOGRAPHIC **Exploring Our World**

About 7,000 windmills stand on an 80-square-mile patch of hilly land near San Francisco. They turn in the strong winds that blow through a nearby pass in California's mountains. Why were they put there? These wind vanes generate electricity. In fact, they churn out enough electricity every year to meet the needs of all the homes in San Francisco.

Natural Resources

As you learned in Section 2, people settle in some areas to gain access to resources. **Natural resources** are products of the earth that people use to meet their needs. Wind, water, and oil are resources that provide energy to power machines. Good soil and fish are resources that people use to produce food. Stones like granite and ores like iron ore are resources people can use for making products.

The value of resources changes as people discover new technology. Trees, for example, have been a valuable resource throughout history. People used wood to stay warm, cook food, and build homes. Oil, on the other hand, was a gooey nuisance until the Industrial Revolution. People soon began to use oil products to run cars and heat homes. Today many countries in Southwest Asia have great pools of underground oil. As a result, they are among the richest countries on the earth.

Renewable Resources People can use some natural resources as much as they want. These **renewable resources** cannot be used up or can be replaced naturally or grown again. Wind and sun cannot be used up—the wind will continue to blow even if we use a windmill to catch some of its power. Forests, grasslands, plants and animals, and soil can be replaced—*if* people manage them carefully. A lumber company concerned about future growth can plant as many new trees as it cuts. Fishing fleets can limit the number of fish they catch to make sure that enough fish remain to reproduce.

Today many countries are trying to find efficient ways of using renewable energy sources. Some produce *hydroelectric power,* the energy generated by falling water. Even if a river does not flow quickly, it is possible to turn it into hydroelectric power. Engineers can build a dam and then release the water in a powerful stream.

Do you have a solar-powered calculator? If so, you know that the sun can provide energy to run people's machines. *Solar energy* is power produced by the heat of the sun. Making use of this energy on a large scale requires huge pieces of equipment. As a result, this energy source is not yet economical to use.

Nonrenewable Resources Humans use a great variety of minerals. They make steel from iron and aluminum from bauxite. Can you think of other examples? Metals and other minerals found in the earth's crust are also resources. They are **nonrenewable resources** because the earth provides limited supplies of them and they cannot be replaced. These resources were formed over millions of years by forces within the earth. Thus, it simply takes too long to generate new supplies.

One major nonrenewable source of energy is *fossil fuels*—coal, oil, and natural gas. People burn oil and gas to heat homes or run cars. They burn fossil fuels to generate electricity. Oil and coal are also used as raw materials to make plastics and medicines.

Another nonrenewable energy source is nuclear energy. *Nuclear energy* is power made by creating a controlled atomic reaction. Nuclear energy can be used to produce electricity, but some people fear its use. Nuclear reactions produce dangerous waste products that are difficult to dispose of. They need thousands of years to become safe. Some people worry that there is no safe way to transport and store this waste. Still, some countries rely on nuclear energy to generate power. France, Japan, South Korea, and Taiwan are examples.

✓Reading Check **What are three fossil fuels?**

World Trade

Resources, like people, are not distributed evenly around the world. Some areas have large amounts of one resource. Others have none of that resource but are rich in another one. These differences affect the economies of the world's countries.

Saffron—A Valuable Resource

A resource does not have to produce energy to be valued. The people in the Indian region of Kashmir are picking a resource that is precious to cooks—crocus flowers. Inside each crocus are three tiny orange stalks. When dried, the stalks become a spice called saffron. Cooks use it to add a delicate orange color and flavor to food. Saffron—the world's most expensive spice—is in short supply, though. Producers need nearly 4,700 flowers to produce just 1 ounce (28 g) of saffron.

NATIONAL GEOGRAPHIC

World Economic Activity

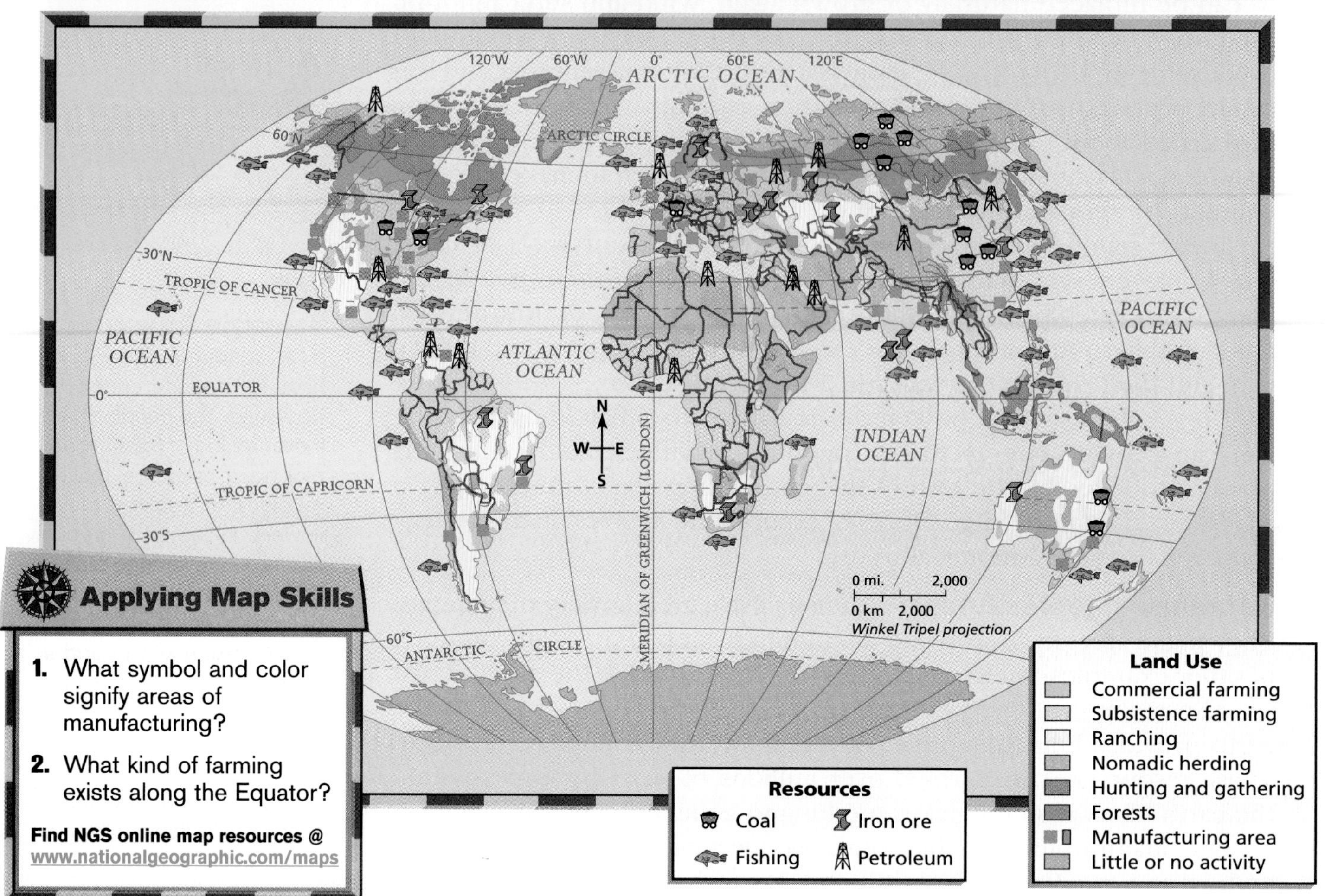

Applying Map Skills

1. What symbol and color signify areas of manufacturing?
2. What kind of farming exists along the Equator?

Find NGS online map resources @ www.nationalgeographic.com/maps

Look at the map above. Do you see the centers of manufacturing in the northern and eastern United States? There are large supplies of coal in the region and deposits of iron ore nearby. These areas became industrial centers because the people here took advantage of the resources they had.

In the western United States, you see another picture. People use much of the land for ranching. The soil and climate are well suited to raising livestock. *Commercial farming*—or growing food for sale in markets—occurs throughout much of the United States.

These examples show how the world's people respond to the unequal distribution of resources. They *specialize,* or focus on the economic activities best suited to their resources. Parts of **Brazil** have the perfect soil and climate for growing coffee. As a result, Brazil produces more coffee beans than any other country. Cotton grows well in parts of **China,** the world's top producer of that product.

Countries often cannot use all that they produce. What do they do with the extra? They export what they do not need, trading it to other countries. When they cannot produce as much as they need of a good, they **import** it, or buy it from another country. The world's countries, then, are connected with one another in a complex web of trade.

Barriers to Trade Governments try to manage their country's trade to benefit their country's economy. Some charge a **tariff,** or a tax added to the price of goods that are imported. If there is a tariff on cars, for instance, all people who buy an imported car pay more than just the purchase price. Governments often create tariffs hoping to persuade their own people to buy products made in their own country instead of buying imported goods.

Governments sometimes create other barriers to trade. They might put a strict **quota,** or number limit, on how many items of a particular product can be imported from a particular country. A government may even stop trading with another country altogether as a way to punish it.

Free Trade In recent years, governments around the world have moved toward free trade. **Free trade** means taking down trade barriers so that goods flow freely among countries. Several countries have joined together to create free trade agreements in certain parts of the world. For instance, the United States, Mexico, and Canada have agreed to eliminate all trade barriers to one another's goods. These three countries set up the North American Free Trade Agreement (NAFTA). The largest free trade agreement—the European Union (EU)—includes most of the countries of Europe.

Reading Check **What are three kinds of barriers to trade?**

Earning a Living

Factory workers in China sew clothes (left). Most people still farm in Kenya (above). In the United States, more jobs are in service or technology industries.

Region **What regions are considered developed?**

Differences in Development

Look again at the economic activity map on page 92. You see that countries differ in how much manufacturing they have. Countries that have a great deal of manufacturing are called **developed countries.** The countries of Europe and North America are developed countries. So are Australia and Japan. Other countries have only a few—or no—manufacturing centers. Many people in these countries practice *subsistence farming,* or grow only enough food for their own families. These countries, which are working toward industrialization, are called **developing countries.** Developing countries are found throughout Africa, Asia, and Latin America.

Why do countries want manufacturing? Workers in industry typically earn more than farmers. Industrial companies can generally charge more for their products than food companies can. As a result, industrial countries are wealthier than agricultural countries.

In recent decades, the economies of many countries have changed dramatically. Developing countries have invited large companies from developed countries to build factories in their lands. The companies find that developing countries have a valuable resource—people. The spread of industry has created booming economies in places like Hong Kong, Singapore, South Korea, Taiwan, and China.

✓Reading Check **Why do developing countries want more industry?**

Assessment

Defining Terms

1. **Define** natural resource, renewable resource, nonrenewable resource, export, import, tariff, quota, free trade, developed country, developing country.

Recalling Facts

2. **History** How can the value of resources change over time?
3. **Economics** What is the difference between commercial farming and subsistence farming?
4. **Economics** Why do countries specialize in producing certain goods?
5. **Economics** What is the difference between a developing country and a developed country?

Critical Thinking

6. **Drawing Conclusions** Why are tariffs and quotas called "barriers" to trade?
7. **Analyzing Information** How has the world's economy changed in recent decades?

Graphic Organizer

8. **Organizing Information** Draw a chart like this one, listing three examples for each type of resource.

Renewable resources	Nonrenewable resources

Applying Geography Skills

9. **Analyzing Maps** Look at the economic activity map on page 92. What two types of farming are shown on the map?

Section 4 People and the Environment

Guide to Reading

Main Idea

The actions that people take have a huge effect on the environment.

Terms to Know

- desalinization
- conservation
- pesticide
- ecosystem
- crop rotation
- irrigation
- erosion
- deforestation
- acid rain

Places to Locate

- Saudi Arabia

Reading Strategy

Draw a diagram like this one. On the lines write at least two problems that arise with human use of water, land, and air.

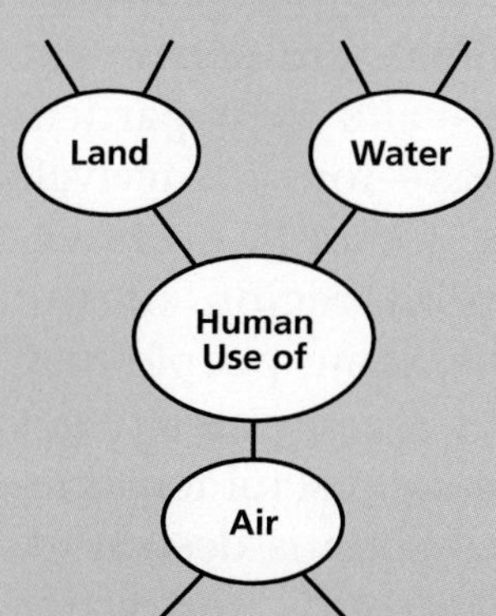

What happens when we harm the environment? Some plants and animals might be gone forever. This scientist hopes to prevent that. She works at a seed bank. Behind her, stored at −4°F (−20°C), are jars of plant seeds from around the world. Should any of these 4,000 types of plants become extinct, these seeds can start growing them again.

The rapidly growing number of people threatens the delicate balance of life in the world. More and more people use more water. They need more land to live on and to grow more food. Spreading industry fouls the air. Humans must act carefully to be sure not to destroy the earth that gives us life.

Water Use

As you recall from Chapter 2, people, plants, and animals need freshwater to live. People need clean water to drink. They also need water for their crops and their animals. In fact, as much as 70 percent of the water used is for farming. Only a small fraction of the world's water is freshwater, though. Some countries, such as **Saudi Arabia,** obtain drinkable water through **desalinization**—or removing salt from seawater. This is a process in which seawater is boiled in huge chambers, and the resulting steam is condensed as freshwater. For now, though, this process is expensive and cannot be widely used. Because the earth's supply of water is limited, people must manage freshwater carefully.

Water Management Some regions receive heavy rainfall in some months of the year and little, or none, in other months. They can manage their water supply by building storage areas to hold the heavy rains for later use. People have to build these storage areas carefully to prevent too much of the water from evaporating.

Managing water supplies involves two main steps. The first step is **conservation,** or the careful use of resources so they are not wasted. Did you know that 6 or 7 gallons (23 to 27 liters) of water go down the drain every *minute* that you shower? Taking shorter showers is an easy way to prevent wasting water.

The second approach to managing the water supply is to avoid polluting water. Some manufacturing processes use water. Sometimes those processes result in dangerous chemicals or dirt entering the water supply. Many farmers use fertilizers to help their crops grow. Many also use **pesticides,** or powerful chemicals that kill crop-destroying insects. These substances can seep into the water supply and cause harm.

Reading Check How can manufacturing and farming harm the water supply?

NATIONAL GEOGRAPHIC On Location

Disappearing Rain Forests

A bulldozer knocks down trees in a rain forest in Ecuador.

Human/Environment Interaction Why is cutting down the rain forests a problem?

Land Use

In addition to managing water resources, people must carefully manage the land they use. As humans expand their communities, they invade **ecosystems.** These are places where the plants and animals are dependent upon one another—and their particular surroundings—for survival. Ecosystems can be found in every climate and vegetation region of the world. For example, some people may want to drain a wet, marshy area to get rid of disease-carrying mosquitoes and make the soil useful for farming. When the area is drained, however, the ecosystem is destroyed. The delicate balance among the insects, reptiles, birds, and water plants is torn apart. In managing land, humans must recognize that some soils are not suited for growing certain crops—and some land is not useful for growing any crops at all.

Soil To grow food, soil needs to have certain minerals. Farmers add fertilizers to the soil to supply some of these minerals. Some also practice crop rotation, or changing what they plant in a field to avoid using up all the minerals in the soil. Some crops—like beans—actually restore valuable minerals to the soil. Many farmers now plant bean crops every three years to build the soil back up.

In many dry areas, farmers use irrigation to deliver water to their crops. Over time, the small amounts of salt in this freshwater can build up on the land. Once that happens, the land is no longer fertile.

If people do not carefully manage the soil, it can erode away. In erosion, wind or water carries soil away, leaving the land less fertile than before. Have you ever seen a group of trees alongside a farmer's field? The farmer may have planted those trees to block the wind and prevent erosion. In the tropics, erosion by water presents a problem—especially if farmers plant their crops on sloping land. When heavy rains come, the soil may simply wash down the hillside.

Forests Some areas of the world have thick forests of tall trees. Growing populations in these countries often turn to these lush forests as a source of land to grow food. Yet deforestation, or cutting down forests, is a problem—especially in the tropics. Rains in these areas are extremely heavy. When the tree roots are no longer there to hold the soil, the water can wash it away. Often, the cleared land is fertile for just a few years. Then farmers have to move to a new area and cut the trees in that section of forest. As a result, more and more of the forest is lost over time.

✓Reading Check **What problem can result from irrigation?**

Burning fossil fuels adds harmful chemicals to the air.

Human/Environment Interaction What are some effects of air pollution?

Air Pollution

Industries and vehicles that burn fossil fuels are the main sources of air pollution. Throughout the world, fumes from cars and other vehicles pollute the air. The chemicals in air pollution can seriously damage people's health.

These chemicals also combine with precipitation. They then fall as acid rain, or rain containing high amounts of chemical pollutants. Acid rain kills fish and eats away at the surfaces of buildings. It can even destroy entire forests.

Some scientists believe that increasing amounts of pollutants in the atmosphere will cause the earth to warm. You learned about this greenhouse effect in Chapter 2. While not all experts agree, some scientists say that the increase in temperature can have disastrous effects. Glaciers and ice caps may melt, raising the level of the world's seas. Higher seas could flood coastal cities. Warmer temperatures can also make some land no longer able to produce food.

Reading Check **What causes acid rain?**

Balancing People and Resources

Water, land, and air are among people's most precious resources. We need water and air to live. We need land to grow food. Only by caring for these resources can we be sure that we will still have them to use in the future.

Sometimes, though, protecting the environment for the future seems to clash with feeding people in the present. For example, farmers destroy the rain forests not because they want to but because they need to feed their families. They dislike being told by people in other countries that they should save the rain forests. Before they stop cutting down the rain forests, these farmers will need to find new ways to meet their needs.

Reading Check **How does saving the rain forests clash with current human needs?**

Assessment

Defining Terms

1. **Define** desalinization, conservation, pesticide, ecosystem, crop rotation, irrigation, erosion, deforestation, acid rain.

Recalling Facts

2. **Human/Environment Interaction** How do human activities affect ecosystems?
3. **Human/Environment Interaction** What are three ways of managing water?
4. **Economics** Why do farmers practice crop rotation?

Critical Thinking

5. **Making Comparisons** Which resource—water, soil, or air—do you think is most precious to people? Why?
6. **Analyzing Information** What ecosystems were affected by the growth of your community?

Graphic Organizer

7. **Organizing Information** Draw a diagram like this one and list three results of global warming.

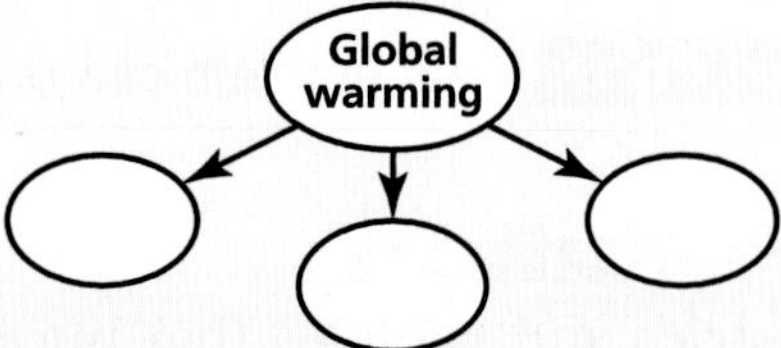

Applying Geography Skills

8. **Analyzing Maps** Look at the vegetation map in Chapter 2 on page 66. In what parts of the world do you see tropical rain forests?

Reading Review

Section 1 Culture

Terms to Know

- culture
- ethnic group
- dialect
- monarchy
- dictator
- democracy
- economic system
- cultural diffusion
- civilization
- culture region

Main Idea

People usually live with others who follow similar beliefs learned from the past.

✓Culture *Culture* is the way of life of a group of people who share similar beliefs and customs.

✓Culture Culture includes eight elements or traits: social groups, language, religion, daily life, history, arts, a government system, and an economic system.

✓Culture Cultures change over time and influence other regions.

Section 2 Population

Terms to Know

- death rate
- birthrate
- famine
- population density
- urbanization
- emigrate
- refugee

Main Idea

The world's population is growing rapidly, and how and where people live are changing, too.

✓History In the past 200 years, the world's population has grown at a very rapid rate.

✓Movement Some areas are more densely populated than others.

✓Culture About 50 percent of the world's people live in cities.

Section 3 Resources and World Trade

Terms to Know

- natural resource
- renewable resource
- nonrenewable resource
- export
- import
- tariff
- quota
- free trade
- developed country
- developing country

Main Idea

Because many resources are limited and distributed unevenly, countries must trade for goods.

✓Human/Environment Interaction Renewable resources cannot be used up or can be replaced fairly quickly.

✓Human/Environment Interaction Some resources—such as fossil fuels and minerals—are nonrenewable.

✓Economics Countries specialize by producing what they can produce best with the resources they have.

✓Economics Countries export their specialized products and import what they need.

Section 4 People and the Environment

Terms to Know

- desalinization
- conservation
- pesticide
- ecosystem
- crop rotation
- irrigation
- erosion
- deforestation
- acid rain

Main Idea

The actions that people take have a profound effect on the environment.

✓Human/Environment Interaction People need to manage water resources because freshwater is not available everywhere.

✓Human/Environment Interaction Air pollution has damaging effects on the land and on people's health.

Chapter 3

Assessment and Activities

Using Key Terms

Match the terms in Part A with their definitions in Part B.

A.

1. culture
2. developed country
3. irrigation
4. crop rotation
5. population density
6. culture region
7. tariff
8. quota
9. developing country
10. cultural diffusion

B.

a. collecting water and bringing it to crops
b. spreading knowledge to other cultures
c. countries working toward industrialization
d. many different countries with cultural traits in common
e. a number limit on imports from a country
f. the average number of people living in a square mile
g. country where much manufacturing is carried out
h. the way of life of a group of people who share similar beliefs and customs
i. a tax added to the price of imported goods
j. alternating what is planted in a field

Reviewing the Main Ideas

Section 1 Culture

11. **Culture** What are the major religions?
12. **Economics** What is the difference between a market economy and socialism?
13. **Movement** Give an example of cultural diffusion.

Section 2 Population

14. **Culture** What has created rapid population growth?
15. **Culture** How do you calculate population density?
16. **Movement** Why have many people moved to cities?

Section 3 Resources and World Trade

17. **Human/Environment Interaction** What are three kinds of renewable energy sources?
18. **Economics** How do countries respond to the unequal distribution of resources?

Section 4 People and the Environment

19. **Human/Environment Interaction** How can farmers restore the minerals in the soil?
20. **Human/Environment Interaction** What two problems can result from air pollution?

World Culture Regions

Place Location Activity

On a separate sheet of paper, match the letters on the map with the numbered places listed below.

1. Latin America
2. North Africa, Southwest Asia, and Central Asia
3. Europe
4. Russia
5. East Asia
6. United States and Canada
7. Australia, Oceania, and Antarctica
8. Africa South of the Sahara

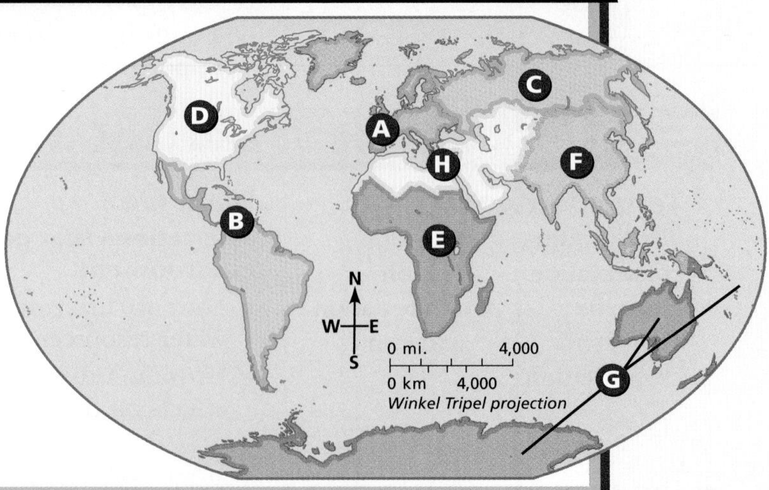

Self-Check Quiz Visit the ***Geography: The World and Its People*** Web site at gwip.glencoe.com and click on **Chapter 3—Self-Check Quizzes** to prepare for the Chapter Test.

 Critical Thinking

21. **Making Predictions** In what ways do you think a company investing in a developing country could help the people there? How could that same company harm the culture?
22. **Sequencing Information** Make a chart like the one below, and list the ways you use electricity from the moment you wake up until you go to sleep. In the second column, write how you would perform the same activity if you had no electricity to rely on.

Activities With Electricity	Without Electricity

 GeoJournal Activity 

23. **Writing a Paragraph** Write a paragraph about the settlement of your community. Answer such questions as: Why did people originally settle in the area? How has the culture of your area changed?

 Mental Mapping Activity

24. **Focusing on the Region** Draw a simple outline map of the United States. On your map, label the areas where the following activities take place:
    - Commercial farming
    - Manufacturing
    - Raising livestock
    - Fishing
    - Obtaining oil

 Technology Skills Activity 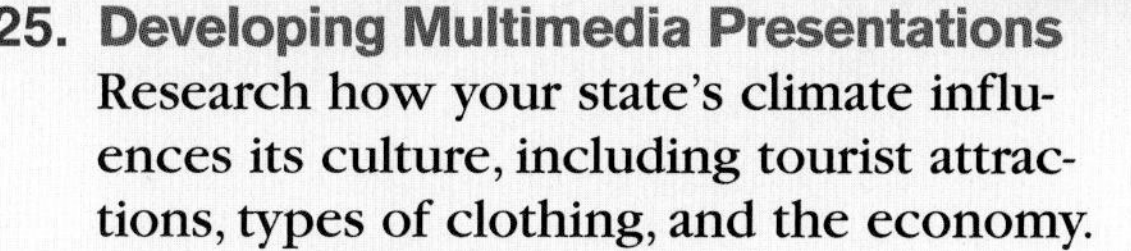 

25. **Developing Multimedia Presentations** Research how your state's climate influences its culture, including tourist attractions, types of clothing, and the economy. Use your research to develop a commercial promoting your state.

Standardized Test Practice

Directions: Study the graph, then answer the following question.

Source: *Britannica Book of the Year,* 1999.

1. According to the graph, how much do the United States and Canada export?

A $1,005,900,000,000

B $1,005,900,000

C $1,005,900

D $1,005

Test-Taking Tip: In order to understand any type of graph, look carefully around the graph for keys that show how it is organized. On this bar graph, the numbers along the left side represent billions of dollars. Therefore, you need to multiply the number on the graph by 1,000,000,000 to get your answer.

Unit 2

◀ Skier in Idaho's stretch of the Rocky Mountains

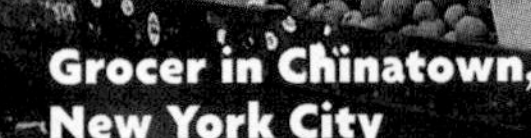
Grocer in Chinatown, New York City

Farm on the Manitoba plains

The United States and Canada

Which of the world's culture regions do you call home? It is probably the United States and Canada. If you look at a globe, you will see that the United States and Canada cover most of North America. These two nations share many of the same landforms, including rugged mountains in the west, rounded mountains in the east, and rolling plains in the center.

NGS ONLINE
www.nationalgeographic.com/education

Focus on:

The United States and Canada

SPANNING MORE THAN 7 MILLION square miles (18 million sq. km), the United States and Canada cover much of North America. These huge countries share many of the same landscapes, climates, and natural resources.

The Land

The United States and Canada make up a region bordered by the very cold Arctic Ocean in the north and bathed by the Gulf of Mexico's warm currents in the south. The western coast faces the Pacific Ocean. Eastern shores are edged by the Atlantic.

Rugged mountains are found in the western part of each country. The Pacific ranges follow the coastline. Farther inland are the massive, jagged peaks of the Rocky Mountains. Relatively young as mountains go, the Rockies stretch more than 3,000 miles (4,828 km) from Alaska to the southwestern United States.

East of the Rockies are the wide and windswept Great Plains. This gently rolling landscape covers the central part of both the United States and Canada. In the United States, the Mississippi River—the largest river system in North America—flows through the heart of these plains.

The Appalachian range, much older than the Rockies, is the dominant landform in the eastern part of the region. East and south of the Appalachians' low, rounded peaks are coastal plains that end at the Atlantic shores.

The Climate

This region's vast size and varied landforms help give it great diversity in climate and vegetation. In the far northern parts of Alaska and Canada, amid the treeless tundra and dense evergreen forests, brief summers and bitterly cold winters prevail. The Pacific coast, from southern Alaska to northern California, has a mild, wet climate. Rain clouds blowing in from the ocean are blocked by the Pacific ranges. Robbed of moisture, the land immediately east of these mountains is dry.

Hot, humid summers and cold, snowy winters are the rule on the Great Plains. This humid continental climate extends from the plains across southeastern Canada and the northeastern United States. The southeastern states, however, enjoy much milder winters. The mildest of all are found on Florida's southern tip, the only part of the mainland that has a tropical climate.

UNIT 2

Parachutist plunging toward the Appalachian Mountains, West Virginia ▶

◀ Polar bear snoozing in the Canadian Arctic

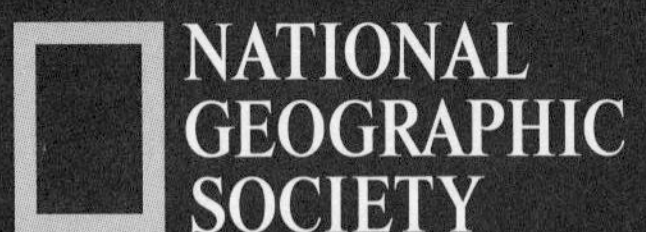

Regional Atlas

The Economy

The United States and Canada are prosperous countries. Abundant natural resources and plenty of skilled workers have been key ingredients in creating two of the most successful economies in the world. Both countries operate under the free enterprise system, in which individuals and groups—not the government—control businesses and industries.

The region's strong economy was built on agriculture, which remains important today. Fertile soil, numerous waterways, a favorable climate, and high-tech equipment have made the United States and Canada two of the world's top food producers. Livestock, grains, vegetables, and fruits all are raised by the region's farmers.

Rich oil, coal, and natural gas deposits occur in this region. So do deposits of valuable minerals, including copper, iron ore, nickel, silver, and gold. These energy sources and raw materials have made it possible for the United States and Canada to develop large industrial economies. Today, however, people are more likely to work in offices than in factories. Service industries such as banking, communications, entertainment, insurance, and health care employ most people in the region.

The People

The United States and Canada have a rich mix of cultures. Native Americans were the nations' first inhabitants. Centuries later, settlers from Europe arrived. Immigrants from Africa, Asia, Latin America, and almost every other part of the world eventually followed. Some came looking for religious or political freedom. Some came as enslaved laborers. Some came for a fresh start in these immense lands of boundless opportunity.

Today more than 310 million people call this region home. Thirty-one million of them live in Canada, while the remaining 281 million live in the United States. On either side of the border, most people live in urban areas. Toronto, Vancouver, and Montreal are among Canada's largest cities. In the United States, New York City, Los Angeles, and Chicago are the most populous cities.

◀ **Worker in sterile gown manufacturing computer chips in Texas**

Exploring the Region

1. **Which oceans border the region?**
2. **Why is the climate dry just east of the Pacific ranges?**
3. **What factors have helped make the region prosperous?**
4. **In which country do most of the region's people live?**

Unit 2

Inuit boys examining a Native American sculpture ▶

The United States and Canada

Physical

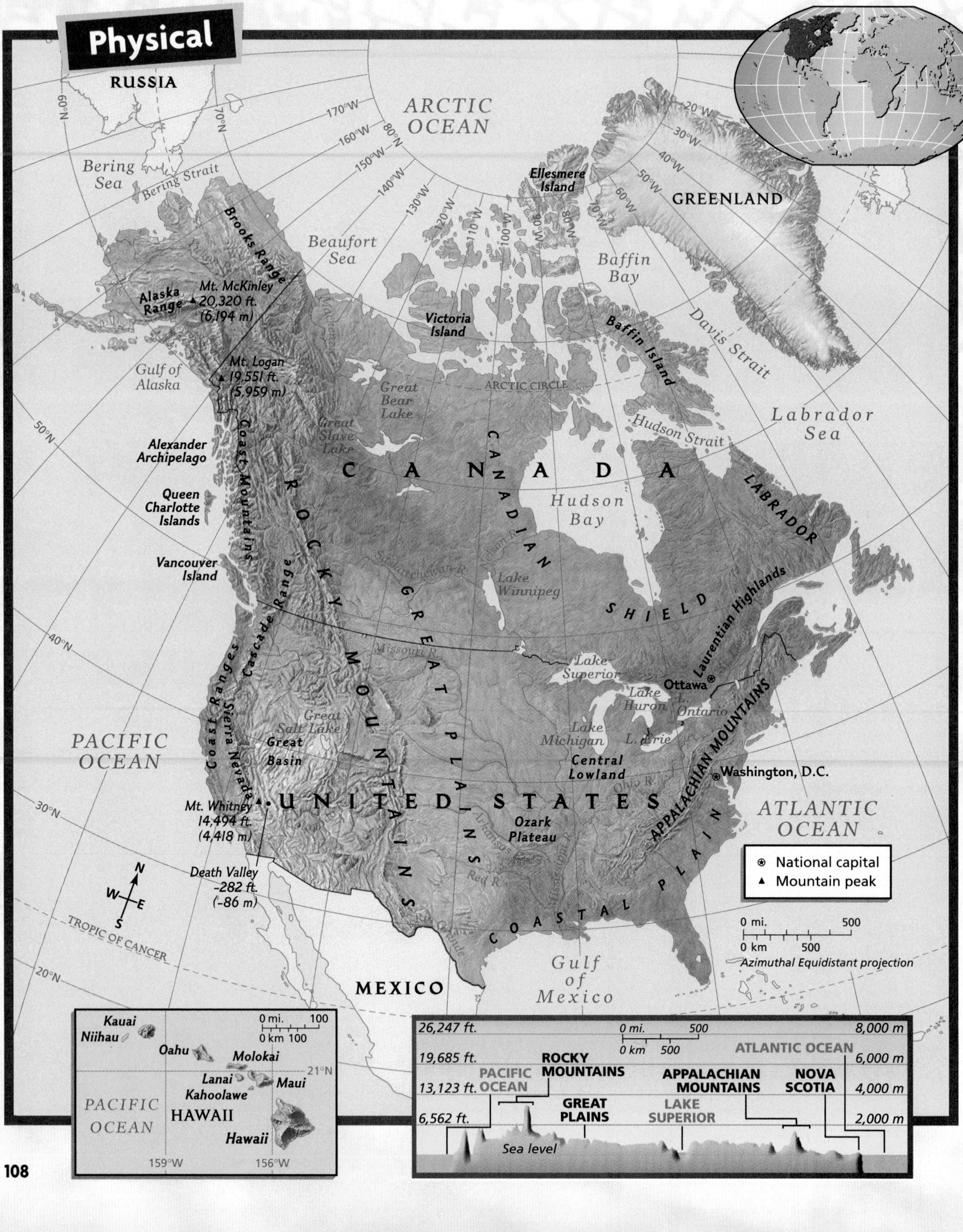

RUSSIA

ARCTIC OCEAN

Bering Sea

Bering Strait

GREENLAND

Ellesmere Island

Beaufort Sea

Baffin Bay

Brooks Range

Alaska Range

Mt. McKinley 20,320 ft. (6,194 m)

Victoria Island

Baffin Island

Davis Strait

Gulf of Alaska

Mt. Logan 19,551 ft. (5,959 m)

Great Bear Lake

ARCTIC CIRCLE

Labrador Sea

Hudson Strait

Great Slave Lake

Alexander Archipelago

Coast Mountains

C A N A D A

LABRADOR

Queen Charlotte Islands

Hudson Bay

CANADIAN SHIELD

ROCKY MOUNTAINS

Vancouver Island

Lake Winnipeg

Laurentian Highlands

Cascade Range

GREAT PLAINS

Lake Superior

Ottawa

Coast Ranges

Sierra Nevada

Lake Huron

L. Ontario

Great Salt Lake

PACIFIC OCEAN

Great Basin

Lake Michigan

L. Erie

APPALACHIAN MOUNTAINS

Central Lowland

Washington, D.C.

Mt. Whitney 14,494 ft. (4,418 m)

UNITED STATES

Ozark Plateau

ATLANTIC OCEAN

Death Valley −282 ft. (−86 m)

COASTAL PLAIN

TROPIC OF CANCER

MEXICO

Gulf of Mexico

0 mi. 500
0 km 500
Azimuthal Equidistant projection

⊛ National capital
▲ Mountain peak

N S E W

60°N 70°N 50°N 40°N 30°N 20°N
170°W 160°W 150°W 140°W 130°W 120°W 110°W 100°W 90°W 80°W 70°W 60°W 50°W 40°W 30°W 20°W

Kauai
Niihau
Oahu
Molokai
Lanai
Maui
Kahoolawe
HAWAII
Hawaii
PACIFIC OCEAN
0 mi. 100
0 km 100
21°N
159°W 156°W

26,247 ft. — 8,000 m
19,685 ft. — 6,000 m
13,123 ft. — 4,000 m
6,562 ft. — 2,000 m
Sea level
0 mi. 500
0 km 500
PACIFIC OCEAN
ROCKY MOUNTAINS
GREAT PLAINS
LAKE SUPERIOR
APPALACHIAN MOUNTAINS
NOVA SCOTIA
ATLANTIC OCEAN

UNIT 2

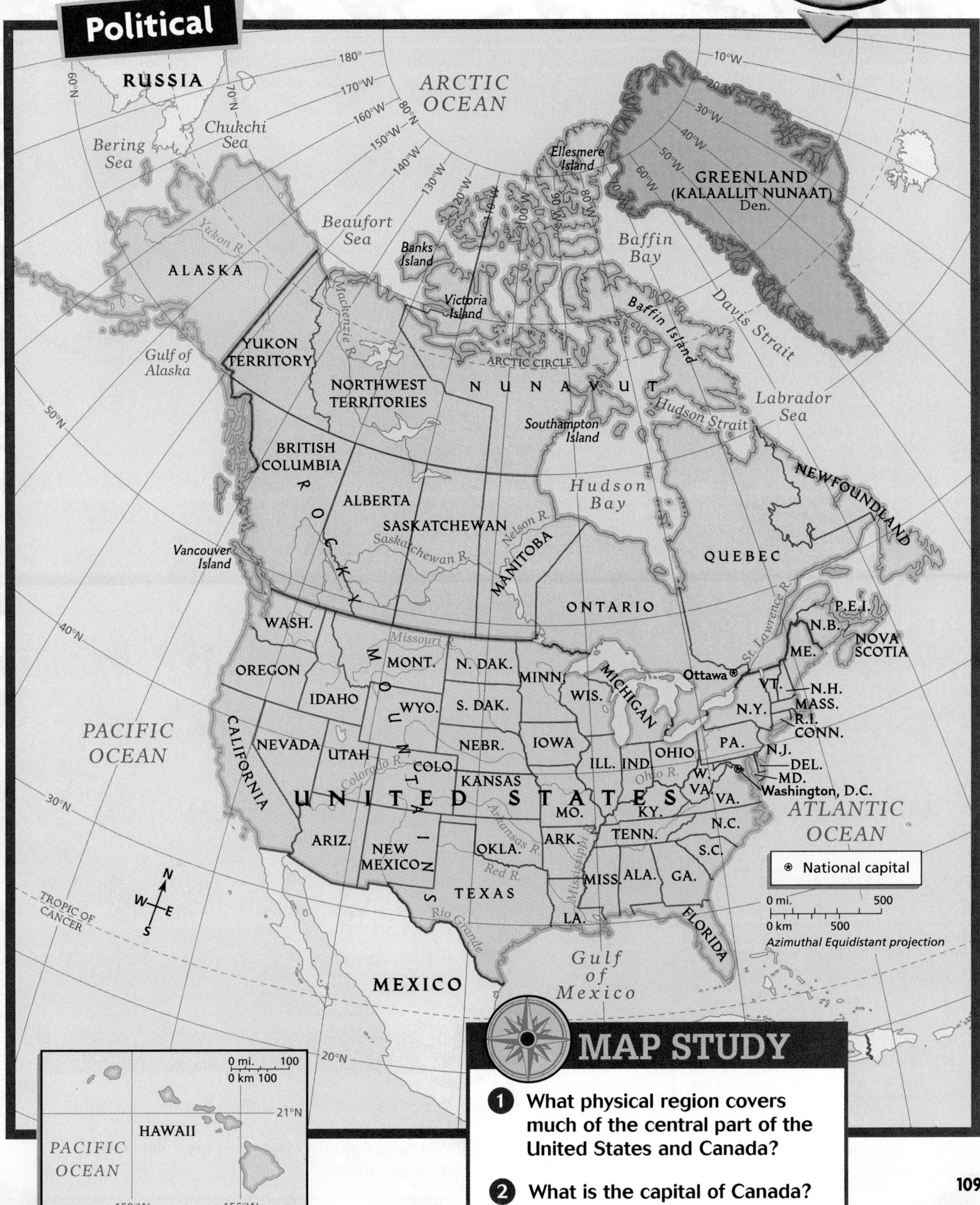

MAP STUDY

1. What physical region covers much of the central part of the United States and Canada?
2. What is the capital of Canada?

The United States and Canada

Food Production

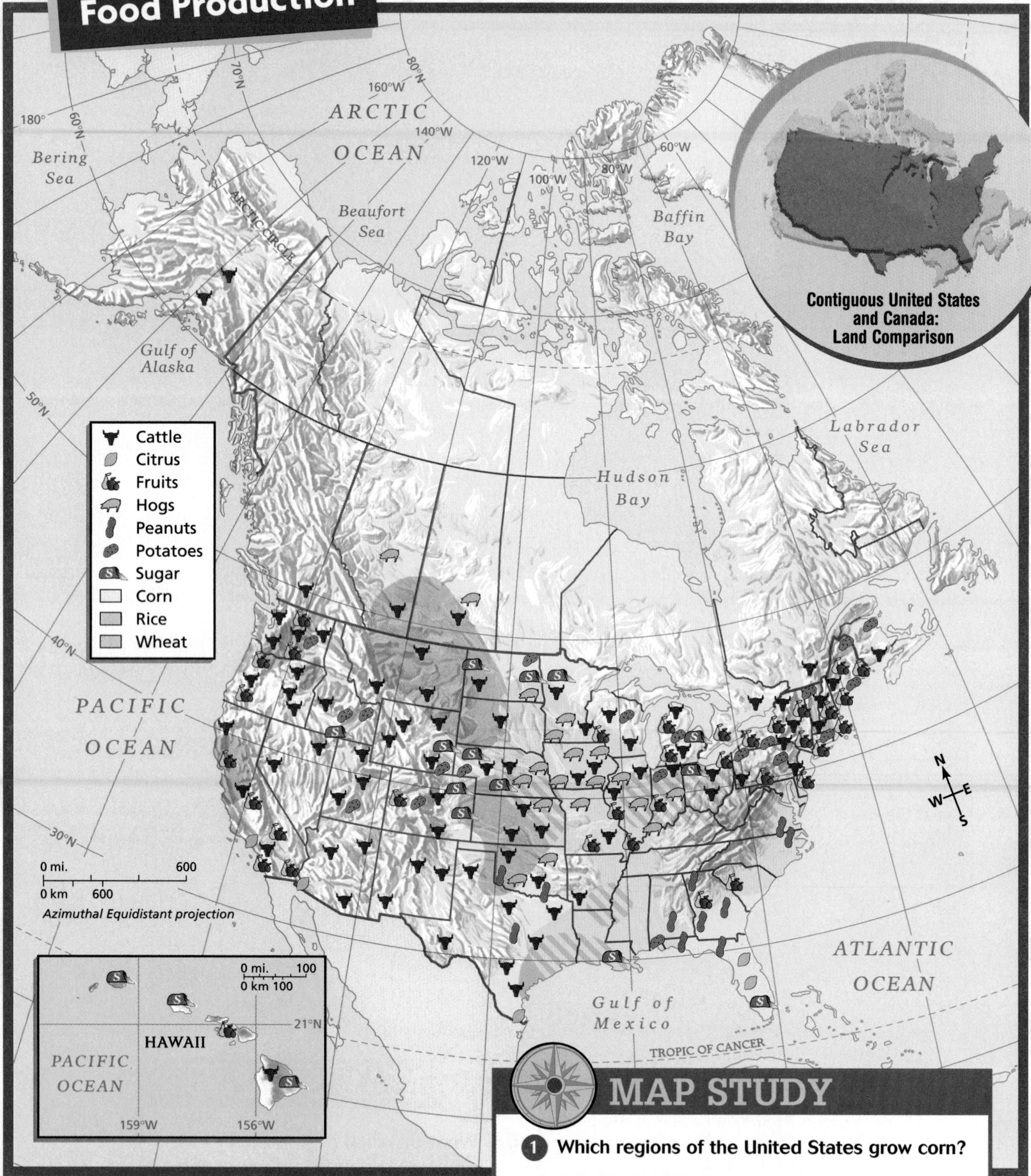

MAP STUDY

1. Which regions of the United States grow corn?
2. Where in Canada would you most likely want to raise cattle?

Geo Extremes

① **HIGHEST POINT**
Mount McKinley (Alaska)
20,320 ft. (6,194 m) high

② **LOWEST POINT**
Death Valley (California)
282 ft. (86 m)
below sea level

③ **LONGEST RIVER**
Mississippi-Missouri
(United States)
3,710 mi. (5,971 km) long

④ **LARGEST LAKE**
Lake Superior
31,700 sq. mi.
(82,103 sq. km)

⑤ **LARGEST CANYON**
Grand Canyon (Arizona)
277 mi. (446 km) long
1 mi. (1.6 km) deep

⑥ **GREATEST TIDES**
Bay of Fundy (Nova Scotia)
52 ft. (16 m)

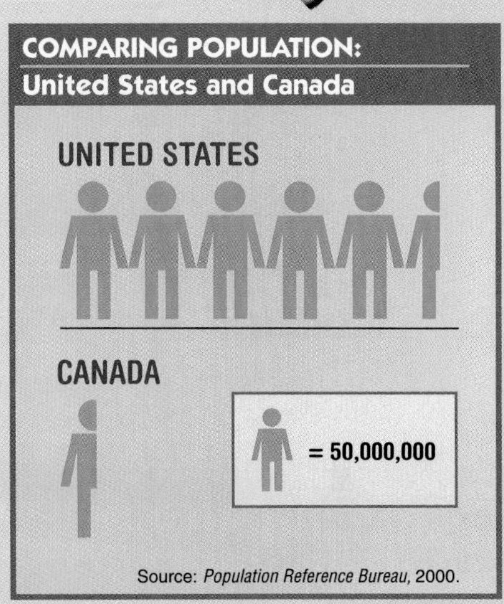

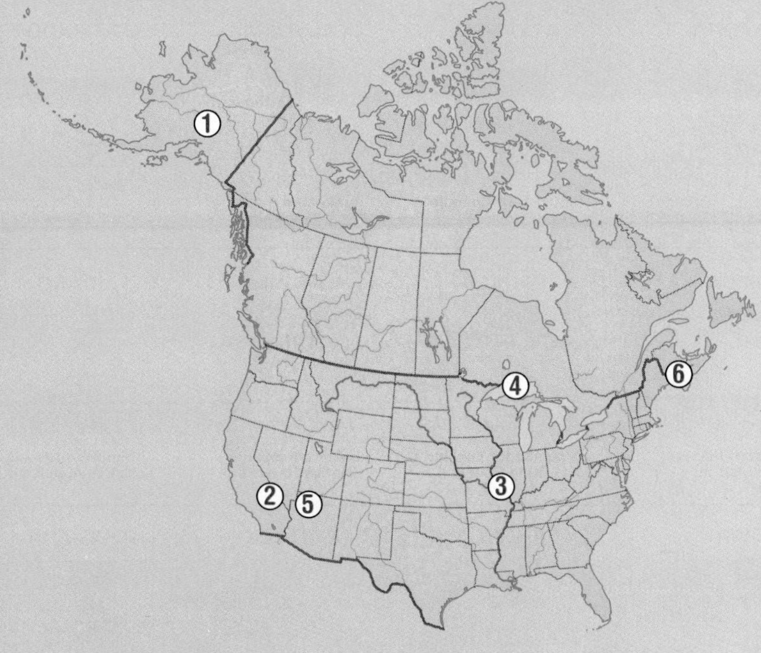

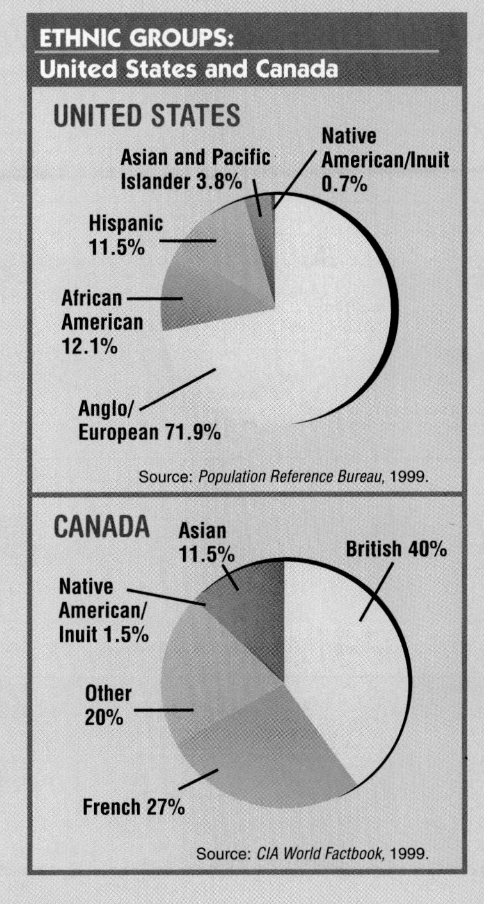

GRAPHIC STUDY

1. In what area of the United States do you find both the lowest point and largest canyon?
2. How does the percentage of Native American/Inuit population in the United States compare with their percentage of the population in Canada?

REGIONAL ATLAS

Country Profiles

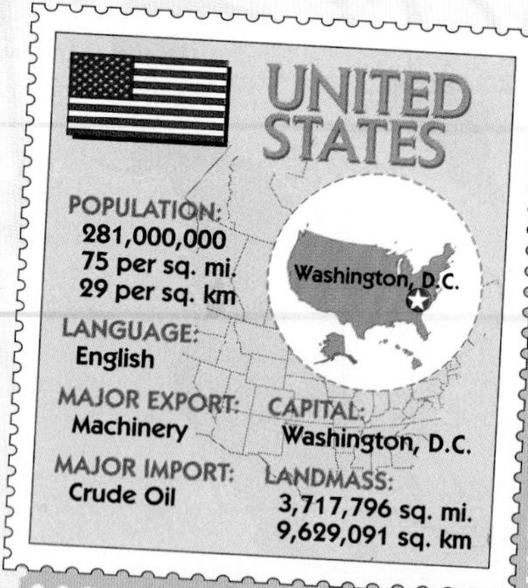

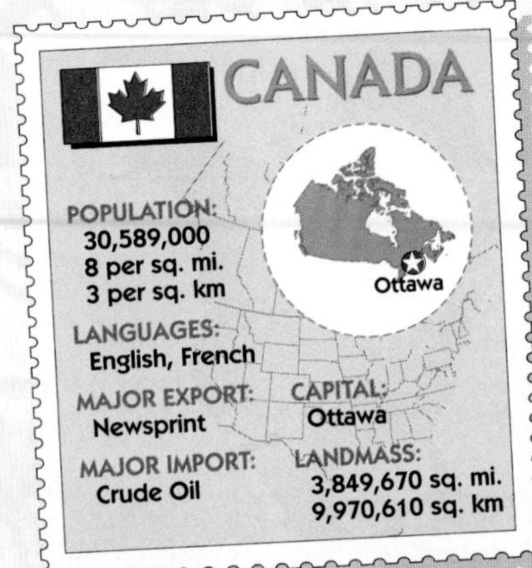

U.S. State Names: Meaning and Origin

State	Capital	Meaning and Origin
ALABAMA	Montgomery	"thicket clearers" (Choctaw)
ALASKA	Juneau	"the great land" (Aleut)
ARIZONA	Phoenix	"little spring" (Papago), or "dry land" (Spanish)
ARKANSAS	Little Rock	"downstream people" (Quapaw)
CALIFORNIA	Sacramento	unknown meaning (Spanish)
COLORADO	Denver	"red" (Spanish)
CONNECTICUT	Hartford	"beside the long tidal river" (Native American)
DELAWARE	Dover	named for Virginia's colonial governor, Baron De La Warr
FLORIDA	Tallahassee	"feast of flowers" (Spanish)
GEORGIA	Atlanta	named for England's King George II
HAWAII	Honolulu	unknown meaning (Native Hawaiian)
IDAHO	Boise	unknown meaning (Native American)
ILLINOIS	Springfield	"tribe of superior men" (Native American)
INDIANA	Indianapolis	"land of Indians" (European American)
IOWA	Des Moines	unknown meaning (Native American)
KANSAS	Topeka	"people of the south wind" (Sioux)
KENTUCKY	Frankfort	"land of tomorrow" (Iroquoian)
LOUISIANA	Baton Rouge	named for France's King Louis XIV
MAINE	Augusta	named for an ancient French province
MARYLAND	Annapolis	named in honor of the wife of England's King Charles I
MASSACHUSETTS	Boston	"great mountain place" (Native American)
MICHIGAN	Lansing	"great lake" (Ojibway)
MINNESOTA	Saint Paul	"sky-tinted water" (Sioux)
MISSISSIPPI	Jackson	"father of the waters" (Native American)

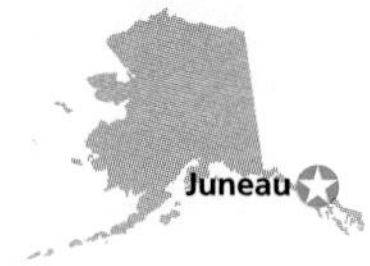

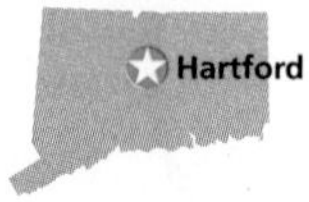

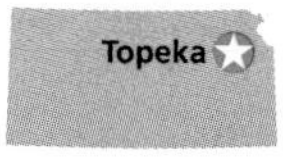

Countries, states, provinces, and flags not drawn to scale

State	Capital	Meaning and Origin
MISSOURI	Jefferson City	"town of the large canoes" (Native American)
MONTANA	Helena	"mountainous" (Spanish)
NEBRASKA	Lincoln	"flat water" (Native American)
NEVADA	Carson City	"snowcapped" (Spanish)
NEW HAMPSHIRE	Concord	named for Hampshire, a county in England
NEW JERSEY	Trenton	named for Isle of Jersey, a British territory
NEW MEXICO	Santa Fe	named for the state's former colonial ruler, Mexico
NEW YORK	Albany	named in honor of the English Duke of York
NORTH CAROLINA	Raleigh	named in honor of England's King Charles I
NORTH DAKOTA	Bismarck	named for the Dakota, a Native American group
OHIO	Columbus	"great river" (Native American)
OKLAHOMA	Oklahoma City	"red people" (Choctaw)
OREGON	Salem	unknown meaning and origin
PENNSYLVANIA	Harrisburg	"Penn's woodland," named for the father of Pennsylvania's founder, William Penn
RHODE ISLAND	Providence	unknown meaning and origin
SOUTH CAROLINA	Columbia	named for England's King Charles I
SOUTH DAKOTA	Pierre	named for the Dakota, a Native American group
TENNESSEE	Nashville	named for tana-see, "the meeting place" (Yuchi)
TEXAS	Austin	"friends" (Tejas)
UTAH	Salt Lake City	"people of the mountains" (Ute)
VERMONT	Montpelier	"green mountain" (French)
VIRGINIA	Richmond	named for the unmarried Queen Elizabeth I of England, known as "the Virgin Queen"
WASHINGTON	Olympia	named in honor of George Washington
WEST VIRGINIA	Charleston	began as the western part of Virginia before becoming a state in 1863
WISCONSIN	Madison	"grassy place" (Chippewa)
WYOMING	Cheyenne	"upon the great plain" (Delaware)

Canadian Province and Territory Names: Meaning and Origin

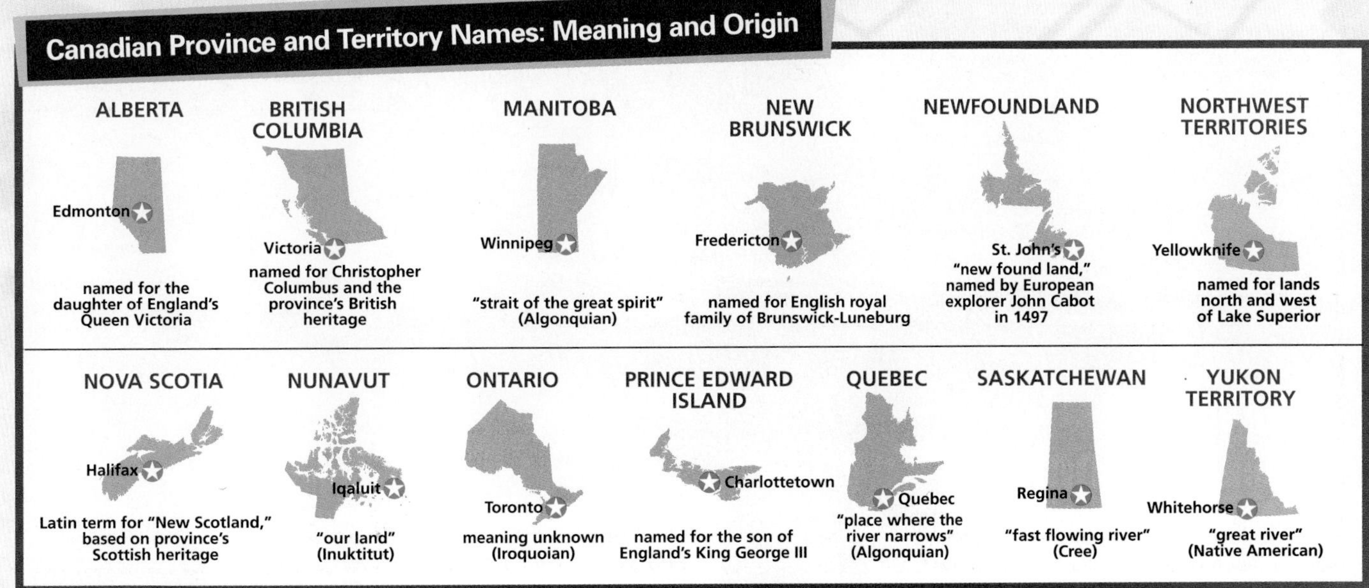

The United States

To learn more about the people and places of the United States, view ***The World and Its People*** **Chapter 4** video.

Geography online

Chapter Overview Visit the ***Geography: The World and Its People*** Web site at gwip.glencoe.com and click on **Chapter 4–Chapter Overviews** to preview information about the United States.

A Vast, Scenic Land

Guide to Reading

Main Idea

The United States has a great variety of landforms and climates.

Terms to Know

- contiguous
- megalopolis
- coral reef

Places to Locate

- Atlantic Coastal Plain
- Gulf Coastal Plain
- Appalachian Mountains
- Central Lowland
- Mississippi River
- Great Lakes
- Great Plains
- Rocky Mountains
- Mt. McKinley

Reading Strategy

Make a chart like the one below. Fill in details about each of the seven physical regions of the United States.

Region	Details

◀ Monument Valley, Utah

NATIONAL GEOGRAPHIC **Exploring Our World**

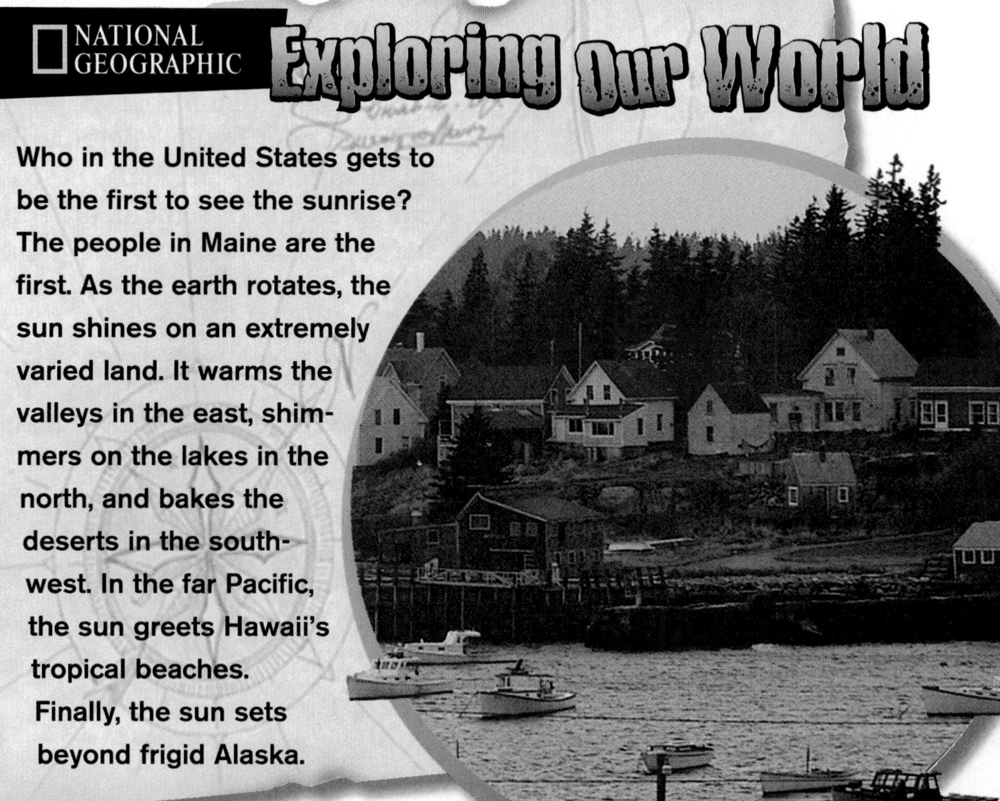

Who in the United States gets to be the first to see the sunrise? The people in Maine are the first. As the earth rotates, the sun shines on an extremely varied land. It warms the valleys in the east, shimmers on the lakes in the north, and bakes the deserts in the southwest. In the far Pacific, the sun greets Hawaii's tropical beaches. Finally, the sun sets beyond frigid Alaska.

The United States stretches 2,807 miles (4,517 km) across the middle part of North America. The 48 states in this part of the country are **contiguous,** or joined together inside a common boundary. These states touch the Atlantic Ocean, the Gulf of Mexico, and the Pacific Ocean. Our neighbors are Canada to the north and Mexico to the south.

Two states lie apart from the other 48. Alaska—the largest state—lies in the northwestern portion of North America. Hawaii is in the Pacific Ocean, about 2,400 miles (3,862 km) southwest of California.

From Sea to Shining Sea

The United States ranks as the fourth-largest country in the world. Only Russia, Canada, and China are larger. Like a patchwork quilt, the United States has regional patterns of different landscapes. You can see swamps and deserts, tall mountains and flat plains.

The contiguous states have five main physical regions: the Coastal Plains, the Appalachian Mountains, the Interior Plains, the Mountains and Basins, and the Pacific Coast. Alaska and Hawaii each have their own unique set of physical landforms.

The Coastal Plains A broad lowland runs along the eastern and southeastern coasts of the United States. The eastern lowlands are called the **Atlantic Coastal Plain.** The lowlands in the southeast border the Gulf of Mexico and are called the **Gulf Coastal Plain.**

Find the Atlantic Coastal Plain on the map on page 117. Stretching from Massachusetts to Florida, it widens the farther south you go. Excellent harbors along the Atlantic Coastal Plain led to the growth of shipping ports like New York City. The soil in the northern part of this region tends to be thin and rocky.

Boston, New York City, Philadelphia, Baltimore, and Washington, D.C., all lie in the Atlantic Coastal Plain. These cities and their suburbs form an almost continuous line of settlement. Geographers call this kind of huge urban area a **megalopolis.** Find these cities on the map on page 133.

Applying Map Skills

1. What is the national capital of the United States?
2. Which states do not lie within the 48 contiguous states?

Find NGS online map resources @
www.nationalgeographic.com/maps

Find the Gulf Coastal Plain on the map below. This plain is wider than the Atlantic plain. Soils in this region are better than those along the Atlantic coast. Texas and Louisiana both have rich deposits of oil and natural gas. The large cities of the Gulf Coastal Plain include Houston and New Orleans, which are shown on the map on page 133.

The Appalachian Mountains Along the western edge of the Atlantic Coastal Plain rise the **Appalachian** (A•puh•LAY•chuhn) **Mountains.** The second-longest range in North America, the Appalachians run almost 1,500 miles (2,414 km) from eastern Canada to Alabama. They are the oldest mountains on the continent. How can you tell? Their rounded peaks show their age. Erosion has worn them down over time. The highest peak, Mount Mitchell in North Carolina, reaches 6,684 feet (2,037 m).

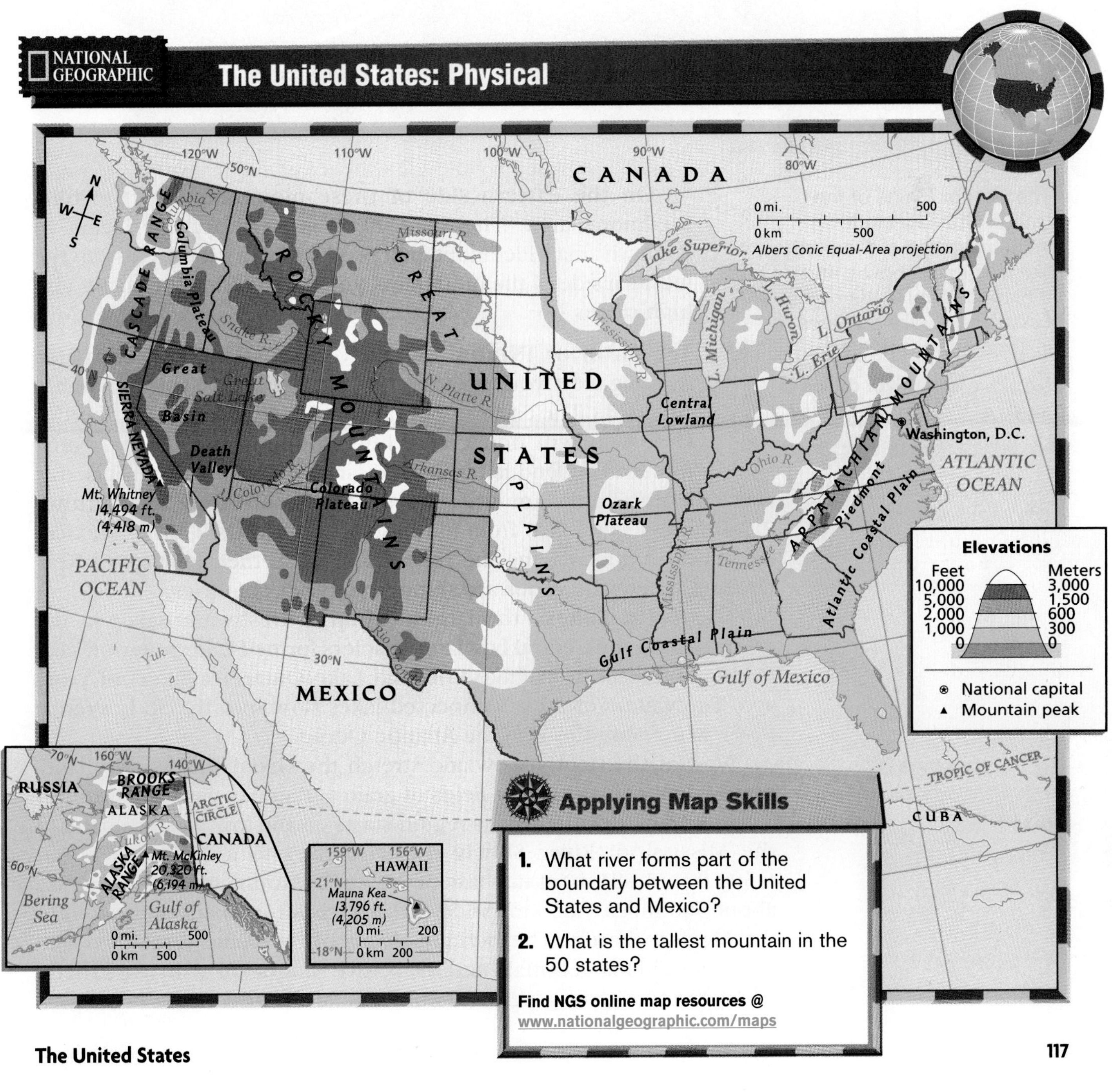

Applying Map Skills

1. What river forms part of the boundary between the United States and Mexico?
2. What is the tallest mountain in the 50 states?

Find NGS online map resources @ www.nationalgeographic.com/maps

City and Country

The Interior Plains of the United States include industrial cities of the north, like Chicago (above), and the agricultural lands of the Great Plains, like this area in Texas (above right).

Region **What river drains much of the Interior Plains?**

On the eastern side of these mountains lies the hilly Piedmont area. The land here is very fertile. Farms in Pennsylvania's Piedmont area produce high crop yields. On the western side of the mountains, you find a system of valleys and high ridges.

The Interior Plains When you cross the Appalachians, heading west, you enter the vast Interior Plains. This region has two parts. The eastern section is called the **Central Lowland.** Here you will find grassy hills, rolling flatlands, and thick forests. The land is fertile, and farms are productive. This area also contains important waterways. The **Mississippi River** flows 2,340 miles (3,766 km) from Minnesota south to the Gulf of Mexico. Barges carry goods along the river. Many finish their journey in New Orleans, where the goods are shipped to other countries.

The **Great Lakes**—the largest group of freshwater lakes in the world—lie in the Central Lowland. Glaciers formed Lake Superior, Lake Michigan, Lake Huron, Lake Erie, and Lake Ontario millions of years ago. The waters of these connected lakes flow into the St. Lawrence River, which empties into the Atlantic Ocean.

West of the Central Lowland stretch the **Great Plains.** The landscape, blanketed with neat fields of grain and grassy pastures, takes on a checkerboard pattern. This region starts on the low western bank of the Mississippi River. Slowly the land rises to a height of about 6,500 feet (1,981 m) at the base of the Rocky Mountains. The Plains are about 500 miles (805 km) wide and stretch into Canada and down to the Mexican border. The rich grasslands of the Plains once provided food for millions of buffalo and the Native Americans who lived there. Today farmers grow grains and ranchers raise cattle.

Mountains and Basins West of the Great Plains rise the majestic **Rocky Mountains**—the longest mountain range in North America. This range begins in Alaska and runs all the way south to Mexico.

As you read in Chapter 1, the surface of the earth rides on huge sheets of rock called tectonic plates. Sometimes these plates collide with such force that they push the land up very high. That is how the Rocky Mountains were formed. The force of this collision has raised some peaks more than 14,000 feet (4,267 m). Running along these mountains is a ridge called the Continental Divide. This ridge separates rivers that flow west—toward the Pacific Ocean—from those that flow east—toward the Mississippi River. Many important rivers begin in the high, snowy peaks of the Rockies. The Rio Grande, Missouri, Platte, Arkansas, and Red Rivers all flow east. The Colorado, Snake, and Columbia Rivers flow west.

As you move west of the Rocky Mountains, you find three large plateaus. Find the northernmost one—the Columbia Plateau—on the map on page 117. South of it you see another plateau called the Great Basin, which includes the Great Salt Lake. The lake's high salt levels make it easy for you to float in it. The third plateau farther south is the Colorado Plateau. Here is where you find the brilliant orange and red rocks shown in the photograph on page 114. The Grand Canyon is also part of the magnificent scenery of this plateau.

The Pacific Coast Near the Pacific coast rise two other mountain ranges. Like the Rockies, the peaks in these ranges are very high. The Cascade Range reaches from Washington State south to California. Volcanoes formed these high peaks—and some of them still erupt. Along California's eastern side runs the Sierra Nevada. The name *Nevada* means "snow covered" in Spanish. Even in a place as far south as California, these high mountains remain covered with snow.

To the west of these Pacific ranges lie fertile valleys. The Willamette Valley in Oregon and the Central Valley in California both produce abundant crops. Many of the fruits and vegetables you eat may come from these valleys.

Alaska Mountain ranges form a semicircle over the northern, eastern, and south-central parts of Alaska. **Mt. McKinley**—the tallest mountain in North America—stands 20,320 feet (6,194 m) high in the Alaska Range. The northern part of the state borders on the frigid Arctic Ocean, and you can almost see Russia from Alaska's western shores. Most people in Alaska live along the southern coastal plain or in the central Yukon River valley.

Hawaii Eight large islands and more than 120 smaller islands make up Hawaii, our western state in the Pacific Ocean. Volcanoes on the ocean floor erupted and formed these islands. Some of the islands have **coral reefs,** formed by the skeletons of small sea animals. These structures lie just above or submerged just below the surface of the water.

✓Reading Check **How were the Rocky Mountains formed?**

A Variety of Climates

Because the United States is such a large country, you probably expect it to have a variety of climates. You are right! Most of the country lies squarely in the middle latitude region—from 30°N to 60°N latitude. As you remember from Chapter 2, this part of the earth has the greatest variety of climates. With Alaska and Hawaii, our country also has high latitude and tropical climates.

Mid-Latitude Climates Look at the climate map below. As you can see, the area from the northern Great Plains to the northern Atlantic coast has a humid continental climate. Winters in this region are cold, and summers are hot and long. Rain falls on and off throughout the year. Snow often blankets the area during the winter—especially around the Great Lakes.

The southern part of the Great Plains and the southeastern states have a humid subtropical climate. Winters are milder than in the north, and summers are hot and humid. Being close to the Gulf of Mexico and the Caribbean Sea often means that summer months bring violent thunderstorms, hurricanes, and tornadoes.

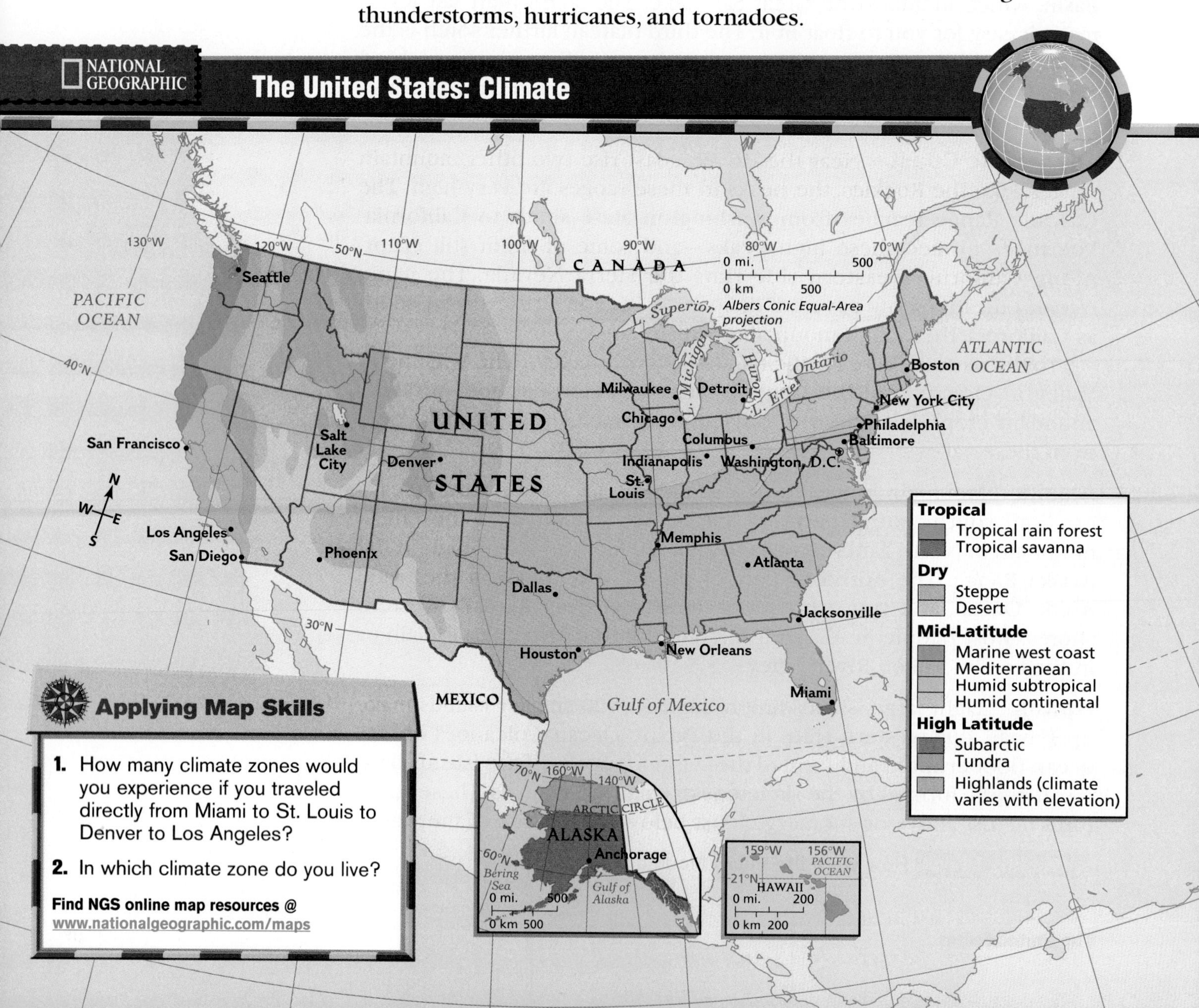

NATIONAL GEOGRAPHIC On Location

Seasons in Vermont

As these views of a country lane in Vermont show, the humid continental climate region has four distinct seasons of the year.

Region **How does a humid continental climate differ from a humid subtropical climate?**

The Pacific coast from northern California up to Washington has a marine west coast climate. Temperatures are mild year-round, and winds from the Pacific bring plenty of rainfall. Huge forests of tall trees grow in these areas.

Southern California has a Mediterranean climate. People in this area enjoy dry, warm summers and mild, rainy winters. Fruits and vegetables, including grapes for wine, thrive in the Mediterranean climate of this region.

Dry Climates Much of the western Great Plains has a dry steppe climate. This region is dry much of the year, but enough rain falls to support the growth of thick grasses. You also find steppe climates on the plateaus west of the Rockies. Why are these areas dry? The Pacific mountain ranges block the humid ocean winds. Therefore, hot, dry air gets trapped in the plateaus and basins between the Pacific mountain ranges and the Rockies.

In the southwest, even less rain falls. This arid region has a desert climate, and temperatures climb very high. In southeastern California's Death Valley, the lowest point in the United States, temperatures soar as high as 125°F (52°C) in the summer. Turn to the vegetation map on page 66 of Chapter 2 and the photograph on page 69 to see what types of vegetation grow in the dry climate zones.

NATIONAL GEOGRAPHIC On Location

Hawaii

Lush tropical growth is found in Hawaii, our 50th state.

Location **In what ocean is Hawaii located?**

High Latitude Climates People in Alaska experience the cold climates of high latitude regions. The southern two-thirds of the state has a subarctic climate, with cool summers and freezing winters. Rainfall is heavy in coastal regions and lighter in the interior. Only small bushes can grow in the far north's tundra climate.

As you recall from Chapter 2, mountains have cool climates. Look at the climate map on page 120. Compare the highland climate areas to the physical map on page 117 to see which mountain ranges have highland climates.

Tropical Climates The southern tip of Florida is the only part of the contiguous United States with a tropical climate. This area has heavy rainfall and warm temperatures all year long. However, Hawaii is the wettest state in the nation. It lies within the tropics, yet cooling breezes from the ocean keep temperatures moderate. Average temperatures in Honolulu range from 72°F (22°C) in the cool months to 78°F (26°C) in the warm months.

✓Reading Check **Why are dry climates found in the western United States?**

Section 1 Assessment

Defining Terms

1. **Define** contiguous, megalopolis, coral reef.

Recalling Facts

2. **Place** How does the United States rank in size among all the countries of the world?
3. **History** Which region once supported millions of buffalo and the Native Americans who depended on them?
4. **Place** What is the Continental Divide?

Critical Thinking

5. **Understanding Cause and Effect** What evidence indicates that the Appalachians are the oldest mountains in North America?
6. **Drawing Conclusions** What challenges do you think result from the distance between Alaska, Hawaii, and the other states?

Graphic Organizer

7. **Organizing Information** Create a diagram like this one to compare the Atlantic and Gulf Coastal Plains. In the overlapping area, write the characteristics that the two areas share. In the separate outer parts of the ovals, write the qualities that make each region unique.

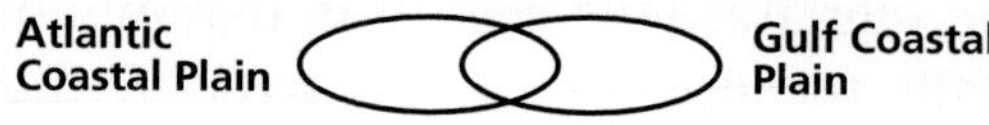

Applying Geography Skills

8. **Analyzing Maps** Look at the physical map on page 117 and the climate map on page 120. At what elevation does the city of Denver lie? What climate zone do you find just west of Denver?

An Economic Leader

Guide to Reading

Main Idea

The powerful United States economy runs on abundant resources and the hard work of Americans.

Terms to Know

- free enterprise system
- service industry
- navigable
- fossil fuels
- acid rain
- landfill
- recycling
- free trade

Places to Locate

- New York City
- Washington, D.C.
- Los Angeles

Reading Strategy

Complete a chart like this one. First, list the five economic regions of the United States. In the right column, list the economic activities carried out in each region.

Region	Economic Activities

NATIONAL GEOGRAPHIC **Exploring Our World**

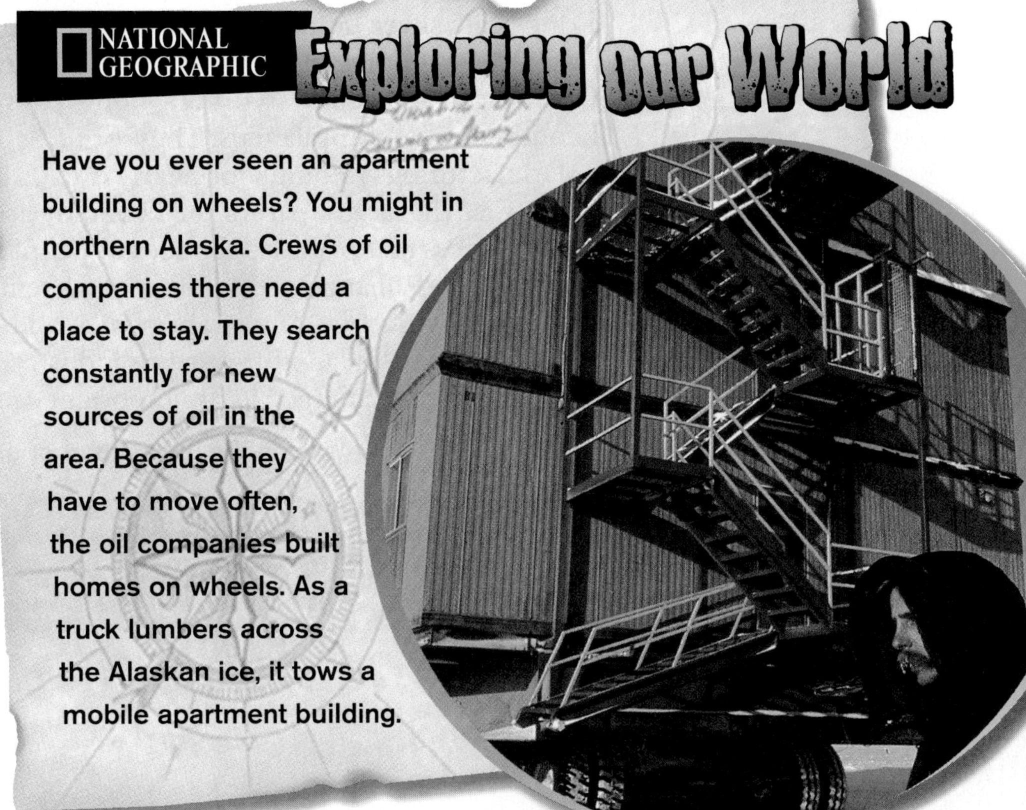

Have you ever seen an apartment building on wheels? You might in northern Alaska. Crews of oil companies there need a place to stay. They search constantly for new sources of oil in the area. Because they have to move often, the oil companies built homes on wheels. As a truck lumbers across the Alaskan ice, it tows a mobile apartment building.

The United States has a large, energetic, and growing economy. Fueling all of this economic activity is freedom. As you recall from Chapter 3, the **free enterprise system** is built on the idea that individual people have the right to run businesses to make a profit with limited interference from the government. Americans are free to start their own businesses and to keep the profits they earn. They are free to work in whatever jobs they want—and for whatever employers they want. This has helped create great economic success.

The World's Economic Leader

The United States is rich in resources and has a hardworking labor force. As a result, the country has built the world's largest economy—in terms of how much money is made from the sale of its goods and services. In fact, the American economy is larger than the next two largest economies—China's and Japan's—combined.

Farms in the United States produce about one-half of the world's corn and about one-tenth of its wheat. American farmers raise about 20 percent of the world's beef, pork, and lamb. The country exports more food than any other nation. Yet agriculture is only a small part of the American economy. Food makes up less than 2 percent of the value of all goods produced in the country.

The United States has rich mineral resources. About one-fifth of the world's coal and copper and one-tenth of the world's petroleum come from the United States. The country also has large amounts of iron ore, zinc, lead, silver, gold, and many other minerals. Mining, though, makes up little more than 1 percent of the nation's economy.

American factory workers build cars and airplanes. They make computers and appliances. They process foods and make medicines. Manufacturing accounts for nearly one-fifth of the American economy.

By far, the largest part of the economy is services. A **service industry** is a business that provides services to people instead of producing goods. Banking and finance are services. So is entertainment—and people all over the world buy American movies and CDs. The United States is a leader in tourism, another service industry. Computer-based, online services have also emerged as an important American service industry.

✓Reading Check **What is the largest part of the United States economy?**

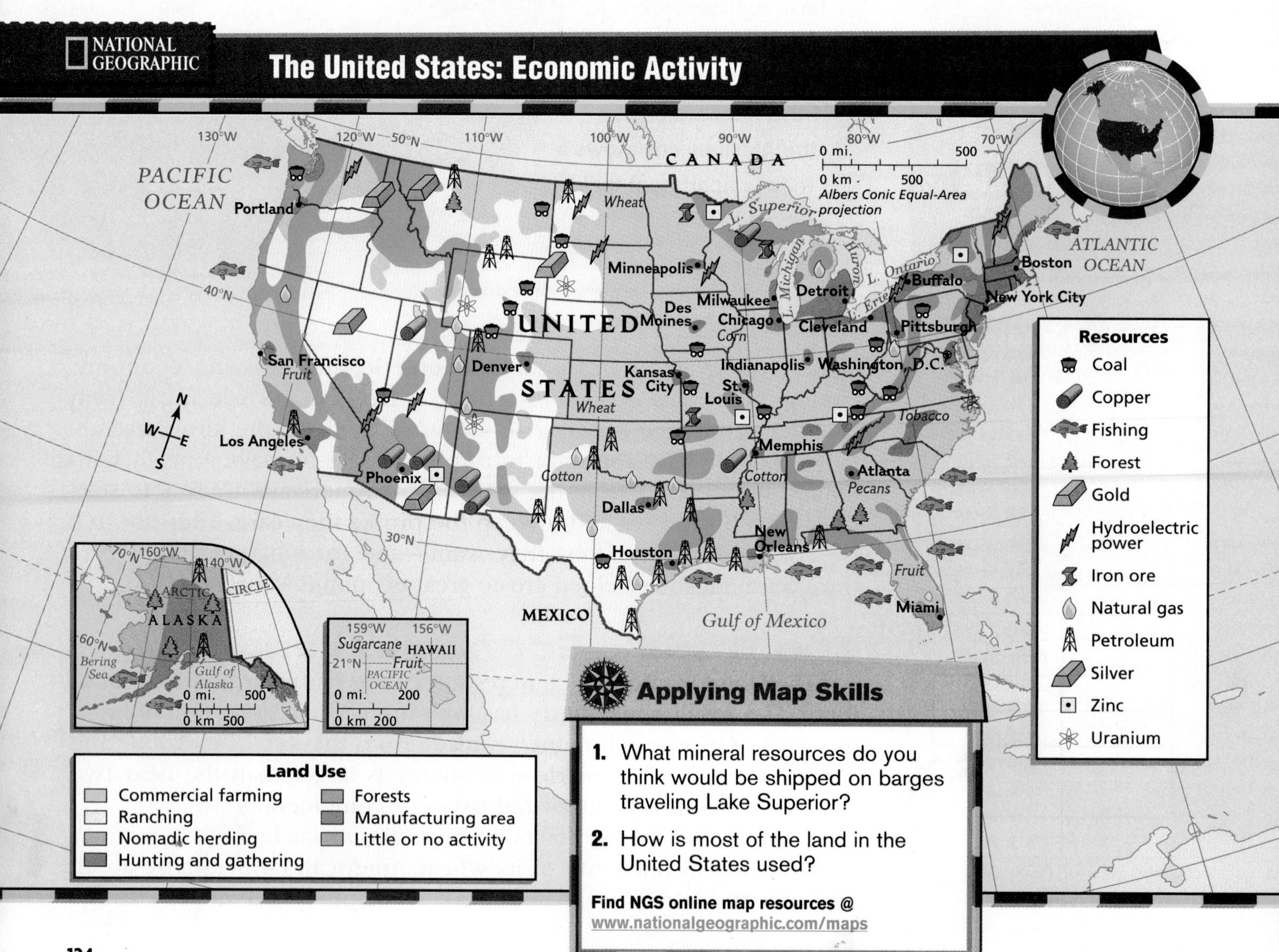

Applying Map Skills

1. What mineral resources do you think would be shipped on barges traveling Lake Superior?
2. How is most of the land in the United States used?

Find NGS online map resources @ www.nationalgeographic.com/maps

America's Economic Regions

Geographers group states together into five economic regions—the Northeast, the South, the Midwest, the Interior West, and the Pacific.

The Northeast Some farmers in central Pennsylvania and western New York grow grains and fruits. Yet as you read in Section 1, the rocky soil and steep hills in this region are a challenge to the farmers. The area boasts plenty of deep water ports and swiftly moving rivers, though. As a result, manufacturing, trade, and fishing are the heartbeat of this region. In fact, the Northeast was home to the first mills powered by running water and coal. Look at the economic activity map on page 124. As you can see, coal mining takes place in Pennsylvania and West Virginia.

With their deep, natural harbors, Boston, New York City, Philadelphia, and Baltimore all are important ports. Goods are shipped all over the world to and from these ports. These cities filled with skyscrapers are also important centers of banking, insurance, and finance. **New York City** is one of the financial capitals of the world. It is also a world center in the fashion, entertainment, and communications industries. Farther south, the nation's capital—**Washington, D.C.**—employs hundreds of thousands in government and tourism services.

The South With rich soil on most of the Coastal Plains, agriculture flourishes in the Southern states. Because of the region's warm, wet climate, farmers in Louisiana and Arkansas grow rice and sugarcane. Tobacco flourishes in Virginia and the Carolinas. In Florida you can sample the citrus fruits that farmers grow. Peanuts and pecans are found in Georgia. You also see cotton growing in several Southern states, including Texas. Texas, in fact, has more farms than any other state in the country. The people of Texas grow cotton, sorghum, and wheat and raise livestock as well.

The traditional image of the South as an agricultural region is changing, however. As you tour the South, you see expanding cities, growing industries, and diverse populations. New manufacturing centers have drawn new businesses and people to the South from the Northeast and elsewhere. Workers make textiles, electrical equipment, and airplane parts. Oil is found in Texas and Louisiana. As a result, they produce petroleum-based products.

Service industries are important in the South as well. Florida is a major tourist center. People come to enjoy amusement parks in Orlando, the Kennedy Space Center at Cape Canaveral, and the beautiful beaches on both coasts. Millions of people flock to New Orleans each year to taste its spicy food and hear its lively music. Houston, Dallas, Atlanta, and Miami are just a few of this region's major centers of business and finance.

The Midwest This part of the United States has been called "America's breadbasket." Miles and miles of grain and soybean fields greet you as you travel over flat land and fertile soil. In this farm belt, farmers grow corn, soybeans, oats, and wheat to feed animals and people all over the world. Dairy farms in the upper

Surf's Up!

Fourteen-year-old Shawn Kilgore lives on Florida's Captiva Island, along the Gulf of Mexico. "I really like warm weather," he says. "Who needs snow? My dog Sunny and I couldn't go surfing if we lived in Ohio where my cousins are." Shawn's parents manage a resort for tourists. "My mom and dad are always reminding me that we live in one of the world's richest countries. So my older sister and I volunteer to grocery-shop for people around here who can't do it themselves."

NATIONAL GEOGRAPHIC On Location

Farms

A farmer harvests alfalfa. America's economy was originally built on agriculture.

Region **What economic region do you think this farm is in? How can you tell?**

Midwest produce milk and cheese. However, technology has changed many farms from small family-owned acres to big businesses. The graph in the **Geography Handbook** on page 15 shows you the decrease in the number of farms over the past few decades.

Many of the region's rivers are **navigable,** or wide and deep enough to allow the passage of ships. As a result, many cities here are major ports—even though they are far from an ocean. Businesses in Cincinnati and Louisville send goods down the Ohio River. St. Louis and Memphis serve as centers of trade along the Mississippi River. Chicago's and Cleveland's industries ship goods through the Great Lakes and St. Lawrence Seaway to ports around the world.

Because of their abundant coal and iron resources, many cities in the Midwest are manufacturing centers. A complex network of railroads also helps the region's many industries. Detroit is called Motown (short for Motor Town) because the country's auto industry started and grew here. Other major industries include steel, heavy machinery, and auto parts.

The Interior West Magnificent landscapes greet visitors to this region. However, this area is short on an important resource—water. With its dry climate, the region discourages farming. Yet grasses thrive in much of the land, and where the land is irrigated, you find agriculture. Large areas are used for raising cattle and sheep. Ranches here may be huge—as large as 4,000 acres (1,619 ha). In the past, cowhands worked the range on horseback. Although they still use horses today, you are just as likely to see them driving a sturdy truck.

Look at the map on page 124. You see rich deposits of minerals and energy resources in the Interior West. The discovery of gold and silver in the mountains and riverbeds drew settlers here 150 years ago. Mining still plays an important role in the economy.

Many people work in service industries, too. Every year tourists travel to Denver, Salt Lake City, Albuquerque, and Phoenix. They use these cities as starting points for trips to sites such as Yellowstone National Park or the Grand Canyon. Some visit the ruins of ancient Native American settlements, such as those found at Mesa Verde in southwestern Colorado.

The Pacific The Pacific region includes the states on the western coast plus Alaska and Hawaii. The fertile valleys of California, Oregon, and Washington produce large amounts of food. As you learned in

Section 1, many of the fruits and vegetables you enjoy every day come from these states. Do you like pineapple? If so, it may have come from Hawaii. This state also grows sugarcane, coffee, and rice in its tropical climate and rich volcanic soil.

In this region, just like the Atlantic coast, fishing is a major industry. The states of Washington and Oregon draw many people to work in the lumber industry. Mineral resources are important in the Pacific region, too. California has gold, lead, and copper. Alaska has vast reserves of oil.

Factory workers in California and Washington make planes. The areas around San Francisco and Seattle are world-famous centers of research in computers and software. **Los Angeles** is the world capital of the movie industry. These states also attract millions of tourists who plan to visit California's redwood forests, Hawaii's tropical beaches, or the stunning glaciers of Alaska.

✓Reading Check **What goods are manufactured in the Pacific states?**

Entering the Twenty-First Century

The American economy, although strong, faces challenges in the twenty-first century. One of these challenges is how to clean up pollution and trash. Americans burn **fossil fuels**—coal, oil, and natural gas—to power their factories and run their cars. Burning these fuels pollutes the air, endangering all who breathe it. The pollution also mixes with water vapor in the air to make **acid rain,** or rain containing high amounts of chemical pollutants. Acid rain damages trees and harms rivers and lakes.

The fast-paced American way of life creates another problem. People generate huge amounts of trash. **Landfills,** the areas where trash companies dump the waste they collect, grow higher and higher

NATIONAL GEOGRAPHIC On Location

Factories

A worker inspects computer components. Along with agriculture, America's economy is strong in technology, science, education, and medicine.

Place **What areas in the United States are important software centers?**

each year. Many communities now promote **recycling,** or reusing materials instead of throwing them out. Recycling cuts down on the amount of trash.

New Technology The ability to develop new technology has been a major source of strength for the American economy. Researchers work constantly to find new products to make people's lives easier, healthier—and more fun. Success has helped the country become a world leader in satellites, computers, medicine, and many other fields. Keeping our number one position will require just as much creative thinking and hard work. You will need to learn and use these new technologies to stay productive in your future jobs.

World Trade The United States leads the world in the value of all its imports and exports. Millions of Americans depend on trade for their jobs. American leaders have worked hard to promote free trade. **Free trade** means taking down trade barriers such as tariffs or quotas so that goods flow freely among countries. In 1993 the United States joined Mexico and Canada in the North American Free Trade Agreement (NAFTA). This agreement promised to remove all barriers to trade among those three countries.

✓Reading Check **How do factories and cars harm the environment in the United States?**

Section 2 Assessment

Defining Terms

1. **Define** free enterprise system, service industry, navigable, fossil fuels, acid rain, landfill, recycling, free trade.

Recalling Facts

2. **Economics** Why is the Midwest called "America's breadbasket"?
3. **History** The discovery of which resources first brought settlers to the Interior West?
4. **Economics** What was the goal of the North American Free Trade Agreement (NAFTA)?

Critical Thinking

5. **Analyzing Information** Describe two characteristics of the United States that have helped it become a world leader.
6. **Understanding Cause and Effect** What reasons can you give for the economic changes taking place in the South?

Graphic Organizer

7. **Organizing Information** Draw a diagram like this one. Name one economic region of the United States in the center oval. In the outer ovals write one specific example of each subtopic under their headings.

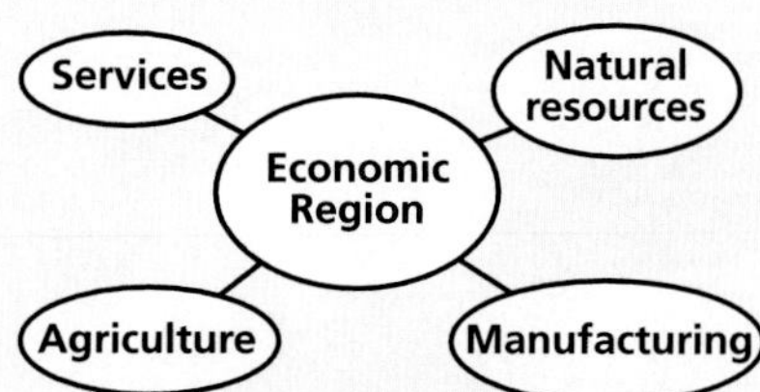

Applying Geography Skills

8. **Analyzing Maps** Study the economic activity map on page 124 and the climate map on page 120. Then explain why there is little economic activity southwest of Phoenix, Arizona.

Geography Skill

Using Scale

Model cars or airplanes are like the real versions, except for size. Models are made to scale—for example, 1 inch on a model may stand for 1 foot in the real vehicle.

Learning the Skill

Scale is also used to represent size and distance on maps. For example, 1 inch on a map may represent 100 miles (161 km) on the earth's surface. On another map, 1 inch may represent 1,000 miles. A map scale is usually shown with a **scale bar.** This bar shows you how much real distance on the earth is shown by a measurement on the map. To use scale, follow these steps:

- On the scale bar, find the unit of measurement.
- Note the distance in miles or kilometers that the unit represents (1 inch = 5 miles? 1 inch = 100 miles?).
- Measure the distance between two points on the map.
- Multiply that number by the miles or kilometers each unit stands for.

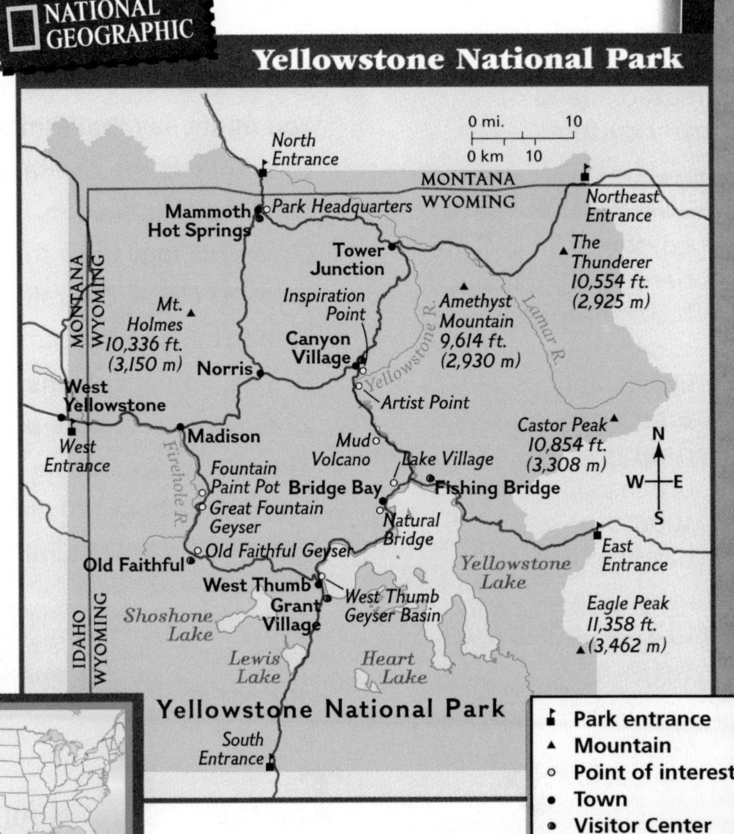

Practicing the Skill

Look at the map to answer the following questions.

1. What is the scale of miles on this map?
2. What is the scale of kilometers on this map?
3. About how many inches long is the map in a direct line from the North Entrance to the South Entrance? How many miles is this measurement?
4. By road, about how far is the North Entrance from West Thumb?
5. How much farther by road is it from Old Faithful Geyser to the South Entrance than from the geyser to Bridge Bay?

Applying the Skill

Look at the economic activity map of the United States on page 124. About how many miles does 1 inch represent on the contiguous states? What is the scale of miles on the inset map of Hawaii?

GO TO

Practice key skills with **Glencoe Skillbuilder Interactive Workbook, Level 1.**

Section 3

The Americans

Guide to Reading

Main Idea

The United States has attracted people from all over the world who have created a land of many cultures.

Terms to Know

- colony
- democracy
- federal republic
- secede
- immigrant
- ethnic group
- rural
- urban
- suburbs
- national park

Places to Locate

- Texas
- California
- Georgia
- Massachusetts

Reading Strategy

Create a diagram like this one. In each outer oval, write under the heading one fact about American society as it relates to the topic given.

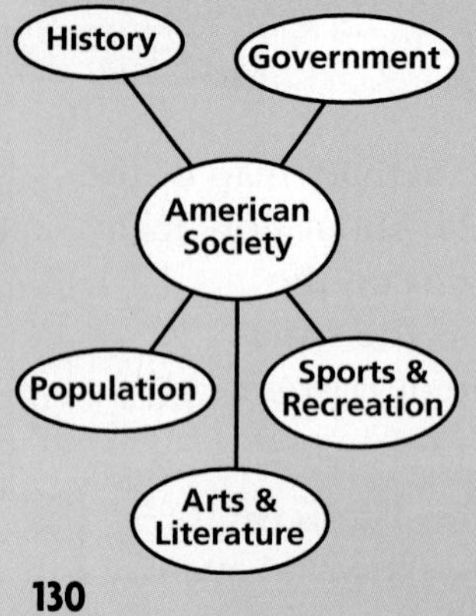

NATIONAL GEOGRAPHIC **Exploring Our World**

The United States has often been called a nation of immigrants. You might say that Elmhurst, New York, is the capital of this immigrant nation. (This area may have the greatest ethnic diversity in the country.) Elmhurst is a section of Queens, one of the boroughs of New York City. People from more than 120 different nations live in Elmhurst.

The United States is full of people from many different lands. What attracts people to the United States? One reason is the freedom that Americans enjoy. Economic opportunity is another reason. The United States gives people in many other lands hope that they and their children can enjoy better lives.

A Rich History

The United States is a young country compared to many others. The country became independent a little more than 200 years ago. Before it became a country, however, the land's history stretched back thousands of years. Experts have long believed that the first people to settle in the Americas came from Asia. At the time, the earth's climate was much colder than it is now. Huge sheets of ice covered much of the Northern Hemisphere. As a result, sea levels were lower, and a land bridge connected Asia and Alaska. Herd animals crossed this bridge—and the people who hunted them followed.

These people fanned out over the Americas. Over time, they developed different ways of life using local resources. In the Northeast of the present-day United States, the people hunted deer and fished. In the Southeast and Mississippi Valley, they grew corn and other crops. On the Great Plains, they hunted buffalo. In the dry Southwest, they irrigated the land to grow corn and beans. In the Northwest, they fished.

Around A.D. 1500, Europeans learned of the existence of the Americas. The raw materials they saw—forests, animal furs, and rich soils—soon led them to set up colonies, or overseas settlements tied to a parent country. The French built trading posts around the Great Lakes. The Spanish made communities in the area from **Texas** to **California.** British colonists settled along the Atlantic coast from **Georgia** to **Massachusetts.**

A Democratic Republic By the mid-1700s, the people living in the British colonies had started to see themselves as Americans—different from the British. They resented certain actions of the British government, believing that these actions abused their rights. From 1775 to 1781, the new Americans fought a war that freed the colonies from British rule. With the help of France, they won the war and formed a new nation—the United States of America.

In 1787 a group of leaders, including George Washington and James Madison, met to create a new form of government. They wrote the document called the Constitution of the United States that set the form of government still used today. Our government is based on the principle of democracy, a form of government in which the people rule. We have a *representative democracy,* in which voters choose leaders who make and enforce the laws.

The 13 former British colonies became the first 13 states. Each state had its own government, but people chosen by the voters of each state also served in a national government. In this way, the United States was a federal republic, or a government divided between national and state powers with a president who leads the national government. As you can see from the chart on page 132, the national government is divided into three branches.

A Period of Growth From 1800 to 1900, the United States experienced tremendous growth. It grew from the 13 states along the Atlantic coast to include 45 states that reached to the Pacific Ocean. The population boomed as millions of people settled here from other lands. They cleared forests, farmed, and often fought with Native Americans who were being pushed out of the way. Farmers grew corn in the Midwest and cotton in the South. Some people mined gold and silver in the Rocky Mountains and California.

In the mid-1800s, the nation experienced a crisis. The South had built its economy on slavery. Hundreds of thousands of enslaved Africans had been forced to work in the agricultural South. Over time, slavery divided the country. In 1861 several Southern states seceded, or withdrew from the national government. For four years, the North and the South fought a bitter civil war. In the end, the Southern states were brought back into the Union, and slavery was abolished.

San Xavier del Bac

Is this Catholic church in Spain? In Mexico? No, this Spanish-style church, called San Xavier del Bac, stands near Tucson, Arizona. Settlers built the church in 1797, when the area was part of Spain's colonial empire. In fact, many Spanish settlements in the American Southwest were founded in the 1500s, long before the English Pilgrims sailed to the Americas on the *Mayflower.*

Branches of the United States Government

Analyzing the Diagram

The United States government has three main branches.

Place **Which branch makes the laws?**

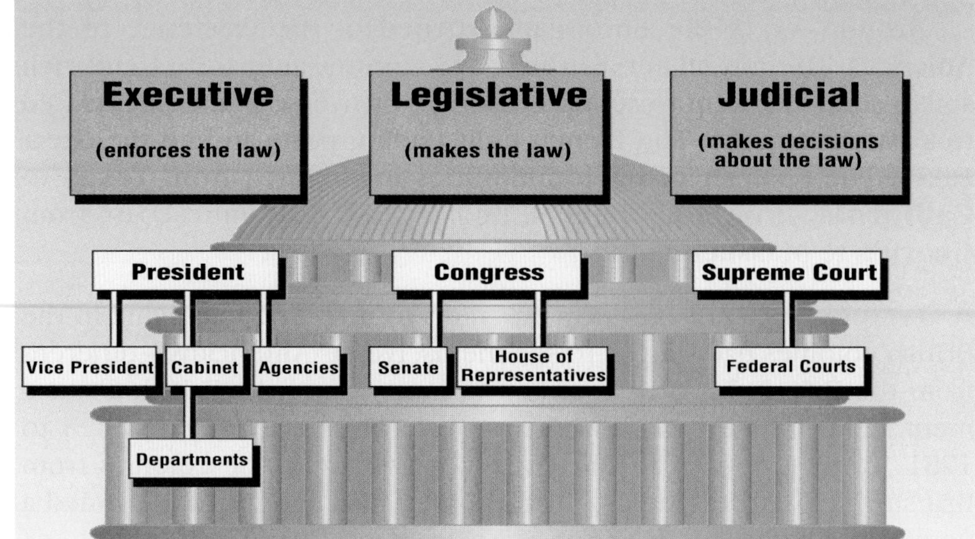

The Civil War did more than end slavery. It also launched the country into a period of great economic growth. Railroads crisscrossed the land, and factories sprang up, especially in the Northeast and Midwest. This economic growth attracted another great wave of **immigrants,** or people who move to a new country to make a permanent home.

A World Leader During the early 1900s, the United States became one of the leading economies in the world. Automobiles rolled off assembly lines, electricity became common, and other technologies—the telephone and radio, for example—entered daily life.

The world plunged into two World Wars in the 1910s and 1940s. The United States took part in these wars. Our country's leaders urged the world's people to fight for freedom and to defeat dangerous dictators. American factories built tanks and airplanes, while American soldiers helped win the wars.

After World War II, the United States enjoyed great influence around the world. American companies shipped their products to all continents. American leaders pushed for democracy and free enterprise in other countries. American culture spread around the globe.

At home, however, tensions existed among groups within American society. Many of the Americans who had fought in the two World Wars or had taken care of the home front were women, African Americans, and Hispanic Americans. After World War II, these groups wanted equal rights. Because the United States was often not tolerant toward minorities, many people, including such men as Martin Luther King, Jr., began to push for change. The poems on page 136 describe two views of Americans struggling to be accepted.

✓ Reading Check **How is our country a democracy and a federal republic?**

One Out of Many

About 280 million people live in the United States, making it the third most populous country in the world. Compared with people in most other countries, Americans enjoy a high standard of living. Americans, on the average, can expect to live about 76 years. Medical advances have helped people achieve longer lives.

Because it is a nation of immigrants, the United States has a diverse population with various ethnic groups. An **ethnic group** is a group of people who share a culture, language, or history. Almost three-fourths of the people in our country are descended from European ethnic groups. African American ethnic groups form about 12 percent of the population. The fastest-growing ethnic groups are the Hispanic, who trace their heritage to the countries of Latin America and Spain.

Today many immigrants to the United States come from China, India, other Asian countries, and the Pacific islands. The smallest ethnic groups have lived in the country the longest—Native Americans who

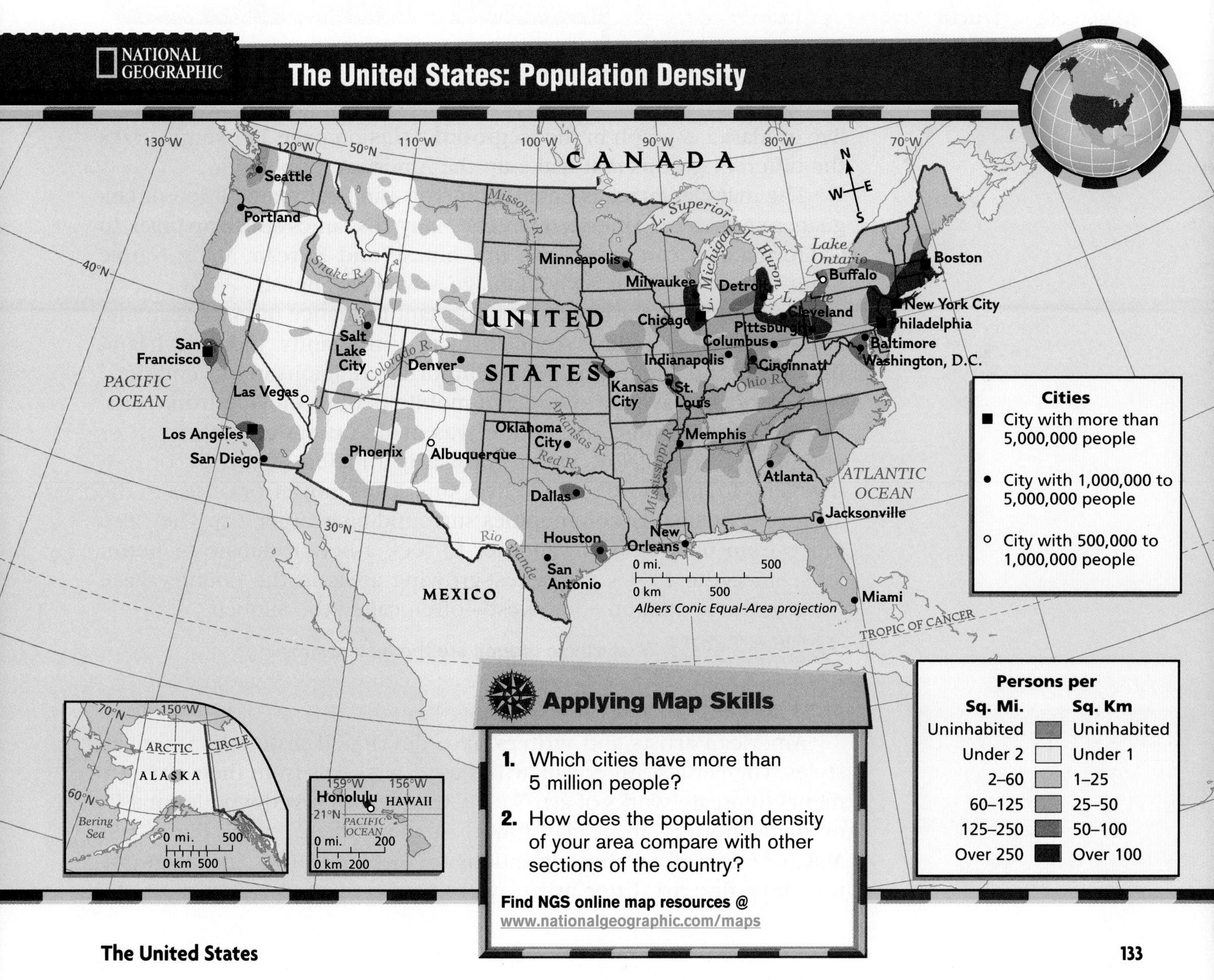

Applying Map Skills

1. Which cities have more than 5 million people?
2. How does the population density of your area compare with other sections of the country?

Find NGS online map resources @ www.nationalgeographic.com/maps

Music

The music of North America stems from Native American, European, and African influences. This Native American flute was developed by peoples on the Great Plains. When you blow into the flute, the air turns upward and travels through an outside tube. Then the air goes back *into* the flute and passes over a sharp edge, which creates the sound. In addition to five or six playing holes, four "direction" holes are added. This allows the music to be heard to the north, south, east, and west.

Looking Closer How does the flute player "amplify" his music in a natural way?

GO TO **World Music: A Cultural Legacy**
Hear music of this region on Disc 1, Track 4.

live in Alaska. A graph in the **Regional Atlas** on page 111 summarizes the different groups that make up the American population.

The main language is English, but you can hear many different languages spoken on American streets. Many Hispanics speak Spanish. In California you can read signs in Chinese and Korean. Many Native Americans speak their own language as well as English.

Religion has always been an important influence on American life. Most Americans follow some form of Christianity. Judaism, Islam, Buddhism, and Hinduism are also important religions in our country.

Americans have always been a mobile people, moving from place to place. At one time, our nation was made up entirely of **rural,** or countryside, areas. Now we are primarily a nation of **urban,** or city, dwellers. To find more room to live, Americans move from cities to the **suburbs,** or smaller communities surrounding a larger city. They also move from one region to another to seek a better climate or better jobs. Since the 1970s, the fastest-growing areas in the country have been in the South and Southwest—often called the Sunbelt.

Reading Check **What ethnic groups are the fastest-growing?**

American Culture

American artists and writers have developed distinctly American styles. The earliest American artists used materials from their environments to create works of art. Native Americans carved wooden masks or made pottery from clay found in their areas. Artists like Maria Martinez carried on these traditions by turning Native American pottery into fine art. Later artists were attracted to the beauty of the

American land. Winslow Homer painted the stormy waters of the North Atlantic. Georgia O'Keeffe painted the colorful cliffs and deserts of the Southwest. Artists like Thomas Eakins painted scenes of city life.

Two themes are common to American literature. One theme focuses on the rich diversity of the people in the United States. The poetry of Langston Hughes and the novels of Toni Morrison portray the triumphs and sorrows of African Americans. The novels of Amy Tan examine the lives of Chinese Americans. Oscar Hijuelos and Sandra Cisneros write about the country's Hispanics.

A second theme focuses on the landscape and history of particular regions. Mark Twain's humorous books relate life along the Mississippi River in the mid-1800s. Nathaniel Hawthorne wrote about the people of New England. Willa Cather portrayed the struggles people faced in settling the Great Plains. William Faulkner examined life in the South.

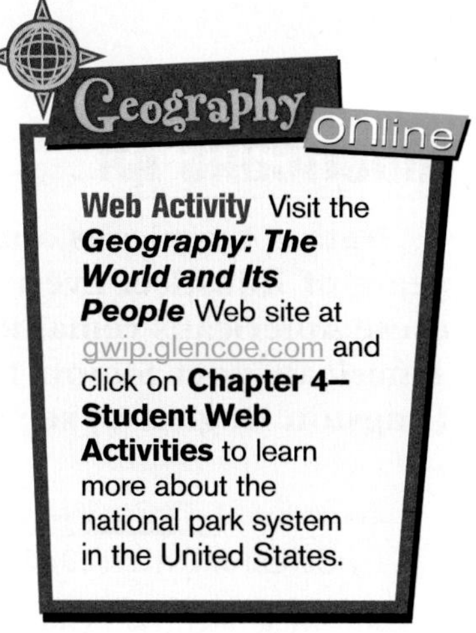

Sports and Recreation Many Americans spend their leisure time at home, watching television, playing video games, or using a computer. Many also pursue active lives outdoors. They bike and hike, ski and skate, shoot baskets and kick soccer balls. Many enjoy spectator sports such as baseball and football. Stock-car races and rodeos also attract large crowds. Millions each year travel to **national parks,** or areas set aside to protect wilderness and wildlife and for recreation.

Reading Check What are two common themes in American literature?

Assessment

Defining Terms

1. **Define** colony, democracy, federal republic, secede, immigrant, ethnic group, rural, urban, suburbs, national park.

Recalling Facts

2. **History** What route do experts think the first Americans took to reach North America?
3. **Government** What document explains the form of government used in the United States?
4. **Culture** What theme do the works of Langston Hughes and Toni Morrison share?

Critical Thinking

5. **Analyzing Information** After World War II, what tensions existed within society?
6. **Drawing Conclusions** How does climate and culture influence the popularity of sports in your area?

Graphic Organizer

7. **Organizing Information** Draw a diagram like the one below. At the tops of the three arrows, complete the diagram by listing three reasons that Americans today are moving more frequently than ever.

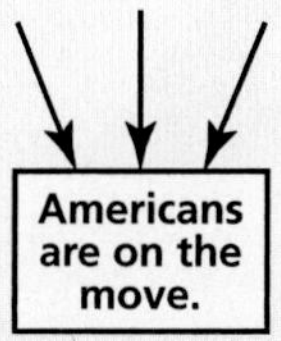

Applying Geography Skills

8. **Analyzing Maps** According to the population density map on page 133, what are the two largest cities in the Pacific Northwest?

Making Connections

ART | SCIENCE | LITERATURE | TECHNOLOGY

▲ Picking cotton near Dallas, Texas, 1907

Americans All

Native Americans and African Americans endured many years of injustice. Even so, the pride and determination of these Americans remained strong. Read the poems by Native American poet Simon J. Ortiz and African American poet Langston Hughes to see how they express these feelings.

Survival This Way

by Simon J. Ortiz (1941–)

Survival, I know how this way.
This way, I know.
It rains.
Mountains and canyons and plants
grow.
We travelled this way,
gauged our distance by stories
and loved our children.
We taught them
to love their births.
We told ourselves over and over
again, "We shall survive
this way."

▲ Native Americans on the Great Plains, 1891

I, Too

by Langston Hughes (1902–1967)

I, too, sing America.

I am the darker brother.
They send me to eat in the kitchen
When company comes,
But I laugh,
And eat well,
And grow strong.

Tomorrow,
I'll be at the table
When company comes.
Nobody'll dare
Say to me,
"Eat in the kitchen,"
Then.

Besides,
They'll see how beautiful I am
And be ashamed—

I, too, am America.

Making the Connection

1. How does the poem "Survival This Way" tell how Native Americans feel about their children?
2. What does Langston Hughes mean by the phrase "I, too, sing America"?
3. **Making Comparisons** In what way do both poems convey a message of hope?

Reading Review

Section 1 A Vast, Scenic Land

Terms to Know
contiguous
megalopolis
coral reef

Main Idea
The United States has a great variety of landforms and climates.

✓ Region The United States has five main physical regions: the Coastal Plains, the Appalachian Mountains, the Interior Plains, the Mountains and Basins region, and the Pacific Coast. Alaska and Hawaii make up two additional regions.

✓ Place Northeastern coastal lowlands have poor soil but are densely populated.

✓ Economics The Central Lowland is well suited to agriculture, as are western coastal valleys.

✓ Place The high Rocky Mountains and nearby basins have rich mineral deposits.

Section 2 An Economic Leader

Terms to Know
free enterprise system
service industry
navigable
fossil fuels
acid rain
landfill
recycling
free trade

Main Idea
The powerful United States economy runs on abundant resources and the hard work of Americans.

✓ Economics Because of many natural resources and a hardworking labor force, the United States has the world's most productive economy.

✓ Economics Service industries contribute the most to the American economy, followed by manufacturing, agriculture, and mining.

✓ Economics The United States has five economic regions—the Northeast, the South, the Midwest, the Interior West, and the Pacific.

✓ Economics Creativity and hard work are needed to continue to develop new technologies and help the American economy grow.

Section 3 The Americans

Terms to Know
colony
democracy
federal republic
secede
immigrant
ethnic group
rural
urban
suburbs
national park

Main Idea
The United States has attracted people from all over the world who have created a land of many cultures.

✓ History The American people are immigrants or the descendants of immigrants who came from all over the world.

✓ Government The United States has a representative democratic government with power shared by the states and the national government.

✓ Culture Ethnic groups in America are descendants of five main peoples: Europeans, Africans, Hispanics, Asians and Pacific Islanders, and Native Americans and Inuit.

✓ Culture American arts celebrate the country's ethnic and regional diversity.

Chapter 4

Assessment and Activities

Using Key Terms

Match the terms in Part A with their definitions in Part B.

A.

1. contiguous
2. megalopolis
3. free enterprise system
4. fossil fuels
5. navigable
6. immigrant
7. colony
8. democracy
9. ethnic group
10. suburb

B.

a. oil, natural gas, and coal
b. smaller community surrounding a city
c. areas joined inside a common boundary
d. government by the people
e. limited government control over the economy
f. group of people who share a common culture, language, and history
g. a "supercity"
h. person who moves to a new country
i. wide and deep enough for ships to pass
j. overseas settlement tied to a parent country

Reviewing the Main Ideas

Section 1 A Vast, Scenic Land

11. **Region** What are the two parts of the Interior Plains?
12. **Place** Which part of the contiguous United States has a tropical climate?
13. **Region** Name four of the mountain ranges found in the United States.

Section 2 An Economic Leader

14. **Place** Name four of the mineral resources found in the United States.
15. **Economics** Name four of the South's agricultural products.
16. **Human/Environment Interaction** What is happening to America's landfills?

Section 3 The Americans

17. **History** Why did the American colonists want independence from Britain?
18. **Culture** Which two ethnic groups have grown the fastest in the United States?
19. **Culture** Which part of the United States did Georgia O'Keeffe show in her paintings?

The United States

Place Location Activity

On a separate sheet of paper, match the letters on the map with the numbered places listed below.

1. Rocky Mountains
2. Mississippi River
3. Appalachian Mountains
4. Washington, D.C.
5. Chicago
6. Lake Superior
7. Ohio River
8. Gulf of Mexico
9. Texas
10. Los Angeles

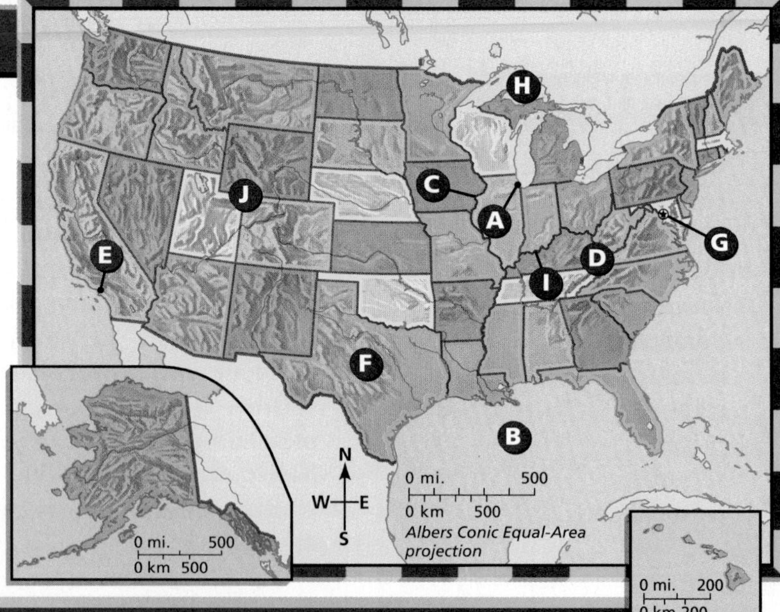

Self-Check Quiz Visit the ***Geography: The World and Its People*** Web site at gwip.glencoe.com and click on **Chapter 4—Self-Check Quizzes** to prepare for the Chapter Test.

Critical Thinking

20. Understanding Cause and Effect What physical features in the Midwest have affected the economy of that region?

21. Categorizing Information Draw a diagram like the one below. In each outer oval, write two facts about the United States under each heading.

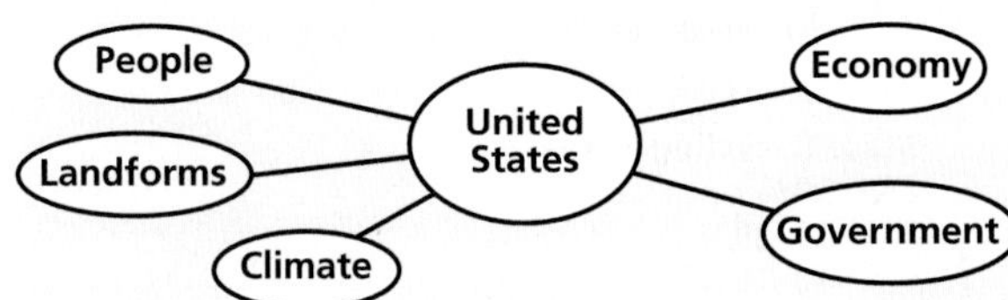

GeoJournal Activity

22. Writing a Paragraph Write a paragraph describing the economic region in which you live. Explain what people in your area generally do for a living.

Mental Mapping Activity

23. Focusing on the Region Draw a simple outline map of the United States, then label the following:

- Appalachian Mountains
- Rocky Mountains
- Mississippi River
- Atlantic Ocean
- Great Plains
- Great Lakes
- Alaska
- Hawaii
- Pacific Ocean
- Gulf of Mexico

Technology Skills Activity

24. Using a Spreadsheet Choose one of the physical regions of the United States. List the names of the states in that region in a spreadsheet beginning with cell A2 and continuing down column A. List the populations of each state in column B, beginning with cell B2. Then make a bar graph that shows the populations of the states in that region.

Standardized Test Practice

Directions: Study the graph, then answer the following questions.

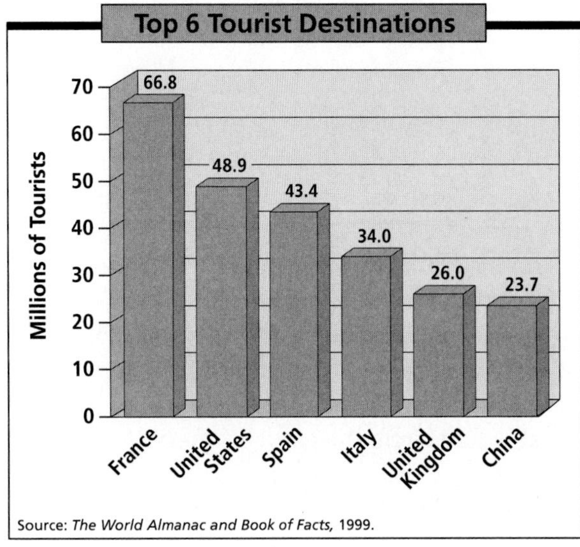

1. According to the graph, about how many tourists visited the United States in 1999?

A 48.9

B 66.8

C 48,900

D 48,900,000

2. Which country on the graph had the <u>least</u> number of tourists?

F France

G China

H Spain

J Italy

Test-Taking Tip: A common error when reading graphs is overlooking the information on the bottom and the side of the graph. Check the sides of the graph to see what the numbers mean.

EYE on the Environment

TOO MUCH Trash

Tons of Trash If you are an average American, you throw away about 4 pounds (2 kg) of trash each day. Not much, right? Think again. That is 1,460 pounds (663 kg) a year. By age 13, you have produced almost 10 tons (9 t) of trash!

Americans create more than a third of the world's trash—200 million tons (181 million t) each year. That is enough to fill a line of garbage trucks that would circle the earth 8 times!

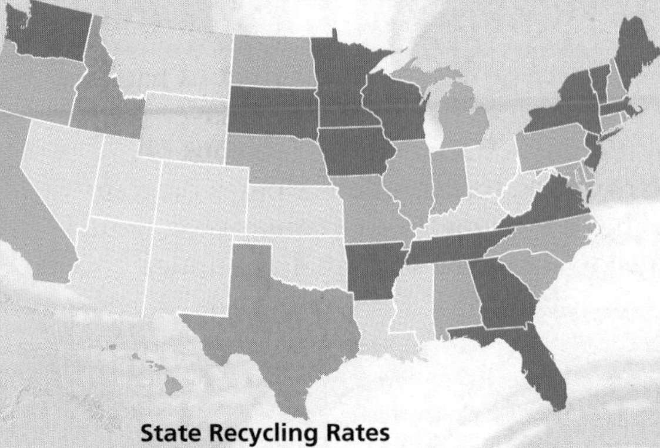

State Recycling Rates
- 30% or greater
- 20–29%
- 10–19%
- Less than 10%
- Unavailable

Source: U.S. EPA Municipal Solid Waste Handbook—Internet Version.

What happens to trash?

- Most ends up in landfills.
- Some is burned in incinerators.
- Some is dumped into lakes, rivers, and oceans.

All of these disposal methods create pollution and harm living things. When landfills fill up, new ones must be created. But sites for new landfills are getting hard to find. Would you want to live near one?

The Three R's Surprisingly, the solution to too much trash is simple. We need to produce less waste. How? By following the three R's—reduce, reuse, and recycle.

- REDUCE the amount of trash you throw away each day.
- REUSE products and containers.
- RECYCLE some of your trash. About 80 percent of household trash can be recycled.

If we reduce, reuse, and recycle, we can win the war against trash.

Trash piles up at a landfill in New Jersey.

Making a Difference

Dig It! You are at the ball game. You toss part of your hot dog into a trash can. Eventually, the hot dog goes to a landfill. How long will it take the hot dog to decay in a landfill?

In 1973 archaeologist William Rathje began the Garbage Project. He wanted to "dig up" facts about the trash Americans throw away. Rathje and his University of Arizona students spent years studying garbage from landfills across the United States. His research results are full of surprises. In some landfills, team members found foods such as steaks and hot dogs that were 15 to 20 years old! Lack of air, light, and moisture prevents wastes from breaking down. Another surprise: About a third of the trash in landfills is paper. Yard waste, food scraps, plastics, construction materials, and furniture are some of the other items we throw away.

William Rathje

Recycling to the Max Linda Munn and her husband, Frank Schiavo, are teachers in California. They have not set out a curbside garbage can in more than 20 years. That is because they recycle or compost almost everything they use. They produce only about two handfuls of trash a week—and that goes to a recycling center, too.

What Can You Do?

Make Toys From Trash

Create toys from discarded clean paper, cardboard, or plastic. Have a class contest and award prizes to students who reuse trash in the most creative ways.

Campaign Against Waste

Investigate products used every day. Which ones have too much packaging—layers of plastic or paper thrown away once the product is used? Can you think of ways to eliminate the excess? Identify companies that make these products and send them a letter or an e-mail outlining your packaging changes.

Use the Internet

Click the Games option at *www.edf.org/Earth2Kids* to learn more about recycling. Also check out the Environmental Protection Agency's kids' page at *www.epa.gov/epaoswer/osw/kids.htm*

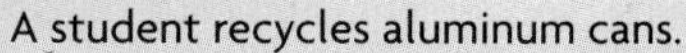
A student recycles aluminum cans.

Canada

The World and Its People NATIONAL GEOGRAPHIC

To learn more about Canada's people and places, view ***The World and Its People*** **Chapter 5** video.

Geography online

Chapter Overview Visit the ***Geography: The World and Its People*** Web site at gwip.glencoe.com and click on **Chapter 5–Chapter Overviews** to preview information about Canada.

Section 1 Landforms of the North

Guide to Reading

Main Idea

Canada is a vast country with many landforms and climates.

Terms to Know

- province
- glacier
- peninsula
- tundra
- prairie
- cordillera

Places to Locate

- Laurentian Highlands
- St. Lawrence River
- Hudson Bay
- Canadian Shield
- Interior Plains
- Rocky Mountains
- Coast Mountains

Reading Strategy

Create a chart like this one. In each space write the name of one of Canada's six physical regions and a fact about it.

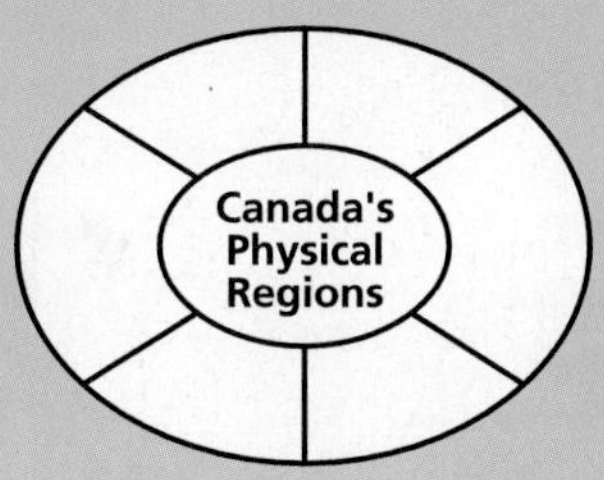

◀ Vancouver, British Columbia

NATIONAL GEOGRAPHIC **Exploring Our World**

Have you ever seen up close and personal a lumbering, snarling grizzly bear? Many tourists come to Banff National Park in western Canada hoping to spot such a creature. Located in the Rocky Mountains, Banff is Canada's oldest, best-loved, and busiest national park. More than 4 million visitors a year are drawn to its spectacular mountain scenery.

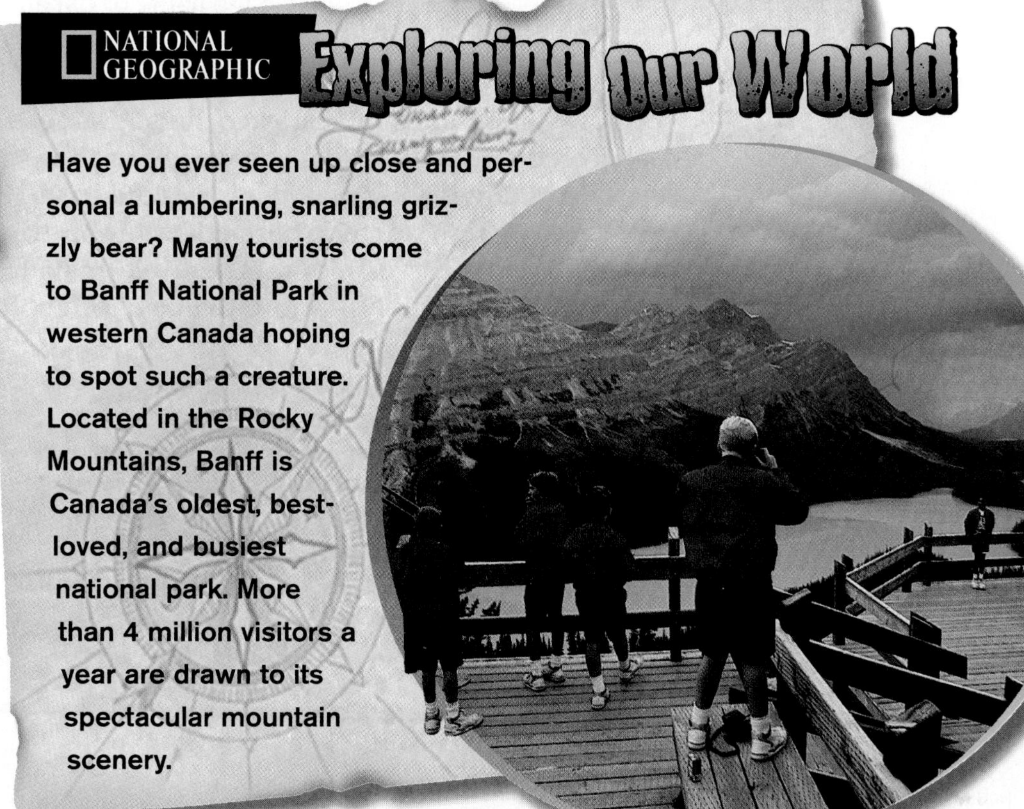

Vikings first landed their longboats on its eastern coast around A.D. 1000. Niagara Falls thunders in the southeast. Grizzly bears roam its western regions. What country are we describing? It is Canada.

From Atlantic to Pacific

The political map on page 144 shows you that Canada is located north of the contiguous United States. Between the two countries lies the world's longest undefended border, which stretches 5,522 miles (8,887 km) across North America. No military troops try to halt the thousands of people who cross this border every day. Like the United States, Canada has the Atlantic Ocean on its eastern coast and the Pacific Ocean on its western coast. The Arctic Ocean lies to the far north.

Canada is the world's second-largest country in land area. Only Russia is larger. Instead of being made up of states, Canada has 10 **provinces,** or regional political divisions. It also includes 3 territories.

Look at the map below to find the provinces of Newfoundland (NOO•fuhn•luhnd), Nova Scotia, New Brunswick, Prince Edward Island, Quebec (kwih•BEHK), Ontario, Manitoba, Saskatchewan (suh•SKA•chuh•wuhn), Alberta, and British Columbia. Now find the Yukon Territory and the Northwest Territories. In 1999 a third territory—Nunavut (NOO•nuh•vuht)—was carved out of part of the Northwest Territories. This area is the homeland of the Inuit, a Native American people.

✓ Reading Check **What is the name of Canada's newest territory?**

Canada's Landforms

Thousands of years ago, huge **glaciers,** or giant sheets of ice, covered most of Canada. The weight of these glaciers pushed much of the land down and created a large low basin. Highlands rose on the western, eastern, and northern edges of this basin. Water filled the land that was pushed very low. As a result, Canada today has many lakes and inland waterways—more than any other country in the world.

Geographers divide Canada's vast water-studded land into six physical regions. These regions are the Eastern Highlands, the St. Lawrence and Great Lakes Lowlands, the Canadian Shield and Arctic Islands, the Interior Plains, the Rocky Mountains, and the Pacific Coast.

The Eastern Highlands Along Canada's southeastern Atlantic coast stretch the Appalachian Highlands. They continue farther south through the eastern United States as the Appalachian Mountains. In Canada's northeast, across the St. Lawrence River, lies another highland area—the **Laurentian** (law•REHN•chuhn) **Highlands.** Traveling through both of these parts of Canada, you see rolling hills and low mountains. The valleys between are dotted with tidy farms. Forests blanket much of the landscape. Many deepwater harbors nestle along the jagged, rocky coasts.

The St. Lawrence and Great Lakes Lowlands Cutting through the eastern highland areas are the lowlands of the **St. Lawrence River.** These lowlands continue west to the Great Lakes region. The St. Lawrence River and the Great Lakes form the major waterway

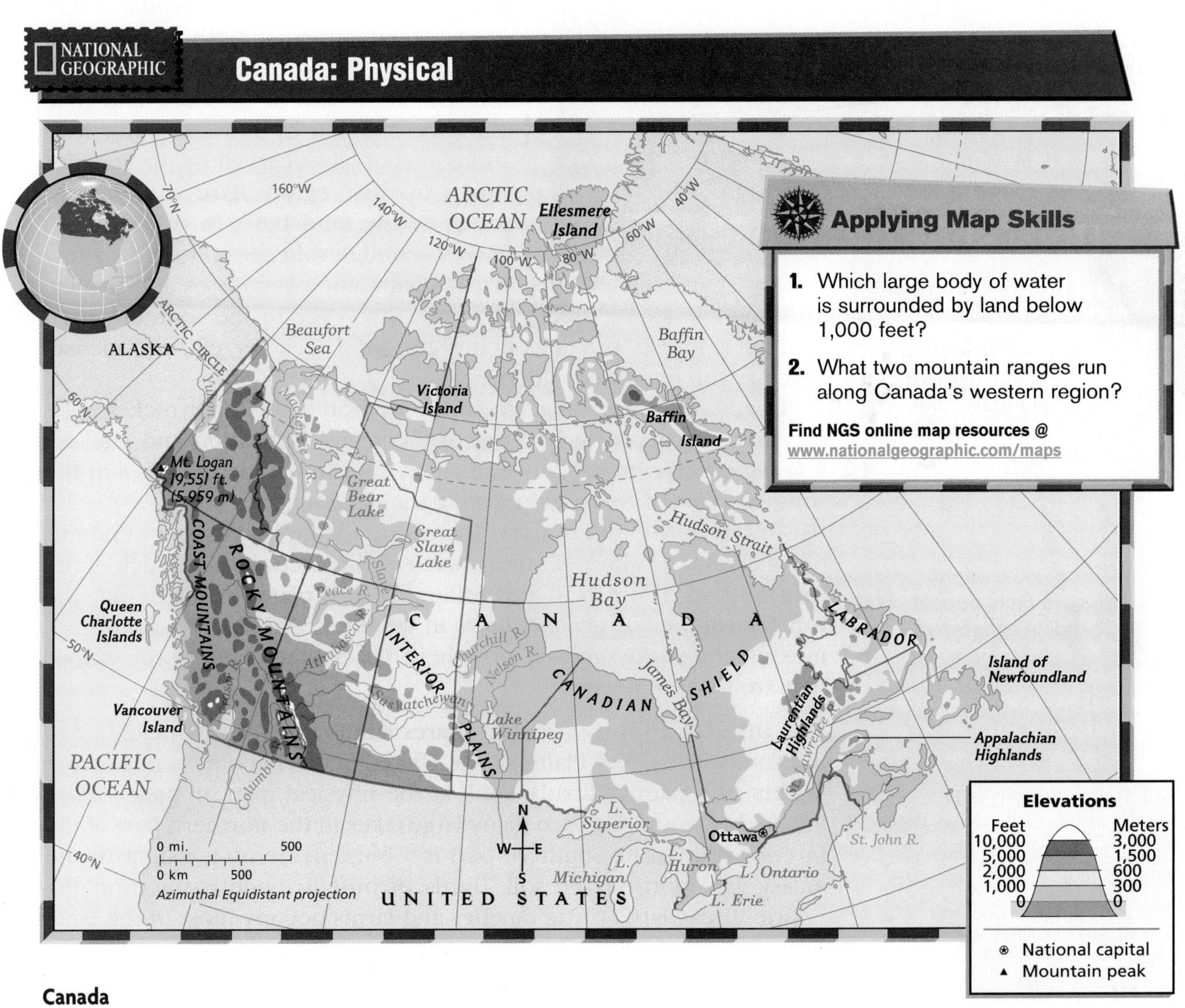

Horseshoe Falls, Canada

Canada's Horseshoe Falls—one of the two waterfalls that make up Niagara Falls—lies on the Niagara River, which flows from Lake Erie into Lake Ontario.

Place How might Niagara Falls benefit Canada's economy?

linking the Atlantic coast and central Canada. Huge, slow-moving barges carrying grain, ore, coal, and other resources course through this waterway that Canada shares with the United States.

Find the St. Lawrence River valley on the physical map on page 145. Now find the peninsula in Ontario that is bordered by Lake Ontario, Lake Erie, and Lake Huron. A peninsula is a piece of land with water on three sides. The St. Lawrence River valley and this peninsula have rich soil, good transportation routes, and sprawling urban centers. You find most of Canada's people, industries, and farms here.

The Canadian Shield and the Arctic Islands Wrapped around **Hudson Bay** is the huge, horseshoe-shaped region known as the **Canadian Shield.** It includes about half of Canada's land area. Hills worn down by erosion along with thousands of lakes carved by glaciers dot much of this region. Bare rock covers much of the land here. In other places there is enough thin soil to support a few hardy plants, such as mosses and shrubs. This soil cannot be used for farming, however. In the southern part, evergreen forests provide shelter and food for deer, elk, and moose. Much of the region is wilderness.

Deep within the Canadian Shield are iron ore, copper, nickel, gold, and uranium deposits. Because of the region's location and climate, few people live here. Many Canadians vacation along the lakes in the southern part of this region during the summer.

To the north lie the Arctic Islands. Ten large islands and hundreds of small ones lie almost entirely north of the Arctic Circle. Much of the land consists of tundra—vast rolling, treeless plains in which only the top few inches of ground thaw in summer. Only low-lying bushes, mosses, and sturdy grasses grow here. Glacial ice blankets the islands that are farthest north.

The Interior Plains Canada shares landforms with its neighbor to the south. The Great Plains of the United States become the **Interior Plains** of western Canada. Look at the physical map on page 145 to locate this region. You see many large lakes in the northern part of the Interior Plains. The southern part is a huge prairie—a rolling, inland grassy area with fertile soil. Herds of buffalo once roamed on the prairie. Today large cattle ranches and farms occupy most of the land.

The Rocky Mountains Another landform shared by Canada and the United States is the **Rocky Mountains,** part of an area called the cordillera (KAWR•duhl•YEHR•uh). A **cordillera** is a group of mountain ranges that run side by side. The Canadian Rockies are known for their scenic beauty and rich mineral resources. Tourists from around the world are drawn to this area, particularly to Banff and Jasper National Parks.

The Pacific Coast West of the Rockies you cross high plateaus until you reach the **Coast Mountains.** These mountains skirt Canada's Pacific shore and form another part of the cordillera. Like the Rockies, they cross into the United States.

A string of islands off Canada's west coast are actually partly underwater peaks of the Coast Mountains. The Inside Passage—a waterway that is 1,000 miles (1,609 km) long—separates these islands from the mainland Coast ranges. You can use the Inside Passage to travel by boat between the city of Seattle in Washington State and ports on Alaska's southeastern tail. Along the way, narrow fingers of the sea snake inland between steep mountainsides.

Near Canada's border with Alaska, several mountains soar more than 15,000 feet (4,572 m). Mount Logan—Canada's highest peak—even reaches 19,551 feet (5,959 m). Most of the people in the Pacific Coast region live along the coast and in river valleys that cut through the mountains.

✓Reading Check **What are two landforms that Canada shares with the United States?**

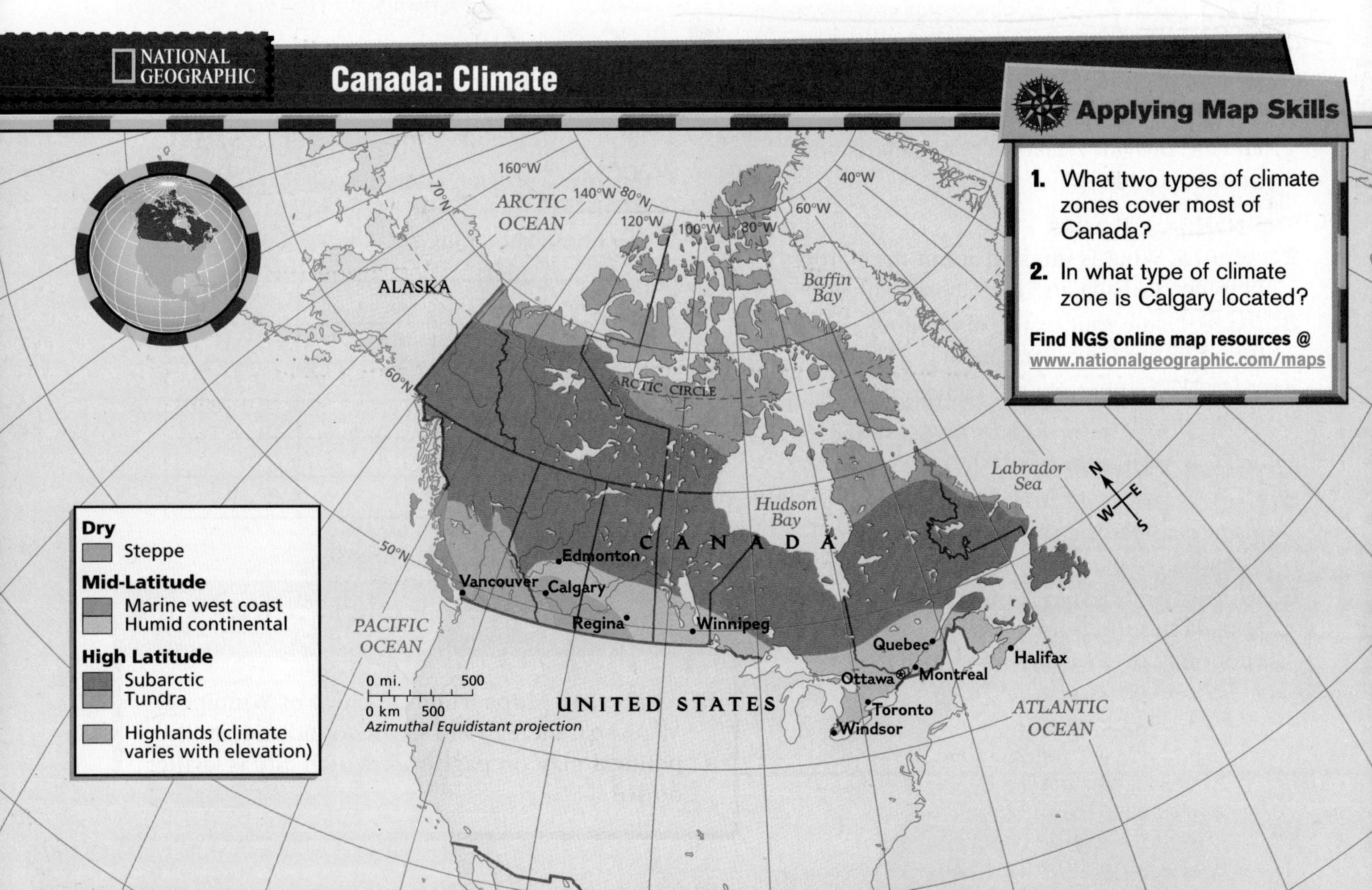

The Climate

One feature that Canada does not share with the United States is climate. The map on page 147 shows you that Canada generally has a cool or cold climate. In Canada's far north, people shiver in the cold tundra climate. Farther south, between 70°N and 50°N latitude, you find a subarctic climate with short, cool summers and long, cold winters.

Southeastern Canada has a humid continental climate. Winters can be long, cold, and snowy here. Summers are short and sometimes hot. As you might guess, most Canadians live in this area.

The humid continental climate continues west of the Great Lakes to the Interior Plains. The western part of the Plains has similar temperatures but less rainfall, making for a dry steppe climate. Rainfall here is low because of the rain shadow effect of the Rocky Mountains.

The southwestern Pacific coast, with its marine west coast climate, is the only area in Canada that has wet, mild winters. The Coast Mountains in this region cause warm winds from the Pacific Ocean to release moisture. The western, or windward, side of the mountains gets more rain and has warmer temperatures than any other part of Canada. In fact, British Columbia's capital—Victoria—is known for its well-kept gardens that bloom year-round.

✓Reading Check **Which part of Canada has wet, mild winters?**

Assessment

Defining Terms

1. **Define** province, glacier, peninsula, tundra, prairie, cordillera.

Recalling Facts

2. **Region** What is unusual about the border between Canada and the United States?
3. **Place** Name four of the mineral resources found in the Canadian Shield.
4. **Region** In what type of climate do most Canadians live?

Critical Thinking

5. **Understanding Cause and Effect** How did glaciers affect the physical landscape of Canada?
6. **Analyzing Information** What region in Canada has the most people and the most economic activity?

Graphic Organizer

7. **Organizing Information** Draw a chart like this one. For each climate type listed, write where in Canada that climate exists and one fact about the climate.

Climate	Region	Fact
Tundra		
Subarctic		
Humid Continental		
Steppe		
Marine West Coast		

Applying Geography Skills

8. **Analyzing Maps** Find the cities of Winnipeg, Manitoba, and St. John's, Newfoundland, on the political map on page 144. Which city is farther north?

Geography Skill

Reading a Physical Map

A map that shows the different heights of the land is called a **physical map.** Physical maps use colors and shading to also show *relief*—or how flat or rugged the land surface is. Colors are also used to show the land's *elevation*—or height above sea level. Green often shows the lowest elevations (closest to sea level). Yellows, oranges, browns, and reds usually mean higher elevations. Sometimes the highest areas, such as mountain peaks, are white.

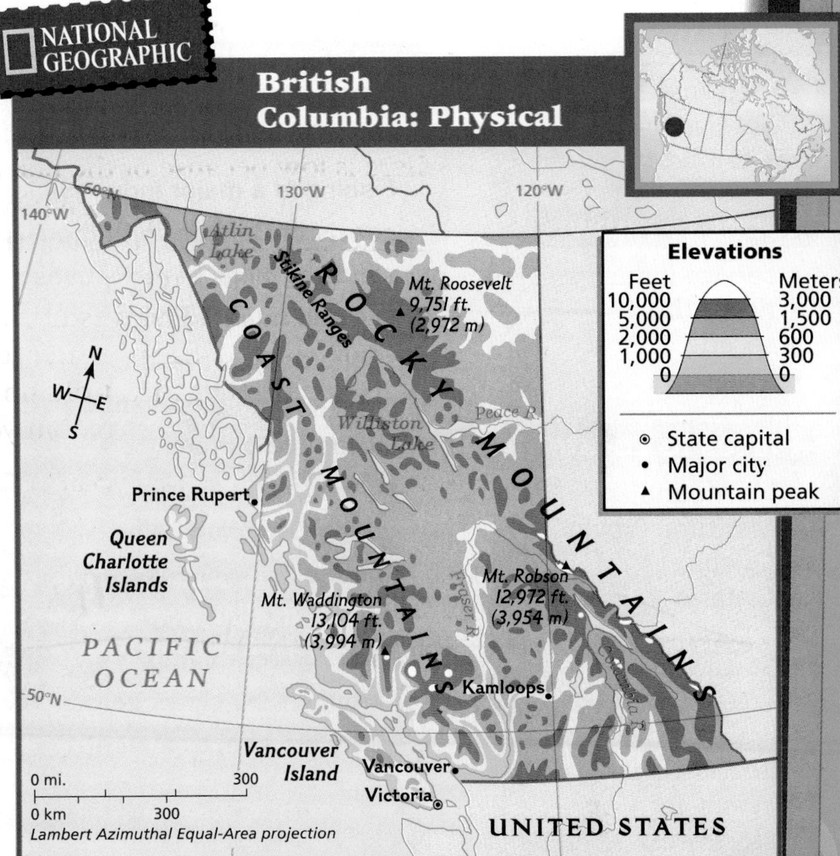

Learning the Skill

To read a physical map, apply these steps:

- Read the map title to identify the region shown on the map.
- Use the map key to find the meaning of colors and symbols.
- Identify the areas of highest and lowest elevation on the map.
- Find important physical features, including mountains, rivers, and coastlines.
- Mentally map the actual shape of the land.

Practicing the Skill

Look at the map to answer the following:

1. What province is highlighted on the map?
2. What mountain ranges are labeled?
3. What is the elevation of the green areas on the map (in feet and meters)?
4. What color on the map means 2,000–5,000 feet (600–1,500 m)?
5. Briefly describe the physical landscape of the area shown on the map, moving from west to east.

Applying the Skill

Look at the physical map of Canada on page 145. Describe the physical landscape of the country, moving from east to west.

GO TO Practice key skills with **Glencoe Skillbuilder Interactive Workbook, Level 1.**

Section 2

A Resource-Rich Country

Guide to Reading

Main Idea

Canada's economy benefits from rich natural resources, skilled workers, and close trading ties with the United States.

Terms to Know

- service industry
- newsprint
- secede
- acid rain

Places to Locate

- Newfoundland
- Maritime Provinces
- Quebec
- Ontario
- Ottawa
- St. Lawrence Seaway
- Prairie Provinces
- British Columbia
- Yukon Territory
- Northwest Territories
- Nunavut

Reading Strategy

Create a chart like this one and list Canada's six economic regions in the left column. In the right column, list the main economic activities in each region.

Economic Regions	Economic Activities

NATIONAL GEOGRAPHIC **Exploring Our World**

Fishing is a major industry along the coasts of Canada. With thousands of miles of rocky coastline and hundreds of sheltered harbors, the provinces on the Atlantic Ocean are perfectly suited to this activity. A young Canadian helps the family business by banding lobsters—placing thick bands around their claws before they are sent to market.

Fishing is Canada's oldest industry. Yet it is only one of many economic activities that Canadians carry on today. Productive farms, forests, mines, and businesses have turned Canada into one of the world's most advanced economies.

Canada's Economic Regions

Canada's economy is similar to that of the United States. Canada is known for fertile farmland, rich natural resources, and skilled workers. Manufacturing, farming, and service industries are the country's major economic activities. **Service industries** are businesses that provide services to people instead of producing goods. Fishing, mining, and lumbering are also important to the Canadian economy.

Canada, like the United States, has a free market economy in which people start and run businesses with limited government involvement. Canada's government, however, plays a more direct role in the

Canadian economy. For example, Canada's national and provincial governments provide health care for citizens. Broadcasting, transportation, and electric power companies are also government-owned. These public services might not have been available in Canada's remote areas without government support.

Geographers group Canada's provinces and territories into six economic regions: Newfoundland and the Maritime Provinces, Quebec, Ontario, the Prairie Provinces, British Columbia, and the North.

Newfoundland and the Maritime Provinces Canada's easternmost economic region is formed by **Newfoundland** and the **Maritime Provinces.** The Maritime Provinces are Nova Scotia, New Brunswick, and Prince Edward Island. Fishing has long been a major economic activity here. The Grand Banks, off the coast of Newfoundland, is known as one of the best fishing grounds in the world. As a result of overfishing, however, fishing has been regulated. Today fewer Canadians make a living from the sea.

Farming is limited in this region. A short growing season and thin, rocky soil discourage large-scale agriculture. Yet small farms throughout the Maritime Provinces grow crops such as potatoes and apples.

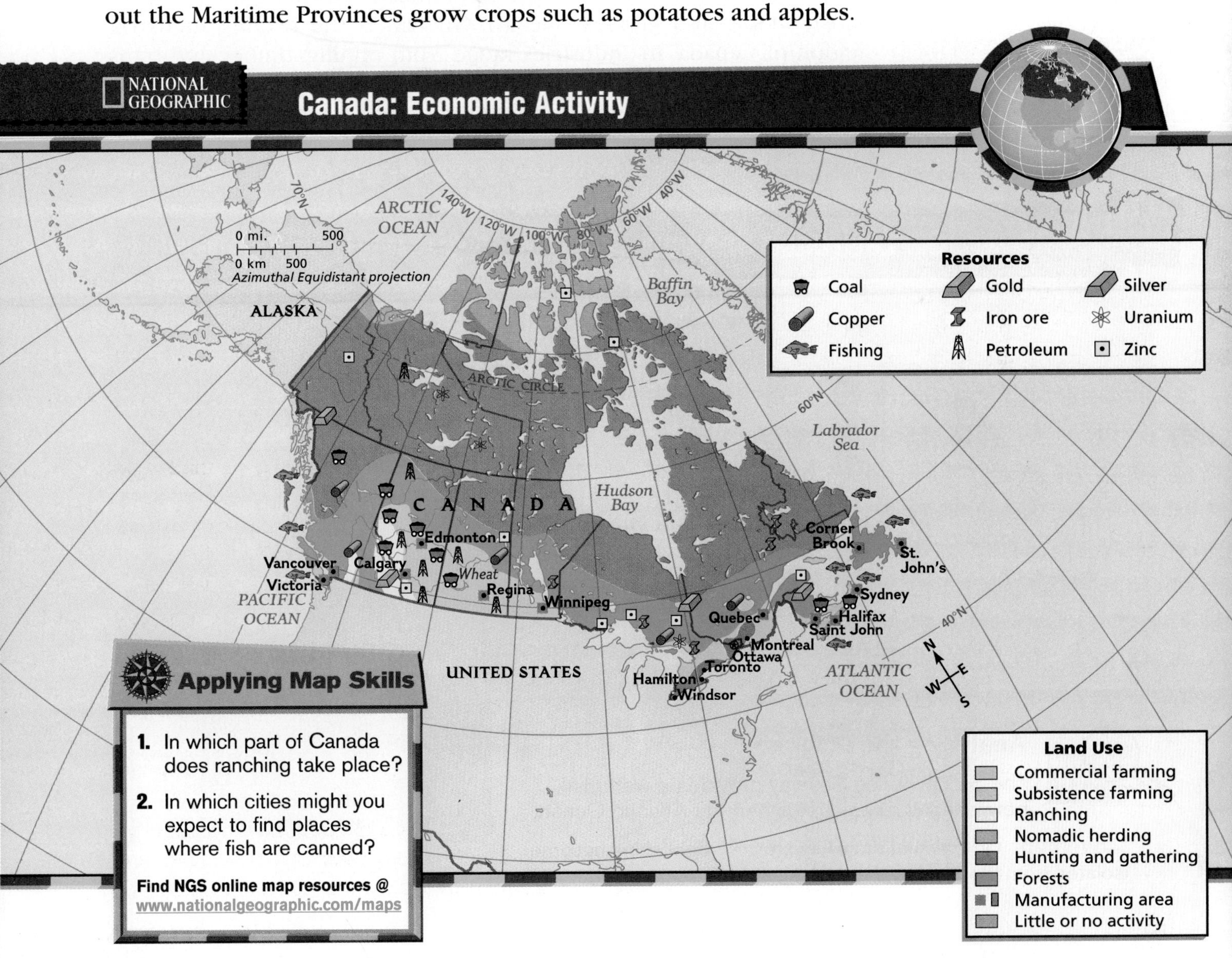

Applying Map Skills

1. In which part of Canada does ranching take place?
2. In which cities might you expect to find places where fish are canned?

Find NGS online map resources @ www.nationalgeographic.com/maps

Manufacturing and mining provide jobs for most people in this region. Tourism is increasingly important, too. In 1997 Canada opened a bridge connecting Prince Edward Island to the mainland. Since then, the number of visitors to the island has doubled. Halifax is a major shipping center. Its harbor remains open in winter when ice closes most other eastern Canadian ports.

Quebec Canada's largest province in land area is **Quebec.** It is home to almost 25 percent of Canadians. Most of Quebec's people live in cities in and around the St. Lawrence River valley. Montreal, an important port on the St. Lawrence River, is Canada's second-largest city and a major financial and industrial center. The city of Quebec, founded by the French in 1608, is the capital of the province. Many historic sites and a European charm make it popular with tourists.

Manufacturing and service industries are dominant in Quebec's economy. To the north, you find miners providing the province with iron ore, copper, and gold. Other economic activities in Quebec include agriculture and fishing.

Ontario Canada's second-largest province is **Ontario,** but it has the most people and greatest wealth. Ontario is the leading industrial region of Canada. Its industries range from mining, timber, and transport equipment to oil, gas, and chemicals. The region produces more than half of Canada's manufactured goods.

NATIONAL GEOGRAPHIC

St. Lawrence Seaway

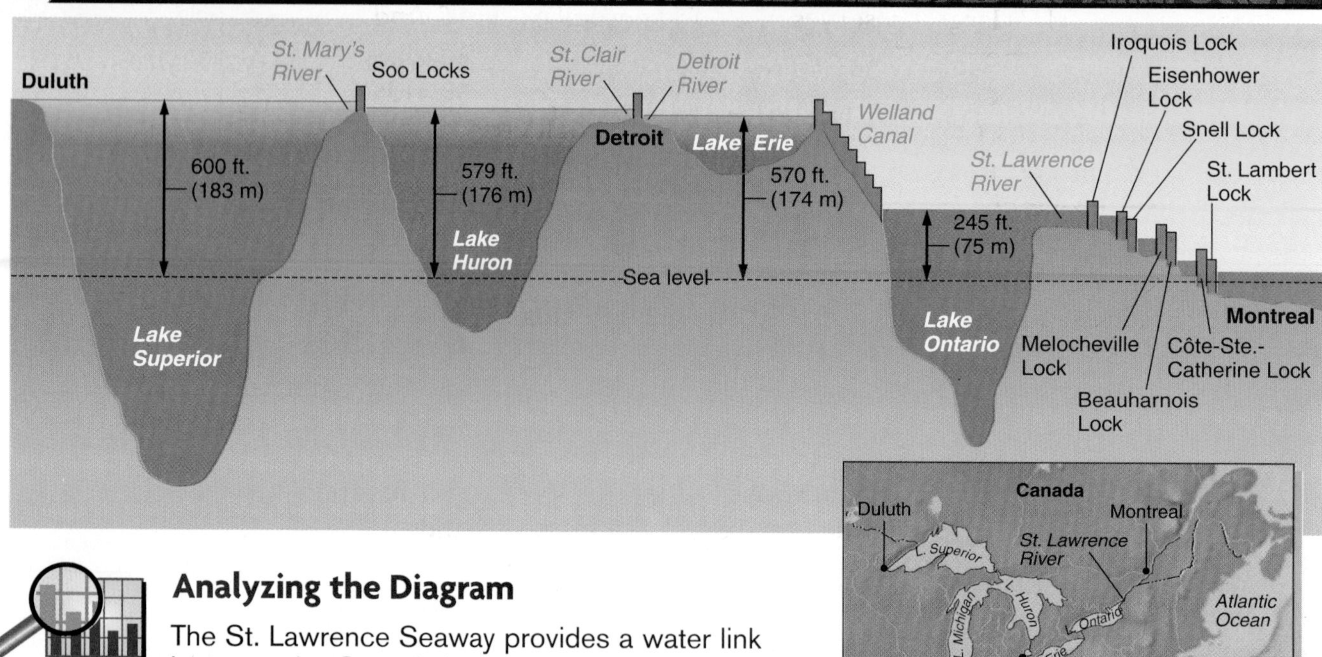

Analyzing the Diagram

The St. Lawrence Seaway provides a water link between the Great Lakes and the Atlantic Ocean.

Movement On which of the lakes shown would ships become isolated from the Seaway if the lake level dropped sharply?

Southern Ontario also has fertile land and a growing season long enough for commercial farming. Farmers here grow grains, fruits, and vegetables and raise beef and dairy cattle.

Toronto, the capital of Ontario, is Canada's largest city. It is also the country's chief manufacturing, financial, and communications center. Most of Canada's large corporations have their headquarters here. **Ottawa,** the capital city of Canada, lies in Ontario near the border with Quebec. Many Canadians work in government offices in Ottawa.

Ontario borders the Great Lakes and the St. Lawrence River. To open the Great Lakes to ocean shipping, the United States and Canada built the **St. Lawrence Seaway.** Look at the diagram on page 152. It shows how a system of locks and canals allows ships to pass between the Great Lakes and the Atlantic Ocean. Turn to page 164 to learn more about the St. Lawrence Seaway.

Nighttime Harvest

At harvest time in southern Saskatchewan, the work goes on around the clock. The farms in the Prairie Provinces are large and depend on machinery.

Region **What other economic activities take place in the Prairie Provinces?**

The Prairie Provinces The **Prairie Provinces**—Manitoba, Saskatchewan, and Alberta—spread between the Canadian Shield and the Rocky Mountains. Farming and ranching are major economic activities here. Canada is one of the world's biggest producers of wheat, most of which is exported to Europe and Asia. Ranchers in Alberta raise most of Canada's cattle.

Some of the world's largest reserves of oil and natural gas are found in Alberta and Saskatchewan. These resources contribute to Canada's wealth. Huge pipelines carry the oil and gas to other parts of Canada and to the United States. Canada's fossil fuels and hydroelectric power make it the fifth-largest producer of energy in the world.

The Prairie Provinces have some of the fastest-growing cities in Canada. Calgary and Edmonton, both in Alberta, are leading oil and agricultural centers. Winnipeg, in Manitoba, is a major transportation and business center that links eastern and western Canada.

British Columbia Thick forests blanket much of **British Columbia.** As you might guess, timber, pulp, and paper industries provide much of British Columbia's income. The province helps make Canada the world's leading producer of **newsprint,** the type of paper used for printing newspapers. The mining of coal, copper, and lead also adds to the wealth of British Columbia.

Agriculture and fishing are strong economic activities in British Columbia. In river valleys between mountains, farmers raise cattle and poultry. They also grow fruits and vegetables. Fishing fleets sail out into the Pacific Ocean to catch salmon and other kinds of fish. Vancouver is a bustling trade center and the nation's main Pacific port.

The North Geese, moose, bears, and caribou are the main inhabitants of many of Canada's northern regions. This area includes the **Yukon Territory,** the **Northwest Territories,** and **Nunavut.** The North accounts for 40 percent of Canada's land, but few people live here. Most are Inuit and other Native Americans who follow traditional hunting and gathering ways of life. The far north is Arctic wilderness. Many resources are thought to lie hidden beneath the frozen ground. The harsh climate and lack of roads make it very costly to mine these resources.

Web Activity Visit the ***Geography: The World and Its People*** Web site at gwip.glencoe.com and click on **Chapter 5—Student Web Activities** to learn more about Quebec's French culture.

Economic Issues Canada's economy faces a number of issues. One issue concerns Quebec. About 80 percent of Quebec's population is French-speaking. The rest of Canada is largely English-speaking. Many people in Quebec want to **secede,** or withdraw, from Canada. If that happens, the province's economy would suffer.

Experts also worry about **acid rain,** or rain containing high amounts of chemical pollutants. This rain is damaging Canada's lakes and forests. Below-normal water levels on the Great Lakes are also causing concern.

A third issue involves the United States. About $1 billion worth of trade passes between Canada and the United States each day. In 1994 Canada, the United States, and Mexico created the North American Free Trade Agreement (NAFTA) to remove trade barriers among the three countries. Some Canadians fear that their economy is too dependent on the United States. They worry that the American economy is so large that it will dominate the partnership.

Reading Check **Which economic region is Canada's main wheat-growing area?**

Assessment

Defining Terms

1. **Define** service industry, newsprint, secede, acid rain.

Recalling Facts

2. **Economics** What are the results of overfishing the Grand Banks?
3. **Place** Identify five facts about Toronto.
4. **Economics** Which province is the world's leading producer of newsprint?

Critical Thinking

5. **Making Inferences** Why is Vancouver a useful port for Canadian trade with Asian countries?
6. **Drawing Conclusions** Explain why some Canadians fear NAFTA.

Graphic Organizer

7. **Organizing Information** Draw a chart like this one. Then list each province or territory, what economic region it is in, what resources are found in it, and major cities, if any.

Province or Territory	Economic Region	Resources	Cities

Applying Geography Skills

8. **Analyzing Maps** Look at the economic activity map on page 151. Name the types of economic activity that take place north of the Arctic Circle.

Section 3 The Canadians

Guide to Reading

Main Idea

Canadians of many different backgrounds live in towns and cities close to the United States border.

Terms to Know

- colony
- dominion
- parliamentary democracy
- prime minister
- bilingual

Places to Locate

- Quebec
- Montreal
- Nova Scotia
- New Brunswick
- Prince Edward Island
- Toronto

Reading Strategy

Draw a chart like this one and give at least two facts about Canada for each topic.

History		
Population		
Culture		

NATIONAL GEOGRAPHIC **Exploring Our World**

Arrêt or Stop? People living in Quebec need to know both words when they cross the street. Canada has two official languages—English and French. All government documents are printed in both languages. In Quebec, even the school system is divided into French and English.

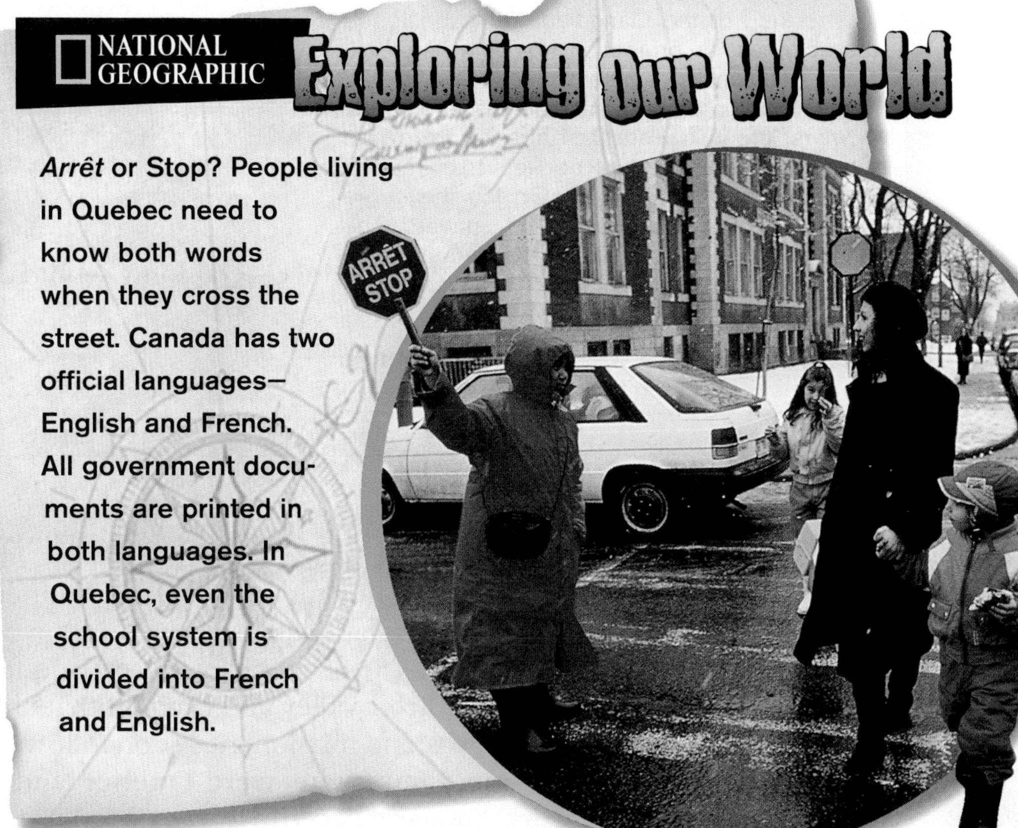

Like the United States, Canada's population is made up of many different cultures. The largest group of Canadians has a European heritage, but the country is home to people from all continents. Yet unlike the United States, Canada has had difficulty achieving a strong sense of being one nation. The country's vast distances and largely separate cultures have made Canadians feel more closely attached to their own region or culture than to Canada as a whole.

Canada's History

Canada's first peoples—the Inuit and other Native Americans—adjusted to the environment in a number of different ways. As a result, they developed a great variety of cultures. Some lived in coastal fishing villages. Others were hunters and gatherers constantly on the move. Still others founded permanent settlements near rivers where they raised crops on fertile land.

Thousands of years passed before European settlers arrived. The first Europeans in Canada were Viking explorers from northern Europe who landed in about A.D. 1000. They lived for a while on the

Clothing

The Inuit of the Canadian Arctic designed their clothes for protection from the harsh climate. Traditional clothing was made up of a caribou or sealskin parka, pants, mittens, and boots. In winter the Inuit wore their furs facing toward the skin. This created air pockets that trapped warm air close to the body. On top they wore another layer with the fur facing outward. The clothing flapped as the wearer moved, creating a breeze that kept the person from overheating while running or working.

Looking Closer How does traditional clothing protect the Inuit from the harsh climate?

Newfoundland coast but eventually left. In 1497 John Cabot, an Italian who was exploring for England, landed near Newfoundland. He claimed the area for England.

Then in 1534 French explorer Jacques Cartier sailed into the St. Lawrence River valley and claimed that area for France. French explorers, settlers, and missionaries soon followed and founded several cities. The most important were **Quebec** and **Montreal.** For almost 230 years, France ruled the area around the St. Lawrence River and the Great Lakes. This region was called New France.

During the 1600s and 1700s, England and France fought each other for territory around the globe. The British battled the French in several wars to win control of eastern North America. The last war, known in the United States as the French and Indian War, ended with a treaty signed in 1763. In that treaty, France gave Britain all of its land in Canada. During this time, European warfare and diseases were destroying the Native American cultures.

From Colony to Nation *Where* Europeans settled reflected their sharp cultural differences. For about 100 years, Great Britain held Canada as a colony. A **colony** is an overseas territory with ties to the parent country. The Atlantic coast and what is today Ontario became home to mostly English-speaking people. Between them lay the largely French-speaking region, which was called Quebec. The British kept Canada's English and French areas separate, with each region having its own colonial government.

Like the American colonists, Canadians wanted to have more control over their lives. In 1867 the British backed Canadian wishes by uniting the territories of Ontario, Quebec, **Nova Scotia,** and **New Brunswick** into one large nation known as the Dominion of Canada. As a **dominion,**

Canada had its own government to run local affairs. British officials in London, however, still controlled Canada's relations with other countries.

The new Canadian government promised continued protection for the French language and culture. Yet many English-speaking Canadians did not always keep to this promise. French speakers often claimed that they were treated unfairly because of their heritage. Canada often was torn apart by disputes between the two ethnic groups.

After Canada's founding, it gradually expanded its territory. In the late 1860s, Britain handed over to Canada a large area of land in western North America. In 1885 the Canadian government completed a railroad that crossed the continent from the Atlantic to the Pacific coast. This encouraged people from abroad and from other parts of Canada to settle in the west. On the vast expanse of prairies, settlers grew grain and raised cattle. Over the next 65 years, these lands—as well as the eastern territories of **Prince Edward Island** and Newfoundland—joined Canada as provinces.

During the 1900s, Canadians fought side by side with the British in two world wars. Canada's loyal support in these conflicts gradually led to the nation's full independence. In 1982 Canadians finally won the right to change their constitution without British approval. Today only one major link between Canada and Britain remains. The British king or queen still reigns as king or queen of Canada, but this is a ceremonial position with no real power.

Canada's Government The Canadians have a British-style parliamentary democracy. In a **parliamentary democracy,** voters elect representatives to a lawmaking body called Parliament. These representatives then choose an official named the **prime minister** to head the government. Since the British king or queen visits Canada only once in a while, a Canadian official called the governor-general carries out most of the government's ceremonial duties.

As you read in Section 2, some people in largely French-speaking Quebec want to pull out of Canada and form their own country. The majority of Quebec's people voted twice against a measure that would lead to independence. Those who favor the move still support independence, however. Only a free Quebec, they claim, can successfully protect French culture in a largely English-speaking North America. As a result, Canada's future as a united country is uncertain.

In recent years, Canada's Native Americans have strengthened their influence as well. In response, the Canadian government has given these peoples more control over land. In 1999 the new territory of Nunavut was created for the Inuit who live in the north. *Nunavut* means "our land" in one of the Inuit languages. The Inuit have formed their own government and also gained control over the minerals in the region.

Reading Check **What kind of government do Canadians have?**

Time to Play

Fifteen-year-old Natalie Menard has been playing ice hockey since she was five years old. Winters are long in Quebec, so Natalie enjoys plenty of time on the ice. Most of her friends are of French descent, and all of their school classes are conducted in French. Natalie also enjoys visiting her cousin Angela, who lives in Toronto, Ontario. More than 6 miles (10 km) of covered walkways and underground tunnels in downtown Toronto connect subways with shops, offices, hotels, and restaurants. Natalie and Angela walk from place to place without even thinking of the weather.

Canada's People and Culture

Although Canada is large in land area, it has only about 30.6 million people. This compares with a population of about 280 million in the United States. Look at the population density map below. It shows you that most Canadians live within 100 miles (161 km) of the United States border.

Canada is a **bilingual** country, or a country that has two official languages—English and French. Yet a growing number of Canadians speak Ukrainian and Chinese. Because of heavy immigration and a high birthrate, Canada's population has grown rapidly since World War II. Today the population is extremely diverse, as you can see from the graph of Canada's ethnic groups on page 111. It also has a long history of religious diversity. Most Canadians are Roman Catholic or Protestant. Still, many Canadians follow Judaism, Buddhism, Hinduism, and Islam.

The Arts and Literature From poetry to novels to drama, Canadian authors write either in English or French about many subjects. The painter-writer Emily Carr portrayed the dark green forests and the Native American cultures of the Pacific Coast in her works. A group of artists, known together as the Group of Seven, used lavish colors and unusual shapes to portray the wild beauty of the Canadian north.

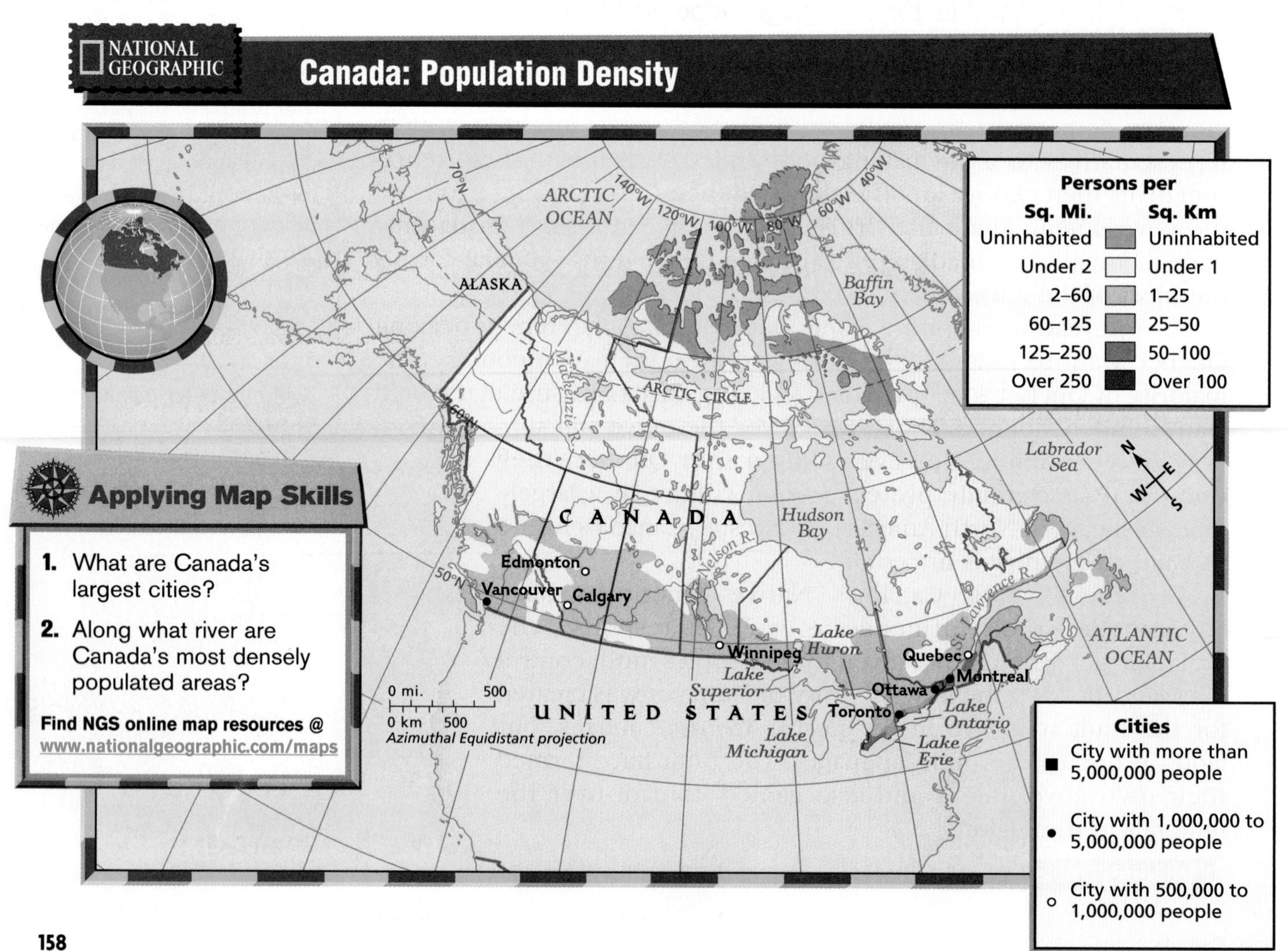

Food, Sports, and Recreation

Because Canada has such ethnic diversity, people here can enjoy a variety of tasty foods. People from many different groups have settled in cities like **Toronto.** You can walk down the street and sample the foods of Ukraine, Greece, Italy, the Caribbean, and China all in the same day.

Canadians enjoy a variety of activities, especially outdoor sports. You will find local parks and national parks crowded with people exercising and having fun. Many young Canadians enjoy playing ice hockey. They also take part in other winter sports, including skiing, skating, and snowboarding. During the summer, they might go sailing on Lake Ontario. Professional football and hockey are tremendous spectator sports. Many Canadian sports fans also flock to see the baseball games played in Toronto's large indoor stadium.

How does Canada's population compare with that of the United States?

Toronto and its suburbs have well over 4 million people, making the area by far Canada's largest urban area.

Location **On what body of water is Toronto located?**

Section 3 Assessment

Defining Terms

1. Define colony, dominion, parliamentary democracy, prime minister, bilingual.

Recalling Facts

2. History Who were the first people to live in Canada?
3. Government What new territory was created in 1999 and what does its name mean?
4. Movement What led to the settlement of western Canada?

Critical Thinking

5. Analyzing Information What is the link between Canada and Great Britain?
6. Summarizing Information What are two reasons for Canada's population growth?

Graphic Organizer

7. Organizing Information Draw a diagram like this one, and list two examples under each heading in the outer ovals.

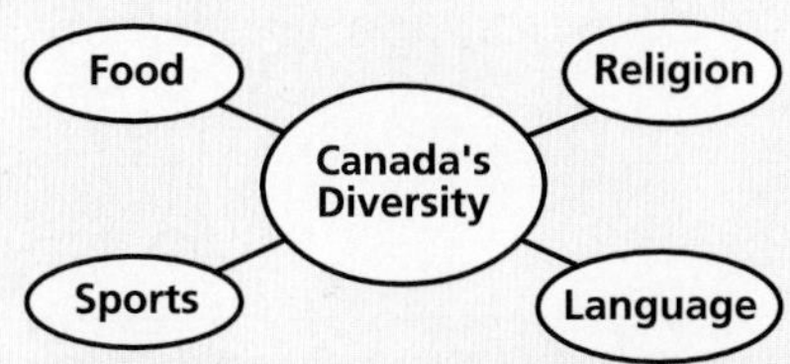

Applying Geography Skills

8. Analyzing Maps Study the population density map on page 158. Which cities have populations between 500,000 and 1,000,000?

Making Connections

ART SCIENCE LITERATURE TECHNOLOGY

Snow and Ice Sculpting

While some art forms can exist almost anywhere, that is not the case for ice and snow sculptures. Both of these art forms find the support and weather they need at the city of Quebec's Winter Carnival. Each year more than 1 million people come to this two-week-long festival to enjoy the arts and to celebrate winter.

A Tradition in Ice Sculpture

Quebec held its first Winter Carnival in 1894 to lift the spirits of local people during the long winter months. A local artist carved likenesses of political leaders out of ice. Since then, ice and snow sculpture have become important features of the Winter Carnival. The centerpiece of the Winter Carnival is its glistening ice palace, home to *Bonhomme,* the snowman mascot of the Winter Carnival. Artists work for months creating the impressive castle, which is bathed in colored lights.

◀ **Quebec's Ice Palace**

A giant snow sculpture ▶

Snow Sculpture

The International Snow Sculpture competition is another annual tradition of the Quebec Winter Carnival. Teams of sculptors from about 20 countries compete to create the winning snow sculpture. Each team begins with a huge block of packed snow weighing between 30 and 40 tons (27 and 36 t). It reaches about 12 feet (4 m) high. Working just as they might with stone or wood, sculptors chisel figures into the snow. This time, however, their work could melt away with only a few days of warm weather. At the high point of the competition, during the Night of the Long Knives, the sculptors work day and night to finish their creations.

Carnival visitors can see other examples of ice and snow sculpture in front of shops and restaurants around the city. They can spend the night in a traditional snow igloo and slide down an icy toboggan run. Other activities include dogsled racing, a snow swim, and a canoe race down the ice-filled St. Lawrence River. With so many unique sights and activities, it is easy to understand how the Quebec Winter Carnival has become the world's largest winter festival.

Making the Connection

1. How did the tradition of snow and ice sculpture start at the Quebec Winter Carnival?
2. How is the art of the Quebec Winter Carnival dependent upon the weather?
3. **Sequencing Information** Describe how artists make snow sculptures in the competition.

Reading Review

Section 1 Landforms of the North

Terms to Know
province
glacier
peninsula
tundra
prairie
cordillera

Main Idea

Canada is a vast country with many landforms and climates.

✓Region Canada, the second-largest country in the world, is rich in natural resources.

✓Region Canada has a variety of landforms, including mountains, lowlands, Arctic wilderness, and prairies.

✓Economics The lowlands of the St. Lawrence River and the Great Lakes region have rich soil and good transportation routes.

✓Region The Canadian Shield, covering half of Canada's land area, is rocky and unsuitable for farming but has mineral resources and water power.

✓Region Most of Canada has a cool or cold climate. Milder temperatures are found in the southern part of the country and the southwest.

Section 2 A Resource-Rich Economy

Terms to Know
service industry
newsprint
secede
acid rain

Main Idea

Canada's economy benefits from rich natural resources, skilled workers, and close trading ties with the United States.

✓Economics Canada is one of the world's most economically advanced countries.

✓Economics Most people in the east make a living in manufacturing, mining, and service industries. Some work in fishing and farming.

✓Culture Quebec and Ontario have Canada's largest cities and most of its people.

✓Economics Farming, ranching, oil, and forestry are major economic activities in the west.

✓Economics Economic challenges include settling regional differences, working out Canada's relationship with the United States, and solving environmental problems.

Section 3 The Canadians

Terms to Know
colony
dominion
parliamentary democracy
prime minister
bilingual

Main Idea

Canadians of many different backgrounds live in towns and cities close to the United States border.

✓History Native Americans were the first Canadians. French and British settlers later built homes in Canada. Large numbers of immigrants have recently come from Asia and Eastern Europe.

✓Government Canada's government is a parliamentary democracy headed by a prime minister.

✓Culture Some people in French-speaking Quebec want to separate from the rest of Canada.

✓Culture Canada's population is made up of many different ethnic groups. English and French are the country's two official languages.

Chapter 5

Assessment and Activities

Using Key Terms

Match the terms in Part A with their definitions in Part B.

A.

1. province
2. glacier
3. tundra
4. secede
5. newsprint
6. acid rain
7. peninsula
8. bilingual
9. prime minister
10. parliamentary democracy

B.

a. having or speaking two languages
b. giant sheet of ice
c. land surrounded by water on three sides
d. voters elect representatives to a lawmaking body called Parliament
e. government leader chosen by members of Parliament
f. vast, dry, treeless plain in the high latitudes
g. type of paper used for printing newspapers
h. regional political division
i. to withdraw
j. precipitation with large amounts of chemicals

Reviewing the Main Ideas

Section 1 Landforms of the North

11. **Location** What three oceans border Canada?
12. **Region** Name three natural resources found in the Interior Plains.
13. **Location** In which physical region do most Canadians live?

Section 2 A Resource-Rich Economy

14. **Government** Describe two ways in which Canada's government plays a role in the nation's economy.
15. **Economics** Why did the United States and Canada build the St. Lawrence Seaway?
16. **Economics** Name three economic activities found in British Columbia.
17. **Human/Environment Interaction** What are two problems affecting Canada's economy?

Section 3 The Canadians

18. **History** Who was the first explorer to claim part of Canada for France?
19. **Culture** Why do some of Quebec's people want independence from Canada?
20. **Culture** What are Canada's two official languages?

Canada

Place Location Activity

On a separate sheet of paper, match the letters on the map with the numbered places listed below.

1. Hudson Bay
2. Nunavut
3. British Columbia
4. Ottawa
5. Quebec (province)
6. St. Lawrence River
7. Rocky Mountains
8. Winnipeg
9. Ontario
10. Nova Scotia

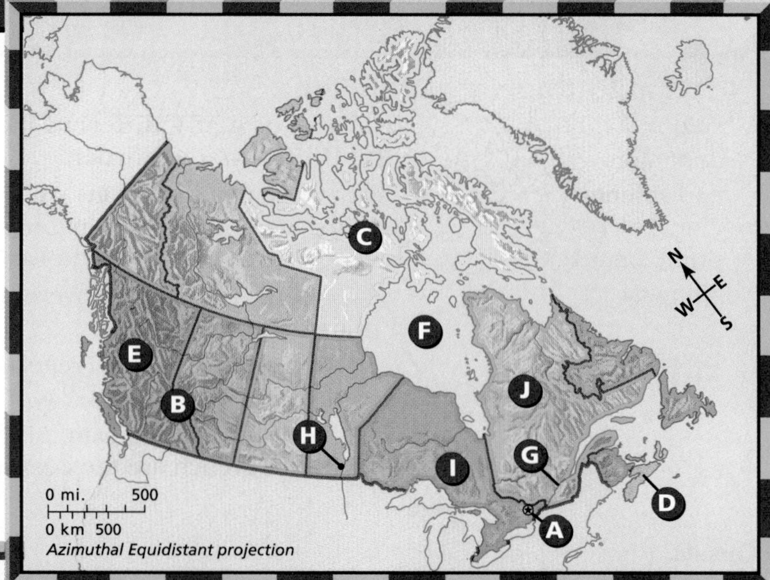

Self-Check Quiz Visit the ***Geography: The World and Its People*** Web site at gwip.glencoe.com and click on **Chapter 5–Self-Check Quizzes** to prepare for the Chapter Test.

 Critical Thinking

21. **Making Comparisons** Compare the overall climate of Canada with the overall climate of the United States.
22. **Analyzing Information** Why do most Canadians live near the United States border?
23. **Categorizing Information** Choose one of Canada's provinces or territories. Complete a chart like the one below with at least two facts or examples under the headings in each section.

Province or Territory	Landforms	Resources
	Major Cities	Products

 GeoJournal Activity 

24. **Writing a Speech** List what you know about how people can use forests and forest products. Then take the role of an environmental leader. Write a short speech explaining how Canada's forests are useful and why they need to be protected.

 Mental Mapping Activity

25. **Focusing on the Region** Draw a simple outline map of Canada, then label the following on your map:
    - Arctic Ocean
    - Pacific Ocean
    - Atlantic Ocean
    - Rocky Mountains
    - Hudson Bay
    - Quebec (province)
    - Ontario
    - British Columbia
    - Nunavut
    - Ottawa

 Technology Skills Activity 

26. **Using the Internet** Access the Internet and search for information on the Inuit and the new territory of Nunavut. Create an illustrated time line that shows the steps leading to the creation of the new territory.

Standardized Test Practice

Directions: Study the graph, then answer the following questions.

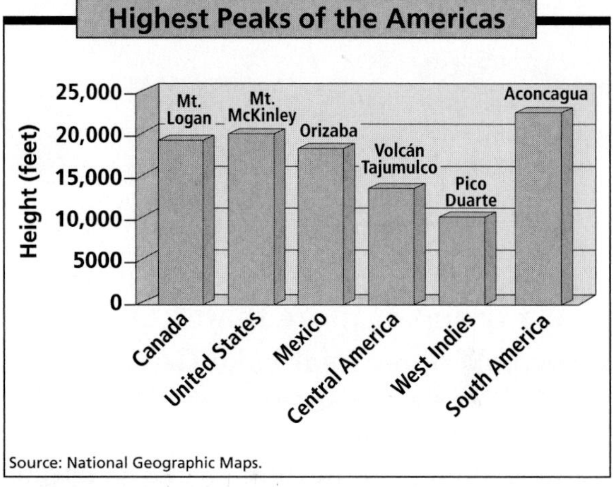

1. **What is the tallest mountain in the Americas?**
   - **A** Mt. Logan
   - **B** Mt. McKinley
   - **C** Orizaba
   - **D** Aconcagua
2. **Which mountain in North America is the tallest?**
   - **F** Mt. Logan
   - **G** Mt. McKinley
   - **H** Aconcagua
   - **J** Orizaba

Test-Taking Tip: When you are not sure of an answer, use the process of elimination. On question 2, for example, you know that the United States and Canada are both in North America. You have not yet learned that Mexico is also part of North America. Even so, Mexico's highest peak is shorter than the highest peak in both Canada and the United States.

GEOGRAPHY & HISTORY

Iroquois greeting Cartier

THE ST. LAWRENCE: A River of Trade

A cargo ship winds its way through the Thousand Islands (right), a group of more than 1,500 islands that lie in the St. Lawrence River near Lake Ontario.

Along with a system of lakes, locks, dams, and canals, the river forms the St. Lawrence Seaway, a busy highway for international trade. More than a thousand ships travel the waterway each year, hauling about 50 million tons (45 million t) of cargo. Yet the river was not always so easy to navigate. When French explorer Jacques Cartier sailed upriver in 1535, he thought he had found a shortcut to Asia. His dreams were ruined, however, when he was stopped by swift rapids near present-day Montreal. Many changes had to occur before the river would be tamed.

The Seaway's History

To the Iroquois Indians, who greeted Cartier upon his arrival, the St. Lawrence was "the river without end." In their birchbark canoes, they paddled far into the interior, bringing back beaver, lynx, and other furs to trade with the Europeans. In 1608 Samuel de Champlain of France founded the first trading post on the river, later known as the city of Quebec.

Early explorers and settlers, however, could not get their boats through many parts of the St. Lawrence. In 1680 a canal was begun around the Montreal rapids. As more canals were built, the river became a major Canadian shipping route. In 1833 Canada opened the Welland Canal, which bypasses Niagara Falls and links Lake Erie with Lake Ontario.

By the early 1900s, Canada and the United States were planning to widen and deepen sections of the St. Lawrence to allow for larger ships. Construction of the St. Lawrence Seaway, as the waterway was called, began in 1954. The project called for building miles of canals, plus 15 locks, 3 dams, and several hydroelectric power stations. The seaway opened in 1959. For the first time, ships could travel between the Atlantic Ocean and inland ports such as Chicago, Illinois, on Lake Michigan, and Duluth, Minnesota, on Lake Superior.

The Seaway Today

Today the St. Lawrence Seaway is still an important avenue of trade. Ships carry iron ore from Labrador to ports on the Great Lakes. The ships return with wheat and other grains. Many products travel from North American ports to countries overseas. In winter, thick ice closes sections of the seaway for months.

QUESTIONS

1. Why is the St. Lawrence Seaway important to the United States and Canada?
2. How did building the seaway help ships?

The busy St. Lawrence Seaway ▶

NATIONAL GEOGRAPHIC SOCIETY
The Great Lakes and St. Lawrence Seaway
CANADA
N
S
W
E
Duluth
Lake Superior
Lake Huron
Lake Michigan
Chicago
Niagara Falls
Lake Ontario
Lake Erie
St. Lawrence R.
Quebec
Montreal
Gulf of St. Lawrence
ATLANTIC OCEAN
UNITED STATES
0 mi.
500
0 km
500

SPECIAL REPORT

FOCUS

◂ Tennessee's capitol in Nashville

◂ Kayaker on the Ocoee River

NATIONAL GEOGRAPHIC SOCIETY

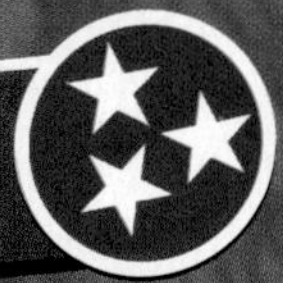

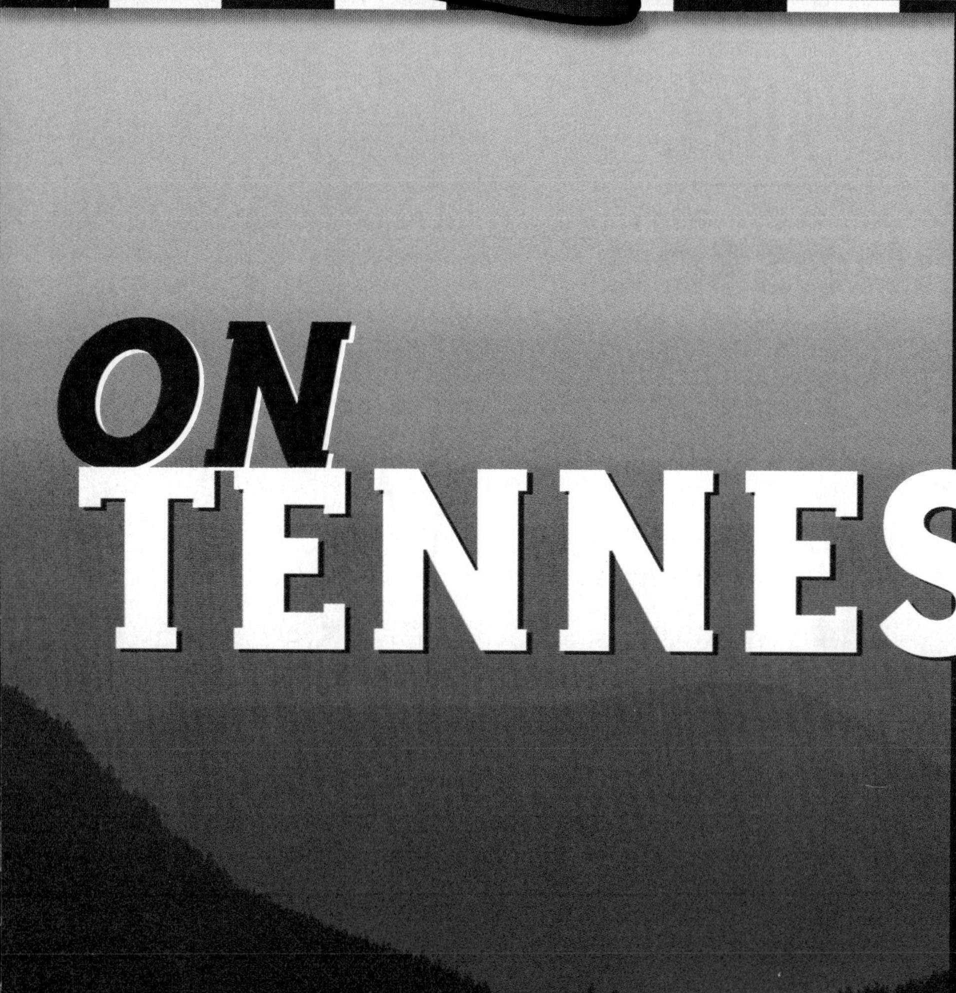

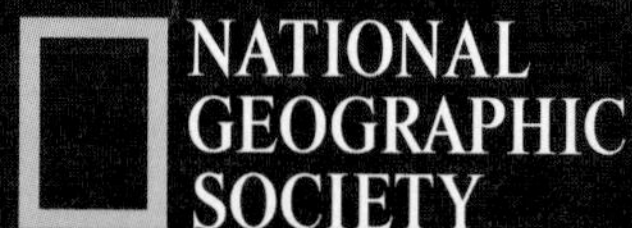

ON TENNESSEE

Where can you see a bluish haze surrounding the Great Smoky Mountains? Where can you zip wildly over the white-water rapids of the Ocoee River in a kayak? Where do the past and the present come together on the ancient floodplain of the Mississippi River? You can experience these wonders in the state of Tennessee.

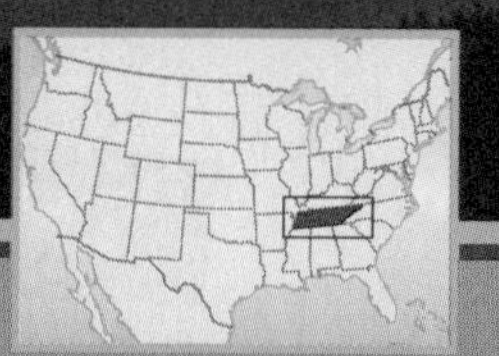

Author

Theodore H. Schmudde, Ph.D., *is Professor of Geography (Emeritus) at the University of Tennessee in Knoxville. He was co-coordinator of the Tennessee Geographic Alliance for 11 years and the director of its summer institute programs. His 38-year career in education includes teaching undergraduate and graduate courses at Southern Illinois University and the University of Tennessee.*

Reviewers

Donna Jett
Social Sciences Teacher
Powell Middle School
Powell, Tennessee

Ida Haskew Smith
Teacher/Assistant Principal
South Pittsburg Elementary
South Pittsburg, Tennessee

NGS ONLINE
www.nationalgeographic.com/education

Regional Atlas: Tennessee

TENNESSEE EXTENDS ABOUT 500 MILES (805 km) from the tree-covered Smoky Mountains on the east to the Mississippi River on the west. From early settlement until about 100 years ago, most people in Tennessee depended on farming and forest industries for their livelihoods. Today manufacturing, tourism, and service industries provide the incomes for most of the population.

The Land

The physical landscape of Tennessee—a diverse surface of mountains, hills, and plains—has been shaped by nature over millions of years. Along the eastern edge of the state are the Blue Ridge Mountains, which are separated from the Cumberland Plateau (an upland area) to the west by the Great Valley of Tennessee. West of the Cumberland Plateau lies a large lowland area of plains and hills called the Nashville Basin. Surrounding the basin is an elevated landscape called the Highland Rim. The Western Highland Rim, a broad north-south area of low hills, separates the Nashville Basin from the lowlands of the Gulf Coastal Plain. The floodplain bordering the Mississippi River is a distinctive flat landscape along Tennessee's western edge.

◀ **Big South Fork National Recreation Area**

The Climate

Climates across Tennessee are appropriately described as having long, warm (even hot) summers and shorter, moderate winters. Precipitation is usually ample in all seasons of the year to support an abundant growth of vegetation and field crops of all kinds. This precipitation also creates a well-developed surface system of rivers and smaller streams and large reserves of groundwater. Tennessee's major rivers generally flow from east to west. This pattern was a key factor in shaping the early settlement of the state. How? The westward flow of these rivers, with their origins in Virginia and North Carolina, provided easy inland movement.

The Economy

The early role of the rivers as avenues of trade and movement of people is no longer very significant, although there is still some transport of goods by barge on the Tennessee and Cumberland Rivers. The Mississippi River, in contrast, is still used extensively by barge traffic carrying such cargo as grains, fuels, and rock. Today Tennessee's rivers and lakes are sources for generating hydroelectric power, supplying water for homes and industries, and recreational uses.

Agriculture is still an important source of income, but it no longer employs large numbers of people. Soybeans, tobacco, corn, and cotton are major crops. Cattle are the major source of livestock income.

A century ago, industry in Tennessee involved small factories that crafted items for use on farms, processed raw materials, or produced textiles. In the last 50 years, however, manufacturing has grown to include national and international companies and is now the second-most important source of employment after service industries. Products range from pencils and computers to automobiles, trucks, and boats.

Tourism plays a major role in the economy of Tennessee. The mountain areas of East Tennessee attract large numbers of tourists. The state's lakes also attract people who boat and fish. Another draw for tourists are the state's Civil War battlefields.

The People

The census of 2000 counted 5.6 million people in Tennessee. The population has steadily increased over the past two centuries. In the past 100 years, this growth has shaped the cultural geography of the state in three important ways. First, the population has shifted from mostly rural locations to mostly urban places. Second, the population is now very much concentrated in and around the state's five largest urban areas. The third change is the substantial movement of people from other parts of the country into Tennessee, especially in the last 30 years. Tennessee's largest cities are usually the destination for most of these people. However, areas of East and Middle Tennessee—with their scenic mountains, upland landscapes, and many lakes—have also attracted many of the state's newcomers.

A riverboat ▲ in Memphis

Exploring the Region

1. **How does Tennessee's landscape differ going from east to west?**
2. **Describe the state's climate.**
3. **What types of products make up Tennessee's economy?**
4. **How have Tennessee's population patterns changed in the past 100 years?**

Focus On Tennessee

NATIONAL GEOGRAPHIC

Tennessee: Political

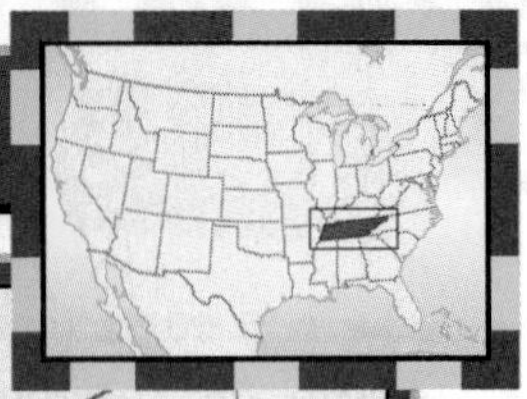

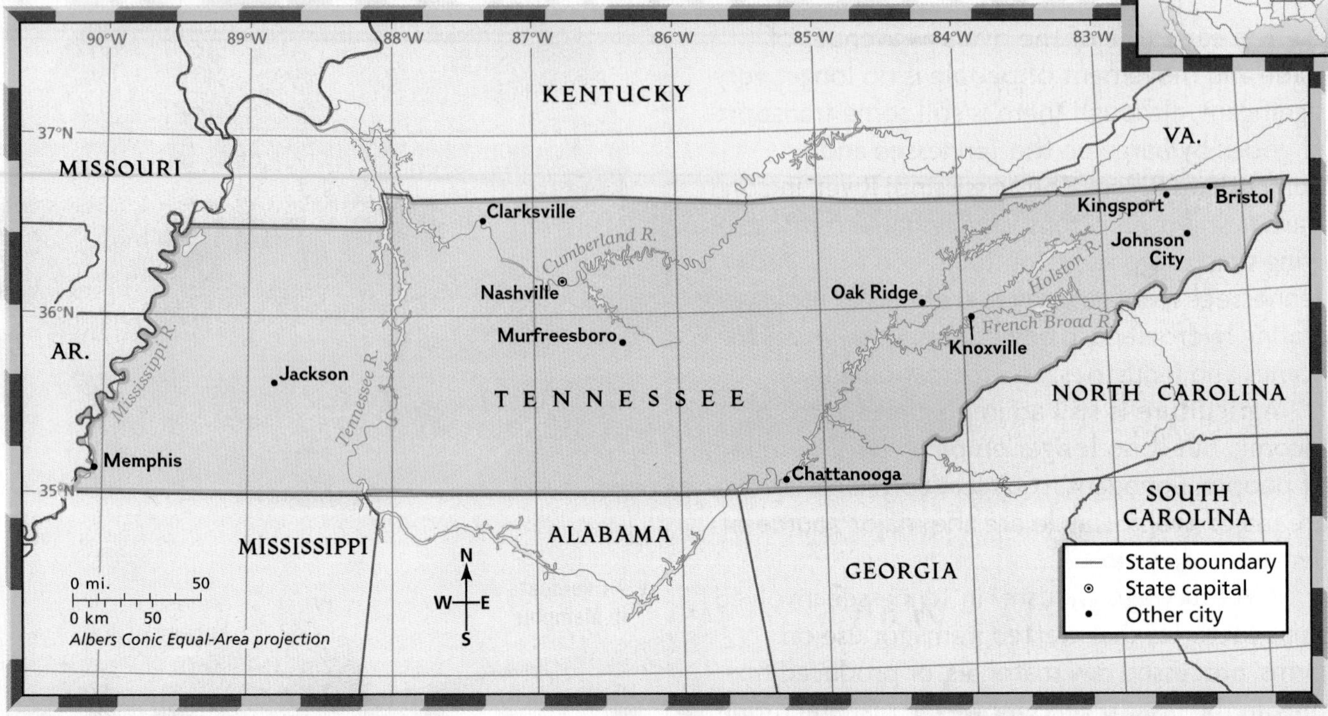

90°W 89°W 88°W 87°W 86°W 85°W 84°W 83°W
37°N 36°N 35°N
KENTUCKY
VA.
MISSOURI
AR.
TENNESSEE
NORTH CAROLINA
SOUTH CAROLINA
MISSISSIPPI
ALABAMA
GEORGIA
Clarksville
Cumberland R.
Nashville
Murfreesboro
Jackson
Memphis
Mississippi R.
Tennessee R.
Chattanooga
Oak Ridge
Knoxville
French Broad R.
Holston R.
Kingsport
Bristol
Johnson City
N W E S
0 mi. 50
0 km 50
Albers Conic Equal-Area projection
State boundary
State capital
Other city

NATIONAL GEOGRAPHIC

Tennessee: Physical

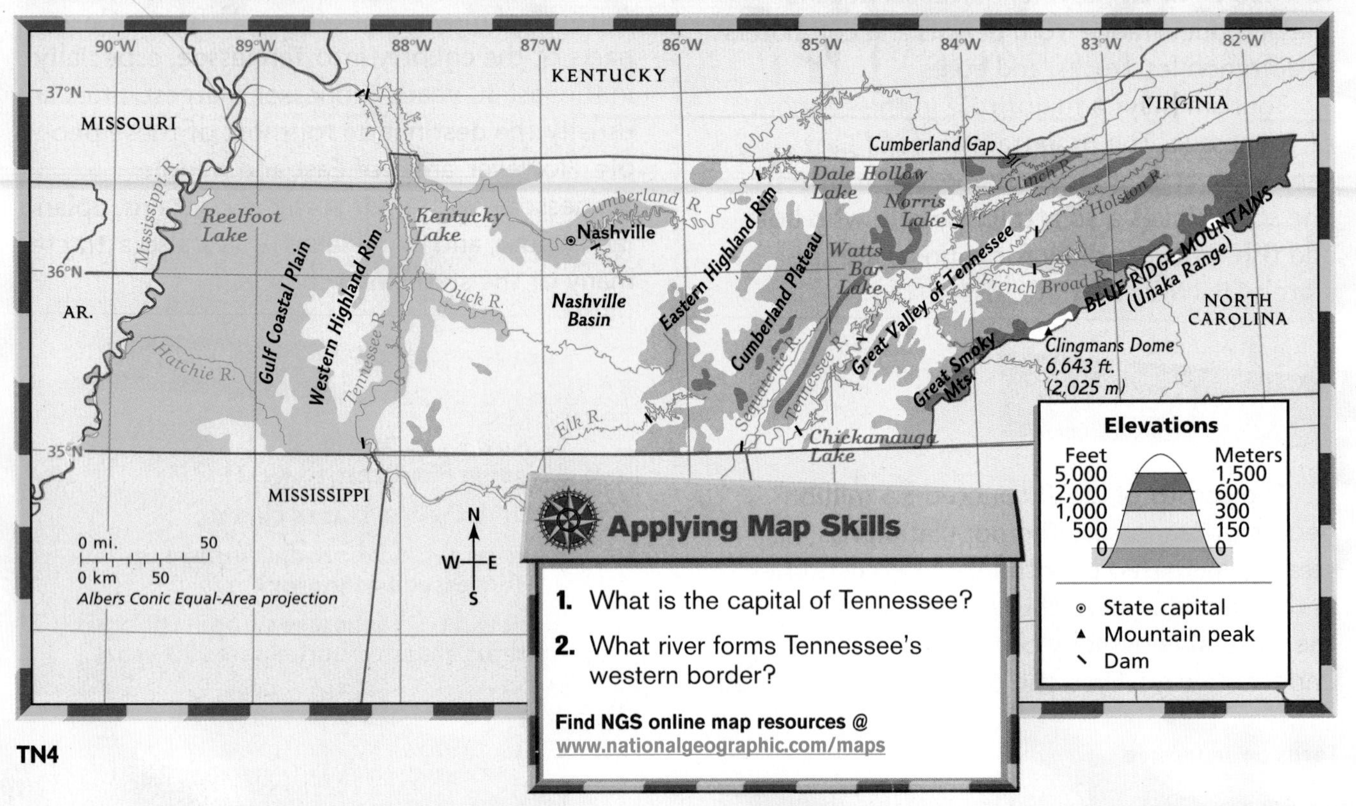

Applying Map Skills

1. What is the capital of Tennessee?
2. What river forms Tennessee's western border?

Find NGS online map resources @ www.nationalgeographic.com/maps

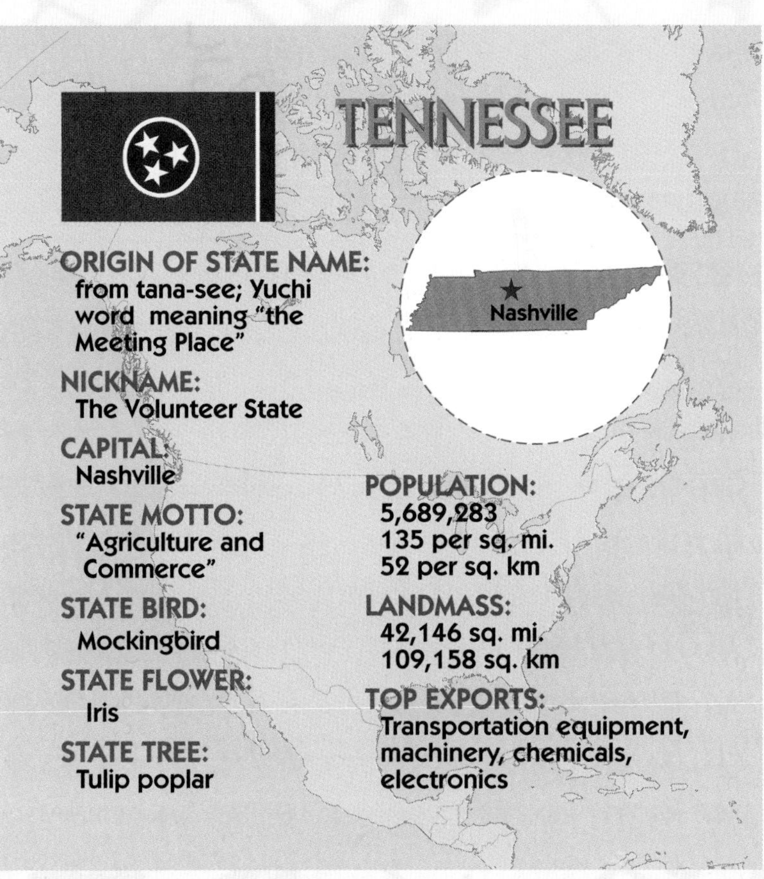

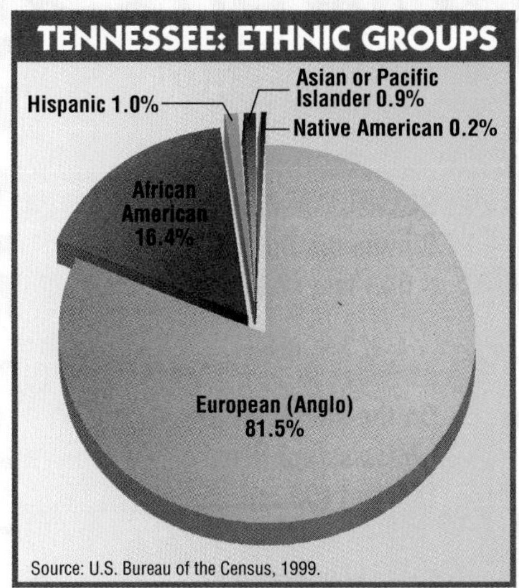

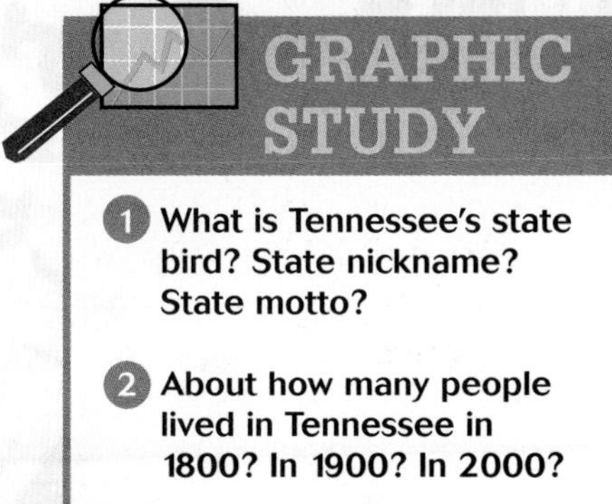

1. What is Tennessee's state bird? State nickname? State motto?
2. About how many people lived in Tennessee in 1800? In 1900? In 2000?

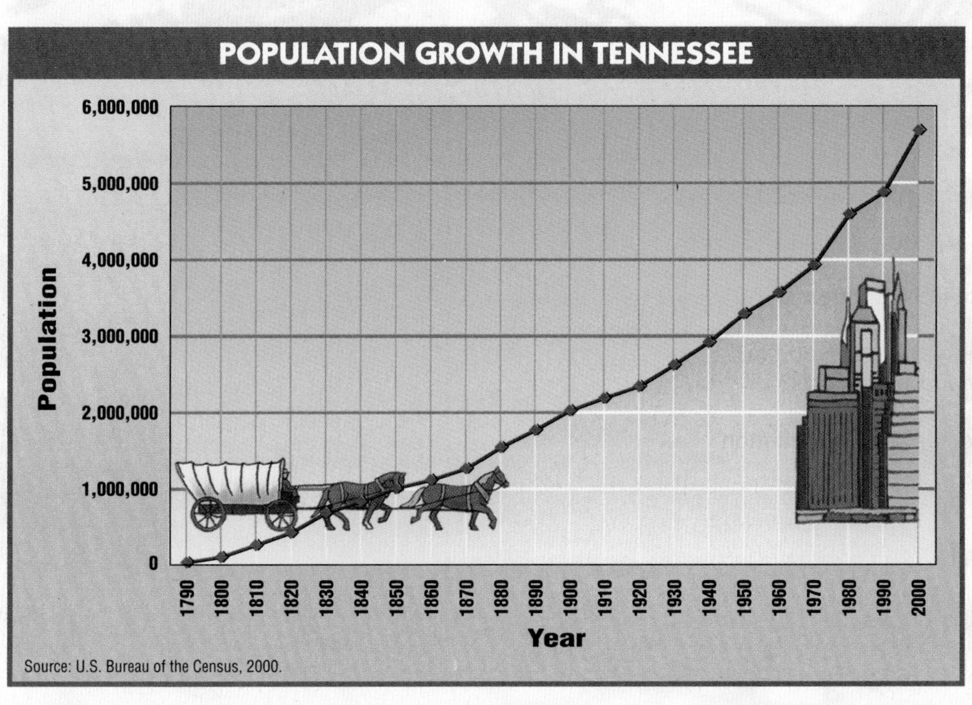

Focus On Tennessee

Geo Extremes

① HIGHEST POINT
Clingmans Dome
6,643 feet (2,025 m)

② LOWEST POINT
On the shores of the Mississippi River
182 feet (55 m)

③ LONGEST RIVER
Tennessee River
652 miles (1,049 km) in total length

④ LARGEST NATURAL LAKE
Reelfoot Lake
24 sq. mi. (62 sq. km)

⑤ LARGEST CAVERNS
Cumberland Caverns
32.5 miles (52.3 km) of passages

⑥ HIGHEST WATERFALL
Fall Creek Falls
256 feet (78 m)

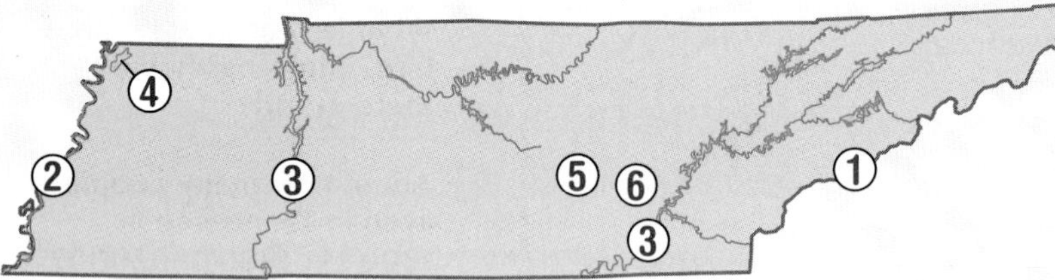

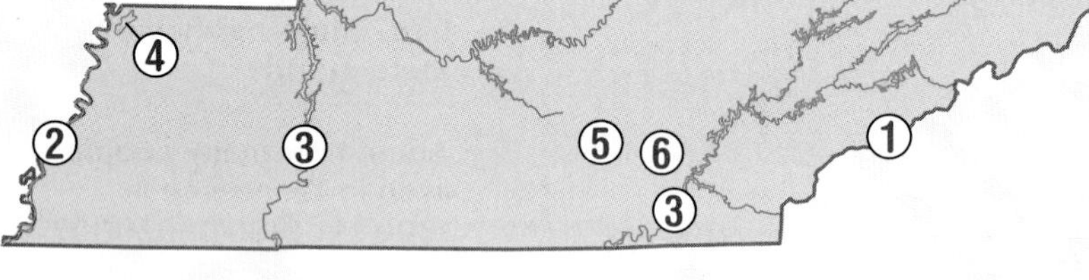

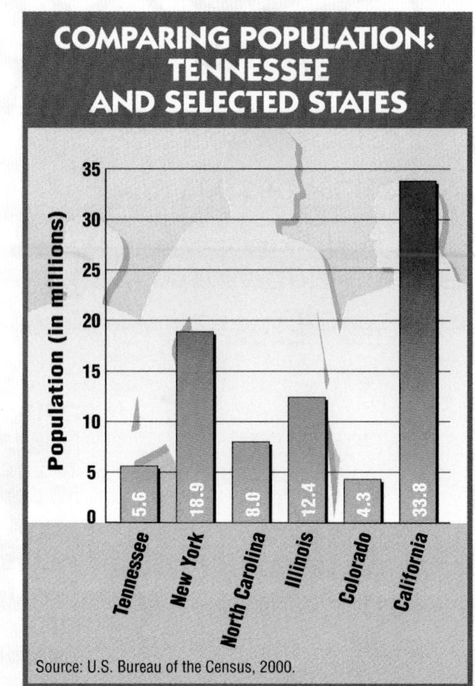

GRAPHIC STUDY

1. What is the highest point in Tennessee?
2. In what regions of Tennessee do you find the state's highest and lowest points?
3. How does Memphis compare in population to Chattanooga?

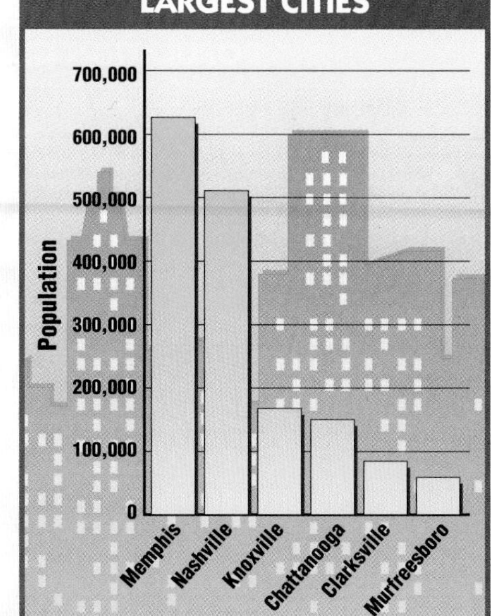

Tennessee's Geography

Guide to Reading

Main Idea

Tennessee has three grand divisions and six main physical regions.

Terms to Know

- ridge
- bluff
- alluvial plain
- tributary

Places to Locate

- Blue Ridge Mountains
- Great Valley of Tennessee
- Tennessee River
- Cumberland Plateau
- Nashville Basin
- Eastern Highland Rim
- Western Highland Rim
- Gulf Coastal Plain
- Mississippi River
- Cumberland River

Reading Strategy

Draw a chart like the one below. List the six physical regions of Tennessee and write two facts about each.

Region	Facts

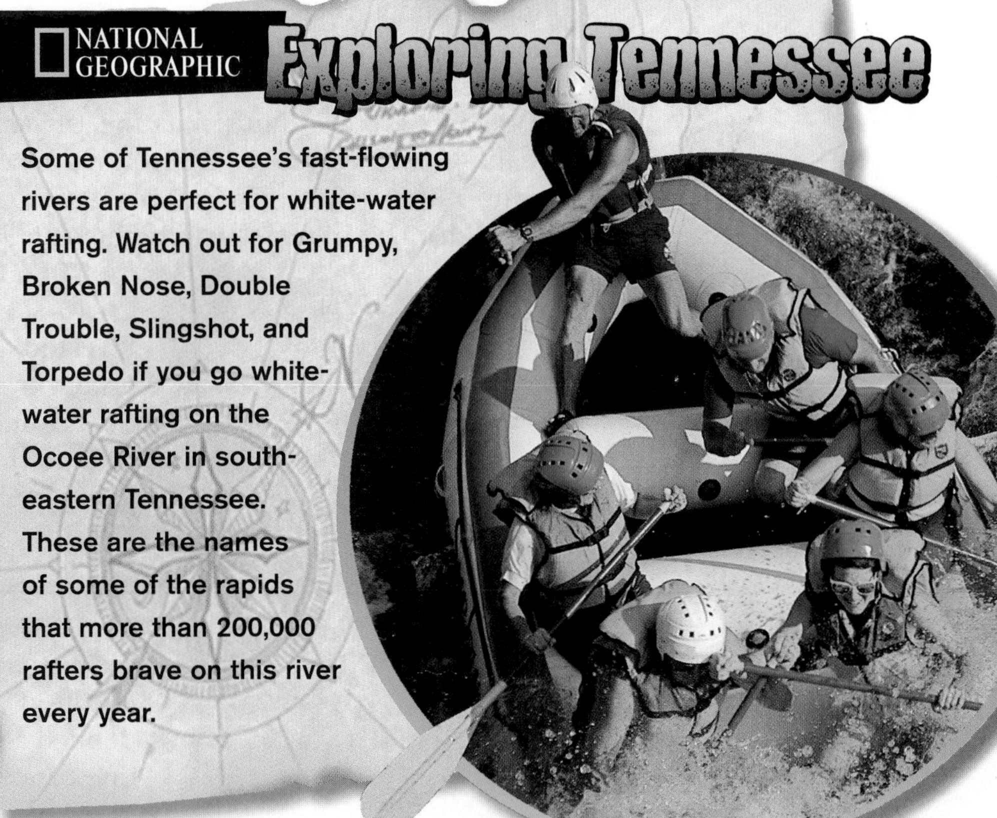

NATIONAL GEOGRAPHIC **Exploring Tennessee**

Some of Tennessee's fast-flowing rivers are perfect for white-water rafting. Watch out for Grumpy, Broken Nose, Double Trouble, Slingshot, and Torpedo if you go white-water rafting on the Ocoee River in southeastern Tennessee. These are the names of some of the rapids that more than 200,000 rafters brave on this river every year.

Tennessee covers 42,146 square miles (109,158 sq. km), making it 34th in size among the states of the United States. The political map on page TN4 shows you that Tennessee borders eight states. These are North Carolina on the east, Arkansas and Missouri on the west, Kentucky and Virginia on the north, and Mississippi, Alabama, and Georgia on the south.

The Land

It is a tradition that Tennessee has three grand divisions: East Tennessee, Middle Tennessee, and West Tennessee. The three stars on the state flag represent these three divisions. In terms of landforms, six major physical regions can be defined for the state. Starting on the east, these are the Blue Ridge Mountains, the Great Valley of Tennessee, the Cumberland Plateau, the Nashville Basin, the Highland Rim (with eastern and western parts), and the Gulf Coastal Plain. Refer to the physical map on page TN4 as we look at Tennessee's physical regions.

Blue Ridge Mountains Running along the eastern border of Tennessee are the **Blue Ridge Mountains,** part of the Appalachian Mountains that run from Maine to Georgia and Alabama. The Blue Ridge Mountains take their name from the bluish haze that hangs over their tree-covered sides. The Great Smoky Mountains is a name applied to the southern part of the Blue Ridge Mountains in Tennessee. These mountains are also known as the Unaka, which is a Cherokee word meaning "white smoke." The elevation of these mountains averages about 5,000 feet (1,524 m), but a few peaks reach over 6,000 feet (1,829 m). The highest peak in the state is Clingmans Dome.

The Blue Ridge Mountains have great scenic beauty and are well-forested with hardwood and evergreen trees and colorful flowering bushes. In fact, there are more kinds of trees in the Blue Ridge Mountains than there are in all of Europe.

Knoxville is located on the Tennessee River. It was the state's first capital, from 1796 to 1812.

Location In which physical region is Knoxville located?

Great Valley of Tennessee West of the mountains lies the **Great Valley of Tennessee.** The landscape here includes both ridges and valleys. The elevated ridges are usually sharply defined and narrow and run parallel to one another. The valley lowlands between the ridges range from narrow to wide. The Clinch River and the Holston River occupy the northern part of the Great Valley and were routes for early pioneers into East Tennessee. The **Tennessee River,** which begins near Knoxville by the joining of the Holston and French Broad Rivers, is the main waterway in the middle and southern parts of the Great Valley.

Most of the population of East Tennessee is concentrated in the Great Valley. Early settlers found the soils here good for crops, and the rivers provided transportation. The major cities here are Knoxville, Chattanooga, and the Tri-Cities of Johnson City, Kingsport, and Bristol.

Cumberland Plateau West of the Great Valley lies the **Cumberland Plateau,** a rather flat-topped upland bounded on the east and west by steep slopes. The Cumberland Plateau does not have good soils for

farming, but it does contain rich seams of coal in places. The plateau was originally covered with forests, most of which were cleared for timber from the 1880s to the 1920s. The Sequatchie River is located within a steep-sided lowland in the southern part of the plateau.

Nashville Basin West of the Cumberland Plateau is the core area of Middle Tennessee—the **Nashville Basin.** The physical map on page TN4 shows you that the area east and west of Nashville is a low area surrounded by higher lands. This basin region has been a major area for agricultural settlement. Soils here, however, tend to be shallow and have been badly eroded over the past 150 years. Today this is no longer a dominant area for crop production.

Agriculture

Cotton fields are a common sight in West Tennessee's Gulf Coastal Plain.

Human/Environment Interaction **Why are Tennessee's largest farms located in this region?**

Highland Rim Surrounding the Nashville Basin is the Highland Rim. This region is usually defined as two parts—the **Eastern Highland Rim** and the **Western Highland Rim.** The Eastern Highland Rim is a plateaulike upland that is lower than the Cumberland Plateau but higher than the Nashville Basin. The Western Highland Rim is mostly low hills. In both rim areas, you can explore underground caves hollowed out by water. Much of the soil on these rims is either rocky or thin and not easily farmed.

Gulf Coastal Plain West Tennessee is covered by a plains area that makes up the state's sixth physical region. This area is part of the **Gulf Coastal Plain,** which stretches northward from the Gulf of Mexico along both sides of the **Mississippi River.** A series of **bluffs,** or steep cliffs, drop sharply to the floodplain of the river. This lowland area is an **alluvial plain,** or an area built up from soil left by river floods. In some places, there is little floodplain. In other places, such as northwest Tennessee, the floodplain can be miles wide. This section of the Coastal Plain—the lowest part of the state—is often called the Mississippi Bottoms.

West Tennessee's Gulf Coastal Plain forms the state's major agricultural region. The soils covering the Coastal Plain can be quite fertile but are prone to rapid erosion. Tennessee's largest farms are found here.

✓Reading Check **What are Tennessee's six physical regions?**

NATIONAL GEOGRAPHIC On Location

Water Recreation

Tennessee's rivers and lakes provide drinking water and water for industrial use. In addition, Tennesseans use them to enjoy many different outdoor sports.

Human/Environment Interaction **Why were dams built along the Tennessee River and its tributaries?**

Rivers and Lakes

Although Tennessee has only one natural lake, the state has a plentiful water supply from mountain streams and dam-created lakes. Three large rivers and more than eighteen smaller rivers and tributaries eventually drain into the Gulf of Mexico.

The three largest rivers of the state are the Mississippi River, the Tennessee River, and the **Cumberland River.** The Mississippi River and its **tributaries,** or small rivers that flow into it, drain the Coastal Plains area of the state. The other two rivers form systems of drainage for most of the rest of Tennessee. Trace the course of the Tennessee River on the map on page TN4. Note that it begins in the eastern part of the state, loops into Alabama and Mississippi on the south, and then flows north through the Western Highland Rim into Kentucky.

Starting in the 1930s, the federal government built a series of dams along the Tennessee River and some of its tributaries. The dams were built for flood control and to provide hydroelectricity to the Tennessee Valley. The system of dams and lakes is also a major resource for water recreation and fishing.

Tennessee's only natural lake, Reelfoot Lake, is unusual. Located on the floodplain of the Mississippi River in far northwestern Tennessee, it formed as the result of very strong earthquakes along the New Madrid fault line in 1811–1812. Reelfoot Lake is a shallow lake that is gradually filling with silt. It is a tourist attraction because of its swampy environment and abundance of fish.

✓ Reading Check **What river flows through Tennessee twice?**

The Climate

The long warm season found throughout the state provides a long growing season for crops and is ideal for all types of outdoor activities. Summer temperatures usually range from 85°F to 95°F (29°C to 35°C). Low temperatures rarely fall below 10°F (–12°C), and the coldest winter month, January, averages above freezing.

Winds coming to Tennessee generally are from the Gulf of Mexico. These warm winds carry much moisture. Thus, the state receives year-round precipitation. Annual precipitation averages about 50 inches (127 cm). Most precipitation comes as rain, but almost all parts of the state will get some snow each winter.

Reading Check **Why does Tennessee receive year-round precipitation?**

Climograph: Memphis

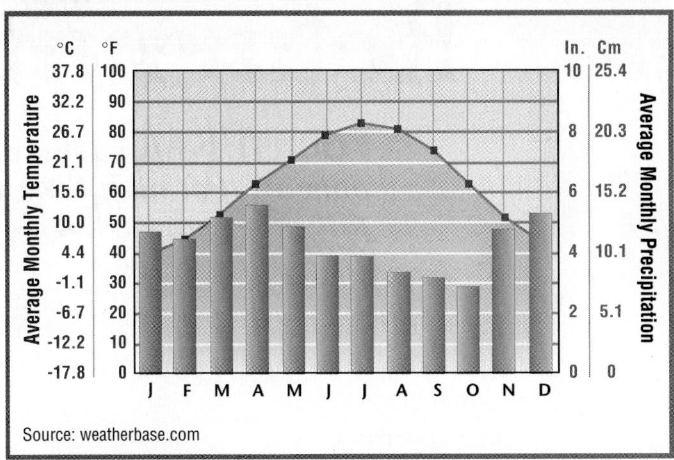

Analyzing the Graph

A climograph shows average monthly temperatures (line graph) and average monthly precipitation (bar graph).

Place In which month does Memphis receive the most precipitation?

Assessment

Defining Terms

1. **Define** ridge, bluff, alluvial plain, tributary.

Recalling Facts

2. **Region** What states border Tennessee?
3. **Region** In what physical region can you explore underground caves?
4. **Place** What major rivers flow through Tennessee?

Critical Thinking

5. **Making Comparisons** How do East Tennessee and West Tennessee differ?
6. **Drawing Conclusions** Which of Tennessee's three grand divisions would you expect to produce the most crops? Why?

Graphic Organizer

7. **Organizing Information** Draw a diagram like the one below. List one example of each kind of landform in Tennessee. Then identify in which of the state's physical regions it appears.

Landform	Example	Location
Highland		
Lowland		
River		

Applying Geography Skills

8. **Analyzing Maps** Look at the physical map on page TN4. Name three lakes shown on the map that were formed by building dams.

CASE STUDY: Returning Animals

FOCUS: ***People debate whether—and how—to bring back animals that once roamed Tennessee. As some experiments fail, others are tried.***

In the 1800s and early 1900s, the national government and state governments set aside some lands as national and state parks. In recent years, people have debated what purpose these parks should serve. Some say we should use parks to preserve the wilderness as it used to be. They hope to make natural lands thrive with the plants and animals that once lived in them. Others argue that parks should be set aside for people to use for recreation. Bringing back certain animals, they say, causes problems.

▲ Great Smoky Mountains National Park

Loss of Wildlife

Tennessee was once home to a wide variety of animals. Some—such as black bears, deer, raccoons, and rabbits—still live in the state today. Others are long gone. In the 1800s, bison and elk grazed in the forests and meadows. Cougars and red wolves hunted them. As settlers moved into Tennessee, bison and elk were hunted for their meat and hides. Farmers killed the cougars and wolves to protect their own livestock from these hunting animals. As a result, these species disappeared from the state.

Bringing Animals Back

In the past decade, scientists and park rangers have tried to bring back animals that have disappeared from Tennessee. Some projects have worked well. Peregrine falcons once more swoop through the skies. River otters again dive into Tennessee's fast-flowing streams. Scientists have also brought

◀ Elk being released at the Royal Blue Wildlife Reserve near Caryville, Tennessee

three species of freshwater fish back to the swift waters of Abrams Creek in Great Smoky Mountains National Park.

Other plans have not worked. Despite many years of effort, the return of red wolves did not succeed. In the early and mid-1990s, park officials released nearly 40 wolves into Great Smoky Mountains National Park. Most died or had to be recaptured after they moved onto privately owned land. In 1998 the government dropped the plan to reintroduce wolves.

The Return of the Elk

In late 2000, 50 elk were released into the Royal Blue Wildlife Reserve near Caryville, Tennessee. The elk are expected to become accustomed to a migratory life in the reserve's forested areas. After a few months, they will be released into the wild and watched. If the herd thrives, the plan calls for some 400 elk to be brought into the Tennessee wilderness area over the next four years.

Some people oppose this plan. They argue that the elk could wander out of the designated area to feed on and damage the crops in nearby fields. They also point out that the elk could bring diseases into the region, which could harm livestock that graze nearby. To prevent this problem, scientists are careful to test the animals to be sure they are free of disease before they are brought into the reserve.

Using the Case Study

1. **Movement** **Why were bison and elk hunted in Tennessee?**
2. **Human/Environment Interaction** **What happened to the plan to bring back red wolves? Why?**
3. **Forming an Opinion** **Do you think elk should have been reintroduced to Tennessee? Why or why not?**
4. **Skillbuilder Activity** **Write a letter to the managers of Great Smoky Mountains National Park explaining your position on whether animals should or should not be reintroduced to the park.**

Tennessee's History

Guide to Reading

Main Idea

The people of Tennessee have played important roles in history.

Terms to Know

- clan
- constitution
- secede

Places to Locate

- Watauga River
- Knoxville
- Nashville
- Chattanooga
- Memphis

Reading Strategy

Draw a diagram like the one below. Then list three key events from Tennessee's history for each period.

Period	Events
Before 1800	
1800s	
1900s	

NATIONAL GEOGRAPHIC Exploring Tennessee

Native Americans once lived throughout Tennessee. About 15,000 live here today, and their ancestors left behind reminders of their lives. Farmers often find Native American artifacts in their fields. There are larger reminders, however. Pinson Mounds State Park in West Tennessee includes at least 15 mounds that Native Americans used for religious ceremonies and burials.

Tennessee's Native Americans

Prehistoric Native Americans were the first people to live in Tennessee. From about 15,000 to 12,000 years ago, bands of hunters moved into the area to hunt herds of mastodons, an elephant-like animal, and caribou, a kind of deer. Living in caves and rock shelters, these people used arrows and spears with points made of stone.

Over thousands of years, the climate slowly warmed. Mastodons and other animals died out, and forests spread. The Native Americans settled along rivers, where they hunted smaller game and collected nuts, wild plants, and shellfish. About 5,000 years ago, they began to farm.

Mound Builders As time passed, these Native Americans developed a more complex society. They began to make pottery and to live in towns. They also built earthen mounds, which they used for burials.

Several mounds are found throughout the Ohio and Mississippi River valleys. Tennessee's Pinson Mounds—now a state archaeological park—is the largest mound complex in the United States from the years A.D. 1 to 500. Later mounds were built for religious purposes as well as for burials.

Over time, the Mound Builders developed new kinds of corn and beans, their chief crops. These new strains produced bigger harvests, which could feed more people. As a result, the population grew.

The Cherokee and Other Groups Around 1540, four main groups of Native Americans lived in Tennessee—the Cherokee, the Chickasaw, the Yuchi, and the Shawnee. The Cherokee and the Chickasaw were the two stronger groups and eventually forced out the remaining Yuchi and Shawnee. After 1714, Middle Tennessee remained a hunting ground used by both the Cherokee and the Chickasaw.

The Cherokee developed a complex civilization. They had seven **clans,** or groups of people related to one another. Only men could hold the important post of chief, but women had a part in deciding matters of war and peace. Each settlement had from 12 to more than 200 dwellings. An open square in the center was used for religious

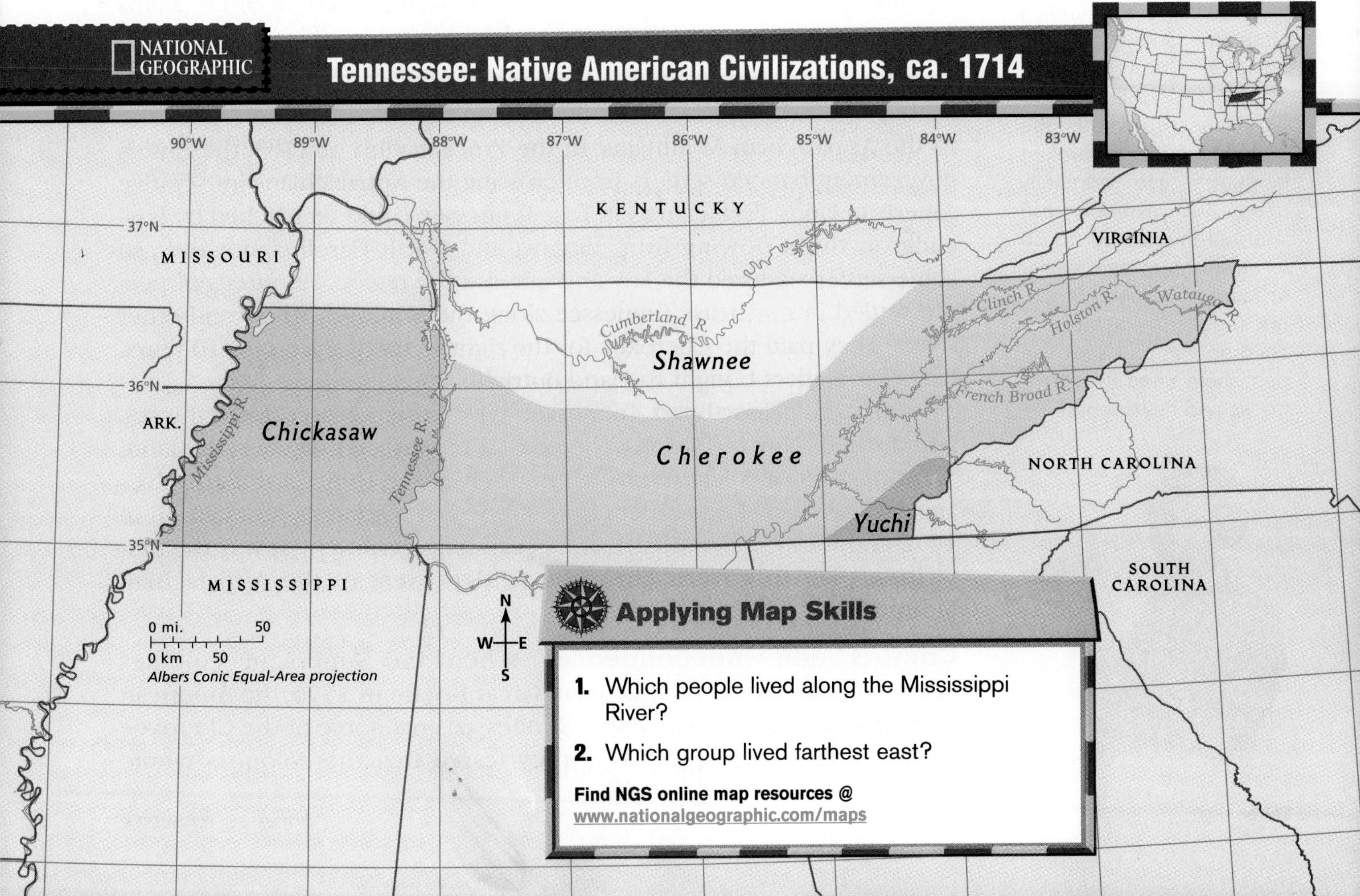

Applying Map Skills

1. Which people lived along the Mississippi River?
2. Which group lived farthest east?

Find NGS online map resources @
www.nationalgeographic.com/maps

ceremonies and war dances. The Cherokee hunted wild game for food, but they were mainly farmers who cultivated corn.

Reading Check **Why did the Native American population grow during the time of the Mound Builders?**

European Settlement

In 1541 Spaniards led by Hernando de Soto became the first Europeans to reach Tennessee. More than 100 years would elapse before both English and French explorers arrived in the region. In 1673 James Needham and Gabriel Arthur crossed the Appalachian Mountains into Tennessee. They hoped to establish trade between the Cherokee and the English. That same year, French missionaries Jacques Marquette and Louis Joliet explored the Mississippi River valley south past Tennessee's present-day borders. In 1682 French explorer Robert Cavelier, known as Sieur de La Salle, claimed the entire Mississippi River valley for the king of France and named it Louisiana.

For the next decades, England and France traded with Native Americans for beaver furs and deer hides. They also built forts in the area and struggled for control of the region and Native American allies. This struggle eventually erupted into the French and Indian War. Great Britain won the war in 1763, and France surrendered all of its claims in North America, including Tennessee.

The Watauga Association During this British colonial era, European settlers and African Americans lived along the Atlantic coast and inland to the Appalachian Mountains. In the Proclamation of 1763, the British government banned settlers from crossing the Appalachians into Native American lands. Fertile areas in East Tennessee could be reached by traveling on rivers flowing from Virginia and North Carolina, however, so some settlers ignored the law and entered the region. Hundreds of people settled in northeast Tennessee along the **Watauga River** and other rivers. They paid the Cherokee for the right to use the land for 10 years. Later, the settlers bought the land outright.

This area of northeast Tennessee was rather isolated from the settled areas of North Carolina, the coastal colony that claimed the land. Wanting a set of rules to govern themselves and to defend themselves against the Cherokee, settlers here formed the Watauga Association in 1772 and wrote a **constitution,** or plan of government. It was the first written plan to govern European settlers west of the Appalachian Mountains.

Conflict and Independence When the American colonies declared their independence from Great Britain in 1776, the American Revolutionary War began. In the Tennessee area, some of the Cherokee sided with the British because they feared that the colonists would

Sequoyah

What if your language did not have a written form? How could you send messages to another person? A Cherokee named Sequoyah faced that problem—and solved it. In the early 1800s, he invented a way to write the Cherokee language. Sequoyah used symbols from English, Greek, and Hebrew writings to represent the sounds of the Cherokee language. He originally used 200 symbols but later cut the number to 86 to make the system easier to learn. Cherokee teachers taught the system to children, and Cherokee publishers used it to print books and newspapers.

take more of their land. The Watauga settlers—led by John Sevier—defeated the Cherokee in several fights. Four years later, Sevier led Tennessee settlers again in helping to defeat the British at the battle of Kings Mountain in North Carolina, a major turning point in the American Revolution.

That same year—1780—about 300 settlers moved into the Nashville Basin. Most of the men came with James Robertson, following an overland route. Here they began building Fort Nashborough and planting crops. The men's wives and children, under the leadership of John Donelson, made the hazardous journey to the fort down the Tennessee River and up the Cumberland River. The entire central region of Tennessee began to be settled.

In 1783 the United States won its independence from Great Britain. The people living in the Tennessee area quickly declared that they wanted to become the new state of Franklin. The United States government did not agree, however, and the area remained a territory. President George Washington appointed William Blount as the territorial governor.

Reading Check **Why did settlers move into Tennessee even though they were banned from doing so?**

NATIONAL GEOGRAPHIC

Tennessee: Early Settlements and Roads, ca. 1800

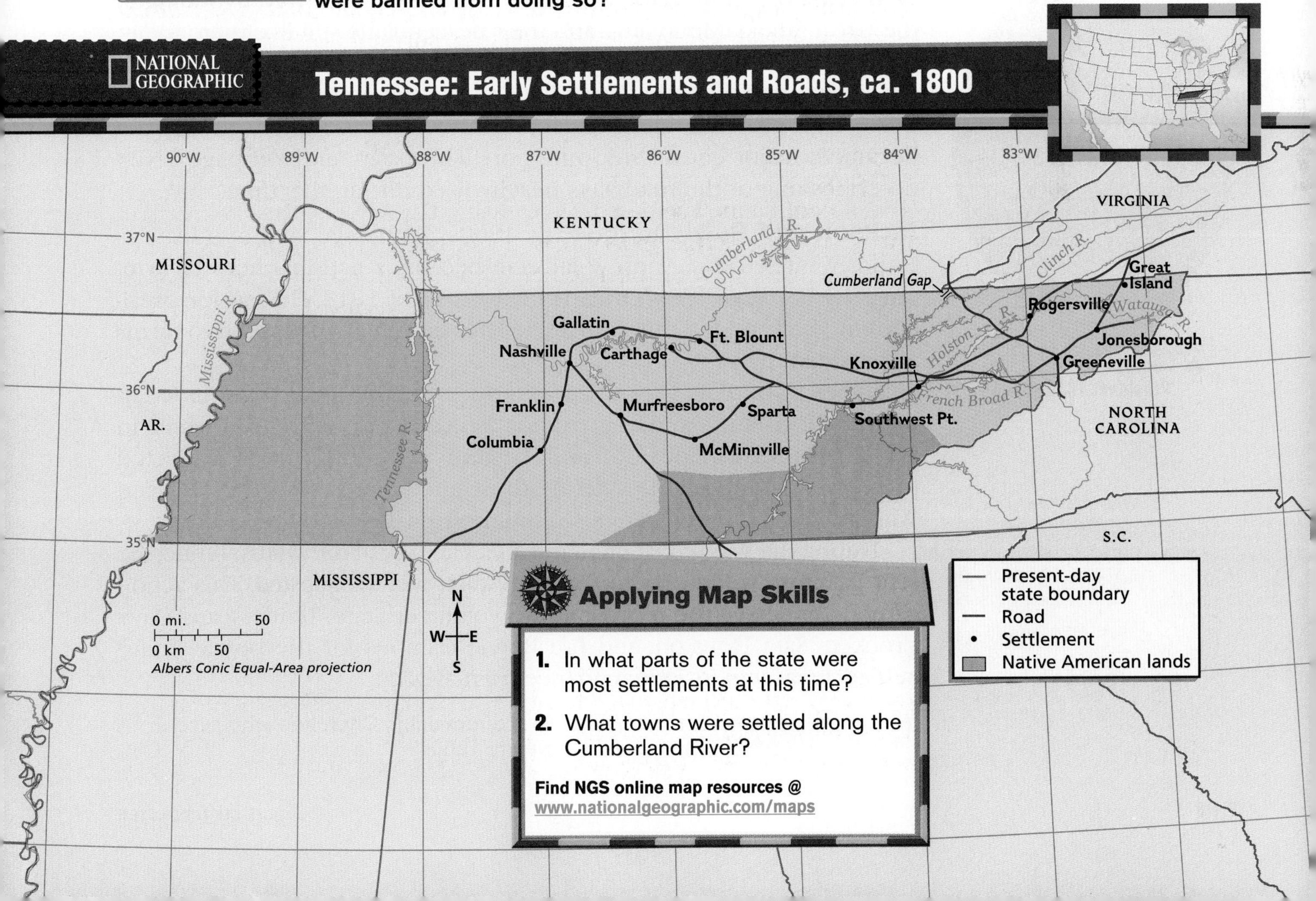

Applying Map Skills

1. In what parts of the state were most settlements at this time?
2. What towns were settled along the Cumberland River?

Find NGS online map resources @ www.nationalgeographic.com/maps

Statehood and Growth

By 1795 the territory had enough people to apply for statehood. On June 1, 1796, Congress approved Tennessee as the country's sixteenth state—the first state to be created out of a territory. John Sevier was elected governor and served in the capital, which was then located at **Knoxville.** The state legislature sent Andrew Jackson to the national House of Representatives and William Blount and William Cocke to the Senate.

▼ Andrew Jackson, President 1829–1837

▲ James Knox Polk, President 1845–1849

The population of Tennessee grew steadily and was mostly people of English, Scots-Irish, German, French, or African heritage. By 1830 nearly 700,000 people lived in the state. Farmers grew corn, cotton, and tobacco and raised pigs. With the spread of the population to the west, **Nashville** was made the state capital.

In the early 1800s, nearly two-thirds of the state's land was held by Native Americans. By 1819 the Cherokee held only a small amount of land near **Chattanooga.** Then in 1838 the United States Army, under orders of Andrew Jackson, forcibly moved the Cherokee remaining here and in other states to Indian Territory in present-day Oklahoma. So many Cherokee died along the way that the journey became known as the Trail of Tears. About 1,000 Cherokee avoided being moved by hiding in the Great Smoky Mountains, and their descendants still live there today.

By the early 1850s, steamboats were plying the rivers, and the state's first railroad—the Nashville and Chattanooga Line—connected these two growing cities. Business and trade boomed. **Memphis** became a major cotton shipping port. The Case Study on page TN24 describes one of the roadways heavily used during this time.

Jackson and Polk In the early 1800s, Tennessee sent two leaders to the White House. Andrew Jackson became a national hero by winning the Battle of New Orleans in the War of 1812. He ran for president in 1824 and lost, but four years later ran again and won two terms as president.

James Knox Polk was a strong supporter of Jackson. Polk served in the state legislature and as governor. He also represented Tennessee in the United States House of Representatives. In 1844 he was elected president. During his presidency, the United States won the Mexican War and acquired new lands stretching from Texas to California.

During the War of 1812 and the Mexican War of the 1840s, Tennessee sent far more volunteers to the army than were requested. This action earned Tennessee the nickname the Volunteer State. Tennesseans Davy Crockett, Sam Houston, and Jim Bowie (famous for the bowie knife) helped Texas win its independence from Mexico.

✓Reading Check **What happened to the remaining Cherokee who lived in Tennessee in the early 1800s?**

Civil War and Reconstruction

Tennessee became part of the sectional tension that caused the Civil War and split the United States in the mid-1800s. Some plantation owners in West Tennessee, as in states of the Lower South, used enslaved Africans to raise cotton and tobacco and defended the institution of slavery. The majority of people in East Tennessee were culturally tied to people in the Northern states and generally lived on small farms that did not use enslaved Africans.

Secession In 1860 Abraham Lincoln was elected president. He opposed the spread of slavery in new territories. In addition, throughout the Northern states there was rising opposition to *all* slavery. As a result, several Southern states **seceded,** or withdrew, from the United States and formed the Confederate States of America.

With economic and cultural ties to the Southern states, most of Middle and West Tennessee's people supported slavery but not secession. They had a long history of loyalty to the Union. However, on June 8, 1861, Tennessee voters were asked to decide whether or not to leave the Union. People of East Tennessee voted not to secede. In Middle and West Tennessee, the vote was to secede. The state joined the Confederacy and was the last state to secede from the Union.

The Civil War in Tennessee With their cultural differences, Tennesseans remained divided in their loyalties during the Civil War. Volunteers joined the Confederate Army and the Union Army in large numbers. In fact, Tennessee provided more soldiers than any other state.

The Battle of Shiloh

More men were killed in the Battle of Shiloh than in all of America's previous wars. Together the two armies suffered more than 23,000 casualties—people killed or wounded.

Place **Who won the Battle of Shiloh?**

Tennessee's central location between the Lower South and the North, its railroad lines, and its rivers were of great value to both sides. As a result, important battles were fought in the state. One of the bloodiest and most critical battles took place at Shiloh along the Tennessee River. In 1862 a large Union army defeated Confederate forces here and gained control of Middle and West Tennessee. The several battles for control of Chattanooga, which the Union eventually won, were also key engagements. By 1864 the Union had control of the whole state. Turn to page TN26 to learn more about Civil War battles in Tennessee.

Lincoln named Tennessee's Andrew Johnson as the state's military governor. Johnson had served in the United States Senate during the war and was elected vice president when Lincoln ran for reelection in 1864. The Civil War ended in April 1865, with the Confederacy's defeat. Several weeks later, Lincoln was assassinated, and Andrew Johnson became the third Tennessean to become president of the country.

Reconstruction The period after the Civil War is called Reconstruction because the Confederate states had to reconstruct, or build, new governments to rejoin the Union. Tennessee reentered the Union in July 1866, sooner than any other seceded state. The following decades were difficult for Tennessee, though. Thousands of Tennesseans had died in the fighting or from diseases like yellow fever. The war had left parts of the state in ruins, thousands of people were homeless, and families were devastated.

Reading Check When did Tennessee reenter the Union?

Time Line of Tennessee History

9500 B.C. to A.D. 1700

9500 B.C. Ancestors of Native Americans live in Tennessee

500 B.C. Mound Builder culture in Tennessee begins

A.D. 1500s Chickasaw, Yuchi, and Cherokee peoples inhabit the Tennessee area

1541 Spain's Hernando de Soto becomes first European to enter Tennessee

1673 Marquette and Joliet explore the Mississippi River valley

1701 to 1800

1763 British gain control of Tennessee at end of French and Indian War

1772 Settlers of North Carolina form Watauga Association

1779 Fort Nashborough founded at site of modern Nashville

1785 Settlers of Tennessee declare state of Franklin

1796 Tennessee enters the Union as a state

The Twentieth Century

In the late 1800s, Tennessee's economy gradually expanded and became tied to the economy of the nation. Railways spread across the state, and new factories opened. Timber harvesting and coal mining also became important sources of employment in the early 1900s.

After the United States entered World War I in 1917, about 100,000 people from Tennessee served in the armed forces. The most famous soldier in World War I was from Tennessee—Sergeant Alvin C. York of Fentress County. He won the Congressional Medal of Honor—the nation's highest military honor—and became a symbol of patriotism throughout the country.

▲ **Alvin York, winner of the Congressional Medal of Honor**

After the war, the United States Congress approved the Nineteenth Amendment to the Constitution, which would give women the right to vote. After 35 states voted in favor of the amendment, one more state vote was needed to make it official. Anne Dallas Dudley, a state and national leader in the woman suffrage movement, urged members of the Tennessee state legislature to pass the amendment. In 1920 Tennessee became the 36th state to approve the Nineteenth Amendment, and women across the country could vote.

Depression and Recovery Tennessee's economy continued to grow after World War I, although the state's farmers faced hardships with the high cost of modernizing their equipment and low prices for their crops. In 1929 the Great Depression began, a sharp national economic collapse that cost many people their jobs and their way of life.

1815 Chattanooga founded as a trading post run by Cherokee

1819 Memphis founded

1861 Tennessee secedes from Union; Civil War begins

1801 to 1900

1861–1865 Civil War brings many battles to Tennessee

1866 Tennessee readmitted to Union

1880s New laws begin to restrain African Americans' voting rights

1918 Sergeant Alvin York fights heroically in World War I

1933 Federal government creates Tennessee Valley Authority (TVA)

1940s Oak Ridge built as part of effort to develop atomic bomb

1960 African American college students in Nashville begin sit-ins for civil rights

1901 to 2000

1968 Martin Luther King, Jr., shot to death in Memphis

1980 Japanese automaker begins building factory in Tennessee

1987 General Motors auto plant opens near Spring Hill

2000 Tennessee named "State of the Year" for tremendous economic growth in 1999

Nashville

During the early 1960s, students from Fisk University staged sit-ins at restaurants in Nashville to protest segregation.

History **Why do you think the owner of this restaurant placed packages of napkins on stools near this student?**

In 1933 President Franklin D. Roosevelt launched his New Deal, a program that aimed to rebuild the country's economy. One of his plans called for creating the Tennessee Valley Authority (TVA). He hoped that the TVA's dams could provide hydroelectric energy to Tennessee and surrounding states, as well as prevent the state's rivers from flooding and damaging nearby areas. Today the TVA is a major producer of electricity in the southeastern United States, although most of that electricity now comes from coal- and nuclear-powered plants. Turn to page TN46 to learn more about the TVA.

World War II During World War II, hundreds of thousands of Tennesseans joined the armed forces. Tennessee also had a unique role in the weapons research of World War II. The development and production of the atomic bomb took place in secret facilities at a newly built town called Oak Ridge, near Knoxville. Today Oak Ridge remains a major research center, although bomb production is no longer important.

A Tennessean, Cordell Hull, was secretary of state during World War II and the postwar period. One of the leaders that founded the United Nations in 1945, he received the Nobel Peace Prize for his role in setting up this organization.

The Later Years World War II can be seen as a turning point in the economy of Tennessee. The mechanization of farming methods resulted in larger farms but fewer workers on farms. Industries outside the state were locating branches in many Tennessee towns, offering rural populations new sources of income and opportunities. However, many young, rural Tennesseans migrated outside the state, especially to Michigan and Ohio, to find jobs.

Tennessee also made advances in civil rights for African Americans. In 1956, after years of separate and unequal education, African Americans began attending schools with white students. African American students from Fisk University in Nashville staged sit-ins that helped them win equal rights in restaurants and other public places. Their nonviolent tactics became role models for other civil rights groups fighting segregation throughout the country.

Memphis was the scene of one of the saddest days of the civil rights struggle. In April 1968, Reverend Martin Luther King, Jr.—the foremost leader of the civil rights movement—was visiting the city to support local workers who were seeking better working conditions. He was shot to death while standing with friends on the balcony of the Lorraine Motel, in which he was staying. Today that motel is a national museum showcasing the struggle for civil rights.

By the 1970s, manufacturing had become a major source of employment in Tennessee. Automobile-assembly factories were built in the early 1980s, followed by manufacturers of parts needed by the assembly plants. Memphis became an air-shipping hub when Federal Express made the city the center for its overnight letter and package services.

Tennessee leaders played important roles in national politics. Senator Howard Baker, Jr., was a leading figure in the United States Senate. Al Gore, Jr., served two terms as a United States senator and as vice president of the United States. The government, economy, and culture of Tennessee today are discussed in the next three sections.

Reading Check What city was the site of atomic research?

Section 2 Assessment

Defining Key Terms

1. **Define** clan, constitution, secede.

Recalling Facts

2. **History** For what were the mounds created by the Mound Builders used?
3. **Location** Why was Tennessee important to both sides during the Civil War?
4. **Government** How did Tennessee contribute to equal rights for women?

Critical Thinking

5. **Understanding Cause and Effect** In which area was slavery more extensive, East Tennessee or West Tennessee? Why?
6. **Summarizing Information** Why were the Reconstruction years difficult for Tennessee?

Graphic Organizer

7. **Organizing Information** Create a chart like the one below. Then explain how each Tennessean named on the chart contributed to the United States.

Sequoyah	Andrew Jackson	James Knox Polk
Anne Dallas Dudley	Cordell Hull	Fisk University students

Applying Geography Skills

8. **Analyzing a Time Line** Look at the time line on pages TN20–TN21. What city was founded by the Cherokee in the 1800s? What manufacturing industry moved into Tennessee in the 1980s?

Case Study:

The Natchez Trace

Focus: ***An ancient trail blazed by Native Americans became a well-worn pathway in the early years of the United States. Today it serves as a highway and a park.***

What do a Native American trader, a flatboat worker of the 1800s, and a modern family driving a car have in common? If they traveled from southern Mississippi to Tennessee, they probably took the same road. That road is the Natchez Trace, which covers about 450 miles (724 km) from Natchez, Mississippi, to Nashville, Tennessee.

▲ **The Natchez Trace Parkway today**

Origins of the Natchez Trace

Why is this route called a "trace"? The name comes from an old French word for "a line of footprints." Native Americans, you see, first created the road the hard way—by foot. Avoiding swamps, they cut the trail through dense oak and hickory forests to bring trade goods from the lower Mississippi River valley to the North. Over time, Native Americans wore down a clear path that stretched hundreds of miles.

Pioneer Highway

In the late 1700s, settlers streamed over the Appalachian Mountains. They settled along the Ohio and Mississippi Rivers and in places such as Tennessee. With fertile land and backbreaking labor, farmers produced abundant crops. Carting those goods back over the Appalachians to towns on the Atlantic coast was difficult, though. Farmers found it much easier to use the Ohio and Mississippi Rivers to ship their harvests on flatboats. These boats relied on the river currents to carry goods to large ports in the South.

The Mississippi River has a strong south-flowing current, which made it difficult for the flatboats to move back to the North. After the goods were unloaded in the South, the flatboat workers went back to the North on land. They created the Natchez Trace by following the old Native American trails. This walkway was narrow—only 8 feet (2.4 m) wide at its widest—and covered by dirt. Still, every month thousands of people used it. From

about 1800 to 1830, the Trace was a major American roadway.

Over time, facilities sprang up to care for the travelers. Business people built "stands," which were like inns. Conditions were crowded at these stands. Visitors to the stand in Mount Locust, Mississippi, had to sleep three to a bed. The Choctaws who lived along the Trace also sold food to travelers who needed it.

The journey along the Trace was difficult. In the South, the country was low and swampy, with clouds of mosquitoes. In the North, it was hilly, and many weary travelers had to walk uphill for long stretches.

A Period of Decline

In the 1820s and 1830s, new technology came into use. Steamboats plied the waters of the Mississippi River. Their powerful engines made it possible to move north, upstream, with ease. Railroads later crossed the region, enabling people to travel by boat or by rail. The Trace was no longer needed, and for many decades, it was simply ignored.

Though farms spread through the region crossed by the Trace, the road was not turned into farmland. Long stretches of the pathway were on high, rocky ground that farmers could not plow. As a result, fields never covered the roadway.

The Trace Today

Today the Trace is a park—a very long, very thin national park. The Natchez Trace Parkway follows the old footpath on a winding route from Natchez to Nashville. Though the road stretches 450 miles (724 km) long, it ranges only 90 feet (27 m) to 300 feet (91 m) wide.

The roadway is dotted with places where drivers can visit remains of Native American mound villages or see what is left of the old travelers' stands. At night, with the stars shining overhead and the crickets chirping, they can feel like those earlier travelers did, but without the sore feet!

Using the Case Study

1. **Human/Environment Interaction** What are the four stages in the history of the Natchez Trace?
2. **History** When was the Natchez Trace most in use?
3. **Understanding Cause and Effect** Why did the Natchez Trace fall out of use?
4. **Skillbuilder Activity** Write a journal entry explaining what you think it was like to travel along the Natchez Trace in the 1800s.

TENNESSEE: The Battleground

Drummer boy at Shiloh

During the Civil War, more battles were fought in Tennessee than in any other state except Virginia. What made Tennessee such an important battleground?

Tennessee's Importance

Tennessee's location made the state vital for both the Union and the Confederate states. To invade Mississippi, Alabama, and Georgia, Union forces had to go through Tennessee. Confederate armies used Tennessee as a defensive line for other Confederate states.

Tennessee's rivers were also important. Union forces used the Mississippi River to reach deep into the Confederacy. The Tennessee and Cumberland Rivers could also be used to reach the other side's territory.

Finally, railroads connected Nashville, Chattanooga, and Memphis to other Confederate cities. Controlling these cities led to control of rail lines.

Key Battles

In early February 1862, Union forces captured Fort Henry, giving them control of the Tennessee River. About a week later, they fought heavily to take Fort Donelson and gain control of the Cumberland River. By the end of the month, Union troops took over Nashville, and Confederate troops there retreated.

In April 1862, Union General Ulysses S. Grant moved along the Tennessee River into the southwestern part of the state, hoping to seize the railroad connecting Memphis to Confederate cities along the Atlantic coast. The Confederate army attacked Grant's troops at Shiloh. After fierce fighting, the Confederates had to withdraw when 25,000 Union reinforcements arrived. Two months later, Union forces captured Memphis.

Brilliant cavalry raids during the late summer returned control of the southern part of Middle Tennessee to the Confederates. In December, however, the bloody battle at Murfreesboro, or Stones River, produced a Confederate retreat.

In 1863 a Union army took Chattanooga, a rail center. This same army was defeated by Confederate forces at the Battle of Chickamauga and quickly retreated back to Chattanooga. When fresh troops arrived, the Union army struck again and pushed the Confederates out of Tennessee.

The last two battles in Tennessee were fought at Franklin and Nashville. The Confederate army met a costly defeat in December of 1864 and left Tennessee in Union hands.

QUESTIONS

1. What happened at the Battle of Shiloh?

2. Why did the Union army retreat to Chattanooga?

Battle of Nashville, by Howard Pyle, 1906 ▶

NATIONAL GEOGRAPHIC SOCIETY

Civil War Battles in Tennessee

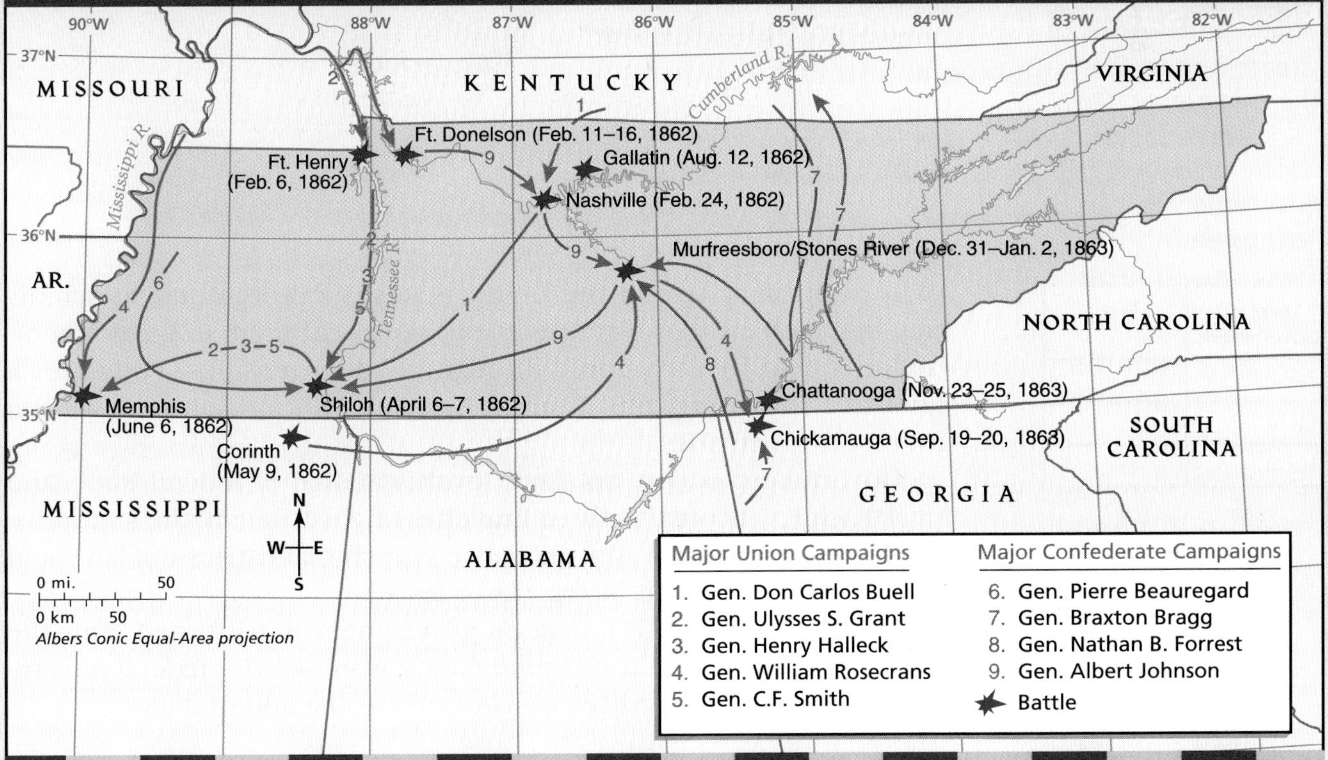

90°W 88°W 87°W 86°W 85°W 84°W 83°W 82°W

37°N 36°N 35°N

MISSOURI

KENTUCKY

VIRGINIA

AR.

NORTH CAROLINA

SOUTH CAROLINA

MISSISSIPPI

ALABAMA

GEORGIA

Mississippi R.

Tennessee R.

Cumberland R.

Ft. Donelson (Feb. 11–16, 1862)

Ft. Henry (Feb. 6, 1862)

Gallatin (Aug. 12, 1862)

Nashville (Feb. 24, 1862)

Murfreesboro/Stones River (Dec. 31–Jan. 2, 1863)

Memphis (June 6, 1862)

Shiloh (April 6–7, 1862)

Corinth (May 9, 1862)

Chattanooga (Nov. 23–25, 1863)

Chickamauga (Sep. 19–20, 1863)

N W E S

0 mi. 50

0 km 50

Albers Conic Equal-Area projection

Major Union Campaigns	Major Confederate Campaigns
1. Gen. Don Carlos Buell	6. Gen. Pierre Beauregard
2. Gen. Ulysses S. Grant	7. Gen. Braxton Bragg
3. Gen. Henry Halleck	8. Gen. Nathan B. Forrest
4. Gen. William Rosecrans	9. Gen. Albert Johnson
5. Gen. C.F. Smith	Battle

Section 3 Tennessee's Government

Guide to Reading

Main Idea

Tennesseans are governed by three levels of government—federal, state, and local.

Terms to Know

- amendment
- legislative branch
- executive branch
- veto
- cabinet
- judicial branch
- criminal case
- civil case
- appellate court
- home rule

Places to Locate

- Davidson County
- Nashville

Reading Strategy

Create a chart like the one below. Then fill in three facts about each level of government in Tennessee.

Level of Government	Facts
Federal	
State	
Local	

NATIONAL GEOGRAPHIC Exploring Tennessee

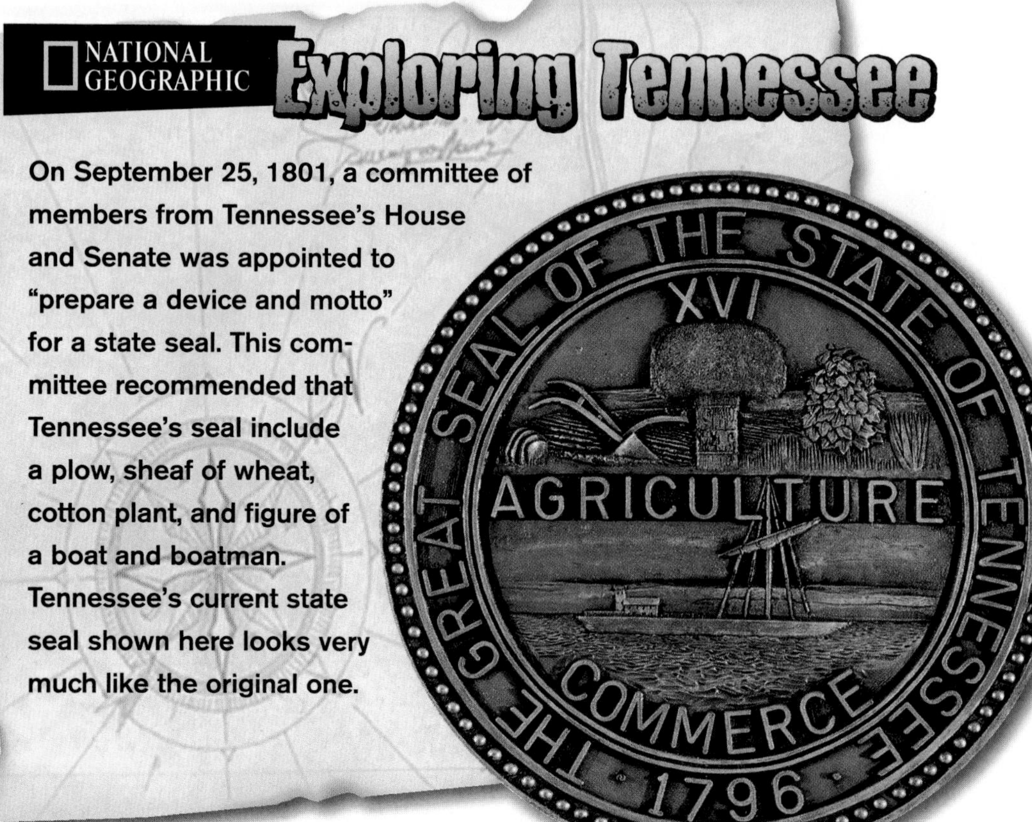

On September 25, 1801, a committee of members from Tennessee's House and Senate was appointed to "prepare a device and motto" for a state seal. This committee recommended that Tennessee's seal include a plow, sheaf of wheat, cotton plant, and figure of a boat and boatman. Tennessee's current state seal shown here looks very much like the original one.

The political system of the United States is a representative democracy in which citizens elect people to represent them in government. Power is held by the people through good citizenship—voting for a candidate that represents them and staying informed about laws and government activities.

Government occurs on three levels: national or federal, state, and local. Each level contains three branches of government: the legislative branch that makes laws, the executive branch that carries out laws, and the judicial branch that interprets or tests laws.

At the state level, Tennessee's government is patterned after the federal government of the United States. Also like the federal government, the state has a written constitution as the adopted law.

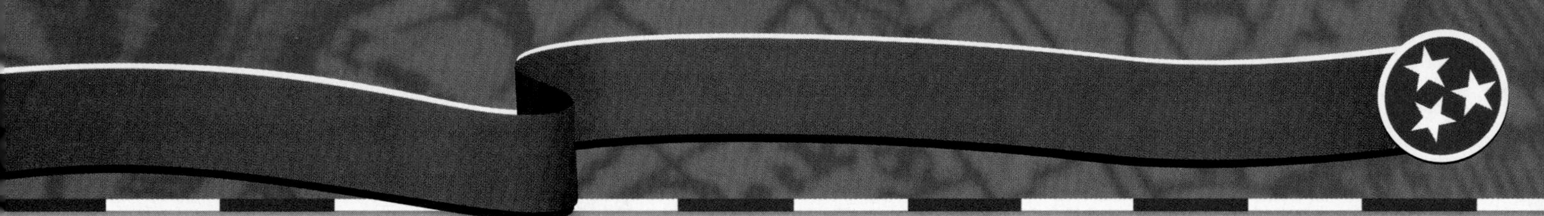

Tennessee's Constitution

Tennessee's present constitution was adopted in 1870. The state had two earlier constitutions, the first of which was adopted in 1796 when Tennessee became a state. The second was adopted in 1835.

Amendments, or changes to the constitution, can be added to this basic law in one of two ways. The state legislature, or lawmakers, can propose an amendment if a majority of the legislators vote for it. For the amendment to take effect, however, two more steps are needed. First, the legislature must again approve it in the following session by a two-thirds majority. Second, a majority of people voting in an election for governor must approve the amendment.

The second way to amend the constitution is through a constitutional convention. If a majority of voters approve, a majority of legislators may call such a convention specifically to propose amendments. Any amendments that this meeting passes must then be approved by a majority of the voters in a statewide election.

✓Reading Check **How many constitutions has Tennessee had?**

▼ Tennessee's state bird is the mockingbird.

▲ The act naming the iris as the state flower did not specify a color. However, by tradition the purple iris is considered Tennessee's state flower.

The Legislative Branch

The **legislative branch** has the power to make state laws based on the people's wishes. Tennessee's legislature, called the General Assembly, is divided into two parts, or houses. As in the national Congress, these houses are called the Senate and the House of Representatives. Voters elect 33 state senators for four-year terms. The 99 members of the House of Representatives are elected for two-year terms.

The General Assembly meets in odd-numbered years on the second Tuesday in January to plan its activities and choose its officers. This organizational session lasts no more than 15 days. The regular session of the assembly starts on the Tuesday after the organizational session ends. Regular sessions are limited to 90 legislative days over a two-year period. In an emergency, the governor can call a special session, as can the leaders of the two houses under certain circumstances. The Case Study on page TN36 describes how the two houses pass a law.

Each house has a leader called the Speaker. The Speaker of the Senate also serves as the state's lieutenant governor, or second in command. If anything happens to the governor, the lieutenant governor runs the state. The Speaker of the House is third in line.

✓Reading Check **What is Tennessee's legislature called?**

The Executive Branch

The **executive branch** of Tennessee's government has the responsibility to implement and enforce laws, collect taxes, and promote the well-being of the state and its citizens. Suppose the legislature

The Organization of Tennessee's State Government

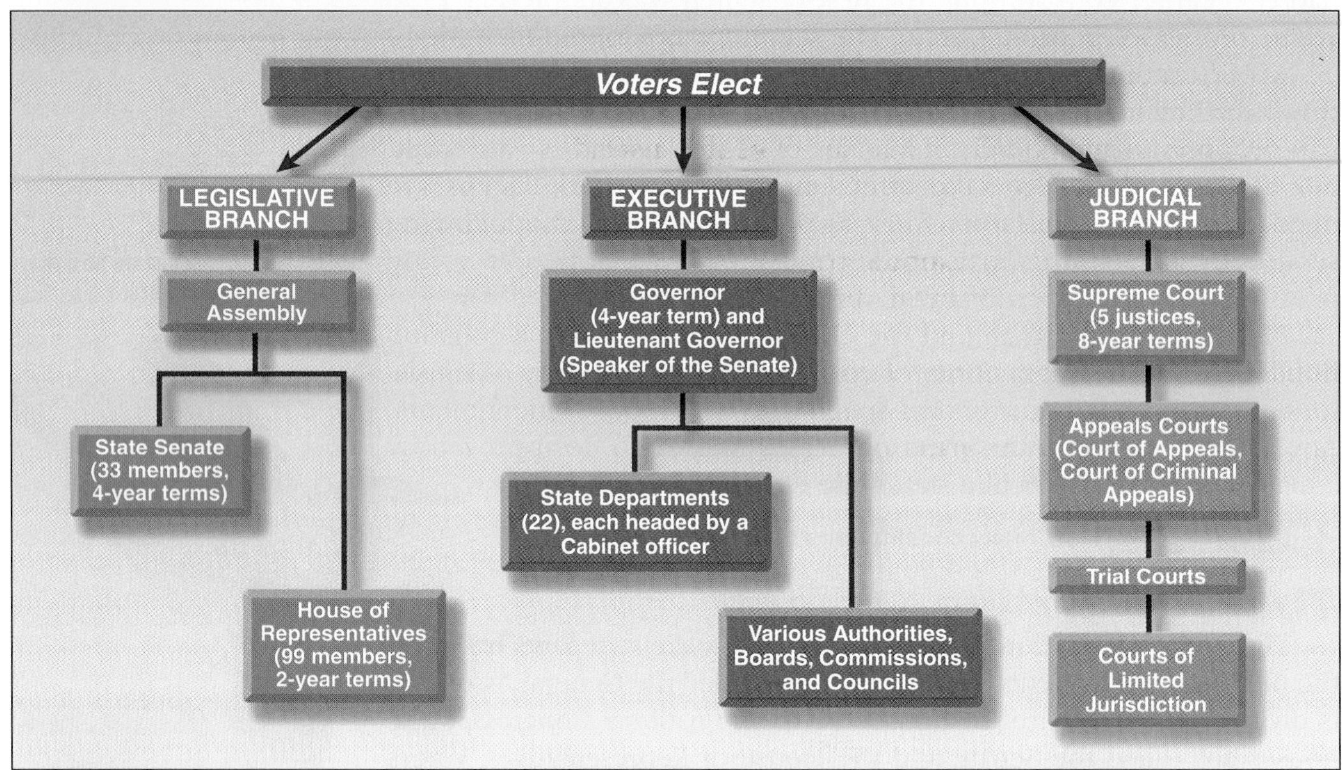

Analyzing the Chart

Tennessee's state government is modeled after the national government.

Place **Who serves as the state's lieutenant governor?**

makes a law that states a person in Tennessee must pass a test to get a driver's license. Workers in the executive branch's Department of Transportation write the test, give it to potential drivers, judge how they perform on the test, and give a driver's license to those who pass it.

The Governor As you can see from the chart above, the governor heads the executive branch. This official is the state's commander in chief. He or she can call the Tennessee National Guard into service if an emergency occurs.

The state's voters elect the governor to a four-year term. A governor may serve an unlimited number of terms but can only hold the office for two terms in a row. The chart on page TN32 lists all of Tennessee's governors.

The governor can recommend potential laws to the legislature and can comment on bills, or proposed laws, that the legislature is considering. Once the General Assembly passes a bill, the governor's actions determine the bill's fate. If the governor signs the bill, it becomes state law. If the governor does not sign the bill in 10 days, it still becomes state law. The governor can also **veto**, or disapprove, a bill, which prevents the bill from becoming a law. However, the General Assembly has

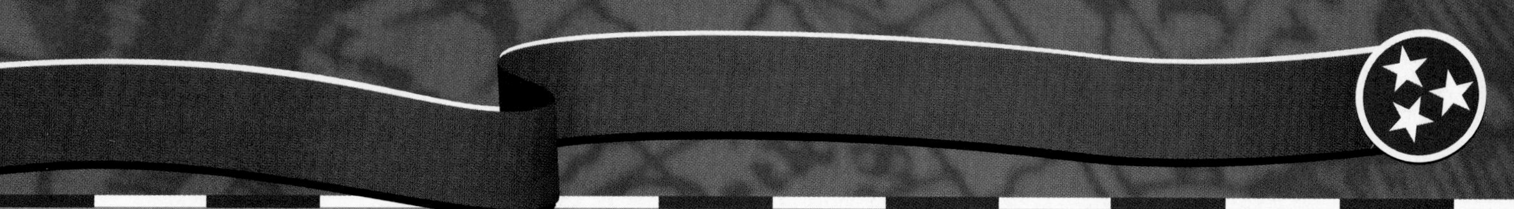

the power to override that veto. This means that if a majority of both houses in the legislature approves the bill once more following a governor's veto, it does become the law of Tennessee.

The Cabinet and Commissions In addition to the governor, the executive branch includes 22 departments plus other agencies. The people who head up these departments are called the **cabinet.** Cabinet members are appointed by the governor instead of elected by voters. Some of Tennessee's departments include the Departments of Agriculture, Health, Labor and Workforce Development, Safety, Education, Tourist Development, Environment and Conservation, and Children's Services.

There are also special commissions, such as the Arts Commission or the Tennessee Bureau of Investigation, that have authority over certain areas. The governor has the power to appoint the members of these commissions and to oversee their work.

Some members of the executive branch are appointed by other parts of the government. The attorney general—the state's chief legal officer—is named by the chief justice of the Tennessee Supreme Court. The legislature chooses the secretary of state and two officers who oversee the state's finances.

On the Job

Governor Don Sundquist heads the executive branch in Tennessee.

Government **What government officials are appointed by the governor?**

Reading Check **What three options does a governor have when the legislature passes a bill?**

The Judicial Branch

Tennessee also has a **judicial branch,** which provides a system to settle civil disputes, to protect the rights of citizens, and to rule on conflicts between laws and the state constitution. The judicial system has four levels of courts. Voters elect all judges in these courts to eight-year terms.

The lowest level includes Courts of Limited Jurisdiction. Municipal Courts, for instance, try cases such as traffic violations. Juvenile Courts only hear cases involving people younger than 18 years of age.

The state's trial courts hear trials in criminal and civil cases. **Criminal cases** involve people charged with breaking the law. **Civil cases** are those in which one person or group charges that another person or group somehow caused injury.

Tennessee's Governors

Name	Party	Occupation	Term of Office
John Sevier	Democrat	Soldier, pioneer	1796–1801
Archibald Roane	Democrat	Lawyer	1801–1803
John Sevier	Democrat	Soldier, pioneer	1803–1809
Willie Blount	Democrat	Lawyer, planter	1809–1815
Joseph McMinn	Democrat	Merchant	1815–1821
William Carroll	Democrat	Merchant, soldier	1821–1827
Sam Houston	Democrat	Lawyer	1827–1829
William Hall	Democrat	Planter, soldier	1829
William Carroll	Democrat	Merchant, soldier	1829–1835
Newton Cannon	Whig	Merchant, lawyer	1835–1839
James K. Polk	Democrat	Lawyer	1839–1841
James C. Jones	Whig	Lawyer	1841–1845
Aaron V. Brown	Democrat	Lawyer	1845–1847
Neill S. Brown	Whig	Lawyer	1847–1849
William Trousdale	Democrat	Lawyer	1849–1851
William B. Campbell	Whig	Lawyer	1851–1853
Andrew Johnson	Democrat	Tailor	1853–1857
Isham G. Harris	Democrat	Lawyer, senator	1857–1862
Andrew Johnson	Democrat	President (military rule)	1862–1865
William G. Brownlow	Whig	Editor, preacher	1865–1869
DeWitt C. Senter	Whig-Republican	Lawyer	1869–1871
John C. Brown	Whig-Democrat	Lawyer	1871–1875
James D. Porter	Democrat	Lawyer, educator	1875–1879
Albert S. Marks	Democrat	Lawyer, chancellor	1879–1881
Alvin Hawkins	Whig-Republican	Lawyer, judge	1881–1883
William B. Bate	Democrat	Lawyer, senator	1883–1887
Robert Love Taylor	Democrat	Lawyer, senator	1887–1891
John P. Buchanan	Democrat	Farmer	1891–1893
Peter Turney	Democrat	Lawyer, judge	1893–1897
Robert Love Taylor	Democrat	Lawyer, senator	1897–1899
Benton McMillin	Democrat	Lawyer, diplomat	1899–1903
James B. Frazier	Democrat	Lawyer, senator	1903–1905
John I. Cox	Democrat	Lawyer	1905–1907
Malcolm R. Patterson	Democrat	Lawyer, judge	1907–1911
Ben W. Hooper	Republican	Lawyer	1911–1915
Tom C. Rye	Democrat	Lawyer, judge	1915–1919
A.H. Roberts	Democrat	Lawyer, judge	1919–1921
Alfred A. Taylor	Republican	Lawyer	1921–1923
Austin Peay	Democrat	Lawyer	1923–1927
Henry H. Horton	Democrat	Lawyer, farmer	1927–1933
Hill McAlister	Democrat	Lawyer	1933–1937
Gordon Browning	Democrat	Lawyer, judge	1937–1939
Prentice Cooper	Democrat	Lawyer	1939–1945
Jim McCord	Democrat	Editor	1945–1949
Gorden Browning	Democrat	Lawyer, judge	1949–1953
Frank G. Clement	Democrat	Lawyer	1953–1959
Buford Ellington	Democrat	Farmer	1959–1963
Frank G. Clement	Democrat	Lawyer	1963–1967
Buford Ellington	Democrat	Farmer	1967–1971
Winfield Dunn	Republican	Dentist	1971–1975
Ray Blanton	Democrat	Farmer, businessman	1975–1979
Lamar Alexander	Republican	Lawyer	1979–1987
Ned McWherter	Democrat	Businessman	1987–1995
Don Sundquist	Republican	Businessman	1995–

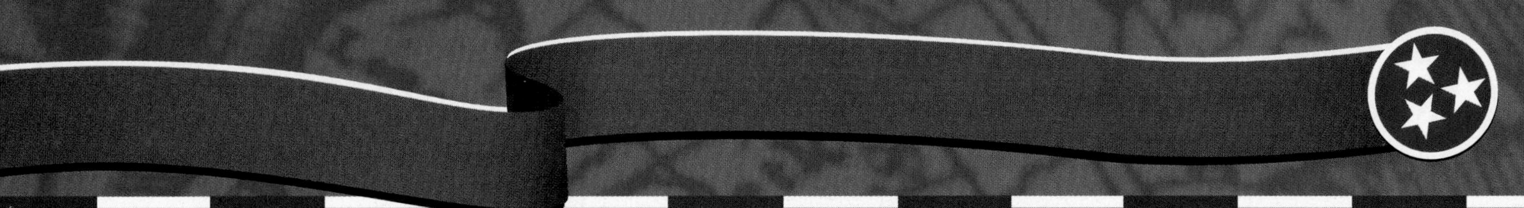

The person who loses in a trial court has the right to appeal the decision to an appellate court. The person might say that his or her rights were violated or that the lower court judge applied the law in the wrong way. The judges of the appellate courts hear the facts and then rule whether the lower court decision should stand or be overturned. Tennessee's Court of Criminal Appeals and the Court of Appeals, which hears civil cases, both have 12 judges.

The highest court in Tennessee is the state Supreme Court. The five justices on this court serve as the final court of appeals for the state. They hear appeals of decisions made by justices of the appellate courts. Parties that lose a case before the state Supreme Court might have one other source of appeal, however. They might be able to take their case to the United States Supreme Court.

✓Reading Check **What is the highest court in Tennessee?**

Local Government

Tennessee has about 335 cities and towns, each with its own government. Some of these cities have adopted home rule, meaning that they have their own charters, or constitutions, that give them the right to govern themselves. Cities without home rule have less freedom to change their practices from the rules set by the state legislature.

Types of Local Government

Analyzing the Chart

Tennessee's cities follow one of three types of local government.

Place **In which type do city council members hire a manager?**

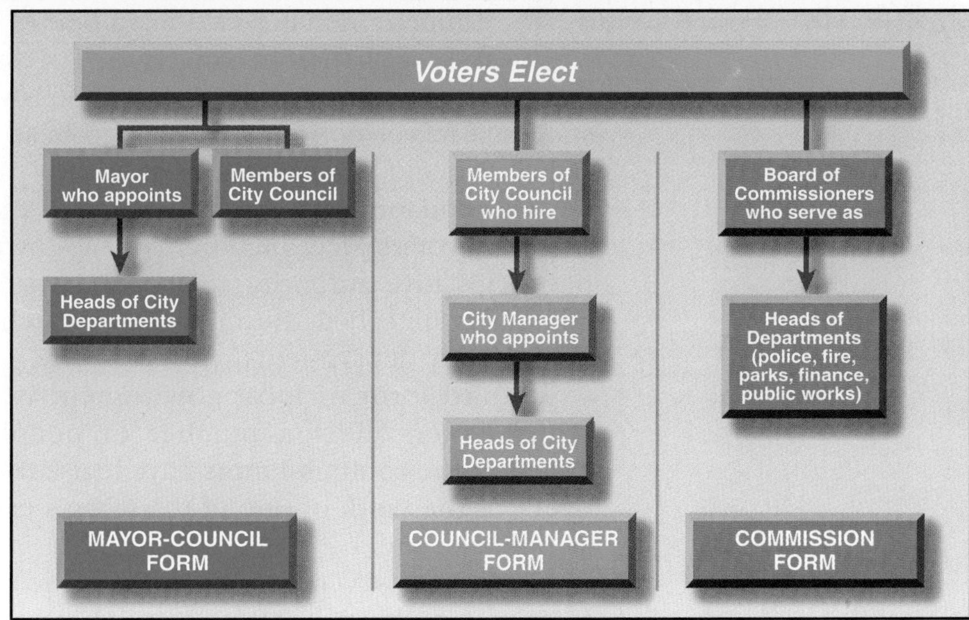

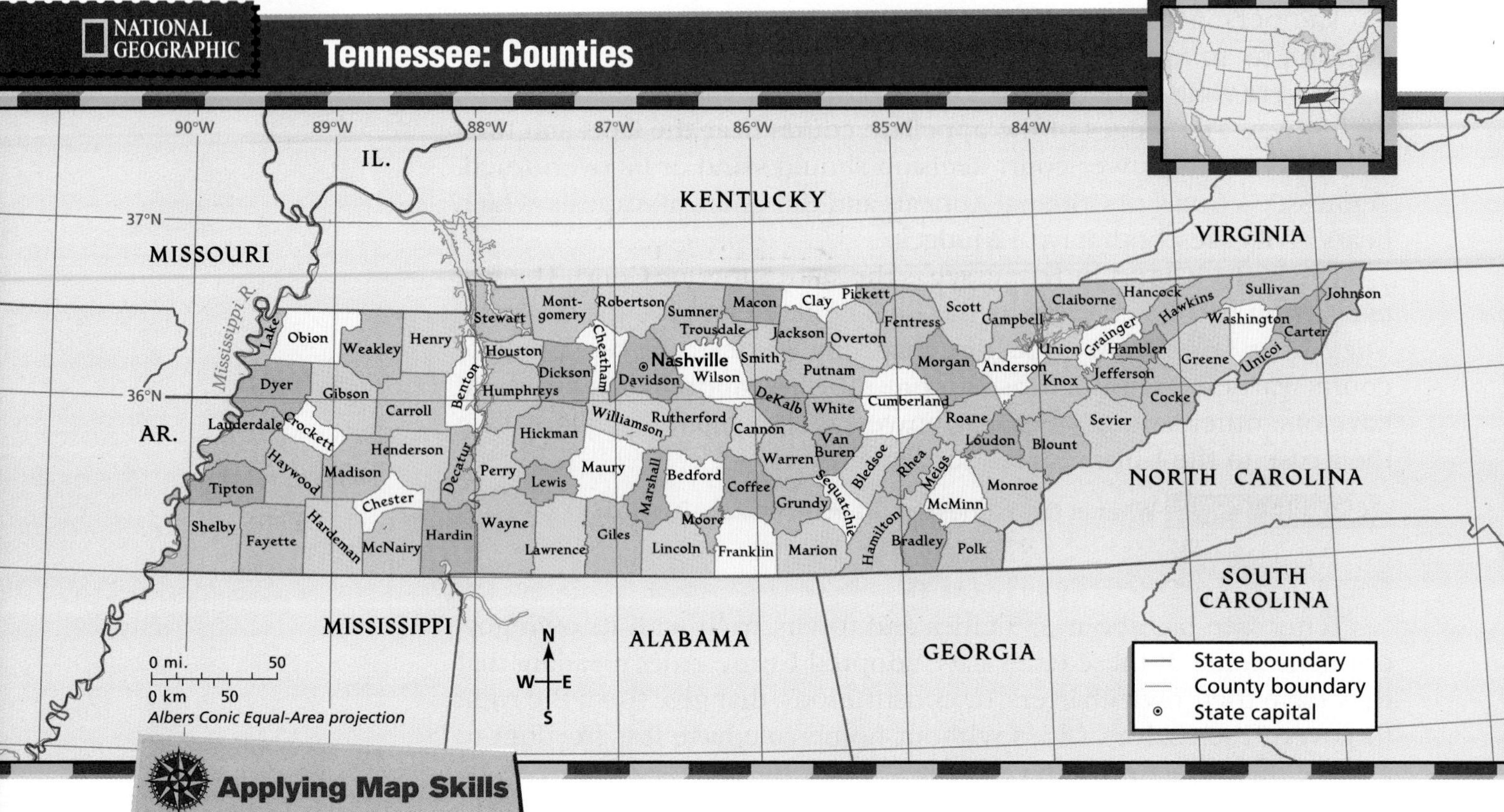

Applying Map Skills

1. In what county is the capital located?
2. What is the easternmost county in the state?

Find NGS online map resources @ www.nationalgeographic.com/maps

Local government can take one of three forms. The structure of each of these forms is shown in the chart on page TN33. In one form—the mayor-council form—the government includes two main bodies. The city council serves as the legislature, making laws. The mayor is the city or town's chief executive, carrying out the laws. Like the governor of the state, the mayor appoints officials to head city departments, such as police, fire, and parks and recreation.

A second form of local government is the council-manager form. In this plan, voters elect members of the town council. These members have legislative authority and make laws. They select a professional administrator called the city manager, who makes sure that all the town or city departments work properly.

A third form of local government is the commission form, in which voters elect a number of people called commissioners. Together, the commissioners have legislative power. Each of them also oversees the work of one of the town's executive departments, such as police or fire.

Sometimes several towns in the same area need to work together to solve a problem or address an issue. In such cases, the towns may

form what is called a *special district* that has the power to address one issue—such as sewage or water treatment—for an area larger than just one town.

County Government The map on page TN34 shows Tennessee's 95 counties. Groups known as county commissions govern almost all of Tennessee's counties. These groups both make and carry out laws. County governments handle elections, collect taxes, issue licenses, and settle wills and estates when people die. They also register property titles and promote public health, education, and library services.

In recent decades, more and more people have moved to suburbs and are no longer subject to city government rules. However, these people still need services such as police and fire protection. County governments have taken on these roles, making county governments more important than they used to be. **Davidson County** and the city of **Nashville** have an unusual arrangement. In 1963 their two governments joined together as one. A mayor and a 40-member council serve as the government of both the city and the county.

Reading Check How many counties does Tennessee have?

Section 3 Assessment

Defining Key Terms

1. **Define** amendment, legislative branch, executive branch, veto, cabinet, judicial branch, criminal case, civil case, appellate court, home rule.

Recalling Facts

2. **Government** What are the three branches of Tennessee's government?
3. **Government** Why are the two highest courts called appellate courts?
4. **Government** What are three examples of departments that a mayor oversees?

Critical Thinking

5. **Analyzing Information** Why does the constitution of Tennessee include the opportunity to make amendments?
6. **Drawing Conclusions** How have population changes affected county government?

Graphic Organizer

7. **Organizing Information** Draw a diagram like this one. Under each arrow, describe the structure of the appropriate branch of Tennessee's state government.

Legislative Branch	Executive Branch	Judicial Branch
↓	↓	↓

Applying Geography Skills

8. **Analyzing Charts** Look at the charts showing the organization of state and local governments on pages TN30 and TN33. What group chooses most of the public officials at each of these levels of government?

CASE STUDY: Bikes and Helmets

FOCUS: ***Early in 2000, the Tennessee legislature changed a law about wearing bicycle safety helmets. How are laws made in the state?***

The General Assembly of Tennessee makes laws—but how? First, a legislator has to decide that a new law is needed. Tennessee had a law saying that children must wear bicycle helmets when they ride their bikes on any "public roadway." Two Tennessee state senators thought this wording was confusing. Did "public roadway" mean highways? What about streets or sidewalks? They decided to make the law clearer.

Introducing a Bill

The path to a new law begins when a member of the state Senate or House makes a proposal called a *bill.* In this case, the two senators wrote a bill proposing that the words "public roadway" be changed to "public highway, street, or sidewalk." They introduced it on January 20. From then on, the proposal was known as SB2794. *SB* stands for "Senate Bill."

In the Senate

The bill was sent to the Senate's Transportation Committee for review. Members of that committee studied the bill and recommended that the full Senate approve it. On February 16, 32 senators voted in favor of the bill. There were no votes against it. As a result, the bill passed the Senate.

▲ Children wearing safety helmets

In the House

The bill was not a law yet, however. It had to pass the House, too. Members of the House introduced their own version of the bill on February 2. That bill was given the number HB3194. *HB* stands for "House Bill." A committee in the House also had to review the bill. As in the Senate, the House committee approved the bill and recommended it for passage.

The House bill was placed on the calendar for March 20. On that day, House leaders introduced the Senate version of the bill. They did so because the two versions of a bill have to use the same language for the bill to become law. When the bill came up for vote in the House, though, some members of the House added three amendments, or changes to the language of the bill. The full House approved the bill with the amendments.

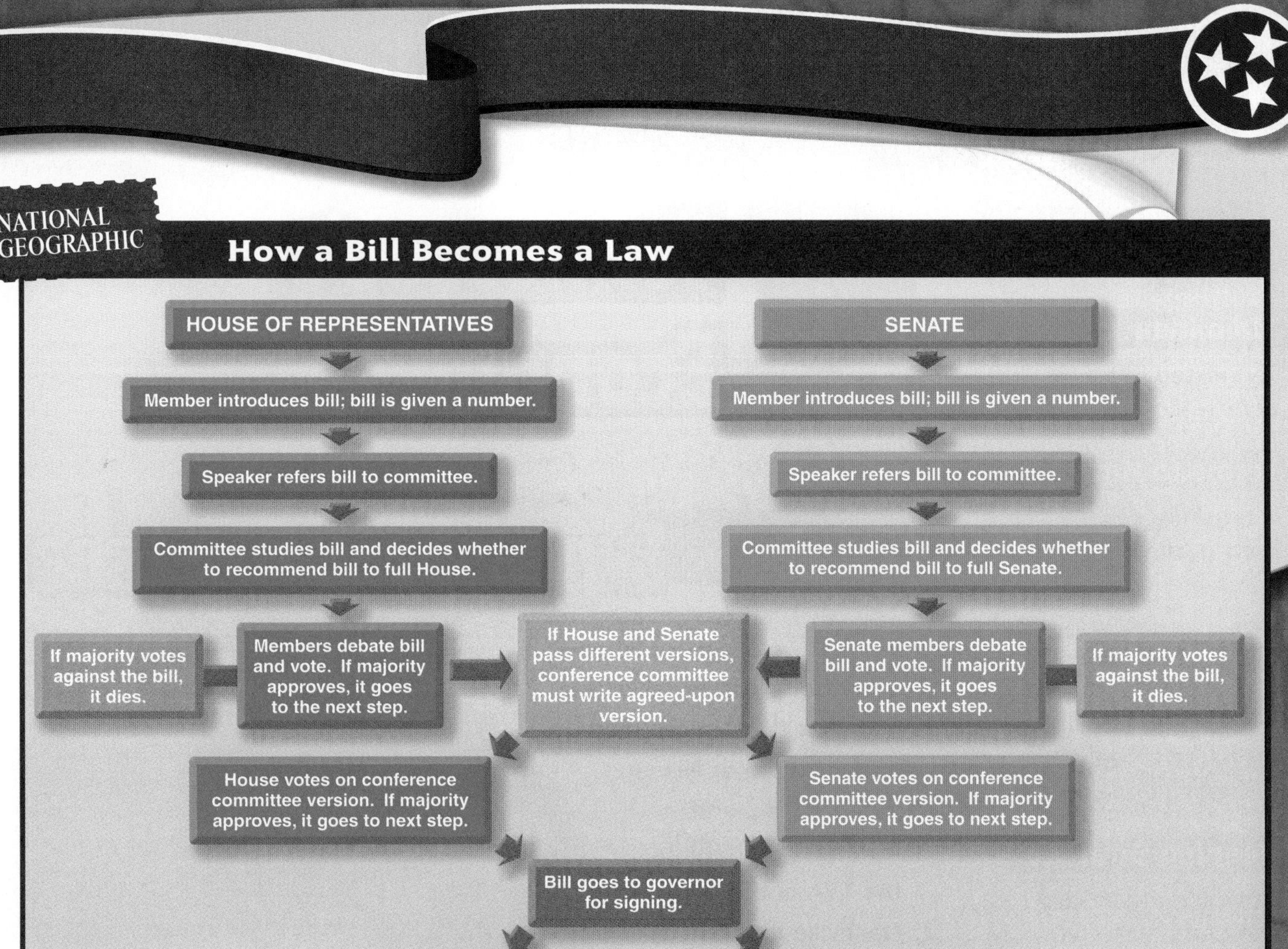

Working Together

Although the bike safety bill had passed both houses, it still was not a law. The House version differed from the Senate version. The Senate voted in favor of two amendments but turned down the third. When the vote went back to the House, its members refused to remove that third amendment.

The bill then went to a conference committee made up of members of both the Senate and the House to work out the differences between the two bills. They agreed to the House version and took the final version of the bill back to their chambers.

On June 5, the Senate approved the bill by a 30-to-0 vote. Four days later, the House passed it 88 to 0. On June 19, 2000, the governor signed the bill into law. It now had a new number—it was Public Chapter 916.

Using the Case Study

1. **Government** What happens to a bill after it is introduced in a house and given a number?
2. **Government** What is an amendment?
3. **Predicting Consequences** What if the members of the conference committee were unable to agree on the language for a bill?
4. **Skillbuilder Activity** Identify an issue that you think is a concern in Tennessee. Write your proposal for a new law to address the issue.

Guide to Reading

Main Idea

Tennessee has a diverse economy.

Terms to Know

- bituminous
- strip mining
- service industry

Places to Locate

- Memphis
- Nashville
- Chattanooga
- Knoxville

Reading Strategy

Draw a diagram like the one below. On the right, list three facts about each area of Tennessee's economy.

Economic Area	Facts
Agriculture	
Mining and Timber	
Manufacturing	
Service Industries	

Section 4 Tennessee's Economy

NATIONAL GEOGRAPHIC **Exploring Tennessee**

What do you think of when you hear the words *Tennessee's economy?* You might think of the Saturn or Nissan automobile plants. Perhaps you think of the TVA or the Nashville music industry. You might even think of walking horses, but probably not *carousel* horses. Here, a worker in Chattanooga carves carousel horses.

Tennessee used to be primarily a state of farms and small towns. In the 1930s, that changed rapidly. The Tennessee Valley Authority (TVA) played a role in this change by supplying low-cost electricity to factories. More and more manufacturing plants moved to rural counties and small towns, especially in the 1960s and 1970s. Tourism also expanded rapidly, and in some parts of the state, it is now a major source of employment. Thus Tennessee's economy is quite diverse.

Agriculture

The best areas for agriculture are found in West Tennessee, the Nashville Basin, and the Great Valley of East Tennessee, where the soils and landscape are most suitable for crop production. Even in these areas, however, the dominance of farming as a full-time livelihood has declined drastically over the last 50 years. As recently as 1950, about 230,000 farms contained roughly 10 million acres (4.1 million ha) devoted to growing crops. Today Tennessee has fewer than 75,000 farms, with approximately 7 million acres (2.8 million ha) devoted to crops. Furthermore, a majority of these are actually part-time farms, which means that their owners earn more income from nonfarm employment than from the sale of agricultural products. Part-time farming is especially prevalent in East and Middle Tennessee.

Still, agriculture remains important for the state as a whole. Livestock income is derived mostly from cattle, but dairy products and poultry are also important in some areas of the state. The Nashville Basin is known nationally for its walking horses.

Income from crop production comes mostly from tobacco, soybeans, cotton, and corn. Tobacco is grown mainly in East and Middle Tennessee. Cotton is almost exclusively found in West Tennessee, which also produces most of the soybeans and corn. Tennessee has some specialty crop areas as well. For example, Warren County on the

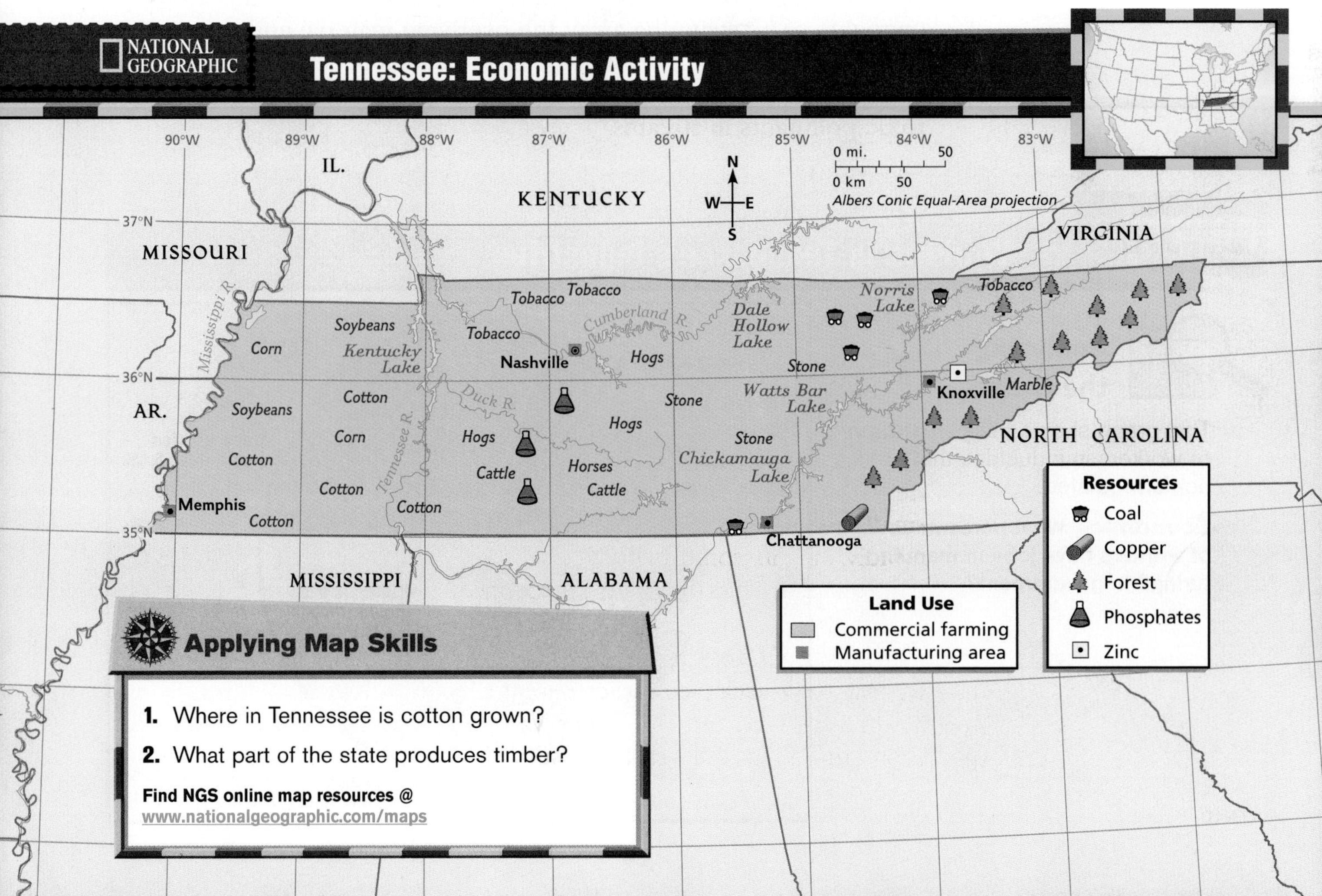

Applying Map Skills

1. Where in Tennessee is cotton grown?
2. What part of the state produces timber?

Find NGS online map resources @ www.nationalgeographic.com/maps

Highland Rim is one of the country's major producing areas of nursery stock—trees, shrubbery, and flowering bushes. Grainger County in East Tennessee is known for its tomatoes.

Reading Check **What are the state's main sources of agricultural income?**

Mining and Timber

Coal and other mineral products are relatively minor in the state's economy. The most widespread product mined today is stone, particularly crushed limestone, which is used in all kinds of construction, including highways. Knoxville used to be the center of marble quarrying, and it still has a thriving but small quarrying industry. The Great Valley of East Tennessee has some zinc mining east of Knoxville. Phosphate, used to make fertilizer, is mined in the Nashville Basin. Special clay for making pottery is taken from northwest Tennessee.

The Cumberland Plateau is a producer of **bituminous** coal, or soft coal. Coal mining became important at the end of the 1800s, and locally it is of some importance today. Seams of coal are exposed along the sides of the valleys eroded into the Cumberland Plateau. The coal is mined either by tunneling into these seams—if the seams are thick enough—or by stripping away the overlying material and then taking the coal. **Strip mining** results in barren bands of land and leaves long scars on the valley sides. It also can be a serious source of erosion and toxic pollutants in streams.

Workers in Tennessee's Industries

Analyzing the Graph

This graph shows the percentage of workers in industries that are nonfarm related.

Economics **What percentage of workers have jobs in manufacturing? In government?**

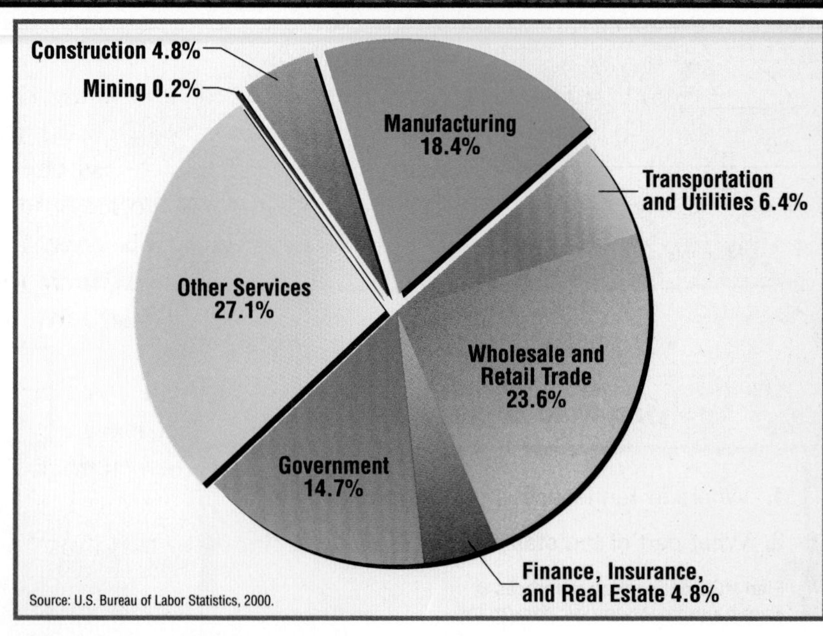

Source: U.S. Bureau of Labor Statistics, 2000.

NATIONAL GEOGRAPHIC On Location

Industry and Agriculture

Spring Hill was selected by General Motors as the site for their Saturn factory (left). Tennessee walking horses are raised and trained throughout the state (above).

Region **How have the types of manufacturing industries in Tennessee changed over time?**

The uplands of the Blue Ridge Mountains, parts of the Cumberland Plateau, and the Highland Rim are sources of timber products. Hardwoods like oak make up the major share of Tennessee's timber. Softer woods like cedar, pine, and hemlock are also harvested. Tennessee is one of the country's main producers of red cedar.

✓Reading Check **What is the most widespread product mined in Tennessee?**

Manufacturing and Transportation

Manufacturing has become increasingly important in Tennessee. In 1900 manufacturing accounted for only 46,000 jobs. Today more than 500,000 Tennesseans work in factories.

The types of manufacturing have changed over time. In the past, factories made textiles, chemicals, clothing, processed foods, and leather goods. Those industries are still found across the state, but today heavy manufacturing is more important. Two automakers—one from Japan and one from the United States—built new factories in Tennessee in the 1980s. These plants brought many new jobs to the state, attracted billions of dollars in foreign investment, and made Tennessee an important car manufacturing center.

Memphis, the state's largest city, is an important center of cotton, chemicals, and paper production. **Nashville** is home to factories that print books and music, make transportation equipment, and produce textiles. Factory workers in **Chattanooga** make metals, textiles, chemicals, and food products. **Knoxville** is a manufacturing center as well.

Tourist Attractions

Nashville's Parthenon was originally built in 1897 to celebrate the state's 100th birthday (above). An incline takes tourists to the top of Lookout Mountain near Chattanooga (right).

Place **What park is the most visited park in the United States?**

Transportation In the past, the people of Tennessee used the state's rivers to move themselves and their goods. Today shipping on waterways is largely limited to barging bulk goods such as fuels (petroleum products and coal), grains, and rock, gravel, and sand. The Mississippi River is a major waterway for shipping, and Memphis is an important river port. The Tennessee River has significant waterway traffic up to Chattanooga. The Cumberland River is the only other waterway in the state with much traffic.

Rail lines, especially north-south links, serve the largest cities for freight, but passenger service is now limited to Memphis and Nashville. Tennessee's position in the interstate highway system is vital, however. North-south interstate highways cross each of the three grand divisions, and I-40 is a heavily used east-west highway from Knoxville to Memphis.

✓Reading Check **By how much did manufacturing jobs grow in Tennessee from 1900 to the present?**

Service Industries

Tennessee's manufacturing centers are also home to important **service industries,** or businesses that provide services to people instead of producing goods. Banking, health care, and tourism are types of service industries. Look at the graph on page TN40. Add up the percentage of jobs in transportation and utilities; wholesale and retail trade; finance, insurance, and real estate; and other services. You will see that these service industries account for more than 60 percent of all the jobs in Tennessee.

Tourism Tennessee's reputation for mountain scenery draws thousands of tourists each year. With its forested mountains, hiking trails, and streams for fishing, Great Smoky Mountains National Park is the country's most visited park. Other beautiful natural areas are found on the Cumberland Plateau. The Chattanooga area also has spectacular scenery and draws many visitors to its unusual freshwater aquarium. Tennessee's rivers and dam-created lakes are used for boating and sport fishing.

Nashville is known as the home of country music, and music lovers come to visit the Grand Ole Opry. Memphis draws large numbers of tourists to Graceland, the home of Elvis Presley. Graceland is the second-most visited house in the United States, after the White House.

Tennessee's historic sites also appeal to tourists. Near Nashville is the Hermitage, the beautiful mansion that was the home of President Andrew Jackson. The city also holds the only full-sized replica of the original Parthenon, a temple built in Greece. The Greeneville area has the homes of President Andrew Johnson and frontier hero Davy Crockett. Several of the state's Civil War battlefields have become national parks, including Shiloh, Lookout Mountain, and Murfreesboro. At Cade's Cove you can visit a restored mountain community as it looked in the early 1900s. Memphis has a museum dedicated to the civil rights movement.

✓Reading Check **What are four tourist attractions in the state?**

Section 4 Assessment

Defining Key Terms

1. Define bituminous, strip mining, service industry.

Recalling Facts

2. Region What leading crop is grown in Middle and East Tennessee?

3. Human/Environment Interaction Why is strip mining a problem?

4. Place What are three places in Tennessee that attract tourists interested in natural beauty?

Critical Thinking

5. Drawing Conclusions Why would a state welcome the building of auto plants?

6. Synthesizing Information How do transportation links contribute to Tennessee's economy?

Graphic Organizer

7. Organizing Information Draw a diagram like the one below. In each outer oval, list three examples under each heading.

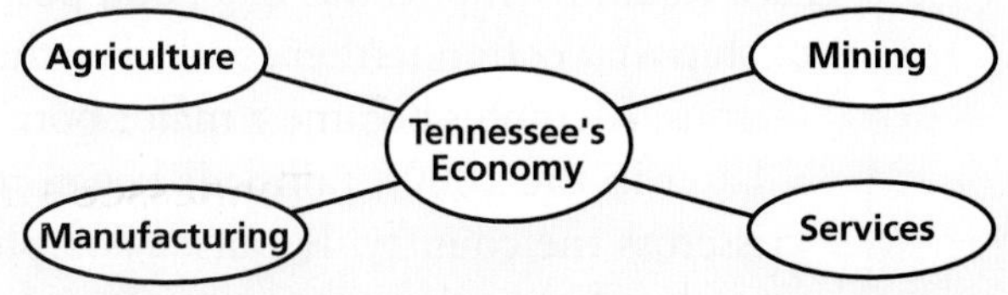

Applying Geography Skills

8. Analyzing Maps Look at the economic activity map on page TN39. What resources are found in East Tennessee?

CASE STUDY: Memphis Shipping Hub

FOCUS: ***For nearly 200 years, Memphis has been one of the country's main centers for shipping goods. Why? The city's location makes it an ideal shipping hub—for many forms of transportation.***

What do giant pandas have to do with Memphis? In December 2000, the pandas were brought from China to their new home at the National Zoo in Washington, D.C. To move them, officials called on Federal Express, a leading shipping company based in Memphis.

It is hardly surprising that people wanting to move something from one place to another should call on Memphis. The city has used its location to become a major shipping center throughout its history.

▲ **Two giant pandas are loaded onto a Federal Express plane in Beijing, China.**

By Water and Rail

When Memphis was founded in 1819, the city's location in the midst of rich cotton-growing land was ideal. In addition, it had a good harbor on the Mississippi River. As a result, Memphis was in a good position to ship that cotton farther south. For these reasons, Memphis became a major port.

Later in the 1800s, railroads began to crisscross the country. Because Memphis was already a major port, several rail lines were connected to it. The railroads increased the value of Memphis as a transportation center. Increased trade led to growth, and by the 1850s, Memphis was among the South's larger cities.

By Land and Air

In the 1940s and 1950s, the city's harbor was improved to increase the city's ability to ship goods. In addition, trucks began to use newly built interstate highways to transport goods between Memphis and other states.

In the 1970s, Memphis became a major center of air transportation. This development resulted from the idea of one man: Fred Smith. Smith believed that American businesses needed a package-delivery service that would guarantee overnight delivery. To deliver packages overnight, Smith had to solve a problem. How could he collect thousands of packages in, say, Chicago, New York,

and Atlanta and make sure they were delivered all over the country?

The solution Smith found was to bring all the packages to the same place, sort them there, and then send them on their way. The place he chose was Memphis. Why? As the map above shows, Memphis sits within 500 miles (805 km) of nearly 20 states. In addition, its mild climate means that the airport rarely has to shut down because of bad weather.

In 1973 Smith's company—Federal Express—began its overnight service. Packages are brought in, sorted, and shipped out at night. The airport at Memphis now handles more air cargo than any other airport in the world.

Using the Case Study

1. **Location** What two benefits of geography did Memphis enjoy in the 1800s?
2. **Economics** What two benefits of geography led Smith to choose Memphis for his new idea in the 1970s?
3. **Making Inferences** If Memphis had not been an important port, would railroads have connected to it? Why or why not?
4. **Skillbuilder Activity** Look at the map above. What major cities are within 500 miles (805 km) of Memphis?

EYE on the Tennessee Environment

IMPACT OF the TVA

Power to the People In most of Tennessee, and in parts of six other states, the Tennessee Valley Authority (TVA) supplies electric power. The country's largest power company, the TVA has 29 dams supplying hydroelectric power, 11 coal-burning power plants, 3 nuclear power plants, and 1 pumped-water plant. What impact do the TVA operations have on the environment?

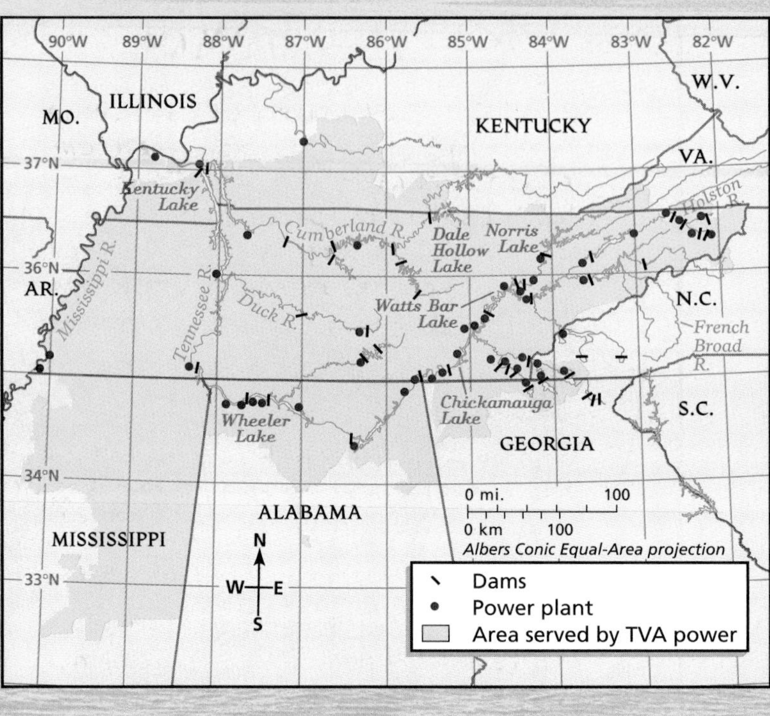

Critics say that the TVA creates several problems:

- Coal-burning plants pump dangerous pollutants into the air.
- Some coal companies harvest the coal by strip mining, which clears the land of valuable trees and leads to water pollution.
- Nuclear power plants produce dangerous radioactive wastes.

TVA's Response The TVA has taken steps to address these problems:

- It has launched an Environmental Research Center to find ways of solving environmental problems.
- The TVA only buys coal from mining companies who repair the land after the coal is gone.
- The TVA has reduced the pollutants emitted by its power plants.

Tellico Dam on the Tennessee River is one of the many dams built by the TVA to control flooding and generate electric power.

Making a Difference

Solar Power In 2000, the TVA announced a Green Power Switch program to begin producing energy using renewable sources such as solar and wind power. In the summer of 2000, the TVA installed solar panels at Dollywood Entertainment Park in Pigeon Forge, Tennessee. These solar panels will collect solar energy and are part of the TVA's Green Power program to offer environmentally friendly energy options to TVA customers.

Local leaders take a closer look at the TVA solar panels installed at a tram stop in Dollywood Entertainment Park.

Wind Power The TVA's Green Power program also will use power generated from the wind. Three wind turbines sit on top of Buffalo Mountain in Oliver Springs, Tennessee. The Tennessee Valley Authority built the windmills on 2 acres (.8 ha) of a reclaimed strip mine in Anderson County. The three windmills together will generate 6 million kilowatt hours of electricity each year.

Wind power is a renewable resource.

What Can You Do?

Become Informed

Read the critics' views of the TVA by visiting *www.tngreen.com/air/*. Choose one issue highlighted by the critics and then visit the TVA's Web site at *www.tva.com* to see how the TVA is addressing the problem.

Save Rivers

A group called American Rivers works to protect rivers from pollution and other problems. Visit its Web site at *www.americanrivers.org* and find the list of "Ten Ways You Can Help Rivers." Use the list to create a bulletin board display.

Conserve Energy

One way of cutting pollution is to use less energy. Research to find simple ways that people can cut the amount of energy they use. Design a poster that urges people to adopt one or a few of these actions.

Guide to Reading

Main Idea

Tennessee's people have created rich cultures, with many contributions to American society.

Terms to Know

- immigrant
- metropolitan area
- revival
- bluegrass
- blues

Places to Locate

- Tri-Cities
- Jonesborough
- Pigeon Forge

Reading Strategy

Make an outline like the one below. Then fill in details about Tennessee's people.

I. Population
II. Urban Centers
III. Religion and Education
IV. Culture

Section 5 Tennessee Today

NATIONAL GEOGRAPHIC **Exploring Tennessee**

Sports are a source of pride for the people of Tennessee. The football team of the University of Tennessee was crowned national champions in 1998. The women's basketball team at the same university won six national championships between 1987 and 1998. In 2000 the NFL's Tennessee Titans played in the Super Bowl.

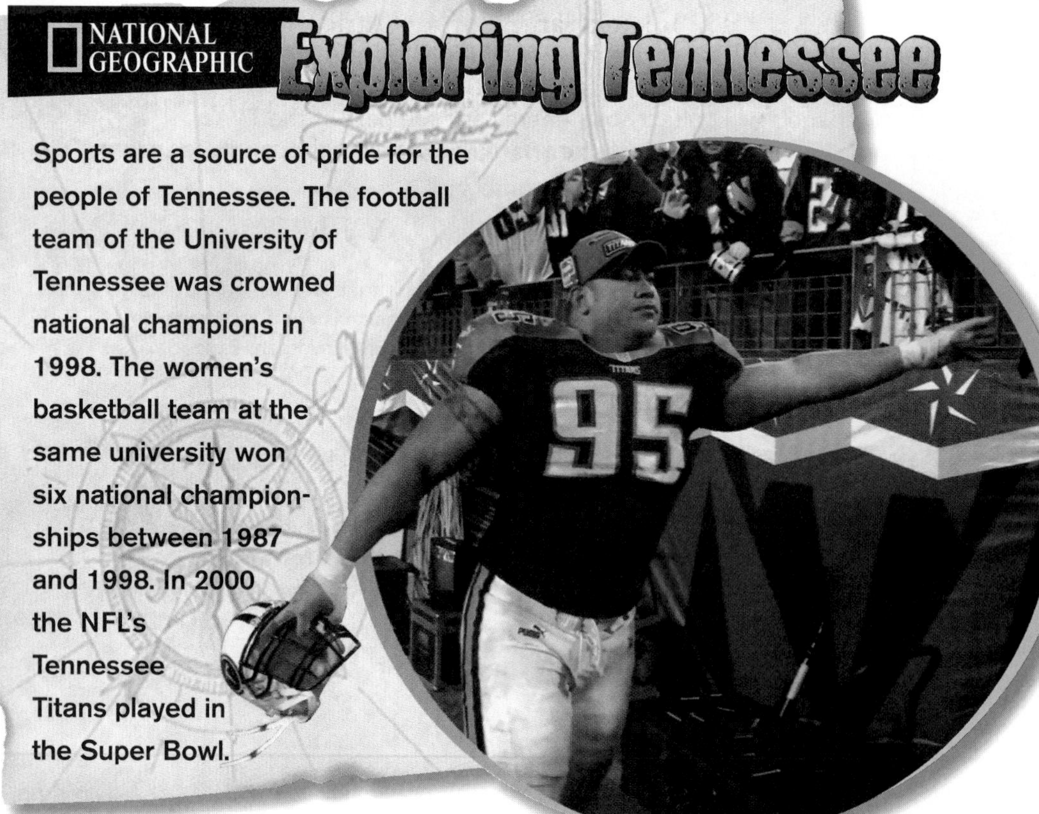

The three grand divisions of Tennessee have heritages of somewhat different ways of life. East Tennessee is known for its mountain heritage and the self-reliance of its people. Middle Tennessee has been an area of prosperous family farms and commerce and a diverse population. West Tennessee has an economy based on agriculture, including cotton, and has cultural ties to the Lower South.

Tennessee's Population

In 1900 just over 2 million people lived in Tennessee. In 1950 the population was roughly 3.3 million. Since then, the population has grown rapidly. Today Tennessee has more than 5.6 million people. The graph on page TN5 shows how the state's population grew from 1790 to 2000.

A large number of Tennessee's people trace their ancestry to the state's early settlers. In fact, Tennessee has a larger percentage of native-born people than the average for all the states. Recently, the state's population growth has come from **immigrants,** or people drawn from other states and countries. This incoming population is attracted to Tennessee's favorable climate and growing economy.

Look at the graph on page TN5, which shows the ethnic makeup of Tennessee's population. About 80 percent of the people are of European descent. The next largest group, African Americans, makes up more than 16 percent of the population. Hispanics, Asians and Pacific Islanders, and Native Americans form smaller groups in Tennessee.

Reading Check What are the two largest ethnic groups in Tennessee?

NATIONAL GEOGRAPHIC

County Population Growth

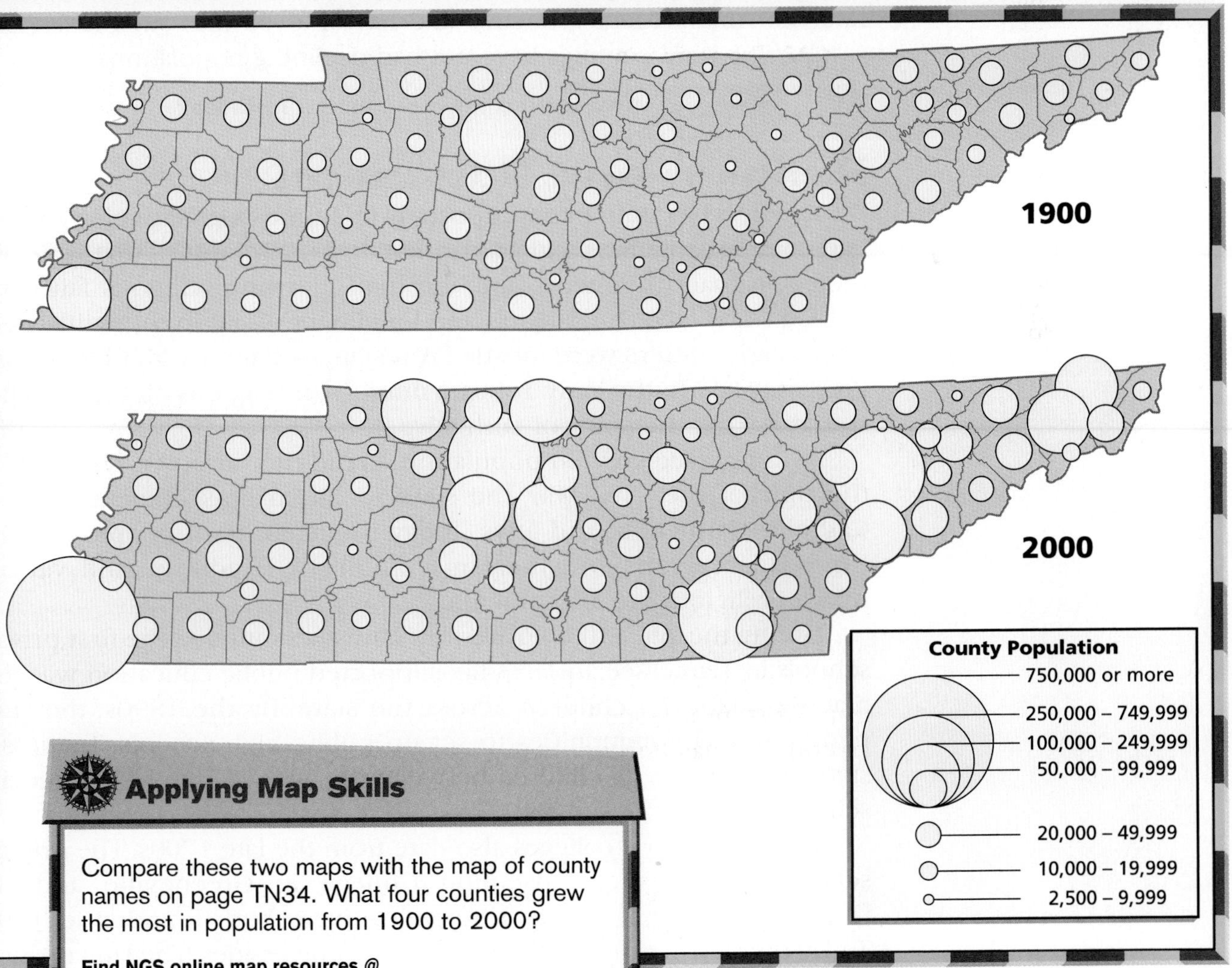

1900

2000

County Population

- 750,000 or more
- 250,000 – 749,999
- 100,000 – 249,999
- 50,000 – 99,999
- 20,000 – 49,999
- 10,000 – 19,999
- 2,500 – 9,999

Applying Map Skills

Compare these two maps with the map of county names on page TN34. What four counties grew the most in population from 1900 to 2000?

Find NGS online map resources @
www.nationalgeographic.com/maps

Source: Adapted from the "Tennessee: 200 Years of Population Growth" map by the Department of Geography and the Cartographic Services Laboratory, University of Tennessee, Knoxville.

Urban Centers

Today nearly two-thirds of Tennessee's people live in urban areas. The fastest-growing areas of the state are suburban communities near the major cities of Nashville, Memphis, and Knoxville. Memphis and Nashville are the two largest metropolitan areas, with more than 1 million people each. A **metropolitan area** includes the population of a city and its surrounding suburbs. The Memphis metro area, at the southwest corner of Tennessee, includes suburbs that are actually in other states.

There are three metropolitan areas in East Tennessee. Knoxville is the largest one, with more than 600,000 people. The other two metro areas are Chattanooga and the **Tri-Cities**—a grouping of Johnson City, Kingsport, and Bristol in northeast Tennessee. Both of these metro areas have close to one-half million people.

Outside the metropolitan areas are thriving towns and rural areas. Many of the people living in these areas are of local origin. However, more and more people from the state's metropolitan areas and outside the state find the rural settings attractive and have moved into such areas. As a result, most rural counties have not had declining populations.

✓Reading Check **What three cities make up the Tri-Cities?**

Religion and Education

Religion has long been important in Tennessee. Native Americans had complex religions and performed many ceremonies that reflected their spirituality. Pioneers later brought a strong religious faith that helped them face the dangers and loneliness of life in the wilderness. These early settlers were mostly Protestants—Baptists, Methodists, and Presbyterians. In the early 1800s, a number of religious meetings called **revivals** kept the spirit of faith alive.

As Tennessee grew in population, so did the variety of religions. By the time of the Civil War, the state included Episcopalians, Roman Catholics, Lutherans, and Jews. Today the majority of people practice Christian religions, but Judaism, Buddhism, Hinduism, and various African religions are also practiced.

During the late 1700s, Protestant ministers founded the first private schools in Tennessee. In 1853 tax-supported public education was first made available to children across the state. By the 1890s, the state required local communities to set up public high schools. Tennessee state law requires all children between the ages of 7 and 17 to receive schooling.

Tennessee's first colleges also date from the late 1700s. The original schools—now called Tusculum College in Greeneville and the University of Tennessee at Knoxville—were both founded in 1794. Today the state has nearly 80 colleges and universities. The University of

Tennessee's Counties

County Name	County Seat	Area in sq. mi. (sq. km)	Population
Anderson	Clinton	338 (875)	71,004
Bedford	Shelbyville	474 (1,228)	34,905
Benton	Camden	394 (1,020)	16,497
Bledsoe	Pikeville	406 (1,052)	10,945
Blount	Maryville	559 (1,448)	102,785
Bradley	Cleveland	329 (852)	84,126
Campbell	Jacksboro	480 (1,243)	38,466
Cannon	Woodbury	266 (689)	12,248
Carroll	Huntingdon	599 (1,551)	29,450
Carter	Elizabethton	341 (883)	53,299
Cheatham	Ashland City	303 (785)	36,128
Chester	Henderson	289 (749)	14,859
Claiborne	Tazewell	434 (1,124)	29,747
Clay	Celina	236 (611)	7,268
Cocke	Newport	434 (1,124)	32,291
Coffee	Manchester	429 (1,111)	46,355
Crockett	Alamo	265 (686)	14,077
Cumberland	Crossville	682 (1,766)	45,326
Davidson	Nashville	502 (1,300)	530,050
Decatur	Decaturville	333 (862)	10,788
DeKalb	Smithville	304 (787)	16,174
Dickson	Charlotte	490 (1,269)	43,017
Dyer	Dyersburg	510 (1,321)	36,725
Fayette	Somerville	705 (1,826)	31,441
Fentress	Jamestown	499 (1,262)	16,357
Franklin	Winchester	553 (1,432)	37,826
Gibson	Trenton	603 (1,562)	48,030
Giles	Pulaski	611 (1,582)	29,036
Grainger	Rutledge	280 (725)	20,219
Greene	Greeneville	622 (1,611)	60,900
Grundy	Altamont	361 (935)	14,046
Hamblen	Morristown	161 (417)	54,201
Hamilton	Chattanooga	543 (1,406)	294,720
Hancock	Sneedville	222 (575)	6,767
Hardeman	Bolivar	668 (1,730)	24,451
Hardin	Savannah	578 (1,497)	25,247
Hawkins	Rogersville	487 (1,261)	50,109
Haywood	Brownsville	533 (1,380)	19,416
Henderson	Lexington	520 (1,347)	24,767
Henry	Paris	562 (1,456)	30,091
Hickman	Centerville	613 (1,588)	21,283
Houston	Erin	200 (518)	7,888
Humphreys	Waverly	532 (1,378)	17,192
Jackson	Gainesboro	309 (800)	9,643
Jefferson	Dandridge	274 (710)	45,104
Johnson	Mountain City	299 (774)	16,736
Knox	Knoxville	509 (1,318)	376,039
Lake	Tiptonville	163 (422)	8,131
Lauderdale	Ripley	471 (1,220)	24,234
Lawrence	Lawrenceburg	617 (1,598)	39,626
Lewis	Hohenwald	282 (730)	11,127
Lincoln	Fayetteville	570 (1,476)	29,773
Loudon	Loudon	229 (593)	39,892
Macon	Lafayette	307 (795)	18,542
Madison	Jackson	557 (1,442)	86,752
Marion	Jasper	500 (1,295)	26,907
Marshall	Lewisburg	375 (971)	26,423
Maury	Columbia	613 (1,588)	70,440
McMinn	Athens	430 (1,114)	46,395
McNairy	Selmer	560 (1,450)	24,312
Meigs	Decatur	195 (505)	10,134
Monroe	Madisonville	635 (1,645)	35,576
Montgomery	Clarksville	539 (1,396)	129,411
Moore	Lynchburg	129 (334)	5,140
Morgan	Wartburg	522 (1,352)	18,689
Obion	Union City	545 (1,412)	32,240
Overton	Livingston	433 (1,121)	19,654
Perry	Linden	415 (1,075)	7,560
Pickett	Byrdstown	163 (422)	4,711
Polk	Benton	435 (1,127)	15,094
Putnam	Cookeville	401 (1,039)	59,735
Rhea	Dayton	316 (818)	28,116
Roane	Kingston	361 (935)	50,008
Robertson	Springfield	477 (1,235)	54,861
Rutherford	Murfreesboro	619 (1,603)	171,401
Scott	Huntsville	532 (1,378)	20,239
Sequatchie	Dunlap	266 (689)	10,846
Sevier	Sevierville	592 (1,533)	65,783
Shelby	Memphis	755 (1,955)	873,000
Smith	Carthage	314 (813)	16,771
Stewart	Dover	458 (1,186)	11,759
Sullivan	Blountville	413 (1,070)	150,231
Sumner	Gallatin	529 (1,370)	126,009
Tipton	Covington	459 (1,189)	48,348
Trousdale	Hartsville	114 (295)	6,971
Unicoi	Erwin	186 (482)	17,310
Union	Maynardville	224 (580)	16,584
Van Buren	Spencer	274 (710)	5,008
Warren	McMinnville	433 (1,121)	36,421
Washington	Jonesborough	326 (844)	102,814
Wayne	Waynesboro	734 (1,901)	16,413
Weakley	Dresden	580 (1,502)	32,952
White	Sparta	377 (976)	22,864
Williamson	Franklin	582 (1,507)	123,793
Wilson	Lebanon	571 (1,479)	86,496

Source: *Tennessee Blue Book*, 1999– 2000 edition, U.S. Bureau of the Census, 2000.

Country Music

Country music stars celebrated the 75th birthday of Nashville's Grand Ole Opry in 2000.

Culture **What other kinds of music originated in Tennessee?**

Tennessee, with its main campus at Knoxville, is the state's largest university and includes campuses at Chattanooga, Tullahoma (the Space Institute), Martin, and the medical school at Memphis. Nashville is home to two famous private universities. Vanderbilt University, founded in 1873, is one of the leading universities in the country. Fisk University, founded in 1867, is a leading university for African Americans. The University of the South, in Sewanee, is another well-known private university. This school publishes the oldest literary magazine in the United States.

✓ Reading Check **When did Tennessee require local communities to create public high schools?**

Culture

Tennessee's people have contributed to literature, music, sports, and the arts. Many of the arts in Tennessee reflect the ways of rural and pioneer life. The state is known for its beautiful quilts, wood furniture, folk carvings, and musical instruments. A stringed instrument known as a dulcimer is still handmade by Tennessee craftspeople.

Literature American literature has many ties to Tennessee. Nashville has long been known as "the Athens of the South" because of its classical Greek buildings and talented thinkers and writers. In the 1920s, a group of poets and writers known as the Fugitives came together to share ideas at Vanderbilt University. The most famous member of this group was Robert Penn Warren. He won the Pulitzer Prize for *All the King's Men,* a novel he wrote about a fictional political leader.

In 1977 tens of millions of Americans were riveted to their television sets to watch *Roots.* This was a miniseries based on a novel that showed the suffering of an enslaved African American family and their joy in freedom. The novel is the dramatic family story of Tennessee author Alex Haley.

Literature in Tennessee is not just a matter of the written word. Each October in **Jonesborough,** the National Storytelling Festival takes place. Here skilled storytellers from the United States and other countries meet to spin their tales before fascinated listeners.

Music Tennessee is famous for the diversity of its music. East Tennessee has given us folk ballads, gospel music, and bluegrass. Folk ballads come from the early Tennessee settlers who brought their music from Europe. Gospel music began in the revivals of the 1800s. **Bluegrass** is a kind of country music with a bright sound of banjos and guitars played rapidly.

West Tennessee was the birthplace of a different form of music. On the cotton plantations of the region, enslaved African Americans developed a type of music known as the **blues.** This music is very rhythmic and sung in a mournful tone. In the early 1900s, blues and jazz from New Orleans came together in Memphis. An African American musician named W.C. Handy wrote many songs here, including "Memphis Blues" and "St. Louis Blues." His work and that of singer Bessie Smith, from Chattanooga, made Memphis the home of the blues.

Another type of music is country music, whose popularity spread with the invention of the radio and the record player. The most famous country music radio program was the Grand Ole Opry, which made Nashville the country music capital of the world. Today the city is home to music recording and publishing and to television production.

Many famous singers and performers have come from Tennessee. One of the best known is Elvis Presley, "the King of Rock and Roll," who called Memphis his home. Another famous singer is Dolly Parton, who came out of rural East Tennessee. She is an accomplished singer,

Music

Memphis was home to two very different—and very popular—musicians. W.C. Handy, "the Father of the Blues," was born in Alabama. A cornet player and a composer, he is noted for making blues a popular music form.

Elvis Presley was born in Mississippi, but he recorded his first songs in Memphis. He helped create rock and roll, which combined Memphis blues with country music.

Looking Closer How did Handy's work influence Presley?

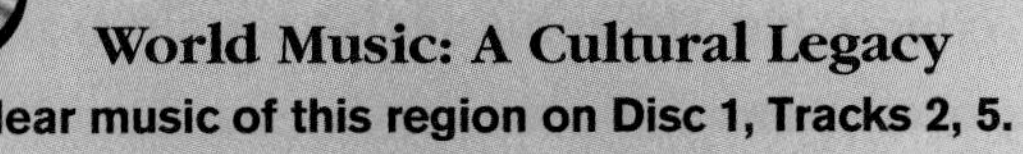

World Music: A Cultural Legacy

Hear music of this region on Disc 1, Tracks 2, 5.

songwriter, and actress. She also has a theme park called Dollywood, which is a major tourist attraction in her hometown of Pigeon Forge near the Great Smoky Mountains.

▲ Wilma Rudolph

Sports An outstanding athlete from Tennessee was Wilma Rudolph. Born in Clarksville, Rudolph overcame childhood paralysis to compete in sports. In the 1960 Olympic Games in Rome, Italy, she won three gold medals.

Today perhaps the best-known female Tennessean in sports is Pat Summitt, coach of women's basketball at the University of Tennessee. She has coached six national championship teams as well as an Olympic championship team.

In the late 1990s, professional football came to the state when the team named the Tennessee Titans moved to Nashville. In January 2000, the team played in the Super Bowl.

✓Reading Check What athlete won three gold medals in the 1960 Olympics?

Section 5 Assessment

Defining Key Terms

1. **Define** immigrant, metropolitan area, revival, bluegrass, blues.

Recalling Facts

2. **Place** What is Tennessee's largest metropolitan area in population?
3. **Culture** What religion do the largest number of Tennesseans practice?
4. **Culture** What famous writers have come from Tennessee?

Critical Thinking

5. **Supporting Generalizations** What details support the generalization that Tennessee has been home to many kinds of music?

Graphic Organizer

6. **Organizing Information** Draw a diagram like the one below and fill in two key facts about Tennessee under each heading.

Population	Religion and Education	Culture

Applying Geography Skills

7. **Analyzing Charts** Look at the chart of Tennessee's counties on page TN51. What county has Memphis as the county seat?

Reading Review

Section 1 Tennessee's Geography

Terms to Know
ridge
bluff
alluvial plain
tributary

Main Idea

Tennessee has three grand divisions and six main physical regions.

✓ Region The three grand divisions are East, Middle, and West Tennessee.

✓ Region Tennessee's six physical regions include the Blue Ridge Mountains, the Great Valley of Tennessee, the Cumberland Plateau, the Nashville Basin, the Highland Rim, and the Gulf Coastal Plain.

Section 2 Tennessee's History

Terms to Know
clan
constitution
secede

Main Idea

The people of Tennessee have played important roles in history.

✓ Movement As European settlers came to Tennessee, the chief Native American groups were the Chickasaw and Cherokee.

✓ Government Tennessee became a state in 1796.

✓ History A border state, Tennessee was a battleground in the Civil War.

Section 3 Tennessee's Government

Terms to Know
criminal case
civil case
appellate court
home rule

Main Idea

Tennesseans are governed by three levels of government—federal, state, and local.

✓ Government Tennessee's government has three branches: the legislative to make laws, the executive to carry out laws, and the judicial to interpret laws.

✓ Government County and local governments oversee many areas of life.

Section 4 Tennessee's Economy

Terms to Know
bituminous
strip mining
service industry

Main Idea

Tennessee has a diverse economy.

✓ Economics After the TVA was started in the 1930s, Tennessee's economy changed from mostly farming to manufacturing.

✓ Movement Tourism plays a major role in the state's economy.

Section 5 Tennessee Today

Terms to Know
metropolitan area
revival
bluegrass
blues

Main Idea

Tennessee's people have created rich cultures, with many contributions to American society.

✓ History Tennessee's population has grown in size and become more urban.

✓ Culture Tennessee is home to many different styles of music.

Assessment and Activities

Using Key Terms

Match the terms in Part A with their definitions in Part B.

A

1. alluvial plain
2. bluegrass
3. blues
4. bluff
5. constitution
6. judicial branch
7. legislative branch
8. executive branch
9. secede
10. strip mining

B

a. steep cliff
b. strongly rhythmic music that is sung in a mournful tone
c. part of government that interprets laws
d. to withdraw from a national government
e. area that is built up from rich fertile soil left by river floods
f. clearing the land to find coal that lies near the surface
g. part of government that makes laws
h. kind of country music with a bright sound of banjos and guitars
i. part of government that enforces laws
j. plan of government

Tennessee

Place Location Activity

On a separate sheet of paper, match the letters on the map with the numbered places listed below.

1. Blue Ridge Mountains
2. Chattanooga
3. Cumberland River
4. Cumberland Plateau
5. Gulf Coastal Plain
6. Knoxville
7. Memphis
8. Mississippi River
9. Nashville
10. Tennessee River

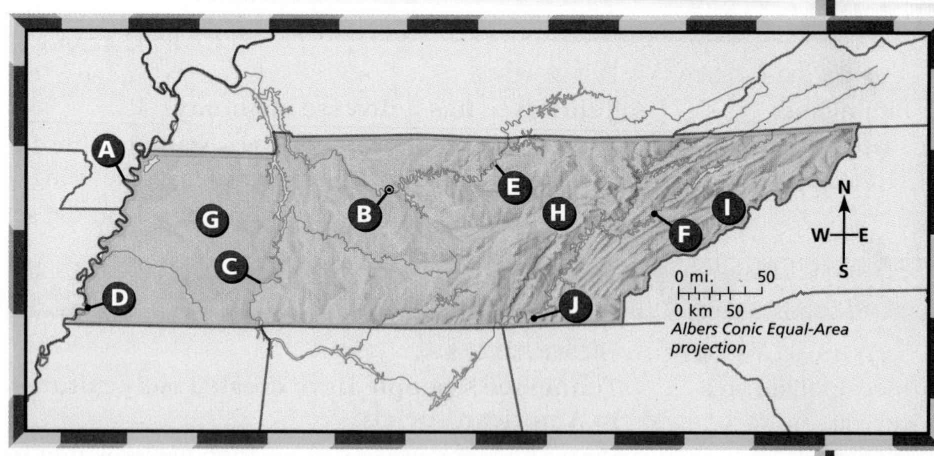

Reviewing the Main Ideas

Section 1 Tennessee's Geography

11. **Region** What are the six physical regions of Tennessee?
12. **Region** What physical region of Tennessee has coal deposits?
13. **Place** About how much precipitation does Tennessee receive each year?
14. **Human/Environment Interaction** How does Tennessee's climate benefit farming?

Section 2 Tennessee's History

15. **Government** Why did early settlers create the Watauga Association?
16. **History** What three presidents have come from Tennessee?
17. **Economics** How did Tennessee's economy change after World War II?

Section 3 Tennessee's Government

18. **Government** In what two ways can Tennessee's constitution be amended?
19. **Government** How long is the term of Tennessee's governor?
20. **Government** What is the difference between a civil and a criminal case?

Section 4 Tennessee's Economy

21. **Economics** What are Tennessee's four most valuable crops?
22. **Region** In which division of Tennessee are most minerals and timber resources found?
23. **Economics** What are Tennessee's chief manufactured products?
24. **Place** What are six sites in Tennessee that attract tourists?

Section 5 Tennessee Today

25. **Movement** What proportion of Tennessee's people live in urban areas?
26. **Place** What is Tennessee's largest city?
27. **Culture** What are three kinds of music that originated in East Tennessee?

Critical Thinking

28. **Understanding Cause and Effect** How has geography affected agriculture in Tennessee?
29. **Synthesizing Information** How has Tennessee's location had an impact on its economy?
30. **Drawing Conclusions** How did Tennessee's location affect it during the Civil War?
31. **Organizing Information** Draw a time line like the one below. Identify five important events and their dates in Tennessee's history.

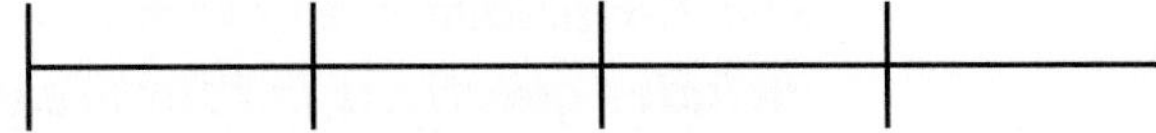

GeoJournal Writing Activity

32. **Describing Tennessee** Imagine that you are traveling across Tennessee from one side of the state to the other—either east to west or west to east. Write a description of what you would see during your travels. Include specific details to convey a sense of Tennessee's variety. Be sure to describe the people you might meet and their activities, as well as the state's natural scenery.

Mental Mapping Activity

33. **Focusing on the Region** Draw a simple outline map of Tennessee. Then label the following features on your map:
    - Blue Ridge Mountains
    - Cumberland Plateau
    - Great Valley of Tennessee
    - Knoxville
    - Memphis
    - Nashville
    - Nashville Basin
    - Eastern Highland Rim
    - Western Highland Rim
    - Chattanooga
    - Tennessee River
    - Mississippi River

Technology Skills Activity

34. **Building a Database** Working in a group, research one of the three grand divisions of the state—East Tennessee, Middle Tennessee, or West Tennessee. Find out what you can about the natural, historical, and cultural attractions of the division. Then create a database that identifies the location of each attraction, what type of attraction it is, and a brief description of the attraction.

TERRANOVA STANDARDIZED TEST PRACTICE

The TerraNova is an exam that tests what you know about social studies. It includes questions in four areas: civics and government, history, geography, and economics.

CIVICS AND GOVERNMENT PERSPECTIVES

Directions

Choose the best answer to each of the following multiple choice questions.

1 **Read the quote below from civil rights leader Martin Luther King, Jr., in the 1960s. Then answer the question that follows.**

"The old law about 'an eye for an eye' leaves everybody blind."

According to this quote from Martin Luther King, Jr., what conclusion can be drawn regarding his beliefs?

A Martin Luther King, Jr., believed that people of different races should continue to be segregated from one another.

B Martin Luther King, Jr., felt that the citizens of the United States must revolt with violent outrage against the government.

C Martin Luther King, Jr., believed that we should never rely on old laws to achieve harmony.

D Martin Luther King, Jr., felt that fighting violence with violence results in injury to all.

2 **Read the passage below, which is an excerpt from the Thirteenth Amendment to the United States Constitution. Then answer the question that follows.**

Neither slavery nor involuntary servitude, except as a punishment for crime whereof the party shall have been duly convicted, shall exist within the United States . . .

Congress shall have power to enforce this article by appropriate legislation.

The main idea of the Thirteenth Amendment is that

F states could not secede from the Union.

G enslaved people convicted of crimes had the right to a fair trial.

H Congress had the right to abolish slavery in whatever state it chose.

J slavery was made illegal in every state of the Union.

Test-Taking Tip: Remember to read each answer choice carefully *before* you mark your answer. Do not forget to use the process of elimination when you are answering the questions. If you first eliminate the answers that you know are wrong, you increase your chances of choosing the correct answer.

Historical and Cultural Perspectives

Directions

Read the chart below. Then answer Questions 3 through 5.

3 **From which country did the majority of these people come?**

A England

B Germany

C Italy

D Poland

4 **If one was a fan of Machiavellian thought, one would most likely be interested in**

F politics.

G art.

H science.

J agriculture.

5 **The Renaissance greatly affected society by reviving ideas and culture. All of the following emerged during this period EXCEPT for**

A Copernicus's theory of Earth's rotation around the sun.

B religious artwork by painters and sculptors.

C writings influenced by the study of classical subjects.

D the overthrow of the Roman Catholic Church.

Test-Taking Tip: When answering questions, look out for key words such as NOT, ONLY, and EXCEPT, which drastically change what the question is asking.

INFLUENTIAL PEOPLE WHO LIVED DURING THE RENAISSANCE		
Baldassare Castiglione	1478–1529	Italian writer; wrote book on rules of behavior for ladies and gentlemen
Benvenuto Cellini	1500–1571	Italian goldsmith; sculptor; wrote about his life and times
Nicolaus Copernicus	1473–1543	Polish astronomer; stated that Earth moves around the sun
Albrecht Dürer	1471–1528	German artist; painted and made woodcuts of religious and classical subjects
Beatrice d'Este **Isabella d'Este**	1475–1497 1474–1539	Italian noblewomen; sisters; honored for their learning; supported writers and artists
Galileo	1564–1642	Italian scientist; did experiments on the motion of objects; used telescope to discover new facts about universe
Niccolò Machiavelli	1469–1527	Italian politician; writer; wrote advice to rulers on how to keep power
Thomas More	1477–1535	English scholar; saint; government official; refused to accept king as Church head
Petrarch	1304–1374	Italian poet; scholar; restored study of classics; collected manuscripts; wrote letters and poems
Raphael	1483–1520	Italian religious painter and architect
Andreas Vesalius	1514–1564	Flemish surgeon; founder of modern medicine; wrote first full description of human body

GEOGRAPHIC PERSPECTIVES

Directions

Study the map below to answer Questions 6 through 8.

6 **Between what two lines of latitude are most of the major digs located?**

F 20°E and 30°E

G 30°N and 40°N

H 40°E and 50°E

J 40°N and 50°N

7 **According to the map, which archaeological site is located on the island of Cyprus?**

A Khirokitia

B Sesklo

C Jarmo

D Jericho

8 **Which of the following is a true statement that can be answered by looking at the map?**

F Archaeologists began expeditions in the late 1900s.

G The majority of the major dig sites are located near a body of water.

H The archaeological digs were conducted in North and South America.

J Artifacts such as clothing and pots were found in Jericho.

Test-Taking Tip: When answering a question that refers to a map or graph, never rely on your memory. Always refer back to the source, and then choose your answer.

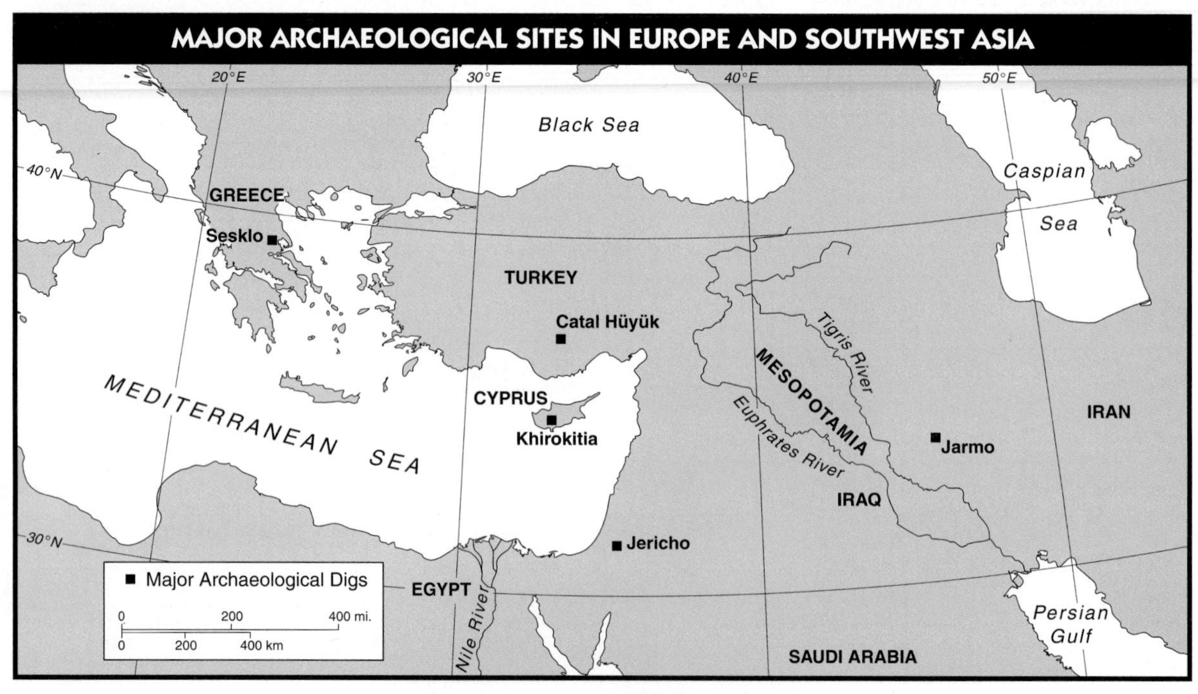

Economic Perspectives

Directions

Use the graph below to determine the answers to Questions 9 through 11.

9 **What do the bars on this graph measure?**

A Years

B Millions of Dollars

C Billions of Dollars

D Years *and* Billions of Dollars

10 **What was the total consumer debt in 2000?**

F about $1,350

G about $1,350,000

H about $1,350,000,000

J about $1,350,000,000,000

11 **Which of the following statements is the BEST summary of the information provided on the bar graph?**

A The amount of consumer debt has remained constant from 1990 to 2000.

B In 1997 the mortgage debt was at an all-time high.

C Millions of dollars each year are invested in the economy.

D The amount of consumer debt has steadily increased over the years.

Test-Taking Tip: In order to understand any type of graph, look carefully around the graph for keys that show how it is organized. On this bar graph, the numbers along the left side represent billions of dollars. Therefore, you need to multiply the number on the graph by 1,000,000,000 to get your answer.

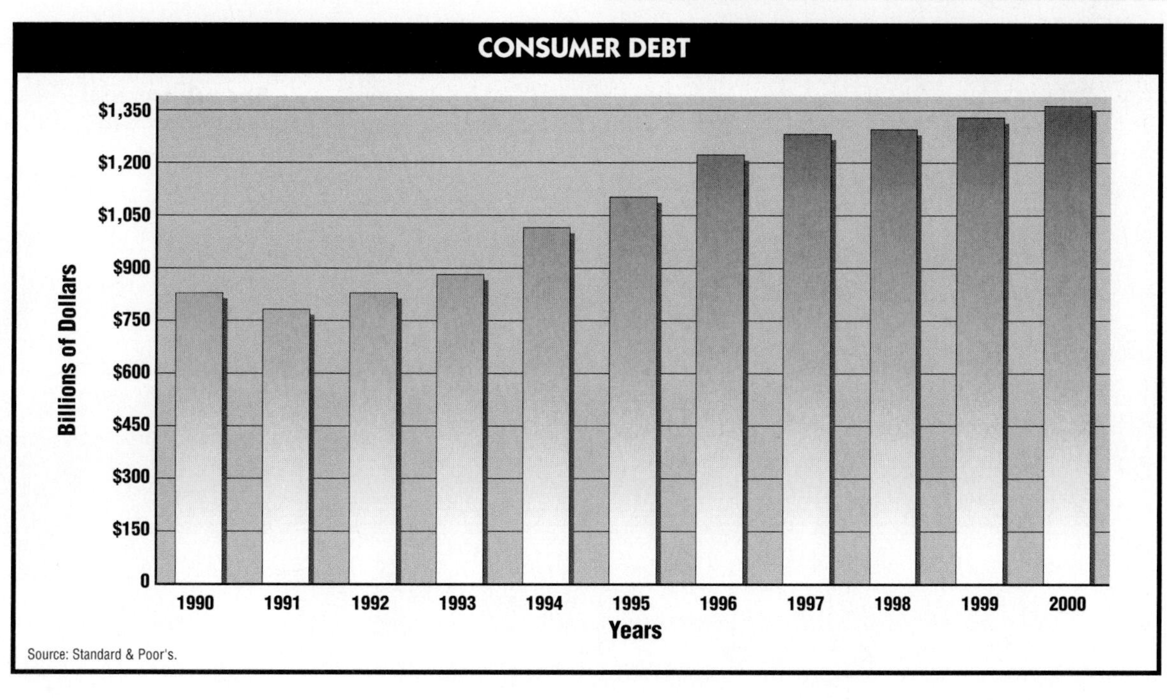

Unit 3

Peruvian Indian woman and child

Spanish colonial architecture in Guatemala

Latin America

Where can you find steamy tropical forests, frigid mountain peaks, thundering waterfalls, and peaceful island beaches? All of these contrasts can be found in Latin America—a huge part of the world made up of 33 nations on two continents. This region stretches from the Mexico–United States border, in North America, to the southernmost tip of South America.

NGS ONLINE
www.nationalgeographic.com/education

Spider monkey and Mayan ruins, Mexico ▲

Focus on:

Latin America

COMMON THREADS OF LANGUAGE AND RELIGION unite this region. Once claimed as European colonies, most Latin American countries still use either Spanish or Portuguese as the official language. These two languages are based on Latin, which is how the region gets its name. Most Latin Americans are Roman Catholic, another influence from colonial times.

The Land

Latin America stretches from the Rio Grande south to Tierra del Fuego, just 600 miles (966 km) from Antarctica's frozen shores. Three times larger than the continental United States, the region includes Mexico, Central America, the Caribbean islands, and South America.

Mountains are prominent features in many parts of Latin America. Some Caribbean islands are actually the exposed tops of ancient, submerged volcanoes. In Mexico, the branches of the Sierra Madre spread like welcoming arms to hug a central highland known as the Mexican Plateau. Mist-covered peaks stretch through the interior of Central America. Most impressive, however, are the Andes. The longest series of mountain ranges in the world, the lofty Andes follow the western coast of South America for 4,500 miles (7,242 km).

Narrow coastal plains line the edges of Mexico and Central America. South America has vast inland plains. These include the pampas of Argentina and the llanos of Colombia and Venezuela. The largest lowland area on this continent is the basin of the Amazon River, the longest river in the Western Hemisphere.

The Climate

Most of this region has a tropical climate. Daily showers drench the rain forests, which thrive in the lowlands. In Brazil the Amazon River and its tributaries snake through the largest area of rain forest regions, which covers roughly one-third of South America. Rain forests contain more species of plants and animals than any other ecosystem on Earth.

The climate tends to be drier and cooler at higher elevations and farther away from the Equator. Under these conditions, tall grasses and scattered trees flourish.

Drier still are parts of northern Mexico and southern Argentina. Here, rainfall is sparse and so is vegetation. Yet even these places are lush compared to the Atacama Desert, along Chile's coast. The barren Atacama is among the world's driest places.

UNIT 3

Three-toed sloth in rain forest, Panama

Peaks of the Andes, Chile

The Economy

Latin America is rich in natural resources. Gold drew many of the first European conquerors. Copper, silver, iron ore, tin, and lead also are abundant in the region. Latin American countries are among the world's leading producers of oil and natural gas.

Agriculture plays an important role in the region's economy. Coffee, bananas, and sugarcane thrive in the moist, fertile lowlands. On higher ground, farmers raise grain and fruit, while cowhands known as gauchos drive huge herds of cattle across rolling grasslands.

Industrialization is increasing in Latin America. However, some countries are moving along this path more quickly than others. In recent years, Mexico, Brazil, and Venezuela have become major producers of manufactured goods. Some things have hindered industrial development in other parts of the region. These include shortages of money, skilled labor, and reliable transportation, along with geographic barriers such as rugged mountains and thick forests.

The People

Long before Europeans crossed the Atlantic Ocean, great Native American civilizations developed in Latin America. The Maya flourished in the Guatemalan lowlands and across Mexico's Yucatán Peninsula. The central highlands of Mexico were the site of the Aztec Empire. In South America, the Inca established an empire that stretched from southern Colombia to central Chile.

Beginning in the 1500s, Spain and Portugal ruled most of Latin America. These European invaders destroyed the Native American civilizations. They also brought enslaved Africans to work alongside Native Americans on plantations.

Independence came for many Latin American countries in the early 1800s. These countries remain a cultural mixture—Native Americans, Europeans, Africans, and others all have left their mark.

Today most Latin Americans live in urban areas along the coasts of South America or in a band reaching from Mexico into Central America. Some of the largest cities in the world are in this region, including Mexico City, Rio de Janeiro, and Buenos Aires.

Exploring the Region

1. **What is Latin America's longest series of mountain ranges?**
2. **What type of climate is found across most of the region?**
3. **What European countries once ruled Latin America?**
4. **Which Latin American countries are industrializing most rapidly?**

◀ **Mexican boy carrying decorated cross for religious celebration**

UNIT 3

Rio de Janeiro, Brazil ▼

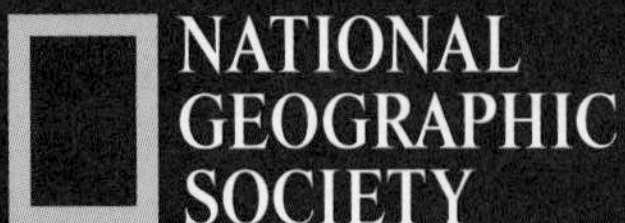

Latin America

Physical

120°W 110°W 100°W 90°W 80°W 70°W 60°W 50°W

30°N 20°N 10°N 0° 10°S 20°S 30°S 40°S

TROPIC OF CANCER
EQUATOR
TROPIC OF CAPRICORN

UNITED STATES
Rio Grande
Gulf of Mexico
Bermuda Is.
BAHAMAS
Baja California
SIERRA MADRE OCCIDENTAL
Plateau of Mexico
SIERRA MADRE ORIENTAL
MEXICO
Sierra Madre del Sur
Yucatán Peninsula
CUBA
Greater Antilles
HAITI
DOM. REP.
JAMAICA
Puerto Rico
WEST INDIES
Lesser Antilles
Caribbean Sea
BELIZE
HONDURAS
GUATEMALA
NICARAGUA
EL SALVADOR
COSTA RICA
Isthmus of Panama
PANAMA
Lake Maracaibo
VENEZUELA
Llanos
Orinoco R.
GUYANA
SURINAME
FRENCH GUIANA
Guiana Highlands
COLOMBIA
ECUADOR
Galápagos Islands
AMAZON BASIN
Amazon R.
PERU
ANDES
BRAZIL
BRAZILIAN HIGHLANDS
Mato Grosso Plateau
Lake Titicaca
BOLIVIA
Altiplano
Atacama Desert
PARAGUAY
Gran Chaco
Paraguay R.
CHILE
ARGENTINA
URUGUAY
Aconcagua 22,834 ft. (6,960 m)
Pampas
Río de la Plata
PATAGONIA
Strait of Magellan
Tierra del Fuego
Cape Horn
Falkland Islands
South Georgia I.
PACIFIC OCEAN
ATLANTIC OCEAN
ATLANTIC OCEAN

N W E S

▲ Mountain peak

0 mi. 1,000
0 km 1,000
Lambert Azimuthal Equal-Area projection

26,247 ft. 8,000 m
19,685 ft. 6,000 m
13,123 ft. 4,000 m
6,562 ft. 2,000 m
0 mi. 500
0 km 500
ANDES
AMAZON BASIN
MATO GROSSO PLATEAU
BRAZILIAN HIGHLANDS
LIMA
Sea level
SALVADOR

UNIT

Political

120°W 110°W 100°W 90°W 80°W 70°W 60°W 50°W 40°W 30°W
30°N 20°N 10°N 0° 10°S 20°S 30°S 40°S

NORTH AMERICA
BERMUDA U.K.
ATLANTIC OCEAN
Rio Grande
Gulf of Mexico
TROPIC OF CANCER
BAHAMAS
Nassau
Havana
CUBA
MEXICO
Mexico City
BELIZE
Cayman Is. U.K.
Port-au-Prince
HAITI
DOMINICAN REPUBLIC
Santo Domingo
Virgin Islands U.S. & U.K.
ANTIGUA AND BARBUDA
Guadeloupe Fr.
DOMINICA
Martinique Fr.
ST. LUCIA
ST. VINCENT AND THE GRENADINES
BARBADOS
GRENADA
TRINIDAD AND TOBAGO
Port-of-Spain
JAMAICA
Kingston
Puerto Rico U.S.
San Juan
ST. KITTS AND NEVIS
Caribbean Sea
Belmopan
GUATEMALA
Guatemala City
HONDURAS
Tegucigalpa
San Salvador
EL SALVADOR
NICARAGUA
Managua
San José
COSTA RICA
Panama City
PANAMA
Caracas
VENEZUELA
Georgetown
GUYANA
Paramaribo
SURINAME
Cayenne
FRENCH GUIANA Fr.
Bogotá
COLOMBIA
N S E W
EQUATOR
Galápagos Islands Ecua.
Quito
ECUADOR
Negro R.
Amazon R.
Madeira R.
SOUTH AMERICA
BRAZIL
PERU
Lima
PACIFIC OCEAN
Lake Titicaca
La Paz
BOLIVIA
Sucre
Brasília
Salvador
PARAGUAY
Paraguay R.
Paraná R.
TROPIC OF CAPRICORN
Asunción
CHILE
ARGENTINA
Santiago
URUGUAY
Buenos Aires
Montevideo
Río de la Plata
ATLANTIC OCEAN
Falkland Islands U.K.
South Georgia Island U.K.

0 mi. 1,000
0 km 1,000
Lambert Azimuthal Equal-Area projection

- National capital
- Territorial capital

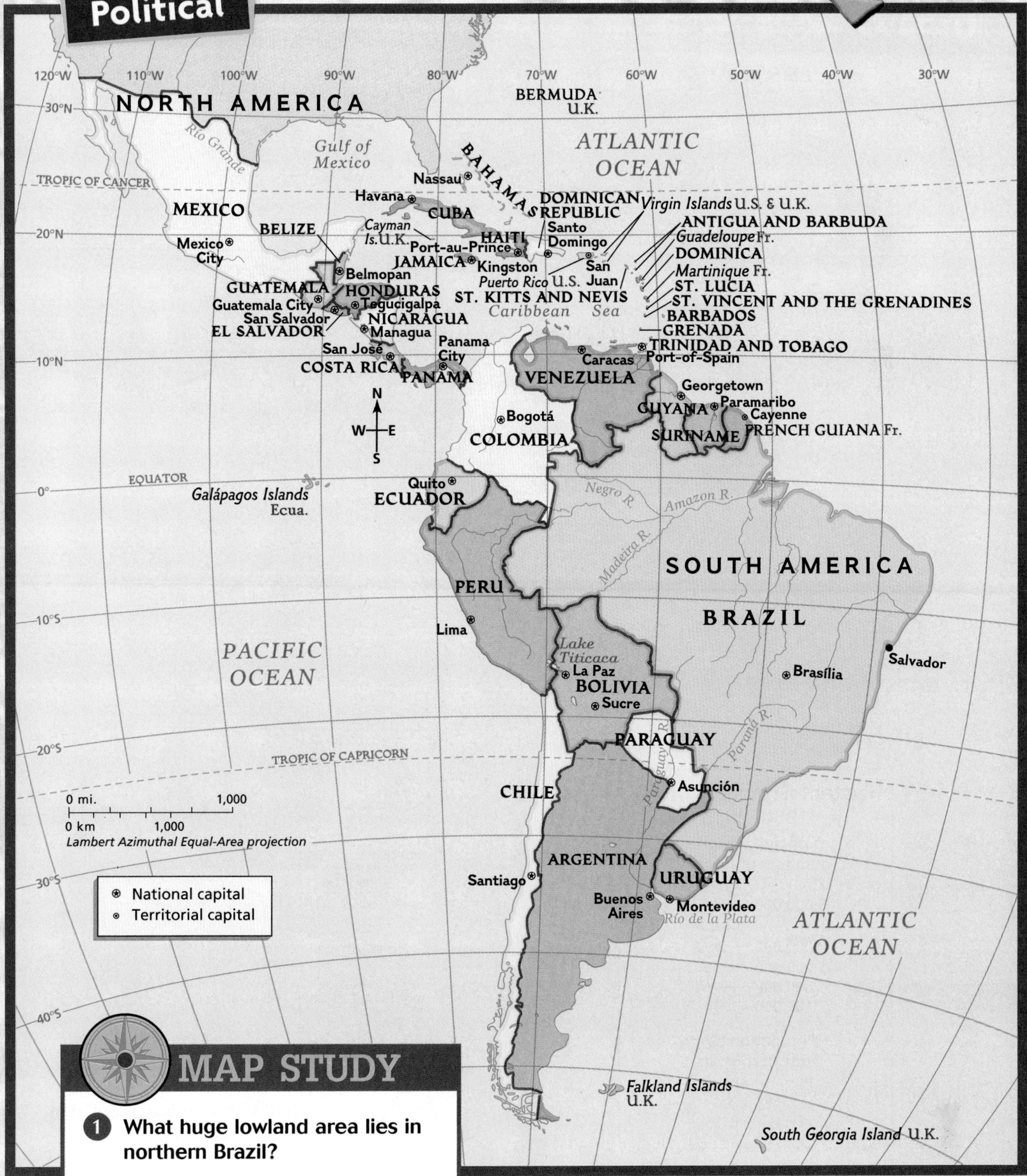

MAP STUDY

1. What huge lowland area lies in northern Brazil?
2. What is the capital of Cuba?

Latin America

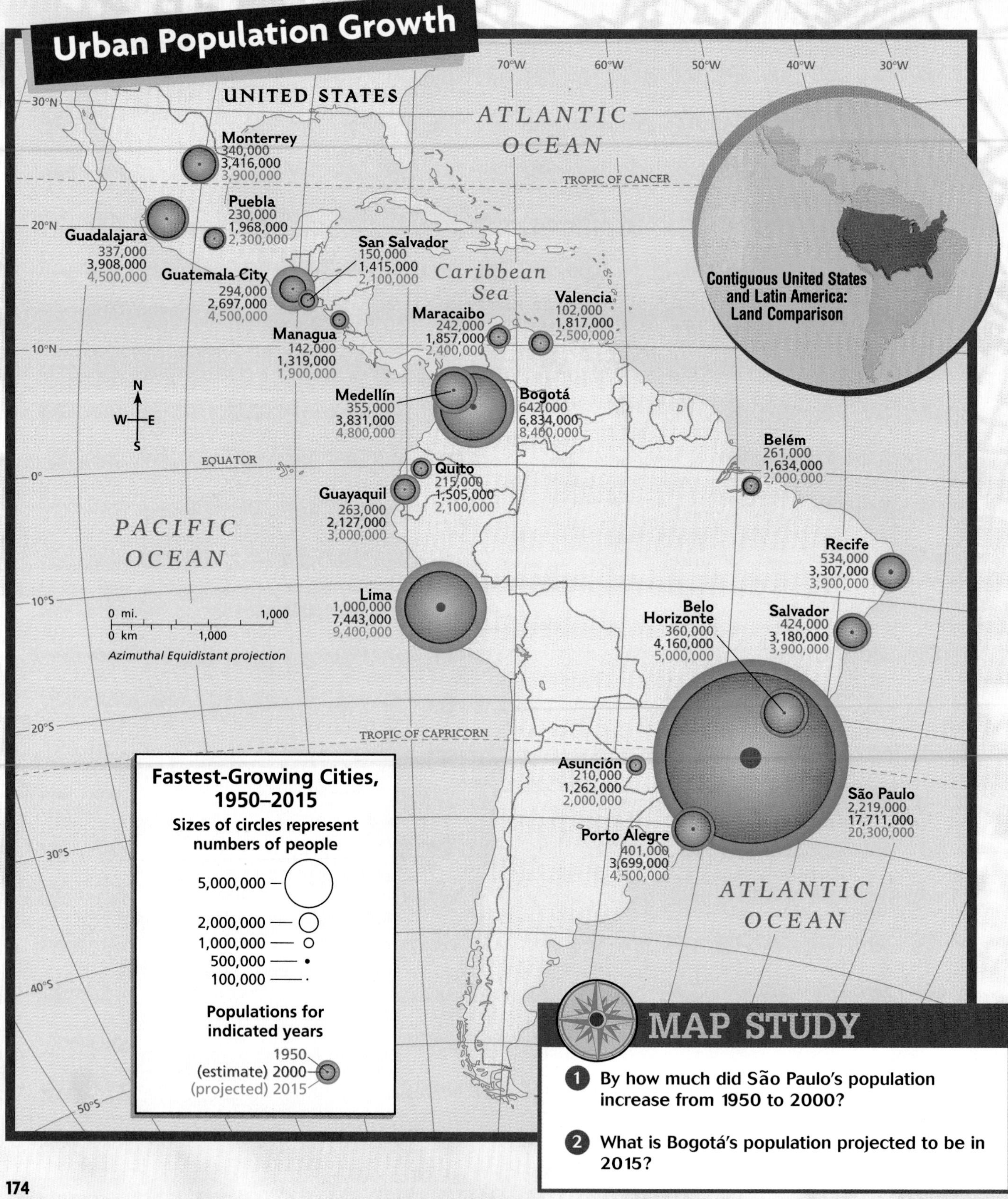

MAP STUDY

1. By how much did São Paulo's population increase from 1950 to 2000?
2. What is Bogotá's population projected to be in 2015?

Geo Extremes

① **HIGHEST POINT**
Aconcagua (Argentina)
22,834 ft. (6,960 m) high

② **LOWEST POINT**
Valdés Peninsula (Argentina)
131 ft. (40 m) below sea level

③ **LONGEST RIVER**
Amazon River
(Brazil and Peru)
4,000 mi. (6,437 km) long

④ **LARGEST LAKE**
Lake Maracaibo (Venezuela)
5,217 sq. mi. (13,512 sq. km)

⑤ **HIGHEST LARGE NAVIGABLE LAKE**
Lake Titicaca
(Peru and Bolivia)
12,500 ft. (3,810 m) high

⑥ **HIGHEST WATERFALL**
Angel Falls (Venezuela)
3,212 ft. (979 m) high

⑦ **DRIEST PLACE**
Atacama Desert (Chile)
rainfall barely measurable

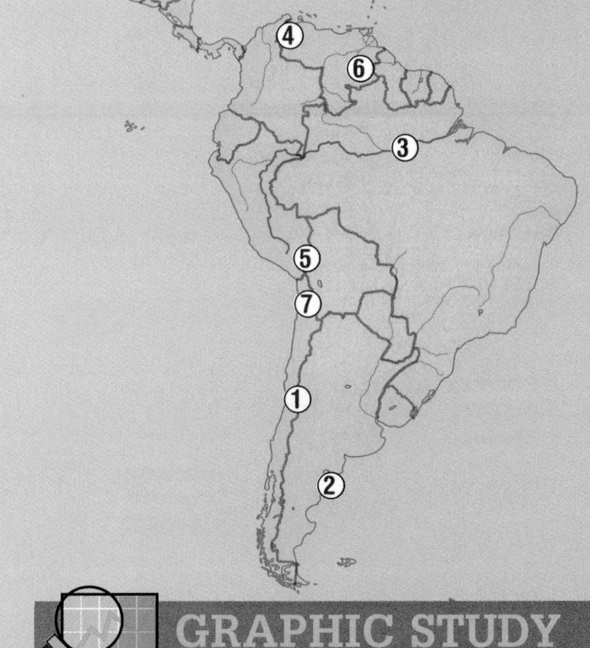

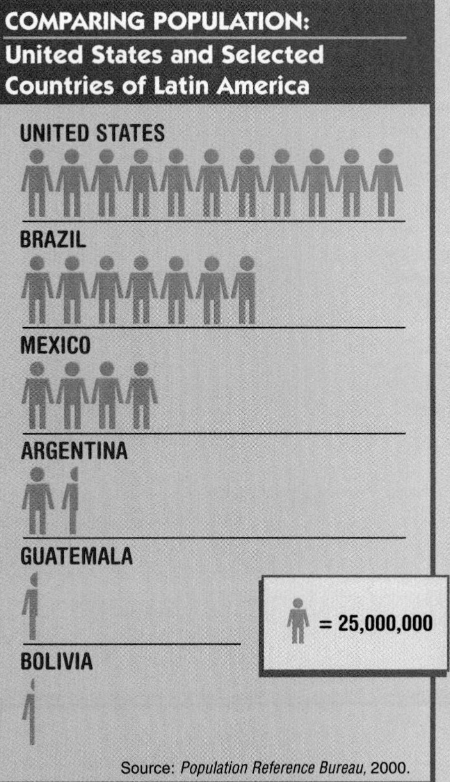

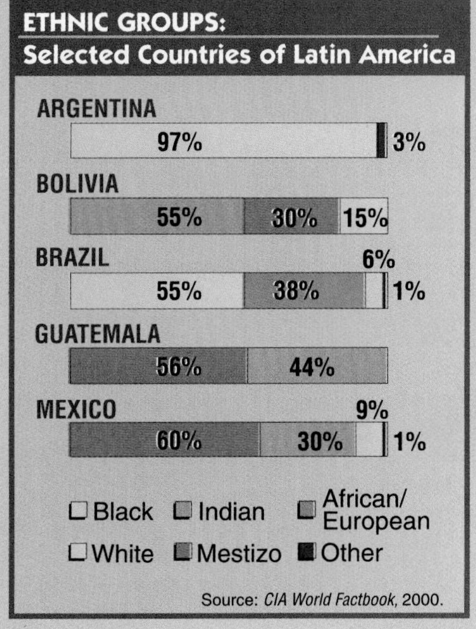

GRAPHIC STUDY

1. What two Latin American "extremes" are found in Venezuela?
2. What countries have a majority of mestizos (people of mixed European and Native American ancestry)?

Country Profiles

ANTIGUA and BARBUDA

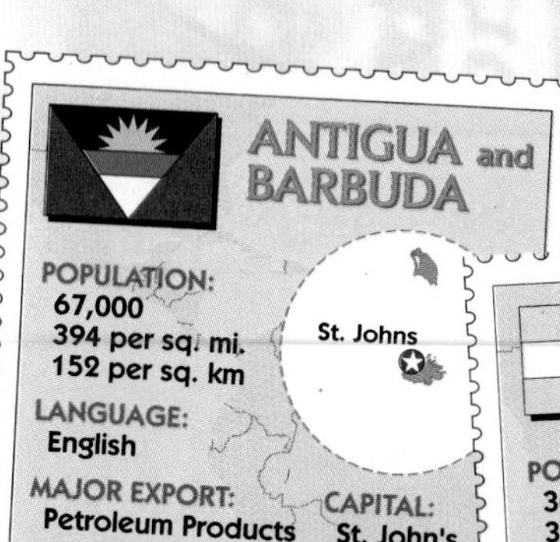

POPULATION:
67,000
394 per sq. mi.
152 per sq. km

LANGUAGE:
English

MAJOR EXPORT:
Petroleum Products

MAJOR IMPORTS:
Foods and Livestock

CAPITAL:
St. John's

LANDMASS:
170 sq. mi.
440 sq. km

ARGENTINA

POPULATION:
36,568,000
34 per sq. mi.
13 per sq. km

LANGUAGE:
Spanish

MAJOR EXPORT:
Meat

MAJOR IMPORT:
Machinery

CAPITAL:
Buenos Aires

LANDMASS:
1,068,302 sq. mi.
2,766,889 sq. km

BAHAMAS

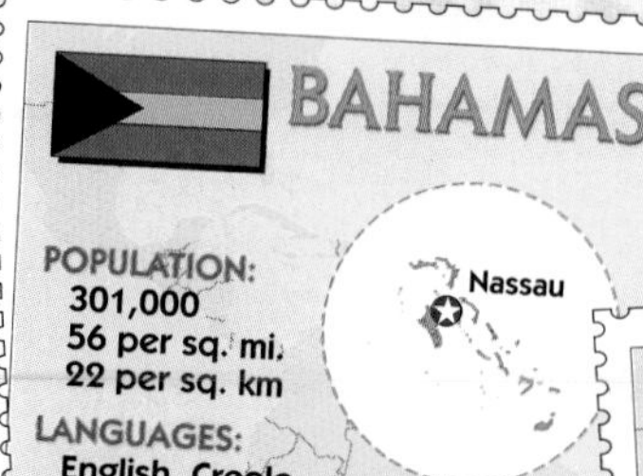

POPULATION:
301,000
56 per sq. mi.
22 per sq. km

LANGUAGES:
English, Creole

MAJOR EXPORT:
Pharmaceuticals

MAJOR IMPORT:
Foods

CAPITAL:
Nassau

LANDMASS:
5,382 sq. mi.
13,939 sq. km

BARBADOS

POPULATION:
269,000
1,620 per sq. mi.
626 per sq. km

LANGUAGE:
English

MAJOR EXPORT:
Sugar

MAJOR IMPORT:
Manufactured Goods

CAPITAL:
Bridgetown

LANDMASS:
166 sq. mi.
430 sq. km

BELIZE

POPULATION:
248,000
28 per sq. mi.
11 per sq. km

LANGUAGE:
English

MAJOR EXPORT:
Sugar

MAJOR IMPORT:
Machinery

CAPITAL:
Belmopan

LANDMASS:
8,867 sq. mi.
22,965 sq. km

BOLIVIA

POPULATION:
8,090,000
19 per sq. mi.
7 per sq. km

LANGUAGES:
Spanish, Quechua, Aymara

MAJOR EXPORT:
Metals

MAJOR IMPORT:
Machinery

CAPITALS:
La Paz, Sucre

LANDMASS:
424,164 sq. mi.
1,098,581 sq. km

BRAZIL

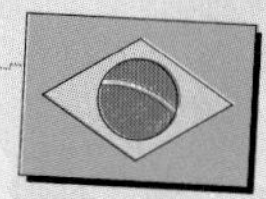

POPULATION:
167,988,000
51 per sq. mi.
20 per sq. km

LANGUAGE:
Portuguese

MAJOR EXPORT:
Iron Ore

MAJOR IMPORT:
Crude Oil

CAPITAL:
Brasília

LANDMASS:
3,286,488 sq. mi.
8,511,965 sq. km

CHILE

POPULATION:
15,018,000
51 per sq. mi.
20 per sq. km

LANGUAGE:
Spanish

MAJOR EXPORT:
Copper

MAJOR IMPORT:
Machinery

CAPITAL:
Santiago

LANDMASS:
292,135 sq. mi.
756,626 sq. km

COLOMBIA

POPULATION:
38,581,000
88 per sq. mi.
34 per sq. km

LANGUAGE:
Spanish

MAJOR EXPORT:
Petroleum

MAJOR IMPORT:
Machinery

CAPITAL:
Bogotá

LANDMASS:
439,737 sq. mi.
1,138,914 sq. km

COSTA RICA

POPULATION:
3,594,000
182 per sq. mi.
70 per sq. km

LANGUAGE:
Spanish

MAJOR EXPORT:
Coffee

MAJOR IMPORT:
Raw Materials

CAPITAL:
San José

LANDMASS:
19,730 sq. mi.
51,100 sq. km

CUBA

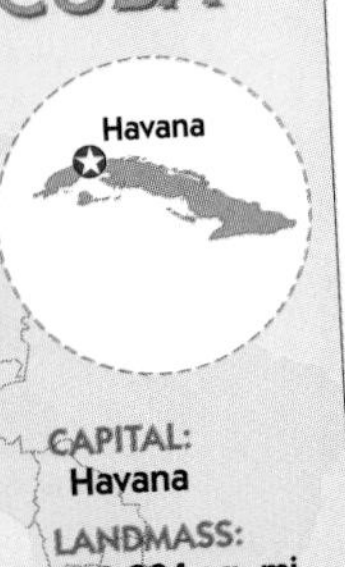

POPULATION:
11,178,000
261 per sq. mi.
101 per sq. km

LANGUAGE:
Spanish

MAJOR EXPORT:
Sugar

MAJOR IMPORT:
Petroleum

CAPITAL:
Havana

LANDMASS:
42,804 sq. mi.
110,861 sq. km

Countries and flags not drawn to scale

DOMINICA

POPULATION: 71,000; 245 per sq. mi.; 95 per sq. km
LANGUAGES: English, French
MAJOR EXPORT: Bananas
MAJOR IMPORT: Manufactured Goods
CAPITAL: Roseau
LANDMASS: 290 sq. mi.; 751 sq. km

DOMINICAN REPUBLIC

POPULATION: 8,299,000; 441 per sq. mi.; 170 per sq. km
LANGUAGE: Spanish
MAJOR EXPORT: Ferronickel
MAJOR IMPORT: Foods
CAPITAL: Santo Domingo
LANDMASS: 18,816 sq. mi.; 48,734 sq. km

ECUADOR

POPULATION: 12,411,000; 113 per sq. mi.; 44 per sq. km
LANGUAGES: Spanish, Quechua
MAJOR EXPORT: Petroleum
MAJOR IMPORT: Transport Equipment
CAPITAL: Quito
LANDMASS: 109,484 sq. mi.; 283,561 sq. km

EL SALVADOR

POPULATION: 5,859,000; 721 per sq. mi.; 278 per sq. km
LANGUAGE: Spanish
MAJOR EXPORT: Coffee
MAJOR IMPORT: Raw Materials
CAPITAL: San Salvador
LANDMASS: 8,124 sq. mi.; 21,041 sq. km

FRENCH GUIANA*

POPULATION: 185,000; 5 per sq. mi.; 2 per sq. km
LANGUAGE: French
MAJOR EXPORT: Shrimp
MAJOR IMPORT: Foods
CAPITAL: Cayenne
LANDMASS: 34,749 sq. mi.; 89,999 sq. km

* Territory of France

GRENADA

POPULATION: 97,000; 729 per sq. mi.; 282 per sq. km
LANGUAGES: English, French
MAJOR EXPORT: Bananas
MAJOR IMPORT: Foods
CAPITAL: St. George's
LANDMASS: 133 sq. mi.; 344 sq. km

GUATEMALA

POPULATION: 12,336,000; 293 per sq. mi.; 113 per sq. km
LANGUAGES: Spanish, Mayan Languages
MAJOR EXPORT: Coffee
MAJOR IMPORT: Petroleum
CAPITAL: Guatemala City
LANDMASS: 42,042 sq. mi.; 108,889 sq. km

GUYANA

POPULATION: 705,000; 8 per sq. mi.; 3 per sq. km
LANGUAGE: English
MAJOR EXPORT: Sugar
MAJOR IMPORT: Manufactured Goods
CAPITAL: Georgetown
LANDMASS: 83,000 sq. mi.; 214,969 sq. km

HAITI

POPULATION: 7,751,000; 723 per sq. mi.; 279 per sq. km
LANGUAGES: French, Creole
MAJOR EXPORT: Manufactured Goods
MAJOR IMPORT: Machinery
CAPITAL: Port-au-Prince
LANDMASS: 10,714 sq. mi.; 27,750 sq. km

HONDURAS

POPULATION: 5,901,000; 136 per sq. mi.; 53 per sq. km
LANGUAGE: Spanish
MAJOR EXPORT: Bananas
MAJOR IMPORT: Machinery
CAPITAL: Tegucigalpa
LANDMASS: 43,277 sq. mi.; 112,088 sq. km

JAMAICA

POPULATION: 2,621,000; 618 per sq. mi.; 238 per sq. km
LANGUAGES: English, Creole
MAJOR EXPORT: Alumina
MAJOR IMPORT: Machinery
CAPITAL: Kingston
LANDMASS: 4,244 sq. mi.; 10,991 sq. km

Country Profiles

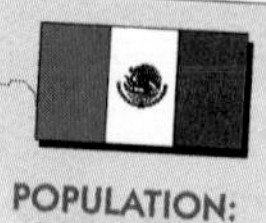

MEXICO

POPULATION:
99,734,000
132 per sq. mi.
51 per sq. km

LANGUAGES:
Spanish, Native American Languages

MAJOR EXPORT:
Crude Oil

MAJOR IMPORT:
Machinery

CAPITAL:
Mexico City

LANDMASS:
756,066 sq. mi.
1,958,201 sq. km

NICARAGUA

POPULATION:
4,952,000
99 per sq. mi.
38 per sq. km

LANGUAGE:
Spanish

MAJOR EXPORT:
Coffee

MAJOR IMPORT:
Manufactured Goods

CAPITAL:
Managua

LANDMASS:
50,193 sq. mi.
129,999 sq. km

PANAMA

POPULATION:
2,809,000
94 per sq. mi.
36 per sq. km

LANGUAGE:
Spanish

MAJOR EXPORT:
Bananas

MAJOR IMPORT:
Machinery

CAPITAL:
Panama City

LANDMASS:
29,762 sq. mi.
77,082 sq. km

PARAGUAY

POPULATION:
5,219,000
33 per sq. mi.
13 per sq. km

LANGUAGES:
Spanish, Guaraní

MAJOR EXPORT:
Cotton

MAJOR IMPORT:
Machinery

CAPITAL:
Asunción

LANDMASS:
157,048 sq. mi.
406,752 sq. km

PERU

POPULATION:
26,624,000
54 per sq. mi.
21 per sq. km

LANGUAGES:
Spanish, Quechua, Aymara

MAJOR EXPORT:
Copper

MAJOR IMPORT:
Machinery

CAPITAL:
Lima

LANDMASS:
496,225 sq. mi.
1,285,217 sq. km

PUERTO RICO*

POPULATION:
3,887,652
1,132 per sq. mi.
437 per sq. km

LANGUAGES:
Spanish, English

MAJOR EXPORT:
Pharmaceuticals

MAJOR IMPORT:
Chemical Products

CAPITAL:
San Juan

LANDMASS:
3,435 sq. mi.
8,897 sq. km

* U.S. Commonwealth

ST. KITTS and NEVIS

POPULATION:
39,000
386 per sq. mi.
149 per sq. km

LANGUAGE:
English

MAJOR EXPORT:
Machinery

MAJOR IMPORT:
Electronic Goods

CAPITAL:
Basseterre

LANDMASS:
101 sq. mi.
261 sq. km

ST. LUCIA

POPULATION:
154,000
647 per sq. mi.
250 per sq. km

LANGUAGES:
English, French

MAJOR EXPORT:
Bananas

MAJOR IMPORT:
Foods

CAPITAL:
Castries

LANDMASS:
238 sq. mi.
617 sq. km

ST. VINCENT and the GRENADINES

POPULATION:
114,000
760 per sq. mi.
294 per sq. km

LANGUAGES:
English, French

MAJOR EXPORT:
Bananas

MAJOR IMPORT:
Foods

CAPITAL:
Kingstown

LANDMASS:
150 sq. mi.
388 sq. km

SURINAME

POPULATION:
431,000
7 per sq. mi.
3 per sq. km

LANGUAGE:
Dutch

MAJOR EXPORT:
Bauxite

MAJOR IMPORT:
Machinery

CAPITAL:
Paramaribo

LANDMASS:
63,037 sq. mi.
163,265 sq. km

TRINIDAD and TOBAGO

POPULATION:
1,285,000
649 per sq. mi.
250 per sq. km

LANGUAGE:
English

MAJOR EXPORT:
Petroleum

MAJOR IMPORT:
Machinery

CAPITAL:
Port-of-Spain

LANDMASS:
1,981 sq. mi.
5,131 sq. km

Countries and flags not drawn to scale

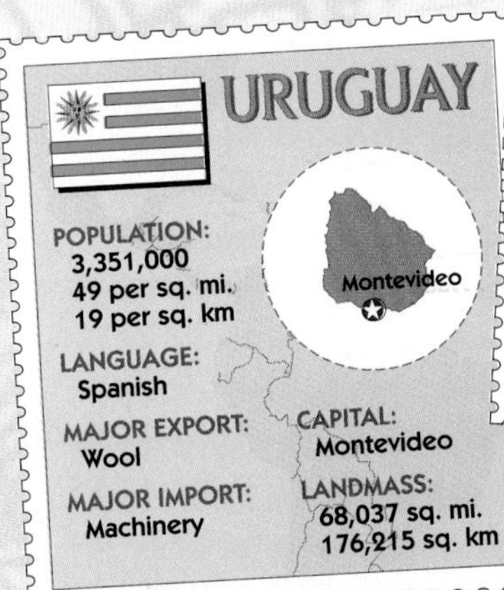

* Territory of U.S.

Questions From Buzz Bee!

The following questions are taken from National Geographic GeoBees. Use your textbook, the Internet, and other library resources to find the answers.

1. In 1911 Hiram Bingham found the site of a major Incan city in the Peruvian Andes. Name this site.
2. Marajó Island, which is just south of the Equator and about the same size as Denmark, is bordered on the northwest by what river?
3. Cowhands who tend cattle on the grasslands of Argentina are part of the country's folklore. What are these cowhands called?
4. Name the world's most populous Spanish-speaking country.
5. Bananas grown on coastal lowlands north of Tegucigalpa are a major export of which Central American country?

Chapter 6

Mexico

The World and Its People NATIONAL GEOGRAPHIC

To learn more about the people and places of Mexico, view ***The World and Its People*** **Chapter 6** video.

Geography Online

Chapter Overview Visit the ***Geography: The World and Its People*** Web site at gwip.glencoe.com and click on **Chapter 6–Chapter Overviews** to preview information about Mexico.

Section 1 Mexico's Land and Economy

Guide to Reading

Main Idea

Mexico's mountainous landscape and varied climate create different economic regions.

Terms to Know

- land bridge
- peninsula
- latitude
- altitude
- hurricane
- vaquero
- *maquiladora*
- subsistence farm
- plantation

Places to Locate

- Pacific Ocean
- Gulf of Mexico
- Baja California
- Yucatán Peninsula
- Sierra Madre
- Mexico City
- Plateau of Mexico
- Monterrey
- Tijuana
- Ciudad Juárez
- Guadalajara

Reading Strategy

Make three charts like this one to show how Mexico's northern, central, and southern regions differ.

Region →	
Landscape →	
Climate →	
Economy →	

NATIONAL GEOGRAPHIC **Exploring Our World**

Mexican farmer Dionisio Pulido was plowing his cornfield one day. Suddenly his son heard a rumble in the ground. Then white smoke began to spew into the air. When they awoke the next day, they saw a volcano 30 feet (9 m) high. Today, more than 50 years later, the volcano named Paricutín soars nearly 8,990 feet (2,740 m) high.

Paricutín and other volcanoes are scattered throughout Mexico because the country sits where three plates in the earth's crust collide. Sometimes the movement of these plates can bring disastrous results. Hot magma, or melted rock, might shoot through a volcano. The ground might shift violently in an earthquake. Do you see why Native Americans once called Mexico "the land of the shaking earth"?

Bridging Two Continents

Mexico forms part of a land bridge, or narrow strip of land that joins two larger landmasses. This land bridge connects North America and South America. Look at the map on page 172. You can see that Mexico, part of North America, borders the southern United States. Farther south, Mexico reaches its narrowest point at the Isthmus of Tehuantepec (tay•WAHN•tah•PEHK). Here, only 140 miles (225 km) separate the **Pacific Ocean** from the **Gulf of Mexico.**

◀ The Lighthouse of Commerce stands guard over Monterrey and Saddle Mountain.

The Pacific Ocean borders Mexico on the west. Extending south along this western coast is **Baja** (BAH•hah) **California.** It is a long, thin **peninsula,** or piece of land with water on three sides. On Mexico's eastern side, the Gulf of Mexico and the Caribbean Sea border the shores. Between the Gulf and the Caribbean Sea is another peninsula—the **Yucatán** (YOO•kah•TAHN) **Peninsula.**

Mexico is a rugged land. If you saw it from space, you might think that the country looked like a crumpled piece of paper with deep folds. Towering mountain ranges and a huge, high plateau occupy the center of the country.

The Sierra Madre Three different mountain ranges in Mexico make up the **Sierra Madre** (SYEHR•rah MAH•thray), or "mother range." The Sierra Madre Occidental runs down the western coast. The Sierra Madre Oriental extends along the eastern coast. The steep ridges of the Sierra Madre del Sur rise in southwestern Mexico. Because of the rugged terrain, few people live in the Sierra Madre. The mountains are rich in resources, though. They hold copper, zinc, silver, and timber.

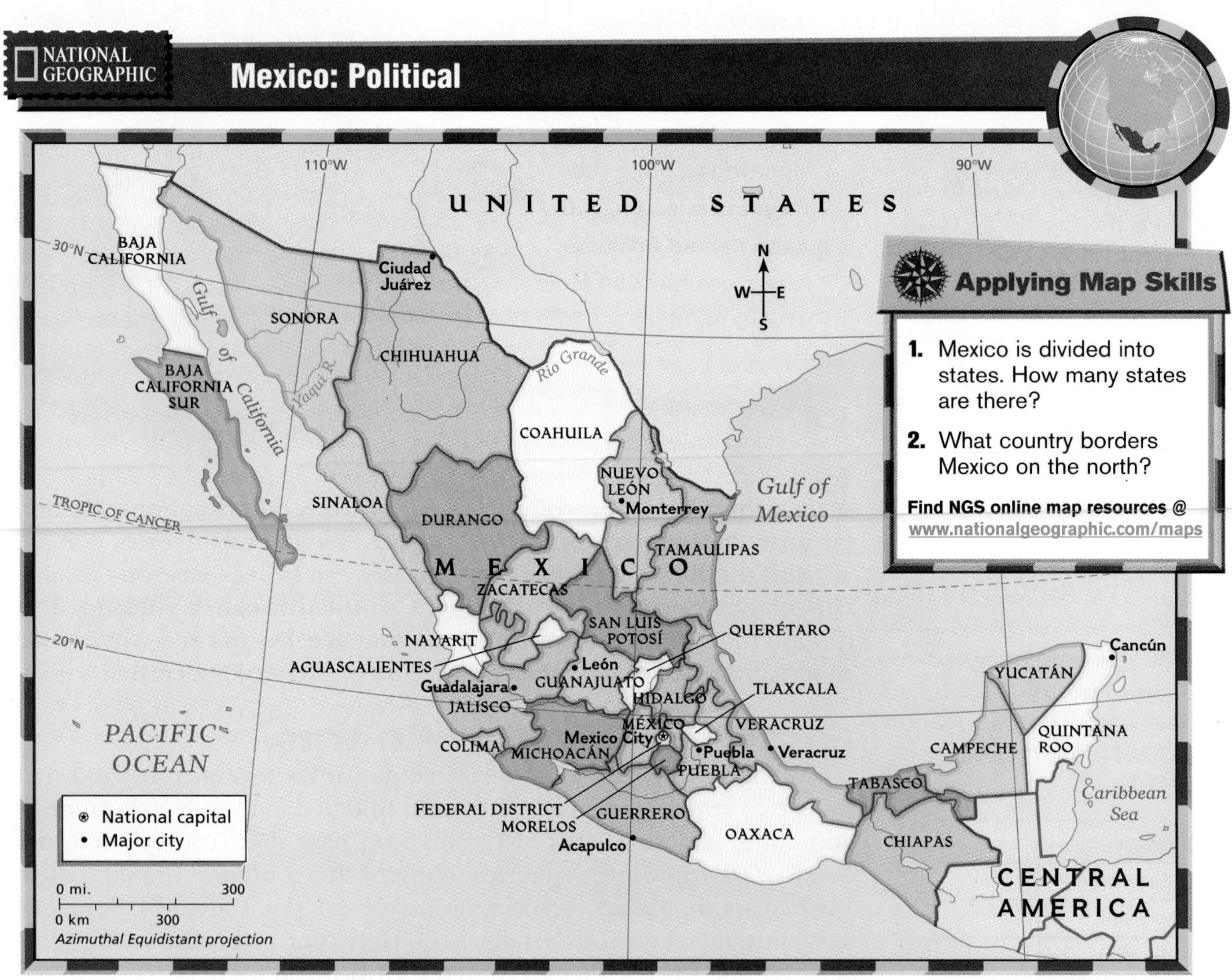

Applying Map Skills

1. Mexico is divided into states. How many states are there?
2. What country borders Mexico on the north?

Find NGS online map resources @ www.nationalgeographic.com/maps

Many of Mexico's mountains are volcanoes. Popocatépetl (POH•puh•KAT•uh•PEHT•uhl), or "El Popo," as Mexicans call it, erupted violently centuries ago. In December 2000, El Popo erupted again, hurling molten rock into the sky. About 30,000 people from surrounding areas were forced to temporarily leave their homes. Tens of millions of people live 50 miles (80 km) or less from the mountain and could face even worse eruptions in the future.

Mexicans face another danger from the land. Earthquakes can destroy their cities and homes. A 1985 quake killed nearly 10,000 people in Mexico's capital, **Mexico City,** even though the earthquake's center was about 185 miles (298 km) away.

The Plateau of Mexico The Sierra Madre surround the large, flat center of the country, the **Plateau of Mexico.** You find mostly deserts and grassy plains in the northern part of the Plateau. Broad, flat valleys that slice through the center hold many of the country's chief cities and most of its people. To the south, the Plateau steadily rises until it meets with the high, snowcapped mountains of the Sierra Madre del Sur.

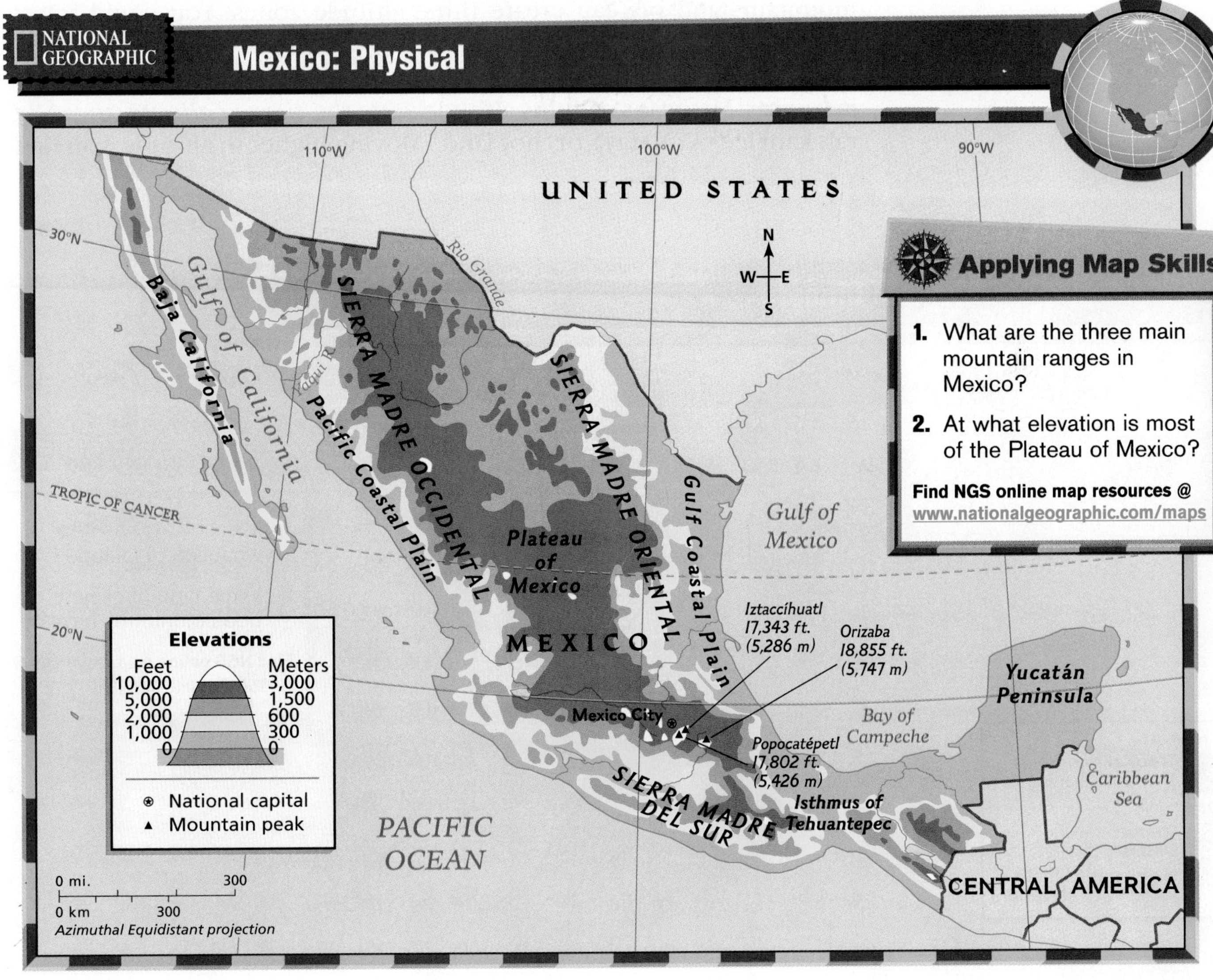

Coastal Lowlands Mexico's lowland plains squeeze between the mountains and the sea. The Pacific Coastal Plain begins with a hot, largely empty desert in the north. As you move farther south, better soil and rainfall allow ranching and farming along this plain. On the other side of the country, the Gulf Coastal Plain has more rain and fertile soil for growing crops and raising animals.

Reading Check **What two dangers from the land do Mexicans face?**

Land of Many Climates

Mexico has many different climates. Why? As you read in Chapter 2, **latitude**—or location north or south of the Equator—affects temperature. The Tropic of Cancer, which cuts across the center of Mexico at 23½°N latitude, marks the northern edge of the tropics. Areas south of this line have warm temperatures throughout the year. Areas north of this line are warm in summer and cooler in winter.

Altitude, or height above sea level, affects temperature in Mexico as well. The higher up you go, the cooler the temperatures—even within the tropics. The diagram on page 185 shows that Mexico's mountains and plateau create three altitude zones. You could travel through all of these zones in a day's trip across the Sierra Madre.

Because they are near sea level, the coastal lowlands have high temperatures. Mexicans call this altitude zone the *tierra caliente* (tee•AY•rah kah•lee•AYN•tay), or "hot land." Moving higher in altitude, you find

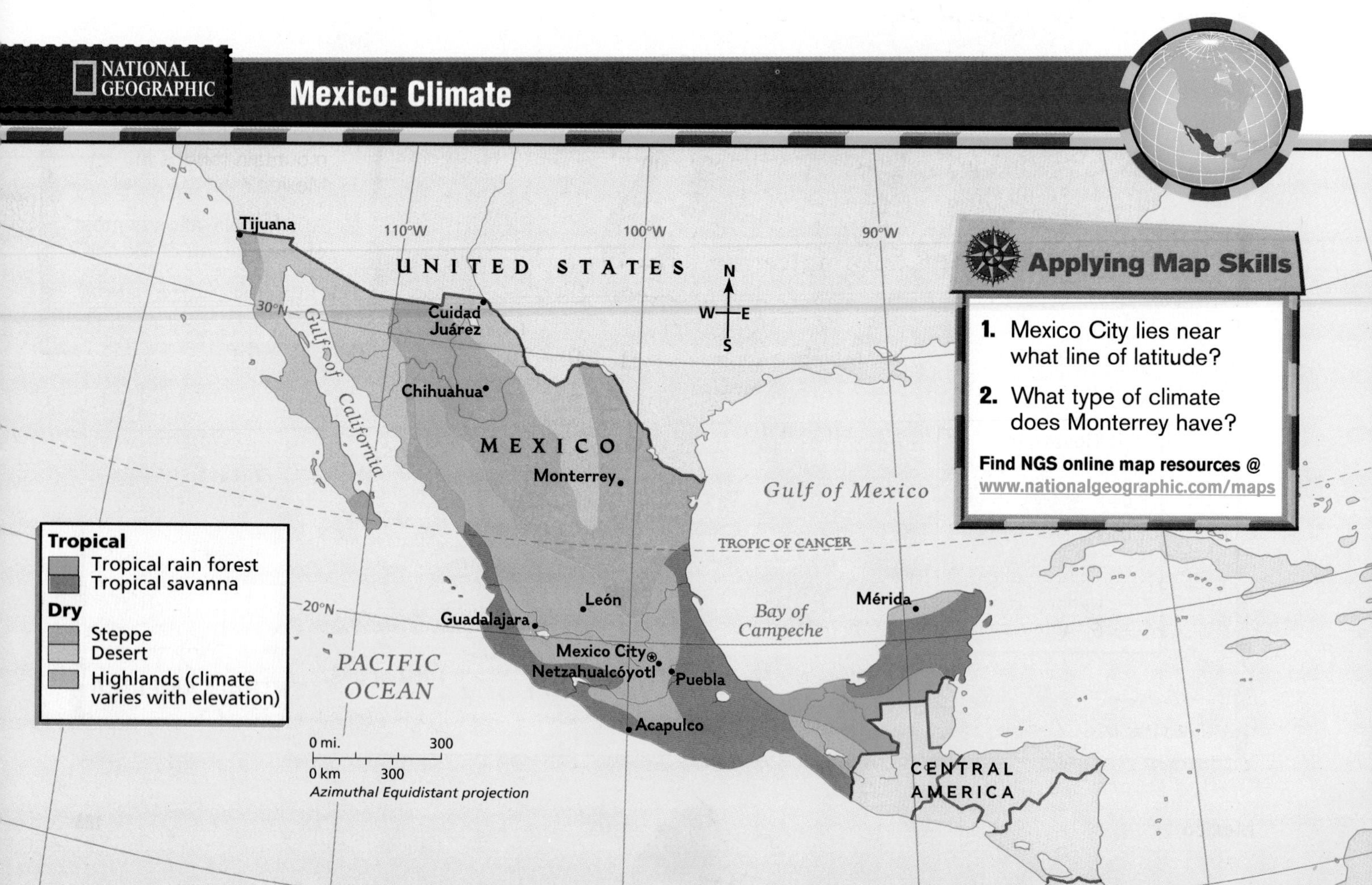

Mexico's Altitude Zones

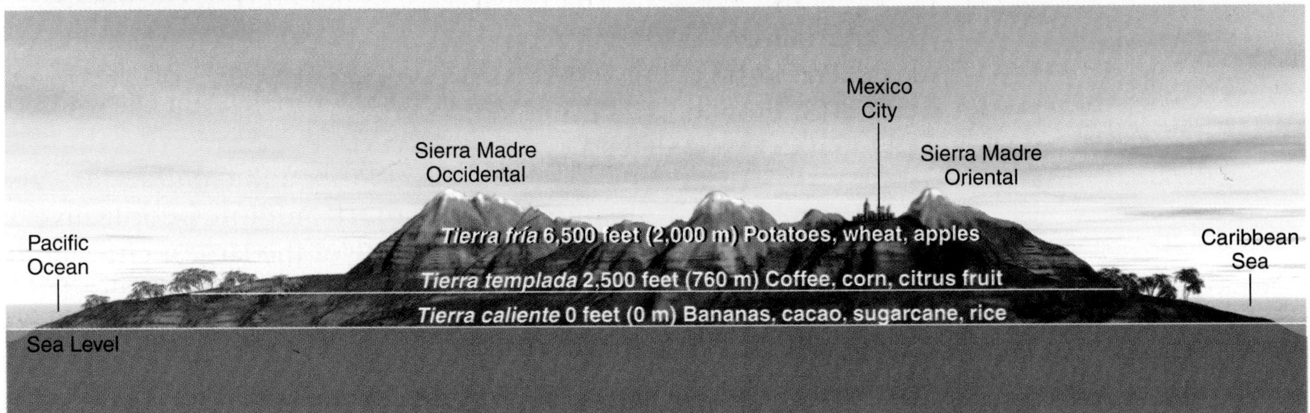

the *tierra templada* (taym•PLAH•dah), or "temperate land." Here the climate becomes more moderate. In the highest zone, the climate becomes even cooler. Mexicans call this the *tierra fría* (FREE•ah), or "cold land."

Rainfall varies throughout Mexico. Baja California and northern Mexico receive very little precipitation. Other regions receive more, mostly in the summer and early fall. From June to October, Mexico can be hit by **hurricanes.** These fierce tropical storms with high winds and heavy rains form over the warm waters of the Atlantic or Pacific Oceans. They can strike Mexico with fury.

Analyzing the Diagram

Mexico has zones of different climates that result from different altitudes.

Location **In which altitude zone is Mexico City located?**

Reading Check **What is Mexico's warmest altitude zone?**

Mexico's Economic Regions

Mexico's physical geography and climate together give Mexico three distinct economic regions: the north, central Mexico, and the south. Large stretches of northern Mexico are too dry and rocky to farm without irrigation. By building canals to carry water to their fields, people can grow cotton, fruits, grains, and vegetables.

Did you know that the skills used by American cowhands originated in Mexico? Cowhands called **vaqueros** (vah•KEHR•ohs) developed the tools and techniques for herding, roping, and branding cattle. Vaqueros in northern Mexico carry on this work today.

Northern Mexico has seen an economic boom. **Monterrey,** Mexico's main producer of steel and cement, has long been an important industrial city. In this and other cities, many companies from the United States and elsewhere have built ***maquiladoras*** (mah•KEEL•ah•DOHR•as), or factories that assemble parts made in other countries. As a result, thousands of Mexicans have flocked to cities such as **Tijuana** (tee•WAH•nah) and **Ciudad Juárez** (see•ooh•DAHD HWAH•rayz). Their growth has raised concerns about damage to the environment and dangers to the health and safety of workers. Still, factory work and increased trade have raised the standard of living in northern cities.

More than half of Mexico's people live in the central region, the country's heartland. Why do they call this area home? The climate is one reason. Although central Mexico lies in the tropics, its high elevation keeps it from being hot and humid. Temperatures are mild, and the climate is pleasant year-round. A second reason is the fertile soil created by volcanic eruptions over the centuries. This allows good production for farming and ranching.

Large industrial cities such as Mexico City and **Guadalajara** also prosper in central Mexico. More than 18 million people live in Mexico City and its suburbs, making it one of the largest cities in the world.

The south is the poorest economic region of the country. The mountains towering in the center of this region have poor soil. **Subsistence farms,** or small plots where farmers grow only enough food to feed their families, are common here. In contrast, the coastal lowlands of this area have good soil and plentiful rain. Wealthy farmers grow sugarcane or bananas on **plantations,** large farms that raise a single crop for sale.

Both coasts also have beautiful beaches and a warm climate. Tourists from all over the world flock to such resorts as Acapulco and Puerto Vallarta on the Pacific coast and Cancún on the Yucatán Peninsula.

Reading Check **How does the economic region of northern Mexico differ from that of southern Mexico?**

Section 1 Assessment

Defining Terms

1. **Define** land bridge, peninsula, latitude, altitude, hurricane, vaquero, *maquiladora*, subsistence farm, plantation.

Recalling Facts

2. **Place** What bodies of water border Mexico?
3. **Location** What are the names of Mexico's three mountain ranges and where are they located?
4. **Economics** Why have many Mexicans moved to the cities of the north?

Critical Thinking

5. **Analyzing Information** Why is Mexico sometimes referred to as "the land of the shaking earth"?
6. **Understanding Cause and Effect** What two factors have the greatest effect on the climate of Mexico?

Graphic Organizer

7. **Organizing Information** Draw a diagram like this one, then list two facts that explain the large population growth of central Mexico.

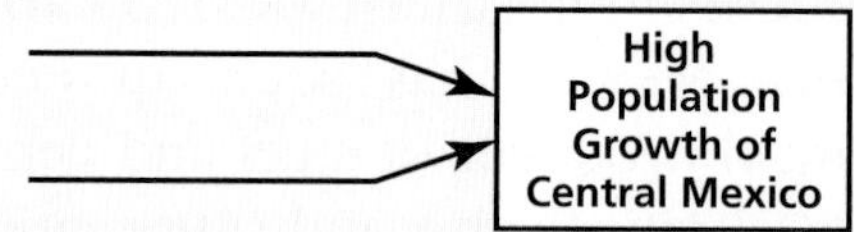

Applying Geography Skills

8. **Analyzing Maps** Refer to the physical map of Mexico on page 183. What is the elevation of the Yucatán Peninsula?

Technology Skill

Using the Internet

To learn more about almost any topic imaginable, use the **Internet**—a global network of computers. Many features, such as e-mail, interactive educational classes, and shopping services are offered on the Net.

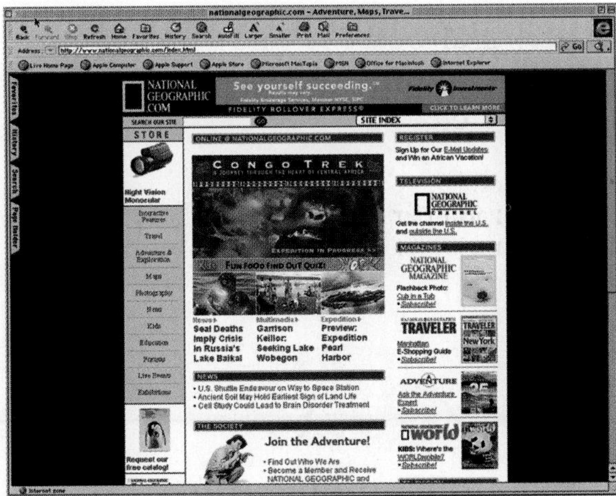

▲ **The National Geographic Society's Web site**

Learning the Skill

To get on the Internet, you need three things: (a) a personal computer, (b) a *modem*—or device that connects your computer to a telephone line, and (c) an account with an Internet service provider (ISP). An ISP is a company that enables you to log on to the Internet, usually for a fee.

After you are connected, the easiest way to access Internet sites is to use a "Web browser," a program that lets you view and explore information on the World Wide Web. The Web consists of many documents called "Web sites," each of which has its own address, or Uniform Resource Locator (URL). Many URLs start with the keystrokes *http://*

If you do not know the exact URL of a site, commercial "search engines" such as Yahoo! or AltaVista can help you find information. Type a subject or name into the "search" box, then press Enter. The search engine lists available sites that may have the information you are looking for.

Practicing the Skill

Follow these steps to learn how the Internet can help you find information about Mexico's Sierra Madre.

1. Log on to the Internet and access a search engine.
2. Search by typing "Sierra Madre" in the search box.
3. Scroll the list of Web sites that appears when the search is complete. Select a site to bring up and read or print.
4. If you get "lost" on the Internet, click on the back arrow key at the top of the screen until you find a familiar site.
5. Continue selecting sites until you have enough information to write a short report on minerals found in the Sierra Madre.

Applying the Skill

Follow the above steps to locate information about *maquiladoras.* Use the information you gather to create a chart or graph showing how the number of workers hired by *maquiladoras* has increased over the past 10 years.

Section 2

Mexico's History and Government

Guide to Reading

Main Idea

Mexico's culture reflects a blend of its Native American and Spanish past.

Terms to Know

- hieroglyphics
- mural
- colony
- hacienda
- mestizo
- federal republic

Places to Locate

- Yucatán Peninsula
- Tenochtitlán
- Mexico City

Reading Strategy

Draw a chart like this one, then provide one example of how Native Americans and Europeans influenced Mexican culture.

Ethnic groups	Influence on Mexican Culture
Native American	
European	

NATIONAL GEOGRAPHIC **Exploring Our World**

Thousands of people visit an ancient temple in Mexico's Yucatán Peninsula on the spring and fall equinoxes. On those two days, the setting sun casts a shadow on the stairs of the temple's north face. The area that is not shadowed looks like the ancient Native American god called Kukulcan, or the Feathered Serpent, going down the temple stairs.

The first people to arrive in Mexico were the ancestors of today's Native Americans. Mexico's Native American heritage shapes the country's culture. So does Mexico's European heritage, brought by the Spaniards who conquered the area in the 1500s.

Native American Civilizations

Native Americans came to Mexico thousands of years ago. From about 1200 B.C. to the A.D. 1500s, these people built a series of brilliant, highly advanced civilizations on Mexican soil. Of these, the Mayan and Aztec civilizations are the best known. Look at the map on page 189 to see where the Mayan and Aztec civilizations thrived.

The Maya The people called the Maya lived in the rain forests of the **Yucatán Peninsula** and surrounding areas from about A.D. 250 to A.D. 900. Religion held Mayan society together. Mayan priests needed to measure time accurately to hold religious ceremonies at the correct moment. They studied the heavens and developed a calendar of 365 days.

The Maya were the first to grow corn. They also built huge stone temples in the shape of pyramids with steps. One of these structures, the temple of Kukulcan, showed careful planning. Each side of Kukulcan had 91 steps, totaling 364. The platform at the temple's top made one more step for a grand total of 365—just like the days in the year.

The Maya also developed **hieroglyphics,** a form of writing that uses signs and symbols. They had a complex number system. Artists decorated temples and tombs with elaborate **murals,** or wall paintings.

Around A.D. 900, Mayan civilization declined. Why? Historians do not know. Some suggest that the Maya overused the land and could not grow enough food. Others suggest that warfare or the spread of disease caused their decline. The Maya did not disappear, however. Their descendants still live in the same area and speak the Mayan language.

The Aztec Around A.D. 1200, a people called the Mexica moved into central Mexico from the north. The Spanish later called these people Aztec. The Aztec conquered a large empire in central Mexico. Their capital, **Tenochtitlán** (tay•NAWCH•teet•LAHN) was magnificent. Today **Mexico City**—Mexico's capital—stands on this ancient site.

Tenochtitlán was originally built on two islands in the middle of Lake Texcoco. Long dikes connected it to land. The city had huge stepped pyramids. Merchants traded gold, silver, and pottery in busy marketplaces. Farmers grew their crops in structures called "floating gardens," or rafts filled with mud. The rafts eventually sank to the lake bottom and piled up, forming fertile islands.

Reading Check What two Native American cultures flourished in Mexico?

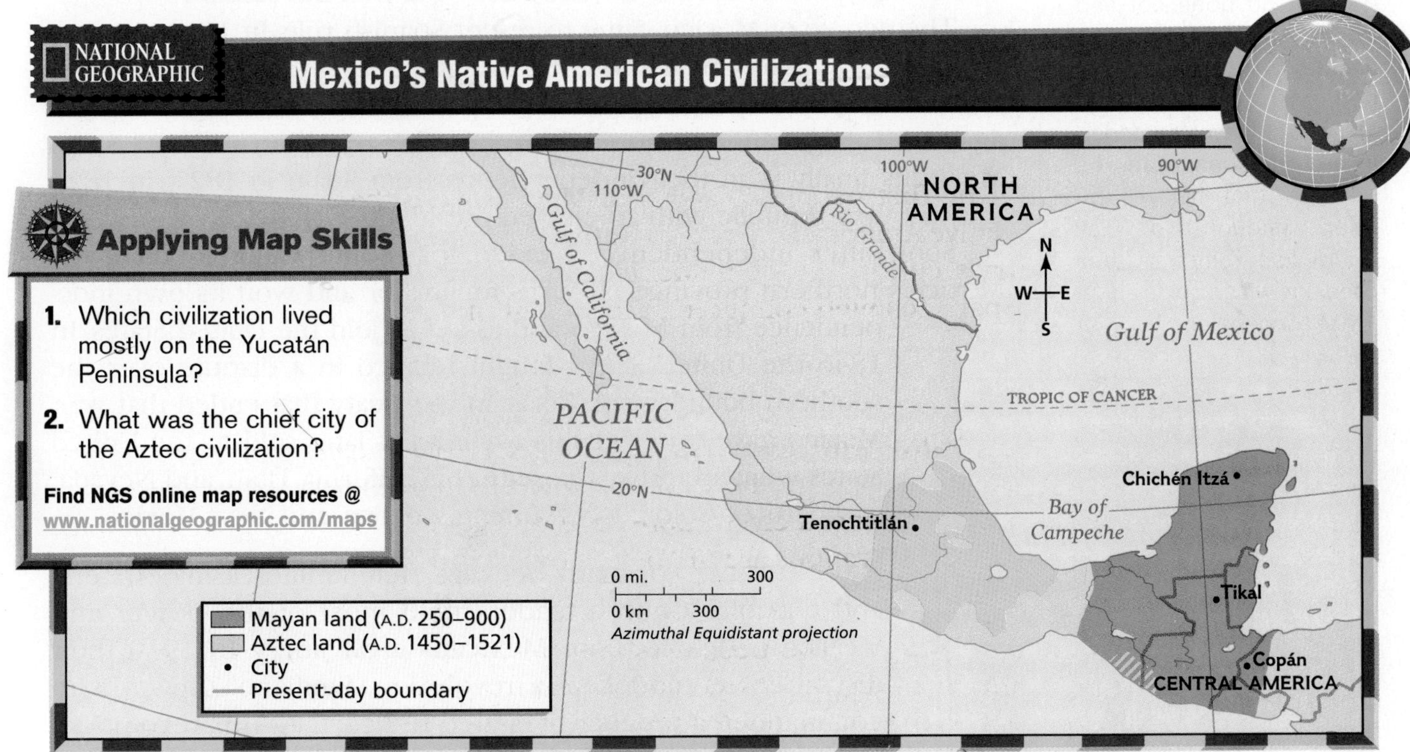

Spanish Mexico

In 1519 Mexico's history changed dramatically. A Spanish army led by Hernán Cortés landed on Mexico's Gulf coast. He and about 600 soldiers marched to Tenochtitlán, which they heard was filled with gold. Some Native Americans who resented the harsh rule of the Aztec joined the Spanish. With their weapons, the Spaniards defeated the Aztec within two years.

Spain made Mexico a **colony,** or an overseas territory, because Mexico's rocky land held rich deposits of gold and silver. Many Spanish settlers came to live in Mexico. Some raised cattle on large ranches called **haciendas** (ah•see•AYN•dahs). Others started gold and silver mines. The Spaniards made Native Americans work on the ranches and in the mines. Thousands of Native Americans died from mistreatment. Many thousands more died of diseases like the common cold and smallpox caught from the Europeans. Spanish priests came to Mexico and in their own way tried to improve the lives of the Native Americans. Because of their work, many Native Americans accepted the priests' teachings. Today about 90 percent of Mexico's people follow the Roman Catholic religion.

A Mixing of Cultures Over time, the Spanish and Native American cultures mixed. Modern Mexicans reflect this blending of peoples. About 60 percent are **mestizos** (mays•TEE•zohs), having mixed Spanish and Native American heritage. Another 30 percent of the population are completely Native American, while the remaining 10 percent are descended from Europeans, especially the Spaniards.

Reading Check **Why was Mexico a valuable colony for Spain?**

Digging for Treasure

Fourteen-year-old Benito is on a quest. He has joined his father and uncle in an archaeological dig, hoping to discover ruins from an ancient Aztec civilization. Although digging is hard and dirty work, Benito is excited to do it. His mother told him that he is a direct descendant of the Aztec. Perhaps he will be the one to find their fabled "city of gold." If he does not find riches, though, he has another plan. He hopes to become a famous baseball or soccer player someday. If he practices hard, he believes that he will be good enough to play in Mexico City's Azteca Stadium, which holds about 100,000 people.

Independence and Revolution

The people of Mexico came to resent Spanish rule. In 1810 they rallied behind a Catholic priest, Miguel Hidalgo (mee•GAYL ee•DAHL•goh). He led an army of peasants in revolt. Spanish officials brought charges against Hidalgo and executed him, but the rebellion did not stop. Mexicans finally won their independence from Spain in 1821. In 1824 they set up a republic with an elected president.

Soon after independence, Mexico lost some valuable territory. Mexico's northern province of Texas fought for and won its own independence from Mexico and asked to join the United States. In 1846 the United States fought Mexico in a dispute over the southern boundary of Texas. In the treaty that ended that war, Mexico gave up its claims to Texas. It later sold to the United States what are today the states of California, Utah, and Nevada, and parts of Colorado, Wyoming, Arizona, and New Mexico.

Revolution For many decades, rich families, army officers, and Catholic Church leaders held most of the power and wealth in Mexico. Poor Mexicans grew angry. In 1910 their discontent exploded in a revolution. Emiliano Zapata, who commanded a rebel army, stated the goals of this revolution.

He wanted to give to the poor "the lands, woods, and water that the landlords or bosses have taken from us." Zapata's forces swooped down and seized many large haciendas. They divided the land among the poor.

Reading Check Who led the 1910 revolution against Spanish rule?

Mexico's Government

Mexico, like the United States, is a **federal republic** because power is divided between national and state governments, and a strong president leads the national government. Mexico's national government differs in that it has much more power than the states. The Mexican president, who can serve only one six-year term, also has more power than the legislative and judicial branches.

For many decades, one political party called the Institutional Revolutionary Party led Mexico. All the presidents and most other elected officials came from this party. In recent years, economic troubles and the people's lack of political power led to growing frustration. In the year 2000, the newly elected president of Mexico, Vicente Fox, came from a different political party—for the first time in 70 years.

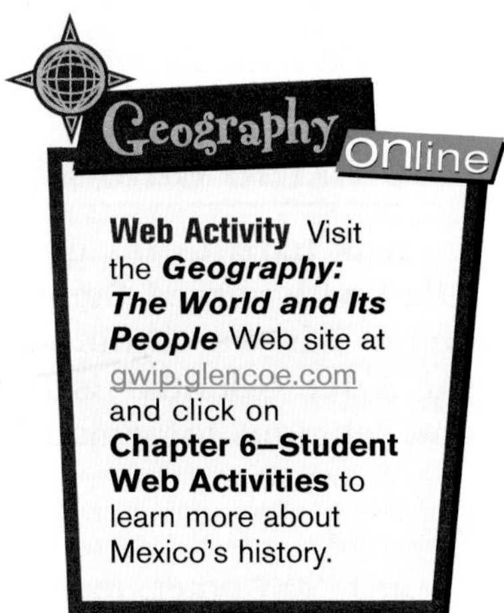

Reading Check What form of government does Mexico have?

Assessment

Defining Terms

1. **Define** hieroglyphics, mural, colony, hacienda, mestizo, federal republic.

Recalling Facts

2. **History** Describe three achievements of the ancient Maya.
3. **History** Which European country conquered and colonized Mexico?
4. **History** What were Emiliano Zapata's goals?

Critical Thinking

5. **Sequencing Information** Put the following events in the correct chronological order: Cortés conquers the Aztec, Hidalgo leads peasants in revolt, the Mexica move into central Mexico, Zapata leads a revolution.
6. **Understanding Cause and Effect** How did the arrival of Europeans affect the Native Americans in Mexico?

Graphic Organizer

7. **Organizing Information** Draw a diagram like this one. In one circle list facts about the Mexican government. In the other put information about the U.S. government. In the overlapping area write facts that are true about both.

Mexico's Government | U.S. Government

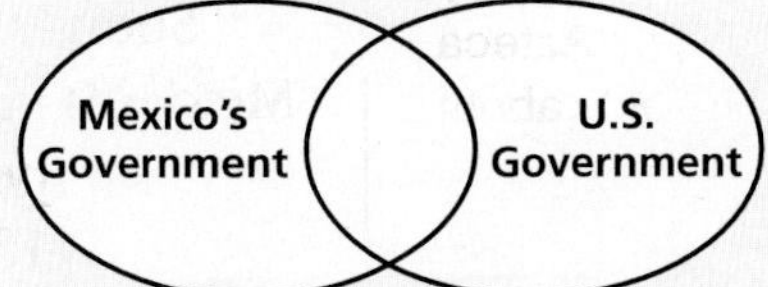

Applying Geography Skills

8. **Analyzing Maps** Refer to the map of Mexico's Native American civilizations on page 189. Which Native American group settled the farthest south?

Making Connections

ART | SCIENCE | LITERATURE | TECHNOLOGY

The Aztec Calendar Stone

It is hard to imagine how a huge stone filled with carved figures can serve as a calendar. Known commonly as the Sun Stone, the Aztec calendar is full of both scientific and religious information.

History

In 1790 workers in the heart of the *zocalo,* or main square, of Mexico City uncovered a massive circular stone. Mexico City sits on top of Tenochtitlán, the ancient capital of the Aztec Empire. Some 300 years earlier, the Aztec at Tenochtitlán had carved the 25-ton (23-t) basalt rock calendar. Using stone tools, they created a monument that measured 12 feet (3.6 m) in diameter and 3 feet (.9 m) thick.

The face of the Aztec sun god appears at the center of the calendar stone. The sun god was thought to be one of the most important Aztec gods. Seven rings surround the sun god. In the closest ring are four squarelike spaces, each with a symbol that represents the four past ages of the world—the time that existed before humans appeared. Circling these symbols is a ring with signs representing the 20 days of the Aztec month.

Meaning of the Calendar

The Aztec calendar stone is actually two calendars in one. One calendar is a religious calendar based on a 260-day cycle. The Aztec believed that their lives depended on fulfilling their gods' demands. The calendar told Aztec priests when to make offerings and hold rituals for each god. It also divided the days among the gods. According to the Aztec view, this kept the universe in balance. An imbalance could lead to a power struggle among the gods and bring about the end of the world.

The second calendar is an agricultural calendar based on a 365-day solar cycle. The Aztec were very efficient farmers. They used this calendar to keep track of the seasons and ceremonies related to agricultural cycles.

Making the Connection

1. What does the Aztec agricultural calendar reveal about the scientific understanding of the Aztec?
2. Why was it important for the Aztec to divide the days among the gods?
3. **Making Comparisons** How do the two calendar systems of the Aztec differ?

◄ **Today the Aztec calendar stone is displayed in the National Museum of Anthropology in Mexico City.**

Section 3

Mexico Today

Guide to Reading

Main Idea

Mexicans enjoy a rich and lively culture but face many serious challenges.

Terms to Know

- plaza
- adobe
- industrialized
- service industry
- migrant worker
- smog

Places to Locate

- Gulf of Mexico
- Rio Grande

Reading Strategy

Draw a diagram like this one. In each of the smaller ovals, write an example of Mexican culture. Create as many smaller ovals as you need.

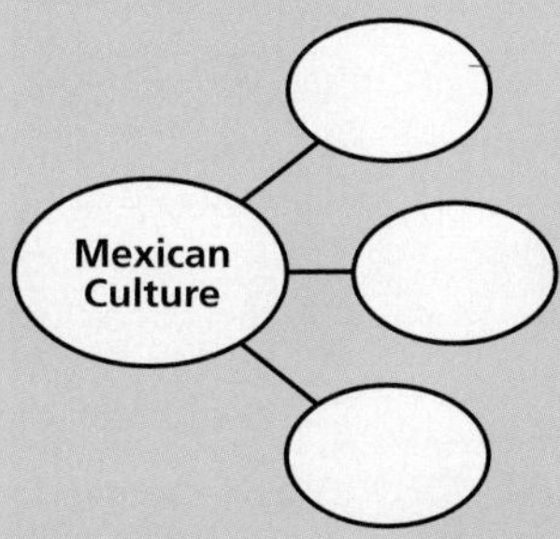

NATIONAL GEOGRAPHIC **Exploring Our World**

Mexican art reveals the pride that the people take in their rich heritage. The people of Taxco (TAHS•koh) call their city the "silver capital of the world." Though the nearby hills no longer hold any silver, the city remains a home to craftspeople who make silver jewelry, cups, and trays. Here, a designer and silversmith examine a new pitcher design.

Mexico—the third-largest country in size in Latin America, after Brazil and Argentina—has a large and dynamic population. More than 70 percent of all Mexicans live in the country's bustling cities.

Mexico's Cities and Villages

In the center of Mexico's cities, you often find large **plazas,** or public squares. Around each city's plaza stand important buildings such as a church and a government center. When you look at the buildings, you can see the architectural style of Spanish colonial times. Newer sections of the cities have a mix of towering glass office buildings and modern houses. In the poorer sections of town, people build small homes out of whatever materials they can find. This may include boards, sheet metal, or even cardboard.

Rural villages also have central plazas. Streets lead from the plazas to residential areas. Many homes are made of **adobe** (uh•DOH•bee), or sun-dried clay bricks. The roofs might be made of straw or of colored tile, in the Spanish style.

✓Reading Check **What do you find in the center of Mexico's cities and villages?**

Mexican Culture

Mexican artists and writers have created many national treasures. In the early 1900s, Mexican painters produced beautiful murals—just as Native American painters had done centuries before. Among the most famous of these mural painters were José Clemente Orozco and Diego Rivera. Rivera's wife Frida Kahlo became well known for her paintings that revealed her inner feelings. Modern writers such as Carlos Fuentes and Octavio Paz have written poems and stories that reflect the values of Mexico's people.

Food If you have tasted Mexican food, you know that it is a rich blend of flavors. Corn—first grown in Mexico—continues to be an important part of the Mexican diet. Chocolate, tomatoes, and chilies were all Native American foods as well. When the Spanish came, they brought beef, chicken, cheese, and olive oil, which Mexicans added to their cooking.

Today Mexicans combine these different cooking traditions in popular foods like tacos and enchiladas. Both dishes combine a flat bread called a tortilla with meat or beans, vegetables, cheese, and spicy chilies.

Celebrations Throughout the year, Mexicans enjoy several special celebrations called fiestas (fee•EHS•tuhs). These special days include parades, fireworks, music, and dancing. Mariachi (MAHR•ee•AH•chee) bands may play such traditional instruments as the violin, guitar, horn, and bass at fiestas. More likely, however, you will hear the fast-paced rhythms and singing of Latino bands, which have influenced the United States.

National holidays include Independence Day (September 16) and Cinco de Mayo (May 5). This holiday celebrates the day in 1862 that Mexicans defeated an invading French army in battle. November 2 is a

Art

Mexican artist Diego Rivera is one of the most famous mural painters of the twentieth century. He believed that art belonged to the people. In Mexico City, Rivera's murals line the courtyard of the Ministry of Education building and cover the walls of the National Palace. With their characteristically vivid colors and distinctive style, Rivera's murals tell the story of the work, culture, and history of the Mexican people.

Looking Closer How did Rivera's work support his belief that art belongs to the people?

Mexico Through the Centuries ▶

NATIONAL GEOGRAPHIC **On Location**

Work and Play

A skilled seamstress (left) makes clothing in a *maquiladora* in northern Mexico. On September 16, parades celebrate the women and men who helped win Mexican independence (above).

Place **What is the purpose of fiestas?**

special religious celebration called the Day of the Dead. On this day, families gather in cemeteries where they honor their departed loved ones by laying down food and flowers.

Reading Check **What are some important celebrations in Mexico?**

Mexico's Economy Today

With many resources and workers, Mexico has a growing economy. Did you know that Mexico's economy ranks among the top 12 in the world? As in the past, agriculture is still important. Farmers raise food to feed people at home—and also to ship around the world. Corn, beans, wheat, and rice are the main crops grown for food. Exports include coffee, cotton, vegetables, fruit, livestock, and tobacco.

In recent years, Mexico has **industrialized,** or changed its economy to rely less on farming and more on manufacturing. Factories in Mexico now make cars, consumer goods, and steel. The labels on your clothing may even say "Made in Mexico."

Mexico has large deposits of petroleum and natural gas in the **Gulf of Mexico** and along the southern coast. As a result, Mexico numbers among the world's major oil-producing nations.

Mexico is also home to important service industries. **Service industries,** you recall, are businesses that provide services to people rather than produce goods. Banking is a major service industry in Mexico, as is tourism.

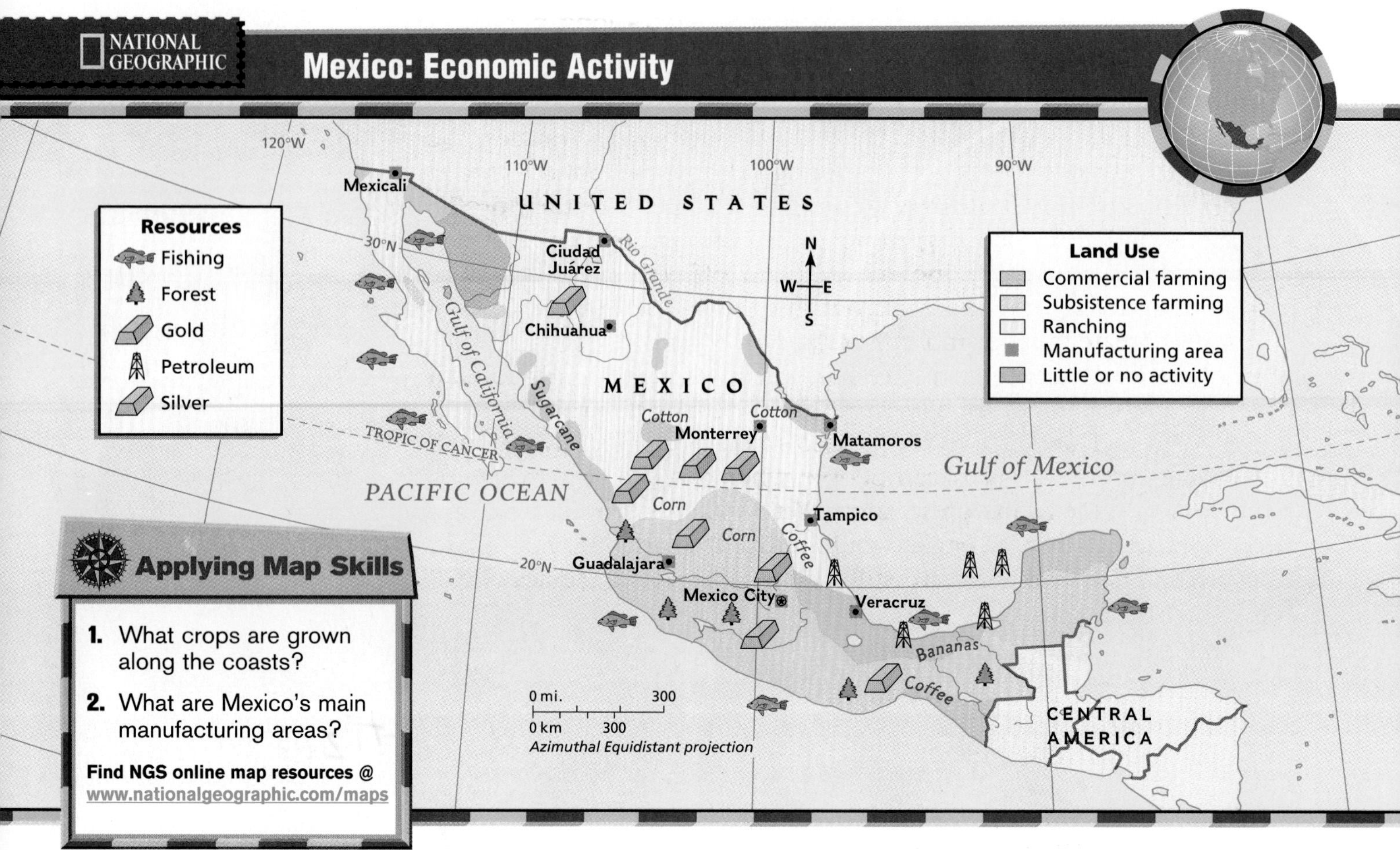

Free Trade To promote economic growth, the government of Mexico has moved to break down barriers to trade with other countries. In the mid-1990s, Mexico, Canada, and the United States signed the North American Free Trade Agreement, or NAFTA. Mexico's leaders hoped that free trade would encourage companies to open factories in Mexico, creating jobs. In 1999 Mexico signed a similar agreement with many countries in Europe.

✓Reading Check **Where are most of Mexico's oil fields located?**

Mexico's Challenges

Mexico has tried to use its resources to improve the lives of its people. These actions have had strong effects on Mexican life—and created some challenges for the future.

Population Mexico's population has increased rapidly in recent decades. Because many people have moved to the cities to find jobs, the cities have grown quickly. Many people have been forced to take jobs that pay low wages. As a result, thousands of people crowd together in poor sections of the cities.

Those Mexicans who cannot find any work in their country may become **migrant workers.** These are people who travel from place to place when extra workers are needed to plant or harvest crops.

They legally and sometimes illegally cross Mexico's long border to work in the United States. Though the pay is low, the migrant workers can earn more in the United States than in Mexico.

Foreign Investment and Foreign Debt For many decades, the Mexican government refused to let foreign companies build factories in Mexico. Leaders feared that the companies would take their profits to their own country, draining money out of Mexico. In the 1990s, the government changed this policy. Mexican officials were still concerned that money would be lost, but they hoped that the new factories would create jobs for more Mexicans.

To help its economy grow, Mexico borrowed money from foreign banks. The government then had to use any money it earned in taxes to pay back the loans. As a result, Mexico's leaders did not have enough funds to spend on the Mexican people when the economy began to struggle. Many Mexicans grew angry. Yet if the government did not make the loan payments, banks would refuse to lend more money for future plans. Because there are still loans to be repaid, Mexicans will face this situation for many years.

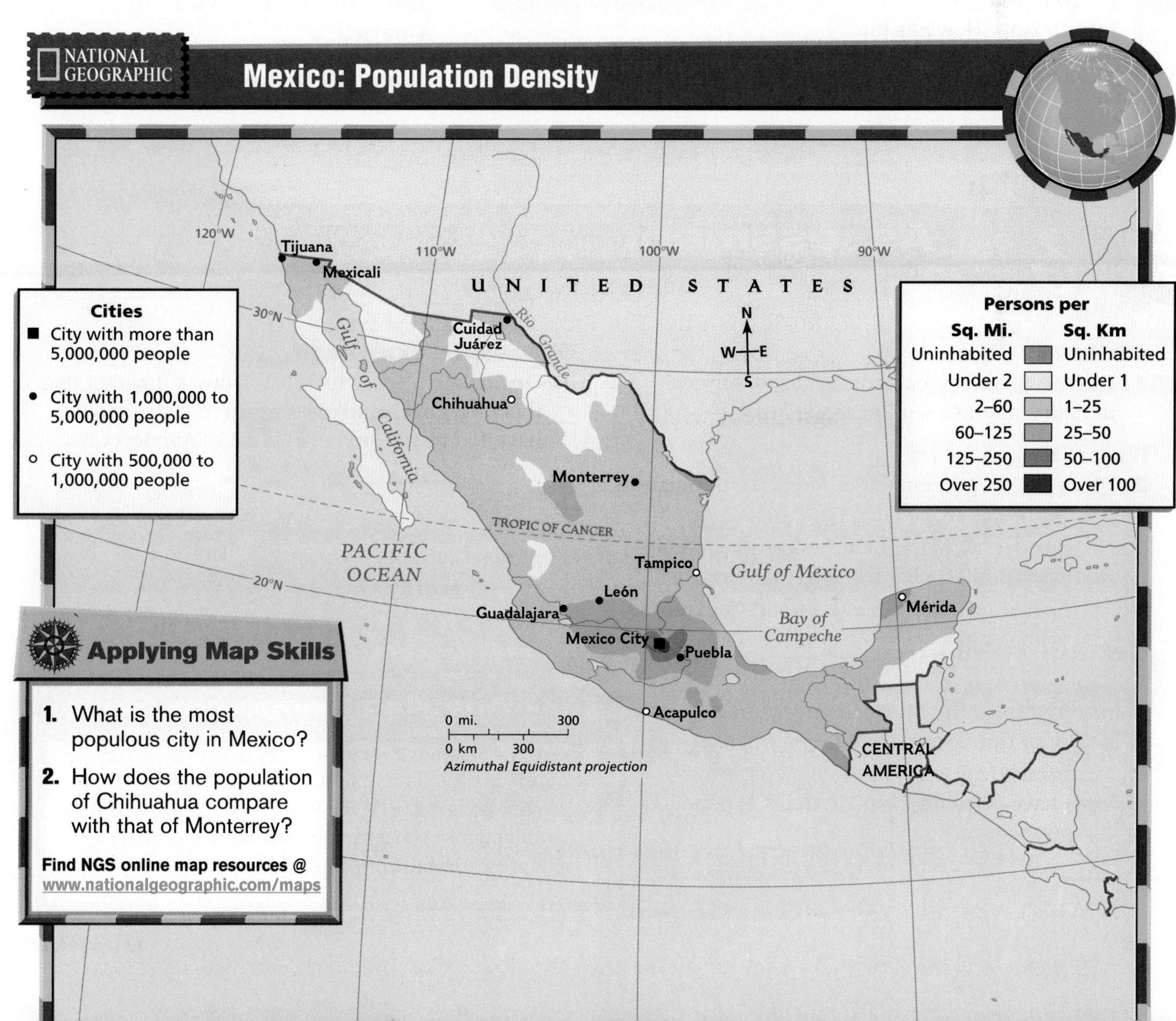

Applying Map Skills

1. What is the most populous city in Mexico?
2. How does the population of Chihuahua compare with that of Monterrey?

Find NGS online map resources @ www.nationalgeographic.com/maps

Hazy smog fills the sky over Mexico City.

Human/Environment Interaction How has the landscape contributed to air pollution in Mexico City?

Pollution As Mexico's population boomed, its cities grew very large. At the same time, the economy industrialized. Both of these changes contributed to rising pollution in Mexico.

The mountains that surround Mexico City trap the exhaust fumes from hundreds of thousands of cars. People wake each day to a thick haze of fog and chemicals called **smog.** Many people wear masks when they leave their homes to go to work or school. In northern Mexico, many factories release dangerous chemicals into the air or water. One environmental group says that the **Rio Grande** is now one of the most polluted rivers in North America.

Reading Check What challenges does Mexico face?

Section 3 Assessment

Defining Terms

1. **Define** plaza, adobe, industrialized, service industry, migrant worker, smog.

Recalling Facts

2. **Place** What percentage of Mexico's population lives in urban areas?
3. **Economics** What agricultural product was first grown in Mexico by Native Americans?
4. **Economics** Name three of Mexico's exports.

Critical Thinking

5. **Analyzing Information** What has resulted from the Mexican government's policy of borrowing from foreign banks?
6. **Summarizing Information** What problems have resulted from Mexico's expanding population?

Graphic Organizer

7. **Organizing Information** Draw a diagram like this one. On the arrows list three factors that have led to the smog problem of Mexico City.

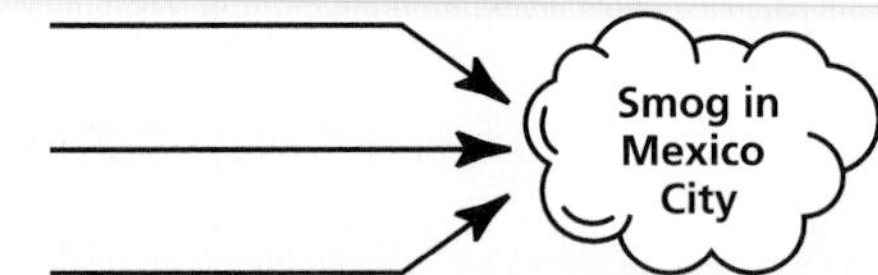

Applying Geography Skills

8. **Analyzing Maps** Look at the population density map on page 197. What is the population of Guadalajara? What is the population density of the area surrounding Mérida?

Reading Review

Section 1 Mexico's Land and Economy

Terms to Know

land bridge
peninsula
latitude
altitude
hurricane
vaquero
maquiladora
subsistence farm
plantation

Main Idea

Mexico's mountainous landscape and varied climate create different economic regions.

✓ **Location** Mexico connects North and South America.

✓ **Region** Mexico has three mountain ranges, a large central plateau, and coastal lowlands.

✓ **Location** Much of Mexico lies in the tropics, but the climate in some areas is cool because of high elevation.

✓ **Region** Landforms and climate combine to create three economic zones in Mexico.

Section 2 Mexico's History and Government

Terms to Know

hieroglyphics
mural
colony
hacienda
mestizo
federal republic

Main Idea

Mexico's culture reflects a blend of its Native American and Spanish past.

✓ **History** Mexico's Native American civilizations—the Maya and Aztec—made many contributions to Mexico's culture.

✓ **Culture** Mexico's people reflect the country's Native American and Spanish roots. The main language is Spanish, and the main religion is Catholicism.

✓ **History** The Spanish ruled Mexico from the 1500s to 1821, when Mexico won its independence.

✓ **Government** Mexico is a federal republic with a strong central government and a system of state governments.

Section 3 Mexico Today

Terms to Know

plaza
adobe
industrialized
service industry
migrant worker
smog

Main Idea

Mexicans enjoy a rich and lively culture but face many serious challenges.

✓ **Culture** More than 70 percent of Mexicans live in cities today.

✓ **Economics** Farming is still important in Mexico, but manufacturing, service industries, and oil refining play larger roles in the economy.

✓ **Culture** Challenges facing Mexico include problems caused by population growth, foreign investment and debt, and pollution.

Chapter 6 Assessment and Activities

Using Key Terms

Match the terms in Part A with their definitions in Part B.

A.

1. altitude
2. hurricane
3. vaquero
4. *maquiladora*
5. mestizo
6. adobe
7. plaza
8. smog
9. mural
10. subsistence farm

B.

a. factories that assemble parts from other countries
b. cowhand
c. sun-dried clay bricks
d. wall painting
e. height above sea level
f. fog mixed with smoke
g. produces only enough to support a family's needs
h. fierce tropical storm
i. public square
j. a person of Native American and Spanish ancestry

Reviewing the Main Ideas

Section 1 Mexico's Land and Economy

11. **Location** How does Mexico's latitude affect its climate?
12. **Place** Name three mineral resources found in the mountains of Mexico.
13. **Movement** How have *maquiladoras* affected northern Mexico's cities?

Section 2 Mexico's History and Government

14. **History** What was the capital of the ancient Aztec?
15. **Movement** What effects did Spanish conquest have on Native Americans?
16. **History** When did Mexico win its independence from Spain?

Section 3 Mexico Today

17. **Culture** Who are two of Mexico's famous mural painters?
18. **Culture** What does Cinco de Mayo celebrate?

Mexico

Place Location Activity

On a separate sheet of paper, match the letters on the map with the numbered places listed below.

1. Sierra Madre Occidental
2. Mexico City
3. Plateau of Mexico
4. Yucatán Peninsula
5. Baja California
6. Rio Grande
7. Gulf of Mexico
8. Guadalajara
9. Monterrey
10. Sierra Madre del Sur

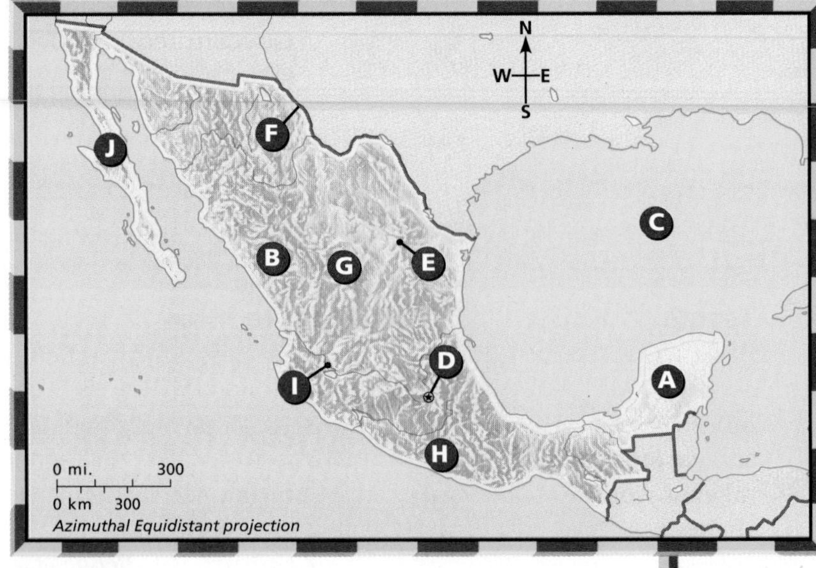

Self-Check Quiz Visit the ***Geography: The World and Its People*** Web site at gwip.glencoe.com and click on **Chapter 6—Self-Check Quizzes** to prepare for the Chapter Test.

Critical Thinking

19. **Understanding Cause and Effect** Why have Mexico's leaders encouraged free trade agreements with other countries?
20. **Sequencing Information** Choose eight events and their dates from Mexico's history and place them in the correct order on a time line like the one below.

GeoJournal Activity

21. **Writing a Brochure** In this chapter, you learned about Mexico's economic and environmental challenges. Research the economy of your city or town. Include the types of industries, trading partners, and environmental effects of the industries. Share the information you gather by making a brochure. Include a map of your area.

Mental Mapping Activity

22. **Focusing on the Region** Draw a simple outline map of Mexico, then label the following:

- Pacific Ocean
- Gulf of Mexico
- Yucatán Peninsula
- Baja California
- Sierra Madre Occidental
- Sierra Madre Oriental
- Sierra Madre del Sur
- Plateau of Mexico
- Mexico City
- Rio Grande

Technology Skills Activity

23. **Developing a Multimedia Presentation** Imagine that you work for Mexico's Economic Development Office. Create a multimedia presentation to present to a group of foreign investors. Use a software application such as PowerPoint® to showcase positive features like climate, resources, and labor supply.

Standardized Test Practice

Directions: Read the paragraph below, then answer the question that follows.

The Aztec civilization was organized into classes. At the top was the emperor. His power came from his control of the army and the religious beliefs of the people. Next came the nobles, followed by commoners. Commoners included priests, merchants, and artists. Below commoners were the serfs, or workers who farmed the nobles' fields. Slaves, the lowest class, included criminals and people in debt, as well as female and children prisoners of war. Male prisoners of war were sacrificed to the Aztec gods. The Aztec believed that live human sacrifices were needed to keep the gods pleased and to prevent floods and other disasters.

1. Which of the following statements is an opinion about the information given above?

F The Aztec civilization was organized into classes.

G Male prisoners of war were sacrificed to the Aztec gods.

H Slaves included children.

J The Aztec should not have sacrificed people to the gods.

Test-Taking Tip: This question asks you to identify an opinion. An opinion is a person's belief. It is not a proven fact (such as answer F). Opinions often contain subjective words, like *easier,* or *best,* or *should.*

GeoLAB ACTIVITY

Built on Solid Ground?

1 Background

The earth's surface seems solid and stable. The outer layer of our planet, however, is split into large pieces called *plates.* Plates are like pieces of a puzzle—an enormous puzzle in which the pieces slowly move together, apart, and past one another. Where the edges of plates bump together, as they do in the region around Mexico, earthquakes can occur. The type of land on which buildings are constructed helps determine how much damage an earthquake will cause. If you lived in a part of the world where earthquakes occur, where would you want to build your house?

2 Materials

- **2 widemouthed clear jars**
- **1 funnel**
- **1 measuring cup full of water**
- **sand (enough to fill half of one jar)**
- **gravel (enough to fill half of one jar)**
- **2 rocks (rocks should be larger than the gravel but small enough to fit inside the jars)**

Earthquake Damage in Mexico City

Believe It or Not!

The incredible power of earthquakes was seen in the western states of Montana and Wyoming in 1959. An earthquake vibrated 500,000 square miles of wilderness area, ripping off enormous chunks of 8,257-foot Mount Jackson in Yellowstone National Park. A new lake was created, and 160 geysers roared to life.

3 What to Do

1. Fill one jar halfway with gravel. Put one rock on top of the gravel.
2. Fill the second jar halfway with sand. Push the funnel into the edge of the sand so that it is standing upright against the side of the jar. Then put one rock on top of the sand.
3. Slowly pour water from the measuring cup into the funnel. Add water until it is just below the level of the top of the sand. Remove the funnel.
4. Compare the two jars. Make a sketch of each one.
5. Now make an "earthquake" by giving the table or jars several quick shakes.
6. Compare the two jars again, and make a second sketch of each one.

4 LAB ACTIVITY REPORT

1. Describe what you saw when you added water to the sand through the funnel.
2. Compare the sketches you made before and after you shook the jar holding the gravel.
3. In which jar did the rock move most during the "earthquake"?
4. **Drawing Conclusions** On which of these surfaces would it be safest to build a house? Why?

Sand mixed with water represents loosely packed soil, which is found in much of the United States. ▼

5 Extending the Lab

Activity

Using construction paper and tape, make a model of a building you think could withstand an earthquake. Consider such details as the number of walls; how wide and tall the building is; and the size, number, and type of support columns between floors. When your model is completed, place it on a table. See how well your model withstands an "earthquake" by shaking the table in different ways and with differing amounts of force.

Chapter 7

Central America and the West Indies

The World and Its People NATIONAL GEOGRAPHIC

To learn more about the people and places of Central America and the West Indies, view ***The World and Its People*** **Chapter 7** video.

Geography Online

Chapter Overview Visit the ***Geography: The World and Its People*** Web site at gwip.glencoe.com and click on **Chapter 7–Chapter Overviews** to preview information about Central America and the West Indies.

Section 1 Central America

Guide to Reading

Main Idea

Rich soil and a warm climate make Central America largely a farming region.

Terms to Know

- isthmus
- hurricane
- plantation
- subsistence farm
- canopy
- eco-tourist
- literacy rate
- republic
- parliamentary democracy

Places to Locate

- Belize
- Guatemala
- El Salvador
- Honduras
- Nicaragua
- Costa Rica
- Panama

Reading Strategy

Make a chart like this one, listing each country in Central America and key facts about each country.

Country	Key Facts

NATIONAL GEOGRAPHIC Exploring Our World

Unusual animals found nowhere else on the earth roam among the floor and canopy of Central America's rain forests. The small frog here seems like it would be a snack for other, larger animals. Do not be fooled by the enlargement of the photo, however. Many frogs like this one hold a deadly poison in their skin, which would quickly kill anything that tried to eat it.

Home to many different animals and plants, Central America is an **isthmus**, or a narrow piece of land that links two larger areas of land—North America and South America. Most of the countries on the isthmus have two coastlines—one on the Pacific Ocean and one on the Caribbean Sea. This narrow region (actually part of North America) stretches more than 1,000 miles (1,609 km) from Mexico southeast to the South American continent. Seven countries make up Central America: **Belize, Guatemala, El Salvador, Honduras, Nicaragua, Costa Rica,** and **Panama.** In Panama, the isthmus is only about 37 miles (60 km) wide.

A Rugged Land

Like Mexico, Central America sits where plates in the earth's crust meet. The collision of these plates produces volcanoes and earthquakes in the region. The Central Highlands, which curve like a backbone through inland Central America, are actually a chain of volcanic mountains. Because of their ruggedness, the Central Highlands are difficult to cross. This causes serious problems for transportation and has also kept many of the region's people isolated from one another. The

◄ Guadeloupe, an island in the Lesser Antilles

volcanoes of the Central Highlands do bring some benefits to farmers, though. Volcanic material has made the soil very fertile.

The map on page 207 shows you coastal plains on either side of the Central Highlands. These plains are named for the bodies of water they meet—the Pacific Lowlands on the west and the Caribbean Lowlands on the east. The Pacific Lowlands in Nicaragua hold several freshwater lakes. Oval-shaped Lake Nicaragua covers 3,100 square miles (8,029 sq. km), making it Central America's largest lake.

Climate Central America's climate is mostly tropical, but there are some differences from place to place. Mountainous areas are cool year-round, and they also block the movement of winds and moisture.

In the Pacific Lowlands, a tropical savanna climate prevails. Temperatures are warm, and rain is plentiful from May through November. From December through April, the climate is hot and drier.

In contrast, the Caribbean Lowlands have a hot, tropical rain forest climate throughout the year. Here you can expect about 100 inches (254 cm) of rain each year. Breezes from the Caribbean Sea provide

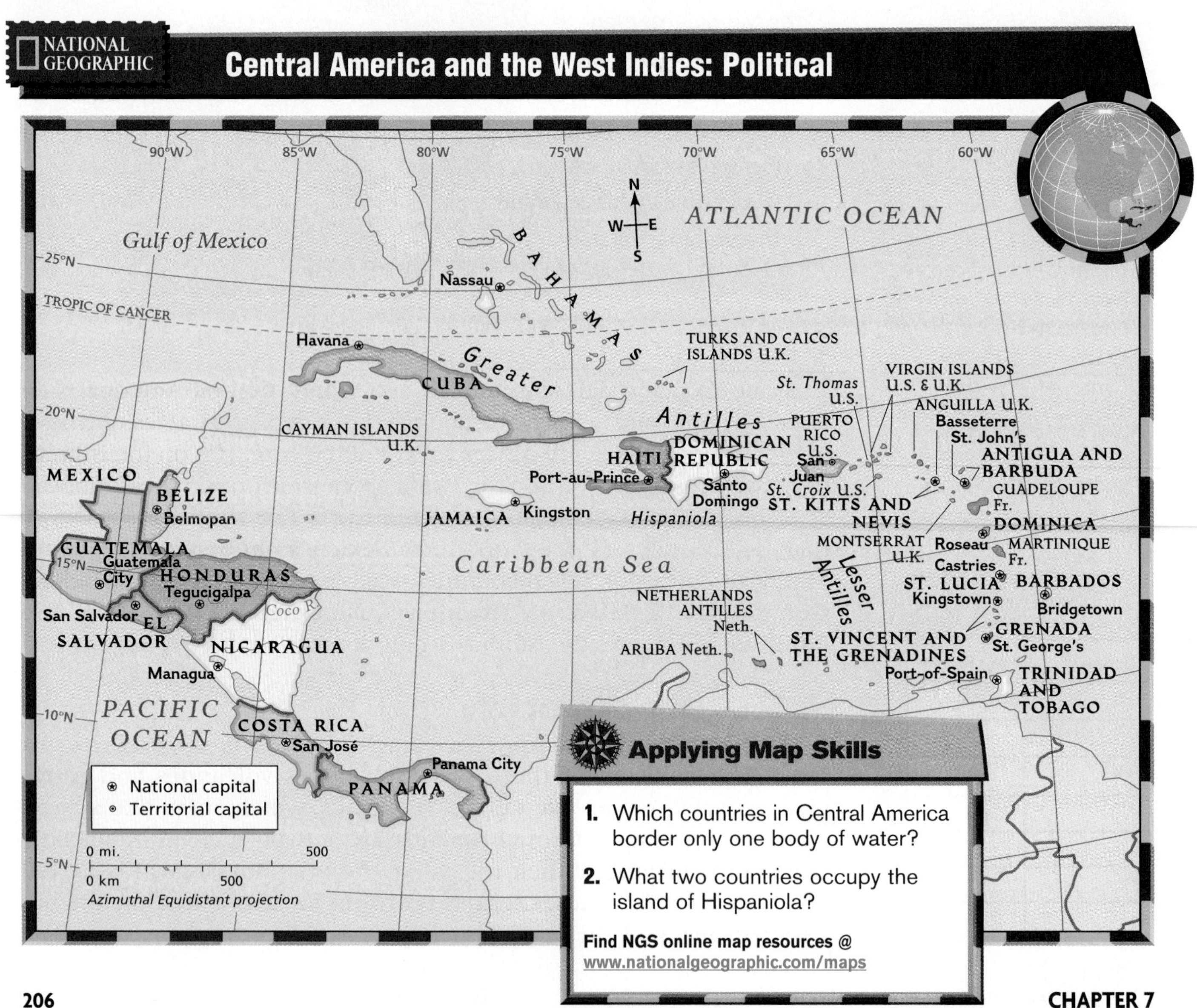

Applying Map Skills

1. Which countries in Central America border only one body of water?
2. What two countries occupy the island of Hispaniola?

Find NGS online map resources @ www.nationalgeographic.com/maps

some cooling relief. These breezes can be replaced by deadly hurricanes during the summer and fall, though. **Hurricanes** are fierce storms with winds of more than 74 miles (119 km) per hour.

Reading Check **How have the volcanoes in Central America been helpful?**

The Economy

The economies of the Central American countries depend on farming and harvesting wood from their rain forests. Central America has two kinds of farms. Wealthy people and companies own **plantations**—commercial farms that grow crops for sale. Major crops include coffee, bananas, cotton, and sugarcane. Plantations export their harvest to the United States and other parts of the world. Farmers in Guatemala and Costa Rica also grow flowers and ornamental plants for export.

Many farms in Central America are not plantations but **subsistence farms,** or small plots of land where poor farmers grow only enough food to feed their families. Subsistence farmers typically raise livestock and grow corn, beans, and rice.

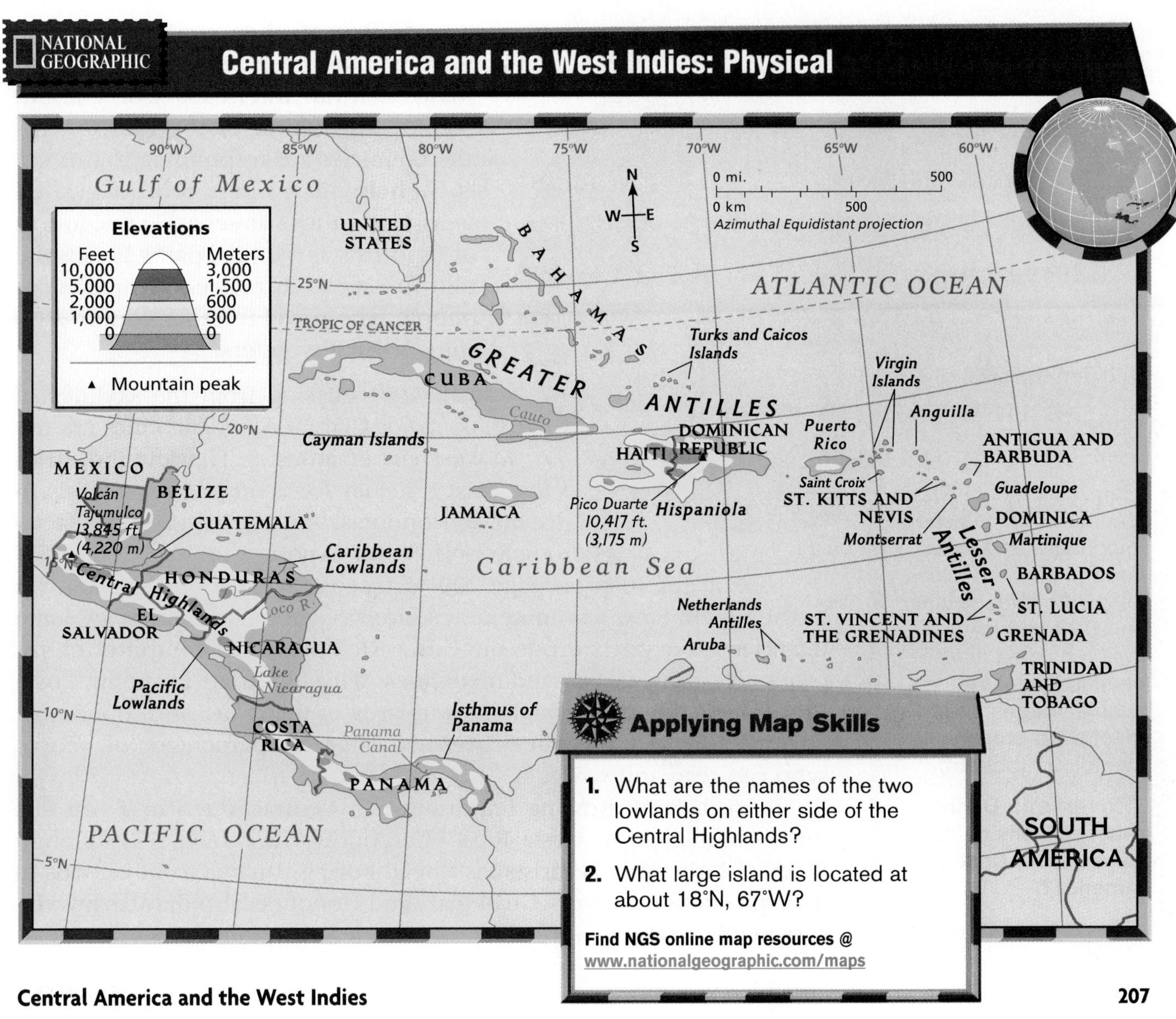

Applying Map Skills

1. What are the names of the two lowlands on either side of the Central Highlands?
2. What large island is located at about 18°N, 67°W?

Find NGS online map resources @ www.nationalgeographic.com/maps

Economic Highs and Lows

San José, Costa Rica's capital (top), has shopping malls and fast-food chains like many North American cities. In 1998 Hurricane Mitch caused massive mudslides that buried whole villages and destroyed crops in Honduras (bottom).

Movement During what seasons do hurricanes strike Central America?

Rain Forests Under Central America's green **canopy,** or topmost layer of the rain forest that shades the forest floor, valuable resources can be found. The dense forests offer expensive woods—mahogany and rosewood, for example. Unusual animal and plant species also thrive here. Scientists research the plants to develop new medicines.

Both local and foreign-owned companies have set up large-scale operations in the rain forests. Lumber companies cut down and export the valuable trees. Other companies and local farmers also cut or burn the trees to clear land for farming. Without trees to hold the soil in place, heavy rains wash it and its nutrients away. As a result, the land becomes poor just a few years after being cleared. The businesses and farmers then move on, clearing trees from another piece of land.

Many Central Americans worry about the rapid destruction of the rain forests. Some countries are responding to this crisis by helping workers replant cleared areas. Costa Rica has set aside one-fourth of its forests as national parks. It uses the rain forests to attract **eco-tourists,** or people who travel to other countries to enjoy natural wonders.

Industry Missing from the skylines of most major Central American cities are the smokestacks of industry. The few industries that exist generally focus on preparing foods. In Guatemala, Honduras, and Nicaragua, some factories produce clothing for export.

Look at the map on page 209. You see that most of the countries in the region have few mineral resources. Guatemala, which has some oil reserves, exports crude oil. Costa Rica produces computer chips, other electronic goods, and medicines. With its varied economy, Costa Rica enjoys one of the highest standards of living in Latin America. It also has one of the highest **literacy rates,** or percentage of people who can read and write.

Tourism is of growing importance in Central America. If you like bird-watching, go to Costa Rica. The country has about 850 different kinds of birds. Many tourists visit neighboring Panama to buy goods in its large tax-free markets. Guatemala and Honduras also draw many visitors to the magnificent ruins of their ancient Mayan culture.

The Panama Canal The economy in Panama is based on farming—as the economy is throughout Central America—but Panama also earns money from its canal. The Panama Canal stretches across the narrow Isthmus of Panama. Ships pay a fee to use the canal to shorten travel time between the Atlantic and Pacific Oceans. Turn to page 212 to see how the canal works.

The United States built the canal and owned it for more than 80 years. In 2000 Panama was given control of the canal. Panama hopes to use this important waterway to build its economy. Nearly half of Panama's 2.8 million people live and work in the canal area.

✓Reading Check **What are the major crops grown on Central America's plantations?**

The History and People of Central America

Native Americans settled Central America thousands of years ago. The Maya flourished in the rain forests of the north from about A.D. 250 to A.D. 900. Look at the Native American civilizations map on

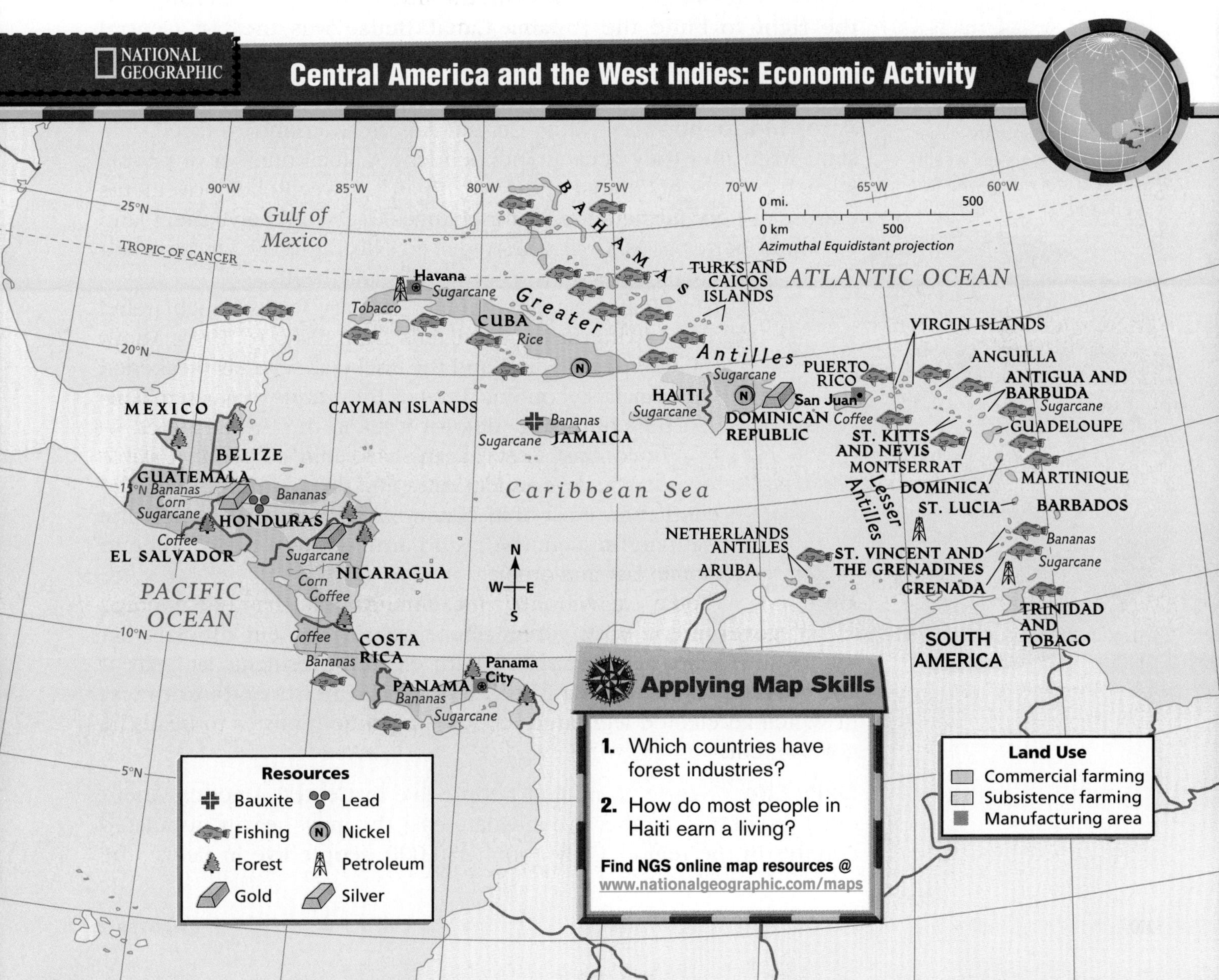

page 189. In Tikal (tee•KAHL), Guatemala, and Copán (koh•PAHN), Honduras, the Maya created impressive temples and sculptures. Then they mysteriously left their cities. Many of their descendants still live in the area today.

In the 1500s, Spaniards established settlements in Central America. For the next 300 years, Spanish landowners forced Native Americans to work on plantations. The two cultures gradually blended. Native Americans started to speak the Spanish language and follow the Roman Catholic faith. Native American traditions, in turn, affected the Spanish settlers.

One Central American country has a different history. The area that today is Belize was a British colony from the 1600s to the late 1900s. Early British settlers brought enslaved Africans to cut trees for their valuable woods. In Belize, African and British influences are strong.

Most Central American countries gained independence from Spain by 1821. The two exceptions are Panama and Belize. Panama was part of the South American country of Colombia for decades. In 1903 the United States helped Panama win its independence in exchange for the right to build the Panama Canal. Belize was the last Central American country to gain independence. It ceased to be a British colony in 1981.

What a Catch!

The deep blue waters of Lake Nicaragua are home to the world's only freshwater sharks and swordfish. Now the lake holds one less swordfish. Amadeo Robelo, who lives in Granada, Nicaragua, just spent three hours battling the powerful fish. Amadeo enjoys fishing with his father on weekends. After years of fighting in Nicaragua's civil war, his father wants to see the peace last and spend time with his children. He also wants Amadeo to become part of Nicaragua's middle class—something new in a region where you are either one of the few with wealth or one of the many who live in poverty.

After Independence Most Central American countries faced constant strife after they became independent. A small number of people in each country held most of the wealth and power. Rebel movements arose as poor farmers fought for changes that would give them land and better lives. Civil wars raged in Nicaragua, El Salvador, and Guatemala as recently as the 1980s and 1990s.

In Guatemala, government military forces fought rebel groups living in the highlands from 1960 to 1996. About 150,000 people died, and the civil war severely weakened Guatemala's economy. Tens of thousands of Guatemalans left the country to look for work in the United States.

In contrast, Costa Ricans have enjoyed peace. A stable democratic government rules, and the country has avoided conflict for most of its history. As a result of these peaceful relations, the country has no army—only a police force to maintain law and order.

Today each country in Central America has a democratic government, with voters choosing government officials. Six countries are also **republics** with elected presidents as head of the government. Belize is a British-style **parliamentary democracy,** in which an elected legislature chooses a prime minister to head the government.

Daily Life Nearly 36 million people live in Central America. About one-third of this number live in Guatemala, the most heavily populated country in the region. Only about 250,000 people live in Belize, the least populous country. Spanish is the official language throughout the region, except for English-speaking Belize. Many Central Americans also speak Native American languages, such as Mayan. Guatemala's population, for instance, is largely Native American and has 21 different Native American languages. Most Central Americans follow the Roman Catholic religion.

About 50 percent of all Central Americans live on farms or in small villages. At least one major city, usually the capital, is densely populated in each country. Guatemala's capital, Guatemala City, ranks highest in population with about 2,200,000 people. People living in urban areas hold manufacturing or service industry jobs, or they work on farms outside the cities. Those living in coastal areas may harvest shrimp, lobster, and other seafood to sell in city markets or for export.

Whether rural or urban, most people enjoy a major celebration called Carnival. This festival comes before Lent, a solemn period of prayer and soul-searching before the Christian celebration of Easter. During Carnival—and at other times—bands play salsa, a mixture of Latin American popular music, jazz, and rock. Do you like baseball? It is a national sport in Nicaragua and very popular in Panama, too. Most people throughout the region also enjoy *fútbol,* or soccer.

✓Reading Check **Why is the government of Belize different from that of other countries in Central America?**

Assessment

Defining Terms

1. **Define** isthmus, hurricane, plantation, subsistence farm, canopy, eco-tourist, literacy rate, republic, parliamentary democracy.

Recalling Facts

2. **Location** Why does Central America experience earthquakes and volcanoes?
3. **Culture** What is the major religion and language of Central America?
4. **Place** Which country in Central America is the most heavily populated? The most sparsely populated?

Critical Thinking

5. **Making Comparisons** How have the differences in government stability affected the citizens of Guatemala and Costa Rica?
6. **Analyzing Cause and Effect** How do the Central Highlands affect climate?

Graphic Organizer

7. **Organizing Information** Draw a diagram like this one. On the lines list the major products and industries of Central America.

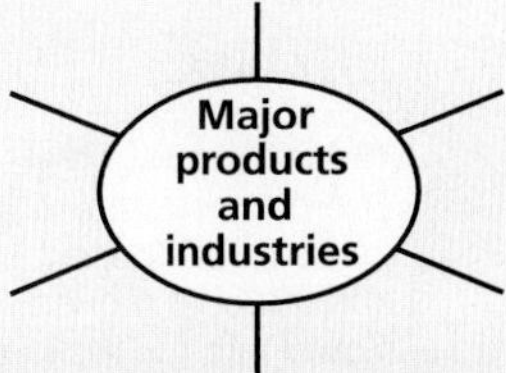

Applying Geography Skills

8. **Analyzing Maps** Refer to the political map on page 206. Which countries of Central America border Mexico? Which border the Pacific Ocean?

Making Connections

ART · SCIENCE · LITERATURE · TECHNOLOGY

The Panama Canal Locks

Before the Panama Canal was built, it took 60 days for a ship to sail around the southern tip of South America. Now about 35 oceangoing vessels can travel each day through the canal in about eight hours.

Digging the Canal

The first attempts to build a canal across Panama were begun in 1881 by a private French company. Huge expenses, poor planning, and the effects of diseases such as malaria and yellow fever stopped construction. In 1904 the United States government took over. Doctors had recently learned that bites from infected mosquitoes caused malaria and yellow fever. Workers drained swamps and cleared brush to remove the mosquitoes' breeding grounds. Then the digging began. The canal's course ran through hills of soft volcanic soil. Massive landslides regularly occurred before the 50-mile (80-km) canal was completed in 1914.

An Engineering Masterpiece

To move ships through the canal, engineers designed three sets of locks—the largest concrete structures on the earth. They allow ships to move from one water level to another by changing the amount of water in the locks. Together, the locks can raise or lower ships about 85 feet (26 m)—the height of a seven-story building. The diagram below shows you how these locks work.

Making the Connection

1. Why was a canal through Panama desirable?
2. What function do locks perform?
3. **Understanding Cause and Effect** How did medical advances affect the construction of the Panama Canal?

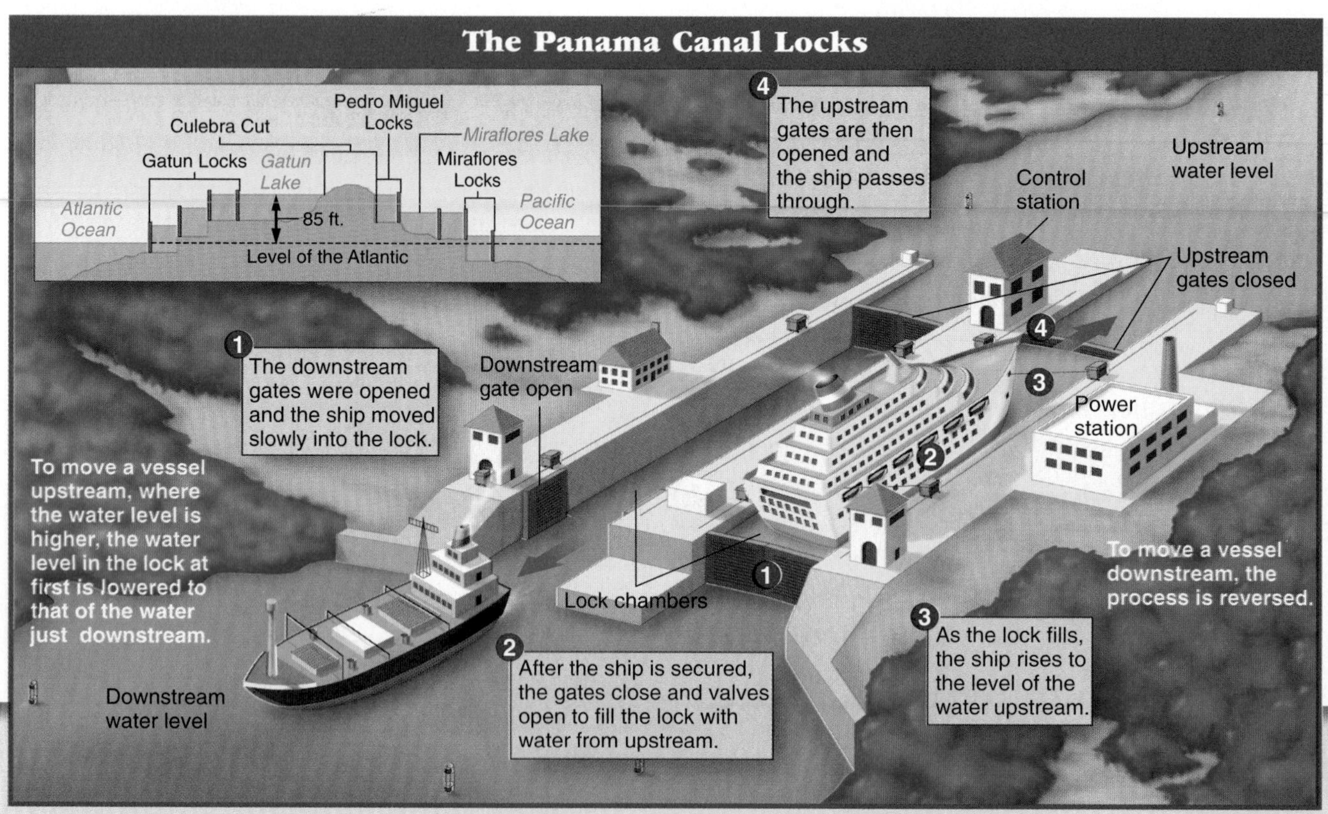

Section 2

The West Indies

Guide to Reading

Main Idea

The islands of the West Indies rely on tourism to support their economies.

Terms to Know

- archipelago
- bauxite
- colony
- communist state
- cooperative
- embargo
- free trade zone
- commonwealth

Places to Locate

- Caribbean Sea
- Greater Antilles
- Cuba
- Jamaica
- Hispaniola
- Puerto Rico
- Lesser Antilles
- Haiti
- Dominican Republic

Reading Strategy

Draw a diagram like this one. In each circle, list a country in the West Indies and features that are unique to it. Where the circles overlap, list features that are similar to both countries.

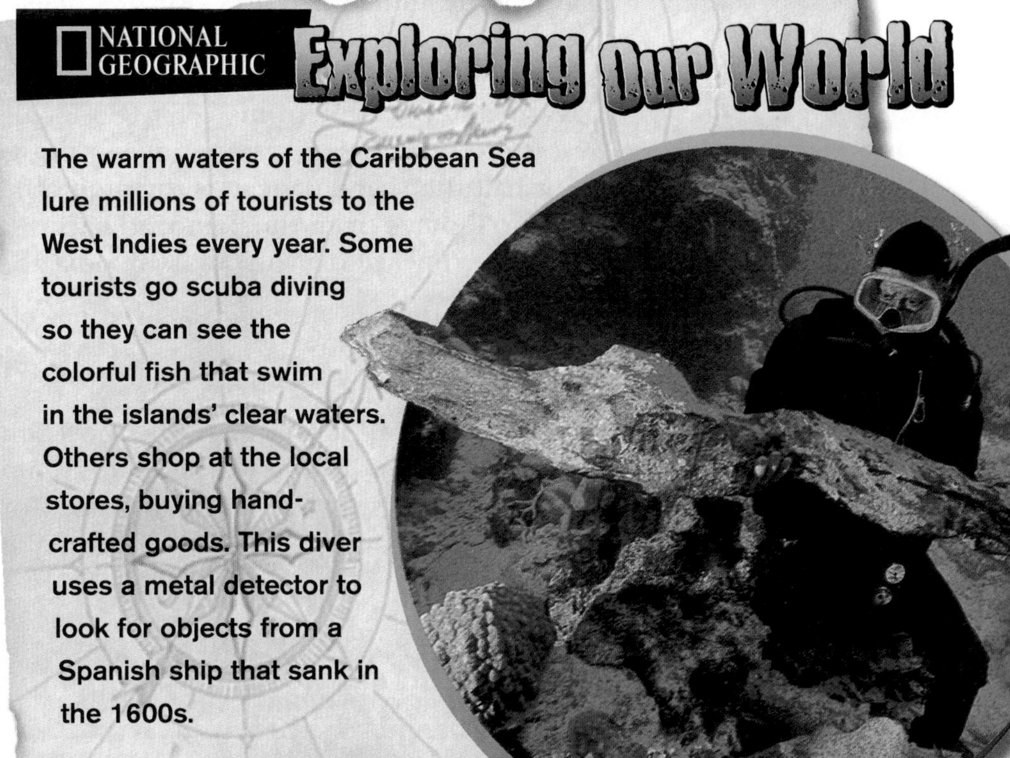

The warm waters of the Caribbean Sea lure millions of tourists to the West Indies every year. Some tourists go scuba diving so they can see the colorful fish that swim in the islands' clear waters. Others shop at the local stores, buying hand-crafted goods. This diver uses a metal detector to look for objects from a Spanish ship that sank in the 1600s.

Several **archipelagos** (AHR•kuh•PEH•luh•GOHS), or groups of islands, dot the **Caribbean Sea.** These island groups are known as the West Indies. East of Florida are the Bahamas, an archipelago of nearly 700 islands. South of Florida you find the **Greater Antilles** (an•TIH•leez). This group includes the large islands of **Cuba, Jamaica, Hispaniola** (HIHS•puhn•YOH•luh), and **Puerto Rico.** To the southeast are smaller islands called the **Lesser Antilles.**

Mountaintop Islands

When you look at the islands of the West Indies, you are really looking at the tops of mountains. Many West Indian islands are part of an underwater chain of mountains formed by volcanoes. A typical volcanic island has central highlands ringed by coastal plains. The volcanic soil in the highlands is rich.

Other islands are limestone mountains pushed up from the ocean floor by pressures under the earth's crust. Limestone islands generally are flatter than volcanic islands. The sandy soil found on many limestone islands is not good for farming.

The islands of the West Indies vary in size. Cuba, the largest island, is slightly smaller than the state of Pennsylvania. Among the smallest islands is Montserrat, slightly smaller than the city of Miami, Florida.

Climate The West Indies lie in the tropics. Most islands have a fairly constant tropical savanna climate. Sea and wind, more than elevation, affect the climate here. Cool northeast breezes sweep across the Caribbean Sea. They take on the temperature of the cooler water beneath them. When the winds blow onshore, they keep temperatures warm and pleasant, from 70°F to 85°F (21°C to 30°C).

Caribbean breezes sometimes bring gentle rains, but not *always.* For half the year, hurricanes threaten the West Indies. The word "hurricane" comes from the Taíno, an early Native American people who lived on the islands. They worshiped a god of storms named Hurakan.

✓Reading Check **What formed the islands of the West Indies?**

The Economy of the West Indies

Tourism and farming are the most important economic activities in the West Indies. A warm, sunny climate and beautiful beaches attract millions of tourists each year. Tourism is the region's major industry. Airlines and cruise ships make regular stops at different islands.

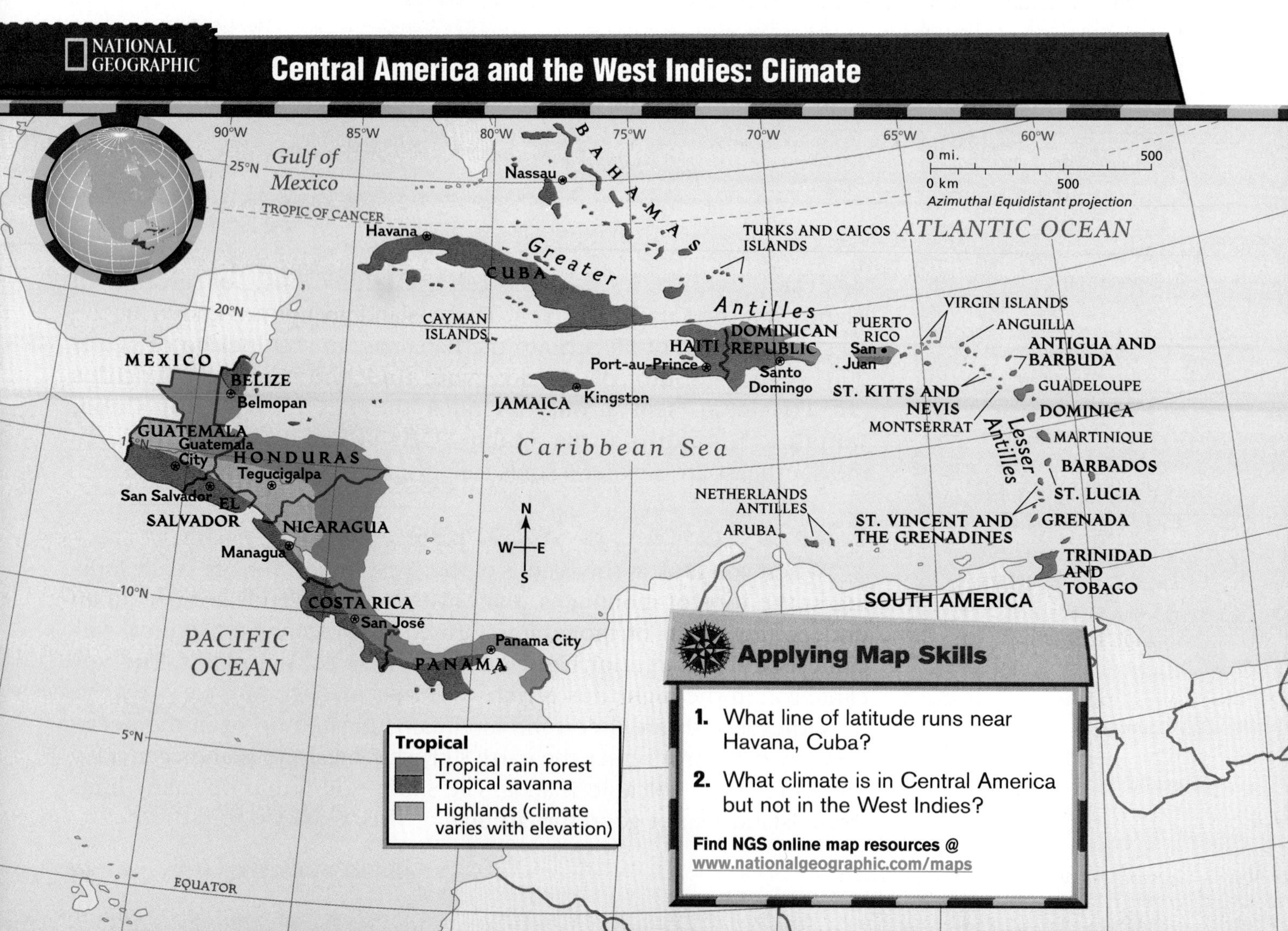

Wealthy landowners grow crops such as sugarcane, bananas, coffee, and tobacco for export. Many laborers work on the plantations that grow these commercial crops. Some areas are used for subsistence farming. People may own small plots of land or rent it from someone else. They grow rice and beans, which are basic parts of the diet in this region, as well as fruits and vegetables. Puerto Rico has dairy and livestock industries as well.

The Caribbean islands face an economic danger by depending on one crop. If the crop fails, no income is earned. If too much of the crop is produced worldwide, overall prices fall and the economy is in serious trouble. Another economic challenge is that many West Indians cannot find jobs when the growing season is over, or they have to work for low pay. Workers often pack up and head to other West Indian islands, Central America, or the United States.

Mining, Manufacturing, and Trade Most of the islands do not have large amounts of minerals, although several islands have some resources. Jamaica, for example, mines **bauxite,** a mineral used to make aluminum. The country of Trinidad and Tobago exports oil products. In Puerto Rico, companies make chemicals and machinery. Haiti and the Dominican Republic have textile factories where workers make cloth. Workers in Jamaica also make clothing.

Several islands have banking and financial industries. The Panama Canal has also increased business in the region. Since the 1500s, trading ships have sailed to the West Indies. Turn to page 224 to learn more about this trade, known as the Columbian Exchange.

Reading Check **What is the major industry in the West Indies?**

Bee Hummingbird

How small is this bird? The bee hummingbird of Cuba measures only 2 inches (5.1 cm) from head to tail. That is small enough to make it the tiniest bird in the world. People walking through the swamps where it lives sometimes mistake the bird for an insect. The bird's wings move so fast—80 beats per second—that the human eye cannot see them. At two grams, the bee hummingbird weighs less than a penny.

History and Culture

When Christopher Columbus reached San Salvador—now known as Hispaniola—in 1492, who met him? As you probably guessed, it was a Native American group—the Taíno. The Taíno and other Native Americans lived in the islands long before the coming of Europeans.

The Spaniards established the first permanent European settlement in the Western Hemisphere in 1496. That settlement is now the city of Santo Domingo, capital of the Dominican Republic. During the next 200 years, the Spaniards, the English, the French, and the Dutch also founded **colonies,** or overseas settlements, on many of the islands. They found the soil and climate perfect for growing sugarcane.

By the mid-1600s, most Native Americans had died from European diseases and harsh treatment. The Europeans then brought enslaved Africans to work on sugar plantations. When the slave trade ended in the early 1800s, plantation owners still in need of workers brought them from Asia, particularly India. The Asians agreed to work a set number of years in return for free travel to the West Indies.

Independence During the 1800s and 1900s, many Caribbean islands won their freedom from European rule. The first to become independent were the larger island countries, such as Haiti, the

Dominican Republic, and Cuba. Later, smaller islands such as Barbados and Grenada became countries. Many countries—like Haiti and the Dominican Republic—are republics. Others—like Jamaica and the Bahamas—are British-style parliamentary democracies.

Cuba is the only country in the Western Hemisphere with a government based on the ideas of communism. In a **communist state,** government leaders have strong control of the economy and society as a whole.

Some Caribbean islands still are not independent. Two large islands—Martinique and Guadeloupe—have ties to France. Puerto Rico and some of the Virgin Islands are linked to the United States. Other small islands in the Lesser Antilles are owned by the British or the Dutch.

Daily Life Although many people in Central America have Native American ancestors, the peoples of the West Indies have African or mixed African and European ancestry. Large Asian populations live in Trinidad and Jamaica as well.

More than 37 million people live in the West Indies. Cuba, with about 11.2 million people, has the largest population in the region. Saint Kitts and Nevis has only about 40,000 people. Most people speak a European language and follow the Roman Catholic or Protestant faiths.

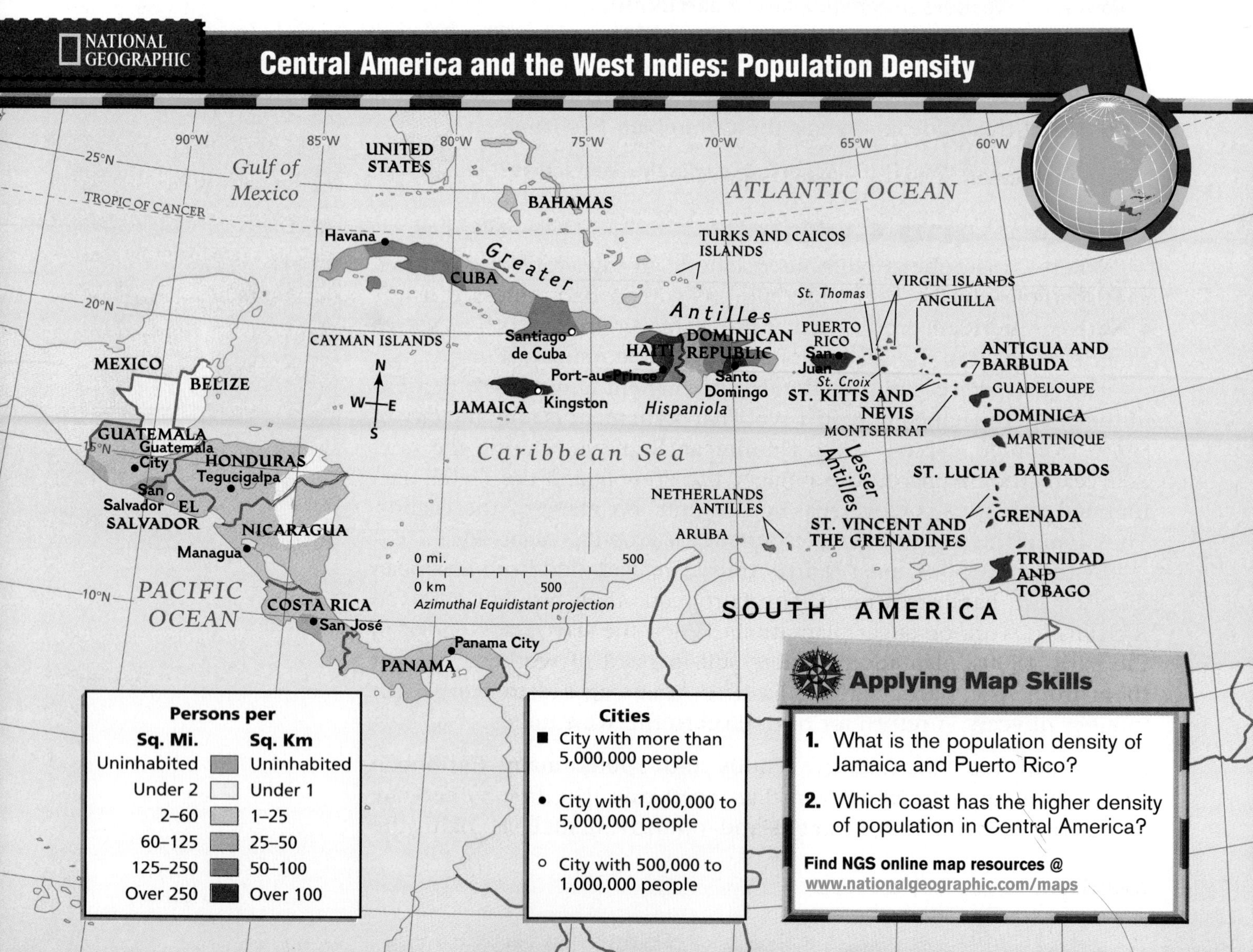

Economic Activities

Schoolgirls walk past vast sugar plantations on Barbados that European countries started in the colonial period (left). A steel-drum band entertains tourists in Trinidad (above).

Region **What attracts so many tourists to the islands of the West Indies?**

About 60 percent of West Indians live in cities and villages. The other 40 percent live and work in the countryside. Many islanders have jobs in the hotels or restaurants that serve the tourist industry.

If you visit the Caribbean, you are likely to hear lively music. The bell-like tones of the steel drum, developed in Trinidad, are part of the rich musical heritage of the region. Enslaved Africans created a kind of music called calypso. Jamaica's reggae music combines African rhythms and American popular music. Cuban salsa blends African rhythms, Spanish styles, and jazz.

On several islands, you will hear a different sound—the crack of a baseball bat. People in Puerto Rico, the Dominican Republic, and Cuba have a passion for baseball. Soccer is another popular sport.

✓Reading Check **Where was the first permanent European settlement in the West Indies?**

Island Profiles

The islands of the West Indies share many similarities, but they also have differences. Some of these differences can be seen in Cuba, Jamaica, Haiti, the Dominican Republic, and Puerto Rico.

Cuba One of the world's top sugar producers, Cuba lies about 90 miles (145 km) south of Florida. Most farmers work on **cooperatives,** or farms owned and operated by the government. In addition to growing sugarcane, they grow coffee, tobacco, rice, and fruits. In Havana, Cuba's capital and the largest city in the West Indies, workers make food products, cigars, and household goods.

Cuba is a communist state led by a dictator, President Fidel Castro. Cuba won its independence from Spain in 1898. The country had a democratic government, although military leaders sometimes seized power. In 1959 Castro led a revolution that took control of the government. He set up a communist state and turned to the Soviet Union for support. When he seized property belonging to American companies, the United States government responded. It put in place an **embargo,** or a ban on trade, against Cuba.

Cuba relied on aid from the Soviet Union. When the Soviet Union broke apart in 1989, it stopped giving economic support to the island. The Cuban economy is struggling, and many Cubans live in poverty.

Jamaica What languages would you hear if you visited Jamaica? Officially, English is the spoken language. Yet many Jamaicans speak Creole, which is a mixture of African languages and English, French, and Spanish. Creole is a musical-sounding language with a characteristic Jamaican rhythm. Almost all of Jamaica's 2.6 million people are of African or mixed African and European backgrounds. A small number are of Asian ancestry.

Once a British colony, Jamaica became independent in 1962. Kingston is the country's capital and largest city. With misty blue mountains and sunny beaches, Jamaica attracts thousands of tourists every year. The country is also one of the world's leading producers of bauxite. The main export crops are sugar, coffee, and bananas.

Haiti On the western half of the island of Hispaniola, you will find the country of **Haiti.** Led by a formerly enslaved man, Francois-Dominique Toussaint-Louverture, Haiti fought for and won its independence from France in 1804. It was the second independent republic in the Western Hemisphere (after the United States). It became the first nation in the history of the world to be founded by formerly enslaved persons. About 95 percent of Haiti's 7.8 million people are of African ancestry. Civil war has left Haiti's economy in ruins, and most Haitians are poor. Coffee and sugar, the main export crops, are shipped through Port-au-Prince, the country's capital.

Dominican Republic The **Dominican Republic** shares the island of Hispaniola with Haiti, filling the eastern part. Though they share the same island, the two countries have different histories and little contact. Haiti was a French colony. The Dominican Republic was settled by Spaniards, who brought enslaved Africans to work on sugar plantations. Sugar is still an important crop to the Dominicans. Tourism is growing, too, and many Dominicans sell goods in the country's free trade zone. **Free trade zones** are areas where people can buy goods from other countries without paying taxes.

The government of the Dominican Republic hopes to build up the country's electrical power so the economy can grow more quickly.

Poverty remains a problem, though. As a result, many Dominicans have left the country. Thousands have come to the United States looking for work.

Puerto Rico To be or not to be a state in the United States, that is the question that Puerto Ricans ask themselves every few years. The last time they voted on the question, they said no. How did Puerto Rico become part of the United States? The island was a Spanish colony from 1508 to 1898. After the Spanish-American War in 1898, the United States won control of Puerto Rico. Since 1952 the island has been a **commonwealth**, or a partly self-governing territory, under American protection. By law, Puerto Ricans are citizens of the United States. They can come and go from the island to the United States as they wish. Today nearly 3 million Puerto Ricans live in the United States. The island itself holds about 3.9 million.

Puerto Rico has a high standard of living compared to most other Caribbean islands. It also boasts more industry, with factories producing chemicals, machinery, clothing, and other products. San Juan, the capital and largest city, is home to about 1 million people. In rural areas, farmers grow sugarcane and coffee. Puerto Rico makes more money from tourism than any country in the region.

Web Activity Visit the ***Geography: The World and Its People*** Web site at gwip.glencoe.com and click on **Chapter 7—Student Web Activities** to learn more about Puerto Rico.

Reading Check What is a commonwealth?

Assessment

Defining Terms

1. **Define** archipelago, bauxite, colony, communist state, cooperative, embargo, free trade zone, commonwealth.

Recalling Facts

2. **Region** What three archipelagos make up the West Indies?
3. **History** Name four groups who have influenced the culture of the Caribbean region.
4. **Government** How is Cuba different from every other country in the Western Hemisphere?

Critical Thinking

5. **Drawing Conclusions** Describe two reasons Puerto Ricans might be satisfied remaining a commonwealth, rather than becoming a state.
6. **Making Predictions** What is the danger of a country depending on only one crop?

Graphic Organizer

7. **Organizing Information** Complete a chart like the one below with facts about Haiti and the Dominican Republic.

Country	Haiti	Dominican Republic
Colonized by		
Products		
Problems		

Applying Geography Skills

8. **Analyzing Maps** Refer to the population density map on page 216. What cities in the West Indies have more than 1 million people?

Geography Skill

Interpreting an Elevation Profile

You have learned that differences in land elevation are often shown on physical or relief maps. Another way to show elevation is on **elevation profiles.** When you view a person's profile, you see a side view. An elevation profile is a diagram that shows a side view of the landforms in an area.

Learning the Skill

Suppose you could slice right through a country from top to bottom and could look at the inside, or *cross section.* The cross section, or elevation profile, below pictures the island of Jamaica. It shows how far Jamaica's landforms extend below or above sea level.

Follow these steps to understand an elevation profile:

- Read the title of the profile to find out what country you are viewing.
- Look at the line of latitude written along the bottom of the profile. On a separate map, find the country and where this line of latitude runs through it.
- Look at the measurements along the sides of the profile. Note where sea level is located and the height in feet or meters.
- Now read the labels on the profile to identify the heights of the different landforms shown along with their elevation.
- Compare the highest and lowest points.

Practicing the Skill

Use the elevation profile below to answer the following questions.

1. At what elevation is Kingston?
2. What are the highest mountains, and where are they located?
3. Where are the lowest regions?
4. Along what line of latitude was this cross section taken?

Applying the Skill

Turn to page 17 in the **Geography Handbook.** Use the elevation profile of Africa to answer questions 2–4 above about *that* continent.

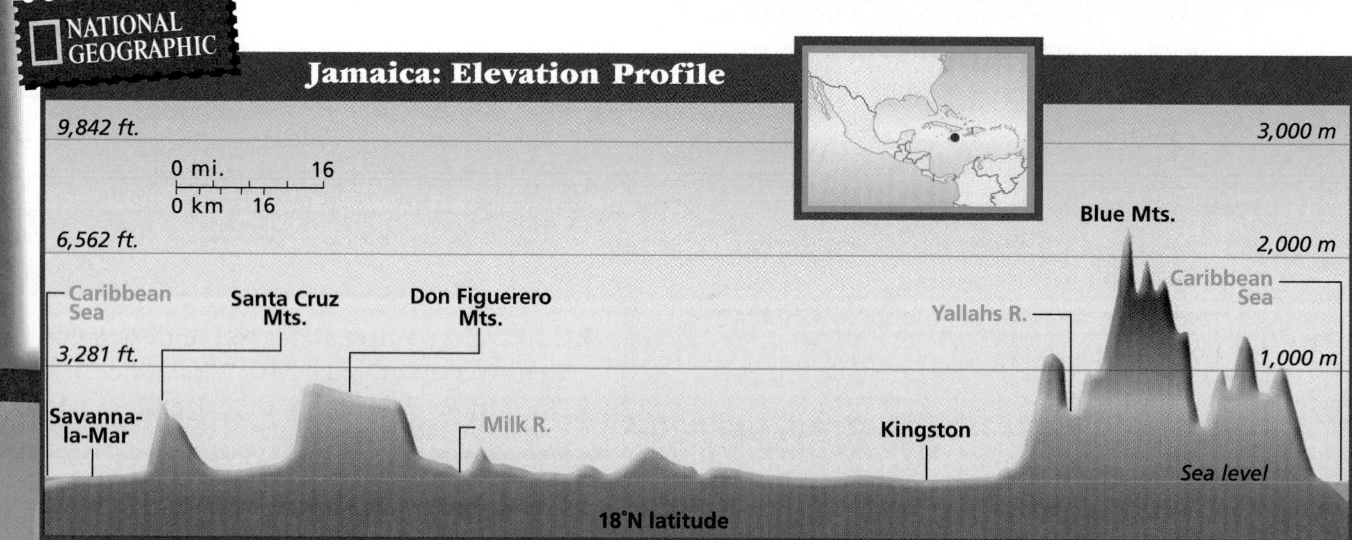

Chapter 7 Reading Review

Section 1 Central America

Terms to Know

isthmus
hurricane
plantation
subsistence farm
canopy
eco-tourist
literacy rate
republic
parliamentary democracy

Main Idea

Rich soil and a warm climate make Central America largely a farming region.

✓ Region Central America includes seven countries: Belize, Guatemala, Honduras, El Salvador, Nicaragua, Costa Rica, and Panama.

✓ Region Volcanic mountains run down the center of Central America with coastal lowlands on either side.

✓ Economics Most people in the region farm—either on plantations or subsistence farms.

✓ Culture Most countries in Central America have a blend of Native American and Spanish cultures.

Section 2 The West Indies

Terms to Know

archipelago
bauxite
colony
communist state
cooperative
embargo
free trade zone
commonwealth

Main Idea

The islands of the West Indies rely on tourism to support their economies.

✓ Region The West Indies include three different island groups: the Bahamas, the Greater Antilles, and the Lesser Antilles.

✓ History Most of the islands were at one time colonies of European countries.

✓ Economics Farming and tourism are the major economic activities in the West Indies.

✓ Culture The cultures of the West Indies mix Native American, European, African, and Asian influences.

✓ Government Most governments in the West Indies are democratic, but a dictator rules Communist Cuba.

◀ The Panama Canal

Chapter 7

Assessment and Activities

Using Key Terms

Match the terms in Part A with their definitions in Part B.

A.

1. isthmus
2. literacy rate
3. plantation
4. eco-tourist
5. archipelago
6. bauxite
7. commonwealth
8. embargo
9. free trade zone
10. republic

B.

a. large commercial farm
b. mineral ore from which aluminum is made
c. ban on trade
d. narrow piece of land connecting two larger pieces of land
e. area where people can buy goods from other countries without paying taxes
f. a person who travels to another country to enjoy its natural wonders
g. country with an elected president
h. percentage of adults who can read and write
i. partly self-governing territory
j. group of islands

Reviewing the Main Ideas

Section 1 Central America

11. **Region** What seven countries make up Central America?
12. **Place** How do the climates of the Pacific Lowlands and the Caribbean Lowlands differ?
13. **History** In what Central American countries did the Maya live?
14. **Culture** What percentage of Central Americans live in cities and small villages?

Section 2 The West Indies

15. **Economics** What two activities form the basis of the West Indian economies?
16. **Region** Many of the Caribbean islands were formed by what type of tectonic activity?
17. **Movement** Why do many West Indians move to other countries?
18. **History** What was the first nation in the world to be founded by formerly enslaved people?
19. **History** When did the United States gain control of Puerto Rico?

Central America and the West Indies

Place Location Activity

On a separate sheet of paper, match the letters on the map with the numbered places listed below.

1. Guatemala
2. Caribbean Sea
3. Cuba
4. Puerto Rico
5. Costa Rica
6. Panama
7. Bahamas
8. Haiti
9. Jamaica
10. Honduras

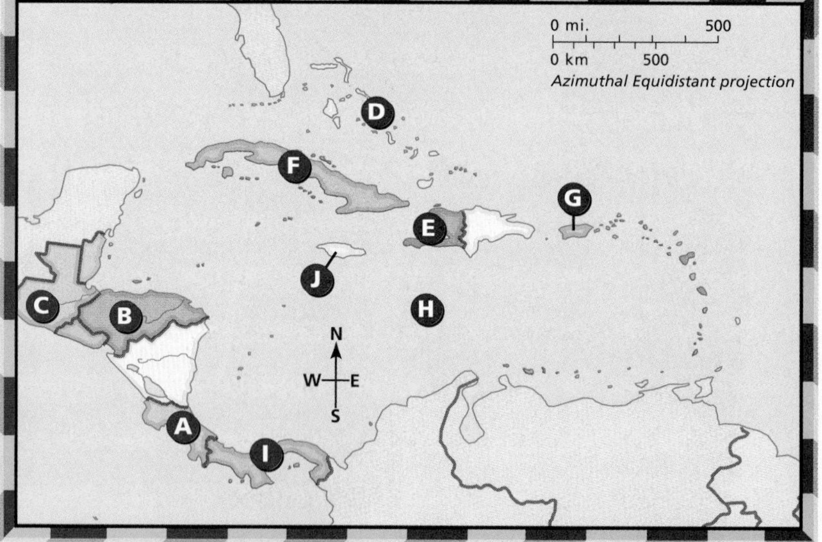

Self-Check Quiz Visit the ***Geography: The World and Its People*** Web site at gwip.glencoe.com and click on **Chapter 7—Self-Check Quizzes** to prepare for the Chapter Test.

 Critical Thinking

20. **Analyzing Information** Explain why Cuba's location is an important factor in the United States's relationship with that nation.
21. **Categorizing Information** Create a diagram like this with details about the people, history, and economy of a country in Chapter 7.

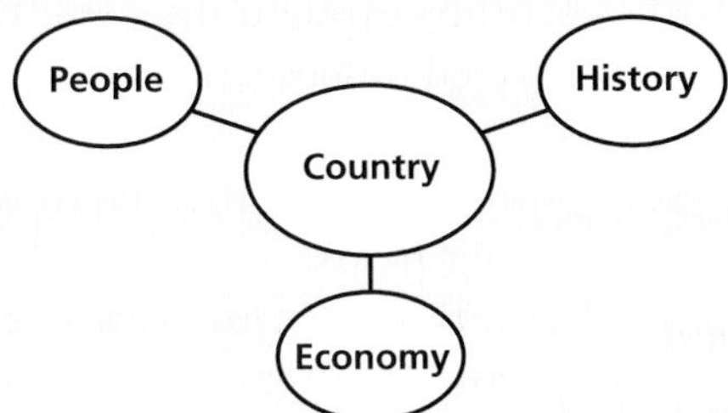

 GeoJournal Activity 

22. **Writing an Itinerary** Write an itinerary, or travel plan, for a cruise through the Caribbean. Your ship should make five stops. Include a map showing the route and descriptions of the sites and activities at each stop.

 Mental Mapping Activity

23. **Focusing on the Region** Draw an outline map of Central America and the West Indies, then label the following:

- Pacific Ocean
- Caribbean Sea
- Guatemala
- Panama
- Cuba
- Puerto Rico
- Lesser Antilles
- Bahamas

 Technology Skills Activity 

24. **Building a Database** Create a database about Central America. Your database should have a record for each country. Each record should have a field for the following: population, per capita GDP, and capital city. Sort the records from largest to smallest for per capita GDP. What generalizations can you make based on these data?

Standardized Test Practice

Directions: Study the graph, then answer the question that follows.

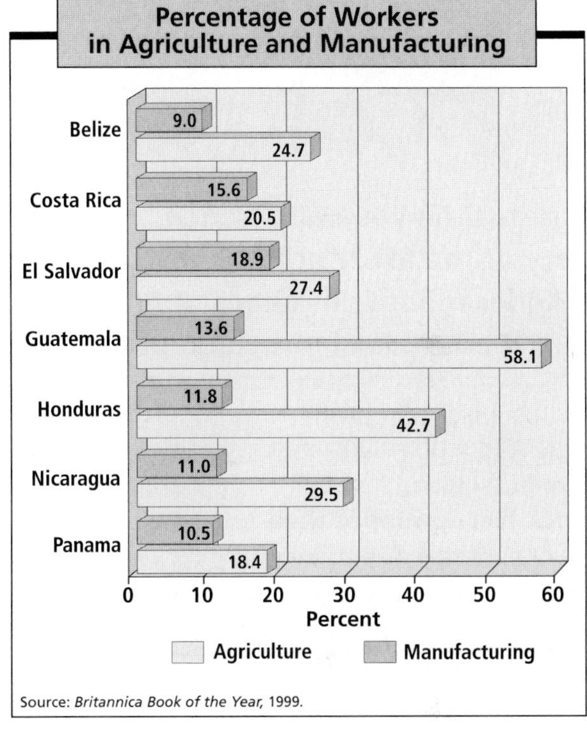

1. Of the countries shown on the graph, which has the lowest percentage of workers in manufacturing?

A Belize
B Honduras
C Nicaragua
D Panama

Test-Taking Tip: The process of elimination can be helpful here. First look at the key to see which of the bars represents manufacturing. Then look at the four answer choices and compare their percentages.

GEOGRAPHY

Columbus with King Ferdinand and Queen Isabella of Spain

The Columbian Exchange

The next time you eat a french fry, think about the long history of the lowly potato. The story begins high in the Andes mountain ranges of Bolivia and Peru (right), where thousands of years ago potatoes grew wild.

By the 1400s the Inca, an early people who ruled a vast empire in western South America, had developed thousands of varieties of potatoes. Yet how potatoes got from such a faraway time and place to be part of our everyday diet is a story that began even before the Inca.

Two Separate Worlds

Before the 1400s, people living in the world's Eastern Hemisphere were unknown to those living in the Western Hemisphere. This changed on October 12, 1492, when explorer Christopher Columbus, who had sailed from Spain, landed in the Bahamas in the Americas. Believing he had reached the Indies of Asia, Columbus named the people on the islands "Indians" and claimed the land for Spain. Columbus returned to the Americas the following year, bringing more than a thousand men in 17 ships. With his second trip, Columbus began what became known as "the Columbian exchange"—an exchange of people, animals, plants, and even diseases between the two hemispheres.

For Better and for Worse

The Europeans brought many new things to the Americas. Columbus brought horses, which helped the Native Americans with labor, hunting, and transportation. European farm animals such as sheep, pigs, and cattle created new sources of income. Explorers brought crops—oats, wheat, rye, and barley—that eventually covered North America's Great Plains. The sugarcane brought by Europeans flourished on plantations in Central and South America.

Some parts of the exchange were disastrous, however. Europeans brought diseases that killed millions of Native Americans. Plantation owners put enslaved Africans to work in their fields.

From the Americas, explorers returned home with a wide variety of plants. Spanish sailors carried potatoes to Europe. Nutritious and easy to grow, the potato became one of Europe's most important foods. (European immigrants then brought the potato to North America.) Corn from the Americas fed European cattle and pigs. Tobacco grown there became as valuable as gold. Peanuts, tomatoes, hot peppers, and cacao seeds (from which chocolate is made) changed the landscapes, eating habits, and cooking styles in Europe, Asia, and Africa.

QUESTIONS

1. **What is "the Columbian exchange"?**
2. **Exchanges continue today. What are some present-day exchanges among the world's hemispheres?**

Women in Peru tend a potato field. ▶

NATIONAL
GEOGRAPHIC
SOCIETY

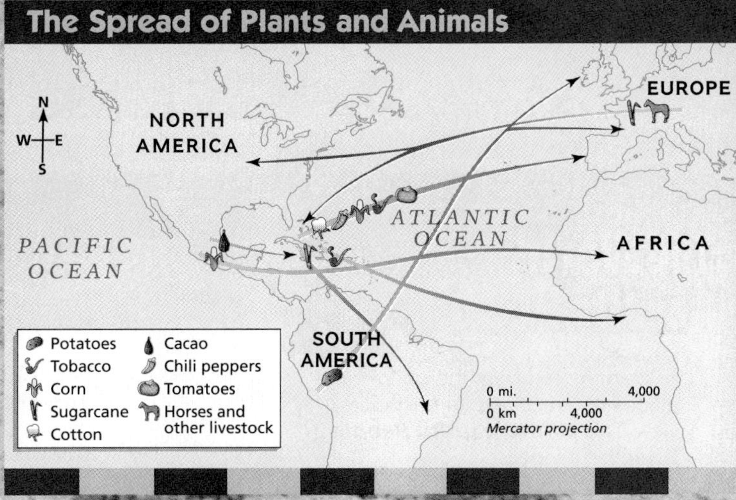
The Spread of Plants and Animals
N
S
W
E
NORTH AMERICA
EUROPE
PACIFIC OCEAN
ATLANTIC OCEAN
AFRICA
SOUTH AMERICA
Potatoes
Tobacco
Corn
Sugarcane
Cotton
Cacao
Chili peppers
Tomatoes
Horses and other livestock
0 mi.
4,000
0 km
4,000
Mercator projection

Brazil and Its Neighbors

The World and Its People — NATIONAL GEOGRAPHIC

To learn more about the people and places of Brazil and its neighbors, view ***The World and Its People*** **Chapter 8** video.

Geography Online

Chapter Overview Visit the ***Geography: The World and Its People*** Web site at gwip.glencoe.com and click on **Chapter 8—Chapter Overviews** to preview information about Brazil and its neighbors.

Section 1 Brazil

Guide to Reading

Main Idea

Brazil is a large country with many resources, a lively culture, and serious economic challenges.

Terms to Know

- basin
- *selva*
- escarpment
- favela
- inflation
- republic

Places to Locate

- Amazon River
- Paraná River
- São Francisco River
- Brazilian Highlands
- Brasília
- Rio de Janeiro
- São Paulo

Reading Strategy

Create a chart like the one below and fill in at least one key fact about Brazil in each category.

Brazil	
Land	
Climate	
History	
Economy	
Government	
People	

◀ Iguazú Falls, Brazil

NATIONAL GEOGRAPHIC **Exploring Our World**

Some of the world's largest freshwater fish swim in the mighty Amazon River in Brazil. Called pirarucu (pih•RAHR•uh•KEW), these fish can grow up to 15 feet (4.6 m) long. What a catch! The people who catch these huge fish often make the fish scales into souvenir key chains for tourists.

Like the pirarucu fish, Brazil is BIG. With a land area of 3,286,488 square miles (8,511,964 sq. km), Brazil is the fifth-largest country in the world and the largest in South America. In fact, Brazil makes up almost half of South America. It borders every South American country except Chile and Ecuador.

Brazil's Land and Climate

Because Brazil covers such a large area, it has many different types of landforms. The map on page 229 shows you that Brazil has narrow coastal plains, highland areas, and lowland river valleys.

The **Amazon River** is the world's second-longest river, winding almost 4,000 miles (6,437 km) from the Andes mountain ranges to the Atlantic Ocean. The river has such a powerful current at its mouth that it carries soil 60 miles (97 km) out to sea. On its journey to the Atlantic, the Amazon drains water from a wide, flat basin. A **basin** is a low area surrounded by higher land. In the Amazon Basin, heavy rain falls in the summer and autumn. Rainfall can reach as much as 120 inches (305 cm) a year. These rains support the growth of thick tropical rain forests, which Brazilians call *selvas.* Turn to page 252 to learn more about this rain forest, which covers one-third of Brazil.

Brazil has lowlands along the **Paraná River** and the **São Francisco River.** Both rivers begin in southeast Brazil. The Paraná flows to the southwest and the São Francisco to the northeast.

In addition to lowlands, Brazil has highlands. The **Brazilian Highlands** cover about half of the country, including much of the east and south. The highlands drop sharply to the Atlantic Ocean. This drop is called the Great Escarpment. An escarpment, as you remember, is a steep cliff between higher and lower land.

Applying Map Skills

1. What is the capital of Brazil?
2. What country in this region is a territory of France?

Find NGS online map resources @ www.nationalgeographic.com/maps

Varied Climate Different climates exist in Brazil due to the country's huge size and varied landforms. Traveling in the Amazon Basin, you would feel the steamy temperatures and heavy rains of a tropical rain forest. In the highlands and on much of the coast, you would enjoy a tropical savanna climate, with hot temperatures and wet and dry seasons. In the south, you would have the warm temperatures of a humid subtropical zone. The capital, **Brasília,** is closer to the Equator than the coastal city of **Rio de Janeiro** (REE•oh DAY zhuh•NEHR•oh) but has milder temperatures. Why? Brasília is located at a higher altitude.

Reading Check **What causes Brazil to have different climates?**

Applying Map Skills

1. Which area of Brazil—the north or the south—has the highest elevation?
2. Name two rivers that flow into the Amazon River.

Find NGS online map resources @ www.nationalgeographic.com/maps

Brazil's Economy

How do Brazilians earn a living? Agriculture, mining, and forestry have been important for centuries. Today Brazil's economy is diverse and productive, yet the country still faces serious economic challenges.

The North For centuries the Amazon Basin was a mysterious region whose secrets were guarded by the Native Americans living there. This began to change in the mid-1800s. World demand skyrocketed for the rubber harvested from the basin's trees, and new settlers streamed to Brazil's interior. In recent years, government-built roads have brought even more people to the Amazon Basin. Mining companies dig for minerals such as bauxite, tin, and iron ore. Logging companies harvest mahogany and other woods from the rain forest. Farmers use the cleared land to grow soybeans and tobacco and to graze cattle.

Farmers along the Atlantic coastal plain grow tobacco, sugarcane, bananas, and cacao for export. Several large port cities—including Recife and Salvador—are located along the coast. Farther inland, thinly populated plateaus and highlands receive less than 40 inches (102 cm) of rain a year. Farmers in this area must use irrigation to bring water to their fields of beans, corn, and cotton.

The South In the southern part of Brazil are rich mineral resources and fertile farmland. This region boasts one of the largest iron-ore deposits in the world, and the highlands are perfect for growing coffee. As the graph below shows, Brazil produces far more coffee than other countries. Brazil also exports large amounts of another popular breakfast drink—orange juice. Rice and bananas flourish as well.

The towering forests of the north are matched by the towering skyscrapers of the southeast. Here stand Brazil's major cities and centers of industry. Tourists flock to Rio de Janeiro, which has more than

Leading Coffee-Producing Countries

Analyzing the Graph

Brazil's highlands have the right soil and climate to grow coffee.

Region Which leading coffee-producing countries are in Latin America?

Visit gwip.glencoe.com and click on **Chapter 8—Textbook Updates.**

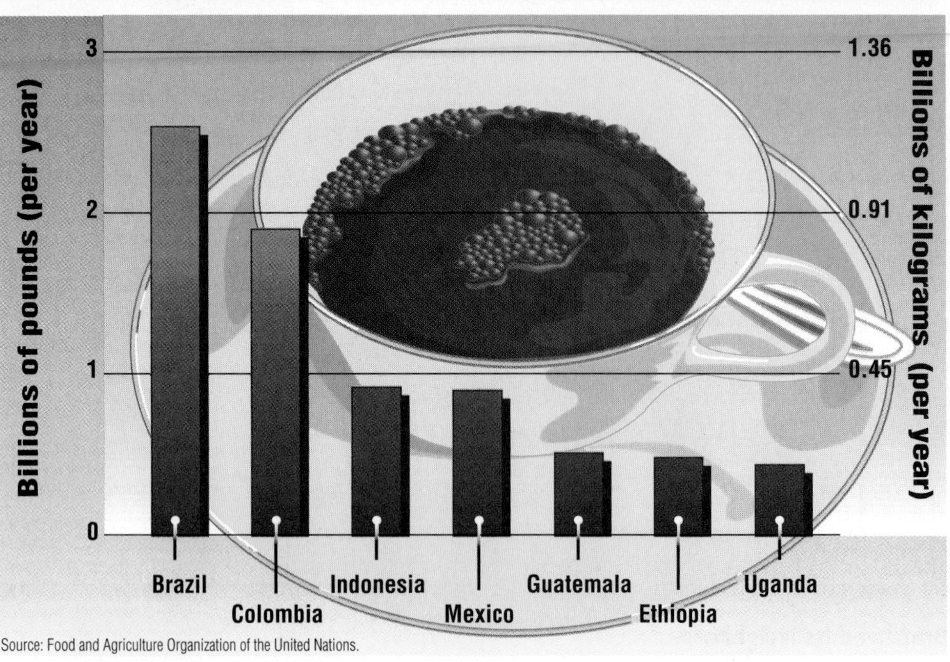

Source: Food and Agriculture Organization of the United Nations.

10 million people. If you visited Rio, you might enjoy the city's beautiful coastline, sandy beaches, and annual celebration of the holiday called Carnival. **São Paulo** (SAH•oh POW•loh), home to more than 16.5 million people, is one of the fastest-growing urban areas in the world. It is also Brazil's leading trade and industrial center. Vehicles, electronic products, steel, and more are manufactured here.

Farther south along the coast are more large cities, such as Curitiba (KUR•uh•TEE•buh) and Porto Alegre—each humming with industry. As you move west from the coast, you find cattle grazing on grasslands. Brazil—the leading cattle producer in South America—exports beef all over the world.

Brazil's Economic Challenges Brazil's economy has brought wealth to many Brazilians and built a large and strong middle class. Yet as many as one-fifth of Brazil's people live in extreme poverty. Many Brazilian cities are surrounded by **favelas,** or slum areas. Thousands of poor people move here looking for work in the urban factories. They live in crude shacks with neither running water nor sewage systems. City governments have tried to clean up these areas, but people continue to settle here because they have no money to pay for housing. Many children as young as 10 go to work to help earn money.

To increase jobs and products for export, the government has encouraged mining, logging, and farming in the rain forest. However, these activities cause problems. First, they damage the land. Mining often results in dangerous levels of mercury building up in streams and lakes. Logging and the deliberate burning of trees to clear land for farming destroy large amounts of forest. In addition, these activities threaten the Native Americans who live in the rain forest. As more people settle in the Amazon Basin, Native Americans find it difficult to follow traditional ways of life. In the 1990s, the government announced plans to set aside 10 percent of the Amazon forest as parks. Another 10 percent will be set aside for native peoples.

✓Reading Check **What city is Brazil's leading trade and industrial center?**

Brazil's History and Culture

With about 168 million people, Brazil has the largest population of all Latin American nations. Unlike most of Latin America, Brazil's culture is largely Portuguese rather than Spanish. The Portuguese were the first and largest European group to colonize Brazil. Today Brazilians are of European, African, Native American, Asian, or mixed ancestry. Almost all of them speak a Brazilian form of Portuguese, which includes many words from Native American and African languages. Most of the population follow the Roman Catholic religion, but many Brazilians combine Catholicism with beliefs and practices from African and Native American religions.

Influence of History Native Americans were the first people to live in Brazil. In the 1500s, the Portuguese took control of fertile coastal areas. They forced Native Americans to work on large plantations that

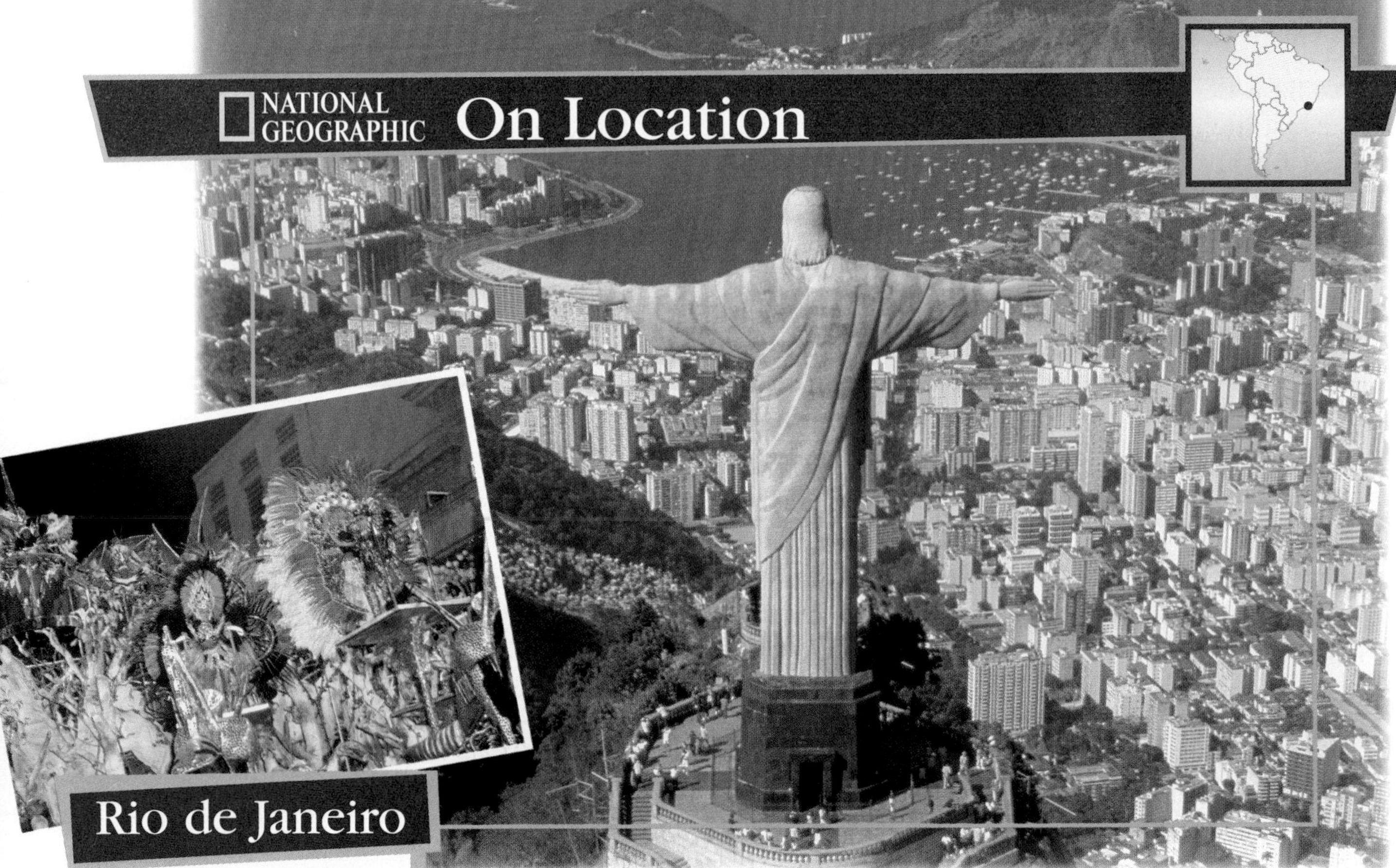

A huge statue of Christ overlooks Rio de Janeiro (right). Crowds of people in Rio de Janeiro celebrate Carnival wearing brightly colored costumes (above).

Place **What groups make up Brazil's population?**

grew tobacco and, later, sugarcane. Many Native Americans died from disease or overwork. To replace them, early Portuguese settlers brought people from Africa and enslaved them. Slavery finally was banned in 1888, but Africans remained in Brazil, most of them living in the northeastern part of the country. Over the years, African traditions have influenced Brazilian religion, music, dance, and food.

In the 1980s, economic problems created hard times for Brazil's people. Inflation soared. **Inflation** is an overall increase in the prices of goods across the entire economy. In the early 1990s, prices rose at a rate of 7,000 percent a year. This means that something costing $1 in January would cost about $70 in December. A new president ordered economic reforms that quickly slowed the rate of price increases, and Brazil's economy began to recover.

Moving to the Cities Look at the population map on page 246. You see that much of Brazil is sparsely populated. Millions of people have moved from rural areas to coastal cities in hopes of finding better jobs. The government has tried to encourage people to move from crowded coastal areas to less populated inland areas. Highways now crisscross the country and reach many once remote regions. In 1960 Brazil moved its capital from coastal Rio de Janeiro 600 miles (966 km) inland to the newly built city of Brasília. With more than 1.7 million people, Brasília is a modern and rapidly growing city.

The Government Brazil declared independence from Portugal in 1822. At first the new nation was an empire, with emperors ruling from 1822 to 1889. Like other Latin American countries, Brazil then experienced periods of military dictatorship. Today Brazil is a democratic **republic,** where people elect a president and other leaders. In Brazil, though, citizens cannot choose whether to vote or not vote. People from ages 18 to 70 are required by law to vote. Brazil has more than a dozen political parties—not just two main ones, as in the United States.

The national government of Brazil is much stronger than its 26 state governments. Brazil's president has more power over the country than an American president does in the United States.

Leisure Time Brazilians live for soccer, which they call *fútbol.* Every village has a soccer field, and the larger cities have stadiums. Maracana Stadium in Rio de Janeiro seats 220,000 fans.

Brazil is also famous for Carnival. This festival is celebrated just before the beginning of Lent, the Christian holy season that comes before Easter. The most spectacular Carnival is held each year in Rio de Janeiro. The celebration includes Brazilian music and showy parades.

Brazil has one of the largest television networks in the world. This network produces prime-time soap operas called *telenovelas.* These programs are wildly popular in Brazil—and viewers in more than 60 other nations enjoy them too.

✓Reading Check **Why do most Brazilians speak Portuguese?**

Assessment

Defining Terms

1. **Define** basin, *selva,* escarpment, favela, inflation, republic.

Recalling Facts

2. **Location** Where is the source of the Amazon River located?
3. **Economics** What resources attract companies to the Amazon Basin?
4. **Culture** What is the major religion of Brazil?

Critical Thinking

5. **Making Comparisons** How does the economy in northern Brazil differ from the economy in southern Brazil?
6. **Summarizing Information** What economic challenges face Brazilians?

Graphic Organizer

7. **Organizing Information** Draw a diagram like this one. Beside the left arrow, write the cause of the government action. On the right, list results of this action.

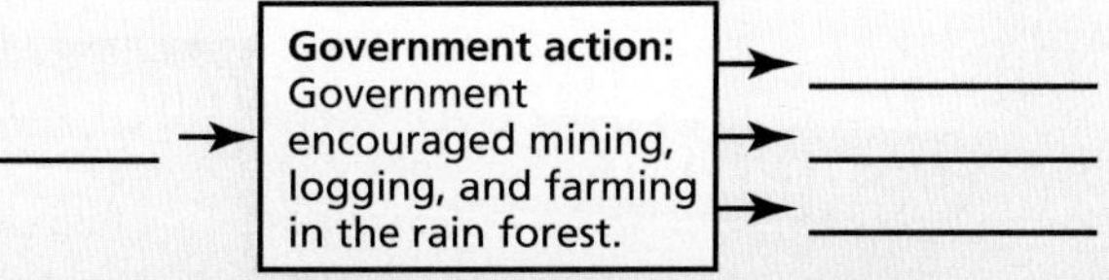

Applying Geography Skills

8. **Analyzing Maps and Graphs** Look at the maps on page 229 and page 238, and the graph on page 230. At what elevation is most coffee in Brazil grown? How much coffee does Brazil produce in a year?

Critical Thinking Skill

Sequencing and Categorizing Information

Sequencing means placing facts in the order in which they occurred. *Categorizing* means organizing information into groups of related facts and ideas. Both actions help you deal with large quantities of information in an understandable way.

Learning the Skill

Follow these steps to learn sequencing and categorizing skills:

- Look for dates or clue words that provide you with a chronological order: *in 2004, the late 1990s, first, then, finally, after the Great Depression,* and so on.
- If the sequence of events is not important, you may want to categorize the information instead. Categories might include economic activities or cultural traits.
- List these characteristics, or categories, as the headings on a chart.
- As you read, fill in details under the proper category on the chart.

Brasília

Practicing the Skill

Read the sentences below, then answer the questions that follow.

After Brazil's independence from Portugal in 1823, a bill was presented to build a new capital named Brasília. More than 100 years later, in 1955, a planning committee chose the site for the new capital. The first streets were paved in 1958. On April 20, 1960, the festivities to officially "open" the new capital started at 4:00 P.M.

Brasília has both positive and negative aspects. The positive include virtually no air pollution, no threat of natural disasters, many green areas, and a pleasant climate. The negative aspects of the capital include very high housing prices, inefficient public transportation, few parking spaces, and long distances between the various government buildings.

1. What information can be organized sequentially?
2. What categories can you use to organize the information? What facts could be placed under each category?

Applying the Skill

Find two newspaper or magazine articles about Brazil or another South American country. Sequence or categorize the information on note cards or in a chart.

GO TO Practice key skills with **Glencoe Skillbuilder Interactive Workbook, Level 1.**

Argentina

Guide to Reading

Main Idea

Argentina is a large nation with diverse landforms, a strong economy, and a vibrant culture.

Terms to Know

- tannin
- *estancia*
- gaucho

Places to Locate

- Andes
- Aconcagua
- Patagonia
- pampas
- Buenos Aires
- Río de la Plata
- Gran Chaco

Reading Strategy

Draw a time line like this one and list at least five key dates and events in Argentina's history.

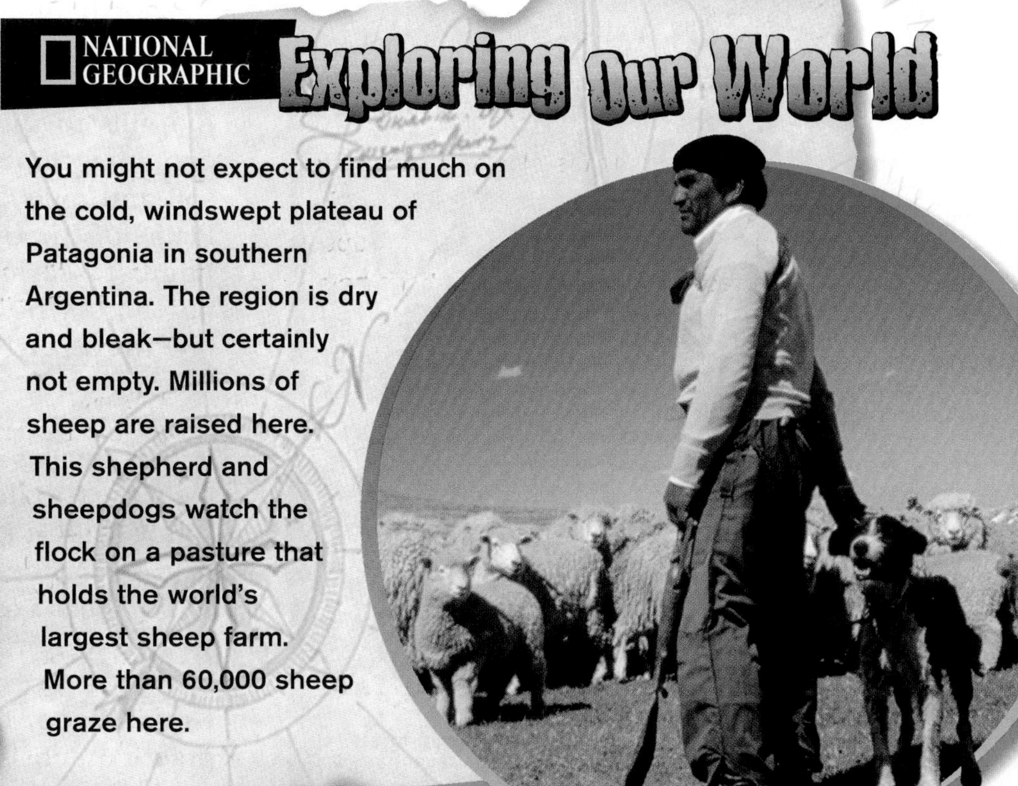

You might not expect to find much on the cold, windswept plateau of Patagonia in southern Argentina. The region is dry and bleak—but certainly not empty. Millions of sheep are raised here. This shepherd and sheepdogs watch the flock on a pasture that holds the world's largest sheep farm. More than 60,000 sheep graze here.

South of Brazil lies Argentina. It shares a long border with Chile to the west, touches Bolivia and Paraguay to the north, and borders on Brazil and Uruguay to the northeast. Argentina's eastern side is a long coast along the Atlantic Ocean. Its southern tip reaches almost to the continent of Antarctica.

Mountains, Plateaus, and Plains

Argentina's land area of 1,068,302 square miles (2,766,889 sq. km) makes it South America's second-largest country, after Brazil. Argentina is about the size of the United States east of the Mississippi River. Within this vast area, you can find mountains, deserts, plains, and forests.

The **Andes** tower over the western part of Argentina. Snowcapped peaks and clear blue lakes draw tourists for skiing and hiking. **Aconcagua** (AH•kohn•KAH•gwah) soars to a height of 22,834 feet (6,960 m), making it the highest mountain in the Western Hemisphere. On the eastern edge of the Andes are foothills. Through this area flow mountain streams, which farmers use to grow grains, cotton, and grapes.

Applying Map Skills

1. What types of climates does Argentina have?
2. In which climate zone is the capital of Argentina?

Find NGS online map resources @ www.nationalgeographic.com/maps

South and east of the Andes lies a dry, windswept plateau called **Patagonia.** Most of Patagonia gets little rain and has poor soil. As a result, sheep raising is the only major economic activity. Find Patagonia on the physical map on page 229.

North of Patagonia, in the center of Argentina, are vast treeless plains known as the **pampas.** They stretch from the Andes foothills to the Atlantic coast. Argentina's economy depends on this region's fertile soil and mild climate. Similar to the Great Plains of the United States, the pampas are home to farmers who grow grains and ranchers who raise livestock. More than two-thirds of the country's people live in this region.

Buenos Aires, Argentina's capital and largest city, lies in the area where the pampas meet the **Río de la Plata.** The Río de la Plata is not really a river but a funnel-shaped bay that enters the Atlantic Ocean. It is formed by the Paraná and Uruguay Rivers.

In the northwest, heavy summer rains help great forests grow in the area called the **Gran Chaco.** The few people who live here practice subsistence farming and harvest quebracho (kay•BRAH•choh) trees. These hardwood trees produce **tannin,** a substance used in processing leather. To the east, hot, humid grasslands lie between the Uruguay and Paraná Rivers. Farmers graze livestock and grow crops on this fertile soil.

✓Reading Check **Why are the pampas an important region of Argentina?**

Argentina's Economy

Argentina has vast grasslands, so it is not surprising that Argentina's economy depends on farming and ranching. The country's major farm products include beef, sugarcane, wheat, soybeans, and corn. Most of these products are grown throughout the pampas and the northeastern part of the country. Huge ***estancias*** (ay•STAHN•see•ahs), or ranches, cover the pampas. Owners of these ranches hire **gauchos** (GOW•chohs), or cowhands, to take care of the livestock. Gauchos are the national symbol of Argentina, admired for their independence and horse-riding skills. The livestock that the gauchos herd and tend are a vital part of the country's economy.

Beef and food products are Argentina's chief exports. Turn to page 240 to read more about gaucho life on the pampas.

Manufacturing Argentina is one of the most industrialized countries in South America. As you can see from the map on page 238, most of the country's factories are in or near Buenos Aires. Argentina's leading manufactured goods are food products, automobiles, chemicals, textiles, books, and magazines.

Petroleum is Argentina's most valuable mineral resource. The country's major oil fields are in Patagonia and the Andes. Other minerals—zinc, iron, copper, tin, and uranium—are mined in the Andes as well.

Reading Check **What are Argentina's chief exports?**

Argentina's People

Look at the population density map on page 246. Note that the most densely settled area is in and around Buenos Aires. Many people also live on the pampas. Why is this? The Andean region and Patagonia have harsh climates, so settlement in those areas is sparse. Buenos Aires and the pampas have a mild—although sometimes humid—climate that makes these areas more attractive to settlers.

Early History Before the arrival of the Europeans, Native Americans farmed and hunted on the land. In the late 1500s, the Spaniards settled

Buenos Aires

This broad street in Buenos Aires is the Avenida 9 de Julio—or Avenue of the Ninth of July. Nearly 450 feet (137 m) wide, the street is named in honor of the day Argentina won independence from Spain.

Place **Who led Argentina's fight for freedom from Spain?**

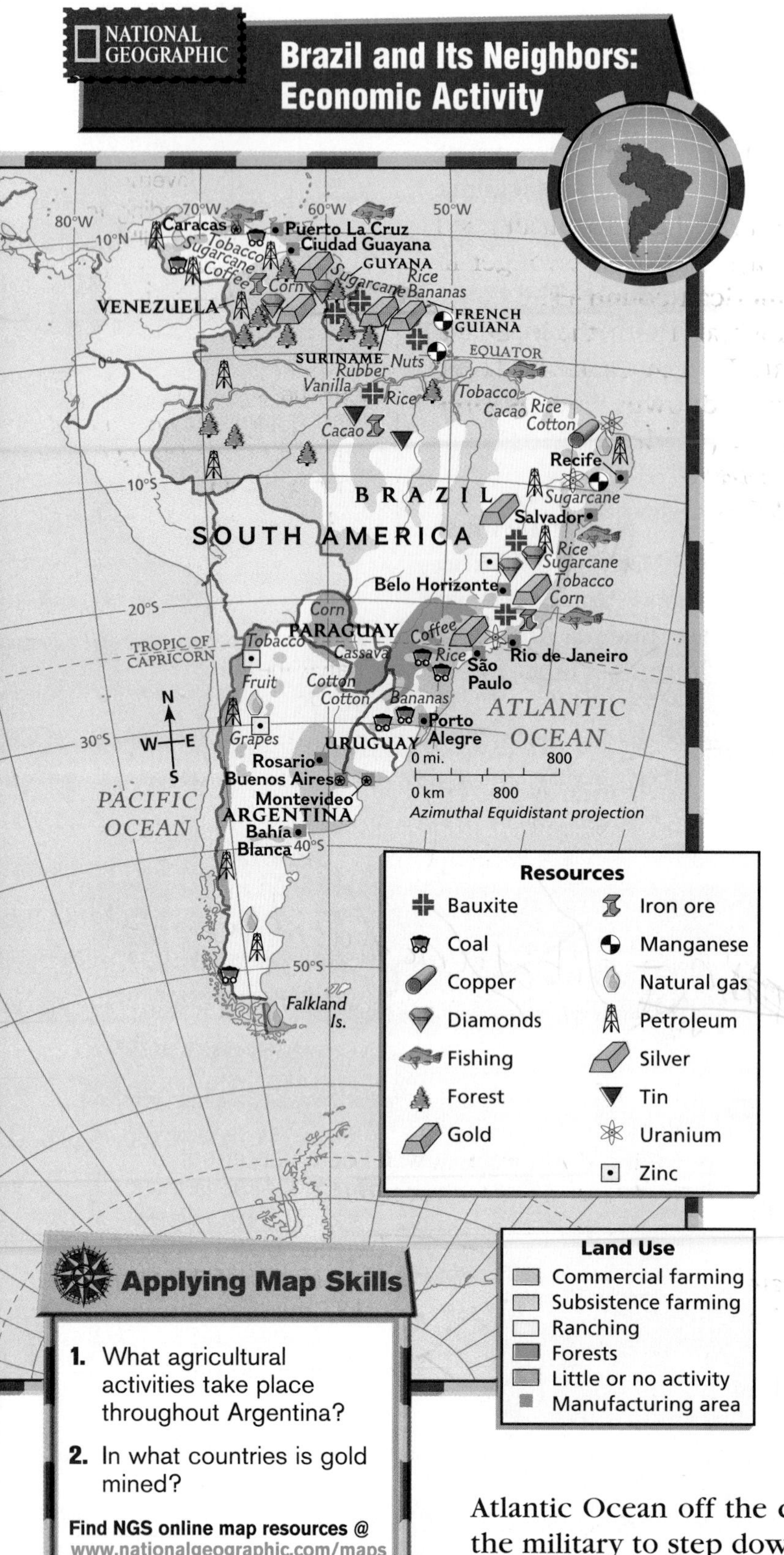

Applying Map Skills

1. What agricultural activities take place throughout Argentina?
2. In what countries is gold mined?

Find NGS online map resources @ www.nationalgeographic.com/maps

the area that is now Buenos Aires. By 1800 Buenos Aires was a flourishing port. Unfortunately, most of the Native Americans in the region had died from disease or were killed by Europeans.

In 1816 a general named José de San Martín led Argentina in its fight for freedom from Spain. After independence, the country was torn apart by conflict between the national government in Buenos Aires and various outlying regions. By the mid-1850s, a strong national government had emerged. Argentina entered a time of prosperity that lasted until the end of the 1800s. The growth of livestock raising and other industries brought wealth to some of Argentina's people. Still, because it was hard to make a living, many poor farmers migrated to the cities.

Political Unrest During the first half of the 1900s, Argentina entered a period of political unrest. Elected leaders governed poorly, the economy suffered, and the military took over. One of these military leaders, Juan Perón, became a dictator in the late 1940s. With his popular wife Eva at his side, Perón tried to improve the economy and give more help to workers. His crackdown on freedom of speech and the press made people unhappy, however. In 1955 a revolt drove Perón from power, and democracy returned.

Military officers again took control of Argentina in the 1970s. They ruled harshly, and political violence resulted in the deaths of many people. In 1982 Argentina suffered defeat in a war with the United Kingdom for control of the Falkland Islands. The Falklands, known in Argentina as the Malvinas, lie in the Atlantic Ocean off the coast of Argentina. Argentina's loss forced the military to step down, and elected leaders regained control of the government.

Today Argentina is a democratic republic. A powerful elected president leads the nation for a four-year term. A legislature with two houses makes the laws. As in the United States, nine judges appointed by the president sit on the country's highest court.

The country is also divided into 23 provinces and the federal district—which is Buenos Aires, the capital. The national government is much stronger than the provincial governments.

Argentina's Culture About 85 percent of Argentina's people are of European ancestry. During the late 1800s, immigrants in large numbers came to Argentina from Spain and Italy. Their arrival greatly influenced Argentina's society and culture. European ways of life are stronger in Argentina today than in most other Latin American countries.

The official language of Argentina is Spanish, although the language includes many Italian words. Most people are Roman Catholic. About 80 percent of Argentina's people live in cities and towns. Buenos Aires and its suburbs hold more than 12 million people. Buenos Aires has wide streets, European-style buildings, and shops and theaters. Its citizens call themselves *porteños* (pohr•TAY•nyohs), which means "people of the port." They have a passion for the national dance of Argentina, the tango.

✓Reading Check **Why does Argentina have a strong European culture?**

I Protest!

Argentina's government wants to cut spending for schools, so Guillermo Larzabal intends to protest with his teachers in front of the congress building in Buenos Aires. "This is exciting!" he says. "I'm usually busy going to school and practicing *fútbol.* During the summer, from December to February, I spend all day kicking a *fútbol* with my friends. Sometimes our parents let us walk along the Avenida 9 de Julio. We watch the people and eat *helado*—ice cream."

Assessment

Defining Terms

1. **Define** tannin, *estancia,* gaucho.

Recalling Facts

2. **Location** Near what other continent is South America's Argentina located?
3. **Region** Describe two ways in which the pampas are similar to the Great Plains of the United States.
4. **Economics** List four of Argentina's mineral resources.

Critical Thinking

5. **Analyzing Cause and Effect** Which of Juan Perón's policies led to his removal from office?
6. **Making Comparisons** How do the economic activities in Patagonia, the pampas, and the Gran Chaco differ?

Graphic Organizer

7. **Organizing Information** Draw a diagram like this one, then write one fact about Argentina in each section of the "pie."

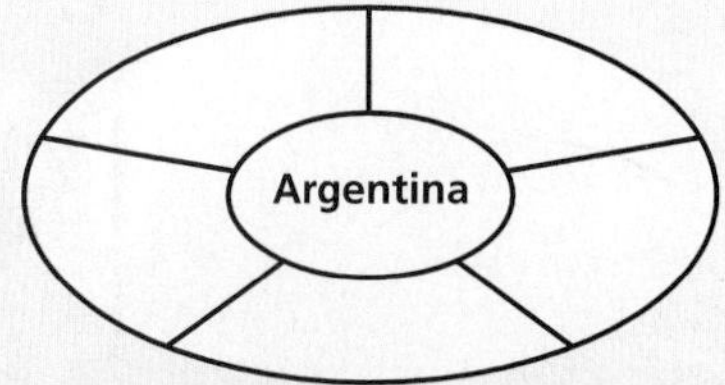

Applying Geography Skills

8. **Analyzing Maps** Study the physical map on page 229. What body of water separates the southern tip of Argentina from the mainland? What body of water borders Argentina on the east?

Making Connections

ART SCIENCE LITERATURE TECHNOLOGY

Poetry on the Pampas

As you learned in Section 2, gauchos herd cattle on the pampas. In 1872 José Hernández wrote the epic poem *El Gaucho Martín Fierro.* The poem tells the story of Martín Fierro, who recalls his life as a gaucho on the pampas. The following lines were translated from the poem.

El Gaucho Martín Fierro
by José Hernández (1834–1886)

A son am I of the rolling plain,
A gaucho born and bred;
For me the whole great world is small,
Believe me, my heart can hold it all;
The snake strikes not at my passing foot,
The sun burns not my head.

. . . .

Ah, my mind goes back and I see again
The gaucho I knew of old;
He picked his mount, and was ready aye,
To sing or fight, and for work or play,
And even the poorest one was rich
In the things not bought with gold.

The neediest gaucho in the land,
That had least of goods and gear,
Could show a troop of a single strain,
And rode with a silver-studded rein,
The plains were brown with the grazing herds,
And everywhere was cheer.

And when the time of the branding came,
It did one good to see
How the hand was quick and the eye was true,
When the steers they threw with the long lassoo [lasso],
And the merry band that the years have swept
Like leaves from the autumn tree.

Gauchos on Argentina's pampas ▲

Making the Connection

1. How does the poet describe the land on which the gaucho lives?
2. How can you tell from the poem that a gaucho is often on the move?
3. **Drawing Conclusions** What evidence does the poem give that the gaucho's way of life was a proud and happy one?

Section 3

Caribbean South America

Guide to Reading

Main Idea

Each nation in Caribbean South America has a unique culture, depending on who settled the country.

Terms to Know

- llanos
- hydroelectric power
- altitude
- caudillo

Places to Locate

- Venezuela
- Lake Maracaibo
- Caracas
- Orinoco River
- Guiana Highlands
- Guyana
- Suriname
- French Guiana

Reading Strategy

Create a chart like this one, then list the names of the groups of people who live in each land.

Country	Groups
Venezuela	
Guyana	
French Guiana	
Suriname	

NATIONAL GEOGRAPHIC **Exploring Our World**

Thick rain forests cover much of the countries north of Brazil. Scientists try all kinds of ways to study the many plants and animals that live hundreds of feet above the ground in the rain forest canopy. Some use elaborate ropes and pulleys. Another scientist designed a raft nearly as large as a baseball diamond that could be dropped by a blimp on top of the canopy.

Four lands make up Caribbean South America: Venezuela, Guyana, Suriname, and French Guiana. They all border Brazil and either the Caribbean Sea or the Atlantic Ocean.

Venezuela: An Oil-Rich Land

Venezuela (VEH•nuh•ZWAY•luh) is the westernmost country of Caribbean South America. In the northwest lie the lowland coastal areas surrounding **Lake Maracaibo** (MAH•rah•KY•boh), the largest lake in South America. Swamps fill much of this area, and few people live here. The great number of towering oil wells, however, gives you a clue that rich oil fields lie under the lake and along its shores. Venezuela has more oil reserves than any other country in the Americas.

The Andean highlands begin south of the lake and are part of the Andes mountain ranges. This area includes most of the nation's cities,

Angel Falls—the highest waterfall in the world at 3,212 feet (979 m)—roars over a cliff in Venezuela. It would take 11 football fields stacked end-to-end to reach the top.

Place What is one of the rivers that provides Venezuela with hydroelectric power?

including **Caracas** (kah•RAH•kahs), the capital and largest city.

East of the highlands, you see grassy plains known as the **llanos** (LAH•nohs). The llanos have many ranches, farms, and oil fields. Venezuela's most important river—the **Orinoco**—flows across the llanos. This river is a valuable source of **hydroelectric power,** or water-generated electricity, for Venezuela's cities.

South and east of the llanos rise the **Guiana Highlands,** deeply cut by rivers. Angel Falls—the world's highest waterfall—spills over a bluff in this region.

The Climate Because it is close to the Equator, Venezuela has a mostly tropical climate. In the Guiana Highlands to the south, you enter a steamy rain forest. In the grassy llanos, a tropical savanna climate brings you hot temperatures but less rain. Much of the Caribbean coast is dry, with some areas receiving only 16 inches (41 cm) of rainfall yearly. As in Mexico, temperatures in Venezuela differ with **altitude,** or height above sea level. In the Andean highlands you are usually warm in the daytime but cool at night.

The Economy Venezuelans once depended on crops such as coffee and cacao to earn a living. Since the 1920s, petroleum has changed the country's economy. Venezuela is a world leader in oil production and one of the chief suppliers of oil to the United States. Because the government owns the oil industry, oil provides nearly half of the government's income. Iron ore, limestone, bauxite, gold, diamonds, and emeralds also are mined. Factories make steel, chemicals, and food products. About 10 percent of the people farm, growing sugarcane and bananas or raising cattle.

History and Government Originally settled by Native Americans, Venezuela became a Spanish colony in the early 1500s. The Spanish gave the country its name. With its many rivers, the land in South America reminded Spanish explorers of Venice, Italy, which is full of canals. They named the area *Venezuela,* which means "Little Venice."

In the early 1800s, rebellion swept across the Spanish colonial empire. Simón Bolívar (see•MOHN boh•LEE•VAHR)—born in Venezuela—became one of the leaders of this revolt. He and his soldiers freed Venezuela and neighboring regions from Spanish rule. In 1830 Venezuela became independent.

During most of the 1800s and 1900s, the country was governed by military rulers called **caudillos** (kow•THEE•yohz). Their rule was often harsh. Since 1958, Venezuela has been a democracy led by a president and a two-house legislature.

Rising oil prices during the 1970s brought more money to the country. The middle class grew, and many people prospered. When oil prices fell in the 1990s, the country suffered. The government did not have the money to give the poor and unemployed the services they needed. In 1998 Venezuelans showed their impatience with the government. They elected a former military leader, Hugo Chavez, as president. Chavez proposed major changes to the country's constitution and economy. In December 1999, the Venezuelan people voted to accept the new constitution.

The People Most of Venezuela's 23.8 million people have a mix of European, African, and Native American backgrounds. Spanish is the major language of the country, and the major religion is Roman Catholicism. Nearly 90 percent of Venezuelans live in cities. More than 3.6 million people live in Caracas, which holds towering skyscrapers surrounded by mountains.

✓Reading Check **What product changed Venezuela's economy?**

The Guianas

Caribbean South America also includes the countries of **Guyana** (gy•AH•nuh) and **Suriname** (SUR•uh•NAH•muh) and the territory of **French Guiana** (gee•A•nuh). Guyana was a British colony called British Guiana. Suriname, once a colony of the Netherlands, was called Dutch Guiana. As a result, these three lands are called "the Guianas."

The Guianas have similar landforms. Highlands in the interiors are covered by thick rain forests. As you move toward the Caribbean coast, the land descends to low coastal plains. The climate is hot and tropical. Two rainy seasons bring heavy rain, which causes the growth of rain forests. Most people live on the coastal plains because of the cooling ocean winds. The map on page 238 shows that sugarcane grows in Guyana and French Guiana, while rice and bananas flourish in Suriname. Many people also earn their living mining gold and bauxite.

Guyana In the early 1600s, the Dutch were the first Europeans to settle in Guyana. They forced Native Americans and Africans to work on tobacco, coffee, and cotton farms and, later, on sugarcane plantations. Great Britain won possession of the Dutch colonies in the early 1800s and ended slavery. Still needing workers, the British paid Indians from Asia to move here. Today people from India make up most of Guyana's population. Another one-third are of African ancestry. Small numbers of Native Americans and Europeans also live here. Christianity and Hinduism are the chief religions. Most people speak English. Georgetown, the capital, is the major city.

Guyana won its independence from Britain in 1966. Guyana remains a very poor country, however, and depends on aid from the United Kingdom.

Roping a Capybara

Capybaras are the world's largest rodents. They may grow to be 2 feet tall and 4 feet long, and weigh more than 100 pounds. Found in Central and South America, the capybara (KA•pih•BAR•uh) lives along rivers and lakes, and eats vegetation. Here, a gaucho ropes a dog-sized capybara in Venezuela. Some Venezuelans eat capybara during the Easter season.

Suriname The British were the first Europeans to settle Suriname, but the Dutch gained control in 1667. As in Guyana, the Dutch brought enslaved Africans to work on large sugar plantations. Because of harsh treatment, many Africans fled into the isolated interior of the country. Their descendants still live there today. Later the Dutch hired workers from the Asian lands of India and Indonesia.

Asians form a large part of Suriname's population. About half of Suriname's people practice Christianity. The rest follow Hinduism or Islam. The main language is Dutch. Paramaribo (PAH•rah•MAH•ree•boh) is the capital and chief port. In 1975 Suriname won its independence from the Dutch. The country is poor, so it still relies on Dutch aid.

French Guiana French Guiana became a colony of France in the 1600s and remains one today. The country is headed by a French official called a *prefect,* who lives in the capital, Cayenne (ky•EHN). The French government provides jobs and aid to many of French Guiana's people.

Most people in French Guiana are of African or mixed African and European ancestry. They speak French and are Roman Catholic. In Cayenne, you see sidewalk cafés, police in French uniforms, and shoppers using francs, the French currency—just as you would in Paris, France. You also see local influences, such as Carnival, Native American woodcarving, and Caribbean music and dance.

✓Reading Check **What European countries influenced the development of Guyana, Suriname, and French Guiana?**

Assessment

Defining Terms

1. **Define** llanos, hydroelectric power, altitude, caudillo.

Recalling Facts

2. **Place** What is the largest lake in South America?
3. **History** Who was Simón Bolívar?
4. **Economics** Name fou\ of Venezuela's mineral resources.

Critical Thinking

5. **Drawing Conclusions** Why is Hinduism one of the major religions of Guyana?
6. **Understanding Cause and Effect** Why does a drop in oil prices hurt Venezuela's poor and unemployed?

Graphic Organizer

7. **Organizing Information** Draw a diagram like this one. In the top box, under the heading list similarities about the Guianas. In the smaller boxes, under the headings write facts about each country that show their differences.

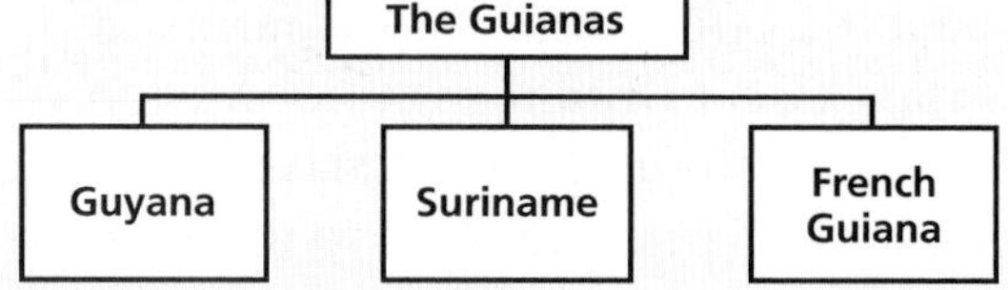

Applying Geography Skills

8. **Analyzing Maps** Look at the population density map on page 246. What is the population of Caracas? What is the population density of the area surrounding Caracas?

Section 4

Uruguay and Paraguay

Guide to Reading

Main Idea

Farming and ranching form the economic base of Uruguay and Paraguay.

Terms to Know

- welfare state
- landlocked

Places to Locate

- Uruguay
- Montevideo
- Paraguay
- Paraguay River
- Gran Chaco
- Paraná River
- Asunción

Reading Strategy

Create a diagram like this one. Under each heading fill each circle with facts about these two countries. Put statements that are true of both countries in the area where the circles overlap.

NATIONAL GEOGRAPHIC **Exploring Our World**

The traditional music of Paraguay seems to be out of place with the rest of its culture. The harp is the country's national instrument, and Paraguayans are famous for their slow, mournful guitar playing. In contrast, the traditional dances are much livelier. Here, a woman performs the bottle dance—a difficult feat even though the bottles are attached to one another.

In the 1800s, European settlers built ranches on the vast plains of Uruguay and Paraguay, Brazil's southern neighbors. Raising livestock and manufacturing products from livestock form the economic base of these two countries.

Uruguay

Uruguay shares a border with southeastern Brazil. It touches water on the other three sides, with the Atlantic Ocean on the east, the Uruguay River on the west, and the Río de la Plata on the south. If you traveled in Uruguay, you would see grass blanketing its rolling, hilly plains. The hills descend to a low, narrow, fertile plain along the Atlantic coast.

You would enjoy the country's generally mild climate. Temperatures are moderate and rarely fall below freezing. Sometimes, though, a cold and violent wind rises in Argentina and blows north.

NATIONAL GEOGRAPHIC

Brazil and Its Neighbors: Population Density

Applying Map Skills

1. What is the most densely populated area of Uruguay?
2. What cities in this region have more than 5 million people?

Find NGS online map resources @ www.nationalgeographic.com/maps

The Economy Uruguay's grasslands support sheep and cattle raising, the country's main economic activities. In fact, both Uruguay and Paraguay are covered with plains that are perfect for raising livestock. Cowhands are as common here as they are in our state of Texas. Animal products—meat, wool, and hides—top all exports. As you might expect, the major industries—textiles, footwear, and leather goods—use the products of the vast animal herds. Making tires and cement and refining petroleum play smaller roles in the economy. The economic health of Uruguay depends on the economies of its neighbors, Argentina and Brazil. Uruguay trades mainly with these countries but also with the United States and the European Union.

History and Government Uruguay joined Argentina in declaring independence from Spain in 1811. Later the Portuguese in Brazil took control of Uruguay. Not until 1828, with Argentina's help, did Uruguay win complete independence. Stable civilian governments led the country for most of its history. For many years, the government spent more on education than it did on defense. Uruguay's prosperity allowed it to become a **welfare state,** a country that uses tax money to support people who are sick, needy, jobless, or retired. Falling world demand for meat and wool and high government spending hurt the economy in the 1950s and 1960s, though. In addition, because of political troubles, military leaders took control of the government.

In 1985 democratic government returned to Uruguay. New leaders tried various economic changes to bring back prosperity. Many people resisted efforts to cut government spending, however. They feared losing their welfare benefits and suffering a lower standard of living. Reform efforts continue at a slow pace.

The People Most of Uruguay's 3.4 million people are of European ancestry. Only a small number have African or mixed ancestry. Very few Native Americans remain in the country. Spanish is the official language, and the Roman Catholic faith is the major religion. More

Itaipu Dam

About 40,000 workers labored to build Paraguay's Itaipu Dam. Brazil funded its construction. In return, Brazil pays low prices for the electricity it buys from Paraguay.

Human/Environment Interaction
How do both Paraguay and Brazil benefit from this arrangement?

than 90 percent of the people live in cities and towns. Nearly 1.4 million Uruguayans live in the coastal city of **Montevideo** (MAHN•tuh•vuh•DAY•oh), the country's capital.

Many people in rural areas own or rent small farms. Others work as gauchos on huge ranches. Legends about the gauchos have inspired Uruguay's folk music and literature. Uruguayans still flock to see gaucho rodeos.

✓Reading Check **What is a welfare state?**

Paraguay

Paraguay sits near the center of South America. Paraguay is landlocked because it has no seacoast. The **Paraguay River** divides Paraguay into east and west regions. Rolling hills, forests, rivers, and a humid subtropical climate make the eastern region a pleasant place to live. Most of Paraguay's people live here.

To the west is a plains region called the **Gran Chaco,** which you may remember is shared with Argentina. This area is home to less than 5 percent of Paraguay's people. Droughts in winter and floods in summer discourage people from living there. In Gran Chaco's tropical savanna climate, grasses, palm trees, and quebracho trees thrive. Quebracho trees provide tannin, a chemical used to process leather.

The Economy Forestry and farming are the major economic activities in Paraguay. Large cattle ranches cover much of the country. Most farmers, however, use small plots of land to grow grains, soybeans, and cassava. Cassava roots can be ground up and eaten or used to make tapioca. They can also be sliced and fried just like potatoes.

Paraguay also exports electricity. The country has the world's largest hydroelectric power generator at the Itaipu (ee•TY•poo) Dam, on the **Paraná River.** Paraguay sells nearly 90 percent of the electricity it produces to neighboring countries.

> **Geography Online**
>
> **Web Activity** Visit the ***Geography: The World and Its People*** Web site at gwip.glencoe.com and click on **Chapter 8–Student Web Activities** to learn more about Paraguay.

History and Government A Native American group called the Guaraní were the first people to live in Paraguay. By the 1500s, settlers and Roman Catholic missionaries from Spain arrived in the country. Paraguay was a colony of Spain until it became independent in 1811.

Paraguay has had a troubled history. Several wars in the 1800s left the nation very poor. Leaders had to invite investors from Argentina and Brazil to buy land to help the economy recover. Foreigners still own much of Paraguay's land. In addition, military leaders ruled harshly, punishing those who criticized them. In the 1990s, the country adopted a new constitution. Today the people of Paraguay elect their leaders.

The People Paraguayans today are mostly of mixed Guaraní and Spanish ancestry. Both Spanish and Guaraní are official languages, but more people speak Guaraní. Most people practice the Roman Catholic faith. About one-half of the people live in cities. **Asunción** (ah•SOON•see•OHN) is the capital and largest city.

Paraguayan arts are influenced by Guaraní culture. Guaraní lace is Paraguay's most famous handicraft. Like people in Uruguay, the people of Paraguay enjoy meat dishes and sip *yerba maté,* a tealike drink.

Reading Check **What are the main economic activities in Paraguay?**

Section 4 Assessment

Defining Terms

1. Define welfare state, landlocked.

Recalling Facts

2. Economics List three of Uruguay's major products.

3. Culture What percentage of Uruguay's people live in cities and towns?

4. Human/Environment Interaction What is the significance of the Itaipu Dam?

Critical Thinking

5. Making Predictions How can being landlocked affect a country's economy?

6. Making Comparisons How do Uruguay and Paraguay differ in regard to their Native American populations?

Graphic Organizer

7. Organizing Information Draw a diagram like this one, then on the lines list facts about the two regions of Paraguay.

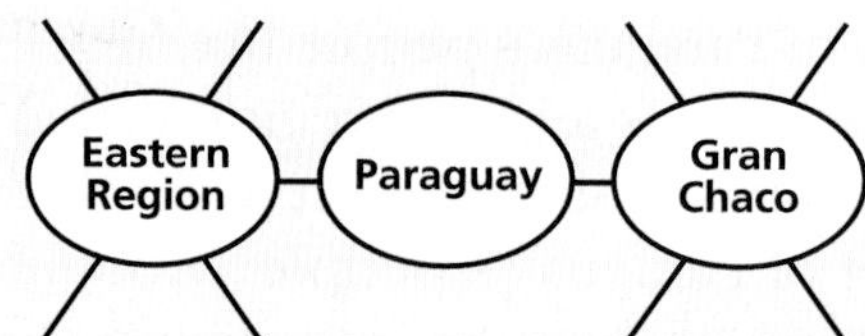

Applying Geography Skills

8. Analyzing Maps Refer to the population density map on page 246. About how many people live in Uruguay's capital city?

Chapter 8

Reading Review

Section 1 Brazil

Terms to Know
basin
selva
escarpment
favela
inflation
republic

Main Idea

Brazil is a large country with many resources, a lively culture, and serious economic challenges.

✓ **Economics** Brazil's prosperous economy includes mining, forestry, growing coffee and sugarcane, and manufacturing goods.

✓ **Economics** Brazil is trying to reduce its number of poor people and balance the use of resources with the preservation of its rain forests.

✓ **Culture** Most Brazilians are of mixed Portuguese, African, and Native American ancestry. Most live along the Atlantic coast and the Amazon River.

Section 2 Argentina

Terms to Know
tannin
estancia
gaucho

Main Idea

Argentina is a large nation with diverse landforms, a strong economy, and a vibrant culture.

✓ **Region** Few people live in Argentina's Andes region, Patagonia, or Gran Chaco. The most populous area is the vast grassland called the pampas.

✓ **Economics** Argentina's strong economy includes mining, farming, ranching, and manufacturing.

✓ **Culture** Argentina's capital, Buenos Aires, is a huge city with European style.

Section 3 Caribbean South America

Terms to Know
llanos
hydroelectric power
altitude
caudillo

Main Idea

Each nation in Caribbean South America has a unique culture, depending in part on who settled the country.

✓ **Culture** Most Venezuelans are of mixed European, African, and Native American ancestry. Most live in cities in the central highlands.

✓ **Culture** Guyana and Suriname have large numbers of people descended from workers who were brought from Africa and Asia.

✓ **Government** French Guiana is a territory of France.

Section 4 Uruguay and Paraguay

Terms to Know
welfare state
landlocked

Main Idea

Farming and ranching form the economic base of Uruguay and Paraguay.

✓ **Place** Uruguay and Paraguay have large areas of grass-covered plains that support ranching and industries that depend on raising livestock.

✓ **Economics** Paraguay grows grains, soybeans, and cassava, and the country exports electricity.

Chapter 8 Assessment and Activities

Using Key Terms

Match the terms in Part A with their definitions in Part B.

A.

1. basin
2. *estancia*
3. escarpment
4. caudillo
5. landlocked
6. gaucho
7. *selva*
8. inflation
9. llanos
10. tannin

B.

a. steep cliff separating two flat land surfaces, one higher than the other
b. cowhand
c. overall increase in prices across an entire economy
d. military dictator
e. large, grassy plains region of Latin America
f. a country that has no border on a sea or an ocean
g. broad, flat lowland surrounded by higher land
h. substance from tree bark used in turning hides into leather
i. rain forest in Brazil
j. large ranch in Argentina

Reviewing the Main Ideas

Section 1 Brazil

11. **Place** Describe the Amazon River.
12. **Location** Why are Brazil's inland areas sparsely populated?
13. **Government** What are the voting requirements in Brazil?

Section 2 Argentina

14. **Place** What is Argentina's capital?
15. **Place** How is Patagonia different from the pampas?
16. **Culture** Why does Argentina have only a small percentage of Native Americans?

Section 3 Caribbean South America

17. **Economics** Which of Venezuela's resources is its main source of income?
18. **Culture** Where do most of the people of the Guianas live?

Section 4 Uruguay and Paraguay

19. **Culture** What are the major language and religion of Uruguay?
20. **Economics** What are the major economic activities of Paraguay?

Brazil and Its Neighbors

Place Location Activity

On a separate sheet of paper, match the letters on the map with the numbered places listed below.

1. Brazil
2. Amazon River
3. Argentina
4. Rio de Janeiro
5. Paraguay
6. Orinoco River
7. Río de la Plata
8. Venezuela
9. Brasília
10. Suriname

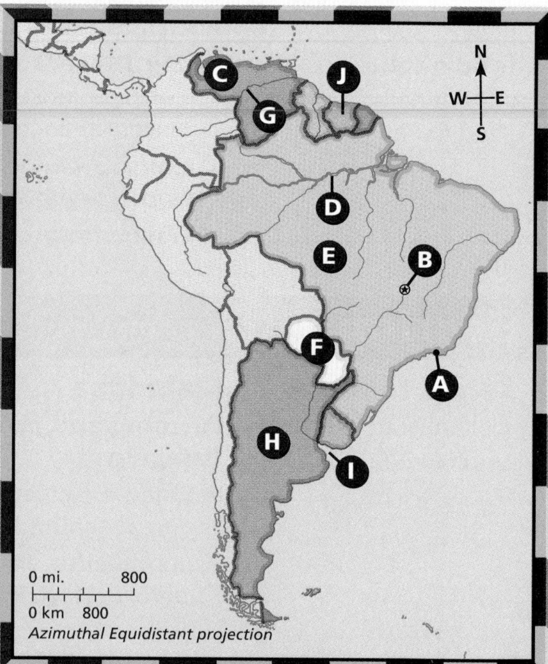

Self-Check Quiz Visit the ***Geography: The World and Its People*** Web site at gwip.glencoe.com and click on **Chapter 8—Self-Check Quizzes** to prepare for the Chapter Test.

 Critical Thinking

21. **Analyzing Information** What facts support the statement "Argentina is one of the most industrialized countries in South America"?
22. **Identifying Points of View** In a chart like the one below, identify arguments for and against the cutting down of the rain forest.

Cutting Down the Rain Forest	
For	Against

 GeoJournal Activity

23. **Writing a Research Report** Research the way coffee is grown, processed, and transported to the market and consumer. Write a report on your findings. Include a map of the areas where coffee is grown, a diagram with information about how it is grown and harvested, and a flowchart that shows how the coffee gets from harvest to consumer.

 Mental Mapping Activity

24. **Focusing on the Region** Draw a simple outline map of South America, then label the following:
    - Caribbean Sea
    - Atlantic Ocean
    - Pacific Ocean
    - Amazon River
    - Venezuela
    - Brazil
    - Argentina
    - Brazilian Highlands
    - Río de la Plata
    - Guiana Highlands

 Technology Skills Activity

25. **Using the Internet** Conduct a search for information about the Amazon rain forest and create an annotated bibliography of five useful Web sites. Your bibliography should contain the Web address, a brief summary of the information found on the site, and whether or not you feel the site is useful.

Standardized Test Practice

Directions: Read the passage below and answer the question that follows.

The Amazon Basin is a gigantic system of rivers and rain forests, covering half of Brazil and extending into neighboring countries. Much of the Amazon is still unexplored, and the rain forest holds many secrets. Some of the animals found here include the jaguar, tapir, spider monkey, sloth, river dolphin, and boa constrictor. Forest birds include toucans, parrots, hummingbirds, and hawks. More than 1,800 species of butterflies and 200 species of mosquitoes give you an idea about the insect population. In addition, the fish—such as piranha, pirarucu, and electric eel—are very unusual. Biologists cannot identify much of the catch found in markets.

1. **Based on this passage, which of the following generalizations is most accurate?**

   F The Amazon rain forest covers about one-third of the South American continent.

   G Native Americans living in the Amazon rain forest are losing their traditional way of life.

   H The Amazon Basin is huge, and its rain forests hold thousands of animal species.

   J The Amazon Basin is located only in Brazil.

Test-Taking Tip: This question asks you to make a generalization about the Amazon Basin. A *generalization* is a broad statement. Look for facts and the main idea *in the passage* to support your answer. Do not rely only on your memory. The main idea can help you eliminate answers that do not fit. Also, look for the statement that is true AND that is covered in the paragraph.

EYE on the Environment

VANISHING Rain Forests

Rain Forest Riches Imagine never tasting chocolate. Think about never eating a banana, chewing gum, or munching cashews. If there were no rain forests, we would have none of these foods. We also would not have many of the drugs used to treat malaria, multiple sclerosis, and leukemia. In fact, rain forest plants provide a fourth of the world's medicines.

Millions of kinds of plants and animals live in rain forests—more than half of all species on Earth. Scientists have studied only a fraction of these species. So no one really knows what new foods, medicines, or animals are there, just waiting to be discovered.

Rain Forest Destruction Yet we may never know. Why? Because a chunk of rain forest the size of two football fields vanishes every second! The forests are being destroyed for many reasons.

- Loggers cut trees and sell the lumber worldwide.
- Ranchers and farmers clear land for cattle and crops.
- Miners level acres of forest to get at valuable minerals.

Settlers clear trees for a home in the rain forest.

People are trying to find ways to use rain forests without destroying them. Changing farming practices and developing different forest industries are possible solutions. However, time is running out. Can we afford to lose rain forests and all their treasures?

Male golden toad

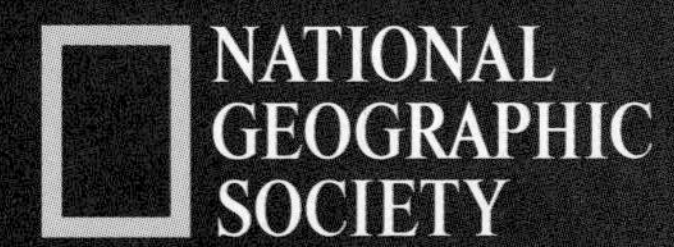

Making a Difference

New species *Callithrix humilis,* a dwarf marmoset

Discovering New Monkeys How would it feel to discover an animal that no one knew existed? Dutch scientist Marc van Roosmalen knows. He recently discovered a new species of monkey (photo, at right) in Brazil.

Van Roosmalen runs an orphanage for abandoned monkeys. One day, a man showed up with a tiny monkey van Roosmalen had never seen before. He spent about a year tracking down a wild population of the monkeys deep in the Amazon rain forest. Of some 250 kinds of monkeys known worldwide, about 80 live in Brazil. At least 7 new species have been discovered since 1990.

Rain Forest Field Trip With help from the Children's Environmental Trust Foundation, students from Millbrook, New York, traveled to Peru's Yarapa River region, deep in the Amazon rain forest. Students studied the forest from platforms built in the canopy, and they soared among the tall trees using ropes. The students met rain forest creatures at night, went bird-watching at dawn, and swam in the Yarapa River—home to crocodiles called caimans.

Back in Millbrook, the students educate others about saving rain forests. They also raise money to help support a Peruvian zoo that protects rain forest animals.

Millbrook student traps insects for study.

What Can You Do?

Write a Note

Write to your government representatives and encourage them to support plans that help save rain forests.

Check Out Your Community

What environmental problems face your community? What can you do to help solve the problems? For example, does your community have problems with water pollution or water shortages? What steps does your community take to make sure you have clean water to drink?

Use the Internet

Learn more about efforts to save rain forests. Check out the Rainforest Action Network at *www.ran.org* or search National Geographic's Web site at *www.nationalgeographic.com*

Chapter 9

The Andean Countries

The World and Its People NATIONAL GEOGRAPHIC

To learn more about the people and places of the Andean countries, view ***The World and Its People*** **Chapter 9** video.

Geography Online

Chapter Overview Visit the ***Geography: The World and Its People*** Web site at gwip.glencoe.com and click on **Chapter 9—Chapter Overviews** to preview information about the Andean countries.

Section 1 Colombia

Guide to Reading

Main Idea

Although it has many resources, Colombia faces political and economic turmoil.

Terms to Know

- cordillera
- llanos
- cash crop
- mestizo
- republic
- campesino

Places to Locate

- Colombia
- Andes
- Magdalena River
- Bogotá
- Cartagena
- Medellín
- Cali

Reading Strategy

Create a chart like the one below and list advantages that Colombia enjoys in the left column. In the right column, list the challenges that it faces.

Colombia	
Advantages	Challenges

NATIONAL GEOGRAPHIC **Exploring Our World**

In a thin vein of black shale, a miner in Colombia spots a glistening green stone. He is not the first Colombian to mine the precious gemstones we call emeralds. The Colombian mine called Muzo has been producing top-quality emeralds for a thousand years. Early Native American rulers would offer these gems—more rare than diamonds—to their gods.

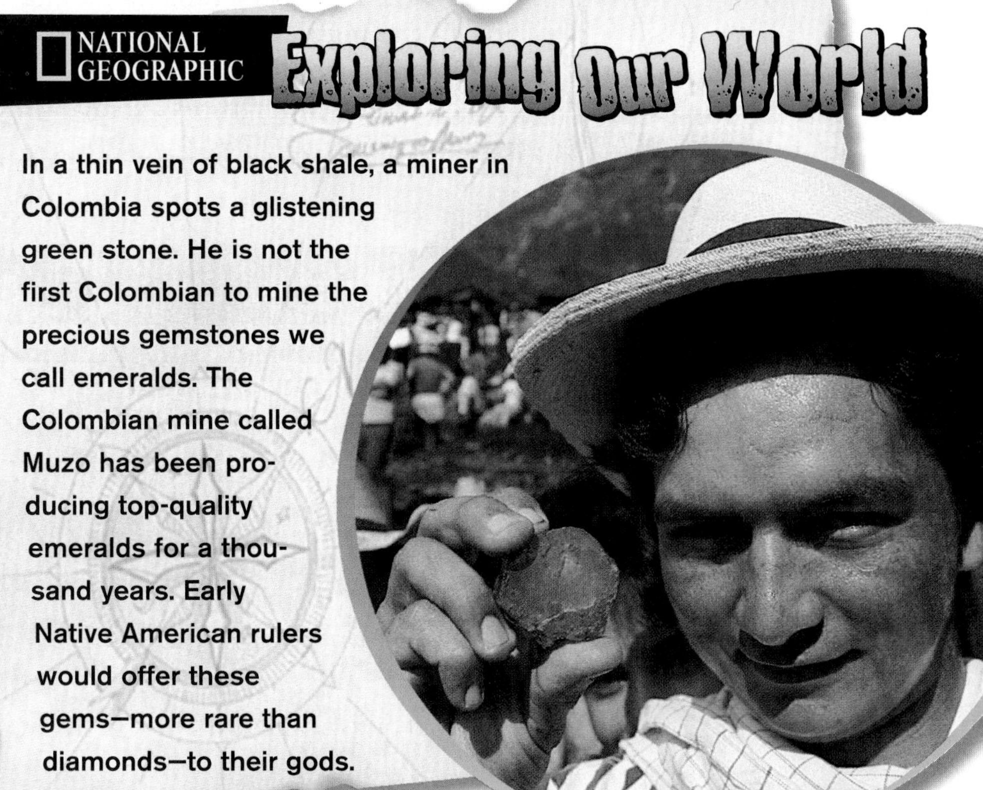

Colombia—named after Christopher Columbus—sits astride the lofty **Andes** mountain ranges at the northwestern edge of South America. These mountains continue south through five other countries—Ecuador, Peru, Bolivia, Chile, and Argentina.

Colombia's Land and Climate

Colombia—almost three times larger than Montana—has coasts on both the Caribbean Sea and the Pacific Ocean. The Andes sweep through the western part of Colombia. Here they become a **cordillera** (KAWR•duhl•YEHR•uh), or a group of mountain ranges that run side by side. Colombia's major river, the **Magdalena River,** flows between the central and eastern Andes to the Caribbean Sea. Nearly 80 percent of Colombia's people live in the valleys and highland plateaus of the Andes. **Bogotá** (BOH•goh•TAH), Colombia's capital and largest city, is located on a high Andean plateau.

Busy ports, such as **Cartagena** (KAHR•tah•HAY•nah), handle Colombia's trade on the Caribbean coast. In the west, thick forests spread over the lowlands along the Pacific coast. Few people live there.

◀ Mount Cotopaxi overlooks Quito, Ecuador

Tropical rain forests spread across the southeastern plain into the Amazon Basin. Only a few Native American groups live in this hot, steamy region. In the northeast you find hot grasslands called the **llanos.** Here, ranchers drive their cattle across the rolling plains.

Colombia lies entirely within the tropics. Temperatures in places are very hot, and heavy rains fall along the coasts and in the interior plains. In the high elevations of the Andes, however, temperatures are very cool for a tropical area. Bogotá lies at 8,355 feet (2,547 m) above sea level. High temperatures average only 67°F (19°C).

Reading Check **Where do most of Colombia's people live?**

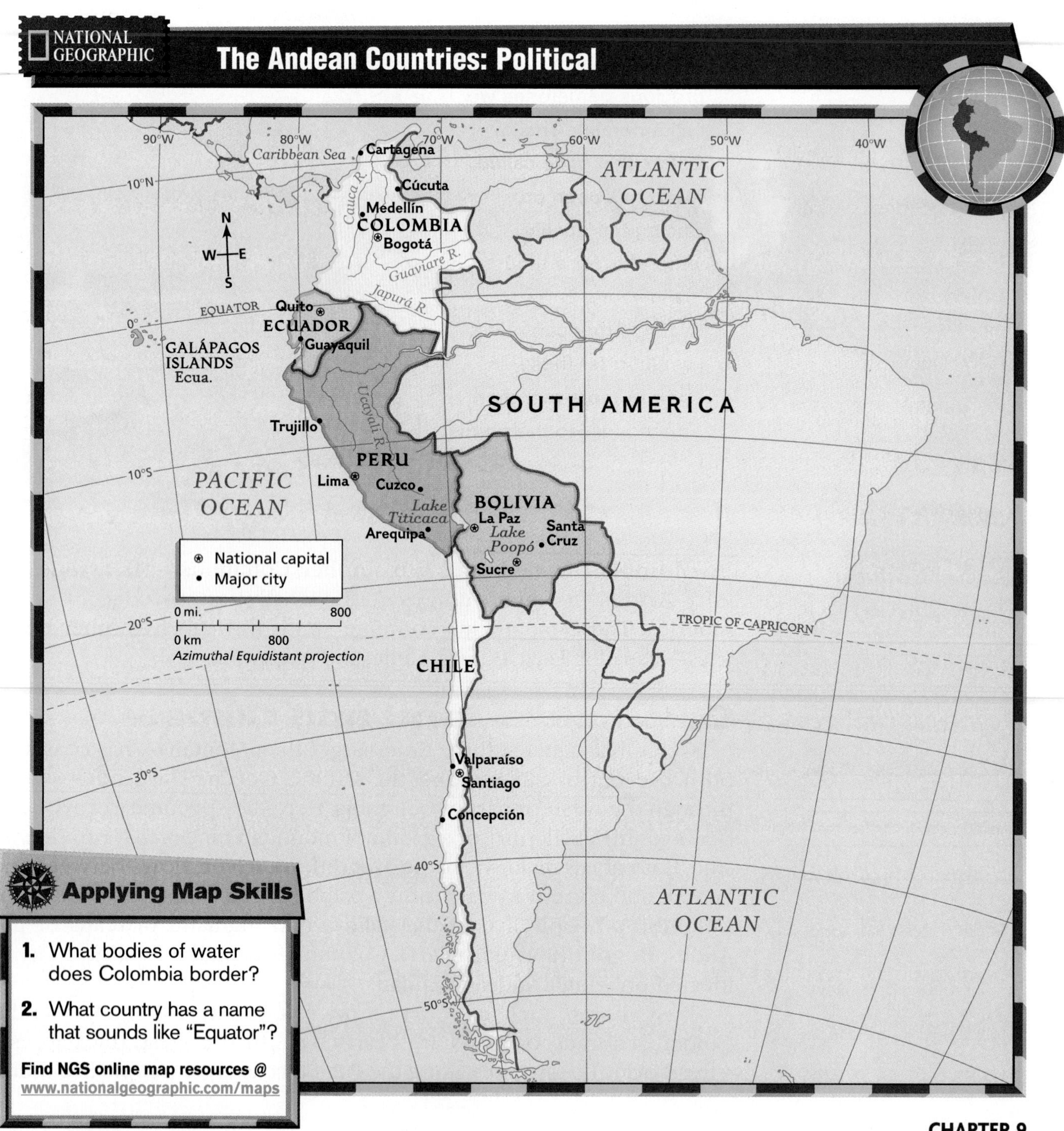

Applying Map Skills

1. What bodies of water does Colombia border?
2. What country has a name that sounds like "Equator"?

Find NGS online map resources @ www.nationalgeographic.com/maps

Colombia's Economy

Colombia has many natural resources. The mountains hold valuable minerals and precious stones, and Colombia has more coal than any other country in South America. Second only to Brazil in its potential hydroelectric power, Colombia also has large petroleum reserves in the lowlands. In addition, the country is a major supplier of gold and the world's number one source of emeralds.

In regard to manufacturing, factories in Colombia produce a variety of products. Workers make clothing, leather goods, food products, paper, chemicals, and iron and steel products.

NATIONAL GEOGRAPHIC

The Andean Countries: Physical

Applying Map Skills

1. What are the inland plains of Colombia called?
2. What physical feature runs through all of these countries?

Find NGS online map resources @ www.nationalgeographic.com/maps

Colombian Coffee

Many historians believe that coffee was "discovered" in Ethiopia, Africa. Eventually Spanish missionaries brought the first coffee plants to Colombia.

Region **What other crops does Colombia export?**

Agriculture The coastal regions and the highlands have good soil for growing crops. In fact, the differences in land elevation allow Colombians to grow a variety of crops. Coffee is the country's major **cash crop**—a product sold for export. Colombian coffee—grown on large plantations and small farms—is known all over the world for its rich flavor.

Did you know that the average American eats about 28 pounds (13 kg) of bananas a year? Colombia exports bananas as well as cacao, sugarcane, rice, and cotton. Huge herds of cattle roam large *estancias* in the llanos. The rain forests of the eastern plains also supply a valuable resource—lumber.

Economic Challenges Despite many natural resources, Colombia faces economic challenges. In the 1980s, drug dealers became a major force in Colombia. The dealers paid farmers more to grow coca leaves—which are used to make the drug cocaine—than the farmers could earn growing coffee. At the same time, the drug dealers used their immense profits to build private armies. They threatened—and even killed—government officials who tried to stop them.

The government of Colombia has stepped up its efforts to break the power of the drug dealers. It has had some success, but drug dealers continue to flourish. In addition, the government has tried to persuade thousands of farmers to switch back to growing other crops.

✓Reading Check **What crop has been a problem in Colombia? Why?**

Colombia's History and People

About 38.6 million people live in Colombia. Nearly all Colombians are **mestizos** (meh•STEE•zohs), meaning they have mixed European and Native American or African backgrounds. Most speak Spanish and follow the Roman Catholic faith.

In 1810 Colombia was one of the first Spanish colonies in the Americas to declare independence. Simón Bolívar, whom you read about in Chapter 8, led this struggle for independence. In 1819 Colombia became part of New Granada, an independent country that included Venezuela, Ecuador, and Panama. Later, these other regions broke away and became separate countries.

Colombia today is a **republic** with an elected president. Political violence has scarred the country's history, though. During the late 1800s alone, Colombia suffered through more than 50 revolts and 8 civil wars. Fighting broke out again in 1948. About 300,000 people died in this conflict, which ended in the late 1960s.

To prevent further turmoil, the two main political parties agreed to govern the country together. Efforts were made to improve the lives of poor farmers by giving them more land. Factories and industrial jobs opened up. Still, a wide gap between rich and poor remained, causing further troubles.

In the 1960s, groups of rebels in the countryside began fighting the government. This latest civil war has lasted more than 35 years and left more than 100,000 people dead. In late 1999, more than 13 million Colombians joined in a massive protest across the country, urging an end to the fighting.

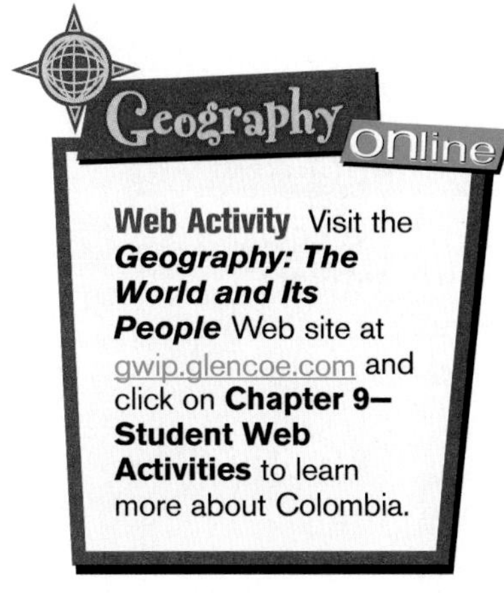

A Diverse Culture Colombia has a rapidly growing urban population. Colombian farmers, or **campesinos,** and their families have journeyed to cities to look for work or to flee the fighting in the countryside. Thirty cities have more than 100,000 people each. The largest ones are Bogotá, **Medellín** (MAY•thay•YEEN), and **Cali** (KAH•lee).

You can see Colombia's Spanish, Native American, and African heritages reflected in its culture. Native American skills in weaving and pottery date back before the arrival of Columbus. Caribbean African rhythms blend with Spanish-influenced music. The Colombian writer Gabriel García Márquez is one of Latin America's most famous authors. His novels blend legends and fantasy with events of everyday life.

✓Reading Check **What is a mestizo?**

Section 1 Assessment

Defining Terms

1. **Define** cordillera, llanos, cash crop, mestizo, republic, campesino.

Recalling Facts

2. **Economics** Colombia is the world's number one source of what mineral?
3. **Movement** What are two reasons campesinos and their families have moved to the cities?
4. **Economics** What are four agricultural products of Colombia?

Critical Thinking

5. **Analyzing Cause and Effect** Why does Bogotá, which is located in the tropics, have an average temperature of only 67°F (19°C)?
6. **Drawing Conclusions** Why do you think it is so difficult for Colombian farmers to stop growing coca?

Graphic Organizer

7. **Organizing Information** Draw a time line like this one, then put the following events and their dates in the correct order on it: Massive protest held by more than 13 million Colombians, Native Americans settle the region, Colombia declares independence from Spain, Colombia suffers 50 revolts and 8 civil wars, Colombia becomes part of New Granada.

Applying Geography Skills

8. **Analyzing Maps** Study the physical map on page 257. What rivers run through Colombia? Which side of the country is mountainous?

Section 2

Peru and Ecuador

Guide to Reading

Main Idea

Peru and Ecuador share similar landscapes, climates, and history.

Terms to Know

- altiplano
- navigable
- foothill
- subsistence farm
- empire

Places to Locate

- Peru
- Ecuador
- Lake Titicaca
- Lima
- Galápagos Islands
- Guayaquil
- Quito

Reading Strategy

Draw two ovals like these. Under each heading list facts about Peru and Ecuador in the outer parts of the ovals. Where the ovals overlap, write facts that apply to both countries.

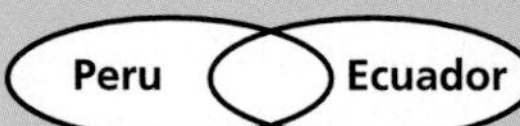

NATIONAL GEOGRAPHIC **Exploring Our World**

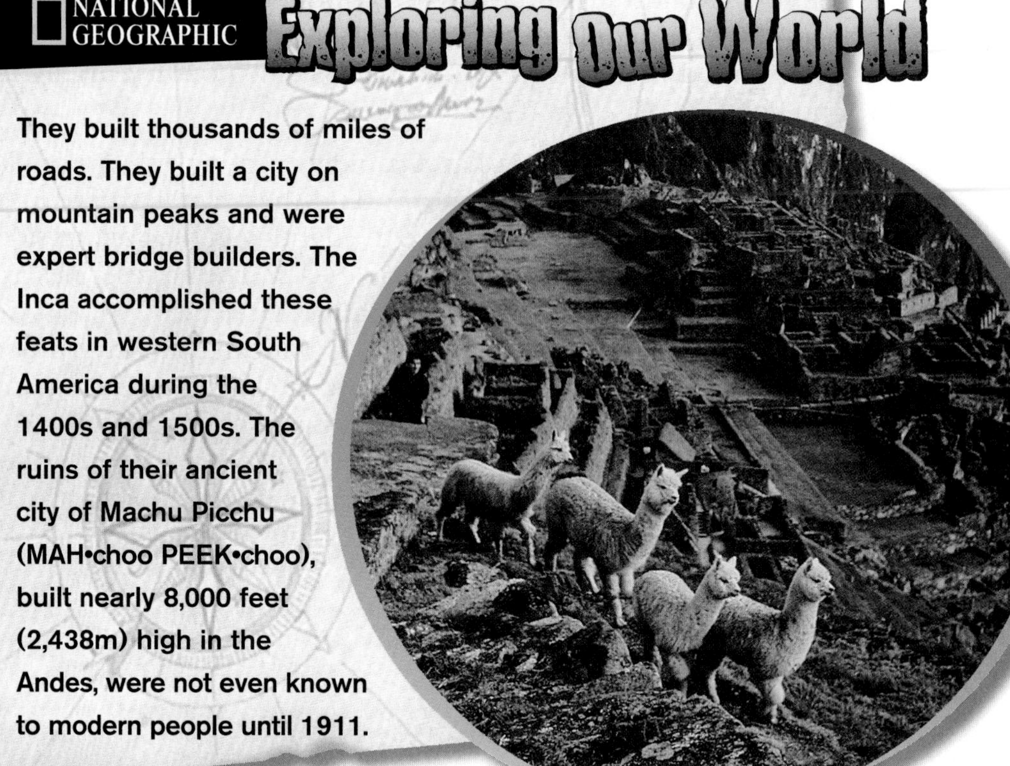

They built thousands of miles of roads. They built a city on mountain peaks and were expert bridge builders. The Inca accomplished these feats in western South America during the 1400s and 1500s. The ruins of their ancient city of Machu Picchu (MAH•choo PEEK•choo), built nearly 8,000 feet (2,438m) high in the Andes, were not even known to modern people until 1911.

Peru and **Ecuador** lie along the Pacific coast of South America west of Brazil and south of Colombia. The Andes form the spine of these countries. *Peru*—a Native American word that means "land of abundance"—is rich in mineral resources.

Peru

Dry deserts, snowcapped mountains, and hot, humid rain forests greet you in Peru. Most of Peru's farms and cities lie on a narrow coastal strip of plains and deserts. The cold Peru Current in the Pacific Ocean keeps temperatures here fairly mild even though the area is very near the Equator. Find the Peru Current on the map on page 58.

The Andes, with their highland valleys and plateaus, sweep through the center of Peru. South-central Peru contains a large highland plateau called the **altiplano.** Here you can see **Lake Titicaca** (TEE•tee•KAH•kah), the highest navigable lake in the world. **Navigable** means that a body of water is wide and deep enough to allow ships to travel in it. The altiplano continues south into Bolivia, which you will learn about in Section 3.

East of the Andes you descend to the foothills and flat plains of the Amazon Basin. **Foothills** are the low hills at the base of a mountain range. Rainfall is plentiful here, and temperatures remain high throughout the year. Thick rain forests cover almost all of the plains area.

Peru's Economy Peru's economy relies on a variety of natural resources. The Andes contain many minerals, including copper, silver, gold, and iron ore. Peru's biggest export is copper from mines in the south. The second-largest export—fish—comes from the Peru Current, the cool Pacific Ocean current that parallels the coast.

About a third of Peru's people farm the land. Some grow sugarcane, cotton, and coffee for export. Like Colombia, Peru grows coca leaves. Most people, however, work on **subsistence farms,** where they grow enough food to meet their family's needs. The chief crops are rice, plantains (a kind of banana), and corn. Do you enjoy eating potatoes? Thank the Native Americans of the Andes. Thousands of years ago, they were the first to grow this food. Potatoes are still Peru's main food crop, and farmers grow hundreds of varieties in different colors and shapes.

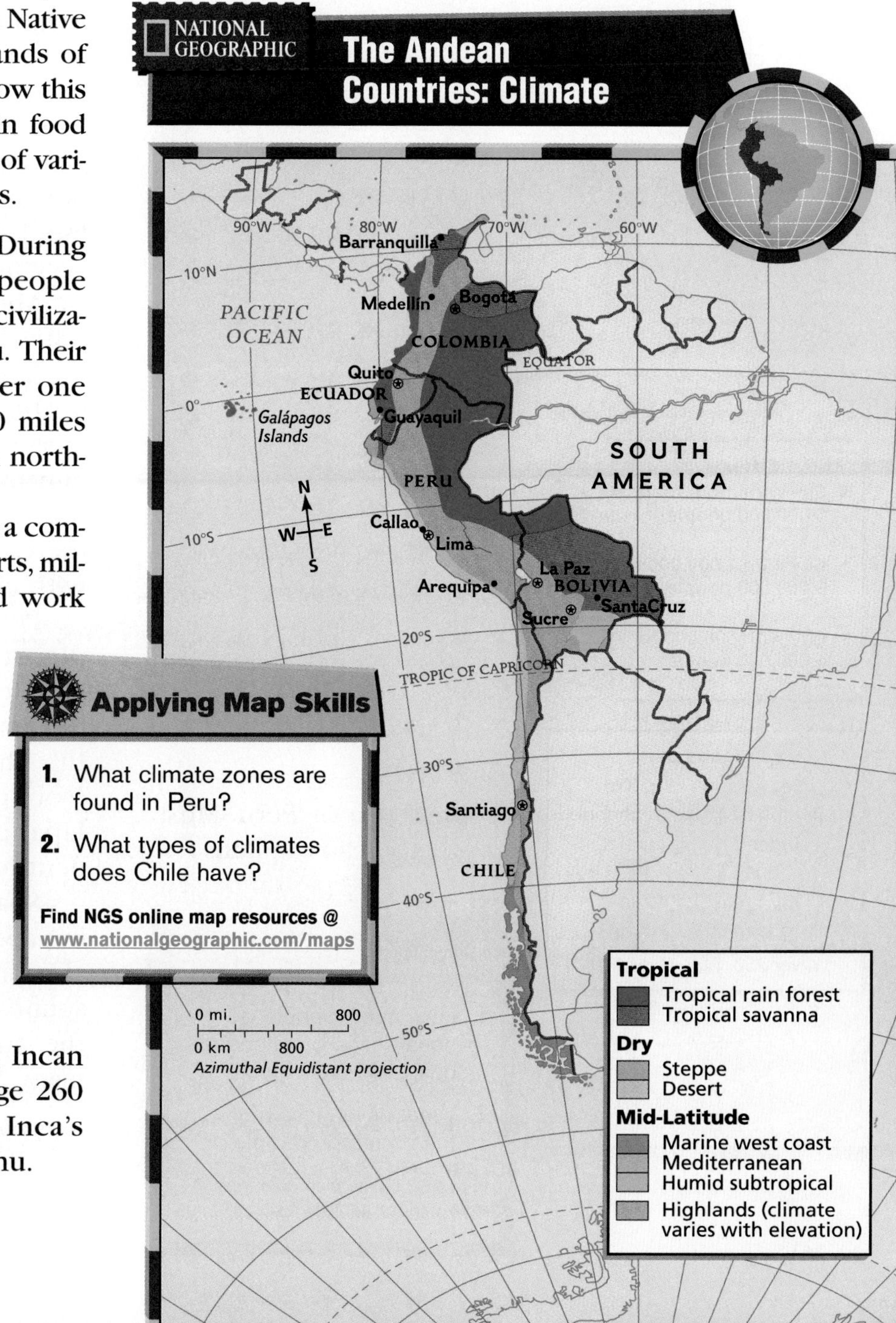

Applying Map Skills

1. What climate zones are found in Peru?
2. What types of climates does Chile have?

Find NGS online map resources @ www.nationalgeographic.com/maps

From Empire to Republic During the 1400s, a Native American people called the Inca had a powerful civilization in the area that is now Peru. Their **empire,** or group of lands under one ruler, stretched more than 2,500 miles (4,023 km) along the Andes from northern Ecuador to central Chile.

The Incan emperor developed a complex system of tax collection, courts, military posts, trade inspections, and work rules. Officials kept records by using quipu, or rope with knotted cords of different lengths and colors. Each knot meant a different item or number. Work crews built irrigation systems, roads, and suspension bridges that linked the regions of the empire to Cuzco, the capital city of the Inca. You can still see the remains of magnificent fortresses and buildings erected centuries ago by skilled Incan builders. The photograph on page 260 shows the ruins of one of the Inca's most famous cities—Machu Picchu.

In the early 1500s, Spaniards arrived in Peru, craving the gold and silver found here. They defeated the Inca and made Peru a Spanish territory. Peru gained its freedom from Spain in the 1820s. After independence, Peru fought wars with neighboring Chile and Ecuador over land.

Peru is now a republic with an elected president. In recent years, the country's economy has grown very rapidly. Many of Peru's people, however, still live in poverty and cannot find steady jobs.

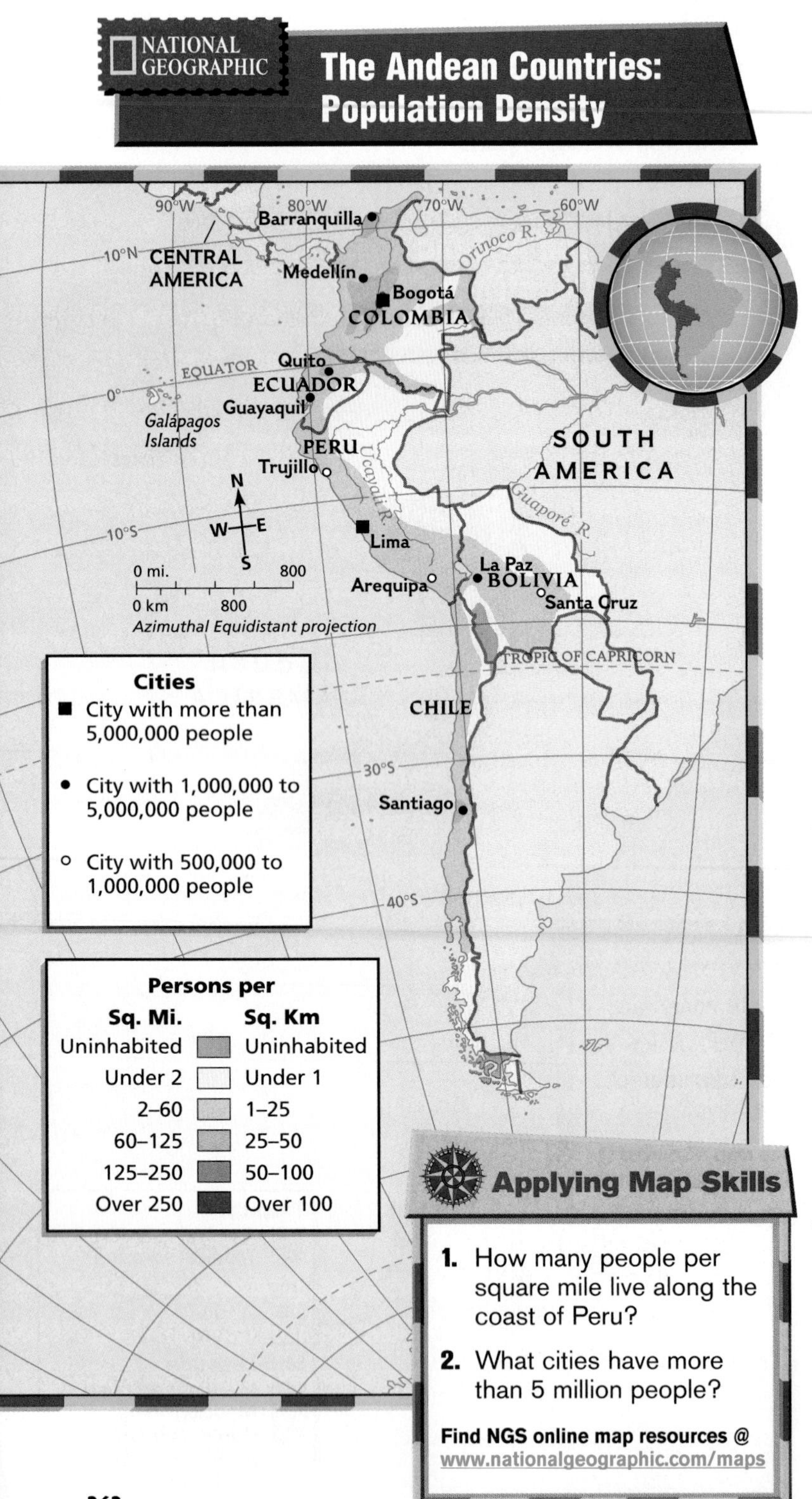

Peru's Culture Peru has 26.6 million people, making it the fourth-most populous country in South America. The people of Peru live mostly in cities or towns in or near the plain along the Pacific coast. **Lima** (LEE•mah), with more than 6 million people, is the capital and largest city. In recent years, many people from the countryside have moved to Lima in search of work. Because of this sudden rise in population, the city has become overcrowded, noisy, and polluted. Many people live in barrios, or very poor neighborhoods.

About half of Peru's people are Native American. In fact, Peru has one of the largest Native American populations in the Western Hemisphere. Many live in the Andean highlands or the eastern rain forests where they follow a traditional way of life. Most of them blend the Catholic faith, Peru's main religion, with beliefs of their ancestors.

Peruvians also include many people of mixed or European ancestry. People of Asian heritage form a small but important part of the population. In the 1990s, Alberto Fujimori (FOO•jee•MAW•ree), a Peruvian of Japanese ancestry, was Peru's president for 10 years.

Spanish is Peru's official language, but about 70 Native American languages also are spoken. You can hear the sounds of Quechua (KEH•chuh•wuh), the ancient language of the Inca, in many Native American villages.

Reading Check **Who built a huge empire centered in Peru?**

Cultural Close-Up

Music

Dating back thousands of years, the panpipe is one of the most common musical instruments from the Andes region. Panpipes are made of bamboo in various sizes. Individual bamboo stalks are carefully cut and lashed together with strips of bamboo and woolen string. The notes often alternate from one set of pipes to another. To play a complete melody, then, the two rows of pipes are often stacked one on top of the other.

Looking Closer Which do you think produces a higher note—a short or long stalk? Explain.

GO TO

World Music: A Cultural Legacy
Hear music of this region on Disc 1, Track 10.

Ecuador

Ecuador is one of the smallest countries in South America. In fact, the entire country is no bigger than the state of Nevada in the United States. Can you guess how it got its name? *Ecuador* is the Spanish word for "Equator," which runs right through Ecuador. Find the country on the map on page 256. Located between Colombia and Peru, Ecuador looks like a grinning face gazing westward across the Pacific Ocean at the **Galápagos Islands.** Owned by Ecuador since 1832, these scattered islands are known for their rich plant and animal life. Turn to page 265 to learn more about the unique Galápagos Islands.

Ecuador's land and climate are similar to Peru's. Swamps and fertile plains stretch along Ecuador's Pacific coast. The Peru Current in the Pacific Ocean keeps coastal temperatures mild. The Andes run through the center of the country. The higher you climb up these mountains, the colder the climate gets. In contrast, hot, humid rain forests cover the lowlands of eastern Ecuador.

Ecuador's Economy Agriculture is Ecuador's most important economic activity. Bananas, cacao, coffee, rice, sugarcane, and other export crops grow in the coastal lowlands. Here you will find **Guayaquil** (GWY•ah•KEEL), Ecuador's most important port city. Farther inland, farms in the Andean highlands grow coffee, beans, corn, potatoes, and wheat. The eastern lowlands yield petroleum, Ecuador's major mineral export.

Andean Dig

Why is this man upside down? He is trying to recover a hard-to-reach frozen mummy in the Andes. This archaeological site lies more than 22,000 feet (6,706 m) above sea level. In 1999 scientists found the frozen bodies of three young Native Americans who were sacrificed 500 years ago to persuade the gods to bring good weather.

Ecuador's People Of Ecuador's 12.4 million people, about 40 percent are mestizos and another 40 percent are Native Americans. African Americans are a small part of the population. Spanish is Ecuador's official language, but many Native Americans speak their traditional languages. Most people are Roman Catholic.

About half of Ecuador's people live along the coast. Guayaquil is the most populous city. The other half of the population live in the valleys and plateaus of the Andes. **Quito** (KEE•toh), Ecuador's capital, lies more than 9,000 feet (2,743 m) above sea level. The city's historic center has Spanish colonial churches and old whitewashed houses with red-tiled roofs built around central courtyards. You will not find flashing neon signs here because the building of modern structures has been strictly controlled since 1978. In that year, the United Nations Educational, Scientific, and Cultural Organization (UNESCO) declared the "old town" section of Quito a protected world cultural heritage site. Quito does have a "new town" section, though, in the north. This area contains modern offices, embassies, and shopping centers. From the heart of Quito, you can see several snowcapped volcanoes looming in the distance. Very few people live in the lowlands of the east.

Why are Ecuador's eastern lowlands important economically?

Assessment

Defining Terms

1. **Define** altiplano, navigable, foothill, subsistence farm, empire.

Recalling Facts

2. **Place** Describe the foothills east of the Andes.
3. **History** Who were the first people to grow potatoes?
4. **Economics** What is Ecuador's major mineral export?

Critical Thinking

5. **Analyzing Information** Why is Peru's name, which means "land of abundance," appropriate? Why is it also inappropriate?
6. **Analyzing Cause and Effect** What effect does the Peru Current have on the coastal areas of Peru and Ecuador?

Graphic Organizer

7. **Organizing Information** Draw two diagrams like this one. Under each heading list facts about each category for Peru and Ecuador.

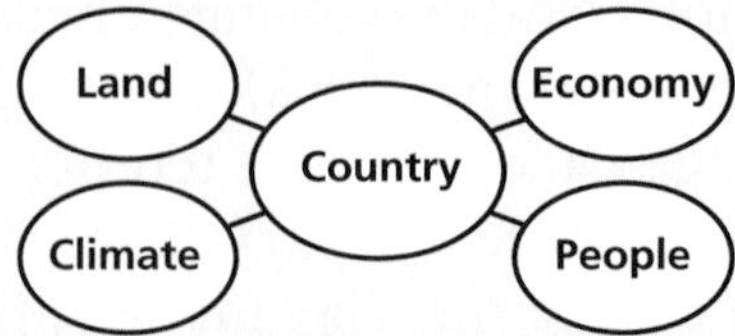

Applying Geography Skills

8. **Analyzing Maps** Turn to the climate map on page 261. In what climate zone is Quito, Ecuador, located? Lima, the capital of Peru, is located in which climate zone?

Making Connections

The Galápagos Islands

The Galápagos Islands are located in the eastern Pacific Ocean about 600 miles (966 km) west of mainland Ecuador. Since 1959 about 95 percent of the islands has been maintained as a national park.

History of Exploration

From the first documented visit to the Galápagos Islands in 1535, people have commented on the islands' unusual wildlife. Sailors, including pirates and whalers, stopped on the islands to collect water and to trap the huge *galápagos*, or tortoises, found on the islands. Sailors valued the tortoises as a source of fresh meat because the giant tortoises could live on ships for months without food or water.

Charles Darwin

The most famous visitor to the Galápagos Islands was Charles Darwin, a scientist from England. He was studying animals all over the world. In 1835 Darwin spent five weeks visiting four of the biggest islands in the Galápagos. He carefully studied the volcanic landscape and the plant and animal life that he saw. He took notes on the differences between animals such as finches, mockingbirds, and iguanas from island to island. Darwin believed that these differences showed how populations of the same species change to fit their environment.

▲ Giant Galápagos tortoise

A Fragile Environment

Today the Galápagos Islands are still prized for their amazing variety of animal and plant life. Many of the species found here exist nowhere else on the earth. For instance, the Marine iguana that lives here is the only seagoing lizard in the world.

Unfortunately, years of contact between the islands and humans have had serious effects. Three of the 14 types of tortoises are extinct, and others are seriously threatened. Populations of goats, pigs, dogs, rats, and some types of plants, brought by visitors, have grown so large that they threaten the survival of native plants and animals. Demand for exotic marine life, including sharks and sea cucumbers, has led to overfishing. The government of Ecuador, along with environmentalists worldwide, is now working to protect the islands.

Making the Connection

1. Why did sailors long ago stop at the islands?
2. What did Darwin observe about the islands?
3. **Drawing Conclusions** Why are environmentalists and the government of Ecuador working to protect the Galápagos Islands?

Section 3

Bolivia and Chile

Guide to Reading

Main Idea

Bolivia and Chile share the Andes, but their economies and people are different.

Terms to Know

- landlocked
- sodium nitrate

Places to Locate

- Bolivia
- Chile
- Sucre
- La Paz
- Atacama Desert
- Santiago
- Cape Horn

Reading Strategy

Create a chart like the one below. In each row, write at least one fact about Bolivia and one about Chile.

	Bolivia	Chile
Land		
Climate		
Economy		
People		

NATIONAL GEOGRAPHIC **Exploring Our World**

The woman hides her face from the gusting wind as she follows her herd of sheep across the plains of Bolivia. She worries about her teenage children, who want to leave their home to find work in the city. The woman is part of a Native American group called the Chipaya, who raise sheep and farm in the dusty altiplano of Bolivia.

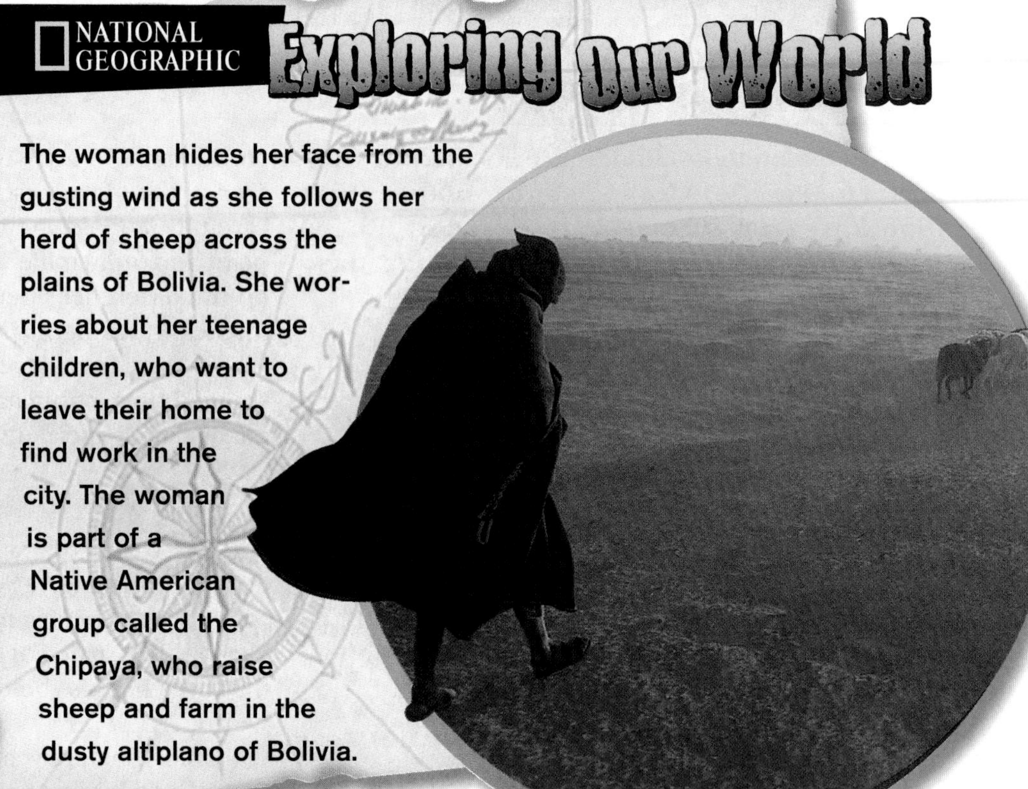

At first glance, **Bolivia** and **Chile** seem very different. Bolivia lacks a seacoast, while Chile has a long coastline on the Pacific Ocean. The Andes, however, affect the climate and cultures of both countries.

Bolivia

Bolivia lies near the center of South America. It is a **landlocked** country, having no land that touches a sea or an ocean. Bolivia also is the highest and most isolated country in Latin America. Why? The Andes dominate Bolivia's landscape. Look at the physical map on page 257. You see that in western Bolivia, the Andes surround a high plateau called the altiplano. Because of the high elevation, the altiplano has a cool climate. Unless you were born in this area, you would find that the cold, thin air at 12,000 feet (3,658 m) makes it difficult to breathe. Few trees grow on the altiplano, and most of the land is too dry to farm. Still, the vast majority of Bolivians live on this high plateau. Those areas that have water have been farmed for many centuries.

Bolivia also has lowland plains and tropical rain forests. A vast lowland plain spreads over northern and eastern Bolivia. Tropical rain forests cover the northern end of the plain. Grasslands and swamps sweep across the rest of the plain. Most of this area has a hot, humid climate. South-central Bolivia, however, has gently sloping hills and broad valleys. The land is more fertile here, and many farms dot this region.

Bolivia's Economy Bolivia is rich in minerals such as tin, silver, and zinc. Miners remove these minerals from high in the Andes. Workers in the eastern lowlands draw out gold, petroleum, and natural gas.

Still, Bolivia is a poor country. About two-thirds of the people live in poverty. Throughout the highlands, many villagers practice subsistence farming. They struggle to grow wheat, potatoes, and barley. At higher elevations, herders raise animals such as alpacas and llamas for wool and for carrying goods. In the south, farmers plant soybeans, a growing export. Timber is another important export.

Bolivian leaders hope that some new projects will expand the economy. Peru and Bolivia are building a highway to the Pacific coast. Bolivia also made an agreement with Brazil that calls for a pipeline to carry natural gas to Brazil. Increased trade from these projects is expected to spark economic growth in Bolivia.

Bolivia's People What is unusual about Bolivia's capital? There is not just one capital city, but two. The official capital is **Sucre** (SOO•kray). The administrative capital and largest city is **La Paz** (lah•PAHZ). Both capital cities are located in the altiplano. La Paz—at 12,000 feet (3,658 m)—is the highest capital city in the world.

Most of Bolivia's more than 8 million people live in the Andean highlands. About half are of Native American ancestry, and another 40 percent are mestizos. In the cities, most people follow modern ways of living. In the country, you may hear traditional sounds—music played with flutelike instruments.

Reading Check **What is the altiplano?**

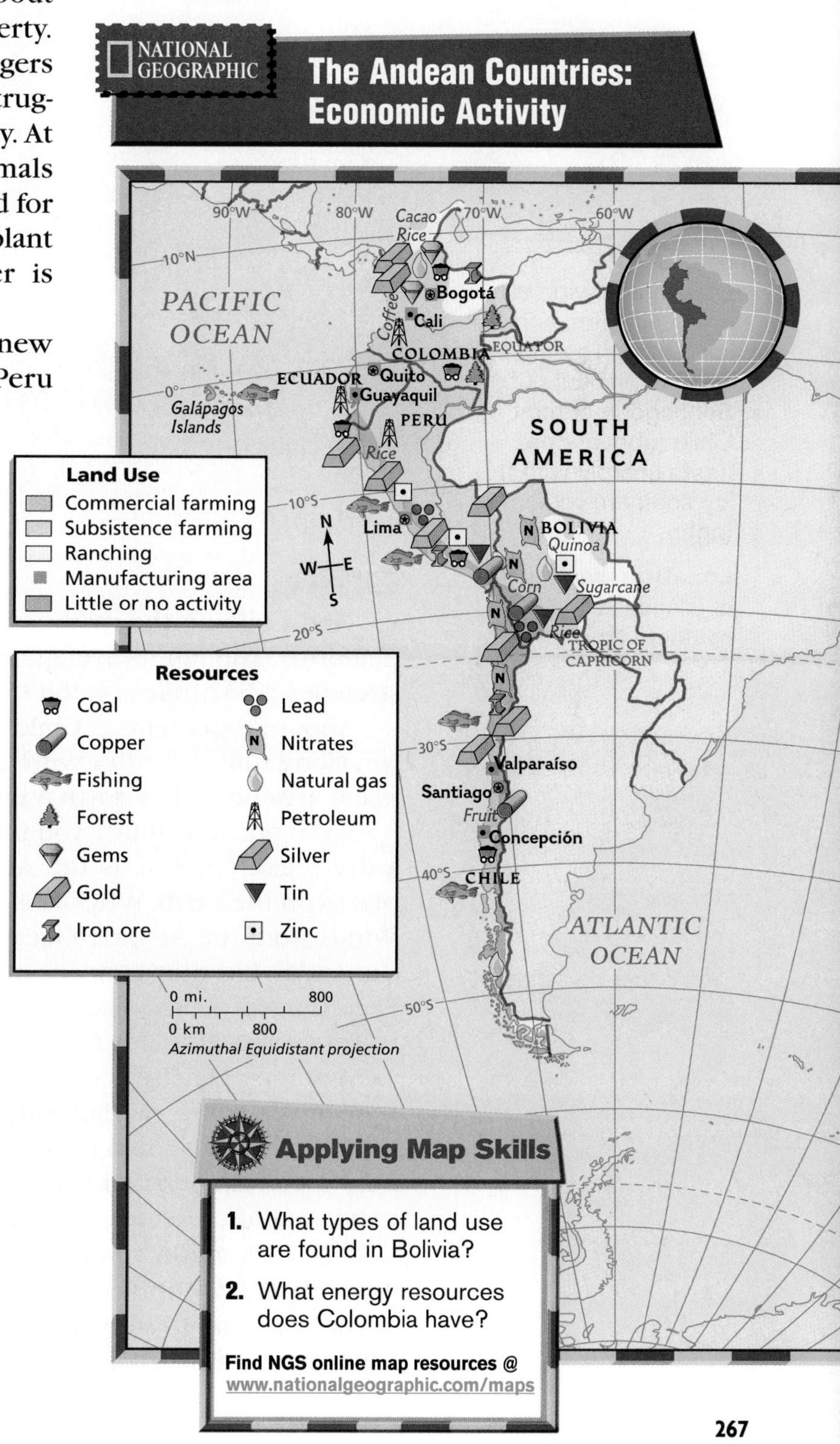

Chile's Contrasts

Chile has a wide variety of climates and landforms. The moderate capital city of Santiago in central Chile (above) contrasts sharply with the icy southern region (right).

Location What group of islands lies at the southern tip of Chile?

Chile

Find Chile on the map on page 256. It is almost twice the size of California. Though its average width is only 110 miles (177 km), Chile stretches 2,652 miles (4,268 km) along the Pacific Ocean.

About 80 percent of Chile's land is mountainous. The high Andes run along Chile's border with Bolivia and Argentina. Except in the altiplano area of Chile's north, very few Chileans live in the Andes.

From north to south, you find different regions in Chile. The first is a dry region known as the **Atacama Desert.** It is one of the driest places on the earth. Why? This area is in the rain shadow of the Andes. Winds from the Atlantic Ocean bring precipitation to regions east of the Andes, but they carry no moisture past them. In addition, the cold Peru Current in the Pacific Ocean does not evaporate as much as a warm current does. As a result, only dry air hits the coast.

A steppe climate zone lies just north of **Santiago,** Chile's capital. It receives some rainfall and has moderate temperatures. Most of Chile's people live in a central region called the Central Valley. With a mild Mediterranean climate, the fertile valleys here have the largest concentration of cities, industries, and farms.

The lake region, also known as "the south," has a marine west coast climate that supports thick forests. Chile's far south is a stormy, windswept region of snowcapped volcanoes, thick forests, and huge glaciers. The Strait of Magellan separates mainland Chile from a group of islands known as Tierra del Fuego (FWAY•goh)—or "Land of Fire." This region is shared by both Chile and Argentina. Cold ocean waters batter the rugged coast around **Cape Horn,** the southernmost point of South America.

Chile's Economy In recent years, Chile has enjoyed high economic growth, and the number of people living below the poverty line has fallen by half. Mining forms the backbone of Chile's economy. The Atacama region is rich in minerals. Chile ranks as the world's leading copper producer. The country also mines and exports gold, silver, iron ore, and sodium nitrate—used as a fertilizer and in explosives.

Agriculture is also a major economic activity. Farmers produce wheat, corn, beans, sugar, and potatoes. The grapes and apples you eat in winter may come from Chile's summer harvest. Many people also raise cattle, sheep, and other livestock.

Chile has factories that process fish and other foods. Other workers make wood products, iron, steel, vehicles, cement, and textiles. Service industries such as banking and tourism also thrive.

Chile's Culture Of the 15 million people in Chile, most are mestizos. A large minority are of European descent, and some Native American groups live in the altiplano and "the south." Nearly all the people speak Spanish, and most are Roman Catholic. Some 80 percent of Chile's population live in urban areas. Chile has been a democratic republic since the end of strict military rule in 1989.

Reading Check **What percentage of Chileans live in urban areas?**

Assessment

Defining Terms

1. **Define** landlocked, sodium nitrate.

Recalling Facts

2. **Economics** What percentage of Bolivia's population lives in poverty?
3. **Geography** What makes La Paz unique?
4. **Economics** Chile is the world's leading producer of what mineral?

Critical Thinking

5. **Analyzing Cause and Effect** Why is the Atacama Desert one of the driest places?
6. **Making Comparisons** What are differences and similarities between the economies of Bolivia and Chile?

Graphic Organizer

7. **Organizing Information** Draw a diagram like this one. Under each arrow list supporting facts for the main idea given.

Main Idea: Bolivia is rich in minerals but is still a poor country.
↑ ↑ ↑ ↑

Applying Geography Skills

8. **Analyzing Maps** Study the physical map on page 257. The southernmost tip of South America is part of what country?

Technology Skill

Using a Database

An electronic **database** is a collection of data—names, facts, and statistics—that is stored in a file on the computer. Databases are useful for organizing large amounts of information. The information in a database can be sorted and presented in different ways.

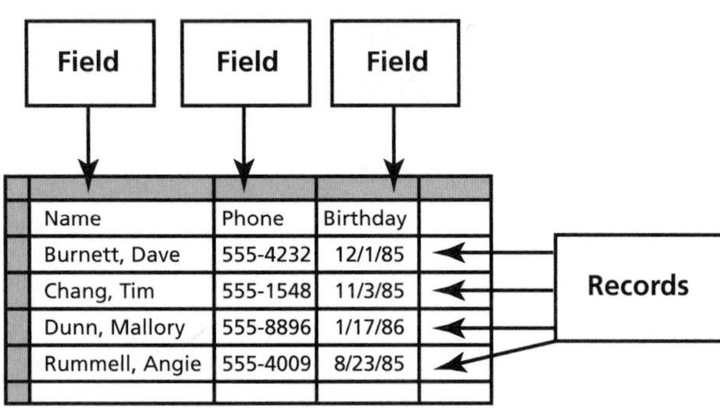

▲ **Using a database can help organize statistics, names and addresses, and even baseball card collections.**

Learning the Skill

The database organizes information in categories called *fields*. For example, a database of your friends might include the fields **Name, Address, Telephone Number,** and **Birthday.** Each person you enter into the database is called a *record*. After entering the records, you might create a list sorted by birthdays or use the records to create address labels. Together, all the records make up the database.

Geographers use databases for many purposes. They often have large amounts of data that they need to analyze. For example, a geographer might want to compare and contrast certain information about the Andean countries. A database would be a good place to sort and compare information about the land, economies, and people of these countries.

Practicing the Skill

Follow these steps to build a database about the Andean countries.

1. Determine what facts you want to include in your database and research to collect that information.
2. Follow the instructions in the database that you are using to set up fields. Then enter each item of data in its assigned field.
3. Determine how you want to organize the facts in the database—chronologically by the date, alphabetically, or by some other category.
4. Follow the instructions in your computer program to sort the information.
5. Check that all the information in your database is correct. If necessary, add, delete, or change information or fields.

Applying the Skill

Research and build a database that organizes information about an Andean country of your choice. Explain why the database is organized the way it is.

Chapter 9

Reading Review

Section 1 Colombia

Terms to Know
cordillera
llanos
cash crop
mestizo
republic
campesino

Main Idea
Although it has many resources, Colombia faces political and economic turmoil.

✓ Place Colombia, in the northwestern corner of South America, has central highlands, two coastal lowlands, and an interior plain with few people.

✓ Economics Colombia is rich in coal, hydroelectric power, gold, and emeralds.

✓ Government The government of Colombia is struggling to combat the power of drug dealers who make huge fortunes from selling cocaine, which comes from the coca plant.

✓ History Civil war has led many people to leave the countryside for Colombia's cities.

Section 2 Peru and Ecuador

Terms to Know
altiplano
navigable
foothill
subsistence farm
empire

Main Idea
Peru and Ecuador share similar landscapes, climates, and history.

✓ Place Peru and Ecuador have narrow coastal plains with mild temperatures; the high Andes in the center; and hot, rainy lowlands in the interior.

✓ Economics Peru's main exports are copper and fish. Many people farm. Ecuador's economy is focused on agriculture.

✓ Culture Most people in Peru and Ecuador are Native Americans or mestizos.

▲ Dancers in Peru

Section 3 Bolivia and Chile

Terms to Know
landlocked
sodium nitrate

Main Idea
Bolivia and Chile share the Andes, but their economies and people are different.

✓ Human/Environment Interaction Bolivia is a poor country consisting mainly of the towering Andes and a high plateau that is difficult to farm.

✓ Region In addition to its mountains, Chile has five different regions. Most people live in the fertile Central Valley.

✓ Economics Chile has a diverse economy that includes mining—especially copper and sodium nitrate—farming, and manufacturing.

Chapter 9 Assessment and Activities

Using Key Terms

Match the terms in Part A with their definitions in Part B.

A.

1. cordillera
2. campesino
3. cash crop
4. altiplano
5. navigable
6. foothill
7. empire
8. sodium nitrate
9. landlocked
10. mestizo

B.

a. person of mixed Native American and European ancestry
b. crop grown to be sold, often for export
c. mineral used in making fertilizer
d. group of lands under one ruler
e. group of mountain ranges that run side by side
f. a body of water wide and deep enough for ships to pass through
g. a country that has no land on a sea or an ocean
h. low hills at the base of a mountain range
i. farmer in Colombia
j. high plateau region of the Andes

Reviewing the Main Ideas

Section 1 Colombia

11. **Location** Colombia borders which two major bodies of water?
12. **Place** List four of Colombia's natural resources.
13. **Culture** What is the heritage of most of Colombia's people?

Section 2 Peru and Ecuador

14. **Place** What is the highest navigable lake in the world?
15. **History** What ancient Native American civilization of the Andean countries lived in Peru?
16. **Place** Who owns the Galápagos Islands?

Section 3 Bolivia and Chile

17. **Location** Why is it difficult for visitors to breathe when visiting the altiplano?
18. **Economics** What types of projects does Bolivia have planned that it hopes will expand its economy?
19. **Government** What type of government does Chile have?

The Andean Countries

Place Location Activity

On a separate sheet of paper, match the letters on the map with the numbered places listed below.

1. Colombia
2. Peru
3. Chile
4. Andes
5. Lake Titicaca
6. Quito
7. Bogotá
8. Strait of Magellan
9. Lima
10. Bolivia

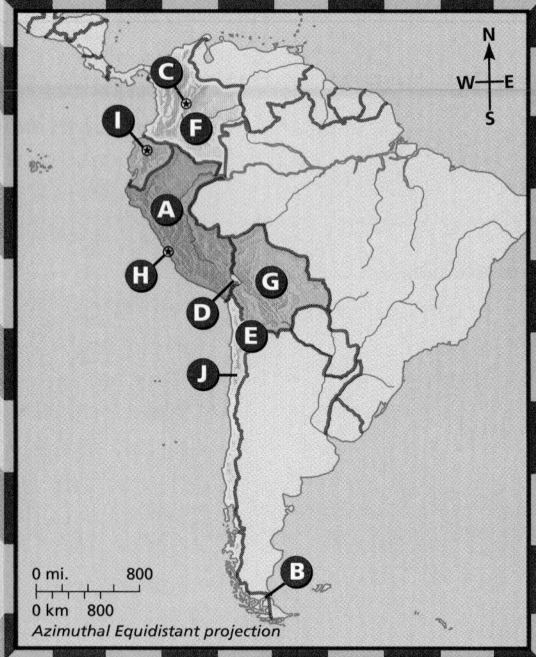

Self-Check Quiz Visit the ***Geography: The World and Its People*** Web site at gwip.glencoe.com and click on **Chapter 9—Self-Check Quizzes** to prepare for the Chapter Test.

Critical Thinking

20. **Making Inferences** Why are Native Americans who live in the Andean highlands more likely to follow a traditional way of life than those who live in the cities?
21. **Analyzing Cause and Effect** On a diagram like the one below, list factors that have led to political violence during Colombia's history.

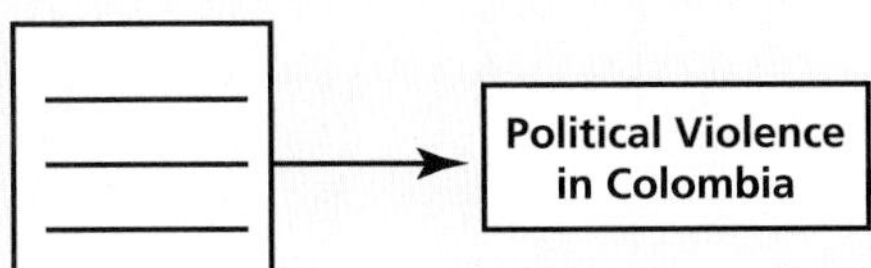

GeoJournal Activity

22. **Writing About Cities** Research one of the major cities of the Andean countries. Prepare a report that includes a map, fact bank, pictures, and a T-shirt design that shows a famous landmark of the city.

Mental Mapping Activity

23. **Focusing on the Region** Draw a simple outline map of South America, then label the following:

- Pacific Ocean
- Andes
- Atacama Desert
- Strait of Magellan
- Chile
- Peru
- Colombia
- Galápagos Islands
- Lake Titicaca
- Ecuador

Technology Skills Activity

24. **Building a Database** Create a fact sheet about the Andean countries by building a database. Create fields for such categories as physical features, natural resources, capital cities, population, and type of government. When you have entered data for each field, print your fact sheet.

Standardized Test Practice

Directions: Read the paragraphs below, then answer the question that follows.

Simón Bolívar, an aristocrat from Venezuela, led many of South America's lands to independence. He believed in equality and saw liberty as "the only object worth a man's life." Called "the Liberator," Bolívar devoted his life to freedom for Latin Americans.

Bolívar was the son of a rich family in New Granada, or what is today Colombia, Venezuela, Panama, and Ecuador. In 1805 he went to Europe. There, he learned about the French Revolution and its ideas of democracy. He returned home, vowing to free his people from Spanish rule. In 1810 Bolívar started a revolt against the Spaniards in Venezuela. Spanish officials soon crushed the movement, but Bolívar escaped and trained an army. During the next 20 years, Bolívar and his forces won freedom for the present-day countries of Venezuela, Colombia, Panama, Bolivia, and Ecuador.

1. What is the main idea of the paragraphs above?

A Bolívar was the son of a rich family.
B Bolívar traveled to Europe and learned about democracy.
C Simón Bolívar was called "the Liberator."
D Bolívar devoted his life to freedom for Latin Americans.

Test-Taking Tip: This question asks you to find the main idea, or to make a generalization. Most of the answer choices provide specific details, not a general idea. Which of the answers is more of a general statement?

Unit 4

Woman in Hungary creating folk art

Ancient ruins in Delphi, Greece

Europe

You have learned about the Americas. Now let us spin the globe and travel to the Eastern Hemisphere. The first region you will learn about is Europe—relatively small as continents go, but rich in history and culture. Like the United States, most nations in Europe are industrialized and have high standards of living. Unlike the United States, however, the people of Europe do not share a common language or government.

▲ The Louvre museum, Paris, France

NGS ONLINE
www.nationalgeographic.com/education

Focus on:

Europe

BOTH A CONTINENT and a region, Europe has a wide range of cultures—and a history of conflict among its people. Recently, connections in trade, communication, and transportation have helped to create greater unity among European nations.

The Land

Jutting westward from Asia, Europe is a great peninsula that breaks into smaller peninsulas and is bordered by several large islands. Europe's long, jagged coastline is washed by many bodies of water, including the Arctic and Atlantic Oceans, and the North, Baltic, and Mediterranean Seas. Deep bays and well-protected inlets shelter fine harbors.

Mountains sweep across much of the continent. Those in the British Isles and large parts of northern Europe are low and rounded. Higher and more rugged are the Pyrenees, between France and Spain, and the Carpathians, in eastern Europe. The snow-capped Alps are Europe's highest mountains, towering over the central and southern parts of the continent.

Curving around these mountain ranges are broad, fertile plains. In the north, the North European Plain stretches from the British Isles to the Russian border. Cities, towns, and farms dot the gently rolling landscape.

For centuries, Europe's rivers have provided links between coastal ports and inland population centers. In western Europe, the Rhine flows northwest from the Alps until it empties into the North Sea. The Danube winds through eastern Europe, bound for the Black Sea.

The Climate

Despite its northern location, Europe enjoys a relatively mild climate. The secret lies in the region's closeness to the Atlantic. An ocean current known as the North Atlantic Current brings warm waters and winds to bathe Europe's western shores. As a result, northwestern Europe enjoys mild temperatures all year, along with plentiful rainfall. Farther south, countries along the Mediterranean Sea have hot, dry summers and mild winters. The region's northernmost countries have longer, colder winters than their southern neighbors. Winters are also cold in Europe's interior, which lies far from the influence of the Atlantic.

The vegetation varies from one climate zone to another. In Scandinavia's far north, you would find mostly mosses and small shrubs blanketing a tundra-like landscape. In northwestern and eastern Europe, grasslands and forests cover the rolling land. Farther south, drought-resistant shrubs and small trees cover rugged hills.

Village at the foot of the Alps, Switzerland ▼

◀ Fisherman mending nets in Malta

The Economy

An abundance of key natural resources, waterways, and ports has helped make Europe a global economic power. Agriculture, manufacturing, and service industries dominate the region's economies.

Some of the most productive farmland in the world can be found on the European continent. From the fertile black soil, farmers gather bountiful harvests of grains, fruits, and vegetables. Cattle and sheep graze through lush European pastures.

Vast reserves of oil and natural gas lie offshore. Rich deposits of iron ore, coal, and other minerals have provided the raw materials for heavy industry and manufacturing. Europe was the birthplace of the Industrial Revolution, which transformed the region from an agricultural society into an industrial one. Today, countries such as France, Germany, Italy, Poland, and the United Kingdom rank among the world's top manufacturing centers.

The People

After Asia, Europe is the most densely populated continent on the earth. In some European countries, such as Sweden, most people belong to the same ethnic group. The populations of other countries, however, are made up of several ethnic groups. Some ethnic groups live together peacefully. Other groups often face tension and conflict.

Europeans enjoy a rich cultural heritage that stretches back thousands of years. Walk through the heart of any large European city and you might see ancient Roman ruins, Gothic cathedrals built in the Middle Ages, and sculptures created by Renaissance masters.

Throughout their long history, Europeans have explored and settled other lands. They have spread their culture to every part of the globe. Competition among European nations in the past century led to two world wars and a bitter division into Communist and non-Communist areas. Setting aside their differences, many European nations have recently joined the European Union. They are moving into the new century as a united economic force.

Exploring the Region

1. **What bodies of water border Europe?**
2. **Why is Europe's climate relatively mild?**
3. **What has helped make Europe a global economic power?**
4. **How did European culture spread to other parts of the world?**

◀ **Cargo lining the docks of Rotterdam, a port city in the Netherlands**

UNIT 4

Children by road signs in Ireland ▼

Europe

Physical

20°W
10°W
0°
10°E
20°E
30°E
60°N
50°N
40°N

▲ Mountain peak

0 mi. 500
0 km 500
Lambert Azimuthal Equal-Area projection

ARCTIC CIRCLE
MERIDIAN OF GREENWICH (LONDON)
ICELAND
Faroe Is.
Shetland Is.
Orkney Is.
Norwegian Sea
NORWAY
SCANDINAVIA
SWEDEN
FINLAND
RUSSIA
ESTONIA
LATVIA
LITHUANIA
RUSSIA
BELARUS
ATLANTIC OCEAN
UNITED KINGDOM
IRELAND
British Isles
Thames R.
North Sea
Jutland
DENMARK
Baltic Sea
NORTH EUROPEAN PLAIN
Elbe R.
NETH.
GERMANY
POLAND
Oder R.
Vistula R.
BELG.
LUX.
Rhine R.
Seine R.
Loire R.
CZECH REP.
Carpathian Mountains
SLOVAKIA
UKRAINE
Dnieper R.
MOLDOVA
FRANCE
LIECH.
AUSTRIA
SWITZ.
ALPS
Hungarian Plain
HUNGARY
Bay of Biscay
Mt. Blanc 15,771 ft. (4,807 m)
Matterhorn 14,690 ft. (4,478 m)
SLOV.
CROATIA
ROMANIA
ANDORRA
Pyrenees
Ebro R.
SAN MARINO
BOSN. & HERZG.
YUG.
Danube R.
Black Sea
PORTUGAL
Douro R.
SPAIN
Tagus R.
IBERIAN PENINSULA
MONACO
Corsica
Apennines
Adriatic Sea
Balkan Peninsula
BULGARIA
ITALY
MACED.
Sardinia
ALBANIA
Strait of Gibraltar
Mediterranean Sea
GREECE
Aegean Sea
Sicily
MALTA
Crete
CYPRUS

26,247 ft. 8,000 m
0 mi. 500
0 km 500
19,685 ft. 6,000 m
PYRENEES
ALPS
13,123 ft. 4,000 m
6,562 ft. 2,000 m
LISBON
Sea level
WARSAW

UNIT 4

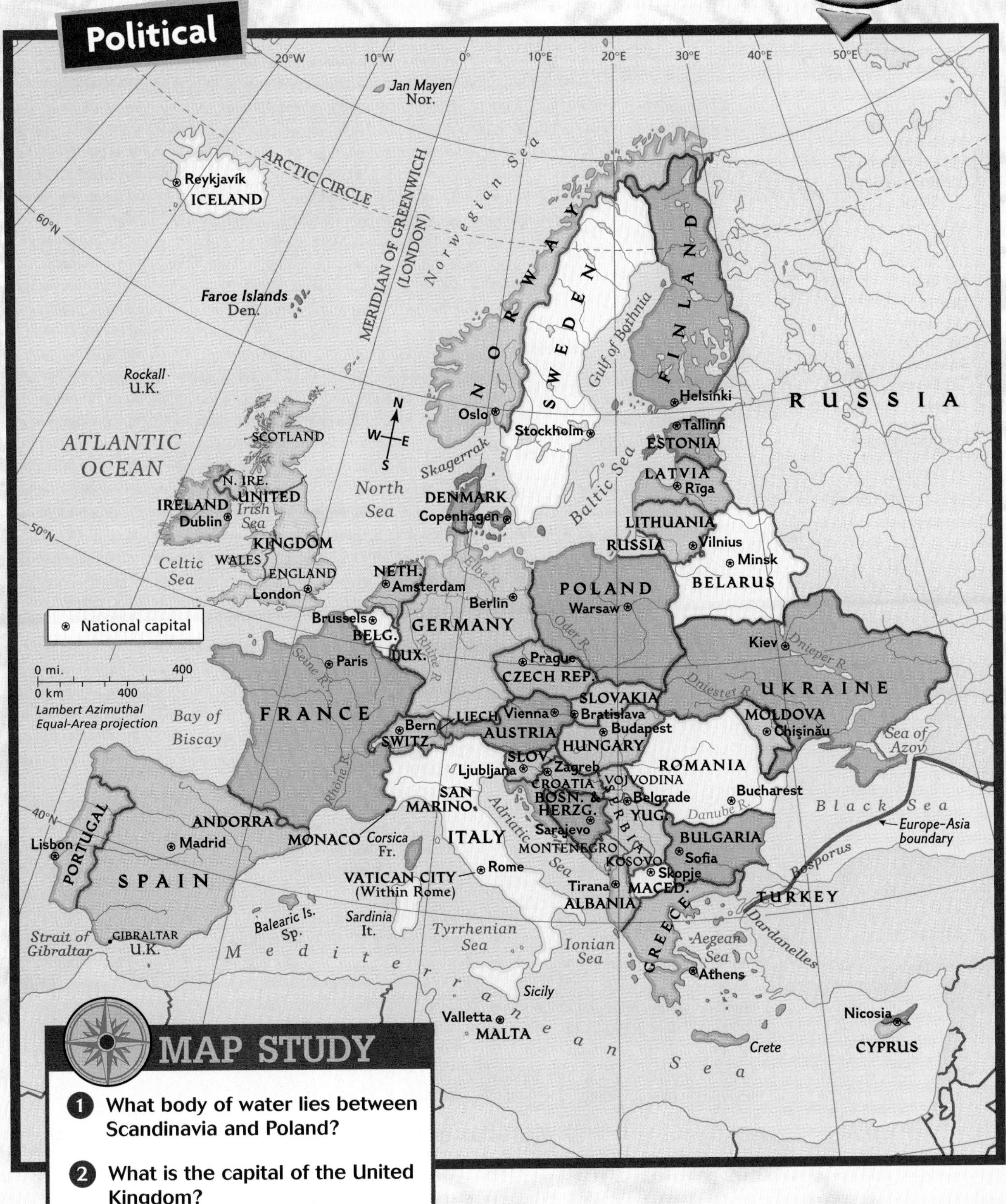

MAP STUDY

1. What body of water lies between Scandinavia and Poland?
2. What is the capital of the United Kingdom?

REGIONAL ATLAS

Europe

Languages

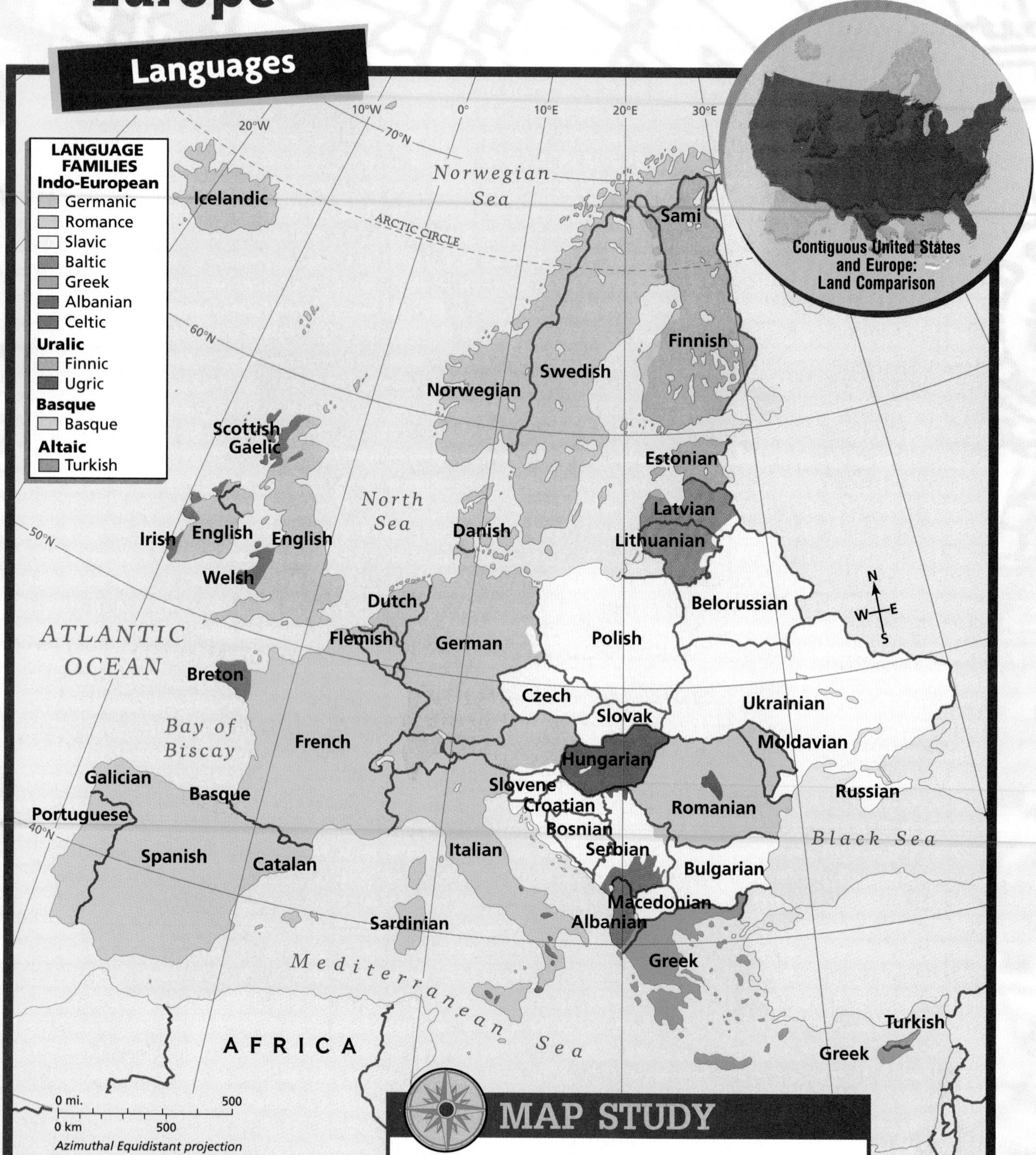

LANGUAGE FAMILIES

Indo-European
- Germanic
- Romance
- Slavic
- Baltic
- Greek
- Albanian
- Celtic

Uralic
- Finnic
- Ugric

Basque
- Basque

Altaic
- Turkish

10°W 0° 10°E 20°E 30°E 20°W 70°N 60°N 50°N 40°N

ARCTIC CIRCLE

Norwegian Sea
North Sea
ATLANTIC OCEAN
Bay of Biscay
Mediterranean Sea
Black Sea
AFRICA

Icelandic
Sami
Finnish
Swedish
Norwegian
Scottish Gaelic
Estonian
Latvian
Lithuanian
Irish
English
English
Danish
Welsh
Dutch
Belorussian
Flemish
German
Polish
Breton
Czech
Slovak
Ukrainian
French
Moldavian
Hungarian
Galician
Slovene
Basque
Russian
Portuguese
Croatian
Romanian
Bosnian
Serbian
Spanish
Catalan
Italian
Bulgarian
Macedonian
Sardinian
Albanian
Greek
Turkish
Greek

N E S W

Contiguous United States and Europe: Land Comparison

0 mi. 500
0 km 500
Azimuthal Equidistant projection

MAP STUDY

1. What language family is found in the most northern part of Europe?
2. What are three Romance languages?

Geo Extremes

① HIGHEST POINT
Mont Blanc (France and Italy)
15,771 ft. (4,807 m) high

② LOWEST POINT
Nieuwerkerk aan den IJssel (Netherlands)
22 ft. (7 m) below sea level

③ LONGEST RIVER
Danube (central Europe)
1,776 mi. (2,858 km) long

④ LARGEST LAKE
Lake Vänern (Sweden)
2,156 sq. mi. (5,584 sq. km)

⑤ HIGHEST WATERFALL
Mardalsfossen, Southern (Norway)
2,149 ft. (655 m) high

⑥ LARGEST ISLAND
Great Britain
84,210 sq. mi.
(218,103 sq. km)

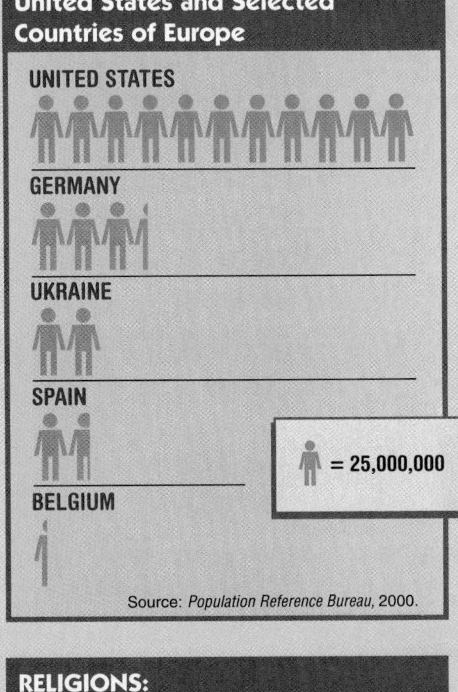

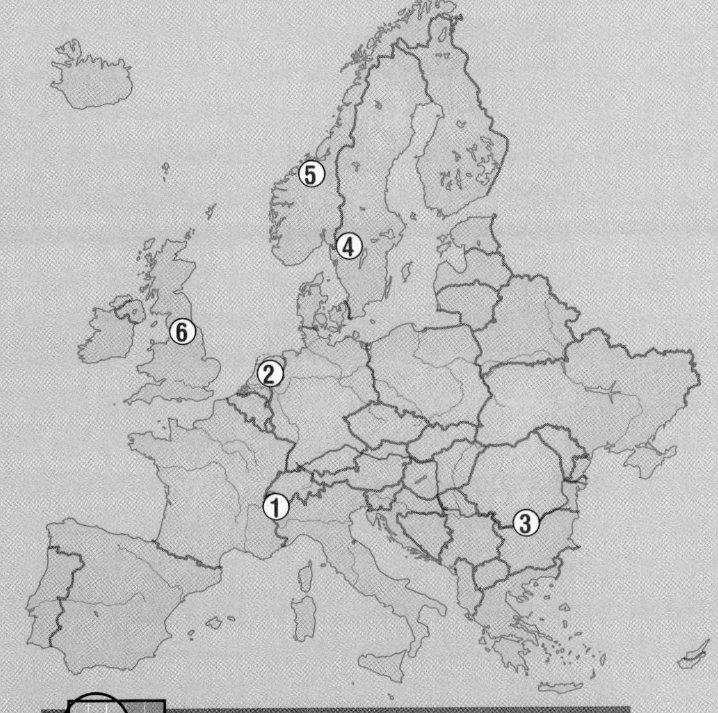

RELIGIONS: Selected Countries of Europe

BOSNIA AND HERZEGOVINA: 40% | 31% | 15% | 4% | 10%

GERMANY: 38% | 34% | 1.7% | 26.3%

MOLDOVA: 98.5% | 1.5%

SPAIN: 99% | 1%

UNITED KINGDOM: 72% | 23% | 2.5% | 2.5%

■ Eastern Orthodox □ Jewish □ Protestant
■ Roman Catholic □ Muslim ■ Other

Source: *CIA World Factbook*, 2000.

GRAPHIC STUDY

1. What two countries share the highest point in Europe?
2. Roughly what is the population of Germany? What percentage of the population is Protestant?

Country Profiles

ALBANIA

POPULATION:
3,460,000
312 per sq. mi.
120 per sq. km

LANGUAGE:
Albanian

MAJOR EXPORT:
Asphalt

MAJOR IMPORT:
Machinery

CAPITAL:
Tirana

LANDMASS:
11,100 sq. mi.
28,748 sq. km

ANDORRA

POPULATION:
66,000
377 per sq. mi.
146 per sq. km

LANGUAGES:
Catalan, French, Spanish

MAJOR EXPORT:
Electricity

MAJOR IMPORT:
Manufactured Goods

CAPITAL:
Andorra la Vella

LANDMASS:
175 sq. mi.
453 sq. km

AUSTRIA

POPULATION:
8,087,000
250 per sq. mi.
96 per sq. km

LANGUAGE:
German

MAJOR EXPORT:
Machinery

MAJOR IMPORT:
Petroleum

CAPITAL:
Vienna

LANDMASS:
32,377 sq. mi.
83,856 sq. km

BELARUS

POPULATION:
10,167,000
127 per sq. mi.
49 per sq. km

LANGUAGES:
Belarussian, Russian

MAJOR EXPORT:
Machinery

MAJOR IMPORT:
Fuels

CAPITAL:
Minsk

LANDMASS:
80,154 sq. mi.
207,598 sq. km

BELGIUM

POPULATION:
10,225,000
868 per sq. mi.
335 per sq. km

LANGUAGES:
Flemish, French

MAJOR EXPORTS:
Iron and Steel

MAJOR IMPORT:
Fuels

CAPITAL:
Brussels

LANDMASS:
11,783 sq. mi.
30,518 sq. km

BOSNIA and HERZEGOVINA

POPULATION:
3,839,000
194 per sq. mi.
75 per sq. km

LANGUAGE:
Serbo-Croatian

MAJOR EXPORT:
N/A

MAJOR IMPORT:
N/A

CAPITAL:
Sarajevo

LANDMASS:
19,741 sq. mi.
51,129 sq. km

BULGARIA

POPULATION:
8,188,000
191 per sq. mi.
74 per sq. km

LANGUAGE:
Bulgarian

MAJOR EXPORT:
Machinery

MAJOR IMPORT:
Fuels

CAPITAL:
Sofia

LANDMASS:
42,823 sq. mi.
110,912 sq. km

CROATIA

POPULATION:
4,600,000
211 per sq. mi.
81 per sq. km

LANGUAGE:
Serbo-Croatian

MAJOR EXPORT:
Transport Equipment

MAJOR IMPORT:
Machinery

CAPITAL:
Zagreb

LANDMASS:
21,829 sq. mi.
56,538 sq. km

CYPRUS

POPULATION:
875,000
384 per sq. mi.
148 per sq. km

LANGUAGES:
Greek, Turkish

MAJOR EXPORT:
Citrus Fruits

MAJOR IMPORT:
Manufactured Goods

CAPITAL:
Nicosia

LANDMASS:
2,277 sq. mi.
5,897 sq. km

CZECH REPUBLIC

POPULATION:
10,284,000
338 per sq. mi.
130 per sq. km

LANGUAGES:
Czech, Slovak

MAJOR EXPORT:
Machinery

MAJOR IMPORT:
Crude Oil

CAPITAL:
Prague

LANDMASS:
30,450 sq. mi.
78,864 sq. km

DENMARK

POPULATION:
5,325,000
320 per sq. mi.
124 per sq. km

LANGUAGE:
Danish

MAJOR EXPORT:
Machinery

MAJOR IMPORT:
Machinery

CAPITAL:
Copenhagen

LANDMASS:
16,638 sq. mi.
43,092 sq. km

ESTONIA

POPULATION:
1,441,000
83 per sq. mi.
32 per sq. km

LANGUAGE:
Estonian

MAJOR EXPORT:
Textiles

MAJOR IMPORT:
Machinery

CAPITAL:
Tallinn

LANDMASS:
17,413 sq. mi.
45,099 sq. km

Countries and flags not drawn to scale

UNIT 4

FINLAND

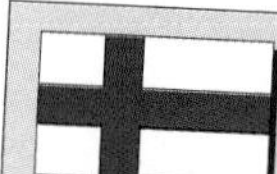

Helsinki

POPULATION:
5,170,000
40 per sq. mi.
15 per sq. km

LANGUAGES:
Finnish, Swedish

MAJOR EXPORT:
Paper

MAJOR IMPORT:
Foods

CAPITAL:
Helsinki

LANDMASS:
130,558 sq. mi.
338,145 sq. km

FRANCE

POPULATION:
59,067,000
281 per sq. mi.
109 per sq. km

LANGUAGE:
French

MAJOR EXPORT:
Machinery

MAJOR IMPORT:
Crude Oil

CAPITAL:
Paris

LANDMASS:
210,026 sq. mi.
543,965 sq. km

GERMANY

POPULATION:
81,950,000
594 per sq. mi.
230 per sq. km

LANGUAGE:
German

MAJOR EXPORT:
Machinery

MAJOR IMPORT:
Machinery

CAPITAL:
Berlin

LANDMASS:
137,857 sq. mi.
357,046 sq. km

GREECE

POPULATION:
10,539,000
207 per sq. mi.
80 per sq. km

LANGUAGE:
Greek

MAJOR EXPORT:
Foods

MAJOR IMPORT:
Machinery

CAPITAL:
Athens

LANDMASS:
50,962 sq. mi.
131,990 sq. km

HUNGARY

Budapest

POPULATION:
10,076,000
281 per sq. mi.
108 per sq. km

LANGUAGE:
Hungarian

MAJOR EXPORT:
Machinery

MAJOR IMPORT:
Crude Oil

CAPITAL:
Budapest

LANDMASS:
35,919 sq. mi.
93,030 sq. km

ICELAND

Reykjavík

POPULATION:
277,000
7 per sq. mi.
3 per sq. km

LANGUAGE:
Icelandic

MAJOR EXPORT:
Fish

MAJOR IMPORT:
Machinery

CAPITAL:
Reykjavík

LANDMASS:
39,769 sq. mi.
103,001 sq. km

IRELAND

Dublin

POPULATION:
3,734,000
138 per sq. mi.
53 per sq. km

LANGUAGES:
English, Irish Gaelic

MAJOR EXPORT:
Chemical Products

MAJOR IMPORT:
Foods

CAPITAL:
Dublin

LANDMASS:
27,137 sq. mi.
70,284 sq. km

ITALY

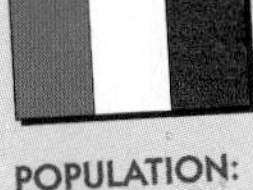

POPULATION:
57,717,000
496 per sq. mi.
192 per sq. km

LANGUAGE:
Italian

MAJOR EXPORT:
Metals

MAJOR IMPORT:
Machinery

CAPITAL:
Rome

LANDMASS:
116,324 sq. mi.
301,277 sq. km

LATVIA

POPULATION:
2,430,000
97 per sq. mi.
38 per sq. km

LANGUAGES:
Latvian, Russian

MAJOR EXPORT:
Wood

MAJOR IMPORT:
Fuels

CAPITAL:
Rīga

LANDMASS:
24,942 sq. mi.
64,599 sq. km

LIECHTENSTEIN

Vaduz

POPULATION:
32,000
516 per sq. mi.
200 per sq. km

LANGUAGE:
German

MAJOR EXPORT:
Machinery

MAJOR IMPORT:
Machinery

CAPITAL:
Vaduz

LANDMASS:
62 sq. mi.
160 sq. km

LITHUANIA

POPULATION:
3,700,000
147 per sq. mi.
57 per sq. km

LANGUAGES:
Lithuanian, Polish, Russian

MAJOR EXPORTS:
Foods and Livestock

MAJOR IMPORT:
Minerals

CAPITAL:
Vilnius

LANDMASS:
25,174 sq. mi.
65,200 sq. km

LUXEMBOURG

POPULATION:
432,000
433 per sq. mi.
167 per sq. km

LANGUAGES:
Luxembourgian, German, French

MAJOR EXPORT:
Steel Products

MAJOR IMPORT:
Minerals

CAPITAL:
Luxembourg

LANDMASS:
998 sq. mi.
2,586 sq. km

Country Profiles

MACEDONIA, Former Yugoslav Republic of

POPULATION:
2,019,000
203 per sq. mi.
79 per sq. km

LANGUAGES:
Macedonian, Albanian

MAJOR EXPORT:
Manufactured Goods

MAJOR IMPORT:
Fuels

CAPITAL:
Skopje

LANDMASS:
9,928 sq. mi.
25,713 sq. km

MALTA

POPULATION:
380,000
3,115 per sq. mi.
1,203 per sq. km

LANGUAGES:
Maltese, English

MAJOR EXPORT:
Machinery

MAJOR IMPORT:
Foods

CAPITAL:
Valletta

LANDMASS:
122 sq. mi.
316 sq. km

MOLDOVA

POPULATION:
4,284,000
324 per sq. mi.
126 per sq. km

LANGUAGES:
Moldovan, Russian

MAJOR EXPORT:
Foods

MAJOR IMPORT:
Petroleum

CAPITAL:
Chişinău

LANDMASS:
13,217 sq. mi.
33,999 sq. km

MONACO

POPULATION:
33,000
55,000 per sq. mi.
17,368 per sq. km

LANGUAGE:
French

MAJOR EXPORT:
N/A

MAJOR IMPORT:
N/A

CAPITAL:
Monaco

LANDMASS:
0.6 sq. mi.
1.9 sq. km

NETHERLANDS

POPULATION:
15,799,000
986 per sq. mi.
381 per sq. km

LANGUAGE:
Dutch

MAJOR EXPORT:
Manufactured Goods

MAJOR IMPORT:
Raw Materials

CAPITAL:
Amsterdam

LANDMASS:
16,023 sq. mi.
41,499 sq. km

NORWAY

POPULATION:
4,462,000
36 per sq. mi.
14 per sq. km

LANGUAGE:
Norwegian

MAJOR EXPORT:
Petroleum

MAJOR IMPORT:
Machinery

CAPITAL:
Oslo

LANDMASS:
125,182 sq. mi.
324,220 sq. km

POLAND

POPULATION:
38,674,000
320 per sq. mi.
124 per sq. km

LANGUAGE:
Polish

MAJOR EXPORT:
Manufactured Goods

MAJOR IMPORT:
Machinery

CAPITAL:
Warsaw

LANDMASS:
120,725 sq. mi.
312,677 sq. km

PORTUGAL

POPULATION:
9,992,000
280 per sq. mi.
108 per sq. km

LANGUAGE:
Portuguese

MAJOR EXPORT:
Clothing

MAJOR IMPORT:
Machinery

CAPITAL:
Lisbon

LANDMASS:
35,672 sq. mi.
92,389 sq. km

ROMANIA

POPULATION:
22,460,000
245 per sq. mi.
95 per sq. km

LANGUAGES:
Romanian, Hungarian, German

MAJOR EXPORT:
Textiles

MAJOR IMPORT:
Fuels

CAPITAL:
Bucharest

LANDMASS:
91,699 sq. mi.
237,499 sq. km

SAN MARINO

POPULATION:
26,000
1,083 per sq. mi.
426 per sq. km

LANGUAGE:
Italian

MAJOR EXPORT:
Building Stone

MAJOR IMPORT:
Manufactured Goods

CAPITAL:
San Marino

LANDMASS:
24 sq. mi.
61 sq. km

SLOVAKIA

POPULATION:
5,401,000
285 per sq. mi.
110 per sq. km

LANGUAGES:
Slovak, Hungarian

MAJOR EXPORT:
Transport Equipment

MAJOR IMPORT:
Machinery

CAPITAL:
Bratislava

LANDMASS:
18,921 sq. mi.
49,006 sq. km

SLOVENIA

POPULATION:
1,978,000
253 per sq. mi.
98 per sq. km

LANGUAGES:
Slovene, Serbo-Croatian

MAJOR EXPORT:
Transport Equipment

MAJOR IMPORT:
Machinery

CAPITAL:
Ljubljana

LANDMASS:
7,819 sq. mi.
20,251 sq. km

Countries and flags not drawn to scale

UNIT 4

SPAIN

POPULATION:
39,418,000
202 per sq. mi.
78 per sq. km

LANGUAGES:
Spanish, Catalan, Galician, Basque

MAJOR EXPORTS:
Cars and Trucks

MAJOR IMPORT:
Machinery

CAPITAL:
Madrid

LANDMASS:
194,897 sq. mi.
504,782 sq. km

SWEDEN

POPULATION:
8,856,000
51 per sq. mi.
20 per sq. km

LANGUAGE:
Swedish

MAJOR EXPORT:
Paper Products

MAJOR IMPORT:
Crude Oil

CAPITAL:
Stockholm

LANDMASS:
173,732 sq. mi.
449,964 sq. km

SWITZERLAND

POPULATION:
7,119,000
447 per sq. mi.
172 per sq. km

LANGUAGES:
German, French, Italian, Romansch

MAJOR EXPORT:
Precision Instruments

MAJOR IMPORT:
Machinery

CAPITAL:
Bern

LANDMASS:
15,941 sq. mi.
41,288 sq. km

UKRAINE

POPULATION:
49,910,000
214 per sq. mi.
83 per sq. km

LANGUAGES:
Ukrainian, Russian

MAJOR EXPORT:
Metals

MAJOR IMPORT:
Machinery

CAPITAL:
Kiev

LANDMASS:
233,206 sq. mi.
604,001 sq. km

UNITED KINGDOM

POPULATION:
59,364,000
630 per sq. mi.
243 per sq. km

LANGUAGES:
English, Welsh, Scottish Gaelic

MAJOR EXPORT:
Manufactured Goods

MAJOR IMPORT:
Foods

CAPITAL:
London

LANDMASS:
94,248 sq. mi.
244,101 sq. km

VATICAN CITY

POPULATION:
1,000

LANGUAGES:
Italian, Latin

MAJOR EXPORT:
N/A

MAJOR IMPORT:
N/A

CAPITAL:
N/A

LANDMASS:
0.2 sq. mi.
0.4 sq. km

YUGOSLAVIA
(Serbia and Montenegro)

POPULATION:
10,646,000
270 per sq. mi.
104 per sq. km

LANGUAGES:
Serbo-Croatian, Albanian

MAJOR EXPORT:
Manufactured Goods

MAJOR IMPORT:
Machinery

CAPITAL:
Belgrade

LANDMASS:
39,450 sq. mi.
102,173 sq. km

GEO BEE

Questions From Buzz Bee!

The following questions are taken from National Geographic GeoBees. Use your textbook, the Internet, and other library resources to find the answers.

1. Which European capital city located on the Seine River is known as the City of Light?
2. Which country leased Hong Kong from China for 99 years?
3. Slovakia and which other present-day central European country became independent in 1993?

Chapter 10

Western Europe

The World and Its People NATIONAL GEOGRAPHIC

To learn more about the people and places of Western Europe, view ***The World and Its People*** **Chapter 10** video.

Geography Online

Chapter Overview Visit the ***Geography: The World and Its People*** Web site at gwip.glencoe.com and click on **Chapter 10—Chapter Overviews** to preview information about Western Europe.

Section 1

The United Kingdom

Guide to Reading

Main Idea

The United Kingdom is a major industrial country that once ruled a vast global empire.

Terms to Know

- moor
- loch
- currency
- parliamentary democracy
- constitutional monarchy
- devolution

Places to Locate

- United Kingdom
- England
- Wales
- Scotland
- Great Britain
- Northern Ireland
- Ireland
- London
- Thames River

Reading Strategy

Create a diagram like this one, filling in the names of the four regions that make up the United Kingdom and one fact about each.

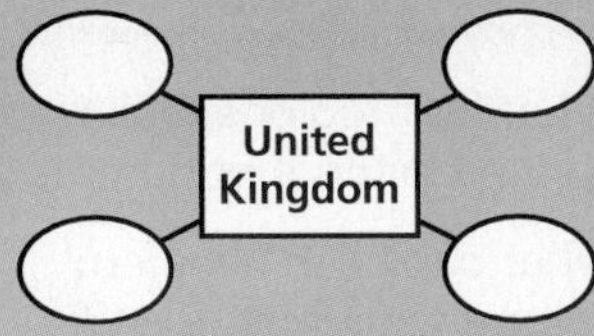

NATIONAL GEOGRAPHIC **Exploring Our World**

Every year millions of tourists visit London, England. They come to see the crown jewels or dungeons in the Tower of London. They also visit the Houses of Parliament and the tall clock known as Big Ben. You cannot be afraid of heights if you ride one of London's newest attractions. Known as the London Eye, it is the tallest Ferris wheel in the world.

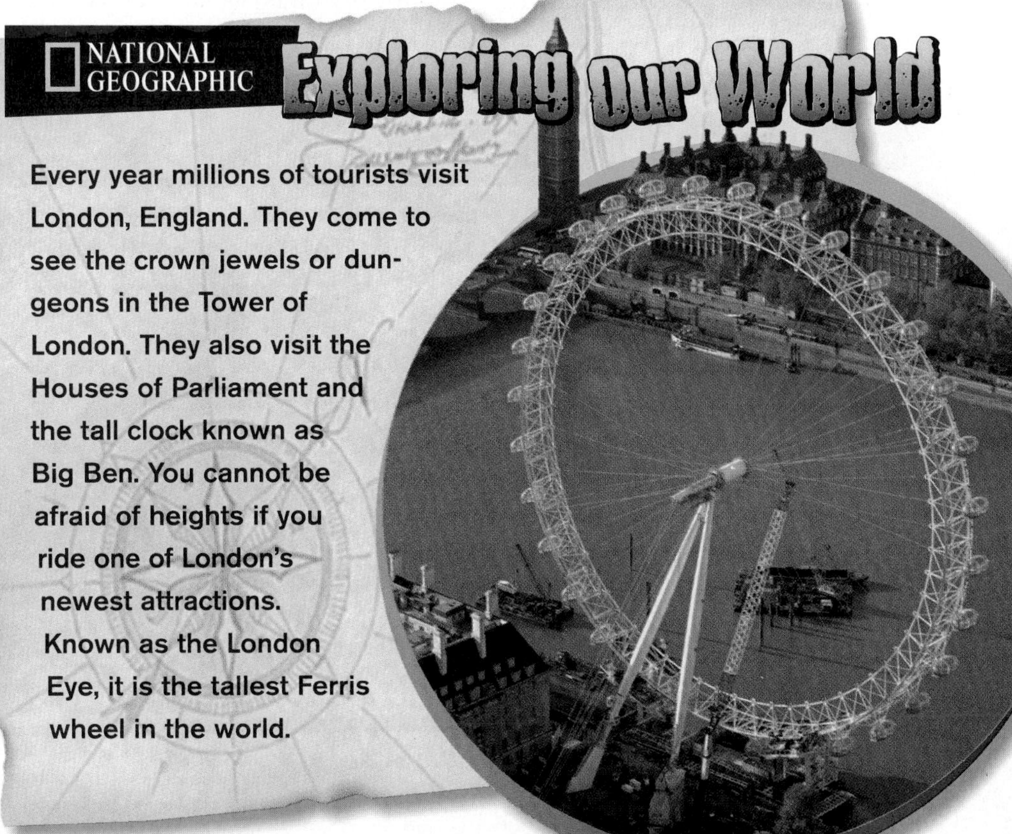

About the size of Oregon, the **United Kingdom** lies just northwest of the continent of Europe. Four regions make up this country. **England, Wales,** and **Scotland** are located on the island of **Great Britain.** The United Kingdom's fourth region—**Northern Ireland**—shares a different island with the Republic of **Ireland.**

The Land and Climate

Find the English Channel on the map on page 291. If you entered Great Britain from this body of water, you would be standing on rolling plains covered by a patchwork of fertile fields and meadows. Soon, however, vast urban areas—such as **London** and Birmingham—would come into view. This is a reminder that the south and east of Great Britain contain the most crowded areas in the United Kingdom.

As you travel west and north—in northern England, Wales, and Scotland—highland areas come into view. Here you see rugged hills

◀ The Eiffel Tower in Paris, France

and low mountain ranges. You also cross **moors**—treeless, windy highland areas that have damp ground. Water is never far away. Northwest England holds the beautiful blue waters of the Lake District. Farther north, in Scotland, narrow bays called **lochs** cut into the highland coasts and reach far inland. A lowland area in central Scotland contains two large cities—Glasgow and Edinburgh—and most of Scotland's people, farmland, and industry. Across the Irish Sea is Northern Ireland, with its landscape of gentle mountains, valleys, and fertile lowlands. Belfast is the region's major city and port.

Applying Map Skills

1. What four regions make up the United Kingdom?
2. What capital in Western Europe is farthest east?

Find NGS online map resources @ www.nationalgeographic.com/maps

The climate map on page 297 shows you that the United Kingdom has a mild climate even though it lies as far north as Canada. Why is this so? The North Atlantic Current carries warm waters from the Caribbean Sea and Gulf of Mexico to Great Britain. Winds blowing over these waters warm the United Kingdom in winter and cool it in summer.

The ocean winds also bring plenty of rain, which is good for agriculture but not for tourists. If you visit the United Kingdom, take your raincoat. Clouds fill the sky more than half the days of the year.

Reading Check **Why is the United Kingdom's climate mild even though it lies as far north as Canada?**

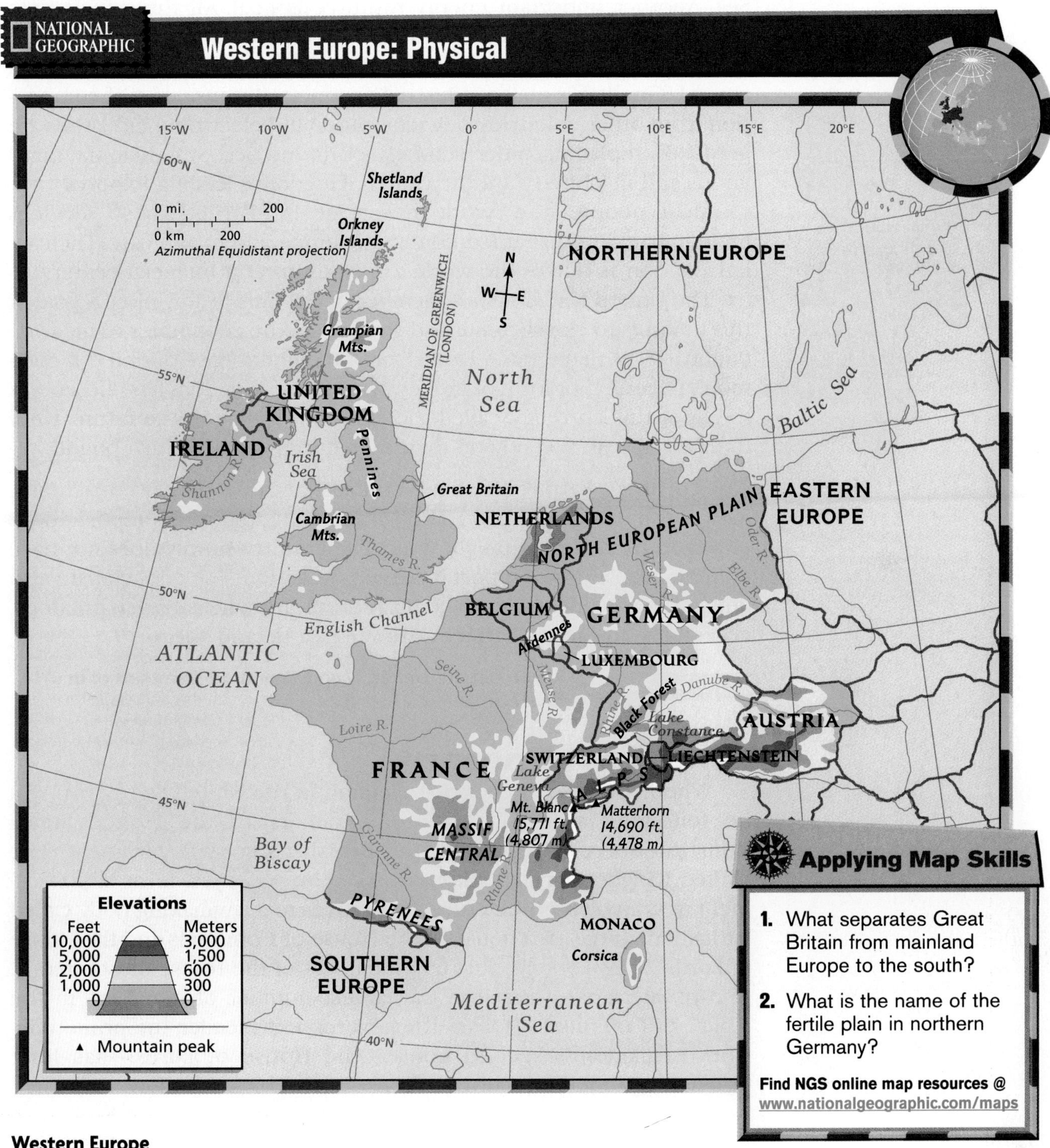

Applying Map Skills

1. What separates Great Britain from mainland Europe to the south?
2. What is the name of the fertile plain in northern Germany?

Find NGS online map resources @ www.nationalgeographic.com/maps

The Economy

More than 200 years ago, inventors and scientists in the United Kingdom sparked the Industrial Revolution. Fuel-powered machines in factories began producing more goods than ever before. The Industrial Revolution helped make the United Kingdom the world's leading economic power during the 1800s. Although the country's economic influence declined during the 1900s, the United Kingdom is still a major industrial and trading country.

Resources and Manufacturing The United Kingdom is rich in energy resources. It pumps oil and natural gas from under the North Sea. Another important energy resource is coal. All three fuels help power the country and are exported to other countries.

Heavy machinery, ships, textiles, and automobiles were once the United Kingdom's major industrial products. Because of stiff competition from other countries, new computer and electronic industries are gradually replacing older smokestack industries. Still, manufactured goods and machinery are the United Kingdom's leading exports.

Most people now work in service industries. These services include banking, insurance, communications, and health care. The capital, London, is one of the world's most important financial centers.

The United Kingdom is a member of the European Union. A goal of this union is to closely unite and strengthen the economies of member countries. To make trade easier, some members have adopted a common **currency**, or form of money. The United Kingdom has chosen *not* to adopt this currency, called the euro, but it may in the future. Until then, the British will rely on their own currency, the British pound.

Agriculture Farmers here are efficient because they use machines. As a result, yields are high. The United Kingdom must import about one-third of its food, though. Why? The country simply does not have enough farmland to support its large population. The cool climate also limits the growing season. The main crops are wheat, barley, potatoes, vegetables, and fruits. Farmers also raise cattle and sheep.

✓Reading Check **Why must the United Kingdom import one-third of its food?**

The Government

When you vote in your first election in the United States, you will be following a British tradition. Framers of the United States Constitution copied parts of the British form of government. The United Kingdom is a **parliamentary democracy**, a form of government in which voters elect representatives to a lawmaking body called Parliament. It has two houses—the House of Commons and the House of Lords. British voters elect 651 members of the House of Commons. The political party that has the largest number of members in the House of Commons chooses the government's leader, the prime minister. Parliament's second house—the House of Lords—has little power. Most members of this House are nobles who have inherited their titles. The House of Lords cannot block any laws that the House of Commons wants to pass, but it can help in revising laws.

The United Kingdom's government is also a **constitutional monarchy,** in which a queen or king is the official head of state. The monarch represents the country at public events but has little power. The prime minister and other elected officials make government decisions.

Devolution In the late 1990s, the British government began a new policy called devolution. **Devolution** involves the transfer of certain powers from the central government to regional governments. New regional governments were created for Scotland, Wales, and Northern Ireland. The goals of devolution are to give the regions more power over their own affairs and to help them preserve their cultures.

Reading Check How is the prime minister chosen?

Loch Ness

Castle ruins overlook Loch Ness in Scotland.

Movement Who were among the first people to settle in Great Britain?

History and Culture

More than 59 million people live in the United Kingdom. Many people in the United States and other parts of the world have ancestors from here. The British people speak English, although you can hear two older languages—Welsh and Scottish Gaelic—spoken in outlying areas of the country. Most people are Protestant Christians, although immigrants from former British colonies practice Islam and other religions.

The British people are descendants of various groups. Among early arrivals were the Celts (KEHLTS), who sailed to Great Britain and Ireland from the European mainland around 500 B.C. Their descendants live today in Scotland, Wales, Ireland, and in the southwest corner of England. The Romans invaded Great Britain in 55 B.C. In the A.D. 400s and 500s, the Anglos, Saxons, and Jutes came from mainland Europe. In 1066 the Normans from France conquered England.

In the late 1500s, England became a major European power. In 1707 England, Wales, and Scotland united to form Great Britain. When Ireland joined in 1801, the country's name became the United Kingdom. Traders, soldiers, and settlers set sail to distant lands and won control of large areas throughout the world. By the mid-1800s, the United Kingdom governed the world's largest overseas empire. The United States, Canada, India, and Australia all once belonged to it.

In the 1900s, the United Kingdom fought and was victorious in the two World Wars. During World War II, the nation's leader was Prime Minister Winston Churchill. His rousing speeches gave the British people courage during the war's darkest days. Despite victory, the United Kingdom was weakened by both conflicts. After World War II, nearly all of the countries in the British Empire became independent nations.

Culture The United Kingdom is a densely populated country. About 90 percent of the people live in cities and towns. With more than 7 million people, the city of London is one of Europe's most heavily populated cities.

Ancient and modern meet in London. In the heart of the city is Westminster Abbey, where Britain's kings and queens have been crowned since 1066. Farther down the **Thames** (TEHMZ) **River,** you can see the Tower of London. The crown jewels that belong to the British monarchs have been kept there since 1303. People get around London by riding colorful double-decker buses or by using the subway, which they call "the Tube."

What do the Beatles, Led Zeppelin, and Ewan MacGregor have in common? All of these performers come from the United Kingdom. For centuries, the people of the United Kingdom have left their mark on world culture. British writers include William Shakespeare, Charles Dickens, Charlotte and Emily Brontë, and Jane Austen. Visitors flock to the West End, London's famous theater district, to see the plays of Shakespeare or the modern musicals of Andrew Lloyd Webber.

✓Reading Check **What percentage of the United Kingdom's people live in towns and cities?**

Assessment

Defining Terms

1. **Define** moor, loch, currency, parliamentary democracy, constitutional monarchy, devolution.

Recalling Facts

2. **Place** What is the largest city in the United Kingdom?
3. **Economics** What resources does the United Kingdom take from under the North Sea?
4. **History** How did Winston Churchill encourage the people of Britain during World War II?

Critical Thinking

5. **Analyzing Information** What are three facts that support the statement "Ancient and modern meet in London"?
6. **Understanding Cause and Effect** As a result of devolution, regional governments were created in which parts of the United Kingdom?

Graphic Organizer

7. **Organizing Information** Complete a chart like the one below by writing two facts about the United Kingdom under each category heading.

The United Kingdom		
Climate	Resources	Products
Government	History	Culture

Applying Geography Skills

8. **Analyzing Maps** Look at the physical map on page 291. Name the three mountain ranges found on the island of Great Britain.

Making Connections

ART SCIENCE LITERATURE TECHNOLOGY

Stonehenge

Stonehenge, one of the world's best-known and most puzzling ancient monuments, stands in southern England.

History of Stonehenge

The most noticeable part of Stonehenge is its huge stones set up in four circular patterns. A circular ditch and mound form a border around the site. Shallow dirt holes also circle the stones.

Stonehenge was built over a period of more than 2,000 years. The earliest construction, that of the circular ditch and mound, probably began about 3100 B.C. The outer ring of large pillars, topped with horizontal rocks, was built about 2000 B.C. An inner ring of stone pillars also supports horizontal stones.

There was no local source of stone, so workers carried it from an area that was about 20 miles (32 km) north. The stones are huge—up to 30 feet (9 m) long and 50 tons (45,359 kg) in weight. Before setting the stones in place, workers smoothed and shaped them. They carved joints into the stones so that they would fit together perfectly. Then the builders probably used levers and wooden supports to raise the blocks into position.

About 500 years later, builders added the third and fourth rings of stones. This time they used bluestone, which an earlier group of people had transported 240 miles (386 km) from the Preseli Mountains of Wales.

What Does It Mean?

Although much is known about when people built Stonehenge, experts do not agree who built it. Early theories suggested that an ancient group known as Druids or the Romans built the monument. Now archaeologists believe that the monument was completed long before either of these groups came to the area.

▲ Stonehenge

An even greater mystery is *why* Stonehenge was built. Most experts agree that Stonehenge was probably used as a place of worship. Some believe that the series of holes, stones, and archways were used as a calendar. By lining up particular holes and stones, people could note the summer and winter solstices. They could also keep track of the months. Some scientists think that early people used the site to predict solar and lunar eclipses.

Making the Connection

1. About how old is Stonehenge?
2. From where did the stones used at Stonehenge come?
3. **Sequencing Information** Describe the order in which Stonehenge was built.

Section 2

The Republic of Ireland

Guide to Reading

Main Idea

Once a war-torn, agricultural country, the Republic of Ireland is now enjoying economic growth.

Terms to Know

- peat
- bog

Places to Locate

- Ireland
- Shannon River
- Dublin

Reading Strategy

Create a chart like this one and fill in at least one key fact about the Republic of Ireland in each category.

Ireland	
Land	
Climate	
Economy	
People	

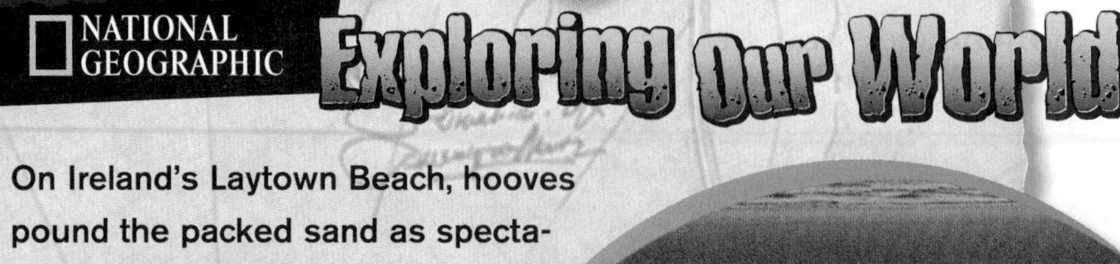

On Ireland's Laytown Beach, hooves pound the packed sand as spectators cheer on their favorite horse. Ireland's fascination with fast horses dates back to about 500 B.C. That is when the Celts—who loved chariot racing—first reached the island. Ireland's green pastures are rich in calcium, helping horses build strong bones.

The way of life in **Ireland** (officially called the Republic of Ireland) differs from that in the United Kingdom. One key difference is in religion. More than 90 percent of Ireland's people are Catholic. Another difference is in the size of its population. Only 3.7 million people live in Ireland, compared to more than 59 million in the United Kingdom.

The Emerald Isle

Surrounded by the blue waters of the Atlantic Ocean and the Irish Sea, Ireland's lush green meadows and tree-covered hills stand out. As a result, it is called the Emerald Isle.

In western Ireland, the land rises to rocky cliffs that overlook the sea. At Ireland's center lies a wide, rolling plain covered with forests and farmland. Much of the area is rich in **peat,** or wet ground with decaying plants, which can be dried and used for fuel. Peat is dug from **bogs,** or low swampy lands. The **Shannon River** flows southwest through the plain. **Dublin,** Ireland's capital and largest city, lies in the east.

No part of Ireland is more than 70 miles (113 km) from the sea. As a result, Ireland is warmed by moist winds that blow over the North Atlantic Current. These winds, along with frequent rain and mist, keep Ireland's landscape green all year. Because the island is small and the mountains are not high, the entire island has the same climate.

Reading Check **Why is Ireland called the Emerald Isle?**

Agriculture and Industry

If you look at the map on page 302, you will see that Ireland has few mineral resources. The country does have rich soil and pastureland, however. In the mid-1800s, Irish farmers grew potatoes as their main food. Then disaster struck. Too much rain allowed a disease to spread among the plants. Potatoes began to rot in the fields. The Irish—with little else to eat—suffered terribly. A million or more died during what was known as the Potato Famine. An equal number moved to other countries, especially the United States. Ireland's farmers still grow potatoes, but they also grow barley, wheat, sugar beets, and turnips. They raise beef and dairy cattle as well.

Although farming is still important, manufacturing employs more people and contributes more to the country's economy. Ireland has attracted foreign companies to set up operations. At the same time,

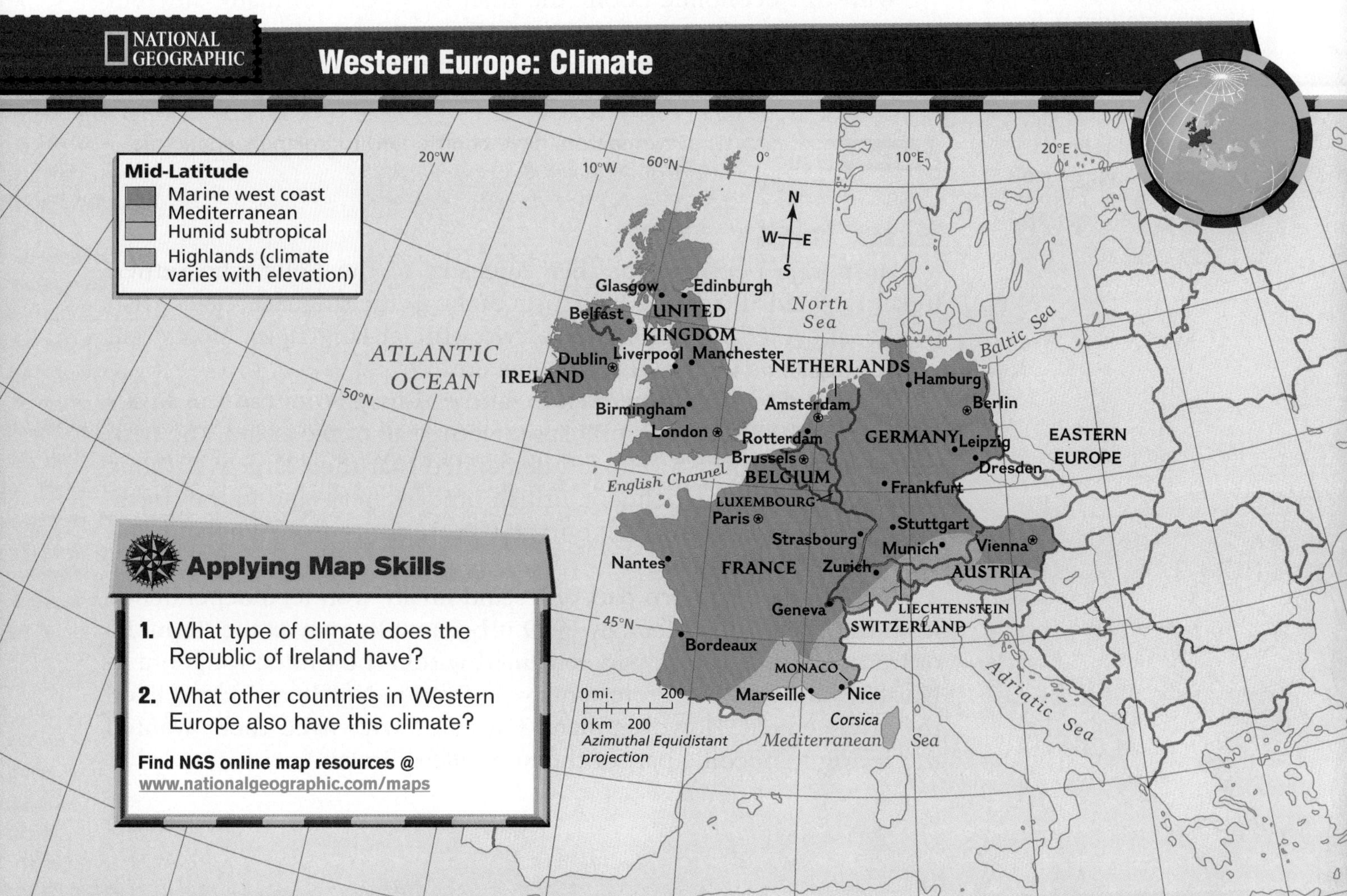

Applying Map Skills

1. What type of climate does the Republic of Ireland have?
2. What other countries in Western Europe also have this climate?

Find NGS online map resources @ www.nationalgeographic.com/maps

NATIONAL GEOGRAPHIC **On Location**

Rural and Urban Life

Bright green meadows greet people who venture into Ireland's countryside (right). In Dublin, a sidewalk artist shows her own bright colors (above).

Place **What religion do most Irish practice?**

Ireland joined the European Union so it could market its products more widely.

With this economic boom, the Irish now work in many different manufacturing industries. Some have jobs processing foods and beverages. Others make textiles, clothing, pharmaceuticals, and computer equipment.

Reading Check **What two factors have contributed to Ireland's economic growth?**

The Irish

Most Irish people trace their ancestry to the Celts who settled Ireland around 500 B.C. Today a form of the Celtic language, called Irish Gaelic, and English are Ireland's two official languages. Most Irish speak English as their everyday language.

Political conflict has marked Ireland's history. From the A.D. 1100s to the early 1900s, English officials governed all of the island. The Irish people resisted British rule and demanded that their largely Catholic country become independent. British officials held land in the northern part of Ireland and encouraged Protestants from England and Scotland to move there.

In 1922 the southern part of Ireland finally won its independence from the United Kingdom. In 1949 it became known as the Republic of Ireland. The northern part remained within the United Kingdom as Northern Ireland. The Protestants who lived in Northern Ireland liked the arrangement. However, many Catholics who lived there wanted the region to become part of the Republic of Ireland.

The Northern Ireland Conflict Disagreement over Northern Ireland exploded into violence in the 1960s through the 1990s. Thousands died in ongoing attacks by Protestants or Catholics on people of the other faith. In 1998 officials of the United Kingdom and the Republic of Ireland met with leaders of the different sides in Northern Ireland. They all signed an agreement to end the political violence. The agreement gave Northern Ireland its own elected assembly. The assembly—with both Catholic and Protestant members—has the power to govern Northern Ireland. At the same time, the Republic of Ireland dropped the claim that it had the right to rule Northern Ireland and agreed to cooperate with the new assembly. The next year, the new government took office. Although disagreements continue to occur, many people hope that the new peace will last.

Irish Life and Culture In the past, most Irish lived in the countryside, but today Ireland is an urban nation. About 58 percent of Ireland's people live in cities and towns. Nearly one-third live in and around Dublin, the capital. Life often centers on the neighborhood church.

You may think that rock groups like the Cranberries, the Pogues, and U2 are Ireland's most famous cultural export. Irish music, both modern and traditional, is performed around the world. Of all the arts, however, the Irish have had the greatest influence on literature. Playwright George Bernard Shaw, poet William Butler Yeats, and novelist James Joyce are some of the country's best-known writers.

✓ Reading Check **What are the two official languages of Ireland?**

Time to Perform!

Ann McBriarty is carrying on a long-held tradition of Irish step dancing. She has learned the four basic step dances: the reel, the light jig, the slip jig, and the hornpipe. Ann wears the costume of her dancing school now. She says, "After I reach a certain level, I may wear a dress that is different from the other dancers."

Assessment

Defining Terms

1. **Define** peat, bog.

Recalling Facts

2. **Place** What is the major influence on Ireland's climate?
3. **Economics** Why did Ireland join the European Union?
4. **History** Who were the Celts?

Critical Thinking

5. **Understanding Cause and Effect** What event in the mid-1800s led many Irish people to move to the United States?
6. **Drawing Conclusions** What conclusions can be drawn from the fact that no part of Ireland is more than 70 miles from the sea?

Graphic Organizer

7. **Organizing Information** Place the following events and their dates in order on a time line like the one below: (a) Celts arrive in Ireland; (b) Officials sign peace agreement; (c) British officials encourage Protestants to settle in Northern Ireland; (d) Southern Ireland becomes known as the Republic of Ireland.

Applying Geography Skills

8. **Analyzing Maps** Turn to the physical map on page 291. What bodies of water surround Ireland?

Section 3 France

Guide to Reading

Main Idea

A center of European culture, France is also a major agricultural and manufacturing country.

Terms to Know

- navigable
- republic

Places to Locate

- France
- Pyrenees
- Alps
- Massif Central
- Rhône River
- North European Plain
- Seine River
- Paris
- Rhine River

Reading Strategy

Draw a diagram like this. Then list three French agricultural and manufacturing products in the small ovals.

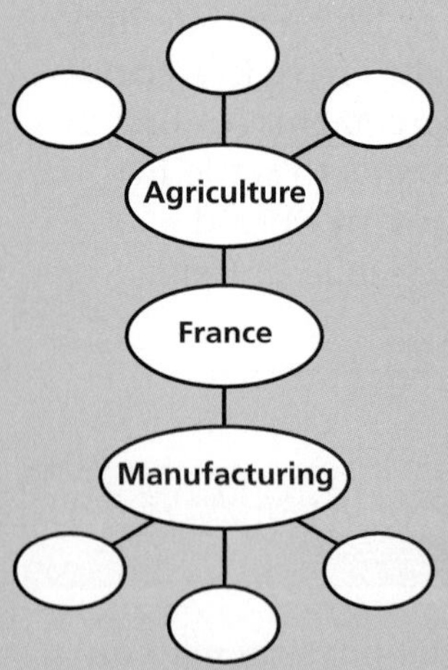

NATIONAL GEOGRAPHIC **Exploring Our World**

France has won fame around the world for its masterpieces in art and architecture, and for the skill of its chefs. Tourists flock to France's top restaurants to savor the unusual and delicious creations. Soon these plates will be carried to the dining room, where they will undoubtedly be greeted with cries of delight.

France and its neighbors in Western Europe rank as major economic and cultural centers of the world. For centuries, these countries struggled with one another for power and land. In the first half of the 1900s, warfare among them tore apart the European continent. Since the end of World War II, however, these countries have set aside their differences. Joined in economic partnership in the European Union, they look forward to a peaceful and prosperous twenty-first century.

France's Land and Climate

The largest country in Western Europe, **France** is slightly smaller than the state of Texas. On its southwestern and eastern borders, France touches several European countries. Look at the map on page 281 to see which seven countries are France's neighbors.

The map also shows that seas wash the other half of France's borders. If you like to swim, beaches beckon on the Mediterranean Sea, the Atlantic Ocean, and the English Channel. Since the mid-1990s, a tunnel—called the Chunnel—runs under the English Channel. People and goods now move rapidly between France and Great Britain.

Mountains and Highlands In the southwest, the **Pyrenees** (PIHR•uh•NEEZ) mountain range separates France from Spain. In the southeast, the **Alps** divide France from Italy and Switzerland. The soaring, icy peaks of the French Alps include Mont Blanc. At 15,771 feet (4,807 m), Mont Blanc is one of the highest mountains in Europe. Another highland region—the **Massif Central** (ma•SEEF sahn•TRAHL)—rises in south-central France. The long **Rhône** (ROHN) **River** flows through a wide valley that separates the Massif from the Alps.

Plains and Rivers Most of northern France is part of the vast **North European Plain.** The rich soil in this flat lowland area makes France a major agricultural country. In many French towns, you can find open-air markets displaying an abundance of fresh farm produce.

A network of rivers connects the different regions of France. Most of these rivers are **navigable,** or wide and deep enough to allow the passage of ships. The **Seine** (SAYN) **River** flows through **Paris,** the capital of France. Most of the country's major roads, railways, and canals meet in Paris. From the Paris area, barges transport goods by river and canal to Marseille, France's busiest Mediterranean port, and from there to other countries. Other important French rivers are the Loire (LWAHR), Rhône, Garonne, and the Rhine. The **Rhine River,** a major inland waterway of Europe, forms part of France's eastern border.

Climate Regions Most of France has a marine west coast climate with cool summers, mild winters, and plenty of rainfall. This climate is ideal for agriculture. The

Views of France

Tourists in Nice (NEES) enjoy the Mediterranean Sea (left). Wine grapes are harvested in one of France's grape-growing valleys (right).

Place What details in the photos suggest that France has a mild climate?

NATIONAL GEOGRAPHIC **On Location**

mountain areas have a highland climate. Along the Mediterranean coast, summers are hot and winters are mild. Blue skies, rocky cliffs, and lovely beaches draw many tourists to this region.

Reading Check **What bodies of water border France?**

France's Economy

France's well-developed economy relies on agriculture and manufacturing. Most people, however, work in service industries such as banking, commerce, communications, and tourism. Tourists from all over the world flock to visit France's historic and cultural sites, such as palaces and museums.

Agriculture France produces more food than any other nation in Europe. In fact, it ranks as the second-largest food exporter in the world, after the United States. Yet only 5 percent of French workers labor on farms. Their success is a tribute to France's fertile soil and good climate.

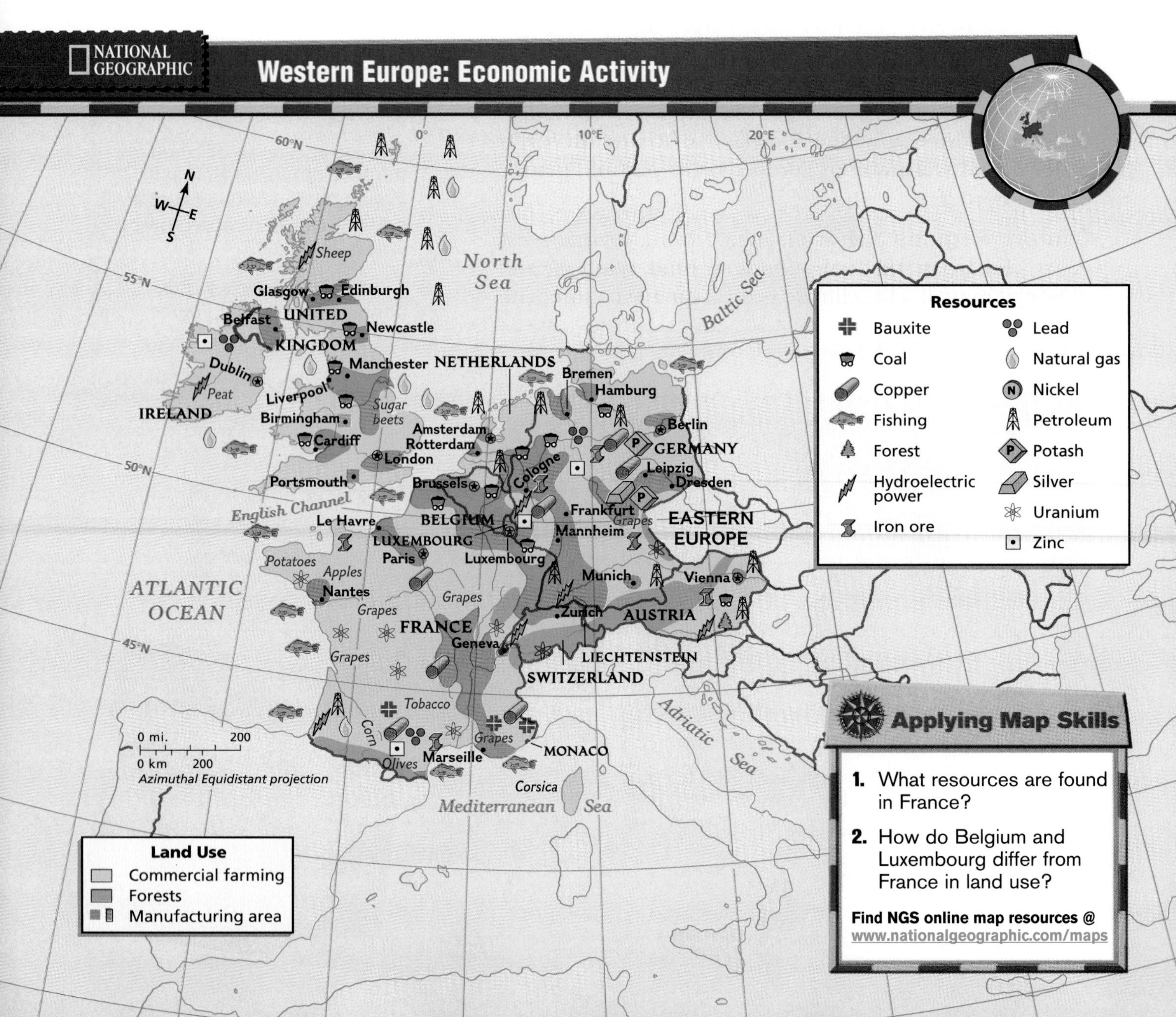

Applying Map Skills

1. What resources are found in France?
2. How do Belgium and Luxembourg differ from France in land use?

Find NGS online map resources @ www.nationalgeographic.com/maps

French farmers grow grains, sugar beets, fruits, and vegetables. They also raise beef and dairy cattle. In addition, vineyards are a common sight. The grapes are used to make famous French wines. Olives are grown along the warm, dry Mediterranean coast. Most French food exports go to other members of the European Union. The United States imports mainly wine and cheese.

Mining and Manufacturing France's natural resources include bauxite, iron ore, and coal. France has small petroleum reserves and little hydroelectric power. How does the nation power its industries? About 80 percent of France's energy comes from nuclear power plants.

Workers produce a variety of manufactured goods, including steel, chemicals, textiles, airplanes, cars, and computers. France is also a leading center of commerce, with an international reputation in fashion.

✓Reading Check **From where does most of France's energy come?**

The French People

"Liberté . . . Egalité . . . Fraternité" (Liberty, Equality, Fraternity)—France's national motto—describes the spirit of the French people. Although they have regional differences, the French share a strong national loyalty. Most French trace their ancestry to the Celts, Romans, and Franks of early Europe. They speak French, and about 90 percent of them are Roman Catholic.

History and Government During the 50s B.C., the area that is now France came under Roman rule. Then in the A.D. 400s, a group called the Franks arrived from central Europe and gave France its name. By A.D. 800, the Frankish ruler Charlemagne (SHAR•luh•MAYN) had created an empire that stretched across much of Western Europe. After Charlemagne's death, France emerged as a separate kingdom.

Kings ruled France for nearly 800 years and made the nation a major European power. Royalty and nobles built elegant country houses along the Loire River. King Louis XIV, the "Sun King," erected a magnificent palace at Versailles (vehr•SY) in the 1600s, when France was at a peak of its cultural and political influence.

In 1789 the French people overthrew their king in the bloody French Revolution. They set up a **republic,** a strong national government headed by elected leaders. In 1799 General Napoleon Bonaparte seized power. He conquered much of Europe before armies from a group of European countries defeated him.

In the 1900s, France was a battleground during the two world wars. The country survived and today plays an important role in world affairs. France has been a strong supporter of the European Union.

France's government is known as the Fifth Republic. A powerful president, elected for a seven-year term, leads the nation. The French president manages the country's foreign affairs. He or she appoints a prime minister to run the day-to-day affairs of government. France also has a legislature with two parts: the Senate and the more powerful National Assembly. Under certain conditions, the French president can

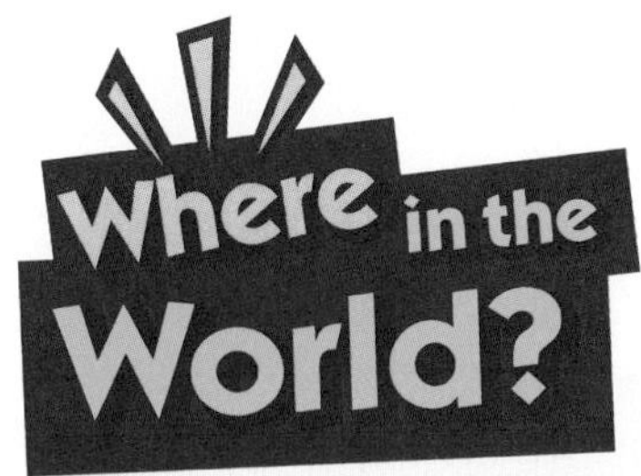

Reims Cathedral

Majestic Gothic cathedrals like this one at Reims draw tourists to France. Several features characterize Gothic architecture. One is the pointed arch. Another is the use of ribbed vaults, or stone "ribs" that hold the vaulted roof. A third is the use of flying buttresses, or stone archways that extend from the main part of the church to an outer part.

The cathedral at Reims was begun in 1211 and took 80 years to complete, although the decorations continued for centuries. It is almost 500 feet long, making it one and a half times the length of a football field. Twenty-five kings of France received their crowns here.

disband the National Assembly and order new elections. This gives him or her more power over France than the president of the United States holds over America.

An Urban Population About three-fourths of France's 59.1 million people live in cities and towns. Paris, the capital, is the largest city and the main transportation and communications center. Other large cities include Lyon, Marseille, Bourdeaux, and Toulouse. A superb railroad system connects these and other cities. French passenger trains are among the fastest in the world. *Trains à Grande Vitesse* (TGVs) or "trains of great speed" can go as fast as 168 miles (270 km) per hour.

The city of Paris was founded more than 2,000 years ago on a small island in the Seine River. Gradually the city spread onto both banks of the river. Today Paris and its suburbs have a population of more than 9 million people. The city is home to many universities, museums, and other cultural sites. Outstanding cultural figures who lived in Paris include the writer Victor Hugo and the painters Claude Monet and Pierre-Auguste Renoir. Each year, millions of tourists flock to the City of Light, as Paris is called. They visit such sites as the Eiffel Tower, the cathedral of Notre Dame, and the Louvre (LOOV), one of the world's most famous art museums.

Reading Check What is the main religion in France?

Assessment

Defining Terms

1. **Define** navigable, republic.

Recalling Facts

2. **Movement** What structural innovation makes it possible for goods and people to move quickly between France and England?
3. **Economics** Name five of France's agricultural products.
4. **Culture** What are three famous landmarks found in Paris?

Critical Thinking

5. **Analyzing Information** What characteristics have created a strong sense of national loyalty in France?
6. **Drawing Conclusions** France is the second-largest food exporter in the world. Why is that remarkable?

Graphic Organizer

7. **Organizing Information** Draw a diagram like the one below. At the end of each arrow, list a fact that indicates a power of the French president.

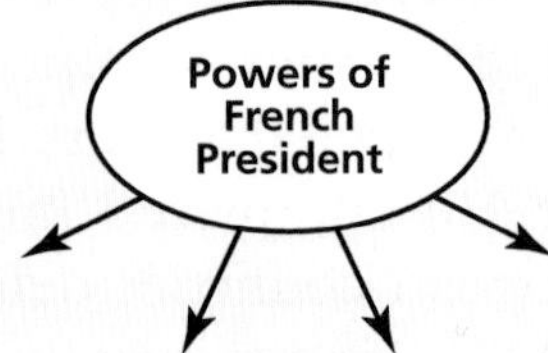

Applying Geography Skills

8. **Analyzing Maps** Turn to the physical map on page 291. What river in France empties into the English Channel?

Geography Skill

Reading a Vegetation Map

Vegetation maps show the kinds of plants that naturally grow in a given area. Climate largely determines the vegetation of an area. For example, evergreen trees (also called *coniferous*) such as firs and spruces grow in cool climates. In the year-round warmth of the tropics, evergreens with broad leaves, such as palm trees and rubber trees, can grow. Between these two extremes, broad-leaved *deciduous* trees are common. Deciduous trees have broad leaves, but they shed them in autumn. In dry or Mediterranean climates, grasses and shrubs are found because there is not enough water to support tree growth. Highland climates may have *alpine* vegetation—small shrubs and wildflowers. Extremely cold or dry climates may have little or no vegetation.

Learning the Skill

To read a vegetation map, follow these steps:

- Read the title of the map.
- Study the map key.
- Find examples of each vegetation zone on the map.
- Look at other aspects of the area's geography, such as rivers, oceans, and landforms to explain the vegetation patterns.

Practicing the Skill

Look at the map above to answer the following questions.

1. What vegetation covers most of France?
2. What type of vegetation is found along France's Mediterranean coast?
3. From the map, what conclusions can you draw about the amount of rain the regions of France receive?

Applying the Skill

Find a vegetation map of your state. What types of vegetation are common in your part of the country?

Section 4

Germany, Switzerland, and Austria

Guide to Reading

Main Idea

Germany, Switzerland, and Austria are known for their mountain scenery and prosperous economies.

Terms to Know

- autobahn
- Holocaust
- communist state
- federal republic
- reunification
- infrastructure
- neutrality

Places to Locate

- Germany
- Switzerland
- Austria
- Danube River
- Liechtenstein

Reading Strategy

Create a diagram like this one. Under the headings fill each oval with facts about each country. Put statements that are true of all three countries where the ovals overlap.

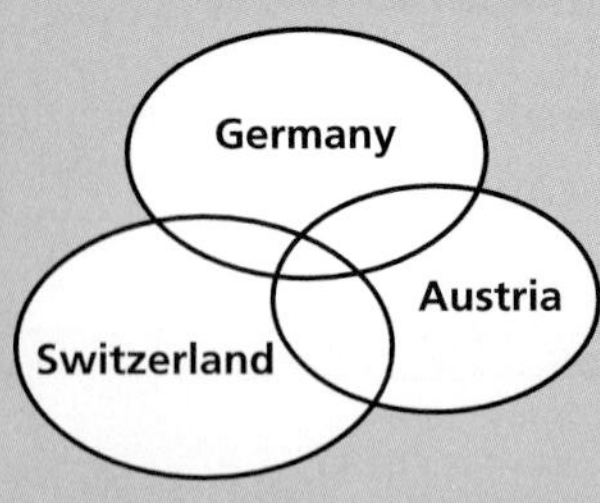

NATIONAL GEOGRAPHIC **Exploring Our World**

For nearly 30 years, armed guards patrolled a 103-mile (166-km) wall that divided the German city of Berlin into eastern and western halves. During that time, the citizens of East Berlin were not allowed to travel freely to West Berlin. In late 1989, the wall finally came down. Germans from both parts of the city came together and celebrated.

From the 1940s to the late 1980s, the countries of **Germany, Switzerland,** and **Austria** lay on—or close to—the "iron curtain." This was the name given after World War II to the imaginary barrier that separated Communist Eastern Europe from democratic Western Europe. Today all three countries are adjusting to the changes sweeping Europe since the fall of communism's iron curtain.

Germany

About the size of Montana, Germany lies in the heart of Europe. Mountains in the south and plains in the north form the physical landscape of Germany. The Alps rise in the southern German state of Bavaria. The lower slopes of these mountains—a favorite destination for skiers—are covered with forests. Mountain peaks, many capped with snow year-round, tower above the trees. Below the mountains and their foothills are dairy farms, bogs, and sparkling lakes.

Have you ever heard a cuckoo clock announce the hour? That clock may have come from Germany's Black Forest. Lying just north of the Alps, this region is famous for its beautiful scenery and for its wood products. Is the forest really black? No, but in places the trees grow so close together that the forest appears to be black. In recent decades the Black Forest has suffered severe damage from acid rain. Smoke containing sulfur and other chemicals from factories and automobiles causes this problem. The Germans have not yet found a solution to the acid rain problem, because much of the pollution is formed in other countries.

From the Black Forest area flows one of Europe's most important waterways—the **Danube River.** It winds eastward across southern Germany. Rivers are also important in northern Germany, which is part of the vast North European Plain. The Rhine, Elbe, and Weser Rivers flow across this region. Linked by canals, these rivers transport raw materials and manufactured goods.

On Germany's northern plain, lakes and marshes dot a landscape scattered with deposits of earth and stones left by long-ago glaciers. In places the soil is suitable only for pasture, which supports an important dairy farming industry. The plain's southern edge, however, has fertile soil and small farms. Because of the rivers and productive land, the northern plain has many cities and towns. Berlin, Germany's largest city and capital, is the major center of the northeast. To the west lies Hamburg, Germany's largest port city, located on the Elbe River.

Germany's Climate Westerly Atlantic Ocean winds crossing Europe help keep Germany mild in winter and cool in summer. As you can see from the climate map on page 297, most of Germany has a marine west coast climate. The mountainous southern areas have a highland climate with colder winters.

An Economic Power Germany is a global economic power and a leader in the European Union. In fact, an area in western Germany called the Ruhr ranks as one of the world's most important industrial centers. The Ruhr developed around rich deposits of coal and iron ore. Battles have been fought among Europe's leaders for control of this productive area. Factories here produce high-quality steel, ships, cars, machinery, chemicals, and electrical equipment. Cities such as Cologne (kuh•LAWN), Essen, and Dortmund cover the Ruhr.

In the eastern part of Germany you will find another large industrial urban area. Metals, chemicals, machines, and textiles are produced in cities such as Leipzig (LYP•sik) and Dresden. The explosive growth of factories, service industries, and high technology has used up the supply of workers. Thus, a growing number have come from Turkey, Italy, Greece, and the former Yugoslav republics.

Germany imports about one-third of its food, although it is a leading producer of beer, wine, and cheese. Farmers raise livestock and grow grains, vegetables, and fruits. Superhighways called **autobahns,** along with railroads, rivers, and canals, link Germany's cities.

Bavaria, Germany

The beauty of the Bavarian Alps attracts many tourists.

Location **In what part of Germany are mountains located?**

People and Culture Most of Germany's 82 million people trace their ancestry to groups who settled in Europe from about the A.D.100s to 400s. The people speak German, a language that is related to English. Roman Catholics and Protestants make up most of the population and are fairly evenly represented.

Throughout history, Germans have made important contributions to Europe's cultural heritage. Johann Sebastian Bach (BAHK) and Ludwig van Beethoven (BAY•TOH•vuhn) composed some of the world's greatest classical music. Munich (MYOO•nikh), the largest city in southern Germany, is known for its theaters, museums, and concert halls. Berlin has also emerged as a cultural center.

Influences of History For hundreds of years, Germany was a collection of small territories ruled by princes. During the 1500s, a German priest named Martin Luther tried to reform some of the practices of the Catholic Church. When that failed, he began a new form of Christianity known as Protestantism. Luther's followers, called Protestants, followed forms of worship that they felt were closer to the Bible's teachings. Years of warfare between Protestants and Catholics further divided the German territories.

During the late 1800s, a German leader named Otto von Bismarck finally united the territories into a single nation—Germany. The country's efforts to become a world power helped lead to the European tensions that caused World War I. Germany's defeat in this war caused great anger and distress among the German people.

In 1933 dictator Adolf Hitler and his Nazi Party gained control of the country. Hitler increased German military power and invaded neighboring countries, setting off World War II. One of the horrors of World War II was the **Holocaust,** the systematic murder of more than 6 million Jews by Nazis. Another 6 million people also were murdered. When the Allies—led by the United States, the United Kingdom, and the Soviet Union—defeated Germany, the Holocaust finally ended.

After World War II, the Allies divided Germany. One part—West Germany—became a democracy with close ties to the United States. It built a prosperous free market economy. The other part—East Germany—was a communist state with ties to the Soviet Union. A **communist state** is a country whose government has strong control over the economy and society as a whole.

In 1989 protests calling for democracy swept through the Communist lands of Eastern Europe. The economies of these countries were a disaster, and people were tired of low standards of living. East Germany's government fell, and the two parts of Germany were reunited a year later.

Germany's Government Like the United States, Germany is a **federal republic** in which a national government and state governments share powers. An elected president serves as Germany's head of state, but he or she carries out only ceremonial duties. Another official, the chancellor, is the real head of the government. The chancellor is chosen by one of the two houses of parliament. Usually, the majority party in the parliament selects the chancellor.

Berlin For many years, Berlin was Germany's capital. When Germany was split after World War II, Berlin was divided, too. East Germany made East Berlin its capital. West Berlin was linked to West Germany, but it was entirely surrounded by East German land. West Berlin became a prosperous and exciting place. East Berlin, however, experienced slower growth and became run-down. Meanwhile, West Germany set up a separate capital in the city of Bonn on the Rhine River.

Built by the East Germans in 1961, the Berlin Wall finally came down in 1989. Ten years later, Berlin became the capital of Germany again. The old parliament building, known as the Reichstag, has been rebuilt to hold the government of the new Germany. Companies are putting up new buildings across the city—especially in the eastern part.

Germany Reunited Germans were overjoyed when their country was reunited. Families that had been split by living in the two separate countries could now visit each other. **Reunification**—bringing the two parts together under one government—has been difficult, however. Workers in East Germany had less experience and training in modern technology than workers in West Germany. After reunification, many old and inefficient factories in the east could not compete with the more advanced industries in the west. Having no Communist government to support them, the factories were forced to close. As a result, the number of people without jobs has risen in the eastern part of Germany.

One of the challenges for the united Germany has been to close the economic gap between the two parts of the country. The German government has spent billions of dollars to provide needed training, education, and modernization. Huge amounts of money have also been spent in the east to improve the **infrastructure,** or the transportation and communications networks on which an economy depends.

✓Reading Check **What was the Holocaust?**

Switzerland

The Alps form most of the landscape in Switzerland, Austria, and **Liechtenstein.** That is why they are called the Alpine countries. Switzerland and Austria together cover an area about the size of

Alabama. Sandwiched between them is tiny Liechtenstein, covering only 60 square miles (155 sq. km).

The rugged Swiss Alps have always created a natural barrier to travel between northern and southern Europe. For centuries, landlocked Switzerland guarded the few routes that cut through this barrier.

Because of its location, Switzerland has practiced **neutrality**—refusing to take sides in disagreements and wars between countries. In fact, the Swiss have not been involved in a foreign war since the early 1500s. As a result of Switzerland's peaceful heritage, the Swiss city of Geneva is today the center of many international organizations.

Swiss Chocolate

Switzerland's factories produce some of the best chocolate in the world.

Place **What other products are made in Switzerland?**

Alpine Land and Climate The Alps make Switzerland the continental divide of central Europe. A continental divide is a high place from which rivers flow in different directions. Several rivers, including the Rhine and the Rhône, begin in the Swiss Alps. Dams built on many of Switzerland's rivers produce great amounts of hydroelectric power.

Another mountain range, the Jura Mountains, runs across northwest Switzerland. Between the Jura Mountains and the Alps lies a plateau known as the *Mittelland,* or "Middle Land." Most of Switzerland's industries and its richest farmlands are found here. Bern, Switzerland's capital, and Zurich, its largest city, are also located on this plateau.

The Alps shape Switzerland's climate. Though temperatures differ with elevation, in most parts of the country winters are cold, and summers are warm.

Manufacturing and Service Industries Although it has few natural resources, Switzerland is a thriving industrial nation. Using imported materials, Swiss workers make high-quality goods such as machinery, pharmaceuticals, high-tech electronic equipment, and clocks and watches. They also produce chemicals and gourmet foods such as chocolate and cheese. Tourism is an important industry, as are banking and insurance. Zurich and Geneva are important international financial centers.

Culture and Government As you might expect given its location, Switzerland has many different ethnic groups and religions. Did you know that the country has four national languages? They are German, French, Italian, and Romansch. Most Swiss speak German, and many speak more than one language. Only a tiny percentage speak Romansch, an old language based on Latin.

Just under half of the Swiss people are Catholic. A slightly smaller number are Protestants. The Protestant Reformed faith developed in Switzerland during the 1500s. It later spread to many countries, including the United States.

The Swiss have enjoyed a stable democratic government for more than 700 years. Like Germany, Switzerland is a federal republic. In Switzerland, however, the units of local government—which are called cantons—have a great deal of power. Heading the national government is a seven-member panel called the Federal Council. The council chooses one of its members to be Switzerland's president.

Reading Check **In what part of Switzerland are most of its industries and farmlands found?**

Austria

The political map on page 290 shows you that Austria is a landlocked country lying in the heart of Europe. Small when compared to some other European countries, Austria is slightly larger than the state of Maryland.

Yet, believe it or not, Austria once was one of Europe's largest countries. Under the powerful Hapsburg royal family, the Austrian Empire ruled much of central Europe from the late 1200s to the early 1900s. World War I destroyed that empire. By 1918 Austria had become a small republic, with the borders it has today.

A Mountainous Country The Alps cover three-fourths of Austria. In fact, Austria is one of the most mountainous countries in the world. Have you ever seen the movie *The Sound of Music*? It took place in Austria's spectacular mountains.

NATIONAL GEOGRAPHIC On Location

Vienna, Austria

People enjoy relaxing in one of Vienna's many coffeehouses.

Place **What famous musicians lived or performed in Vienna?**

The Danube River flows from west to east across the country's northern region. Austria's climate is similar to Switzerland's. In winter, lowland areas receive rain, and mountainous regions have snow. Summers are cooler here than they are in Switzerland.

Austria's Economy Austria's economy is strong and varied. The mountains provide valuable timber and hydroelectric power. They yield iron ore and coal as well. The mountains also attract millions of tourists who enjoy the fresh air and fine hiking and skiing.

Austrian factories produce machinery, chemicals, metals, and vehicles. The country also has some petroleum and natural gas. Austrian farmers raise dairy cattle and other livestock, sugar beets, grains, potatoes, and fruits.

Austria's People Austria is home to about 8.1 million people. Most Austrians live in cities and towns and work in manufacturing or service jobs. The majority of people speak German. About 90 percent of the people are Roman Catholic.

Vienna, on the Danube River, is the capital and largest city. It has a rich history as a center of culture and learning. Some of the world's greatest composers, including Mozart, Schubert, and Haydn, lived or performed in Vienna. The city's concert halls, historic palaces and churches, and grand architecture continue to draw musicians today.

✓Reading Check **What economic benefits do Austria's mountains provide?**

Assessment

Defining Terms

1. **Define** autobahn, Holocaust, communist state, federal republic, reunification, infrastructure, neutrality.

Recalling Facts

2. **Human/Environment Interaction** What has damaged the Black Forest?
3. **History** Why have battles been fought over the Ruhr?
4. **Culture** What are Switzerland's four languages?

Critical Thinking

5. **Understanding Cause and Effect** What problems have emerged as a result of German reunification?
6. **Analyzing Information** How have the Alps helped Switzerland maintain its neutrality?

Graphic Organizer

7. **Organizing Information** Draw a diagram like the one below. On the lines list two facts about Austria's physical features, two facts about Austria's people, and four facts about Austria's economy.

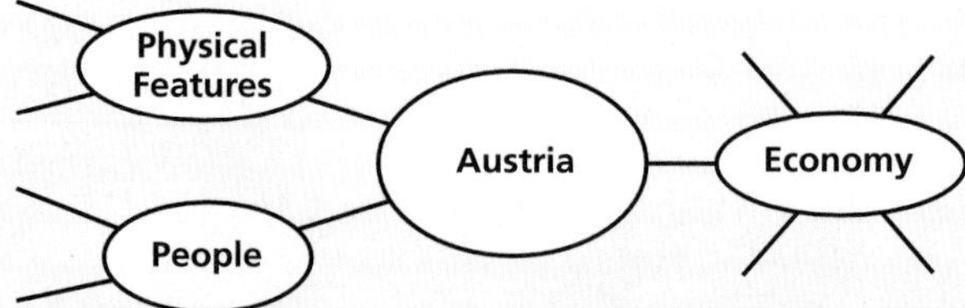

Applying Geography Skills

8. **Analyzing Maps** Look at the political map on page 290. The city of Frankfurt is located at what degree of latitude?

Section 5

The Benelux Countries

Guide to Reading

Main Idea

Belgium, the Netherlands, and Luxembourg are small countries with long histories of international trade.

Terms to Know

- polder
- multinational company
- multilingual

Places to Locate

- Belgium
- Netherlands
- Luxembourg
- Brussels
- North Sea
- Rotterdam
- Amsterdam

Reading Strategy

Create a diagram like this one. Fill in the names of the three Benelux countries and write at least one key fact about the people from each country.

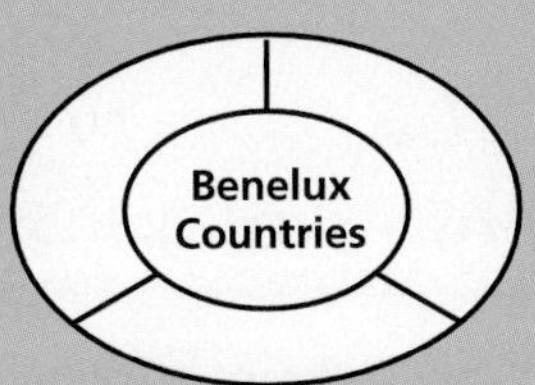

NATIONAL GEOGRAPHIC **Exploring Our World**

Tulips create colorful carpets in the Netherlands every spring. Originally from Asia, these vivid blooms are more than a beautiful sight—they are an important cash crop. Dutch growers export flowers and bulbs around the world. The Dutch have another reason to feel proud of this beautiful display. These flowers grow on land the Dutch reclaimed from the sea.

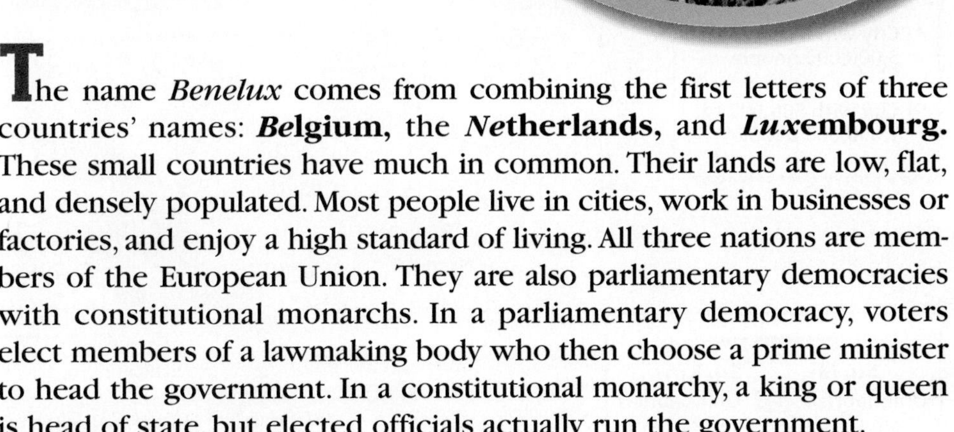

The name *Benelux* comes from combining the first letters of three countries' names: ***Be**lgium,* the ***Ne**therlands,* and ***Lux**embourg.* These small countries have much in common. Their lands are low, flat, and densely populated. Most people live in cities, work in businesses or factories, and enjoy a high standard of living. All three nations are members of the European Union. They are also parliamentary democracies with constitutional monarchs. In a parliamentary democracy, voters elect members of a lawmaking body who then choose a prime minister to head the government. In a constitutional monarchy, a king or queen is head of state, but elected officials actually run the government.

Belgium

About the size of Maryland, Belgium touches France, Luxembourg, Germany, and the Netherlands. From a wide coastal plain, the land rolls gently upward to a hilly, forested region in the interior known as

Ardennes. Because Belgium is centrally located in Western Europe, it has been a battleground over the centuries. Most recently, British and American troops fought the Germans there in World War II. Lying near Western Europe's major industrial regions, Belgium has long been a trade and manufacturing center.

Belgium's Economy Belgian lace, Belgian chocolate, and Belgian diamond-cutting all enjoy a worldwide reputation for excellence. With few natural resources of their own, the Belgian people import metals, fuels, and raw materials. They use these materials to make vehicles, chemicals, and textiles, which are then exported. Belgium's excellent road system also helps its economic success.

Belgium's People Most of the people are Roman Catholic. The country has two main cultural and language groups. The Flemings in the north speak Flemish, a language based on Dutch. The south is home to the French-speaking Walloons. Tensions sometimes arise between the two groups, especially because there is more wealth and industry in the north than in the south.

Most Belgians live in crowded urban areas. **Brussels**—the capital and largest city—is an international center for trade. Many world

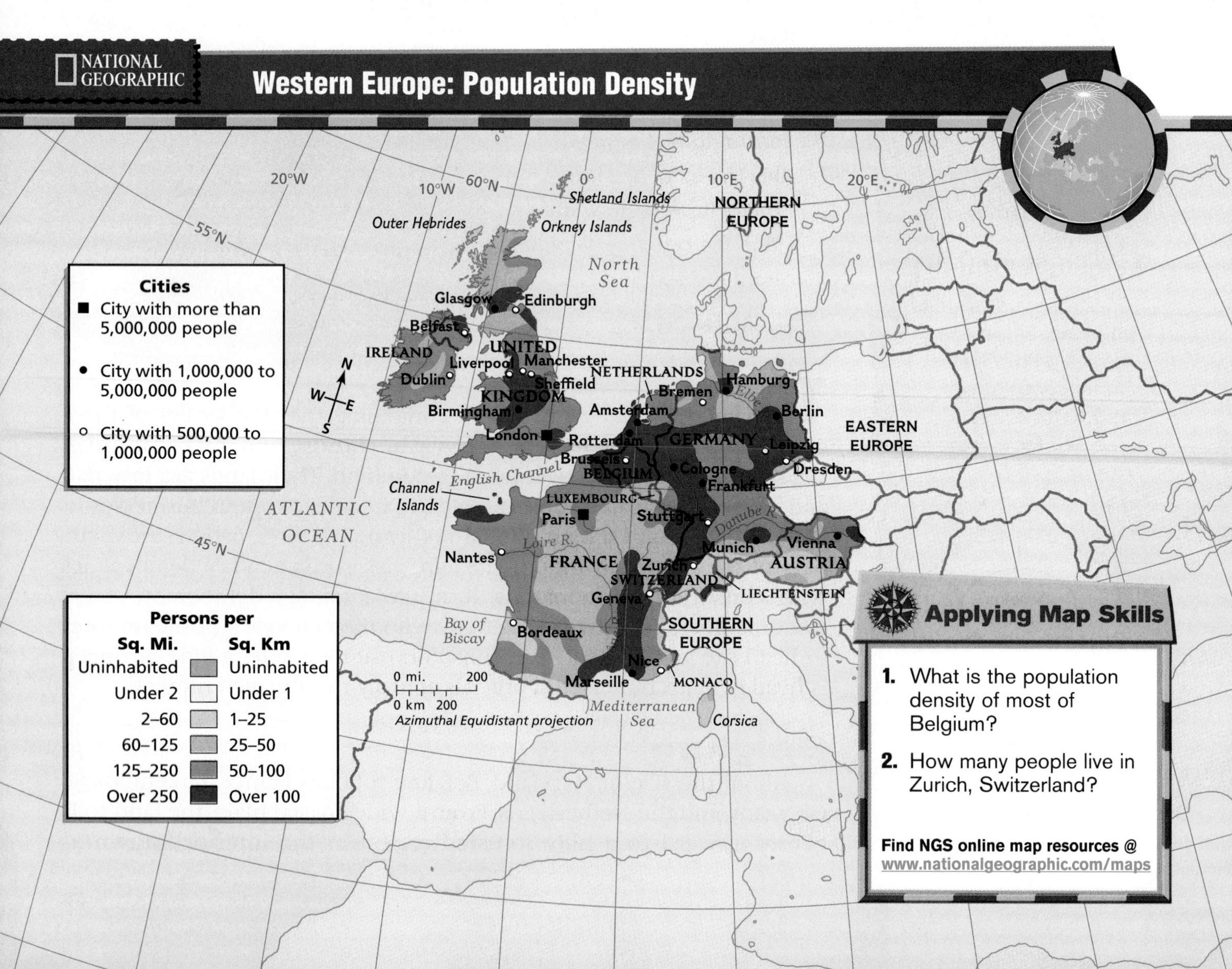

Applying Map Skills

1. What is the population density of most of Belgium?
2. How many people live in Zurich, Switzerland?

Find NGS online map resources @ www.nationalgeographic.com/maps

organizations have located their headquarters here as well. By law, Brussels recognizes both Flemish and French speakers. Its street signs and official documents are printed in both languages.

Reading Check **Why has Belgium's location been an advantage and a disadvantage?**

The Netherlands

The Netherlands—about half the size of Maine—is one of the most densely populated countries in the world. Sometimes called Holland, it is located on the **North Sea** to the northeast of Belgium.

Netherlands means "lowlands." True to its name, nearly half of this small, flat country lies below sea level. Over the centuries, the people of the Netherlands, known as the Dutch, have learned how to protect their land and how to reclaim more from the sea. The Dutch method of reclaiming land is simple, but it takes hard work. First they strengthen sand dunes along the coasts and build dikes, or dams, to keep the sea out. Then they cut ditches and canals for drainage and pump the wetlands dry. Once run by windmills, pumps are now driven by steam or electricity. These drained lands, called **polders,** have rich farming soil. The Dutch also build factories, airports, and even towns on them.

Without defenses against the sea, high tides would flood much of the country twice a day. An engineering feat known as the Delta Plan Project was completed in 1986. It consists of four huge barriers that keep the North Sea from overflowing the countryside during storms.

The Dutch Economy and People On polders, Dutch farmers raise dairy cattle, grow food, and produce tulips and other flowers. They use extremely efficient farming methods. High technology makes small farms so productive that the Dutch can export cheese, vegetables, and flowers. In fact, the Netherlands ranks third in the world—after the United States and France—in the value of its agricultural exports.

Though farming is important, most people work in service industries, manufacturing, and trade. During the 1600s, the Netherlands was a major sea power, and world trade brought the country much wealth. Still active in trading, the Netherlands has one of the world's busiest ports at **Rotterdam,** located near the Rhine River.

About 90 percent of the Dutch live in cities and towns. **Amsterdam** is the capital and largest city. Canals crisscross Amsterdam's historic districts, which preserve the art and architecture of the Dutch "golden age" of the 1600s. Living in a densely populated country, the Dutch make good use of their space. Houses are narrow but tall, and apartments are often built over highways. One of Amsterdam's most famous

Rotterdam's architects are challenged to find ways of cramming more buildings into an already overcrowded city.

Location **Near what river is Rotterdam located?**

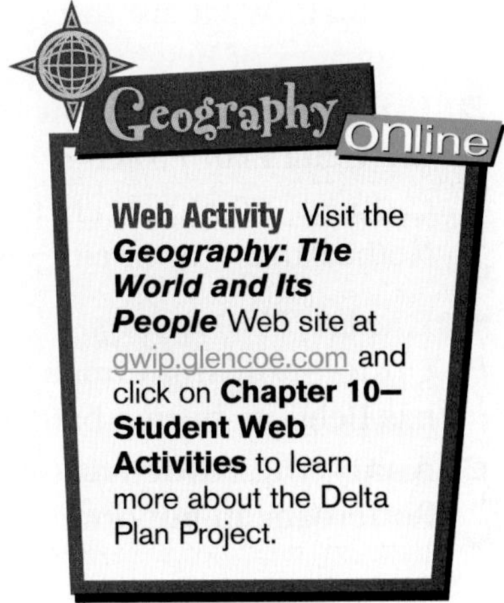

Web Activity Visit the ***Geography: The World and Its People*** Web site at gwip.glencoe.com and click on **Chapter 10—Student Web Activities** to learn more about the Delta Plan Project.

people was Anne Frank. Her diary tells about her life as she and her family hid from the German Nazis during World War II.

About one-third of the Dutch people are Roman Catholic. Others are Protestants, and a small number of immigrants from other lands are Muslims. The people of the Netherlands speak Dutch.

Reading Check **How much of the Netherlands lies below sea level?**

Luxembourg

Southeast of Belgium lies Luxembourg, one of Europe's smallest countries. Its capital and largest city is also called Luxembourg. The entire country is only about 55 miles (89 km) long and about 35 miles (56 km) wide, making it slightly smaller than the state of Rhode Island.

Despite its size, Luxembourg is prosperous. Many **multinational companies,** or firms that do business in several countries, have their headquarters here. It is home to the second-largest steel-producing company in Europe and is a major banking center as well. By the late 1990s, well over 200 banks were operating in Luxembourg.

Why is Luxembourg so attractive to foreign companies? First, the country is centrally located. Second, most people in this tiny land are **multilingual,** or able to speak several languages. They speak Luxembourgian, a blend of old German and French; French, the official language of the law; and German, used in most newspapers. Almost all the people of Luxembourg are Roman Catholic.

Reading Check **What industries are important in Luxembourg?**

Assessment

Defining Terms

1. **Define** polder, multinational company, multilingual.

Recalling Facts

2. **Culture** What are the two major cultures and languages of Belgium?
3. **Human/Environment Interaction** What is the Delta Plan Project?
4. **Culture** What percentage of the people in the Netherlands live in cities and towns?

Critical Thinking

5. **Understanding Cause and Effect** Why has Belgium been a battleground?
6. **Analyzing Information** Why is Rotterdam an important city?

Graphic Organizer

7. **Organizing Information** Draw a diagram like this one. In the center circle list five characteristics that Belgium, the Netherlands, and Luxembourg share.

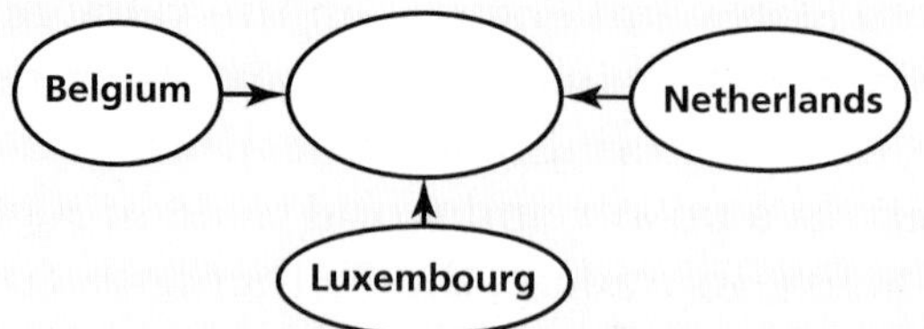

Applying Geography Skills

8. **Analyzing Maps** Turn to the physical map on page 291. What body of water borders Belgium and the Netherlands?

Chapter 10

Reading Review

Section 1 The United Kingdom

Terms to Know
moor
loch
parliamentary democracy
constitutional monarchy
currency
devolution

Main Idea

The United Kingdom is a major industrial country that once ruled a vast global empire.

✓ **Economics** The United Kingdom has a strong economy and is rich in energy resources.

✓ **Government** The government of the United Kingdom recently began to give more power to regional governments.

Section 2 The Republic of Ireland

Terms to Know
peat
bog

Main Idea

Once a war-torn, agricultural country, the Republic of Ireland is now enjoying economic growth.

✓ **Economics** Ireland has attracted foreign investors and improved its economy.

✓ **History** After years of conflict, a peace plan was adopted in Northern Ireland.

Section 3 France

Terms to Know
navigable
republic

Main Idea

A center of European culture, France is also a major agricultural and manufacturing country.

✓ **Economics** France balances agriculture, manufacturing, and service industries.

✓ **Culture** Paris is a world center of art, learning, and culture.

Section 4 Germany, Switzerland, and Austria

Terms to Know
autobahn
Holocaust
communist state
federal republic
reunification
infrastructure
neutrality

Main Idea

Germany, Switzerland, and Austria are known for their mountain scenery and prosperous economies.

✓ **Economics** The German economy is very strong, but the eastern region—reunited with the west in 1990—lags behind the western region.

✓ **Economics** Switzerland produces high-quality manufactured goods.

✓ **Human/Environment Interaction** Austria's strong economy makes good use of its mountainous terrain.

Section 5 The Benelux Countries

Terms to Know
polder
multinational company
multilingual

Main Idea

Belgium, the Netherlands, and Luxembourg are small countries with long histories of international trade.

✓ **Location** Belgium's location has made it an international center for trade.

✓ **Economics** The Dutch grow valuable crops on reclaimed land.

✓ **Economics** Luxembourg is home to many multinational companies.

Chapter 10

Assessment and Activities

Using Key Terms

Match the terms in Part A with their definitions in Part B.

A.

1. moor
2. multilingual
3. neutrality
4. loch
5. polder
6. constitutional monarchy
7. multinational company
8. Holocaust
9. infrastructure
10. currency

B.

a. type of money
b. transportation and communication networks on which an economy depends
c. a king or queen shares power with elected officials
d. land reclaimed from the sea
e. treeless, windy highland area
f. refusing to take sides
g. slaughter of Jews by the Nazis
h. narrow bay cut into highland coasts
i. company that has offices in several countries
j. able to speak several languages

Reviewing the Main Ideas

Section 1 The United Kingdom

11. **Region** What regions make up the United Kingdom?
12. **History** How have the British influenced other parts of the world?

Section 2 The Republic of Ireland

13. **Culture** What is the major language(s) and religion of the Republic of Ireland?
14. **History** What has been the major source of conflict in Northern Ireland?

Section 3 France

15. **Place** Why is Paris an important city?
16. **Government** What is the Fifth Republic?

Section 4 Germany, Switzerland, and Austria

17. **History** Why was Germany divided after World War II?
18. **Location** Why is Geneva the center of many international organizations?

Section 5 The Benelux Countries

19. **Place** What is the capital of Belgium?
20. **Economics** Why do the Dutch reclaim land from the sea?

Western Europe

Place Location Activity

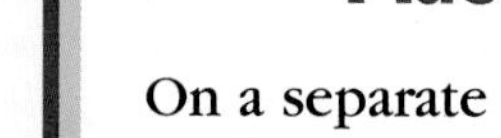

On a separate sheet of paper, match the letters on the map with the numbered places listed below.

1. United Kingdom
2. English Channel
3. France
4. Germany
5. Alps
6. Rhine River
7. Ireland
8. Paris
9. Berlin
10. London

Self-Check Quiz Visit the ***Geography: The World and Its People*** Web site at gwip.glencoe.com and click on **Chapter 10—Self-Check Quizzes** to prepare for the Chapter Test.

Critical Thinking

21. **Making Generalizations** How do you think the Industrial Revolution affected the lives of people who lived during that time? How do you think it has shaped your life today?
22. **Sequencing Information** Draw a time line like this one, then list five events with dates from Germany's history.

GeoJournal Activity

23. **Writing a News Broadcast** Research an important event that took place in one of the countries studied in this chapter. Write a script for a news broadcast about the event. Present the broadcast as a news anchor.

Mental Mapping Activity

24. **Focusing on the Region** Draw a simple outline map of Western Europe, then label the following:
    - United Kingdom
    - Republic of Ireland
    - Rhine River
    - English Channel
    - Switzerland
    - France
    - Germany
    - Austria
    - Alps
    - Paris

Technology Skills Activity

25. **Using a Spreadsheet** List the names of the nine Western European countries in a spreadsheet, beginning with cell A2 and continuing down the column. Find each country's population and record the figures in column B. In column C list each country's area in square miles. Title column D "Population Density." Then divide column B by column C to determine the population density. Print out and share your spreadsheet with the class.

Standardized Test Practice

Directions: Study the map, then answer the question that follows.

1. **In 1945 what country controlled the land surrounding Berlin, Germany's capital?**
   F the United Kingdom
   G the Soviet Union
   H the United States
   J France

Test-Taking Tip: This question asks you to synthesize information on the map with prior knowledge. Notice that the map does not specifically state that the United Kingdom, for example, controlled a portion of Germany. Instead, it refers to this area as the "British" zone.

GEOGRAPHY 

1961—the Wall goes up

GERMANY: Together Again

It was one of the biggest parties in German history. On November 9, 1989, thousands of people poured into the streets—cheering, singing, and hugging each other. The Berlin Wall could no longer keep the German people apart.

The Fall of the Wall

Today there is only one Germany—but after World War II, there were two. After surrendering in 1945, Germany was carved into four parts. The United States, the United Kingdom, and France merged their three parts into one country—West Germany. The Soviet Union's portion became East Germany.

Deep within Soviet territory lay the city of Berlin. It also was divided into four parts. The Soviet section became East Berlin. The remaining sections combined into West Berlin, which became part of West Germany.

In West Germany, the United States and its allies encouraged a democratic government that allowed people to choose their leaders from among competing political parties. The Soviets instituted a one-party, Communist government that gave East Germans no political choices and little control over their own lives.

East Germans soon grew unhappy with their government. During the early 1960s, refugees poured into West Germany through Berlin. Desperate to stop the flow, East Germany's government erected the Berlin Wall in 1961. Built of concrete and topped with barbed wire, the Wall separated West Berlin from East Berlin, blocking the exit route for East Germans. Those caught trying to escape to West Berlin were often shot by guards who had orders to kill.

The Wall held Germans apart for more than 20 years. By 1989, however, people across Eastern Europe were demanding change. East Germans wanted freedom. They forced their leaders to open the Wall on November 9, and Germany reunited within a year.

Growing Pains

However, after 40 years of living under separate political systems, many differences had developed between East Germans and West Germans. Former West Germans support the competition of a market economy. They live a more prosperous lifestyle than do former East Germans.

Former East Germans regret the loss of free health care and the guaranteed jobs that came with communism. Although East Germany was an industrial giant, it lacked modern necessities such as adequate transportation systems and reliable telephone service. Today Germany is investing heavily to improve services for all of its citizens.

QUESTIONS

1. Why was Germany split into two countries?
2. What are some difficulties Germans face in becoming one country?

1989—the Wall comes down ▶

NATIONAL
GEOGRAPHIC
SOCIETY
The Two Germanys: 1945
DENMARK
North
Sea
UNITED
KINGDOM
West
Berlin
East
Berlin
N
W
E
S
NETHERLANDS
POLAND
EAST
GERMANY
WEST
GERMANY
BELGIUM
LUX.
FRANCE
CZECHOSLOVAKIA
0 mi.
200
0 km
200
AUSTRIA
HUNGARY
SWITZ.

Chapter 11 Southern Europe

The World and Its People NATIONAL GEOGRAPHIC

To learn more about the people and places of Southern Europe, view ***The World and Its People*** **Chapter 11** video.

Chapter Overview Visit the ***Geography: The World and Its People*** Web site at gwip.glencoe.com and click on **Chapter 11–Chapter Overviews** to preview information about Southern Europe.

Section 1 Spain and Portugal

Guide to Reading

Main Idea

Spain and Portugal are working toward building prosperous economies.

Terms to Know

- plateau
- dry farming
- navigable
- colony
- parliamentary republic
- dialect

Places to Locate

- Spain
- Portugal
- Andorra
- Iberian Peninsula
- Pyrenees
- Tagus River
- Guadalquivir River
- Madrid
- Barcelona
- Lisbon

Reading Strategy

Draw a diagram like this one. List information about Spain and Portugal under their names in the outer parts of the ovals. Where the ovals overlap, write statements that are true of both countries.

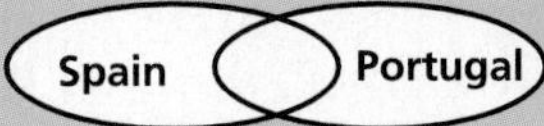

NATIONAL GEOGRAPHIC **Exploring Our World**

The "running of the bulls" is an annual and controversial event in Pamplona, a city in northern Spain. Although animal rights groups object to it, each morning during the weeklong Festival of San Fermín, a half dozen bulls are released to run along the city's narrow streets. Young men risk their lives running ahead of the bulls. Their goal is to stay in the race as long as possible.

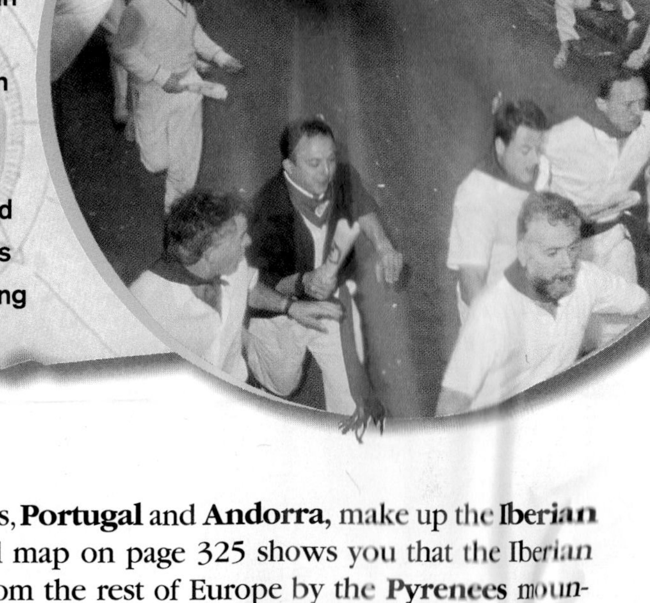

Spain and its neighbors, **Portugal** and **Andorra,** make up the **Iberian Peninsula.** The physical map on page 325 shows you that the Iberian Peninsula is separated from the rest of Europe by the **Pyrenees** mountain range. Off the peninsula's southern tip lies the Strait of Gibraltar, a narrow passageway between the Atlantic Ocean and the Mediterranean Sea. The strait divides the Iberian Peninsula—and Europe—from Africa. Only 9 miles (14 km) separate the two continents at this point.

Spain—about twice the size of Oregon—takes up about 80 percent of the Iberian Peninsula. Portugal—slightly smaller than Indiana—sits on the peninsula's western edge and occupies most of the remaining space. Tiny Andorra, with only 175 square miles (453 sq. km), perches high in the Pyrenees.

The Land and Climate

As you can tell from the physical map, most of the erian Peninsula has high elevation. The Pyrenees forms the borde tween Spain and France. For a long time, these very steep mount isolated the Iberian Peninsula from the rest of Europe. Today, wit vances in

◀ Colorful gondolas parade in the Grand Canal in Venice, Italy

technology and communication, the peninsula's people are closely linked to European events.

A huge central plateau covers about two-thirds of the peninsula. A **plateau,** you may recall, is flat land with high elevation. Because this plateau lies in the rain shadow of the mountains, it is the driest part of the peninsula. In many areas the reddish-yellow soil is poor, and the land is dry-farmed to grow crops such as wheat and vegetables. **Dry farming** is a method in which the land is left unplanted every few years so that it can store moisture. Some farmers also herd sheep, goats, and cattle.

Many of the Iberian Peninsula's major rivers begin in the central plateau. The **Tagus** (TAY•guhs) **River**—the peninsula's longest river—flows from central Spain to the Atlantic Ocean. Most of these rivers are not **navigable,** or wide and deep enough to allow the passage of ships. The **Guadalquivir** (GWAH•thahl•kee•VEER) **River** is one of the few navigable rivers.

On the climate map on page 331, you see that Portugal and most of Spain have a Mediterranean climate. People in these areas generally enjoy mild winters and hot summers. Yet elevation and closeness to

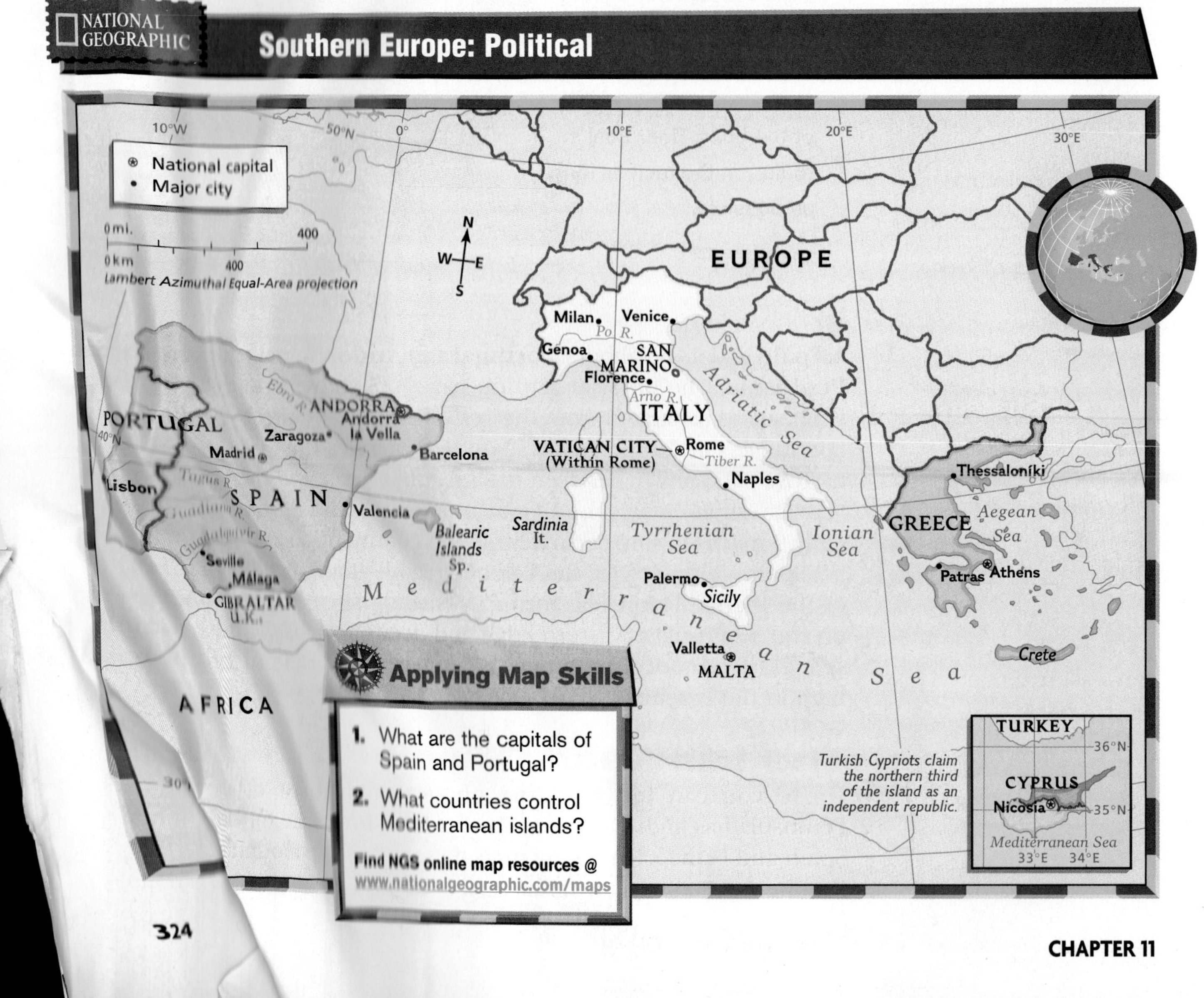

the sea cause differences in climate. In northwestern Spain, warm winds from the Atlantic Ocean drop much rain, and winters are chilly. You find a dry steppe climate in southeastern Spain because of hot winds from North Africa.

Reading Check **What type of landform covers central Spain?**

Growing Economies

Spain and Portugal both belong to the European Union. Once slow in developing manufacturing, the two countries in recent years have worked hard to catch up economically with other European Union nations. Agriculture remains important to Spain and Portugal, but most of their people now work in manufacturing and service industries. Andorra draws millions of tourists each year who flock to its duty-free shops.

Although much of Spain is dry and rugged, Spanish farmers grow a wide variety of grains. On eastern coastal plains, they use irrigation to grow citrus fruits and olive trees. Acres and acres of olive groves make Spain one of the world's leading producers of olive oil. Vegetables and

NATIONAL GEOGRAPHIC

Southern Europe: Physical

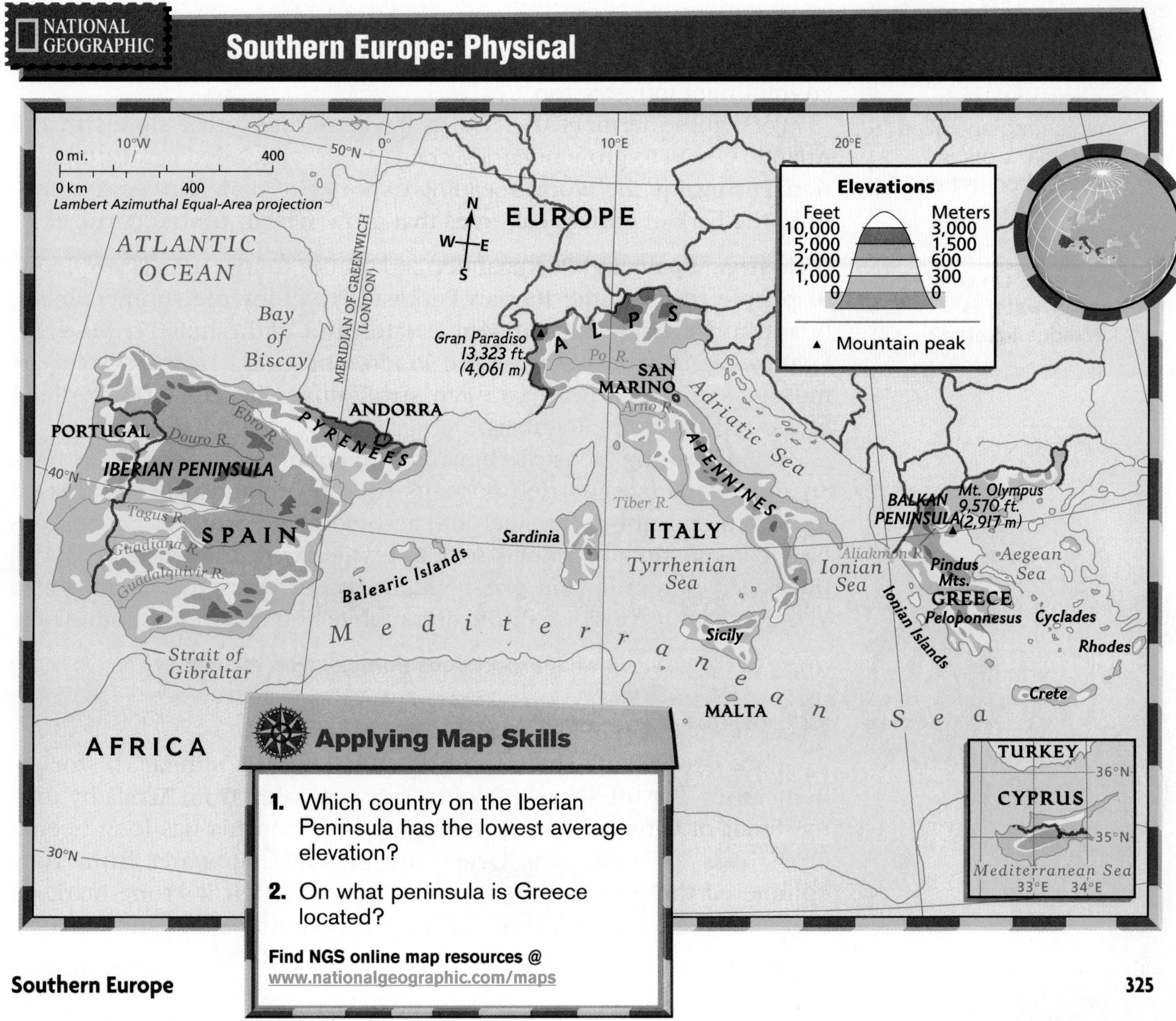

Applying Map Skills

1. Which country on the Iberian Peninsula has the lowest average elevation?
2. On what peninsula is Greece located?

Find NGS online map resources @ www.nationalgeographic.com/maps

Spain and Portugal

Barcelona (above) is the main city of the Spanish region called Catalonia. Cork is stripped from a tree in central Portugal (right).

Location **On what body of water is Barcelona located?**

grapes are other important Spanish crops. Grass grows well in the north, which has more rain. People there raise beef and dairy cattle. Fishing is an important industry, too.

Portuguese farmers use the well-watered land that slopes to the Atlantic Ocean to grow potatoes, grains, fruits, olives, and grapes. In addition, Portugal is the world's leading exporter of cork. The cork comes from the bark of certain oak trees that grow well in central Portugal.

Industry Spain and Portugal depend on the tourist industry. Millions of people travel to the Iberian Peninsula to enjoy the sunny climate, beautiful beaches, and ancient castles and cathedrals. In **Madrid,** Spain's capital, you can visit the Prado, one of the world's great art museums. In **Barcelona** you can stroll along the city's flower-lined boulevard called the Ramblas.

Manufacturing industries benefit both countries' economies as well. Spanish workers mine rich deposits of iron ore and make processed foods, clothing, footwear, steel, and automobiles. Portugal's economy is based on traditional products such as textiles, cork and wood products, beverages, porcelain, and glassware. In recent years, the country also strengthened its position in the automobile and electronics industries.

✓ Reading Check **In what export does Portugal lead the world?**

History and Government

The people of Spain and Portugal share similar histories. Remember that the Iberian Peninsula is separated from Africa by only the Strait of Gibraltar. Because of this, the peninsula has long been a crossroads as well as a target for invaders. Romans from Italy conquered the peninsula in the 100s B.C. They left a strong mark on Iberian life and culture. Most languages spoken in Spain and Portugal are based on Latin, the language of Rome. Roman law forms the basis for law in both countries. In addition, most people in Spain and Portugal are Roman Catholic.

Beginning in the A.D. 700s, Muslims—followers of the religion of Islam—crossed the Strait of Gibraltar from North Africa and conquered much of the Iberian Peninsula. Spanish and Portuguese Christians fought for centuries to drive out the Muslims. The Spanish won their final victory over the Muslims in 1492.

That same year, the Spanish king and queen gave money to an explorer named Christopher Columbus. Columbus sailed west hoping to find a new sea route to Asia. Instead, he touched ground in the Americas. Soon Spain had a vast empire in South America and North America.

Portugal's Prince Henry "the Navigator" likewise encouraged exploration. In the 1500s, the country had become a trading nation and built its own empire. Portuguese merchants and soldiers founded colonies in Africa, South America, India, and Southeast Asia.

These overseas empires brought Spain and Portugal wealth from gold, silver, and trade goods. By the late 1800s, however, Spain had lost most of its **colonies,** or overseas territories. Portugal's power also declined, but it ruled parts of Africa and Asia until the late 1900s.

The Government As their empires crumbled, Spain and Portugal suffered a series of wars and rebellions. From 1936 to 1939, Spain had a violent civil war. General Francisco Franco's forces won, and he ruled as dictator of Spain until his death in 1975. During this same period, Portugal also was under a dictatorship. Today both countries are modern democracies. Spain is a constitutional monarchy, in which a king or queen is head of state, but elected officials run the government. Portugal is a **parliamentary republic,** with a president as head of state. A prime minister, chosen by the legislature, is the head of government. Andorra is a semi-independent principality—a region governed by both Spain and France.

Reading Check **What two things happened in 1492 in this region?**

The People

Despite similar histories, the people of Spain and Portugal have their cultural differences. Portugal developed a unified culture based on the Portuguese language, while Spain remained a "country of different countries." The Spanish people do not all speak the same language or even have a single culture.

The region of Castile, in central Spain, dominated the culture for centuries. The dialect of the Castilian people became the form of Spanish spoken by most Spaniards. A **dialect** is a local form of a language. People in other regions of Spain, however, regard themselves as separate groups. In the Mediterranean region of Catalonia, the people speak Catalan, a language related to French. Galicia in northwestern Spain has its own language—Galician. Andalusia in the south has its unique dialects and cultural traditions.

The Alhambra

The Muslim rule of Spain brought economic success to the Iberian Peninsula. The Muslims brought scientific knowledge, methods of irrigation, and new crops. They also brought literature, music, and art to Spain.

The Alhambra Palace in southern Spain is a spectacular example of Muslim art. Islam forbids art that includes human forms. As a result, Muslim artists created complex patterns and elaborate designs. This is the Court of the Lions. In the center is a fountain where running water cooled the people of the palace in Spain's hot midday sun.

The Basque people in the Pyrenees see themselves as completely separate from Spain. They speak Basque, a language unlike any other in the world. Having lived in Spain longer than any other group, many Basques want independence in order to preserve their way of life. Some Basque groups have even used violence against the Spanish government.

Rural and City Life Almost two-thirds of the people in Portugal live in rural areas. **Lisbon,** with a population of just about 2 million, is Portugal's capital and largest city. Porto is its second-largest city.

In contrast, more than three-fourths of Spain's 39.4 million people live in cities and towns. Madrid has more than 3 million people and ranks as one of Europe's leading cultural centers. Madrid faces the usual urban challenges of heavy traffic and air pollution. Fast-paced Barcelona is Spain's leading seaport and industrial center.

You find some centuries-old traditions even in the modern cities. For example, most Spanish families usually do not eat dinner until 9 or 10 o'clock at night. On special occasions, Spaniards enjoy paella, a traditional dish of shrimp, lobster, chicken, ham, and vegetables mixed with seasoned rice.

Rock and jazz music are popular with young Spaniards and Portuguese, but the people of each region have their own traditional songs and dances as well. Spanish musicians often accompany singers and dancers on guitars, castanets, and tambourines. Spanish dances such as the bolero and flamenco and soulful Portuguese music known as fado have spread throughout the world.

Reading Check What are the five culture regions of Spain?

Assessment

Defining Terms

1. **Define** plateau, dry farming, navigable, colony, parliamentary republic, dialect.

Recalling Facts

2. **Location** What three countries are located on the Iberian Peninsula?
3. **Economics** Name four types of goods manufactured in Portugal.
4. **History** What group controlled Spain from the A.D. 700s until 1492?

Critical Thinking

5. **Drawing Conclusions** Why do you think Spain is more urban than Portugal?
6. **Understanding Cause and Effect** Why do the Basque people feel separate from the rest of Spain?

Graphic Organizer

7. **Organizing Information** In a chart like this one, list facts about Spain and Portugal for each category.

	Spain	Portugal
Land		
Economy		
Cities		
People		

Applying Geography Skills

8. **Analyzing Maps** Turn to the physical map on page 325. What rivers flow through both Spain and Portugal?

Geography Skill

Reading a Population Map

Population density is the number of people living in a square mile or square kilometer. A **population density map** shows you where people live in a given region. Mapmakers use different colors to represent different population densities. The darker the color, the more dense, or crowded, the population is in that particular area. Cities that are shown by dots or squares also represent different population sizes.

Learning the Skill

To read a population density map, follow these steps:

- Read the title of the map.
- Study the map key to determine what the colors mean.
- On the map, find the areas that have the lowest and highest population density.
- Identify what symbols are used to show how heavily populated the cities are.

Practicing the Skill

Look at the map below to answer the following questions.

1. What color stands for 125–250 people per square mile (50–100 per sq. km)?
2. Which cities have more than 1 million people?
3. Which areas have the lowest population density? Why?

Applying the Skill

Obtain a population density map of your state. What is the population density of your area? What is the nearest city with 1 million people?

GO TO Practice key skills with **Glencoe Skillbuilder Interactive Workbook, Level 1.**

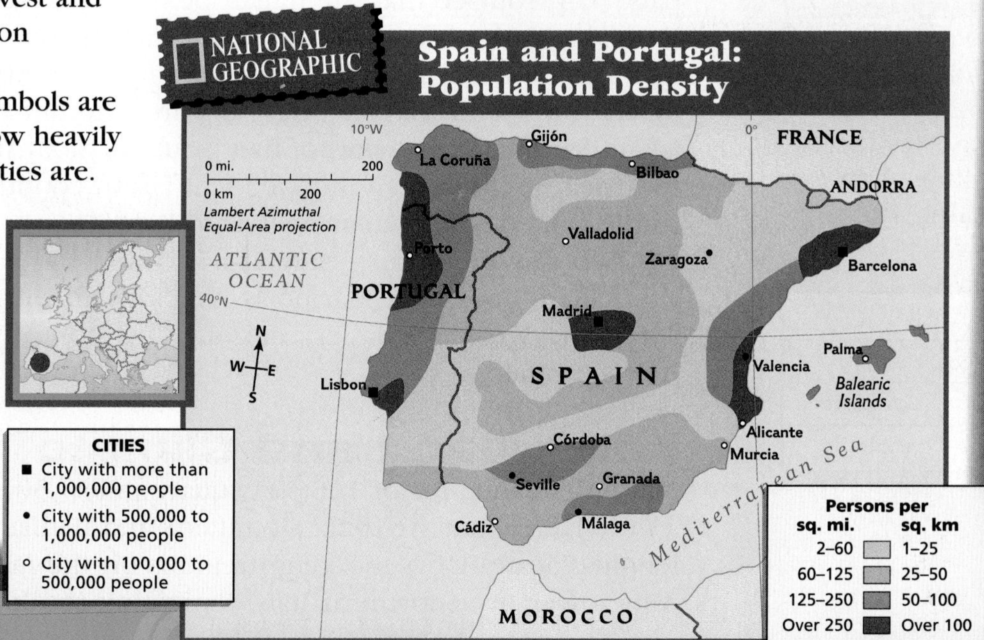

Italy

Guide to Reading

Main Idea

Once the center of a mighty empire, Italy has influenced Europe's religions, cultures, and governments.

Terms to Know

- sirocco
- city-state
- Renaissance
- coalition government
- pope

Places to Locate

- Italy
- Sicily
- Malta
- San Marino
- Vatican City
- Rome
- Apennines
- Po River
- Venice

Reading Strategy

Create a chart like this one and fill in at least one key fact about Italy under each category heading.

Italy	
Land	History
Climate	Government
Economy	People

NATIONAL GEOGRAPHIC **Exploring Our World**

Italy is known for the religious influence it has had on the world. Sometimes even animals are included in religious services. Here a horse and rider leave the church in Siena, Italy, after being blessed before the city's big horse race. The race, known as the Palio, has been held twice a year for more than 300 years.

The country of **Italy** is a land of seacoasts. Look at the map on page 324. You see that the Italian peninsula sticks out from Southern Europe into the center of the Mediterranean Sea. The peninsula looks like a boot about to kick a triangle-shaped football. The "football" is **Sicily,** an island that belongs to Italy. Another large Mediterranean island, Sardinia, is also part of Italy. South of Sicily, just before you come to Africa, lies **Malta,** an independent island country that has close ties to the United Kingdom as well as to Italy.

Two tiny countries—**San Marino** and **Vatican City**—lie within the Italian "boot." San Marino is near the northeastern coast. Vatican City—the world's smallest nation—lies completely within **Rome,** Italy's capital.

Italy's Land and Climate

With a land area of 116,324 square miles (301,277 sq. km), Italy is a little larger than Arizona. Mountains and highlands run down Italy's length. Locate Italy's mountain regions on the map on page 325. The Alps tower over northern Italy, separating the Italian peninsula from

France, Switzerland, Austria, and Slovenia. Another mountain range, the **Apennines** (A•puh•NYNZ), runs down the center of Italy to the toe of the boot. Low hills flank these mountains on the east and west sides.

The rumbling of volcanic mountains echoes through the southern part of the peninsula and the island of Sicily. Mount Etna, Europe's highest active volcano, rises on Sicily's eastern coast. Throughout history, the southern part of Italy has experienced volcanic eruptions and earthquakes.

Although mountains and hills dominate most of Italy, you can also find lowland regions. In the northeast, the largest lowland is the **Po River** valley. The Po, Italy's longest river, flows 400 miles (644 km) from the French border to the Adriatic Sea.

The map below shows you that most of Italy has a mild Mediterranean climate of sunny summers and rainy winters. In spring and summer, hot dry winds called **siroccos** blow across Italy from North Africa. In fall and winter, the land receives cool, moist air from the Atlantic Ocean. Most of Italy receives enough rain to grow crops.

Italy has two other climate regions. The Po River valley has a humid subtropical climate, with warm, humid summers and cool, rainy winters. The Alps in the far north of Italy give this area a highland climate. Temperatures there tend to be cool or cold.

Reading Check **Where are Italy's two main mountain regions located?**

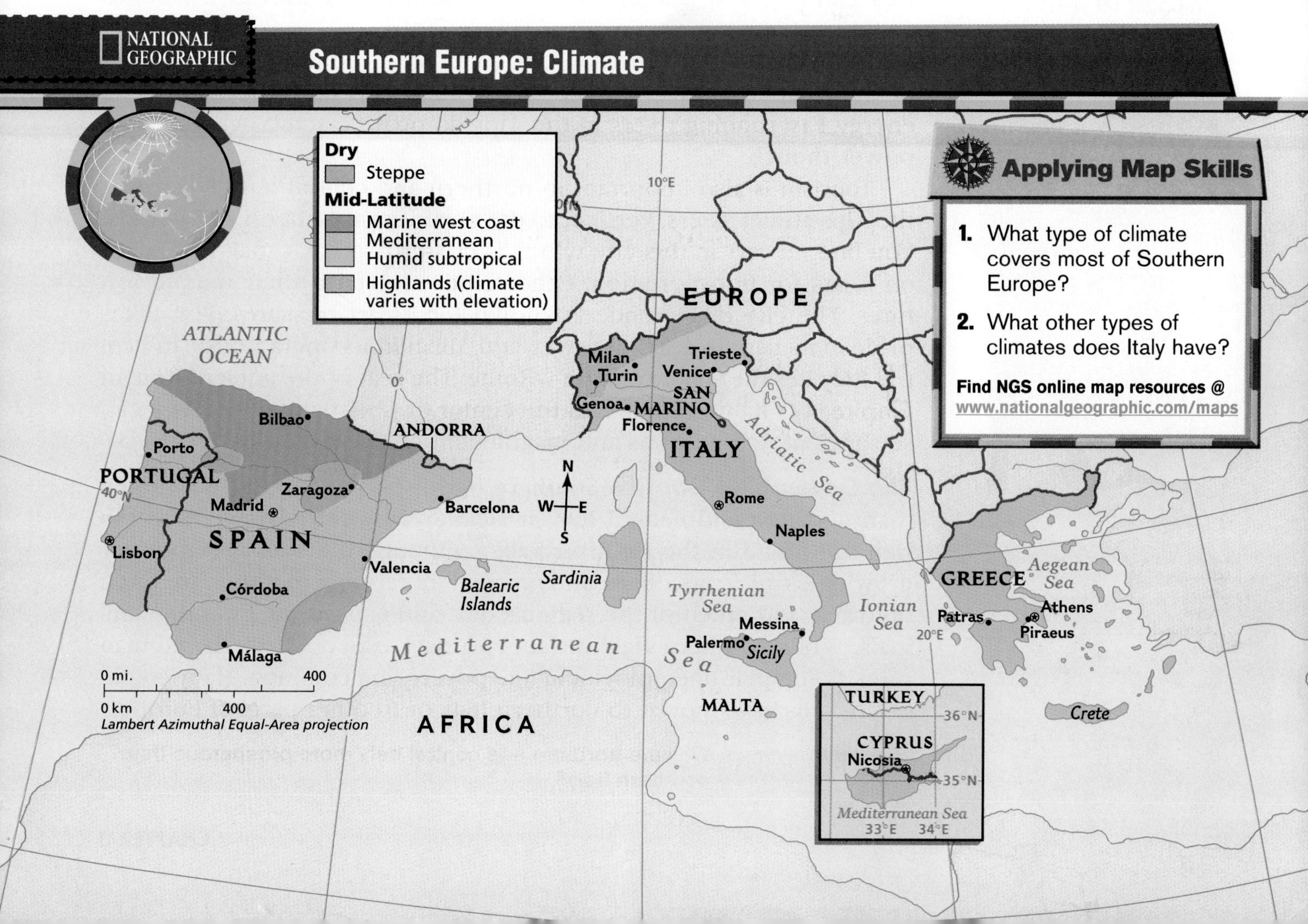

Ancient and Modern

Italy has both the old—Rome's Colosseum—and the new—the stylish models of Milan's fashion industry.

Place **How has Italy's economy changed in the past 50 years?**

Italy's Economy

In the past 50 years, Italy has changed from a mainly agricultural country into one of the world's leading industrial economies. A member of the European Union, Italy has a large market for its goods, which include cars and home appliances. Many of those goods are produced by small, family-owned businesses rather than by large corporations. Italian businesses are known for creating new designs and methods for making products.

Prosperous North and Center Fertile soil and steady, year-round rainfall give northern Italy many benefits. Most of Italy's agriculture centers on the Po River valley. Farmers grow sugar beets, corn, wheat, vegetables, and fruits. In hilly areas of northern and central Italy, farmers grow grapes for wine. Italy is one of the world's major wine-producing countries.

The Po River valley is even more important as a manufacturing center. Factories here produce most of Italy's manufactured goods. Skilled workers in the cities of Milan and Turin make cars, machinery, chemicals, clothing, and leather goods. Genoa, a thriving port city, also has factories.

Italy has few natural resources, so most of the raw materials used in these factories must be imported. Italy also imports most of its energy. Fast-running rivers in the Alps do provide some hydroelectric power, though.

Tourism is also important in northern and central Italy. Resorts in the Alps attract skiers. **Venice,** to the northeast, is built on 117 islands. You find no cars in this city, which is crisscrossed by canals and relies on boats for transportation. Other cities also have their unique features. The city of Florence is known for its art treasures. Pisa takes pride in its famous leaning tower, and Milan in its opera house. In central Italy lies the star attraction—Rome. The seat of the ancient Roman Empire, it is Italy's capital and the center of Christianity. Here you can see ancient Roman ruins and magnificent churches and palaces.

The Developing South Southern Italy is poorer and less developed than northern and central Italy. It lacks hydroelectric power and the rich soil found in the Po River valley, although the soils are good for growing citrus fruits, olives, and grapes. Still, farming methods are often outdated, and much of the region's dry land is used for pasturing animals. While southern Italy attracts tourists, especially to the Roman ruins at Pompeii, unemployment and poverty are common. Many southern Italians have moved to northern Italy or to other parts of Europe.

Reading Check **Why are northern and central Italy more prosperous than southern Italy?**

Italy's History and Culture

For hundreds of years, Italy was the heart of Western civilization. The city of Rome became a powerful force in the Mediterranean in the 200s B.C. Roman armies conquered a huge empire that stretched from the eastern Mediterranean to Spain and from North Africa to the British Isles. Rome influenced the government, arts, and architecture of much of Europe.

After the fall of the Roman Empire in the A.D. 400s, Italy broke into many small territories and city-states. Each **city-state** consisted of a city and its surrounding countryside. In the 1300s, wealthy merchant families arose in many city-states. Their money helped artists and scholars explore new ways of thinking. The result was the **Renaissance**—a French word meaning "rebirth." From the 1300s to 1600, this time of profound cultural achievements in the arts and learning spread throughout Europe.

European powers such as Spain and Austria took control of parts of Italy, however. In addition, rivalry grew among some of Italy's city-states. As a result, Italy did not become a unified nation until the mid-1800s. From the 1920s to the early 1940s, dictator Benito Mussolini ruled the country. He joined with Germany's Adolf Hitler and pulled Italy into World War II. Italy was defeated in the war, and Mussolini was removed from power.

Italy's Government After World War II, Italy became a democratic republic. Yet democracy did not bring a stable government. Since the late 1940s, political power has constantly changed hands. Rivalry between the wealthy north and the poorer south has caused political tensions. In addition, many political parties exist, and no single

Architecture

For 800 years the Leaning Tower of Pisa has stood as a monument to construction mistakes. Begun in 1173, the tower began to tilt even before it was finished. Over time the tower moved even more, until by 1990, it leaned 12 feet (3.7 m) to the south. Fearing the tower would fall over, experts closed it. They added 800 tons (726 t) of lead weights to its base. They also removed 30 tons (27 t) of subsoil from underneath the north side of the tower in hopes that it would sink the opposite way. Visitors have once more returned to the tower.

Looking Closer Why do you think experts fixed the tower's problem but still left it leaning?

Traveling Water Boulevards

Carlo lives in Venice, Italy—a city made up of 117 islands. He gets around by jumping on a *vaporetto* (water bus) or gondola (also called a water taxi). You see, most of the city's streets are canals. For fun, Carlo and his friends cruise the "streets" of Venice by boat.

party has been strong enough to gain control. Instead, Italy has seen many **coalition governments,** where two or more political parties work together to run a country.

Italy's People If you look at the population density map on page 337, you will see that parts of Italy are very crowded. About two-thirds of Italy's 57.7 million people live on only one-fourth of the land. Why? Mountains take up much of the country. The Po River valley is the most densely populated region. Many Italians have moved to northern cities, such as Milan and Turin, from the poorer southern region in order to find jobs.

About 70 percent of Italy's people live in towns and cities, and more than 90 percent of Italians work in manufacturing and service industries. Most Italians—more than 95 percent—are Roman Catholic. Celebrating the church's religious festivals is a widely shared part of Italian life. Vatican City in Rome is the headquarters of the Roman Catholic Church. The **pope,** who is the head of the church, lives and works here. Vatican City has many art treasures as well as the world's largest church, St. Peter's Basilica.

The people of Italy speak Italian, which developed from Latin, the language of ancient Rome. Italian is closely related to French and Spanish. Do you know any Italian words? Many have been adopted into the English language. Pasta, made from flour and water, is the basic dish in Italy. Some pasta dishes are spaghetti, lasagna, and ravioli.

✓Reading Check **Why have coalition governments been necessary in Italy?**

Section 2 Assessment

Defining Terms

1. **Define** sirocco, city-state, Renaissance, coalition government, pope.

Recalling Facts

2. **Place** What is the capital of Italy?
3. **Location** Where is Italy's major agricultural region? Why?
4. **Culture** What is Vatican City?

Critical Thinking

5. **Summarizing Information** What are at least five things tourists can see in Italy?
6. **Understanding Cause and Effect** Why are there no cars in Venice?

Graphic Organizer

7. **Organizing Information** Draw a time line like this one and label it with four important events and dates in Italy's history.

Applying Geography Skills

8. **Analyzing Maps** Look at the climate map on page 331. In which climate zone is the city of Venice located?

Making Connections

ART SCIENCE LITERATURE TECHNOLOGY

Leonardo da Vinci

The Italian Leonardo da Vinci is considered one of the greatest artists of the Renaissance. He painted the *Mona Lisa* and the *Last Supper*, two of the world's best-known paintings. He was also a talented architect, engineer, and inventor.

The Artist

Leonardo da Vinci was born in 1452 in a small town near Florence, Italy. As the son of a wealthy man, he received the best education that Florence could offer. Leonardo became known for his ability to create sculptures and paintings that looked almost lifelike. Much of his success in this area came from his keen interest in nature. He also studied human anatomy and used this knowledge to make his figures realistic.

The Inventor

As a child, Leonardo was fascinated with machines and began to draw his own inventions. The first successful parachute jump was made from the top of a French tower in 1783—but Leonardo had sketched a parachute in 1485. He designed flying machines, armored tanks, and aircraft landing gear. He even drew a diver's suit that used tubes and air chambers to allow a swimmer to remain underwater for long periods of time.

Leonardo's Notebooks

Much of what we know about Leonardo comes from the thousands of pages of notes and sketches he kept in his notebooks. He used mirror, or reverse, writing, starting at the right side of the page and moving across to the left. No one is sure why Leonardo wrote this way. Some think he was trying to keep people from reading and stealing his ideas. He may also have been trying to hide his thoughts from the Roman Catholic Church, whose teachings sometimes conflicted with his ideas. From a practical standpoint, writing in reverse probably helped him avoid smearing wet ink, since he was left-handed.

▲ The *Mona Lisa*

▲ Leonardo da Vinci

Making the Connection

1. What are two of Leonardo's best-known works?
2. Why might Leonardo have written his notebooks in mirror writing?
3. **Understanding Cause and Effect** In what way did Leonardo's interest in the world around him influence his work?

Section 3

Greece

Guide to Reading

Main Idea

With a rugged landscape, Greece relies on sea trade and tourism to build its economy.

Terms to Know

- mainland
- elevation
- suburb

Places to Locate

- Athens
- Greece
- Balkan Peninsula
- Pindus Mountains
- Peloponnesus
- Crete
- Aegean Sea
- Cyprus

Reading Strategy

Create a diagram like this one. In each box give an example of something that would attract tourists to Greece.

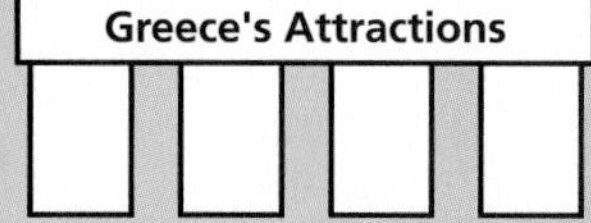

NATIONAL GEOGRAPHIC **Exploring Our World**

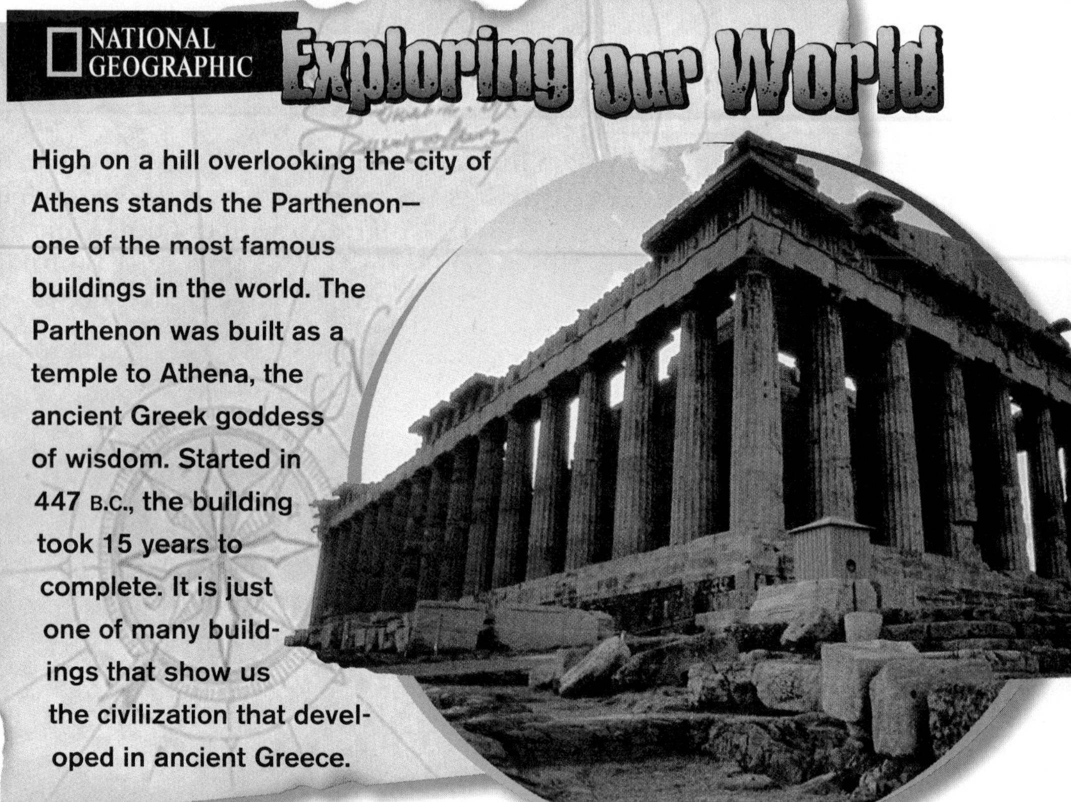

High on a hill overlooking the city of Athens stands the Parthenon—one of the most famous buildings in the world. The Parthenon was built as a temple to Athena, the ancient Greek goddess of wisdom. Started in 447 B.C., the building took 15 years to complete. It is just one of many buildings that show us the civilization that developed in ancient Greece.

In ancient times, **Athens** was a small town. Today the city is a modern urban center that is growing rapidly in size and population. The ancient Greeks would be amazed to see the changes that have taken place in Athens over the centuries. Yet they would find many other places in **Greece** that have changed very little. Outside the large cities, much of Greek life still follows traditional ways.

Rugged Land, Mild Climate

Much of Greece sits on the southern tip of the **Balkan Peninsula** that juts out from Europe into the Mediterranean Sea. This is the Greek **mainland**—the major part of a country connected to a large landmass. Greece also includes 2,000 islands around the mainland. Greece—both mainland and islands—is about the size of Alabama.

Greece has a Mediterranean climate with hot, dry summers and mild, rainy winters. As you learned in Chapter 2, however, climate may vary, depending on **elevation,** or height above sea level. High-elevation areas in Greece are often cooler and wetter than lowlands.

The physical map on page 325 shows you that most of Greece is rocky and mountainous. Rugged ranges separate valleys and plains. Long arms of the sea reach into the coast, forming many smaller peninsulas. Like other Mediterranean areas, Greece is often shaken by earthquakes.

The **Pindus Mountains** run through the center of the Greek mainland. The Pindus and other smaller ranges divide Greece into many separate regions. Historically, this has kept people in one region isolated from people in other regions. Because of the poor, stony soil, most people living in the highlands graze sheep and goats. Constant grazing over the centuries has destroyed natural forests. Scrubby plants continue to grow, but they do little to halt soil erosion.

To the east of the Pindus Mountains lie two fertile lowlands—the Plain of Thessaly and the Macedonia-Thrace Plain. These two plains are Greece's major farming areas. At the southern end of the Pindus range is still another lowland, the Plain of Attica. About one-third of Greece's people live here. Athens, the Greek capital, lies on the Plain of Attica.

Southwest of the Plain of Attica lies the **Peloponnesus** (PEH•luh•puh•NEE•suhs). This large peninsula has rugged mountains and deep valleys. If you had traveled through this region about

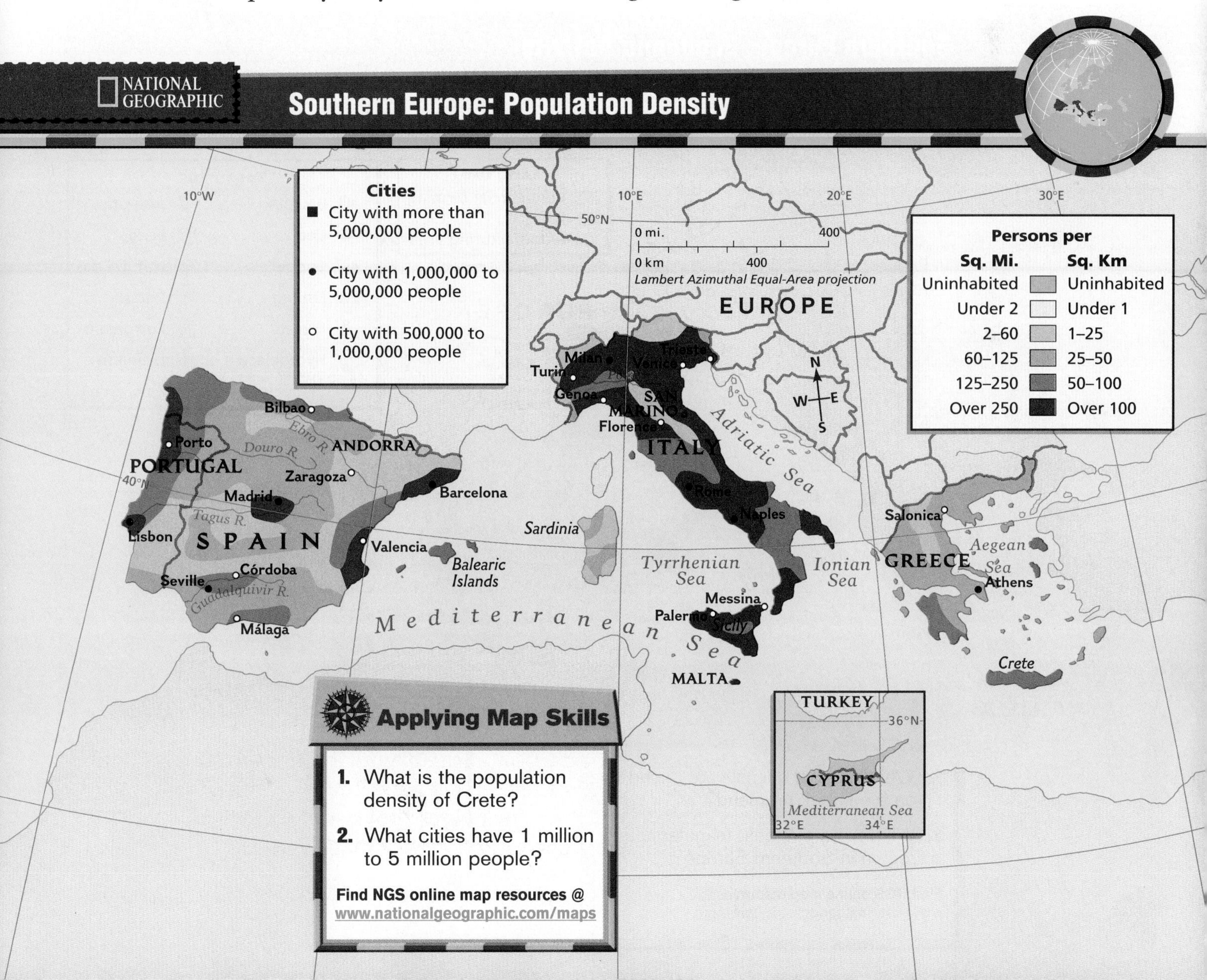

2,600 years ago, you might have heard crowds cheering on athletes competing in the first Olympic games.

The Islands Of the 2,000 Greek islands, only about 170 have people living on them. The largest Greek island, covering more than 3,000 square miles (7,770 sq. km), is **Crete.** Some of the islands are grouped together and named after the body of water in which they are located. The Ionian Islands lie in the Ionian Sea. The Aegean Islands lie in the **Aegean Sea.**

Farther east in the Mediterranean is the island country of **Cyprus.** Once under Turkish and then British rule, Cyprus became independent in 1960. For centuries Greeks and Turks have lived on Cyprus, but fighting between the two groups has resulted in a divided country. A United Nations peacekeeping force patrols a strip of land 112 miles (180 km) long. This strip separates the south (ruled by Greek Cypriots) from the north (controlled by Turkish Cypriots).

Reading Check **Where are Greece's major farming areas?**

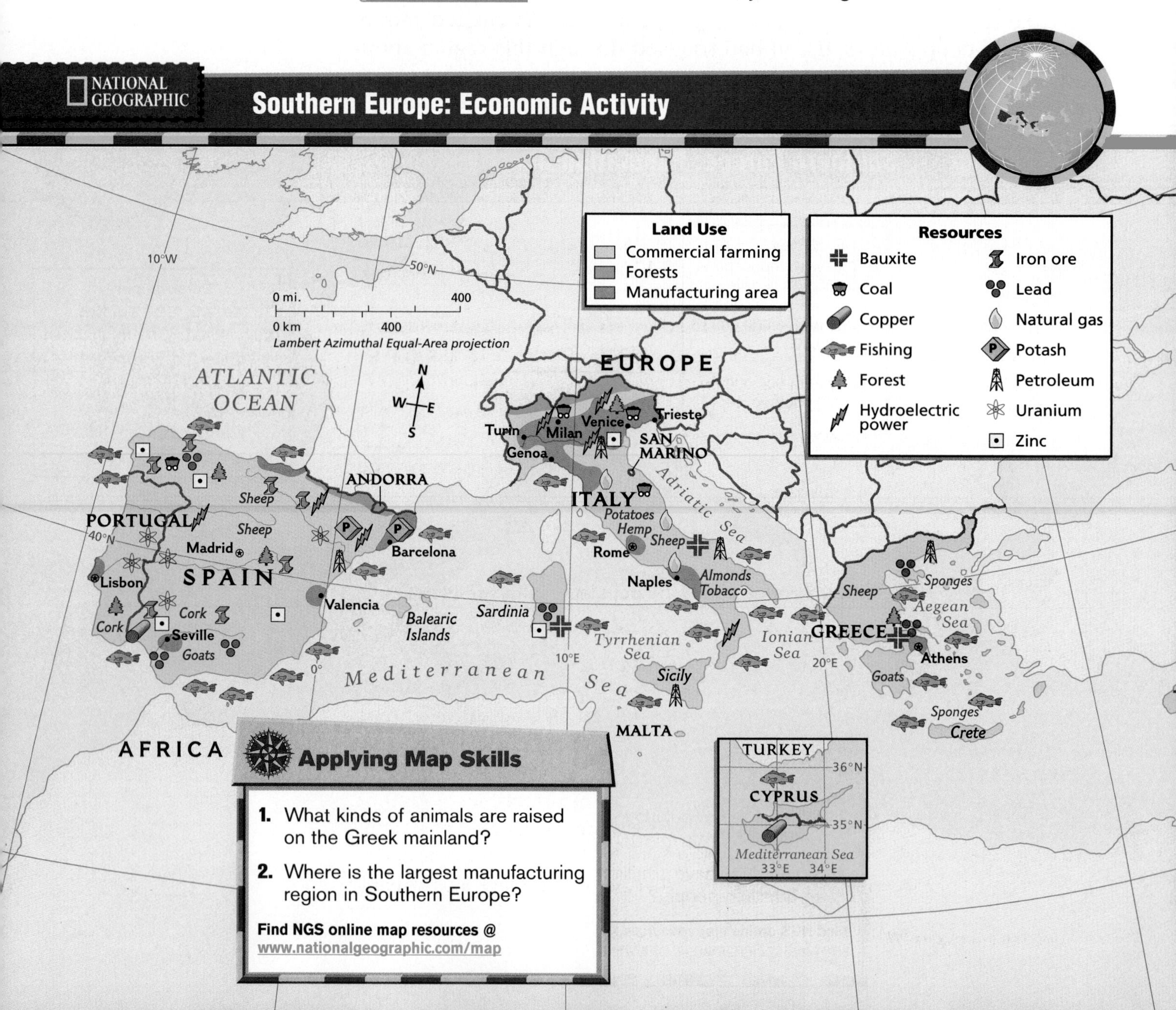

Greece's Economy

Greece belongs to the European Union but has one of the least developed economies in Europe. It must import food, fuels, and many manufactured goods. Because of Greece's rocky soil, only about one-third of the land can be used for farming. Yet almost 20 percent of Greek workers make their living from the land. Most Greek farms are small and lie in valleys, where the land is flat and more fertile. Farmers cultivate sugar beets, grains, citrus fruits, and tobacco. Like the other countries of Southern Europe, Greece has important crops of olives, used for olive oil, and grapes, used for wine.

Manufacturing has grown rapidly in recent years. Greek workers produce food and beverages, tobacco products, cement, textiles, and chemicals. Almost 60 percent of workers have jobs in service industries.

Greek Islands

Sparkling blue waters and brilliant white architecture attract tourists to the Greek islands.

Movement **In what ways does tourism help the Greek economy?**

Shipping and Tourism No part of Greece is more than 85 miles (137 km) from the sea. Have you ever read the famous epic poem, the *Odyssey*? Composed by an early poet named Homer, the *Odyssey* tells of a hero who took a long sea voyage. Greece still has one of the largest shipping fleets in the world, including oil tankers, cargo ships, fishing boats, and passenger vessels. Shipping is vital to the economy.

Tourism is another key industry. Each year millions of visitors come to Greece to visit historic sites such as the Parthenon in Athens and the temple of Apollo at Delphi. Others come to relax on beaches and to enjoy the beautiful island scenery. Cruise ships ferry passengers from island to island, while hotels and restaurants cater to the needs of tourists.

Although Greece and other Mediterranean countries rely on the sea for income, their growing populations threaten the sea's environment. Untreated sewage, garbage, and industrial chemicals often are dumped into the sea. These wastes pollute Mediterranean waters.

✓Reading Check **How has Greece's growing population affected the sea?**

Greece's History and Culture

Many "firsts" mark the history of Greece. The early Greeks developed theories of geometry, medical science, astronomy, physics, and government. In fact, much of Western civilization grew out of the achievements of ancient Greece.

The early Greeks reached the height of their cultural development during the mid-400s B.C.—the Golden Age of Greece. During this time, the city-state of Athens gave birth to the ideals of Western democracy. Our word "democracy" comes from the Greek language and means "power of the people." The ancient Greeks prized freedom and valued the importance of the individual. Greek thinkers such as Plato and Aristotle laid the foundations of Western philosophy and science. Greek writers such as Sophocles (SAH•fuh•KLEEZ) created dramas that explored human thoughts and feelings.

Lying near the crossroads of Europe and Asia, Greece was attacked and conquered by neighboring peoples. Not until 1829 did Greece become an independent country. During World War II, the country was brutally occupied by German forces. After this conflict, a bitter civil war was fought between Greek conservatives and Communists. In 1968 the Greeks set up their present form of government—a parliamentary republic. A president performs ceremonial duties, while a prime minister and cabinet hold actual political power.

> **Geography Online**
>
> **Web Activity** Visit the ***Geography: The World and Its People*** Web site at gwip.glencoe.com and click on **Chapter 11—Student Web Activities** to learn more about Greek culture.

Daily Life About 65 percent of Greece's 10.5 million people live in urban areas. Athens, the capital and largest city, is home to more than 750,000 people. Another 2.5 million live in its **suburbs**—the smaller communities that surround a city. The Greeks of today have much in common with their ancestors. They debate political issues with great enthusiasm, and they value the art of storytelling.

More than 95 percent of Greeks are Greek Orthodox Christians. Religion influences much of Greek life, especially in rural areas. Easter is the most important Greek holiday. Traditional holiday foods include lamb, fish, and feta cheese—made from sheep's or goat's milk.

Reading Check **How are the Greeks of today like their ancestors?**

Section 3 Assessment

Defining Terms

1. **Define** mainland, elevation, suburb.

Recalling Facts

2. **Place** What is the Peloponnesus?

3. **Government** Why does a United Nations peacekeeping force patrol the island of Cyprus?

4. **Economics** Why could one say that Greece's economy is dependent on the sea?

Critical Thinking

5. **Analyzing Information** The mid-400s B.C. is known as the Golden Age of Greece. List facts that support that title.

6. **Understanding Cause and Effect** Why has much of Greece's land suffered from land erosion?

Graphic Organizer

7. **Organizing Information** On a diagram like this one, list facts about Greece under each of the four topic headings.

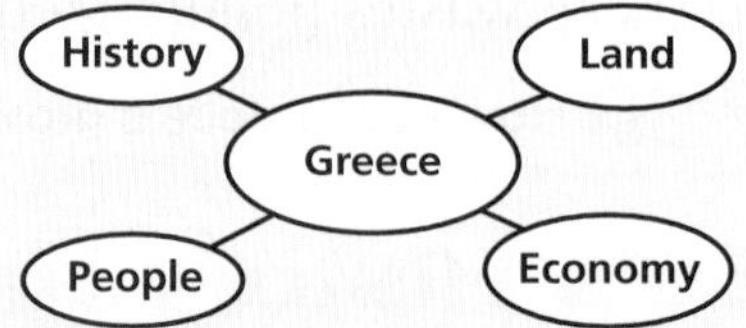

Applying Geography Skills

8. **Analyzing Maps** Study the physical map on page 325. What body of water separates Italy and Greece?

Chapter 11 Reading Review

Section 1 Spain and Portugal

Terms to Know
plateau
dry farming
navigable
colony
parliamentary republic
dialect

Main Idea

Spain and Portugal are working toward building prosperous economies.

✓ **Location** Spain and Portugal occupy the Iberian Peninsula, which is blocked from the rest of Europe by the Pyrenees and dominated by a huge central plateau.

✓ **Economics** Agriculture is still important to both countries, but the majority of people now work in manufacturing and service industries.

✓ **Culture** Spain has several distinct cultural regions, each with its own language or dialect.

Section 2 Italy

Terms to Know
sirocco
city-state
Renaissance
coalition government
pope

Main Idea

Once the center of a mighty empire, Italy has influenced Europe's religions, cultures, and governments.

✓ **Economics** The Po River valley, in the north, is Italy's main agricultural region and its principal industrial center.

✓ **History** The ancient Romans made important contributions to Western civilization in language, government, and architecture.

✓ **History** The Renaissance developed in Italy and spread renewed learning throughout Europe.

✓ **Government** Rome, Italy's capital, surrounds Vatican City, the world's smallest nation and headquarters of the Roman Catholic Church.

Section 3 Greece

Terms to Know
mainland
elevation
suburb

Main Idea

With a rugged landscape, Greece relies on sea trade and tourism to build its economy.

✓ **Place** Greece consists of a mountainous mainland and 2,000 islands.

✓ **Economics** Shipping and tourism are vital to Greece's economy.

✓ **History** Ancient Greeks laid the foundations for Western civilization—including science, art, philosophy, government, and drama.

▲ Mount Athos, Greece

Chapter 11

Assessment and Activities

Using Key Terms

Match the terms in Part A with their definitions in Part B.

A.

1. mainland
2. Renaissance
3. coalition government
4. sirocco
5. dry farming
6. city-state
7. plateau
8. dialect
9. suburb
10. pope

B.

a. rebirth of learning and the arts
b. land is left unplanted every few years
c. head of the Roman Catholic Church
d. the main landmass of a country
e. high, flat land
f. two or more political parties share power to run a country
g. smaller community surrounding a central city
h. local form of a language
i. hot, dry wind from Africa
j. independent city and the lands around it

Reviewing the Main Ideas

Section 1 Spain and Portugal

11. **Location** What narrow body of water separates Africa and the Iberian Peninsula?
12. **Human/Environment Interaction** How do Spain's farmers grow crops on the central plateau?
13. **Culture** Why did the Castilian dialect become the major language of Spain?

Section 2 Italy

14. **Economics** Why is the Po River valley important to Italy?
15. **Place** Why is Rome an important city?
16. **Culture** What does daily life center on in Italy?

Section 3 Greece

17. **Location** Which mountains are located in the center of the Greek mainland?
18. **Human/Environment Interaction** How does the rocky landscape influence Greece's economic activities?
19. **History** Identify three important people of ancient Greece. Why were they important?

NATIONAL GEOGRAPHIC **Southern Europe**

Place Location Activity

On a separate sheet of paper, match the letters on the map with the numbered places listed below.

1. Mediterranean Sea
2. Strait of Gibraltar
3. Portugal
4. Spain
5. Rome
6. Cyprus
7. Adriatic Sea
8. Greece
9. Aegean Sea
10. Pyrenees

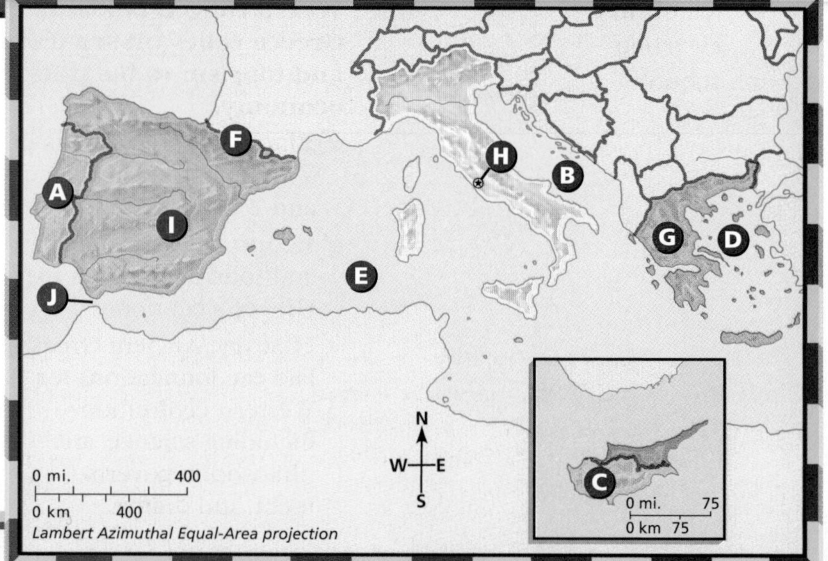

Self-Check Quiz Visit the ***Geography: The World and Its People*** Web site at gwip.glencoe.com and click on **Chapter 11—Self-Check Quizzes** to prepare for the Chapter Test.

Critical Thinking

20. **Drawing Conclusions** Why is the *Odyssey* an appropriate story for a Greek hero?
21. **Making Comparisons** On a diagram like this one, compare the ways in which ancient Greece and Rome influenced Western civilization by writing information under the "Greece" and "Rome" heads.

GeoJournal Activity

22. **Writing and Drawing** Andorra, Vatican City, Malta, and San Marino are four of Europe's smallest countries. The others are Liechtenstein and Monaco. Choose one of these countries and research it. Among other things, these countries are known for their beautiful postage stamps. As part of your research, design a stamp that displays one of the country's important features.

Mental Mapping Activity

23. **Focusing on the Region** Draw a simple outline map of Europe, then label the following:
    - Portugal
    - Spain
    - Pyrenees
    - Italy
    - Po River
    - Greece
    - Rome
    - Crete
    - Sicily
    - Mediterranean Sea

Technology Skills Activity

24. **Developing a Multimedia Presentation** Southern Europe is full of places that attract tourists. Imagine that you have taken a two-week trip to this region. Create a multimedia presentation that showcases the places you have visited and what you have learned about the region.

Standardized Test Practice

Directions: Read the paragraphs below, then answer the question that follows.

The ancient Greeks held the Olympic Games in Olympia every four years. The games were a religious festival in honor of Zeus, the Greeks' chief god. Trading and wars stopped while the games took place. The first Greek calendar began with the supposed date of the first Olympic Games in 776 B.C.

Athletes came from all over the Greek-speaking world to compete. Only male athletes, however, were allowed to take part, and women were not permitted even as spectators. Olympic events at first consisted only of a footrace. Later the broad jump, the discus throw, boxing, and wrestling were added. The Greeks crowned Olympic winners with wreaths of olive leaves and held parades in their honor.

1. **Based on the paragraphs, which of the following statements about Greek culture is NOT correct?**

   F The Greeks valued individual achievements.

   G The Greeks believed in many gods.

   H The Greeks believed in being healthy.

   J The Greeks discouraged individual glory.

Test-Taking Tip: Read all the choices carefully before choosing the one that does NOT describe Greek culture. Eliminate answers that you know are incorrect. For example, all the Olympic events were performed by individuals, not by teams. Therefore, answer F *does* describe Greek culture. The question, however, is asking for the statement that does NOT describe Greek culture.

Chapter 12
Northern Europe
The World and Its People
NATIONAL GEOGRAPHIC
To learn more about the people and places of Northern Europe, view *The World and Its People* Chapter 12 video.
Geography online
Chapter Overview Visit the ***Geography: The World and Its People*** Web site at gwip.glencoe.com and click on **Chapter 12—Chapter Overviews** to preview information about Northern Europe.

Section 1

Norway, Sweden, and Finland

Guide to Reading

Main Idea

The economies of Norway, Sweden, and Finland rely on water, forests, and mineral resources.

Terms to Know

- fjord
- skerry
- emigrate
- welfare state
- heavy industry
- nationalism
- sauna

Places to Locate

- Scandinavia
- Norway
- Sweden
- Finland
- Denmark
- Iceland
- Kjølen Mountains
- Oslo
- Baltic Sea
- Gulf of Bothnia
- Stockholm
- Helsinki

Reading Strategy

Create a diagram like this one and put information about each country in the ovals under the country's name. Where the ovals overlap, write facts that are true of all three countries.

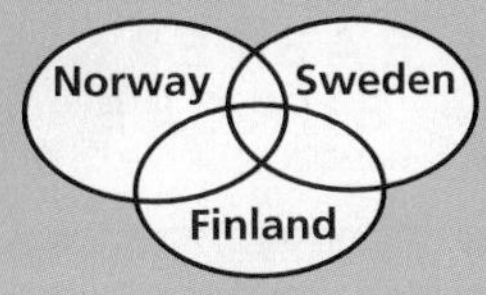

◀ Stockholm, Sweden

NATIONAL GEOGRAPHIC Exploring Our World

An ocean of snow covers northern Sweden in winter, when the sun is above the horizon for only a few hours a day and summer seems light-years away. Here, near Sweden's border with Norway, a footbridge used in summer to cross a ravine is almost buried in snow. Instead of using the footbridge, a hardy Swede zips by on his snowmobile.

The region of Northern Europe—also known as **Scandinavia**—is made up of five countries: **Norway, Sweden, Finland, Denmark,** and **Iceland.** People in these countries have standards of living that are among the highest in the world.

Norway

Jutting out to sea on the Scandinavian peninsula lie Norway and Sweden. Along the peninsula's western edge runs the kingdom of Norway. Its long, jagged coastline on the Atlantic Ocean includes many **fjords** (fee•AWRDS), or steep-sided valleys that are inlets of the sea. Thousands of years ago glaciers slowly moved across the mountainous land. On the seacoast they carved deep, narrow valleys. When the glacial ice eventually melted, the sea level rose. Water then flooded the valleys, producing the fjords. Today the fjords provide Norway with sheltered harbors and beautiful scenery popular with tourists.

The glacier-covered **Kjølen** (CHOO•luhn) **Mountains** tower over northern Norway. Rivers rushing down from mountains provide hydroelectricity to farms, factories, and homes. Only 3 percent of Norway is suitable for agriculture, much of it in the southeast.

Forests cover about 25 percent of Norway. Acid rain is slowly destroying many forested areas, however. Turn to page 362 to learn more about acid rain and its effects on Northern Europe.

About one-third of Norway lies north of the Arctic Circle. This rugged area is often called Land of the Midnight Sun. Here the sun never sets in the midsummer months. In the midwinter months, the sun never rises. Turn to page 352 to find out more about the Midnight Sun.

Norway's far northern location results in a mostly cold climate. However, a mild climate is found along Norway's southern and western coasts, even though this area lies at the same latitude as Alaska. Winds blowing over the North Atlantic Current raise temperatures on the land. Most of Norway's 4.5 million people live in the south within 10 miles (16 km) of the coast, chiefly in urban areas. **Oslo,** the capital and largest city, lies at the end of a fjord on the southern coast.

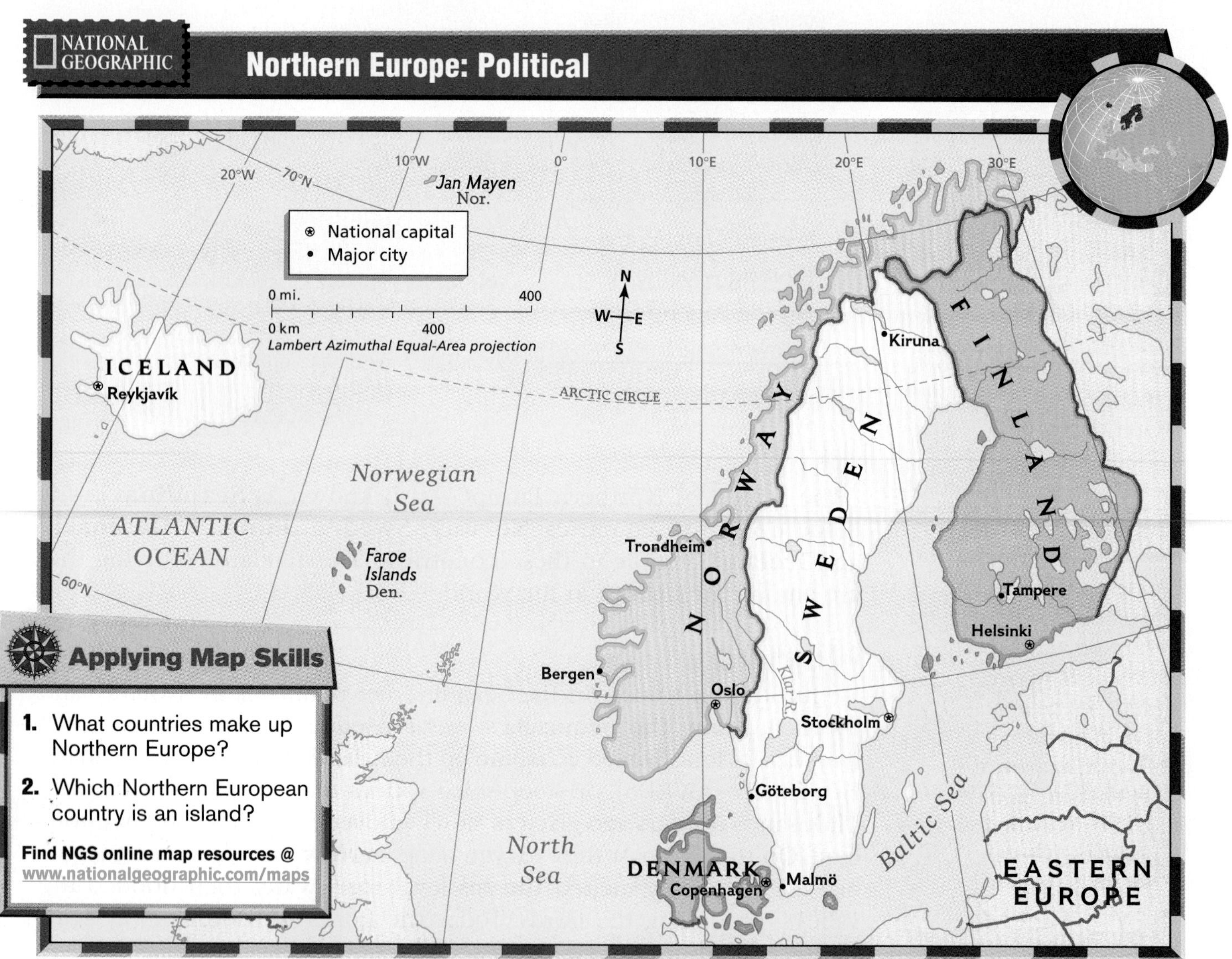

Norway's Economy Norway is a wealthy country, partly because of the seas that lap its coast. Norway began to extract oil and natural gas from beneath the North Sea in the 1970s. Today it is the world's second-largest oil exporter, after Saudi Arabia. The seas themselves provide an important export—fish. The city of Bergen is a major port and fish market. Warm ocean currents keep Bergen and most of Norway's other harbors ice-free all year. Norway's large fleet of commercial ships and cruise ships carries cargo and people around the world.

Norway's History and People Norway's first settlers arrived about 10,000 years ago. They followed herds of reindeer that migrated north as the glaciers retreated. During the A.D. 700s and 800s, Norway's Vikings, seeking land and adventure, raided and traded throughout Europe. They often founded settlements along the way. You can still see unique stave churches that reflect traditions of the Vikings as well as early Christian traditions. These churches are among the world's oldest wooden buildings. About A.D. 1000, a Viking named Leif Eriksson became possibly the first European to explore North America's coast.

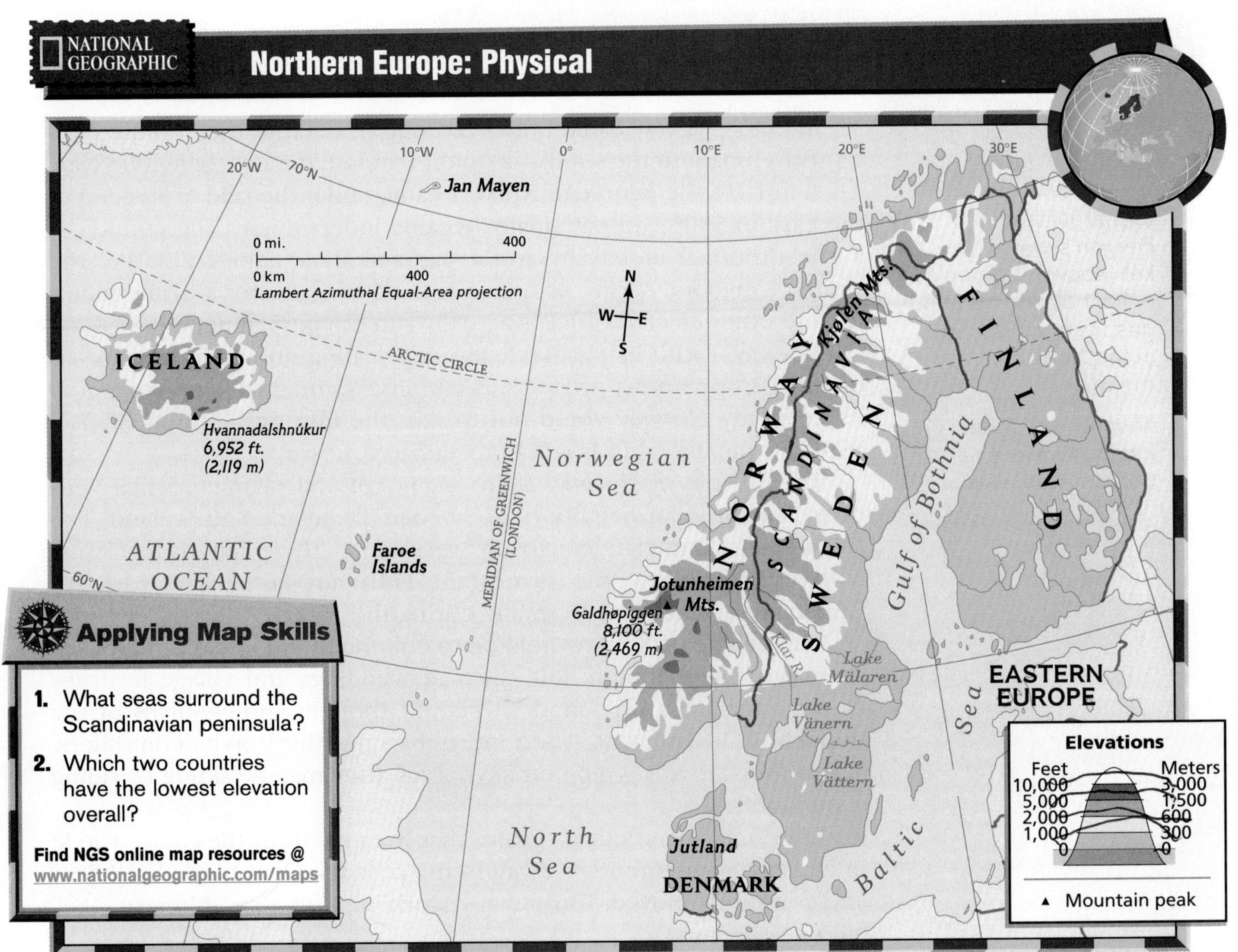

Applying Map Skills

1. What seas surround the Scandinavian peninsula?
2. Which two countries have the lowest elevation overall?

Find NGS online map resources @ www.nationalgeographic.com/maps

Norway's Economy

A shopper goes from boat to boat looking for bargains in Bergen's water market (above). Europe's richest oil and natural gas fields are found in the North Sea (right).

Movement What keeps Norway's harbors ice-free all year?

In 1387 Norway came under the rule of tiny but much more populous Denmark to the south—a union that lasted more than 400 years. Then in 1814 the people of Norway came under the rule of Sweden to the east. In 1905 Norway finally became independent. The country is a constitutional monarchy and a parliamentary democracy, like the United Kingdom. A king or queen is head of state, but a prime minister and other elected officials actually run the government.

Norway—with its profitable farming, fishing, and oil industries—is one of Europe's most prosperous nations. Wanting to keep control of its economy, Norway voted not to join the European Union (EU) in 1994. EU membership is still hotly debated, however.

The people of Norway share many cultural characteristics with their Scandinavian neighbors in Sweden, Denmark, and Iceland. The Norwegian language is closely related to their languages. Most Norwegians follow the Protestant Lutheran faith. This form of Christianity came from Germany during the 1500s.

The people of Norway hold on to cultural traditions. You might see them wearing elaborate folk dress at weddings and village festivals. Norwegians are a very modern people, though. Three-fourths of the population lives in cities, and more than one-third owns computers. When they are not typing on keyboards, they may be skiing or riding snowmobiles.

The Sami are an ethnic group that lives north of the Arctic Circle in Finland, Sweden, and Norway. In the past, the Sami herded reindeer and constantly moved. Today many work in mining and forestry.

✓ Reading Check **What type of government does Norway have?**

Sweden

Sweden is almost the size of California. Inland snow-covered mountains adjoin forested highlands, fertile lowlands, and then coastal **skerries,** or rocky islands. Sweden's long coastline touches the **Baltic Sea,** the **Gulf of Bothnia,** and a narrow arm of the North Sea. The country has about 100,000 lakes, most carved by glaciers.

Sweden is colder than Norway. Why is that? Sweden's mountains block the warm winds of the North Atlantic Current. This causes northern Sweden to have cool summers and cold winters. Many coastal ports are frozen for at least a couple of months during the winter. The North Atlantic winds provide the far south with a milder climate.

Sweden's Economy Sweden is a wealthy, industrial country. Its prosperity comes from abundant natural resources. Sweden's powerful northern rivers produce hydroelectricity. Iron ore deposits in the Arctic region supply steel to factories that manufacture cars, machinery, and ships. Timber from Sweden's forests provides lumber for furniture and wood pulp for newsprint. Exports include machinery, motor vehicles, paper products, wood, and electronic products. Only about 8 percent of Sweden's land can be used for farming. Swedish farmers have developed efficient ways to grow crops, and their farms supply most of the nation's food.

Roads and railroads crisscross the southern region. In 2000 a bridge and tunnel system was opened, joining Sweden and Denmark for the first time. This system is 10 miles (16 km) long and connects Malmö, Sweden, with Copenhagen, Denmark's capital.

Sweden's History and People The Vikings had an important role in Sweden's early history. In 1523 Sweden became a separate kingdom apart from Denmark and Norway. King Gustav Vasa turned Sweden from a Roman Catholic to a Protestant country. During the 1600s, Swedish armies conquered much of the area around the Baltic Sea.

Sweden's agricultural economy suffered during the 1800s. Many Swedes **emigrated,** or moved to other countries. About 1 million Swedes settled in the United States. A turnaround began during the late 1800s. Cities and factories grew, and a new middle class arose.

Sweden's economic wealth enabled it to become a welfare state. A **welfare state** is a country that uses tax money to help people who are sick, needy, jobless, or retired. Since the 1970s, economic slowdowns and high taxes have limited government spending for welfare. To help its economic growth, Sweden joined the European Union in 1995. The country is a parliamentary democracy.

Most of Sweden's almost 9 million people live in cities in the southern lowlands. **Stockholm** is the country's capital and largest city. Most of the people are Swedes and speak Swedish. Sweden's high standard of living has attracted more than 1 million immigrants from nearby Norway and Denmark and distant Turkey and Vietnam.

Reading Check **What three natural resources have helped make Sweden wealthy?**

The Sami

The Sami live in northern Finland, Sweden, and Norway. Experts believe the original Sami came to Finland after the last Ice Age, following herds of reindeer. Many Sami still follow a traditional way of life based on herding reindeer, although many also fish, hunt, and work in manufacturing. How important are reindeer to the Sami culture? The various Sami languages have about 400 names for reindeer according to gender, age, color, shape, and so on. Today about 30,000 Sami live in Norway, 20,000 in Sweden, 6,000 in Finland, and 2,000 in Russia.

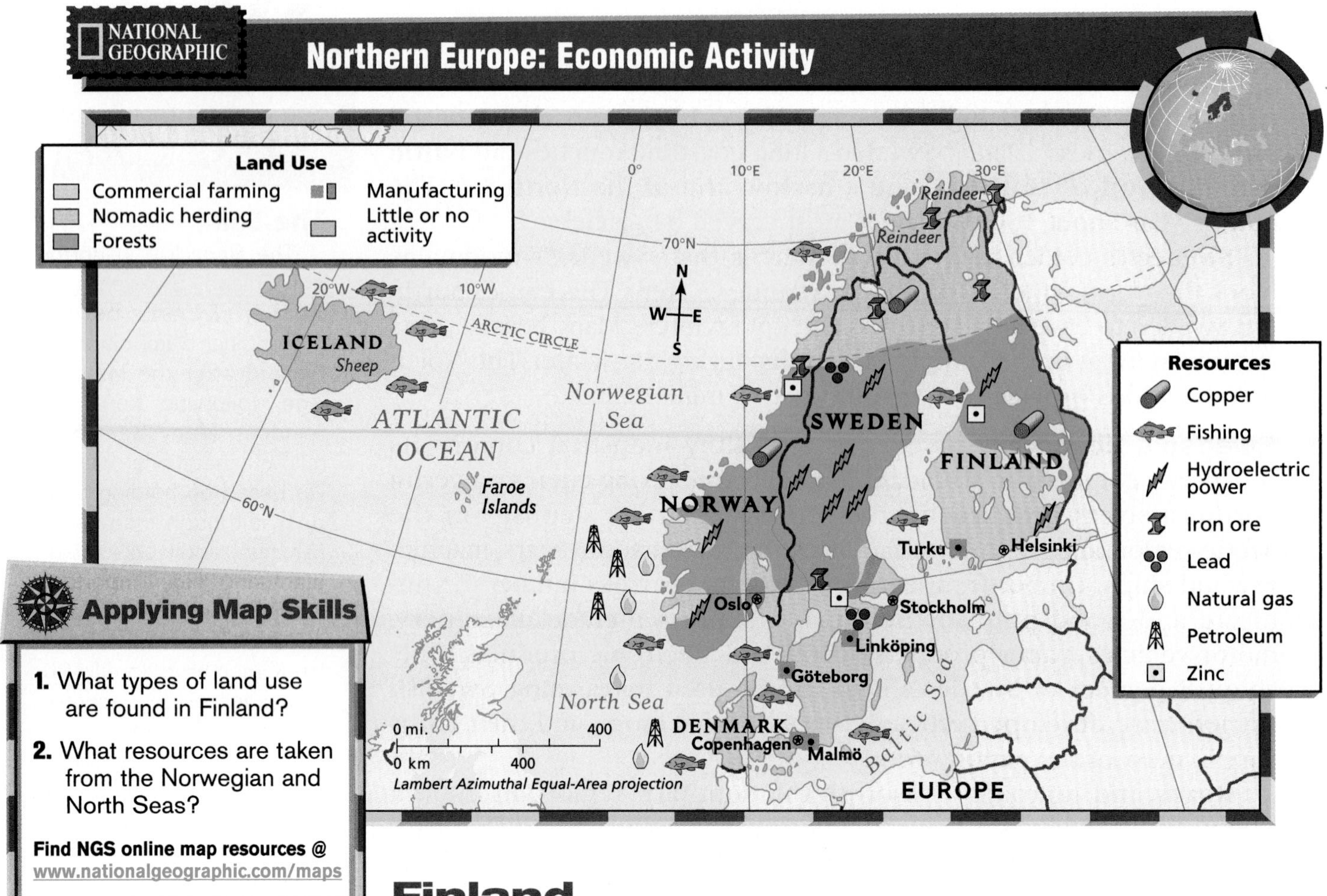

Applying Map Skills

1. What types of land use are found in Finland?
2. What resources are taken from the Norwegian and North Seas?

Find NGS online map resources @ www.nationalgeographic.com/maps

Finland

Finland lies on a flat plateau broken by small hills and valleys. Its inland areas hold some of the largest unspoiled wilderness in Europe. Thick forests cover two-thirds of the country. Thousands of glacier-formed lakes dot the countryside. If you include marshes and bogs, water covers about 10 percent of Finland's land area.

Finland can get extremely cold in winter. Like Sweden, it lies far from the warm North Atlantic Current. As a result, the country has humid continental and subarctic climates.

Finland's Economy Most of Finland's wealth comes from its huge forests of spruce, pine, and birch. Paper and wood production are important exports. As in Ireland, peat bogs provide fuel. Rivers, flowing from Finland's abundant lakes, yield hydroelectric power.

The Finns have long traded with neighboring Russia. Now they are expanding their markets in the west. In 1995 Finland joined the European Union. In recent years, **heavy industry**—or manufactured goods such as machinery—has driven Finland's economy. The Finns are also leaders in the electronic communications industry. In fact, Finns as young as 10 carry mobile phones to school.

Finland's best farmland lies in the southwestern part of the country. Farmers raise livestock for dairy products and meat, meeting all of the country's needs. They also grow potatoes and grains. Because of the short growing season, however, Finland must import fruits and vegetables.

Finland's History and People The ancestors of the Finns settled in the region thousands of years ago. These people probably came from what is now Siberia in eastern Russia. As a result, Finnish language and culture differ from those of Finland's Scandinavian neighbors.

By the A.D. 1000s, Swedish Vikings controlled Finland. For almost 700 years, Finland was part of Sweden. Some Swedish customs remain in the culture. Along with Finnish, Swedish is an official language.

In 1809 the Finns came under the control of Russia. During the 1800s, nationalism, or the desire for an independent country, swept through Finland. With the fall of the Russian Empire in 1917, Finland declared its independence as a republic. Finland then became, and remains, a parliamentary democracy. A president serves as head of state, and a prime minister runs the government.

Most of Finland's more than 5 million people live in towns and cities on the southern coast. **Helsinki,** the capital, has over 900,000 people, but the city has still kept a small-town atmosphere. Helsinki, for example, has no high-rise buildings.

Most Finns belong to the Finnish ethnic group. Their language, Finnish, is a Uralic language. Because of centuries under Swedish rule, most Finns practice the Protestant Lutheran faith. With snow on the ground for about half of the year, Finns enjoy cross-country skiing. After outdoor activities, many Finns enjoy relaxing in saunas, or wooden rooms heated by water sizzling on hot stones.

✓Reading Check **Why is Finnish culture different from the cultures in the rest of Scandinavia?**

Assessment

Defining Terms

1. Define fjord, skerry, emigrate, welfare state, heavy industry, nationalism, sauna.

Recalling Facts

2. Location What countries make up Scandinavia?

3. Movement How was the landscape of Norway created?

4. Economics What resource produces most of Norway's wealth?

Critical Thinking

5. Summarizing Information Why is Sweden called a welfare state?

6. Understanding Cause and Effect Why must Finland import most of its fruits and vegetables?

Graphic Organizer

7. Organizing Information Draw a diagram like the one below. At the end of each of the three arrows, list one way that the sea affects life in Norway.

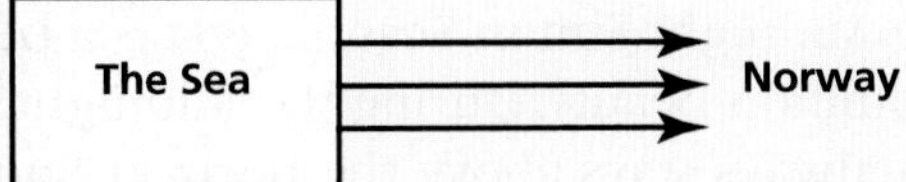

Applying Geography Skills

8. Analyzing Maps Study the physical map on page 347. Which country in this region extends the farthest north? Which country in the region has the lowest overall elevation?

Making Connections

ART | SCIENCE | LITERATURE | TECHNOLOGY

Midnight Sun, Shine On!

At the Equator, the number of hours of daylight is nearly constant year-round. Elsewhere, daylight varies with the latitude and the changing seasons of the year. North of the Arctic Circle, however, the sun shines both night and day for part of the summer. This period is known as the Midnight Sun.

▲ A worker herds the "lawnmowers" for Stockholm's city parks at 3:00 A.M., lit by the Midnight Sun.

Endless Day

The Midnight Sun in Scandinavia is a period of uncommon beauty. During the Midnight Sun, the sun always stays above the horizon. Sunlight shines around the clock, and people can take part in outdoor activities regardless of the time. For many people, the Midnight Sun brings a feeling of celebration. Tourists from around the world flock to the area. The length of the Midnight Sun can vary from a few days to several months, depending on latitude.

Endless Night

In winter, the pattern is reversed. The sun dips below the horizon and stays there. Days or months go by without daylight. Most people continue to carry out their regular routines. Floodlights are turned on to make outdoor activities possible. However, without daylight, the body's own sense of time can be affected. Research has shown that the human body tends to operate on a 24- or 25-hour cycle. Your body's cycle helps keep you alert during the day. It also helps you relax at night. Light and darkness can influence this cycle.

Sunlight and Mood

Although most people are not severely affected by the continuous period of darkness, others develop more serious problems. Some people report trouble falling asleep or difficulty in staying awake during the daytime. Others gain weight. For some, the dark period is a time when they feel continuously depressed. This condition, known as seasonal affective disorder (SAD), also affects people in other parts of the world during winter.

Medical professionals sometimes use lights to help people affected by SAD. Through exposure to special bright lights, patients may be able to adjust their body cycles.

Making the Connection

1. What is the Midnight Sun?
2. What happens to the sun in winter north of the Arctic Circle?
3. **Understanding Cause and Effect** How can one's body be affected by lack of sunlight?

Section 2

Denmark and Iceland

Guide to Reading

Main Idea

Denmark and Iceland have related histories and rely on the sea for their economies.

Terms to Know

- archipelago
- moor
- geyser
- geothermal energy
- fault line
- saga

Places to Locate

- Jutland
- Copenhagen
- Reykjavík

Reading Strategy

Create a chart like this one, filling in at least two key facts for (1) the land, (2) the economy, and (3) the people of each country.

Denmark	(1)
	(2)
	(3)
Iceland	(1)
	(2)
	(3)

NATIONAL GEOGRAPHIC **Exploring Our World**

The island of Iceland is called the Land of Fire and Ice because it has both huge glaciers and live volcanoes. Underground hot springs are used to heat homes, buildings, and even swimming pools. Here, Icelanders swim in a pool heated by a geothermal power station. The electric power is produced by steam from the hot springs.

Iceland lies out in the Atlantic Ocean far from mainland Northern Europe. Despite this remote location, the people of Iceland consider themselves part of Northern Europe. They have close cultural ties with the other Scandinavian countries. Denmark is a small country that extends north from Germany toward the Scandinavian peninsula.

Denmark

South of Norway and Sweden, Denmark guards the channel that connects the North Sea and the Baltic Sea. Only about the size of Maryland, Denmark rules the large island of Greenland off the coast of Canada. It also governs the Faroe **archipelago,** or group of islands, in the North Atlantic between Norway and Iceland.

The map on page 347 shows you that most of Denmark is made up of a peninsula known as **Jutland.** The southern border of Jutland touches Germany, Denmark's only land connection to the European mainland. Denmark also includes nearly 500 islands, only 100 of which have people living on them. **Copenhagen,** Denmark's capital, lies on Zealand, the largest island. Throughout history, Denmark's location has made it a link for people and goods between Scandinavia and the rest of Europe. Ferries and bridges connect Jutland and the islands. A bridge and tunnel now join Denmark's Zealand to Sweden.

Most of Denmark is low, rolling grasslands, green hills, woods, and **moors,** or windy treeless land that is often wet. Unlike Norway and Sweden, Denmark has a relatively flat landscape. Its highest elevation, in Jutland's lake district, is only 568 feet (173 m) above sea level.

The North Atlantic Current sweeps northward along Denmark's western coast. Warm winds from this current give Denmark a mild, damp climate. Winter months are cold, and daylight hours are short. Spring and summer have more sunshine and warmer temperatures.

Denmark's Economy A fairly fertile landscape and a moist, mild climate allow the Danes to farm more than 70 percent of their country. Denmark has some of the richest farmland in Northern Europe. Danish farm products include butter, cheese, bacon, and ham. Food that is exported helps pay for the machinery and raw materials that must be imported. The Danish also export ships, diesel engines, and beautifully designed furniture, silver, and porcelain. Royal Copenhagen porcelain is among the finest in the world. The Danes also invented and export the world-famous Lego toy building blocks.

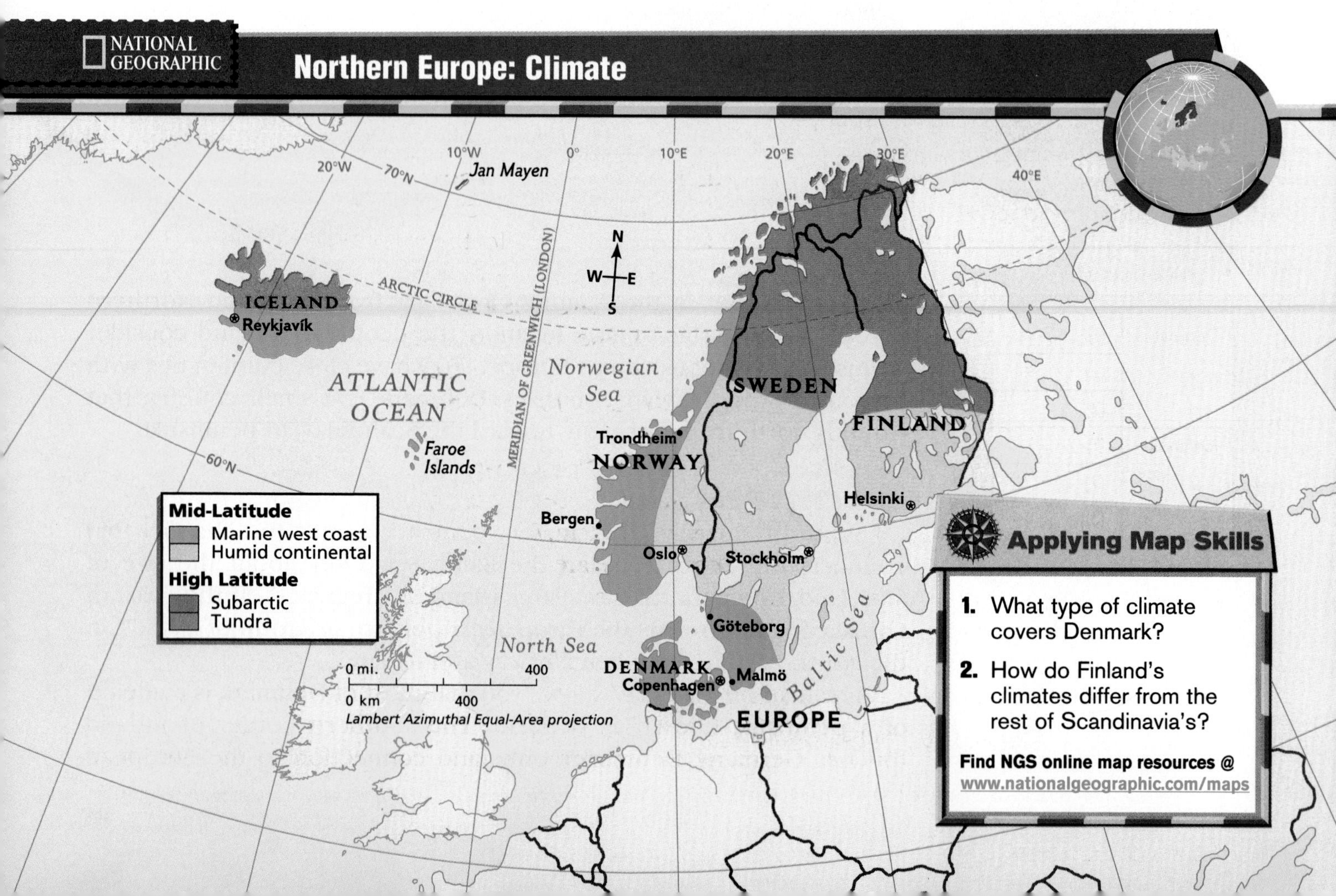

History and Government Historians believe that the Danes came from Sweden and settled the area that is now Denmark around A.D. 500. About 350 years later, Norwegian Viking warriors conquered Jutland. By the 1000s, their descendants had established a kingdom in Denmark and had converted the country to Christianity.

In the late 1300s, Denmark, Norway, and Sweden formed one kingdom under the Danish Queen Margarethe (mahr•GRAY•tuh). Opposed to Danish controls, Sweden and Norway eventually broke away. Today Denmark is a parliamentary democracy, with a king or queen as head of state and elected officials running the government.

Like Norway, Denmark tried to be neutral in the war-torn 1900s. The German Nazis, however, invaded and ran the country's affairs during World War II. After the war, Denmark prospered and set up a welfare state similar to that in Sweden. In 1993 it joined the European Union.

Copenhagen, Denmark

This attractive city is known for its old church spires and red-tiled roofs as well as its modern buildings and parks.

Place **What sites attract tourists to Copenhagen?**

The Danes The more than 5 million Danes enjoy a high standard of living. About 85 percent of them live in cities or towns. Copenhagen, Denmark's capital, is the largest city in Northern Europe. In the center of Copenhagen sits Tivoli Gardens—one of Europe's oldest amusement parks. In Copenhagen's harbor is another famous attraction: a statue of the Little Mermaid. She is a character from a story by the Danish author Hans Christian Andersen. Andersen, who lived and wrote during the 1800s, is Denmark's most famous writer.

The Danish language is similar to Swedish and Norwegian. Like their Scandinavian neighbors, the Danes mostly are Protestant Lutheran in religion. Although traditional customs remain, Danes pride themselves on being thoroughly modern. People here are less inclined to wear historical clothes and celebrate traditional festivals as people often do in other parts of Europe. Instead of noisy, elaborate occasions, Danes prefer quiet, relaxing evenings in their homes or cozy get-togethers with friends in small cafés.

✓ Reading Check **What large Atlantic island does Denmark rule?**

NATIONAL GEOGRAPHIC

Northern Europe: Population Density

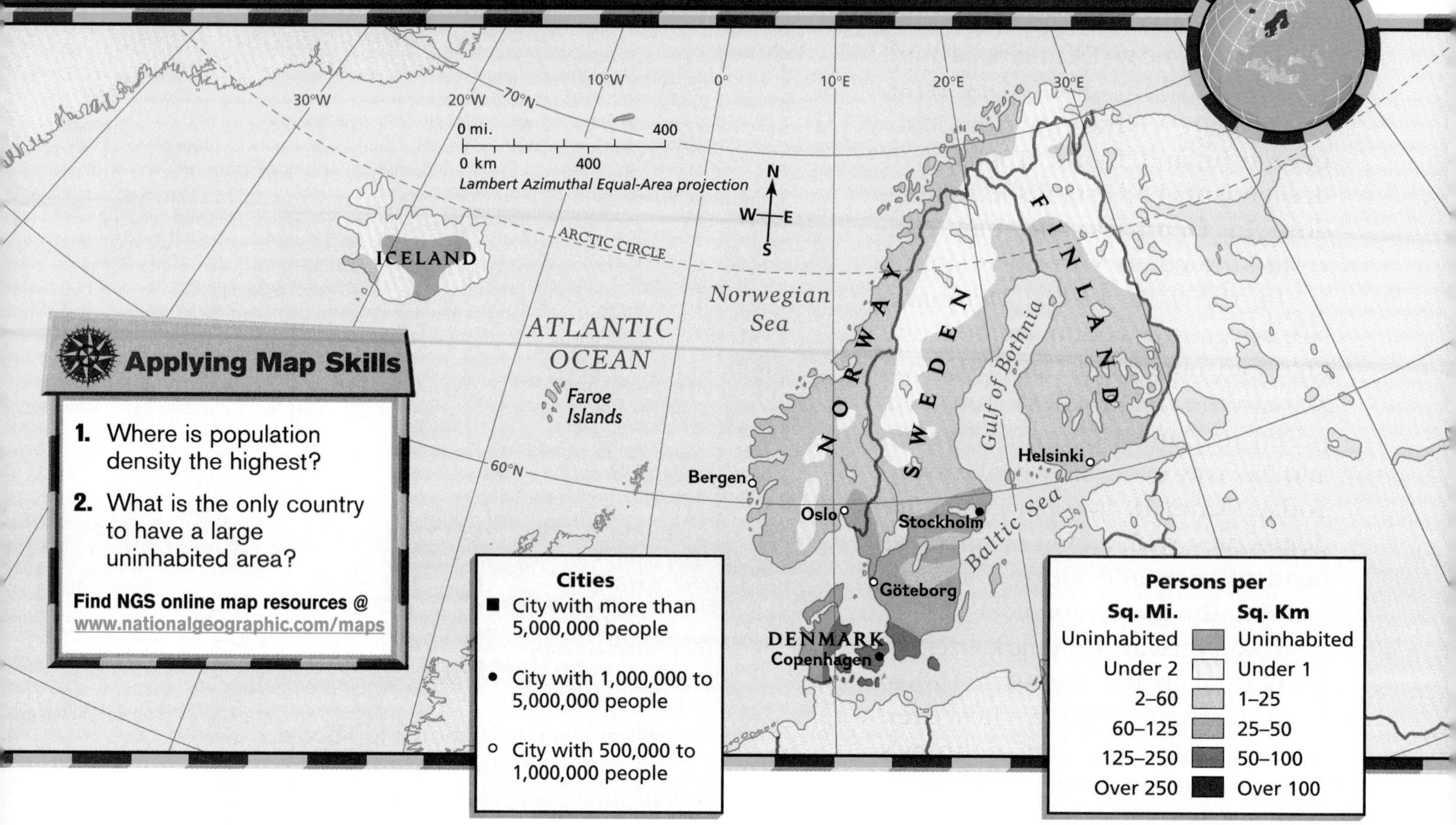

30°W 20°W 10°W 0° 10°E 20°E 30°E 70°N 60°N

0 mi. 400
0 km 400
Lambert Azimuthal Equal-Area projection

N W E S

ARCTIC CIRCLE

ICELAND

ATLANTIC OCEAN

Norwegian Sea

Faroe Islands

NORWAY SWEDEN FINLAND DENMARK

Gulf of Bothnia *Baltic Sea*

Bergen, Oslo, Stockholm, Göteborg, Copenhagen, Helsinki

Applying Map Skills

1. Where is population density the highest?
2. What is the only country to have a large uninhabited area?

Find NGS online map resources @ www.nationalgeographic.com/maps

Cities

- ■ City with more than 5,000,000 people
- ● City with 1,000,000 to 5,000,000 people
- ○ City with 500,000 to 1,000,000 people

Persons per

Sq. Mi.	Sq. Km
Uninhabited	Uninhabited
Under 2	Under 1
2–60	1–25
60–125	25–50
125–250	50–100
Over 250	Over 100

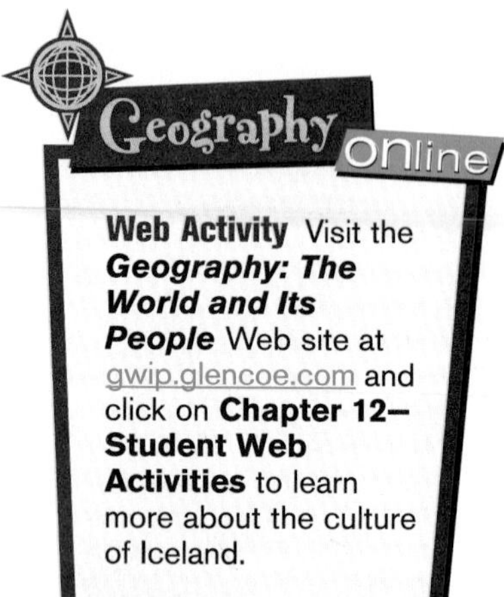

Web Activity Visit the ***Geography: The World and Its People*** Web site at gwip.glencoe.com and click on **Chapter 12—Student Web Activities** to learn more about the culture of Iceland.

Iceland

Iceland was given its chilly name because of its far northern location. Yet in certain places the country's groundwater actually boils. Iceland is a land of hot springs and **geysers**—springs that shoot hot water and steam into the air. The people of Iceland make the most of this unusual environment. They use **geothermal energy,** or heat produced by natural underground sources, to heat most of their homes, buildings, and swimming pools.

What makes such natural wonders possible? In the North Atlantic, an undersea range of mountains runs along a **fault line,** or break in the earth's crust along which movement occurs. Sitting on top of the fault line, Iceland is at the mercy of constant volcanic activity. Every few years, one of the country's 200 volcanoes erupts. The volcanoes heat the springs that appear across the length of Iceland.

Almost 80 percent of Iceland's total land area is made up of glaciers, lakes, and treeless wilderness areas where few people live. Fast-flowing rivers provide a good source for hydroelectric power. The North Atlantic Current warms most of Iceland's coast and keeps temperatures from getting too cold. Iceland has more than its fair share of clouds and rainfall, though. In January, **Reykjavík** (RAY•kyah•veek), the capital, enjoys an average of only three sunny days.

Iceland's Economy The country's economy depends heavily on fishing. Fish exports provide the money for Iceland to buy food and consumer goods from other countries. For this reason, Iceland is concerned that overfishing will reduce the amount of fish available. In the 1970s, Iceland decided to enlarge the ocean area open only to Icelandic fishing boats. British fishing fleets did not agree with this decision. For a few years, British and Icelandic gunboats exchanged rounds of fire during what became known as the Cod Wars. To reduce its dependence on fishing, Iceland has introduced new manufacturing and service industries.

Iceland's People Most Icelanders trace their heritage to Vikings who came from mainland Scandinavia during the A.D. 800s and 900s. **Sagas,** or long tales, written between A.D. 1180 and 1300, celebrate the achievements of Viking heroes and early Icelandic settlers. The country became a parliamentary republic in 1944. A president serves as head of state, and a prime minister is in charge of the government.

About 99 percent of the 300,000 Icelanders live in urban areas. More than half the people live in Reykjavík. The people have a passion for books, magazines, and newspapers. In fact, the literacy rate in Iceland is 100 percent—every adult can read and write.

Reading Check **How do the people of Iceland take advantage of the country's geysers?**

Cozy Ballet?

Helle Oelkers (far right) is a member of Northern Europe's finest ballet—the Royal Danish Ballet. Helle likes to think that her performance encourages audience members to feel *hygge*. *Hygge* means feeling cozy and snug. She explains, "The greatest compliment a Dane can give is to thank someone for a cozy evening."

Assessment

Defining Terms

1. **Define** archipelago, moor, geyser, geothermal energy, fault line, saga.

Recalling Facts

2. **Location** With what other European country does Denmark share a border?
3. **Economics** What are five products made in Denmark?
4. **History** Who are the ancestors of today's Icelanders?

Critical Thinking

5. **Analyzing Information** How has Denmark's location affected its relationship with the rest of Europe?
6. **Understanding Cause and Effect** What events led to the Cod Wars?

Graphic Organizer

7. **Organizing Information** Create a diagram like the one below. In the second box list three effects on Iceland from its location on a fault line.

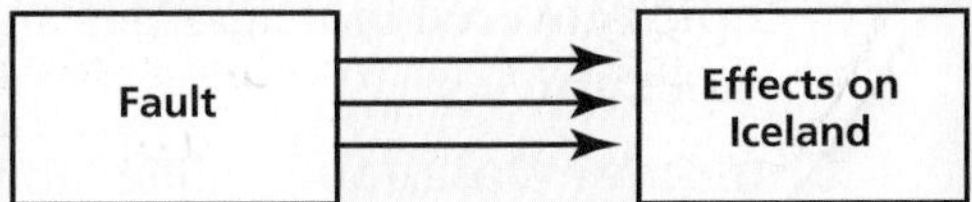

Applying Geography Skills

8. **Analyzing Maps** Study the physical map on page 347. What is Denmark's elevation? At what elevation is central Iceland?

Study and Writing Skill

Using Library Resources

Your teacher has assigned a major research report, so you go to the library. As you wander the aisles surrounded by books, you wonder: Where do I start my research? Which reference tools should I use?

Learning the Skill

Libraries contain many resources. Here are brief descriptions of important ones:

- **Encyclopedia:** set of books containing short articles on many subjects arranged alphabetically
- **Biographical Dictionary:** brief biographies listed alphabetically by last names
- **Atlas:** collection of maps and charts
- **Almanac:** reference updated yearly that provides current statistics and historical information on a wide range of subjects
- **Card Catalog:** listing of every book in the library, either on cards or computerized; search for books by author, subject, or title
- **Periodical Guide:** set of books listing topics covered in magazines and newspaper articles
- **Computer Database:** collections of information organized for rapid search and retrieval
- **World Wide Web:** collection of information on the Internet accessed with a Web browser *(Caution: Some information may not be reliable.)*

Practicing the Skill

Suppose you are assigned a research report dealing with Denmark. Read the questions below, then decide which of the resources on the left you would use to answer each question and why.

1. During which years did Queen Margarethe rule Denmark?
2. What is the current population of Denmark?
3. Besides "The Little Mermaid," what stories did Danish author Hans Christian Andersen write?

Applying the Skill

Using library resources, research the origins and main stories of Icelandic sagas. Find out if the sagas say anything about the land or environment of Iceland. Present the information you find to the class.

◀ The Little Mermaid statue in Copenhagen

Chapter 12 Reading Review

Section 1 Norway, Sweden, and Finland

Terms to Know
fjord
skerry
emigrate
welfare state
heavy industry
nationalism
sauna

Main Idea

The economies of Norway, Sweden, and Finland rely on water, forests, and mineral resources.

✓ **Region** Northern Europe—also known as Scandinavia—includes Norway, Sweden, Finland, Denmark, and Iceland.

✓ **Economics** North Sea oil and gas have made Norway a wealthy nation.

✓ **Human/Environment Interaction** Sweden's prosperity comes from vast forests, rich deposits of iron ore, and waterpower.

✓ **Economics** Sweden is a welfare state, although government spending for welfare has been limited.

✓ **Economics** With its thick forests, Finland is a major producer of wood and paper products.

Urnes Stave Church near Sognefjord, Norway ▶

Section 2 Denmark and Iceland

Terms to Know
archipelago
moor
geyser
geothermal energy
fault line
saga

Main Idea

Denmark and Iceland have related histories and rely on the sea for their economies.

✓ **Movement** Throughout history, Denmark's location has made it a link for people and goods between Scandinavia and the rest of Europe.

✓ **Economics** With rich farmland, Denmark exports butter, cheese, bacon, and ham.

✓ **Government** Denmark and most other Scandinavian countries are parliamentary democracies, with a king or queen as head of state and elected officials running the government.

✓ **Place** Most of Iceland has glaciers, lakes, and treeless wilderness areas where few people live.

✓ **History** Most Icelanders trace their heritage to Vikings who came from mainland Scandinavia during the A.D. 800s and 900s.

Chapter 12 Assessment and Activities

Using Key Terms

Match the terms in Part A with their definitions in Part B.

A.

1. fjord
2. saga
3. emigrate
4. skerry
5. geothermal energy
6. heavy industry
7. geyser
8. fault line
9. nationalism
10. sauna

B.

a. long tale or story
b. heat produced by underground steam
c. rocky island
d. production of industrial goods
e. to move to another country
f. steep-sided inlet of the sea
g. wooden rooms heated by water sizzling on hot stones
h. hot spring that spouts hot water
i. loyalty or pride in one's country
j. cracks in the earth's crust

Reviewing the Main Idea

Section 1 Norway, Sweden, and Finland

11. **Location** Why is part of Norway called the Land of the Midnight Sun?
12. **Human/Environment Interaction** Which of Norway's industries depend on the sea?
13. **Culture** Who are the Sami? Where do they live?
14. **History** Why have so many people from other parts of the world immigrated to Sweden?
15. **Economics** What resource produces most of Finland's wealth?
16. **Location** Why is Finland so cold?

Section 2 Denmark and Iceland

17. **Government** Which North Atlantic islands does Denmark control?
18. **Location** On which peninsula is Denmark located?
19. **Economics** How do Icelanders obtain the money to buy consumer goods and food from other countries?
20. **Culture** What is Iceland's literacy rate?

Northern Europe

Place Location Activity

On a separate sheet of paper, match the letters on the map with the numbered places listed below.

1. North Sea
2. Baltic Sea
3. Iceland
4. Finland
5. Sweden
6. Kjølen Mountains
7. Denmark
8. Norway
9. Helsinki
10. Copenhagen

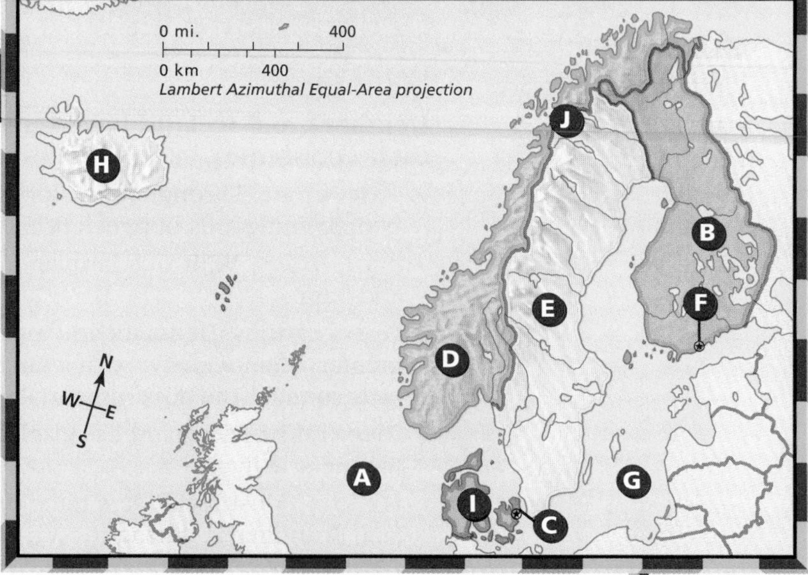

Self-Check Quiz Visit the ***Geography: The World and Its People*** Web site at gwip.glencoe.com and click on **Chapter 12—Self-Check Quizzes** to prepare for the Chapter Test.

Critical Thinking

21. **Analyzing Information** Why is the name Land of Fire and Ice appropriate for Iceland?
22. **Organizing Information** Create an outline of each country in this section. Use the following guide as your base outline.

I. Name of Country
  A. Land
    1. Physical features
    2. Climate
  B. Economy
    1. Agriculture
    2. Manufacturing
  C. People

GeoJournal Activity

23. **Writing a News Article** From 1963 to 1967, the island of Surtsey was born in a series of volcanic eruptions off the southern coast of Iceland. Research this event, and write a newspaper article describing it.

Mental Mapping Activity

24. **Focusing on the Region** Draw a simple outline map of Northern Europe, then label the following:

- Arctic Ocean
- Baltic Sea
- Finland
- Sweden
- Norway
- Denmark
- Iceland
- Copenhagen
- Oslo
- Kjølen Mountains

Technology Skills Activity

25. **Building a Database** Search the Internet to find important facts about one of the countries in this chapter. Use the information to create a database for visitors to the country. Include climate information, currency, foods, and holidays.

Standardized Test Practice

Directions: Study the graph below, then answer the question that follows.

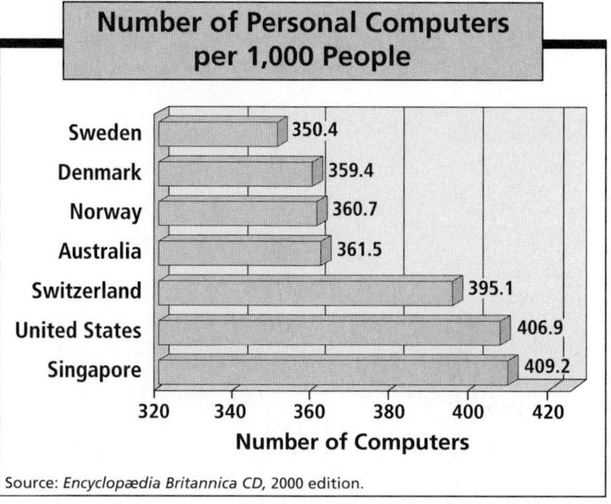

1. Which Scandinavian country has the highest number of personal computers per 1,000 people?

A Singapore
B Switzerland
C Denmark
D Norway

Test-Taking Tip: Use the information on the graph to help you answer this question. Look carefully at the information on the bottom and the side of a bar graph to understand what the bars represent. The important word in the question is *Scandinavian.* Other countries may have more personal computers, but which Scandinavian country listed on the graph has the most personal computers per 1,000 people?

EYE on the Environment

RAIN, RAIN Go Away

Acid Rain Have you ever sucked on a lemon slice? Yow! Lemons make you pucker up because they are high in acid. Rainwater can be acidic, too. Any form of precipitation that contains high amounts of acid is known as acid rain. In some parts of the world, rain or snow falls that is as acidic as lemon juice.

Why does this happen? When cars and trucks burn gasoline, or when factories and power plants burn coal, sulfur and nitrogen compounds are produced. High in the atmosphere, these gases mix with moisture to form sulfuric acid and nitric acid. These acids make rainwater much more acidic than normal. Acid rain is a problem because it

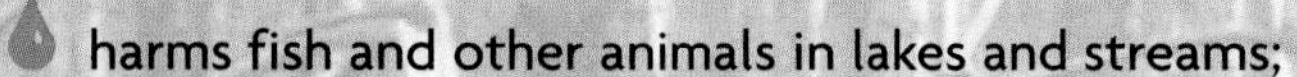

- harms fish and other animals in lakes and streams;
- damages trees and crops;
- washes nutrients out of soils.

Taking Action Europeans are very concerned about acid rain and its effects. Half of the trees in Germany's Black Forest are sick or dying. Forests in Norway, Austria, Poland, France, and the Czech Republic have also been damaged. In Sweden, 20 percent of the lakes contain few or no fish. The same is true of most lakes in southern Norway.

Many European countries are trying to reduce acid rain by

- installing filters on factory smokestacks;
- putting special exhaust systems on motor vehicles;
- building new factories that do not burn coal.

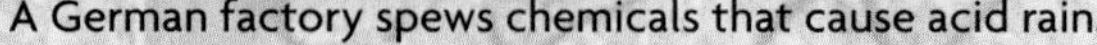
A German factory spews chemicals that cause acid rain.

Acid rain eats away at a statue in Rome.

Making a Difference

Student collects weather data

Acid Rain 2000 A project called Acid Rain 2000 is giving students across Europe a chance to study acid rain and its effects. From 2000 to 2005, participating students will be collecting four kinds of environmental data at study sites in Europe.

- **WEATHER** — Each day, students record the wind direction and the acidity of precipitation.
- **PLANTS** — Once a month, students check the condition of trees and other plants at their sites.
- **SOIL** — Once a month, students test the soil at their sites for acid and plant nutrient levels.
- **LICHENS** — Twice a year, students record the condition of plants called lichens. Since lichens die if the air is too polluted, they are good indicators of a site's air quality.

Acid Rain 2000 participants e-mail the data they collect to Northamptonshire Grammar School, near Northampton, England. There, students and staff process the data and publish the project's findings on the Internet. Acid Rain 2000 hopes to show which areas in Europe are most sensitive to acid rain.

What Can You Do?

Collect Data

Although Acid Rain 2000 is a European project, you can collect similar kinds of data at a study site in your community. For more information about how to set up a site and collect data, contact Acid Rain 2000 at *www.brixworth.demon.co.uk/acidrain2000*

Investigate

Does acid rain affect your community? If so, what impact has acid rain had on the environment? What are local industries doing to combat the problem? Motor vehicle exhaust contributes to acid rain. What can you do to limit vehicle use on a daily basis?

Use the Internet

Learn more about the international problem of acid rain. Good sites include *www.brixworth.demon.co.uk/acidrain2000/sites.htm* and the acid rain home page of the U.S. Environmental Protection Agency at *www.epa.gov/docs/airmarkets/acidrain*

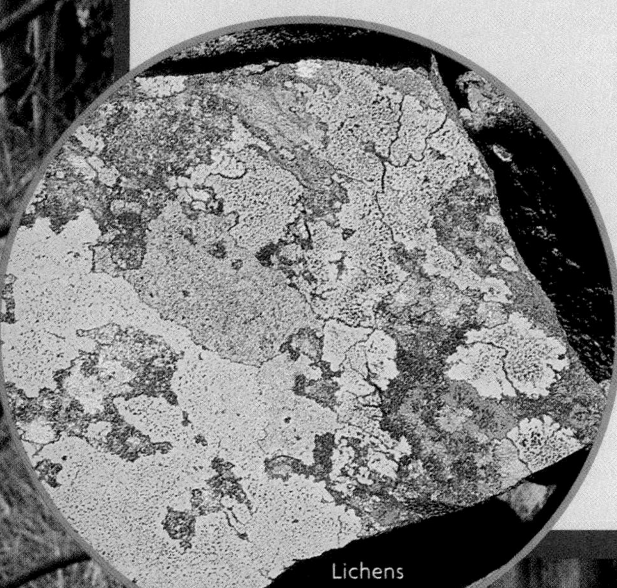

Lichens

Chapter 13 Eastern Europe

The World and Its People NATIONAL GEOGRAPHIC

To learn more about the people and places of Eastern Europe, view ***The World and Its People*** **Chapter 13** video.

Geography Online

Chapter Overview Visit the ***Geography: The World and Its People*** Web site at gwip.glencoe.com and click on **Chapter 13—Chapter Overviews** to preview information about Eastern Europe.

Section 1 Poland

Guide to Reading

Main Idea

Poland, a large country with a rich history, is undergoing many changes.

Terms to Know

- bog
- communist state
- acid rain
- republic
- pope

Places to Locate

- Poland
- North European Plain
- Carpathian Mountains
- Vistula River
- Oder River
- Warta River
- Warsaw

Reading Strategy

Make a chart like this one, writing three facts in the right column for each category in the left column.

Poland	
Land	
Economy	
People	

NATIONAL GEOGRAPHIC **Exploring Our World**

Have you heard the saying "Back to the salt mines"? This means it is time to get back to work, and it came from Wieliczka (vyeh•LEECH•kah), Poland. For about 1,000 years workers have mined salt here, even sculpting it into art. This room lies 331 feet (101 m) beneath the earth's surface. Salt sculptures decorate the walls. Even the chandeliers are made of rock salt.

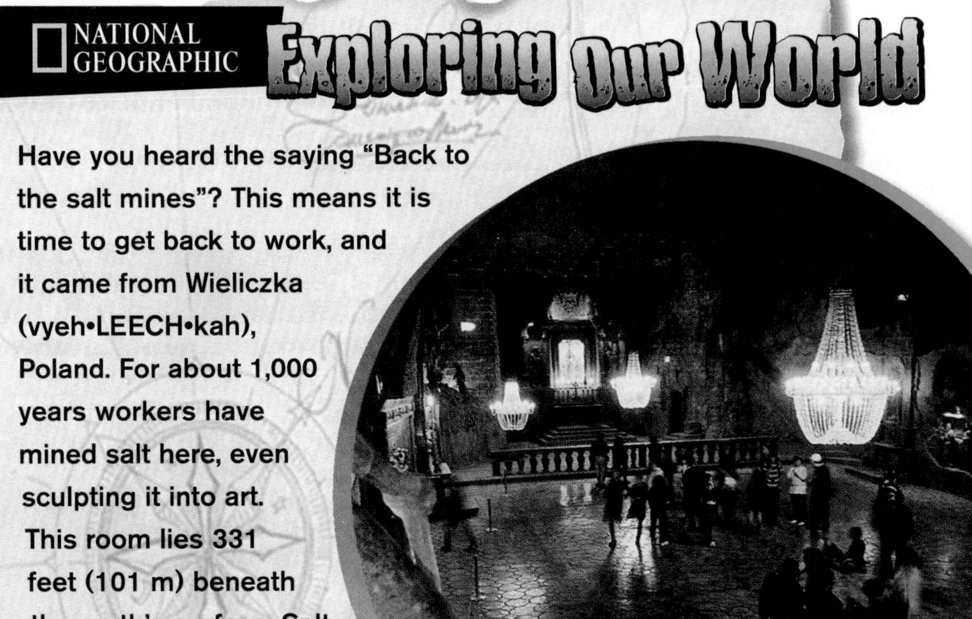

Poland is a large country in Eastern Europe. This was not the case in the late 1700s when Poland disappeared from world maps—gobbled up by larger neighbors. In the late 1900s, Poland became a democracy with a free market economy. Since then, many changes have occurred.

Poland's Land and Climate

Find Poland on the map on page 367. About the size of New Mexico, Poland lies on the huge **North European Plain** that stretches from France to Russia. Thick forests once blanketed this flat landscape, but most of the trees were cut down long ago to create farmland. Many Polish people live in this fertile central region.

North toward the Baltic Sea, you find gently rolling land that cradles several thousand glacier-carved lakes. Forests and **bogs,** or low swampy lands, also dot this northern part of the country. Sandy beaches wind along the Baltic coastline. In the south, the low Sudeten (zoo•DAYT•uhn) Mountains stretch along Poland's border with the Czech Republic. The higher **Carpathian** (kahr•PAY•thee•uhn) **Mountains** form Poland's border with Slovakia.

◀ Prague, capital of the Czech Republic

Poland's rivers begin in the mountains, then twist and turn northward to eventually drain into the Baltic Sea. The **Vistula** (VISH•chuh•luh) **River** begins in the Carpathians and flows more than 680 miles (1,094 km) on an S-shaped course. The **Oder River** and **Warta River** flow through western Poland.

Western Poland has a marine west coast climate. Warm winds blowing across Europe from the Atlantic Ocean bring mild weather year-round. If you like cooler weather, visit eastern Poland. It experiences a humid continental climate of cool summers and cold winters.

Reading Check **What three major rivers flow through Poland?**

A Changing Economy

In the past, Poland was a communist state, or a country in which the government has strong control over the economy and society as a whole. The Polish government decided what, how, and how many goods would be produced. In 1989 Poland started moving to a free market economy. The change has been difficult. In their communist state, workers had jobs for life, even if business was slow. Today businesses lay off workers if they cannot afford to keep a large staff. Poland has met many economic challenges, though. Many people have started businesses, and Poles no longer suffer from shortages of goods.

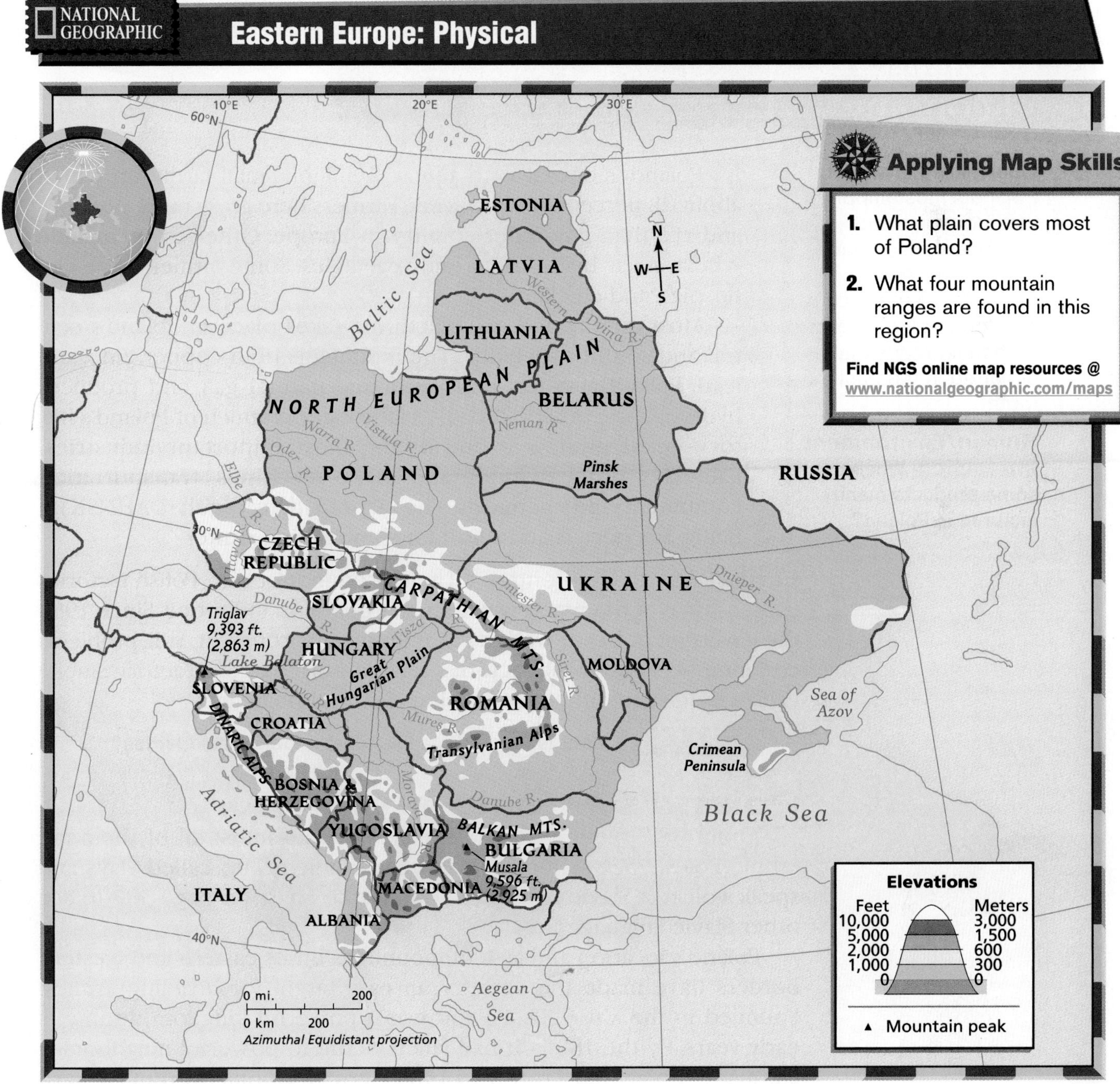

NATIONAL GEOGRAPHIC **On Location**

Poland's Economy

Coal mining is one of Poland's most important industries and is concentrated near the Czech Republic (above). Polish shoppers do not face most of the shortages that occurred in the past (right).

Human/Environment Interaction **What are some products manufactured in Poland?**

Poland is dotted with almost 2 million small farms, on which about 28 percent of Poles work. Farmers here grow more potatoes and rye than any other country in Europe. Other crops include wheat, sugar beets, fruits, and vegetables. Some farmers raise cattle, pigs, and chickens.

Most mining and manufacturing takes place in Poland's central and southern regions. The mountains hold copper, zinc, and lead. Poland also has petroleum and natural gas, and produces hydroelectric power. Today—as throughout much of Poland's history—coal mining is one of the most important industries. Factories process foods and make machines, transportation equipment, and chemicals. The city of Gdańsk (guh•DAHNSK), a Baltic Sea port, is an important shipbuilding center.

Environmental Challenges Under Communist rule, Polish factories caused some of the worst water and air pollution in Europe. Since 1989 the government has moved to clean up the environment. Still, problems continue because Polish factories rely on burning coal. Factory smoke causes **acid rain,** or rain containing chemical pollutants.

✓ Reading Check **What is one of Poland's most important industries?**

Poland's People and History

About 38.7 million people live in Poland. Almost all of them are ethnic Poles. Poles belong to the large ethnic group called Slavs and speak Polish, a Slavic language. Look at the chart on page 388 to see other Slavic languages.

Poland's location and lack of mountains on its eastern and western borders have made the country an easy target for invading armies. Founded in the A.D. 900s, Poland was a powerful kingdom during its early years. By the 1800s, it had fallen victim to powerful neighbors—Germany, Russia, and Austria. In 1939 German troops overran western

Poland, beginning World War II. Poles suffered greatly during the conflict. **Warsaw,** the capital, was bombed to ashes. Some 6 million European Jews and 6 million others were murdered in brutal prison camps set up by the Germans in Poland and elsewhere.

After the war, the Soviet Union swallowed up lands in eastern Poland. In exchange, the Poles gained western areas belonging to defeated Germany. In 1947 a Communist government came to power in Poland. Resisting its rule, workers and farmers in 1980 formed Solidarity, a labor group that struggled peacefully for democratic change. The Communist government finally allowed free elections in 1989, and a new democratic government was formed. A year later, Solidarity leader Lech Walesa (LEHK vah•LEHN•suh) was elected Poland's first democratic president. Today Poland is a democratic **republic,** a government headed by elected leaders. The people vote for a president who serves for five years. They also elect all the lawmakers.

Daily Life Poland is more rural than nations in other parts of Europe. About one-third of the people live in the countryside. As Poland's economy changes, more people are moving to cities such as Warsaw.

Poles feel a deep loyalty to their country. Religion unites Poles as well. Most are Roman Catholic, and religion has a strong influence on daily life. Poles were very proud in 1978 when Karol Wojtyla (voy•TEE•wah) was named **pope,** or head of the Roman Catholic Church. Taking the name John Paul II, he was the first Pole ever to become pope.

✓ Reading Check **What two beliefs or attitudes unite the Polish people?**

Assessment

Defining Terms

1. **Define** bog, communist state, acid rain, republic, pope.

Recalling Facts

2. **Human/Environment Interaction** What happened to most of Poland's forests?

3. **Economics** Why is Gdańsk important?

4. **Culture** What is Poland's language and major religion?

Graphic Organizer

5. **Organizing Information** On a time line like this one, label five important events and their dates in Poland's history.

Critical Thinking

6. **Understanding Cause and Effect** Which of Poland's physical features has made it an easy target for invading armies? Why?

7. **Making Comparisons** What is the difference in job security under a communist state and the new free market economy?

Applying Geography Skills

8. **Analyzing Maps** Refer to the physical map on page 367. The Vistula River empties into what body of water? Now turn to the population density map on page 387. What is the population density of the area surrounding Kraków?

Study and Writing Skill

Taking Notes

Effective note taking involves more than just writing facts in short phrases. It involves breaking up information into meaningful parts so that it can be remembered.

Learning the Skill

To take good notes, follow these steps:

- Write key points and important facts and figures quickly and neatly. Use abbreviations and phrases.
- Copy words, statements, or diagrams drawn on the board.
- Ask the teacher to repeat important points you do not understand.
- When studying textbook material, organize your notes into an outline (see page 758).
- For a research report, take notes on cards. Note cards should include the title, author, and page number of sources.

Practicing the Skill

Suppose you are writing a research report on Eastern Europe. First, identify main idea questions about this topic, such as "Who has ruled Poland?" or "What economic activities are found in the Czech Republic?" Then find material about each question.

Using this textbook as a source, read the material on pages 368 and 378 and prepare notes like this:

Main Idea: Who has ruled Poland?
1. Powerful kingdom founded in A.D. 900s
2. 1800s—taken over by Germany, Russia, Austria
3. 1939—Germans invade
4. After WWII, Soviet Union takes over
Main Idea: What economic activities are found in the Czech Republic?
1.
2.
3.

Applying the Skill

In an encyclopedia or on the Internet, find information about Poland's coal industry and the environmental consequences of burning coal. Take notes by writing the main idea and supporting facts. Then rewrite the article using only your notes.

◄ A Czech teenager displays Soviet souvenirs for tourists who flock to Prague.

Section 2

The Baltic Republics

Guide to Reading

Main Idea

People in Estonia, Latvia, and Lithuania are trying to change their economies, yet keep their cultures.

Terms to Know

- oil shale
- peat

Places to Locate

- Baltic Sea
- Estonia
- Latvia
- Lithuania
- Tallinn
- Rīga
- Vilnius

Reading Strategy

Make a chart like this one, listing ways in which Estonia, Latvia, and Lithuania are similar and different. Write the facts under the correct heading.

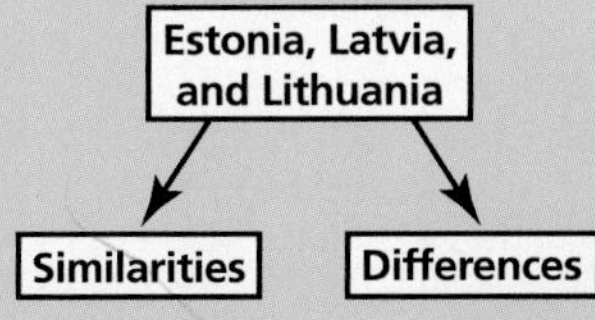

NATIONAL GEOGRAPHIC **Exploring Our World**

The Estonians have a rich tradition of dance, music, and storytelling. Every four years, Estonians stage the Song and Dance Festival to celebrate their people's music. Up to 500,000 people of Estonian descent may take part, many coming from as far away as the United States, Canada, and Australia.

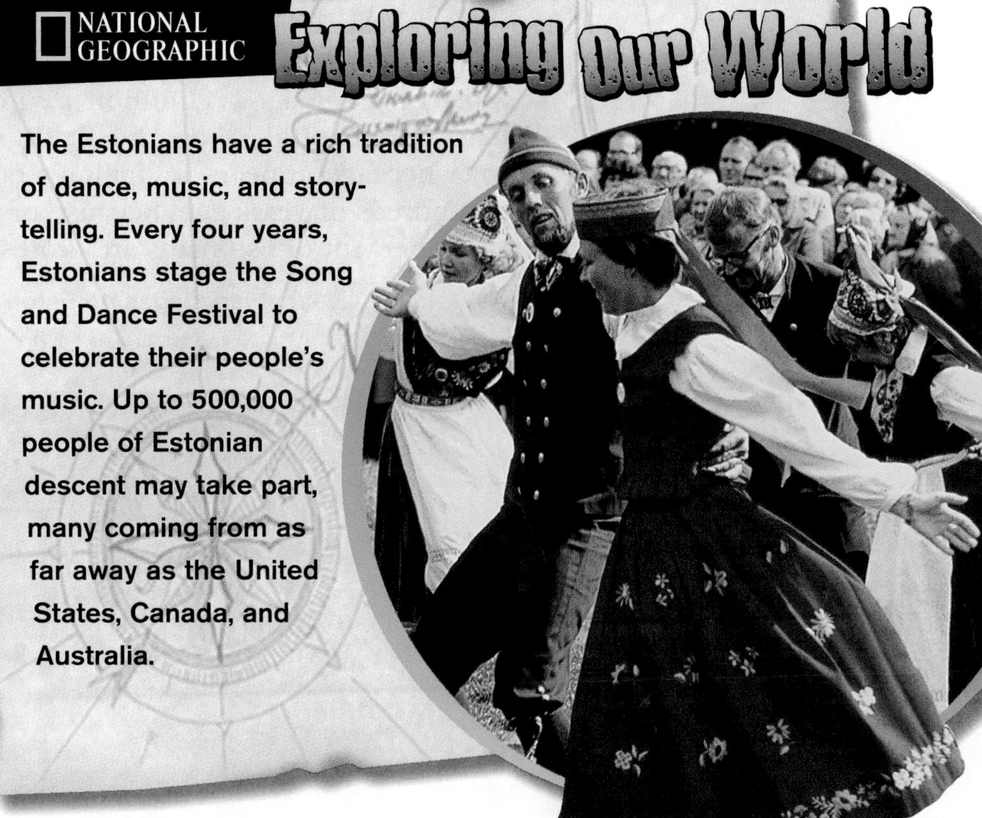

The **Baltic Sea** washes the western shores of three small countries. These lands—**Estonia, Latvia,** and **Lithuania**—have several things in common. In 1940 the Soviet Union took control of all three. Hoping for independence, the countries finally won that freedom in 1991. Today they are all democratic republics with elected leaders. They also have free market economies.

Estonia

The smallest Baltic republic, Estonia is mostly a flat lowland of lakes and rivers. Forests cover about one-third of the land, and about 800 islands dot Baltic coastal areas. Winds from the Baltic Sea give the western part of Estonia cool summers and mild winters. Farther inland, winters can be fairly severe.

Much of Estonia is a wetland and poor for agriculture. On soil that *is* farmable, farmers work hard to grow potatoes and grains. They also raise beef and dairy cattle. Food processing, Estonia's largest manufacturing industry, is followed by textiles, chemicals, cement, and wood products.

Estonia can produce most of the energy it needs. It has large deposits of **oil shale,** a rock that contains oil. Another resource is **peat,** wet ground with decaying plants that can be dried and used for fuel. Some peat bogs are as much as 20 feet (6 m) thick.

The Estonians About two-thirds of Estonia's people are ethnic Estonians. The Estonian language, very different from those of the other Baltic republics, is related to Finnish and Hungarian. Most ethnic Estonians speak Russian as well as Estonian. In fact, about 30 percent of the people are Russian.

Most of Estonia's 1.4 million people live in towns and cities. **Tallinn,** the capital, is on the Baltic coast. Estonia's much older German heritage appears in Tallinn's beautiful churches and castles built hundreds of years ago. Because of historical ties with Germany, about 80 percent of Estonians are Protestant Lutheran.

Reading Check What languages do Estonians speak?

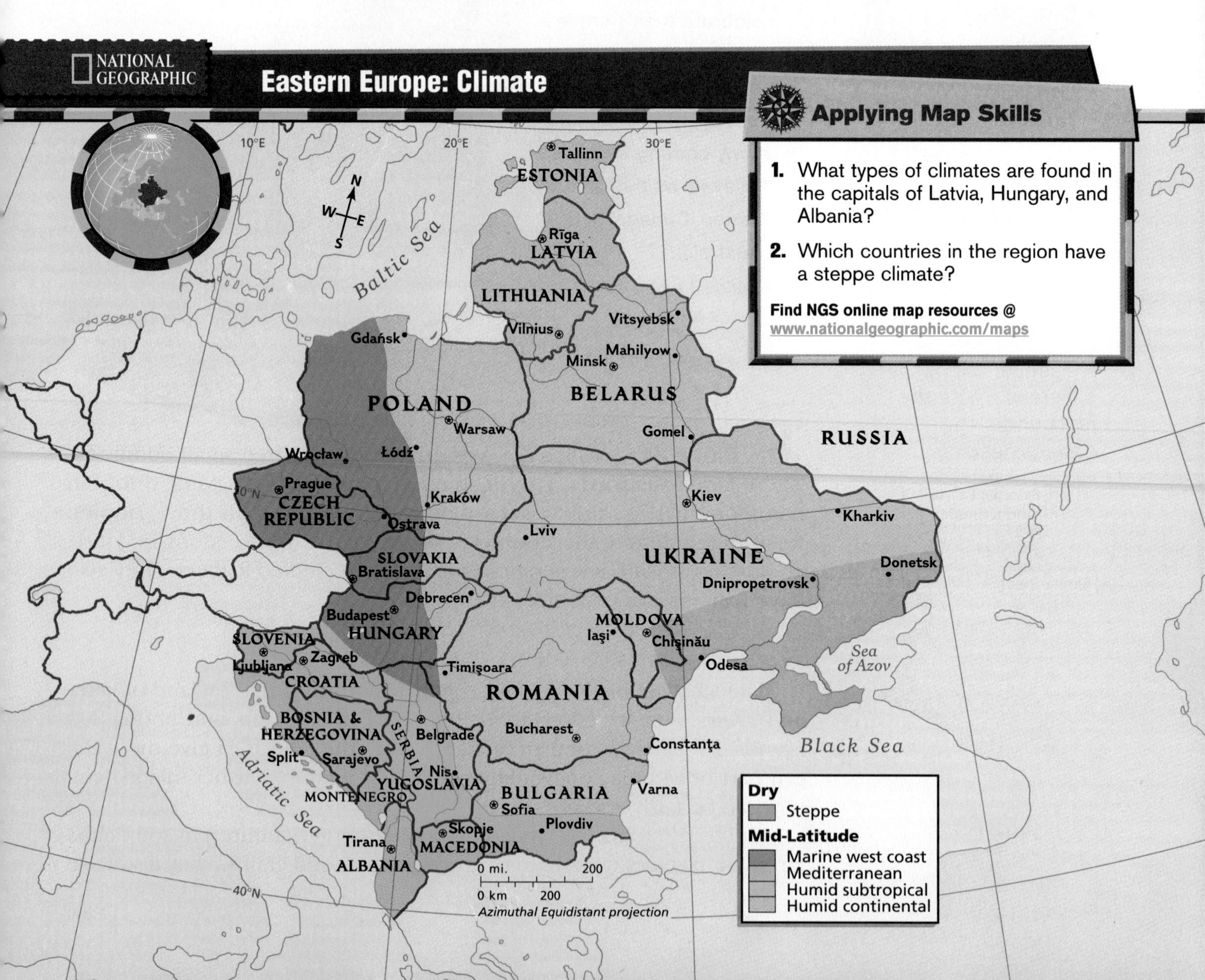

Latvia

South of Estonia lies Latvia, about the size of West Virginia. Crossing Latvia, you see a landscape of coastal plains, low hills, and forests. The Gulf of Rīga pokes into Latvia's northern coast. This Baltic location has helped make Latvia a trading center. It also has given the country a moderate climate of cool summers and mild winters.

After years of Communist rule, Latvia is working hard to create a free market economy. Dairy and livestock farming is at the heart of agriculture. Latvian farmers also grow potatoes, grains, sugar beets, fruits, and vegetables. Workers produce chemicals, vehicles, wood products, electrical machinery, and textiles. **Rīga,** the capital and largest city, is an important shipping and industrial center.

Latvia's Economy

Fish caught in the nearby Baltic Sea are sold in Rīga's Central Market.

Place **What products are manufactured in Latvia?**

Latvia's industry is more developed than industry in the other two Baltic republics. The rapid building of factories during Communist days led to widespread pollution, though. Latvia faces the challenge of cleaning up its environment.

The Latvians Like Estonia, Latvia has been invaded many times throughout its history. The most recent conquerors were the Soviets in the 1940s. At that time, many Latvians fled to the West. More than 200,000 people of Latvian descent live in the United States, the United Kingdom, Canada, and Australia.

Ethnic Latvians now make up only about 56 percent of Latvia's 2.4 million people. Russians—who make up 30 percent—actually outnumber Latvians in the country's largest cities. The government has recently passed a law requiring that all citizens know the Latvian language, which has upset some Russians who do not speak Latvian fluently.

The Latvian language is similar to that of Latvia's southern neighbors, the Lithuanians. Most Latvians are Lutheran like their northern neighbors, the Estonians. In all three countries, large midsummer celebrations begin in late June, when people flock to the countryside to enjoy the lakes and forests.

✓Reading Check **What is the capital of Latvia?**

Lithuania

About the size of Ireland, Lithuania is the largest of the Baltic republics. The country's mostly flat lowlands are crossed by rivers, dotted with lakes, and only lightly forested. Small hills formed by glacial rock deposits rise in the south and east of the country. Thanks to Baltic winds, mild winter and summer temperatures prevail.

Lithuania is the most rural of the Baltic republics. With fertile soil and a mild climate, the country has productive farms that grow potatoes, grains, and sugar beets. Farmers also raise dairy cattle and livestock.

Under Soviet rule, Lithuania developed factories fueled by nuclear power. Workers process foods and make textiles, chemicals, and wood products. Some quarry limestone, a stone often used in making cement. Lithuania is also a major source of amber, the fossilized sap of pine trees, used to make jewelry.

The Lithuanians With 3.7 million people, Lithuania is the most populous of the Baltic republics. Ethnic Lithuanians make up a greater part of their population than do ethnic Estonians or Latvians in their own countries. More than 80 percent of the people are ethnic Lithuanian, while less than 10 percent are Russian. Unlike the other Baltic peoples, Lithuania's people are mostly Roman Catholic. You will find beautiful old Catholic churches in the city of **Vilnius,** the capital.

During its early history, Lithuania had close ties with Poland to the west. In the 1700s, part of Poland and most of Lithuania were absorbed into the Russian Empire. After World War I, the Lithuanians enjoyed a brief period of freedom until the Soviet takeover in the 1940s. With the fall of the Soviet Union in 1991, Lithuania finally became independent.

Reading Check **What percentage of Lithuania's people are ethnic Lithuanians?**

Assessment

Defining Terms

1. **Define** oil shale, peat.

Recalling Facts

2. **Human/Environment Interaction** What resources enable Estonia to meet most of its own energy needs?
3. **History** Why are only 56 percent of Latvia's people of Latvian descent?
4. **Culture** What is the difference between the religion of Lithuania and that of the other Baltic Republics?

Critical Thinking

5. **Understanding Cause and Effect** What results of Estonia's years of rule by other countries are still visible today?
6. **Analyzing Information** How does Latvia's location help make it a trading center?

Graphic Organizer

7. **Organizing Information** Create a diagram like this one. Then list three resources or products for each country at the end of each line.

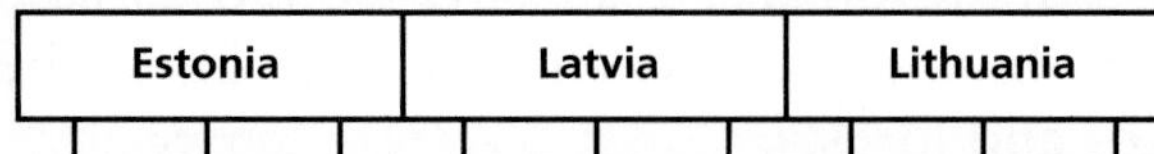

Applying Geography Skills

8. **Analyzing Maps** Refer to the political map on page 366. Which city is farther west, Tallinn, Estonia, or Vilnius, Lithuania?

Section 3 Hungary, the Czech Republic, and Slovakia

Guide to Reading

Main Idea

Hungary, the Czech Republic, and Slovakia are changing to free market economies.

Terms to Know

- landlocked
- bauxite
- nomad
- spa
- nature preserve
- privatize

Places to Locate

- Hungary
- Czech Republic
- Slovakia
- Danube River
- Great Hungarian Plain
- Budapest
- Prague
- Bratislava

Reading Strategy

Fill in three charts like this one with facts about the past and present of each of the following countries: Hungary, the Czech Republic, and Slovakia.

Country	
Past	
Present	

NATIONAL GEOGRAPHIC **Exploring Our World**

The end of Communist rule in 1989 brought many changes to Eastern Europe. In the Czech Republic, factory workers now labor to convert weapons no longer needed to new uses. In this factory, they remove the cannons from tanks, make other changes, and paint the vehicles red and white. Why? They are creating radio-controlled fire fighting vehicles.

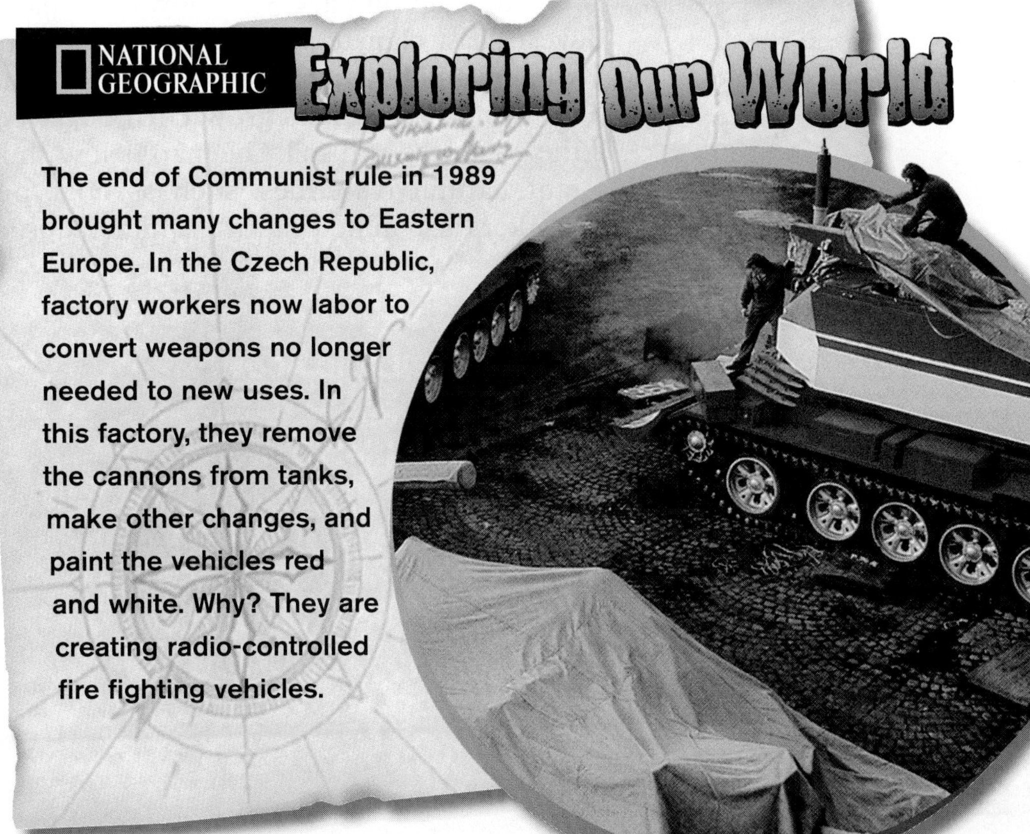

In the center of Eastern Europe, you find **Hungary,** the **Czech** (CHEHK) **Republic,** and **Slovakia** (sloh•VAH•kee•uh). The Czech Republic and Slovakia once were partners in a larger country known as Czechoslovakia.

Hungary

Hungary, almost the size of Indiana, is **landlocked,** meaning it has no land bordering a sea or an ocean. Hungary depends on the **Danube River** for trade and transportation. This mighty river twists and turns through Hungary and several other countries. Its waters flow 1,776 miles (2,858 km) before emptying into the Black Sea.

The **Great Hungarian Plain** runs through eastern Hungary. This vast lowland area, dotted with farms, has excellent soil for farming and for grazing animals. Many Hungarians here also raise horses. The Danube River separates the Great Hungarian Plain from a very different region to the west. This region is called Transdanubia because it lies "across the Danube." Rolling hills, wide valleys, and forests cover the landscape. Lake Balaton, one of Europe's largest lakes, also lies in Transdanubia. Many Hungarians spend their vacations in this part of the country.

The Carpathian Mountains rise in northern Hungary. In this scenic area, you can wander through thick forests, find strange rock formations, and explore underground caves.

The map on page 372 shows that parts of Hungary have a marine west coast climate and others a humid continental climate with cold winters and hot summers. Western Hungary receives the most rainfall.

Hungary's farmers grow corn, sugar beets, wheat, and potatoes in the country's rich soil. The map below shows that Hungary has important natural resources, such as coal, petroleum, and natural gas. Workers also mine **bauxite,** a mineral used to make aluminum. Foods,

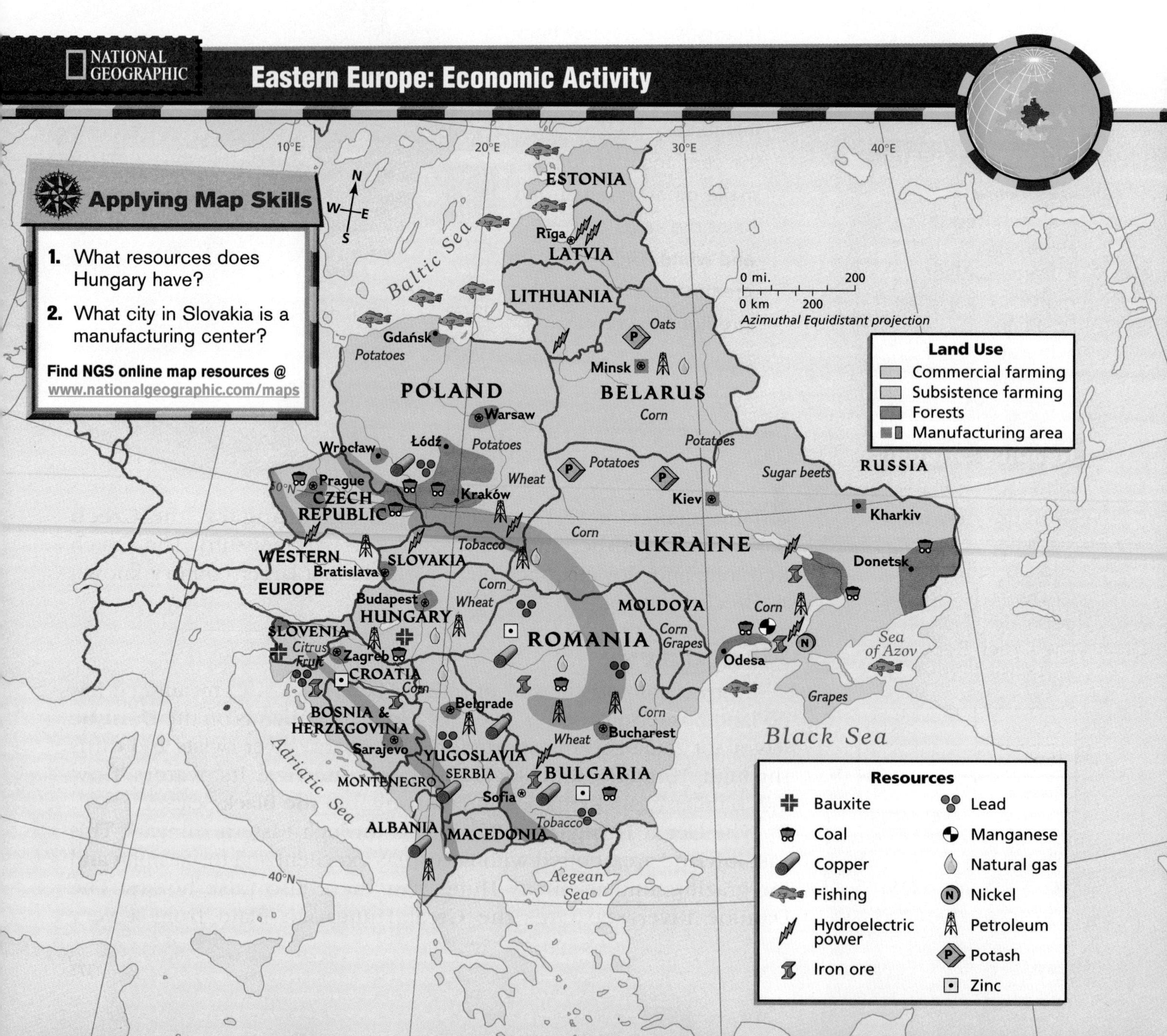

Budapest, Hungary

Hungary's capital extends along both banks of the Danube River.

Place **What two physical regions does the Danube River separate?**

beverages, and tobacco products are manufactured, as well as machines, chemicals, and metals.

In the late 1940s, Hungary's economy came under Communist control. Industry was rapidly increased to meet military needs. When communism collapsed in the 1980s, a free market economy returned. Service industries, such as financial services and tourism, now thrive.

The Hungarians Magyars came to the Danube River valley from central Asia about 1,000 years ago. They were **nomads,** or people who move from place to place with herds of animals. Skilled horse riders, the Magyars used the grassy plains to feed their animals. They set up a large kingdom in Eastern Europe and adopted Catholicism.

Hungarians value their unique Magyar culture. They struggled to protect it even when they lost their freedom to other peoples. Beginning in the 1500s, the Ottoman Turks and later the Austrians ruled most or all of Hungary.

In 1867 Hungary and Austria became partners in a large empire. When this empire was defeated in World War I, Hungary lost much of its territory and became the small, landlocked nation it is today. Hungary became Communist under the control of the Soviet Union after World War II. In 1956 Hungarians revolted, but Soviet tanks crushed the revolt, killing many people. In 1989 Hungarians finally ended Communist rule and set up a democracy.

About 90 percent of Hungary's 10 million people are descended from the Magyars. Almost all speak the Hungarian language. About two-thirds are Roman Catholic, while another one-fourth are Protestant. Two-thirds of Hungarians live in towns and cities. **Budapest** (BOO•duh•PEHST), the capital and largest city, is called "the Paris of Eastern Europe." It is actually two different cities divided by the Danube River. On the western bank lies the old city of Buda, full of beautiful churches and palaces. Bridges link this older settlement to the newer city of Pest, which has factories and tall, modern buildings.

✓Reading Check **What river is important to Hungary, and why?**

The Czech Republic

The Czech Republic is a landlocked country. About the size of South Carolina, it includes two historic political regions—Bohemia, in the west, and Moravia, in the east. Many areas are known for their natural beauty. In the mountains to the north and south, you can visit **spas,** or resorts with hot mineral springs that people bathe in to regain their health. You may explore **nature preserves,** or protected areas for plants and animals. The mountains also show scars caused by Czech industries. You can see the bare trunks of trees killed by pollution and acid rain.

The Czechs enjoy a high standard of living compared to other Eastern European countries. Large fertile areas make the Czech Republic a major agricultural producer. Farmers grow grains, sugar beets, potatoes, and other foods. Manufacturing forms the backbone of the country's economy, however. Factories make machinery, vehicles, metals, and textiles. Food processing is an important industry as well. **Prague** (PRAHG), the capital, is a center of service industries, tourism, and high-technology manufacturing.

The country has some petroleum and natural gas. Minerals include limestone, coal, and kaolin, a fine clay used for pottery. The brown coal that powers factories creates heavy smoke, though, so Czech leaders are trying to move toward nuclear energy.

Before 1989 the Czech Republic had a government-controlled economy based on communism. Since then, it has moved toward a free market. Yet the Communist past continues to haunt the present. Many factories are old, inefficient, and harmful to the environment. The Czechs are trying to modernize them to continue their prosperity.

The Czechs The ancestors of the Czechs were Slavic groups that settled much of Eastern Europe in the A.D. 400s and 500s. By 900, the Czechs had accepted Christianity. They also had formed a kingdom called Bohemia that lasted 600 years. Bohemia became part of the Austrian Empire in the 1500s.

Austrian rule lasted until 1918, when Czechoslovakia was created. Czechoslovakia was under Communist rule from 1948 until 1989, when a new democratic government peacefully voted the Communists out of office. In 1993 the Czechs and Slovaks agreed to split into the Czech Republic and the Republic of Slovakia. Today the Czech Republic is a parliamentary democracy, with a powerful president assisted by a prime minister.

Most of the Czech Republic's 10.3 million people belong to a Slavic ethnic group called Czechs and speak the Czech language. About two-thirds live in cities, many in crowded high-rise apartment buildings. Prague, with about 1.2 million people, is often called "the city of a hundred spires" because of its many church steeples. The entire country is famous for the architectural splendor of its historic buildings and monuments. Musical contributions range from classical to punk. More recently, the country has been a leading European center of jazz.

The Czechs also have produced great literature. Even government leaders are known for their writing skills. The first president of the Czech Republic, Vaclav Havel (VAHT•slahf HAH•vehl), is a noted author of plays.

✓Reading Check **What country ruled Czechoslovakia from the early 1500s until 1918?**

Slovakia

About twice the size of New Hampshire, Slovakia is largely a mountainous land. The Carpathian Mountains tower over the northern region. Rugged peaks, thick forests, and blue lakes make this area a popular vacation spot. Farther south, vineyards and farms spread across fertile lowlands that stretch to the Danube River. Farmers grow barley, corn, potatoes, sugar beets, and wine grapes. Under Communist rule, factories were built for heavy industry. Although communism is

Music

Early European shepherds were probably the first to play bagpipes. The bag is made from an animal's hide or stomach. To inflate the bag, air is blown through a tube or pumped with a bellows—a small air pump—under one arm. This air escapes through hollow sticks or bones in a controlled way to make different notes. The "drone" pipes produce a steady note, while the "chanter" pipes produce the melody.

Looking Closer **Do you think drone or chanter pipes would be more difficult to control? Why?**

GO TO
World Music: A Cultural Legacy
Hear music of this region on Disc 1, Track 17.

now gone, the push to develop industries continues. The Carpathian Mountains are rich in iron ore, lead, zinc, and copper. Factories use these minerals to produce iron and steel products. Workers also make cement, plastics, textiles, and processed foods.

Slovakia has had difficulty moving to a free market economy. Leaders set out to **privatize** businesses, or transfer the ownership of factories from the government to individual citizens. Some government officials acted corruptly, giving advantages to themselves or to their friends. This made few foreign companies willing to start new businesses here. Slovak factories also suffer from outdated technology that contributes to air and water pollution.

The Slovaks From the 900s to the early 1900s, Hungary ruled Slovakia. After Hungary's defeat in World War I, the Slovaks joined with the Czechs to form Czechoslovakia. In 1993 rising tensions between the two peoples led them to set up separate countries.

Slovaks make up most of the population. They have a language and culture different from the Czechs. Most Slovaks are Roman Catholic. Nearly 60 percent of Slovakia's 5.4 million people live in modern towns and cities. **Bratislava** (BRAH•tih•SLAH•vuh), a port on the Danube, is Slovakia's capital and largest city. Tourists visit villages to see people dress in traditional clothes for festivals. You might even see musicians playing folk music on shepherds' flutes and bagpipes.

✓Reading Check **What mineral resources does Slovakia have?**

Assessment

Defining Terms

1. **Define** landlocked, bauxite, nomad, spa, nature preserve, privatize.

Recalling Facts

2. **Culture** To what ethnic group do most Hungarians belong?
3. **Place** What are three of the Czech Republic's natural resources?
4. **Economics** Why has Slovakia had difficulty in moving to a free market economy?

Critical Thinking

5. **Analyzing Information** Why do the Czechs have a high standard of living?
6. **Understanding Cause and Effect** How do years of Communist control still affect the Czech Republic and Slovakia today?

Graphic Organizer

7. **Organizing Information** Draw a diagram like the one below. Then add at least two facts under the headings in each outer oval.

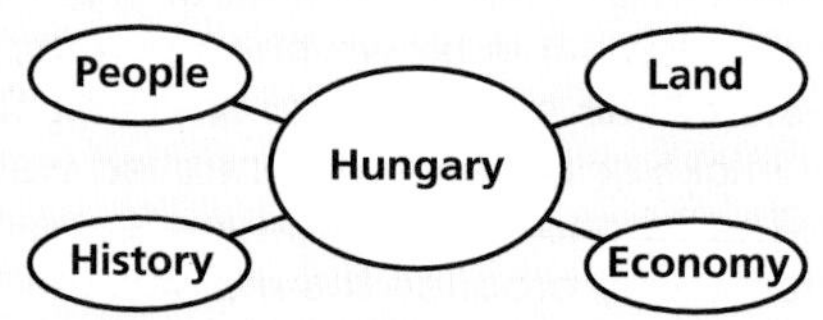

Applying Geography Skills

8. **Analyzing Maps** Turn to the political map on page 366. What countries border Hungary to the north? To the east?

Section 4

The Balkan Countries

Guide to Reading

Main Idea

The Balkan countries have greatly suffered from ethnic conflicts and economic setbacks.

Terms to Know

- consumer goods
- ethnic cleansing
- refugee
- mosque

Places to Locate

- Romania
- Bulgaria
- Albania
- Slovenia
- Croatia
- Bosnia and Herzegovina
- Yugoslavia (Serbia and Montenegro)
- Macedonia

Reading Strategy

Make a chart like this one. For each Balkan country, write a fact or cause in the left box. Then write an effect that results from that fact in the right box.

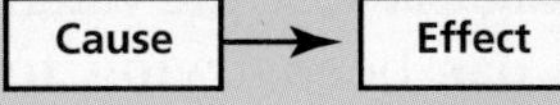

NATIONAL GEOGRAPHIC **Exploring Our World**

Traditional dress, folk music, and dancing enliven outdoor festivals in Romania. Many of these traditions come from the Roma people who have lived here for centuries. If you expect to see folk dress in Romania's capital, however, teenagers there might think you are old-fashioned. These teens in Bucharest listen to rock music and watch TV just as you do.

Europe's Balkan Peninsula lies between the Adriatic Sea and the Black Sea. The political map on page 366 shows you that several countries make up this Balkan region. They are **Romania, Bulgaria,** the former Yugoslav republics, and **Albania.**

Romania

Romania sits on the northeastern edge of the Balkan Peninsula. The Carpathian Mountains—home to bears, wolves, and other wildlife—take up about one-third of the country's land area. A vast plateau covers central Romania. A coastal region along the Black Sea includes the mouth of the Danube River. Many different birds and fish live in lakes and marshes here. Winters can be very cold and foggy, with much snow. Summers are hot and sunny, but rainfall is abundant.

Romania's economic activities include farming, manufacturing, and mining. The forested mountains and central plateau contain deposits of coal, petroleum, and natural gas. Oil wells stand in the south. Orchards and vineyards stretch along Romania's western, eastern, and southern borders. Farmers also grow grains, vegetables, and herbs here.

Despite abundant resources, Romania's economy has been held back by the Communist policies of the past. Under communism, Romania's factories produced steel, chemicals, and machinery. Few **consumer goods**—clothing, shoes, and other products made for people—were manufactured. Romania now has a free market economy to supply these goods, but aging factories must be updated for Romania's economy to grow. In addition, the country needs to heal an environment widely damaged by air and water pollution.

The Romanians About 56 percent of Romania's people live in towns and cities. Bucharest, the capital and largest city, has more than 2 million people. What does Romania's name tell you about its history? If you guessed that the Romans once ruled this region, you are correct. Most of Romania's 22.5 million people are descended from the Romans. The Romanian language is closer to French, Italian, and Spanish—which are all Romance languages—than it is to other Eastern European languages. In other ways, the Romanians are more like their Slavic neighbors. Many Romanians are Eastern Orthodox Christians.

After centuries of rule by the Ottoman Turks and the Austrians, Romania finally emerged as an independent kingdom in the 1800s. During the 1900s, Romanians suffered through two world wars and, later, Communist rule. In 1989 they violently overthrew their Communist dictator. Romania then became a democratic republic and moved toward a free market economy.

Reading Check To what other languages is Romanian related?

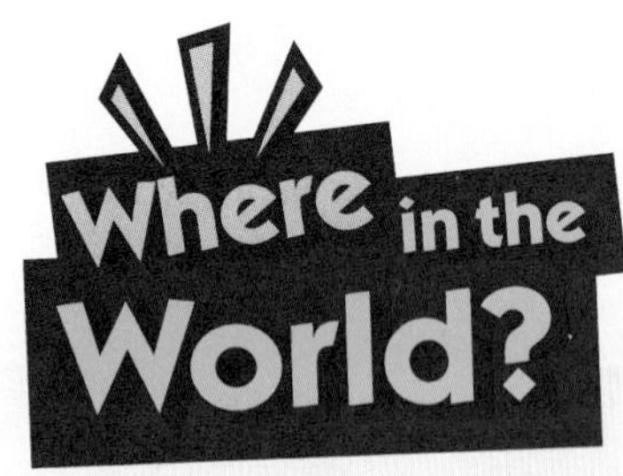

Transylvania

The region of central Romania known as Transylvania has long grabbed our imaginations. Transylvania's mountains and eerie cliff-hanging castles were the setting for English author Bram Stoker's novel *Dracula,* a story about a vampire. Recently, a Spanish doctor noticed that many myths about vampires matched the symptoms of rabies, including pain from bright lights. The doctor discovered that rabies had spread through the region at the same time that the vampire tales began.

Bulgaria

Mountainous Bulgaria lies south of Romania. Two ranges—the Balkan Mountains and the Rhodope (RAH•duh•pee) Mountains—span most of the country. Fertile valleys and plains are tucked among these mountains. Bulgaria's coast along the Black Sea has warmer year-round temperatures than the mountainous inland areas.

Bulgaria's economy rests on both agriculture and manufacturing. Wheat, corn, and sugar beets grow in the fertile valleys. Roses are grown in the central Valley of the Roses. Their sweet-smelling oil is used in perfumes.

When the Soviet Union collapsed, Bulgaria lost the main market for its goods. The government has been trying to rebuild the economy ever since. Manufacturing depends on the country's deposits of zinc and coal. Factories produce machinery, metals, textiles, and processed foods. Tourism is growing as visitors flock to Bulgaria's resorts on the Black Sea.

The Bulgarians Most of Bulgaria's 8.2 million people trace their ancestry to the Slavs and other groups from central Asia. Most Slavic people use the Cyrillic (suh•RIH•lihk) alphabet, which was first created to write the Russian language. The Bulgarian language, similar to Russian, is written in this Cyrillic alphabet. Most Bulgarians practice the Eastern Orthodox Christian religion. About 9 percent of the people are Muslim Turks.

For centuries Turkish officials ruled Bulgaria. In the late 1800s, the Bulgarians won their freedom with Russian help. After World War II, Bulgaria's strong ties to Russia made it easy for Communists to take power. Communism in Bulgaria ended in 1989. High joblessness, crime, and rising prices have troubled the change to democracy.

Sofia, with over 1 million people, is the capital and largest city. During the summer, Bulgarians join vacationers from other countries at resorts on the Black Sea coast. Here, modern hotels line wide, sandy beaches.

✓Reading Check **What alphabet is used in many Slavic languages?**

Former Yugoslav Republics

The former Yugoslav republics used to be one country called Yugoslavia. For years, a Communist dictator named Joseph Broz Tito held the country together. He died in 1980, and communism itself collapsed about 10 years later. In the early 1990s, long-simmering disputes among ethnic groups boiled to the surface and tore the country apart. Five countries emerged: **Slovenia, Croatia, Bosnia and Herzegovina** (HEHRT•seh•GAW•vee•nah), **Yugoslavia** (made up of **Serbia and Montenegro**), and **Macedonia,** also known as the Former Yugoslav Republic of Macedonia (or F.Y.R.O.M.).

After the breakup, Serbia, the strongest country, kept the name of Yugoslavia. It wished to regain control of the other former Yugoslav republics. Serbia also wanted to make sure that Serbs living in the other republics would not lose their rights. As a result, wars erupted throughout the 1990s. Some countries forced people from other ethnic groups to leave their homes, a policy called **ethnic cleansing.** Hundreds of thousands of people died. About the same number became **refugees,** or people who flee to another country to escape danger or disaster. These wars left the region badly scarred without promise of long-term peace.

Find the former Yugoslav republics on the physical map on page 367. You see that mountains form the backbone of the landscape. Plains lie in the north where the Danube River flows. The southwest borders the Adriatic Sea. Inland areas are warm in summer and cold in winter. The long coastal strip has warm summers and cool winters.

Slovenia Slovenia, in the northwest of the Balkans region, has rugged mountains and fertile, densely populated valleys. Of all the countries of the old Yugoslavia, Slovenia is the most peaceful and prosperous. With many factories and service industries, it also has the region's highest standard of living. About 52 percent of the 2 million Slovenians live in towns and cities. Most are Roman Catholic.

Croatia Croatia spreads along the island-studded coast of the Adriatic Sea. Then it suddenly swings inland, encompassing rugged mountains and a fertile plain. Zagreb, the capital and largest city, lies in this inland area. An industrialized republic, Croatia supports agriculture as well. Tourists once flocked to Croatia's beautiful Adriatic beaches, but war has damaged many places.

The Croats, a Slavic group, make up 78 percent of Croatia's 4.6 million people. Another 12 percent are Serbs. Both Croats and Serbs speak the same Serbo-Croatian language, but they use different alphabets. The Croats use the Latin alphabet, the same one that you use for English. The Serbs write with the Cyrillic alphabet. Religion also divides Croats and Serbs. Croats are mainly Roman Catholic, while Serbs are Eastern Orthodox Christians.

Albania

Rugged mountains have isolated Albania from neighboring countries.

Movement **Why have many Albanians fled the country in recent years?**

Bosnia and Herzegovina Mountainous and poor, Bosnia and Herzegovina has an economy based mainly on crops and livestock. Sarajevo (SAR•uh•YAY•voh), the capital, has the look of an Asian city, with its marketplaces and **mosques,** or Muslim houses of worship. Many of the Bosnian people are Muslims, followers of the religion of Islam. Others are Eastern Orthodox Serbs or Roman Catholic Croats. Serbs began a bitter war after Bosnia's independence in 1992. The Dayton Peace Accords divided Bosnia into two regions under one government in 1995. American and other troops came as peacekeepers.

Yugoslavia (Serbia and Montenegro) All that is left of Yugoslavia is Serbia and its reluctant partner, Montenegro. Inland plains and mountains cover the area. The economies of these two republics are based on agriculture and industry. The region's largest city is Belgrade. The 10.6 million Serbs and Montenegrins practice the Eastern Orthodox faith.

Serbia has faced growing unrest in some of its local provinces. Muslim Albanians living in the province of Kosovo want independence from Serbia. Also living in Kosovo is a smaller group of Eastern Orthodox Serbs. For centuries, Albanians and Serbs here have felt a deep anger toward each other. In 1999 Serb forces tried to push the Albanians out of Kosovo. The United States and other nations bombed Serbia to force it to withdraw its troops. Peace in Kosovo remains shaky.

Macedonia (F.Y.R.O.M.) Macedonia's 2 million people, mostly farmers, are a mix of different ethnic groups from the Balkans. In Skopje (SKAW•pyeh), Macedonia's capital, there is an amazing mix of ancient Christian churches, timeworn Turkish markets, and modern shopping centers. Close to Kosovo, Macedonia handled a huge wave of ethnic Albanian refugees from Kosovo, who fled Serb forces in 1999.

✓Reading Check **What nations were formed from the former Yugoslavia?**

Albania

Bordering the Adriatic Sea, Albania is slightly larger than the state of Maryland. Mountains cover most of the country, contributing to Albania's isolation from neighboring countries. A small coastal plain runs along the Adriatic Sea. Most of Albania has a Mediterranean climate.

Albania is a very poor country. Although the country has valuable mineral resources, it lacks the money to mine them. Most Albanians farm, growing corn, grapes, olives, potatoes, sugar beets, and wheat in mountain valleys.

The Albanians Almost two-thirds of Albanians live in the countryside. The capital and largest city, Tirana, and its suburbs have a population of more than 500,000. Although 3.5 million people live in Albania, another 3.2 million Albanians live in nearby countries. These refugees fled Albania to escape the violence that swept the country after communism's fall in the early 1990s.

About 70 percent of Albanians are Muslims. The rest are Christian—either Eastern Orthodox or Roman Catholic. While the Communists opposed religion, Albania's democratic government has allowed people to practice their faith. As a result, many mosques and churches have opened across the country. The most famous Albanian in recent times was the Catholic nun Mother Teresa, who served the poor in Calcutta, India.

✓Reading Check **What is the main religion in Albania?**

Assessment

Defining Terms

1. **Define** consumer goods, ethnic cleansing, refugee, mosque.

Recalling Facts

2. **Place** What is the capital of Romania?
3. **Economics** How are roses used in Bulgaria?
4. **History** Which of the former Yugoslav republics is most prosperous?

Critical Thinking

5. **Drawing Conclusions** How do you think people in the Balkans feel about the recent changes in their countries?
6. **Understanding Cause and Effect** What factors have contributed to the recent conflicts in the Balkans?

Graphic Organizer

7. **Organizing Information** Draw a chart like the one below and complete it by filling in two facts under each country name.

Romania	Bulgaria	Slovenia	Croatia
Bosnia and Herzegovina	Yugoslavia	Macedonia	Albania

Applying Geography Skills

8. **Analyzing Maps** Study the physical map on page 367. What mountain range is found on the east coast of the Adriatic Sea?

Section 5

Ukraine, Belarus, and Moldova

Guide to Reading

Main Idea

Past ties to Russia have had different effects on the economies and societies of Ukraine, Belarus, and Moldova.

Terms to Know

- steppe
- potash

Places to Locate

- Ukraine
- Belarus
- Moldova
- Dnieper River
- Crimean Peninsula
- Kiev
- Minsk
- Chişinău

Reading Strategy

Make a diagram like this one. List at least one fact that shows the Soviet Union's effect on these countries under the correct country name.

On April 26, 1986, Reactor 4 of the Chernobyl (chuhr•NOH•buhl) Nuclear Power Plant in Ukraine exploded. An estimated 5,000 people died, and about 30,000 were disabled by exposure to radiation. Some 30,000 square miles of good farmland were poisoned. These vehicles have been permanently scrapped after being used to clean up after the explosion.

Ukraine, Belarus (BEE•luh•ROOS), and **Moldova** (mawl•DAW•vuh) once belonged to the Soviet Union. When the Soviet Union broke apart in late 1991, Ukraine, Belarus, and Moldova became independent. Since then, they have struggled to build new economies.

Ukraine

Slightly smaller than Texas, Ukraine is by far the largest Eastern European country. The Carpathian Mountains rise along its southwestern border. Farther east, a vast steppe, or gently rolling, partly wooded plains, makes up the country. Nearly 23,000 rivers twist across the steppe. The most important waterway, the **Dnieper** (NEE•puhr) **River,** has been made navigable so ships can carry goods to distant markets. The **Crimean Peninsula** juts into the Black Sea. Most of Ukraine has a humid continental climate with cold winters and warm summers.

Rich dark soil covers nearly two-thirds of Ukraine. Farms are very productive, earning the country the name "breadbasket of Europe." Farmers grow sugar beets, potatoes, and grains and raise cattle and sheep. Factories make machinery, processed foods, and chemicals.

The Ukrainians Early Slavic groups settled and traded along the rivers of the region. During the A.D. 800s, warriors from Scandinavia united these groups into a large state centered on the city of **Kiev** (KEE•ihf). A century later, the people of Kiev accepted the Eastern Orthodox faith and built one of Europe's most prosperous civilizations. After 300 years of freedom, the people of Kiev were conquered by Mongols, then Lithuanians and Poles, and finally the Russians.

In the 1930s, Soviet dictator Joseph Stalin brought Ukraine's farms under government control. This action caused a famine in which millions of Ukrainians starved. Millions more died when Germans invaded

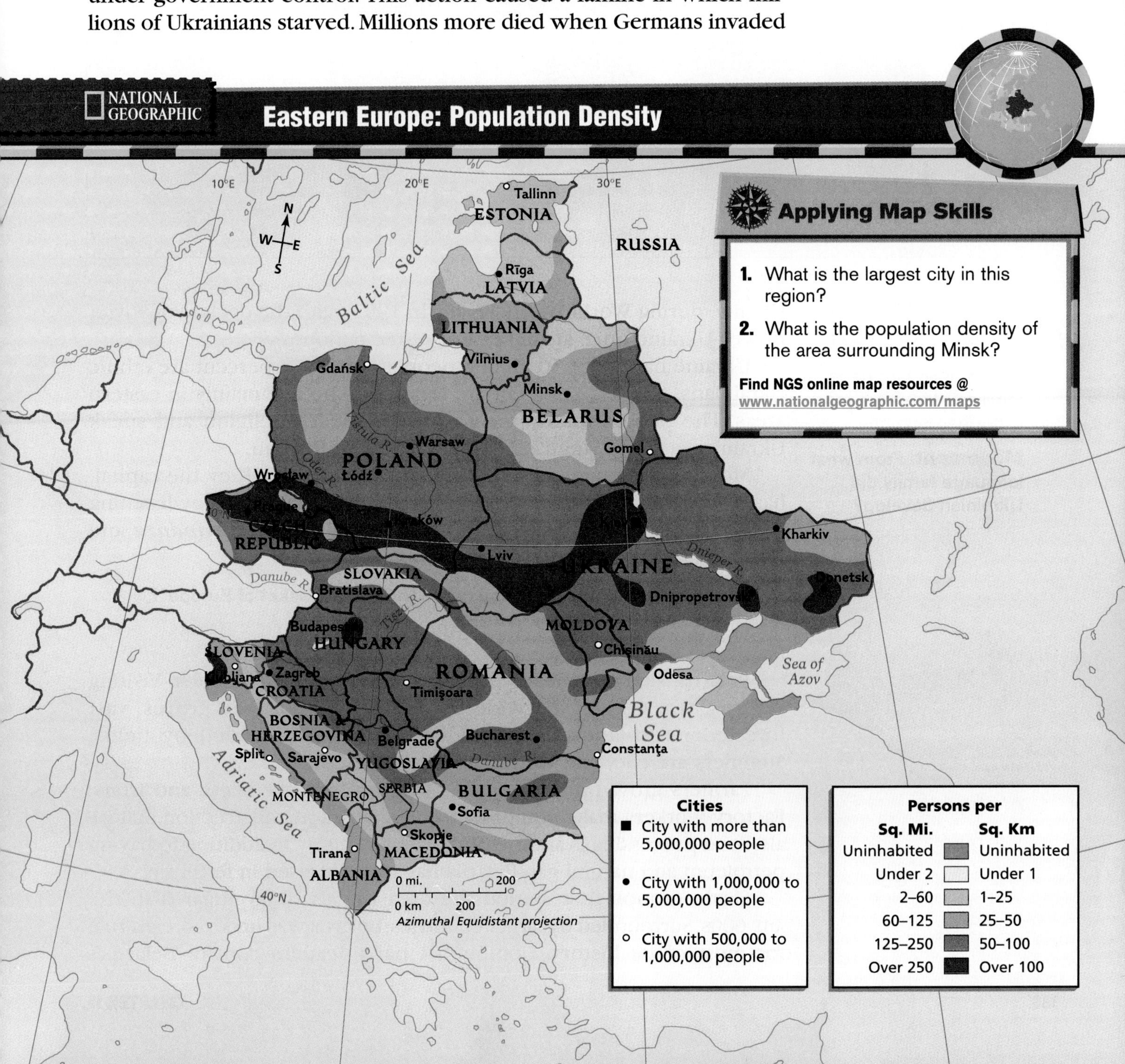

Language Families of Europe

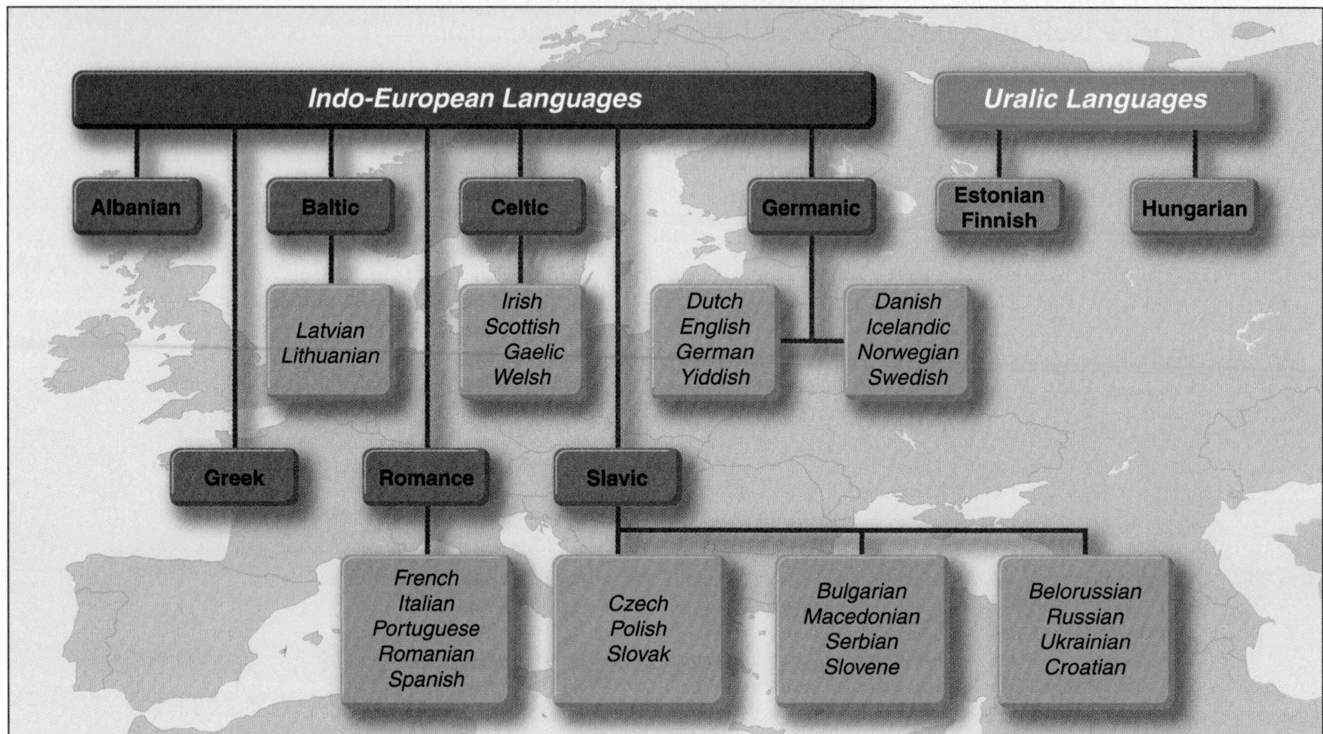

Analyzing the Chart

Seven main language families stem from Indo-European origins.

Movement From what language family did Ukrainian develop?

Ukraine during World War II. Finally in 1991, with the decline of Soviet power, Ukraine once again became a free nation.

Ukraine has about 50 million people. Nearly 75 percent are ethnic Ukrainians. About 22 percent are Russians who live mainly in eastern areas. The people follow the Eastern Orthodox religion and speak Ukrainian, a Slavic language closely related to Russian.

More than 70 percent of the people live in cities. Kiev, the capital, has over 5 million. Modern Ukrainians, even teenagers, enjoy listening to folk music played on a stringed instrument called a *bandura* and watching the acrobatic leaps of the *hopak* dance.

✓Reading Check **Why is Ukraine called the "breadbasket of Europe"?**

Belarus and Moldova

Belarus, slightly smaller than Kansas, is largely lowlands. Visiting Belarus, you would see wide stretches of birch tree groves, vast forested marshlands, and wooden villages surrounded by fields. Summers are cool and wet, and winters are cold.

Farmers grow potatoes, grains, vegetables, sugar beets, and fruits. Factory workers make equipment, chemicals, and construction materials. Food processing is another important industry. In addition to having petroleum and natural gas, Belarus has **potash,** used in fertilizer.

Slavic groups first settled the area that is today Belarus in the A.D. 600s. Surrounded by larger countries, Belarus was under foreign rule for most of its history. Communist party leaders control Belarus's government and have maintained close ties with Russia. Foreign companies have been unwilling to do business here. In addition, Belarus is still linked to neighboring Russia's weak economy. For these reasons, the Belarussians have faced many hardships in recent years.

The 10.2 million people of Belarus are mostly Eastern Orthodox Slavs. Their Belarussian language is closely related to Russian and Ukrainian and is written in Cyrillic. Two-thirds of Belarus's people live in cities. **Minsk,** the largest city, is the capital.

Moldova Moldova is mostly a rolling hilly plain sliced by rivers. These waterways form valleys that hold rich fertile soil. This soil, along with mild winters and warm summers, provides productive farmland. Farmers grow sugar beets, grains, potatoes, apples, and tobacco. Some grow grapes used to make wine. Factories turn out processed foods, machinery, metals, construction materials, and textiles.

Moldova's flag looks similar to Romania's flag. Why? Moldova once was part of Romania. About two-thirds of the people trace their language and culture to that country. Moldova's eastern region, home to many Russians, Ukrainians, and Turks, recently declared independence. This is an important issue to Moldova, because that region also produces about 80 percent of the country's electricity.

Moldova has 4.3 million people. About half live in cities, but much of Moldova's culture is still based on a rural way of life. Villagers celebrate special occasions with lamb, cornmeal pudding, and goat's milk cheese. The chief city is the capital, **Chişinău** (KEE•shee•NOW).

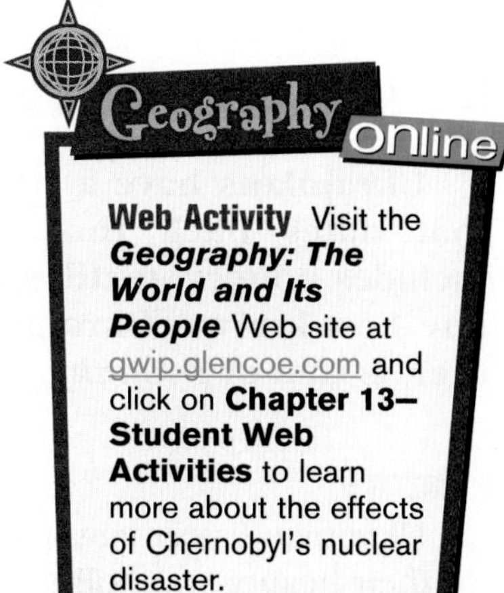

Web Activity Visit the ***Geography: The World and Its People*** Web site at gwip.glencoe.com and click on **Chapter 13—Student Web Activities** to learn more about the effects of Chernobyl's nuclear disaster.

Reading Check **With what nation does Belarus have close ties?**

Assessment

Defining Terms

1. Define steppe, potash.

Recalling Facts

2. Location Where is the Crimean Peninsula located?

3. Government What type of government does Belarus have?

4. Economics Name three of Moldova's agricultural products.

Critical Thinking

5. Categorizing Information List four agricultural products and three manufactured products of Ukraine.

6. Understanding Cause and Effect Why is the culture of Moldova similar to that of Romania?

Graphic Organizer

7. Organizing Information Draw a time line like this one. Then label five important periods or events and dates in Ukraine's history.

Applying Geography Skills

8. Analyzing Maps Compare the physical and population maps on pages 367 and 387. What is the population density around Ukraine's Dniester River?

Making Connections

ART | SCIENCE | LITERATURE | TECHNOLOGY

Ukrainian Easter Eggs

Ukrainians have a rich folk art tradition that dates back thousands of years. It includes pottery, textiles, and woodworking. The best-known Ukrainian art form, however, is that of *pysanky,* or decorated eggs.

History

Ukrainian Easter eggs are known worldwide for their beauty and skillful designs. Many of the designs date back to a time when people in the region worshiped a sun god. According to legend, the sun god preferred birds over all other creatures. Birds' eggs became a symbol of birth and new life, and people believed the eggs could ward off evil and bring good luck. Eggs were decorated with sun symbols and used in ceremonies that marked the beginning of spring.

When Christianity took hold in Ukraine in A.D. 988, the tradition of decorative eggs continued. The egg came to represent religious rebirth and new life. People decorated eggs in the days before Easter, then gave them as gifts on Easter morning.

Technique

The word *pysanky* comes from Ukrainian words meaning "things that are written upon." This phrase helps explain the wax process used to decorate the eggs. An artist uses a pin or a tool called a *kistka* to "write" a design in hot wax onto the egg. The egg is then dipped into yellow dye, leaving the wax-covered portion of the eggshell white. After removing the egg from the dye, the artist writes with hot wax over another section of the egg. This portion stays yellow as the egg is dipped into a second dye color. The process continues, with the artist adding wax and dipping the egg into a darker and darker color. At the end, the artist removes the wax layers to reveal the multicolored design.

Making the Connection

1. What is *pysanky* and when did it originate?
2. What role does placing wax onto the eggshell play in creating a decorative egg?
3. **Drawing Conclusions** What purposes, other than entertainment, might folk art accomplish?

◄ Ukrainian Easter eggs

Chapter 13 Reading Review

Section 1 Poland

Terms to Know
bog
communist state
acid rain
republic
pope

Main Idea
Poland, a large country with a rich history, is undergoing many changes.

✓ Place Poland is a large country with southern mountains and northern plains.
✓ Economics The change to a free market economy has brought challenges.
✓ Culture The Poles feel deep loyalty to their country and the Catholic Church.

Section 2 The Baltic Republics

Terms to Know
oil shale
peat

Main Idea
People in Estonia, Latvia, and Lithuania are trying to change their economies yet keep their cultures.

✓ Place The Baltic countries of Estonia, Latvia, and Lithuania are working to increase manufacturing and service industries.
✓ History These countries are trying to strengthen their ethnic heritage.

Section 3 Hungary, the Czech Republic, and Slovakia

Terms to Know
nomad
spa
landlocked
bauxite
nature preserve
privatize

Main Idea
Hungary, the Czech Republic, and Slovakia are changing to free market economies.

✓ Economics The Czech Republic is prosperous but must modernize its factories.
✓ Economics Because of corruption, Slovakia has had difficulty moving to a free market economy.

Section 4 The Balkan Countries

Terms to Know
consumer goods
ethnic cleansing
refugee
mosque

Main Idea
The Balkan countries have greatly suffered from ethnic conflicts and economic setbacks.

✓ Culture The people of Romania are not related to the Slavic peoples who form the populations of most Eastern European countries.
✓ History Ethnic conflicts have torn apart the former Yugoslav republics.
✓ Economics Albania is rich in minerals but is too poor to develop them.

Section 5 Ukraine, Belarus, and Moldova

Terms to Know
steppe
potash

Main Idea
Past ties to Russia have had different effects on the economies and societies of Ukraine, Belarus, and Moldova.

✓ Geography Ukraine's rich soil allows it to grow large amounts of food.
✓ Culture The people of Belarus want to maintain ties with Russia.
✓ Culture Moldova suffers from disagreements among different ethnic groups.

Chapter 13

Assessment and Activities

Using Key Terms

Match the terms in Part A with their definitions in Part B.

A.

1. spa
2. ethnic cleansing
3. nomad
4. pope
5. steppe
6. privatize
7. mosque
8. bog
9. refugee
10. oil shale

B.

a. head of the Roman Catholic Church
b. resort with hot mineral springs
c. layered rock that contains oil
d. government transfers ownership of businesses to individuals
e. low-lying marshy land
f. Muslim house of worship
g. people who move from place to place
h. forcing people from other groups to leave their homes
i. person who must flee to another country
j. dry, treeless grasslands

Reviewing the Main Ideas

Section 1 Poland

11. **Location** Poland borders what large body of water?
12. **Economics** What is Poland's most important industry?

Section 2 The Baltic Republics

13. **History** Who controlled the Baltic Republics from 1940 to 1991?
14. **Region** Which Baltic Republic is most industrialized?

Section 3 Hungary, the Czech Republic, and Slovakia

15. **Place** What river divides Hungary?
16. **Place** What is the Czech Republic's capital?

Section 4 The Balkan Countries

17. **Government** What problems have accompanied Bulgaria's transition to democracy?
18. **History** What caused Yugoslavia to fall apart?

Section 5 Ukraine, Belarus, and Moldova

19. **Place** What is the capital of Ukraine?
20. **Government** What is unusual about Belarus's government?

Eastern Europe

Place Location Activity

On a separate sheet of paper, match the letters on the map with the numbered places listed below.

1. Danube River
2. Black Sea
3. Croatia
4. Albania
5. Latvia
6. Hungary
7. Warsaw
8. Carpathian Mountains
9. Baltic Sea
10. Ukraine

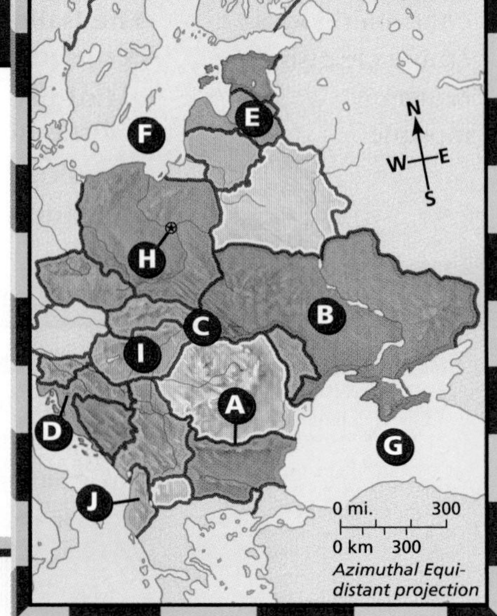

Self-Check Quiz Visit the ***Geography: The World and Its People*** Web site at gwip.glencoe.com and click on **Chapter 13—Self-Check Quizzes** to prepare for the Chapter Test.

Critical Thinking

21. **Understanding Cause and Effect** How have the Balkan Mountains contributed to the ethnic diversity of that region?
22. **Categorizing Information** In a chart like the one below, identify Eastern European countries that are succeeding and ones that continue to struggle economically. Include one fact that explains each situation.

Countries That Are Succeeding	Countries That Are Struggling

GeoJournal Activity

23. **Writing a Poem** A cinquain is a poem with five lines. The first line is a one-word title. Line two has two words that describe the title. Line three has three action words that describe the title. Line four is a four-word phrase that expresses a feeling about the subject. Line five is one word that is a synonym or restatement of the title. Write a cinquain about one Eastern European country.

Mental Mapping Activity

24. **Focusing on the Region** Draw a map of Eastern Europe, then label the following:

- Poland
- Czech Republic
- Hungary
- Black Sea
- Ukraine
- Albania
- Serbia
- Lithuania
- Danube River
- Adriatic Sea

Technology Skills Activity

25. **Building a Database** Create a database of Eastern European countries. Include fields for capital, size, population, government, and products. After analyzing your database, predict which countries have a better chance of improving their standards of living.

Standardized Test Practice

Directions: Study the map below, then answer the question that follows.

1. **Which of these Eastern European countries is NOT being considered for membership in the European Union?**
   A Ukraine
   B Poland
   C Estonia
   D Czech Republic

Test-Taking Tip: This is a tricky question because all the choices are Eastern European countries. You need to study the map to see which answer choice is not listed on the map. Use the process of elimination to narrow your answer choices.

Workers on the statue *Motherland Calls*, Volgograd

Russians in front of St. Basil's Cathedral, Moscow

Russia

If you had to describe Russia in one word, that word would be "BIG"! Russia is the largest country in the world in area. Its almost 6.6 million square miles (17 million sq. km) are spread across two continents—Europe and Asia. As you can imagine, such a large country faces equally large challenges. Since 1991, when Russia emerged as an independent country, it has been struggling to unite its many ethnic groups, set up a democratic government, and build a stable economy.

◀ Siberian tiger in a forest in eastern Russia

NGS ONLINE
www.nationalgeographic.com/education

Focus on:

Russia

RUSSIA IS THE WORLD'S LARGEST COUNTRY. Spanning 11 time zones, it is almost twice the size of the United States. Russia's far northern location affects its climate and the lifestyle of its people. Being somewhat isolated from the rest of the world has played a major role in the country's history, politics, and economic development.

The Land

Stretching nearly halfway around the globe, Russia sprawls from the Bering Sea in the east to the Baltic Sea in the west. Its northernmost lands lie above the Arctic Circle; its southern border winds through the middle of Asia.

Russia is a land of sweeping plains and plateaus interrupted by mountain ranges. The Ural Mountains run north to south, dividing the country into a European region and a much larger Asian region. West of the Urals is the fertile North European Plain—home to three-fourths of the country's population. East of the Urals lies Siberia, which means "sleeping land." Immense and sparsely populated, Siberia is an area of harsh, forbidding landscapes. Although rich in natural resources, much of it remains a wilderness.

The Caspian Sea—actually a saltwater lake—lies at the base of the Caucasus Mountains in Russia's southwest. It is the largest inland body of water in the world. Farther east is Lake Baikal, the world's deepest lake. Many rivers wind through Russian landscapes. The Volga flows southward to empty into the Caspian Sea. The Lena, Yenisey, and Ob Rivers all flow north to the Arctic Ocean.

The Climate

Most of Russia has a cold climate due to its northern location. In Siberia's far north, the landscape is dominated by tundra, a treeless plain. Winters on the tundra are long, dark, and fiercely cold. During the brief summers, only the top few inches of soil thaw out. Deeper down is permafrost—permanently frozen ground.

South of the tundra are immense evergreen forests. This vast woodland area, known as the taiga, is the largest continuous expanse of forest on the earth. Snow blankets the taiga for as much as eight months of the year.

Farther south, the taiga gives way to flat, grass-covered plains, or steppes. Here the climate is less harsh, and the soil quite rich. The steppes make up Russia's most productive agricultural area.

UNIT 5

Wildflowers and wooden churches on the North European Plain, in northwestern Russia ▼

◀ Reindeer pulling sled across the tundra, Siberia

Regional Atlas

The Economy

For nearly 70 years in the twentieth century, Russia and the other republics of the Soviet Union shared a single economy that was controlled by Communist authorities. Wheat and other crops were grown on huge government-owned farms. The top economic priority was heavy industry—the manufacturing of goods such as machinery and military equipment. Russia's rich deposits of minerals, coal, and oil supplied the raw materials and energy for many of its industries. The push to industrialize, however, led to widespread pollution of the air, soil, and water. Industrial growth also was more important than the needs of the people. Shortages of consumer goods—clothing and household products, for example—were common.

In the 1990s, when Russia and the other republics of the Soviet Union became independent countries, each took charge of its own economy. Today Russia is struggling to make the transition to a free enterprise system, in which people run their own businesses and farms.

The People

Roughly 147 million people live in Russia. Most live west of the Ural Mountains, where the climate is mildest and the land most fertile. Moscow and St. Petersburg are the region's largest cities.

Although people of many ethnic groups can be found within Russia's borders, most Russians are descendants of Slavic peoples, or Slavs. Centuries ago, Slavs from northeastern Europe settled in what is now western Russia. Their settlements grew into city-states ruled by princes. By the 1400s, these states were united under the rule of a czar. For more than 400 years, Russia was governed by a series of powerful, and often ruthless, czars. Their armies conquered surrounding lands to gradually create a huge Russian Empire.

In 1917 the last czar was overthrown, and a Communist dictatorship emerged. The Russian Empire became the Union of Soviet Socialist Republics. The Communists made the Soviet Union an industrial power but denied the people basic freedoms. In 1991 the Communists fell from power, and the Soviet Union disintegrated.

Exploring the Region

1. **Why might Russia's north-flowing rivers be difficult to travel in winter?**
2. **Why would it be hard to grow crops on the tundra?**
3. **What was the top economic priority of Communist authorities?**
4. **To what ethnic group do most Russians belong?**

◀ **Russian worker inspecting tractors in a factory**

▲ Young people strolling and singing in St. Petersburg

Russia

Physical

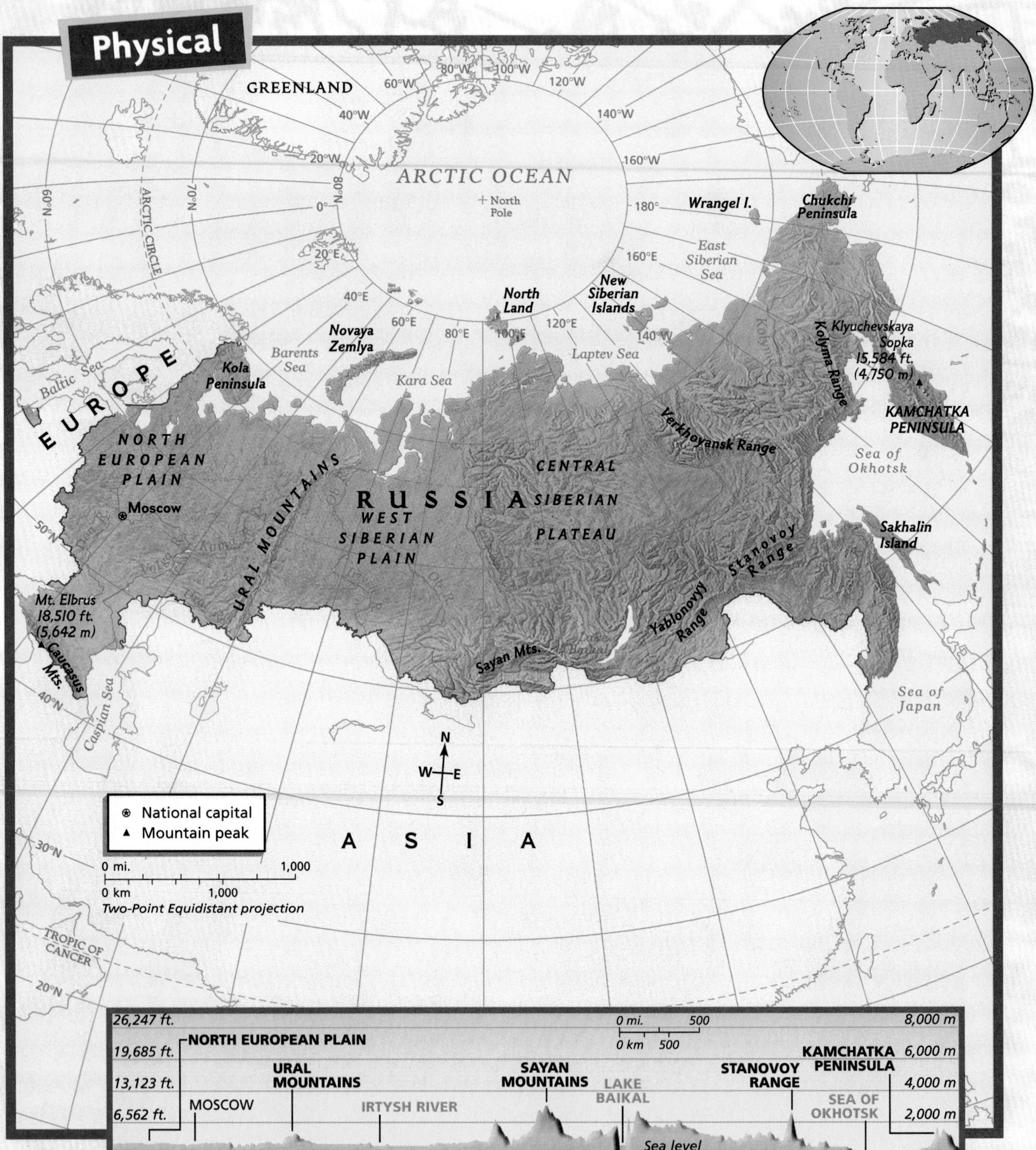

GREENLAND
ARCTIC OCEAN
North Pole
60°W
80°W
100°W
120°W
40°W
140°W
20°W
160°W
0°
180°
20°E
160°E
40°E
60°E
80°E
100°E
120°E
140°E
60°N
70°N
80°N
50°N
40°N
30°N
20°N
ARCTIC CIRCLE
TROPIC OF CANCER
Wrangel I.
Chukchi Peninsula
East Siberian Sea
New Siberian Islands
North Land
Novaya Zemlya
Barents Sea
Kara Sea
Laptev Sea
Kola Peninsula
Baltic Sea
EUROPE
NORTH EUROPEAN PLAIN
Moscow
URAL MOUNTAINS
RUSSIA
WEST SIBERIAN PLAIN
CENTRAL SIBERIAN PLATEAU
Verkhoyansk Range
Kolyma Range
Klyuchevskaya Sopka 15,584 ft. (4,750 m)
KAMCHATKA PENINSULA
Sea of Okhotsk
Sakhalin Island
Stanovoy Range
Yablonovyy Range
Sayan Mts.
Lake Baikal
Mt. Elbrus 18,510 ft. (5,642 m)
Caucasus Mts.
Caspian Sea
Sea of Japan
ASIA

N
W
E
S

- ⊛ National capital
- ▲ Mountain peak

0 mi. 1,000
0 km 1,000
Two-Point Equidistant projection

26,247 ft.
19,685 ft.
13,123 ft.
6,562 ft.
8,000 m
6,000 m
4,000 m
2,000 m
0 mi. 500
0 km 500
NORTH EUROPEAN PLAIN
MOSCOW
URAL MOUNTAINS
IRTYSH RIVER
SAYAN MOUNTAINS
LAKE BAIKAL
STANOVOY RANGE
SEA OF OKHOTSK
KAMCHATKA PENINSULA
Sea level

UNIT

Political

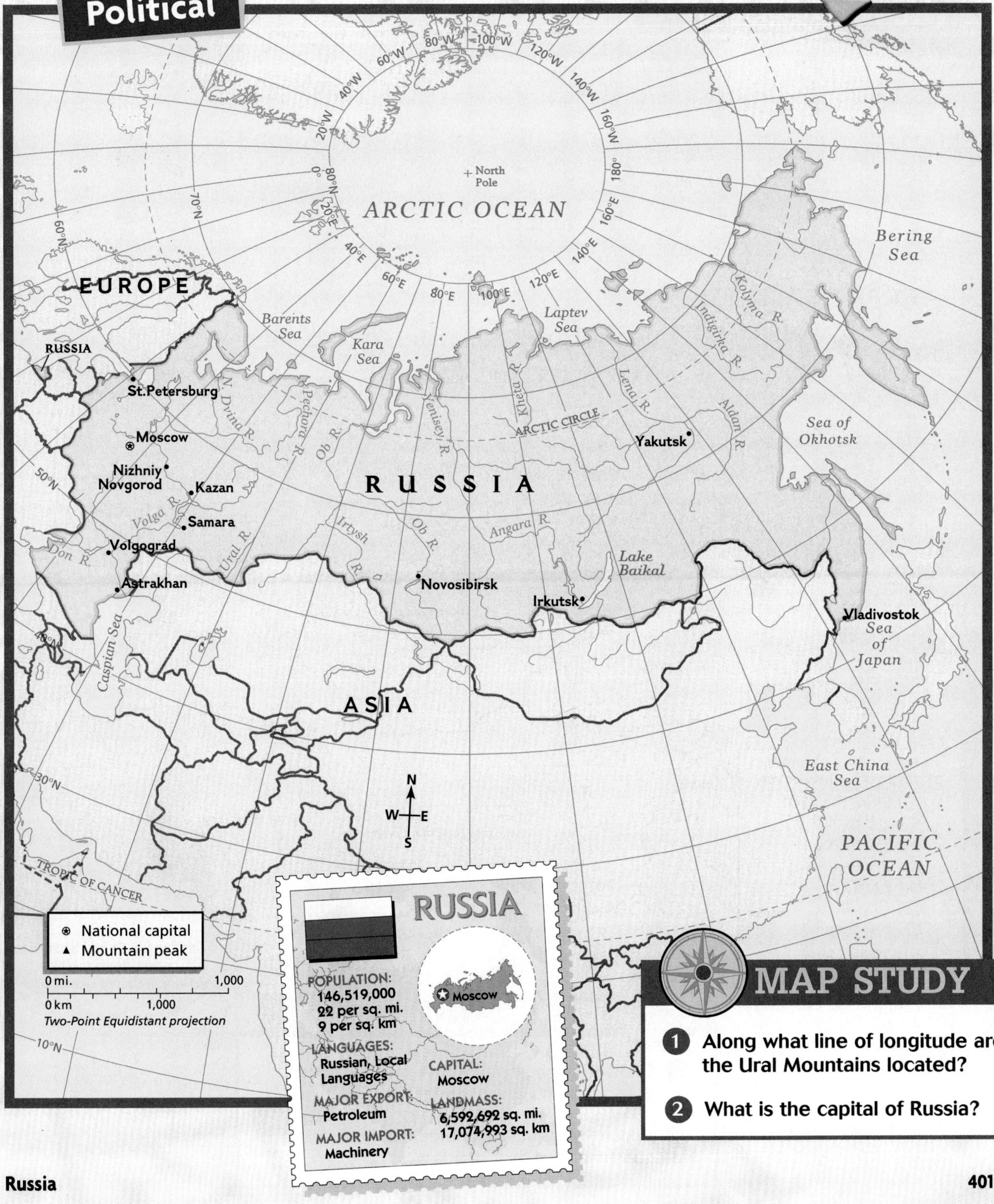

North Pole
ARCTIC OCEAN
EUROPE
RUSSIA
Barents Sea
Kara Sea
Laptev Sea
Bering Sea
Sea of Okhotsk
St.Petersburg
Moscow
Nizhniy Novgorod
Kazan
Samara
Volgograd
Astrakhan
Novosibirsk
Irkutsk
Yakutsk
Vladivostok
Lake Baikal
Sea of Japan
East China Sea
PACIFIC OCEAN
ASIA
Caspian Sea
ARCTIC CIRCLE
TROPIC OF CANCER
N. Dvina R.
Pechora R.
Ob R.
Yenisey R.
Kheta R.
Lena R.
Aldan R.
Indigirka R.
Kolyma R.
Volga R.
Don R.
Ural R.
Irtysh R.
Angara R.
0° 20°W 40°W 60°W 80°W 100°W 120°W 140°W 160°W 180° 160°E 140°E 120°E 100°E 80°E 60°E 40°E 20°E
80°N 70°N 60°N 50°N 40°N 30°N 10°N
N S E W

⊛ National capital
▲ Mountain peak

0 mi. 1,000
0 km 1,000
Two-Point Equidistant projection

RUSSIA

POPULATION:
146,519,000
22 per sq. mi.
9 per sq. km

LANGUAGES:
Russian, Local Languages

CAPITAL:
Moscow

MAJOR EXPORT:
Petroleum

LANDMASS:
6,592,692 sq. mi.
17,074,993 sq. km

MAJOR IMPORT:
Machinery

Moscow

MAP STUDY

1. Along what line of longitude are the Ural Mountains located?
2. What is the capital of Russia?

Regional Atlas

Russia

The Russian Winter

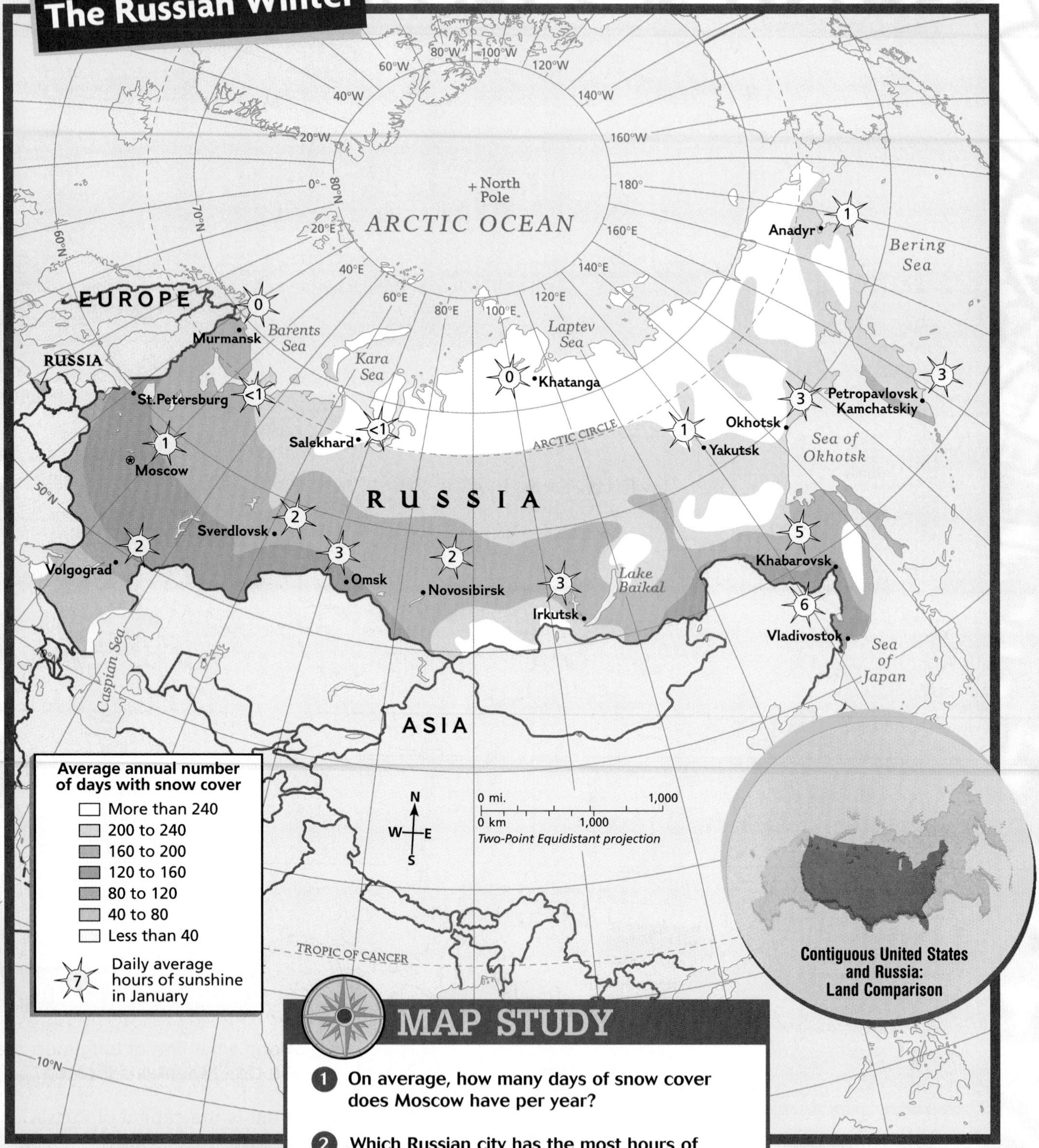

ARCTIC OCEAN

North Pole

EUROPE

RUSSIA

ASIA

Barents Sea

Kara Sea

Laptev Sea

Bering Sea

Sea of Okhotsk

Sea of Japan

Caspian Sea

Lake Baikal

ARCTIC CIRCLE

TROPIC OF CANCER

Murmansk 0

St. Petersburg <1

Moscow 1

Volgograd 2

Sverdlovsk 2

Salekhard <1

Omsk 3

Novosibirsk 2

Khatanga 0

Irkutsk 3

Yakutsk 1

Okhotsk 3

Anadyr 1

Petropavlovsk Kamchatskiy 3

Khabarovsk 5

Vladivostok 6

Average annual number of days with snow cover

- More than 240
- 200 to 240
- 160 to 200
- 120 to 160
- 80 to 120
- 40 to 80
- Less than 40

Daily average hours of sunshine in January

0 mi. 1,000

0 km 1,000

Two-Point Equidistant projection

Contiguous United States and Russia: Land Comparison

MAP STUDY

1. On average, how many days of snow cover does Moscow have per year?
2. Which Russian city has the most hours of sunshine per day in January?

Geo Extremes

① HIGHEST POINT
Mount Elbrus
18,510 ft.
(5,642 m) high

② LOWEST POINT
Caspian Sea
92 ft. (28 m)
below sea level

③ LONGEST RIVER
Ob-Irtysh
3,362 mi.
(5,411 km) long

④ LARGEST LAKE
Caspian Sea
143,244 sq. mi.
(371,000 sq. km)

⑤ DEEPEST LAKE
Lake Baikal
5,315 ft.
(1,620 m) deep

⑥ LARGEST ISLAND
Sakhalin
29,500 sq.mi.
(76,405 sq. km)

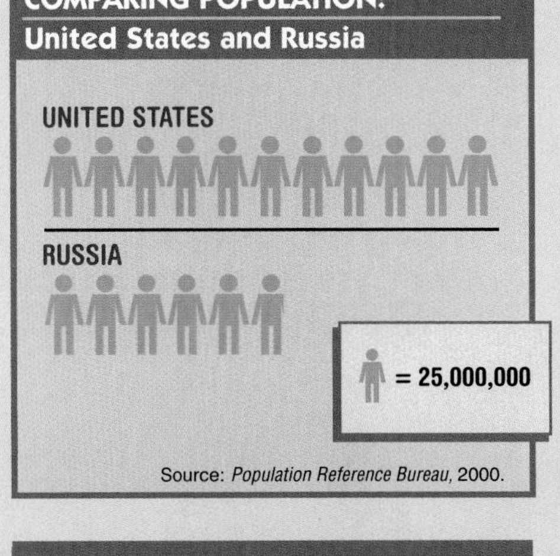

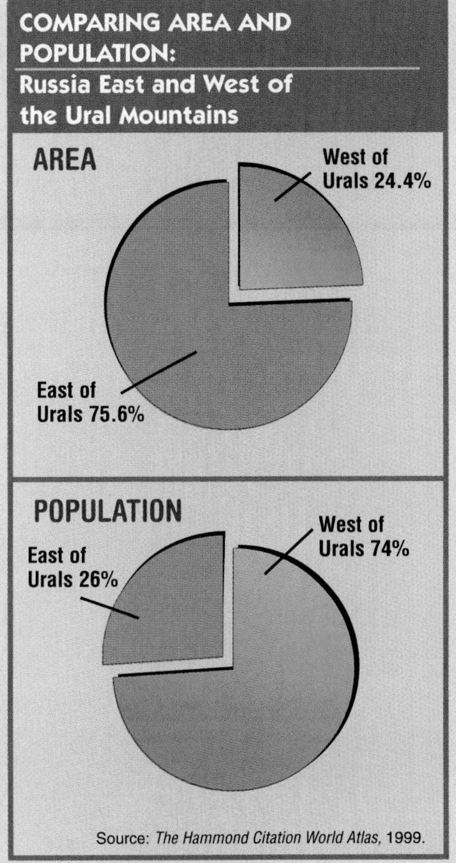

GRAPHIC STUDY

1. What two "extremes" does the Caspian Sea lay claim to?
2. What percentage of Russia's people live west of the Ural Mountains?

Russia—A Eurasian Country

The World and Its People NATIONAL GEOGRAPHIC

To learn more about Russia's land and economy, view ***The World and Its People*** **Chapter 14** video.

Geography Online

Chapter Overview Visit the ***Geography: The World and Its People*** Web site at gwip.glencoe.com and click on **Chapter 14—Chapter Overviews** to preview information about Russia.

Section 1 The Russian Land

Guide to Reading

Main Idea

Russia is a huge country with a cold climate due to its far northern location.

Terms to Know

- steppe
- peninsula
- taiga
- tundra
- permafrost

Places to Locate

- Ural Mountains
- North European Plain
- Moscow
- St. Petersburg
- Volgograd
- West Siberian Plain
- Siberia
- Caucasus Mountains

Reading Strategy

Draw a chart like this one. List two specific names of each type of physical feature given.

Russia	
Plains	
Mountains	
Plateaus	
Rivers	

Siberian tigers hunt in the eastern forests of Russia—sometimes even climbing trees to find food. Only a few hundred now live in the wild, though. The animals they hunt—elk, deer, and wild boar—are dwindling, and the tigers themselves are hunted by people. Poachers who kill the tigers illegally can sell a skin for $15,000. Russia is enforcing laws more strictly to save these animals.

Russia is the world's largest country. Nearly twice as big as the United States, Russia is called a *Eurasian* country because its lands lie on two continents—Europe and Asia. The western part of Russia borders Eastern European countries such as Belarus and Ukraine. As you move east, you run into the **Ural Mountains**—the dividing line between Europe and Asia. The rest of Russia stretches across Asia to the Pacific Ocean. Along the way, it shares borders with 14 other countries. Russia is so wide that it includes 11 time zones from east to west. When it is 12:00 noon in eastern Russia, it is 1:00 A.M. in western Russia.

Russia is also a northern country. As you can see from the map on page 406, its southern border is in the middle latitudes but the north reaches past the Arctic Circle. Russia has a long coastline along the Arctic Ocean. Ice makes shipping difficult or impossible most of the year. Even many of Russia's ports on the Baltic Sea and Pacific Ocean are closed by ice part of the year.

Russia's gigantic size and harsh climates make transportation difficult within the country as well. If you visited Russia, you would

◄ Red Square in Moscow, Russia

discover that, unlike in the United States, railroads still are an important means of getting around. With 93,771 miles (151,000 km) of track, railroads are the leading movers of people and goods in Russia.

Plains Areas

Two large lowland plains cover the western half of Russia. The Ural Mountains divide these plains. Find the Ural Mountains on the map on page 407. To the west of the Urals, you find the **North European Plain.** You may recall that this fertile plain begins in France in Western Europe. This plain has Russia's mildest climate, and about 75 percent of the population live here. This region holds Russia's capital, **Moscow,** and other important cities, such as **St. Petersburg** and **Volgograd.** Much of Russia's industry is also found here. Good farmland lies to the south, along the Don and Volga Rivers. This area is part of the steppe, the nearly treeless grassy plain that stretches through Ukraine.

East of the Urals lies the **West Siberian Plain.** This huge lowland—the world's largest area of flat land—is part of **Siberia.** Because

Applying Map Skills

1. On what two continents is Russia located?
2. Where are most of Russia's cities located?

Find NGS online map resources @ www.nationalgeographic.com/maps

of its many rivers—and the fact that these rivers often flow over ground that is frozen—much of the West Siberian Plain is marshy. Many people live in the southern part of this plain, which is for the most part drier and warmer than the plain to the north.

✓Reading Check **Which part of Russia is home to most of its cities and industries? Why?**

Mountains and Plateaus

Two mountain ranges rise in western Russia—the Urals and the Caucasus (KAW•kuh•suhs). The Ural Mountains, very old and worn by erosion, do not reach very high. Their length is extensive, though, running about 2,500 miles (4,023 km) from the Arctic Ocean to Russia's southern border. As you read earlier, these mountains form the boundary between the continents of Europe and Asia.

The **Caucasus Mountains** separate southwestern Russia from Southwest Asia. Thickly covered with pines and other trees, the Caucasus are much taller than the Urals. They include Mt. Elbrus,

Applying Map Skills

1. What is the elevation on the northern shore of the Caspian Sea?
2. What two plains are divided by the Ural Mountains?

Find NGS online map resources @
www.nationalgeographic.com/maps

The Steppes

Many Russians earn their living by farming and ranching on the plains near the Caucasus Mountains.

Place **What type of vegetation grows on the steppes?**

which is 18,510 feet (5,642 m) high and the tallest peak on the European continent.

Moving to the eastern, or Siberian, side of Russia, you see plateaus, highlands, and even more mountains. Find the Central Siberian Plateau and the various eastern ranges on the map on page 407. These areas stair-step to ever higher mountain ranges in the south. Eastern Russia is home to the majestic Siberian tiger, now an endangered species. Other wildlife in the region include bear, reindeer, lynx, wolf, wildcat, elk, and wild boar.

Mountains also rise on the far eastern Kamchatka (kuhm•CHAHT•kuh) Peninsula. A **peninsula,** you recall, is a piece of land with water on three sides. Many of the mountains in Kamchatka are part of the Ring of Fire. This name is used to describe the active volcanic zone that forms the western, northern, and eastern edges of the Pacific Ocean. Volcanic eruptions and earthquakes sometimes occur on this peninsula.

✓Reading Check **What is the Ring of Fire?**

Inland Water Areas

Russia borders many inland bodies of water. In the southwest, it borders on the Black Sea. Through this sea, Russia gains access to the Mediterranean Sea. If you look at the physical map on page 407, you will find another large sea in southwestern Russia—the Caspian Sea.

About the size of California, the Caspian Sea is actually the largest inland body of water in the world. Like the Great Salt Lake in Utah, the Caspian Sea has salt water, not freshwater. Russia shares this sea with four other countries.

High in the Central Siberian Plateau, you find Lake Baikal. This is the world's deepest freshwater lake. In fact, Lake Baikal holds almost 20 percent of the world's supply of unfrozen freshwater. Tourists travel by train to see the lake's shimmering blue waters.

Russia has several important rivers. The Volga—the longest river in Europe—is an important transportation route. It and other rivers of European Russia are connected by canals. Many rivers also flow through the Asian side of Russia. Most of these rivers begin in the mountains of southern Siberia and flow north across the lowlands to empty into the frigid Arctic Ocean. The Lena (LEE•nuh), the Yenisey (YIH•nih•SAY), and the Ob (AHB) are among the longest rivers in the world.

✓Reading Check **How do the waters of the Caspian Sea and Lake Baikal differ?**

Applying Map Skills

1. What high latitude climate zones cover much of Russia?
2. What type of climate does Moscow have?

Find NGS online map resources @ www.nationalgeographic.com/maps

Skiing the Strait

Dmitry Shparo and his son Matvey (shown below) skied across the icy Bering Strait in 1998. This 55-mile-wide body of water separates Siberia from Alaska. Crossing on floating chunks of ice, their journey took 21 days.

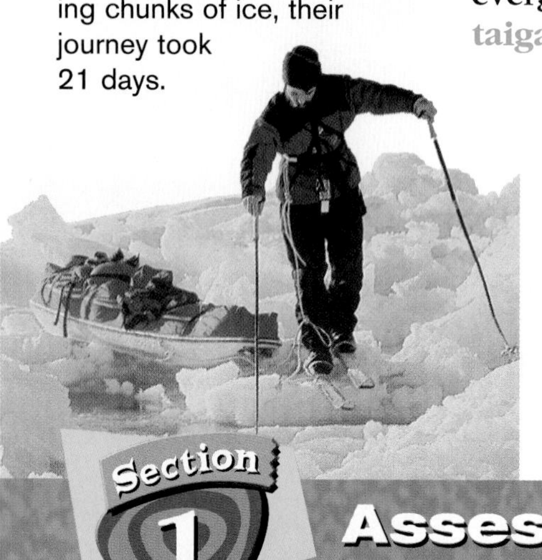

Russia's Climate

European Russia generally enjoys warmer temperatures than Asian Russia. Most of the European region has a humid continental climate. Summers are warm and rainy, while winters are cold and snowy. Moscow can have snow five months out of the year.

Areas near the Black Sea in southern Russia enjoy mild temperatures with a steppe climate throughout the year. Less rain falls—the amount varies from year to year. In years of plentiful rain, farmers can produce abundant crops. In dry years, though, the wheat crop fails.

In contrast, Siberia has high latitude climates. In the south, summers are short and cool, and winters are long and very snowy. Siberia may receive snow as much as eight months of the year. Huge forests of evergreen trees grow in this cool climate. These forests—called the **taiga** (TY•guh)—cover southern Siberia.

Northern Siberia has one of the coldest climates in the world. Not even hardy evergreens can grow there. Instead, you find **tundra,** a vast and rolling treeless plain in which only the top few inches of ground thaw out in summer. The permanently frozen lower layers of soil are called **permafrost** and cover 40 percent of Russia.

✓Reading Check **What are the evergreen forests of Siberia called?**

Section 1 Assessment

Defining Terms

1. **Define** steppe, peninsula, taiga, tundra, permafrost.

Recalling Facts

2. **Place** What is the largest area of flat land in the world?

3. **Location** What mountain range separates Europe and Asia?

4. **Region** How many countries does Russia border?

Critical Thinking

5. **Analyzing Information** Why do you think trains are more important than other kinds of vehicles for moving people and goods across Russia?

6. **Drawing Conclusions** How do you think permafrost contributes to the marshy lands of the West Siberian Plain?

Graphic Organizer

7. **Organizing Information** Create a chart like this one. Then place each of the following items into the column in which it is located: Moscow, Lake Baikal, Yakutsk, Kamchatka Peninsula, St. Petersburg, Vladivostok, Yenisey River, and Ob River.

North European Plain	West Siberian Plain	Eastern Russia

Applying Geography Skills

8. **Analyzing Maps** Turn to the political map on page 406. Name a Russian city located north of the Arctic Circle. Now look at the climate map on page 409. What type of climate does the city north of the Arctic Circle experience?

Making Connections

ART | SCIENCE | LITERATURE | TECHNOLOGY

Russian Poetry

Boris Pasternak is one of Russia's best-known writers. He wrote both poetry and fiction, and in 1958 he won the Nobel Prize for Literature for his novel *Doctor Zhivago.* Officials in what was then the Soviet Union did not approve of the work. Today, however, the Russian government recognizes Pasternak's great contribution to Russian literature.

Is It Not Time for the Birds to Sing
by Boris Pasternak (1890–1960)

The wind pokes about
With a branch of wet lilac
Like a tiny wet sparrow:
Is it not time for the birds to sing?

Raindrops heavy as cuff links
And the garden all shiny
Like a pond dotted
With a million blue tears.

Nursed by grief
And still prickly with pain
The garden revives
Filled with whispers and scents.

All through the night
It had knocked at the window.
Suddenly clothes
Smell musty and wet.

Awakened by the magic
Roll call of other days and names,
Today looks out
With eyes like anemones [flowers].

▲ **Springtime arrives in a Russian garden.**

Making the Connection

1. What lines in the poem hint that the garden wants to bloom?
2. Given the Russian climate, why is the coming of spring significant?
3. **Making Inferences** Is the poet saying it is or is not time for the birds to sing? Explain.

Section 2

Russia's Economic Regions

Guide to Reading

Main Idea

With many resources, Russia could have a large and diverse economy.

Terms to Know

- heavy industry
- light industry
- consumer goods
- hydroelectric power
- bauxite

Places to Locate

- Kaliningrad
- St. Petersburg
- Baltic Sea
- Murmansk
- Vladivostok
- Astrakhan
- Caspian Sea
- Volga River

Reading Strategy

Create a chart like this one, then list at least two facts about the economy of each region.

Region	Facts
Moscow	
Port Cities	
Volga & Urals	
Siberia	

NATIONAL GEOGRAPHIC **Exploring Our World**

Do you see people selling food or other goods on the street where you live? Many older Russians live on small pensions, or payments made by the government to retired workers. To earn extra money, these resourceful people grow food or bake bread. Then they sell their goods in busy areas of the city, often using baby carriages as food carts.

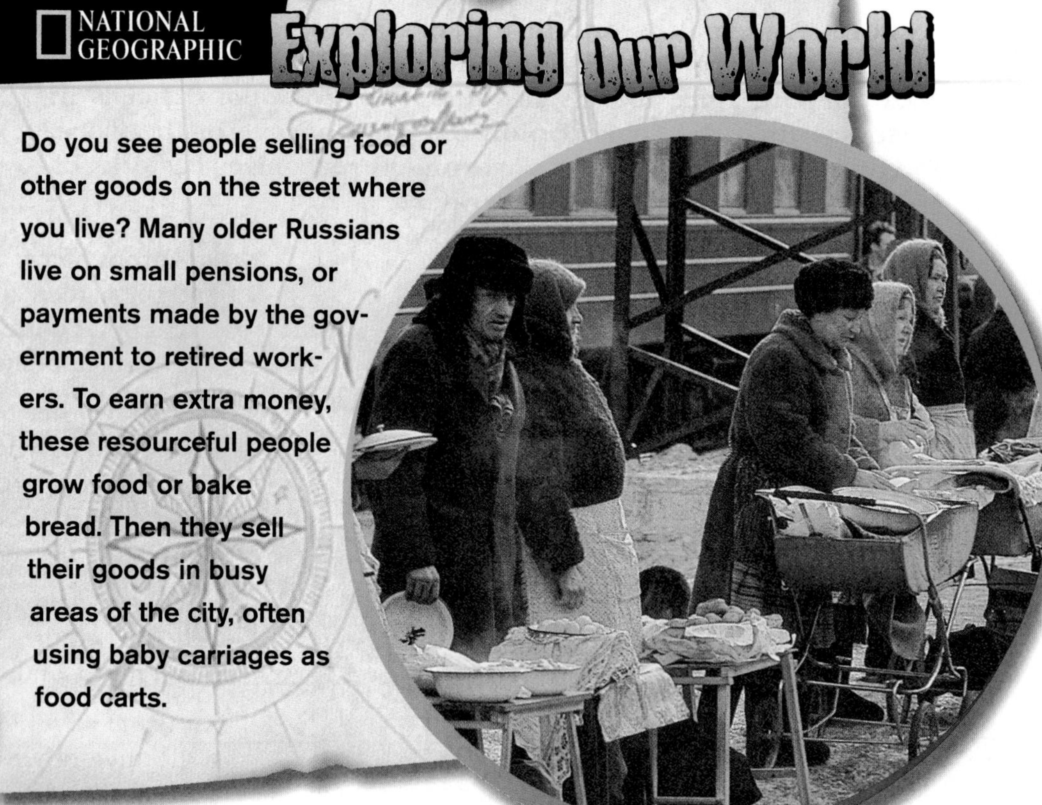

With its many resources, Russia could have a growing economy. It has large deposits of coal, oil, and gas. It also has many minerals, including nickel, iron ore, tin, and gold. The southwestern area can produce rich yields of grains. Russia's fishing industry is among the largest in the world. The vast forests of Siberia provide plenty of timber.

Despite all these advantages, Russia's economy has struggled in recent decades. You will learn why in Chapter 15. For now, you will see what Russia's economy produces. Geographers divide Russia into four different economic regions: the Moscow Region, Port Cities, the Volga and Urals Region, and Siberia.

The Moscow Region

About 800 years old, Moscow is the political and cultural center of Russia. The largest city in Russia, Moscow is the country's economic center and largest transportation hub as well. Look at the economic activity map below. Many of Russia's manufacturing centers are located in the western part of Russia. In the past, many of the country's factories focused on **heavy industry,** or making goods such as machinery, mining equipment, and steel. In recent years, more factories have shifted to **light industry,** or the making of such goods as clothing, shoes, furniture, and household products.

These economic changes are reflected in Moscow. Its older industries include textiles, electrical equipment, and automobiles. Today factories make more **consumer goods,** or household and electronics products. High-technology services have also emerged in the city. Many people in Moscow travel to their jobs by taking the Metro, the name for Moscow's subway system.

Some farming also takes place in the Moscow region. Farmers raise dairy cattle and such grains as barley and oats. They also grow potatoes, corn, and sugar beets. Other crops include flax, which is used to make textiles.

✓Reading Check **What is the difference between heavy industry and light industry?**

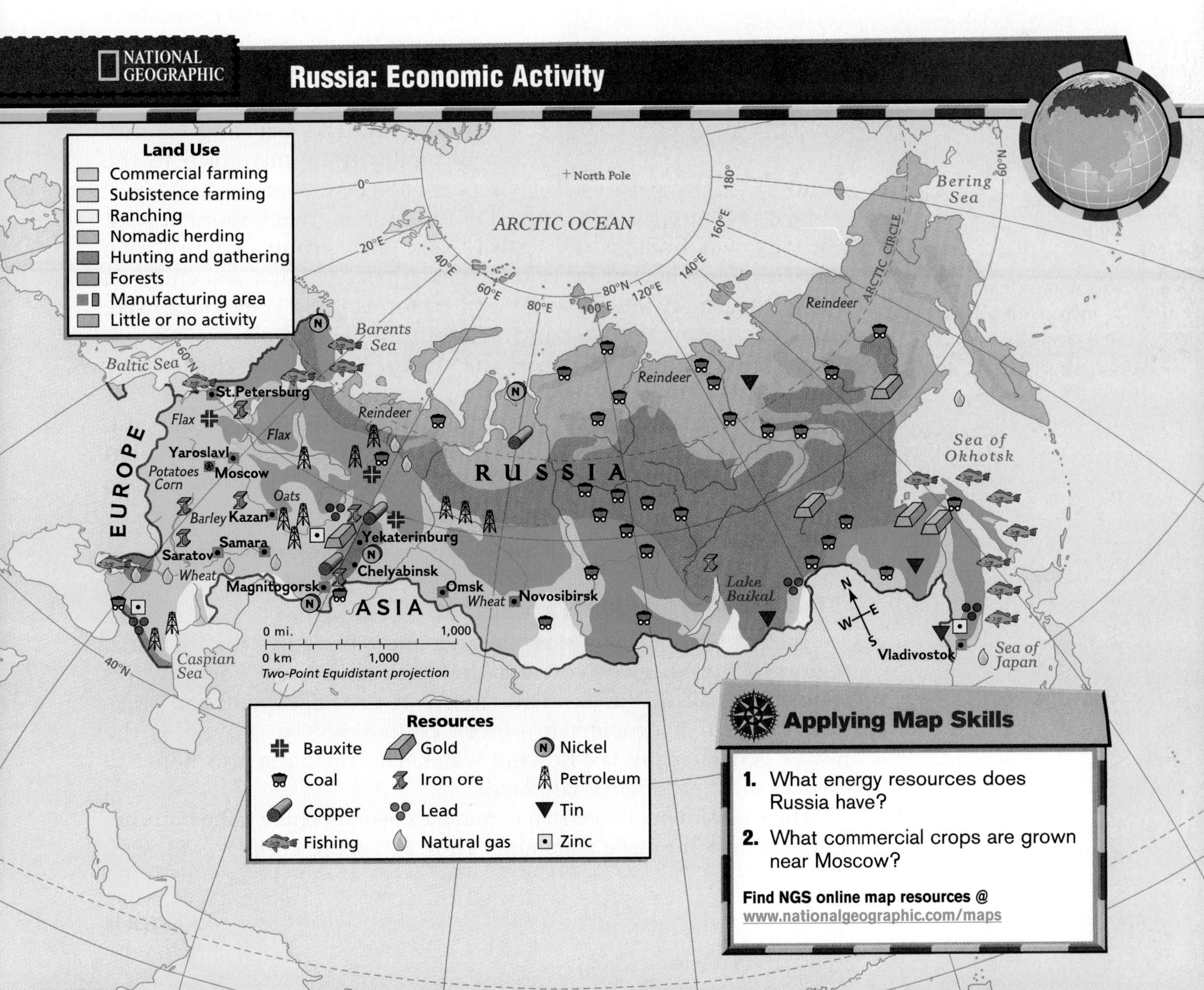

Applying Map Skills

1. What energy resources does Russia have?
2. What commercial crops are grown near Moscow?

Find NGS online map resources @ www.nationalgeographic.com/maps

Tall cranes dot the harbor of Kaliningrad.

Movement **How are Russian officials trying to increase trade in this city?**

Port Cities

Russia has two important northwestern ports—**Kaliningrad** and **St. Petersburg.** Look at the map on page 416. Do you see that Russia owns a small piece of land on the **Baltic Sea** separated from the rest of the country? The port of Kaliningrad is located on this land. This city is Russia's only Baltic port that remains free of ice yearround. Russian officials, hoping to increase trade here, have eliminated all taxes on foreign goods brought to this city. Still, companies that deliver goods to this port face an obstacle. They must transport their goods another 200 miles (322 km) through other countries to reach the nearest inland part of Russia. In summer, they have the choice of keeping the goods on their ships and traveling another 500 miles (805 km) north to the port of St. Petersburg.

St. Petersburg, once the capital of Russia, is another important port. The city was built in the early 1700s on a group of more than 100 islands connected by bridges. Large palaces stand gracefully on public squares in this beautiful city. Factories in St. Petersburg make light machinery, textiles, and scientific and medical equipment. Located on the Neva River near the Gulf of Finland, the city is also a shipbuilding center.

Murmansk, in Russia's far north, and **Vladivostok,** in the east, are other important port cities. So is **Astrakhan,** on the **Caspian Sea.** Trade in these port cities brings needed goods to the Russian people.

✓Reading Check **What are the two main ports in northwestern Russia?**

The Volga and Urals Region

Tucked between the Moscow area and Siberia lies the industrial region of the **Volga River** and Ural Mountains. The Volga carries almost one-half of Russia's river traffic. It provides water for irrigation—and for hydroelectric power. **Hydroelectric power** is the power generated by fast-flowing water. The region is also home to Russia's most productive farmlands.

The Ural Mountains are rich in minerals. Workers here mine **bauxite,** a mineral used to make aluminum. They also mine copper, gold, lead, and nickel. The mountains have such energy resources as coal, oil, and natural gas as well. Find these resources on the economic activity map on page 413.

Reading Check What energy resources are found in the Volga and Urals region?

Web Activity Visit the **Geography: The World and Its People** Web site at gwip.glencoe.com and click on **Chapter 14—Student Web Activities** to learn more about Siberia.

Siberia

East of the Urals lies Siberia. This region has the largest supply of minerals in Russia, including iron ore, uranium, gold, diamonds, and coal. Huge deposits of oil and natural gas lie beneath the permafrost of northern Siberia. About two-thirds of Siberia is covered with trees that could support a timber industry.

Tapping all these resources is very difficult, however. Siberia is mostly undeveloped because of its harsh climate. Another problem is isolation—it can take eight or more days to travel across all of Russia by train. Finding a way to obtain these resources is important to Russia's future economic success, though. Many of the minerals and fuels of western Russia have been used up. The industrial centers there need the resources from Siberia.

Reading Check Why are Siberia's mineral resources important?

Assessment

Defining Terms

1. **Define** heavy industry, light industry, consumer goods, hydroelectric power, bauxite.

Recalling Facts

2. **Location** Why is Moscow the economic center of Russia?
3. **Location** Why is Kaliningrad a very important city?
4. **Economics** What are five mineral resources found in the Ural Mountains?

Critical Thinking

5. **Drawing Conclusions** Why would consumers want the Russian economy to change from relying on heavy industry to a greater emphasis on light industry?
6. **Understanding Cause and Effect** How would eliminating taxes on foreign goods brought through Kaliningrad increase trade with other countries?

Graphic Organizer

7. **Organizing Information** Draw a chart like the one below. On your chart, fill in at least three examples of heavy industry and three examples of light industry.

Heavy Industry	Light Industry
1.	1.
2.	2.
3.	3.

Applying Geography Skills

8. **Analyzing Maps** Look at the transportation map on page 416. What three major ports are located on Russia's eastern borders? What two cities signify the start and end stations of the Trans-Siberian Railroad?

Geography Skill

Reading a Transportation Map

Transportation maps show how people and goods move throughout a region. Lines, colors, and symbols represent different types of transportation. A route normally follows the least difficult path between cities. Because of the physical landscape, though, the least difficult route may not be the shortest route.

Learning the Skill

When reading a transportation map, follow these steps:

- Read the map title and the map key.
- Locate major population centers.
- Identify the routes on the map and points of connection between the routes.
- Draw conclusions about how the physical landscape affects transportation and trade.

Practicing the Skill

Study the map below, then answer the following questions.

1. What kinds of transportation are shown?
2. Which major railroad extends to the far eastern part of Russia? Why does this railroad not follow a straight line?
3. Which general region of Russia has the most trade, industry, and people? How can you tell?

Applying the Skill

On a road map of your state, select a city in the north and another city in the south. Find the quickest route you would take to get from one city to the other.

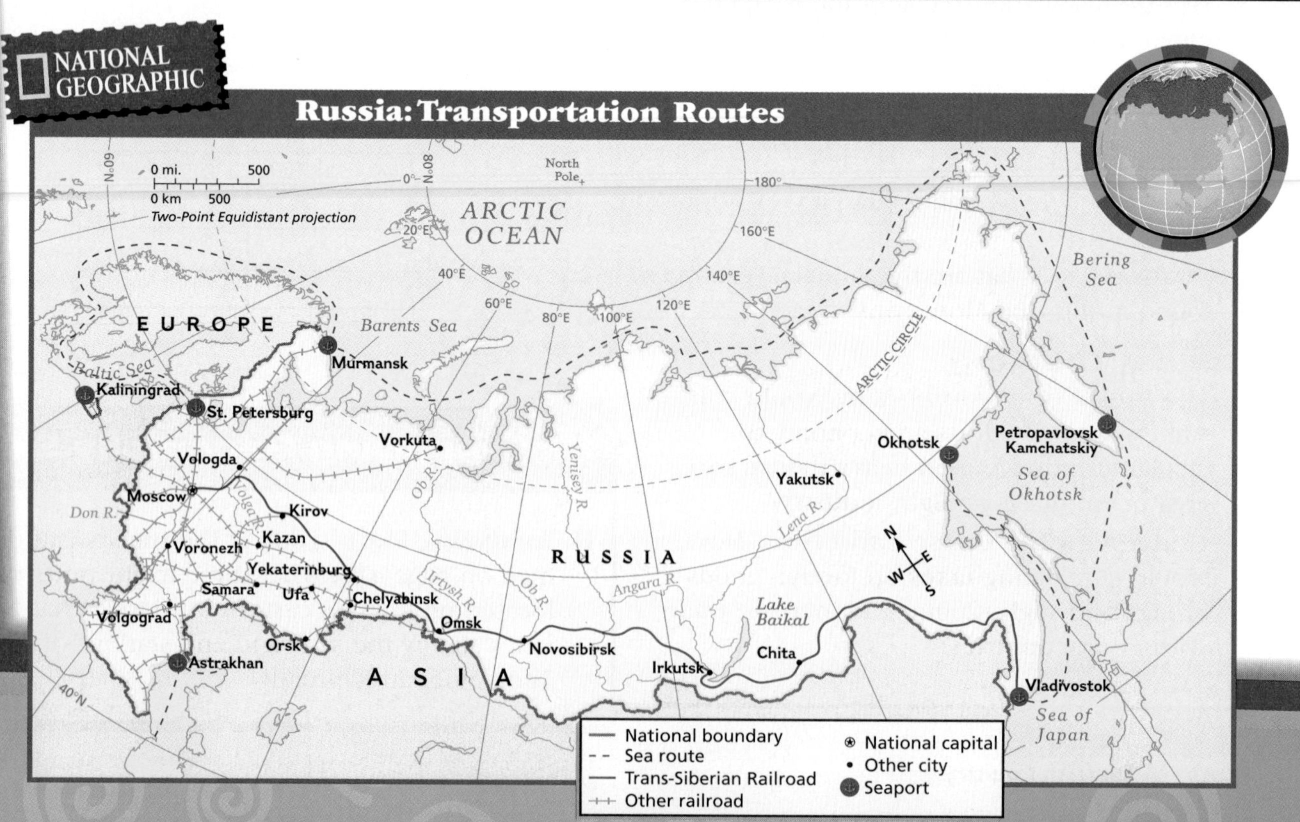

Chapter 14 Reading Review

Section 1 The Russian Land

Terms to Know
steppe
peninsula
taiga
tundra
permafrost

Main Idea

Russia is a huge country with a cold climate due to its far northern location.

✓ Location Spanning two continents—Europe and Asia—Russia is the world's largest country.

✓ Region The western half of Russia is mostly lowland. The eastern half is covered with mountains and plateaus.

✓ Movement Inland waterways are important for moving goods through Russia, but many long rivers drain north into the frigid Arctic Ocean and freeze in winter.

✓ Region European Russia has the mildest climate, while most of Siberia, or Asian Russia, has cold high-latitude climate zones.

Section 2 Russia's Economic Regions

Terms to Know
heavy industry
light industry
consumer goods
hydroelectric power
bauxite

Main Idea

With many resources, Russia could have a large and diverse economy.

✓ History Russia has many resources, but its economy has struggled in recent years.

✓ Economics Moscow, with many industries, is the economic center of Russia.

✓ Movement Ports in the northwest, southwest, and east carry on trade between Russia and other countries.

✓ Location Siberia has many resources, but the area is so cold and remote that it is difficult to tap these resources.

◄ A train of the Trans-Siberian Railroad zips along Lake Baikal.

Chapter 14 Assessment and Activities

Using Key Terms

Match the terms in Part A with their definitions in Part B.

A.

1. permafrost
2. light industry
3. bauxite
4. steppe
5. consumer goods
6. taiga
7. hydroelectric power
8. peninsula
9. heavy industry
10. tundra

B.

a. huge, subarctic evergreen forests
b. dry, treeless plains in the high latitudes
c. dry, treeless grasslands
d. permanently frozen lower layers of soil
e. land with water on three sides
f. production of consumer goods
g. electricity generated by water
h. production of industrial goods
i. mineral from which aluminum is made
j. products for personal use, such as clothing

Reviewing the Main Ideas

Section 1 The Russian Land

11. **Human/Environment Interaction** Why is Russia unable to use ports along its Arctic coast for most of the year?
12. **Location** Which area of Russia has the mildest climate?
13. **Place** In what way is Mt. Elbrus significant?
14. **Region** Why is the Kamchatka Peninsula considered part of the Ring of Fire?
15. **Place** What is the longest river in Europe?

Section 2 Russia's Economic Regions

16. **Place** What city is the political and cultural center of Russia?
17. **Economics** Name four agricultural products from the Moscow region.
18. **Economics** Name four mineral resources found in Siberia.
19. **Movement** What is an important means of transportation for people in Russia?
20. **Economics** Which of Russia's economic regions is the greatest potential source of minerals for the country?

Russia—A Eurasian Country

Place Location Activity

On a separate sheet of paper, match the letters on the map with the numbered places listed below.

1. Ural Mountains
2. Kamchatka Peninsula
3. Lake Baikal
4. Volga River
5. Moscow
6. Lena River
7. West Siberian Plain
8. Caspian Sea
9. Caucasus Mountains
10. Sakhalin Island

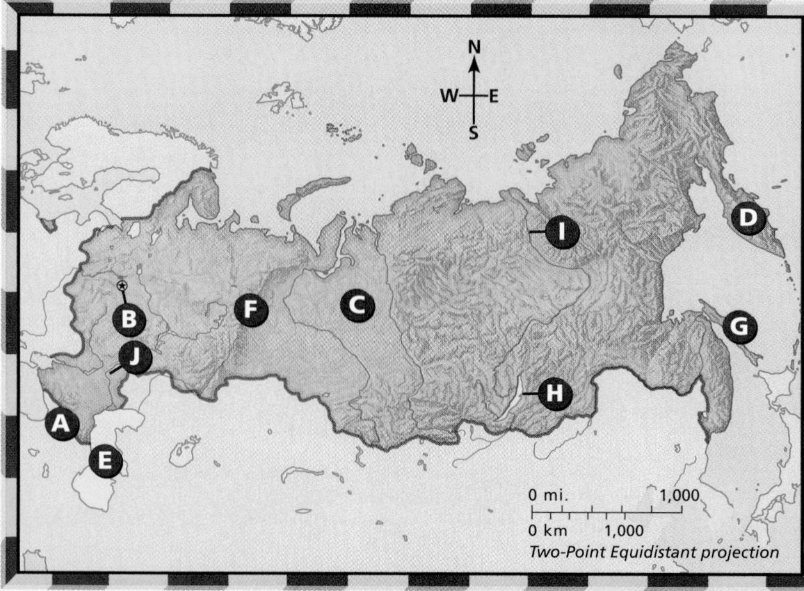

Self-Check Quiz Visit the ***Geography: The World and Its People*** Web site at gwip.glencoe.com and click on **Chapter 14—Self-Check Quizzes** to prepare for the Chapter Test.

Critical Thinking

21. **Making Generalizations** How have recent changes in Russia affected its economy?
22. **Understanding Cause and Effect** On a diagram like the one below, label factors that contribute to Siberia's climate.

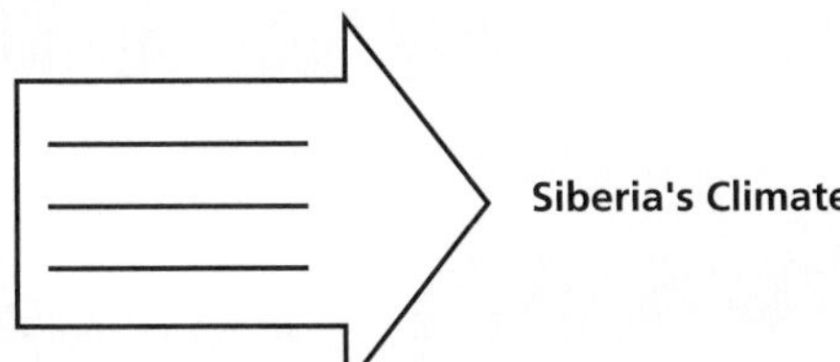

GeoJournal Activity

23. **Writing a Paragraph** Choose one of the photographs from this chapter or the Unit Regional Atlas on pages 394–399 and imagine yourself in the scene. Write a description using vivid words to portray the sights, sounds, and smells you would encounter. What is the temperature? What things can you touch? How do they feel? Describe what is happening.

Mental Mapping Activity

24. **Focusing on the Region** Draw a simple outline map of Russia, then label the following:
    - Arctic Ocean
    - Pacific Ocean
    - Caspian Sea
    - Ural Mountains
    - Lake Baikal
    - Caucasus Mountains
    - Volga River
    - Barents Sea
    - Yenisey River
    - Kamchatka Peninsula

Technology Skills Activity

25. **Using the Internet** Search the Internet for information on Siberian tigers. Create a display that includes a map showing the habitats, pictures, and facts about these endangered animals.

Standardized Test Practice

Directions: Read the paragraph below, then answer the following question.

For 70 years, the Communist government of the Soviet Union stopped at nothing to industrialize the country. Soviet leaders gave little thought to the health of the people or to the land they were ruining. From St. Petersburg to Vladivostok, across more than 8 million square miles, the Russian environment shows decay. Today Russia's great rivers are sewers of chemicals and human waste. Air in more than 100 cities is at least five times more polluted than standards allow, putting millions at risk of lung diseases. Tons of nuclear waste lie under Arctic waters, and the use of toxic fertilizers has poisoned the soil.

Adapted from "The U.S.S.R.'s Lethal Legacy" by Mike Edwards, *National Geographic,* August 1994.

1. Which of the following best explains why the Russian environment is so polluted today?

- **F** Soviet leaders did not care about the health of the people.
- **G** Soviet leaders wanted to industrialize the country at all costs.
- **H** Farmers were careless about the chemicals they spread on their fields.
- **J** Eastern Russia is not as polluted as western Russia.

Test-Taking Tip: Notice that the question asks for the *best* explanation. Read all the choices carefully before choosing the best one. Although all of the answer statements may be true, you need to find the best answer to the question.

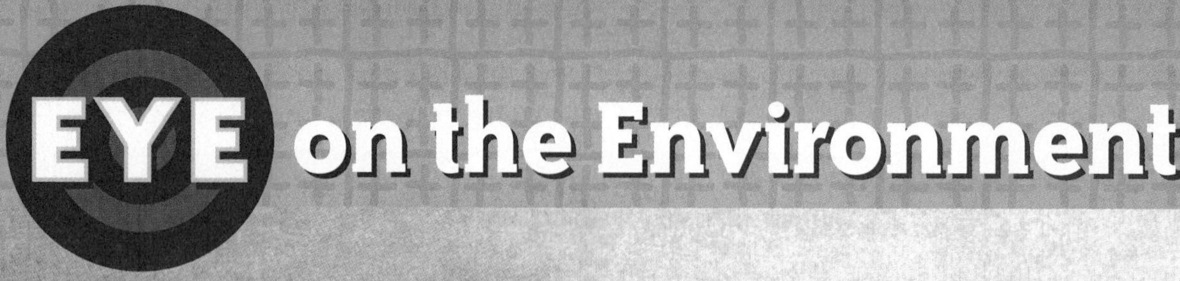

RUSSIA'S Lethal Legacy

Polluted Empire When you turn on a faucet, you expect clean, safe drinking water to come out. Unfortunately, many Russians do not enjoy this simple luxury. People in Russia and the former Soviet Republics are struggling with pollution—a tragic reminder of the days of Communist rule.

For decades, Soviet leaders were determined to turn the USSR into a mighty industrial power. They did not care what happened to the environment. The results of their actions are an environmental nightmare.

Kola Peninsula
St. Petersburg
RUSSIA
Severe pollution
Acid rain
Polluted river

- Coal-burning factories puffed chemicals into the air. Russian city dwellers endure some of the worst air pollution in the world.
- Toxic wastes and untreated sewage were dumped into rivers, resulting in polluted drinking water.
- Pesticides and heavy metals poisoned the soil in many areas.
- Radioactive wastes were emptied into seas and rivers.
- Large oil spills were common and were not cleaned up.

Cleaning Up Since the fall of communism, people in Russia have been trying to clean up their polluted air, land, and water. Yet little money is available, and progress is slow.

A steel plant in Siberia pollutes the air.

Worker cleans up an oil spill in Russian waters.

Making a Difference

Tough Trees Many young Russians are growing up in environmental disaster zones created by past generations. Nevertheless, some students are working to find solutions.

Maria Pestova and Andrey Ignashov live on Russia's Kola Peninsula, near a human-made wasteland called the Kuzomenskikh Desert. They spent two years determining that planting a local pine tree could best turn the desert back into a forest. Then they devised a new planting method to increase the young pines' chances of survival.

Maria Pestova

Detergents for a Clean Environment Ulya Loginova and Natalia Skorohodova live in St. Petersburg, Russia. The Neva River, which flows through the city, is heavily polluted. Household detergents contribute to the problem. Ulya and Natalia studied the effects of several detergents and shampoos and identified which ones caused the least environmental damage.

Ulya and Natalia, along with Maria and Andrey, each won an environmental award for their research.

Ulya Loginova and Natalia Skorohodova

What Can You Do?

Check Out Your Community

Does your community have any pollution problems? What laws or restrictions does your community have concerning pollution? Create an information pamphlet about these laws.

Save Lake Baikal

Russia's Lake Baikal is the world's oldest and deepest lake. A group called Baikal Watch is working to protect the environment of the lake. Find out more about Baikal Watch at www.earthisland.org/baikal

Use the Internet

Learn more about pollution around the world by reading *Pollution Magazine* online at www.gtonline.net/private/pmag. Also read about a project closer to home called Keep America Beautiful at www.kab.org. Suggest a way for your class to become involved.

Chapter 15

Russia—Past and Present

The World and Its People NATIONAL GEOGRAPHIC

To learn more about Russia's past and present, view ***The World and Its People*** **Chapter 15** video.

Geography Online

Chapter Overview Visit the ***Geography: The World and Its People*** Web site at gwip.glencoe.com and click on **Chapter 15—Chapter Overviews** to preview information about Russia's history.

Section 1

A Troubled History

Guide to Reading

Main Idea

The harsh rule of powerful leaders has often sparked violent uprisings in Russia.

Terms to Know

- czar
- serf
- industrialize
- communist state
- cold war
- ethnic group

Places to Locate

- Moscow
- St. Petersburg
- Vladivostok
- Siberia

Reading Strategy

Make a time line like this one. Then list five important years in Russian history and describe what happened in those years.

NATIONAL GEOGRAPHIC **Exploring Our World**

How old is the school you attend? Russian art students enjoy one reminder of Russia's past. In 1764 the empress Catherine the Great enlarged the Russian Academy of Fine Arts to train Russian artists. The empress hoped they would develop the skills shown by artists in Western Europe. The school, now known as the Repin Institute, remains open.

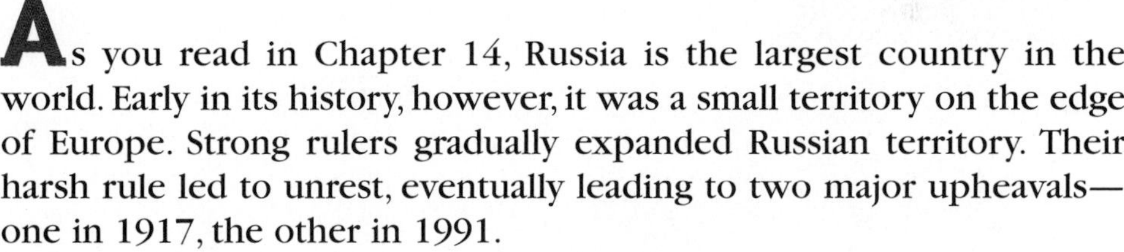

As you read in Chapter 14, Russia is the largest country in the world. Early in its history, however, it was a small territory on the edge of Europe. Strong rulers gradually expanded Russian territory. Their harsh rule led to unrest, eventually leading to two major upheavals—one in 1917, the other in 1991.

The History of Russia

To understand the challenges facing Russia today, let us go back through Russia's history. Modern Russians descend from early groups of Slavs who settled along the rivers of what is today Ukraine and Russia. During the A.D. 800s, these early Slavs built a civilization around the city of Kiev, today the capital of Ukraine. This civilization was called Kievan Rus (kee•AY•vuhn ROOS). By the A.D. 1000s, the ruler and people of Kievan Rus had accepted Eastern Orthodox Christianity. They prospered from trade with the Mediterranean world and Western Europe.

Then Mongols swept in from central Asia in the 1200s. They took control of Kiev and its surrounding lands. Mongol rule, which lasted about 200 years, greatly reduced Kiev's wealth and power. Meanwhile,

◀ Church of the Resurrection in St. Petersburg, Russia

Moscow—a town to the north—became the center of a new Slavic territory called Muscovy (muh•SKOH•vee). In 1480 Ivan III, a prince of Muscovy, drove out the Mongols and made the territory independent.

Rise of the Czars Muscovy slowly developed into the country we know today as Russia. Russian rulers expanded their power, built up their armies, and seized land and other resources. They called themselves **czars,** or emperors. They had complete and total control over the government. As a citizen of Muscovy, you would have feared Czar Ivan IV, who ruled during the 1500s. Known as "the Terrible" or "the Awesome," Ivan used a secret police force to tighten his iron grip on the people and control their lives.

As the map on page 424 shows, the czars gradually conquered surrounding territories. As a result, many non-Russian peoples became part of the growing Russian Empire. Czars, such as Peter I and Catherine II, pushed the empire's borders southward and westward. They also tried to make Russia modern and more like Europe. Peter built a new capital—**St. Petersburg**—in the early 1700s. Built close to Europe near the Baltic coast, St. Petersburg was designed like a European city with its elegant palaces, public squares, and canals. If you had been a Russian noble at this time, you would have spoken French as well as Russian. You also would have put aside traditional Russian dress, worn European clothes, and attended fancy balls and parties.

The czar and the nobles enjoyed rich, comfortable lives. At the bottom of society, however, were the great masses of people. Most were **serfs,** or farm laborers who could be bought and sold along with the land. These people lived hard lives, working on the nobles' country estates or in city palaces. Few could read and write. They remained fiercely loyal to traditional Russian ways and practiced the Eastern Orthodox religion.

Dramatic Changes In 1812 a French army led by Napoleon Bonaparte invaded Russia. Brave Russian soldiers and the fierce winter weather finally forced the French to retreat. The year 1812 became a symbol of Russian patriotism. Have you ever heard the *1812 Overture,* with its dramatic ending that includes the ringing of bells and the bursts of cannon fire? Written by the Russian composer Peter Tchaikovsky (chy•KAWF•skee), this musical masterpiece celebrates the Russian victory over Napoleon.

In the late 1800s, Russia entered a period of economic and social change. In 1861 Czar Alexander II, known as the Czar-Liberator, freed the serfs from being tied to the land. His new law did little to lift them out of poverty, though. Russia began to **industrialize,** or change its economy to rely more on manufacturing and less on farming. Railroads, including the famous Trans-Siberian Railroad, spread across the country. It linked Moscow in the west with **Vladivostok** on Russia's Pacific coast.

Yet Russia did not progress politically. Educated Russians in the cities were stirred by democratic ideas from Western Europe. They pushed for freedom, equality, and a share in governing the country. The czars ignored these demands and continued to rule harshly.

✓Reading Check **What was the name of the civilization that early Slavs built in the area that is today Ukraine?**

The Soviet Era

In 1914 World War I broke out in Europe. Russian and German armies met and fought bloody battles in Eastern Europe. Unprepared for war, Russia suffered many defeats and few victories. As the fighting dragged on, shortages of food in Russian cities caused much starvation. Discontent grew among the Russian people.

Peter the Great

In 1698 Peter I, known as Peter the Great, came to the Russian throne. Nearly 7 feet (2 m) tall, Peter had boundless energy. After becoming czar, he took an 18-month tour of England and the Netherlands. He visited shipyards, factories, and laboratories. He learned carpentry and enough skill in surgery and dentistry to want to practice on others. When he returned home, Peter forced the Russian nobility to adopt the ways of Western Europe. In fact, those who refused to study math and geometry were not allowed to get married.

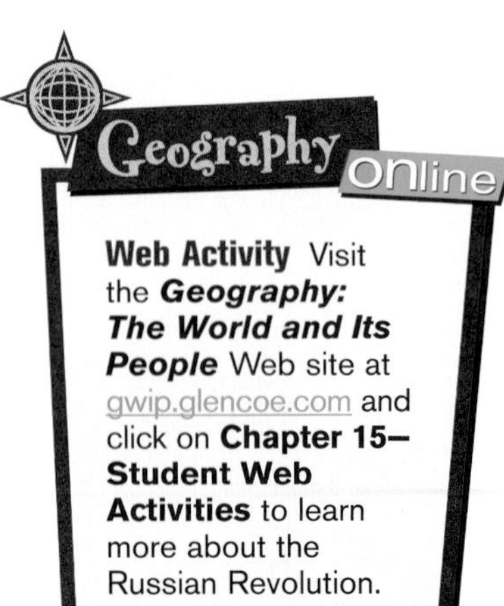

The Russian Revolution In 1917 political leaders, soldiers, and factory workers forced Czar Nicholas II to give up the throne. Later that year, a political rebel named Vladimir Lenin led the Russian Revolution and seized control. He and his followers set up a **communist state,** a country whose government has strong control over the economy and society as a whole. Threatened at first by outside invasion, the Communists moved Russia's capital from coastal St. Petersburg to Moscow in the heart of the country.

Growth of Soviet Power By 1922 Russia's Communist leaders were securely in power. In that year, they formed the Union of Soviet Socialist Republics (U.S.S.R.), or the Soviet Union. This vast territory included Russia and most of the conquered territories of the old Russian Empire. After Lenin died in 1924, Communist officials disagreed over who was to lead the country.

Within a few years, Joseph Stalin had won out over the others and became the Soviet Union's leader. Under Stalin's orders, the government took control of all farming. Stalin also set up five-year plans to industrialize the country. These were programs that set economic goals for a five-year period. They led to an amazing growth of cities. Factory managers were told what to make and how to make it. The government took complete control over the economy. Those who opposed Stalin's actions were killed or sent to remote prison camps deep in the vast forests of icy **Siberia.** Millions of people suffered under Stalin's rule.

In 1941 Nazi Germany invaded the Soviet Union, bringing the country into World War II. During the conflict, the Soviets joined with Great Britain and the United States to defeat the Germans. Millions of Russians—soldiers and civilians—died in what Russians call the Great Patriotic War.

Art

Peter Carl Fabergé was no ordinary Russian jeweler. His successful workshop designed extravagant jeweled flowers, figures, and animals. He is most famous for crafting priceless gold Easter eggs for the czar of Russia and other royalty in Europe and Asia. Each egg was unique and took nearly a year to create. Lifting the lid of the egg revealed a tiny surprise. One egg Fabergé created (shown here) held an intricate ship inside.

Looking Closer Why do you think Fabergé's workshop closed after the Russian Revolution of 1917?

Fabergé egg ▶

Soviet Control

Czechoslovakia tried to throw off Soviet control in 1968. Soviet tanks and troops poured into Bratislava to crush the revolt.

Movement **Why did Stalin set up Communist governments in Eastern European countries?**

A Superpower When World War II ended, Stalin wanted to protect the Soviet Union from any more invasions. He sent troops to set up Communist governments in neighboring Eastern European countries. Stalin and the leaders who followed him strengthened the military and built powerful nuclear weapons. The Soviet Union became one of the two most powerful nations in the world. The other superpower—the United States—opposed Soviet actions. From the late 1940s to the late 1980s, these two nations waged a **cold war.** They competed for world influence without actually fighting each other. They even competed in areas *outside* the world. Both the Soviet Union and the United States launched rockets in a bid to be first in outer space.

The Cold War Years During the Cold War years, the Soviet economy faced many problems. Under government control and with no competition, factories became inefficient and produced poor-quality goods. The government focused on making tanks and airplanes, not cars and refrigerators. As a result, people had few consumer goods to buy. Food often became scarce, and people had to wait in long lines to buy bread, milk, and other basics. Once again, discontent spread among the Russian people and those living in Soviet-controlled areas.

The Soviet Union had another challenge. This vast empire included not only Russians but also people from many other **ethnic groups,** or people who share a common culture, language, or history. Instead of being scattered throughout the country, people in each of these other groups generally lived together in the same area. They resented the control of the government in Moscow, which they believed favored ethnic Russians. They wanted to leave the Soviet Union and form their own countries.

Soviet Collapse In 1985 Mikhail Gorbachev (GAWR•buh•CHAWF) became the leader of the Soviet Union. Without totally abandoning communism, Gorbachev hoped to lessen the government's control of the economy and society. He tried to allow farmers and factory managers to make their own decisions. He allowed people to speak freely about the government and important issues, a policy called *glasnost,* or "openness." Instead of strengthening the country, however, his policies only made people doubt the communist system even more. People's demands for more and more changes eventually led to the collapse of both communism and the Soviet Union.

In late 1991, each of the 15 republics that made up the Soviet Union declared its independence. The Soviet Union no longer existed. Russia emerged as the largest and most powerful of those republics. Although a rough road lay ahead, many Russians were thrilled by the end of communism and the chance to enjoy freedom.

Reading Check **What two superpowers struggled in the Cold War?**

Assessment

Defining Terms

1. Define czar, serf, industrialize, communist state, cold war, ethnic group.

Recalling Facts

2. History Why is Czar Alexander II known as the Czar-Liberator?

3. History Who led the 1917 revolution in Russia?

4. History What happened to the Soviet Union in 1991?

Critical Thinking

5. Understanding Cause and Effect How did the enormous size of the Soviet Union create problems for that nation?

6. Analyzing Information How did a lack of competition affect the economy of the Soviet Union?

Graphic Organizer

7. Organizing Information In a chart like this one, write facts that show the contrast between the nobles and the serfs of Russia.

Nobles	Serfs

Applying Geography Skills

8. Analyzing Maps Study the historical map on page 424. When did Russia give up control of Alaska? In what present-day countries was Kievan Rus located?

Making Connections

ART | SCIENCE | LITERATURE | TECHNOLOGY

Living in Space

In 1986 the Russian space station *Mir* began to orbit Earth. Since that time *Mir* has been home to more than 60 cosmonauts—Russian astronauts—and astronauts from more than a dozen countries.

History

The Soviet Union built the space station *Mir,* the Russian word for "peace," to establish a permanently staffed laboratory in space. Each mission to *Mir* lasted an average of six months to a year. Other spacecraft delivered fresh food, new equipment, and mail from home.

Mir cosmonauts and astronauts spent most of their day in the core module, which contained the living quarters and work compartment. Other modules provided equipment for producing oxygen, recycling water, and performing science experiments. The experiments focused on the long-term effects of weightlessness on plants and animals, including humans. Crew members also checked ozone levels in Earth's atmosphere, recorded changes in the oceans, and observed distant galaxies.

In 1993 the United States and Russia decided to build an International Space Station. The Russian government decided to scrap *Mir* and let it burn up in the atmosphere in 2001.

Making the Connection

1. What was *Mir* and when was it first launched?
2. What kind of scientific research did the *Mir* crew conduct?
3. **Drawing Conclusions** What value do you think a permanent space station can offer?

NATIONAL GEOGRAPHIC

***Mir* Space Station Core Module**

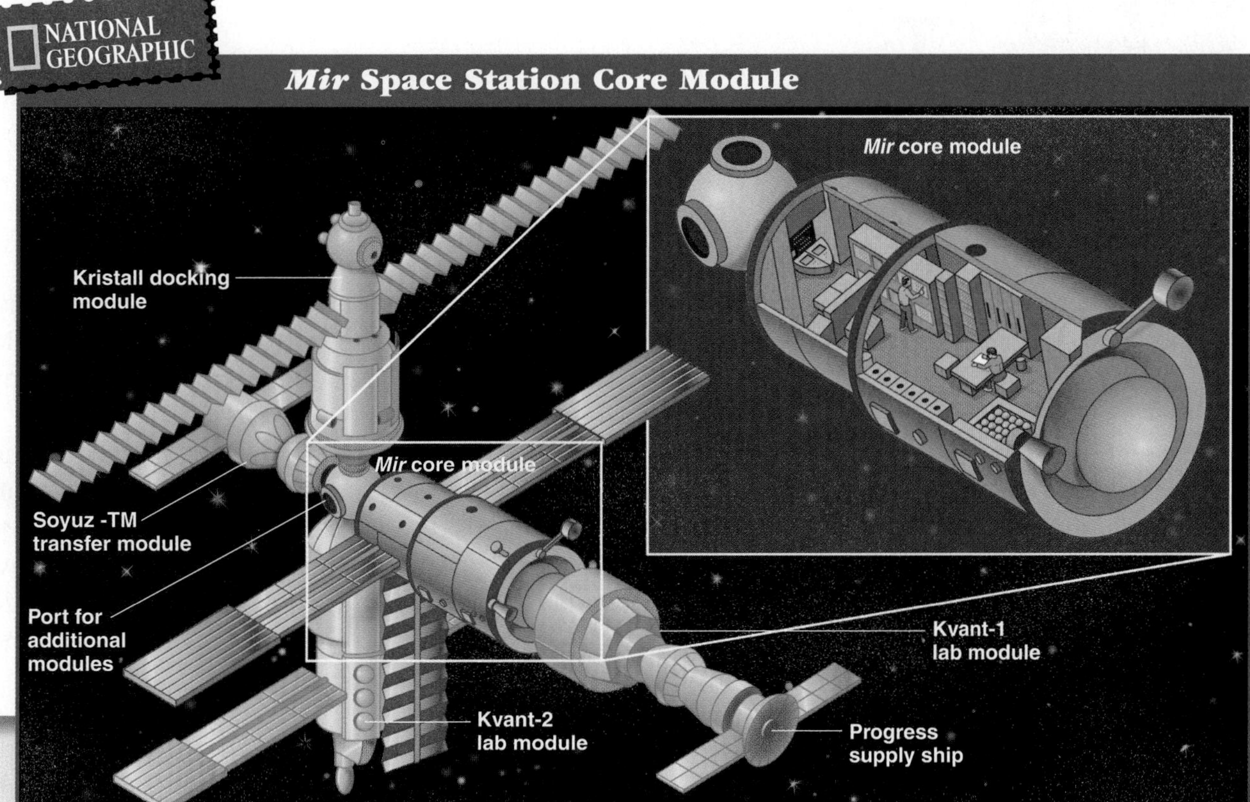

Section 2

A New Russia

Guide to Reading

Main Idea

Russia has a rich cultural heritage, but faces challenges in adopting a new economic system and government.

Terms to Know

- free enterprise system
- nuclear energy
- life expectancy
- democracy
- federal republic
- urban
- suburb
- rural

Places to Locate

- Chechnya
- Caspian Sea
- Moscow
- St. Petersburg

Reading Strategy

Draw a diagram like this one. Then write four challenges facing Russia.

NATIONAL GEOGRAPHIC **Exploring Our World**

When an aging, rusty oil pipeline in Russia broke, 25 million gallons (95 million liters) of oil leaked to the surface. Russia did not have the correct disaster cleanup equipment. Cleanup crews had to burn the oil, further polluting the air. Here, a worker fixes a broken pipeline in freezing Siberia.

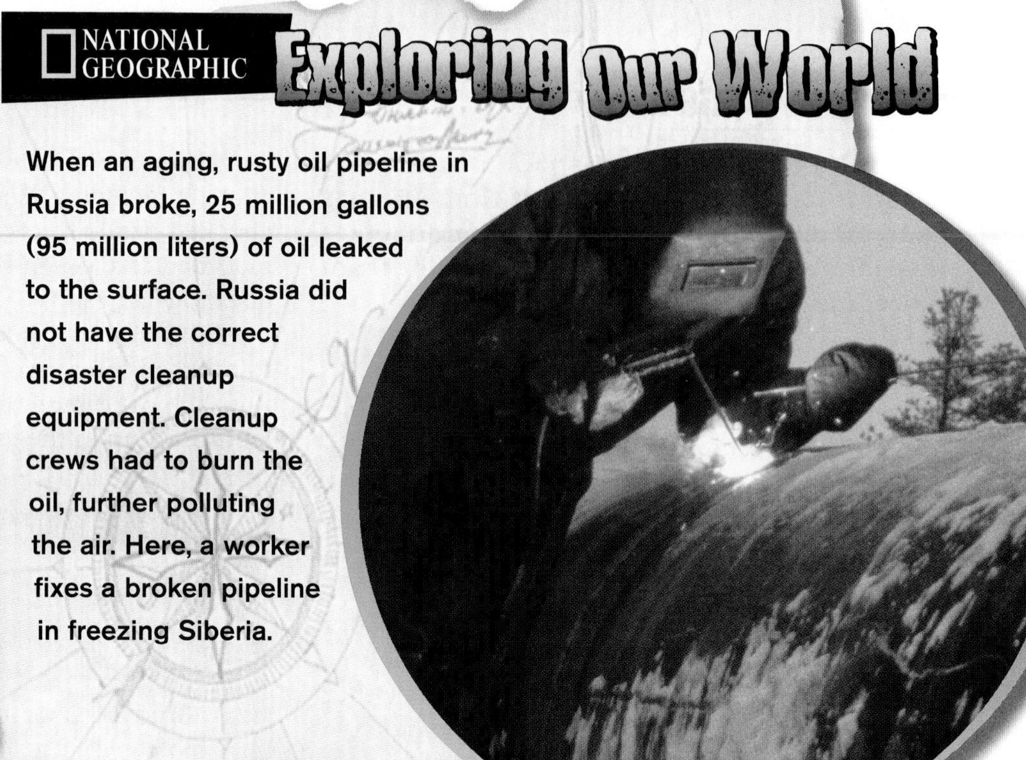

The Russian people have been working to move from the strict, tightly controlled rule of the past toward an open and free economy and government. They have found that these changes do not come easily.

From Communism to Free Enterprise

Under communism, the government controlled Russia's economy. Government officials decided what—and how much—farmers should grow. They told factory managers what products to make, how many to make, and to whom they could sell them.

The fall of communism turned Russia's economy upside down. The Russian government adopted a market economy, the economic system followed in the United States. Under a market economy, or **free enterprise system,** people start and run businesses with little government intervention. Today Russian factory managers can decide what products to make. People can open businesses—restaurants, stores, or computer companies—and choose their own careers.

The Russian people gained freedom, but that has not always helped them. People now can make their own decisions, but those decisions do not always lead to success. They may become unemployed. Under communism, everybody had jobs. Workers today can lose their jobs when a business declines.

In addition, the government no longer sets prices for food and other goods. When prices were set low, the Russian people could afford the goods but often faced shortages. Why? Producers would not supply goods if they could not make a profit. Without government controls, prices have risen. Higher prices make it harder to buy necessities like food and clothing. It is hoped that, in the future, factories will start producing more goods and services. Now that manufacturers know they can receive higher prices and more profits for their goods, supplies should increase.

Environmental Issues The old Communist government did little to protect the environment. Factories belched dirty smoke into the air and dumped poisons into rivers and lakes. Pollution fouled the air, water, and land. The government also built plants to make **nuclear energy,** or power made by creating a controlled atomic reaction. Although nuclear power plants do not belch dirty smoke, they do leave dangerous by-products. In addition, if uncontrolled like the nuclear explosion at Chernobyl, the consequences are disastrous. Turn to page 386 to find out more about Chernobyl.

Pollution has harmed the health of the Russian people, too. Air pollution has caused many people to suffer from diseases of the lungs. Rising numbers of people have cancer, and life expectancy in Russia has fallen. **Life expectancy** is the number of years that an average person is expected to live. Falling life expectancy reveals that the population is growing less healthy.

Food Shortages

Under communism, prices were low, but people faced shortages and had to wait in line to buy goods.

Place **Why can many Russians today not afford goods and services?**

✓Reading Check **Who made economic decisions under Communist rule?**

Political Challenges

Under communism, members of the Communist Party controlled Russia's government and told people how to vote. Today Russia is a **democracy,** a government in which people freely elect their leaders. Russia also is a **federal republic.** This means that power is divided between national and state governments with a president who leads the nation.

Living in a Changed City

Olga lives in Yekaterinburg, a city in the Ural Mountains. When she is not swimming or going to school, Olga hikes and skis in the forests near her home. Olga's mother tells her that life is different now. The city used to be called Sverdlovsk and was officially closed to the outside world until 1990. It did not even appear on maps because Soviet officials wanted to keep the city and its defense industries a secret from the United States and its allies. Her mother's education centered on the Communist point of view. Olga, however, enjoys a variety of classes and plans to take business management courses in college.

A Russian president has stronger powers than an American president. For example, the Russian president can issue orders that become laws even if they are not passed by the legislature. Russia's first two presidents—Boris Yeltsin (BOH•rehs YEHL•tzehn) and Vladimir Putin (VLAH•deh•meehr POO•tihn)—used their powers to push for economic changes in Russia.

In adjusting to a new form of government, Russians face important political challenges. They have to learn how to act in a democracy. Democracy is built on the idea of the rule of law. This means that laws govern not just ordinary people but also government officials. In the past, Russian leaders did what they wanted to do. In the new system, they must learn to follow the law. Also, past governments punished people who criticized their decisions. Now officials have to learn to accept disagreements over government policies.

Another challenge results from the fact that Russia is home to many different ethnic groups. Some of these groups want to form their own countries. Among these groups are the Chechens (CHEH•chehnz), who live in **Chechnya** (CHEHCH•nee•uh) near the **Caspian Sea** in southern Russia. Find Chechnya on the map on page 439. Russian troops have fought Chechen forces to keep Chechnya a part of Russia.

✓Reading Check **Why is being home to different ethnic groups a challenge for Russia?**

The Russian People

Russia is one of the most populous countries in the world, with 146.5 million people. Most of them are ethnic Russians, but the country includes many other groups as well. About 90 percent of the people speak the Russian language. Look at the map on page 433. You will find western Russia, especially around **Moscow,** to be the most densely populated area of the country. About 75 percent of Russia's people live in cities.

Living in the City Russia's urban, or city, areas are large and modern with stone or concrete buildings and wide streets. Tall buildings hold apartments for hundreds of families. Many of these apartments are small and cramped, however. When people in cities relax, they spend time with their families and friends, take walks through parks, or attend concerts, movies, and the circus.

Russian cities have changed in recent years. Some people have benefited from the economic changes sweeping the country. Many of these prosperous people have clustered in Moscow. Their new cars speed down the city's streets. They are building large houses outside the city limits, where few people lived before. As a result, Russia is developing its first suburbs, or smaller communities that surround a city.

Yet a large number of Russia's city dwellers remain poor. These people lack the money to buy the consumer goods that are now more and more available. Many survive only by standing in long lines to receive food given away by government agencies. Some of the poor resent the success of the newly wealthy people.

Living in the Country In Russia's rural areas, or countryside, most people live in houses built of wood. The quality of health care and education is lower in rural areas than in the cities. Over the years, many people have left rural areas to find work in Russia's cities.

✓Reading Check **What percentage of Russia's people live in cities?**

Culture in Russia

Russia has a rich tradition of art, music, and literature. Russians view these cultural achievements with pride. Some of their most beloved works of art are based on religious, historical, or folk themes.

Religion The Soviet Union's Communist rulers put severe limits on the practice of religion. They closed many houses of worship and persecuted outspoken religious leaders. Since the fall of communism, many Russians have returned to religious traditions, including Judaism, Islam,

Applying Map Skills

1. What general area of Russia has the highest population density?
2. What is the population density of most of eastern Russia?

Find NGS online map resources @ www.nationalgeographic.com/maps

NATIONAL GEOGRAPHIC On Location

Urban vs. Rural

The GUM state department store (above) is very similar to modern malls in the United States. In some rural areas, however, people still live without heat, electricity, or plumbing (right).

Movement How have economic changes affected where Russia's people live?

and Christianity. The largest number practices a Russian form of the Eastern Orthodox Christian faith. Tourists enjoy seeing the onion-shaped domes and elaborate decorations of Russian Orthodox churches.

Music, Art, and Literature If you wanted to see Russian culture at its best, where would you go? You might visit **St. Petersburg's** Mariinsky (MAH•ree•IHN•skee) Theater. One of Russia's top ballet companies dances here, and Russian ballet dancers are famous around the world. Composer Peter Tchaikovsky wrote some of the world's favorite ballets, including *Sleeping Beauty* and *The Nutcracker Suite.* You remember that his *1812 Overture* celebrated the Russian defeat of the French invasion of 1812. Nikolay Rimsky-Korsakov used Russian folktales and tunes in his operas and other works. Igor Stravinsky's *Firebird Suite* came from a Russian legend.

If you enjoy painting, you would like to stroll through St. Petersburg's Hermitage Museum. Originally built to hold the art collection of the czars, the museum now displays these works for the public. It has paintings by Russian and European painters and sculptors.

The great works of Russian literature also reflect Russian themes. Poet Alexander Pushkin protested the lack of freedom under the czars. Leo Tolstoy's novel *War and Peace* recounts how Russians rallied to defeat the French in 1812. Fyodor Dostoyevsky (DAHS•tuh•YEHF•skee) wrote many novels that explored Russian life during the late 1800s. In the 1970s, Alexander Solzhenitsyn (SOHL•zhuh•NEET•suhn) wrote novels that revealed the harsh conditions of Communist society.

Celebrations Russians enjoy small family get-togethers as well as national holidays. New Year's Eve is the most festive nonreligious holiday for Russians. Children decorate a fir tree and exchange presents with others in their families. Russians also celebrate the first day of May with parades and speeches. May Day honors Russian workers.

Food If you have dinner with a Russian family, you might begin with a big bowl of borscht, a soup made from beets, or *shchi,* a soup made from cabbage. Next, you might have meat turnovers called piroshki. For the main course, you are likely to eat meat, poultry, or fish with boiled potatoes. On special occasions, Russians like to eat caviar. This delicacy is eggs of the sturgeon, a fish from the Caspian Sea.

Sports and Recreation Russians love soccer and tennis. They also enjoy hiking, camping, and mountain climbing. With Russia's cold climate, winter sports are popular. Russians like to ski, skate, and play ice hockey. Have you ever watched the Olympics? If so, you probably have seen Russian hockey players, figure skaters, and gymnasts standing on the victory podium. They thrill spectators with their skill and grace.

✓Reading Check **Which Russian author wrote about the harsh conditions of Communist society?**

Assessment

Defining Terms

1. Define free enterprise system, nuclear energy, life expectancy, democracy, federal republic, urban, suburb, rural.

Recalling Facts

2. Government What is one power of the Russian president?
3. Government Why has there been fighting with Chechnya?
4. Culture What is the major religion of Russia?

Critical Thinking

5. Synthesizing Information Describe the problems Russians face living in a free society after years of Communist rule.
6. Making Predictions Art ideas are frequently drawn from life. What themes do you think you will see in future Russian arts?

Graphic Organizer

7. Organizing Information Draw a diagram like this one, and list two facts for each topic in the four outer ovals.

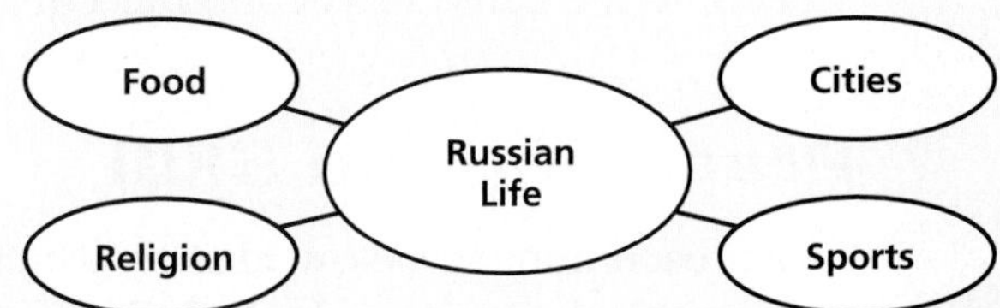

Applying Geography Skills

8. Analyzing Maps Look at the population density map on page 433. What city is located at about 38°E longitude and 55°N latitude? What is the estimated population of this city?

Critical Thinking Skill

Understanding Cause and Effect

Understanding cause and effect involves considering *why* an event occurred. A *cause* is the action or situation that produces an event. What happens as a result of a cause is an *effect.*

Learning the Skill

To identify cause-and-effect relationships, follow these steps:

- Identify two or more events or developments.
- Decide whether one event caused the other. Look for "clue words" such as *because, led to, brought about, produced, as a result of, so that, since,* and *therefore*.
- Look for logical relationships between events, such as "She overslept, and then she missed her bus."
- Identify the outcomes of events. Remember that some effects have more than one cause, and some causes lead to more than one effect. Also, an effect can become the cause of yet another effect.

Practicing the Skill

For each number below, identify which statement is the cause and which is the effect.

1. (A) The Communists moved Russia's capital from coastal St. Petersburg to Moscow in the heart of the country.
   (B) The capital of Russia was threatened by an outside invasion.

▲ Revolutionary leaders and philosophers Lenin, Engels, and Marx

2. (A) Revolutionary leaders seized control of the Russian government.
   (B) During World War I, shortages of food in Russian cities caused much starvation.
   (C) Discontent grew among the Russian people.
3. (A) The Soviet government kept prices for goods and services very low.
   (B) Many goods and services were in short supply in the Soviet Union.

Applying the Skill

In your local newspaper, read an article describing a current event. Determine at least one cause and one effect of that event. Show the cause-and-effect relationship in a diagram like the one here:

GO TO Practice key skills with **Glencoe Skillbuilder Interactive Workbook, Level 1.**

Chapter 15 Reading Review

Section 1 A Troubled History

Terms to Know
czar
serf
industrialize
communist state
cold war
ethnic group

Main Idea

The harsh rule of powerful leaders has often sparked violent uprisings in Russia.

✓History Emperors called czars ruled the Russian Empire from 1480 to 1917.

✓Movement The czars expanded Russian territory to reach from Europe to the Pacific.

✓Government Under the Communists, Russia became part of the Soviet Union.

✓History In 1991 the Soviet Union broke apart, and Russia became an independent republic.

Section 2 A New Russia

Terms to Know
free enterprise system
nuclear energy
life expectancy
democracy
federal republic
urban
suburb
rural

Main Idea

Russia has a rich cultural heritage, but faces challenges in adopting a new economic system and government.

✓Economics The change to a free enterprise economy has been a challenge for Russians as they face rising unemployment and rising prices.

✓Government Russians have had to learn how to live in a democracy.

✓Government Some non-Russian ethnic groups want to create independent nations out of Russia.

✓Culture Russians practice many different religions, but more follow Russian Orthodox Christianity than any other faith.

✓Culture Russian artists, composers, and writers often used themes based on Russian history or traditions.

◀ The Hermitage in St. Petersburg

Chapter 15 Assessment and Activities

Using Key Terms

Match the terms in Part A with their definitions in Part B.

A.

1. cold war
2. nuclear energy
3. rural
4. czar
5. life expectancy
6. industrialize
7. suburb
8. serf
9. urban
10. communist state

B.

a. smaller community surrounding a city
b. changing an economy to manufacturing
c. farm laborers bound to the land they worked
d. period of tension without actual fighting
e. relating to a city
f. former emperor of Russia
g. power from a controlled atomic reaction
h. relating to the countryside
i. number of years that the average person is expected to live
j. government with strong control over the economy and society as a whole

Reviewing the Main Ideas

Section 1 A Troubled History

11. **History** Which czar used a secret police force to maintain strict control over the people?
12. **History** When was the Union of Soviet Socialist Republics formed?
13. **Government** Why did Stalin send people to Siberia?
14. **History** What took place in 1991?

Section 2 A New Russia

15. **Economics** What type of economic system has the new Russia adopted?
16. **Culture** What does falling life expectancy reveal?
17. **Government** Who were Russia's first two presidents?
18. **Culture** What do the *1812 Overture* and *War and Peace* have in common?
19. **Culture** Who wrote *The Nutcracker Suite*?
20. **Human/Environment Interaction** Give at least four examples of the environmental damage that occurred under the Soviet Communist government.

Russia—Past and Present

Place Location Activity

On a separate sheet of paper, match the letters on the map with the numbered places listed below.

1. St. Petersburg
2. Caspian Sea
3. Moscow
4. Baltic Sea
5. Vladivostok
6. Irkutsk
7. Omsk
8. Sea of Japan

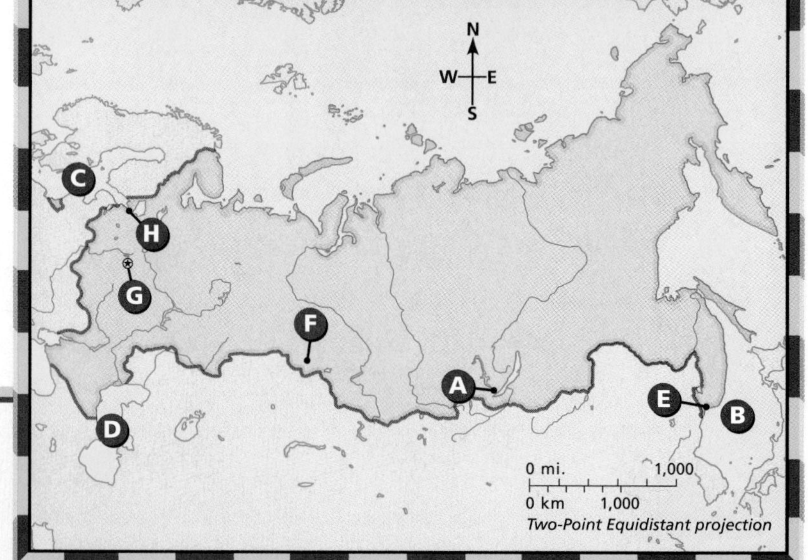

Self-Check Quiz Visit the ***Geography: The World and Its People*** Web site at gwip.glencoe.com and click on **Chapter 15–Self-Check Quizzes** to prepare for the Chapter Test.

Critical Thinking

21. **Understanding Cause and Effect** How did World War I help lead to the Russian Revolution?
22. **Organizing Information** Draw a diagram like this one. Complete it with four characteristics of the free enterprise system in Russia.

Free enterprise in Russia

GeoJournal Activity

23. **Writing a News Article** Learn more about the nuclear disaster at Chernobyl. Find out what happened and its effects on the local people, animals, and land. Write a news article that might have appeared a few days after the explosion. Then write a follow-up article on the long-term effects of the nuclear explosion on neighboring countries.

Mental Mapping Activity

24. **Focusing on the Region** Draw a simple outline map of Russia, then label the following:
    - Arctic Ocean
    - Pacific Ocean
    - Vladivostok
    - Moscow
    - Bering Sea
    - St. Petersburg
    - Siberia
    - Baltic Sea

Technology Skills Activity

25. **Developing Multimedia Presentations** Choose one of the czars of Russia. Research your choice and create a multimedia presentation on this person. Include information on when he or she lived, what he or she accomplished (or did not accomplish), and other interesting facts. Use pictures, maps, and time lines to make your presentation more visual.

Standardized Test Practice

Directions: Study the map below, then answer the question that follows.

1. Which of the following statements about this map is NOT true?

F Chechnya lies along Russia's southern border.

G Chechnya is situated between the Black and Caspian Seas.

H Chechnya's landscape is mostly flat, fertile farmland.

J Chechnya's nearest neighbor is Georgia.

Test-Taking Tip: Be careful when you see the words NOT or EXCEPT in a question. Read all the answer choices and choose the one that *does not* fit with the question. Quickly eliminate answers that are true. Make sure that your answer choice is supported by information *on the map.*

Napoleon and troops retreat from Russia.

RUSSIA'S STRATEGY: Freeze Your Foes

Winter weather can cancel school, bring flu outbreaks, and stop traffic. It can even change history. Such was the case when French ruler Napoleon thought he had conquered the Russian Empire.

In fact, Napoleon did not want to conquer Russia. His real enemy was Great Britain. Napoleon wanted Russia and other countries to stop trading with Great Britain. Yet Russia's czar, Alexander I, refused. By 1812, Napoleon was determined to change Alexander's mind. In June, leading an army of more than half a million soldiers, Napoleon invaded Russia. To reach Moscow and the czar, Napoleon had to fight his way across the Russian countryside.

By the time Napoleon's battle-weary forces reached Moscow, supplies were scarce. All along the route, Russians had burned villages as they retreated, leaving no food or shelter. Reaching Moscow, Napoleon found the city in flames and nearly empty of people. The czar had moved to St. Petersburg. Napoleon took Moscow without a fight, but most of the city was in ashes.

Winter Wins a War

With winter approaching, Napoleon waited in Moscow for Alexander I to offer peace. The czar remained silent, however. With dwindling supplies and many of his troops lacking winter clothes, Napoleon was forced to retreat. He tried to take a new way back, but the Russians made Napoleon use the same ruined route he had used before. Armed bands of Russians attacked at every turn. Starving and desperate to escape the bitter cold, several of Napoleon's soldiers threw themselves into burning buildings. Most of Napoleon's troops never made it out of Russia.

History Repeats

More than a century later, during World War II, Russia's winter was again a mighty foe. On June 22, 1941, Adolf Hitler's German army invaded Russia, then part of the Soviet Union. As the German army fought its way to Moscow, Soviet leader Joseph Stalin issued his own "scorched-earth policy." Soviet citizens burned anything of use to the invaders. By December, German troops were within sight of the Kremlin, Moscow's government center, when winter struck.

Snow buried the invaders. Temperatures fell below freezing. Grease in guns and oil in vehicles froze solid. German soldiers suffered frostbite and died. The Soviets were better clothed and had winterized their tanks and trucks. Stalin's troops pushed back the German army. Once again the Russians triumphed with help from "General Winter."

QUESTIONS

1. **After Napoleon conquered Moscow in 1812, why did he retreat?**
2. **How did Russia's winter affect fighting in World War II?**

German prisoners of Russia's winter ▶

Average Winter Temperatures

EUROPE
Moscow
RUSSIA
ASIA
N
W
E
S

Napoleon's Advance, June–October 1812
German Forces Front Line, December 1941

< -40°F
-40° to -31°F
-30° to -21°F
-20° to -11°F
-10° to 0°F
0° to 10°F
11° to 20°F
21° to 30°F
> 30°F

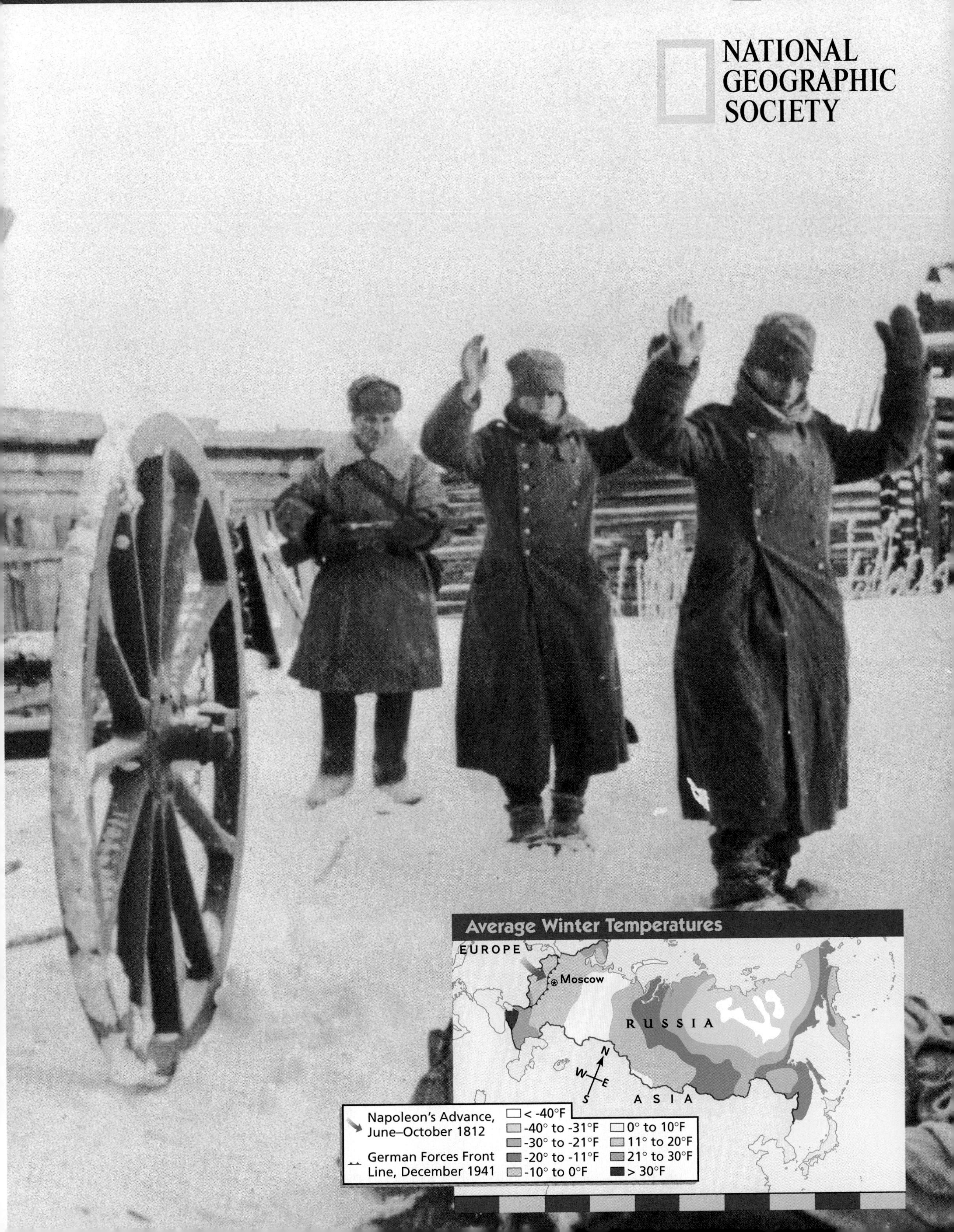

Business district at dusk, Dubai, United Arab Emirates

Young woman in national dress, Turkmenistan ▶

North Africa, Southwest Asia, and Central Asia

Ancient Egyptian pyramids overlook industrial smokestacks. Three-thousand-year-old stone temples tower over sparkling new oil derricks. Remote mountain villages and endless desert seas of sand and gravel contrast with modern beaches overrun by tourists. All of these extremes can be found within the culture region of North Africa, Southwest Asia, and Central Asia.

NGS ONLINE
www.nationalgeographic.com/education

Shepherd tending sheep,
Atlas Mountains, Morocco

Focus on:

North Africa, Southwest Asia, and Central Asia

LYING AT THE INTERSECTION of Europe, Asia, and Africa, this sprawling region has long been a meeting place for diverse peoples and cultures. Troubled by bitter conflicts and plagued by a scarcity of water, the region also is extremely rich in oil and other natural resources.

The Land

Glance at a physical map of this region and you will see a jumble of mountain chains. In the west, the Atlas Mountains—Africa's longest range—run through Morocco and Algeria. The Caucasus Mountains span the land between the Black and Caspian Seas and form the northern border of Georgia and Azerbaijan. Slanting southeast through Turkey and Iran are the Zagros Mountains, where earthquakes frequently occur. Farther east are the Hindu Kush in Afghanistan and the Tian Shan, or "heavenly mountains," in Kyrgyzstan—home to some of the world's largest glaciers.

Mountains block moist winds, helping to create vast deserts across much of the region. The Sahara, in North Africa, is the world's largest hot desert. The Rub' al Khali, or Empty Quarter, covers about one-fourth of the Arabian Peninsula. The Garagum and Qizilqum lie in Turkmenistan and Uzbekistan.

Through these arid landscapes flow great rivers that bring life-giving water. The world's longest river, the Nile, runs 4,241 miles (6,825 km) through Egypt to the Mediterranean Sea. The Tigris and Euphrates Rivers flow southeast through Turkey, Syria, and Iraq.

The Climate

Water is precious in much of this region. Most areas receive a meager 10 inches (25 cm) or less of rainfall each year. In such arid lands, agriculture is only possible along rivers and canals or in places where natural springs bubble to the surface to create lush but isolated oases.

In areas with a steppe climate, where enough rain falls to support grasses, people raise livestock such as sheep, camels, and goats. Steppes cover parts of many Southwest and Central Asian countries. A narrow band of steppe runs along the northern edge of the Sahara, too.

The areas that border the Mediterranean, Black, and Caspian Seas enjoy a milder Mediterranean climate. Although summers are hot and dry, winters bring enough precipitation to turn coastal lowlands into green landscapes.

UNIT 6

Nile River flowing through Aswan, Egypt

◀ Man gazing out across the vast expanses of the Sahara

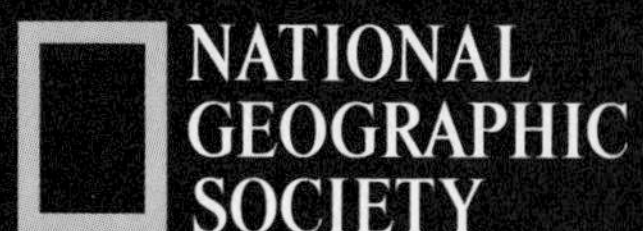

Regional Atlas

The Economy

Like water, natural resources are distributed unevenly across the region. This helps to create great differences in living standards. The region includes some of the world's wealthiest nations—and some of its poorest. Enormous reserves of oil and natural gas lie in certain areas, including lands in central North Africa, along the Persian Gulf, and around the Caspian Sea. Countries such as Saudi Arabia and Kuwait, which export petroleum products to fuel-hungry societies, generally enjoy high standards of living.

On the other hand, those countries with economies based on agriculture have much lower standards of living. Only a small percentage of the region's land is suitable for growing crops. In river valleys and along the coasts, where there is water and fertile soil, farmers raise citrus fruits, grapes, dates, grains, and cotton. Nomadic herding is common across the large expanses of this region that are too dry for crops.

The People

Great pyramids, built as tombs for Egyptian rulers, rise above desert sands. They are a reminder that some of the world's oldest civilizations developed in this region. Roughly 5,000 years ago, the ancient Egyptians built a kingdom along the life-giving Nile River. The Sumerian civilization, an even older society, flourished in the fertile valley between the Tigris and Euphrates Rivers.

Water still dictates where people settle in this region. Most cities lie along seacoasts or rivers, or near desert oases. Among the largest cities are Cairo, Egypt; Istanbul, Turkey; and Tehran, Iran.

In North Africa and Southwest Asia, most of the people are Arabs. Turkic ethnic groups are the majority in Central Asia. Many other ethnic groups also live in the region. Despite the ethnic diversity, many who live here are united by religion. Most people practice Islam, which developed in this region centuries ago. Two other major religions, Judaism and Christianity, also began here. Georgia and Armenia are two of the world's oldest Christian countries, and the country of Israel is the Jewish national homeland.

Exploring the Region

1. **How do mountains help create deserts across much of the region?**
2. **What parts of the region receive the most rainfall?**
3. **How do most people in the region make their living?**
4. **What religion do most people in the region practice?**

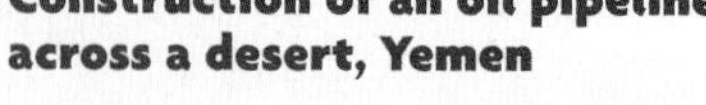

◀ **Construction of an oil pipeline across a desert, Yemen**

UNIT 6

Desert dwellers sharing a meal, Saudi Arabia ▶

North Africa, Southwest Asia, and Central Asia

Physical

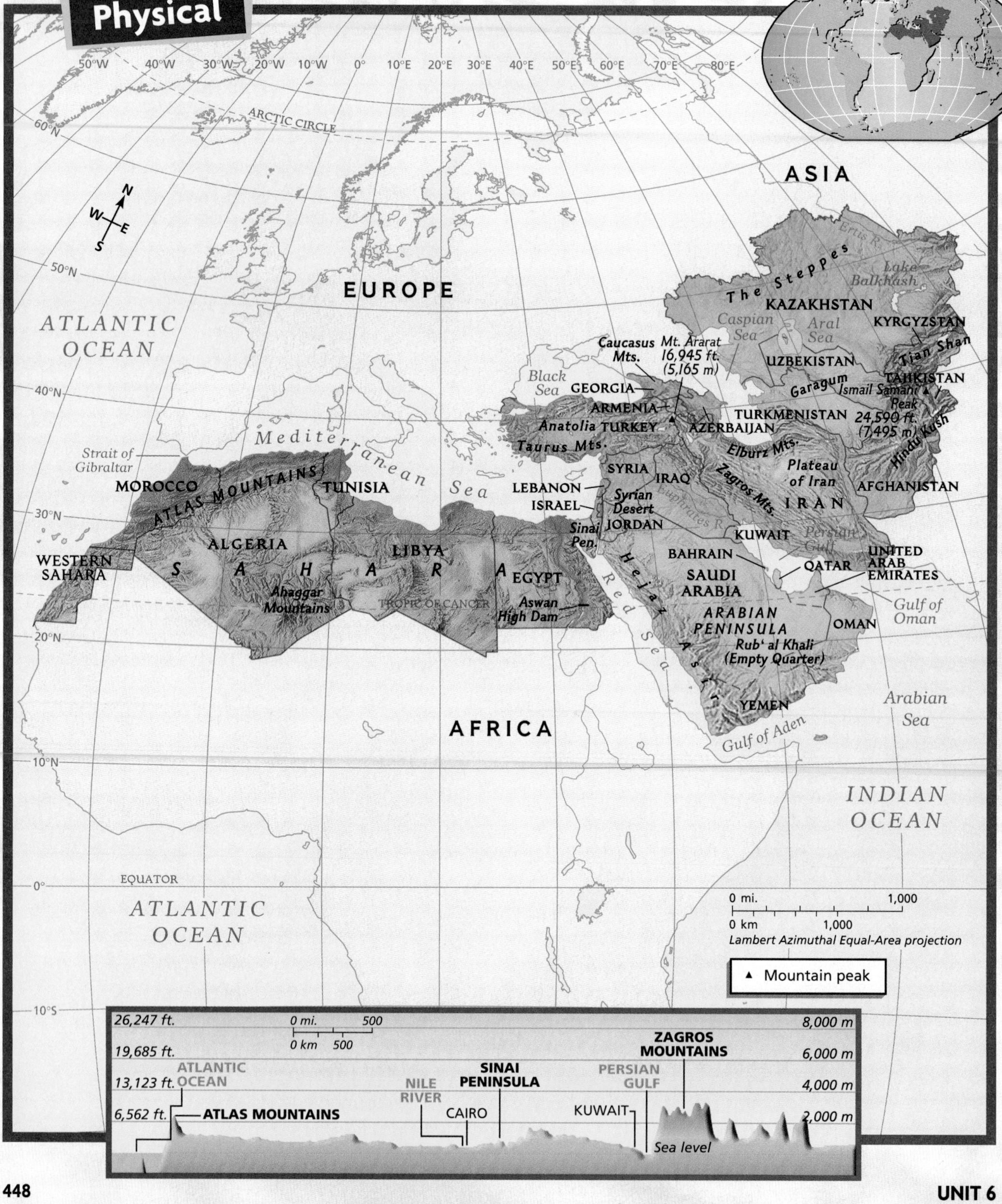

UNIT 6

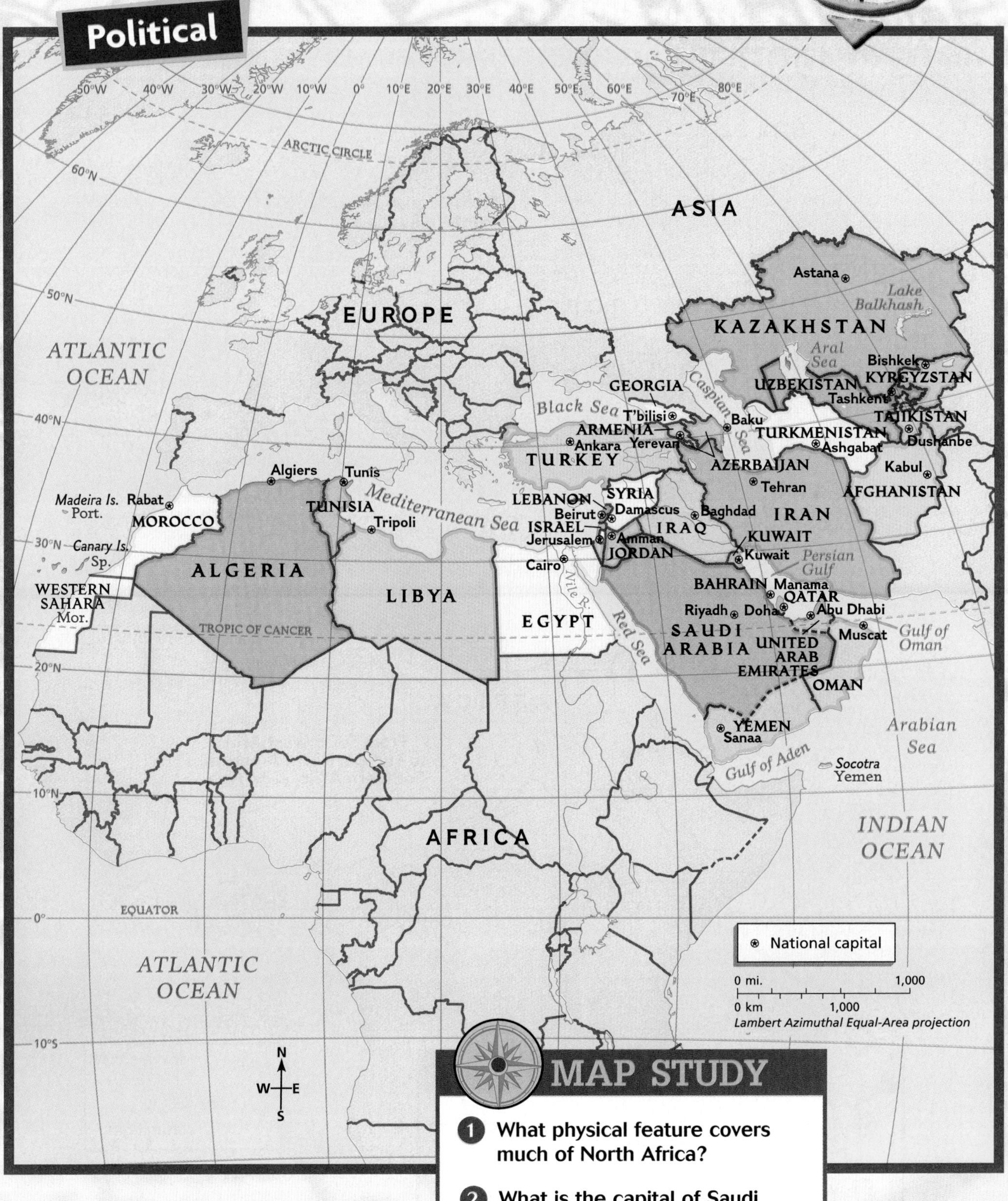

MAP STUDY

1. What physical feature covers much of North Africa?
2. What is the capital of Saudi Arabia?

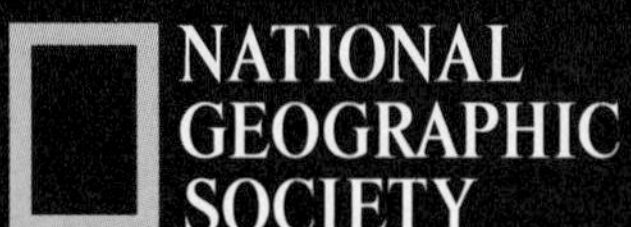

North Africa, Southwest Asia, and Central Asia

Oil and Gas Production and Distribution

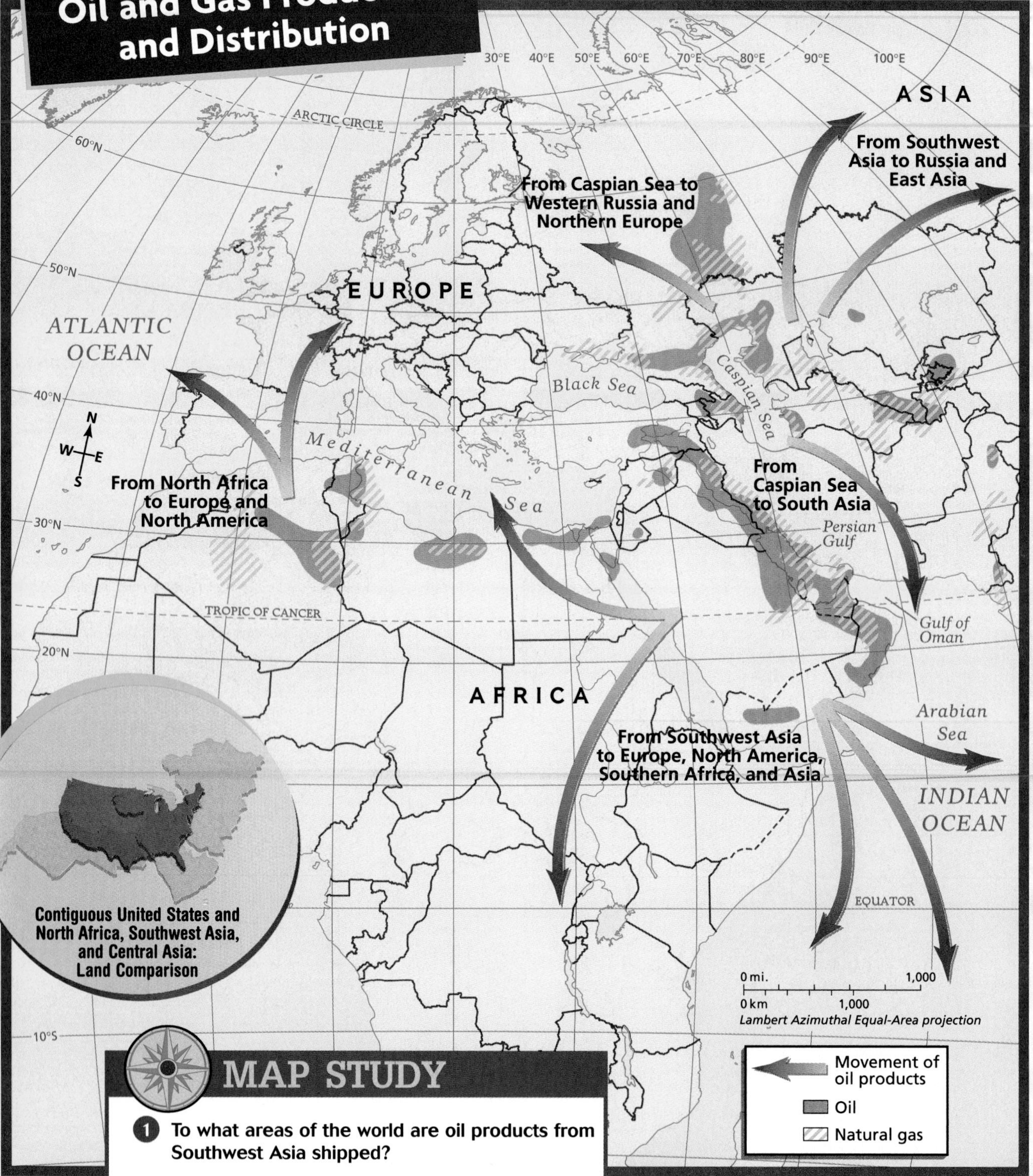

30°E 40°E 50°E 60°E 70°E 80°E 90°E 100°E

ARCTIC CIRCLE

60°N

50°N

40°N

30°N

20°N

10°S

TROPIC OF CANCER

EQUATOR

ASIA

EUROPE

AFRICA

ATLANTIC OCEAN

Black Sea

Caspian Sea

Mediterranean Sea

Persian Gulf

Gulf of Oman

Arabian Sea

INDIAN OCEAN

From Southwest Asia to Russia and East Asia

From Caspian Sea to Western Russia and Northern Europe

From North Africa to Europe and North America

From Caspian Sea to South Asia

From Southwest Asia to Europe, North America, Southern Africa, and Asia

N W E S

0 mi. 1,000

0 km 1,000

Lambert Azimuthal Equal-Area projection

Contiguous United States and North Africa, Southwest Asia, and Central Asia: Land Comparison

Movement of oil products

Oil

Natural gas

MAP STUDY

1. To what areas of the world are oil products from Southwest Asia shipped?
2. What oil regions supply oil products to Russia?

Geo Extremes

① **HIGHEST POINT**
Ismail Samani Peak (Tajikistan)
24,590 ft. (7,495 m) high

② **LOWEST POINT**
Dead Sea (Israel and Jordan)
1,349 ft. (411 m) below sea level

③ **LONGEST RIVER**
Nile River
4,241 mi. (6,825 km) long

④ **LARGEST LAKE**
Caspian Sea
143,244 sq. mi. (371,000 sq. km)

⑤ **LARGEST DESERT**
Sahara (northern Africa)
3,475,000 sq. mi. (9,000,208 sq. km)

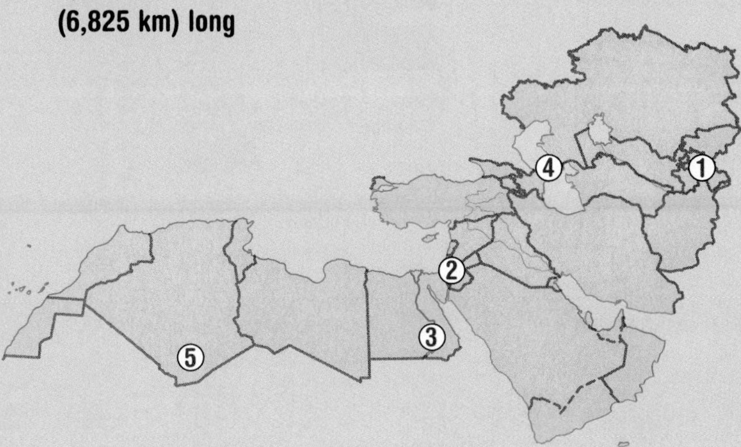

COMPARING POPULATION:
United States and Selected Countries of North Africa, Southwest Asia, and Central Asia

UNITED STATES

EGYPT

AFGHANISTAN

KAZAKHSTAN

ISRAEL

(one figure) = 20,000,000

Source: *Population Reference Bureau,* 2000.

URBAN POPULATIONS:
Selected Cities of North Africa, Southwest Asia, and Central Asia

CAIRO, EGYPT

TEHRAN, IRAN

ALEXANDRIA, EGYPT

ANKARA, TURKEY

ISTANBUL, TURKEY

(one figure) = 500,000

Source: *National Geographic Atlas of the World,* 7th Edition, 1999.

GRAPHIC STUDY

1. The lowest point on the earth is found in this region. Where is it?
2. How does the population of Cairo compare to that of Tehran? How does the population of Ankara compare to that of Cairo?

Country Profiles

AFGHANISTAN
POPULATION: 25,825,000; 103 per sq. mi.; 40 per sq. km
LANGUAGES: Pashto, Dari
MAJOR EXPORTS: Fruits and Nuts
MAJOR IMPORT: Foods
CAPITAL: Kabul
LANDMASS: 251,773 sq. mi.; 652,090 sq. km

ALGERIA
POPULATION: 30,774,000; 33 per sq. mi.; 13 per sq. km
LANGUAGES: Arabic, French, Berber
MAJOR EXPORT: Petroleum
MAJOR IMPORT: Machinery
CAPITAL: Algiers
LANDMASS: 919,595 sq. mi.; 2,381,741 sq. km

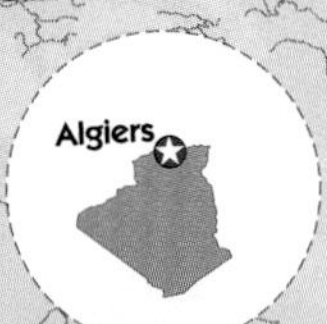

ARMENIA
POPULATION: 3,802,000; 328 per sq. mi.; 127 per sq. km
LANGUAGES: Armenian, Russian
MAJOR EXPORT: Gold
MAJOR IMPORT: Grain
CAPITAL: Yerevan
LANDMASS: 11,583 sq. mi.; 30,000 sq. km

AZERBAIJAN
POPULATION: 7,734,000; 230 per sq. mi.; 89 per sq. km
LANGUAGES: Azeri, Russian, Armenian
MAJOR EXPORT: Petroleum
MAJOR IMPORT: Machinery
CAPITAL: Baku
LANDMASS: 33,591 sq. mi.; 87,000 sq. km

BAHRAIN
POPULATION: 661,000; 2,476 per sq. mi.; 957 per sq. km
LANGUAGE: Arabic
MAJOR EXPORT: Petroleum
MAJOR IMPORT: Machinery
CAPITAL: Manama
LANDMASS: 267 sq. mi.; 691 sq. km

EGYPT
POPULATION: 66,924,000; 173 per sq. mi.; 67 per sq. km
LANGUAGE: Arabic
MAJOR EXPORT: Crude Oil
MAJOR IMPORT: Machinery
CAPITAL: Cairo
LANDMASS: 386,662 sq. mi.; 1,001,449 sq. km

GEORGIA
POPULATION: 5,448,000; 202 per sq. mi.; 78 per sq. km
LANGUAGES: Georgian, Russian
MAJOR EXPORT: Citrus Fruits
MAJOR IMPORT: Fuels
CAPITAL: T'bilisi
LANDMASS: 27,027 sq. mi.; 70,000 sq. km

IRAN
POPULATION: 66,208,000; 104 per sq. mi.; 40 per sq. km
LANGUAGES: Persian, Kurdish
MAJOR EXPORT: Petroleum
MAJOR IMPORT: Machinery
CAPITAL: Tehran
LANDMASS: 636,296 sq. mi.; 1,647,999 sq. km

IRAQ
POPULATION: 22,450,000; 133 per sq. mi.; 51 per sq. km
LANGUAGES: Arabic, Kurdish
MAJOR EXPORT: Crude Oil
MAJOR IMPORT: Machinery
CAPITAL: Baghdad
LANDMASS: 169,235 sq. mi.; 438,317 sq. km

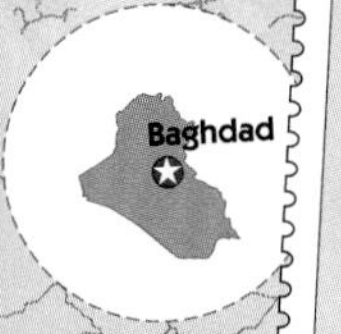

ISRAEL
POPULATION: 6,135,000; 765 per sq. mi.; 295 per sq. km
LANGUAGES: Hebrew, Arabic
MAJOR EXPORT: Polished Diamonds
MAJOR IMPORT: Chemicals
CAPITAL: Jerusalem *
LANDMASS: 8,019 sq. mi.; 20,770 sq. km

* Israel has proclaimed Jerusalem as its capital, but many countries' embassies are located in Tel Aviv.

JORDAN
POPULATION: 4,731,000; 133 per sq. mi.; 52 per sq. km
LANGUAGE: Arabic
MAJOR EXPORT: Phosphates
MAJOR IMPORT: Crude Oil
CAPITAL: Amman
LANDMASS: 35,467 sq. mi.; 91,860 sq. km

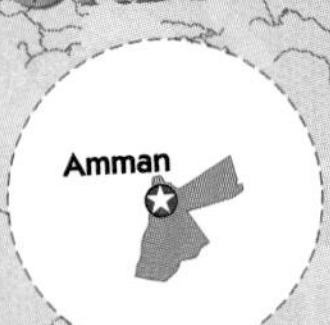

Countries and flags not drawn to scale

UNIT 6

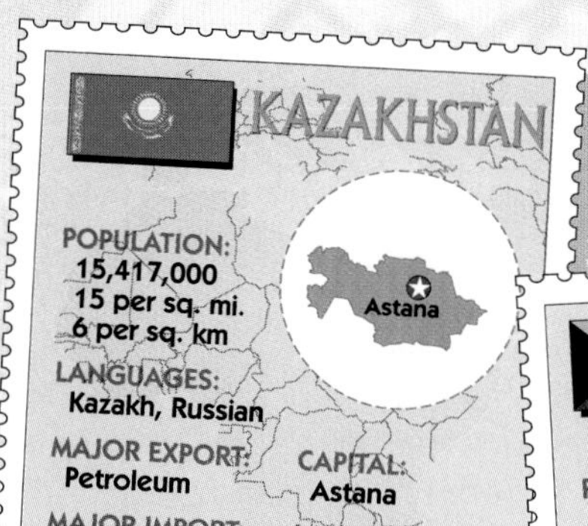
KAZAKHSTAN
POPULATION:
15,417,000
15 per sq. mi.
6 per sq. km
LANGUAGES:
Kazakh, Russian
MAJOR EXPORT:
Petroleum
MAJOR IMPORT:
Machinery
CAPITAL:
Astana
LANDMASS:
1,049,039 sq. mi.
2,716,998 sq. km
Astana

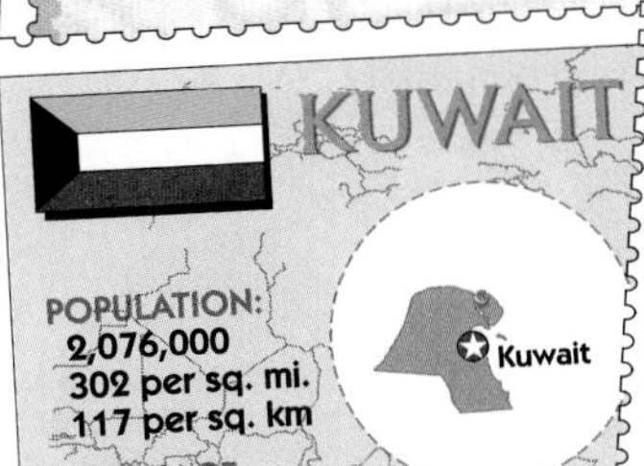
KUWAIT
POPULATION:
2,076,000
302 per sq. mi.
117 per sq. km
LANGUAGE:
Arabic
MAJOR EXPORT:
Petroleum
MAJOR IMPORT:
Foods
CAPITAL:
Kuwait
LANDMASS:
6,880 sq. mi.
17,818 sq. km
Kuwait

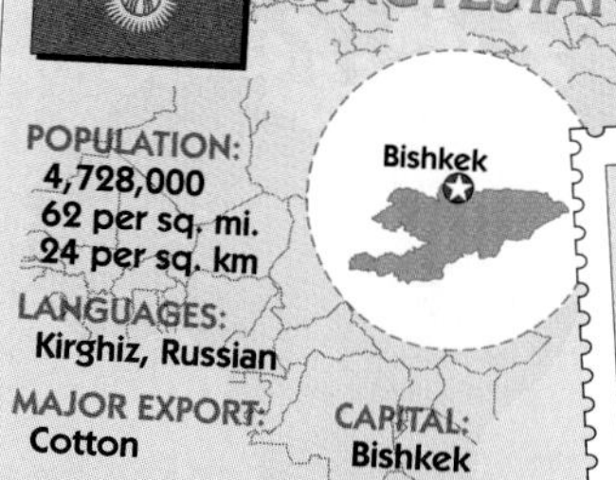
KYRGYZSTAN
POPULATION:
4,728,000
62 per sq. mi.
24 per sq. km
LANGUAGES:
Kirghiz, Russian
MAJOR EXPORT:
Cotton
MAJOR IMPORT:
Grain
CAPITAL:
Bishkek
LANDMASS:
76,834 sq. mi.
198,999 sq. km
Bishkek

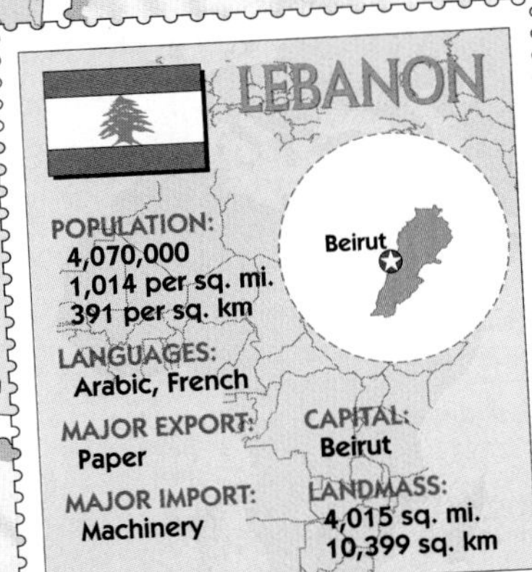
LEBANON
POPULATION:
4,070,000
1,014 per sq. mi.
391 per sq. km
LANGUAGES:
Arabic, French
MAJOR EXPORT:
Paper
MAJOR IMPORT:
Machinery
CAPITAL:
Beirut
LANDMASS:
4,015 sq. mi.
10,399 sq. km
Beirut

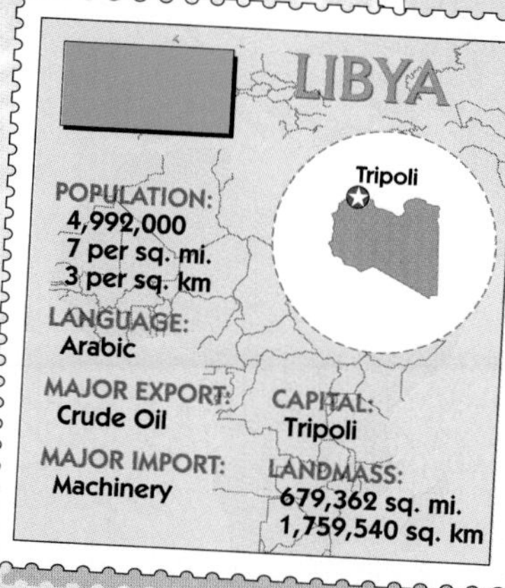
LIBYA
POPULATION:
4,992,000
7 per sq. mi.
3 per sq. km
LANGUAGE:
Arabic
MAJOR EXPORT:
Crude Oil
MAJOR IMPORT:
Machinery
CAPITAL:
Tripoli
LANDMASS:
679,362 sq. mi.
1,759,540 sq. km
Tripoli

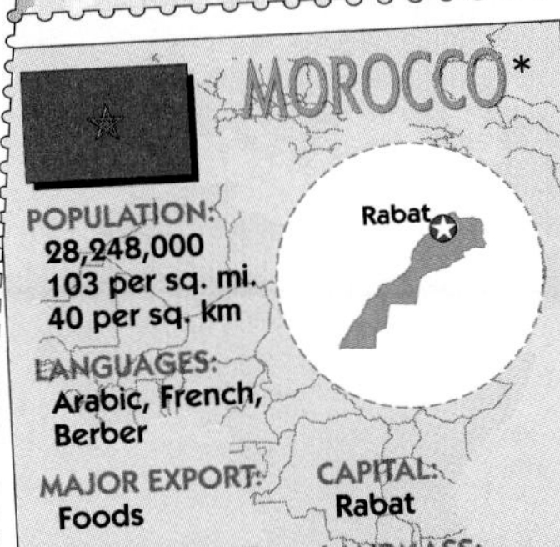
MOROCCO*
POPULATION:
28,248,000
103 per sq. mi.
40 per sq. km
LANGUAGES:
Arabic, French,
Berber
MAJOR EXPORT:
Foods
MAJOR IMPORT:
Manufactured
Goods
CAPITAL:
Rabat
LANDMASS:
275,117 sq. mi.
712,550 sq. km
Rabat

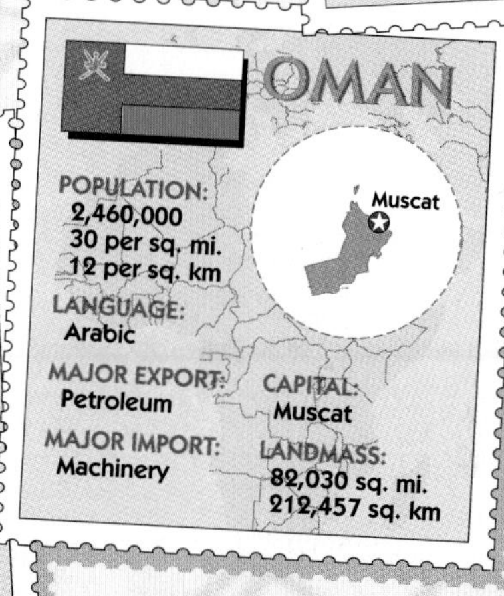
OMAN
POPULATION:
2,460,000
30 per sq. mi.
12 per sq. km
LANGUAGE:
Arabic
MAJOR EXPORT:
Petroleum
MAJOR IMPORT:
Machinery
CAPITAL:
Muscat
LANDMASS:
82,030 sq. mi.
212,457 sq. km
Muscat

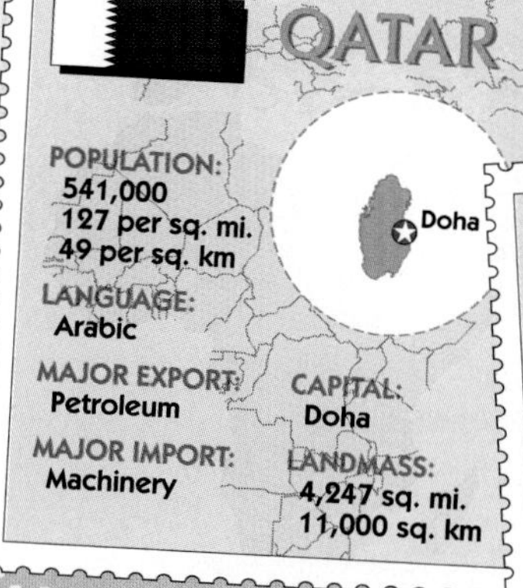
QATAR
POPULATION:
541,000
127 per sq. mi.
49 per sq. km
LANGUAGE:
Arabic
MAJOR EXPORT:
Petroleum
MAJOR IMPORT:
Machinery
CAPITAL:
Doha
LANDMASS:
4,247 sq. mi.
11,000 sq. km
Doha

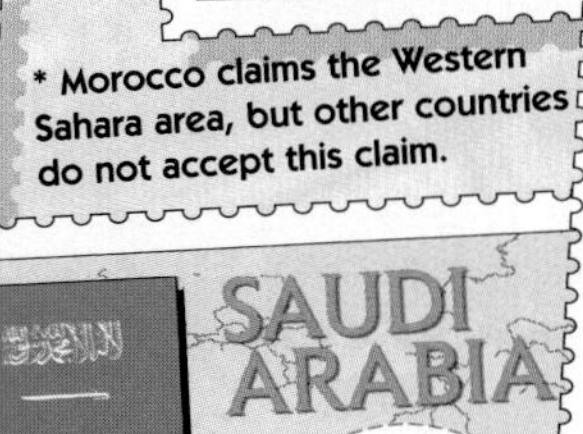
* Morocco claims the Western Sahara area, but other countries do not accept this claim.

SAUDI ARABIA
POPULATION:
20,899,000
25 per sq. mi.
10 per sq. km
LANGUAGE:
Arabic
MAJOR EXPORT:
Petroleum
MAJOR IMPORT:
Machinery
CAPITAL:
Riyadh
LANDMASS:
830,000 sq. mi.
2,149,690 sq. km
Riyadh

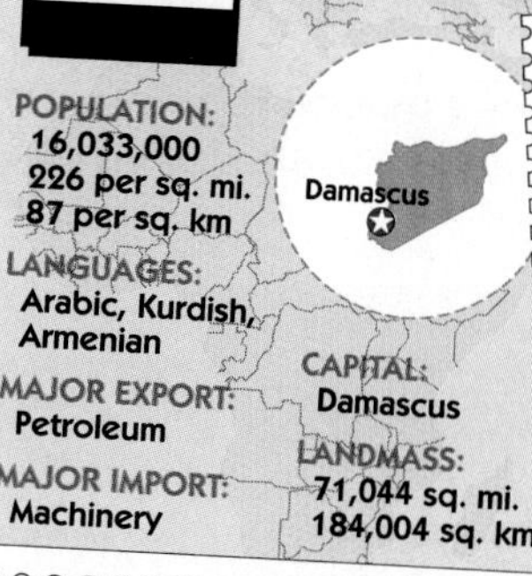
SYRIA
POPULATION:
16,033,000
226 per sq. mi.
87 per sq. km
LANGUAGES:
Arabic, Kurdish,
Armenian
MAJOR EXPORT:
Petroleum
MAJOR IMPORT:
Machinery
CAPITAL:
Damascus
LANDMASS:
71,044 sq. mi.
184,004 sq. km
Damascus

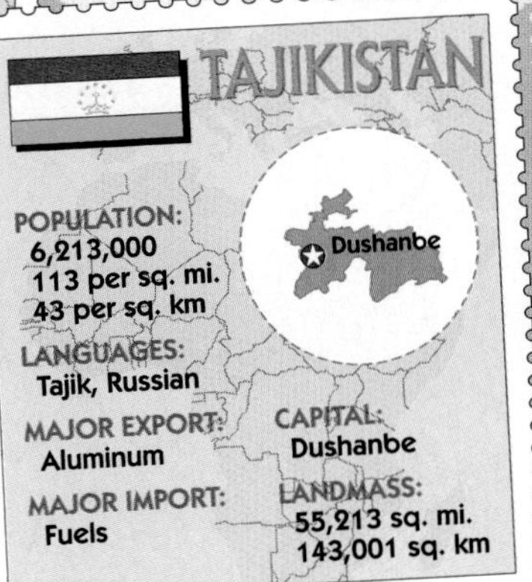
TAJIKISTAN
POPULATION:
6,213,000
113 per sq. mi.
43 per sq. km
LANGUAGES:
Tajik, Russian
MAJOR EXPORT:
Aluminum
MAJOR IMPORT:
Fuels
CAPITAL:
Dushanbe
LANDMASS:
55,213 sq. mi.
143,001 sq. km
Dushanbe

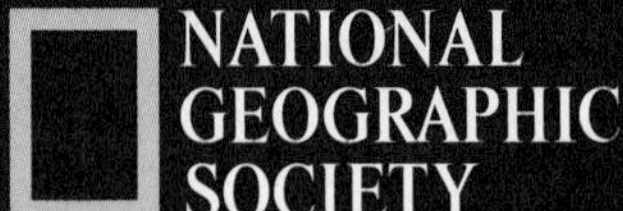

REGIONAL ATLAS

Country Profiles

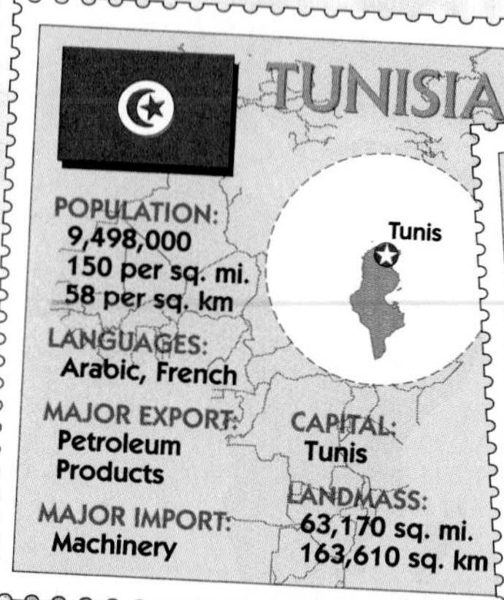

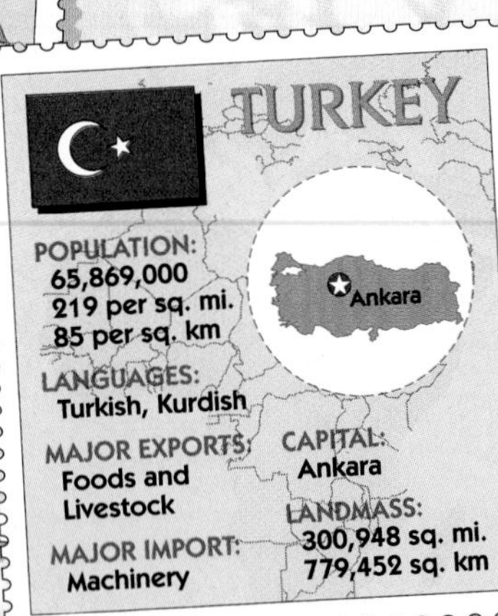

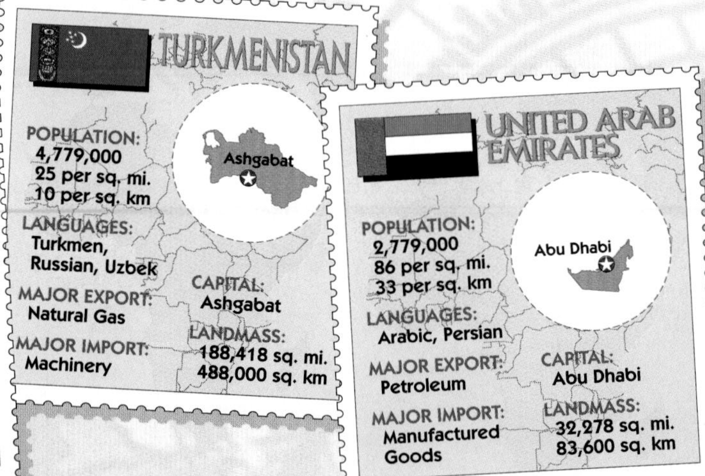

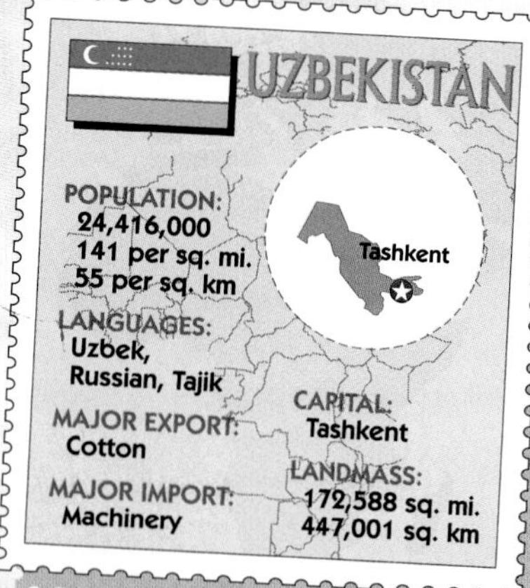

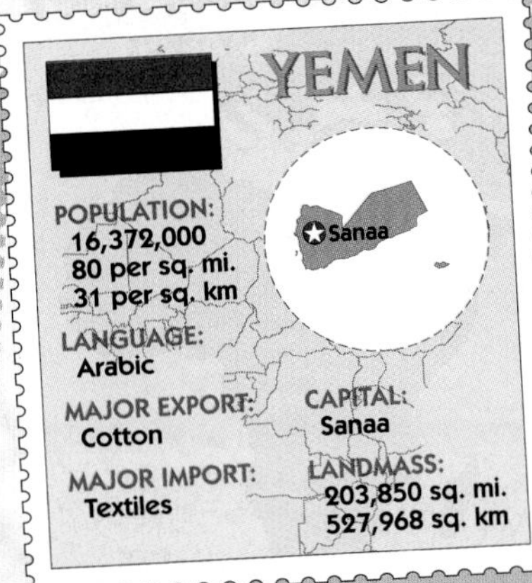

GEO BEE Questions From Buzz Bee!

The following questions are taken from National Geographic GeoBees. Use your textbook, the Internet, and other library resources to find the answers.

1. Which of the countries in North Africa has a king as head of state?
2. Which African capital city is only 150 miles (241 km) from Sicily?
3. The name of a group of people who have traditionally been nomadic herders comes from an Arabic word that means "desert dwellers." Name this group.

Anthias fish and coral reef,
Red Sea, Egypt

Chapter 16

North Africa

The World and Its People NATIONAL GEOGRAPHIC

To learn more about the people and places of North Africa, view ***The World and Its People*** **Chapter 16** video.

Geography Online

Chapter Overview Visit the ***Geography: The World and Its People*** Web site at gwip.glencoe.com and click on **Chapter 16–Chapter Overviews** to preview information about North Africa.

Section 1 Egypt

Guide to Reading

Main Idea

Egypt's Nile River and desert landscape have shaped the lives of the Egyptian people for centuries.

Terms to Know

- delta
- silt
- oasis
- phosphate
- hieroglyphics
- republic
- fellahin
- bazaar
- mosque

Places to Locate

- Nile River
- Sinai Peninsula
- Suez Canal
- Red Sea
- Eastern Desert
- Libyan Desert
- Sahara
- Cairo
- Alexandria

Reading Strategy

Draw a chart like this. Then list five physical features of Egypt and their effects on life in Egypt.

Physical Feature	Effect on Egyptians
→	
→	
→	
→	
→	

◀ The pyramids at El Giza, Egypt

NATIONAL GEOGRAPHIC **Exploring Our World**

What do you think of when you hear the name "Egypt"? Many people think of the ancient pyramids, the Nile River, or King "Tut." The Egyptian ruler Tutankhamun, or "Tut," lived for only about 18 years. Because his tomb was discovered in 1922 untouched by grave robbers, he is the ruler most people remember. This magnificent gold mask was found in his tomb.

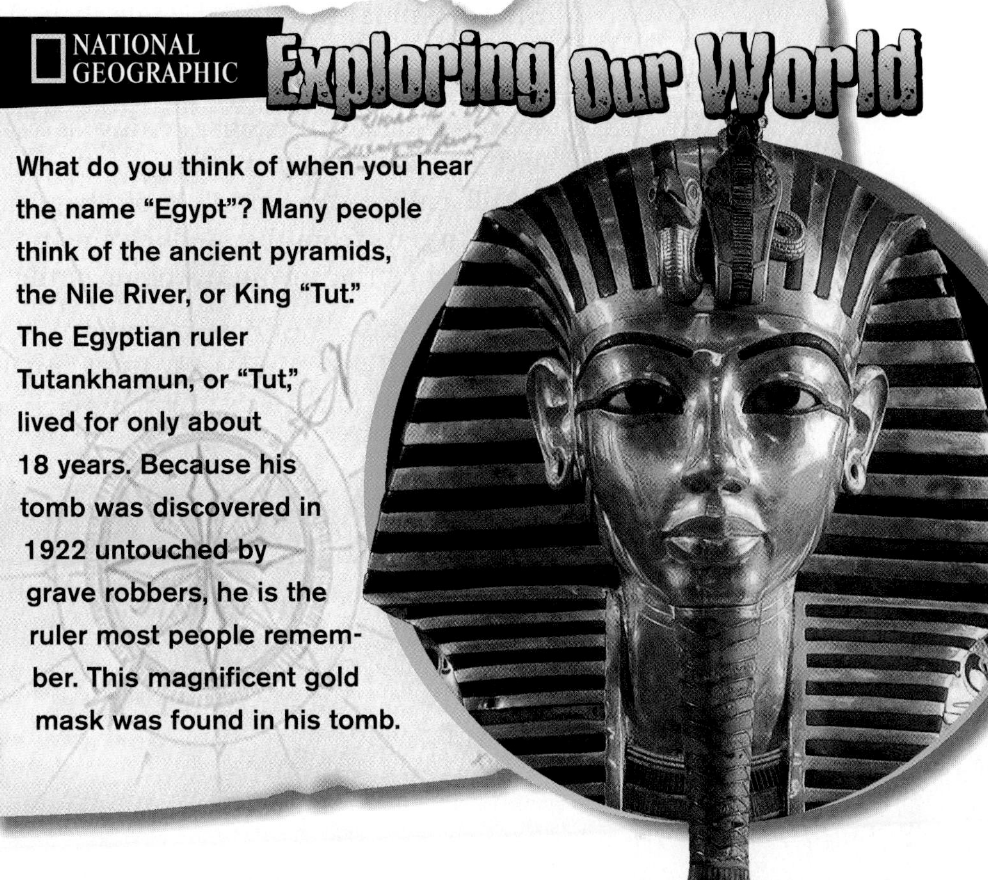

Egypt lies in Africa's northeast corner. Vast deserts sweep over most of the country. On the map on page 459, notice the blue line running through Egypt. This is the **Nile River.** Egypt's location, deserts, and above all, the Nile have shaped life in Egypt for thousands of years.

Egypt's Land and Climate

Egypt is a large country about the same size as Texas and New Mexico together. Yet most of it is desert. So Egypt's people crowd into less than 4 percent of the land, or an area a little larger than the size of Maryland. The lifeline of Egypt is the Nile River, which supplies 85 percent of the country's water. From its sources in East Africa, the river flows 4,241 miles (6,825 km) north to the Mediterranean Sea. This long journey makes the Nile the world's longest river. Along the Nile's banks, you can see mud-brick villages, ancient ruins, and, once in a while, a city or town of modern buildings. Where the river empties into the Mediterranean Sea, you find the Nile's delta. A **delta** is the area formed from soil deposited by a river at its mouth. The Nile delta is a fan-shaped area where the Nile splits into several smaller waterways.

For centuries, the Nile's waters would rise in the spring. The swollen river carried **silt,** or small particles of rich soil. When it reached Egypt, the Nile flooded its banks. As the floodwaters receded, the silt was left behind and made the land good for farming. Today dams and channels control the river's flow and the irrigation of farmland.

Sinai Peninsula The triangle-shaped **Sinai** (SY•NY) **Peninsula** lies southeast of the Nile delta. This area is a major crossroads between Africa and Southwest Asia. A human-made waterway called the **Suez Canal** separates the Sinai Peninsula from the rest of Egypt. Egyptians and Europeans built the canal in the mid-1860s. Today the Suez Canal is still one of the world's most important waterways. Ships use the canal to pass from the Mediterranean Sea to the **Red Sea.** In making this journey, they avoid traveling all the way around Africa.

Desert Areas Vast deserts cover most of Egypt. East of the Nile River spreads the **Eastern Desert,** also known as the Arabian Desert. West of the Nile is the much larger **Libyan** (LIH•bee•uhn) **Desert,** which covers

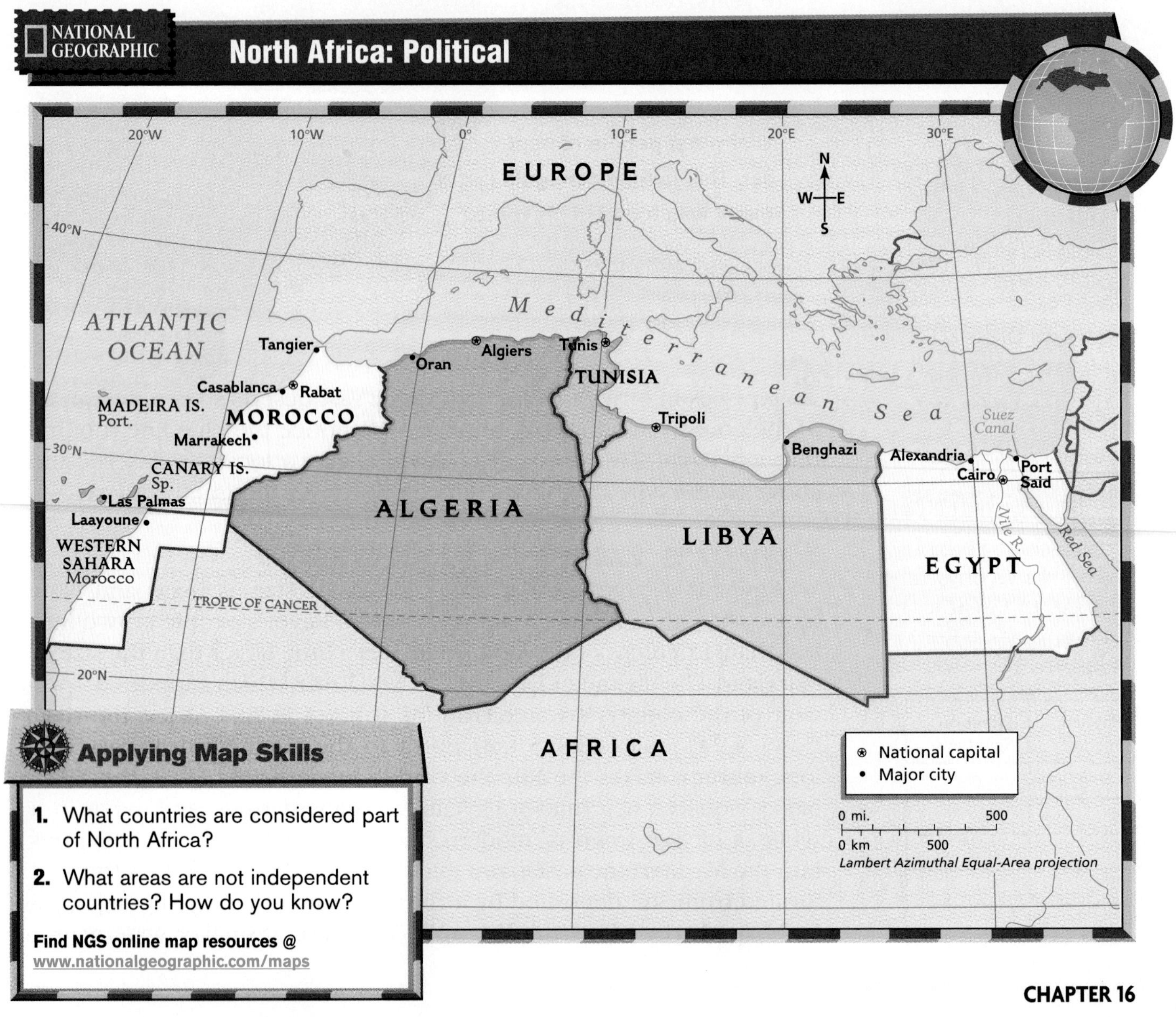

Applying Map Skills

1. What countries are considered part of North Africa?
2. What areas are not independent countries? How do you know?

Find NGS online map resources @ www.nationalgeographic.com/maps

about two-thirds of the country. Dotting both deserts are oases, or areas fed by underground water. The water allows plants to grow, giving these spots lush green growth in the midst of the hot sands.

The Eastern and Libyan Deserts are part of the **Sahara**—one of the largest desert areas in the world. *Sahara* comes from the Arabic word meaning "desert." The Sahara—about the size of the United States—stretches from Egypt westward across North Africa to the Atlantic Ocean.

Climate Wherever you go in Egypt, you find a dry desert climate of hot summers and mild winters. Egypt as a whole receives little rainfall. **Cairo,** the capital, averages only about 0.4 inch (1 cm) a year. In fact, some areas receive no rain for years at a time.

Springtime in Egypt brings hot winds instead of cooling rains. These winds move west across Egypt, reaching up to 87 miles (140 km) per hour. The powerful winds can harm crops and damage houses.

✓Reading Check **Why is the Suez Canal one of the world's most important waterways?**

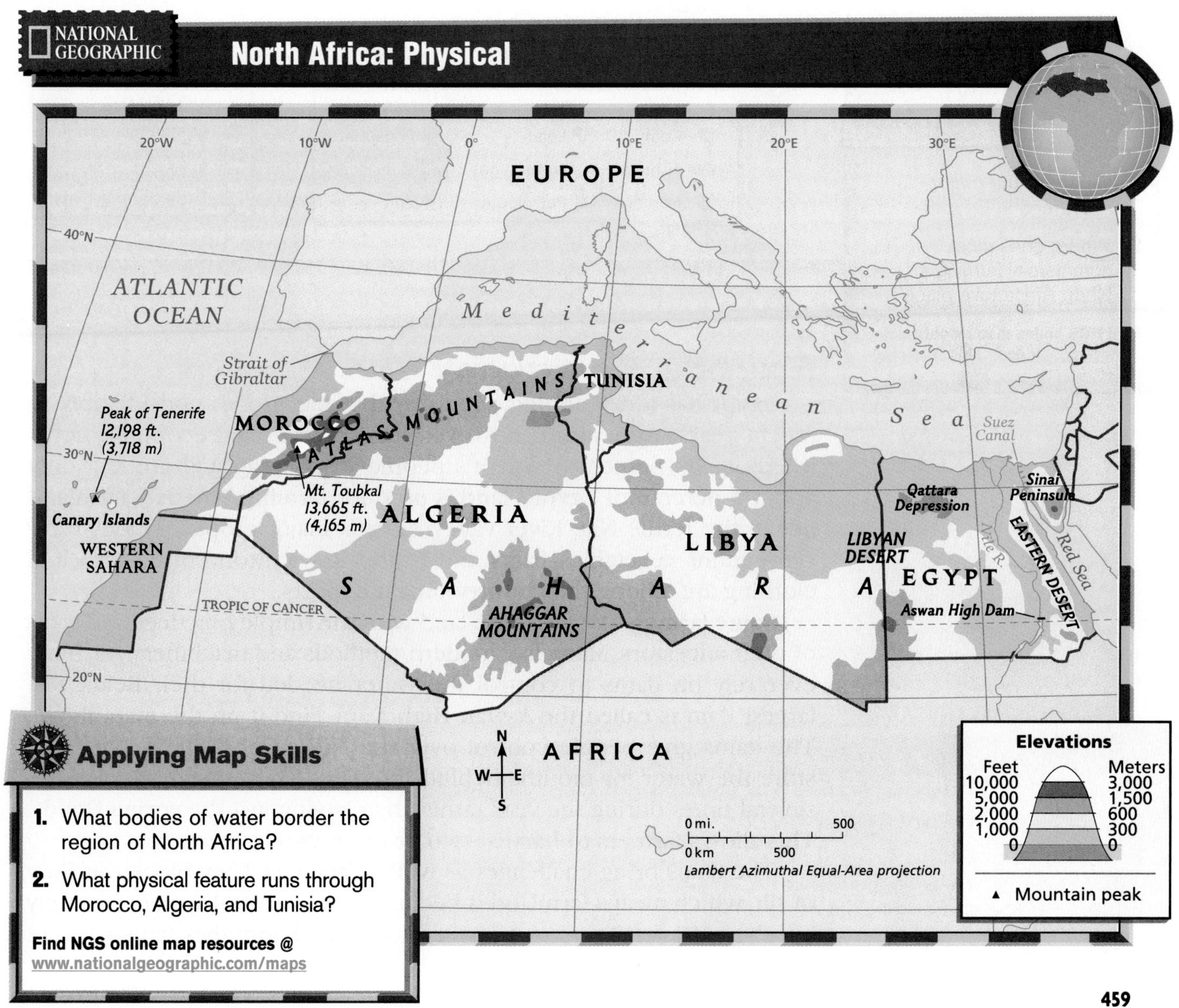

Applying Map Skills

1. What bodies of water border the region of North Africa?
2. What physical feature runs through Morocco, Algeria, and Tunisia?

Find NGS online map resources @ www.nationalgeographic.com/maps

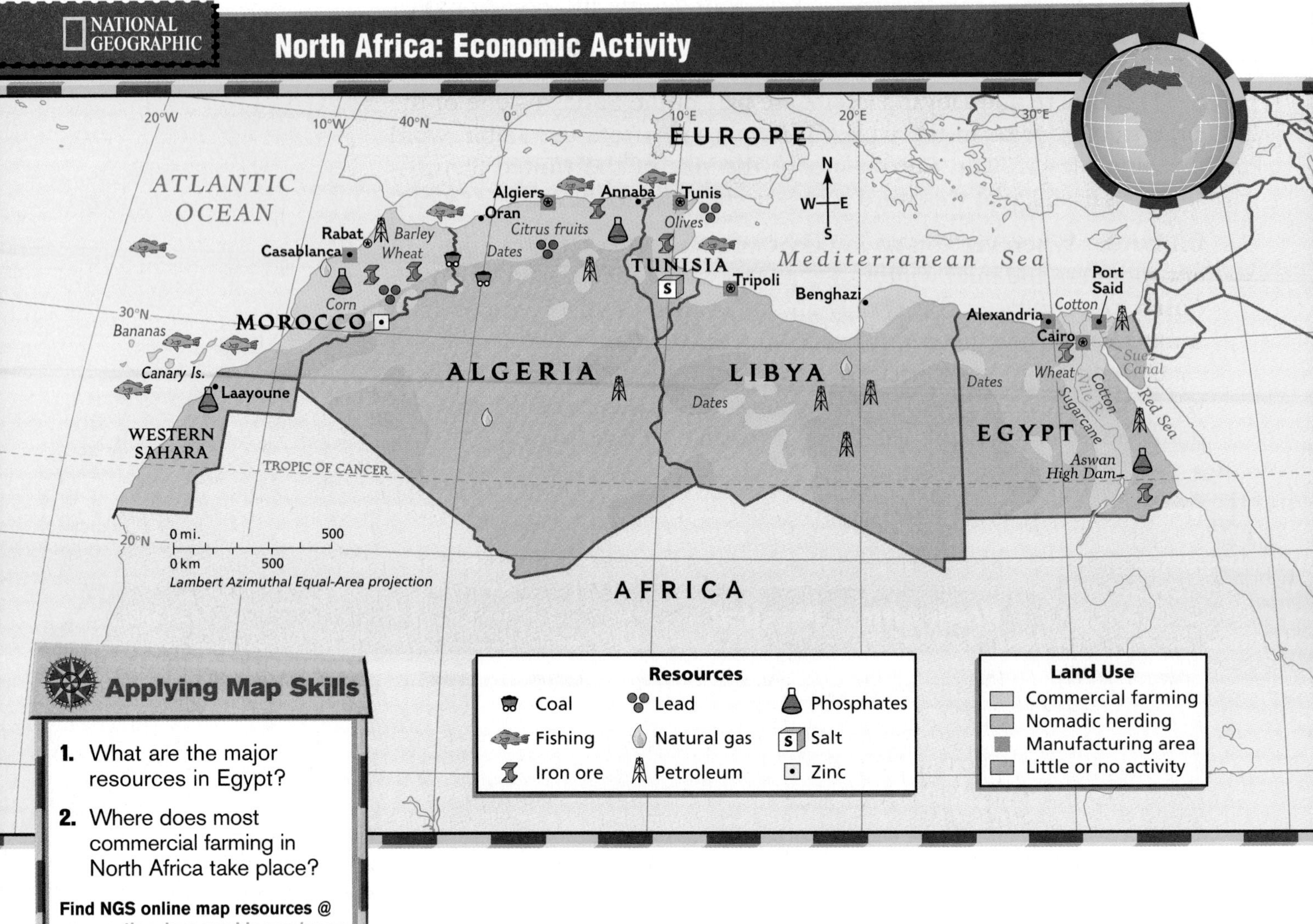

Applying Map Skills

1. What are the major resources in Egypt?
2. Where does most commercial farming in North Africa take place?

Find NGS online map resources @ www.nationalgeographic.com/maps

Egypt's Economy

Egypt has a developing economy that has grown considerably in recent years. Agriculture, however, remains the main economic activity. About 40 percent of Egypt's people work in agriculture, but only about 4 percent of Egypt's land is used for farming. The best farmland lies in the fertile Nile River valley. Egypt's major crops include sugarcane, grains, vegetables, fruits, and cotton. Raw cotton, cotton yarn, and clothing are among the country's main exports.

Some farmers still work the land with the simple practices and tools of their ancestors. Many use modern methods and machinery. All, however, rely on dams to control the water needed for their fields. The largest dam is called the Aswan High Dam. Find it on the map above. The dams give people control over the Nile's floodwaters. They can store the water for months behind the dams. Then they can release it several times during the year, rather than having just the spring floods. This allows farmers to harvest two or three crops a year.

The dams bring challenges as well as benefits. They block the flow of silt, which means farmland is becoming less fertile. Farmers now rely on chemical fertilizers to grow crops. In addition, the dams prevent quantities of freshwater from reaching the delta. So salt water from the Mediterranean Sea now flows deeper into the delta, making the land less fertile.

Industry The Aswan High Dam provides hydroelectric power, which Egypt uses to run its growing industries. The largest industrial centers are the capital city of Cairo and the seaport of **Alexandria.** Egyptian factories make food products, textiles, and consumer goods.

Egypt's main energy resource is oil, found in and around the Red Sea. Petroleum products make up almost half the value of Egypt's exports. The country also has iron ore and phosphates. **Phosphate** is a mineral salt used in fertilizers. Another important industry is tourism. Visitors come to see the magnificent ruins of ancient Egypt.

✓Reading Check **On what crop are many of Egypt's exports based?**

Ramses II

When the Aswan High Dam was built, it blocked the flow of the Nile River and created a reservoir 300 miles (483 km) long. This reservoir, called Lake Nasser, covered land on which 50,000 Egyptians lived. They were moved to a new location. The lake waters also would have covered four colossal statues of Ramses II built into a cliff temple. These statues, measuring 66 feet (20 m) in height, were moved as well. An international team of engineers and scientists dug away the top of the cliff and took apart the statues and temple. They rebuilt them on high ground 200 feet (61 m) above their original location. In all, some 16,000 blocks were moved.

Egypt's History and People

Egypt's fascinating past began about 8,000 years ago, when people first settled along the Nile to farm. In about 3100 B.C., one king brought several small kingdoms together under one rule. Egypt emerged as a powerful nation. For most of the next 3,000 years, Egypt was ruled by a line of pharaohs, or kings. To show the pharaohs' wealth and power, stonecutters and laborers built huge pyramids and majestic temples. Turn to page 463 to learn how the magnificent pyramids were built.

The people of early Egypt created one of the world's most advanced civilizations. They wrote using **hieroglyphics,** or picture signs and symbols. They made paper from papyrus, a reed that grew along the banks of the Nile. Other Egyptian achievements were the invention of a calendar to keep track of the growing season and medical skills to treat injuries and diseases.

From 300 B.C. to A.D. 300, Egypt fell under the influence of Greece and Rome. You may have heard of Cleopatra, an Egyptian queen who ruled during the time of Rome's rise as a Mediterranean power. In A.D. 641, Arabs from Southwest Asia took control of Egypt. They practiced Islam, a religion based on the belief in one God known as Allah. Most of Egypt's people began to speak the Arabic language and became Muslims, as the followers of Islam are called. Today about 94 percent of Egypt's people are Muslims.

Egypt's Modern History By the end of the 1800s, all of Egypt, including the Suez Canal, had become part of the British Empire. Unhappy with British rule, the people of Egypt protested many times. Finally, in 1952 a group of army officers overthrew the British-supported king, and Egypt became independent. One of the army leaders, Gamal Abdel Nasser (guh•MAHL AHB•duhl NAH•suhr), was Egypt's president from 1954 to 1970. Nasser made Egypt one of the most powerful countries in the Muslim world.

Egypt is a **republic,** or a government headed by a president. A legislature makes the laws, but the president has broad powers in running the country. In recent years, various political groups have opposed the government. These groups have used armed attacks in an effort to reach their political goals. The government has tried to stop this violence.

Web Activity Visit the ***Geography: The World and Its People*** Web site at gwip.glencoe.com and click on **Chapter 16–Student Web Activities** to learn more about Egypt's history.

Rural and Urban Life Look at the population density map on page 467. Most of Egypt's 66.9 million people live within 20 miles (32 km) of the Nile River. More than half of Egypt's people live in rural areas. Most are farmers called **fellahin** (FEHL•uh•HEEN). They live in villages and farm small plots of land that they rent from landowners. Many fellahin raise only enough food to feed their families. Any food left over is sold in towns at a **bazaar,** or marketplace.

Life is more modern in Egypt's cities. Many city dwellers have jobs in service, manufacturing, or construction industries. In bustling ports like Alexandria and Port Said (sah•EED), people engage in trade. Cairo is a huge and rapidly growing city. Almost 7 million people are crowded into its central area, with another 6 million living in its suburbs. It is the largest city in Africa. For centuries, Cairo has been a leading center of the Muslim world. Throughout the city you see schools, universities, and **mosques,** or places of worship for followers of Islam.

Cairo's population is increasing at a rapid rate. Why? First, Egypt is a country with a high birthrate. Second, many fellahin have moved to Cairo to find work. The crowded city cannot provide enough houses, schools, and hospitals for all of its people.

Reading Check **When did Egypt become fully independent?**

Assessment

Defining Terms

1. **Define** delta, silt, oasis, phosphate, hieroglyphics, republic, fellahin, bazaar, mosque.

Recalling Facts

2. **Human/Environment Interaction** Why is the Nile River important to Egypt?
3. **History** What were three achievements of the ancient Egyptians?
4. **Culture** What are the major language and religion of Egypt?

Critical Thinking

5. **Understanding Cause and Effect** How has the Aswan High Dam affected farmers?
6. **Making Predictions** If violence in Egypt continues, what effect do you think it could have on the economy?

Graphic Organizer

7. **Organizing Information** In a chart like the one below, fill in three facts about Egypt for each category.

Agriculture	Industry
1.	1.
2.	2.
3.	3.

Applying Geography Skills

8. **Analyzing Maps** Study the political map on page 458. What direction is Alexandria from Cairo?

Making Connections

ART SCIENCE LITERATURE TECHNOLOGY

The Egyptian Pyramids

The ancient Egyptians viewed the pharaoh, or king, as the most important person on the earth. They believed he was a god who would continue to guide them after his death. A pyramid served as a tomb for the pharaoh and provided a place where the body would safely pass into the afterlife. Rooms inside the pyramid held food, clothing, weapons, furniture, jewels, and everything else the pharaoh might need in the afterlife.

The Great Pyramid at El Giza

The largest of Egypt's pyramids is the Great Pyramid of El Giza, built nearly 5,000 years ago. When the pyramid was new, it stood 481 feet (147 m) high—as tall as a 50-story building. The square base of the pyramid covers 13 acres (5 ha). More than 2 million limestone and granite blocks were used in building it. These are no ordinary-sized blocks, however. The huge stones weigh an average of 2.5 tons (2.3 t) each.

Construction

For thousands of years, people have wondered how the Egyptians built the pyramids without modern tools or machinery. In 500 B.C., a Greek historian thought it took 100,000 people to build the Great Pyramid. Today archaeologists believe a workforce of about 20,000 did the job in about 20 years. Barges carried supplies and building materials for the pyramid down the Nile River. Nearby quarries supplied most of the stone. Skilled stonecutters carved the stones into the precise size and shape so that no mortar, or cementing material, was needed to hold the stones together.

Engineers think that workers built ramps and used papyrus twine to drag the huge stones to the pyramid. They formed ramps up all four sides of the pyramid and made the ramps higher and longer as the pyramid rose. They then dragged the stones up the ramps. Once finished, the ramps were cleared away. Then stonemasons smoothed and polished the stone, and the finished pyramid towered over the surrounding desert.

Making the Connection

1. Why did the Egyptians build the pyramids?
2. How many workers did both ancient historians and modern archaeologists think it took to build the Great Pyramid?
3. **Sequencing Information** Describe the process experts think Egyptians used to build the pyramids.

◄ The Great Pyramid at El Giza, Egypt

Section 2

Libya and the Maghreb

Guide to Reading

Main Idea

The countries of Libya, Tunisia, Algeria, and Morocco share a desert environment and a mostly Arab culture.

Terms to Know

- aquifer
- dictatorship
- erg
- civil war
- secular
- casbah
- constitutional monarchy

Places to Locate

- Libya
- Tunisia
- Atlas Mountains
- Algeria
- Morocco
- Strait of Gibraltar
- Western Sahara

Reading Strategy

Draw a diagram like this one. In the four outer ovals, list facts about each country under their headings. In the center oval, write three facts that all four countries have in common.

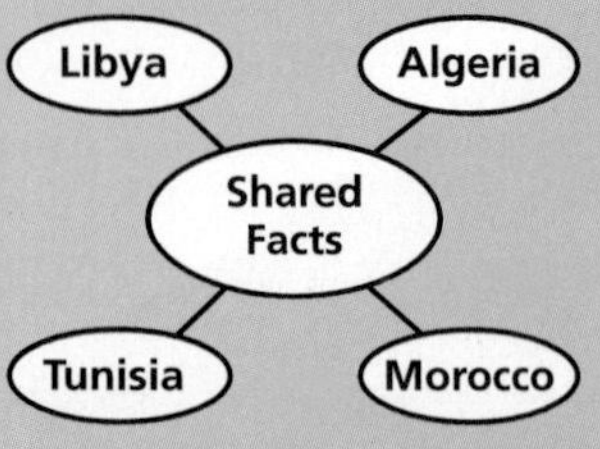

NATIONAL GEOGRAPHIC **Exploring Our World**

The Sahara is the world's largest hot desert. Some of its sand dunes reach 1,000 feet (305 m) high. Thousands of years ago, however, it was not a desert at all. Grass and trees covered the region. Evidence of this can be seen in 7,000-year-old rock carvings of giraffes found in the Sahara. Giraffes eat leaves on tall, healthy trees that need water to grow.

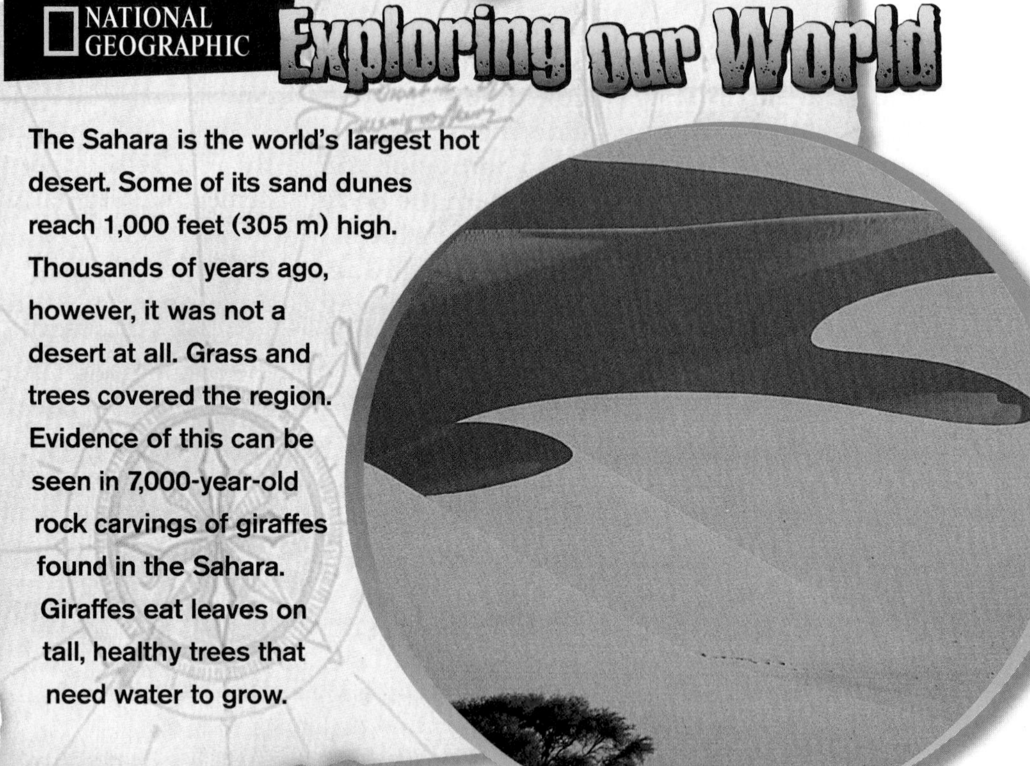

Tunisia, Algeria, and Morocco make up a region of North Africa commonly called the Maghreb (MUH•gruhb). Like Egypt, these countries plus Libya have economies based on oil and other resources in the Sahara. Unlike Egypt, however, none of these nations enjoys the benefits of a life-giving river such as the Nile.

Libya

Libya is slightly larger than Alaska. Two narrow strips of lowland stretch along Libya's Mediterranean coast. As you move about 50 miles (80 km) inland, the lowlands rise to a plateau in the center of the country. This lofty flatland climbs even higher to mountains in the south.

Except for the coastal lowlands, Libya is a desert area with only a few oases. In fact, the Sahara covers more than 90 percent of Libya. During the spring and fall, dust-heavy winds blow from the desert. When these fierce winds strike, temperatures in coastal areas can reach 110°F (43°C).

Libya has no permanent rivers, but aquifers lie beneath the vast desert. **Aquifers** are underground rock layers that store large amounts of water. In the 1990s, the government built pipelines to carry underground water from the desert to coastal areas.

Poor soil and a hot climate mean that Libya has to import about three-fourths of its food. The discovery of oil in Libya in 1959 brought the country great wealth. Libya's government uses oil money to buy food, build schools and hospitals, and maintain a strong military.

Libya's People and History Almost all of Libya's 5 million people have mixed Arab and Berber heritage. The Berbers were the first people known to live in North Africa. During the A.D. 600s, the Arabs brought Islam and the Arabic language to North Africa. Since then, Libya has been a Muslim country, and most of its people speak Arabic.

About 86 percent of Libyans live along the Mediterranean coast. Most live in two modern cities—Tripoli, the capital, and Benghazi (behn•GAH•zee). Libya became independent in 1951 under a king. In 1969 a military officer named Muammar al-Qaddhafi (kuh•DAH•fee) gained power and overthrew the king. Qaddhafi set up a **dictatorship**, or a government under the control of one all-powerful leader.

Reading Check How has Libya been governed since 1969?

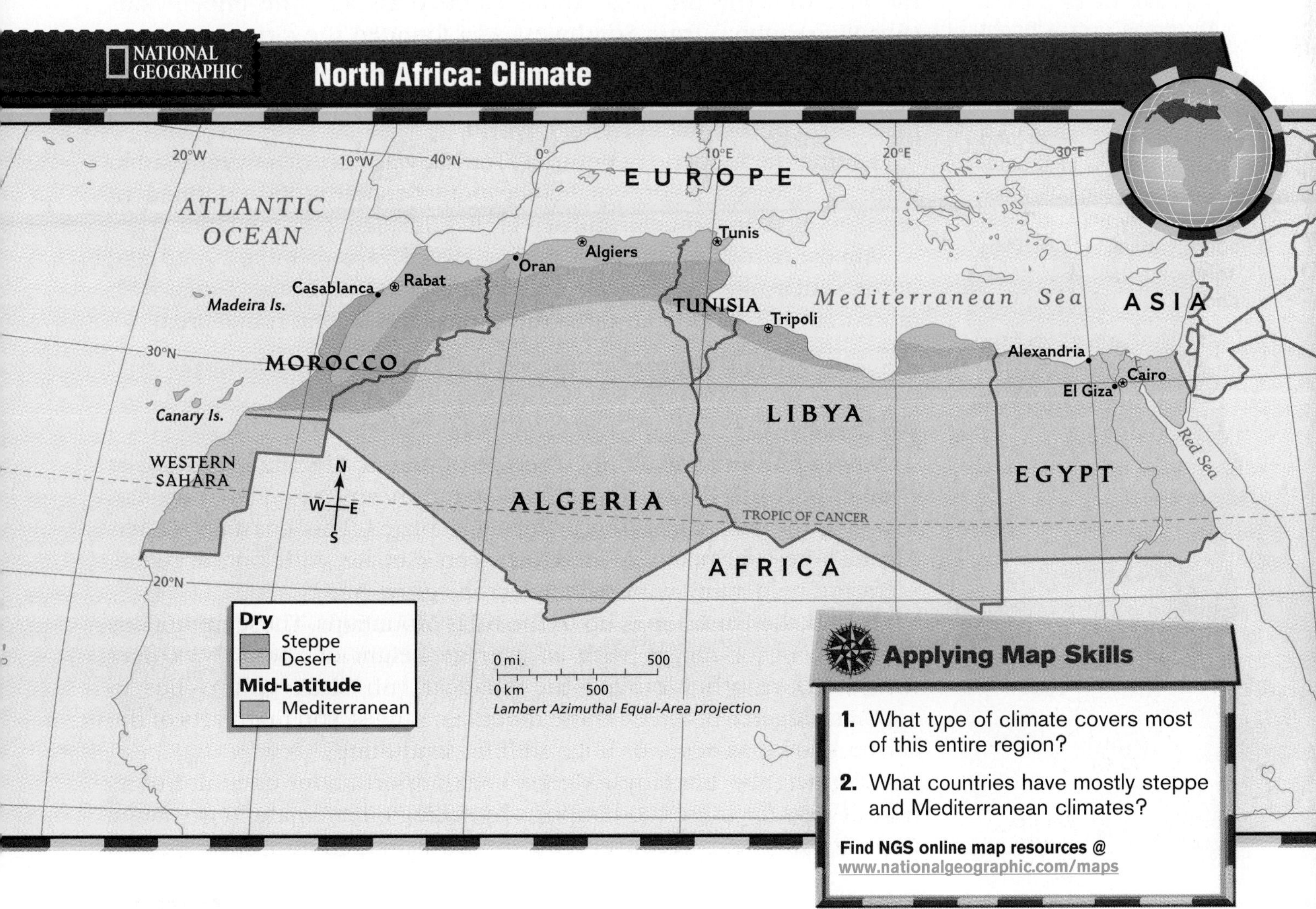

Applying Map Skills

1. What type of climate covers most of this entire region?
2. What countries have mostly steppe and Mediterranean climates?

Find NGS online map resources @ www.nationalgeographic.com/maps

Tunisia

Tunisia, Algeria, and Morocco form a region known as the Maghreb. *Maghreb* means "the land farthest west" in Arabic. These three countries were given this name because they are the westernmost part of the Arabic-speaking Muslim world.

About the size of the state of Georgia, **Tunisia** is North Africa's smallest country. Tunisia has a long Mediterranean coastline and desert areas. Low plains cover the coast and central part of the country. The **Atlas Mountains** reach into the northwest.

Farming and herding take place in much of Tunisia. The climate map on page 465 shows why this is so. Northern and central areas have Mediterranean or steppe climates, which provide some rainfall. Along the fertile eastern coast, farmers grow wheat, olives, fruits, and vegetables. Fishing is an important industry as well.

The country's major resources include phosphates, iron, oil, and natural gas. Tunisian factories produce food products, textiles, and oil products. In addition, tourism is a growing industry. Many visitors enjoy Tunisia's sunny shores and explore its Roman ruins and outdoor markets.

Bazaar!

Taha Hammam makes pottery to sell at the bazaar. "Going to the bazaar is a lot like going to an American mall," he says. "It's a big party where everyone talks and eats and buys and sells things." Taha lives in Algiers. Although Taha wears jeans and sneakers, his parents dress in traditional clothes. His mother wears a black outer dress over a bright housedress, and covers her hair with a long veil that reaches the ground. Taha's father dresses in a long robe. In school, Taha studies Arabic, religious studies, arithmetic, social studies, science, and art.

Tunisia's History and People Tunisia's coastal location has drawn people, ideas, and trade throughout the centuries. The Berbers were the first to settle the area. About 2,800 years ago, the Phoenicians (fih•NEE•shuhnz) from Southwest Asia founded the city of Carthage in the northern part of the country. This city was the center of a powerful trading empire. Carthage later fought unsuccessfully with Rome for control of the Mediterranean world.

During the following centuries, Tunisia was part of several Muslim empires. It was a colony of France until becoming an independent republic in 1956. You can still see French influence in the cities.

Almost all of Tunisia's 9.5 million people are of mixed Arab and Berber ancestry. They speak Arabic and practice Islam. Tunis, with more than 1,000,000 people, is the capital and largest urban area.

✓Reading Check **Why can farming and herding take place in Tunisia?**

Algeria

About one and a half times the size of Alaska, **Algeria** is the largest country in North Africa. Along the Mediterranean coast, you find a narrow strip of land consisting of hills and plains. This coastal area has Algeria's best farmland. A Mediterranean climate with hot, dry summers and mild, rainy winters helps crops grow here.

Inland, the land slopes up to the Atlas Mountains. These mountains form two major ranges with an average height of about 7,000 feet (2,134 m). Another range—the Ahaggar (uh•HAH•guhr)—lies in southern Algeria. Between these mountain ranges, you find parts of the Sahara known as **ergs,** or huge shifting sand dunes.

Like neighboring Libya, Algeria must import about one-third of its food. It pays for these food imports by selling oil and natural gas. Large deposits of these resources lie in the Sahara. They have helped

Algeria's industrial growth, but widespread poverty and lack of jobs still exist. Many Algerians have moved to France and other European countries to find work.

Algeria's History and People About 30.8 million people live in Algeria. The people here—as in Libya and Tunisia—have mixed Arab and Berber heritage. Most of them are Muslim and speak Arabic. If you visited Algeria, you would discover centuries-old Muslim traditions blending with those of France. Why? From 1834 to 1962, Algeria was a French colony. In 1954, Algerian Arabs wanting freedom rose up against the French. A bloody **civil war,** or conflict between different groups inside a country, erupted. When the fighting ended in 1962, Algeria won independence. Many of the French fled to France.

Today Algeria is a republic, with a strong president and a legislature. In the early 1990s, Muslim political parties formed that opposed many of the government's **secular,** or nonreligious, policies. The Muslims gained enough support to win a national election. The government, however, rejected the election results and imprisoned many Muslim opponents. A civil war began that has taken many lives.

Algiers is the country's capital and largest city. Nearly 2.2 million people live here. Many of them live in the newer sections of the city,

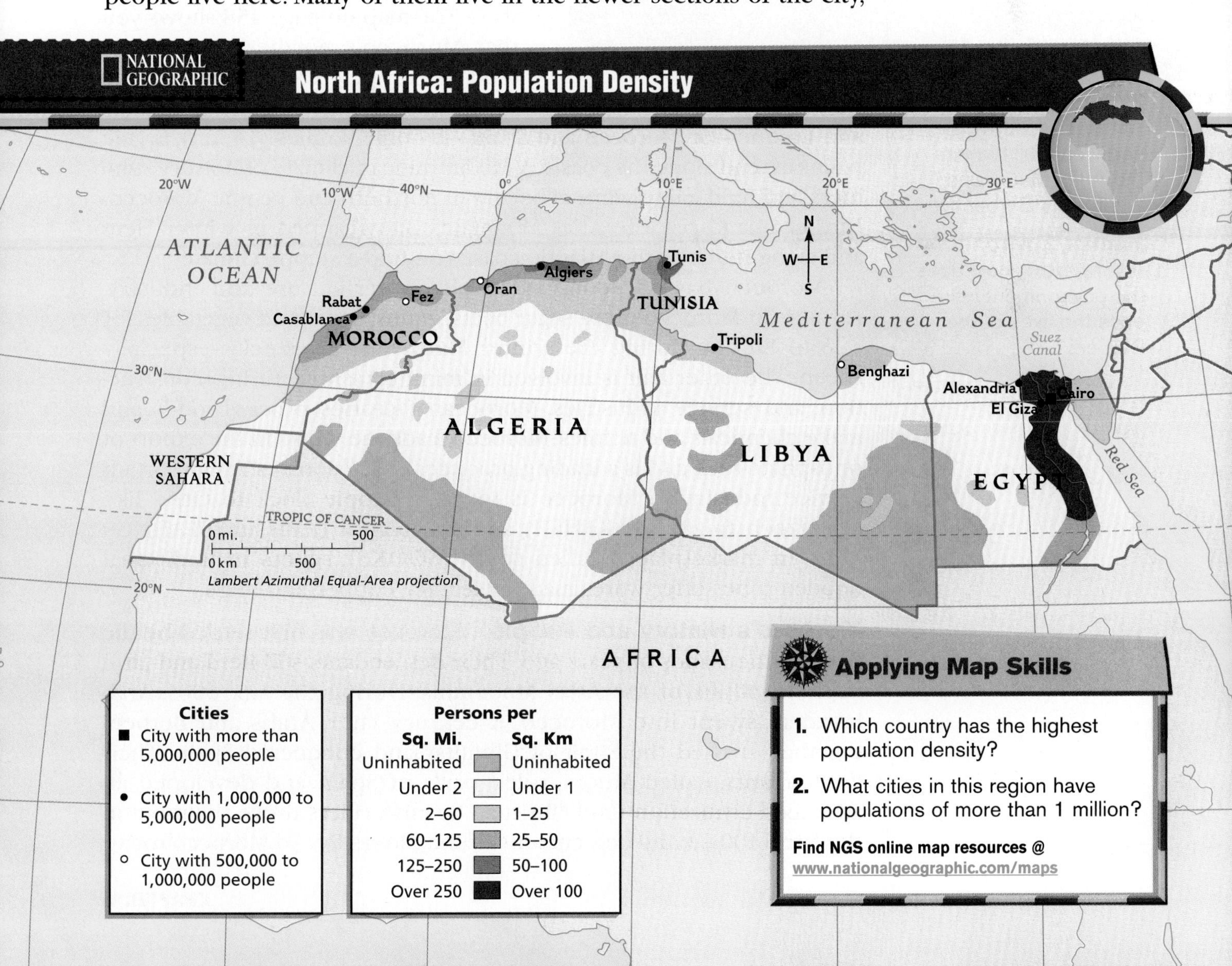

Applying Map Skills

1. Which country has the highest population density?
2. What cities in this region have populations of more than 1 million?

Find NGS online map resources @ www.nationalgeographic.com/maps

Even though North Africa is mostly hot, snow can fall high in the Atlas Mountains where this Berber lives.

Human/Environment Interaction How does the environment influence the lives of the Berbers?

with modern buildings and broad streets. They enjoy visiting the older sections of the city, though, which are called **casbahs.** There they walk down narrow streets, sometimes stopping to bargain with merchants in shops and bazaars. They might step into a historic mosque for their daily prayers. Many people in Algeria's cities speak French as well as Arabic.

✓ Reading Check **What conflict has affected life in Algeria since the early 1990s?**

Morocco

Slightly larger than the state of California, **Morocco** has a long coastline that borders two bodies of water—the Mediterranean Sea on the north and the Atlantic Ocean on the west. The map on page 458 shows you that Morocco's northern tip almost touches Europe. Here you will find the **Strait of Gibraltar.** It separates Africa and Europe—or Morocco and Spain—by only 9 miles (14 km). Fertile plains extend along the coasts. A Mediterranean climate of hot, dry summers and mild, rainy winters occurs in northern and central Morocco. Farther inland rise the Atlas Mountains, snowcapped in winter. Here and along much of the Atlantic coast, you find a steppe climate.

Morocco has an economy based on agriculture and industry. Farmers in Morocco grow sugar beets, grains, fruits, and vegetables for sale to Europe during the winter. Many raise livestock—especially sheep. The other half is involved in mining, manufacturing, construction, and service industries. Moroccan factories process foods and make chemicals and textiles. Morocco leads the world in the export of phosphate rock and is a leading producer of phosphates. An important service industry in Morocco is tourism. People flock to cities like Marrakech (mahr•uh•KEHSH) and Casablanca (KAH•suh•BLAHNG•kuh). In marketplaces called souks (SOOKS), sellers in traditional hooded robes offer wares made of leather, copper, and brass.

Morocco's History and People Morocco was first settled by the Berbers thousands of years ago. Their descendants still herd and farm in the foothills of the Atlas Mountains. During the A.D. 600s, Arab invaders swept into Morocco. A century later, Arabs and Berbers together crossed the Strait of Gibraltar and conquered Spain. Their descendants, called Moors, ruled parts of Spain and developed an advanced civilization until Christian Spanish rulers drove them out in the late 1400s. Many descendants of the Moors live in Morocco today.

As the Moors flourished in Spain, a Muslim kingdom prospered and ruled much of Morocco. In the early 1900s, the Moroccan kingdom weakened, and France and Spain gained control. In 1956 Morocco became independent once again. Today the country is a **constitutional monarchy.** In this form of government, a king or queen is head of state, but elected officials run the government. In Morocco, the monarch still holds many powers, however.

Beginning in the 1970s, Morocco claimed the desert region of **Western Sahara.** The discovery of phosphates there sparked a costly war between Morocco and a rebel group wanting Western Sahara to be independent. The United Nations wants to hold a vote that would allow the people of Western Sahara to decide their own future.

Morocco has about 28.2 million people. Most of them live in the coastal regions, but many also follow a traditional herding way of life in the mountains. Casablanca is Morocco's largest city, home to about 3 million people. Rabat, with a population of 1.2 million, is Morocco's capital.

Morocco's traditional culture is based on Arab, Berber, and African traditions. Moroccan music today blends the rhythms of these groups, sometimes with a dash of European pop and rock. Morocco also is known for its skilled artisans who make a variety of goods, such as carpets, pottery, jewelry, brassware, and woodwork.

Reading Check **Who were the Moors?**

Section 2 Assessment

Defining Terms

1. **Define** aquifer, dictatorship, erg, civil war, secular, casbah, constitutional monarchy.

Recalling Facts

2. **History** Who were the Berbers?
3. **Culture** Why do many Algerians speak French?
4. **History** Why is there a dispute over control of Western Sahara?

Critical Thinking

5. **Making Generalizations** How have the physical features of North Africa affected where people live?
6. **Analyzing Information** How might the countries studied in this section improve their economies?

Graphic Organizer

7. **Organizing Information** Draw a diagram like the one below. Choose one country from this section and fill in each outer part of the diagram with a fact about that country.

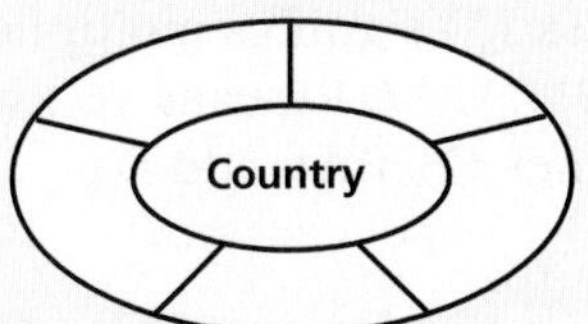

Applying Geography Skills

8. **Analyzing Maps** Study the political map on page 458. Rabat is located on the coast of which country? Along what body of water is it located?

Technology Skill

Using a Spreadsheet

A **spreadsheet** is an electronic worksheet that can manage numbers quickly and easily. Spreadsheets are powerful tools because you can change or update information, and the spreadsheet automatically performs the calculations.

Learning the Skill

All spreadsheets follow a basic design of rows and columns. Each column is assigned a letter, and each row is assigned a number. Each point where a column and a row intersect is called a *cell.* The cell's position on the spreadsheet is labeled according to its corresponding column and row—*A1* is column A, row 1; *B2* is column B, row 2, and so on.

Spreadsheets use *formulas* to calculate numbers. To create a formula, highlight the cell you want the results in. Type an equal sign (=) and then build the formula, step-by-step. If you type the formula *=B4+B5+B6* in cell B7, the numbers in these cells are added together, and the sum shows up in cell B7.

To use division, the formula would look like this: *=A5/C2.* This divides A5 by C2. An asterisk (*) signifies multiplication: *=(B2*C3)+D1* means you want to multiply B2 times C3, then add D1.

Practicing the Skill

Use these steps to create a spreadsheet.

1. In cells B1, C1, and D1, type the years 1980, 1990, and 2000. In cell E1, type the word *Total.*
2. In cells A2 through A6, type the names of North Africa's countries. In cell A7, type the word *Total.*
3. In row 2, enter the number of tons of oil produced by Algeria in 1980, 1990, and 2000.
4. Repeat step 3 in rows 3 through 6 for each country. You can find the information you need for each country in a world almanac or an encyclopedia.
5. Create a formula that tells which cells to add together so the computer can calculate the number of tons of oil for each country. For example, in cell E2, you should type *=B2+C2+D2* to find the total amount of oil Algeria produced in those years.

B2 =

	A	B	C	D	E
1		1980	1990	2000	Total
2	Algeria				
3	Egypt				
4	Libya				
5	Morocco				
6	Tunisia				
7	Total				
8					

▲ **The computer highlights the cell in which you are working.**

Applying the Skill

Use the spreadsheet you have created to answer these questions: Which country is the largest producer of oil? Has it always been number one? Are countries in North Africa together producing more oil or less oil today than they did 20 years ago?

Chapter 16

Reading Review

Section 1 Egypt

Terms to Know

delta
silt
oasis
phosphate
hieroglyphics
republic
fellahin
bazaar
mosque

Main Idea

Egypt's Nile River and desert landscape have shaped the lives of the Egyptian people for centuries.

✓ Location Most people of Egypt live along the Nile River or in its delta.

✓ Economics Forty percent of Egypt's workers live by farming, but industry has grown in recent years.

✓ History The people of ancient Egypt built a rich and highly accomplished civilization.

✓ Culture Today most people in Egypt are Muslims who follow the religion of Islam.

✓ Culture More people in Egypt live in rural areas than in cities, but Cairo is the largest city in Africa.

Section 2 Libya and the Maghreb

Terms to Know

aquifer
dictatorship
erg
civil war
secular
casbah
constitutional monarchy

Main Idea

The countries of Libya, Tunisia, Algeria, and Morocco share a desert environment and a mostly Arab culture.

✓ Region North Africa includes Libya and the three countries called the Maghreb—Tunisia, Algeria, and Morocco.

✓ Location These countries are all located on the Mediterranean Sea. Morocco also has a coast along the Atlantic Ocean.

✓ Region The landscape of this region is mostly desert and mountains.

✓ Economics Oil, natural gas, and phosphates are among the important resources in these countries.

✓ Culture Most of the people in these countries are Muslims and speak Arabic. Most also are of mixed Arab and Berber heritage.

◀ Desert areas begin where the fertile Nile River Valley ends.

Chapter 16

Assessment and Activities

Using Key Terms

Match the terms in Part A with their definitions in Part B.

A.

1. oasis
2. secular
3. delta
4. casbah
5. bazaar
6. dictatorship
7. silt
8. erg
9. aquifer
10. hieroglyphics

B.

a. government under a single leader
b. underground rock layer that stores water
c. old area of cities with narrow streets and small shops
d. marketplace
e. area formed by soil at a river's mouth
f. water and vegetation surrounded by desert
g. nonreligious
h. desert region of shifting sand dunes
i. particles of soil deposited by water
j. ancient form of Egyptian writing

Reviewing the Main Ideas

Section 1 Egypt

11. **Place** What is the capital of Egypt?
12. **Movement** What two bodies of water does the Suez Canal connect?
13. **Economics** Name four of Egypt's agricultural products.
14. **Culture** What huge monuments are a symbol of Egypt?
15. **Government** What type of government does Egypt have today?

Section 2 Libya and the Maghreb

16. **Human/Environment Interaction** Why must Libya depend on aquifers for water?
17. **Region** What does *maghreb* mean?
18. **History** Who founded the city of Carthage in Tunisia?
19. **History** What foreign country controlled Algeria from 1834 to 1962?
20. **Economics** What energy resource is important to almost all of North Africa's countries?

NATIONAL GEOGRAPHIC **North Africa**

Place Location Activity

On a separate sheet of paper, match the letters on the map with the numbered places listed below.

1. Red Sea
2. Morocco
3. Libya
4. Algeria
5. Atlas Mountains
6. Nile River
7. Cairo
8. Tunisia
9. Tripoli
10. Sinai Peninsula

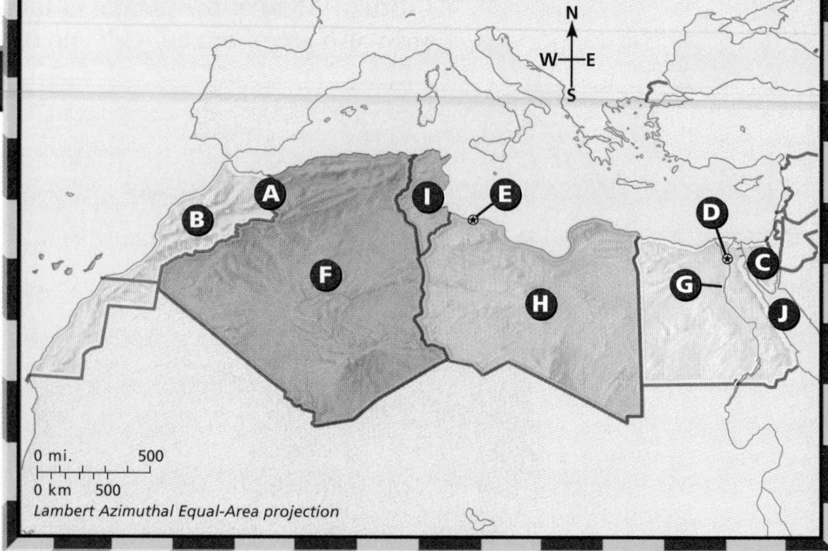

Self-Check Quiz Visit the ***Geography: The World and Its People*** Web site at gwip.glencoe.com and click on **Chapter 16—Self-Check Quizzes** to prepare for the Chapter Test.

Critical Thinking

21. **Understanding Cause and Effect** Why are the most densely populated areas of North Africa along the Mediterranean Sea and the Nile River?
22. **Sequencing Information** On a time line like the one below, label five events or eras in Egyptian history. Include their dates.

GeoJournal Activity

23. **Writing a Dialogue** Imagine that one of the pharaohs of ancient Egypt is able to visit modern times. Write down the conversation you might have as you take him on a tour of Egypt today. Describe the places you would visit. Explain the contrasts between the way people in Egypt live today and the past. What similarities between the past and present will the pharaoh find?

Mental Mapping Activity

24. **Focusing on the Region** Draw a simple outline map of North Africa, then label the following:

- Mediterranean Sea
- Red Sea
- Atlantic Ocean
- Nile River
- Atlas Mountains
- Egypt
- Libya
- Morocco
- Tunisia
- Algeria

Technology Skills Activity

25. **Using the Internet** Use the Internet to research life in the desert. Besides the Sahara, what other large deserts are there in the world? What kinds of life do deserts support? How do humans adapt to life in the desert? Are deserts changing in size and shape? Why? Use your research to create a bulletin board display on "Desert Life."

Standardized Test Practice

Directions: Study the graph, then answer the following question.

Percentage of North Africa's People Living in Each Country

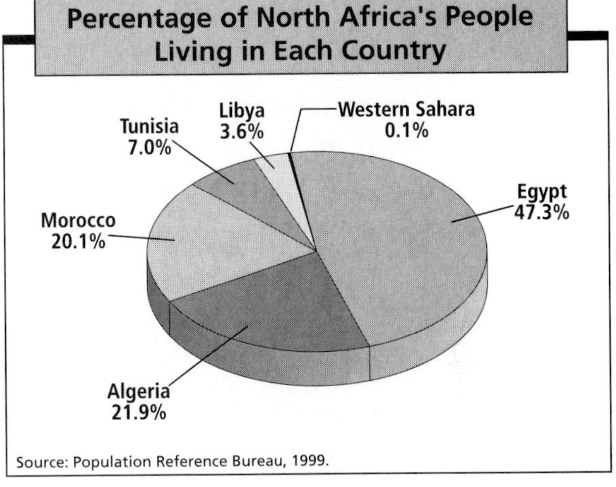

Source: Population Reference Bureau, 1999.

1. **According to the graph above, which one of the following statements is true?**

F Almost half of the people of North Africa live in Egypt.

G Almost half of the people of North Africa live in Algeria.

H Egypt's land area is much larger than Algeria's land area.

J Algeria's land area is much larger than Libya's land area.

Test-Taking Tip: When analyzing circle or pie graphs, first look at the title to see what the graph shows. Next read each section of the "pie" and compare the sections to one another. Notice that no actual population figures are given on the pie graph, only percentages. All the pie sections are different sizes, but together they add up to 100 percent.

GeoLAB ACTIVITY

Oil on the Ocean

1 Background

How did a place that is more than 90 percent desert become one of the richest countries in North Africa? The discovery of oil in the 1950s changed and helped Libya's economy, but it also created possible environmental problems. Libya's oil is shipped across the Mediterranean Sea to Europe and Asia. Whenever oil is transported by ship, there is a risk that it can leak or spill. This activity will demonstrate the far-reaching effects caused by a small amount of oil spilled in water.

2 Materials

- **1 large, shallow pan**
- **water**
- **small amount of motor oil**
- **1 medicine dropper**
- **string**
- **a piece of paper**

Oil Freighter in the Port of Tripoli, Libya

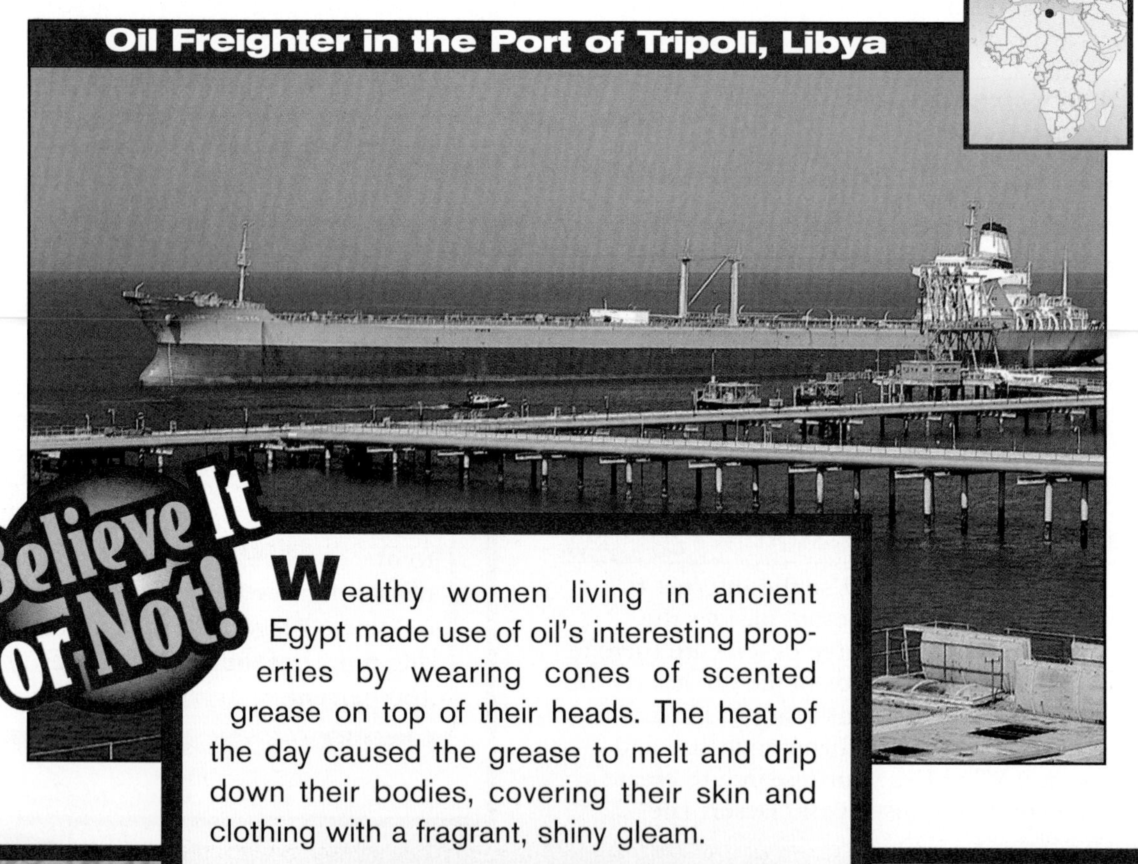

Believe It or Not!

Wealthy women living in ancient Egypt made use of oil's interesting properties by wearing cones of scented grease on top of their heads. The heat of the day caused the grease to melt and drip down their bodies, covering their skin and clothing with a fragrant, shiny gleam.

What to Do

1. Fill the pan two-thirds full with water.
2. Create an oil spill by gently adding one dropperful of motor oil to the center of the pan of water.
3. Loop the string around the edges of the "spill."
4. Remove the string. Mark, measure, and record the length of the string that circled the spill.
5. Wait three minutes, then loop the string around the spill and measure again. Repeat the measurement after another three minutes. Record a total of five different measurements after each three-minute waiting period.
6. Gently shake the pan. Record your observations of the oil spill.
7. Use the paper to gently fan the water's surface. Record your observations of what happens to the oil in the water.

LAB ACTIVITY REPORT

1. How did the oil spill's size change during the 15-minute measuring period?
2. What happened when you shook the pan? Does this occur in the ocean?
3. What did you demonstrate when you fanned the water's surface with the sheet of paper?
4. **Drawing Conclusions** If left alone, what will happen to the oil in the pan over time?

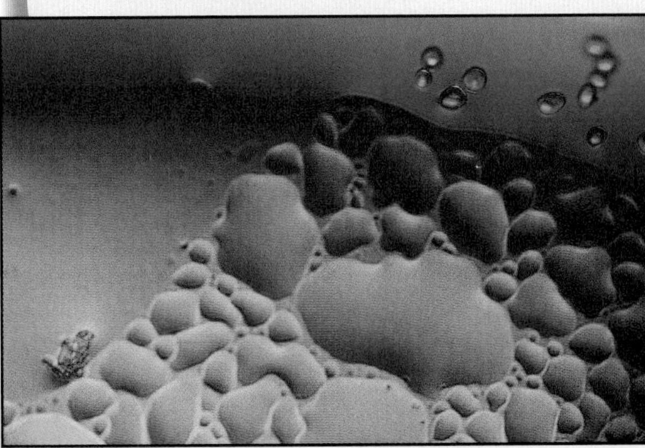

▲ **This is what oil and water look like under a microscope.**

5 Extending the Lab

Activity

Dip several feathers (which symbolize wildlife) into the oil spill. Use different cleaners (dish detergent, clothes detergent, hand soap, and so on) to clean the feathers. Are the cleaners effective? Which cleaner works best? How are the feathers affected by the cleaning? Summarize your findings in a written report.

Chapter 17

Southwest Asia

The World and Its People NATIONAL GEOGRAPHIC

To learn more about the people and places of Southwest Asia, view ***The World and Its People*** **Chapter 17** video.

Chapter Overview Visit the ***Geography: The World and Its People*** Web site at gwip.glencoe.com and click on **Chapter 17—Chapter Overviews** to preview information about Southwest Asia.

Turkey

Guide to Reading

Main Idea

Rapidly modernizing Turkey is a link between Asia and Europe.

Terms to Know

- mosque
- migrate
- secular

Places to Locate

- Bosporus
- Sea of Marmara
- Dardanelles
- Anatolia
- Pontic Mountains
- Taurus Mountains
- Black Sea
- Istanbul
- Ankara

Reading Strategy

Make a chart like this one, filling in at least two key facts about Turkey in each category.

Turkey	Fact #1	Fact #2
Land		
Economy		
People		

NATIONAL GEOGRAPHIC **Exploring Our World**

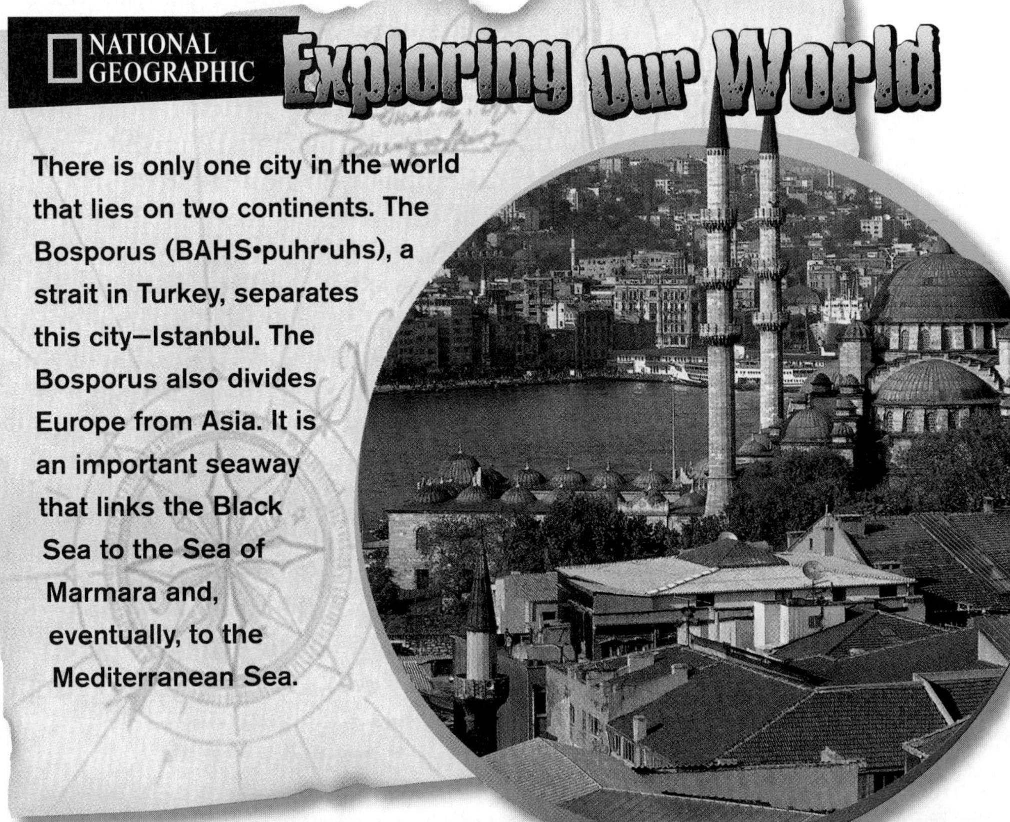

There is only one city in the world that lies on two continents. The Bosporus (BAHS•puhr•uhs), a strait in Turkey, separates this city—Istanbul. The Bosporus also divides Europe from Asia. It is an important seaway that links the Black Sea to the Sea of Marmara and, eventually, to the Mediterranean Sea.

A little larger than the state of Texas, Turkey has a unique location—it bridges the continents of Asia and Europe. The large Asian part of Turkey occupies the peninsula once known as Asia Minor. The much smaller European part lies on Europe's Balkan Peninsula. Three important waterways—the **Bosporus,** the **Sea of Marmara** (MAHR•muh•ruh), and the **Dardanelles** (DAHRD•uhn•EHLZ) separate the Asian and European parts of Turkey. Together, these waterways are called the Turkish Straits. Find these bodies of water on page RA21 of the Reference Atlas.

Turkey's Land and Economy

The center of Turkey is **Anatolia** (A•nuh•TOH•lee•uh), a plateau region rimmed by mountains. The **Pontic Mountains** border the plateau on the north. The **Taurus Mountains** tower over it on the south. Earthquakes often strike the region, causing much damage and death. Lowland plains curve along Turkey's three coasts. Grassy plains cover the northern part along the **Black Sea.** On the western coast, you find broad, fertile river valleys extending inland from the Aegean Sea. In the south, coastal plains stretch along the Mediterranean Sea.

◀ Village in Oman

Turkey's climate varies throughout the country. If you lived on the Anatolian plateau, you would experience the hot, dry summers and cold, snowy winters of the steppe climate. People living in the coastal areas enjoy a Mediterranean climate—hot, dry summers and mild, rainy winters.

Nearly half of Turkey's people are farmers. Many live in the mild coastal areas, where they raise livestock and plant crops such as cotton, tobacco, fruits, and nuts for export. On the drier inland plateau, farmers grow mostly wheat and barley for use at home. In eastern Turkey, grains and goats are raised in mountain valleys.

Turkey has rich mineral resources of coal, copper, and iron. The most important industrial activities are oil refining and the making of textiles and clothing. Turkish factory workers also process foods and make cars, steel, and building materials. About one-third of Turkey's people work in service industries. The country's beautiful beaches and historic sites have made tourism another growing industry.

✓Reading Check **What are Turkey's most important industrial activities?**

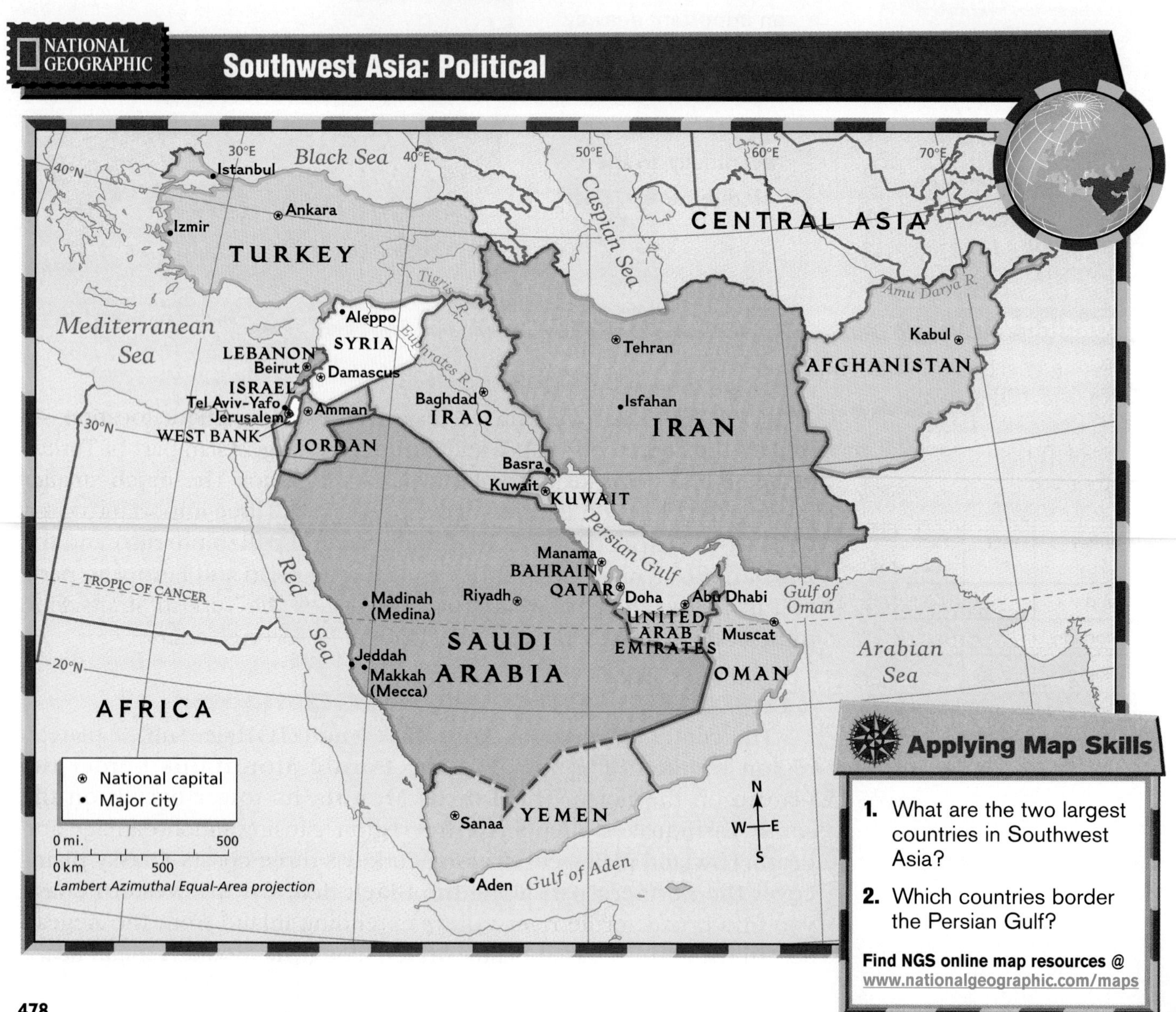

Applying Map Skills

1. What are the two largest countries in Southwest Asia?
2. Which countries border the Persian Gulf?

Find NGS online map resources @ www.nationalgeographic.com/maps

Turkey's People

Most of Turkey's 65.9 million people live in the northern part of Anatolia, on coastal plains, or in valleys. About 98 percent are Muslims, or followers of Islam. Turkish is the official language, but Kurdish and Arabic are also spoken. Kurdish is the language of the Kurds, an ethnic group who make up about 20 percent of Turkey's people. The Turkish government has tried to turn the Kurds away from Kurdish culture and language. Unwilling to abandon their identity, the Kurds have demanded their own independent state. Tensions between the two groups have resulted in violent clashes.

Almost 70 percent of Turkey's people live in cities or towns. **Istanbul** is Turkey's largest city with nearly 8 million people. It is the only city in the world located on two continents. Istanbul is known for its beautiful palaces, museums, and mosques. **Mosques** are places of worship for followers of Islam. Thanks to its location at the entrance to the Black Sea, Istanbul is a major trading center. Turkey's capital and second-largest city is **Ankara.**

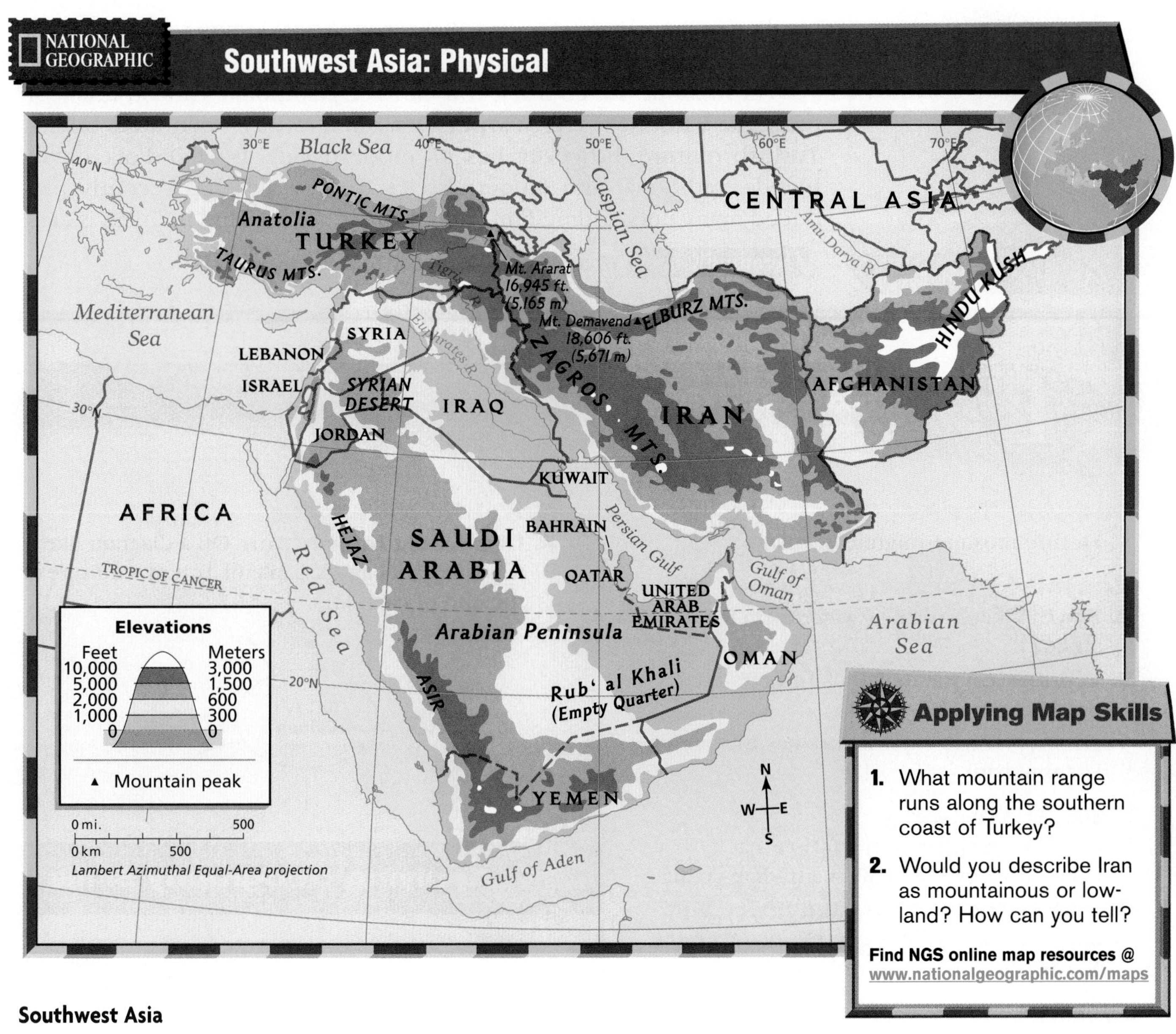

Applying Map Skills

1. What mountain range runs along the southern coast of Turkey?
2. Would you describe Iran as mountainous or lowland? How can you tell?

Find NGS online map resources @ www.nationalgeographic.com/maps

Festival Time

Kudret Özal lives in Söğüt, Turkey. Every year, she and her family attend a festival that honors a warrior ancestor. She says, "At night everyone gathers to sing, dance, and tell jokes and stories." According to custom, Kudret wears clothing that covers her head, arms, shoulders, and legs.

History and Culture Istanbul began as a Greek port called Byzantium more than 2,500 years ago. Later the Romans expanded the city and renamed it Constantinople. For hundreds of years, the city was the glittering capital of the Byzantine Empire.

Many of Turkey's people today are descendants of an Asian people called Turks. These people migrated to Anatolia during the A.D. 900s. **Migrating** means moving from one place to another. One group of Turks—the Ottomans—conquered Constantinople in the 1400s. They, too, renamed the city, calling it Istanbul. The city served as the brilliant capital of a powerful Muslim empire called the Ottoman Empire. At its height, this empire ruled much of southeastern Europe, North Africa, and Southwest Asia.

The Ottomans' defeat in World War I led to the breakup of the empire. During most of the 1920s and 1930s, Kemal Atatürk, a military hero, served as Turkey's first president. Atatürk introduced many political and social changes to modernize the country. Turkey soon began to consider itself European as well as Asian. Many Turkish people, however, continued to value the Muslim faith. During the 1990s, Muslim and **secular,** or nonreligious, political groups struggled for control of Turkey's government.

Throughout the country, you can see traditional Turkish arts: colored tiles, finely woven carpets, and beautifully decorated books. Turkish culture, however, has its modern side as well. Folk music blends traditional and modern styles. Turkey also has recently produced many outstanding films that deal with social and political issues.

Reading Check **What is unusual about Turkey's largest city?**

Assessment

Defining Terms

1. **Define** mosque, migrate, secular.

Recalling Facts

2. **Place** What bodies of water form the Turkish Straits?
3. **Economics** Name five of Turkey's agricultural products.
4. **History** What other names has the city of Istanbul had?

Critical Thinking

5. **Analyzing Information** How has Istanbul's location made it a trading center?
6. **Understanding Cause and Effect** Why have violent clashes occurred between the Kurds and Turkey's government?

Graphic Organizer

7. **Organizing Information** On a diagram like this one, label an example of Turkey's culture at the end of each line.

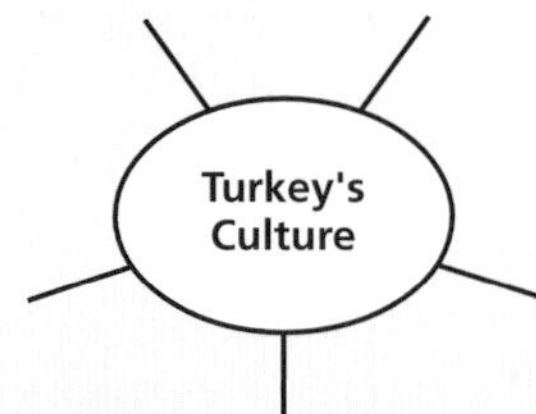

Applying Geography Skills

8. **Analyzing Maps** Study the physical map on page 479. What large body of water borders Turkey on the north? On the south?

Making Connections

ART SCIENCE LITERATURE TECHNOLOGY

A Poem of Freedom

Through many of his poems, Turk Nazim Hikmet criticized actions of the Turkish government. In 1938 he was arrested and sent to prison for about 10 years. Hikmet wrote some of his finest poems there, including the following one.

The World, My Friends, My Enemies, You, and the Earth

by Nazim Hikmet (1902–1963)

I'm wonderfully happy I came into the world,
I love its earth, its light, its struggle, and its bread.
Even though I know its dimensions from pole to pole to the centimeter,
and while I'm not unaware that it's a mere toy next to the sun,
the world for me is unbelievably big.
I would have liked to go around the world
and see the fish, the fruits, and the stars that I haven't seen.
However,
I made my European trip only in books and pictures.
In all my life I never got one letter
with its blue stamp canceled in Asia.
Me and our corner grocer,
we're both mightily unknown in America.
Nevertheless,
from China to Spain, from the Cape of Good Hope to Alaska,
in every nautical mile, in every kilometer, I have friends and enemies.
Such friends that we haven't met even once—
we can die for the same bread, the same freedom, the same dream.
And such enemies that they're thirsty for my blood,
I am thirsty for their blood.
My strength
is that I'm not alone in this big world.
The world and its people are no secret in my heart,
no mystery in my science.
Calmly and openly
I took my place
in the great struggle.
And without it,
you and the earth
are not enough for me.
And yet you are astonishingly beautiful,
the earth is warm and beautiful.

▲ **Old-fashioned outdoor market in Urfa, Turkey**

Making the Connection

1. What does Hikmet say he loves about the world?
2. How has Hikmet "traveled" to Europe?
3. **Drawing Conclusions** What feelings toward life do you get from the poem?

Israel

Guide to Reading

Main Idea

After years of conflict, the Jewish nation of Israel and neighboring Arab countries are trying to achieve peace.

Terms to Know

- kibbutz
- moshav
- Diaspora
- Holocaust
- monotheism

Places to Locate

- Golan Heights
- Dead Sea
- Tel Aviv-Yafo
- Jerusalem
- West Bank
- Gaza Strip

Reading Strategy

Create a time line like this one to track four key events with dates in Israel since its founding in 1948.

NATIONAL GEOGRAPHIC **Exploring Our World**

Modern and traditional cultures exist side by side throughout Israel. Israel was established as an independent country in 1948 after many years of trying to create a homeland for Jews. Since then, Jewish people from more than 100 countries have migrated to this small country. At this market in Tel Aviv-Yafo, buyers and sellers talk about current events and sports.

Israel lies at the eastern end of the Mediterranean Sea. Slightly smaller than the state of New Jersey, it is 256 miles (412 km) long from north to south and only 68 miles (109 km) wide from east to west.

Israel's Land and Climate

The mountains of Galilee lie in Israel's far north. East of these mountains is a plateau called the **Golan Heights.** South of the Golan Heights, between Israel and Jordan, is the **Dead Sea.** At 1,349 feet (411 m) below sea level, the shores of the Dead Sea are the lowest place on the earth's surface. The Dead Sea is also the earth's saltiest body of water—about nine times saltier than ocean water. The map on page 485 shows you where the Golan Heights and the Dead Sea are located.

In southern Israel, a desert called the Negev (NEH•gehv) covers almost half the country. A fertile plain no more than 20 miles (32 km) wide lies along the country's Mediterranean coast. To the east, the Jordan River cuts through the floor of a long, narrow valley before flowing into the Dead Sea.

Northern Israel has a Mediterranean climate with hot, dry summers and mild winters. About 40 inches (102 cm) of rain fall in the north each year. Southern Israel has a desert climate. Summer temperatures soar higher than 120°F (49°C), and annual rainfall is less than 1 inch (2.5 cm).

Reading Check **What plateau is found in northeastern Israel?**

Israel's Economy

Israel's best farmland stretches along the Mediterranean coastal plain. For centuries, farmers here have grown citrus fruits, such as oranges, grapefruits, and lemons. Citrus fruits are still Israel's major agricultural export. Farther inland, you find that the desert actually blooms. This is possible because farmers add fertilizers to the soil and carefully use scarce water resources. In very dry areas, crops are grown with drip irrigation. This method uses computers to release specific amounts of water from underground tubes to the roots of plants. As a result of technology, Israel's farmers not only feed the country's people—they even export some food to other countries.

About 9 percent of Israelis live and work on farm settlements. Many join together to grow and sell crops. People in one type of settlement called a **kibbutz** (kih•BUTS) share all of the property and may also produce goods such as clothing and electronic equipment. Another

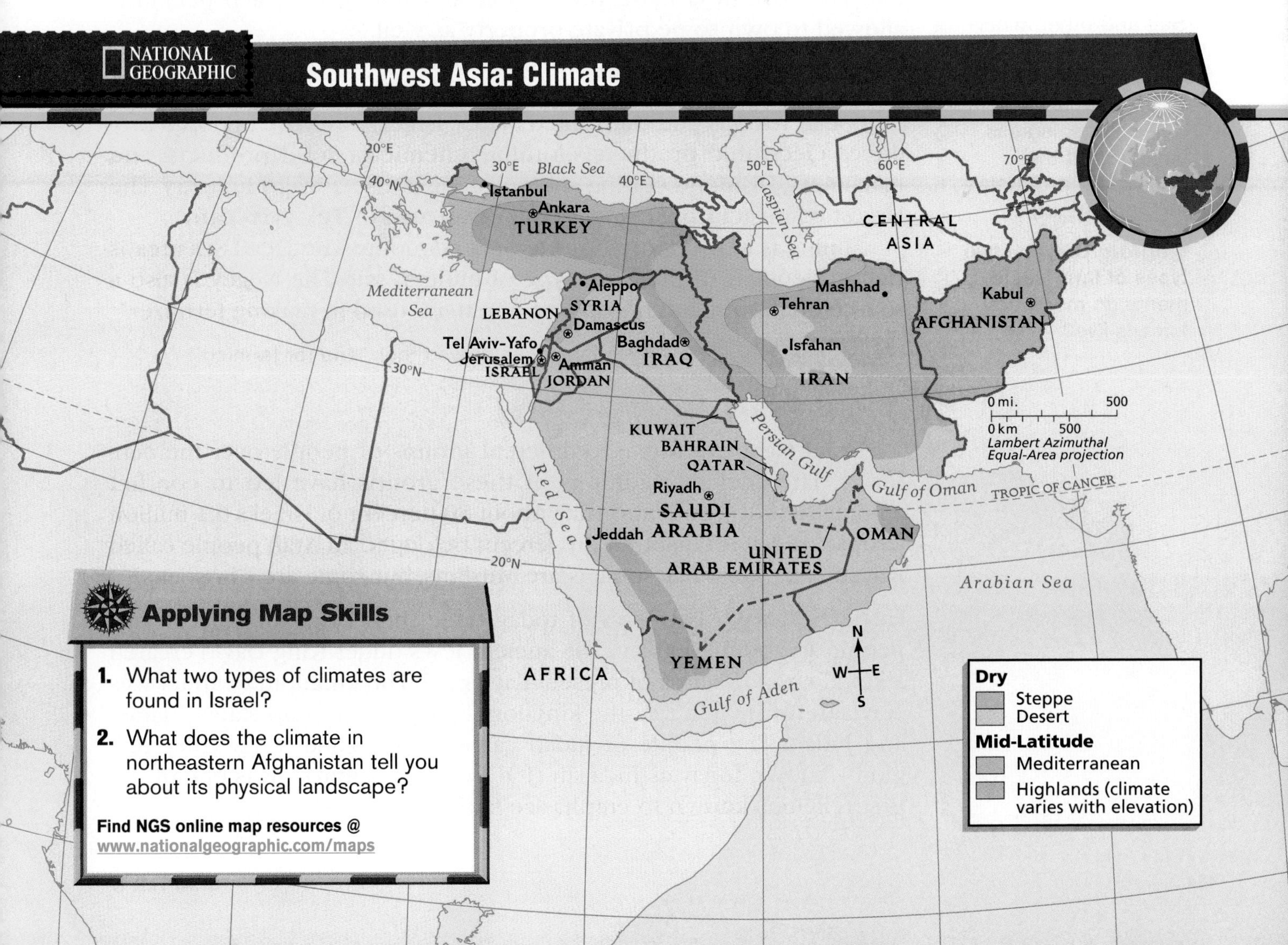

Applying Map Skills

1. What two types of climates are found in Israel?
2. What does the climate in northeastern Afghanistan tell you about its physical landscape?

Find NGS online map resources @ www.nationalgeographic.com/maps

Israel's Landscapes

Salt and other minerals have crystallized on the shores of the Dead Sea (above). In other areas, Israelis have turned the desert into productive farmland (right).

Region On what two types of farm settlements do most rural Israelis live?

kind of settlement is called a **moshav** (moh•SHAHV). People in a moshav share in farming, production, and selling, but each person is allowed to own some private property as well.

Israel is the most industrialized country in Southwest Asia. Its economic development has been supported by large amounts of aid from European nations and the United States. Israel's skilled workforce produces electronic products, clothing, chemicals, food products, and machinery. Diamond cutting and polishing is also a major industry. The largest manufacturing center is the urban area of **Tel Aviv-Yafo.**

Mining is also important to Israel's economy. The Dead Sea area is rich in deposits of potash, a type of mineral salt. The Negev is also a source of copper and phosphate, a mineral used in making fertilizer.

✓Reading Check **How have Israelis improved their land for farming?**

The Israeli People

Israel has been home to different groups of people over the centuries. The ancient traditions of these groups have led to conflict among their descendants today. About 80 percent of Israel's 6.1 million people are Jews. The other 20 percent belong to an Arab people called Palestinians. Most Palestinians are Muslims, but some are Christians.

Early History The Jews of today trace their origins to an ancient people. In about 1000 B.C., the ancient Jews under King David created a kingdom in the area of present-day Israel. The kingdom's capital was **Jerusalem.** By 922 B.C., the kingdom had split into two states—Israel and Judah. The people of Judah came to be called Jews. Their religion—known today as Judaism (JOO•duh•IH•zuhm)—was one of the first religions known to emphasize faith in one God.

Over time, the region was ruled by Greeks, Romans, Byzantines, Arabs, and Ottoman Turks. Under the Romans, the area was called Palestine. The Jews twice revolted against Roman rule but failed to win their freedom. In response, the Romans ordered all Jews out of the land.

During the next 1,900 years, Jews lived in settlements scattered around the world. These settlements were known together as the **Diaspora** (dy•AS•puh•ruh), or scattering of a people. Prejudice against the Jews caused them much hardship. In the late 1800s, some European Jews began to move back to Palestine. These settlers, known as Zionists, had planned to set up a safe homeland for Jews in their ancestral land.

The Birth of Israel During World War I, the British won control of Palestine. They supported a Jewish homeland there. Most of the people living in Palestine, however, were Arabs who also claimed the area as their homeland. To keep peace with the local Arab population, the British began to limit the number of Jews entering Palestine.

During World War II, Germans killed millions of Europe's Jews and others. The mass imprisonment and slaughter of European Jews is known as the **Holocaust.** It brought worldwide attention to Jews. In 1947 the United Nations voted to divide Palestine into a Jewish and an Arab state. The Arabs in Palestine and in neighboring countries disagreed with this division. In 1948 the British left the area, and the Jews immediately declared an independent country called Israel. David Ben-Gurion (BEHN•gur•YAWN) became Israel's first leader.

War soon broke out between Israel and its Arab neighbors. The war ended with Israel's victory. It also brought about significant changes in the area's population. The fighting made many Palestinian Arabs flee to neighboring Arab countries. Jews began arriving from Europe and other areas.

After its war of independence, Israel fought three more wars with its Arab neighbors. In these conflicts, Israel won control of some of its neighbors' land. Palestinian Arabs, now left homeless, demanded their own country. During the 1970s and 1980s, many Palestinians and Israelis died fighting each other. Steps toward peace began when Israel and Egypt signed a treaty in 1979. Agreements made between Israel and Palestinian Arab leaders in 1993 and between Israel and Jordan in 1994 also moved toward peace.

In the 1993 agreement, Israel agreed to turn over two areas to the Palestinians. The **West Bank** lies on the western bank of the

Applying Map Skills

1. Along what sea is the Gaza Strip located?
2. What city is located within the West Bank?

Find NGS online map resources @ www.nationalgeographic.com/maps

Jordan River and surrounds Jerusalem. The **Gaza Strip** is located on the Mediterranean coast and shares a border with Egypt. Find these areas on the map on page 485. Palestinians now have limited control of some of these areas. Yet some Jews still live in these two regions, and tensions between the two groups remain. Many issues—particularly control of Jerusalem—need to be settled before Palestinians achieve independence. In addition, Palestinian Arabs have fewer freedoms and economic opportunities than their Jewish neighbors. In late 2000, violence erupted again because of the inability to resolve these issues.

Israel Today Israel is a democratic republic, a government headed by elected officials. A president represents the country at national events. A prime minister heads the government. The Israeli parliament, or Knesset, meets in a modern building in Jerusalem.

A single law—the Law of Return—increased Israel's population more than any other factor. Passed in 1950, the law states that Jews anywhere in the world can come to Israel to live. As a result, Jewish people have moved to Israel from many countries.

More than 90 percent of Israel's people live in urban areas. The largest cities are Jerusalem, Tel Aviv-Yafo, and Haifa (HY•fuh). Israel proclaimed Jerusalem as its capital in 1950. Turn to page 504 to see why Jerusalem is a holy city for Christians and Muslims as well as Jews. All three religions began in Southwest Asia centuries ago. They all practice **monotheism,** or the belief in one God.

✓Reading Check **Over what two areas do Palestinians have limited control?**

Assessment

Defining Terms

1. **Define** kibbutz, moshav, Diaspora, Holocaust, monotheism.

Recalling Facts

2. **Location** What is the lowest place on the earth's surface? What is its elevation?
3. **History** What was a Zionist?
4. **Place** Why is Jerusalem important?

Critical Thinking

5. **Analyzing Information** What is the major disagreement between Israel and the Palestinians?
6. **Drawing Conclusions** Why do you think Israel has worked so hard to develop its agricultural and manufacturing industries?

Graphic Organizer

7. **Organizing Information** On a diagram like this one, list three things that helped Israel's agricultural success.

Applying Geography Skills

8. **Analyzing Maps** Study the political map on page 478. What country borders Israel to the north? To the northeast? To the east?

Geography Skill

Reading a Time Zones Map

The earth rotates 360° in 24 hours. The earth's surface has been divided into 24 time zones. Each time zone represents 15° longitude, or the distance that the earth rotates in 1 hour.

Learning the Skill

The Prime Meridian, or 0° longitude, is the starting point for figuring out time around the world. Traveling west from 0° longitude, it becomes 1 hour earlier for each time zone crossed. Traveling east, it becomes 1 hour later for each time zone crossed. The international date line is set at the 180° line of longitude. Traveling west across this imaginary line, you add a day. Traveling east, you subtract a day. To read a time zones map:

- Choose a place for which you already know the time and locate it on the map.
- Locate another place and determine if it is east or west of the first place.
- Count the time zones between the two.
- Calculate the time by either adding (going east) or subtracting (going west) an hour for each time zone.
- Determine whether you have crossed the date line, and identify the day of the week.

Practicing the Skill

1. On the map below, if it is 4 P.M. in Rio de Janeiro, what time is it in Honolulu?
2. If it is 10:00 A.M. in Tokyo on Tuesday, what day and time is it in Moscow?

Applying the Skill

Imagine you have a friend living in Rome, Italy. What time (your time) would you call if you wanted to talk to your friend after 7:00 P.M.?

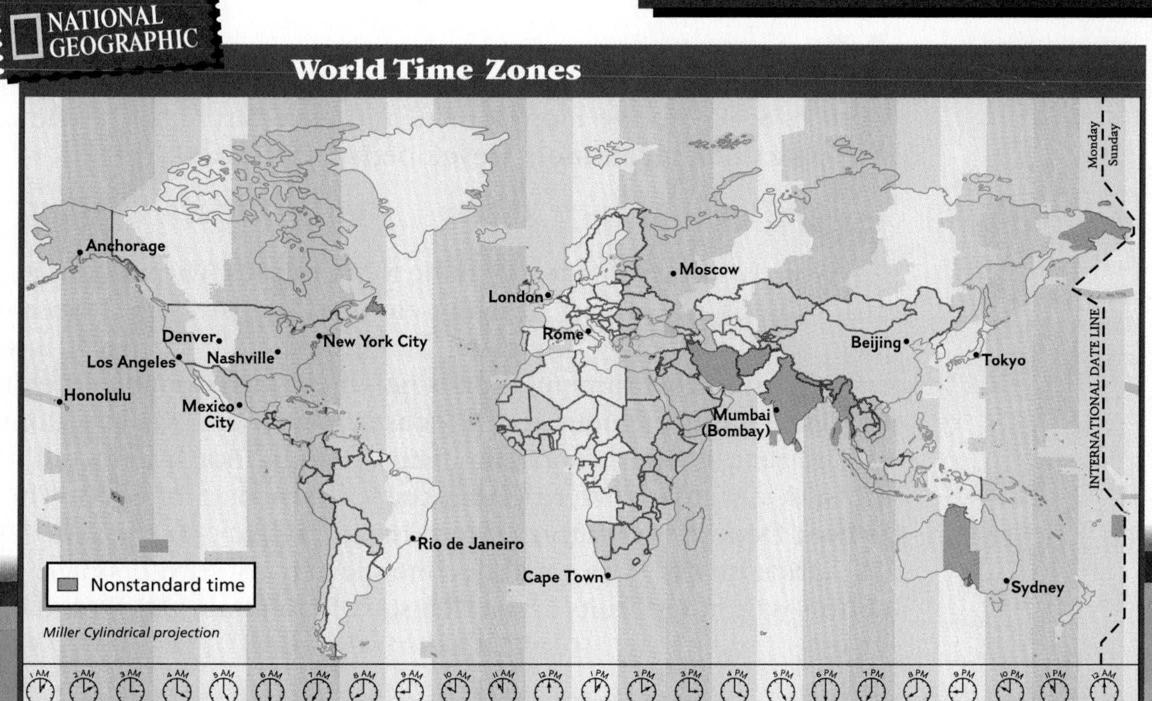

Section 3

Syria, Lebanon, and Jordan

Guide to Reading

Main Idea

Syria, Lebanon, and Jordan have largely Arab populations but have different economies and forms of government.

Terms to Know

- Bedouins
- civil war
- constitutional monarchy

Places to Locate

- Syria
- Syrian Desert
- Euphrates River
- Damascus
- Lebanon
- Beirut
- Jordan
- Jordan River
- Amman

Reading Strategy

Create a chart like this one, listing three key economic activities for each country.

Country	Economic Activities
Syria	
Lebanon	
Jordan	

NATIONAL GEOGRAPHIC **Exploring Our World**

Nomads known as Bedouins survive harsh conditions in the Southwest Asian deserts of Syria, Jordan, Saudi Arabia, and Iraq. Most herd such animals as camels, goats, sheep, and cattle. With water nearly always in short supply, Bedouins may use sand to bathe themselves and eat mainly dried fruits, dates, and milk-based products like cheese and buttermilk.

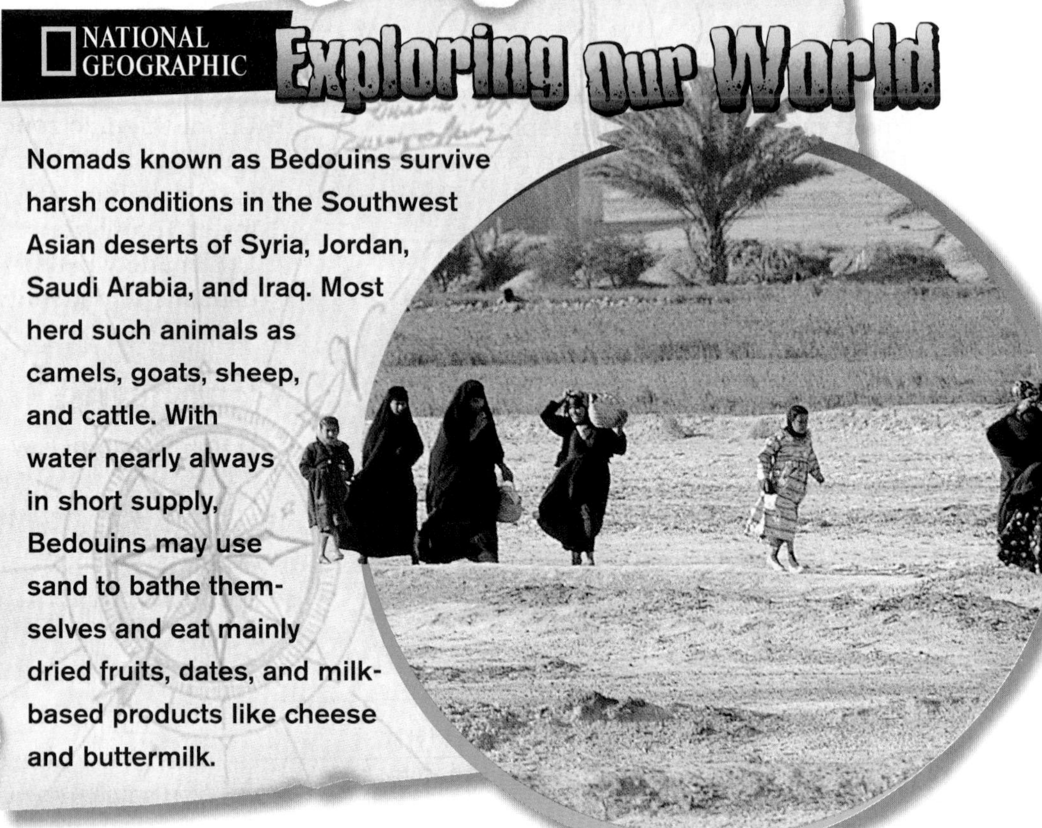

Much of Jordan and large parts of Syria are desert. Lebanon and western Syria receive more rainfall and have fertile soil. Some of the world's earliest civilizations developed in this area.

Syria

Syria has been a center of trade for centuries. Throughout its early history, Syria was a part of many empires, but in 1946 it became an independent country. Since the 1960s, one political party has controlled Syria's government. It does not allow many political freedoms.

Syria's land includes fertile coastal plains and valleys along the Mediterranean Sea. Inland mountains running north and south keep moist sea winds from reaching the eastern part of Syria. The vast **Syrian Desert** covers this eastern region.

Agriculture is Syria's main economic activity. Farmers raise mostly cotton, wheat, and fruits in the rich soil of mountain valleys and coastal plains. In the dry northeast, farmers rely on irrigation. The Syrian government has built dams on the **Euphrates River,** which flows through the country. These dams provide water for irrigation as well as hydroelectric power for cities and industries. Future conflict over Euphrates water is a possibility. Turkey, Syria's upstream neighbor, is building a huge dam that will reduce the flow of water to Syria. Iraq, Syria's downstream neighbor, is concerned about the reduced flow of water that will make its way there.

Like many other countries of Southwest Asia, Syria has reserves of oil—the country's main export. Other industries are food processing and textiles. Syrian fabrics have been highly valued since ancient times.

Syria's People Almost half of Syria's 16 million people live in rural areas. A few are **Bedouins**—nomadic desert peoples who follow a traditional way of life. The word *bedouin* means "desert dweller" in Arabic. Most other Syrians live in cities. The two largest cities are Aleppo, in the north, and **Damascus,** the capital, in the south. Damascus is one of the oldest continuously inhabited cities in the world. It was founded as a trading center more than 5,000 years ago.

Like many other Southwest Asians, the people of Syria are mostly Arab Muslims. Islam has deeply influenced Syria's traditional arts and buildings. In many Syrian cities, you can see spectacular mosques and palaces. As in other Arab countries, hospitality is a major part of life in Syria. Group meals are a popular way of strengthening family ties and friendships. The most favored foods are lamb, flat bread, and bean dishes flavored with garlic and lemon.

Reading Check **On what river has Syria built dams?**

Music

The most common stringed instrument of Southwest Asia is the oud. Often pear-shaped, its neck bends sharply backward. Music from this region uses semitones that are not heard in Western music. Semitones are the "invisible" notes that lie between the black and white keys of a piano. Legend says that the oud owes its special tones to the birdsongs absorbed by the wood from which the oud was made.

Looking Closer What instrument in our culture do you think came from the oud?

GO TO

World Music: A Cultural Legacy
Hear music of this region on Disc 1, Track 25.

Lebanon

Lebanon is about half the size of New Jersey. Sandy beaches and a narrow plain run along its Mediterranean coast. Rugged mountains rise east of the plain and along Lebanon's eastern border. A fertile valley lies between the two mountain ranges. Because the country is so small, you can swim in the warm Mediterranean Sea, then throw snowballs in the mountains—all in the same day.

Cedar trees once covered Lebanon. Now only a few lonely groves survive on mountaintops. Still, Lebanon is the most densely wooded of all the Southwest Asian countries. Many kinds of pine trees thrive on the mountains. Fruit trees flourish on the coastal land.

More than 60 percent of Lebanon's people work in service industries such as banking and insurance. Manufactured products include food, cement, textiles, chemicals, and metal products. Lebanese farmers grow citrus fruits, vegetables, grains, olives, and grapes. Shrimp is harvested from the Mediterranean.

The Lebanese People More than 80 percent of Lebanon's nearly 4.1 million people live in coastal urban areas. **Beirut** (bay•ROOT), the capital and largest city, was once a major banking and business center. European tourists called Beirut "the Paris of the East" because of its elegant shops and sidewalk cafés. Today, however, Beirut is still rebuilding after a civil war that lasted from 1975 to 1991.

A **civil war** is a fight among different groups within a country. Lebanon's civil war arose between groups of Muslims and Christians. About 70 percent of the Lebanese are Arab Muslims and most of the rest are Arab Christians. Many lives were lost in the war, and Lebanon's economy was almost destroyed. Israel invaded Lebanon during the war, finally withdrawing its troops from the south in 2000.

Arabic is the most widely spoken language in Lebanon. French is also an official language. Why? France ruled Lebanon before the country became independent in the 1940s. Local foods reflect a blend of Arab, Turkish, and French influences.

Reading Check Why is Beirut in the process of rebuilding?

Petra

One of Jordan's major tourist attractions, Petra was built by an Arab ruling family during the 300s B.C. The city's temples and monuments were carved out of cliffs in the Valley of Moses in Jordan. It was a major center of the spice trade that reached as far as China, Egypt, Greece, and India. When the trade route bypassed Petra, the city gradually faded in importance. It became unknown to the Western world until it was rediscovered in 1812. Archaeologists have found dams, rock-carved channels, and ceramic pipes that brought water to the 30,000 people who once lived here.

Jordan

Slightly larger than Kentucky, **Jordan** lies south of Syria and east of Israel. From 1948 to 1967, Jordan's borders included land west of the **Jordan River.** This area—the West Bank—was occupied by Israel during the 1967 war between Israel and its neighbors.

A land of contrasts, Jordan stretches from the fertile Jordan River valley in the west to dry, rugged country in the east. Jordan lacks water resources. Small amounts of irrigated farmland lie in the Jordan River valley, however. Here farmers grow wheat, fruits, and vegetables. Jordan's desert is home to tent-dwelling Bedouins, who raise livestock. In recent years, many Bedouins have settled in towns to find work.

Jordan also lacks energy resources. The majority of its people work in service and manufacturing industries. The leading manufactured goods are phosphates, potash, pottery, chemicals, and processed foods. Phosphate and potash are mined near the Dead Sea and made into fertilizer at a plant in Aqaba (AH•kah•buh), Jordan's only port.

Jordan's People Most of Jordan's 4.7 million people are Arab Muslims. They include more than 1 million Palestinian Arabs who fled Israel or the West Bank. **Amman** is the capital and largest city. At least 5,000 years old, Amman is sprinkled with Roman ruins. Petra, another ancient city, was carved completely from a cliff face.

During the early 1900s, the Ottoman Empire ruled this area. After the Ottoman defeat in World War I, the British set up a territory under the Hashemites, a ruling family from the Arabian Peninsula. This territory, later known as Jordan, became independent in 1946. The Hashemite family still rules Jordan today. The country has a **constitutional monarchy.** Elected leaders govern, but a king or queen is the official head of state. From 1952 to 1999, King Hussein (hoo•SAYN) I ruled Jordan. He worked to blend the country's traditions with modern ways of life. The present ruler of Jordan is Hussein's son, King Abdullah (uhb•dul•LAH) II.

Reading Check **What are Jordan's leading manufactured goods?**

Defining Terms

1. **Define** Bedouins, civil war, constitutional monarchy.

Recalling Facts

2. **Location** What landform covers the eastern part of Syria?
3. **Place** What is the capital of Lebanon?
4. **History** What is Petra?

Critical Thinking

5. **Understanding Cause and Effect** How could a dam on the Euphrates River cause a conflict among Turkey, Syria, and Iraq?
6. **Analyzing Information** How and why did Jordan's borders change in 1967?

Graphic Organizer

7. **Organizing Information** Draw a diagram like this one. Inside the large oval, list characteristics that Syria, Lebanon, and Jordan share.

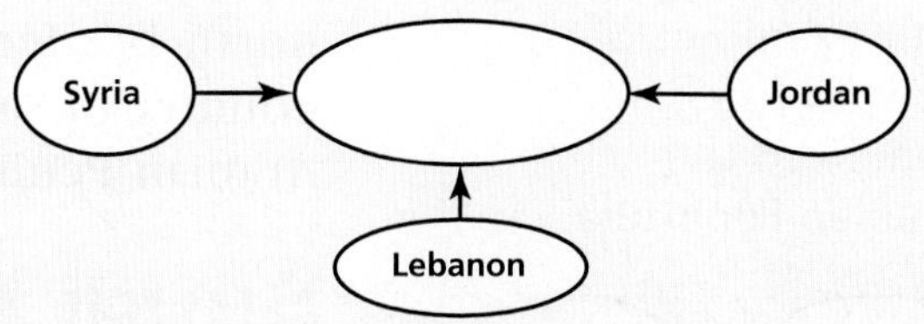

Applying Geography Skills

8. **Analyzing Maps** Study the maps on pages 485 and 479. Jordan's only port, Aqaba, is located on the Gulf of Aqaba. This gulf is part of what larger body of water?

Section 4

The Arabian Peninsula

Guide to Reading

Main Idea

Money from oil exports has boosted standards of living in most countries of the Arabian Peninsula.

Terms to Know

- wadi
- oasis
- desalinization
- hajj

Places to Locate

- Persian Gulf
- Saudi Arabia
- Riyadh
- Makkah
- Kuwait
- Bahrain
- Qatar
- United Arab Emirates
- Oman
- Yemen
- Arabian Sea

Reading Strategy

Create a diagram like this one and give four examples of how oil has benefited the Arabian Peninsula.

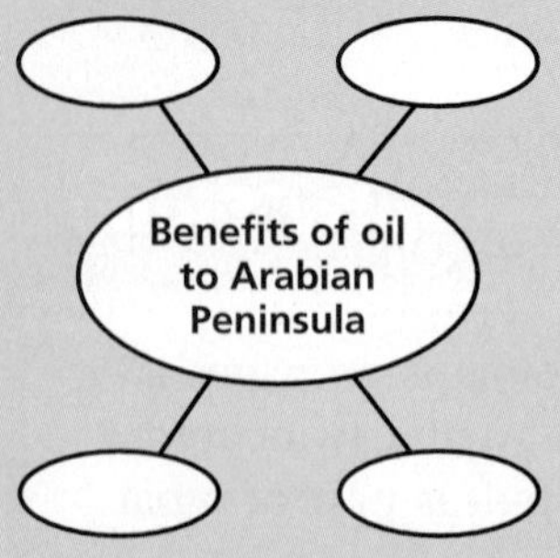

Thousands of years ago, nomads in Arabia and Africa tamed camels. They were the only animals that could make the long journey across the desert, thanks to their ability to go for days without food or water. For centuries, camels were the main source of transport, milk, and meat in the desert. Today they are also valued for their racing speed.

Find the Arabian Peninsula on the map on page 479. Notice that its highest elevations are in the south. The mostly desert land in the north borders Iraq, then it slopes toward the **Persian Gulf.** The country of Saudi Arabia takes up about 80 percent of the quite large Arabian Peninsula.

Saudi Arabia

Saudi Arabia, the largest country in Southwest Asia, is about the size of the eastern half of the United States. Vast deserts cover this region. The largest and harshest desert is the Rub' al Khali, or Empty Quarter, in the southeast. The Empty Quarter has mountains of sand that reach heights of more than 1,000 feet (305 m).

Because of the generally dry, desert climate, Saudi Arabia has no rivers or permanent bodies of water. Highlands dominate the southwest, however, and rainfall there irrigates fertile croplands in the valleys. Water for farming sometimes comes from seasonal **wadis,** or dry riverbeds filled by rainwater from rare downpours. The desert also has **oases**—green areas in the desert fed by underground water.

An Oil-Based Economy Saudi Arabia holds a major share of the world's oil. This entire region is by far the world's leading producer of oil. The graph on page 494 compares the amount of oil reserves in Southwest Asia with those of other regions.

Since 1960 Saudi Arabia and some other oil producers have formed the Organization of Petroleum Exporting Countries (OPEC). Together they work to increase income from the sale of oil. Today OPEC countries supply more than 40 percent of the world's oil. By increasing or reducing supply, they are able to influence world oil prices.

Oil has helped Saudi Arabia boost its standard of living. Money earned by selling oil has built schools, hospitals, roads, and airports. Aware that someday its oil will run out, Saudi Arabia's government has been trying to broaden its economy. In recent years, it has given more emphasis to industry and agriculture. Agriculture in Saudi Arabia has not developed greatly because of the limited amount of water and farmland. To get more water and grow more food, the government of Saudi Arabia has spent much money on irrigation and another process. This process—**desalinization**—takes salt out of seawater.

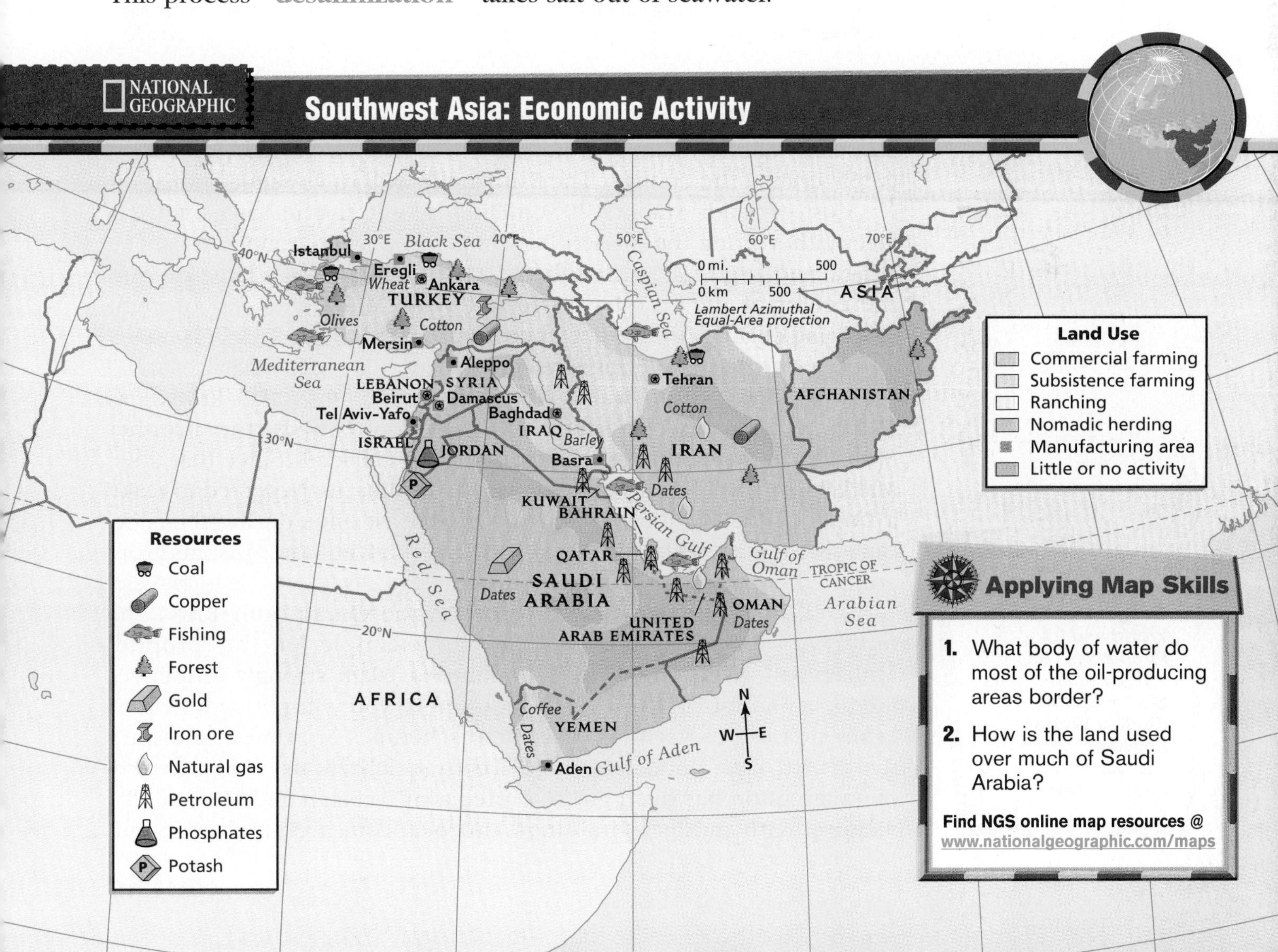

World Oil Production

Analyzing the Graph

Southwest Asia has more known oil than all other regions of the world combined.

Region **What percentage of the world's known oil reserves does Southwest Asia hold?**

Visit gwip.glencoe.com and click on **Chapter 17—Textbook Updates.**

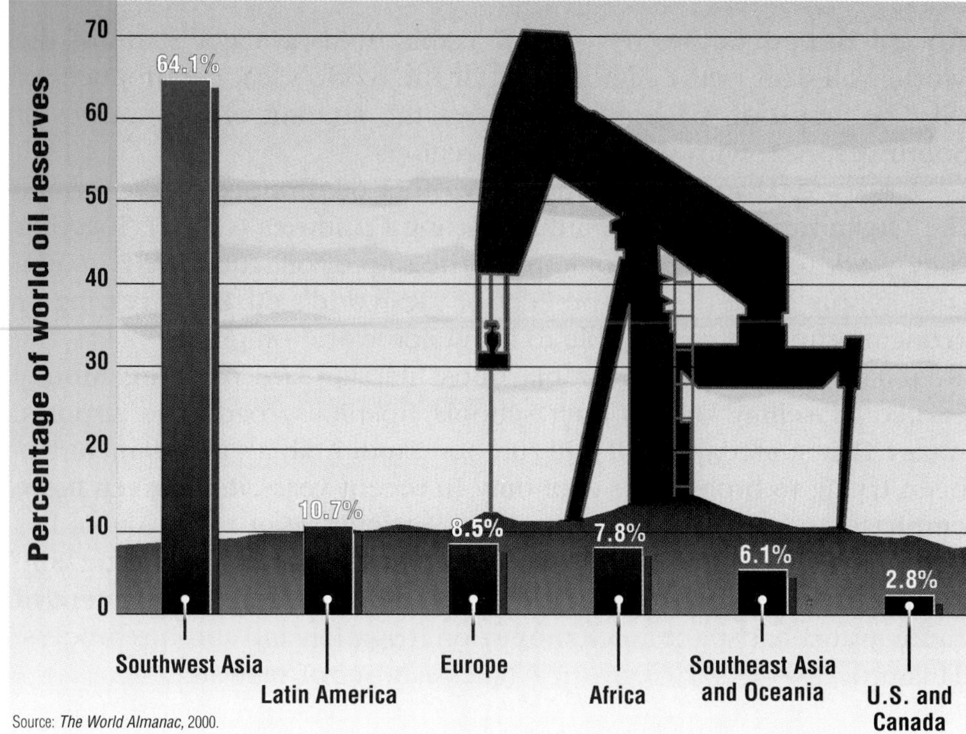

Source: *The World Almanac*, 2000.

History and People The people of Saudi Arabia were once divided into many different family groups. In 1932 a monarchy led by the Saud family unified the country. The Saud family still rules Saudi Arabia.

Most of Saudi Arabia's 20.9 million people live in towns and villages either along the oil-rich Persian Gulf coast or around oases. The capital and largest city, **Riyadh** (ree•YAHD), sits amid a large oasis in the center of the country. In recent years, oil wealth has brought sweeping changes to Riyadh. Once a small rural town, Riyadh is now a modern city with towering skyscrapers and busy highways.

In western Saudi Arabia **Makkah** (MAH•kuh), also known as Mecca, is another important city. In the A.D. 600s, the prophet Muhammad preached the religion of Islam in Makkah. Since that time, Makkah has been Islam's holiest city. All Muslims are expected to make a **hajj,** or religious journey, to Makkah at least once during their lifetime, if they are able to do so. Today several million Muslims from around the world visit Makkah each year.

Saudi Arabia's customs are based on the Quran (kuh•RAN), the holy writings of Islam, and on the example of the prophet Muhammad. As in other Muslim countries, Islam strongly influences life in Saudi Arabia. If you visit Saudi Arabia, you will notice how government, business, school, and home schedules are timed to Islam's five daily prayers and two major yearly celebrations. Much government attention has been given to preparing Makkah and Madinah for visitors, with modern buildings and beautiful architecture. Saudi

Web Activity Visit the ***Geography: The World and Its People*** Web site at gwip.glencoe.com and click on **Chapter 17—Student Web Activities** to learn more about the Islamic religion.

customs concerning the roles of men and women in public life are stricter than in most other Muslim countries. Some Saudi women do not drive cars. They may work outside the home but only in jobs in which they avoid close contact with men.

Reading Check What influences almost every part of Saudi Arabian culture?

The Persian Gulf States

Kuwait (ku•WAYT), **Bahrain** (bah•RAYN), **Qatar** (KAH•tuhr), and the **United Arab Emirates** are located along the Persian Gulf. Beneath their flat deserts and offshore areas lie vast deposits of oil. The Persian Gulf states have used profits from oil exports to build prosperous economies. Political and business leaders, however, are aware that oil revenues depend on constantly changing world oil prices. As a result, they have encouraged the growth of other industries. Their goal is to build a more varied economy.

The people of the Persian Gulf states once made a living from activities such as pearl diving, fishing, and camel herding. Now they have modern jobs in the oil and natural gas industries. They also enjoy a high standard of living. Using income from oil, their governments provide free education, health care, and other services. Many workers from other countries have settled in these countries to work in the modern cities and oil fields and to benefit from the economic boom.

Reading Check How have the economies of the Persian Gulf states changed since the discovery of oil?

Makkah, Saudi Arabia

The Kaaba, the most sacred Islamic shrine, is in the courtyard of Makkah's Grand Mosque.

Place On what are Saudi Arabia's customs based?

Oman and Yemen

At the southeastern and southern ends of the Arabian Peninsula are the countries of **Oman** and **Yemen.** Oman is largely desert, but its bare land yields oil—the basis of the country's economy. Until recently, most of the people of Oman lived in rural villages. The oil industry has drawn many of these people—and foreigners—to Muscat, the country's capital. Other natural resources include natural gas, copper, marble, and limestone. Agricultural products include dates, bananas, camels, and cattle.

Oman's location also has made the country important to world oil markets. The northern part of Oman guards the strategic Strait of Hormuz. Oil-bearing tankers have to go through this narrow waterway to pass from the Persian Gulf into the **Arabian Sea.**

Southwest of Oman lies Yemen, which is made up of a narrow coastal plain and inland mountains. In ancient times, Yemen was famous for its rich trade in fragrant tree resins such as myrrh (MUHR) and frankincense. Yemen's capital, the walled city of Sanaa (sahn•AH), was once a crossroads for camel caravans that carried goods from as far away as China.

Today Yemen is the only country of the Arabian Peninsula that does not have large deposits of oil. Most of the people are farmers or herd sheep and cattle. They live in the high fertile interior where Sanaa is located. Farther south lies Aden (AH•duhn), a major port for ships traveling between the Arabian Sea and the Red Sea.

✓Reading Check **What makes Yemen different from other countries in the Arabian Peninsula?**

Assessment

Defining Terms

1. Define wadi, oasis, desalinization, hajj.

Recalling Facts

2. Place What is the Empty Quarter?
3. Government Who rules Saudi Arabia and what is its form of government?
4. Culture What is the significance of the city of Makkah?

Critical Thinking

5. Analyzing Information Why is the Strait of Hormuz considered to be of such strategic importance?
6. Drawing Conclusions How do the nations of OPEC affect your life?

Graphic Organizer

7. Organizing Information On a diagram like this one, compare your life to the life of a woman in Saudi Arabia. Put facts about your daily life and a Saudi woman's daily life in the outer circles. In the overlapping area, put things that you have in common.

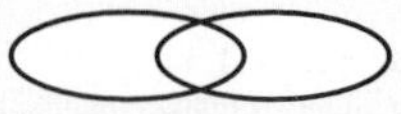

Applying Geography Skills

8. Analyzing Maps Study the political map on page 478. What capital city is located on the Tropic of Cancer?

Section 5

Iraq, Iran, and Afghanistan

Guide to Reading

Main Idea

Iraq, Iran, and Afghanistan have recently fought in wars and undergone sweeping political changes.

Terms to Know

- alluvial plain
- embargo
- shah
- Islamic republic

Places to Locate

- Tigris River
- Euphrates River
- Iraq
- Persian Gulf
- Baghdad
- Iran
- Elburz Mountains
- Zagros Mountains
- Caspian Sea
- Tehran
- Afghanistan
- Hindu Kush
- Kabul

Reading Strategy

Create a chart like this one and list the main landforms in each country.

Country	Landforms
Iraq	
Iran	
Afghanistan	

NATIONAL GEOGRAPHIC **Exploring Our World**

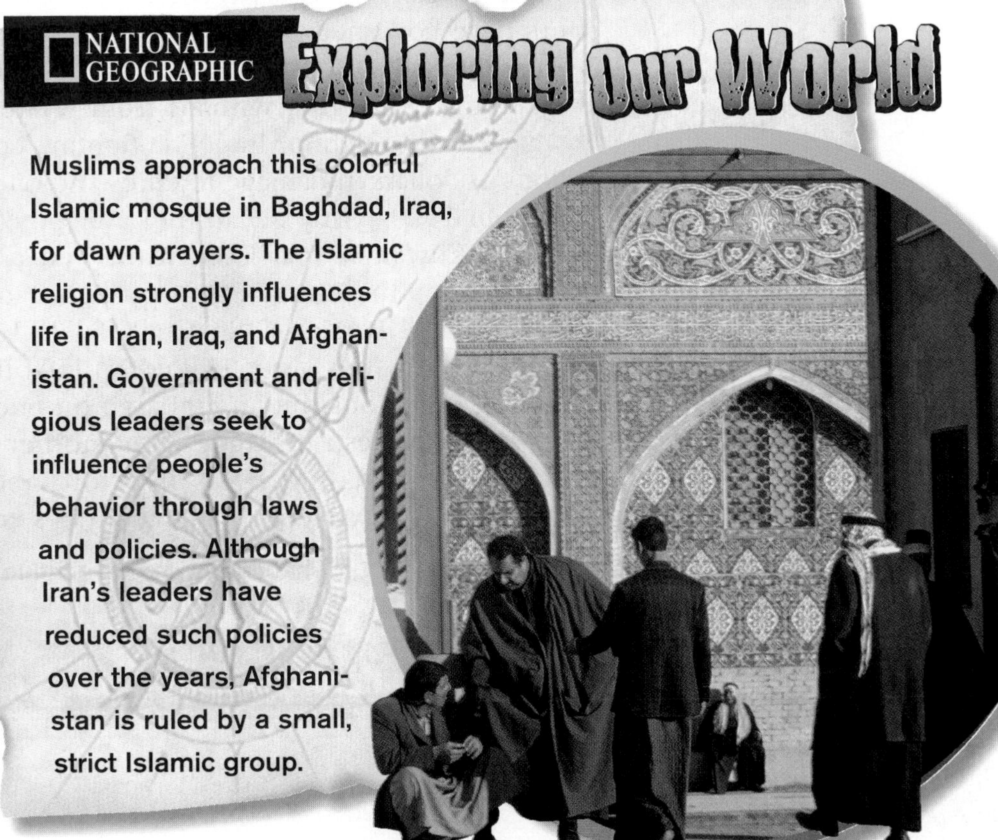

Muslims approach this colorful Islamic mosque in Baghdad, Iraq, for dawn prayers. The Islamic religion strongly influences life in Iran, Iraq, and Afghanistan. Government and religious leaders seek to influence people's behavior through laws and policies. Although Iran's leaders have reduced such policies over the years, Afghanistan is ruled by a small, strict Islamic group.

Iraq, Iran, and Afghanistan are located in a region where some of the world's oldest civilizations developed. This region has experienced turmoil throughout history and even today.

Iraq

More than 4,000 years ago, a people known as the Sumerians built the world's first known cities between the **Tigris** and **Euphrates Rivers.** These rivers are the major geographic features of **Iraq.** They flow through Iraq's northern highlands before entering the **Persian Gulf.** Between the two rivers is an alluvial plain—an area that is built up by rich fertile soil left by river floods. Most farming takes place here. Farmers grow wheat, barley, dates, cotton, and rice.

Oil is the country's major export. Manufacturing has also developed in the past few years. Iraq's factories process foods and make textiles, chemicals, and construction materials.

The Iraqi People About 70 percent of Iraq's 22.5 million people live in urban areas. **Baghdad,** the capital, is the largest city. From the A.D. 700s to 1200s, Baghdad was the center of a large Muslim empire that made many advances in the arts and sciences. Muslim Arabs make up the largest group in Iraq's population. The second-largest group consists of another Muslim people, the Kurds. As you learned in Section 1, the Kurds want to form their own country.

Modern Iraq gained its independence as a kingdom in 1932. In 1958 the last king was overthrown in a revolt. Since then, military leaders have governed Iraq as a dictatorship. The current leader, Saddam Hussein (sah•DAHM hoo•SAYN), rules with an iron hand.

In the 1980s, Iraq, with aid from Western countries, fought a bloody war with its neighbor Iran. The fighting cost thousands of lives and billions of dollars in damage to cities and oil-shipping ports in the Persian Gulf. In 1990, partly because of a dispute over oil, Iraq invaded neighboring Kuwait. A year later, in the Persian Gulf War, a United Nations force led by the United States pushed Iraqi troops out of Kuwait.

After the Persian Gulf War, Saddam Hussein refused to cooperate with the demands of the United Nations. In response, the United States and other nations put an embargo on trade with Iraq. An **embargo** is an order that restricts trade with another country. Since then, Iraq has not exported as much oil as before and could not import certain goods. This has severely damaged Iraq's economy and cost many lives.

Reading Check What two rivers have influenced the history of Iraq?

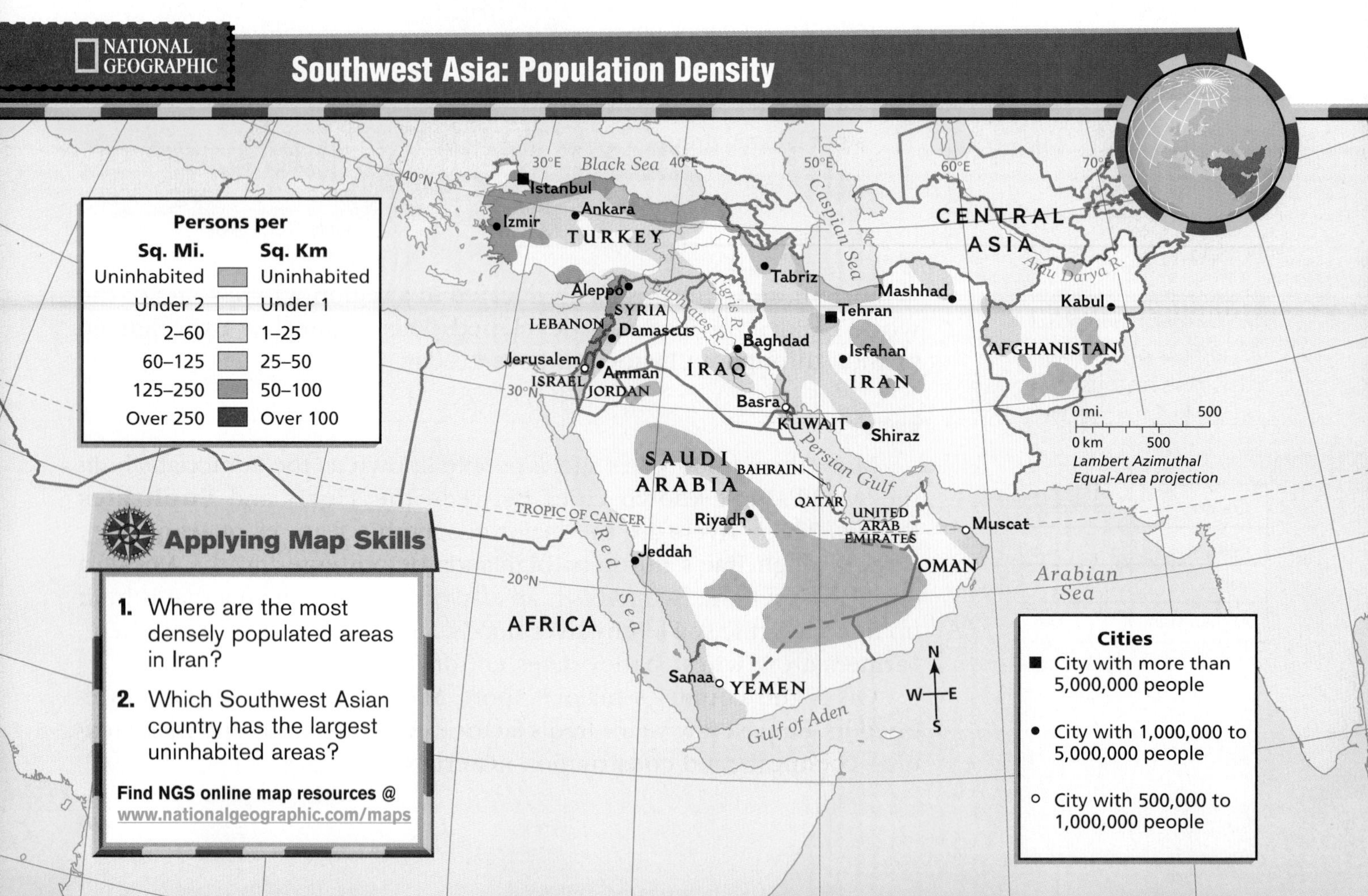

Iran and Afghanistan

An Iranian family picnics in the hills above Tehran (left). Under the Taliban, women in Afghanistan were rarely allowed in public (above).

Place **What form of government does Iran have? What group leads Afghanistan?**

Iran

Once known as Persia, **Iran** is about the size of Alaska. In the center of the country you find a high plateau of deserts and salt flats. Two vast ranges—the **Elburz Mountains** in the north and the **Zagros Mountains** in the west—surround the plateau. Coastal plains wind along the **Caspian Sea** in the north and the Persian Gulf in the south.

Iran is an oil-rich nation where the first oil wells in Southwest Asia were drilled in 1908. The country is trying to promote other industries to make Iran depend less on oil earnings. Major Iranian industries produce textiles, metal goods, and construction materials. The beautiful carpets woven in Iran are valued around the world.

With limited supplies of water, less than 12 percent of Iran's land can be farmed. Some farmers use ancient underground channels to bring water to their fields. They grow wheat, rice, sugar beets, and cotton. Iran is also the world's largest producer of pistachio nuts.

The Iranian People Iran's 66.2 million people differ from those of other Southwest Asian countries. More than one-half are Persians, not Arabs or Turks. The Persians' ancestors migrated from Central Asia centuries ago. They speak Farsi, or Persian, the official language of Iran. Other languages include Kurdish, Arabic, and Turkish. About 60 percent of Iranians live in urban areas. **Tehran,** located in northern Iran, is the largest city and the capital. Iran is also home to about 2 million people from Iraq and Afghanistan who have fled recent wars. Nearly 98 percent of Iran's people practice some form of Islam.

About 2,000 years ago, Iran was the center of the powerful Persian Empire ruled by kings known as **shahs.** In 1979 Muslim religious leaders led a movement that successfully overthrew the last monarchy. Iran has an **Islamic republic,** a government run by Muslim religious leaders.

The government has introduced laws based on its understanding of the Quran, the Muslim sacred writings. Many Western customs seen as a threat to Islam are now forbidden.

✓Reading Check **How do Iranians differ from most other Southwest Asians?**

Afghanistan

A landlocked nation, **Afghanistan** (af•GA•nuh•STAN) is mostly covered with the rugged peaks of the **Hindu Kush** mountain range. Its peaks are as high as 25,000 feet (7,620 m). The Khyber (KY•buhr) Pass cuts through the Hindu Kush. For centuries, this passageway has been a major trade route linking Southwest Asia with other parts of Asia. Rolling grasslands and low deserts make up the other areas.

Almost 70 percent of the people farm. They grow wheat, fruits, and nuts as well as herd sheep and goats. Afghanistan is rich in minerals but has little industry. A few mills produce textiles, and skilled crafts-people produce beautiful jewelry and handwoven carpets.

Most Afghans live in the fertile valleys of the Hindu Kush. The capital city, **Kabul** (KAH•buhl), lies in one of these valleys. The country's 25.8 million people are divided into about 20 different ethnic groups. The two largest groups are the Pashtuns (PUHSH•TOONS) and the Tajiks (tah•JIHKS).

Since ancient times, foreign powers have invaded the country. It has also been torn apart by civil wars among its many ethnic groups. Now a group called the Taliban is in charge. It strictly enforces Islamic religious laws. It also limits individual freedoms, especially for women.

✓Reading Check **What do most Afghans do for a living?**

Assessment

Defining Terms

1. **Define** alluvial plain, embargo, shah, Islamic republic.

Recalling Facts

2. **Economics** What is Iraq's major export?
3. **Place** Describe the physical features of Iran.
4. **History** What has been the significance of the Khyber Pass?

Critical Thinking

5. **Understanding Cause and Effect** Why have Iraq and the United States continued to treat each other with hostility?
6. **Drawing Conclusions** Why would Iran's leaders see Western customs as a threat?

Graphic Organizer

7. **Organizing Information** Draw a chart like this one, then write one fact about Afghanistan under each heading.

Afghanistan		
Capital	Landforms	Agriculture
Crafts	People	Government

Applying Geography Skills

8. **Analyzing Maps** Study the physical map on page 479. Between what two bodies of water is Iran located?

Chapter 17

Reading Review

Section 1 Turkey

Terms to Know

mosque
migrate
secular

Main Idea

Rapidly modernizing Turkey is a link between Asia and Europe.

✓ Location Turkey lies in both Europe and Asia.

✓ Economics Turkey is becoming more industrialized, with textiles and clothing as major industries.

✓ Culture Most of Turkey's people now live in cities or towns.

Section 2 Israel

Terms to Know

kibbutz
moshav
Diaspora
Holocaust
monotheism

Main Idea

After years of conflict, the Jewish nation of Israel and neighboring Arab countries are trying to achieve peace.

✓ Culture About 80 percent of Israel's population are Jews. They have moved to Israel from many countries.

✓ History Israel and its Arab neighbors continue to work toward a peaceful settlement of issues that divide them.

Section 3 Syria, Lebanon, and Jordan

Terms to Know

Bedouins
civil war
constitutional monarchy

Main Idea

Syria, Lebanon, and Jordan have largely Arab populations but have different economies and forms of government.

✓ Economics Farming is the main economic activity in Syria.

✓ History Lebanon is rebuilding and recovering after a civil war.

✓ Place Water shortages in Jordan restrict the land available for farming.

Section 4 The Arabian Peninsula

Terms to Know

wadi
oasis
desalinization
hajj

Main Idea

Money from oil exports has boosted standards of living in most countries of the Arabian Peninsula.

✓ Economics Saudi Arabia is the world's leading oil producer.

✓ Culture The Islamic religion affects almost all aspects of life in Saudi Arabia.

✓ Economics The Persian Gulf states have strong economies based on oil.

Section 5 Iraq, Iran, and Afghanistan

Terms to Know

alluvial plain
embargo
shah
Islamic republic

Main Idea

Iraq, Iran, and Afghanistan have recently fought in wars and undergone sweeping political changes.

✓ Economics Iraq is suffering because of an international trade embargo.

✓ Culture Oil-rich Iran is ruled by Muslim religious leaders.

✓ Place Afghanistan is mountainous and relatively undeveloped.

Chapter 17 Assessment and Activities

Using Key Terms

Match the terms in Part A with their definitions in Part B.

A.

1. monotheism
2. desalinization
3. alluvial plain
4. mosque
5. hajj
6. Bedouins
7. Holocaust
8. secular
9. embargo
10. Diaspora

B.

a. taking salt out of seawater
b. scattering of a people
c. mass slaughter of European Jews
d. nomadic, desert people
e. belief in one god
f. plain built up from soil deposited by a river
g. nonreligious
h. restriction on trade
i. Islamic place of worship
j. religious journey to Makkah

Reviewing the Main Ideas

Section 1 Turkey

11. **Place** What is Turkey's largest city?
12. **Economics** Name five of Turkey's products.

Section 2 Israel

13. **History** When was the modern nation of Israel created?
14. **Government** What is the Law of Return?

Section 3 Syria, Lebanon, and Jordan

15. **Place** What makes Damascus an important city?
16. **History** What area of land did Jordan lose to Israel during the 1967 war?

Section 4 The Arabian Peninsula

17. **Economics** What is OPEC?
18. **Place** What is the capital of Saudi Arabia?

Section 5 Iraq, Iran, and Afghanistan

19. **Economics** Where does most of the farming in Iraq take place?
20. **Culture** How do the people of Iran differ from other Southwest Asian peoples?
21. **Place** What landform makes up Afghanistan?

Southwest Asia

Place Location Activity

On a separate sheet of paper, match the letters on the map with the numbered places listed below.

1. Persian Gulf
2. Zagros Mountains
3. Euphrates River
4. Turkey
5. Iran
6. Israel
7. Iraq
8. Saudi Arabia
9. Makkah
10. Jerusalem

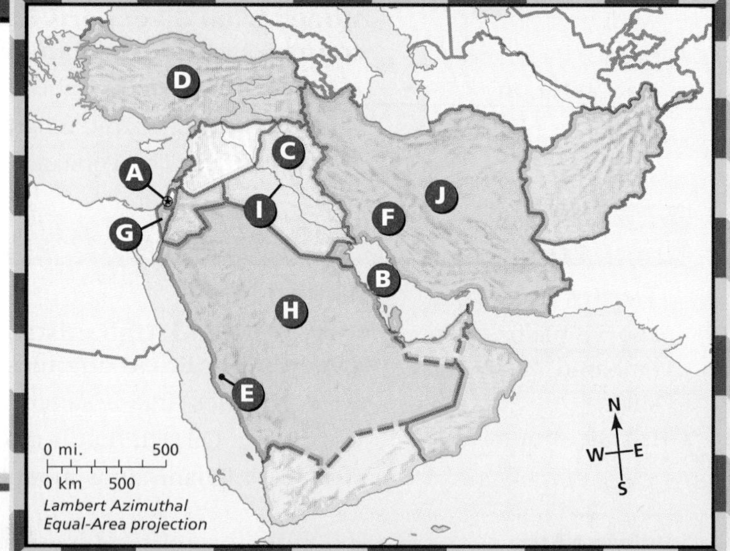

Self-Check Quiz Visit the ***Geography: The World and Its People*** Web site at gwip.glencoe.com and click on **Chapter 17—Self-Check Quizzes** to prepare for the Chapter Test.

Critical Thinking

22. **Evaluating Information** Goods were moved from Southwest Asia to other parts of the world through several routes. How are goods brought to your community? Make a list of all the routes a product would take to get from Southwest Asia to your town.
23. **Analyzing Information** On a chart like this, list a reason for the importance of oil and water to Southwest Asia and one result of their abundance or scarcity.

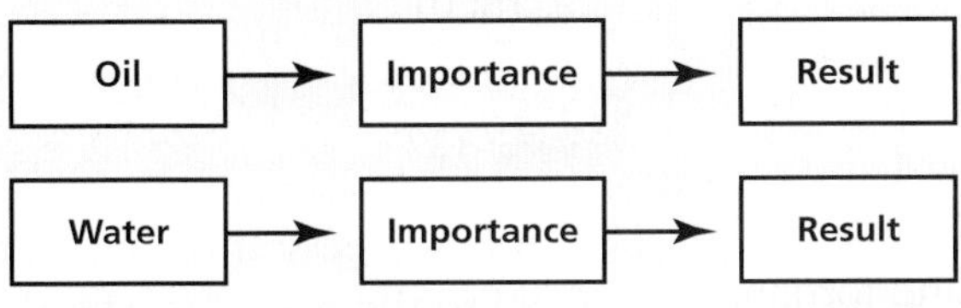

GeoJournal Activity

24. **Writing a Report** Jerusalem is a city holy to three of the world's major religions. Research these religions and identify at least three holy sites you might visit to learn more about them.

Mental Mapping Activity

25. **Focusing on the Region** Draw a simple outline map of Southwest Asia, then label the following:

- Turkey
- Persian Gulf
- Red Sea
- Israel
- Mediterranean Sea
- Iran
- Saudi Arabia
- Yemen
- Iraq
- Afghanistan

Technology Skills Activity

26. **Using the Internet** Search the Internet and find several newspapers that publish current events online. Research an event that took place in one of the countries of Southwest Asia. Create a poster that will inform your class about the event you researched.

Standardized Test Practice

Directions: Study the graph, then answer the question that follows.

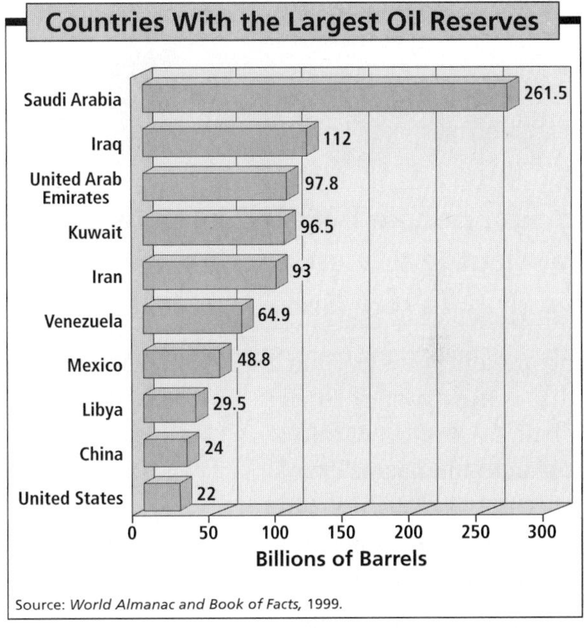

Source: *World Almanac and Book of Facts,* 1999.

1. How many of the 10 countries with the largest oil reserves are located in Southwest Asia?

A one
B three
C five
D seven

Test-Taking Tip: You need to rely on your memory as well as analyze the graph to answer this question. Look at each country, then think back to the countries you studied in Chapter 17. Which of those listed on the graph did you just learn about?

GEOGRAPHY & HISTORY

A painting portrays the life of Jesus.

BIRTHPLACE OF Three Religions

Long ago, people believed in many gods and goddesses. The ancient Jews were the first people known to believe in and pray to one God.

The ancient Jews lived in an area that is now part of Israel. Their beliefs developed into a religion called Judaism. Two other faiths—Christianity and Islam—share many beliefs with Judaism. These three religions all began in Southwest Asia and spread throughout the world.

Judaism, Christianity, and Islam

Judaism traces its beginnings to one man, a herder named Abraham. He lived at least 3,700 years ago in what is now Iraq. According to the Bible, God told Abraham that if he moved to Canaan (later ruled by Abraham's descendants), he would be blessed, and all nations would be blessed through him. Abraham obeyed and did prosper, producing whole nations from his descendants. These descendants suffered great hardships, and their story in the Bible tells how they struggled to remain faithful to the belief in the one powerful and just God.

More than 1,700 years later, a Jew named Jesus began preaching a message of renewal and God's mercy in what is today Israel, the West Bank, and Jordan. Christian scriptures tell that the Roman governor had Jesus put to death in about A.D. 30. Jesus' followers soon proclaimed that Jesus was the world's savior, alive in heaven. The teachings of Jesus became part of a new religion—Christianity. Christian scriptures include the Hebrew Bible in what is called the Old Testament.

About 570 years after Jesus lived, Muhammad was born in the city of Makkah. According to Islamic teachings, he joined the long line of Abrahamic prophets when he first received revelations from God at the age of 40. He soon began preaching to the Arabs, most of whom worshiped idols, and to Christians and Jews living in the Arabian Peninsula. Over the next 23 years, he continued to receive these revelations, which made up the Quran, the holy book of Islam. Islam teaches belief in one God and living a moral life, such as honoring parents, being just to others, and helping the poor.

The Spread of Monotheism

In time, these three religions spread to the rest of the world. Jews settled in other areas and brought Judaism with them. Missionaries, particularly the Christian leader Paul, spread Christianity to Egypt, Greece, Italy, and beyond. Muslim soldiers, scholars, and merchants carried the Islamic faith into Asia, Africa, and Europe. Islam is the faith of the majority of people in Southwest Asia and North Africa today, but all three religions are practiced worldwide.

QUESTIONS

1. In what part of the world did Judaism, Christianity, and Islam begin?
2. How did the three religions spread to other areas?

Muslim, Christian, and Jewish holy sites in Jerusalem ▶

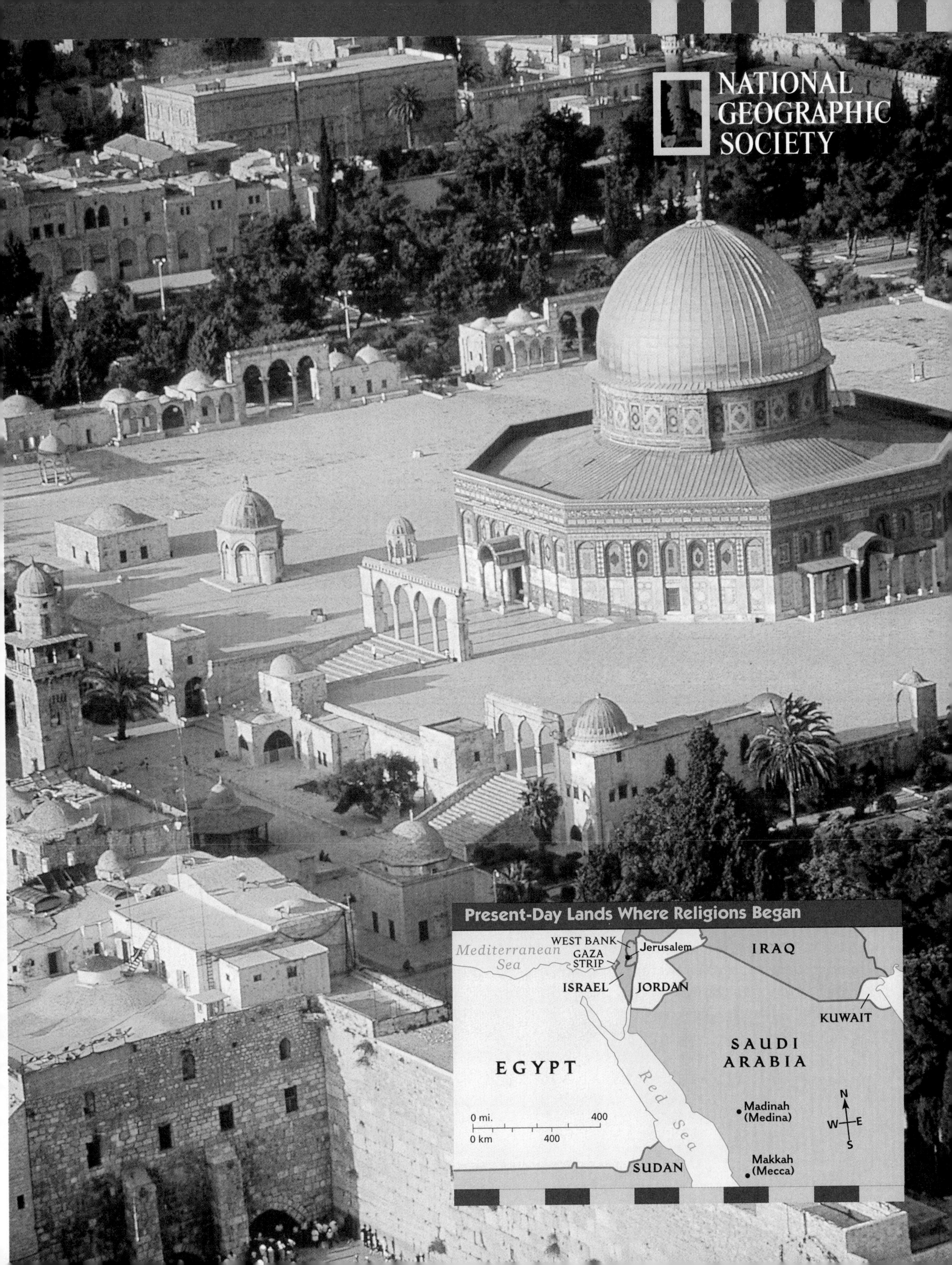
NATIONAL GEOGRAPHIC SOCIETY
Present-Day Lands Where Religions Began
WEST BANK
Jerusalem
Mediterranean Sea
GAZA STRIP
IRAQ
ISRAEL
JORDAN
KUWAIT
SAUDI ARABIA
EGYPT
Red Sea
Madinah (Medina)
Makkah (Mecca)
SUDAN
0 mi. 400
0 km 400
N
W E
S

EYE on the Environment

A Water Crisis

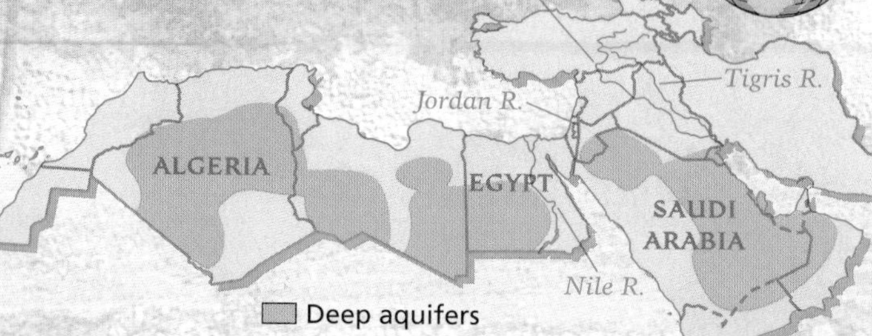

Draining the Rivers The ball game is over. You are hot, sweaty, and thirsty. You press the button on the drinking fountain, but no water comes out. A crisis? Consider this: Many people in Southwest Asia and North Africa never have enough water to meet their needs.

Most of the usable water in this region comes from aquifers—underground areas that store large amounts of water—and from the Jordan, Tigris, Euphrates, and Nile Rivers. Despite these great rivers, water is scarce. The rivers flow through several countries. As each country takes its share of water, less remains for those downstream. A few countries have desalinization plants that turn seawater into fresh water. Desalinization is expensive, though. Water resources are further strained by many factors.

- Population growth — By 2020, about 541 million people will inhabit the region. That is too many people for the existing water supplies.
- Irrigation — About 70 percent of water supplies in Southwest Asia are used to irrigate crops.
- Pollution — River water in many places is polluted by salt, sewage, and chemicals.

Finding Solutions Faced with growing demand and decreasing supplies, countries in this region are looking for creative solutions to the water crisis.

- Some countries are recycling wastewater to use on crops.
- Advances in technology are making desalinization more affordable.
- Countries are building dams to regulate water. They also are constructing pipelines to carry water to where it is most needed.

Camels crossing Egypt's desert drink water piped from the Nile River, 300 miles (483 km) away.

Making a Difference

Wise Water Ways Scientist Sandra Postel is trying to educate others on ways to use water more wisely. In her book, *Last Oasis: Facing Water Scarcity*, Postel argues that we can no longer meet rising demands for water by building larger dams and drilling deeper wells. Instead of reaching out for more water, Postel argues, everyone needs to do more with less water. People need to conserve and recycle water and to use it more efficiently. Through her research, Postel has found that farmers, industries, and cities could cut their water use by as much as 50 percent. Water could be saved by practicing water conservation methods such as drip irrigation and water recycling. Postel hopes that governments around the world will work together to protect one of the earth's most precious resources.

Author Sandra Postel

Meeting Demand A group in Southwest Asia and North Africa is studying ways to ease water shortages in the region. The Water Demand Management Research Network (WDMRN) is made up of scientists and government representatives who are studying ways to meet the growing needs for water. The WDMRN shares information with other water researchers and holds meetings to encourage cooperation between all countries in the region.

Worker takes a drink of water at a desalinization plant, Kuwait.

What Can You Do?

Conserve Water

Saving water is as easy as turning off a faucet. Practice water conservation by taking shorter showers and by turning off the water while brushing your teeth. What other ways can you conserve water at home or at school?

Find Out More

Investigate the pathway drinking water takes in your community. Collaborate with classmates to create a bulletin board display showing how water gets from its source to a drinking fountain in your school.

Use the Internet

The United States has water disputes, too. The Colorado River has been called the "river of contention." Research the Colorado River controversy. A good place to start: the Colorado River Water Users Association at http://crwua.mwd.dst.ca.us. Share what you find with your classmates.

Chapter 18 The Caucasus and Central Asia

The World and Its People — NATIONAL GEOGRAPHIC

To learn more about the people and places of the Caucasus and Central Asia, view ***The World and Its People*** **Chapter 18** video.

Geography Online

Chapter Overview Visit the ***Geography: The World and Its People*** Web site at gwip.glencoe.com and click on **Chapter 18—Chapter Overviews** to preview information about the countries of the Caucasus and Central Asia.

Section 1

Republics of the Caucasus

Guide to Reading

Main Idea

The Caucasus countries have developed their own cultures despite long periods of rule by powerful neighbors.

Terms to Know

- fault
- landlocked
- enclave
- cash crop

Places to Locate

- Armenia
- Georgia
- Azerbaijan
- Caspian Sea
- Black Sea
- Caucasus Mountains
- Yerevan
- T'bilisi
- Baku

Reading Strategy

Make a diagram like this one. Complete the diagram by writing facts about each country's people under the headings.

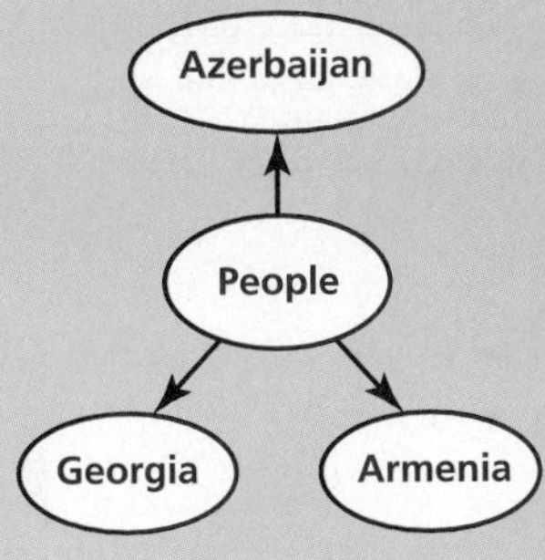

NATIONAL GEOGRAPHIC **Exploring Our World**

Look at the flag of Azerbaijan shown on page 452. Notice that a crescent—a symbol of Islam—appears on the flag. When the Soviet Union invaded Azerbaijan in 1922, most of the country's mosques, or Muslim houses of worship, were forcibly closed. With the Soviet breakup in 1991, mosques like the one shown here have reopened.

The republics of the Caucasus are **Armenia, Georgia,** and **Azerbaijan** (A•zuhr•by•JAHN). They all lie south of Russia between the **Caspian** and **Black Seas.** The towering **Caucasus Mountains,** which give the region its name, run through all three countries. Mt. Kazbek, in Georgia, stands 15,386 feet (4,690 m) high.

The Caucasus Mountains have not been a barrier to the many armies, traders, and settlers who have swept through its valleys over the centuries. Arabs, Turks, Persians, and Russians all have ruled this region at one time or another. Many of these people stayed, making up the different groups living here today. Disagreements among some of these groups have sparked violent conflicts across the region.

The Caucasus republics once were part of the Soviet Union. When the Soviet Union collapsed in 1991, the republics became independent for the first time in centuries. Since then, the region has struggled to move to a free market economy.

◄ Oygaing River and Tian Shan mountain range in Kazakhstan

Armenia

Armenia, about the size of Maryland, sits uneasily on top of many **faults,** or cracks in the earth's crust. It often suffers serious earthquakes. In a 1988 earthquake, about 25,000 people died and another 500,000 lost their homes.

Armenia's 3.8 million people are mostly ethnic Armenians who share a unique language and culture. Nearly 70 percent of the people live in cities. Founded in 782 B.C., **Yerevan** (YEHR•uh•VAHN), the capital, is one of the world's most ancient cities. Armenians are proud of its wide streets, attractive fountains, and colorful buildings made of volcanic stone. An Armenian king made Christianity the official religion in A.D. 301—the first country to do so. About 94 percent of the nation's people belong to the Armenian Orthodox Church.

About 2,000 years ago, Armenia ruled a large empire from the Caspian Sea to the Mediterranean Sea. Today Armenia is not only

Applying Map Skills

1. What country is split into two parts by Armenia?
2. What is the capital of Georgia?

Find NGS online map resources @ www.nationalgeographic.com/maps

smaller but also **landlocked.** It has no land touching a sea or an ocean. One group of Armenians lives in an enclave in neighboring Azerbaijan. An **enclave** is a small territory entirely surrounded by another territory. Cut off from their homeland, these Armenians wish to rejoin Armenia. In the 1990s, newly independent Armenia and Azerbaijan began to fight over the enclave. The shooting has stopped, but the dispute continues.

Armenia paid a high price during the war with Azerbaijan. Officials in Azerbaijan halted the flow of fuel and other resources across their country to landlocked Armenia. This action seriously hurt Armenia's economy and environment. Without any fuel, Armenians cut down trees for firewood. This has led to a massive loss of forests. The drop in industry made agriculture more important to Armenia's economy. Farmers grow wheat, fruits, and vegetables in river valleys. Herders tend sheep and goats that feed on grassy mountain slopes.

Reading Check How has being landlocked recently affected Armenia?

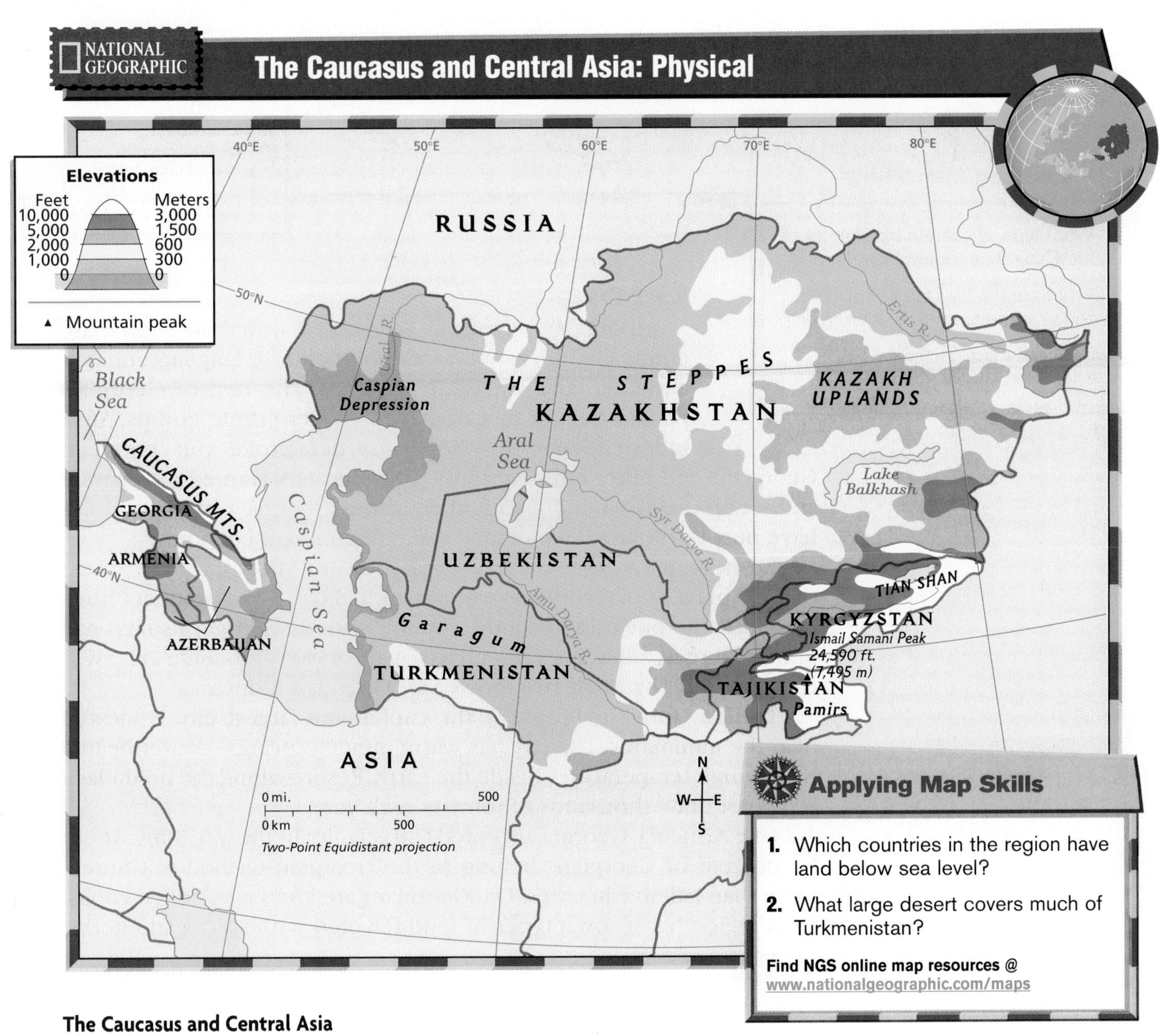

Applying Map Skills

1. Which countries in the region have land below sea level?
2. What large desert covers much of Turkmenistan?

Find NGS online map resources @ www.nationalgeographic.com/maps

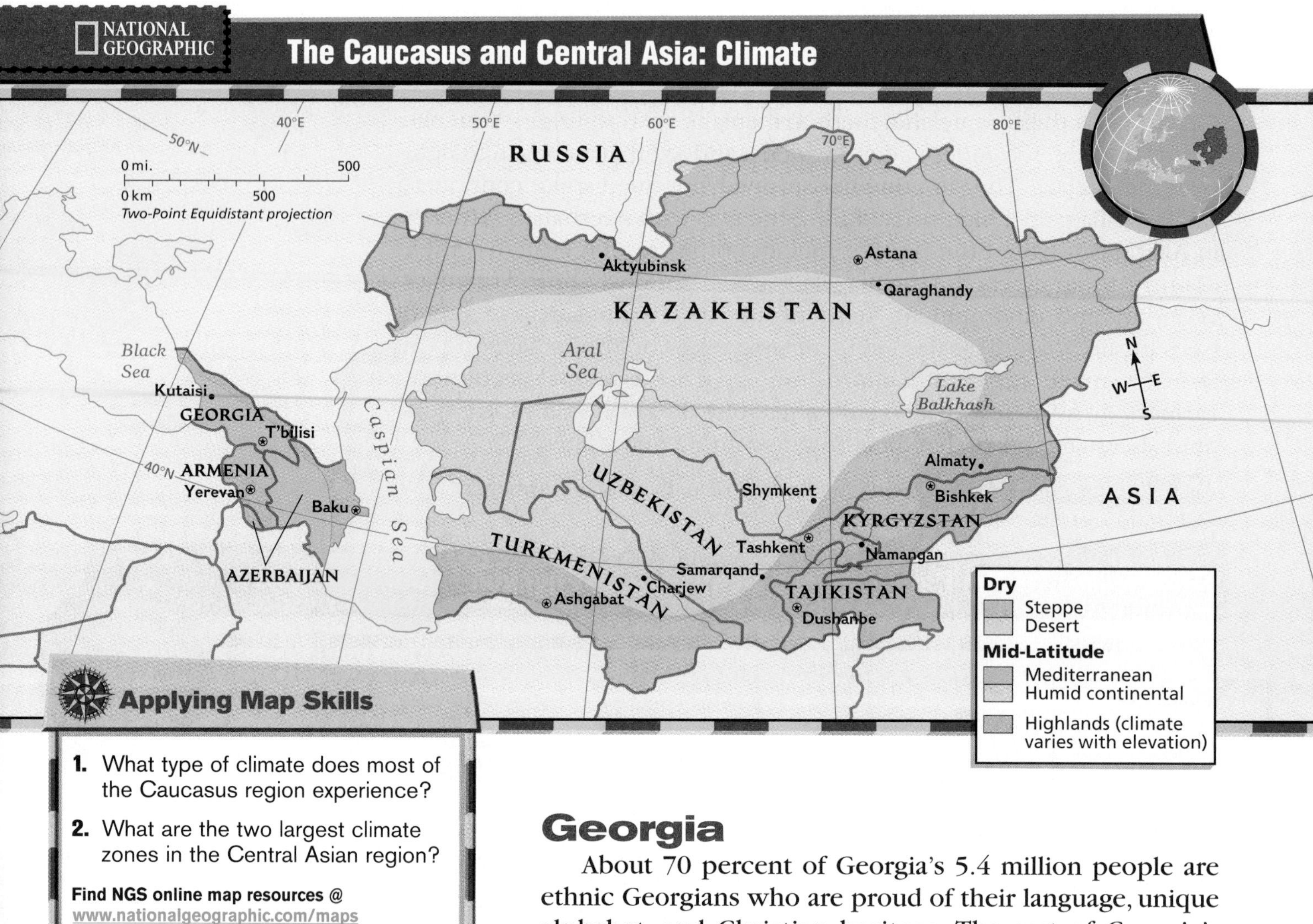

Applying Map Skills

1. What type of climate does most of the Caucasus region experience?
2. What are the two largest climate zones in the Central Asian region?

Find NGS online map resources @ www.nationalgeographic.com/maps

Georgia

About 70 percent of Georgia's 5.4 million people are ethnic Georgians who are proud of their language, unique alphabet, and Christian heritage. The rest of Georgia's people belong to a number of other ethnic groups. After independence in 1991, conflict broke out between Georgians and other ethnic groups. These groups wanted to separate and set up their own independent countries. Georgia's ethnic troubles have hurt its move to democracy and a free market economy.

Farmers in Georgia are few—but they are very productive. Less than 10 percent of Georgians work in agriculture. Farm products, however, make up one-third of all the country's goods. Georgia also has natural resources, such as copper, coal, manganese, and some oil. Swift rivers provide hydroelectric power for Georgia's industries.

T'bilisi (tuh•bih•LEE•see), the capital and largest city, is located near the mountains. The city has warm mineral springs—water heated by the high temperatures inside the earth. Resorts along the mild Black Sea coast draw thousands of tourists each year.

Like Armenia, Georgia accepted Christianity in the A.D. 300s. About 65 percent of Georgians belong to the Georgian Orthodox Church. More than half live in cities. The Georgians are known as skilled cooks. Each region has its own types of food flavored with spices and herbs.

Reading Check **What has hurt Georgia's attempts to become a democracy?**

Azerbaijan

Azerbaijan is split in two by Armenian territory. Most people belong to a group called Azeris. They speak the Azeri language, which is related to Turkish. They also follow the religion of Islam.

About one-third of Azerbaijan's people work in agriculture. Farmers in dry steppe areas use irrigation to grow cotton and tobacco as cash crops, or products grown for sale as exports. The humid climate near the Caspian shore helps farmers grow citrus fruits, grapes, and tea. Oil and natural gas deposits under the Caspian Sea are the most promising part of Azerbaijan's economy. The country has made agreements with foreign companies to develop these resources.

More than half of Azerbaijan's 7.7 million people live in cities. The capital, **Baku** (bah•KOO), is a port on the Caspian Sea. The center of the country's oil industry and manufacturing, Baku is known for the strong winds that blow through the city. In fact, its name comes from the Persian word for "windy town."

Azerbaijan's culture is a blend of Southwest Asian and European influences. The people of Azerbaijan like to eat richly spiced lamb and chicken along with rice and vegetables. The Caspian Sea yields catches of sturgeon, a fish whose eggs are prized as caviar. Craftspeople in Azerbaijan are known for their embroidered textiles. Weavers use colorful threads to create ornate patterns on wool fabric.

✓Reading Check **How does Azerbaijan's religion differ from that in Armenia and Georgia?**

Assessment

Defining Terms

1. Define fault, landlocked, enclave, cash crop.

Recalling Facts

2. Culture What is the official religion of Armenia?
3. Economics Name four of Georgia's natural resources.
4. Place What is the most promising part of Azerbaijan's economy?

Critical Thinking

5. Making Comparisons What common characteristics make the countries of Armenia, Georgia, and Azerbaijan a region?
6. Making Predictions How might the loss of so many trees affect the country of Armenia?

Graphic Organizer

7. Organizing Information Make a diagram like the one below. Then fill in details for each category for the Caucasus republics in the ovals.

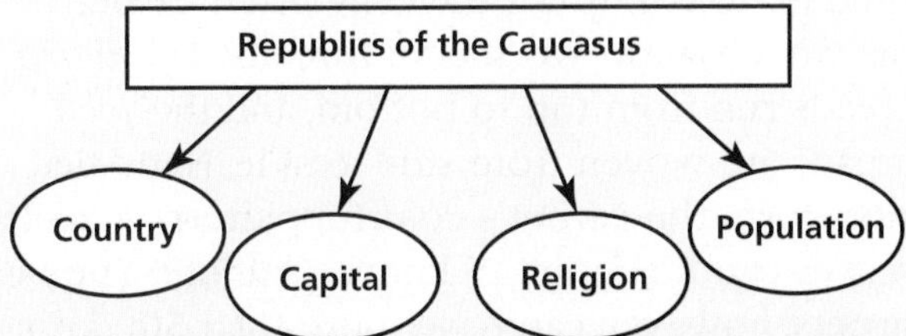

Applying Geography Skills

8. Analyzing Maps Study the political map on page 510. What capital city is located on the Caspian Sea? Now turn to the physical map on page 511. At what elevation does this capital city lie?

Making Connections

ART SCIENCE LITERATURE TECHNOLOGY

Carpet Weaving

For thousands of years, people have been making the hand-knotted floor coverings sometimes called Oriental rugs. Valued for their rich color and intricate design, these handmade rugs are unique works of art.

History

Most experts think that the nomadic peoples of Central Asia were among the first to make hand-knotted carpets. They used their carpets as wall coverings, curtains, and saddlebags, as well as to cover the bare ground in their tents. The soft, thick rugs blocked out the cold and could also be used as a bed or blanket.

As the nomads moved from place to place, they spread the art of carpet-making to new lands and peoples. Throughout the years, the greatest carpet-producing areas have included Turkey, the republics of the Caucasus, Persia, and Turkmenistan. People in other countries, including Afghanistan, Pakistan, Nepal, India, and China, also became skilled carpet weavers.

Weaving and Knotting

Early nomads wove their carpets from sheep's wool on simple wooden looms that could be rolled up for traveling. Each carpet was woven with two sets of threads. The *warp* threads run from top to bottom, and the *weft* threads are woven from side to side. Hand-tied knots form the carpet's colorful pattern. A skillful weaver can tie about 15 knots a minute. The best carpets, however, can have more than 500 knots per square inch!

Color and Design

The beauty of woven carpets comes from the endless combination of colors and designs. Over the years, various regions developed their own carpet patterns. These were passed down from generation to generation. Often the images hold special meanings. For instance, the palm and coconut often symbolize happiness and blessings.

▲ Women weave silk carpets in Uzbekistan.

The very first rugs were colored gray, white, brown, or black—the natural color of the wool. Then people learned to make dyes from plants and animals. The root of the madder plant, as well as certain insects, provided red and pink dye. Turmeric root and saffron supplied shades of yellow, while the indigo plant provided blue.

Making the Connection

1. How did the art of carpet weaving spread from one place to another?
2. What creates the pattern in an Oriental carpet?
3. **Drawing Conclusions** In what way do hand-knotted carpets combine art with usefulness?

Section 2

Central Asian Republics

Guide to Reading

Main Idea

The Muslim countries of Central Asia are trying to build new economies and governments.

Terms to Know

- steppe
- delta
- nomad
- elevation
- clan
- bilingual
- oasis

Places to Locate

- Kazakhstan
- Kyrgyzstan
- Tajikistan
- Uzbekistan
- Turkmenistan
- Aral Sea
- Garagum

Reading Strategy

In a chart like this, write two facts about each country in Central Asia.

Country	Facts
Kazakhstan	
Kyrgyzstan	
Tajikistan	
Uzbekistan	
Turkmenistan	

NATIONAL GEOGRAPHIC **Exploring Our World**

For centuries, the city of Bukhara was a stop along an ancient trading route called the Silk Road, which stretched from China to Europe. In the past, precious Chinese silk was carried on the backs of camels. Silk is still sold in Bukhara's markets. Today, however, international trade occurs through a system of fiber-optic cables laid along the ancient tracks of the Silk Road camels.

Five countries make up the Central Asian republics. They are **Kazakhstan** (kuh•ZAHK•STAHN), **Kyrgyzstan** (KIHR•gih•STAN), **Tajikistan** (tah•JIH•kih•STAN), **Uzbekistan** (uz•BEH•kih•STAN), and **Turkmenistan** (tuhrk•MEH•nuh•STAN). They were part of the Soviet Union. When that nation fell apart in 1991, the republics became independent. In addition, these republics all follow the Islamic religion.

Kazakhstan

Almost four times the size of Texas, Kazakhstan dominates the northern part of Central Asia. The map on page 511 shows you that the Kazakh Uplands make up the eastern part. In this rugged area, you will find the unusual Lake Balkhash. It is so long that there is salt water in its eastern half and freshwater in its western half. Toward the center of Kazakhstan lie the Steppes. A **steppe** is a dry, treeless plain often found on the edges of a desert. In the west, the Caspian Depression lies

Geography Online

Web Activity Visit the ***Geography: The World and Its People*** Web site at gwip.glencoe.com and click on **Chapter 18–Student Web Activities** to learn more about Kazakhstan.

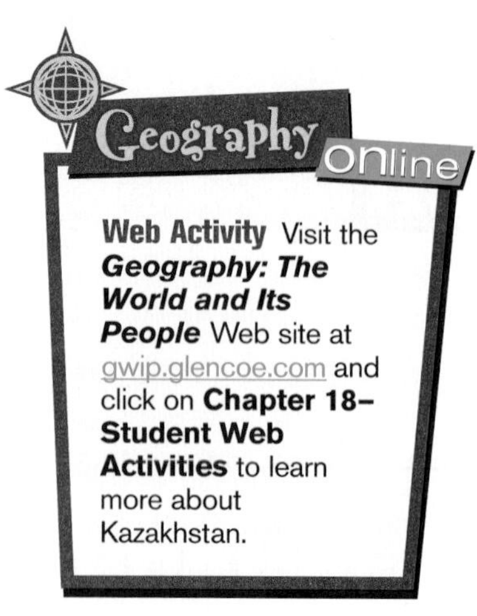

below sea level. Part of this region is the delta of the Ural River. A **delta** is the area where soil has been deposited by a river at its mouth. Two other rivers are important to Kazakhstan. The Ertis (ehr•TIHS) River, called the Irtysh when it flows through Russia, provides water for farmland in the northeast. The Syr Darya (sihr duhr•YAH) River flows across south-central deserts to reach the **Aral Sea.**

Kazakhstan's mineral resources include copper, manganese, gold, zinc, and petroleum. Kazakhstan's factories are very productive. They make machinery and chemicals and process foods. Farming is difficult in the harsh climate, but raising livestock on ranches is an important industry.

Many of Kazakhstan's people are ethnic Kazakhs, whose ancestors were horse-riding warriors called the Mongols. Like the Mongols, the Kazakhs were mostly **nomads,** or people who move from place to place with herds of animals. Under Soviet Communist rule, farms were placed under government control. Kazakh nomads were forced to settle in one place. During this time—in the 1930s—about 1 million Kazakhs died of starvation.

After World War II, the Soviet Union rapidly set up factories, and Russian workers poured into the country. Even today, Kazakhs make up less than one-half of the country's people. Russians form the second-largest group.

NATIONAL GEOGRAPHIC

The Caucasus and Central Asia: Economic Activity

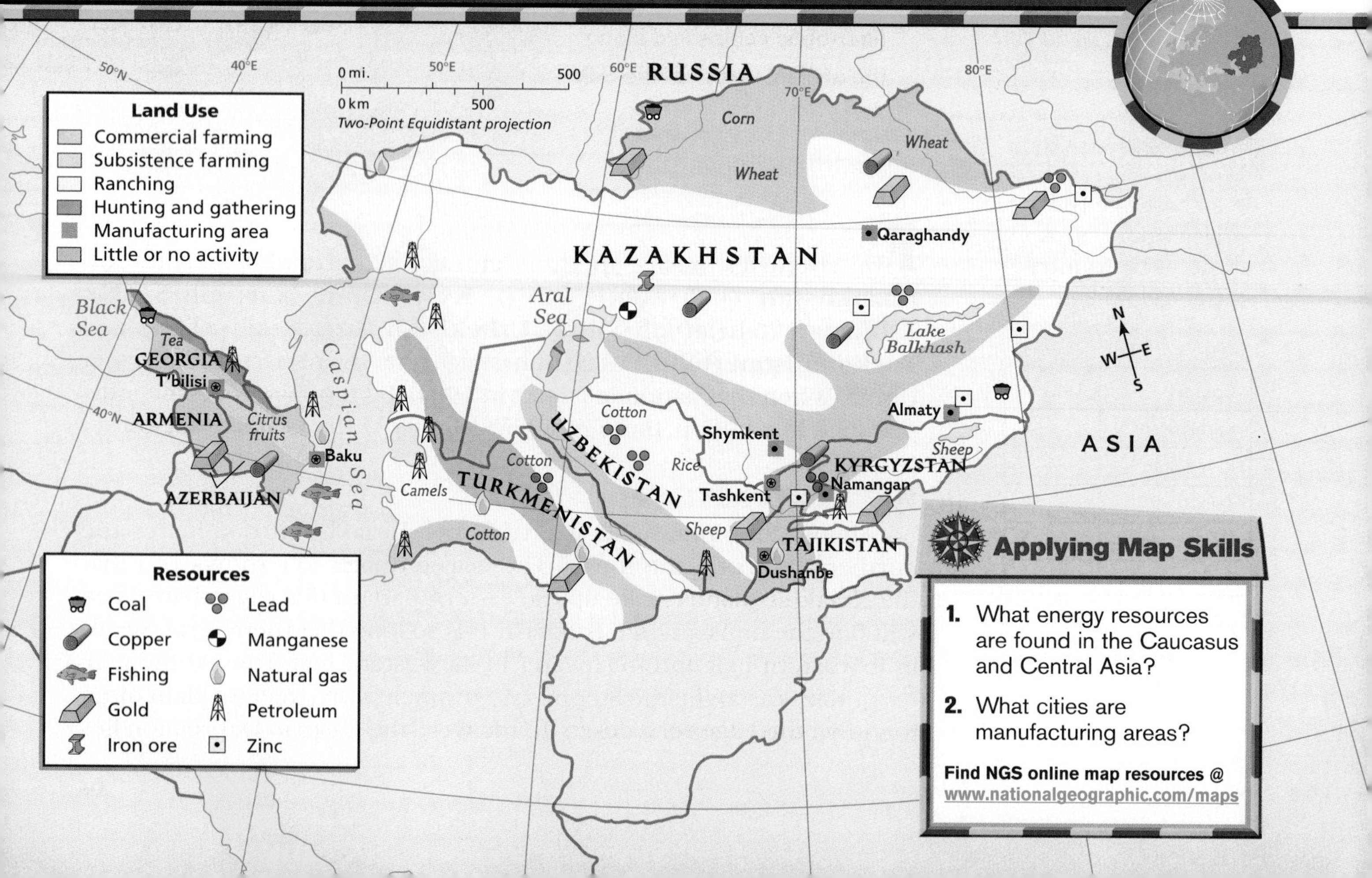

Land Use
Commercial farming
Subsistence farming
Ranching
Hunting and gathering
Manufacturing area
Little or no activity
0 mi. 500
0 km 500
Two-Point Equidistant projection
50°N
40°N
40°E
50°E
60°E
70°E
80°E
RUSSIA
KAZAKHSTAN
Corn
Wheat
Qaraghandy
Aral Sea
Lake Balkhash
Black Sea
Caspian Sea
Tea
GEORGIA
T'bilisi
ARMENIA
Citrus fruits
Baku
AZERBAIJAN
Camels
Cotton
TURKMENISTAN
UZBEKISTAN
Rice
Sheep
Shymkent
Tashkent
Almaty
KYRGYZSTAN
Namangan
TAJIKISTAN
Dushanbe
ASIA
N
E
S
W
Resources
Coal
Copper
Fishing
Gold
Iron ore
Lead
Manganese
Natural gas
Petroleum
Zinc

Applying Map Skills

1. What energy resources are found in the Caucasus and Central Asia?
2. What cities are manufacturing areas?

Find NGS online map resources @ www.nationalgeographic.com/maps

Rapid industrialization has ruined the environment. Diverting water for irrigation has drained rivers, and chemical fertilizers have polluted the soil. Environmental damage also occurred during Soviet testing of nuclear weapons in Kazakhstan. The new Kazakh government has faced the enormous challenge of cleaning up the environment.

Reading Check **What people are ancestors of the Kazakhs?**

Kazakh Nomads

The traditional home of Kazakhs—called a yurt—can be easily taken apart and moved.

Movement **Why would these features be important to the Mongols and early Kazakh people?**

Kyrgyzstan

The lofty Tian Shan (tee•AHN SHAHN) mountain range makes up most of Kyrgyzstan. The climate depends on an area's height above sea level, or **elevation.** Lower valleys and plains have warm, dry summers and chilly winters. Higher areas have cool summers and bitterly cold winters. The harsh climate and lack of fertile soil hinder farmers. They manage to grow cotton, vegetables, and fruits, though. Many also raise sheep or cattle. Kyrgyzstan has few industries, but it does have valuable deposits of mercury and gold.

More than half of the people belong to the Kyrgyz ethnic group. Differences among **clans,** or family groups, often separate one part of the country from another. Kyrgyzstan is a **bilingual** country—one that has two official languages. These are Kirghiz, related to Turkish, and Russian. About 40 percent of the people live in cities, such as the capital, Bishkek.

Reading Check **What are Kyrgyzstan's official languages?**

Tajikistan

Tajikistan is even more mountainous than Kyrgyzstan. Find the mountains known as the Pamirs (puh•MIHRZ) on the map on page 511. Now look for Ismail Samani Peak. Once called Communism Peak, it is the highest mountain in Central Asia.

Agriculture is the most important activity in Tajikistan. Farmers grow cotton, rice, and fruits in fertile river valleys. Mountain streams provide water for irrigation as well as for hydroelectric power.

The largest city is Dushanbe (doo•SHAM•buh), the capital. Most of Tajikistan's people are Tajiks, who are related to the Persians. Another 25 percent are Uzbeks, a group related to the Turks. In 1992 a bitter civil war broke out between rival clans. Many people were killed, and the economy was severely damaged. Despite a peace agreement in 1997, tensions still remain high.

Reading Check **What has recently damaged the economy of Tajikistan?**

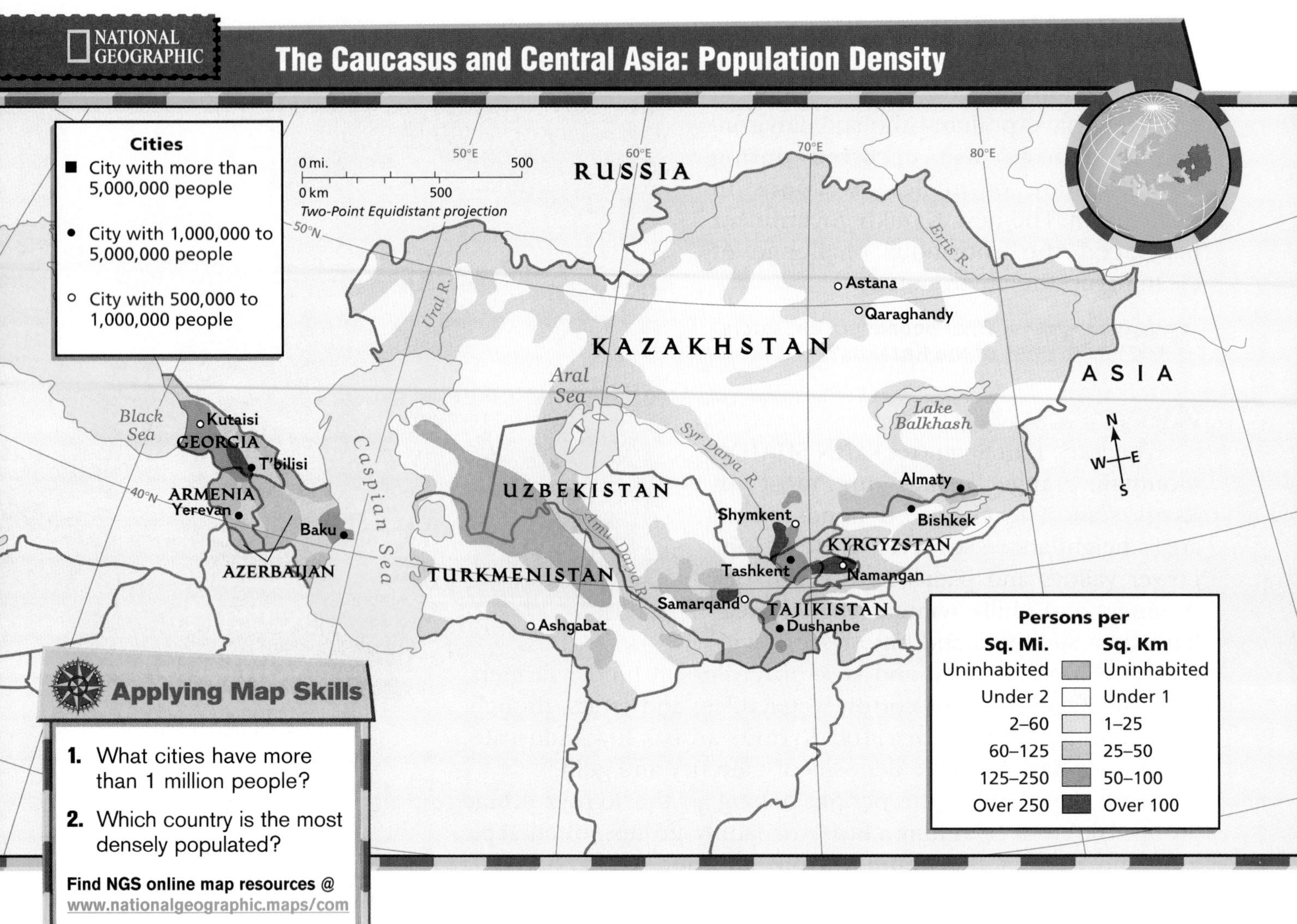

Uzbekistan

Uzbekistan, slightly larger than California, lies between the Amu Darya and the Syr Darya Rivers. Its economy relies on crops grown in fertile river valleys. Uzbekistan is one of the world's largest cotton producers. This boom in cotton, unfortunately, has had disastrous effects on the environment. Large farms needing irrigation have nearly drained away the rivers flowing into the Aral Sea. Receiving less freshwater, the sea has steadily shrunk, and its salt level has increased. Fish and wildlife have disappeared, and salt particles have polluted the air and soil. To create prosperity, Uzbek leaders are now trying to add more variety to the economy. They also want to use newly discovered deposits of oil, gas, and gold.

Most of Uzbekistan's 24.4 million people are Uzbeks who generally live in fertile valleys and oases. An **oasis,** as you recall, is a green area in a desert watered by an underground spring. Tashkent, the capital, is the largest city and industrial center in Central Asia. About 2,000 years ago, the oases of Tashkent, Bukhara, and Samarqand were part of the busy trade route—the Silk Road—that linked China and Europe.

Reading Check **Why has the Aral Sea shrunk in size?**

Turkmenistan

Turkmenistan is larger than neighboring Uzbekistan, but it has far fewer people. Why? Most of this vast land—about 85 percent—is part of a huge desert called the **Garagum** (GAHR•uh•GOOM). Making up the northern and central region, *Garagum* means "black sand." Hidden beneath it are still-to-be-tapped oil and natural gas deposits.

Despite the harshness of the land and climate, agriculture is the leading economic activity. Raising livestock is another important activity. However, not enough produce is available to feed everyone in the country, and much food has to be imported.

More than 75 percent of Turkmenistan's 4.8 million people belong to the Turkmen ethnic group. Ashgabat, the capital, is the country's largest city and leading economic and cultural center. More than one-half of Turkmenistan's people live in rural areas, though. Turkmen villages usually are located near oases formed by mountain streams along Turkmenistan's southern border.

The Turkmen people were nomads who raised camels and other livestock in the desert. Under Soviet rule, the nomads were forced to settle on farms. In the 1950s, Soviet engineers built a large irrigation and shipping canal. This technological feat greatly increased the land area used for growing cotton. However, as in Uzbekistan, cotton growing has helped to dry up the Aral Sea. Turkmenistan is hoping that its oil and natural gas resources will give it a brighter future.

✓Reading Check Why do most Turkmen live along the southern border?

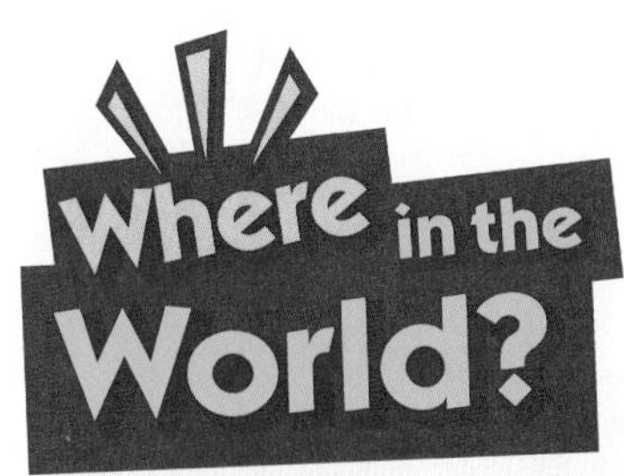

The Aral Sea

This ship once moved along the waters of the Aral Sea. The sea was huge—the fourth-largest inland body of water in the world. To irrigate fields of cotton, Soviet leaders took water from the rivers that flowed into the Aral Sea. The sea shrank to one-half its former size in just 40 years. Now camels walk where fish once swam.

Section 2 Assessment

Defining Terms

1. **Define** steppe, delta, nomad, elevation, clan, bilingual, oasis.

Recalling Facts

2. **Economics** What products are made by factories in Kazakhstan?
3. **Location** What is the highest mountain in Central Asia?
4. **Place** What is unusual about Lake Balkhash?

Critical Thinking

5. **Understanding Cause and Effect** How does a trade route like the Silk Road contribute to the development of civilization?
6. **Drawing Conclusions** How would adding variety to an economy create prosperity?

Graphic Organizer

7. **Organizing Information** Draw a diagram like this and list the results of diverting the rivers that empty into the Aral Sea.

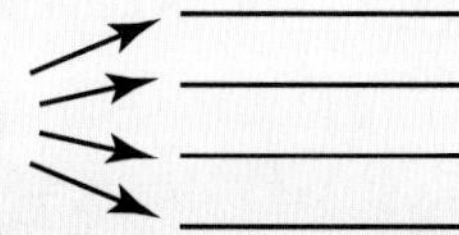

Applying Geography Skills

8. **Analyzing Maps** Study the physical map on page 511. What river forms part of the border between Turkmenistan and Uzbekistan?

Critical Thinking Skill

Analyzing Information

So much information comes our way in today's world. How can you analyze it to decide what is truly useful and accurate?

Learning the Skill

There are two basic types of information sources. *Primary sources* are original records of events made by the people who witnessed them. They include letters, photographs, and artifacts. *Secondary sources* are documents created after an event occurred. They report an event.

When reading sources, try to learn more about the person who wrote the information. Most people have a point of view, or bias. This bias influences the way they write about events.

To analyze information, follow these steps:

- Determine whether the information is a primary or secondary source.
- Identify who created the document and when it was created.
- Read the document. Who and what is it about? What are its purpose and main ideas?
- Determine how the author's point of view, or bias, is reflected in the work.

▼ **A polluted playground in Azerbaijan**

Practicing the Skill

Read the passage below, then answer the questions that follow.

> I went south to Kazakhstan and, at 4:45 A.M., stumbled off a train in Aral and went to the hospital. Beginning in the 1970s the people became ill with hepatitis, typhus, and other diseases. They drank from the rivers, as always, but now the shrunken rivers ran with sewage, industrial metals, and poisons such as DDT. "It wasn't possible to mix infant formula with that water," said a doctor. "It made goo, like soft cheese."
>
> Dust storms often blow for days, sweeping up tons of salts and fertilizers. Doctors brace then to receive children with breathing problems. Kazakhstan, declared a Kazakh writer, was the Soviet Union's "junk heap."

Adapted from "The U.S.S.R.'s Lethal Legacy" by Mike Edwards, *National Geographic,* August 1994.

1. Is this a primary or secondary source?
2. Who is the author of this passage?
3. What is the document about?
4. Where does it take place?
5. What is the purpose of this passage?
6. What, if any, evidence of bias do you find?

Applying the Skill

Analyze one of the letters to the editor in your local newspaper. Summarize the main idea, the writer's purpose, and any primary sources the writer may refer to.

GO TO

Practice key skills with **Glencoe Skillbuilder Interactive Workbook, Level 1.**

Chapter 18

Reading Review

Section 1 Republics of the Caucasus

Terms to Know

fault
landlocked
enclave
cash crop

Main Idea

The Caucasus countries have developed their own cultures despite long periods of rule by powerful neighbors.

✓ Region The tall Caucasus Mountains run through Armenia, Georgia, and Azerbaijan. All three countries were part of the Soviet Union until its breakup in 1991.

✓ Economics Farming is important in all three countries. Georgia and Armenia have industries, including tourism.

✓ History Armenia and Georgia were ancient kingdoms that adopted Christianity many centuries ago.

✓ Economics Azerbaijan, a Muslim country, has an important oil industry.

Section 2 Central Asian Republics

Terms to Know

steppe
delta
nomad
elevation
clan
bilingual
oasis

Main Idea

The Muslim countries of Central Asia are trying to build new economies and governments.

✓ Region Much of the land in the Central Asian republics is covered by desert or grassy steppe. Tall mountains rise in the southeast.

✓ Culture Almost all of the people in the five Central Asian republics are Muslims.

✓ Economics Kazakhstan has rich deposits of oil, copper, and gold.

✓ Economics Most of these countries are poor, and most people engage in farming.

✓ Human/Environment Interaction Uzbekistan and Turkmenistan have thriving cotton production, but the water taken to irrigate their fields is making the Aral Sea shrink.

Republic Square in Yerevan, Armenia ▶

Chapter 18

Assessment and Activities

Using Key Terms

Match the terms in Part A with their definitions in Part B.

A.

1. landlocked
2. oasis
3. bilingual
4. elevation
5. enclave
6. steppe
7. delta
8. fault
9. nomads
10. cash crop

B.

a. dry, treeless grasslands
b. green vegetation surrounded by desert
c. people who move from place to place
d. crack in the earth's crust
e. small region located inside a larger country
f. height above sea level
g. country that has no land on a sea or ocean
h. soil deposited by water at a river's mouth
i. products grown for sale as exports
j. having or speaking two languages

Reviewing the Main Ideas

Section 1 Republics of the Caucasus

11. **Location** Between what two bodies of water are Armenia, Georgia, and Azerbaijan located?
12. **Region** Why do earthquakes occur in Armenia?
13. **Government** What caused Armenia and Azerbaijan to go to war in the 1990s?
14. **Place** What is the capital of Azerbaijan?

Section 2 Central Asian Republics

15. **Region** What are the five countries that make up the Central Asian republics?
16. **History** Why did 1 million Kazakhs die during the 1930s?
17. **Place** What mountain range makes up most of Kyrgyzstan?
18. **Economics** What is the most important economic activity in Tajikistan?
19. **Place** What desert occupies most of Turkmenistan?
20. **Culture** What religion do the people of the Central Asian republics follow?

The Caucasus and Central Asia

Place Location Activity

On a separate sheet of paper, match the letters on the map with the numbered places listed below.

1. Kazakhstan
2. Aral Sea
3. Caspian Sea
4. Turkmenistan
5. Azerbaijan
6. Armenia
7. Tajikistan
8. Baku

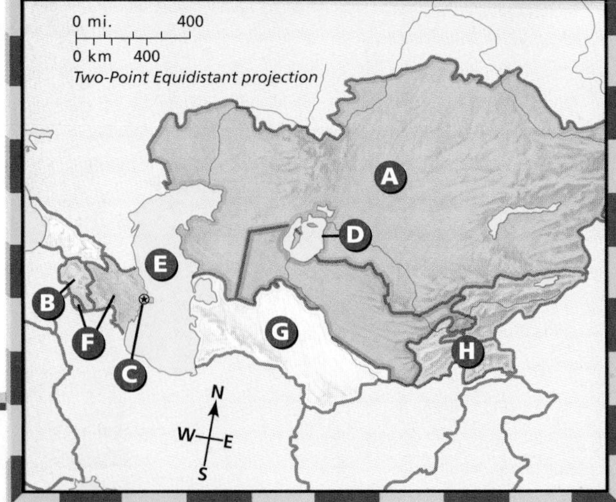

Self-Check Quiz Visit the ***Geography: The World and Its People*** Web site at gwip.glencoe.com and click on **Chapter 18–Self-Check Quizzes** to prepare for the Chapter Test.

 Critical Thinking

21. **Understanding Cause and Effect** Why are there so many Russians living in the countries of Central Asia?
22. **Organizing Information** Make a chart like this one. Then list the similarities and differences between two Central Asian republics' economies.

Country	Similarities	Differences

 GeoJournal Activity 

23. **Writing a Story** Most of the Central Asian republics have a rich tradition of songs, poems, and stories told by word of mouth. Write a story that explains some custom or aspect of your culture. Practice telling your story aloud. Then share it with the class.

 Mental Mapping Activity

24. **Focusing on the Region** Draw a simple outline map of the Caucasus and Central Asia, then label the following:
    - Black Sea
    - Caspian Sea
    - Aral Sea
    - Kazakhstan
    - Caucasus Mountains
    - Georgia
    - Garagum
    - Turkmenistan
    - Lake Balkhash
    - Tashkent

 Technology Skills Activity 

25. **Developing a Multimedia Presentation** Research the Silk Road and create a presentation about it. Your presentation should include a map marked with the route and important cities. Also include examples of the goods that were traded. Try to find the names of any important travelers who may have used the Silk Road.

Standardized Test Practice

Directions: Read the paragraph below, then answer the question that follows.

You may be surprised to know that Kazakhstan was—and still is—important to the exploration of outer space. The Russian space center Baikonur (BY•kuh•NOOR) lies in south-central Kazakhstan. During the Soviet period, Baikonur was used for many space launches. Several historic "firsts in space" occurred here. For example, the first satellite was launched in 1957. The first manned flight took place when cosmonaut Yuri Gagarin orbited the earth in 1961. In addition, the flight of the first woman in space, Valentina Tereshkova, was launched in 1963. After the Soviet collapse, the Russian-owned center remained on independent Kazakh territory.

1. The Soviet space program at Baikonur holds great importance, mostly because

F it is located in south-central Kazakhstan.

G it provides jobs for the people who live near the launch site.

H many "first in space" flights were launched from it.

J Valentina Tereshkova was the first woman in space.

Test-Taking Tip: When a question uses the word *most* or *mostly,* it means that more than one answer may be correct. Your job is to pick the *best* answer. For example, Baikonur's location in Kazakhstan may be important to the people who live near it, which is answer G. Another answer, however, provides a more general reason for Baikonur's importance.

Waterfront of Cape Town, South Africa

Woman making butter in Chad

Giraffe on a plain in Kenya ▼

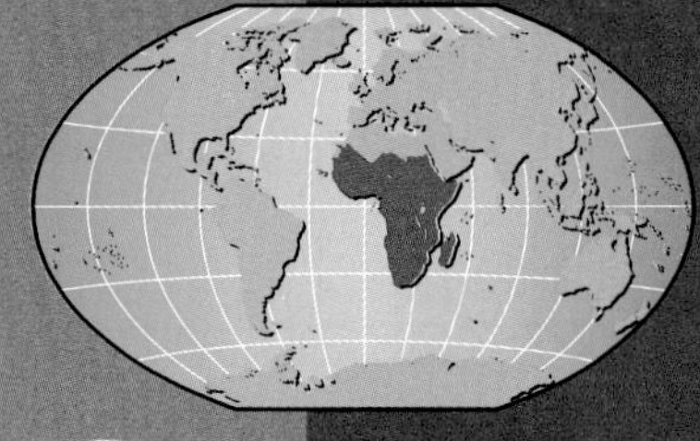

Africa South of the Sahara

The region of Africa south of the Sahara is home to more than 2,000 ethnic groups. Its hot, humid forests and dry grasslands support a variety of wild animals. Both people and animals face tough challenges in this region. The people are struggling to build stable governments and economies. Some animals are threatened with extinction as human activities destroy natural habitats.

NGS ONLINE
www.nationalgeographic.com/education

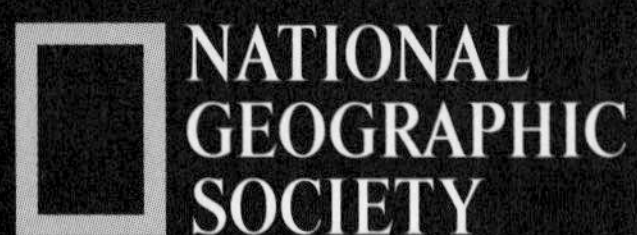

Focus on:

Africa South of the Sahara

STRADDLING THE EQUATOR, Africa south of the Sahara lies almost entirely within the tropics. Famous for its remarkable wildlife, this region also has the world's fastest-growing human population. Settling ethnic rivalries and improving low standards of living are just two of the challenges facing the people in Africa south of the Sahara.

The Land

Africa south of the Sahara has the highest overall elevation of any world region. A narrow band of low plains hugs the coastline. Inland, the land rises from west to east in a series of steplike plateaus. Separating the plateaus are steep cliffs. The region has no long mountain ranges and few towering peaks, although Mt. Kenya and Kilimanjaro are exceptions. At 19,340 feet (5,895 m), Kilimanjaro's summit is the highest point on the African continent.

Great rivers arise in this region's interior highlands. As rivers spill from one plateau to the next, they create thundering waterfalls, such as the spectacular Victoria Falls (right). It is known locally as *Mosi oa Tunya*—"smoke that thunders." Although the Nile River is Africa's longest river, the Congo River is a giant in its own right, winding 2,715 miles (4,370 km) through Africa's heart, near the Equator.

The Great Rift Valley slices through eastern Africa like a steep-walled gash in the continent. Formed by movements of the earth's crust, the valley extends from Southwest Asia southward to the Zambezi River in Mozambique. It cradles a chain of deep lakes.

The Climate

If you started at the Equator and traveled north or south from there, you would pass through four major climate regions, one after the other. Tropical rain forests lie along the Equator and fill the great basin of the Congo River in central and western Africa. Head away from the Equator and you see rain forests give way to tropical savannas. These vast grasslands are home to some of the continent's most famous large mammals, including elephants, lions, rhinoceroses, and giraffes.

As you move farther from the Equator, rainfall becomes scarce, and savannas give way to tropical steppes. Finally you encounter very dry areas where deserts dominate the landscape. Deserts cover more of Africa than any other continent. The largest deserts south of the Sahara are the Namib and the Kalahari.

UNIT 7

Victoria Falls, on the Zambezi River ▼

◀ Elephants browsing near Kilimanjaro, Tanzania

The Economy

Africa south of the Sahara is rich in mineral resources, but these resources are not evenly distributed. Nigeria has huge reserves of oil. South Africa has fabulous deposits of gold and diamonds, making it the wealthiest country in the region. Overall, however, Africa south of the Sahara has the lowest standard of living of any world region.

Manufacturing plays only a small role in the region's economy. In the past, colonial rulers used Africa as a source of raw materials and left the continent largely undeveloped. Today the nations south of the Sahara are struggling to industrialize.

Most people in Africa south of the Sahara still depend on small-scale farming or livestock herding for their livelihoods. They usually are able to raise only enough food to feed their families. Some farmers work on plantations that grow crops for export to other countries. Such crops include coffee, cacao, cotton, peanuts, tea, bananas, and sisal (a fiber). Drought is a constant problem for the region's farmers.

The People

Thousands of years ago, great kingdoms and empires developed in Africa south of the Sahara. In the 1400s and 1500s, Europeans began trading with African societies, carrying away gold, spices, ivory, and enslaved people.

By the late 1800s, European nations had claimed almost all of Africa. For profit and political advantage, they carved up the continent into colonies. In the process, they ripped apart once-unified regions and threw together ethnic groups that did not get along.

Most African nations won their independence in the mid-1900s. Most emerged from colonial rule politically unstable and with crippled economies.

Today more than 625 million people inhabit Africa south of the Sahara. They represent some 2,000 ethnic groups and speak 800 different languages. Nearly three-fourths of the population lives in rural areas. Although Africa is the least urbanized continent, its cities are growing. Lured by the promise of better living conditions, people are flocking to African cities, which are among the fastest-growing urban areas in the world.

Exploring the Region

1. **What happens when Africa's rivers flow from one plateau to another?**
2. **What climate zone is centered on the Equator?**
3. **What makes South Africa the region's most prosperous country?**
4. **How did colonial rule affect Africa south of the Sahara?**

◀ **Woman fertilizing crops in Zimbabwe**

UNIT 7

◀ Crowded market in Lagos, Nigeria

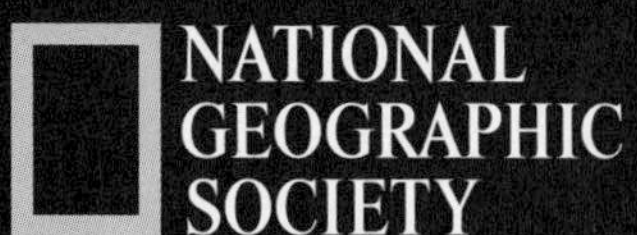

Africa South of the Sahara

Physical

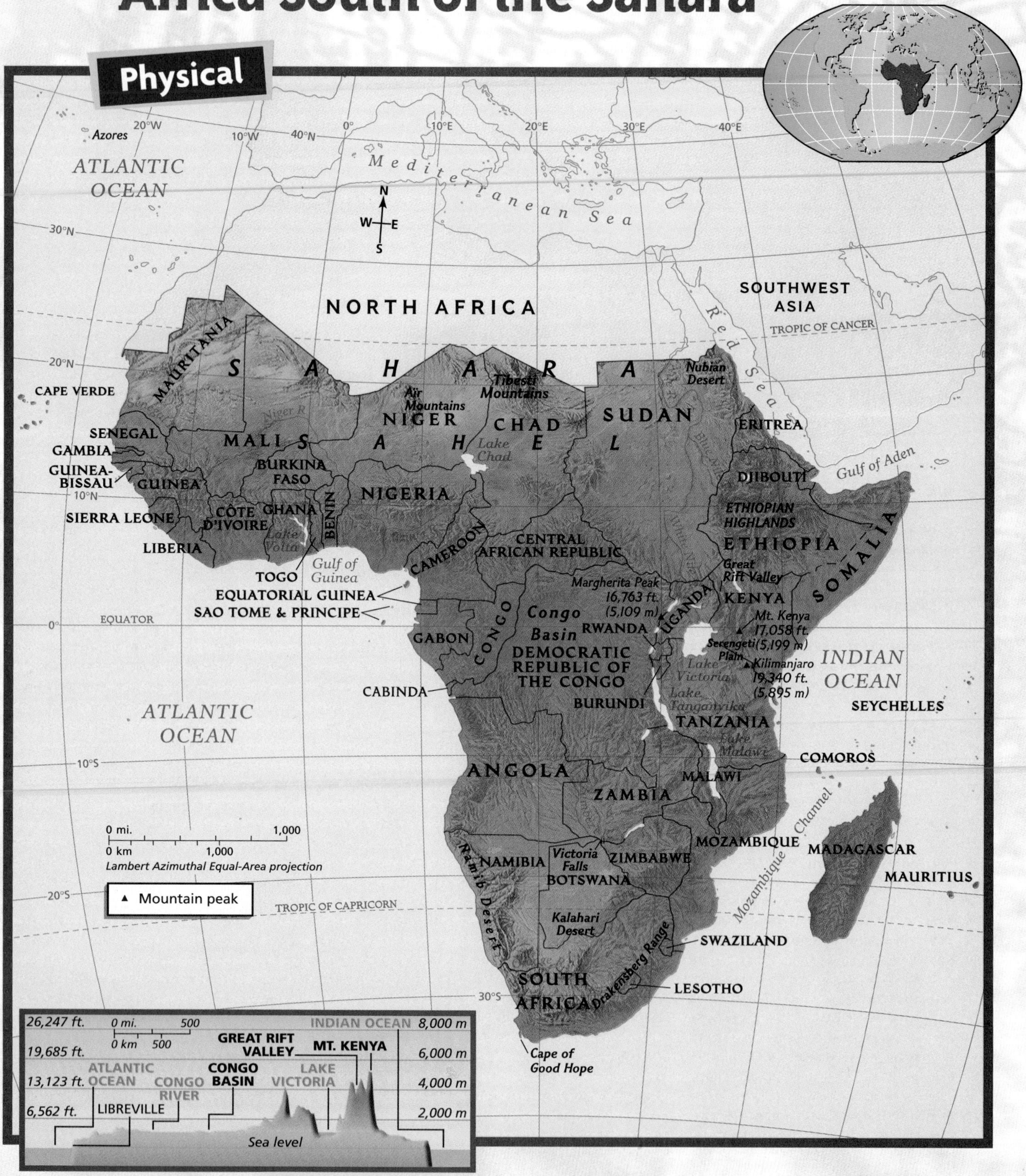

Azores
ATLANTIC OCEAN
Mediterranean Sea
NORTH AFRICA
SOUTHWEST ASIA
TROPIC OF CANCER
Red Sea
Nubian Desert
SAHARA
MAURITANIA
CAPE VERDE
Aïr Mountains
Tibesti Mountains
NIGER
CHAD
SUDAN
ERITREA
SENEGAL
GAMBIA
GUINEA-BISSAU
GUINEA
MALI
SAHEL
Lake Chad
BURKINA FASO
NIGERIA
DJIBOUTI
Gulf of Aden
SIERRA LEONE
CÔTE D'IVOIRE
GHANA
BENIN
LIBERIA
Lake Volta
ETHIOPIAN HIGHLANDS
ETHIOPIA
SOMALIA
CAMEROON
CENTRAL AFRICAN REPUBLIC
Gulf of Guinea
TOGO
EQUATORIAL GUINEA
SAO TOME & PRINCIPE
Great Rift Valley
Margherita Peak 16,763 ft. (5,109 m)
UGANDA
KENYA
EQUATOR
CONGO
Congo Basin
RWANDA
Mt. Kenya 17,058 ft. (5,199 m)
GABON
DEMOCRATIC REPUBLIC OF THE CONGO
Serengeti Plain
Lake Victoria
Kilimanjaro 19,340 ft. (5,895 m)
INDIAN OCEAN
CABINDA
BURUNDI
Lake Tanganyika
SEYCHELLES
ATLANTIC OCEAN
TANZANIA
Lake Malawi
COMOROS
ANGOLA
MALAWI
ZAMBIA
Mozambique Channel
MOZAMBIQUE
MADAGASCAR
Namib Desert
NAMIBIA
Victoria Falls
ZIMBABWE
BOTSWANA
MAURITIUS
TROPIC OF CAPRICORN
Kalahari Desert
Drakensberg Range
SWAZILAND
SOUTH AFRICA
LESOTHO
Cape of Good Hope

0 mi. 1,000
0 km 1,000
Lambert Azimuthal Equal-Area projection

▲ Mountain peak

26,247 ft. | 8,000 m
19,685 ft. | 6,000 m
13,123 ft. | 4,000 m
6,562 ft. | 2,000 m
0 mi. 500
0 km 500
ATLANTIC OCEAN
LIBREVILLE
CONGO RIVER
CONGO BASIN
GREAT RIFT VALLEY
LAKE VICTORIA
MT. KENYA
INDIAN OCEAN
Sea level

UNIT 7

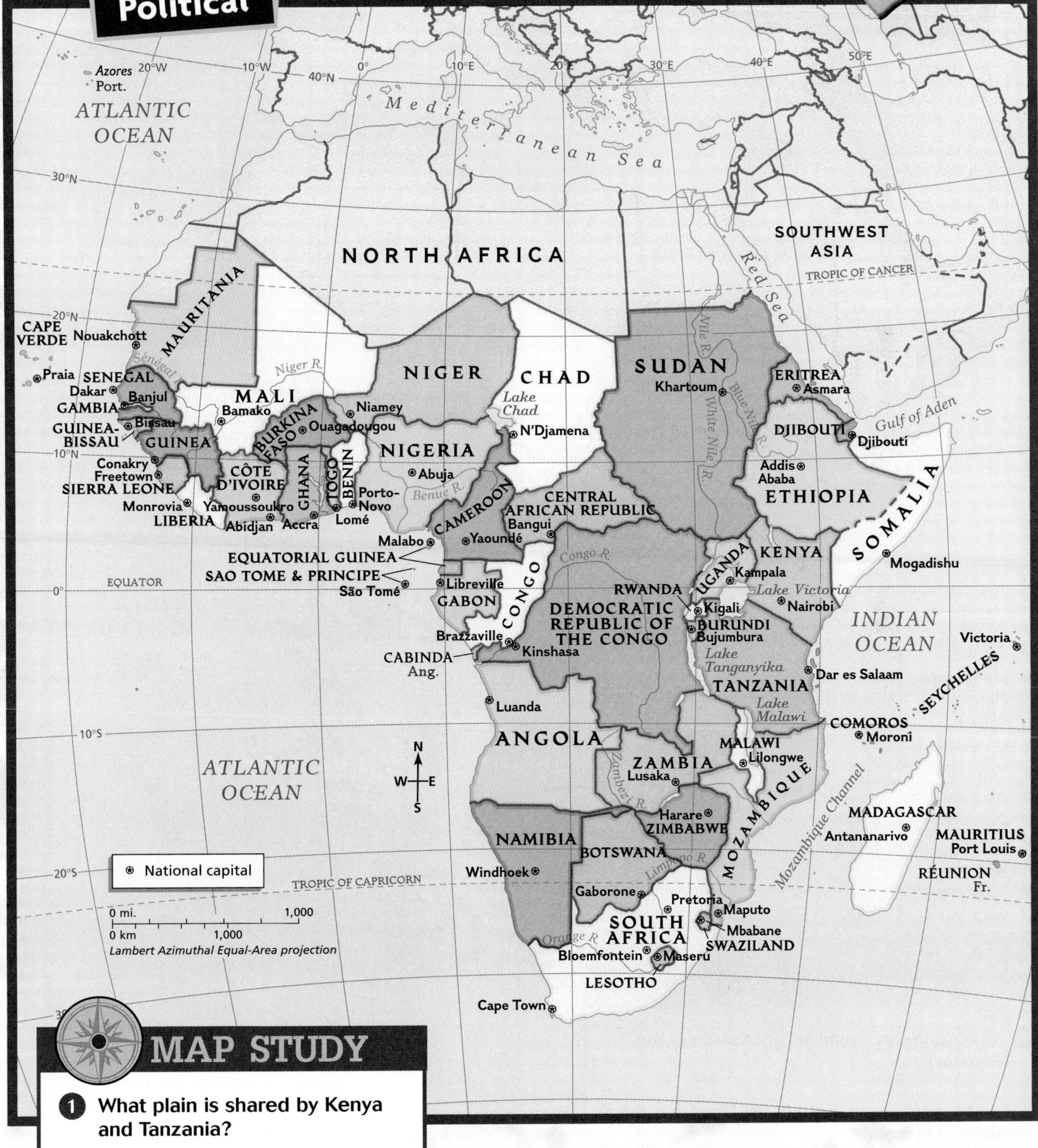

MAP STUDY

1. What plain is shared by Kenya and Tanzania?
2. What is the capital of Nigeria?

NATIONAL GEOGRAPHIC SOCIETY

REGIONAL ATLAS

Africa South of the Sahara

Gems and Minerals

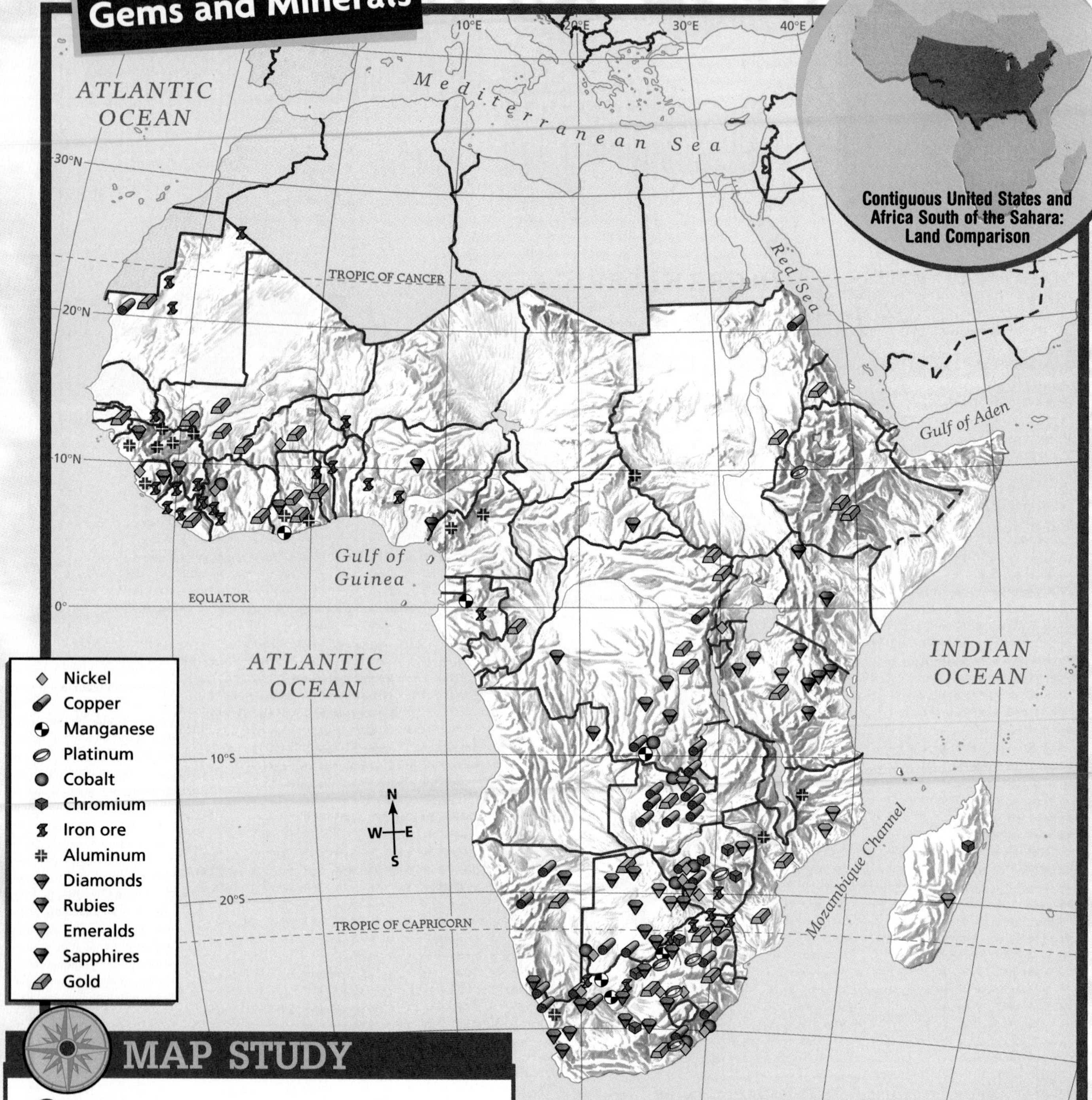

MAP STUDY

1. What gems are found in Africa south of the Equator?
2. Along what ocean north of the Equator is the most gold found?

Geo Extremes

① **HIGHEST POINT**
Kilimanjaro (Tanzania)
19,340 ft. (5,895 m) high

② **LOWEST POINT**
Lake Assal (Djibouti)
512 ft. (156 m)
below sea level

③ **LONGEST RIVER**
Nile River
4,241 mi.
(6,825 km) long

④ **LARGEST LAKE**
Lake Victoria (Kenya, Uganda, and Tanzania)
26,834 sq. mi.
(69,500 sq. km)

⑤ **LARGEST ISLAND**
Madagascar
226,642 sq. mi.
(587,000 sq. km)

⑥ **HOTTEST PLACE**
Dalol, Denakil Depression (Ethiopia)
93°F (34°C) annual average temperature

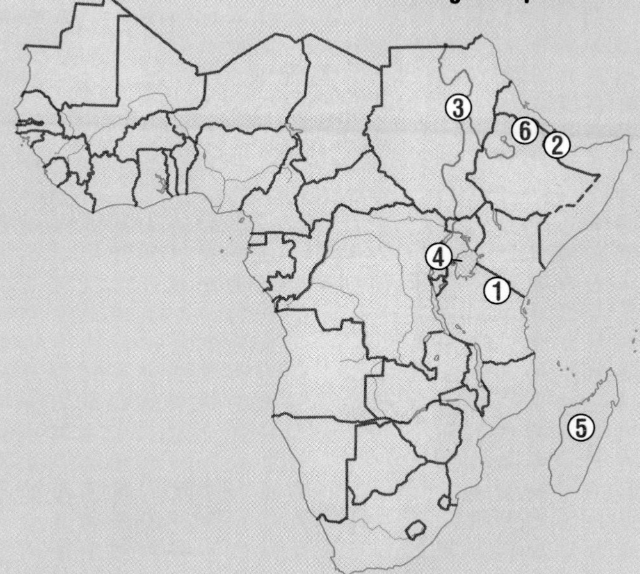

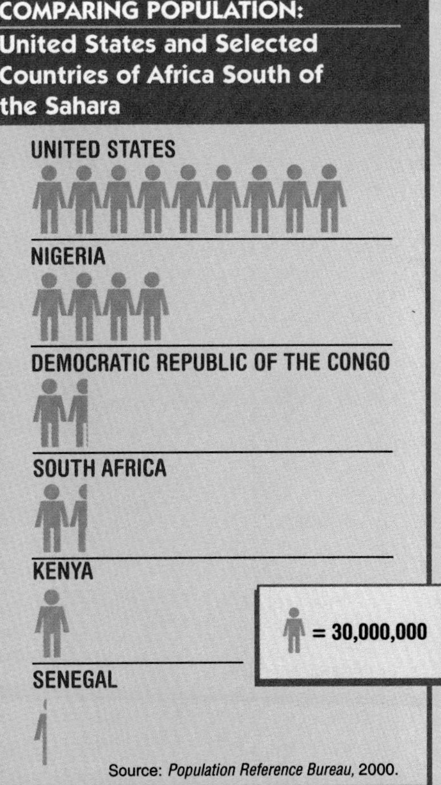

SELECTED RURAL AND URBAN POPULATIONS: Africa South of the Sahara

	Rural	Urban
WEST AFRICA		
Niger	83%	17%
Cape Verde	56%	44%
CENTRAL AFRICA		
Angola	68%	32%
Central African Republic	61%	39%
EAST AFRICA		
Rwanda	95%	5%
Djibouti	17%	83%
SOUTHERN AFRICA		
Lesotho	84%	16%
South Africa	55%	45%

Source: *Population Reference Bureau,* 2000.

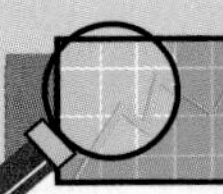

GRAPHIC STUDY

1. What is the longest river in Africa?
2. Of the African countries shown in the chart at lower right, which is least urbanized? Which is most urbanized?

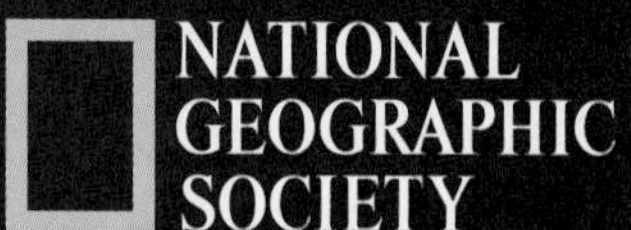

Country Profiles

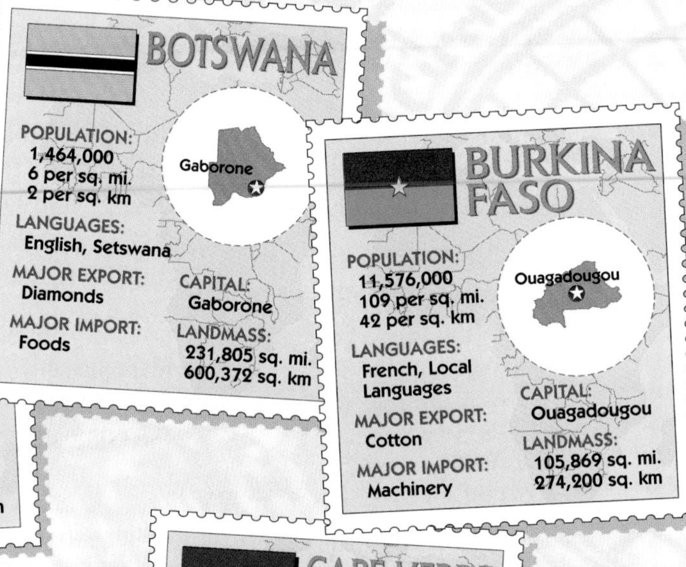

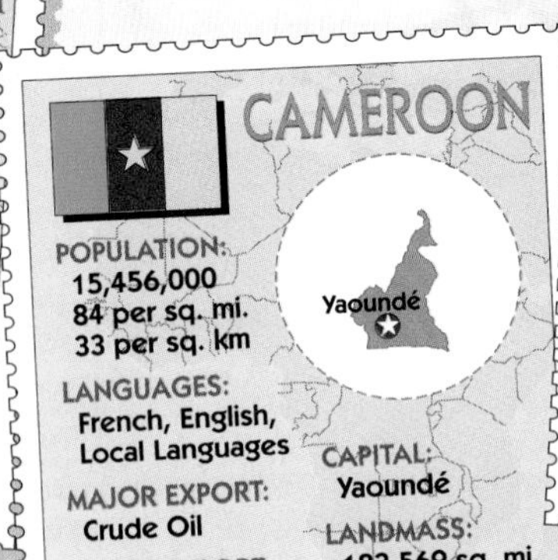

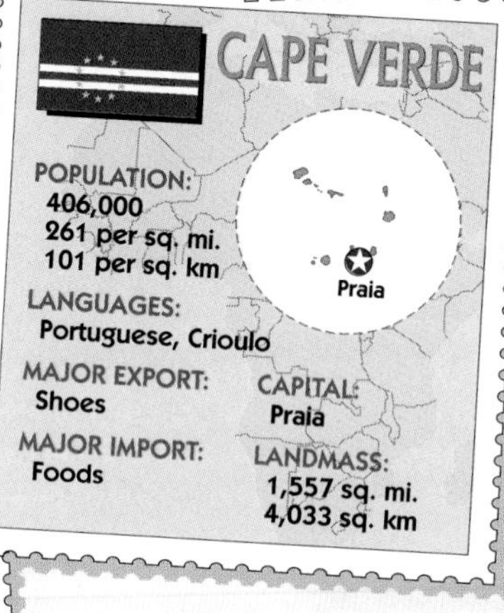

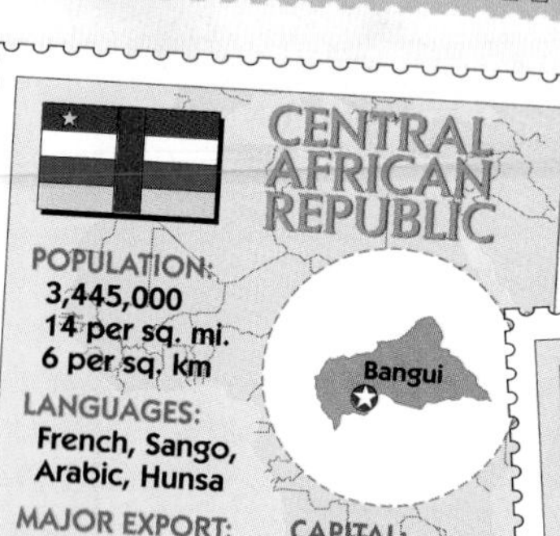

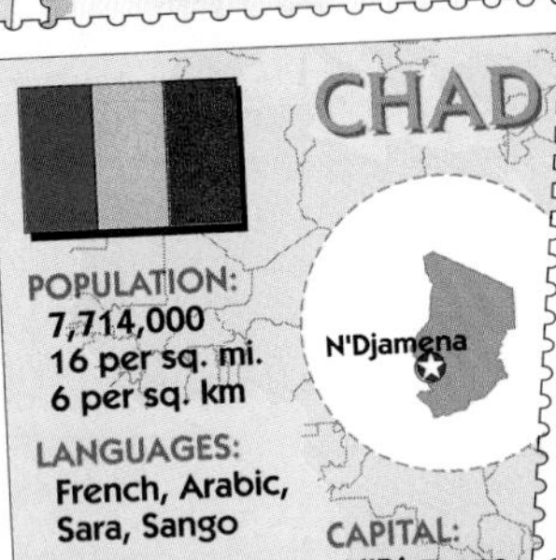

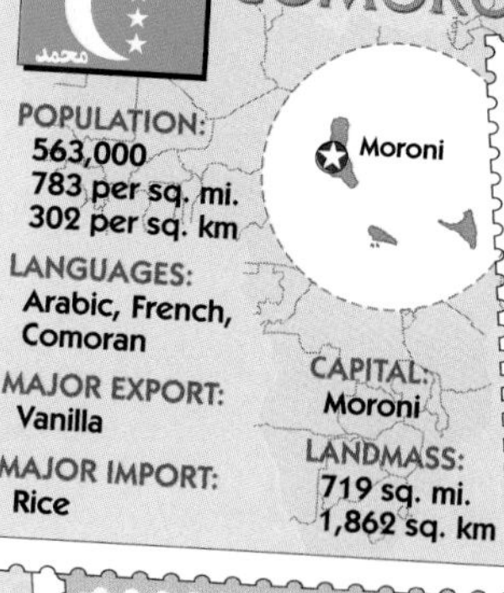

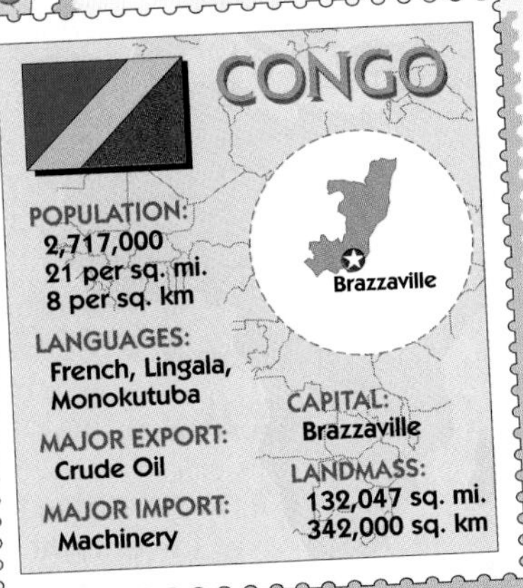

Countries and flags not drawn to scale

UNIT 7

CONGO, Democratic Republic of the

POPULATION: 50,481,000; 56 per sq. mi.; 22 per sq. km

LANGUAGES: French, Lingala, Kingwana

MAJOR EXPORT: Diamonds

MAJOR IMPORT: Manufactured Goods

CAPITAL: Kinshasa

LANDMASS: 905,568 sq. mi.; 2,345,409 sq. km

CÔTE D'IVOIRE

POPULATION: 15,818,000; 127 per sq. mi.; 49 per sq. km

LANGUAGES: French, Dioula

MAJOR EXPORT: Cocoa

MAJOR IMPORT: Foods

CAPITALS: Yamoussoukro, Abidjan

LANDMASS: 124,504 sq. mi.; 322,463 sq. km

DJIBOUTI

POPULATION: 629,000; 70 per sq. mi.; 27 per sq. km

LANGUAGES: French, Arabic

MAJOR EXPORTS: Hides and Skins

MAJOR IMPORT: Foods

CAPITAL: Djibouti

LANDMASS: 8,958 sq. mi.; 23,200 sq. km

EQUATORIAL GUINEA

POPULATION: 442,000; 41 per sq. mi.; 16 per sq. km

LANGUAGES: Spanish, French, Fang, Bubi, Ibo

MAJOR EXPORT: Petroleum

MAJOR IMPORT: Machinery

CAPITAL: Malabo

LANDMASS: 10,831 sq. mi.; 28,051 sq. km

ERITREA

POPULATION: 3,985,000; 85 per sq. mi.; 33 per sq. km

LANGUAGES: Afar, Amharic, Arabic, Tigre

MAJOR EXPORT: Livestock

MAJOR IMPORT: Processed Foods

CAPITAL: Asmara

LANDMASS: 46,842 sq. mi.; 121,320 sq. km

ETHIOPIA

POPULATION: 59,680,000; 140 per sq. mi.; 54 per sq. km

LANGUAGES: Amharic, Tigrinya, Orominga

MAJOR EXPORT: Coffee

MAJOR IMPORTS: Foods and Livestock

CAPITAL: Addis Ababa

LANDMASS: 424,934 sq. mi.; 1,100,574 sq. km

GABON

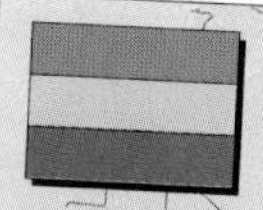

POPULATION: 1,197,000; 12 per sq. mi.; 4 per sq. km

LANGUAGES: French, Local Languages

MAJOR EXPORT: Crude Oil

MAJOR IMPORT: Machinery

CAPITAL: Libreville

LANDMASS: 103,347 sq. mi.; 267,667 sq. km

GAMBIA

POPULATION: 1,268,000; 291 per sq. mi.; 112 per sq. km

LANGUAGES: English, Mandinka, Fula, Wolof

MAJOR EXPORT: Peanuts

MAJOR IMPORT: Foods

CAPITAL: Banjul

LANDMASS: 4,361 sq. mi.; 11,295 sq. km

GHANA

POPULATION: 19,678,000; 214 per sq. mi.; 82 per sq. km

LANGUAGES: English, Local Languages

MAJOR EXPORT: Gold

MAJOR IMPORT: Machinery

CAPITAL: Accra

LANDMASS: 92,100 sq. mi.; 238,537 sq. km

GUINEA

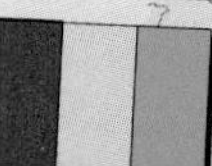

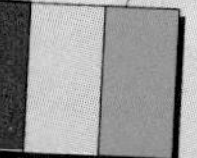

POPULATION: 7,539,000; 79 per sq. mi.; 31 per sq. km

LANGUAGES: French, Local Languages

MAJOR EXPORT: Bauxite

MAJOR IMPORT: Petroleum Products

CAPITAL: Conakry

LANDMASS: 94,926 sq. mi.; 245,857 sq. km

GUINEA-BISSAU

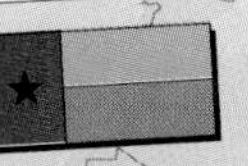

POPULATION: 1,187,000; 85 per sq. mi.; 33 per sq. km

LANGUAGES: Portuguese, Crioulo, Local Languages

MAJOR EXPORT: Cashews

MAJOR IMPORT: Foods

CAPITAL: Bissau

LANDMASS: 13,948 sq. mi.; 36,125 sq. km

Country Profiles

KENYA
POPULATION:
28,809,000
126 per sq. mi.
49 per sq. km
LANGUAGES:
English, Swahili
MAJOR EXPORT:
Tea
MAJOR IMPORT:
Machinery
CAPITAL:
Nairobi
LANDMASS:
228,861 sq. mi.
592,747 sq. km

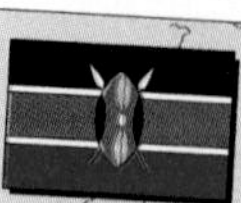

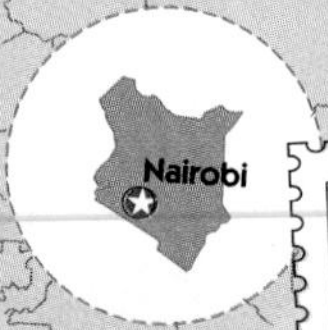

LESOTHO
POPULATION:
2,129,000
182 per sq. mi.
70 per sq. km
LANGUAGES:
English, Sesotho, Zulu, Xhosa
MAJOR EXPORT:
Clothing
MAJOR IMPORT:
Corn
CAPITAL:
Maseru
LANDMASS:
11,720 sq. mi.
30,355 sq. km

LIBERIA
POPULATION:
2,924,000
68 per sq. mi.
26 per sq. km
LANGUAGES:
English, Local Languages
MAJOR EXPORT:
Diamonds
MAJOR IMPORT:
Natural Gas
CAPITAL:
Monrovia
LANDMASS:
43,000 sq. mi.
111,369 sq. km

MADAGASCAR
POPULATION:
14,417,000
64 per sq. mi.
25 per sq. km
LANGUAGES:
French, Malagasy
MAJOR EXPORT:
Coffee
MAJOR IMPORT:
Machinery
CAPITAL:
Antananarivo
LANDMASS:
226,658 sq. mi.
587,041 sq. km

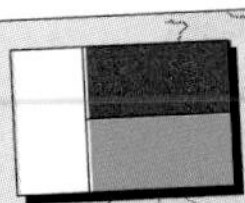

MALAWI
POPULATION:
10,000,000
219 per sq. mi.
84 per sq. km
LANGUAGES:
Chewa, English
MAJOR EXPORT:
Tobacco
MAJOR IMPORT:
Foods
CAPITAL:
Lilongwe
LANDMASS:
45,747 sq. mi.
118,484 sq. km

MALI
POPULATION:
10,960,000
23 per sq. mi.
9 per sq. km
LANGUAGES:
French, Bambara
MAJOR EXPORT:
Cotton
MAJOR IMPORT:
Machinery
CAPITAL:
Bamako
LANDMASS:
478,841 sq. mi.
1,240,192 sq. km

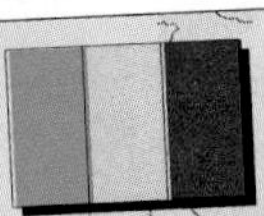

MAURITANIA
POPULATION:
2,598,000
7 per sq. mi.
3 per sq. km
LANGUAGES:
Hasaniya Arabic, Wolof
MAJOR EXPORT:
Fish
MAJOR IMPORT:
Foods
CAPITAL:
Nouakchott
LANDMASS:
397,955 sq. mi.
1,030,700 sq. km

MAURITIUS
POPULATION:
1,172,000
1,487 per sq. mi.
575 per sq. km
LANGUAGES:
English, Creole, Bhojpuri, French
MAJOR EXPORT:
Sugar
MAJOR IMPORT:
Foods
CAPITAL:
Port Louis
LANDMASS:
788 sq. mi.
2,040 sq. km

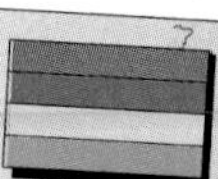

MOZAMBIQUE
POPULATION:
19,124,000
62 per sq. mi.
24 per sq. km
LANGUAGES:
Portuguese, Local Languages
MAJOR EXPORT:
Cashews
MAJOR IMPORT:
Foods
CAPITAL:
Maputo
LANDMASS:
308,642 sq. mi.
799,380 sq. km

NAMIBIA
POPULATION:
1,648,000
5 per sq. mi.
2 per sq. km
LANGUAGES:
English, Local Languages
MAJOR EXPORT:
Diamonds
MAJOR IMPORT:
Construction Materials
CAPITAL:
Windhoek
LANDMASS:
318,261 sq. mi.
824,292 sq. km

NIGER
POPULATION:
9,962,000
20 per sq. mi.
8 per sq. km
LANGUAGES:
French, Hausa, Djerma
MAJOR EXPORT:
Uranium Ore
MAJOR IMPORT:
Manufactured Goods
CAPITAL:
Niamey
LANDMASS:
489,191 sq. mi.
1,267,000 sq. km

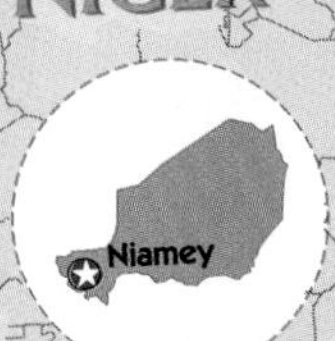

Countries and flags not drawn to scale

UNIT 7

NIGERIA

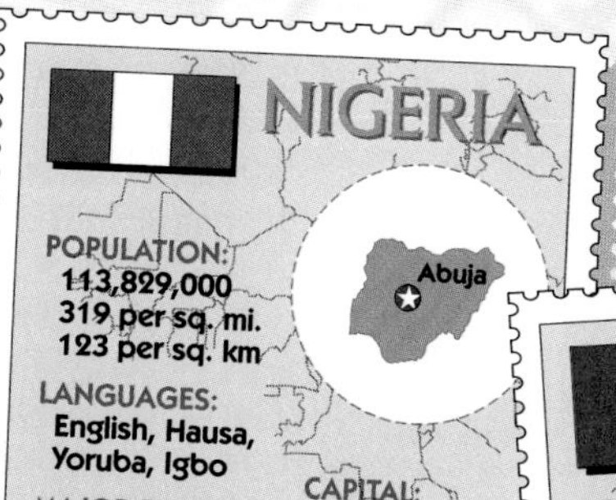

POPULATION:
113,829,000
319 per sq. mi.
123 per sq. km

LANGUAGES:
English, Hausa, Yoruba, Igbo

MAJOR EXPORT:
Petroleum

MAJOR IMPORT:
Machinery

CAPITAL:
Abuja

LANDMASS:
356,669 sq. mi.
923,768 sq. km

RWANDA

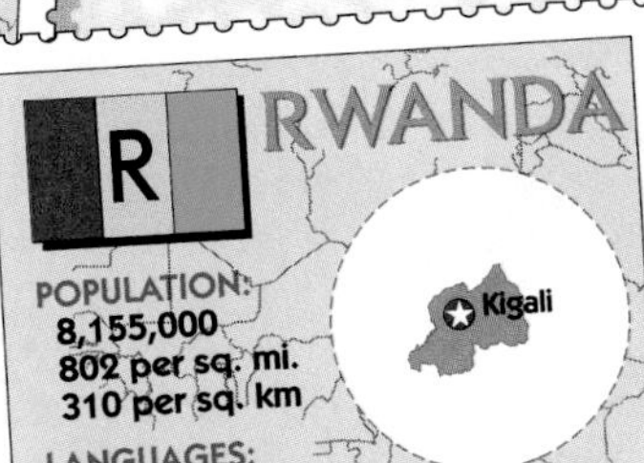

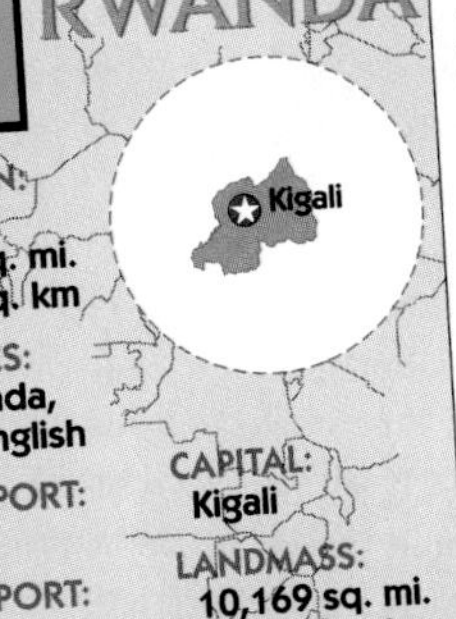

POPULATION:
8,155,000
802 per sq. mi.
310 per sq. km

LANGUAGES:
Kinyarwanda, French, English

MAJOR EXPORT:
Coffee

MAJOR IMPORT:
Foods

CAPITAL:
Kigali

LANDMASS:
10,169 sq. mi.
26,338 sq. km

SAO TOME and PRINCIPE

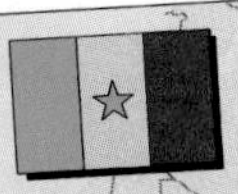

POPULATION:
155,000
417 per sq. mi.
161 per sq. km

LANGUAGES:
Portuguese, Crioulo

MAJOR EXPORT:
Cocoa

MAJOR IMPORT:
Textiles

CAPITAL:
São Tomé

LANDMASS:
372 sq. mi.
964 sq. km

SENEGAL

Dakar

POPULATION:
9,240,000
122 per sq. mi.
47 per sq. km

LANGUAGES:
French, Wolof, Pulaar, Diola

MAJOR EXPORT:
Fish

MAJOR IMPORT:
Foods

CAPITAL:
Dakar

LANDMASS:
75,955 sq. mi.
196,722 sq. km

SEYCHELLES

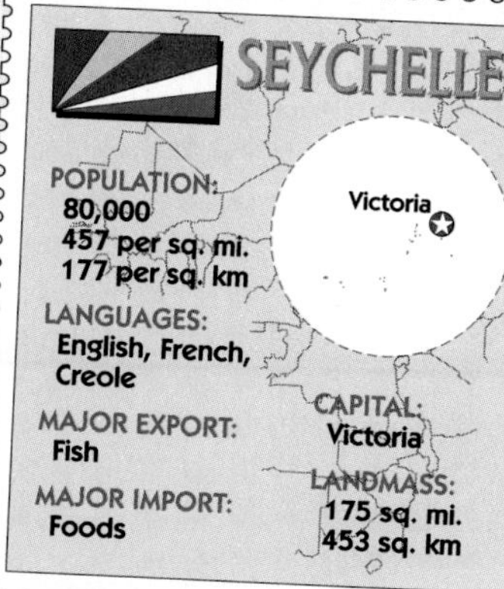

POPULATION:
80,000
457 per sq. mi.
177 per sq. km

LANGUAGES:
English, French, Creole

MAJOR EXPORT:
Fish

MAJOR IMPORT:
Foods

CAPITAL:
Victoria

LANDMASS:
175 sq. mi.
453 sq. km

SIERRA LEONE

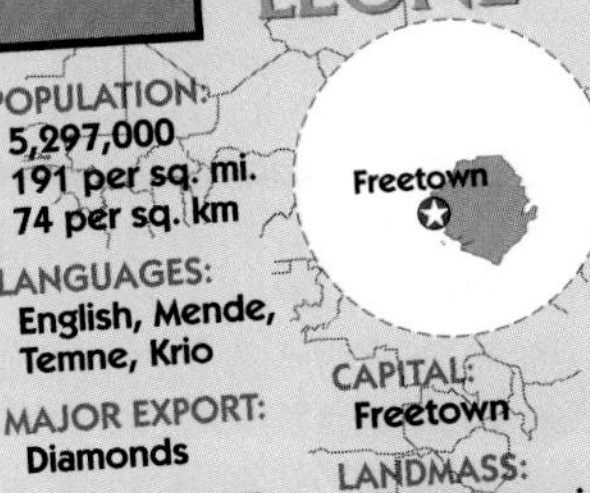

POPULATION:
5,297,000
191 per sq. mi.
74 per sq. km

LANGUAGES:
English, Mende, Temne, Krio

MAJOR EXPORT:
Diamonds

MAJOR IMPORT:
Foods

CAPITAL:
Freetown

LANDMASS:
27,699 sq. mi.
71,740 sq. km

SOMALIA

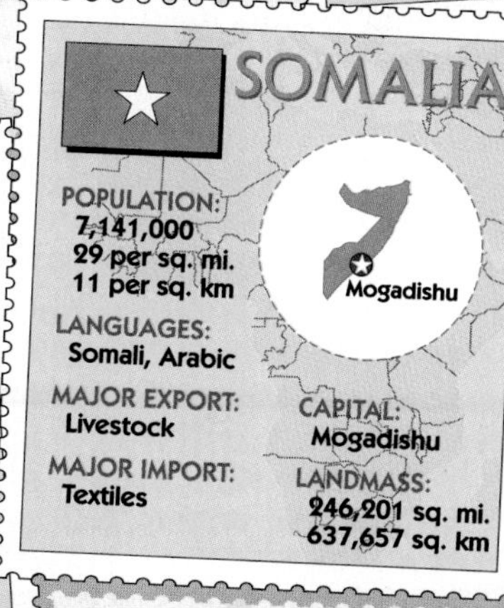

POPULATION:
7,141,000
29 per sq. mi.
11 per sq. km

LANGUAGES:
Somali, Arabic

MAJOR EXPORT:
Livestock

MAJOR IMPORT:
Textiles

CAPITAL:
Mogadishu

LANDMASS:
246,201 sq. mi.
637,657 sq. km

SOUTH AFRICA

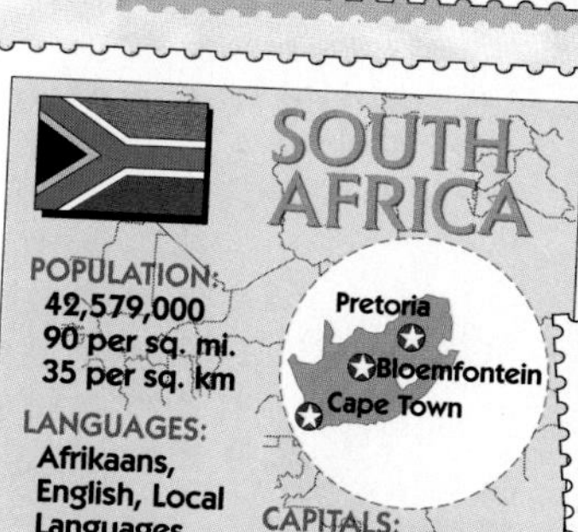

POPULATION:
42,579,000
90 per sq. mi.
35 per sq. km

LANGUAGES:
Afrikaans, English, Local Languages

MAJOR EXPORT:
Gold

MAJOR IMPORT:
Transport Equip.

CAPITALS:
Pretoria, Cape Town, Bloemfontein

LANDMASS:
471,445 sq. mi.
1,221,037 sq. km

SUDAN

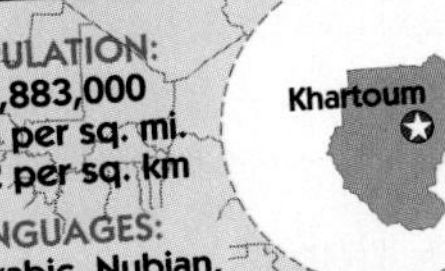

POPULATION:
28,883,000
30 per sq. mi.
12 per sq. km

LANGUAGES:
Arabic, Nubian, Ta Bedawie

MAJOR EXPORT:
Cotton

MAJOR IMPORT:
Petroleum Products

CAPITAL:
Khartoum

LANDMASS:
963,600 sq. mi.
2,495,712 sq. km

SWAZILAND

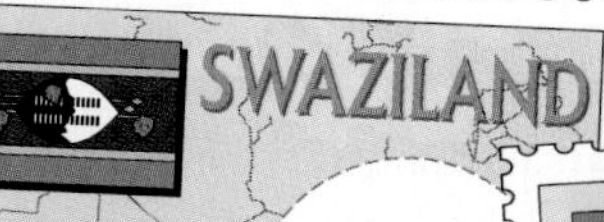

POPULATION:
985,000
147 per sq. mi.
57 per sq. km

LANGUAGES:
English, Swazi

MAJOR EXPORT:
Soft Drink Concentrates

MAJOR IMPORT:
Machinery

CAPITAL:
Mbabane

LANDMASS:
6,704 sq. mi.
17,364 sq. km

TANZANIA

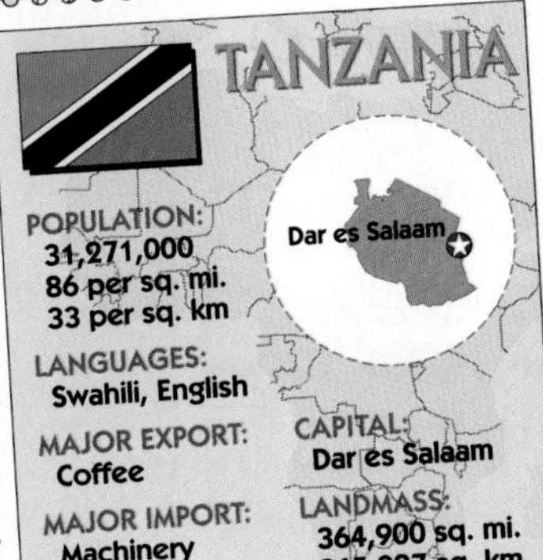

POPULATION:
31,271,000
86 per sq. mi.
33 per sq. km

LANGUAGES:
Swahili, English

MAJOR EXPORT:
Coffee

MAJOR IMPORT:
Machinery

CAPITAL:
Dar es Salaam

LANDMASS:
364,900 sq. mi.
945,087 sq. km

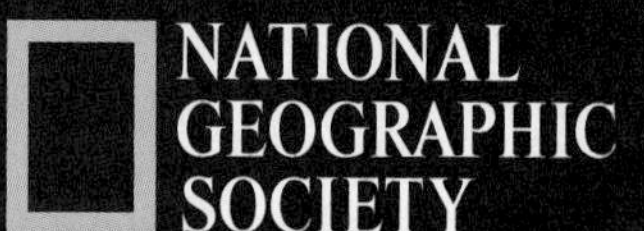

Country Profiles

Countries and flags not drawn to scale

Questions From Buzz Bee!

The following questions are taken from National Geographic GeoBees. Use your textbook, the Internet, and other library resources to find the answers.

1. The Dutch who settled in what is now South Africa became known by a Dutch word that means "farmer." By what name were these settlers known?
2. Volcanic activity created the highest peak along the Great Rift Valley. Name the peak.
3. The Hutu and the Tutsi are ethnic groups that have been fighting for control of two countries. Name these countries.

View over terraced fields and small settlements, Kabale, Uganda

Chapter

19 West Africa

The World and Its People

NATIONAL GEOGRAPHIC

To learn more about the people and places of West Africa, view ***The World and Its People*** **Chapter 19** video.

Geography online

Chapter Overview Visit the ***Geography: The World and Its People*** Web site at gwip.glencoe.com and click on **Chapter 19—Chapter Overviews** to preview information about West Africa.

Section 1 Nigeria

Guide to Reading

Main Idea

A large, oil-rich country, Nigeria has more people than any other African nation.

Terms to Know

- mangrove
- savanna
- harmattan
- subsistence farm
- cacao
- compound
- civil war

Places to Locate

- Nigeria
- Niger River
- Gulf of Guinea
- Kano
- Lagos
- Abuja

Reading Strategy

Create a chart like the one below. Then list two facts about Nigeria in each category.

Nigeria	Fact #1	Fact #2
Land		
Economy		
People		

NATIONAL GEOGRAPHIC **Exploring Our World**

In 1991 Abuja replaced Lagos as Nigeria's capital. The new city was built in an undeveloped region in central Nigeria. Today Abuja has new buildings and a network of roads linking it with other parts of the country. It also has schools. These children prepare to pray at the Islamic Academy in Abuja.

The West African country of **Nigeria** takes its name from the **Niger River,** which flows through western and central Nigeria. One of the largest nations in Africa, Nigeria is more than twice the size of California.

From Tropics to Savanna

Nigeria has a long coastline on the **Gulf of Guinea,** an arm of the Atlantic Ocean. Along Nigeria's coast, the land is covered with mangrove swamps. A **mangrove** is a tropical tree with roots that extend both above and beneath the water.

As you travel inland, the land becomes vast tropical rain forests. Small villages appear in only a few clearings. The forests gradually thin into savannas in central Nigeria. **Savannas** are tropical grasslands with only a few trees. Highlands and plateaus also make up this area. Most of the country has a tropical savanna climate with high average temperatures and seasonal rains. The grasslands of the far north have a dry steppe climate. In the winter months, a dusty wind called the **harmattan** blows south from the Sahara.

✓Reading Check **What kinds of vegetation are found in Nigeria?**

◄ **Colorful side street in Dakar, Senegal**

Economic Challenges

Nigeria is one of the world's major oil-producing countries. More than 90 percent of the country's income comes from oil exports. The government has used money from oil to build highways, schools, skyscrapers, and factories. These factories make food products, textiles, chemicals, machinery, and vehicles. Still, more than one-third of Nigeria's people lack jobs and live in poverty.

Nigeria began to experience economic troubles during the 1980s. As a result of falling world oil prices, Nigeria's income dropped. At the same time, many people left their farms in search of better-paying jobs in the cities. In addition, a few years of low rainfall meant smaller harvests. As a result, food production fell. Nigeria—which had once exported food—had to import food to feed its people.

Despite oil resources, Nigeria's people mainly work as farmers. Most have **subsistence farms,** or small plots that grow just enough

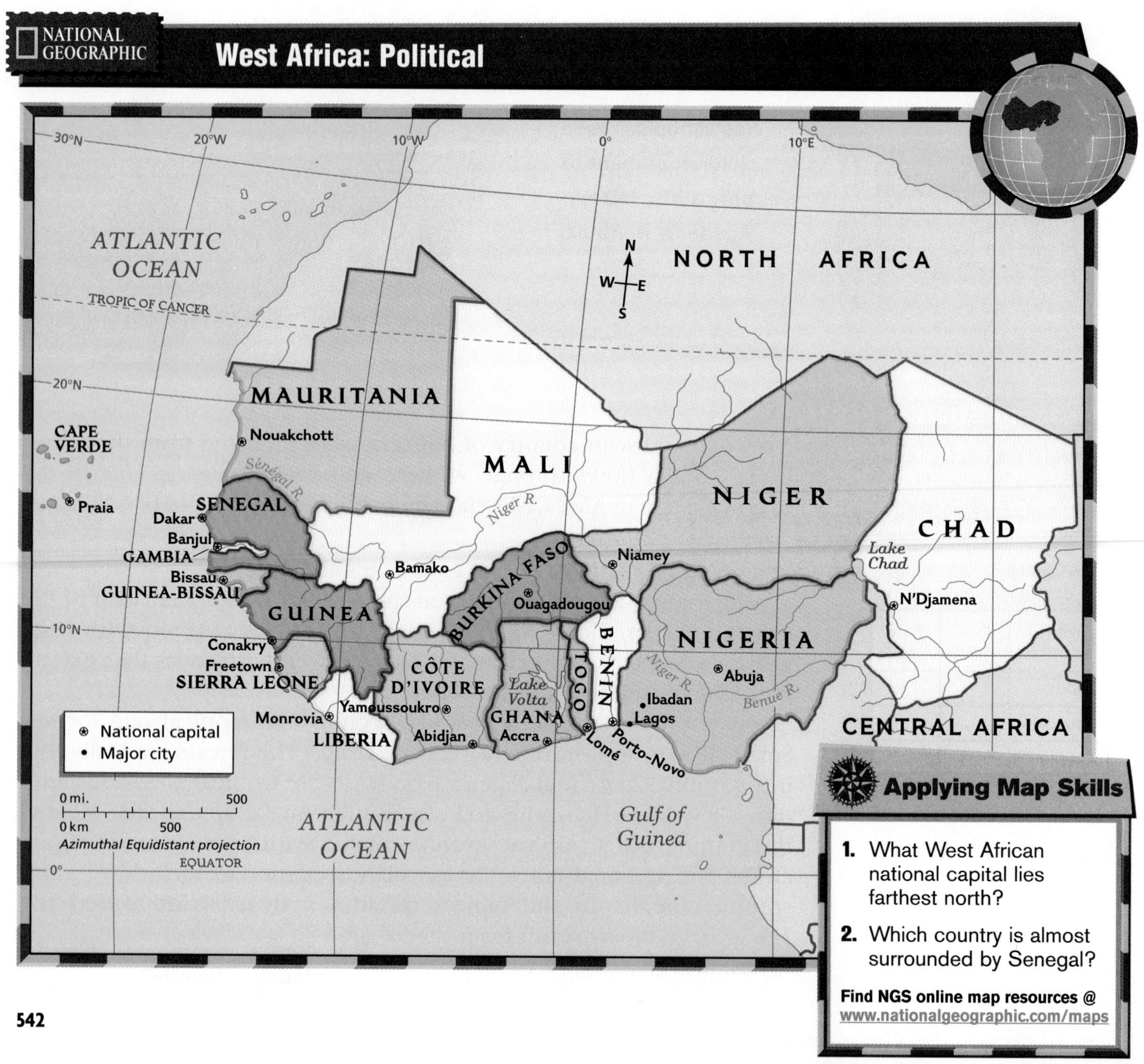

Applying Map Skills

1. What West African national capital lies farthest north?
2. Which country is almost surrounded by Senegal?

Find NGS online map resources @ www.nationalgeographic.com/maps

to feed their families. Some work on larger farms that produce such cash crops as rubber, peanuts, palm oil, and cacao. The **cacao** is a tropical tree whose seeds are used to make chocolate and cocoa. Nigeria is a leading producer of cacao beans.

Reading Check **How has Nigeria's government used money from oil exports?**

Nigeria's People

About 113.8 million people live in Nigeria—more people than in any other country in Africa. The map on page 554 shows that most of the people live along the coast and around the city of **Kano** in the north.

One of the strongest bonds that Africans have is a sense of belonging to a group or family. Nigeria has more than 300 ethnic groups. The four largest are the Hausa (HOW•suh), Fulani (foo•LAH•nee), Yoruba (YAWR•uh•buh), and Ibo (EE•boh). Nigerians speak many different

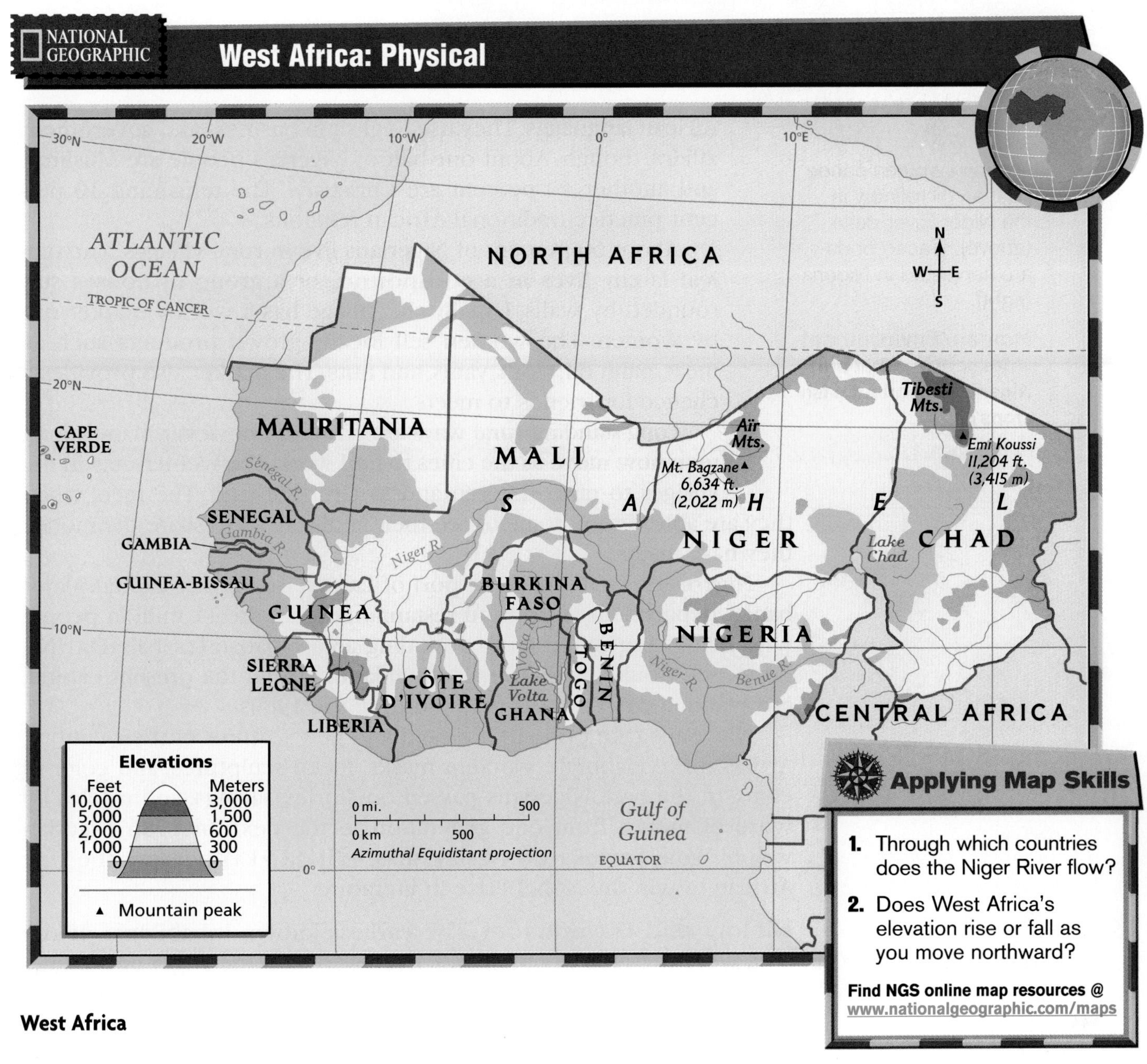

Applying Map Skills

1. Through which countries does the Niger River flow?
2. Does West Africa's elevation rise or fall as you move northward?

Find NGS online map resources @ www.nationalgeographic.com/maps

Nigeria's Economy

Nigerian women canoe past an oil refinery in the Niger River delta (above). Cacao pods are harvested in Nigeria (right).

Human/Environment Interaction What are Nigeria's important cash crops?

African languages. They use English in business and government affairs, though. About one-half of Nigeria's people are Muslims, and another 40 percent are Christians. The remaining 10 percent practice traditional African religions.

About 60 percent of Nigerians live in rural villages. The typical family lives in a compound, or a group of houses surrounded by walls. Usually the village has a weekly market run by women. The women sell locally grown products such as meat, palm oil, cloth, yams, and nuts. The market also provides a chance for friends to meet.

Long-standing rural ways are changing, however. Many young men now move to the cities to find work. The women stay in the villages to raise children and to farm the land. The men, when they are able, return home to see their families and to share the money they have made.

Nigeria's largest city is the port of **Lagos,** the former capital. Major banks, department stores, and restaurants serve the 11 million people who live in Lagos and its surrounding areas. Ibadan (EE•bah•DAHN), Kano, and Abuja (ah•BOO•jah) lie inland. **Abuja,** the present capital, is a planned city that was begun during the 1980s.

Nigerians take pride in both old and new features of their culture. Artists make elaborate wooden masks, metal sculptures, and colorful cloth. In the past, Nigerians passed on stories, sayings, and riddles by word of mouth from one generation to the next. In 1986 Nigerian writer Wole Soyinka (WAW•lay shaw•YIHNG•ka) became the first African to win the Nobel Prize in literature.

History and Government The earliest known inhabitants of the area were the Nok people. They lived between the Niger and Benue

Rivers between 300 B.C. and A.D. 200. The Nok were known as skilled metalworkers and traders.

Over the centuries, powerful city-states and kingdoms became centers of trade and the arts. People in the north came in contact with Muslim cultures and adopted the religion of Islam. People in the south developed cultures based on traditional African religions.

During the 1400s, Europeans arrived in Africa looking for gold and Africans to take overseas as enslaved laborers. In 1884 European leaders divided most of Africa into colonies. The borders of these colonies, however, often sliced through ethnic lands. As a result, many ethnic groups found their members living in two or more separate territories. By the early 1900s, the British had taken control of Nigeria.

In 1960 Nigeria finally became an independent country. Ethnic, religious, and political disputes soon tore it apart, however. One ethnic group, the Ibo, tried to set up their own country. A **civil war**—a fight among different groups within a country—resulted. In this bloody war, starvation and conflict led to 2 million deaths. The Ibo were defeated, and their region remained part of Nigeria.

Nigeria has faced the challenge of building a stable government. Military leaders have often ruled the country. In 1999 Nigerians were able to vote for a president in free elections. Nigeria's democratic government is working to build greater national unity.

Reading Check **What are the four largest ethnic groups in Nigeria?**

Ken Saro-Wiwa

Ken Saro-Wiwa was a Nigerian environmentalist. In the 1990s, he fought to protect farmlands and fisheries on the Niger River from damage caused by oil spills and polluted air. After his death, an international group set up a fund named after Saro-Wiwa. The fund will help people who work to save the environment.

Assessment

Defining Terms

1. **Define** mangrove, savanna, harmattan, subsistence farm, cacao, compound, civil war.

Recalling Facts

2. **Place** Describe the changes in Nigeria's physical geography as you move from the coast inland.
3. **Place** What is the capital of Nigeria?
4. **Culture** How many ethnic groups are represented by the people of Nigeria?

Critical Thinking

5. **Drawing Conclusions** Why do you think government leaders moved the capital city to a new location in the interior of Nigeria?
6. **Understanding Cause and Effect** Why did a drop in oil prices cause an economic depression in Nigeria in the 1980s?

Graphic Organizer

7. **Organizing Information** On a time line like the one below, place the following events and their dates in order: Nigeria becomes independent; Nok people work in metal and trade for goods; Free elections are held; Europeans create colonies in Nigeria.

Applying Geography Skills

8. **Analyzing Maps** Study the physical map on page 543. Into what larger body of water does the Niger River empty?

Critical Thinking Skill

Drawing Inferences and Conclusions

Suppose your teacher brought to class a colorful wooden mask, and a classmate said, "Wow. That's from Nigeria." You might infer that your classmate has an interest in African art and, therefore, recognizes the mask as coming from Nigeria.

Learning the Skill

To *infer* means to evaluate information and arrive at a conclusion. When you make inferences, you "read between the lines" or draw conclusions that are not stated directly in the text. You must use the available facts *and* your own knowledge and experience to form a judgment or opinion about the material.

Use the following steps to help draw inferences and make conclusions:

- Read carefully for stated facts and ideas.
- Summarize the information and list the important facts.
- Apply related information that you may already know to make inferences.
- Use your knowledge and insight to develop some conclusions about these facts.

Practicing the Skill

Read the passage below, then answer the questions that follow.

> Nigerian art forms reflect the people's beliefs in spirits and nature. Yoruba masks are carved out of wood, reflecting the forces of nature and gods. The masks are used in ceremonies to help connect with the spirit of their ancestors. The masks also appear at funerals in order to please the spirits of the dead. Of all the Yoruba masks, the helmet masks of the Epa cult are the most spectacular.

Yoruba wood masks ▲

1. What topic is the writer describing?
2. What facts are presented?
3. What can you infer about the role of masks in Nigerian life?
4. What do you already know about religious ceremonies?
5. What conclusion can you make about traditional religions in Nigeria?

Applying the Skill

Study the photos of Nigerians on page 544. What can you infer about life in Nigeria from the photographs? What evidence supports this inference or conclusion?

GO TO

Practice key skills with **Glencoe Skillbuilder Interactive Workbook, Level 1.**

Section 2

The Sahel Countries

Guide to Reading

Main Idea

The Sahel countries face a continuing struggle to keep grasslands from turning into desert.

Terms to Know

- overgraze
- drought
- desertification

Places to Locate

- Sahel
- Mauritania
- Mali
- Burkina Faso
- Niger
- Chad

Reading Strategy

Create a diagram like this one. Then list two of the factors that have led to the loss of vegetation in the Sahel countries.

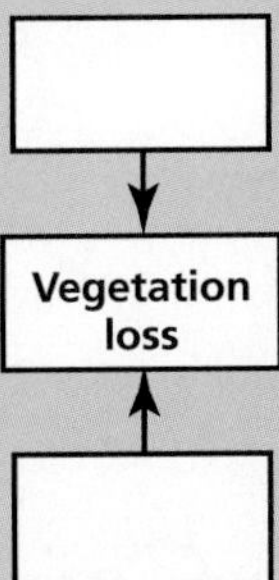

NATIONAL GEOGRAPHIC **Exploring Our World**

Slowly but surely, the desert is creeping into grassy inland areas of West Africa north of Nigeria. Over the past 100 years, a stretch of the Sahara about 100 miles (161 km) wide has swallowed parts of countries in West Africa. This growing desert is like an invading army slowly taking over the countries of the vast Sahel.

Five countries—Mauritania (MAWR•uh•TAY•nee•uh), Mali (MAH•lee), Burkina Faso (bur•KEE•nuh FAH•soh), Niger (NY•juhr), and Chad—are located in an area known as the **Sahel.** The word *Sahel* comes from an Arabic word that means "border." The Sahel in West Africa forms the border between the Sahara to the north and the fertile lands to the south.

The Land and History

The Sahel receives little rainfall, so only short grasses and small trees can support grazing animals. Most people have traditionally herded livestock. Their flocks, unfortunately, have overgrazed the land in some places. When animals **overgraze** land, they strip areas so bare that plants cannot grow back. Then bare soil is blown away by winds.

In the Sahel, dry and wet periods usually follow each other. When the seasonal rains do not fall, drought takes hold. A **drought** is a long period of extreme dryness and water shortages. The latest drought occurred in the 1980s. Rivers dried up, crops failed, and millions of animals died. Thousands of people died of hunger. Millions of others fled to more productive southern areas.

Over the years, both overgrazing and drought have ruined once-productive areas of the Sahel. Many grassland areas have become desert—a process called **desertification.** Scientists believe that the increasing human use of land in the Sahel will only increase damage to the land. More of the Sahel will become desert.

History From the A.D. 500s to 1500s, three great African empires—Ghana (GAH•nuh), Mali, and Songhai (SAWNG•HY)—arose in the Sahel. These empires controlled the trade in gold, salt, and other goods between West Africa and the Arab lands of North Africa and Southwest Asia. To learn more about the salt trade, turn to page 560.

In the early 1300s, Mali's most famous ruler, Mansa Musa, made a journey in grand style to Makkah. This is the holy city of Islam located in the Arabian Peninsula. A faithful Muslim, Mansa Musa made his capital, Tombouctou (TOH•book•TOO), a leading center of Islamic learning. People came from all over the Muslim world to study there.

Invaders from North Africa defeated Songhai—the last of the great empires—in the late 1500s. During the 1800s, the Sahel region came

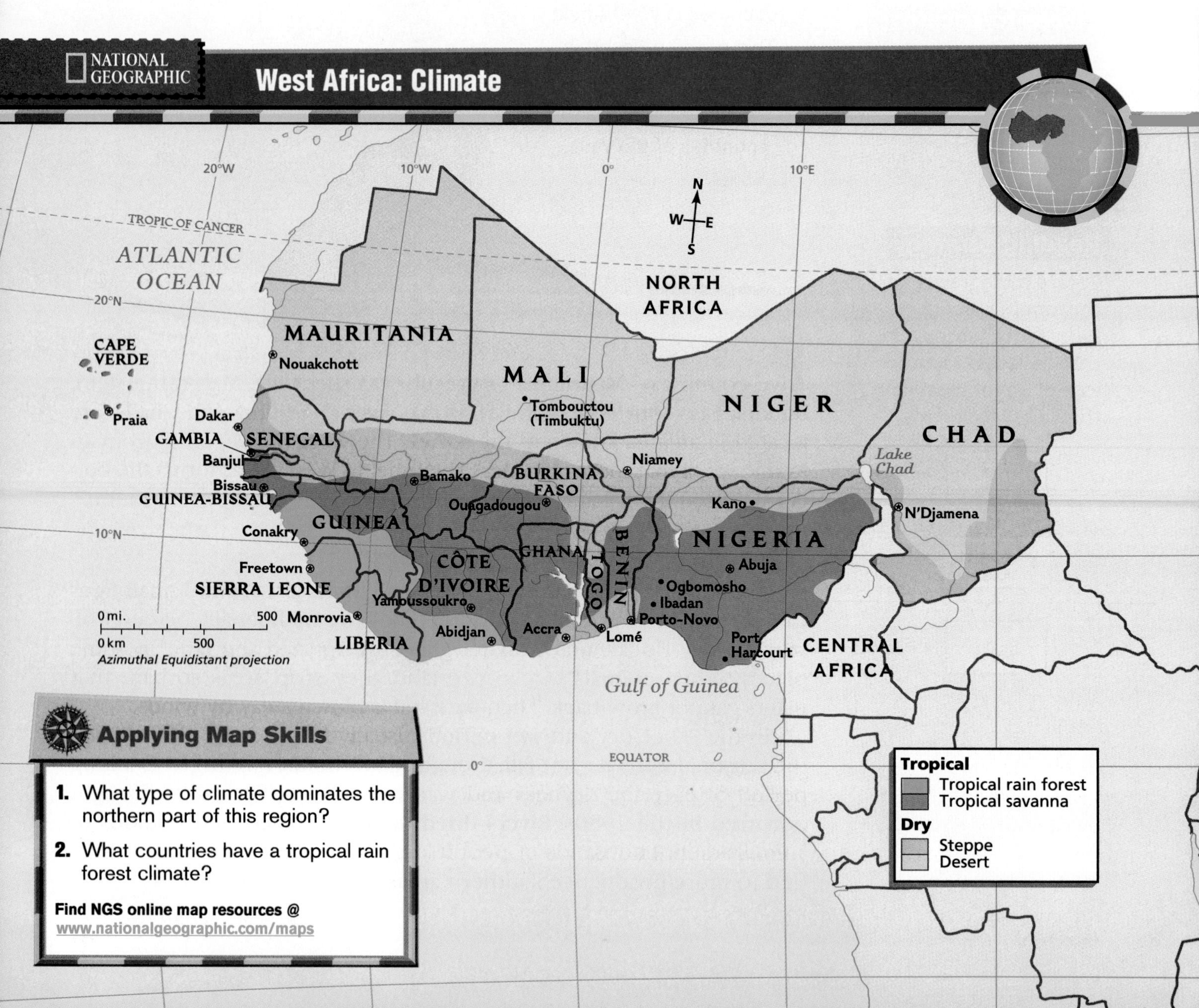

Clothing

To protect themselves from the hot Saharan sun, the Tuareg people wear layers of clothing under their long flowing robes. These loose cotton clothes help slow the evaporation of sweat and conserve body moisture. As a sign of respect for their superiors, Tuareg men cover their mouths and faces with veils. Women usually wear veils only for weddings. The veils are made of blue cloth dyed from crushed indigo. The blue dye easily rubs off onto the skin, earning the Tuareg men the nickname the Blue Men of the Desert.

Looking Closer How is the clothing of the Tuareg appropriate for the land in which they live?

under French rule. The French created five colonies in the area. In 1960 these five colonies became the independent nations of Mauritania, Mali, Upper Volta (now Burkina Faso), Niger, and Chad.

✓Reading Check **What has caused the desertification of the Sahel?**

The People of the Sahel

The Sahel countries are large in size but have small populations. If you look at the map on page 554, you will see that most people live in the southern areas of the Sahel. Rivers flow here, and the land can be farmed or grazed. Yet even these areas do not have enough water and fertile land to support large numbers of people.

Today most people in the Sahel live in small towns. They are subsistence farmers who grow grains, such as millet and sorghum (SAWR•guhm). For years, many people were nomads. Groups such as the Tuareg (TWAH•REHG) and the Fulani, for example, would cross the desert with herds of camels, cattle, goats, and sheep. The recent droughts forced many of them to give up their traditional way of life and move to the towns. Here they often live in crowded camps of tents.

The people of the Sahel practice a mix of African, Arab, and European traditions. Most are Muslims and follow the Islamic religion. They speak Arabic as well as a variety of African languages. In many of the larger cities, French is also spoken.

Mauritania The westernmost Sahel country, **Mauritania** borders the Atlantic Ocean. The waters off the coast are a rich fishing ground, but fishing ships from other countries have overfished these waters. As a result, fewer people can make a living from the sea than in the past. Mauritania's first port suitable for large ships opened in 1986 near the capital, Nouakchott (nu•AHK•SHAHT). Mauritania has rich deposits of iron ore. Fish and iron are the country's chief exports.

Mali and Burkina Faso **Mali** and **Burkina Faso** both are landlocked. They also have to deal with poor soil and frequent droughts. They are among the economically poorest countries in the world.

Mali is a very large country—nearly twice the size of Texas. Yet more than 65 percent of Mali's land area is desert or semidesert. Most of its 11 million people live along the Niger River, and some 80 percent farm or herd livestock for a living. The main cash crop is cotton. One industry that has increased in recent years is gold mining. Mali hopes to become a major exporter of gold in the future.

Most of Burkina Faso's 11.6 million people are subsistence farmers who grow grains. Thousands of people migrate from Burkina Faso every year in search of work. Most travel to nearby Ghana and Côte d'Ivoire.

Niger and Chad **Niger** and **Chad** also are landlocked countries with struggling economies. They suffer from their remote location and from a lack of good transportation. Most of the people live by farming or herding. Niger has 10 million people. Chad has 7.7 million.

Niger has reserves of uranium, a mineral used for making nuclear fuels. This substance has been the country's main export since the 1970s. Chad has petroleum deposits. Yet Chad lacks the money needed to develop oil fields and to build pipelines. A rebellion in the north of Chad has delayed economic improvements as well.

Reading Check **What religion do most people in the Sahel countries follow?**

Assessment

Defining Terms

1. **Define** overgraze, drought, desertification.

Recalling Facts

2. **History** What three great empires ruled in the Sahel from the A.D. 500s to 1500s?
3. **Economics** What are Mauritania's chief exports?
4. **Location** Where do most of Mali's people live?

Critical Thinking

5. **Making Predictions** What problems do you think will arise as people in the Sahel move to more productive areas?
6. **Analyzing Information** Explain how a country with important natural resources, like Chad, can still remain poor.

Graphic Organizer

7. **Organizing Information** On a diagram like this one, list five results of drought.

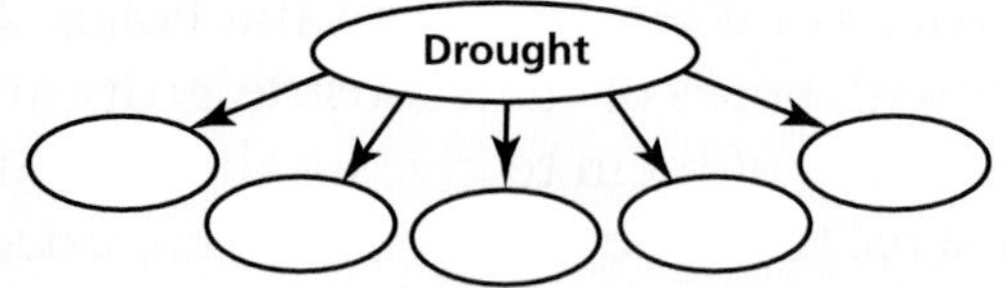

Applying Geography Skills

8. **Analyzing Maps** Study the political map on page 542. Through which West African countries does the Prime Meridian—or 0° longitude—run?

Making Connections

ART SCIENCE LITERATURE TECHNOLOGY

Great Mosque of Djenné

In the West African city of Djenné (jeh•NAY), Mali, stands a huge structure built entirely of mud. It is the Great Mosque of Djenné, and it covers an area the size of a city block. Considered one of Africa's greatest architectural wonders, the existing Great Mosque is actually the third mosque to occupy the location.

Djenné

Located between the Sahara and the African savanna, the city of Djenné was an important crossroads on a trade route connecting northern and southern Africa. Caravans and boats carried gold, salt, and other goods through the city.

During the A.D. 1200s, the ruler of Djenné ordered the construction of the first Great Mosque. Having recently converted to Islam, he had his palace torn down to make room for the huge house of worship. The city became an important Islamic religious center. Over the years, political and religious conflicts led to a decline in the city. People abandoned the Great Mosque, and a second, much smaller one replaced it. Then in 1906, builders began to raise a new Great Mosque. Today the Great Mosque is once more an important part of the religious life of the people of Djenné.

The Great Mosque

Built facing east toward Makkah, the holy city of Islam, the Great Mosque of Djenné is constructed from the same sun-dried mud bricks as most of the rest of the city. The mud walls of the mosque vary in thickness between 16 and 24 inches (41 and 61 cm), providing insulation to keep the interior cool. Roof vents can be removed at night to allow cooler air inside.

With its five stories and three towers, or minarets, the mosque rises above the surrounding buildings. Inside the mosque, the main prayer hall is open to the sky. Although the mosque contains loudspeakers used to issue the call to prayer, there are few other modern improvements.

Maintaining the Mosque

Rain, wind, and heat can damage mud structures, and without care the Great Mosque would soon deteriorate. Each spring the people of Djenné plaster the mosque from top to bottom with fresh mud. It is a great festival day, and nearly everyone volunteers. Workers climb up the sides of the mosque on wooden rods permanently mounted to the walls. They dump mud and water onto the walls, then smooth it with their bare hands. The townspeople know that, with such care, the Great Mosque will remain a place of worship for generations to come.

Making the Connection

1. When was the first Great Mosque built?
2. What elements of the Great Mosque help keep the inside cool?
3. **Making Comparisons** In what way is the Great Mosque like the other buildings in Djenné? In what way is it different?

◄ Great Mosque of Djenné

Section 3

Coastal Countries

Guide to Reading

Main Idea

West Africa's coastal countries have a favorable climate for agriculture.

Terms to Know

- cassava
- bauxite
- phosphate

Places to Locate

- Gambia
- Senegal
- Guinea
- Guinea-Bissau
- Cape Verde
- Liberia
- Sierra Leone
- Côte d'Ivoire
- Ghana

Reading Strategy

Create five charts like this one, filling in at least one key fact about five coastal countries for each category.

Country	
Land	
Economy	
Culture	

NATIONAL GEOGRAPHIC **Exploring Our World**

A royal parade in Ghana is a proud display of wealth. The Ashanti people—who live in this country—have been mining gold since the 1300s. The twenty-fifth anniversary of the reign of their king was a perfect opportunity to celebrate the country's rich history. Skilled goldsmiths created the bracelets, rings, and other jewelry worn by the king and his bearers.

In addition to Nigeria and the Sahel countries, West Africa includes 11 coastal countries. One country—Cape Verde—is a group of islands in the Atlantic Ocean. The other countries, including Togo and Benin, stretch along the Gulf of Guinea and the Atlantic coast.

The Land and Economy

Sandy beaches, thick mangrove swamps, and rain forests cover the shores of West Africa's coastal countries. Highland areas with grasses and trees lie inland. Several major rivers flow from these highlands to the coast. They include the Sénégal, Gambia, Volta, and Niger Rivers. Rapids and shallow waters prevent large ships from traveling far inland.

Because they border the ocean, the coastal countries receive plenty of rainfall. Warm currents in the Gulf of Guinea create a moist, tropical rain forest climate in most coastal lowlands year-round. The highland areas have a tropical savanna climate with dry and wet seasons. Some areas have drier steppe and desert climates.

Most people in the region are subsistence farmers. They grow yams, corn, rice, cassava, and other foods for their families. **Cassava** is a plant whose roots are ground into flour to make bread. Coffee, rubber, cacao, palm oil, and kola nuts are cash crops grown on plantations. Kola nuts help give colas their special flavor.

Despite these rich agricultural resources, coastal West African countries import more in industrial goods than they export in natural products. Why? Agricultural products often rise and fall in price suddenly, and their value is not equal to finished goods. To meet their countries' needs, governments have to borrow money from other countries or international organizations.

Reading Check **What types of climates do the coastal countries have?**

History and People

In early times, the powerful and wealthy kingdoms of Ashanti and Abomey ruled West Africa's coastal region. These kingdoms were centers of trade, learning, and the arts. From the late 1400s to the early 1800s, Europeans set up trading posts along the West African coast. From these posts they traded with Africans for gold, ivory, and other goods that people in Europe wanted.

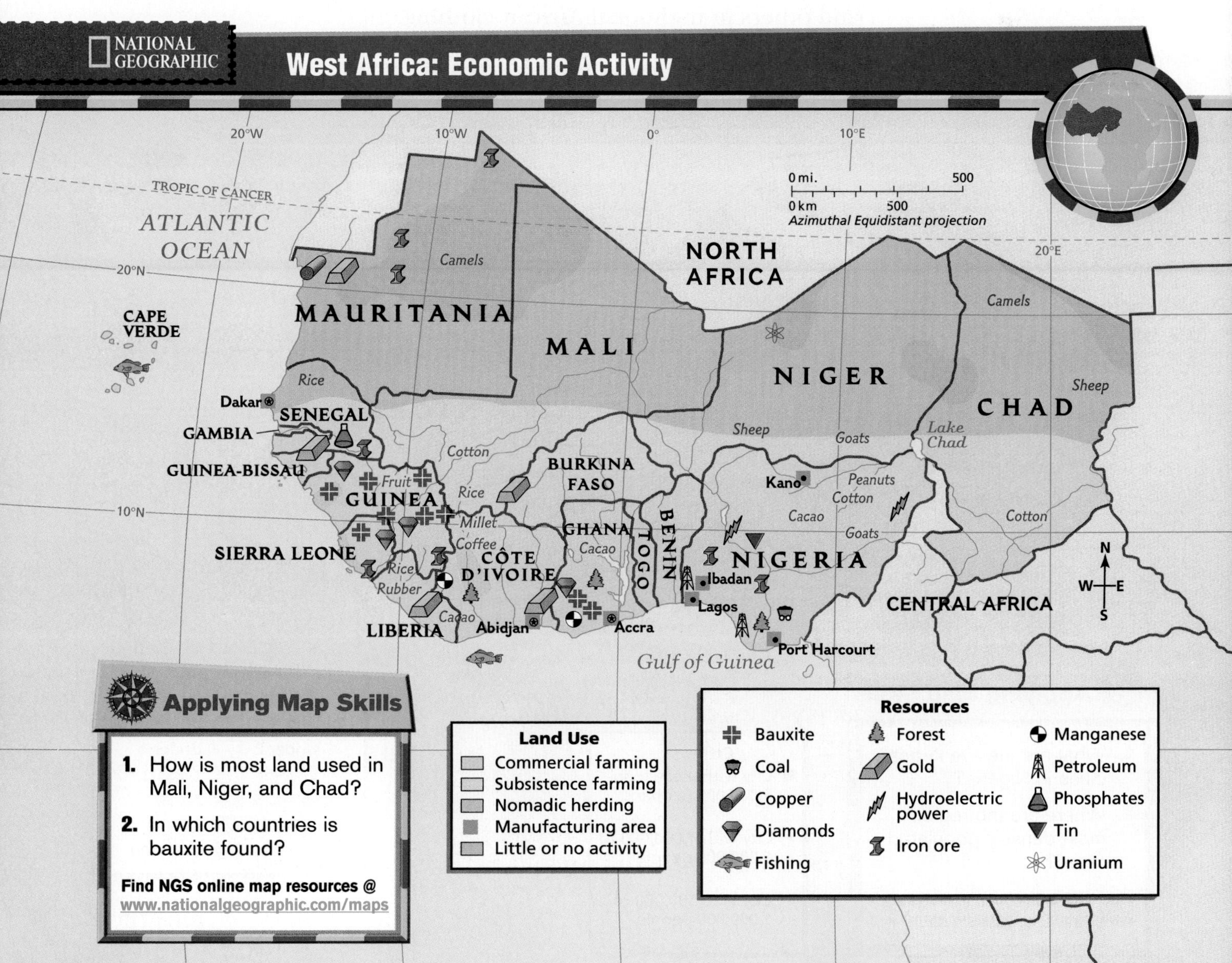

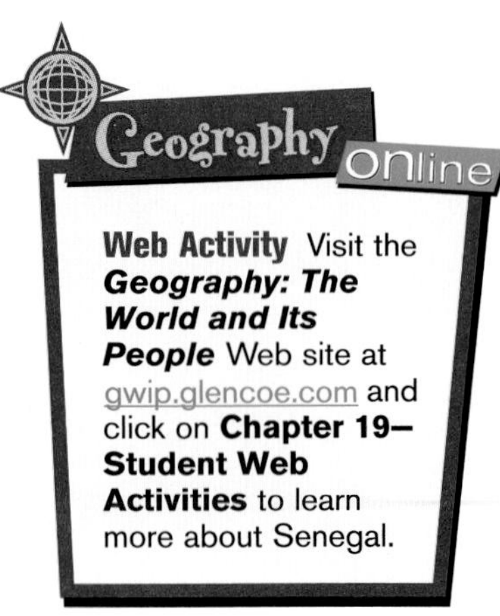

The Europeans also enslaved and forced millions of Africans to migrate to the Americas to work on plantations and in mines. This trade in human beings, which also took place among African countries, was a disaster for West Africa. The removal of so many young and skilled people devastated West African families, villages, and economies.

The French, British, and Portuguese eventually divided up the coastal region and set up colonies to obtain the region's rich resources. In 1957 Ghana became the first country in West Africa to become independent. By the late 1970s, no West African country was under European rule.

People in coastal West Africa cherish family ties. Some practice traditional African religions, whereas others are Christians or Muslims. Local African languages are spoken in everyday conversation. Languages such as French, English, and Portuguese are used in business or government.

Cities in coastal West Africa are modern and growing. If you were to visit cities such as Ghana's capital—Accra (AH•kruh)—or Côte d'Ivoire's capital—Abidjan (AH•bee•JAHN)—you would find busy downtown areas with modern government and office buildings. You would also see some people dressed in Western-style business clothes and others in traditional African clothing.

NATIONAL GEOGRAPHIC

West Africa: Population Density

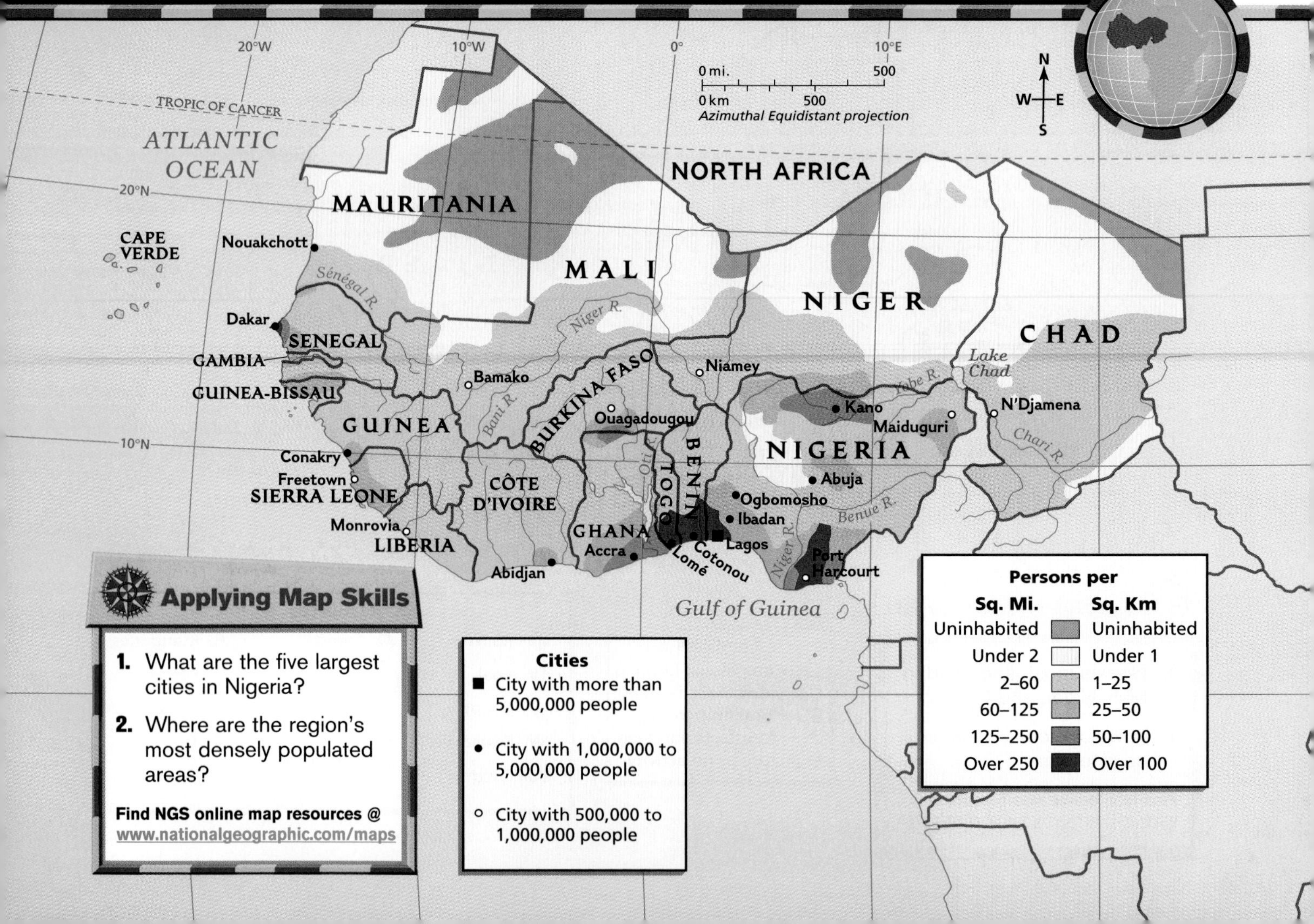

20°W 10°W 0° 10°E
TROPIC OF CANCER
20°N
10°N
0 mi. 500
0 km 500
Azimuthal Equidistant projection
N W E S
ATLANTIC OCEAN
MAURITANIA
NORTH AFRICA
MALI
NIGER
CHAD
CAPE VERDE
Nouakchott
Sénégal R.
Niger R.
Dakar
SENEGAL
GAMBIA
GUINEA-BISSAU
GUINEA
Bamako
Bani R.
BURKINA FASO
Ouagadougou
Niamey
Lake Chad
Yobe R.
N'Djamena
Chari R.
Kano
Maiduguri
NIGERIA
Abuja
Ogbomosho
Ibadan
Lagos
Benue R.
Niger R.
Port Harcourt
Conakry
Freetown
SIERRA LEONE
Monrovia
LIBERIA
CÔTE D'IVOIRE
Abidjan
GHANA
Accra
TOGO
Lomé
BENIN
Cotonou
Gulf of Guinea

Persons per

Sq. Mi.	Sq. Km
Uninhabited	Uninhabited
Under 2	Under 1
2–60	1–25
60–125	25–50
125–250	50–100
Over 250	Over 100

Cities

- ■ City with more than 5,000,000 people
- • City with 1,000,000 to 5,000,000 people
- ○ City with 500,000 to 1,000,000 people

Applying Map Skills

1. What are the five largest cities in Nigeria?
2. Where are the region's most densely populated areas?

Find NGS online map resources @ www.nationalgeographic.com/maps

Gambia, Senegal, and Guinea Most of the people in **Gambia, Senegal,** and **Guinea** work in agriculture. Guinea is also rich in bauxite and diamonds. **Bauxite** is a mineral used to make aluminum. Guinea has about 25 percent of the world's reserves of bauxite. Senegal is an important source of phosphate. **Phosphate** is mineral salt that has phosphorus, which is used in fertilizers.

Gambia proclaimed independence from the British in 1965. Senegal and Guinea were French colonies until becoming independent in 1958 (Guinea) and 1960 (Senegal). Senegal has more people—9.2 million—than the other two countries. About 42 percent live in cities. Dakar (dah•KAHR), Senegal's capital, is a coastal city known for its tree-lined streets, cafés, and markets.

Rivers of West Africa provide not only water but transportation. Here, freight boats on the Niger River deliver goods to Benin's people.

Place What prevents large ships from traveling far inland on West Africa's rivers?

Guinea-Bissau and Cape Verde **Guinea-Bissau** and **Cape Verde** were Portuguese colonies until they won independence in 1975. The 15 volcanic islands of Cape Verde lie about 375 miles (604 km) offshore in the Atlantic Ocean. You will notice a mix of African and Portuguese influences in the languages and cultures of these two countries.

Most of the 1.2 million people in Guinea-Bissau make their living by farming or fishing. Rice—the major crop—is also the basic food item. Do you like to eat cashew nuts? Guinea-Bissau is one of the world's top producers of cashews. Poor soil and low rainfall make the Cape Verde islands unsuitable for farming. Most of the people here work in service industries related to trade, government, and transportation. The islands' 400,000 people must import about 90 percent of their food.

Liberia and Sierra Leone **Liberia** is the only West African nation that was never a colony. African Americans freed from slavery founded Liberia in 1822. Monrovia, Liberia's capital, was named for James Monroe—the president of the United States when Liberia was founded. From 1989 to 1996, a civil war cost many lives and destroyed much of the country's economy.

Like Liberia, **Sierra Leone** was founded as a home for people freed from slavery. The British ruled Sierra Leone from 1787 until 1961. Most of the land is used for farming, but the country also has mineral resources, especially diamonds. As with Liberia, civil war has destroyed recent economic development. Sierra Leone's population of 5.3 million is nearly twice Liberia's 2.9 million.

Côte d'Ivoire **Côte d'Ivoire** has a French name that means "ivory coast." From the late 1400s to the early 1900s, a trade in elephant ivory tusks in Côte d'Ivoire brought profits to European traders. Today the ivory trade is illegal, and the country protects its elephants.

Côte d'Ivoire was a French colony before winning its independence in 1960. It is the world's top producer of cacao beans and also a major producer of coffee and palm oil. The port of Abidjan is the largest urban area and economic center. This busy city has towering office buildings and wide avenues. Abidjan is the official seat of government, but Yamoussoukro (YAH•moo•SOO•kroh), some 137 miles (220 km) inland, has been named the new capital.

Ghana Like Côte d'Ivoire, **Ghana** produces cacao beans for export. Gold and timber are also major sources of income. The country is rich in natural resources, but many people subsistence-farm.

Ghana won its independence from the British in 1957. For a long time, dictators or military leaders ruled the country. Unwise government decisions slowed Ghana's economic growth and brought hardships to its people. In the 1990s, Ghana moved toward democracy.

Ghana's people belong to about 100 ethnic groups. The Ashanti and the Fante are the largest. Many groups still keep their local kings, but these rulers have no political power. The people respect these ceremonial rulers and look to them to keep traditions alive.

About 35 percent of Ghana's people live in cities. Accra, on the coast, is the capital and largest city. A giant dam on the Volta River provides hydroelectric power to urban areas. The dam also has created Lake Volta, the world's largest artificial lake.

✓Reading Check **What are the capitals of Ghana and Côte d'Ivoire?**

Assessment

Defining Terms

1. Define cassava, bauxite, phosphate.

Recalling Facts

2. Economics What types of goods must West African countries import?

3. History Which West African country was never a colony?

4. Government How much political power do the local kings in Ghana have?

Critical Thinking

5. Drawing Conclusions Why is coastal West Africa divided into so many countries?

6. Analyzing Information What West African products do you use?

Graphic Organizer

7. Organizing Information On a diagram like this one, record when each of the coastal countries discussed in this section gained their independence and from whom.

Country	Date of Independence	Independence From Whom?

Applying Geography Skills

8. Analyzing Maps Study the physical map on page 543. Which West African nation has the highest overall elevation? What is that elevation in feet and meters?

Chapter 19 Reading Review

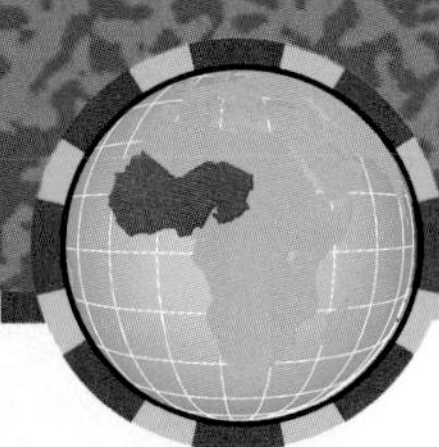

Section 1 Nigeria

Terms to Know
mangrove
savanna
harmattan
subsistence farm
cacao
compound
civil war

Main Idea
A large, oil-rich country, Nigeria has more people than any other African nation.

✓ **Place** Nigeria's major landforms are coastal lowlands, savanna highlands, and partly dry grasslands.

✓ **Economics** More than 90 percent of Nigeria's income comes from oil exports.

✓ **Culture** Nigeria has more than 300 ethnic groups. The government is taking steps to reduce ethnic conflicts.

Section 2 The Sahel Countries

Terms to Know
overgraze
drought
desertification

Main Idea
The Sahel countries face a continuing struggle to keep grasslands from turning into desert.

✓ **Region** The Sahel countries are Mauritania, Mali, Niger, Chad, and Burkina Faso.

✓ **Region** The Sahel forms a border between the Sahara to the north and fertile lands to the south.

✓ **Human/Environment Interaction** Overgrazing and drought have caused many grassland areas in this region to become desert.

✓ **Economics** Most people in the Sahel are subsistence farmers or livestock herders.

Section 3 Coastal Countries

Terms to Know
cassava
bauxite
phosphate

Main Idea
West Africa's coastal countries have a favorable climate for agriculture.

✓ **Region** The 11 countries that make up coastal West Africa are Senegal, Gambia, Guinea, Guinea-Bissau, Cape Verde, Liberia, Sierra Leone, Côte d'Ivoire, Ghana, Togo, and Benin.

✓ **Economics** West Africa's coastal countries have a good climate for agriculture, and most people are farmers.

✓ **History** With the exception of Liberia, the coastal countries were all European colonies. All had gained their independence by the late 1970s.

The port of Abidjan, Côte d'Ivoire ▶

Chapter 19

Assessment and Activities

Using Key Terms

Match the terms in Part A with their definitions in Part B.

A.

1. overgraze
2. cassava
3. drought
4. mangrove
5. compound
6. phosphate
7. desertification
8. cacao
9. subsistence farm
10. savanna

B.

a. process in which deserts expand
b. a group of houses surrounded by a wall
c. plant whose roots are ground into flour and eaten
d. mineral salt used in fertilizers
e. tropical tree whose seeds are used to make cocoa and chocolate
f. tropical grassland with scattered trees
g. produces enough to support a family's needs
h. extended period of extreme dryness
i. when animals strip the land so bare that plants cannot grow
j. tropical tree with roots above and beneath the water

Reviewing the Main Idea

Section 1 Nigeria

11. **Economics** What is Nigeria's major export?
12. **History** Why have there been so many conflicts in Nigeria since 1960?
13. **Culture** Who was the first African to win the Nobel Prize in literature?
14. **Culture** What are the four largest ethnic groups in Nigeria?

Section 2 The Sahel Countries

15. **Region** The Sahel forms the boundary between what two regions in West Africa?
16. **History** Who was Mansa Musa?
17. **Culture** What religion do most people of the Sahel follow?
18. **Economics** Why has fishing declined in Mauritania?

Section 3 Coastal Countries

19. **Movement** Why are ships unable to sail very far inland in coastal West Africa?
20. **Economics** How are kola nuts used?
21. **History** What two kingdoms controlled the coastal area prior to the 1400s?
22. **Economics** What country is one of the world's top producers of cashews?

West Africa

Place Location Activity

On a separate sheet of paper, match the letters on the map with the numbered places listed below.

1. Gulf of Guinea
2. Nigeria
3. Niger River
4. Liberia
5. Cape Verde
6. Lagos
7. Mali
8. Ghana
9. Chad
10. Monrovia

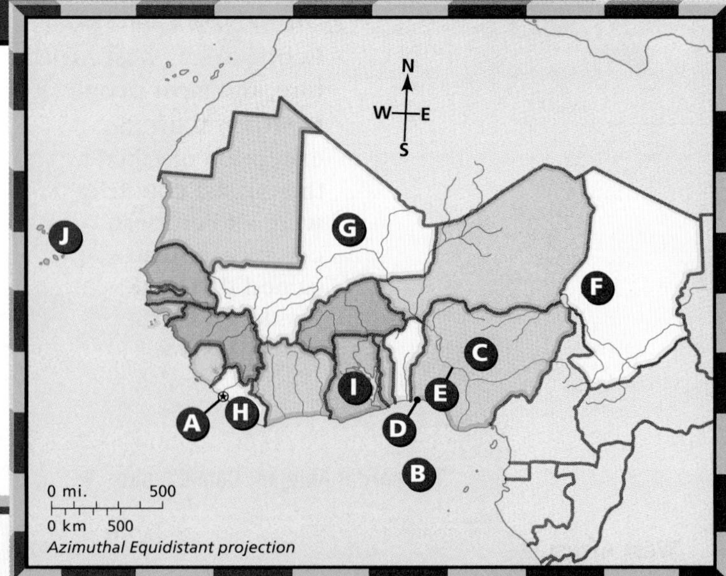

Self-Check Quiz Visit the ***Geography: The World and Its People*** Web site at gwip.glencoe.com and click on **Chapter 19—Self-Check Quizzes** to prepare for the Chapter Test.

Critical Thinking

23. **Evaluating Information** What do you feel is the major challenge facing the countries of West Africa today? Explain your answer.
24. **Sequencing Information** After reviewing the entire chapter, choose what you feel are five of the most important events in the history of West Africa. Place those events and their dates on a time line like this one.

GeoJournal Activity

25. **Writing a Poem** Find out more about one of the countries of West Africa. Imagine that you are there and write an "I am . . ." poem. Begin each line with the words "I am . . ." and then complete it with a description, action, or emotion that you feel relates to the subject. Share your poem with the rest of the class, and ask classmates to identify your poem's subject.

Mental Mapping Activity

26. **Focusing on the Region** Draw a simple outline map of West Africa, then label the following:
    - Niger River
    - Atlantic Ocean
    - Gulf of Guinea
    - Tropic of Cancer
    - Nigeria
    - Niger
    - Senegal
    - Côte d'Ivoire
    - Chad
    - Mali
    - Mauritania
    - Liberia

Technology Skills Activity

27. **Using the Internet** Conduct a search for information about one of the ancient empires or kingdoms of West Africa. Look for maps, pictures, and descriptions of the important rulers. Then write a report using the information you found. Share your report with the rest of the class.

Standardized Test Practice

Directions: Study the graph, then answer the question that follows.

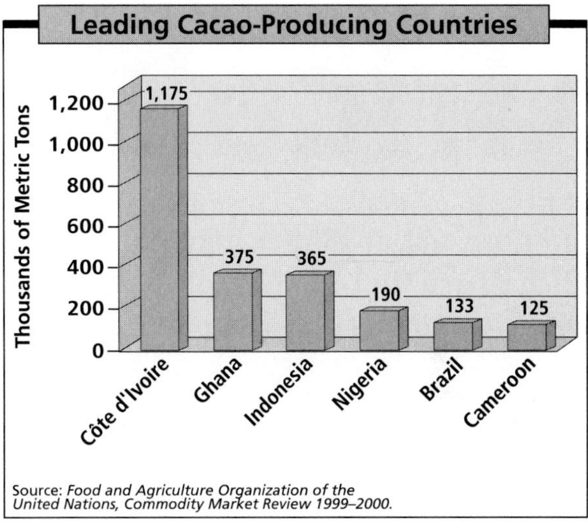

1. What countries on the graph are top cacao-producing countries from West Africa?

A Ghana, Indonesia, and Nigeria
B Côte d'Ivoire, Ghana, and Indonesia
C Côte d'Ivoire, Nigeria, and Cameroon
D Côte d'Ivoire, Ghana, and Nigeria

Test-Taking Tip: The important words in this question are "from West Africa." You need to use information on the graph as well as information you learned in Chapter 19 to answer this question. As with any graph, read the title bar and information along the side and bottom of the graph first. Then analyze and compare the sizes of the bars to one another.

People trade salt and other goods at a market on the Niger River in ancient Africa.

PLEASE PASS THE SALT: Africa's Salt Trade

Passing the salt at dinner may not be a big deal, but in parts of Africa, salt built empires. How did such a basic substance come to play such an important role in Africa?

Good as Gold

Salt is essential for life. Every person contains about 8 ounces (227 g) of salt—enough to fill several saltshakers. Salt helps muscles work, and it aids in digesting food. In hot climates, people need extra salt to replace the salt lost when they sweat. In tropical Africa, salt has always been precious.

Salt is plentiful in the Sahara and scarce in the forests south of the Sahara (in present-day countries such as Ghana and Côte d'Ivoire). These conditions gave rise to Africa's salt trade. Beginning in the A.D. 300s, Berbers drove camels carrying European glassware and weapons from Mediterranean ports into the Sahara. At the desert's great salt deposits, such as those near the ancient sites of Terhazza and Taoudenni, they traded European wares for salt.

The salt did not look like the tiny crystals in a saltshaker. It was in the form of large slabs, as hard as stone. The slabs were pried from hardened salt deposits that were left on the land long ago when landlocked seas evaporated. The salt slabs were loaded onto camels, and the animals were herded south. To people in the south, salt was literally worth its weight in gold. The slabs were cut into equal-sized blocks and exchanged for gold and other products such as ivory and kola nuts. Salt was also traded for enslaved people.

Rise and Decline

Before camels arrived in Africa from Asia in A.D. 300, only a trickle of trade, mostly carried by human porters, made it across the blistering desert. In time, caravans of thousands of camels loaded with tons of salt arrived at southern markets.

Local kings along the trade routes put taxes—payable in gold—on all goods crossing their realms. The ancient empires of Mali, Ghana, and Songhai rose to great power from wealth brought by the salt trade.

Trade routes also provided avenues for spreading ideas and inventions. By the A.D. 800s, Arab traders brought to Africa a system of weights and measures, a written language, and the concept of money. They also brought a new religion: Islam.

Today trucks have replaced many of the camels. Salt no longer dominates trade in the region. However, salt is still important, and the salt trade continues in Mali and in the markets of other West African nations.

QUESTIONS

1 What goods were exchanged in the salt trade?

2 How did the salt trade affect regions south of the Sahara?

A present-day salt caravan in Niger ▶

NATIONAL GEOGRAPHIC SOCIETY
Salt Trade Routes
ATLANTIC OCEAN
Mediterranean Sea
0 mi. 1,000
0 km 1,000
ASIA
N
W
E
S
SAHARA
Terhazza
Taoudenni
NIGER
Nile R.
Red Sea
Lake Chad
CÔTE D'IVOIRE
GHANA
Songhai
Mali
Ghana
Salt deposit
Trade routes
Present boundaries

Chapter 20

Central Africa

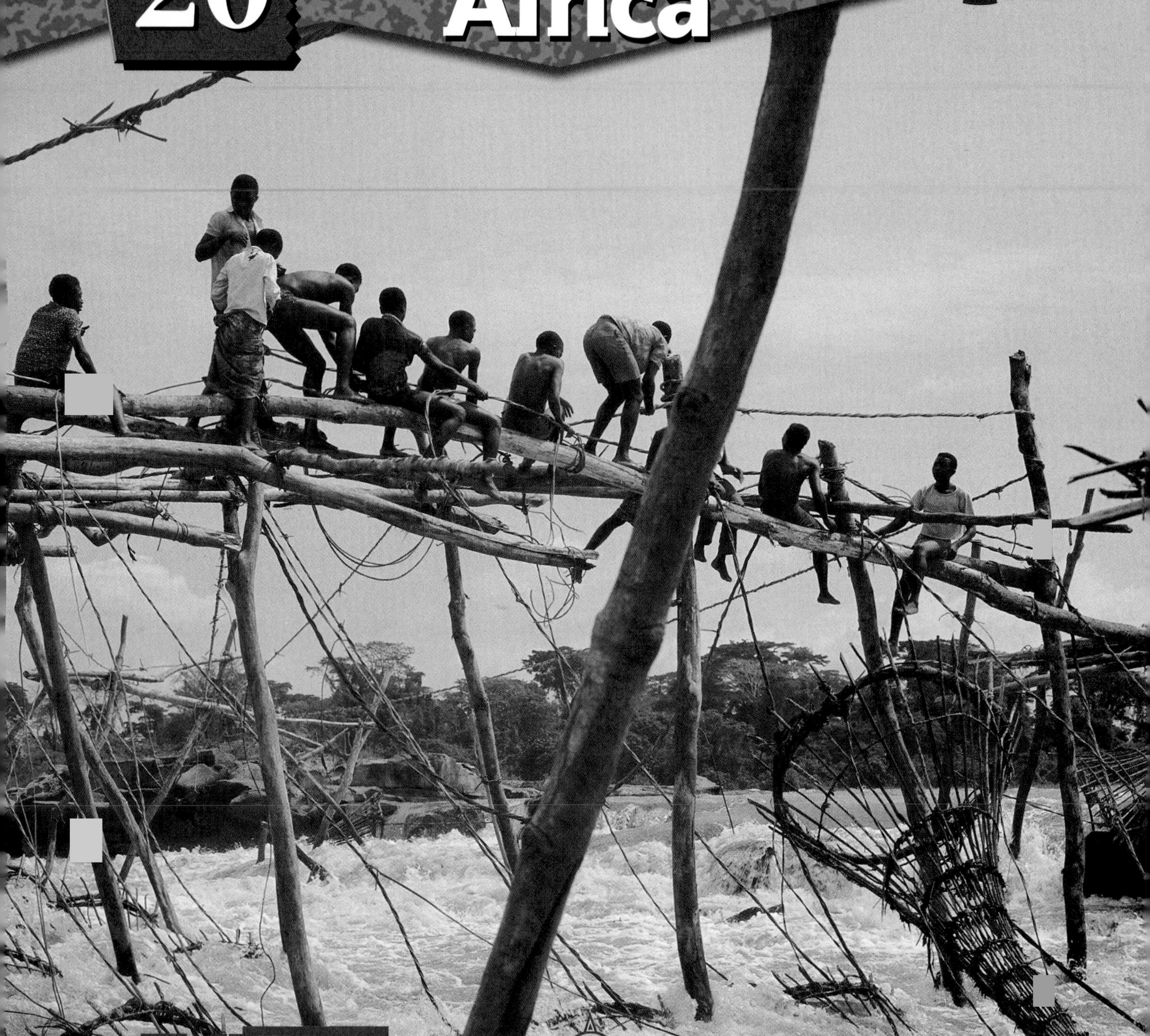

The World and Its People — NATIONAL GEOGRAPHIC

To learn more about the people and places of Central Africa, view ***The World and Its People*** **Chapter 20** video.

Geography online

Chapter Overview Visit the ***Geography: The World and Its People*** Web site at gwip.glencoe.com and click on **Chapter 20–Chapter Overviews** to preview information about Central Africa.

Section 1

Democratic Republic of the Congo

Guide to Reading

Main Idea

The Democratic Republic of the Congo has rich natural resources that are largely undeveloped because of civil war and poor government decisions.

Terms to Know

- savanna
- basin
- canopy
- hydroelectric power
- dictator
- refugee

Places to Locate

- Congo River
- Lake Albert
- Lake Edward
- Lake Kivu
- Lake Tanganyika
- Kinshasa

Reading Strategy

Make a chart like this one. Then list two facts about the Democratic Republic of the Congo for each category.

	Fact #1	Fact #2
Land		
Economy		
People		

NATIONAL GEOGRAPHIC **Exploring Our World**

Barges act as floating malls on the Congo River. They provide goods to areas too remote for overland travel. At each village along the river, local people come to the barge to sell captured animals, crops, or baskets they have woven. Then they buy goods brought upriver from the cities—anything from bread to clothes to cassette tapes.

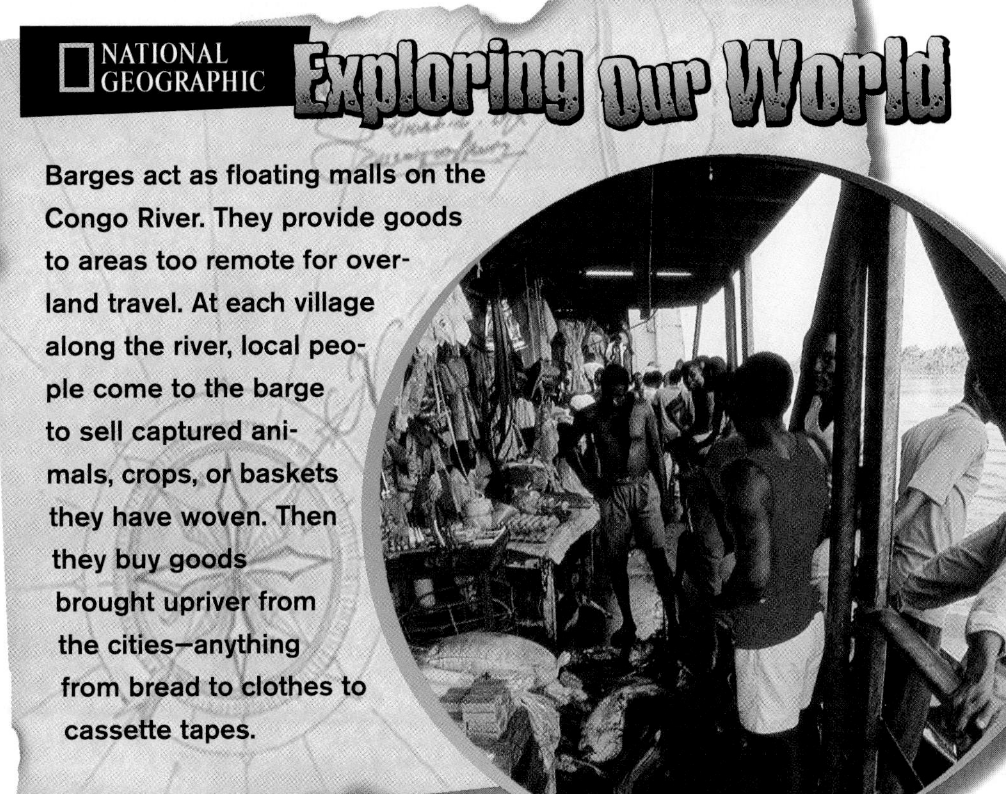

Africa's second-longest river—the **Congo River**—flows through the heart of the Democratic Republic of the Congo. This large country is located on the Equator in the very heart of Africa.

The Land and Climate

One-fourth the size of the United States, the Democratic Republic of the Congo has only about 23 miles (37 km) of coastline. Most of its land borders other African countries—nine in all.

High, rugged mountains rise in the eastern part of the country. Here you will find four large lakes—**Lake Albert, Lake Edward, Lake Kivu,** and **Lake Tanganyika** (TAN•guhn•YEE•kuh). Lake Tanganyika is the longest freshwater lake in the world. It is also the second deepest, after Russia's Lake Baikal. Savannas, or tropical grasslands with few trees, cover the highlands in the far north and south of the country. In these areas, lions and leopards stalk antelopes and zebras for food.

◀ Fishers on the Congo River near Kisangani, Democratic Republic of the Congo

One of the world's largest rain forests covers the central basin of the Democratic Republic of the Congo. A **basin** is a broad flat valley. The treetops form a **canopy,** or an umbrella-like forest covering so thick that sunlight rarely reaches the forest floor. More than 750 different kinds of trees grow here. The rain forests are being destroyed at a rapid rate, however, as they are cleared for timber and farmland.

The mighty Congo River—about 2,800 miles (4,506 km) long—weaves its way through the Congo Basin on its journey to the Atlantic Ocean. The river current is so strong that it carries water

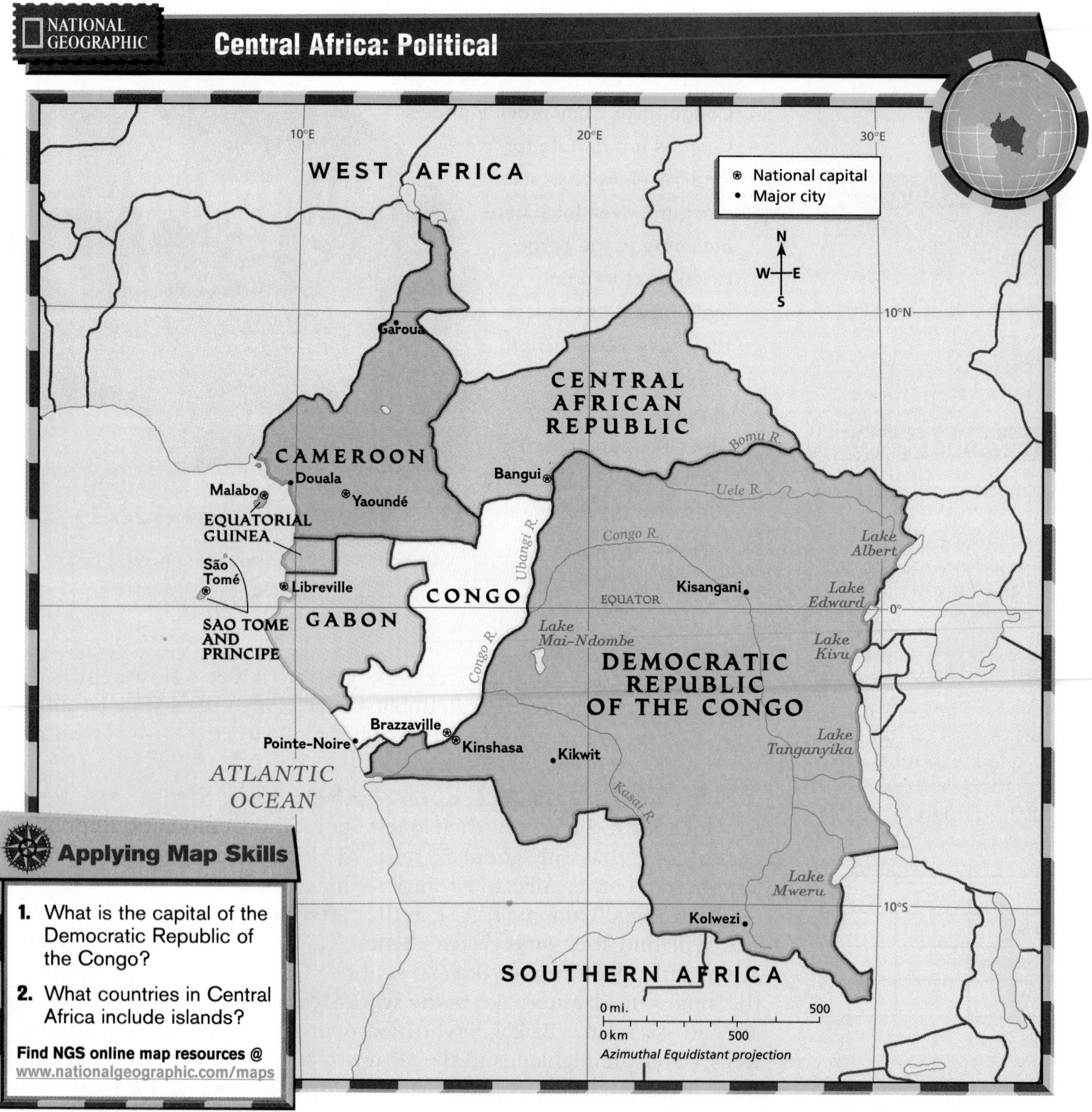

Applying Map Skills

1. What is the capital of the Democratic Republic of the Congo?
2. What countries in Central Africa include islands?

Find NGS online map resources @ www.nationalgeographic.com/maps

about 100 miles (161 km) into the ocean. The Congo River and its tributaries, such as the Kasai River, provide **hydroelectric power,** or electricity generated by flowing water. In fact, these rivers produce more than 10 percent of all the world's hydroelectric power. The Congo is also the country's highway for trade and travel.

A Tropical Climate Because of its location on the Equator, the Democratic Republic of the Congo has a tropical climate. Along the Congo River and in the rain forests, the climate is hot and humid.

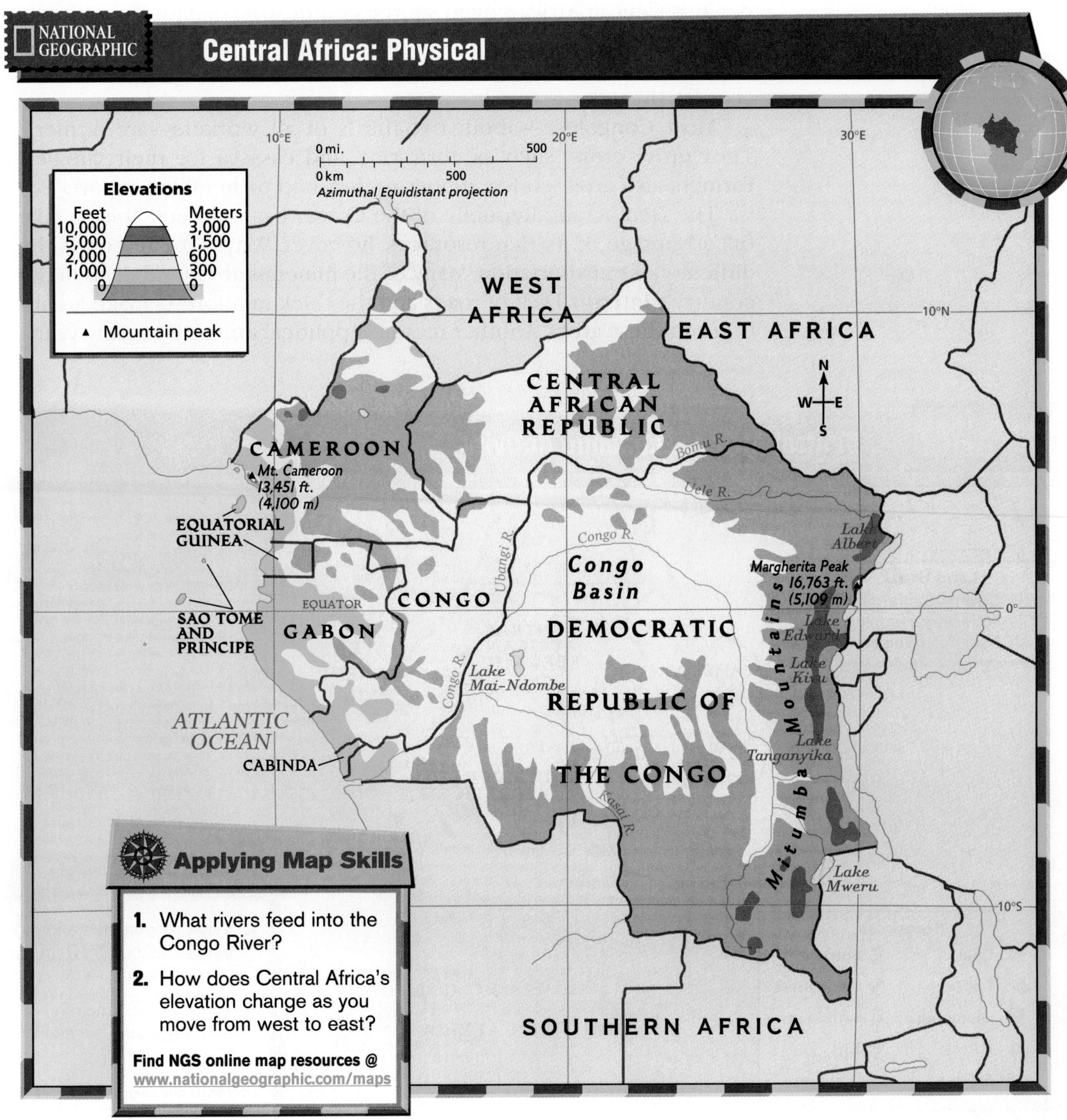

Applying Map Skills

1. What rivers feed into the Congo River?
2. How does Central Africa's elevation change as you move from west to east?

Find NGS online map resources @ www.nationalgeographic.com/maps

Heavy rainstorms bring 80 inches (203 cm) or more of rain each year. In the southern and northern grasslands, rain tends to fall just a few months of the year. The highlands in the east are cooler and drier.

✓Reading Check **Why does the Democratic Republic of the Congo generally have a warm, tropical climate?**

The Economy

The Democratic Republic of the Congo has the opportunity to be a wealthy nation. The map below shows you its many valuable mineral resources. The country exports gold, petroleum, diamonds, and copper. It is Central Africa's main source of industrial diamonds, as shown on the graph on page 567. These diamonds are used in making strong industrial tools that cut metal. The country's factories make steel, cement, tires, shoes, textiles, processed foods, and beverages.

Most Congolese—about two-thirds of all workers—are farmers. They grow crops such as corn, rice, and cassava for their families. Farmers also grow coffee, rubber, cotton, and palm oil for export.

The Democratic Republic of the Congo has not been able to take full advantage of its rich resources, however. Why? One reason is the difficulty of transportation. Many of the minerals are found deep in the country's interior. Lack of roads and the thick rain forests make it hard to reach these areas. Another reason is political unrest. For many years,

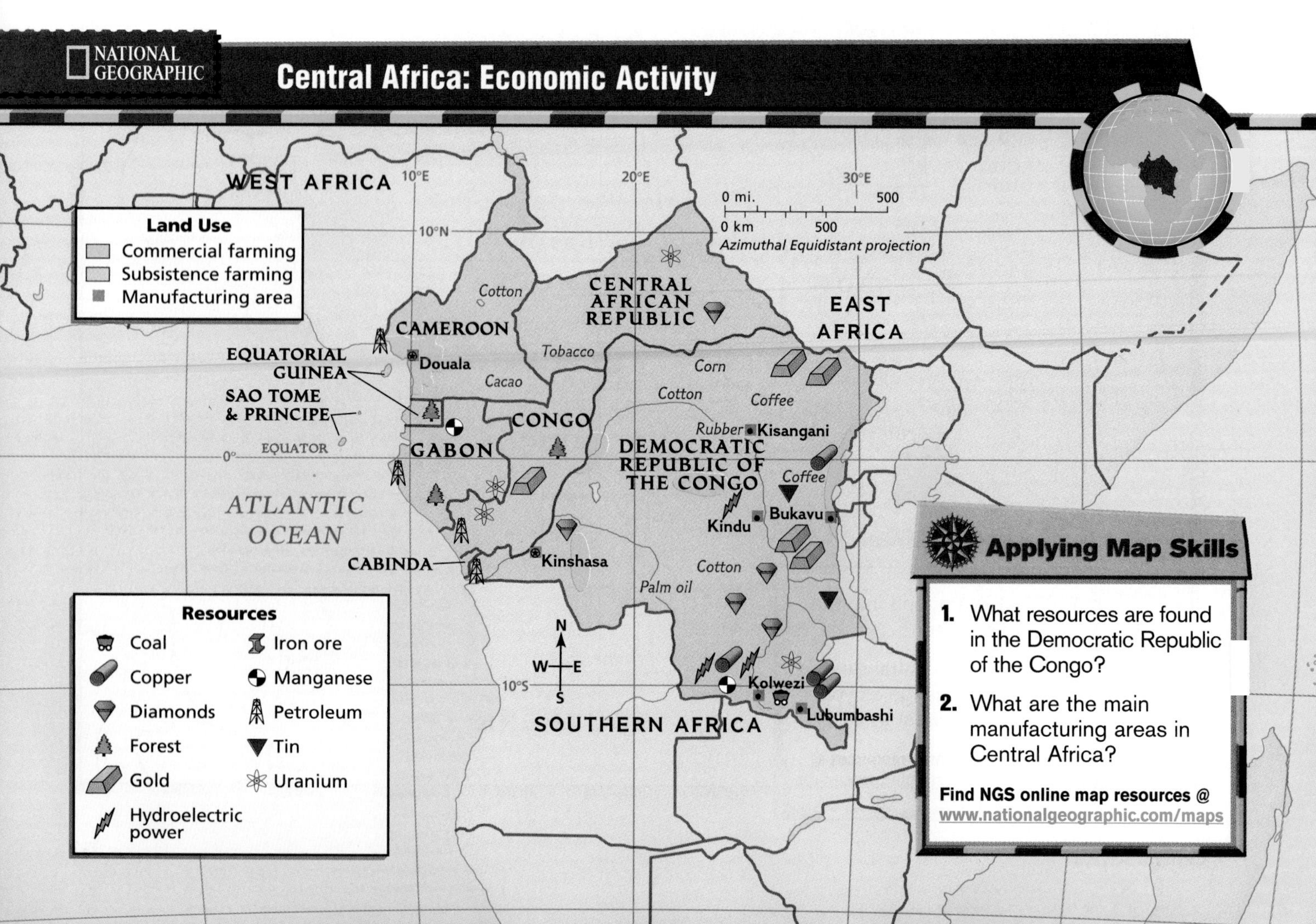

Leading Diamond-Producing Countries

Analyzing the Graph

Three of the world's top diamond-producing countries are in Africa south of the Sahara.

Place **What two countries produce the most diamonds in Africa?**

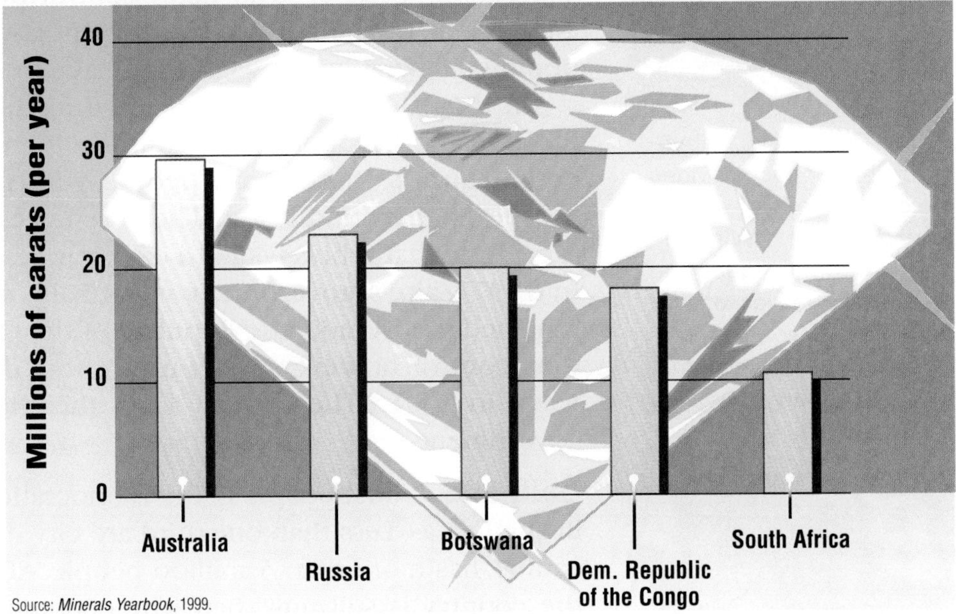

Source: *Minerals Yearbook*, 1999.

Visit gwip.glencoe.com and click on **Chapter 20—Textbook Updates.**

power-hungry leaders kept the nation's wealth for themselves. Then a civil war broke out in the late 1990s. This war has hurt efforts to develop the country's economy.

Reading Check **What mineral resources does the Democratic Republic of the Congo export?**

The People

The Democratic Republic of the Congo's 50.5 million people consists of as many as 250 different ethnic groups. One of these groups is the Kongo people, after whom the country is named. The official language is French, but many people speak local languages, such as Lingala or Kingwana. More than 75 percent of Congolese are Christians. Most of these are Roman Catholic.

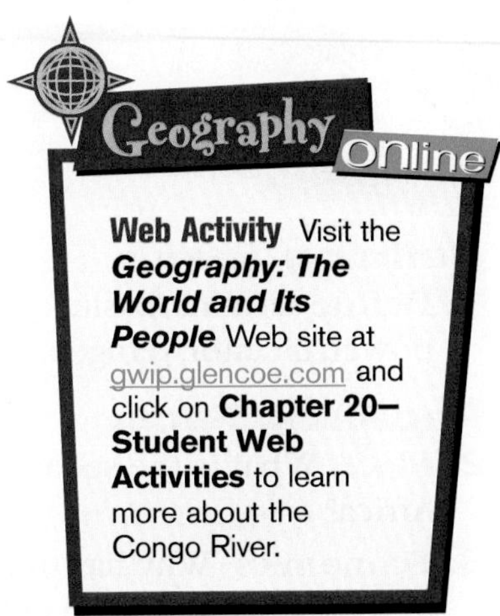

Web Activity Visit the ***Geography: The World and Its People*** Web site at gwip.glencoe.com and click on **Chapter 20—Student Web Activities** to learn more about the Congo River.

History and Government The Congo region was first settled about 10,000 years ago. The Bantu people—ancestors of most of the Congolese people today—moved here from Nigeria around the A.D. 600s and 700s. Several powerful kingdoms arose in the savannas south of the rain forests. The largest of these kingdoms was the Kongo.

In the late 1400s, Portuguese and other European traders arrived in Central Africa. During the next 300 years, they enslaved many people from the Congo region. Most of these Africans were shipped to the Americas. In the late 1800s, King Leopold II of Belgium made the region his personal plantation. Belgium's government took over the area in 1908 and called the colony the Belgian Congo.

After World War II, Africans pushed European governments to end the practice of ruling Africa as colonies. In 1960 the Belgian Congo

The Okapi

The Democratic Republic of the Congo provides the only home for the okapi (oh•KAH•pee). With its long, tough tongue, the okapi pulls leaves off the branches of young trees. Its tongue is so long that the okapi can use it to clean its eyes.

became independent. The country's name was changed to Zaire. From 1965 to 1997, a dictator named Mobutu Sese Seko ruled Zaire. A **dictator** is a leader who takes control of a government and directs affairs as he or she wishes. The corrupt government treated critics and opponents harshly and weakened Zaire's economy.

In the 1990s, civil wars erupted in the neighboring countries of Rwanda and Burundi. These conflicts forced thousands of refugees to enter Zaire. **Refugees** are people who flee to another country to escape danger or disaster. These refugees fought each other at the same time that rebels waged a civil war against Zaire's corrupt leaders. In 1997 Zaire's government was finally overthrown, and Zaire was renamed the Democratic Republic of the Congo. After the rebel leader took control, however, he set up another dictatorship and was assassinated in 2001. The country faces the challenge of building a stable government.

Daily Life Most people in the Democratic Republic of the Congo live in rural areas. Less than one-third are city dwellers. Still, **Kinshasa,** the capital, has more than 5 million people. After years of civil war, life in the country is still unsettled. The economy has nearly collapsed, and many people in the cities are without work.

In rural areas people follow traditional ways of life. They plant seeds, tend fields, and harvest crops. Most of the harvest goes to feeding the family. Any extra goes to the local market—or to the boats moving along the rivers—to sell or trade for goods the people need.

✓Reading Check **What kind of government does the Democratic Republic of the Congo now have?**

Assessment

Defining Terms

1. **Define** savanna, basin, canopy, hydroelectric power, dictator, refugee.

Recalling Facts

2. **Place** What is the second-longest river in Africa?
3. **Economics** Why has the Democratic Republic of the Congo not been able to take full advantage of its resources?
4. **History** When did the Belgian Congo become an independent country?

Critical Thinking

5. **Analyzing Information** Although the Democratic Republic of the Congo is located on the Equator, it does not have the highest temperatures in Africa. Why?
6. **Evaluating Information** Using the Congo River as an example, explain why rivers are so important to economic development.

Graphic Organizer

7. **Organizing Information** On a time line like the one below, label five important events and their dates in the history of the Democratic Republic of the Congo.

Applying Geography Skills

8. **Analyzing Maps** Study the physical map on page 565. What is the highest point in the Democratic Republic of the Congo?

Geography Skill

Mental Mapping

Think about how you get from place to place each day. In your mind you have a picture—or **mental map**—of your route. If necessary, you could probably draw sketch maps like the one below of many familiar places.

Learning the Skill

To develop your mental mapping skills, follow these steps.

- When a country or city name is mentioned, find it on a map to get an idea of where it is and what is near it.
- Draw a sketch map of it and include a compass rose to determine the cardinal directions.
- As you read or hear information about the place, try to picture where on your sketch you would fill in this information.
- Compare your sketch to an actual map of the place. Change your sketch if you need to, thus changing your mental map.

Practicing the Skill

Study the sketch map at right. Picture yourself standing *in* the map, then answer the following questions.

1. If you were facing north, looking at the Chicago Public Library, what route would you take to reach the Chicago Harbor?
2. You are at the Sears Tower, one of the tallest buildings in the world. About how many miles would you have to walk to get to the Medinah Temple?
3. If you met your friend at the public library, would it be too far to walk to the Art Institute? Should you take a taxi? Explain.

Applying the Skill

Think about your own neighborhood. Draw a sketch map of it from your mental map. Which neighborhood streets or roads did you include? What are the three most important features on your map?

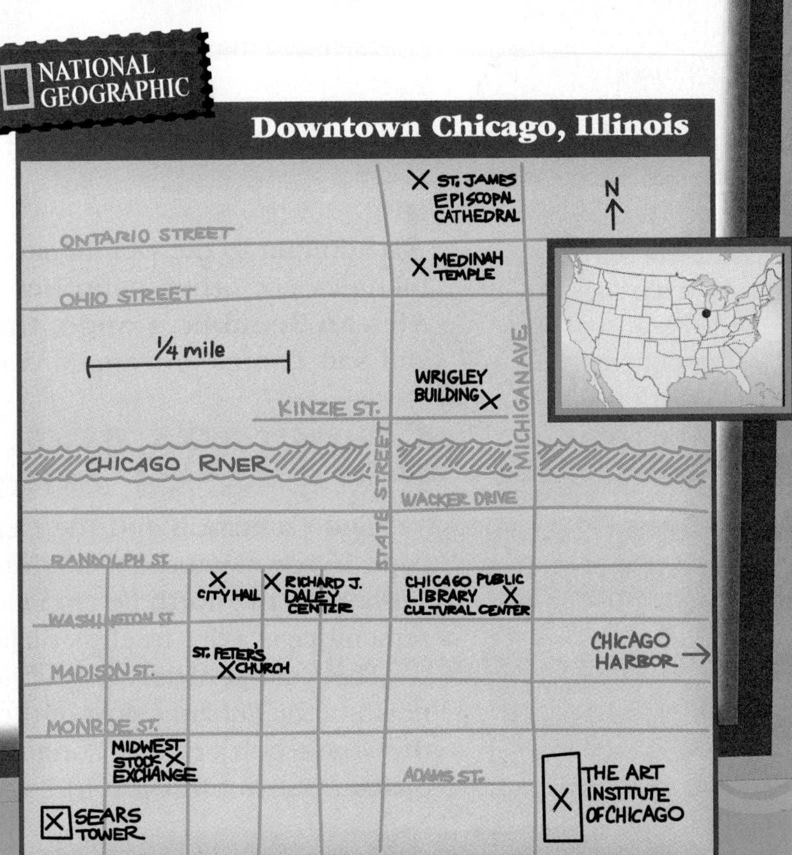

Section 2

Other Countries of Central Africa

Guide to Reading

Main Idea

Other countries in Central Africa have fairly small populations, with most people farming the land.

Terms to Know

- steppe
- tsetse fly
- industrialize
- deforestation

Places to Locate

- Cameroon
- Central African Republic
- Congo
- Gabon
- Equatorial Guinea
- Sao Tome and Principe
- Ubangi River

Reading Strategy

List facts about two countries in Central Africa in the outer parts of ovals like these. Where the ovals overlap, list facts that are true of both countries.

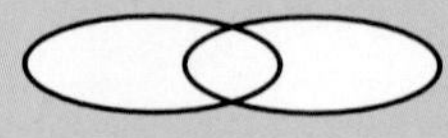

NATIONAL GEOGRAPHIC **Exploring Our World**

In the 2000 Olympic Summer Games, the gold medal in men's soccer went to Cameroon's team, the Indomitable Lions. The streets of Cameroon's capital, Yaoundé, and other cities were jammed with wildly excited fans screaming with joy. Cameroon's president even declared the following Monday a national holiday to celebrate the victory.

In addition to the Democratic Republic of the Congo, Central Africa includes six other countries. They are **Cameroon,** the **Central African Republic, Congo, Gabon** (ga•BOHN), **Equatorial Guinea,** and **Sao Tome** (sow too•MAY) **and Principe** (PREEN•see•pee).

Cameroon and the Central African Republic

Find Cameroon and the Central African Republic on the map on page 565. In Cameroon, hot, humid lowlands stretch along the Gulf of Guinea. To the north lie tropical savannas and steppes. A **steppe,** you remember, is a dry treeless plain often found on the edges of a desert.

The Central African Republic lies deep in the middle of Africa, just north of the Equator. Most of the country lies on a flat plateau, although the south borders the Congo Basin. Savannas make up most of the plateau, but tropical rain forests are found in the south.

The Economy and People Most people in the Central African Republic and Cameroon farm for a living. A few large plantations raise cacao, cotton, tobacco, and rubber for export. Some people herd livestock in areas that are safe from tsetse flies. The bite of the **tsetse** (SEET•see) **fly** causes a deadly disease called sleeping sickness. Turn to page 574 to find out more about sleeping sickness.

These two countries are only beginning to **industrialize,** or base their economies more on manufacturing and less on farming. Cameroon has had greater success in this effort. It has coastal ports and forest products, petroleum, and bauxite. The Central African Republic can claim only diamond mining as an important industry.

A colony of France until 1960, the Central African Republic recognizes French as its official language. Yet most of its people speak Sango, the national African language, to ease communication among the many ethnic groups. Cameroon, divided between the British and the French until 1960, uses both English and French as its official languages. The largest cities are Douala (doo•AH•lah), Yaoundé (yown•DAY), Cameroon's capital, and Bangui (bahng•GEE), the capital of the Central African Republic.

✓Reading Check **Why has Cameroon had greater success than the Central African Republic in industrializing?**

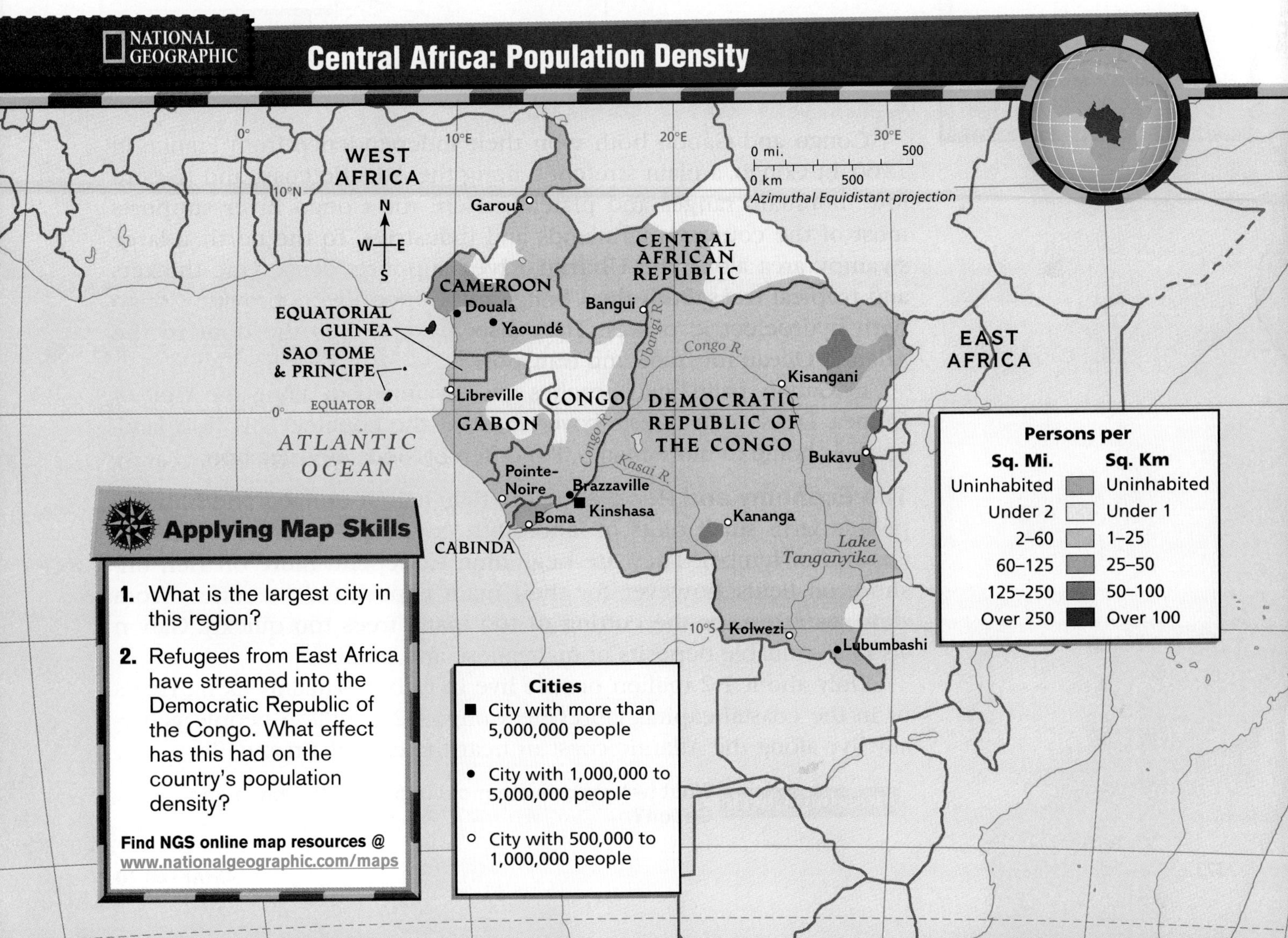

Central Africa: Climate

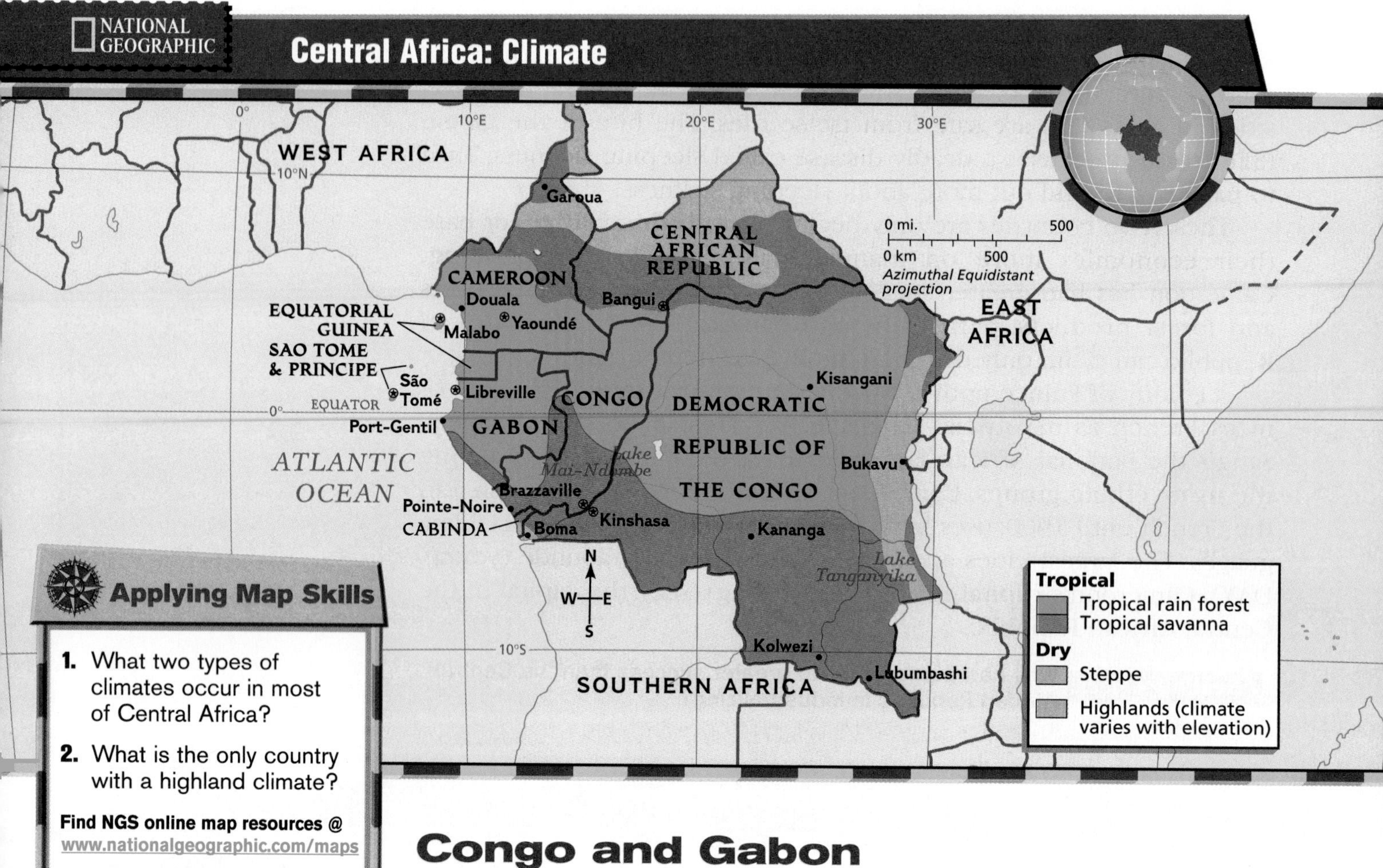

Applying Map Skills

1. What two types of climates occur in most of Central Africa?
2. What is the only country with a highland climate?

Find NGS online map resources @ www.nationalgeographic.com/maps

Congo and Gabon

Congo and Gabon both won their independence from France in 1960. In Congo, a plain stretches along the Atlantic coast and rises to low mountain ranges and plateaus. Here the Congo River supports most of the country's farmlands and industries. To the north, a large swampy area along the **Ubangi River** supports dense vine thickets and tropical trees. Both the Ubangi and Congo Rivers provide Congo with hydroelectric power. They also make Congo the door to the Atlantic Ocean for trade and transport.

In Gabon, palm-lined beaches and swamps run along the Gulf of Guinea. Dense rain forests cover most of the country. This lush landscape is home to more than 3,000 different kinds of vegetation.

The Economy and People More than half of Congo's and Gabon's people farm small plots of land. Both countries' economies rely on exports of lumber. They are beginning to depend more on rich offshore oil fields, however, for their main export. Gabon suffers from **deforestation,** or the cutting of too many trees too quickly. Gabon also has valuable deposits of manganese and uranium.

Only about 1.2 million people live in Gabon—mainly along rivers or in the coastal capital, Libreville. Congo's 2.7 million people generally live along the Atlantic coast or near the capital, Brazzaville.

✓ Reading Check **What two exports are most important to Congo and Gabon?**

Island Countries

The map on page 564 shows you that Equatorial Guinea and Sao Tome and Principe are both island countries. Equatorial Guinea includes land on the mainland of Africa and five islands. Sao Tome and Principe consists of two main islands and several smaller ones.

Equatorial Guinea Once a Spanish colony, Equatorial Guinea won its independence in 1968. Today the country is home to about 400,000 people. Most live on the mainland, although the capital and largest city—Malabo (mah•LAH•boh)—is on the country's largest island.

Farming, fishing, and harvesting wood are the country's main economic activities. For many years, timber and cacao grown in the islands' rich volcanic soil were the main exports. Oil was recently discovered and now leads all other exports.

Sao Tome and Principe The island country of Sao Tome and Principe gained its independence from Portugal in 1975. The Portuguese had first settled here about 300 years earlier. At that time, no people lived on the islands. Today about 200,000 people live here, with almost all living on the main island of Sao Tome.

Sao Tome and Principe are volcanic islands. As a result, the soil is rich and productive. Farmworkers on the islands grow various crops, including coconuts and bananas for export. The biggest export crop, however, is cacao, which makes cocoa.

✓Reading Check **Which of these island countries is also located on the African mainland?**

Assessment

Defining Terms

1. Define steppe, tsetse fly, industrialize, deforestation.

Recalling Facts

2. Place What is the main landform of the Central African Republic?

3. Economics Name three natural resources of Cameroon.

4. Economics What natural resource was recently discovered in Equatorial Guinea?

Critical Thinking

5. Evaluating Information Why do you think Europeans wanted to colonize parts of Africa, like the Congo?

6. Understanding Cause and Effect How could furniture buyers in the United States affect the countries of Central Africa?

Graphic Organizer

7. Organizing Information Complete a chart like this with one fact about each country.

Country	Fact
Cameroon	
Central African Republic	
Congo	
Gabon	
Equatorial Guinea	
Sao Tome & Principe	

Applying Geography Skills

8. Analyzing Maps Study the physical map on page 565. The Ubangi River forms part of the boundaries of what countries?

Making Connections

ART | SCIENCE | LITERATURE | TECHNOLOGY

Battling Sleeping Sickness

Since the 1300s, people in Africa south of the Sahara have battled a disease now commonly called sleeping sickness. Yet it was not until the early 1900s that scientists began to understand the disease and that it was transmitted through the bite of an infected tsetse fly.

The Tsetse Fly

Found only in parts of Africa, the tsetse fly is the common name for any of about 21 species of flies that can transmit sleeping sickness. The flies are larger than the houseflies common to the United States. Tsetse flies thrive in forests and in areas of thick shrubbery and trees near lakes, ponds, and rivers.

Although the bite of a tsetse fly is painful, the bite itself is not necessarily harmful. What gives the tsetse fly its dreadful reputation is the disease-causing parasite it may carry.

Sleeping Sickness

The World Health Organization (WHO) estimates that more than 60 million people in Africa are at risk of being infected with sleeping sickness. As many as 500,000 people carry the disease. If left untreated, the disease leads to a slow breakdown of bodily functions and, eventually, death. Sleeping sickness need not be fatal. When the disease is treated in its early stages, most people recover. Treatment is expensive, however, and many of those infected lack medical care. Even if they are cured, they may become infected again.

Disease Prevention

Stopping sleeping sickness is a major challenge for poor countries struggling to meet the many needs of their people. There is no known vaccine. Controlling the disease involves isolating and treating infected humans. Wild animals with the disease must be removed so that tsetse flies cannot get the parasite in the first place. In addition, woodlands and brush near cities must be cleared. Because the disease is such a threat to human life, it is important that governments and private companies support scientists' efforts to wipe out the disease.

Making the Connection

1. Where do tsetse flies live?
2. What causes sleeping sickness?
3. **Drawing Conclusions** Why is treatment of infected humans only part of the solution to eliminating sleeping sickness?

◄ **Children in Central Africa have learned to report bites of the tsetse fly.**

Chapter 20 Reading Review

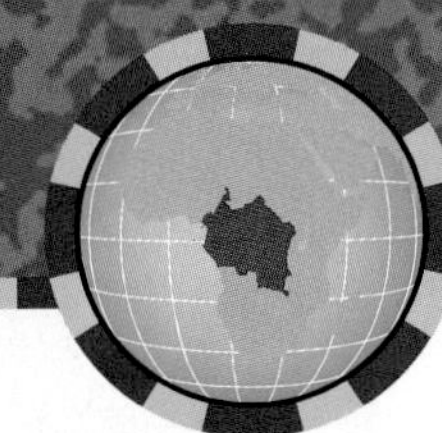

Section 1 Democratic Republic of the Congo

Terms to Know

savanna
basin
canopy
hydroelectric power
dictator
refugee

Main Idea

The Democratic Republic of the Congo has rich natural resources that are largely undeveloped because of civil war and poor government decisions.

✓ **Place** Large areas of rain forests and savannas cover the Democratic Republic of the Congo. It has a warm climate because of its location on the Equator.

✓ **Movement** The Congo River—the second-largest river in Africa—provides transportation and hydroelectric power.

✓ **Place** The Democratic Republic of the Congo has many resources, but most people live in the countryside and farm.

✓ **History** Many years under a corrupt and harsh ruler have prevented the economy from fully developing.

✓ **Government** A recent civil war overthrew a harsh ruler, but an elected government is not yet in place.

Section 2 Other Countries of Central Africa

Terms to Know

steppe
tsetse fly
industrialize
deforestation

Main Idea

Other countries in Central Africa have fairly small populations, with most people farming the land.

✓ **Region** Rain forests cover much of the other countries of Central Africa. The Central African Republic, which receives less rainfall, has only a small area of rain forests.

✓ **Culture** Most people in these countries make their living by farming.

✓ **Economics** Cameroon earns money by exporting oil and bauxite.

✓ **Economics** Congo uses river water to generate hydroelectric power.

✓ **Economics** Gabon exports lumber from its rain forests, but now most of its export earnings come from selling oil.

✓ **Place** Equatorial Guinea—once a Spanish colony—includes land on the African mainland and some islands.

Market in Kinshasa, Democratic Republic of the Congo ▶

Chapter 20 Assessment and Activities

Using Key Terms

Match the terms in Part A with their definitions in Part B.

A.

1. industrialize
2. basin
3. hydroelectric power
4. canopy
5. deforestation
6. dictator
7. tsetse fly
8. savanna
9. steppe
10. refugee

B.

a. insect whose bite causes sleeping sickness
b. economy based on manufacturing
c. dry, treeless grasslands
d. tropical grassland with scattered trees
e. person who flees to another country for safety
f. electric power generated by flowing water
g. a single all-powerful leader
h. loss of forests due to widespread cutting of trees
i. topmost layer of a rain forest
j. broad, flat lowland area surrounded by higher areas

Reviewing the Main Ideas

Section 1 Democratic Republic of the Congo

11. **Location** What important latitude line runs across the Democratic Republic of the Congo?
12. **Human/Environment Interaction** Why are the rain forests in the Democratic Republic of the Congo being destroyed at a rapid rate?
13. **Place** What is the longest freshwater lake in the world?
14. **Economics** What is the major use of the diamonds found in the Democratic Republic of the Congo?
15. **Government** What is the current government of the Democratic Republic of the Congo?

Section 2 Other Countries of Central Africa

16. **Place** Why must Cameroon's people watch where they herd livestock?
17. **Culture** What is the official language of the Central African Republic? Why?
18. **Place** What is the capital of the Congo?
19. **Economics** Name three of Gabon's natural resources.
20. **History** Who originally settled Sao Tome and Principe?

Central Africa

Place Location Activity

On a separate sheet of paper, match the letters on the map with the numbered places listed below.

1. Democratic Republic of the Congo
2. Cameroon
3. Congo River
4. Kinshasa
5. Lake Tanganyika
6. Gabon
7. Central African Republic
8. Equatorial Guinea
9. Kasai River
10. Ubangi River

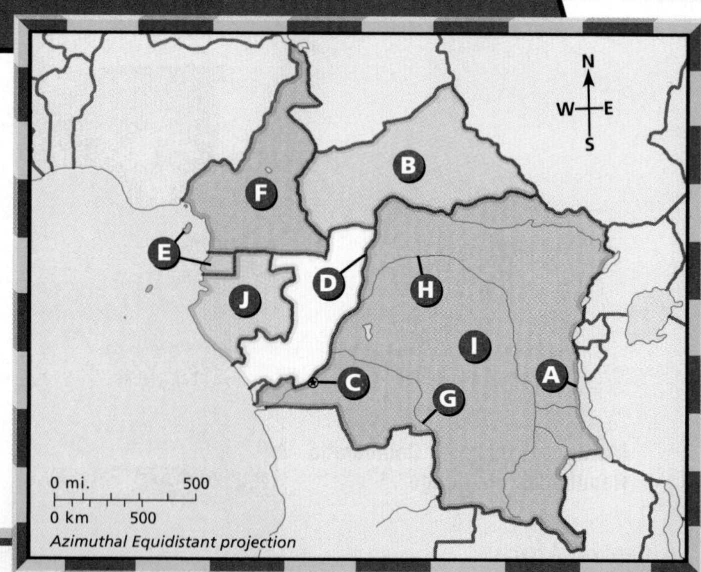

Self-Check Quiz Visit the ***Geography: The World and Its People*** Web site at gwip.glencoe.com and click on **Chapter 20–Self-Check Quizzes** to prepare for the Chapter Test.

Critical Thinking

21. **Synthesizing Information** If you were a government leader in the Democratic Republic of the Congo, what steps would you take to develop the country's resources?
22. **Comparing Information** Compare the economies of the Central African Republic and Cameroon. At the ends of the arrows on a diagram like the one below, list the factors that show which country's economy is the strongest.

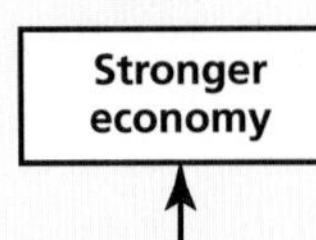

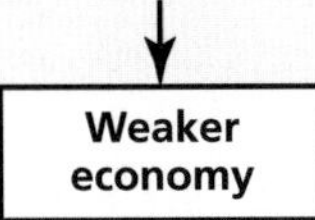

GeoJournal Activity

23. **Writing a Diary** Research the events leading to the overthrow of Mobutu Sese Seko, the former dictator of Zaire. Write at least five diary entries that an eyewitness might have recorded during that turbulent period.

Mental Mapping Activity

24. **Focusing on the Region** Draw a simple outline map of Africa, then label the following:
    - Kinshasa
    - Lake Tanganyika
    - Congo River
    - Gabon
    - Cameroon
    - Congo
    - Democratic Republic of the Congo

Technology Skills Activity

25. **Using a Spreadsheet** Use an almanac or an online source to find the value of the exports for each country of Central Africa. Enter this information and each country's name into a spreadsheet. Then find each country's per capita gross domestic product (GDP) and enter this into the spreadsheet. Create graphs that compare the exports and GDP.

Standardized Test Practice

Directions: Read the paragraph below, then answer the questions that follow.

Gabon is known for its tropical rain forests and savanna grasslands. Both the floor and the canopy of the rain forests are alive with animals. Squirrels, monkeys, baboons, lemurs, and parrots often live their entire lives in the dense branches of the canopy. Pythons, vipers, porcupines, and tortoises move along the rain forest floor. Crocodiles and hippopotamuses live along the riverbanks, while elephants and antelopes roam the savanna. Gorillas, which are endangered in most other places of Africa, are very numerous in Gabon.

1. **Which of the following animals are least likely to live in a tropical rain forest?**
   - **A** elephants
   - **B** baboons
   - **C** pythons
   - **D** parrots
2. **Which of the following would most likely harm Gabon's rain forest habitats?**
   - **F** building a port on the coast
   - **G** discovering oil in the Gulf of Guinea
   - **H** farming small plots of land
   - **J** exporting lumber to furniture makers

Test-Taking Tip: Look in the paragraph to find clues to support your answer. Plus, think about the words *rain forests* and *savanna*. Which has a wet climate and which has a dry climate? As you study for an exam, make note of important words, such as *habitat*. The glossary of your textbook can help you define these words. You may also want to make your own word list as you read new chapters.

GeoLAB ACTIVITY

Water Finds a Way

1 Background

Water flows downhill. Pretty simple, right? Not really. Earth's landforms can pose a challenge to moving water as it winds its way through a *watershed,* or an area that drains into a stream, river, lake, or ocean. In this activity, you will create and experiment with a watershed model. You will learn how landforms like mountains, hills, and valleys channel water into central paths as it moves along.

2 Materials

- **2 sheets of paper (8½" x 11")**
- **1 sheet of cardboard (8½" x 11")**
- **2 water-soluble felt markers (green and blue)**
- **spray bottle filled with water**
- **clear tape**

Watershed of the Nile River

Believe It or Not!

The Nile River in North Africa drains a huge watershed area, with many rivers and streams adding water to it. Just how long is this river? If the Nile were stretched across the United States, it would run almost all the way from New York City to Los Angeles.

What to Do

1. Crumple a sheet of paper into a loose wad, then uncrumple it and place it on the cardboard.
2. Make sure that at least one inch of cardboard can be seen around the edges of the paper. Tape the edges of the paper to the cardboard.
3. Identify hills and mountains on your model. Use the green marker to shade the tops of these features.
4. Identify major locations where you think water will flow or collect. Use the blue marker to color these areas.
5. Use the spray bottle to make it gently "rain" on your model (that is, spray water over your model). Observe and, on the other sheet of paper, draw a diagram showing the paths that the water takes as it moves along your model.

LAB ACTIVITY REPORT

1. Describe the landscape you created when you crumpled and uncrumpled the paper.
2. Name the major landforms found on your model. Does your landscape have valleys, hills, basins, and so on?
3. Where does water tend to collect on your model? Why?
4. **Drawing Conclusions** Where do you think the most populous areas on your model would be? Why?

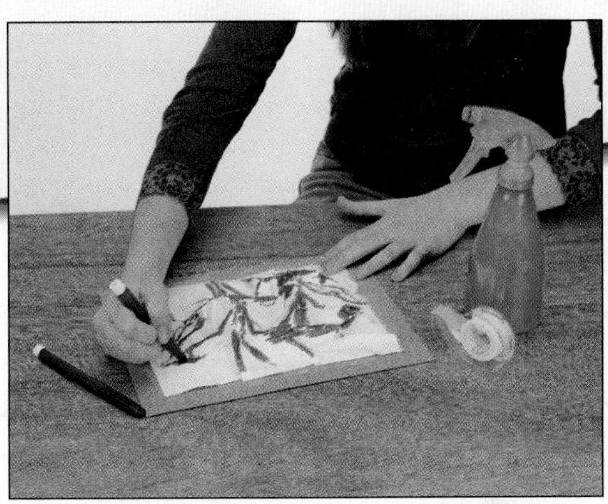

▲ **For your experiment to work properly, make sure you use water-soluble (not permanent) markers.**

Extending the Lab

Activity

Obtain a topographic or relief map of your area. Identify major landforms. Locate streams, rivers, and water bodies. Can you imagine this map as a 3-D model? Write a description or create a model of some part of the watershed in the area in which you live.

Chapter 21

East Africa

The World and Its People NATIONAL GEOGRAPHIC

To learn more about the people and places of East Africa, view ***The World and Its People*** **Chapter 21** video.

Geography Online

Chapter Overview Visit the ***Geography: The World and Its People*** Web site at gwip.glencoe.com and click on **Chapter 21—Chapter Overviews** to preview information about East Africa.

Kenya

Guide to Reading

Main Idea

Kenya is a country of diverse landscapes and peoples.

Terms to Know

- coral reef
- nature preserve
- poaching
- fault
- escarpment
- altitude
- free enterprise system
- cassava

Places to Locate

- Kenya
- Indian Ocean
- Great Rift Valley
- Mt. Kenya
- Nairobi
- Mombasa

Reading Strategy

Draw a diagram like this one. Under each heading in the outer ovals, write two examples of the diversity in Kenya's land, economy, and people.

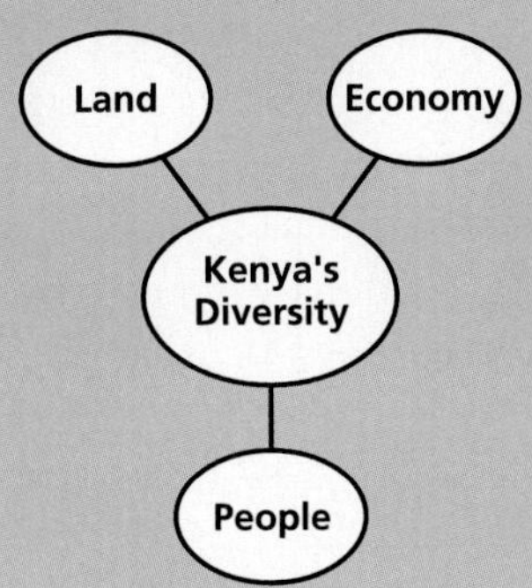

NATIONAL GEOGRAPHIC **Exploring Our World**

The Masai (mah•SY) is one of Kenya's many ethnic groups. Rituals have shaped their lives for hundreds of years. Young men take part in an important four-day ceremony. When it ends, they become elders and help make group decisions. In the ceremony, elders tell them, "Drop your weapons and use your head and wisdom instead."

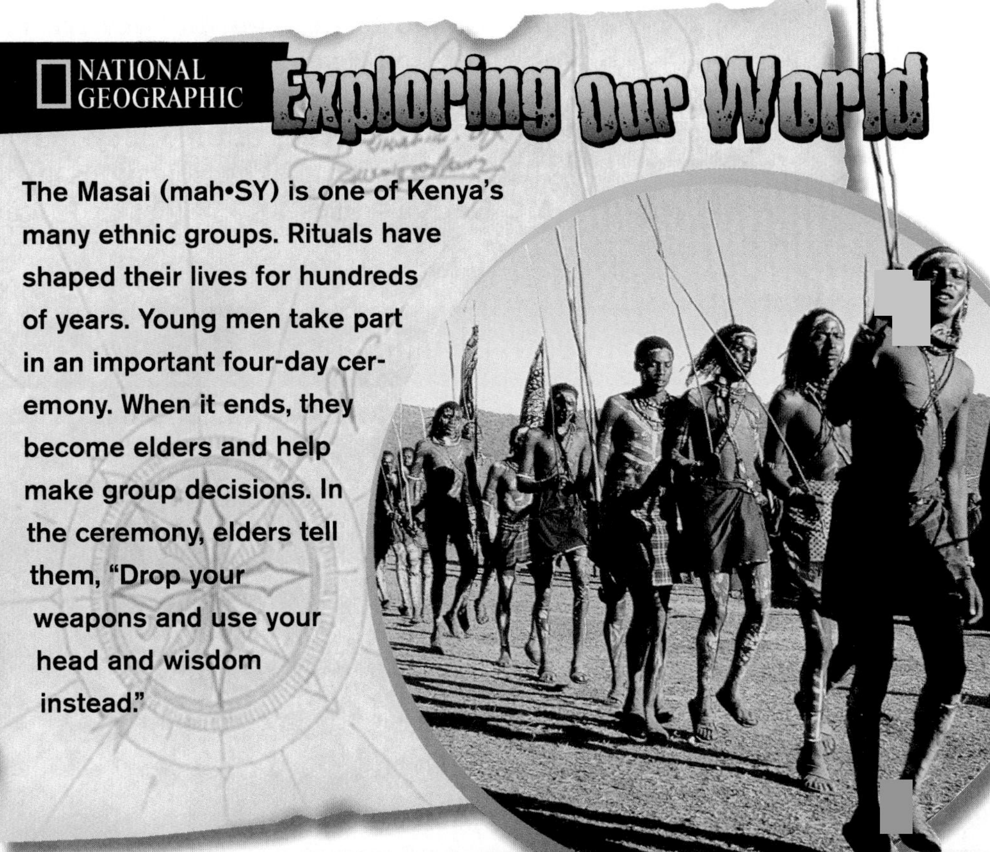

Both traditional and modern cultures meet in **Kenya.** Groups like the Masai follow ways of life similar to their ancestors. People in cities live in apartments and work in offices.

Kenya's Land and Climate

About two times the size of Nevada, Kenya straddles the middle of East Africa. The country's **Indian Ocean** coastline has stretches of white beaches lined with palm trees. Offshore lies a **coral reef,** a natural formation at or near the water's surface that is made of the skeletons of small sea animals. The beautiful beaches and the colorful fish of the coral reef attract tourists from around the world.

West of Kenya's coastal plain, the land rises gently to the central part of the country. Much of this upland plain is dry, but enough rain falls on some hilly areas to support farming. Lions, elephants, rhinoceroses, and other wildlife roam this plain. Millions of acres are designated **nature preserves**—land set aside by a government to protect plants and wildlife. Still, in recent years there has been heavy **poaching,** the illegal hunting of protected animals.

◀ A view of Kilimanjaro in Tanzania, from Kenya

Dominating the western part of the country are highlands and the **Great Rift Valley.** This valley is really a fault—a crack in the earth's crust. The Great Rift Valley begins in southeastern Africa and stretches about 3,500 miles (5,633 km) north to the Red Sea.

The Great Rift Valley actually has two branches. The western branch plows through the western borders of Tanzania, Burundi, Rwanda, and Uganda. The eastern, or Kenyan, branch ranges from 30 to 80 miles (48 to 129 km) wide. Steep cliffs called escarpments tower on both sides of the valley. In many places water has flooded the valley to form lakes. Volcanoes also dot the area. One of them—**Mt. Kenya**—rises 17,058 feet (5,199 m) high.

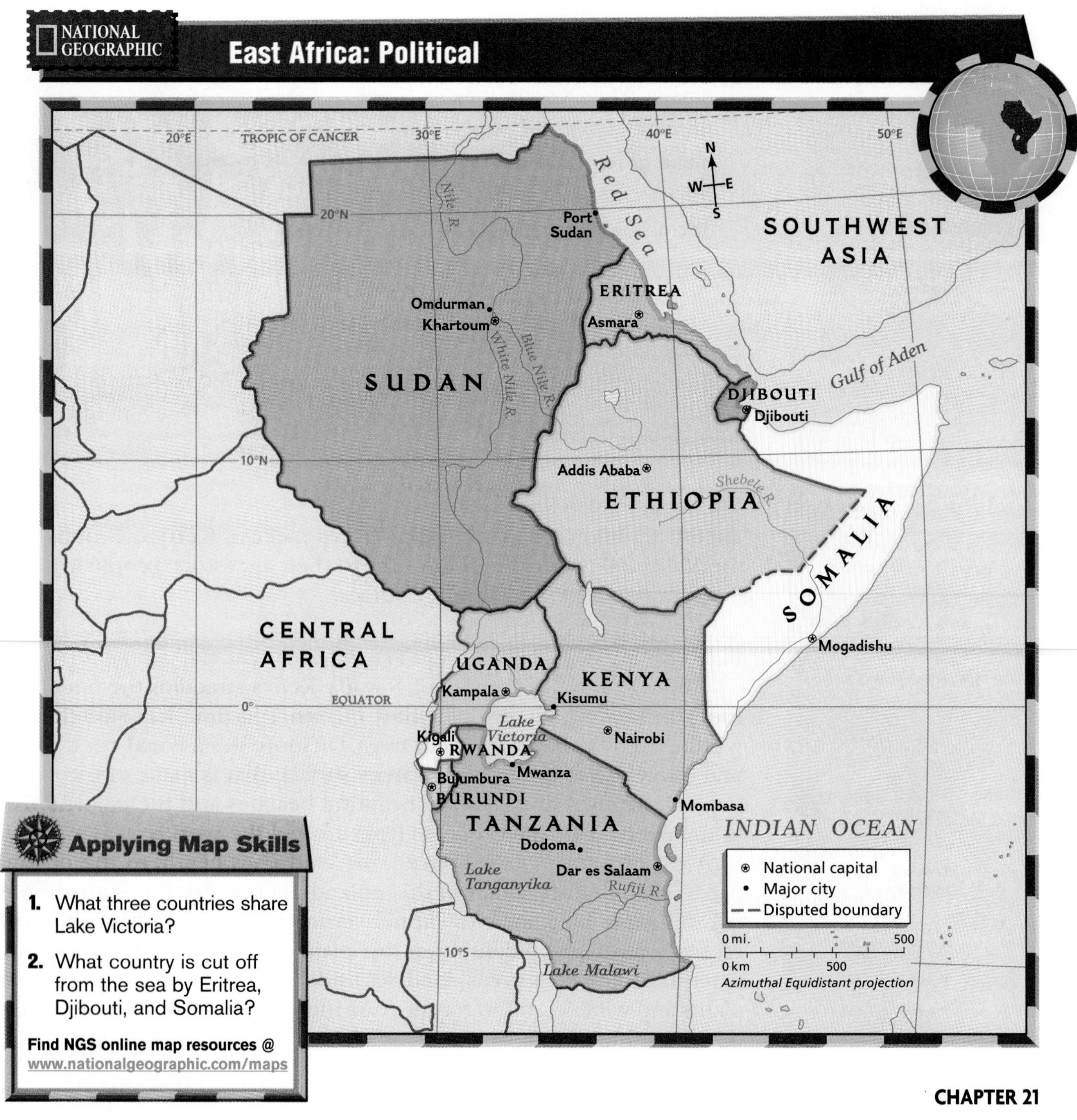

1. What three countries share Lake Victoria?
2. What country is cut off from the sea by Eritrea, Djibouti, and Somalia?

Find NGS online map resources @ www.nationalgeographic.com/maps

Climate Because of its location on the Equator, Kenya has temperatures that tend to be warm year-round. Remember that **altitude,** or height above sea level, also affects climate. The highland regions tend to be cooler than lowlands. The highlands, as well as the coastal regions, also receive more rain than do the central plains. Kenya's best farmland is found in the highlands.

Reading Check **What huge fault runs through East Africa?**

Kenya's Economy

Kenya has a developing economy based on a **free enterprise system.** In this economic system, people can start and run businesses with limited government involvement. Kenya's capital,

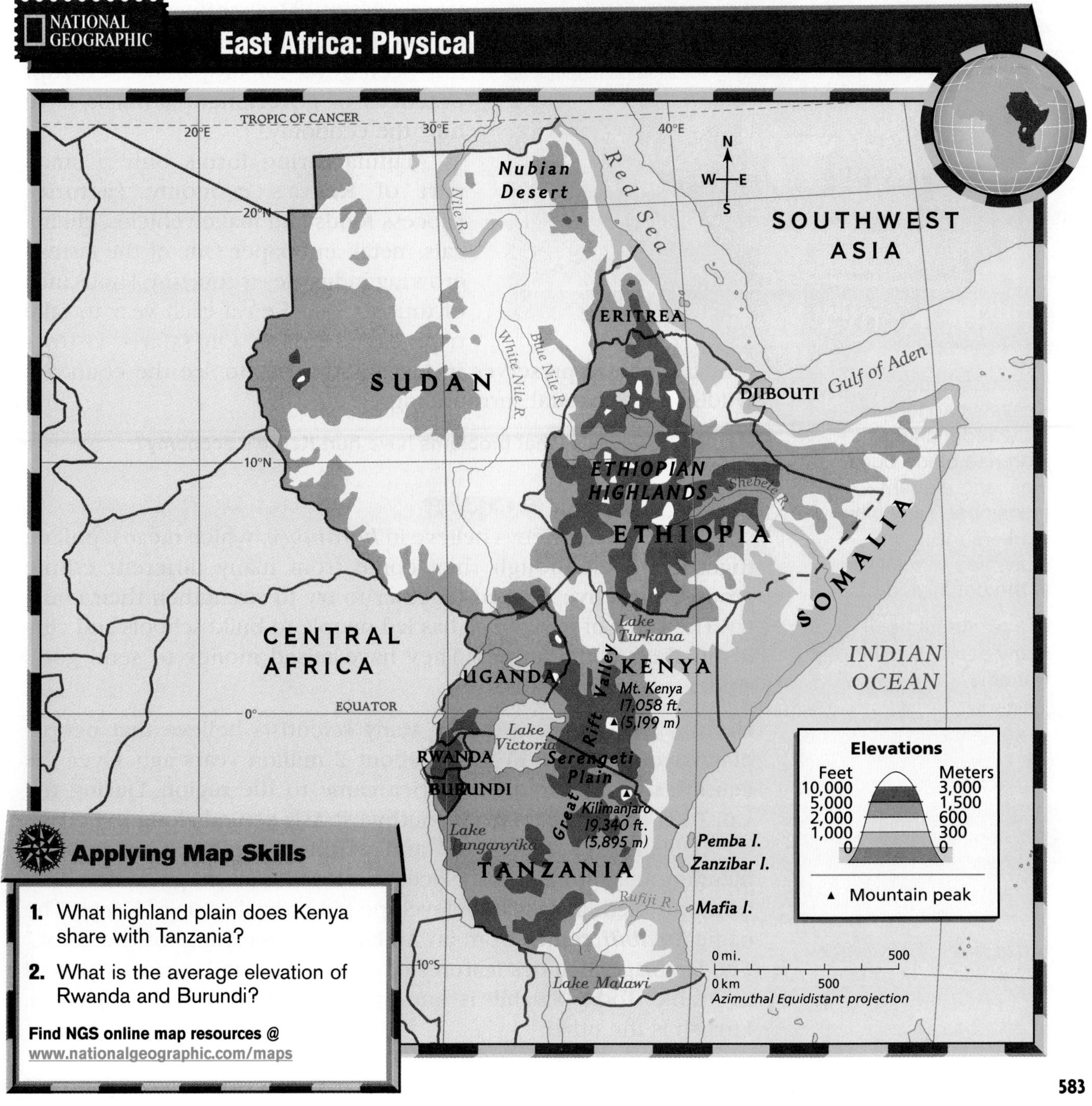

Applying Map Skills

1. What highland plain does Kenya share with Tanzania?
2. What is the average elevation of Rwanda and Burundi?

Find NGS online map resources @ www.nationalgeographic.com/maps

Nairobi, Kenya

Like most cities, Kenya's capital has crowded markets, high-rise office buildings, and elegant mansions. Many city workers maintain close ties to relatives in the countryside.

Place **About how many people live in Nairobi?**

Nairobi (ny•ROH•bee), has become a center of business and commerce for all of East Africa. Foreign companies have set up regional headquarters in this city. Nairobi offers them good transportation and communications systems.

Many Kenyans remain poor, however. Nomadic herding and subsistence farming are still the main economic activities. The main crops are corn, cassava, potatoes, sweet potatoes, and bananas. **Cassava** is a plant whose roots are ground into flour to make bread. Some larger farms raise coffee and tea for export. In recent years, the weather has not been good for crops. Also, corrupt practices of government officials have hurt the economy.

Manufacturing forms only a small part of Kenya's economy. Factories process foods and make vehicles, chemicals, metal, and paper. One of the fastest-growing industries is tourism. Thousands of tourists visit Kenya each year to take trips called safaris. On safaris, visitors tour the nature preserves in jeeps and buses to see the country's wildlife in its natural surroundings.

✓Reading Check **What problems have hurt Kenya's economy?**

Kenya's People

The people of Kenya believe in *harambee,* which means "pulling together." Even though they come from many different ethnic groups, they have worked together to try to strengthen their country. The spirit of *harambee* has led people to build schools and clinics in their communities. They have raised money to send good students to universities.

History and Government Many scientists believe that people may have first lived in Kenya about 2 million years ago. Over the centuries, many groups in Africa came to the region. During the A.D. 700s, Arab traders from Southwest Asia settled along the coast.

Africans and Arabs lived and worked together. As a result, a blending of cultures took place. The Swahili language came about from this blending. Swahili developed in coastal areas of Kenya. The name *Swahili* comes from an Arabic word meaning "of the coast." The language includes features of several African languages as well as Arabic. Today Swahili is one of Kenya's two official languages. English is the other.

The British gained influence in Kenya during the late 1800s and made it a colony after World War I. Attracted by the mild climate and fertile soil, many British people moved to the highlands. They took land from the Africans and set up farms to grow coffee and tea for export.

By the 1940s, Kenya's African groups organized and fought to end British rule. Kenya finally won its independence in 1963 and became a republic. The country's first president, Jomo Kenyatta (JOH•moh kehn•YAHT•uh), won respect as an early leader in Africa's movement for freedom. Under Kenyatta, Kenya enjoyed economic prosperity and had a stable government. In recent years, the economy has weakened under the president who followed Kenyatta. In response, many Kenyans have demanded democratic changes.

Kenya Today Kenya's 28.8 million people are divided among 40 different ethnic groups. The Kikuyu (kee•KOO•yoo) people are Kenya's main group, making up less than one-fourth of the population. If you visited Kenya, you would discover that most Kenyans live in rural areas. With the constant threat of drought, many people struggle to grow crops. In recent years, large numbers of people have moved to cities in search of a better life.

About one-third of Kenya's people live in cities. Nairobi is the largest city, with 1 million people. **Mombasa** (mohm•BAH•sah) is Kenya's chief port on the Indian Ocean. This city has the best harbor in East Africa, making it an ideal site for oceangoing trade.

Reading Check **What city is Kenya's chief port?**

I Am a Samburu

Nimfa Lekuuk is a member of the Samburu of northern Kenya. The word *Samburu* means "the people with the white goats." Nimfa wears the traditional clothes of Samburu women. She is in standard 7 now. "Standard" is the Kenyans' term for *grade.* She studies language, math, history, geography, science, arts and crafts, and religions.

Assessment

Defining Terms

1. Define coral reef, nature preserve, poaching, fault, escarpment, altitude, free enterprise system, cassava.

Recalling Facts

2. Place Describe the Great Rift Valley.
3. Culture What are Kenya's official languages?
4. History Who was Jomo Kenyatta?

Critical Thinking

5. Making Predictions How might a rapidly growing population create problems for Kenya?
6. Evaluating Information Why do you think many African people move from rural areas to urban areas?

Graphic Organizer

7. Organizing Information *Harambee* means "pulling together." On the lines of a diagram like the one below, show examples of *harambee* in Kenya.

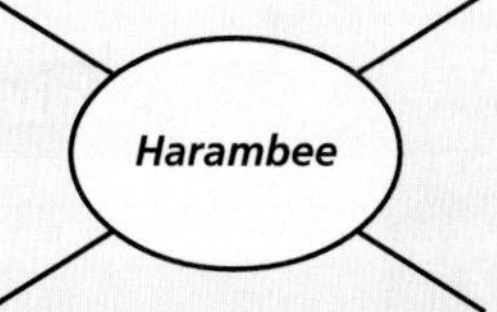

Applying Geography Skills

8. Analyzing Maps Study the political map on page 582. What is Nairobi's latitude and longitude?

Critical Thinking Skill

Making Predictions

Predicting consequences is obviously difficult and sometimes risky. The more information you have, however, the more accurate your predictions will be.

Learning the Skill

Follow these steps to learn how to better predict consequences:

- Gather information about the decision or action you are considering.
- Use your knowledge of history and human behavior to identify what consequences could result.
- Analyze each of the consequences by asking yourself: How likely is it that this will occur?

Practicing the Skill

Study the graph below, then answer these questions:

1. What is measured on this graph? Over what time period?
2. In what year did the fewest tourists visit Kenya?
3. What trend does the graph show?
4. Do you think this trend is likely to continue?
5. On what do you base this prediction?
6. What are three possible consequences of this trend?

Applying the Skill

Analyze three articles in your local newspaper. Predict three consequences of the actions in each of the articles. On what do you base your predictions?

GO TO Practice key skills with **Glencoe Skillbuilder Interactive Workbook, Level 1.**

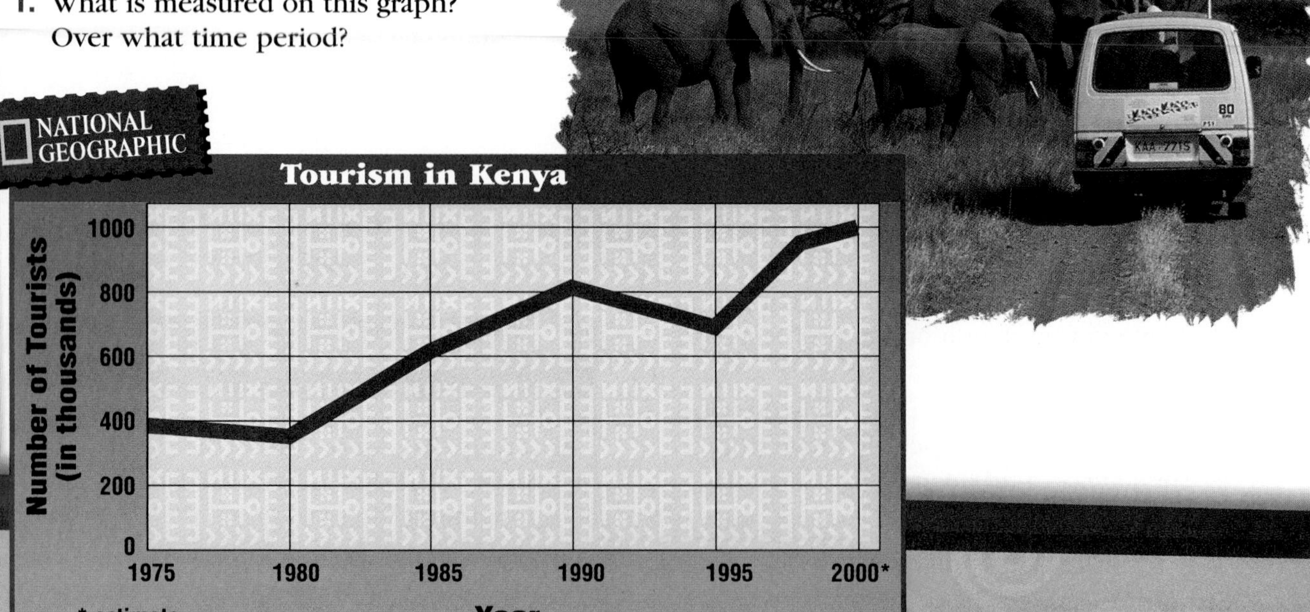

Section 2 Tanzania

Guide to Reading

Main Idea

Tanzania is located on the Indian Ocean and relies on agriculture and tourism.

Terms to Know

- sisal
- habitat
- eco-tourist

Places to Locate

- Tanzania
- Serengeti Plain
- Kilimanjaro
- Great Rift Valley
- Lake Tanganyika
- Lake Victoria
- Dar es Salaam

Reading Strategy

Make a chart like this one. Then list two facts about the land, economy, and people of Tanzania.

Tanzania	Fact #1	Fact #2
Land		
Economy		
People		

NATIONAL GEOGRAPHIC **Exploring Our World**

This red colobus monkey in Tanzania is tired! You would be too if you had spent the day like she did. She usually leaps about 25 feet (8 m) from tree to tree—with a baby hanging on to her. If she were human size, it would be the same as jumping 50 feet (15 m)—without a running start—while carrying an extra 25 pounds (11 kg) of weight.

If you step out into the vast open plains of **Tanzania,** you may suddenly feel very small. You are in the territory of one of the largest wild animal populations in the world. Tanzania includes a large mainland area—once called Tanganyika (TAN•guhn•YEE•kuh)—and three islands—once called Zanzibar. In 1964 these two areas united, forming the country of Tanzania.

Tanzania's Land

About two times the size of California, Tanzania has landforms and climates similar to those in Kenya. The Indian Ocean coastline boasts white beaches and palm trees, bordered by a thin band of humid lowlands. Farther inland, the land gradually slopes upward to a plateau. The **Serengeti** (SEHR•uhn•GEH•tee) **Plain,** with its huge grasslands and patches of trees and shrubs, dominates this plateau. To the north, near the Kenyan border, a snowcapped mountain called **Kilimanjaro** towers over this region. It is the highest point in Africa.

The **Great Rift Valley** cuts two gashes through Tanzania, one in the center of the country and the other along the western border. As in Kenya, parts of the western valley are covered by lakes. Unusual fish swim in the deep, dark waters of **Lake Tanganyika.** You can see another body of water in the northwest corner of Tanzania—**Lake Victoria.** This body of water is Africa's largest lake and one of the sources of the Nile River.

Just east of the mainland lie Tanzania's three islands—Pemba, Zanzibar, and Mafia Island. Find these islands on the map on page 583. They were all formed from coral.

Reading Check **What mountain in Tanzania is the highest point in Africa?**

Tanzania's Economy

More than 80 percent of all Tanzanians work in farming or herding. Most of them grow food on subsistence farms. Some farmers grow coffee, cotton, tea, cashews, and tobacco for export. Another export crop is **sisal,** a plant fiber used to make rope and twine. Do you enjoy eating baked ham? If so, you might have tasted the spice called cloves, often used to flavor ham. The islands of Zanzibar and Pemba produce more cloves than any other places in the world.

The country's few factories process foods or make cement, soap, or textiles. Tanzania has deposits of gold and precious gems like emeralds and diamonds. Yet it does not have enough money to set up large-scale mining operations to get to these resources.

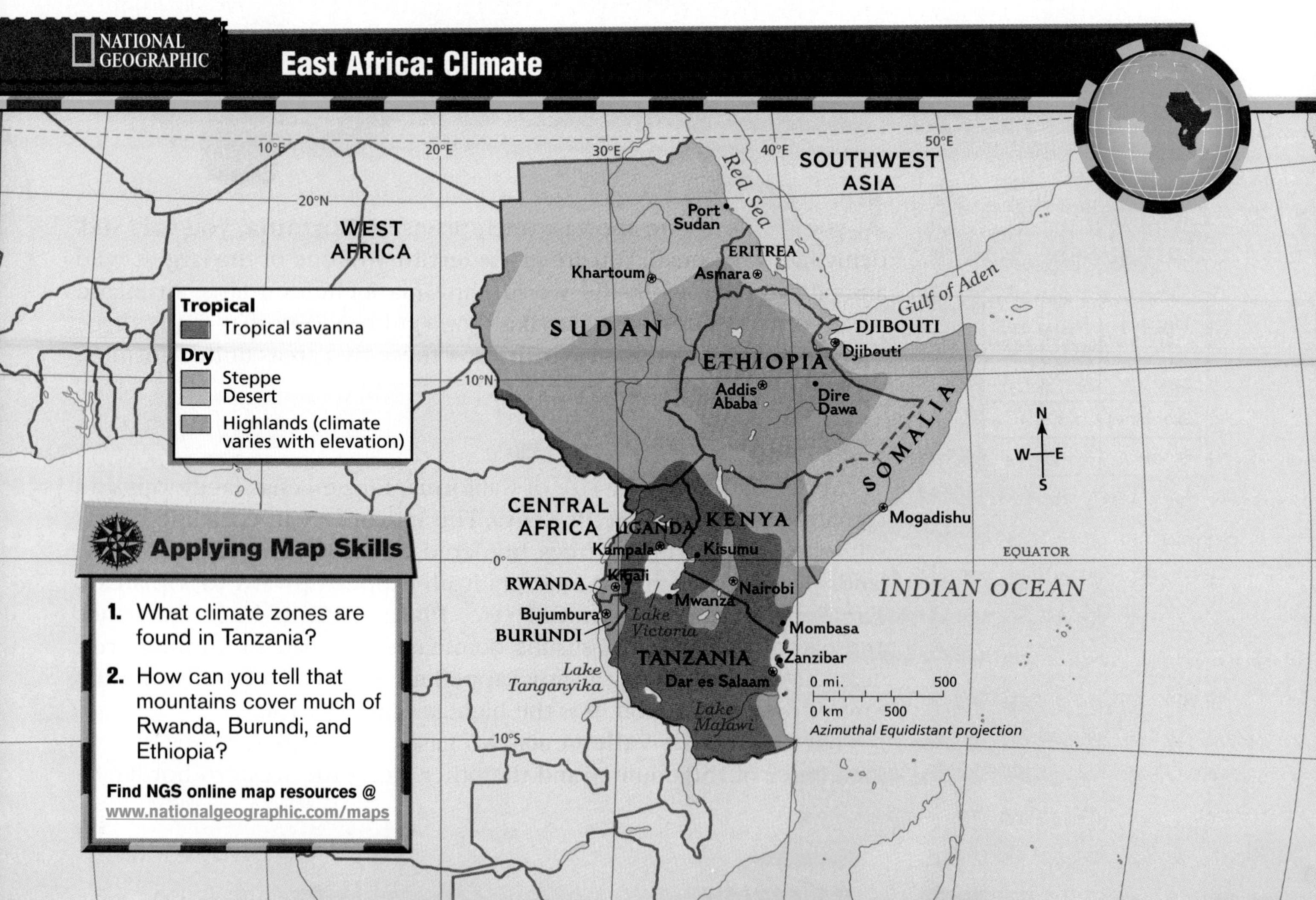

Two Views of Tanzania

Village markets in Tanzania offer both food products and a chance to socialize (above). Zanzibar, once called Spice Island, has a growing tourist industry (left).

Place **Zanzibar leads the world in the production of what spice?**

Tourism is a fast-growing industry in Tanzania. The government has set aside several national parks to protect the habitats of the country's wildlife. A **habitat** is the type of environment in which a particular animal species lives. Serengeti National Park covers about 5,600 square miles (14,504 sq. km). Lions and wild dogs hunt among thousands of zebras, wildebeests, and antelopes. The park attracts many **eco-tourists,** or people who travel to another country to view its natural wonders.

Tanzania's leaders are also taking steps to preserve farmland. In recent years, many trees have been cut down. Without trees, the land cannot hold soil or rainwater in place. As a result, the land dries out, and soil blows away. To prevent the land from becoming desert, the government of Tanzania has announced a new policy. For every tree that is cut down, five new trees should be planted.

✓Reading Check **What is Tanzania doing to try to stop the land from becoming a desert?**

Tanzania's History and Government

Scientists have found what they believe are the remains of some of the earliest human settlements in Tanzania. By about A.D. 500, groups from other parts of Africa had settled in the area. About 200 years later, Arabs from Southwest Asia set up trading centers on Zanzibar and coastal areas. As in Kenya, the Arabs along the coast mixed with the local Africans to form a new culture in which Swahili was spoken.

In the early 1500s, the Portuguese set up a trading post in Zanzibar. Later, in the late 1800s, Germany won control of the southern part of East Africa and set up a colony here. By the early 1900s, tens of thousands of East Africans rebelled against German rule. Many died in fighting, but the rebellion launched a movement for self-rule. After World War I, the British took charge of Zanzibar and mainland Tanganyika. The mainland became independent in 1961, followed by Zanzibar two years later. In 1964 the two countries united as Tanzania. Since then, Tanzania has been one of Africa's most politically stable republics.

During the 1960s, Tanzania's government controlled the economy. By the 1990s, however, it had moved the country toward a free market system. In taking this step, Tanzania's leaders hoped to improve the economy and reduce poverty. Meanwhile, the country's government also became more democratic with more than one political party.

Reading Check **How did Tanzania's economy and government change in the 1990s?**

Tanzania's People

Tanzania's 31.3 million people include more than 120 different ethnic groups. Each group has its own language, but most people also speak Swahili. The two main religions are Christianity and Islam.

About three-fourths of Tanzania's people live in rural areas. **Dar es Salaam,** on the Indian Ocean, is Tanzania's capital and chief port. With nearly 1.4 million people, it is also the country's largest city. The central area of Tanzania has few people. In an effort to encourage people to move there, the Tanzanian government plans to eventually move the capital inland to the city of Dodoma.

Tanzanian music and dance dominate much of East Africa's culture. In Dar es Salaam, you can sway to the music's strong rhythms and Swahili-based sounds performed by local dance bands. In Tanzania, as well as in Kenya, the most popular food is barbecued meat.

Reading Check **Where do three-fourths of Tanzania's people live?**

Assessment

Defining Terms

1. Define sisal, habitat, eco-tourist.

Recalling Facts

2. Place What is the highest mountain in Africa?

3. Economics Why are tourists drawn to Tanzania?

4. Culture What are the two major religions of Tanzania?

Graphic Organizer

5. Organizing Information On a time line like the one below, label five important events and their dates in Tanzania's history.

Critical Thinking

6. Evaluating Information Why do you think two countries such as Tanganyika and Zanzibar would unite?

7. Analyzing Information Why would the government of Tanzania put so much effort into preserving its national parks?

Applying Geography Skills

8. Analyzing Maps Study the physical and political maps on pages 582 and 583. Name the four bodies of water that border Tanzania. On what body of water is Dar es Salaam located?

Making Connections

ART | SCIENCE | LITERATURE | TECHNOLOGY

A Changing Kenya

As developing countries modernize, traditional ways of life often change. In her poem, Kenyan poet and playwright Micere Githae Mugo expresses the challenge of living in a changing world.

Where are those Songs?

by Micere Githae Mugo

Where are those songs
my mother and yours
always sang
fitting rhythms
to the whole
vast span of life?

What was it again
they sang
    harvesting maize, threshing millet, storing
        the grain . . .

What did they sing
bathing us, rocking us to sleep . . .
and the one they sang
stirring the pot
(swallowed in parts by choking smoke)?

What was it
the woods echoed
as in long file
my mother and yours and all the women on
    our ridge
beat out the rhythms
    trudging gaily
    as they carried
    piles of wood
    through those forests
    miles from home

What song was it?

. . . .

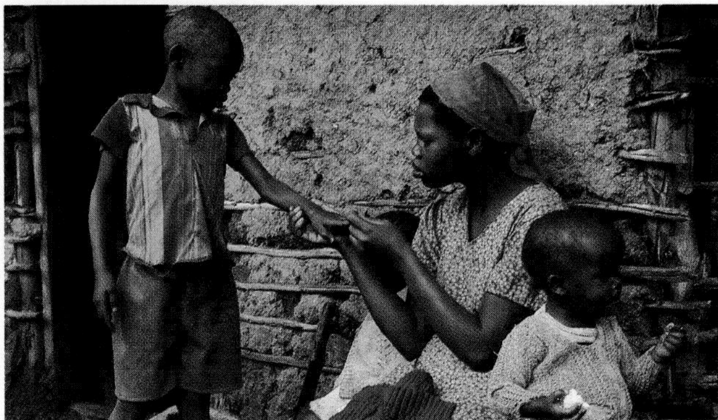

▲ **A mother takes care of her children in Kenya.**

Sing
    I have forgotten
    my mother's song
    my children
    will never know.
This I remember:
    Mother always said
    sing child sing
    make a song
    and sing
    beat out your own rhythms
    the rhythms of your life
    but make the song soulful
    and make life
    sing

. . . .

From "Where are those Songs" by Micere G. Mugo. Reprinted by permission of the author.

Making the Connection

1. Based on the poem, how do you think the poet's mother felt about her responsibilities?
2. How do you think the poet feels about her mother?
3. **Analyzing Information** What do you think the poet's mother meant when she said to "beat out your own rhythms"?

Section 3

Inland East Africa

Guide to Reading

Main Idea

Rwanda, Burundi, and Uganda have suffered much conflict in recent years.

Terms to Know

- plantains
- autonomy
- watershed
- endangered species
- refugee

Places to Locate

- Uganda
- Rwanda
- Burundi
- Lake Victoria
- Nile River
- Kampala

Reading Strategy

Make a chart like this one. On the left, write the cause of conflict in each country under that country's name. Then write the effects of that conflict.

Cause of conflict in:	Effects of conflict
Uganda	
Rwanda	
Burundi	

NATIONAL GEOGRAPHIC **Exploring Our World**

If you walk through the mountain rain forests of Rwanda, you might feel you are being watched. Who's watching you? It could be one of the world's 600 remaining gorillas—the rarest and largest of the great apes. Every day these gorillas face the threat of death from poachers, loss of their habitat, disease, and civil war.

West of Kenya and Tanzania lie **Uganda, Rwanda,** and **Burundi.** All three are landlocked—they have no land touching a sea or an ocean. Instead, they use three large lakes for transportation and trade.

Uganda

Once called "the pearl of Africa," Uganda is a fertile, green land of mountains, lakes, and wild animals. About the size of Oregon, Uganda sits astride the western branch of the Great Rift Valley. Find Uganda on the map on page 583. The country consists mainly of a central plateau. South of the plateau you find **Lake Victoria.** From here, part of the **Nile River** flows through the central plateau to lakes in the west. Although Uganda lies on the Equator, temperatures are mild because of the country's high elevation.

Uganda's rich soil and plentiful rain make the land good for farming. More than 80 percent of Uganda's workers are employed in agriculture. Most farmers work on subsistence farms. They grow **plantains**—a kind of banana—cassava, potatoes, corn, and grains. Some plantations grow coffee, cotton, and tea for export. Coffee makes up nearly three-fourths of the country's exports. Uganda's few factories make cement, soap, sugar, metal, and shoes.

Uganda's People Uganda's 22.8 million people live mainly in rural villages in the southern part of the country. **Kampala,** the capital, lies on the shores of Lake Victoria, making it a port city for local trade.

About two-thirds of Ugandans are Christians. The remaining one-third practice Islam or traditional African religions. At one time there were large numbers of Hindus and Sikhs from South Asia living in the country. A dictator drove them out in 1972. Recently, the Ugandan government has invited them back, and many are now returning.

The people of Uganda belong to more than 40 different ethnic groups. They have a rich cultural heritage of songs, folktales, and poems. In the past, these were passed by word of mouth from one generation to the next. Today they are now in print. For the most part, Ugandans have a very basic diet. Their meals often include beans, beef, goat, mutton, cornmeal, and a variety of tropical fruits.

History and Government For much of the 1900s, the British ruled Uganda. After Uganda won its freedom in 1962, fighting broke out among ethnic groups. These ethnic groups had enjoyed **autonomy,** or self-government, in their local territories under their kings. These kings lost power in 1967, and the ethnic regions were tightly bound to the central government. A period of rule by Idi Amin, a cruel dictator, hurt

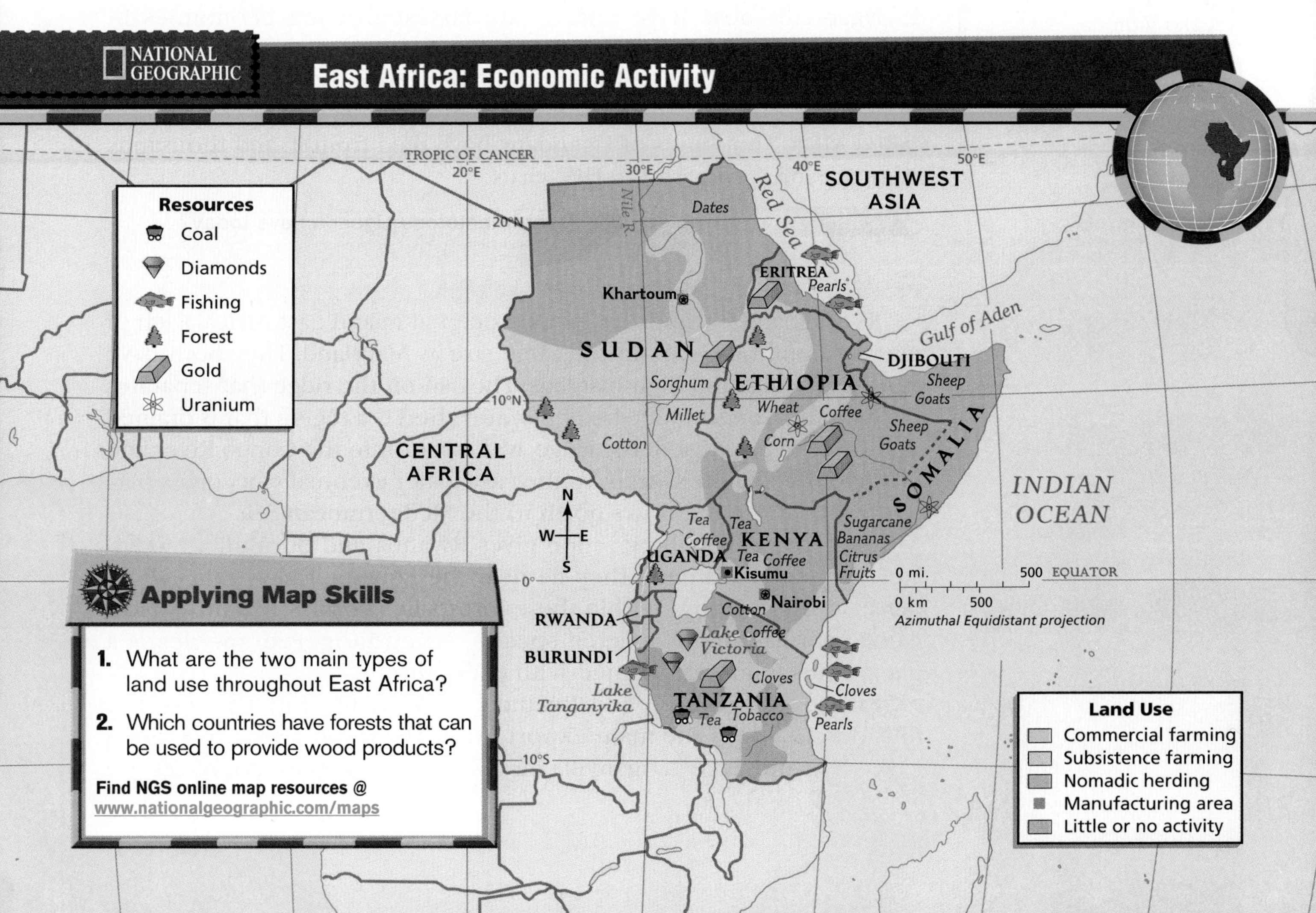

Applying Map Skills

1. What are the two main types of land use throughout East Africa?
2. Which countries have forests that can be used to provide wood products?

Find NGS online map resources @ www.nationalgeographic.com/maps

Kampala, Uganda

Public transportation in Kampala includes passenger boats on Lake Victoria.

Place **Part of what major river flows from Lake Victoria?**

Uganda throughout much of the 1980s. Since the mid-1990s, the national government has allowed ethnic groups to once again have kings, but only as local ceremonial leaders.

Ugandans now have one of the fastest-growing economies in Africa. Uganda also enjoys a stable government. It is a republic with an elected president and legislature. Still, the future is clouded. Uganda, along with other African countries, faces a new threat: the disease called AIDS. Thousands of Ugandans have died from it, and thousands more are infected with the HIV virus.

Reading Check **What kind of government does Uganda have today?**

Rwanda and Burundi

Rwanda and Burundi are located deep in inland East Africa. Each of the two countries is about the same size as Maryland. They both have mountains, hills, and high plateaus. They sit on the ridge that separates the Nile and Congo watersheds. A **watershed** is a region that is drained by a river. To the west of the ridge, water runs into the Congo River and flows to the Atlantic Ocean. To the east, water eventually becomes part of the Nile River and flows north to the Mediterranean Sea.

As in Uganda, high elevation gives Rwanda and Burundi a moderate climate even though they lie near the Equator. Heavy rains allow dense forests to grow. Within these forests live gorillas. Scientists have named gorillas an endangered species. An **endangered species** is a plant or an animal threatened with extinction.

Farmers in Burundi and Rwanda work small plots that dot the hillsides. Coffee is the main export crop. The people who live along Lake Kivu and Lake Tanganyika also fish. Because both countries are landlocked, they have trouble getting their goods to foreign buyers. Few paved roads and no railroads exist. Most goods must be transported by road to Lake Tanganyika, where boats take them to Tanzania or the Democratic Republic of the Congo. Another route is by dirt road to Tanzania and then by rail to Dar es Salaam.

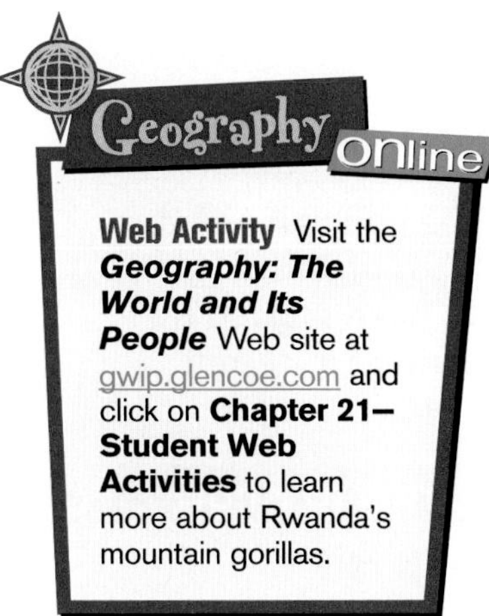

Web Activity Visit the ***Geography: The World and Its People*** Web site at gwip.glencoe.com and click on **Chapter 21—Student Web Activities** to learn more about Rwanda's mountain gorillas.

Ethnic Conflict Rwanda and Burundi have large populations and small areas. As a result, they are among the most densely populated countries in Africa. Rwanda, for example, has an average of 802 people per square mile (310 per sq. km). Yet fewer than 10 percent of the people live in cities.

Two ethnic groups form most of the population of both countries—the Hutu and the Tutsi. The Hutu make up 80 percent or more of the population in both Rwanda and Burundi. Over the years, however, the Tutsi have controlled the governments and economies of these countries. Since the countries became independent in 1962, the Hutu have tried to gain some of this power.

That effort led to a terrible civil war in the 1990s. Hundreds of thousands of people were killed. Two million more became **refugees,** or people who flee to another country to escape persecution or disaster. The fighting between the Hutu and Tutsi has lessened, but both countries face many challenges as they try to rebuild.

✓Reading Check **Which ethnic group makes up the majority of the population in Rwanda and Burundi?**

Section 3 Assessment

Defining Terms

1. **Define** plantains, autonomy, watershed, endangered species, refugee.

Recalling Facts

2. **Location** Explain the factors that affect Uganda's climate.

3. **Place** What is the capital of Uganda?

4. **Region** What endangered species lives in the forests of Rwanda and Burundi?

Critical Thinking

5. **Evaluating Information** How could a deadly epidemic, such as AIDS, affect a country's economy?

6. **Analyzing Information** How do ethnic differences create problems for the countries of East Africa?

Graphic Organizer

7. **Organizing Information** Draw a diagram like the one below. Then write two facts about Uganda under each of the category headings in the outer ovals.

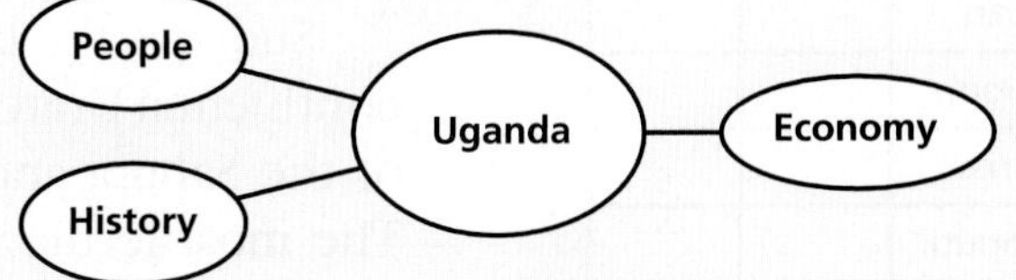

Applying Geography Skills

8. **Analyzing Maps** Study the political map on page 582. What are the four landlocked countries of East Africa?

Section 4

The Horn of Africa

Guide to Reading

Main Idea

The countries of the Horn of Africa have all been scarred by conflict in recent years.

Terms to Know

- drought
- plate
- clan

Places to Locate

- Sudan
- Ethiopia
- Eritrea
- Djibouti
- Somalia
- Blue Nile River
- White Nile River
- Khartoum
- Addis Ababa

Reading Strategy

Make a chart like this one. Then fill in two facts that are true of each country.

Country	Fact #1	Fact #2
Sudan		
Ethiopia		
Eritrea		
Djibouti		
Somalia		

NATIONAL GEOGRAPHIC **Exploring Our World**

In the late 1100s and early 1200s, a king named Lalibela ruled Ethiopia. He had his subjects build Christian churches by carving them out of solid rock. First they cut a huge rectangular trench into the ground. Then they carved the rock inside that trench to form the church. This ancient church is just 1 of 11 ordered built by Lalibela.

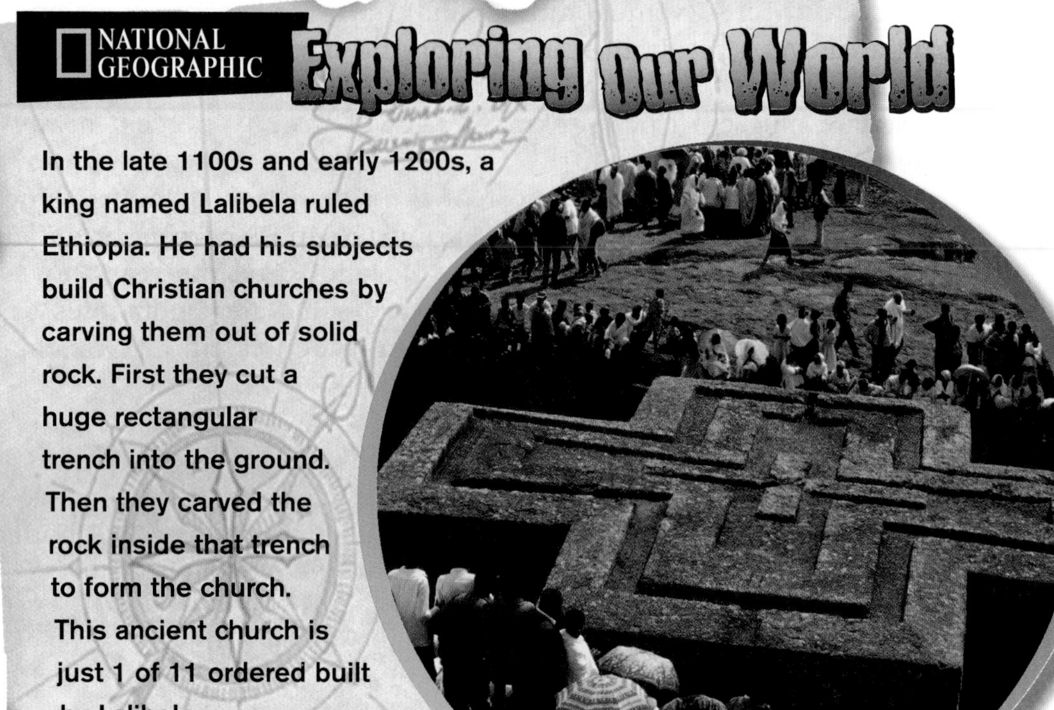

The northern part of East Africa is a region called the Horn of Africa. This region got its name because it is shaped like a horn that juts out into the Indian Ocean. The countries here are **Sudan, Ethiopia, Eritrea** (EHR•uh•TREE•uh), **Djibouti** (jih•BOO•tee), and **Somalia.**

Sudan

Sudan is the largest country in Africa—about one-third the size of the continental United States. The northern part is covered by the sand dunes of the Sahara and Nubian Desert. Nomads raise camels and goats here. The most fertile part of the country is the central region. In this area of grassy plains, the two main tributaries of the Nile River—the **Blue Nile River** and the **White Nile River**—join together at **Khartoum** (kahr•TOOM), Sudan's capital. The southern part of Sudan receives plenty of rain and has some fertile soil. It also holds one of the world's largest swamps, which drains into the White Nile.

Most of Sudan's people live along the Nile River or one of its tributaries. They use water from the Nile to irrigate their fields. Farmers grow sugarcane, grains, nuts, dates, and cotton—the country's leading export. Sheep and gold are other important exports. Recently discovered oil fields in the south offer another possibility of income.

Sudan's People and History Most people in the northern two-thirds of the country are Muslim Arabs. People in the southern one-third come from many different African groups. Most of these southern groups practice Christianity or traditional African religions.

In ancient times, Sudan was the center of a powerful civilization called Kush. The people of Kush had close cultural and trade ties with the Egyptians to the north. During the A.D. 500s, missionaries from Egypt brought Christianity to the area. About 900 years later, Muslim Arabs entered northern Sudan and converted its people to Islam.

From the late 1800s to the 1950s, the British and the Egyptians together ruled the entire country. Sudan became an independent nation in 1956. Since then, military leaders generally have ruled Sudan. Its people have faced an uncertain future. In the 1980s, a fierce civil war broke out between the northern and southern peoples. The fighting has disrupted the economy and caused widespread hunger, especially in the south. A recent **drought**—a long period of extreme

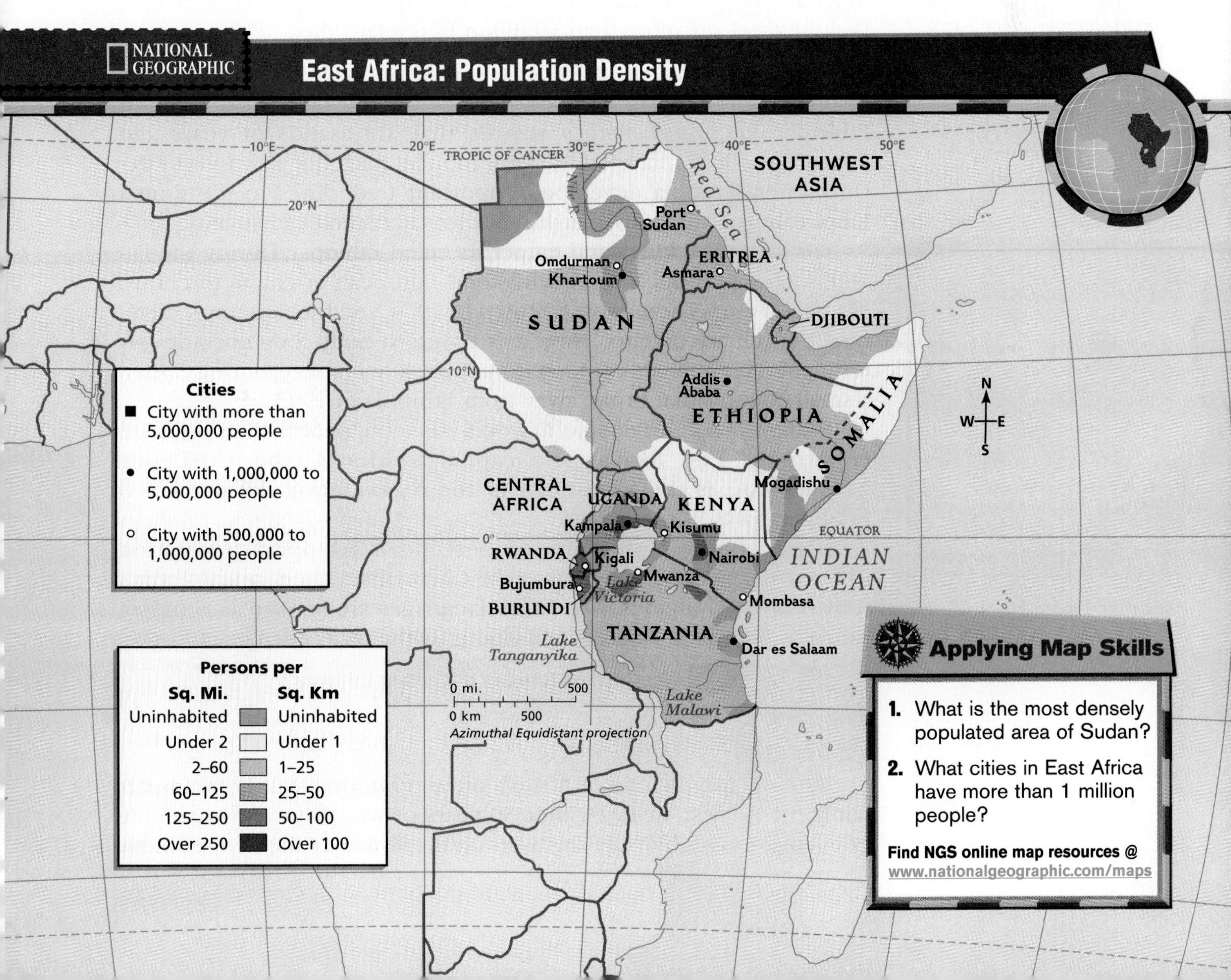

dryness and water shortages—made the situation worse. Millions of people have starved to death, and major outbreaks of diseases have swept through the country. To end the war, the government has announced that it might allow the south to become independent.

Reading Check What is the main export of Sudan?

Casting Votes

In May 2000, Ethiopians voted in their second-ever democratic election. This woman puts her two ballot papers into the ballot box. One ballot was her vote for her region's lawmakers. The other was a vote for the national parliament. People stood in line for hours to exercise their right to vote in a country that has long suffered under military dictators.

Ethiopia

Landlocked Ethiopia is almost twice the size of Texas. Ethiopia's landscape varies from hot lowlands to rugged mountains. The central part of Ethiopia is a highland plateau sliced through by the Great Rift Valley. The valley forms deep river gorges and sparkling waterfalls. Mild temperatures and good soils make the highlands Ethiopia's best farming region. Farmers raise grains, sugarcane, potatoes, and coffee. Coffee is a major export crop. The southern highlands are believed to be the world's original home of coffee.

Rain is not consistent in many parts of Ethiopia, however. Low rainfall in some years brings on drought, and Ethiopia's people suffer. Famine brought Ethiopia to the world's attention in the 1980s. At that time, a drought turned fields once rich in crops into seas of dust. Despite food aid, more than 1 million Ethiopians died.

Ethiopia's History and People Scientists have found what they believe to be the remains of the oldest known human ancestors in Ethiopia. Recorded history reveals that, thousands of years ago, Ethiopian officials traveled to Egypt to meet with the pharaohs of that land. Later, Ethiopia developed important trade links to the Roman Empire. In the A.D. 300s, many Ethiopians accepted Christianity.

For centuries, kings and emperors ruled Ethiopia. During the late 1800s, Ethiopia successfully withstood European attempts to control it. The last emperor was overthrown in 1974, and the country suffered under a military dictator. Now it is trying to build a democratic government. This goal was hindered by warfare with neighboring Eritrea, a small country that broke away from Ethiopia in 1993.

With 59.7 million people, Ethiopia has more people than any other country in East Africa. The capital, **Addis Ababa** (AHD•dihs AH•bah•BAH), is the largest city in the region. About 85 percent of Ethiopians live in rural areas.

Muslims now form about 45 percent of Ethiopia's population. About 40 percent of Ethiopians are Christians. Others practice traditional African religions. Almost 80 languages are spoken in Ethiopia. Amharic, similar to Hebrew and Arabic, is the official language.

Reading Check What makes farming difficult in Ethiopia?

Eritrea

Ethiopia may be one of Africa's oldest countries, but Eritrea is certainly the newest. In 1993, after 30 years of war, Eritrea won its independence from Ethiopia. Eritrea sits on the shores of the Red Sea. It has

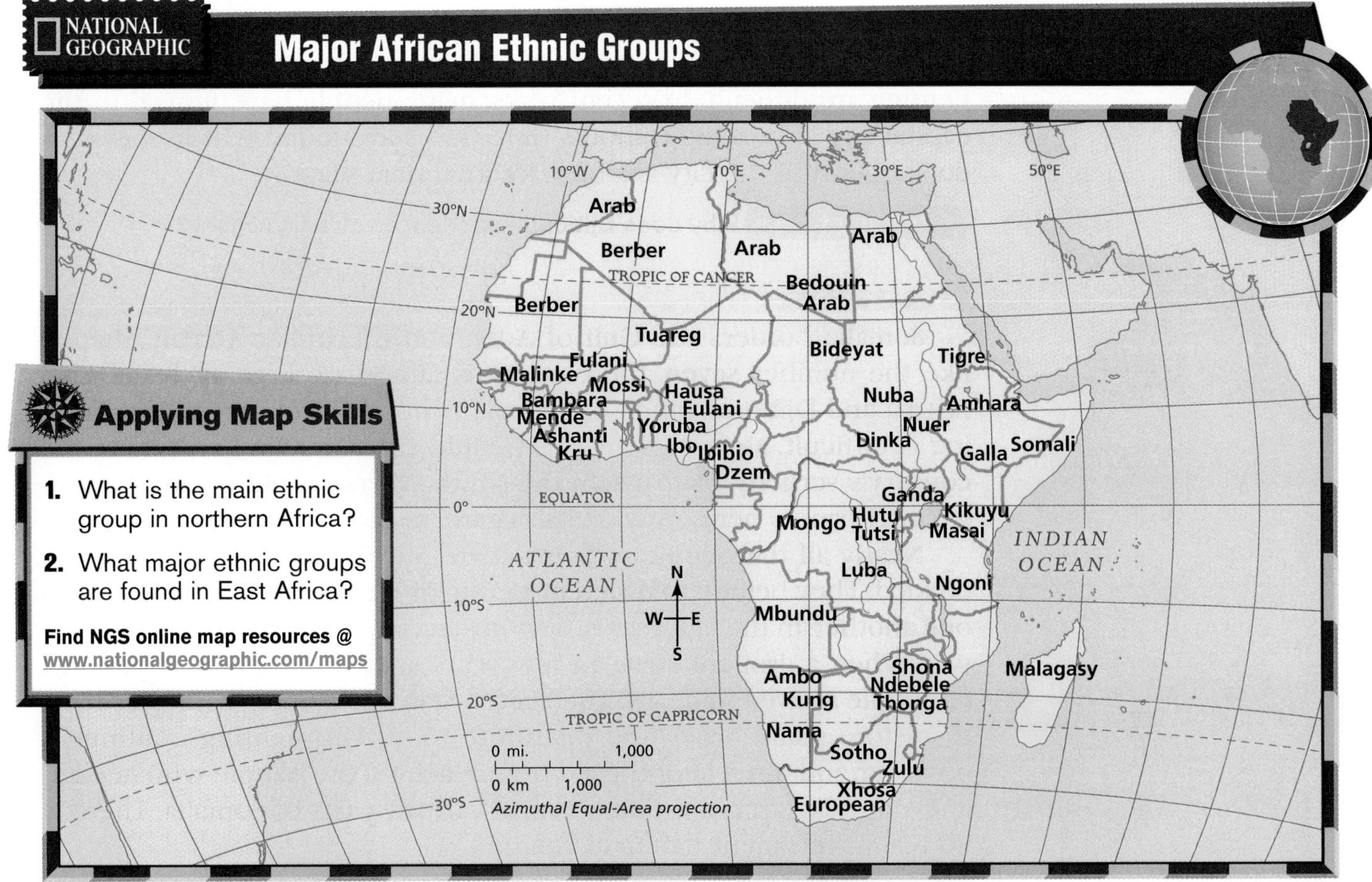

a narrow plain that stretches about 600 miles (966 km) along the coast. When Eritrea became a country, Ethiopia became landlocked.

Most of Eritrea's 4 million people farm the land. Farming is uncertain work because the climate is dry. The long war with Ethiopia also hurt farming. The war did have a positive effect on some of Eritrea's people, however. Women formed about one-third of the army that won the war. After the war ended, the new government passed laws that gave women more rights than they had ever had before.

✓Reading Check **When and from what country did Eritrea win independence?**

Djibouti

To see the earth undergoing change, visit Djibouti. This country lies at the northern tip of the Great Rift Valley, where three of the earth's plates join. **Plates** are huge slabs of rock that make up the earth's crust. In Djibouti, two of these plates are pulling away from each other. As they separate, fiery hot rock rises to the earth's surface, causing volcanic activity.

Djibouti wraps around a natural harbor at the point where the Red Sea meets the Gulf of Aden. This tiny country is one of the hottest, driest places on the earth. Its landscape is covered by rocky desert. Here and there, you will find the desert interrupted by salt lakes and rare patches of grassland.

Djibouti's 600,000 people are mostly Muslims. In the past, they lived a nomadic life of herding. Because of Djibouti's dry climate, farming and herding are difficult. In recent years, many people have moved to the capital city, also called Djibouti. Here they have found jobs in the city's docks, because the city is a busy international seaport.

Reading Check **Why does Djibouti experience volcanic activity?**

Somalia

Somalia borders the Gulf of Aden and the Indian Ocean. Shaped like the number seven, the country is almost as large as Texas. Like Eritrea and Djibouti, much of Somalia is hot, dry country where farming is difficult. Most of Somalia's people are nomadic herders on the country's scrubby plateaus. In the south, rivers provide water for irrigation. Farmers here grow fruits, sugarcane, and bananas.

Nearly all the people of Somalia are Muslims, but they are deeply divided. They belong to different **clans,** or groups of people related to one another. In the late 1980s, disputes between these clans led to civil war. When a drought struck a few years later, hundreds of thousands of people starved to death. The United States and other countries tried to restore some order and distribute food. The fighting continued, however, and often kept the aid from reaching the people who needed it. Even today, armed groups control various parts of Somalia. There is no real government that is in charge.

Reading Check **What kind of conflict led to civil war in Somalia?**

Assessment

Defining Terms

1. **Define** drought, plate, clan.

Recalling Facts

2. **Place** What is the capital of Sudan?
3. **History** What is the only country of East Africa that was never colonized by Europeans?
4. **Government** Describe the current political situation in Somalia.

Critical Thinking

5. **Analyzing Information** What factors do you think might have led to the settlement of Khartoum, Sudan's capital?
6. **Understanding Cause and Effect** How did a war bring increased rights to women in Eritrea?

Graphic Organizer

7. **Organizing Information** On a diagram like the one below, list the major religions practiced by countries of the Horn of Africa. Write the religions under each country's name.

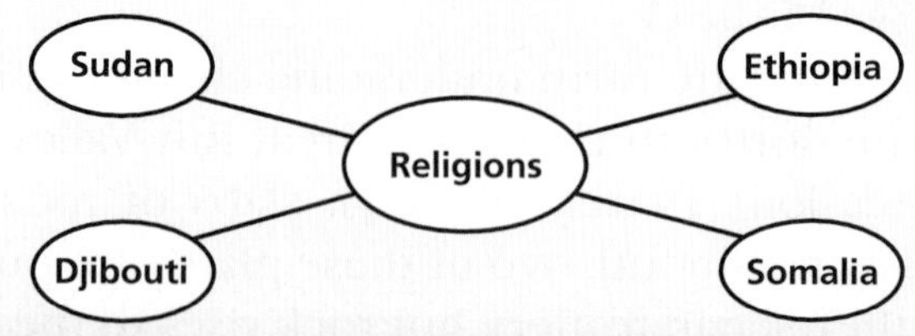

Applying Geography Skills

8. **Analyzing Maps** Study the climate map on page 588. What four types of climates are found in Sudan?

Chapter 21

Reading Review

Section 1 Kenya

Terms to Know
- coral reef
- nature preserve
- poaching
- fault
- escarpment
- altitude
- free enterprise system
- cassava

Main Idea

Kenya is a country of diverse landscapes and peoples.

✓ **Place** Eastern Kenya is covered by lowlands. The western half is marked by highlands and the wide Great Rift Valley.

✓ **Economics** Most people in Kenya carry out subsistence farming. Coffee and tea are grown for export. Tourism is also a major industry in Kenya.

✓ **Culture** Kenya's people come from many different ethnic groups. They speak Swahili, a blended language.

✓ **Government** Since becoming independent in 1963, Kenya has had a mostly stable government.

Section 2 Tanzania

Terms to Know
- sisal
- habitat
- eco-tourist

Main Idea

Tanzania is located on the Indian Ocean and relies on agriculture and tourism.

✓ **Economics** Farming and tourism are the main activities in Tanzania. The country is too poor to develop its mineral resources.

✓ **Government** Tanzania's government has been stable and democratic.

Section 3 Inland East Africa

Terms to Know
- plantains
- autonomy
- watershed
- endangered species
- refugee

Main Idea

Rwanda, Burundi, and Uganda have suffered much conflict in recent years.

✓ **Place** Uganda, Rwanda, and Burundi are landlocked countries with high elevation and rainy, moderate climates.

✓ **Economics** Most people in all three countries practice subsistence farming. Major exports include coffee, tea, and cotton.

✓ **History** Rwanda and Burundi suffered a brutal civil war in the 1990s between the Hutu and the Tutsi ethnic groups.

Section 4 The Horn of Africa

Terms to Know
- drought
- plate
- clan

Main Idea

The countries of the Horn of Africa have all been scarred by conflict in recent years.

✓ **History** Sudan has been torn by a civil war between the northern Muslim Arabs and the southern African peoples.

✓ **Human/Environment Interaction** Ethiopia has good farmland, but scarce rainfall can cause drought.

✓ **Government** Eritrea recently won its independence from Ethiopia.

✓ **History** Fighting between rival clans and drought have caused suffering in Somalia.

Chapter 21 Assessment and Activities

Using Key Terms

Match the terms in Part A with their definitions in Part B.

A.

1. sisal
2. plantains
3. poaching
4. endangered species
5. habitat
6. fault
7. autonomy
8. drought
9. nature preserve
10. eco-tourist

B.

a. self-government
b. extended period of extreme dryness
c. crack in the earth's crust
d. land set aside to protect plants and wildlife
e. hunting and killing animals illegally
f. plant fiber used to make rope
g. people who travel to view natural wonders
h. environment in which an animal species normally lives
i. fruit resembling bananas
j. plant or animal in danger of dying out completely

Reviewing the Main Ideas

Section 1 Kenya

11. **Place** What is the major physical feature of Kenya's interior?
12. **Economics** What are Kenya's major exports?
13. **Place** Why is Mombasa an important city?

Section 2 Tanzania

14. **Place** What is the largest lake in Africa?
15. **Economics** In which part of Tanzania are cloves produced?
16. **Region** Name some of the animals that live on the Serengeti Plain.

Section 3 Inland East Africa

17. **Economics** Name three exports of Uganda.
18. **Economics** How do Burundi and Rwanda get their goods to foreign buyers?
19. **Culture** What two ethnic groups are fighting in Rwanda and Burundi?

Section 4 The Horn of Africa

20. **Place** What is the largest country in Africa?
21. **Economics** Which region of Ethiopia has the best farmland?
22. **Government** What is Africa's newest country?

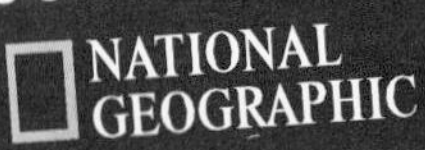

East Africa

Place Location Activity

On a separate sheet of paper, match the letters on the map with the numbered places listed below.

1. Ethiopian Highlands
2. Lake Victoria
3. Kilimanjaro
4. White Nile River
5. Sudan
6. Tanzania
7. Red Sea
8. Somalia
9. Rwanda
10. Nairobi

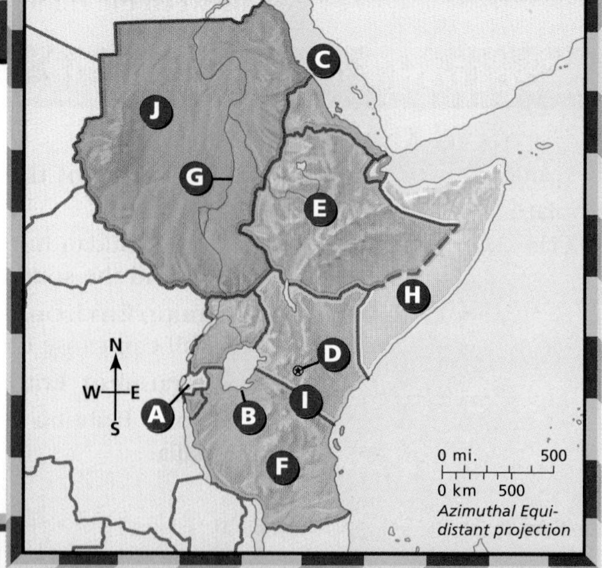

Self-Check Quiz Visit the ***Geography: The World and Its People*** Web site at gwip.glencoe.com and click on **Chapter 21—Self-Check Quizzes** to prepare for the Chapter Test.

Critical Thinking

23. **Analyzing Information** Most of the countries of East Africa depend on agriculture as their main economic activity. Why is a good transportation system important to these agricultural societies?
24. **Sequencing Information** In a diagram like the one below, describe and put in order the steps that can lead to the creation of a desert.

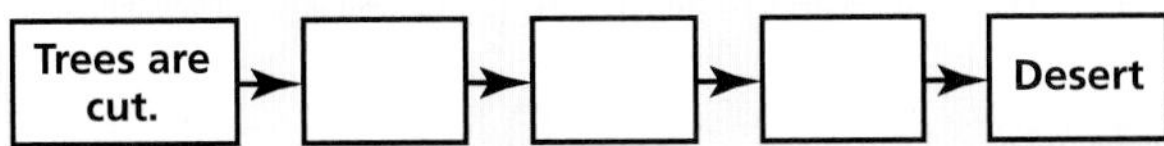

GeoJournal Activity

25. **Writing an Acrostic Poem** To the Masai people, the name *Serengeti* means "a large or extended place." Write an acrostic poem that describes the Serengeti. In an acrostic poem, each line begins with a letter from the word that is the topic. Write SERENGETI vertically down the left margin of your paper. Then write a nine-line poem, with each line starting with the appropriate letter.

Mental Mapping Activity

26. **Focusing on the Region** Draw a simple outline map of Africa, then label the following:
    - Sudan
    - Indian Ocean
    - Ethiopia
    - Kenya
    - Tanzania
    - Great Rift Valley
    - Lake Victoria
    - Uganda
    - Nairobi
    - Nile River

Technology Skills Activity

27. **Developing a Multimedia Presentation** Choose one of Africa's endangered species and create a multimedia presentation about it. Include pictures or video clips of the animal, maps of its habitat area, graphs that show the change in its population, and the steps being taken to protect this animal.

Standardized Test Practice

Directions: Study the map below, then answer the following question.

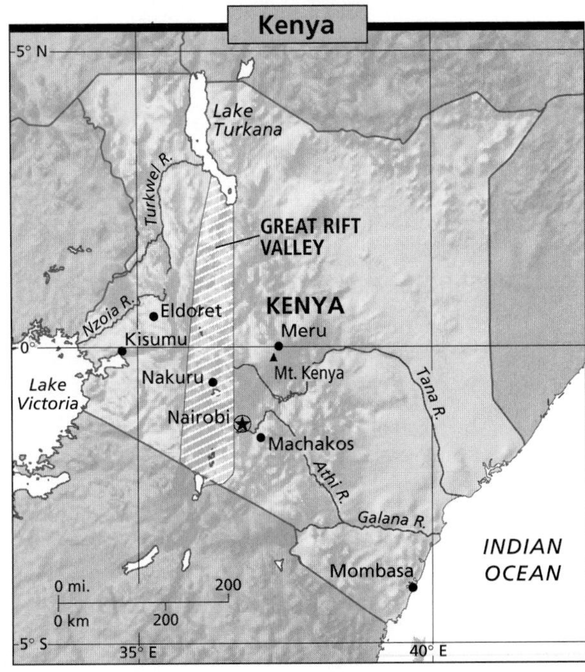

1. **About how many miles is it from Nairobi to Mombasa?**
   F 100 miles
   G 200 miles
   H 300 miles
   J 400 miles

Test-Taking Tip: Look carefully at the map key to understand its *scale,* or distance from one point to another. If you find it hard to judge distances by eye, use a small piece of scrap paper to measure the units described in the key.

EYE on the Environment

Endangered Spaces

Shrinking Habitats When you think of Africa, what images come to mind? Roaring lions? Sprinting cheetahs? Lumbering elephants? Unless conditions change, some wild African animals may soon be only memories. Many are endangered, primarily because their habitats—their grassland and forest homes—are being destroyed in many ways.

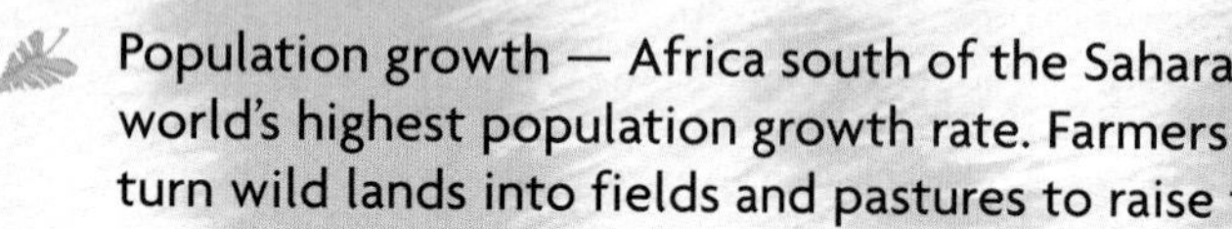

- Population growth — Africa south of the Sahara has the world's highest population growth rate. Farmers and ranchers turn wild lands into fields and pastures to raise food. Urban sprawl also takes over habitats.
- Logging — Logging companies build roads and cut valuable trees, destroying forest habitats.
- Mining — Open pit mines scar the land, pollute waters, and destroy trees.

Cheetahs
Elephants
Mountain Gorillas

As habitats shrink, so do populations of African animals.

- Cheetahs live in Africa's grasslands. As people move into the cheetahs' home, the big cats struggle to survive. Only about 12,000 cheetahs are left in the wild.
- Mountain gorillas live in the misty mountain forests of Central and East Africa. Logging and mining are destroying these forests. Only about 650 mountain gorillas remain.

These and other endangered African animals will survive only if their habitats are saved.

Loggers destroy a forest in the Democratic Republic of the Congo.

Cheetahs are running out of room in Africa.

Making a Difference

Namibian children learn about cheetahs.

The Cheetah Conservation Fund Cheetahs in Africa are getting a helping hand from the Cheetah Conservation Fund (CCF). This organization is based in Namibia, which is home to about 2,500 cheetahs. Namibian ranchers often trap and shoot cheetahs to protect their livestock. The CCF has donated nearly 80 special herding dogs to ranchers. The dogs protect the livestock and keep cheetahs out of harm's way at the same time. The CCF also teaches villagers and schoolchildren about cheetahs and about why it is important to save these big cats and their habitats.

Protecting Gorillas For nearly 18 years, Dian Fossey studied mountain gorillas in Rwanda. Through her book, *Gorillas in the Mist*, which was made into a movie, Fossey told others about mountain gorillas and how their survival was threatened by habitat destruction and poaching. Fossey established the Karisoke Research Center and an international fund to support gorilla conservation.

Dian Fossey fought fiercely to end gorilla poaching. Although Fossey was murdered at Karisoke in 1985, the Dian Fossey Gorilla Fund International continues its work protecting mountain gorillas and their habitat.

A mountain gorilla

What Can You Do?

Adopt a Cheetah

You and your classmates can help save cheetahs in the wild by adopting one. To learn more, contact the Cheetah Conservation Fund at www.cheetah.org

Find Out More

What animal habitats are endangered where you live? Work with a partner to investigate endangered spaces in your area. Summarize your findings in a report to the class.

Use the Internet

How can people help save vanishing habitats? Check The Nature Conservancy's Web site at www.tnc.org to learn how this group works to preserve habitats worldwide.

South Africa and Its Neighbors

The World and Its People NATIONAL GEOGRAPHIC

To learn more about the people and places of South Africa and its neighbors, view ***The World and Its People*** **Chapter 22** video.

Geography Online

Chapter Overview Visit the ***Geography: The World and Its People*** Web site at gwip.glencoe.com and click on **Chapter 22–Chapter Overviews** to preview information about South Africa and its neighbors.

Section 1

Republic of South Africa

Guide to Reading

Main Idea

Rich in resources, South Africa has recently seen major social and political changes.

Terms to Know

- high veld
- escarpment
- developed country
- Boer
- apartheid
- township
- enclave

Places to Locate

- South Africa
- Namib Desert
- Cape of Good Hope
- Drakensberg Range
- Cape Town
- Johannesburg
- Durban
- Pretoria
- Lesotho
- Swaziland

Reading Strategy

Create a time line like this one. Then list five key events and their dates in South Africa's history.

NATIONAL GEOGRAPHIC **Exploring Our World**

Cape Town's Table Mountain is famous for its flat top. A cable car takes people to the top. If you are physically fit and have four hours to spare, you can also climb the mountain. From the top, you can see Cape Town—South Africa's legislative capital. The country's executive capital is Pretoria, while the judicial capital is Bloemfontein.

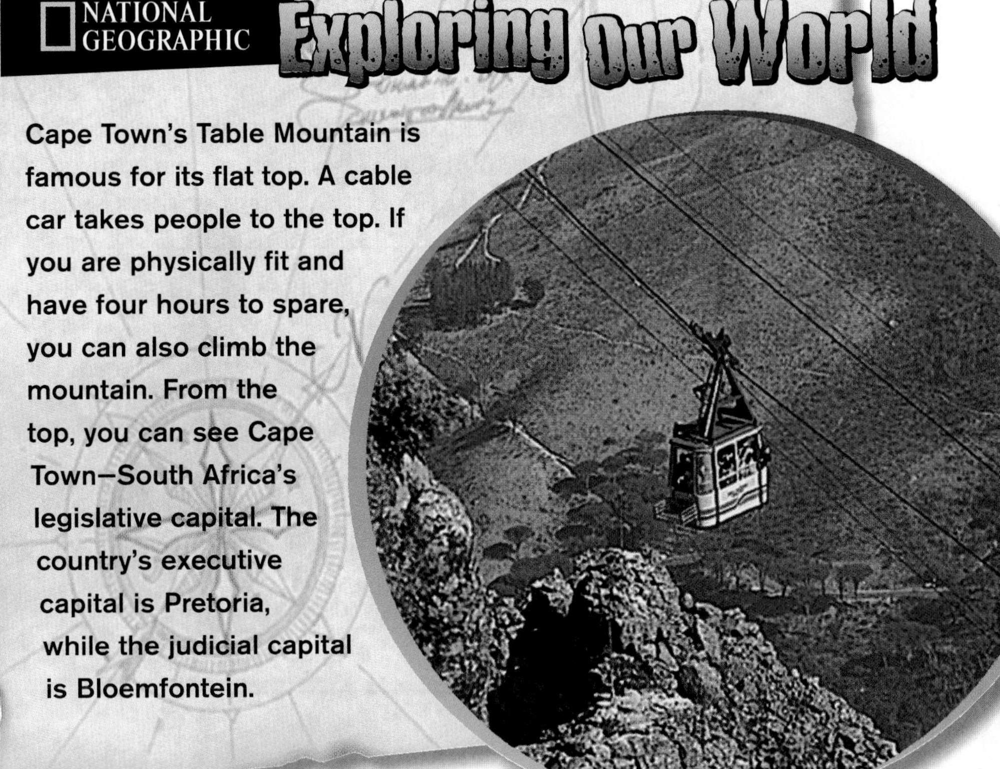

◀ Table Mountain overlooks Cape Town, South Africa.

South Africa (officially called the Republic of South Africa) spreads across the southern end of the African continent. It is a land of beautiful scenery and great mineral wealth. It is also a land of great change.

A Land of Variety

The Republic of South Africa covers an area almost twice the size of Texas. Here you will find the continent's biggest mammal, the African elephant, and smallest mammal, the miniature shrew. To protect these creatures, the government has set aside land as national parks.

South Africa borders the Atlantic Ocean on the west and the Indian Ocean on the south and east. The vast **Namib Desert** reaches into the northwest. Farther south you find the **Cape of Good Hope,** the southernmost point of Africa. Two small plateaus rise above the coastal plain east of the cape. These dry plateaus are the Great Karroo and the Little Karroo. *Karroo* means "land of thirst" in a local African language.

A large plateau spreads through the center of South Africa. Part of this plateau is made up of flat, grass-covered plains called the **high veld.** The high veld has soil too poor for farming, but the grasslands can support grazing livestock. The plateau is separated from coastal areas by the Great Escarpment. An **escarpment** is a steep cliff between higher and lower land. The Great Escarpment reaches its highest elevations in the **Drakensberg Range** in the east.

Climate South Africa lies south of the Equator. As a result, its seasons are opposite to those in the Northern Hemisphere. The climate map on page 615 shows you that South Africa has a variety of climates. On the plateau, winters are cool and sunny with some rainfall. Summers remain mild because of the high elevation. The area around **Cape Town** has a Mediterranean climate of cool, rainy winters and hot, often dry summers. The farther east you go along the coast, the handier an umbrella becomes. Warm winds from the Indian Ocean bring a humid subtropical climate and rain.

Reading Check **Which part of South Africa has a Mediterranean climate?**

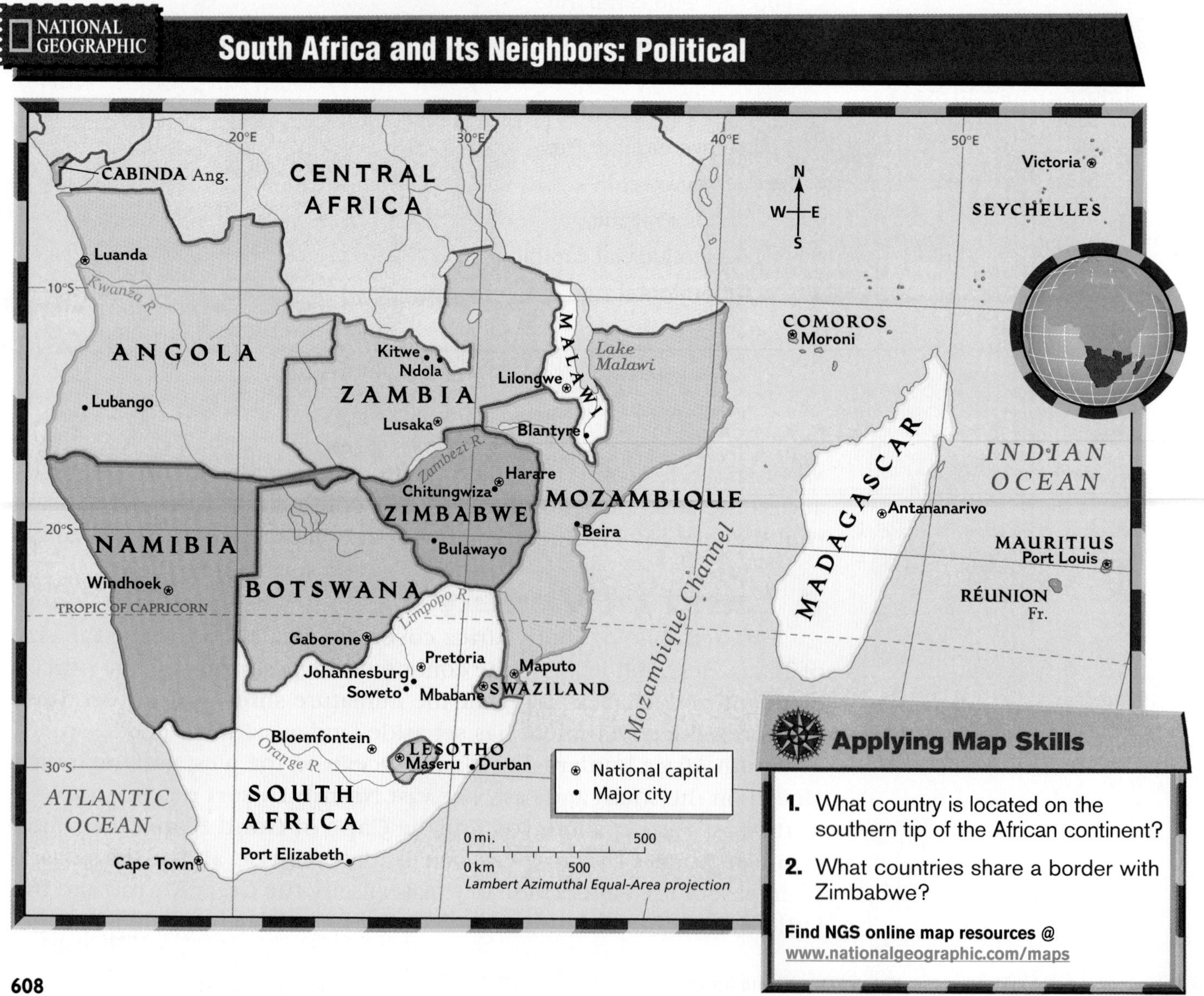

Applying Map Skills

1. What country is located on the southern tip of the African continent?
2. What countries share a border with Zimbabwe?

Find NGS online map resources @ www.nationalgeographic.com/maps

A Developed Economy

South Africa is the most developed country in Africa. As you learned in Chapter 3, a **developed country** is one in which a great deal of manufacturing occurs. Not all South Africans benefit from this prosperous economy, however. In rural areas, many people continue to depend on subsistence farming and live in poverty.

In terms of mineral resources, South Africa is one of the richest countries in the world. It is the world's largest producer and exporter of gold. The Witwatersrand (WIHT•WAW•tuhrz•RAHND)—an area around the city of **Johannesburg**—is the site of the world's largest and richest gold field. South Africa also has large deposits of diamonds, chromite, platinum, and coal. The income earned from these resources has led to the growth of cities, industrial centers, huge cattle and sheep ranches, and high-technology farms.

Factories produce many of the manufactured goods used by South Africans themselves. The country also exports machinery, chemicals, clothing, and processed foods.

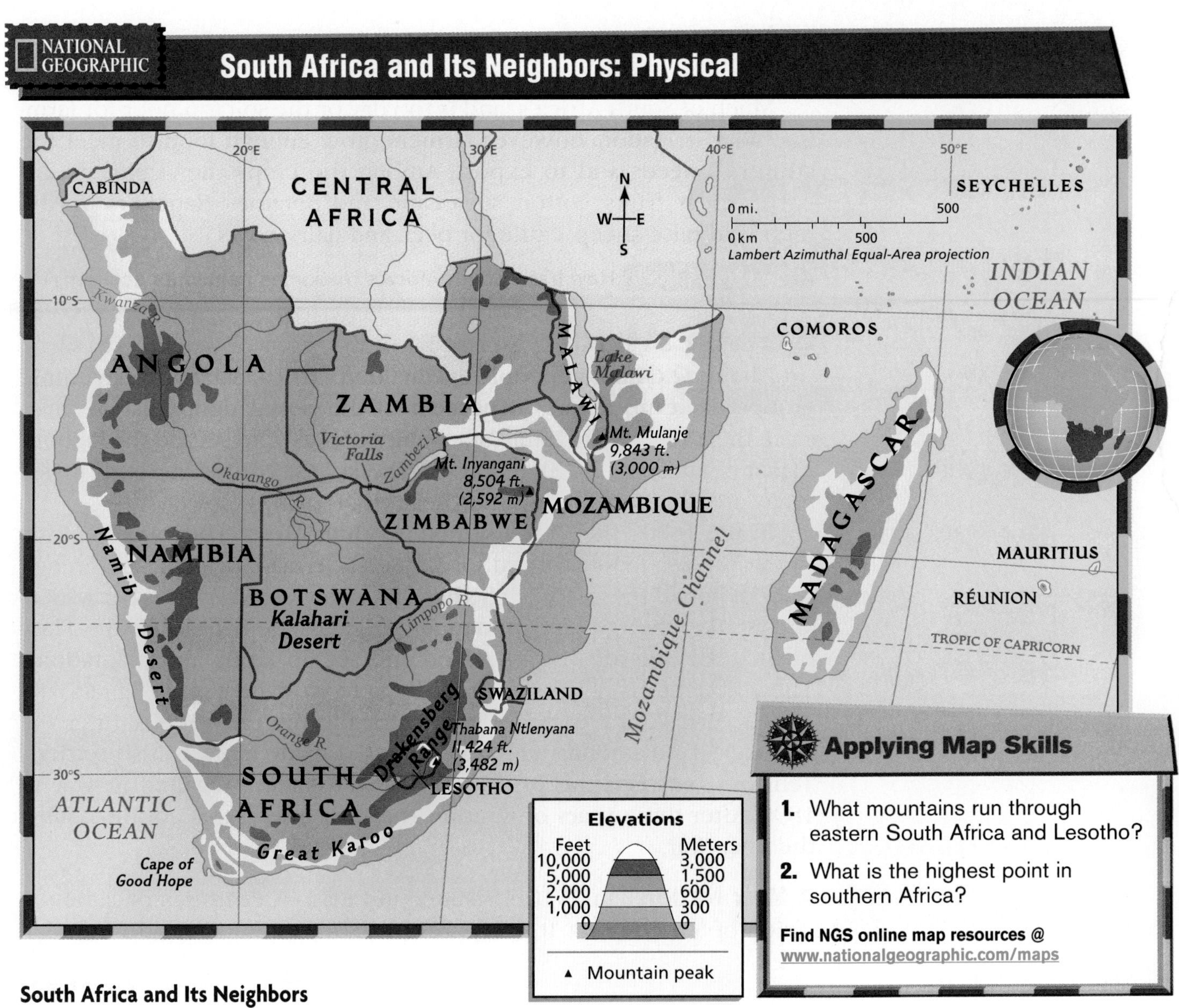

Applying Map Skills

1. What mountains run through eastern South Africa and Lesotho?
2. What is the highest point in southern Africa?

Find NGS online map resources @ www.nationalgeographic.com/maps

Music

The talking drum is a popular instrument in Africa south of the Sahara. Animal skins cover both ends and are held together by strings. While holding the drum under the arm, the musician strikes one skin with a curved wooden mallet. By squeezing down on the strings with the arm, the skins are stretched tighter and the pitch of the drum becomes higher. The loosening and tightening of the strings give the drum its characteristic "talking" sound.

Looking Closer How is the talking drum different from the traditional drums in the United States?

GO TO

World Music: A Cultural Legacy
Hear music of this region on Disk 2, Track 1.

Much of South Africa's land is too dry or the soil too poor for farming. With irrigation, however, farmers grow enough food to meet the country's needs and to export. Among the crops they cultivate are corn, wheat, fruits, cotton, sugarcane, and potatoes. Ranchers on the high veld raise sheep, cattle for beef, and dairy cows.

✓Reading Check **How have South Africa's resources helped its economy?**

South Africa's History and People

About 42.6 million people live in South Africa. Black African ethnic groups make up about 78 percent of the population. Most of them trace their ancestry to Bantu-speaking peoples who settled throughout Africa between A.D. 100 and 1000. The largest groups in South Africa today are the Sotho, Zulu, and Xhosa (KOH•suh).

In the 1600s, the Dutch settled in South Africa. They were known as the **Boers,** a Dutch word for farmers. German, Belgian, and French settlers joined them. Together these groups were known as Afrikaners and spoke their own language—Afrikaans (A•frih•KAHNS). They pushed Africans off the best land and set up farms and plantations. They brought many laborers from India to work on sugar plantations.

The British first came to South Africa in the early 1800s. Later, the discovery of diamonds and gold attracted many more British settlers. Tensions between the British and the Afrikaners resulted in war in 1899. After three years of fighting, the British won this conflict called the Boer War.

A New Nation In 1910 Afrikaner and British territories became the Union of South Africa. It was part of the British Empire and was ruled by whites. Black South Africans founded the African National Congress (ANC) in 1912 in hopes of gaining power.

In the 1930s, the whites set up a system of apartheid, or "apartness." **Apartheid** (uh•PAHR•TAYT) involved laws that separated racial and ethnic groups and limited the rights of blacks. For example, laws forced black South Africans to live in separate areas, called "homelands." People of non-European background were not even allowed to vote.

For more than 40 years, people inside and outside South Africa protested against the practice of apartheid. Many black Africans were jailed for voicing their opposition to apartheid. The United Nations declared that apartheid was "a crime against humanity." Many countries cut off trade with South Africa.

Finally, in 1991 the South African government agreed to end apartheid. In April 1994, South Africa held its first democratic election that allowed all people to vote. South Africans elected their first black president, Nelson Mandela.

The People About 55 percent of South Africans live in urban areas. The largest cities are Cape Town, Johannesburg, **Durban,** and **Pretoria.** South Africa has 11 official languages, including Afrikaans, English, Zulu, Xhosa, and other African ethnic languages. About two-thirds of South Africans are Christians. Almost one-third practice traditional African religions.

One of the challenges facing South Africa today is to develop a better standard of living for its poor people. Most European South Africans live in modern homes and enjoy a high standard of living. Most black African, Asian, and mixed-group South Africans live in rural areas and crowded **townships,** or neighborhoods outside cities. The government has introduced measures to improve education and basic services for these people. It is also working to provide more jobs for the poor.

Another challenge facing South Africa is the AIDS epidemic. Millions of people throughout Africa have been infected with the virus that causes AIDS. South Africa is one of the hardest-hit countries. The government is looking for ways to prevent the spread of the disease and to treat those who have it.

NATIONAL GEOGRAPHIC On Location

Lesotho

Although altitude, soil, and climate make farming difficult in Lesotho, most people are subsistence farmers.

Place **At what elevation does most of Lesotho lie?**

Nelson Mandela

As a young man, Nelson Mandela spoke out against apartheid. He was arrested and jailed. In 1990 he was released after spending a total of 27 years in jail. After becoming president in 1994, Mandela worked hard to maintain peace between the blacks and whites of South Africa.

The country's arts reflect the long struggle for justice and equality. In recent years, musicians have combined traditional African dance rhythms and modern rock music. Since the 1980s, groups such as Ladysmith Black Mambazo have made South African sounds popular worldwide. Other groups preserve traditional instruments and songs.

Reading Check **What has the South African government done to improve the lives of its poor people?**

Lesotho and Swaziland

Look at the political map on page 608. Within South Africa lie two other African nations—**Lesotho** (luh•SOH•toh) and **Swaziland.** They are **enclaves**—small countries located inside a larger country. Both are poor countries that depend heavily on South Africa.

A mountainous kingdom about the size of Maryland, Lesotho's only important natural resource is water. Lesotho sells some of this water to South Africa. Most people subsistence-farm and herd livestock. About one-third of Lesotho's male workers labor in the mines of South Africa. Their wages help support their families in Lesotho.

Swaziland is another tiny kingdom almost completely surrounded by South Africa. It shares a short border with Mozambique. About 60 percent of its people are engaged in subsistence farming. Others work in Swaziland's coal and asbestos mines or travel to South Africa to work in the mines there. Swaziland is ruled by a royal family that has been in power for more than 400 years.

Reading Check **How do Lesotho and Swaziland earn money from South Africa?**

Assessment

Defining Terms

1. **Define** high veld, escarpment, developed country, Boer, apartheid, township, enclave.

Recalling Facts

2. **Place** Name the largest and the smallest mammal in Africa.
3. **Government** Who is Nelson Mandela?
4. **Culture** What challenges face South Africa?

Critical Thinking

5. **Drawing Conclusions** How did the rest of the world view apartheid?
6. **Analyzing Information** Why do you think many of the workers in Lesotho and Swaziland travel to South Africa to find jobs?

Graphic Organizer

7. **Organizing Information** In a chart like the one below, write the resources and products of South Africa in the two boxes.

South Africa	
Resources	Products

Applying Geography Skills

8. **Analyzing Maps** Study the physical map on page 609. Into what body of water does the Orange River empty?

Making Connections

ART | SCIENCE | LITERATURE | TECHNOLOGY

Mining and Cutting Diamonds

A diamond is a mineral made entirely of carbon. It is the hardest-known substance on the earth and the most popular gemstone. Most diamonds formed billions of years ago deep inside the earth's mantle. There, intense pressure and heat transformed carbon into diamond crystal.

Mining

There are two major techniques used for mining diamonds: open pit and underground mining. In open pit mining, the earth is dug out in layers, creating a series of steps or roads that circle down into a pit. After drills and explosives loosen the rock containing diamonds, shovels and trucks remove it. When the pit becomes too deep to reach easily, underground mining may begin.

Underground mining requires sinking a shaft into the ground and tunneling to the rock. Explosives blast the rock loose, and the resulting rubble is crushed and carried to the surface for further processing.

To remove the diamonds, the crushed rock is mixed with water and placed in a washing pan. Heavier minerals, such as diamonds, settle to the bottom, while lighter wastes rise to the top and overflow. Next, the heavier mixture travels to a grease table. Diamonds cling to the grease while other wetted minerals flow past. Workers continue the sorting and separating by hand.

Cutting

The newly mined diamond resembles a piece of glass, not a sparkling jewel. To enhance their brilliance and sparkle, gem-quality diamonds are precisely cut and polished. The cutter uses high-speed diamond-tipped tools to cut facets, or small flat surfaces, into the stone. One of the most popular diamond cuts is the brilliant cut, which has 58 facets. The job of the cutter requires extreme skill, because the angles of the facets must be exactly right to bring out the diamond's beauty.

Making the Connection

1. Of what are diamonds made?
2. Why are gemstone diamonds cut and polished?
3. **Making Comparisons** How are open pit and underground diamond mining techniques alike? How are they different?

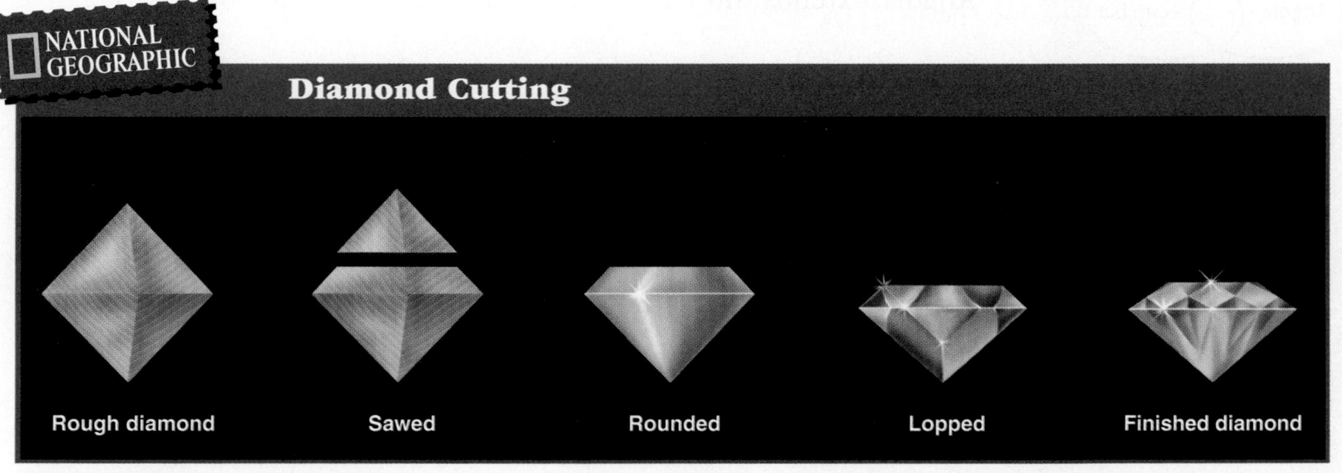

Section 2 Atlantic Countries

Guide to Reading

Main Idea

Angola and Namibia, although rich in resources, are struggling to develop their economies.

Terms to Know

- exclave

Places to Locate

- Angola
- Namibia
- Namib Desert
- Cabinda
- Kalahari Desert

Reading Strategy

Create a diagram like this one. Write facts about Angola and Namibia in the outer ovals under each heading. Where the ovals overlap, write statements that are true of both countries.

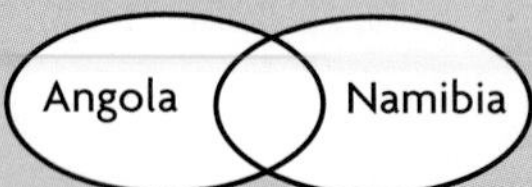

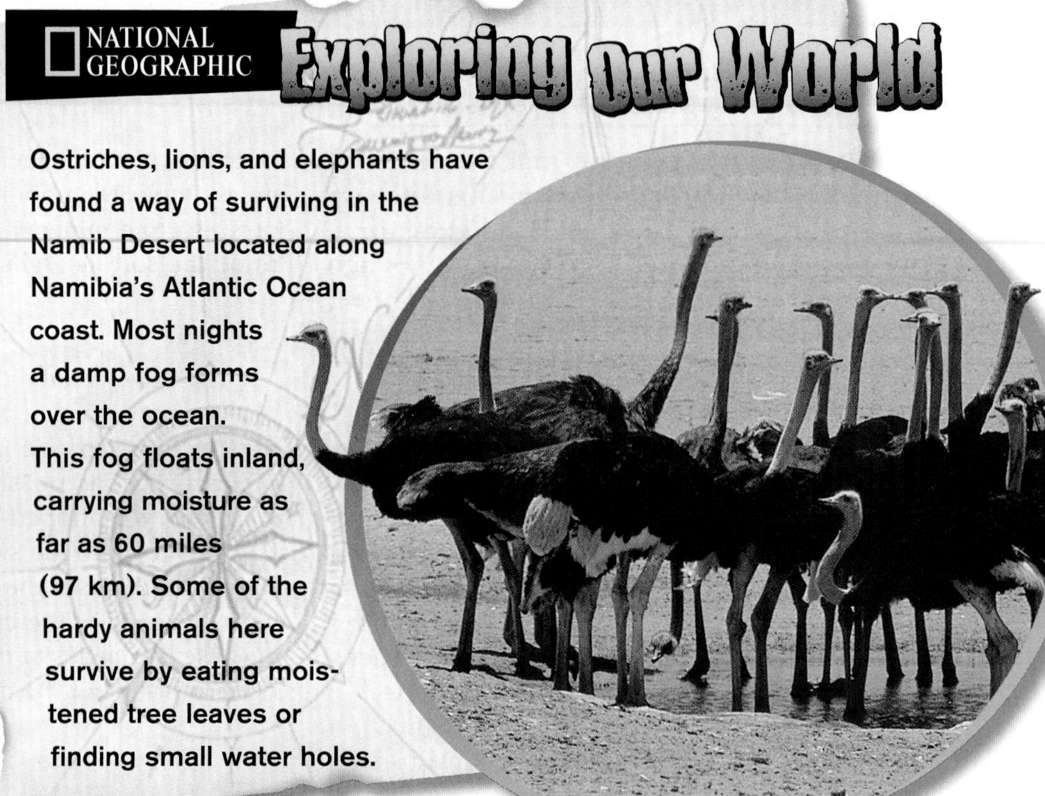

NATIONAL GEOGRAPHIC Exploring Our World

Ostriches, lions, and elephants have found a way of surviving in the Namib Desert located along Namibia's Atlantic Ocean coast. Most nights a damp fog forms over the ocean. This fog floats inland, carrying moisture as far as 60 miles (97 km). Some of the hardy animals here survive by eating moistened tree leaves or finding small water holes.

Angola and **Namibia** have long coastlines on the Atlantic Ocean. For this reason, they are known as southern Africa's Atlantic countries. They share the **Namib Desert**—a vast expanse of sand and rock that stretches north to south about 1,200 miles (1,931 km). It begins in Angola, extends through Namibia, and stretches into South Africa.

Angola

Angola is almost twice the size of Texas. Angola also includes a tiny exclave called **Cabinda.** An **exclave** is a small part of a country that is separated from the main part. Look at the map on page 608. You will see that Cabinda lies just to the north of Angola.

Most of Angola is part of the same inland plateau that sweeps through South Africa. Many rivers cross the country. Some flow into the Congo River in the north. Others flow into the Atlantic Ocean.

Hilly grasslands cover northern Angola. The southern part of the country is a rocky desert. A low strip of land winds along the Atlantic coastline. Most of this lowland area has little natural vegetation. In Cabinda, the exclave to the north, rain forests thrive.

The climate map below shows you that Angola's coastal areas have a desert climate. Inland from the coast, you pass through a narrow stretch of land with a steppe climate. The large inland plateau has a tropical savanna climate of wet and dry seasons. This area receives enough rainfall for farming.

Angola's Economy Angola's main economic activity is agriculture. About 85 percent of the people make their living from subsistence farming. Some farmers grow coffee and cotton for export. Angola's main source of income, however, is oil. Oil deposits off the coast of Cabinda account for 90 percent of Angola's export earnings. Other important industries include diamond mining, fish processing, and textiles. Still, Angola is not a wealthy country. Different groups have struggled for control of the country, which has hurt the economy.

Angola's History Most of Angola's people belong to several African ethnic groups. They trace their ancestry to the Bantu-speaking peoples who spread across much of Africa many centuries ago. In the 1400s, the Kongo kingdom ruled a large part of northern Angola.

From the 1500s until its independence in 1975, Angola was a colony of Portugal. Portugal is still an important trading partner, and Portuguese is the official language. Bantu and other African languages are also widely spoken. Almost 50 percent of Angolans practice the Roman Catholic faith brought to Angola by the Portuguese.

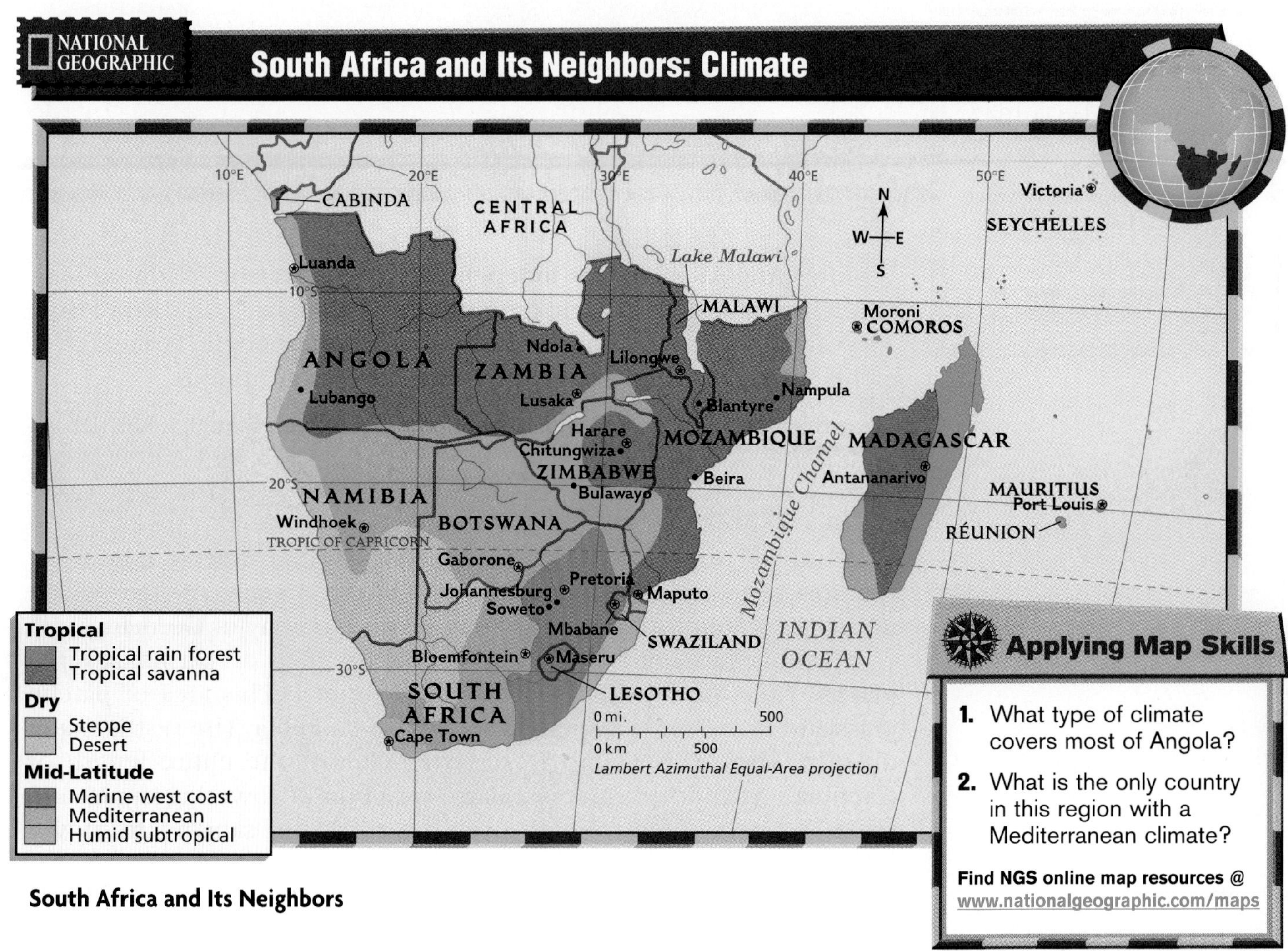

Applying Map Skills

1. What type of climate covers most of Angola?
2. What is the only country in this region with a Mediterranean climate?

Find NGS online map resources @ www.nationalgeographic.com/maps

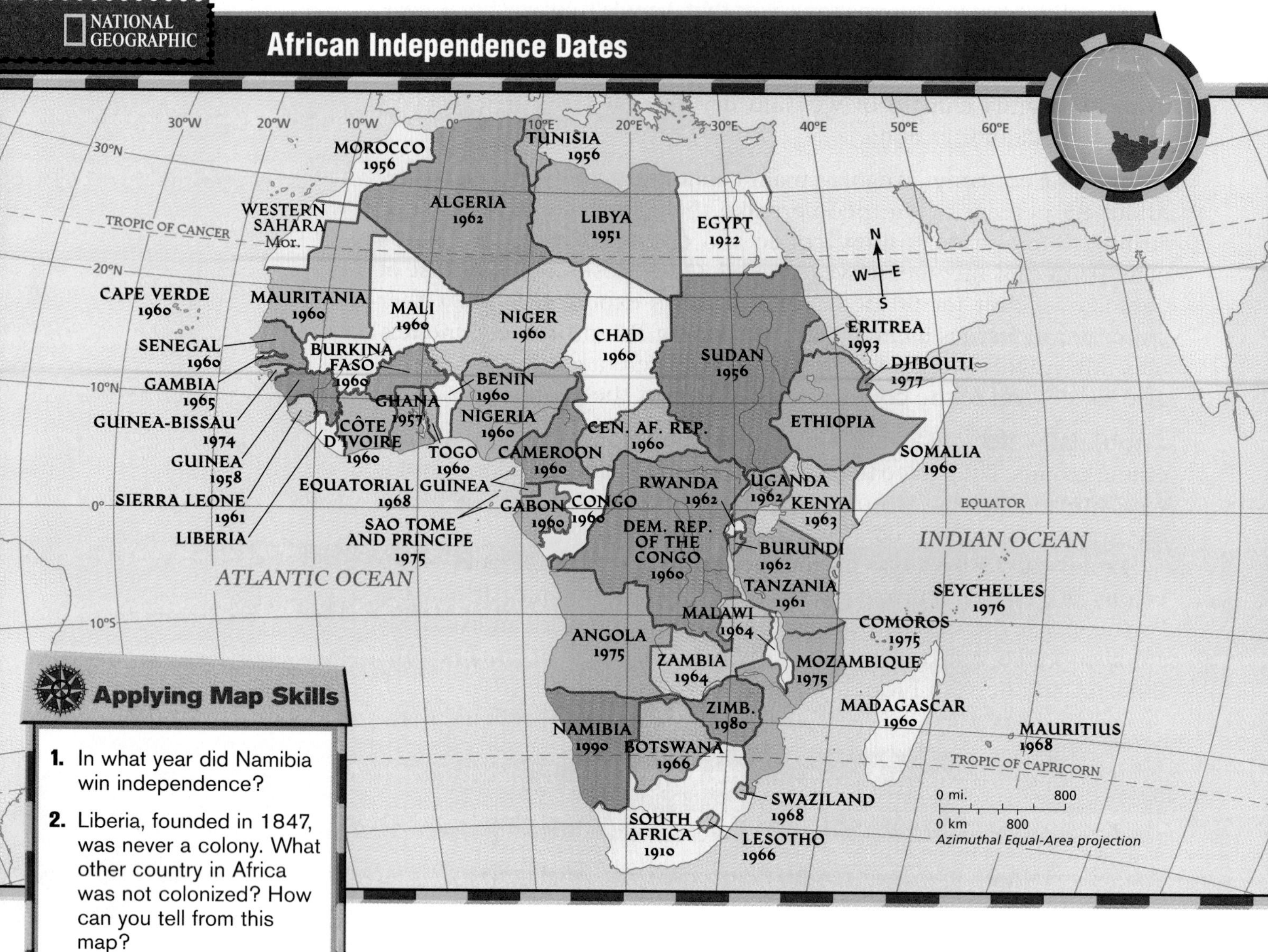

Applying Map Skills

1. In what year did Namibia win independence?
2. Liberia, founded in 1847, was never a colony. What other country in Africa was not colonized? How can you tell from this map?

Find NGS online map resources @ www.nationalgeographic.com/maps

After Angola gained its independence, civil war broke out among different political and ethnic groups. The fighting has lasted more than 25 years and has brought great suffering to the people. Peace agreements have failed to take hold, and the struggle continues.

✓Reading Check **Why is Angola's economy weak, even though it has rich resources?**

Namibia

South of Angola lies Namibia, one of Africa's newest countries. Namibia became independent in 1990 after 75 years of rule by the Republic of South Africa. Before that it was a colony of Germany.

Namibia has a land area about half the size of Alaska. A large plateau runs through the center of the country. This area of patchy grassland is the most populous section of Namibia. The rest is made up of deserts. The Namib Desert runs almost the entire length of Namibia's Atlantic coast. It is a narrow ribbon of towering dunes and rocks. Tourists come from all over the world to "sand-board" down these dunes. Another desert—the **Kalahari Desert**—stretches across the southeastern part of the country. It mainly consists of sand and scrub. As you might guess, most of Namibia has a hot, dry climate.

Namibia's Economy Namibia has rich deposits of diamonds, copper, gold, zinc, silver, and lead. It is the world's fifth-largest producer of uranium, a substance used for making nuclear fuels. The country's economy depends on the mining, processing, and exporting of these minerals. Many people work in Namibia's mines.

Despite this mineral wealth, most of Namibia's people live in poverty. The income from mineral exports stays in the hands of a small group of people. Large amounts also go to the foreign companies that have invested in Namibia's mineral resources. As a result, half of Namibia's people depend on subsistence farming. They also herd cattle, sheep, and goats. Some work in food industries, packing meat and processing fish and dairy products.

Namibia's People Only 1.6 million people live in Namibia. It is one of the most sparsely populated countries in Africa. In fact, in the language of Namibia's Nama ethnic group, *namib* means "the land without people." Most Namibians belong to African ethnic groups. A small number are of European ancestry. Namibians speak African languages, while most of the white population speaks Afrikaans and English.

Reading Check When did Namibia become an independent country?

Assessment

Defining Terms

1. **Define** exclave.

Recalling Facts

2. **Location** Where is the Namib Desert located?
3. **Economics** What is Angola's main source of income?
4. **Place** What two deserts can be found in Namibia?

Critical Thinking

5. **Synthesizing Information** Reread "Exploring Our World" on page 614. Describe another example of animals adapting to a harsh environment.
6. **Understanding Cause and Effect** Why is Namibia one of the most sparsely populated countries in Africa?

Graphic Organizer

7. **Organizing Information** On a chart like the one below, list examples of Namibia's economy in the three categories.

Namibia's Economy		
Resources	Agriculture	Industries

Applying Geography Skills

8. **Analyzing Maps** Study the map of African independence dates on page 616. Which southern African country first achieved independence?

Section 3

Inland Southern Africa

Guide to Reading

Main Idea

Most of inland southern Africa is rich in resources and home to a wide variety of ethnic groups.

Terms to Know

- copper belt
- sorghum

Places to Locate

- Zambia
- Malawi
- Zimbabwe
- Botswana
- Zambezi River
- Victoria Falls
- Lake Malawi
- Harare
- Kalahari Desert
- Okavango River
- Gaborone

Reading Strategy

Create a chart like this one. Then list the main economic activities of each country.

Country	Economic Activities
Zambia	
Malawi	
Zimbabwe	
Botswana	

Hundreds of years ago, southern Africa had powerful, wealthy kingdoms. They traded gold to cities on the eastern coast. The largest kingdom and city was Great Zimbabwe, a Bantu word meaning "stone houses." The city, part of which is shown here, flourished from about A.D. 1100 to 1450. It covered nearly 100 acres (40 ha) and, along with the surrounding valley, was home to nearly 20,000 people.

The four countries of inland southern Africa include **Zambia, Malawi** (mah•LAH•wee), **Zimbabwe,** and **Botswana** (baht•SWAH•nah). They have several things in common. First, they all are landlocked. A high plateau dominates much of their landscape and gives them a mild climate. In addition, about 70 percent of the people practice subsistence farming in rural villages. Thousands move to cities each year to look for work.

Zambia

Zambia is slightly larger than Texas. The **Zambezi** (zam•BEE•zee) **River**—one of southern Africa's longest rivers—crosses the country. The Kariba Dam—one of Africa's largest hydroelectric projects—spans the Zambezi River. Also along the Zambezi River are the spectacular **Victoria Falls,** named in honor of British Queen Victoria, who ruled in the 1800s. The falls are known locally as *Mosi oa Tunya*—or "smoke that thunders."

A large area of copper mines, known as a **copper belt,** stretches across northern Zambia. One of the world's major producers of copper, Zambia relies on it for more than 80 percent of its income. As a result, when world copper prices go down, Zambia's income goes down too. As copper reserves dwindle, the government has encouraged city dwellers to return to farming. Zambia must import much of its food.

Once a British colony, Zambia gained its independence in 1964. The country's 9.7 million people belong to more than 70 ethnic groups and speak many languages. English is the official language. Those who live in urban areas such as Lusaka, the capital, work in mining and service industries. Villagers grow corn, rice, and other crops to support their families. Their main food is porridge made from corn.

✓Reading Check **What happens to Zambia when copper prices go down?**

Malawi

If you travel through narrow Malawi, you see green plains and savanna grasslands in western areas. Vast herds of elephants, zebras, and antelope roam national parks and animal reserves here.

The Great Rift Valley runs through eastern Malawi. In the middle of it lies beautiful **Lake Malawi.** This lake holds about 500 fish species, more than any other inland body of water in the world. Malawi is also famous for its more than 400 orchid species.

Malawi has few mineral resources and little industry. Tobacco, tea, sugar, coffee, and peanuts are exported. Small farmers also grow **sorghum,** a tall grass whose seeds are used as grain and to make syrup. Donations from international organizations support Malawi's people.

Bantu-speaking people arrived in the area about 2,000 years ago, bringing with them knowledge of iron working. The most famous European explorer to reach Malawi was the Scottish missionary David Livingstone during the mid-1800s. Today most people in Malawi are Protestant Christians as a result of missionaries.

In 1964 the British colony became independent. Malawi has recently returned to democratic government after a long period of rule by a dictator. After years of harsh government, the works of many modern writers emphasize themes such as human rights and abuse of power.

Malawi is one of the most densely populated countries in Africa. It has 219 people per square mile (84 people per sq. km). Jobs are scarce, so thousands of men seek work in South Africa and Zambia.

✓Reading Check **What types of landforms cover western Malawi?**

Zimbabwe

Crossing Zimbabwe, you might think you were in the western United States. The vast plateau is studded with large outcrops of rock. The Limpopo River winds through southern lowlands. The Zambezi River crosses the north.

Mining gold, copper, iron ore, and asbestos provides most of the country's income. Some large plantations grow coffee, cotton, and tobacco. Europeans own many of the large plantations, while many

What's for Dinner?

Kabemba Mwape hurries home from the market in Chavuma, Zambia. He carries a live pig on the back of his bike. Although Kabemba's family will enjoy the pig for dinner, they usually eat porridge. Kabemba's family is relatively wealthy. They can afford to pay for meat, bicycles, and the high price of school uniforms and books for Kabemba's education. He knows English, but he speaks his native language of Lozi while at the market.

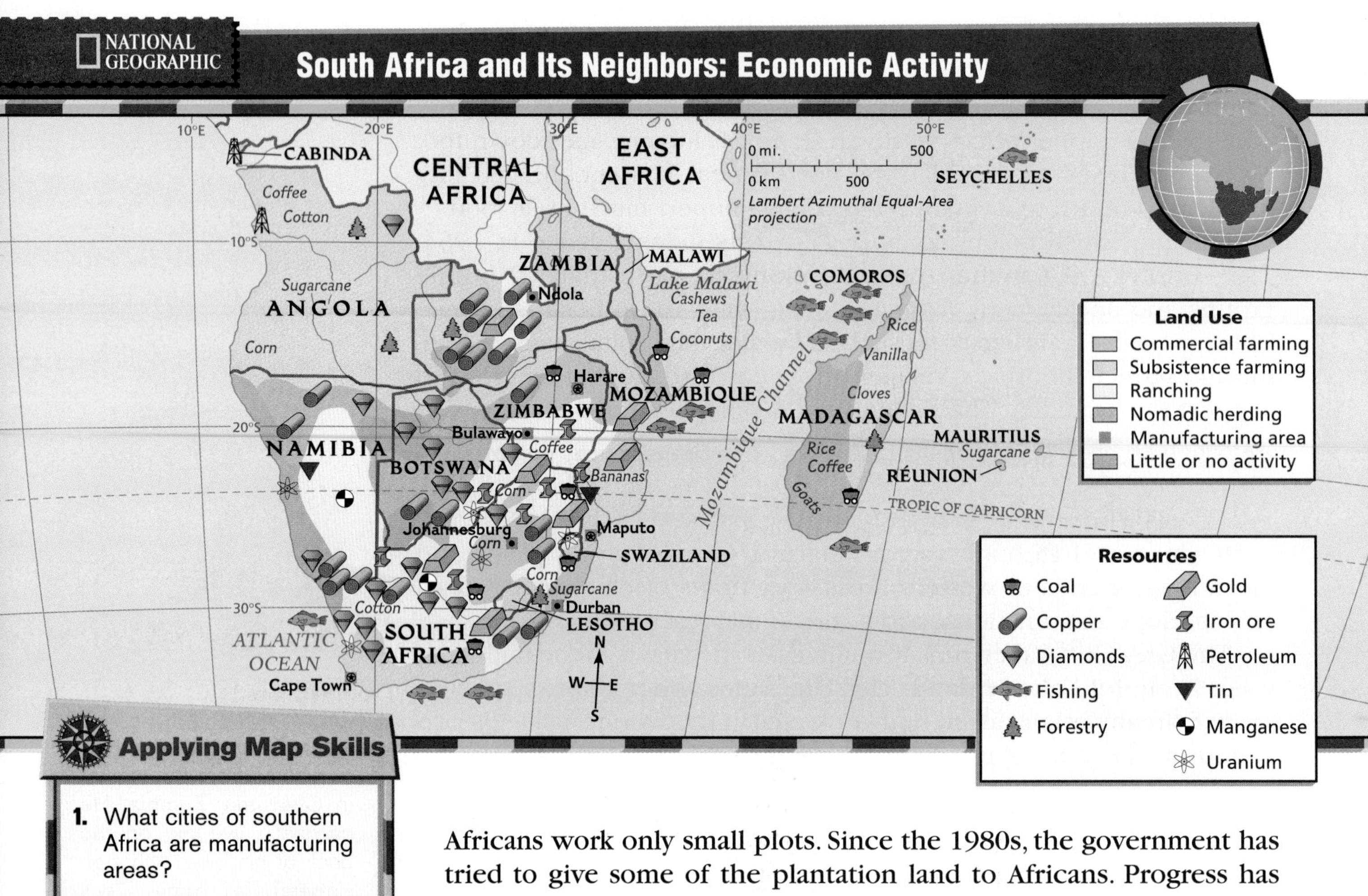

Applying Map Skills

1. What cities of southern Africa are manufacturing areas?
2. What resources are mined in southern Africa?

Find NGS online map resources @ www.nationalgeographic.com/maps

Africans work only small plots. Since the 1980s, the government has tried to give some of the plantation land to Africans. Progress has been slow, and protesters recently took over some European-owned farms to force changes.

Another serious challenge to Zimbabwe's economy comes from the spread of AIDS. People who have the disease often cannot work to support their families. Many children have been orphaned by AIDS. Also, the nation's health care costs have risen sharply.

Zimbabwe takes its name from an ancient African city and trading center—Great Zimbabwe. This remarkable stone fortress was built by an ethnic group called the Shona in the A.D. 1100s to 1400s. The Shona and the Ndebele (ehn•duh•BEH•leh) ruled large stretches of south-central Africa until the late 1800s. In the 1890s, the British controlled the area and called it Rhodesia. They named it after Cecil Rhodes, a British businessman who expanded British rule in Africa.

Europeans ran Rhodesia and owned all the best farmland. In response, the Africans organized into political groups and fought European rule. In 1980 free elections brought an independent African government to power. The country was renamed Zimbabwe.

Today Zimbabwe has about 11.2 million people. Most of them belong to the Shona and Ndebele ethnic groups. About half of the population is Christian. The other half practices traditional African religions. The largest city is **Harare** (hah•RAH•ray), the capital.

✓Reading Check **How has AIDS affected Zimbabwe's economy?**

Botswana

Botswana lies in the center of southern Africa. The map on page 609 shows you that the vast **Kalahari Desert** spreads over southwestern Botswana. This hot, dry area has rolling red sands and low thorny shrubs. The **Okavango River** in the northwest forms one of the largest swamp areas in the world. This area of shifting streams has much wildlife.

Botswana's national emblem has a one-word motto, *Pula,* meaning "rain." The people of Botswana all agree that there is never much of it. From May to October, the sun bakes the land. Droughts strike often, and many years can pass before the rains fall again.

Botswana is rich in mineral resources, especially diamonds and copper. Diamonds account for more than 75 percent of Botswana's export income. Thousands of tourists visit Botswana's game preserves every year. Farming is difficult, and the country grows only about 50 percent of its food needs. It must import the rest. To earn a living, many people work in South Africa for several months a year.

During most of the 1800s, the Tswana ethnic group ruled most of what is today Botswana. Afrikaners from South Africa tried to seize the territory. The Tswana appealed for help to the British, who then took over the land for themselves. After nearly 80 years of British rule, Botswana became independent in 1966. Today it has one of Africa's strongest democracies. Most of Botswana's people are Christians, although a large number practice traditional African religions. The official language is English, but 90 percent of the population speaks an African language called Setswana. **Gaborone** is the capital and largest city.

✓Reading Check **What is Botswana's biggest source of export income?**

Section 3 Assessment

Defining Terms

1. Define copper belt, sorghum.

Recalling Facts

2. Economics What is Zambia's most important export?
3. Place What makes Lake Malawi unique?
4. Culture Where did Zimbabwe get its name?

Graphic Organizer

5. Organizing Information Choose two of the countries in this section. Put the name and facts about each country in the outer ovals. Where the ovals overlap, put facts that are true of both countries.

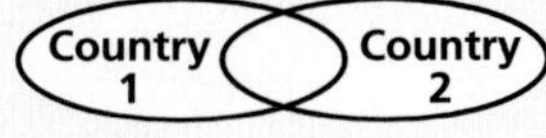

Critical Thinking

6. Synthesizing Information Imagine that someone from Great Zimbabwe traveled to that country today. What do you think he or she would describe as the greatest difference between then and now?
7. Analyzing Information Why do you think the people of Botswana chose *Pula,* or "rain," as their motto?

Applying Geography Skills

8. Analyzing Maps Study the political map on page 608. What five African nations does the Tropic of Capricorn cross?

Technology Skill

Developing Multimedia Presentations

Your geography homework is to make a presentation about Botswana. You want to make your presentation informative but also interesting and fun. How can you do this? One way is to combine several types of media into a **multimedia presentation.**

Learning the Skill

A multimedia presentation involves using several types of media, including photographs, videos, or sound recordings. The equipment can range from simple cassette players to overhead projectors to VCRs to computers and beyond. In your presentation on Botswana, for example, you might show photographs of cheetahs in the Okavango River delta or women fishing. You could also play a recording of local music or find a video of people working in diamond mines. If you have the proper equipment, you can then combine all these items on a computer.

Computer multimedia programs allow you to combine text, video, audio, art or graphics, and animation. The tools you need include computer graphic and drawing programs, animation programs that make certain images move, and systems that tie everything together. Your computer manual will tell you which tools your computer can support.

Practicing the Skill

Use the following questions as a guide when planning your presentation:

1. Which forms of media do I want to include? Video? Sound? Animation? Photographs? Graphics?
2. Which of the media forms does my computer support?
3. Which kinds of media equipment are available at my school or local library?
4. What types of media can I create to enhance my presentation?

Applying the Skill

Plan and create a multimedia presentation on a country discussed in this unit. List three ideas you would like to cover. Use as many multimedia materials as possible and share your presentation with the class.

▼ **Various equipment is needed to make multimedia presentations. For example, photographs and videos of cheetahs will make your report on Botswana more interesting.**

Section 4

Indian Ocean Countries

Guide to Reading

Main Idea

Africa's Indian Ocean countries are mostly farming nations that are struggling to develop more varied economies.

Terms to Know

- cyclone
- slash-and-burn farming
- deforestation

Places to Locate

- Mozambique
- Madagascar
- Comoros
- Seychelles
- Mauritius
- Zambezi River
- Maputo
- Victoria

Reading Strategy

Create a chart like the one below. Then fill in two key facts about each of the Indian Ocean countries.

Country	Fact #1	Fact #2
Mozambique		
Madagascar		
Comoros		
Seychelles		
Mauritius		

NATIONAL GEOGRAPHIC **Exploring Our World**

The island country of Madagascar has wildlife that appears nowhere else on the earth. Lemurs, chameleons, baobabs, geckos, and octopus trees are just a few animals and plants that exist on the island. Ring-tailed lemurs like this one spend their lives in the trees and on the ground, eating fruits, leaves, and seeds.

Mozambique in southern Africa borders the Indian Ocean. Four island countries—**Madagascar** (MA•duh•GAS•kuhr), **Comoros** (KAH•muh•ROHZ), **Seychelles** (say•SHEHL), and **Mauritius** (maw•RIH•shuhs)—also form part of southern Africa's Indian Ocean region.

Mozambique

Sand dunes, swamps, and fine natural harbors line Mozambique's long Indian Ocean coastline. In the center of this Y-shaped country stretches a flat plain covered with grasses and tropical forests. High plateaus and mountains lie along the northwestern border with Malawi. The **Zambezi River** splits Mozambique in two. The Cabora Bassa Dam on this river provides irrigation and electric power.

Most of Mozambique has a tropical savanna climate with wet and dry seasons. Mozambique also experiences deadly cyclones. A **cyclone** is an intense storm system with heavy rain and high winds.

Maputo, Mozambique

A high-rise building is being constructed in Maputo. Hotels and industrial projects are helping the city's economy to grow.

Place What slowed industrial growth in Maputo in the 1980s and 1990s?

Most people in Mozambique are farmers. Some practice **slash-and-burn farming**—a method of clearing land for planting by cutting and burning forest. One result of slash-and-burn farming is **deforestation**, or cutting down of forests. Deforestation can, in turn, lead to flooding during the rainy season. Such floods drove millions of people from their homes in early 2000.

Mozambique's major crops are cashews, cotton, sugarcane, tea, coconuts, and tropical fruits. Fishing provides an income for people who live along the coast. The main source of income, however, comes from its seaports. South Africa, Zimbabwe, Swaziland, and Malawi all pay to use the docks at **Maputo,** the capital, and other ports.

During the 1980s and early 1990s, a fierce civil war slowed industrial growth. In recent years, however, foreign companies have begun to invest in metal production, natural gas, fishing, and transportation services.

About 19.1 million people live here. Nearly all belong to 16 major African ethnic groups. Portuguese is Mozambique's official language, but most people speak African languages. About half of the people practice traditional African religions. Most of the rest are Muslim or Christian.

Reading Check **What is a negative result of slash-and-burn farming?**

Madagascar

Madagascar is the world's fourth-largest island. Madagascar broke away from the African mainland about 160 million years ago. The island's location kept it isolated from other parts of the world. As a result, it has many plants and animals that are not found elsewhere.

If you like vanilla ice cream, thank Madagascar. It produces most of the world's vanilla beans. The main cash crop is coffee, grown on the humid eastern plains. Rice is grown on the central plateau. About 80 percent of the island has been slashed and burned by people who must farm and herd to survive. Rainfall erodes the red clay soil. The government has taken steps to save what forests are left. It has increased the amount of forested land under its protection.

Only about 22 percent of the people are city dwellers. Antananarivo (AHN•tah•NAH•nah•REE•voh), the capital, lies in the central plateau. Called "Tana" for short, this city is known for it colorful street markets, where craftspeople sell a variety of products.

Music revolves around dance rhythms that reflect Madagascar's Southeast Asian and African heritage. The people are known for their rhythmic style of singing accompanied only by hand clapping. Most of the songs have themes about love, poverty, and hope for the future.

Reading Check **What percentage of Madagascar's people live in cities?**

Small Island Countries

Far from Africa in the Indian Ocean are three other island republics—Comoros, Seychelles, and Mauritius. The people of these countries have many different backgrounds.

Comoros Volcanoes formed the Comoros thousands of years ago. Dense tropical forests cover Comoros today. Most of the 600,000 people are farmers. The main crops are rice, vanilla, cloves, coconuts, and bananas. Even though agriculture employs 80 percent of the workforce, Comoros cannot grow enough food for its growing population. The government is trying to encourage industry, including tourism.

The people of Comoros are a mixture of Arabs, Africans, and people from Madagascar. They speak Arabic, French, and Comoran. Most practice Islam. Once ruled by France, the people of Comoros declared their independence in 1975. Since then, they have suffered from fighting among political groups for control of the government.

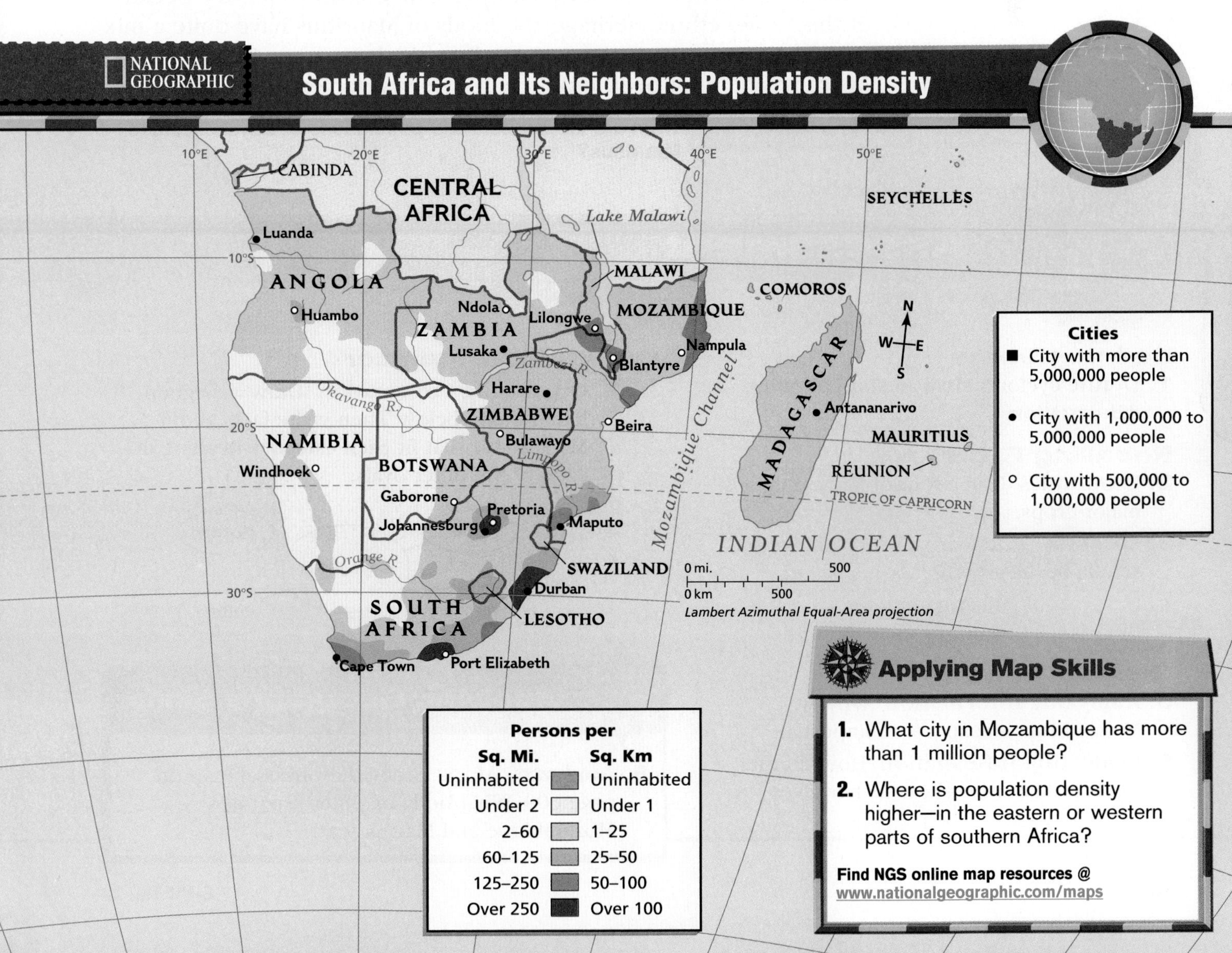

Seychelles About 90 islands form the country of Seychelles. About 40 of the islands are granite with high green peaks. The rest are small, flat coral islands with few people. Nearly 90 percent of the country's 100,000 people live on Mahé, the largest island. Here you will also find the capital, **Victoria.**

Seychelles was not inhabited until the 1700s. Under French and then British rule, it finally became independent in 1976. Most of the country's people are of mixed African, European, and Asian descent. They grow coconuts and cinnamon, the chief cash crops, on the larger islands. Fishing and tourism are important industries as well.

Mauritius Like Comoros, the islands of Mauritius were formed by volcanoes. Bare, black peaks rise sharply above green fields, and palm-dotted white beaches line the coasts. Mauritius has few natural resources, but it has succeeded in building a varied economy. Sugar is its main agricultural export. Major industries are located in Port Louis, the capital. Clothing and textiles account for about half of Mauritius's export earnings. Tourism is an important industry, too.

Mauritius has about 1.2 million people who come from many different backgrounds. About 70 percent are descendants of settlers from India. The rest are of African, European, or Chinese ancestry. Because of this varied ethnic heritage, the foods of Mauritius have quite a mix of ingredients. You can sample Indian chicken curry, Chinese pork, African-made roast beef, and French-style vegetables.

Reading Check **What are the capitals and populations of Seychelles and Mauritius?**

Assessment

Defining Terms

1. **Define** cyclone, slash-and-burn farming, deforestation.

Recalling Facts

2. **Economics** Name four of Mozambique's major crops.
3. **Location** Where are most of the world's vanilla beans grown?
4. **Movement** What natural force created the islands of Comoros and Mauritius?

Critical Thinking

5. **Analyzing Information** Why are Mozambique's seaports so important?
6. **Evaluating Information** How do the foods of Mauritius show its heritage?

Graphic Organizer

7. **Organizing Information** Draw a diagram like the one below. Then write facts about Madagascar that fit each category heading in each of the outer ovals.

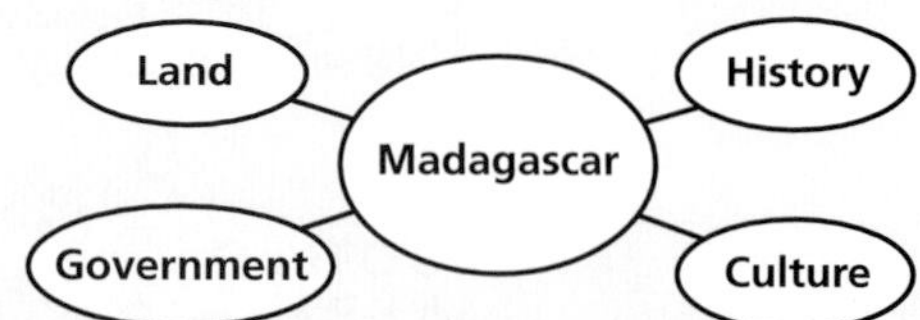

Applying Geography Skills

8. **Analyzing Maps** Study the physical map on page 609. What body of water separates Mozambique and Madagascar?

Chapter 22

Reading Review

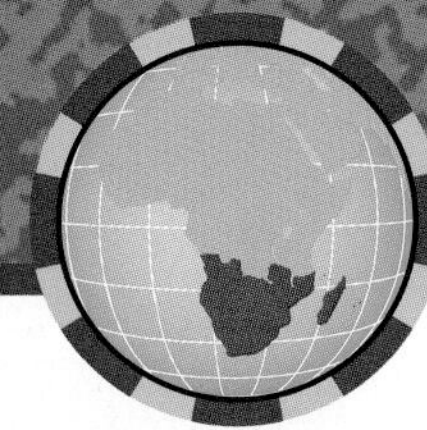

Section 1 Republic of South Africa

Terms to Know
- high veld
- escarpment
- developed country
- Boer
- apartheid
- township
- enclave

Main Idea

Rich in resources, South Africa has recently seen major social and political changes.

✓ Economics Because of its abundant mineral resources, South Africa has the most developed economy in Africa.

✓ Government South Africa held its first democratic election in which people from all ethnic groups could vote in 1994.

✓ Culture South Africa is working to improve the lives of its poorer citizens.

Section 2 Atlantic Countries

Terms to Know
- exclave

Main Idea

Angola and Namibia, although rich in resources, are struggling to develop their economies.

✓ Economics Angola's main source of income is oil.

✓ Culture Few Namibians benefit from the country's rich mineral wealth. The majority live in poverty.

Section 3 Inland Southern Africa

Terms to Know
- copper belt
- sorghum

Main Idea

Most of inland southern Africa is rich in resources and home to a wide variety of ethnic groups.

✓ Economics Zambia is one of the world's largest producers of copper.

✓ Place Zimbabwe has many mineral resources and good farmland.

✓ Economics Mining and tourism earn money for Botswana, but most of its people are farmers.

Section 4 Indian Ocean Countries

Terms to Know
- cyclone
- slash-and-burn farming
- deforestation

Main Idea

Africa's Indian Ocean countries are mostly farming nations that are struggling to develop more varied economies.

✓ Human/Environment Interaction Slash-and-burn farming in Mozambique has led to deforestation and flooding. Neighboring countries pay fees for the use of its ports.

✓ Location Madagascar's island location has resulted in many plants and animals found nowhere else in the world.

✓ Economics Comoros continues to be a mainly agricultural economy, but Mauritius has succeeded in developing a variety of industries.

✓ Place Seychelles's beaches and tropical climate draw many tourists.

Chapter 22
Assessment and Activities

Using Key Terms

Match the terms in Part A with their definitions in Part B.

A.

1. escarpment
2. cyclone
3. exclave
4. slash-and-burn farming
5. township
6. apartheid
7. Boer
8. deforestation
9. sorghum
10. enclave

B.

a. separating racial and ethnic groups
b. storm with high circular winds
c. widespread cutting of trees
d. small nation located inside a larger country
e. steep cliff separating two fairly flat surfaces
f. small part of a nation separated from the main part of the country
g. areas of forest are cleared by burning
h. tall grass used as grain and to make syrup
i. settlements outside cities in South Africa
j. Dutch farmer

Reviewing Main Ideas

Section 1 Republic of South Africa

11. **Location** What is the southernmost point of Africa?
12. **History** When was South Africa's first election allowing all people to vote?
13. **Economics** What is Lesotho's only important natural resource?

Section 2 Atlantic Countries

14. **Region** What desert extends along the Atlantic coast of Angola and Namibia?
15. **History** What European country colonized Angola?
16. **Culture** What does *namib* mean?

Section 3 Inland Southern Africa

17. **Place** What river crosses Zambia?
18. **Economics** Where is the copper belt?
19. **History** What was Great Zimbabwe?

Section 4 Indian Ocean Countries

20. **Economics** What industries does Mozambique hope will help its economy?
21. **Place** What is the capital of Mozambique?
22. **Economics** What is Madagascar's main cash crop?

South Africa and Its Neighbors

Place Location Activity

On a separate sheet of paper, match the letters on the map with the numbered places listed below.

1. Madagascar
2. Lake Malawi
3. Zambezi River
4. Kalahari Desert
5. Angola
6. Zimbabwe
7. Pretoria
8. Mozambique
9. South Africa
10. Namibia

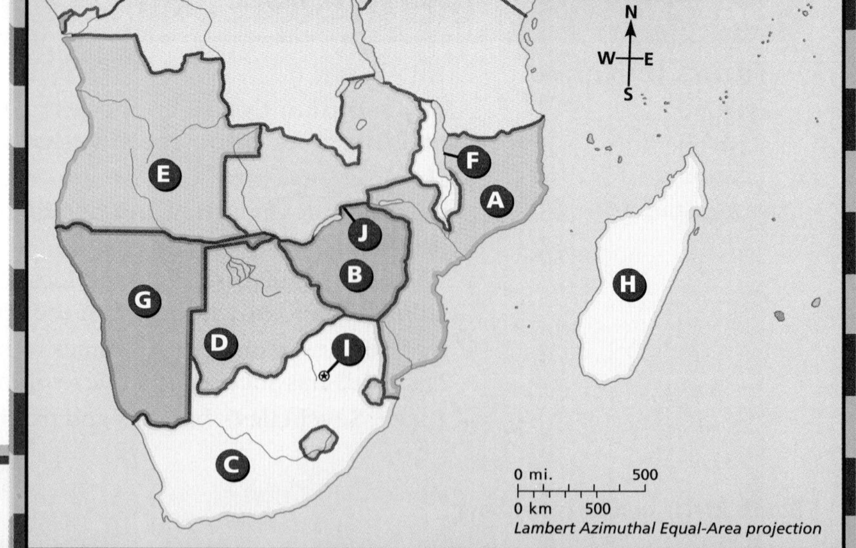

Self-Check Quiz Visit the ***Geography: The World and Its People*** Web site at gwip.glencoe.com and click on **Chapter 22—Self-Check Quizzes** to prepare for the Chapter Test.

 Critical Thinking

23. **Supporting Generalizations** What facts support the statement "South Africa has the most developed economy in Africa"?
24. **Evaluating Information** Many countries of southern Africa are hoping to build and improve their industries. On a chart like the one below, list the positive and negative aspects of industrialization under the correct headings.

Industrialization	
Positives	Negatives

 GeoJournal Activity 

25. **Writing a Myth** Throughout history, different cultures have created myths or stories to explain events in nature, such as thunder and lightning or an eclipse. Write a story that might explain some aspect of African life. Story ideas include how deserts formed, why a zebra has stripes, or why a waterfall has "smoke that thunders."

 Mental Mapping Activity

26. **Focusing on the Region** Draw a simple outline map of Africa, then label the following:
    - Atlantic Ocean
    - Madagascar
    - South Africa
    - Namib Desert
    - Indian Ocean
    - Pretoria
    - Angola
    - Cape Town
    - Mozambique
    - Kalahari Desert

 Technology Skills Activity 

27. **Using the Internet** The Zulu are a well-known ethnic group in Africa. Research this group on the Internet. Write a speech answering these questions: Who are the Zulu? How have they affected the history of southern Africa? Where do they live today?

Standardized Test Practice

Directions: Study the graph below, then answer the question that follows.

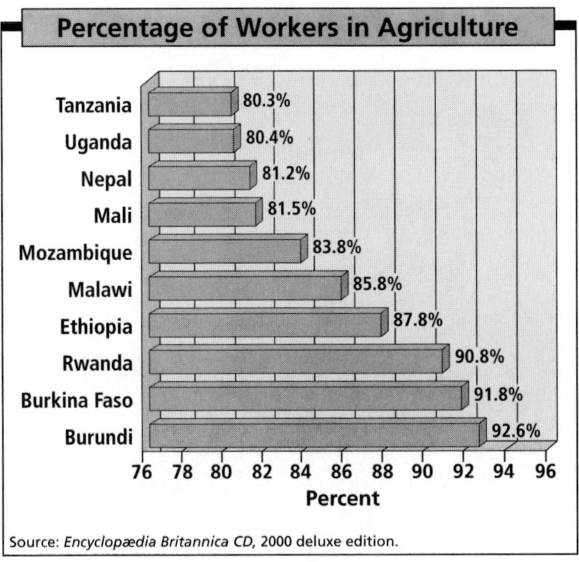

1. What percentage of Malawi's people do NOT work in agriculture?

F 14.2%
G 85.8%
H 81.5%
J 19.7%

Test-Taking Tip: Check your answer by asking yourself, "Did I read the question carefully?" The question is referring to Malawi, so double-check Malawi's percentage of agricultural workers on the graph. Then take another look at the question. Overlooking the word NOT in a question is a common error. If you know the percentage of agricultural workers, how do you find those NOT involved in agriculture?

Unit 8

Taj Mahal, Agra, India

Macaques in a hot spring, Japan

Asia

For many people in the Western Hemisphere, the region of Asia—in the Eastern Hemisphere—brings to mind exotic images. Ancient temples stand in dense rain forests. Farmers work in flooded rice fields. Pandas nibble bamboo shoots. Yet bustling cities, gleaming skyscrapers, and high-technology industries also can be found here. Turn the page to learn more about this region and its 3 billion people.

Monks wrapping statue of Buddha in yellow cloth, Thailand

NGS ONLINE
www.nationalgeographic.com/education

Focus on:

Asia

THE REGION OF ASIA is made up of surprisingly diverse landscapes. It includes a large chunk of the Asian continent, together with island groups that fringe its southern and eastern shores. Some of the world's oldest civilizations and religions had their beginnings in Asia. Now more than 3 billion people call this region home.

The Land

Covering roughly 7.8 million square miles (20.2 sq. km), the Asian region stretches from the mountains of western Pakistan to the eastern shores of Japan. It reaches from the highlands of northeastern China to the tropical islands of Indonesia. The region's long, winding coastlines are washed by two major oceans—the Indian and the Pacific—as well as many seas.

Several mountain ranges slice through central Asia. Most famous are the towering Himalaya, the site of Mt. Everest—the earth's tallest peak. North of the Himalaya lies the vast Plateau of Tibet, so high it has been called the Roof of the World. Beyond the plateau are two immense deserts: the Taklimakan and the Gobi.

Other mountain ranges cut across northeastern China, slant down the Korean Peninsula, and sweep through the peninsulas of Southeast Asia. Offshore, Japan, Indonesia, and other mountainous islands lie along the Ring of Fire. This is an area where adjoining plates of the earth's crust slip and buckle, setting off earthquakes and volcanic eruptions.

Great rivers begin in Asia's lofty center. On their journey to the sea, they flow through fertile plains in several countries. The most important rivers include the Indus in Pakistan, the Ganges and Brahmaputra in India and Bangladesh, the Yangtze and Yellow in China, and the Mekong in Southeast Asia.

The Climate

A person traveling across Asia would need clothes to suit almost every imaginable climate. The snowcapped mountains and high, windswept plateaus of northern and central Asia can be bitterly cold. The deserts can shimmer with heat by day, yet be frosty at night. Lowlands and coastal plains enjoy milder climates. The peninsulas of Southeast Asia and the islands straddling the Equator have mostly tropical climates. They are cloaked in dense rain forests. Seasonal winds called monsoons blow across much of Asia, bringing dry weather in winter and drenching rains in summer.

Unit 8

Terraced rice fields, Bali, Indonesia

Street flooded by monsoon rain, Tamil Nadu, India

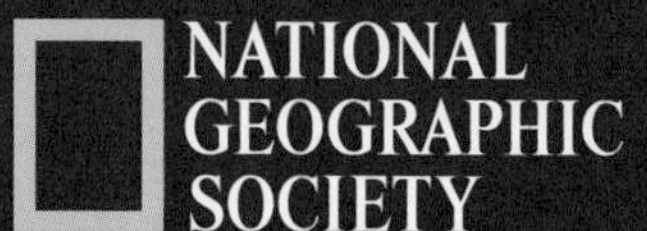

Regional Atlas

The Economy

Agriculture is the major economic activity across most of Asia. The region's rugged mountains and vast deserts mean that only a small amount of the land is suitable for growing crops, however. For example, only about 10 percent of China's land can be used for agriculture. To feed the region's huge population, Asian farmers must make the most of every possible bit of farmland. Terraces allow farmers to grow rice even on steep hillsides. Rice, which grows well in places with warm temperatures and plenty of water, is the most important food crop in Asia. China, India, Indonesia, and Bangladesh are the leading rice producers in the world.

Most of Asia's manufacturing takes place in Japan, South Korea, Taiwan, China, and India. China and India both are rich in coal, iron ore, and other natural resources. Japan, however, has few mineral resources and must import fuel and nearly all the raw materials it needs. Still, Japan has become one of the world's leading manufacturers of cars, electronic products, and other goods. In some of the region's other countries, such as Laos, Vietnam, and Bhutan, industry is less well developed.

The People

Nestled in fertile river valleys, some of the world's oldest civilizations arose in Asia thousands of years ago. Ancient religions took root here as well. Both Hinduism and Buddhism, for example, originated in India. Hindus remain concentrated in India, but over time Buddhism spread throughout the region. The region's most widespread faith—Islam—began in Southwest Asia.

Europeans arrived in the region around 1500, bringing Christianity to some of the people. By the early 1800s, many Asian countries had become European colonies. Most of these countries became independent in the mid-1900s. In many cases, however, independence was followed by political turmoil and conflict between Communist and non-Communist forces. Today China, Vietnam, and North Korea have Communist governments; Nepal is ruled by a monarch; and military leaders control Myanmar. Japan, India, and the Philippines are democracies.

About 3.3 billion people live in Asia, but this huge population is very unevenly distributed. Most people live near the coasts and in the fertile river valleys. As a result, some parts of Asia are among the most crowded places in the world.

Exploring the Region

1. **Why is the Plateau of Tibet called the Roof of the World?**
2. **How do monsoons affect the region?**
3. **What is the most important food crop in Asia?**
4. **What are two religions that originated in the region?**

◀ **Robot welding car bodies in a factory, Japan**

UNIT 8

Three generations of a Chinese family

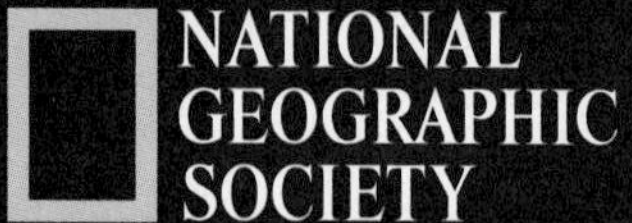

Asia

Physical

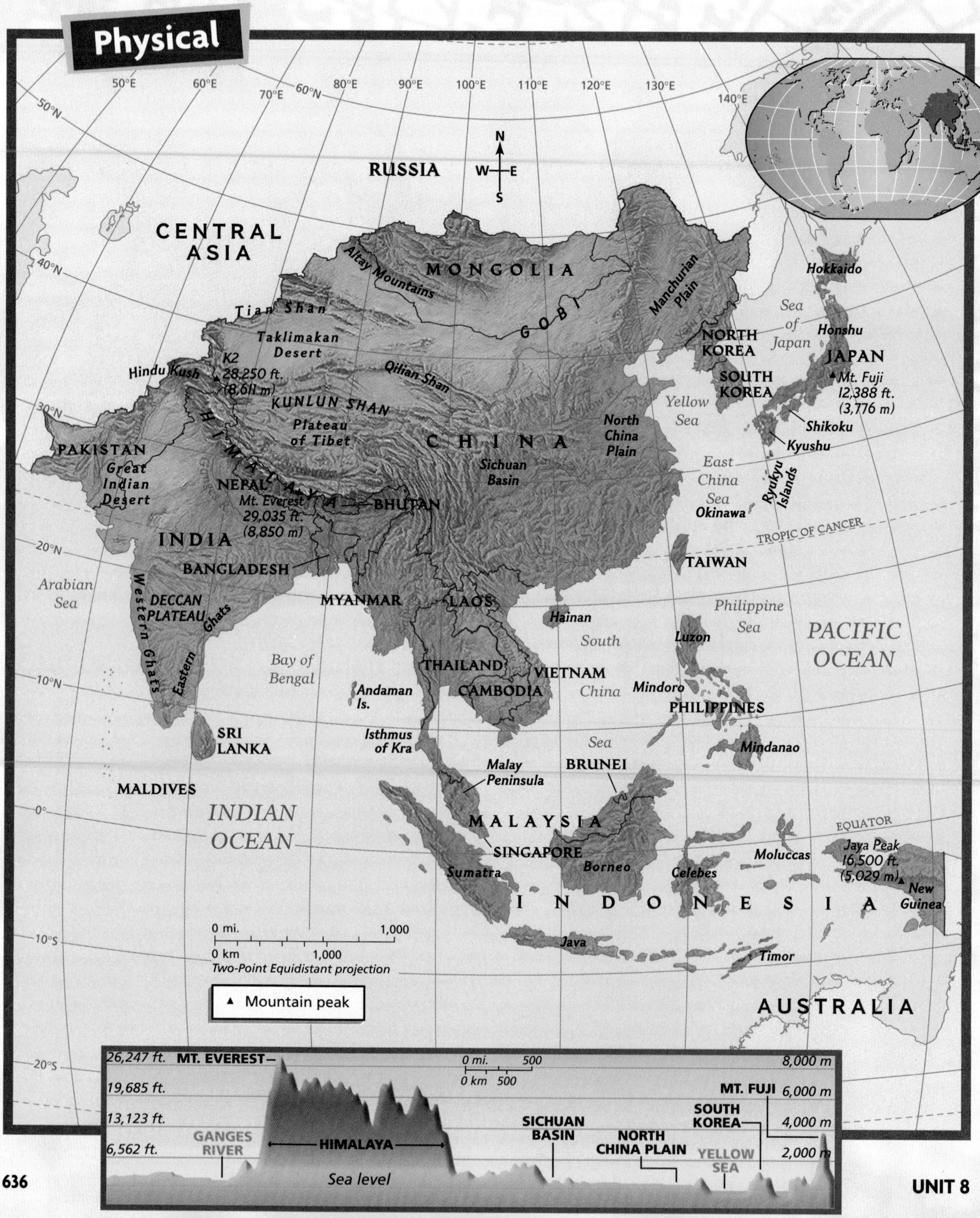

RUSSIA
CENTRAL ASIA
MONGOLIA
Altay Mountains
Tian Shan
Taklimakan Desert
GOBI
Manchurian Plain
Hokkaido
Sea of Japan
Honshu
NORTH KOREA
SOUTH KOREA
JAPAN
Mt. Fuji 12,388 ft. (3,776 m)
Hindu Kush
K2 28,250 ft. (8,611 m)
Qilian Shan
KUNLUN SHAN
Plateau of Tibet
HIMALAYA
CHINA
North China Plain
Yellow Sea
Shikoku
Kyushu
PAKISTAN
Great Indian Desert
NEPAL
Mt. Everest 29,035 ft. (8,850 m)
BHUTAN
Sichuan Basin
East China Sea
Okinawa
Ryukyu Islands
TROPIC OF CANCER
INDIA
BANGLADESH
TAIWAN
Arabian Sea
Western Ghats
DECCAN PLATEAU
Eastern Ghats
MYANMAR
LAOS
Hainan
Philippine Sea
PACIFIC OCEAN
Bay of Bengal
THAILAND
VIETNAM
CAMBODIA
South China Sea
Luzon
Mindoro
PHILIPPINES
Andaman Is.
Isthmus of Kra
SRI LANKA
Malay Peninsula
BRUNEI
Mindanao
MALDIVES
INDIAN OCEAN
MALAYSIA
SINGAPORE
EQUATOR
Sumatra
Borneo
Celebes
Moluccas
Jaya Peak 16,500 ft. (5,029 m)
New Guinea
INDONESIA
Java
Timor
AUSTRALIA

50°E 60°E 70°E 80°E 90°E 100°E 110°E 120°E 130°E 140°E
60°N 50°N 40°N 30°N 20°N 10°N 0° 10°S 20°S

0 mi. 1,000
0 km 1,000
Two-Point Equidistant projection

▲ Mountain peak

26,247 ft. MT. EVEREST
19,685 ft.
13,123 ft.
6,562 ft.
8,000 m
6,000 m
4,000 m
2,000 m
0 mi. 500
0 km 500
GANGES RIVER
HIMALAYA
Sea level
SICHUAN BASIN
NORTH CHINA PLAIN
YELLOW SEA
SOUTH KOREA
MT. FUJI

UNIT 8

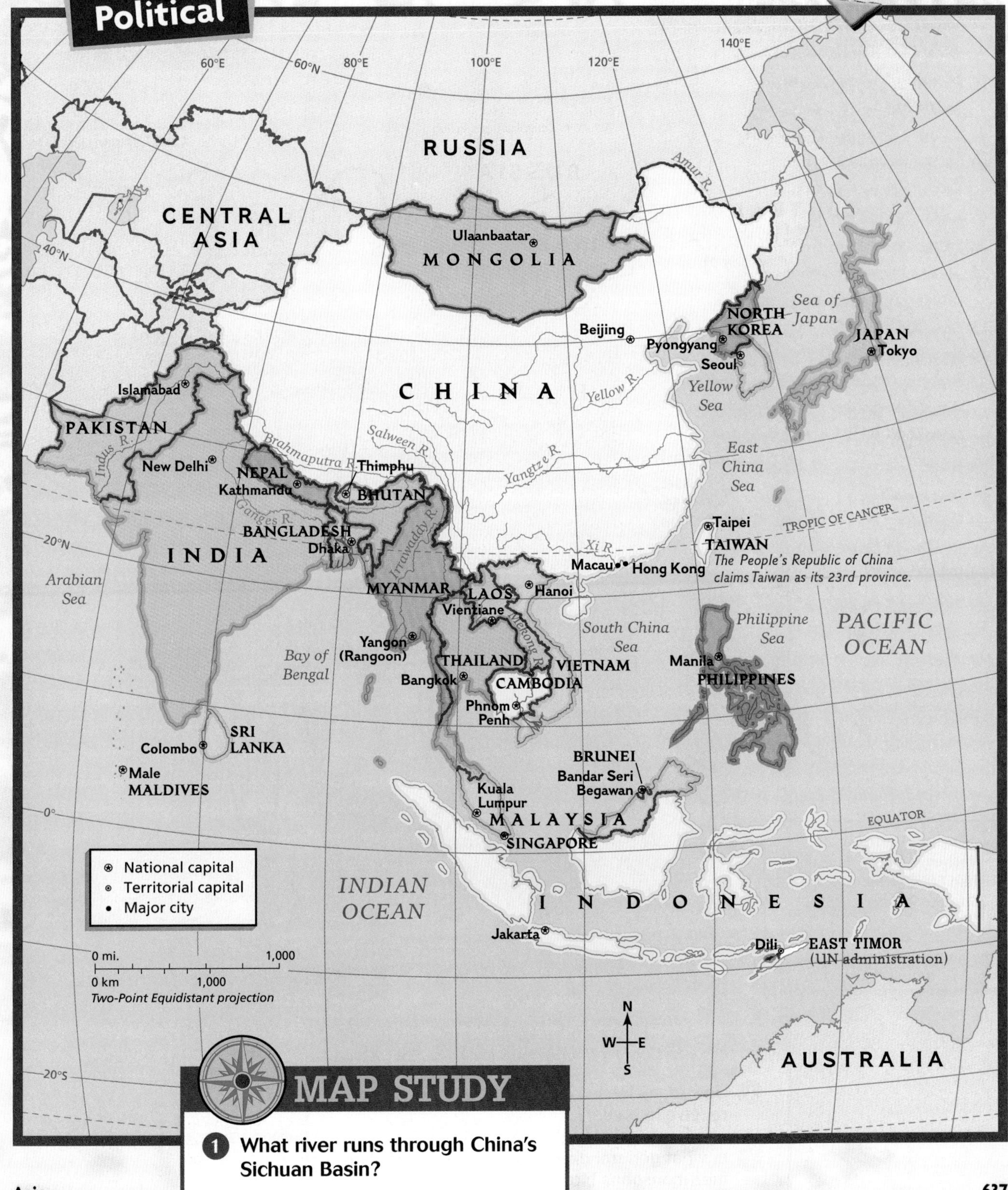

MAP STUDY

1. What river runs through China's Sichuan Basin?
2. What is the capital of Thailand?

Asia

Monsoons

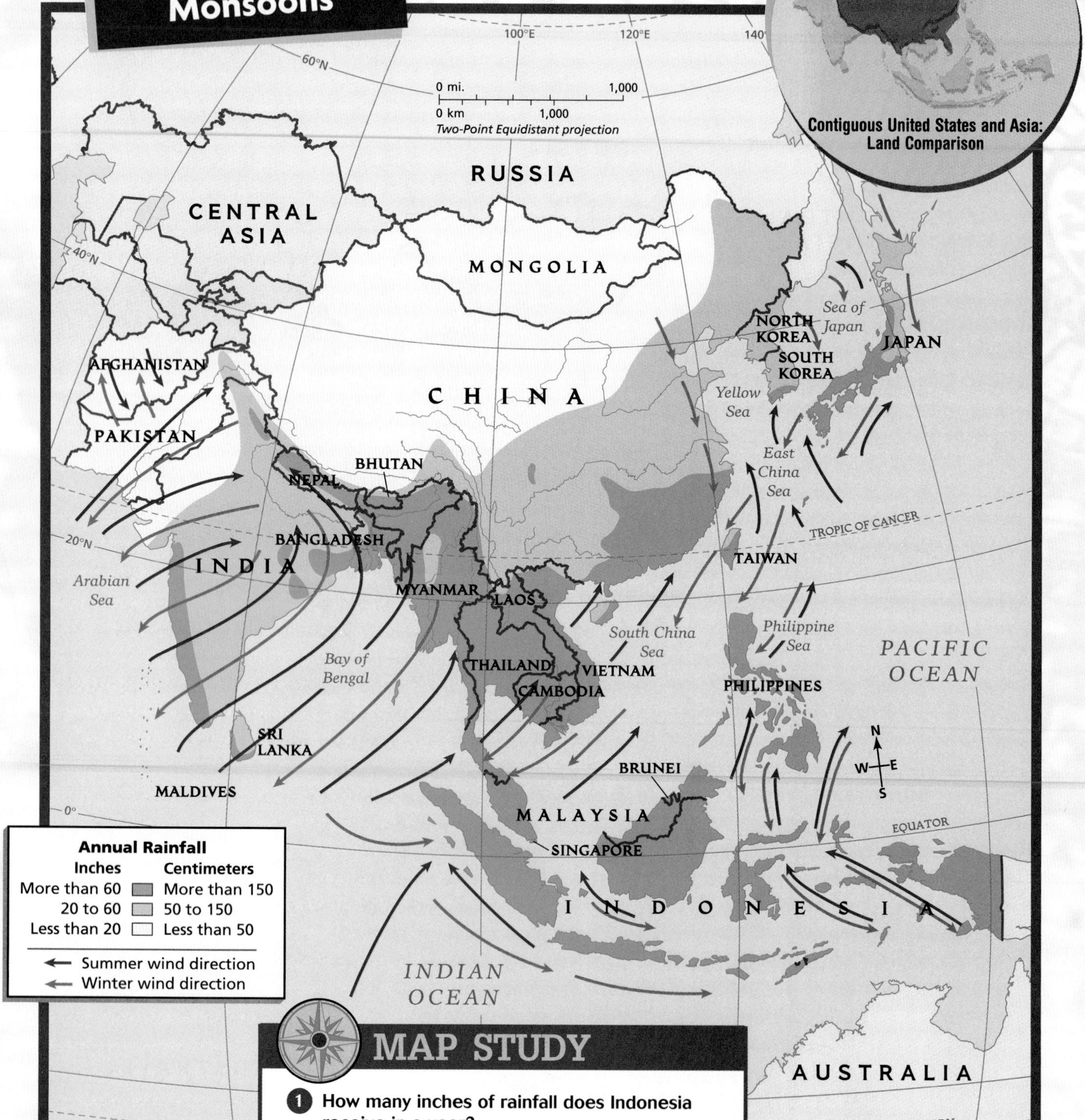

MAP STUDY

1. How many inches of rainfall does Indonesia receive in a year?
2. In what general direction do most of the summer monsoons blow?

Geo Extremes

① HIGHEST POINT
Mt. Everest
(Nepal and Tibet)
29,035 ft. (8,850 m) high

② LOWEST POINT
Turpan Depression (China)
505 ft. (154 m)
below sea level

③ LONGEST RIVER
Yangtze (China)
3,964 mi.
(6,380 km) long

④ LARGEST DESERT
Gobi (Mongolia and China)
500,000 sq. mi.
(1,295,000 sq. km)

⑤ HIGHEST WATERFALL
Mawsmai (India)
1,148 ft. (350 m) high

⑥ LARGEST ISLAND
New Guinea (Indonesia
and Papua New Guinea)
306,000 sq. mi.
(792,536 sq. km)

⑦ WETTEST PLACE
Mawsynram (India)
467 in. (1,186 cm)
average annual rainfall

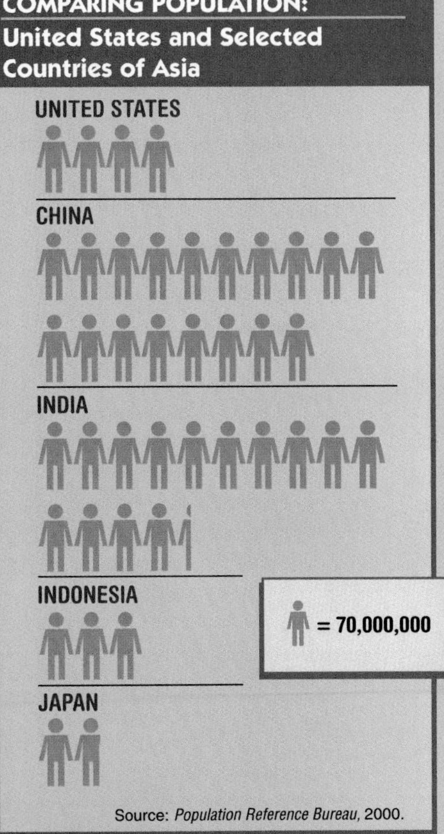

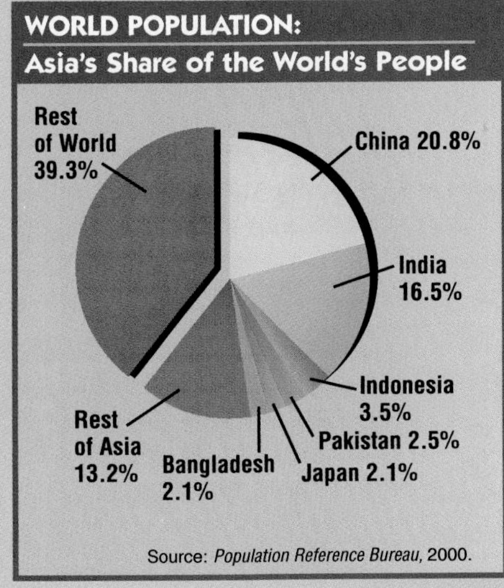

GRAPHIC STUDY

1. The highest point in Asia is also the highest point in the world. What is it?

2. What percentage of the world's population lives in Asia?

Country Profiles

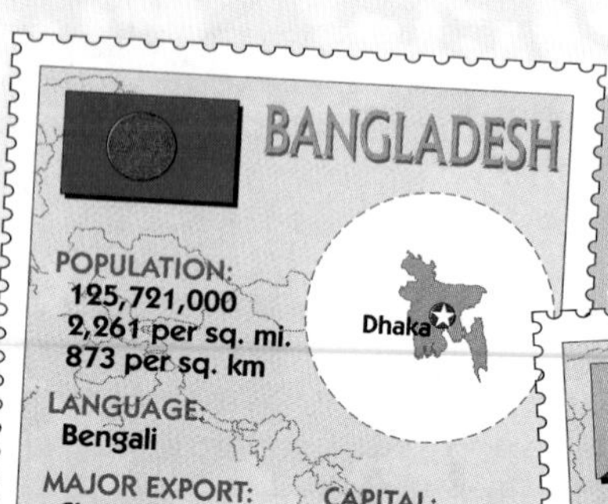

BANGLADESH

POPULATION: 125,721,000; 2,261 per sq. mi.; 873 per sq. km

LANGUAGE: Bengali

MAJOR EXPORT: Clothing

MAJOR IMPORT: Machinery

CAPITAL: Dhaka

LANDMASS: 55,598 sq. mi.; 143,998 sq. km

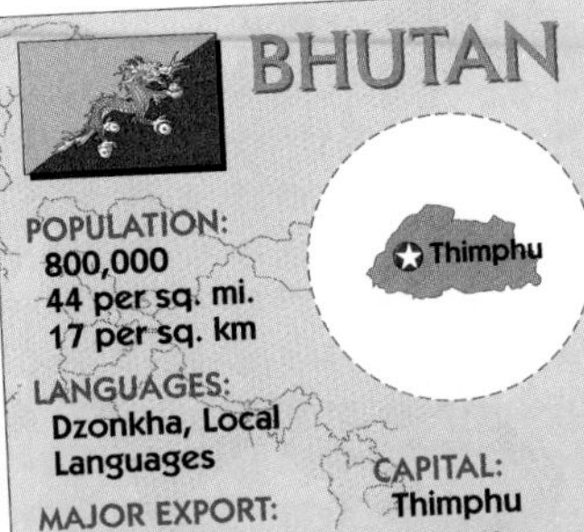

BHUTAN

POPULATION: 800,000; 44 per sq. mi.; 17 per sq. km

LANGUAGES: Dzonkha, Local Languages

MAJOR EXPORT: Cardamom

MAJOR IMPORT: Fuels

CAPITAL: Thimphu

LANDMASS: 18,147 sq. mi.; 47,001 sq. km

BRUNEI

POPULATION: 323,000; 145 per sq. mi.; 56 per sq. km

LANGUAGES: Malay, English, Chinese

MAJOR EXPORT: Crude Oil

MAJOR IMPORT: Machinery

CAPITAL: Bandar Seri Begawan

LANDMASS: 2,226 sq. mi.; 5,765 sq. km

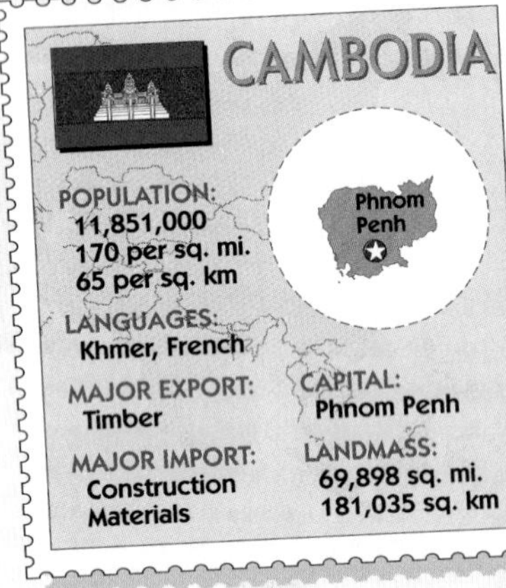

CAMBODIA

POPULATION: 11,851,000; 170 per sq. mi.; 65 per sq. km

LANGUAGES: Khmer, French

MAJOR EXPORT: Timber

MAJOR IMPORT: Construction Materials

CAPITAL: Phnom Penh

LANDMASS: 69,898 sq. mi.; 181,035 sq. km

CHINA

POPULATION: 1,254,062,000; 339 per sq. mi.; 131 per sq. km

LANGUAGE: Mandarin Chinese

MAJOR EXPORT: Machinery

MAJOR IMPORT: Machinery

CAPITAL: Beijing

LANDMASS: 3,705,820 sq. mi.; 9,598,032 sq. km

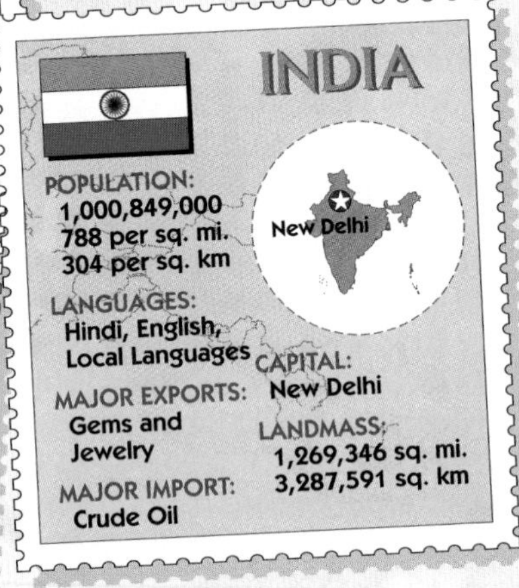

INDIA

POPULATION: 1,000,849,000; 788 per sq. mi.; 304 per sq. km

LANGUAGES: Hindi, English, Local Languages

MAJOR EXPORTS: Gems and Jewelry

MAJOR IMPORT: Crude Oil

CAPITAL: New Delhi

LANDMASS: 1,269,346 sq. mi.; 3,287,591 sq. km

INDONESIA

POPULATION: 211,806,000; 286 per sq. mi.; 110 per sq. km

LANGUAGES: Bahasa Indonesia, Local Languages

MAJOR EXPORT: Textiles

MAJOR IMPORT: Manufactured Goods

CAPITAL: Jakarta

LAND MASS: 741,101 sq. mi.; 1,919,443 sq. km

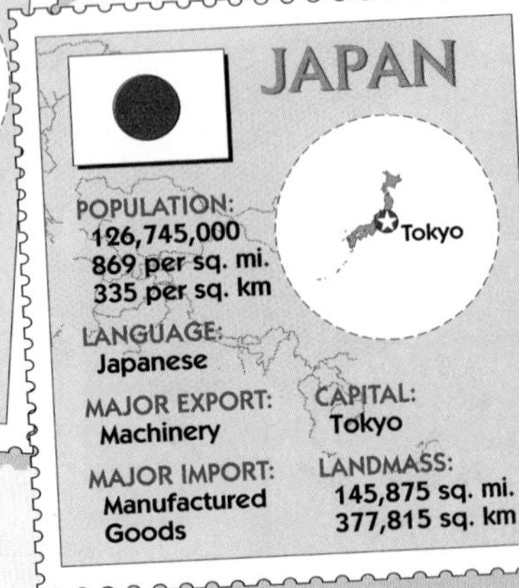

JAPAN

POPULATION: 126,745,000; 869 per sq. mi.; 335 per sq. km

LANGUAGE: Japanese

MAJOR EXPORT: Machinery

MAJOR IMPORT: Manufactured Goods

CAPITAL: Tokyo

LANDMASS: 145,875 sq. mi.; 377,815 sq. km

LAOS

POPULATION: 5,000,000; 55 per sq. mi.; 21 per sq. km

LANGUAGES: Lao, French

MAJOR EXPORT: Wood Products

MAJOR IMPORT: Machinery

CAPITAL: Vientiane

LANDMASS: 91,429 sq. mi.; 236,800 sq. km

Countries and flags not drawn to scale

Unit

MALAYSIA

POPULATION:
22,710,000
178 per sq. mi.
69 per sq. km

LANGUAGES:
Malay, English, Chinese

MAJOR EXPORT:
Electronic Equipment

MAJOR IMPORT:
Machinery

CAPITAL:
Kuala Lumpur

LANDMASS:
127,317 sq. mi.
329,749 sq. km

MALDIVES

POPULATION:
278,000
2,417 per sq. mi.
933 per sq. km

LANGUAGES:
Maldivian Divehi, English

MAJOR EXPORT:
Fish

MAJOR IMPORT:
Machinery

CAPITAL:
Male

LANDMASS:
115 sq. mi.
298 sq. km

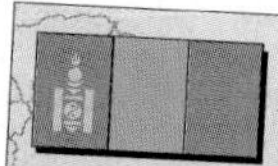

MONGOLIA

POPULATION:
2,438,000
4 per sq. mi.
2 per sq. km

LANGUAGE:
Khalkha Mongol

MAJOR EXPORT:
Copper

MAJOR IMPORT:
Fuels

CAPITAL:
Ulaanbaatar

LANDMASS:
604,250 sq. mi.
1,565,000 sq. km

MYANMAR

POPULATION:
48,081,000
184 per sq. mi.
71 per sq. km

LANGUAGES:
Burmese, Local Languages

MAJOR EXPORT:
Beans

MAJOR IMPORT:
Machinery

CAPITAL:
Yangon (Rangoon)

LANDMASS:
261,218 sq. mi.
676,552 sq. km

NEPAL

POPULATION:
24,303,000
447 per sq. mi.
173 per sq. km

LANGUAGE:
Nepali

MAJOR EXPORT:
Clothing

MAJOR IMPORT:
Petroleum Products

CAPITAL:
Kathmandu

LANDMASS:
54,362 sq. mi.
140,797 sq. km

NORTH KOREA

POPULATION:
21,386,000
460 per sq. mi.
177 per sq. km

LANGUAGE:
Korean

MAJOR EXPORT:
Minerals

MAJOR IMPORT:
Petroleum

CAPITAL:
Pyongyang

LANDMASS:
46,540 sq. mi.
120,538 sq. km

PAKISTAN

POPULATION:
146,488,000
477 per sq. mi.
184 per sq. km

LANGUAGES:
Urdu, English, Punjabi, Sindhi

MAJOR EXPORT:
Cotton

MAJOR IMPORT:
Petroleum

CAPITAL:
Islamabad

LANDMASS:
307,374 sq. mi.
796,095 sq. km

PHILIPPINES

POPULATION:
74,655,000
645 per sq. mi.
249 per sq. km

LANGUAGES:
Tagalog, English

MAJOR EXPORT:
Electronic Equipment

MAJOR IMPORT:
Raw Materials

CAPITAL:
Manila

LANDMASS:
115,831 sq. mi.
300,001 sq. km

SINGAPORE

POPULATION:
3,999,000
16,732 per sq. mi.
6,471 per sq. km

LANGUAGES:
Chinese, Malay, Tamil, English

MAJOR EXPORT:
Computer Equipment

MAJOR IMPORT:
Aircraft

CAPITAL:
Singapore

LANDMASS:
239 sq. mi.
618 sq. km

Country Profiles

* The People's Republic of China claims Taiwan as its 23rd province.

GEO BEE Questions From Buzz Bee!

The following questions are taken from National Geographic GeoBees. Use your textbook, the Internet, and other library resources to find the answers.

1. The Silk Road and modern highways skirt the largest desert in western China, which is characterized by shifting sand dunes. Name this desert.

2. Fortified monasteries called *dzongs* are found throughout the smallest country between China and India. Name this mountainous country.

Unit 8

View over city to Central Plaza at dusk, Wanchai, Hong Kong

Chapter

23 South Asia

The World and Its People NATIONAL GEOGRAPHIC

To learn more about the people and places of South Asia, view ***The World and Its People*** **Chapter 23** video.

Geography online

Chapter Overview Visit the ***Geography: The World and Its People*** Web site at gwip.glencoe.com and click on **Chapter 23—Chapter Overviews** to preview information about South Asia.

India

Guide to Reading

Main Idea

India—the world's most populous democracy—is trying to develop its resources and meet the needs of its rapidly growing population.

Terms to Know

- subcontinent
- monsoon
- jute
- cottage industry
- pesticide
- caste
- coalition government

Places to Locate

- India
- Karakoram Range
- Himalaya
- Satpura Range
- Ganges River
- Great Indian Desert
- Deccan Plateau
- New Delhi
- Mumbai
- Delhi
- Calcutta
- Chennai

Reading Strategy

Create a chart like this one. Then fill in at least two key facts about India under each category.

India	
Land	Economy
History	Religion

◀ Jodhpur, India

NATIONAL GEOGRAPHIC **Exploring Our World**

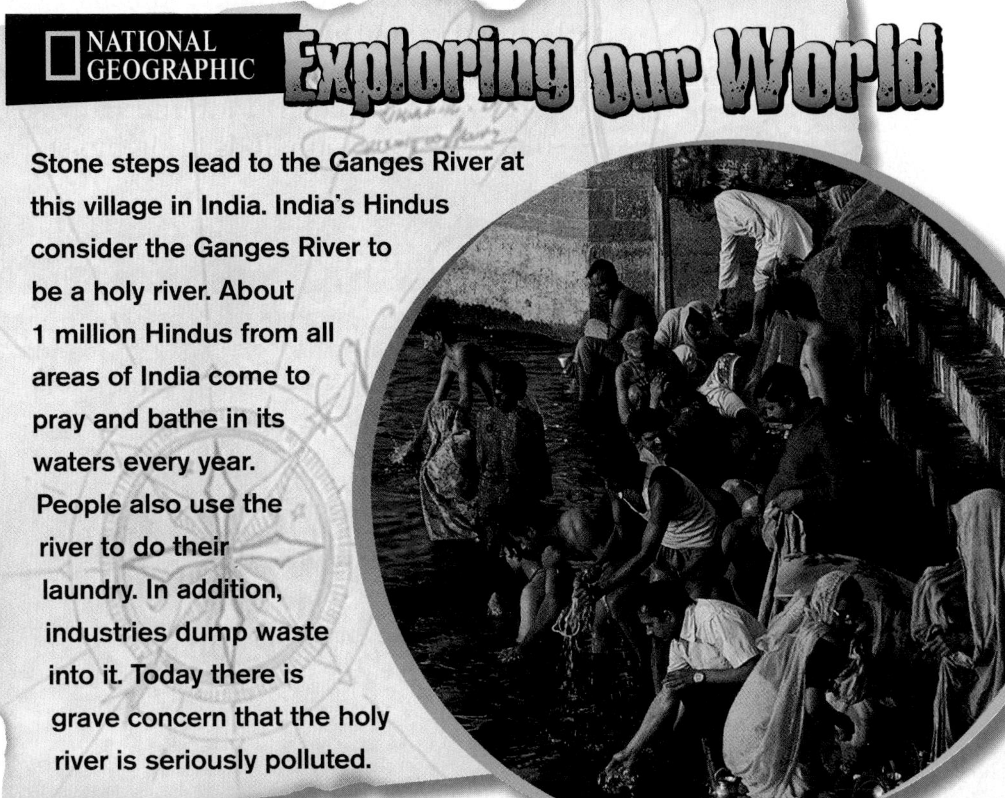

Stone steps lead to the Ganges River at this village in India. India's Hindus consider the Ganges River to be a holy river. About 1 million Hindus from all areas of India come to pray and bathe in its waters every year. People also use the river to do their laundry. In addition, industries dump waste into it. Today there is grave concern that the holy river is seriously polluted.

India and several other countries—Pakistan, Bangladesh (BAHNG•gluh•DEHSH), Nepal, Bhutan, Sri Lanka, and the Maldives—make up the South Asian subcontinent. A **subcontinent** is a large landmass that is part of another continent but distinct from it.

India's Land and Economy

Two huge walls of mountains—the **Karakoram** (KAH•rah•KOHR•ahm) **Range** and the **Himalaya** (HIH•muh•LAY•uh)—form India's northern border and separate South Asia from the rest of Asia. The tallest mountains in the world, the Himalaya's snowcapped peaks average more than 5 miles (8 km) in height. Edging India's southern coasts are the Eastern Ghats and the Western Ghats. These mountains lie just inland from the Bay of Bengal and the Arabian Sea. In central India, the **Satpura** (SAHT•puh•ruh) **Range** divides the country.

North of the Satpura lies the vast Ganges Plain. It boasts some of the most fertile soil in the country and holds about 40 percent of India's people. The **Ganges River** flows through the Ganges Plain to the Bay of Bengal. To the west lies the **Great Indian Desert.** South of the Satpura Range is the **Deccan Plateau.** Forests, farmland, and rich deposits of minerals make the Deccan Plateau a valuable region.

Most of India is warm or hot all year. The Himalaya block cold northern air from sweeping south into the country. **Monsoons,** or seasonal winds that blow steadily from the same direction for months, also influence the climate. Indians experience three seasons—cool, hot, and rainy. During the cool season (November through February) and the hot season (March through April), monsoon winds from the north bring dry air. During the rainy season (May through October), southern monsoon winds bring moist air from the Indian Ocean.

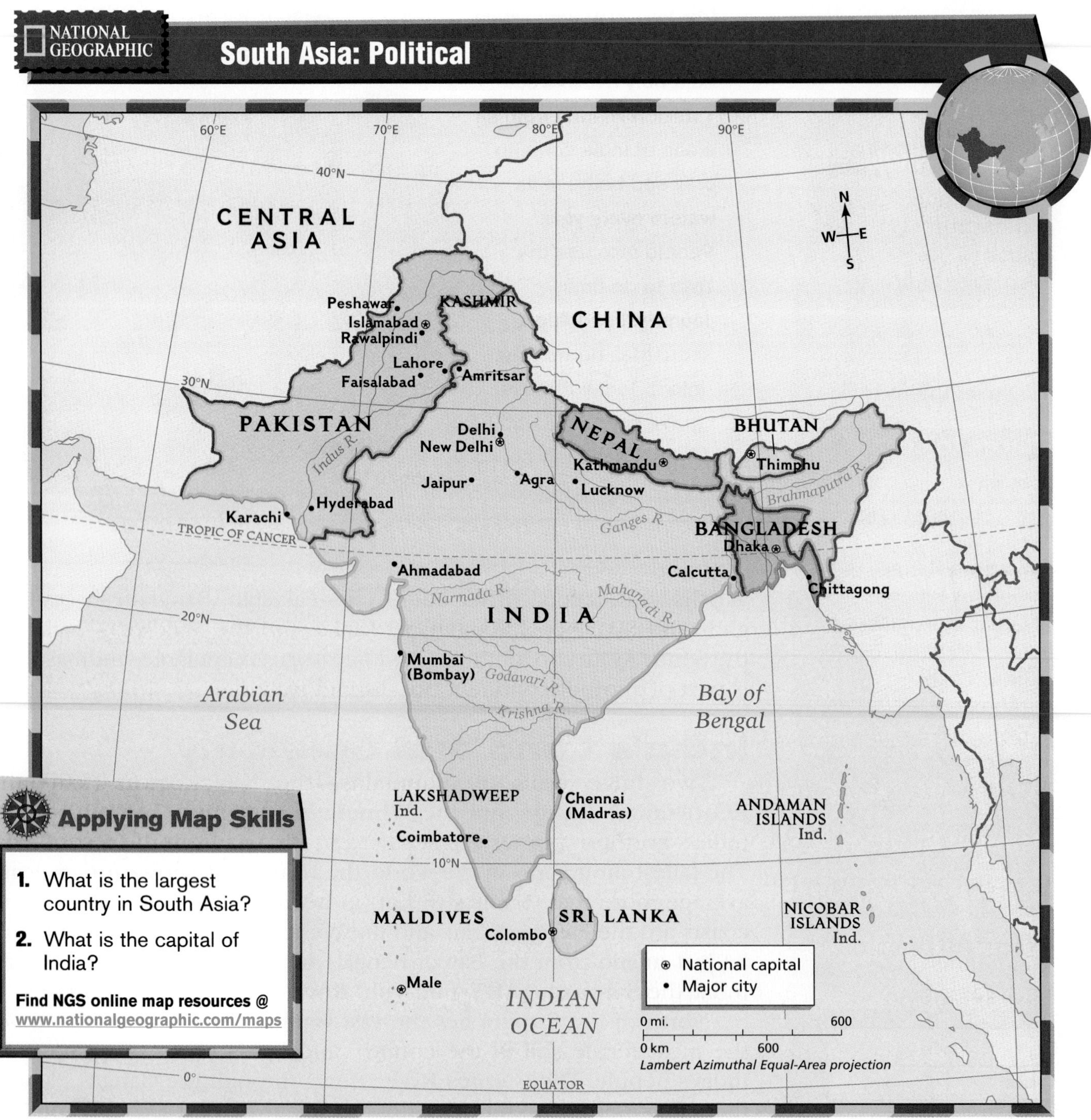

India's Economy Agriculture and industry are equally important to India's economy. The best farmland lies in the Ganges Plain and on the Deccan Plateau. More than two-thirds of India's labor force works in agriculture, mostly on small farms. Many of them cannot afford fertilizer, good seed, or machinery. Still, India's farmers raise a variety of crops, including rice, wheat, cotton, tea, sugarcane, and jute. **Jute** is a plant fiber used for making rope, burlap bags, and carpet backing. India is the world's second-largest rice producer, after China.

Huge factories in India's cities turn out cotton textiles and produce iron and steel. Oil and sugar refineries loom over many urban skylines.

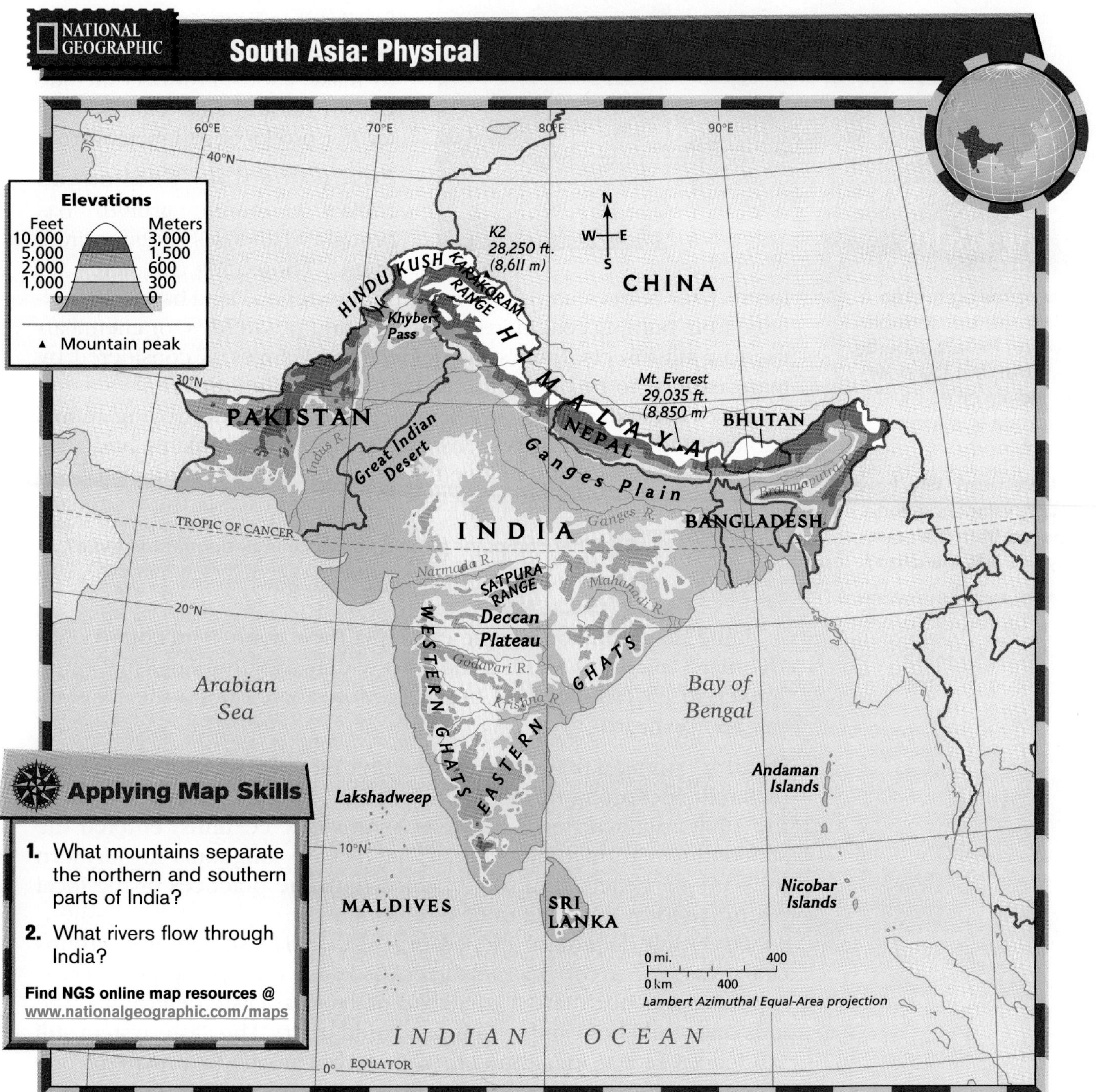

Applying Map Skills

1. What mountains separate the northern and southern parts of India?
2. What rivers flow through India?

Find NGS online map resources @ www.nationalgeographic.com/maps

Two Views of India

The growing middle class live comfortable lives in India's suburbs (above), but the poor in India's cities must struggle to survive (right).

Movement **Why have many villagers in India moved from the countryside into the cities?**

Recently, American computer companies have opened offices in India, making it an important source of computer software. Mining is another major industry. India has rich deposits of coal, iron ore, manganese, and bauxite. Its major exports are gems and jewelry.

Many Indian products are manufactured in cottage industries. A **cottage industry** is a home- or village-based industry in which family members, including children, supply their own equipment to make goods. Products include cotton cloth, silk cloth, rugs, leather products, and metalware.

Environmental Challenges India's economic growth has brought challenges to its environment. Thousands of acres of forests have been cleared for farming. Both water and land have been polluted from burning coal, industrial wastes, and **pesticides,** or chemicals used to kill insects. India's major river, the Ganges, is considered by many experts to be one of the world's most polluted rivers.

All of these developments have played a part in destroying animal habitats. India's elephants, lions, tigers, leopards, monkeys, and panthers have been greatly reduced in number. The government has set up more than 350 national parks and preserves to save these animals.

Reading Check **What computer product is becoming important in India?**

India's People

More than 1 billion people call India their home. The country has 18 official languages. Hindi is the most widely used, but English is often spoken in government and business. More than 1,000 other dialects can also be heard.

History About 4,000 years ago, the first Indian civilization built well-planned cities along the Indus River valley, in present-day Pakistan. In the 1500s B.C., warriors known as Aryans (AR•ee•uhns) entered the subcontinent from Central Asia. They set up kingdoms in northern India. Aryan beliefs gradually blended with the practices of the local people to form the religion of Hinduism.

Over time, Hinduism helped organize India's society into groups called castes. A **caste** was a social class based on a person's ancestry. A person was born into a particular caste. That caste determined the jobs one could hold and whom one could marry. The caste system still influences Indian life, although laws forbid unfair treatment of one group by another.

The religion of Islam also influenced India's history. In the A.D. 700s, Muslims from Southwest Asia brought Islam to India. In the 1500s, they founded the Mogul (MOH•guhl) Empire and ruled India for 200 years.

The British were the last of India's conquerors, ruling from the 1700s to the mid-1900s. They built roads, railroads, and seaports. They also made large profits from the plantations, mines, and factories they set up. An Indian leader named Mohandas Gandhi (moh•HAHN•duhs GAHN•dee) led a nonviolent resistance movement. His efforts brought India independence from the United Kingdom in 1947.

Today India is a federal republic, or a government divided between national and state powers. India has 25 states and 7 territories. The head of state is a president, whose duties are mainly ceremonial. The real power lies with the prime minister. Voters choose from more than 20 major political parties. As a result, the prime minister often leads a coalition government. A **coalition government** is one in which two or more political parties work together to run the country. **New Delhi** was built specifically to be the country's capital.

Religion About 80 percent of India's people are Hindus, or followers of Hinduism. Hindus worship many deities, or gods and goddesses. They believe that after the body dies, the soul is reborn, often in a different form. This process is repeated until the soul reaches perfection. For this reason, many Hindus believe it is wrong to kill any living creature. Cows are particularly sacred. Indians allow them to roam freely.

Islam also has many followers. India's 140 million Muslims form one of the world's largest Muslim populations. Other religions include Christianity, Sikhism (SEE•KIH•zuhm), Buddhism, and

Music

The tabla is a pair of connected drums from India. The drums are made of wood in the shape of a cylinder. Wooden pegs and leather straps hold the skin tightly onto the right-hand drum. The skin on the left-hand drum is kept slightly loose so that players can push down into it. This creates lower and higher pitches. Although the tabla emerged in India 500 years ago, it is now heard in modern pop and jazz music all over the world.

Looking Closer **Which drum do you think has more variation in sound? Why?**

GO TO

World Music: A Cultural Legacy
Hear music of this region on Disc 2, Track 13.

Jainism (JY•NIH•zuhm). Conflict sometimes occurs between Hindus and followers of the other religions. The Sikhs, who practice Sikhism, believe in one God as Christians and Muslims do, yet Sikhs have other beliefs similar to Hindus. Today many Sikhs would like to form their own independent state.

Religion has influenced the arts of India. Ancient Hindu builders constructed temples with hundreds of statues. Hindu writers composed stories about deities. Among Muslim achievements are large mosques, palaces, and forts. One of the finest Muslim buildings in India is the Taj Mahal. Turn to page 651 to learn more about it.

Daily Life About 70 percent of the people live in farming villages. The government has been working to provide villagers with electricity, drinking water, better schools, and paved roads. Many villagers stream to cities to find jobs and a better standard of living.

India's cities are very crowded. **Mumbai** (formerly Bombay), **Delhi, Calcutta,** and **Chennai** (formerly Madras) each have more than 5 million people and are growing rapidly. Modern high-rise buildings tower over slum areas where many live in deep poverty. Bicycles, carts, animals, and people fill the streets.

Many Indians enjoy sports and celebrations. Rugby and soccer are the major sports in India. One of the most popular holidays is Diwali—the Festival of Lights. It is a Hindu celebration marking the coming of winter and the victory of good over evil. Indians also like watching movies. India's movie industry turns out more than 400 movies a year.

✓Reading Check **What percentage of India's people live in rural villages?**

Assessment

Defining Terms

1. Define subcontinent, monsoon, jute, cottage industry, pesticide, caste, coalition government.

Recalling Facts

2. Location What two mountain ranges form India's northern border?
3. Culture What is the most widely used language in India?
4. History What Indian leader led a movement that brought India its independence in 1947?

Critical Thinking

5. Understanding Cause and Effect How do monsoon winds affect India's climate?
6. Drawing Conclusions What challenges do you think having so many languages would present to India?

Graphic Organizer

7. Organizing Information Draw a chart like this one. Then list both modern and traditional aspects of India.

Modern Aspects	Traditional Aspects

Applying Geography Skills

8. Analyzing Maps Look at the population density map on page 661. What are the most densely populated areas of India?

Making Connections

SCIENCE LITERATURE TECHNOLOGY

The Taj Mahal

Considered one of the world's most beautiful buildings, the Taj Mahal was built by the Muslim emperor Shah Jahan of India. He had it built to house the grave of his beloved wife, Mumtaz Mahal. She died in 1631 shortly after giving birth to their fourteenth child.

The Taj Mahal ▲

Background

While they were married, Mumtaz Mahal and Shah Jahan were constant companions. The empress went everywhere with her husband, even on military expeditions. She encouraged her husband to perform great acts of charity toward the poor. This earned her the love and admiration of the Indian people.

After her death, Shah Jahan ordered the construction of the finest monument ever. A team of architects, sculptors, calligraphers, and master builders participated in the design. More than 20,000 laborers and skilled craft workers from India, Persia, the Ottoman Empire, and Europe worked together to build the monument. For 22 years they worked to complete the Taj Mahal, which holds a tomb, mosque, rest house, elaborate garden, and arched gateway.

The Mausoleum

The central part of the Taj Mahal is the domed marble mausoleum, or tomb, built on a square marble platform. The central dome is 213 feet (65 m) tall, and four smaller domed chambers surround it. A high minaret, or tower, marks each corner of the platform.

Inside the central chamber, delicately carved marble screens enclose the caskets of Mumtaz Mahal and Shah Jahan. He was buried next to his wife after his death in 1666. Following Islamic tradition, the caskets face east toward Makkah, the religious capital of Islam.

The white marble from which the mausoleum is built seems to change color throughout the day as it reflects light from the sun and moon. Detailed flower patterns are carved into the marble walls and inlaid with colorful gemstones. Verses from Islamic religious writings are etched in calligraphy into the stone archways.

Making the Connection

1. Who is buried in the Taj Mahal?
2. Who built the Taj Mahal and how long did it take?
3. **Understanding Cause and Effect** How did Shah Jahan's feelings for his wife affect the grave site he built for her?

Section 2

Pakistan and Bangladesh

Guide to Reading

Main Idea

Once a single nation, Pakistan and Bangladesh today are separate countries that border India on the west and east.

Terms to Know

- tributary
- delta
- cyclone

Places to Locate

- Pakistan
- Bangladesh
- Kashmir
- Hindu Kush
- Khyber Pass
- Indus River
- Great Indian Desert
- Karachi
- Islamabad
- Brahmaputra River
- Ganges River
- Dhaka

Reading Strategy

Draw a diagram like this one. In the outer ovals, write statements that are true of each country under the headings. Where the ovals overlap, write statements that are true of both countries.

NATIONAL GEOGRAPHIC **Exploring Our World**

Sorting apricots—what a colorful job! More than 20 kinds of apricots grow in a remote region of Pakistan. Every family here grows at least one apricot tree as well as other crops. The apricots are dried on rooftops, and then workers carefully check and sort them. After that, they are sold to a distributor, who ships them to local and foreign markets.

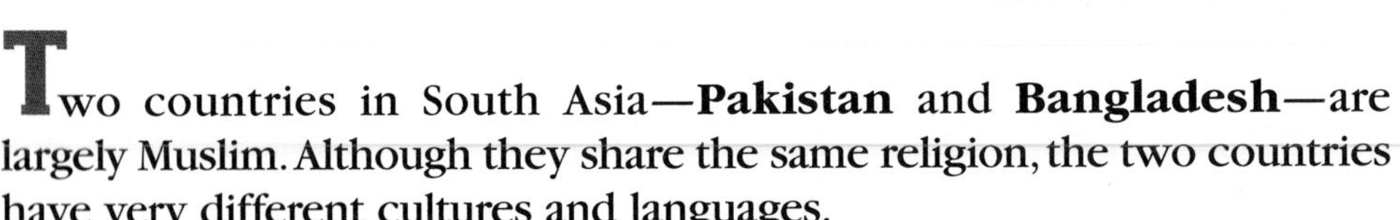

Two countries in South Asia—**Pakistan** and **Bangladesh**—are largely Muslim. Although they share the same religion, the two countries have very different cultures and languages.

For many centuries, both areas were part of India. In 1947 they both separated from largely Hindu India and together formed one Muslim country called Pakistan. The western area was called West Pakistan, and the eastern area, East Pakistan. Cultural and political differences between the two parts led to a violent conflict in 1971. When the war ended, West Pakistan kept the name of Pakistan. East Pakistan became a separate new country called Bangladesh.

Pakistan

Pakistan is about twice the size of California. The country also claims **Kashmir,** a mostly Muslim territory on the northern border of India and Pakistan. Kashmir is currently divided between Pakistan and

India. Both countries want to control the entire region, mainly for its vast water resources. This dispute over Kashmir has sparked three wars between Pakistan and India. In fact, it threatens all of South Asia because both Pakistan and India have nuclear weapons.

Towering mountains occupy most of northern and western Pakistan. The world's second-highest peak, K2, rises 28,250 feet (8,611 m) in the Karakoram Range. Another range, the **Hindu Kush,** lies in the far north. Several passes cut through its rugged peaks. The best known is the **Khyber Pass.** For centuries, it has been used by people traveling through South Asia from the north.

Plains in eastern Pakistan are rich in fertile soil deposited by rivers. The major river system running through these plains is the **Indus River** and its tributaries. A **tributary** is a small river that flows into a larger one. West of the Indus River valley, the land rises to form a mostly dry plateau. Another vast barren area—the **Great Indian Desert**—lies east of the Indus River valley and reaches into India.

Pakistan has mostly desert and steppe climates, with hot summers and cool winters. Rainfall in most areas is less than 10 inches (25 cm) a year. Mountains in the north block cold air from Central Asia.

Pakistan's Economy Pakistan has fertile land and enough energy resources to meet its needs. About half of the people are farmers. A large irrigation system helps them grow crops such as sugarcane, wheat, rice, and cotton. Cotton and textiles are the country's main

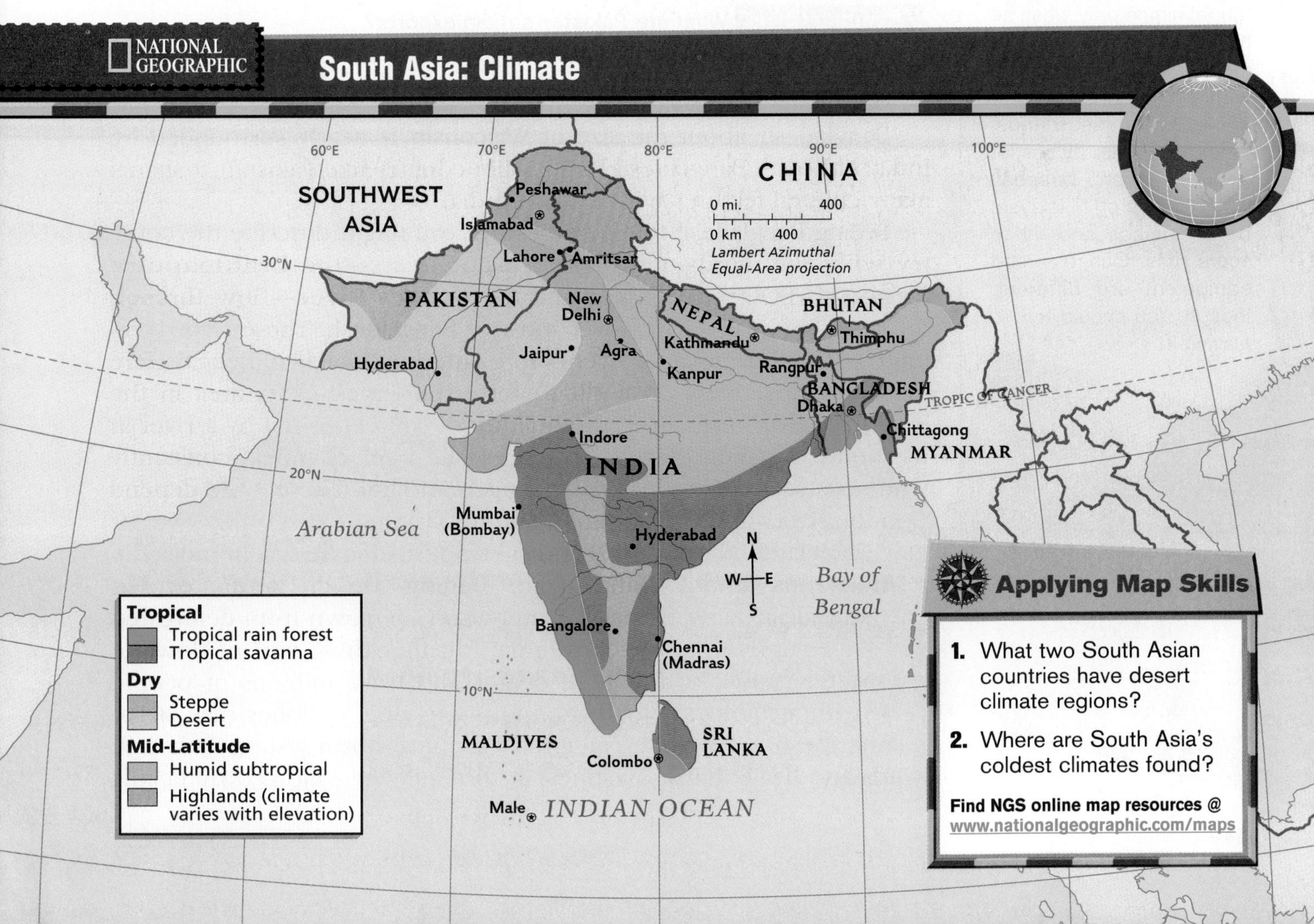

Applying Map Skills

1. What two South Asian countries have desert climate regions?
2. Where are South Asia's coldest climates found?

Find NGS online map resources @ www.nationalgeographic.com/maps

exports. Other important industries include cement, fertilizer, food processing, and chemicals. Many people make metalware, pottery, and carpets in cottage industries. Pakistan's economy is struggling, however, because of frequent changes of government.

Pakistan's People Since independence, Pakistan has had many changes of government. Some of these governments were elected, including a female prime minister, Benazir Bhutto. In other cases, the army seized power from an elected government. The most recent army takeover occurred in 1999, and military leaders still control the country.

About 97 percent of Pakistanis are Muslims. The influence of Islam is seen in large, domed mosques and people bowed in prayer at certain times of the day. Among the major languages are Punjabi and Sindhi. The official language, Urdu, is the first language of only 9 percent of the people. English is widely spoken in government.

Almost 70 percent of Pakistan's people live in rural villages. Most follow traditional customs and live in small homes of clay or sun-dried mud. Pakistanis live in large cities as well. **Karachi,** a seaport on the Arabian Sea, is a sprawling urban area. It has traditional outdoor markets, modern shops, and hotels. In the far north lies **Islamabad,** the capital. The government built this well-planned, modern city to draw people inland from crowded coastal areas. Most people in Pakistan's cities are factory workers, shopkeepers, and craft workers who live in crowded neighborhoods. Wealthier city dwellers live in modern homes.

✓Reading Check **What are Pakistan's main exports?**

School's Out!

Adil Husain is on his way home from middle school. In Pakistan, schooling only goes to grade 10. Adil has only three more years of school before he must decide whether to go to intermediate college (grades 11 and 12) and then the university. Like most Pakistanis, Adil is Muslim. His parents have taught him to pray when he hears the call from the mosque. Afterward, he wants to start a game of cricket with his friends, Kiran and Malik. "It's a lot like American baseball where teams of 11 players bat in innings and try to score runs. Our rules and equipment are different, though. You should try playing it!"

Bangladesh

Bangladesh, about the size of Wisconsin, is nearly surrounded by India. Although Bangladesh is a Muslim country like Pakistan, it shares many cultural features with eastern India.

Seeing Bangladesh for the first time, you might describe the country with one word—water. Two major rivers—the **Brahmaputra** (BRAHM•uh•POO•truh) **River** and the **Ganges River**—flow through the lush, low plains that cover most of Bangladesh. These two rivers unite with a third, smaller river before entering the Bay of Bengal. Here the combined rivers drop silt to form the largest delta area in the world. A **delta** forms from the buildup of soil deposited by a river at its mouth. In Bangladesh's delta area, the river channels constantly shift course, creating many thin fingers of land. The people depend on the rivers for transportation and for farming.

Bangladesh has tropical and subtropical climates. As in India, the monsoons affect Bangladesh. Raging floods often drown Bangladesh's low, flat land. Water also runs down from deforested slopes upriver in northern India. Together, these violent flows of water cause thousands of deaths and leave millions of people without homes. When the monsoons end, cyclones may strike Bangladesh. A **cyclone** is an intense tropical storm system with high winds and heavy rains. Cyclones, in turn, may be followed by deadly tidal waves that surge up from the Bay of Bengal. As deadly as the monsoons and cyclones may be, it is worse if the rains come too late. When this happens, crops often fail and there is widespread hunger.

A Farming Economy Most people of Bangladesh earn their living by farming. Rice is the most important crop. The fertile soil and plentiful water make it possible for rice to be grown and harvested three times a year. Other crops include sugarcane, jute, and wheat. Cash crops of tea grow in hilly regions in the east. Despite good growing conditions, Bangladesh cannot grow enough food for its people. Its farmers have few modern tools and use outdated farming methods. In addition, the disastrous floods can drown crops and cause food shortages.

Bangladesh has an important clothing industry. It exports large amounts of manufactured clothing to other countries. *You* may even be wearing clothes made in Bangladesh.

The People With about 125.7 million people, Bangladesh is one of the most densely populated countries in the world. It is also one of the poorest countries. More than 80 percent of the people live in rural areas. Because of floods, people in rural Bangladesh have to build their houses on platforms. Many people have moved to crowded urban areas to find work in factories. Their most common choice is **Dhaka** (DA•kuh), Bangladesh's capital and major port.

Most of Bangladesh's people speak Bengali. About 88 percent of the people are Muslim, and most of the rest are Hindus. Muslim influences are strong in the country's art, literature, and music.

Ship Breakers

On a beach near Karachi, Pakistan, ship breakers haul an old cargo vessel to shore. Their next task? The men will use hammers, crowbars, and wrenches to pull the ship apart. They will then sell the pipes, chains, portholes, steel plates, and other reusable parts. The work is exhausting, but in this poor country it is a way of making a living.

✓Reading Check **What is an important industry in Bangladesh?**

Assessment

Defining Terms

1. **Define** tributary, delta, cyclone.

Recalling Facts

2. **Region** What region has been the source of conflict between Pakistan and India?
3. **History** Why has the Khyber Pass been important?
4. **Movement** Why was Islamabad built inland?

Critical Thinking

5. **Analyzing Information** Why can rice be grown three times a year in Bangladesh?
6. **Drawing Conclusions** Why are Pakistan's and Bangladesh's economies struggling?

Graphic Organizer

7. **Organizing Information** Draw a diagram like this one. At the ends of the arrows, list three effects on Bangladesh caused by summer monsoon rains.

Applying Geography Skills

8. **Analyzing Maps** Look at the physical map on page 647. What rivers have deltas in Bangladesh?

Geography Skill

Reading a Circle Graph

Have you ever watched someone dish out pieces of pie? When the pie is cut evenly, everybody gets the same size slice. If one slice is cut a little larger, however, someone else gets a smaller piece.

Learning the Skill

A **circle graph** is like a sliced pie. Often it is even called a pie chart. In a circle graph, the complete circle represents a whole group—or 100 percent. The circle is divided into "slices," or wedge-shaped sections representing parts of the whole.

To read a circle graph, follow these steps:

- Read the title of the circle graph to find out what the subject is.
- Study the labels or the key to see what each "slice" represents.
- Compare the sizes of the circle slices.

Practicing the Skill

Look at the graph below to answer the following questions.

1. What is the subject of the circle graph?
2. Which religion in South Asia has the most followers?
3. What percentage practice Islam?
4. What is the combined percentage of Buddhist and Christian followers?

Applying the Skill

Quiz at least 10 friends about the capitals of India, Pakistan, and Bangladesh. Create a circle graph showing what percentage knew (a) all three capitals, (b) two capitals, (c) one capital, or (d) no capitals.

GO TO Practice key skills with **Glencoe Skillbuilder Interactive Workbook, Level 1.**

NATIONAL GEOGRAPHIC

Religions of South Asia

RELIGION	NUMBER OF FOLLOWERS
Hinduism	914,500,000
Islam	366,600,000
Christianity	26,500,000
Buddhism	22,400,000
Sikhism	20,000,000
Other	42,000,000

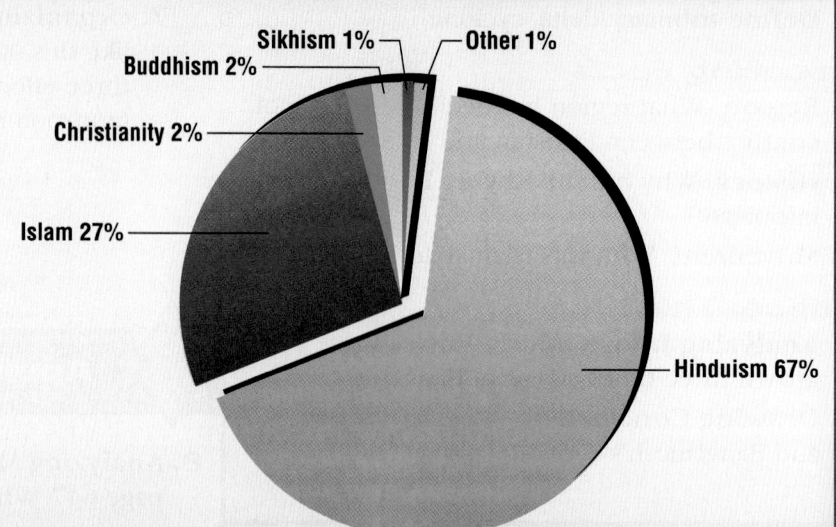

Source: *Time Almanac*, 2000.

Section 3

Other Countries of South Asia

Guide to Reading

Main Idea

The other countries of South Asia include mountainous Nepal and Bhutan and the island countries of Sri Lanka and the Maldives.

Terms to Know

- *dzong*
- atoll
- lagoon

Places to Locate

- Nepal
- Bhutan
- Sri Lanka
- Maldives
- Mount Everest
- Kathmandu
- Thimphu
- Colombo
- Male

Reading Strategy

Fill in a chart like this one by listing the main economic activities in these four countries of South Asia.

Country	Economic Activities
Nepal	
Bhutan	
Sri Lanka	
Maldives	

NATIONAL GEOGRAPHIC **Exploring Our World**

Perched on poles planted into the ocean floor, Sri Lankan fishers await their next catch. Although Sri Lanka is trying to build a modern economy, traditional work still goes on. Some people gave up fishing when Sri Lanka seemed ready to become a major tourist destination. However, years of ethnic warfare have kept tourists away and slowed the economy.

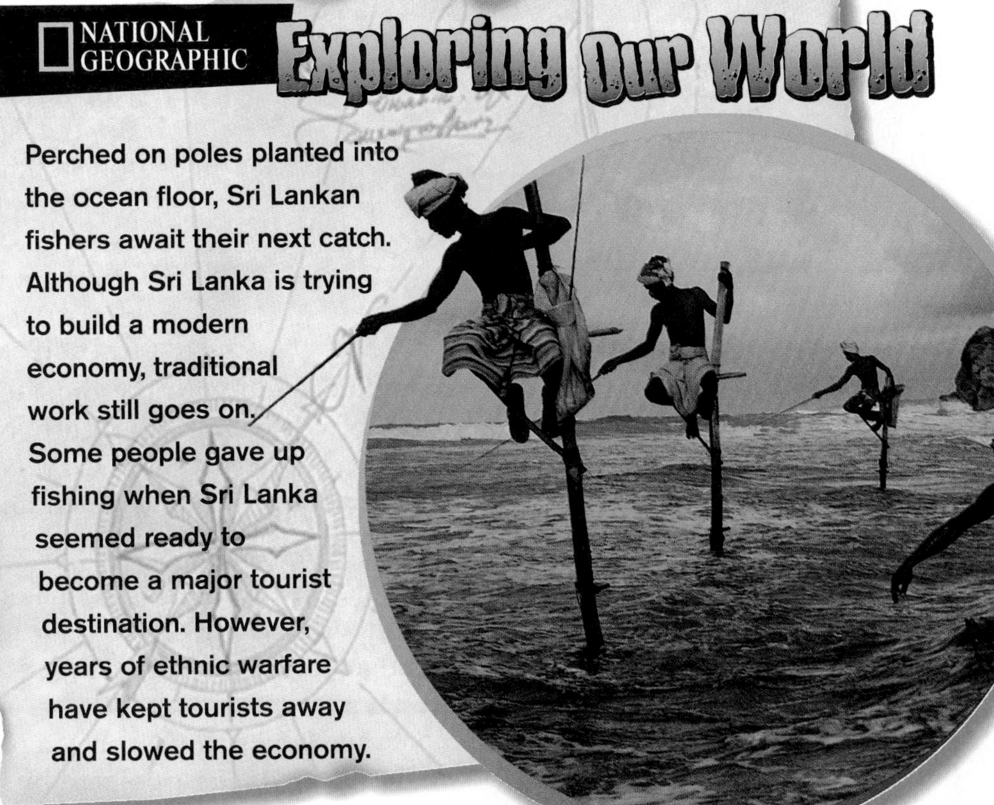

Of the four other countries of South Asia, two are landlocked kingdoms and two are island republics. **Nepal** and **Bhutan** both lie among the towering peaks of the Himalaya. The island countries of **Sri Lanka** and the **Maldives** lie south of India in the Indian Ocean.

Nepal

Nepal—about the size of Arkansas—forms a steep stairway to the world's highest mountain range. The Himalaya, dominating about 80 percent of Nepal's land area, are actually three mountain ranges running side by side. Nepal is home to 8 of the 10 highest mountains in the world. **Mount Everest,** the highest, soars 29,035 feet (8,850 m).

Swift rivers cut through the lower ranges in the south, shaping fertile valleys. A flat, fertile river plain runs along Nepal's southern border with India. The plain includes farmland, swamps, and rain forests. Tigers, elephants, and other wild animals roam these forests.

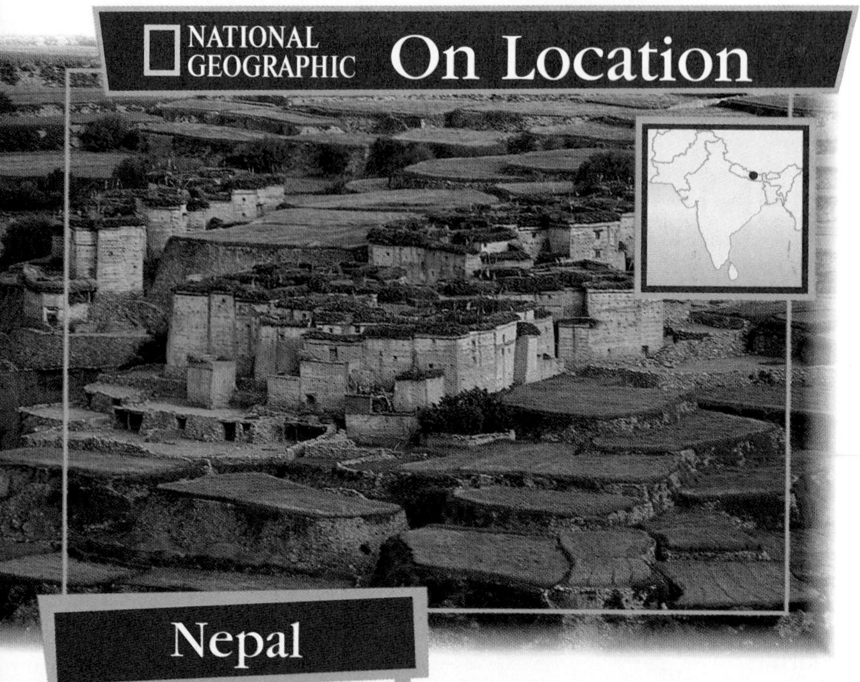

Nepal

Years of hard labor turned mountain slopes into terraced fields in Nepal. Farmers also built channels to bring melting snow from the mountains to the fields.

Place **What mountains dominate Nepal?**

Nepal has a humid subtropical climate in the south and a highland climate in the north. Monsoon rains often flood the southern plains area.

Nepal's economy depends almost entirely on farming. Farmers grow rice, sugarcane, wheat, corn, and potatoes to feed their families. Most fields are located on the southern plains or on the lower mountain slopes.

As the population has increased, Nepalese farmers have moved higher up the slopes. There they clear the forests for new fields and use the cut trees for fuel. Stripped of trees, however, the slopes erode very easily. Valleys often are flooded, fields destroyed, and rivers filled with mud.

With few roads or railroads, Nepal carries on limited trade with the outside world. Herbs, jute, rice, and wheat are exported to India. In return, Nepal imports gasoline, fertilizer, and machinery. Clothing and carpets now make up the country's most valuable exports. Nepal's rugged mountains attract thousands of climbers and hikers each year, creating a growing tourist industry.

Nepal's People Nepal has 24.3 million people. Most are related to peoples in northern India and Tibet. One group—the Sherpa—is known for its skill in guiding mountain climbers. About 85 percent of Nepal's people live in rural villages. A growing number live in **Kathmandu,** Nepal's capital and largest city. Nepal is a parliamentary democracy ruled by a prime minister, who is appointed by Nepal's king.

The founder of Buddhism, Siddartha Gautama (sihd•DAHR•tuh GOW•tuh•muh), was born in the Kathmandu region about 563 B.C. Raised as a prince, Gautama gave up his wealth and became a holy man in India. Known as the Buddha, or "Enlightened One," he taught that people could find peace from life's troubles by living simply, doing good deeds, and praying. Buddhism later spread to other parts of Asia.

Today Hindu is the official religion, but Buddhism is practiced as well. If you visit Nepal, you will find temples and monuments of both religions scattered throughout the country.

✓Reading Check **Why does Nepal have limited trade with other countries?**

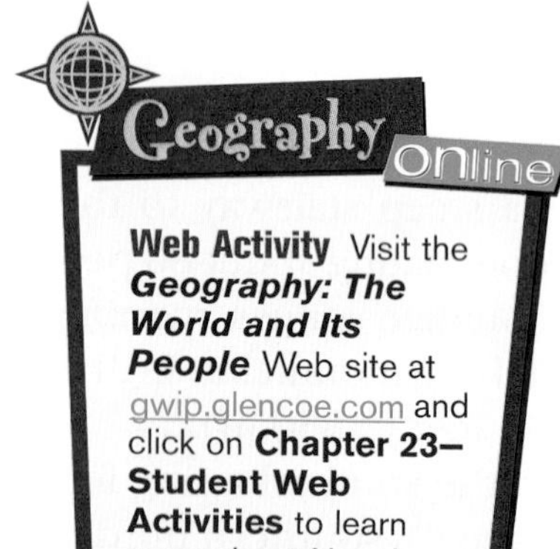

Web Activity Visit the ***Geography: The World and Its People*** Web site at gwip.glencoe.com and click on **Chapter 23—Student Web Activities** to learn more about Nepal.

Bhutan

East of Nepal lies an even smaller kingdom—Bhutan. Bhutan is about half the size of Indiana. The map on page 659 shows you that a small part of India separates Bhutan from Nepal.

As in Nepal, the Himalaya are the major landform of Bhutan. Violent mountain storms are common and are the basis of Bhutan's name, which means "land of the thunder dragon." In the foothills of the Himalaya, the climate is mild. Thick forests cover much of this area. To the south—along Bhutan's border with India—lies an area of subtropical plains and river valleys.

More than 90 percent of Bhutan's people are subsistence farmers. They live in the fertile mountain valleys and grow the spice cardamom, oranges, rice, corn, and potatoes. People also herd cattle and yaks, which are a type of oxen. Bhutan is trying to develop its economy, but the mountains slow progress. Building roads is difficult, and there are no railroads. Bhutan has built hydroelectric plants to create electricity from rushing mountain waters. It now exports electricity to India. Tourism is a new industry. However, the government limits the number of tourists in order to protect Bhutan's cultural traditions.

Bhutan's People Bhutan has about 800,000 people. Most speak the Dzonkha dialect and live in rural villages that dot southern valleys and plains. **Thimphu,** the capital, is located in the southern area.

Bhutan was once called the Hidden Holy Land because of its isolation and its Buddhist religion. In the 1960s, new roads and other connections opened Bhutan to the outside world. Most people remain deeply loyal to Buddhism. In Bhutan, Buddhist centers of prayer and study are called ***dzongs.*** They have shaped the country's art and culture.

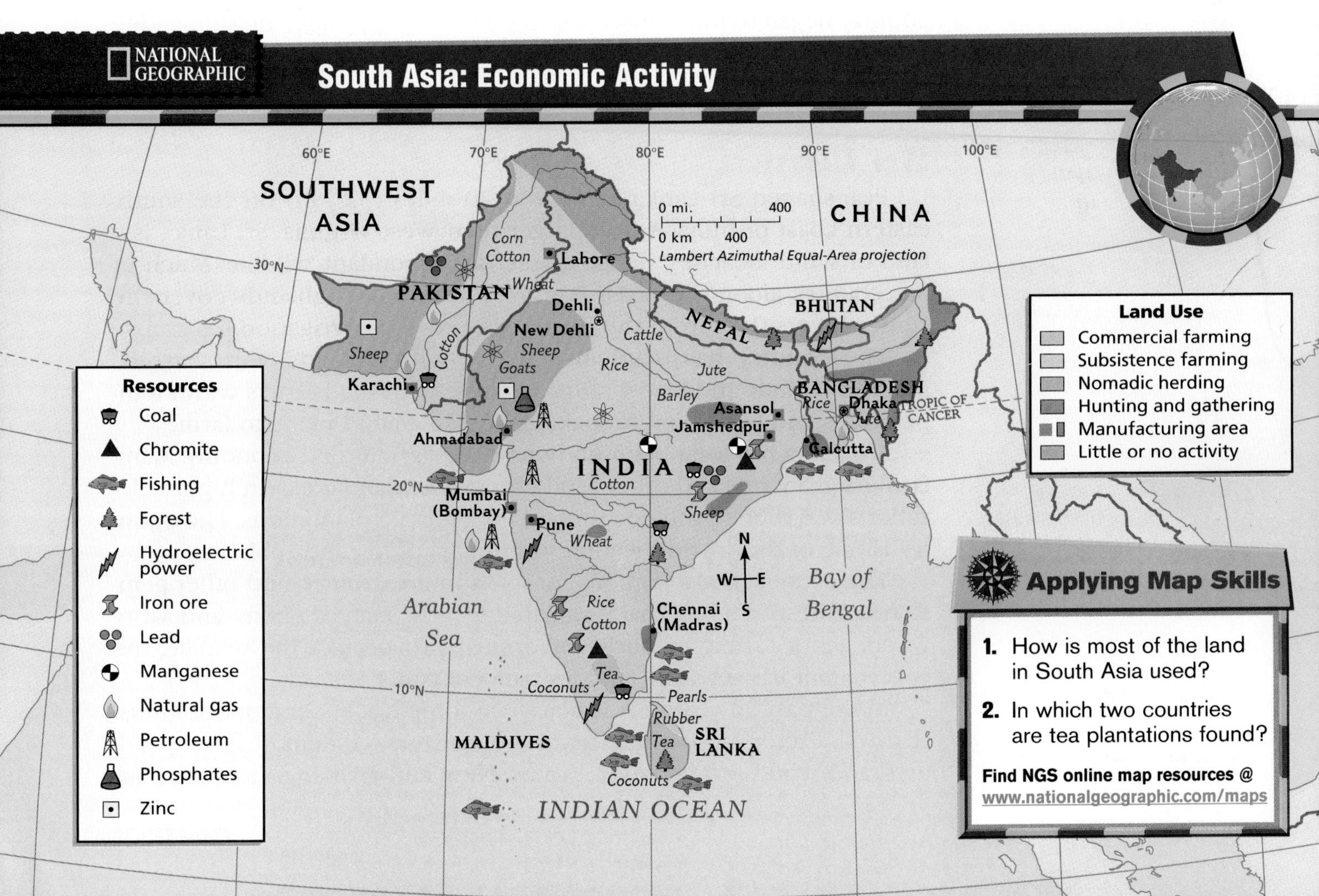

Highest Mountain on Each Continent

Analyzing the Graph

Mount Everest is the tallest mountain on the earth.

Place **What is the tallest mountain in North America?**

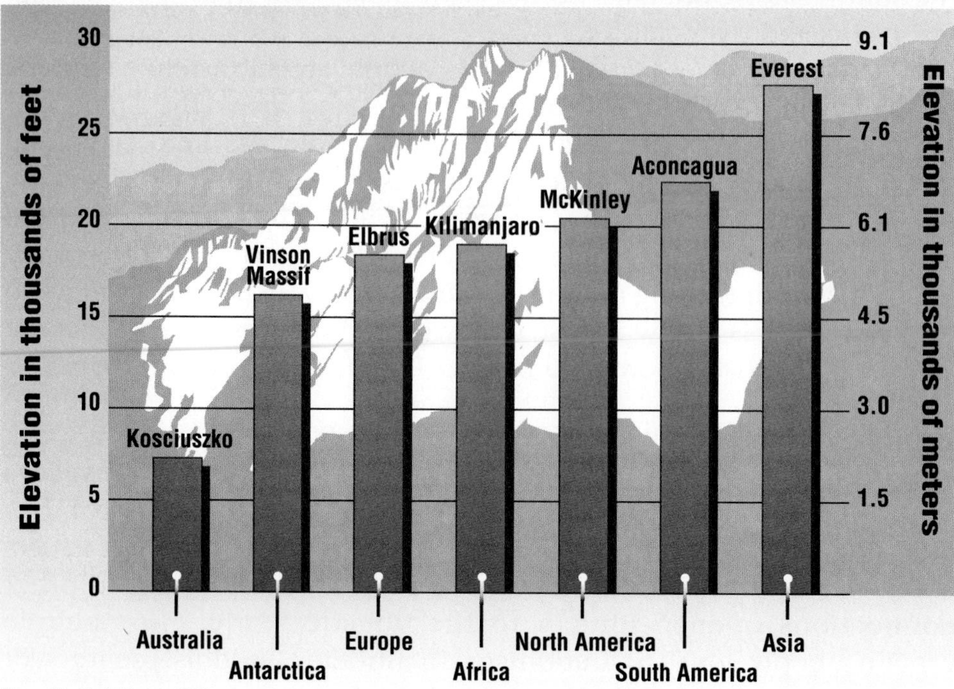

Source: *The World Almanac,* 2000.

For many years, Bhutan was ruled by strong kings. In 1998 the country began to move toward democracy. At that time, the ruling king agreed to share his power with an elected legislature.

✓Reading Check **What is the main religion in Bhutan?**

Sri Lanka

Pear-shaped Sri Lanka lies about 20 miles (32 km) off the southeastern coast of India. A little larger than West Virginia, Sri Lanka is a land of white beaches, dense forests, and abundant wildlife. Much of the country along the coast is rolling lowlands. Highlands cover the center. Rivers flow from the highlands, providing irrigation for crops.

The country has tropical climates with dry and wet seasons. Monsoon winds and heavy rains combine with the island's warm temperatures and fertile soil to make Sri Lanka a good place to farm.

Sri Lanka has long been known for its agricultural economy. Many farmers grow rice and other food crops in lowland areas. In higher elevations, tea, rubber, and coconuts grow on large plantations. The country is one of the world's leading producers of tea and rubber.

The country is also famous for its sapphires, rubies, and other gemstones. Forests contain many valuable woods, such as ebony and satinwood, and a variety of birds and animals. To protect the wildlife, the government has set aside land for national parks.

In the past 20 years, Sri Lanka's economy has become more industrialized. Factories produce textiles, fertilizers, cement, leather products, and wood products for export. New and growing industries are telecommunications, insurance, and banking. **Colombo,** the capital, is a bustling port on the country's western coast.

Sri Lanka's People For centuries, Sri Lanka prospered because of its location on an important ocean route between Africa and Asia. It was a natural stopping place for seagoing traders. Beginning in the 1500s, Sri Lanka—then known as Ceylon—came under the control of European countries. The British ruled the island from 1802 to 1948, when it became independent. In 1972 Ceylon took the name of Sri Lanka, an ancient term meaning "brilliant land." Today Sri Lanka is a republic with a president who carries out ceremonial duties. Real power is held by a prime minister, who is the head of government.

About 19 million people live here. They belong to two major ethnic groups: the Sinhalese (SIHNG•guh•LEEZ) and the Tamils (TA•muhlz). Forming about 74 percent of the population, the Sinhalese live in the southern and western parts of the island. They speak Sinhalese and are mostly Buddhist. The Tamils make up about 18 percent of the population. They live in the north and east, speak Tamil, and are Hindus.

Since 1983 the Tamils and the Sinhalese have fought a violent civil war. The minority Tamils claim they have not been treated justly by the

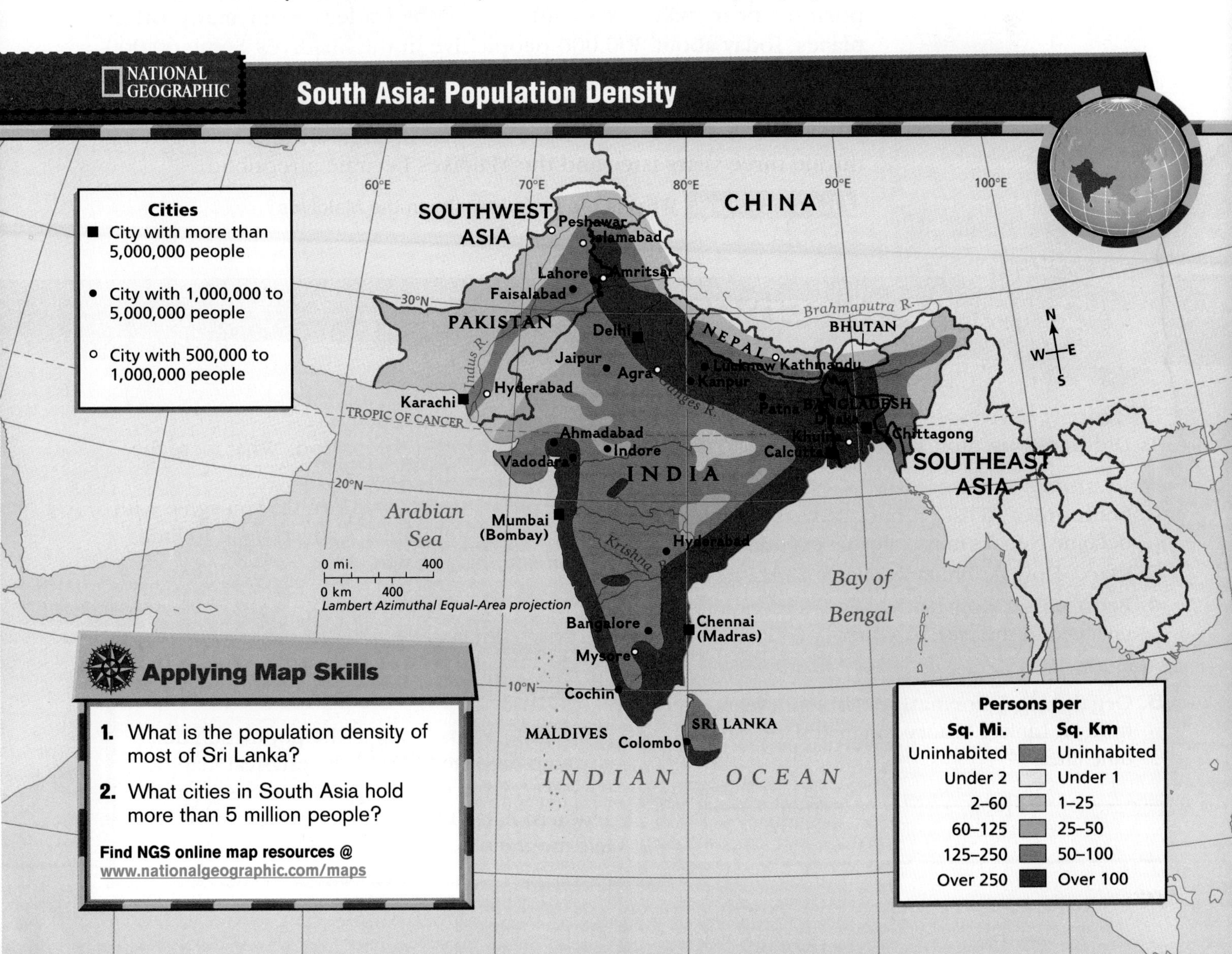

majority Sinhalese. They want to set up a separate Tamil nation in northern Sri Lanka. Thousands of Sri Lankans have lost their lives in the fighting.

Reading Check **What are the two main ethnic groups in Sri Lanka?**

The Maldives

About 370 miles (595 km) south of India lie the Maldives, made up of about 1,200 coral islands. Many of the islands are atolls. An **atoll** is a low-lying, ring-shaped island that surrounds a lagoon. A **lagoon** is a shallow pool of water surrounded by reefs, sandbars, or atolls. Only 200 of the islands are inhabited. The climate of the Maldives is warm and humid throughout the year. Monsoons bring plenty of rain.

Most of the Maldives have poor, sandy soil. Only a limited number of crops can grow, including sweet potatoes, grains, and watermelon. In recent years, the Maldives's palm-lined sandy beaches and coral formations have attracted many tourists. As a result, tourism is now the largest industry. Fishing is the second-largest industry.

The first people to arrive in the Maldives came from southern India and Sri Lanka several thousand years ago. Over the years, the islands' position near major sea routes brought traders from many other places. Today about 300,000 people live in the Maldives. Some 60,000 of them make their home in **Male** (MAH•lay), the capital. Most are Muslims. The islands, which came under British rule during the late 1890s, became independent in 1965. The local traditional ruler lost his throne three years later, and the Maldives became a republic.

Reading Check **What is the main industry in the Maldives?**

Assessment

Defining Terms

1. Define *dzong,* atoll, lagoon.

Recalling Facts

2. Economics What products have recently become Nepal's most valuable exports?

3. Place How do Bhutan's people earn a living?

4. Economics How has Sri Lanka's economy changed in the past 20 years?

Graphic Organizer

5. Organizing Information List four events from Sri Lanka's history and their dates on a time line.

Critical Thinking

6. Summarizing Information What were the teachings of the Buddha?

7. Formulating an Opinion Do you agree with the decision of Bhutan's government to limit tourism? Why or why not?

Applying Geography Skills

8. Analyzing Maps Look at the population density map on page 661 and the physical map on page 647. What is the population density of the southern part of Nepal? The northern part? Explain the difference.

Chapter 23 Reading Review

Section 1 India

Terms to Know
- subcontinent
- monsoon
- jute
- cottage industry
- pesticide
- caste
- coalition government

Main Idea

India—the world's most populous democracy—is trying to develop its resources and meet the needs of its rapidly growing population.

✓**Place** India is the largest country in South Asia in size and population.

✓**Place** The Himalaya and the monsoons affect India's climate.

✓**Economics** India's economy is based on both farming and industry.

✓**Culture** India has many languages and religions, but the majority of Indians are Hindus.

✓**Government** India has a democratic government with many political parties.

Section 2 Pakistan and Bangladesh

Terms to Know
- tributary
- delta
- cyclone

Main Idea

Once a single nation, Pakistan and Bangladesh today are separate countries that border India on the west and east.

✓**History** Cultural and political differences between Pakistan and Bangladesh led to war and separation in 1971.

✓**Economics** Pakistan has fertile land and energy resources, but its economy is not well developed because of a history of unstable governments.

✓**Location** The Ganges and Brahmaputra Rivers form deltas in Bangladesh.

✓**Place** Bangladesh is a densely populated and poor country.

Section 3 Other Countries of South Asia

Terms to Know
- *dzong*
- atoll
- lagoon

Main Idea

The other countries of South Asia include mountainous Nepal and Bhutan and the island countries of Sri Lanka and the Maldives.

✓**Region** The Himalaya are the major landform of Nepal and Bhutan.

✓**Economics** Most people in Nepal are farmers, but the production of textiles and carpets has gained importance in recent years.

✓**Culture** The Buddhist religion has shaped the art and culture of Bhutan.

✓**Economics** Sri Lanka has industrialized, but agriculture is still important.

✓**Economics** Tourism is the biggest industry in the Maldives.

◄ A teacher and his students have classes outdoors on a pleasant day in Bhutan.

Chapter 23 Assessment and Activities

Using Key Terms

Match the terms in Part A with their definitions in Part B.

A.

1. monsoon
2. cyclone
3. atoll
4. jute
5. subcontinent
6. delta
7. lagoon
8. caste
9. *dzong*
10. cottage industry

B.

a. social class based on a person's ancestry
b. seasonal wind
c. family members supply their own equipment to make goods
d. large landmass that is part of another continent but distinct from it
e. Buddhist center for prayer and study
f. shallow pool of water surrounded by reefs
g. intense storm system with high winds
h. ring-shaped island that surrounds a lagoon
i. area formed by soil deposited at the mouth of a river
j. plant fiber used for making rope, burlap bags, and carpet backing

Reviewing the Main Ideas

Section 1 India

11. **Place** What forms a barrier between South Asia and the rest of Asia?
12. **Place** How do the Himalaya affect India's climate?
13. **Economics** What kinds of goods are produced by India's cottage industries?
14. **Culture** What religion do most Indians practice?

Section 2 Pakistan and Bangladesh

15. **Place** What river flows through Pakistan?
16. **Human/Environment Interaction** What kind of damage can a cyclone cause?
17. **Economics** What do most of the people of Bangladesh do for a living?

Section 3 Other Countries of South Asia

18. **History** Why was Bhutan once called the Hidden Holy Land?
19. **Human/Environment Interaction** How do mountains hinder economic development in Bhutan?
20. **History** What is the basis of the civil war in Sri Lanka?
21. **Economics** What is the major industry in the Maldives?

South Asia

Place Location Activity

On a separate sheet of paper, match the letters on the map with the numbered places listed below.

1. Ganges River
2. New Delhi
3. Brahmaputra River
4. Indus River
5. Sri Lanka
6. Himalaya
7. Bangladesh
8. Mumbai
9. Western Ghats
10. Deccan Plateau

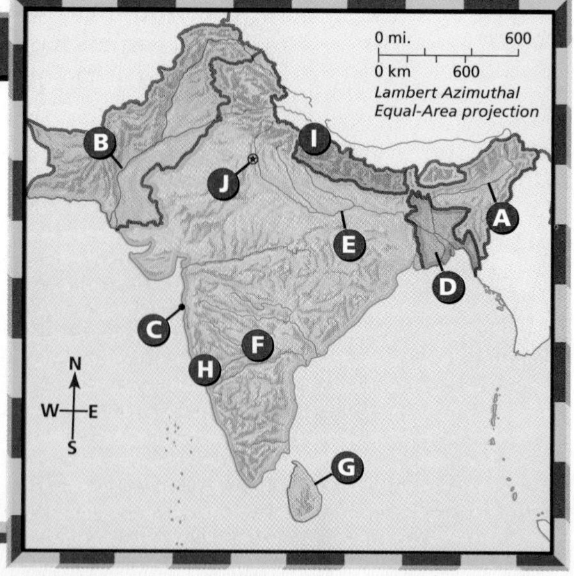

Self-Check Quiz Visit the ***Geography: The World and Its People*** Web site at gwip.glencoe.com and click on **Chapter 23–Self-Check Quizzes** to prepare for the Chapter Test.

Critical Thinking

22. **Identifying Alternatives** In this chapter you read about South Asia, a region with much poverty. What problems do you think a country faces when it has so many poor people? What are some solutions to this poverty?
23. **Understanding Cause and Effect** Draw a diagram like this one. List a physical feature of South Asia in the left-hand box. In the right-hand box, explain how that feature affects people's lives.

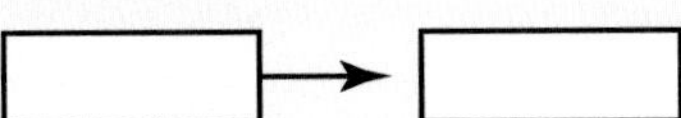

GeoJournal Activity

24. **Writing About Religion** Choose Hinduism, Islam, or Buddhism and research its main beliefs and places of worship. Find out how the religion influences family life. After your research is complete, create a chart or poster that presents your findings.

Mental Mapping Activity

25. **Focusing on the Region** Draw a simple outline map of South Asia, then label the following:
    - Bay of Bengal
    - Kashmir
    - Nepal
    - Bhutan
    - Deccan Plateau
    - Sri Lanka
    - Pakistan
    - Indian Ocean
    - Bangladesh
    - New Delhi

Technology Skills Activity

26. **Using the Internet** Use the Internet to research tourism in one of the following countries: Nepal, the Maldives, India, or Sri Lanka. Find information on the equipment and clothing that is needed, the availability of guides, costs, and so on. Publish your information in a brochure.

Standardized Test Practice

Directions: Study the graph below, then answer the following questions.

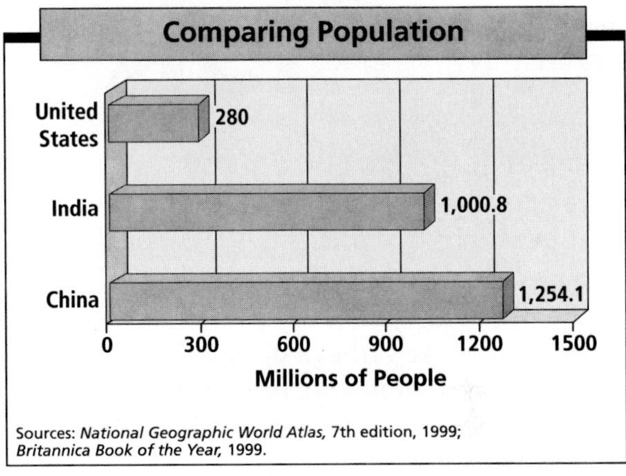

1. **How many people live in India?**
   - **A** 1,000.8
   - **B** 1,000,000.8
   - **C** 1,000,000,000.8
   - **D** 1,000,000,000,000.8
2. **About how many more people live in India than in the United States?**
   - **F** twice as many
   - **G** three times as many
   - **H** four times as many
   - **J** five times as many

Test-Taking Tip: You often need to use math skills in order to understand graphs. Look at the information along the sides and bottom of the graph to find out what the bars on the graph mean. Notice that on the graph above, the numbers represent *millions* of people. Therefore, you need to multiply the number on each bar by 1,000,000 to get the correct answer.

EYE on the Environment

THE HIMALAYA At Risk

HIMALAYA
TIBET
NEPAL
BHUTAN
CHINA
QOMOLANGMA NATURE PRESERVE
Mt. Everest
INDIA
BANGLADESH

Trouble at the Top of the World Have you ever dreamed of climbing Mt. Everest—the highest peak in the world? At 29,035 feet (8,850 m), you would get a terrific view of the Himalaya. Along the way, you would also walk through the world's highest garbage dump. Over the past 50 years, mountaineers have left more than 16 tons (15 t) of discarded oxygen bottles, abandoned tents, leftover food, and other junk on Everest's slopes.

Mt. Everest's trash is only one of many environmental problems facing the Himalayan region. Other problems include:

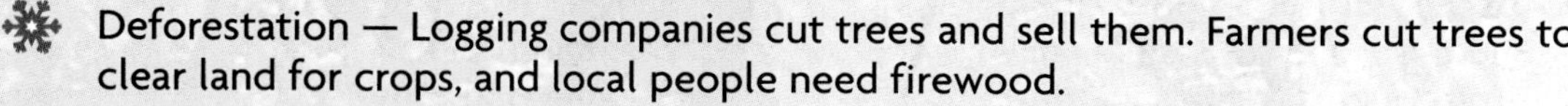

- Deforestation — Logging companies cut trees and sell them. Farmers cut trees to clear land for crops, and local people need firewood.
- Soil Erosion — Each year, wind and rain strip tons of topsoil from deforested lands.
- Tourism — Over the past 30 years, the number of visitors to Nepal each year has increased from 6,000 to 250,000. Tourists consume natural resources and create pollution.

Trash left by Himalayan climbers

Saving the Mountains Some efforts to save the Himalaya are underway.

- Conservation groups and concerned individuals are working to remove the trash on Mt. Everest.
- More national parks are being created in Nepal, Bhutan, and other parts of the region to protect forests and wildlife.

Making a Difference

Qomolangma National Nature Preserve In the late 1980s, the region surrounding Mt. Everest was an environmental disaster in the making. Garbage was piling up. Nearby mountain slopes were being stripped of trees. Uncontrolled hunting was wiping out the wildlife.

Now the situation is a little brighter, thanks to the Tibetan and Chinese governments and an American environmental group, Future Generations. Together they set up the Qomolangma National Nature Preserve. Roughly the size of Denmark, the preserve surrounds Mt. Everest and protects the region's environment.

Citizen takes action against litter in Nepal.

Qomolangma is unique in that local people have a stake in the preserve's success. Instead of paying wardens to patrol the preserve and protect its forests and wildlife, villagers do it themselves. The money that is saved goes to improving health care, education, and other social services for people in the region.

So far, the strategy is working. Future Generations reports that the standard of living for the residents of Qomolangma has been greatly improved since the preserve was established. Deforestation has been sharply reduced, and the area's wildlife is making a comeback.

Local people plant trees.

What Can You Do?

Clean Up Litter

Organize a class field trip to a nearby park or hiking area. Take along gloves and trash bags so you and your classmates can pick up litter you find. How are your cleanup efforts like those taking place on Mt. Everest?

Investigate

Create a time line showing the accomplishments of the organization Future Generations. The Internet address is www.future.org

Use the Internet

Take a virtual field trip to the Himalaya. Start at http://aleph0.clarku.edu/rajs/range.html. Click on parts of the Himalayan map to see individual peaks and regions in detail.

Chapter 24

China

The World and Its People NATIONAL GEOGRAPHIC

To learn more about the people and places of China, view ***The World and Its People*** **Chapter 24** video.

Geography online

Chapter Overview Visit the ***Geography: The World and Its People*** Web site at gwip.glencoe.com and click on **Chapter 24–Chapter Overviews** to preview information about China.

Section 1 China's Land and Climate

Guide to Reading

Main Idea

China—the third-largest country in the world—has very diverse landforms and climates.

Terms to Know

- loess
- dike
- fault
- typhoon

Places to Locate

- China
- Himalaya
- Kunlun Shan
- Plateau of Tibet
- Taklimakan Desert
- Gobi
- Manchurian Plain
- Yangtze River
- Yellow River
- Xi River

Reading Strategy

Draw a diagram like this one. Then list two facts under each heading in the outer ovals.

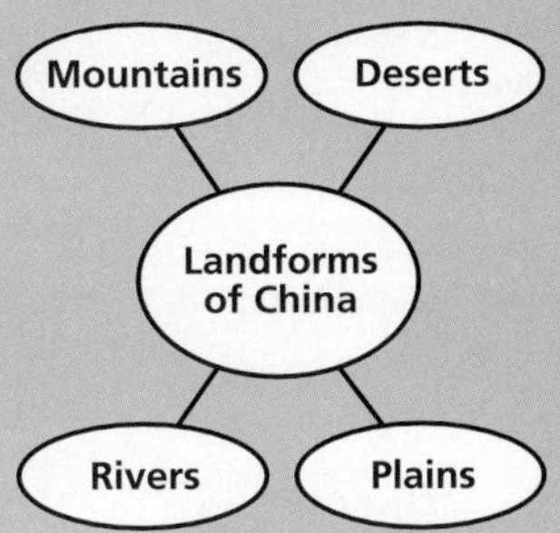

Giant pandas look cute and cuddly, but actually they are somewhat hot-tempered. You would be hot-tempered, too, if your habitat were dwindling in size. Fewer than 1,000 pandas live in the wild, and about 140 live in zoos. The wild pandas make their home on the eastern edge of the Plateau of Tibet. They eat mainly bamboo stems and leaves.

China (officially called the People's Republic of China) lies in the central part of eastern Asia. It is the third-largest country in area, after Russia and Canada. China is just slightly larger than the United States.

China's Land

The physical map on page 671 shows you the many landforms found within China's vast area. Rugged mountains cover about one-third of the country. The mighty **Himalaya** mountain ranges sweep along China's border with India and Nepal. Another towering range—the **Kunlun Shan**—twists and turns from Afghanistan into central China. Farther north you find still more awesome ranges—the Tian Shan and the Altay Mountains.

Between the Himalaya and the Kunlun Shan lies the **Plateau of Tibet.** The world's largest plateau, this high flat land is called the Roof of the World. Its height averages about 13,000 feet (3,962 m) above sea

◄ Part of the Great Wall of China

level. Scattered shrubs and grasses cover the plateau's harsh landscape. Pandas, golden monkeys, and other rare animals roam the thick forests found at the eastern end of this plateau.

In addition to very high elevations, western China has some extremely low areas. The Turpan Depression, east of the Tian Shan, lies about 505 feet (154 m) *below* sea level. It is partly filled with salt lakes. It also is the hottest area of China. Daytime temperatures can reach as high as 122°F (50°C).

In the north of China, mountain ranges circle desert areas. One of these areas is the **Taklimakan Desert.** It is an isolated region with very high temperatures. Sandstorms here may last for days and create huge, drifting sand dunes. Farther east lies another desert, the **Gobi.** Instead of sand, the Gobi has rocks and stones. Temperatures here can be extremely high—and extremely low. On summer days, the thermometer can rise to 110°F (43°C). Because the Gobi is far north and sits at a high elevation, the temperature can plunge as low as −30°F (−34°C) on winter nights.

Applying Map Skills

1. What is the capital of China?
2. What major cities are located along the Yangtze River?

Find NGS online map resources @ www.nationalgeographic.com/maps

The **Manchurian Plain** lies in the center of Manchuria, a region in northeastern China. To the east of the plain lies a heavily forested, hilly area near China's border with North Korea. To the south is the wide, flat North China Plain. The map below shows you that plains also run along the coasts of the South China and East China Seas. These fertile plains are rich in mineral resources. Almost 90 percent of China's people live here.

In the southeast, the land changes from plains to green highlands as you move inland. This region is one of the most scenic areas in China. Tourists come from around the world to see its numerous limestone hills, waterfalls, underground caves, and steep gorges.

Rivers Three of China's major waterways—the **Yangtze** (YANG•SEE), **Yellow,** and **Xi** (SHEE) **Rivers**—flow through the plains and southern highlands. They serve as important transportation routes and also as a source of soil. How? For centuries, these rivers have flooded their banks in the spring. The floodwaters have deposited rich soil to form flat river basins that can be farmed.

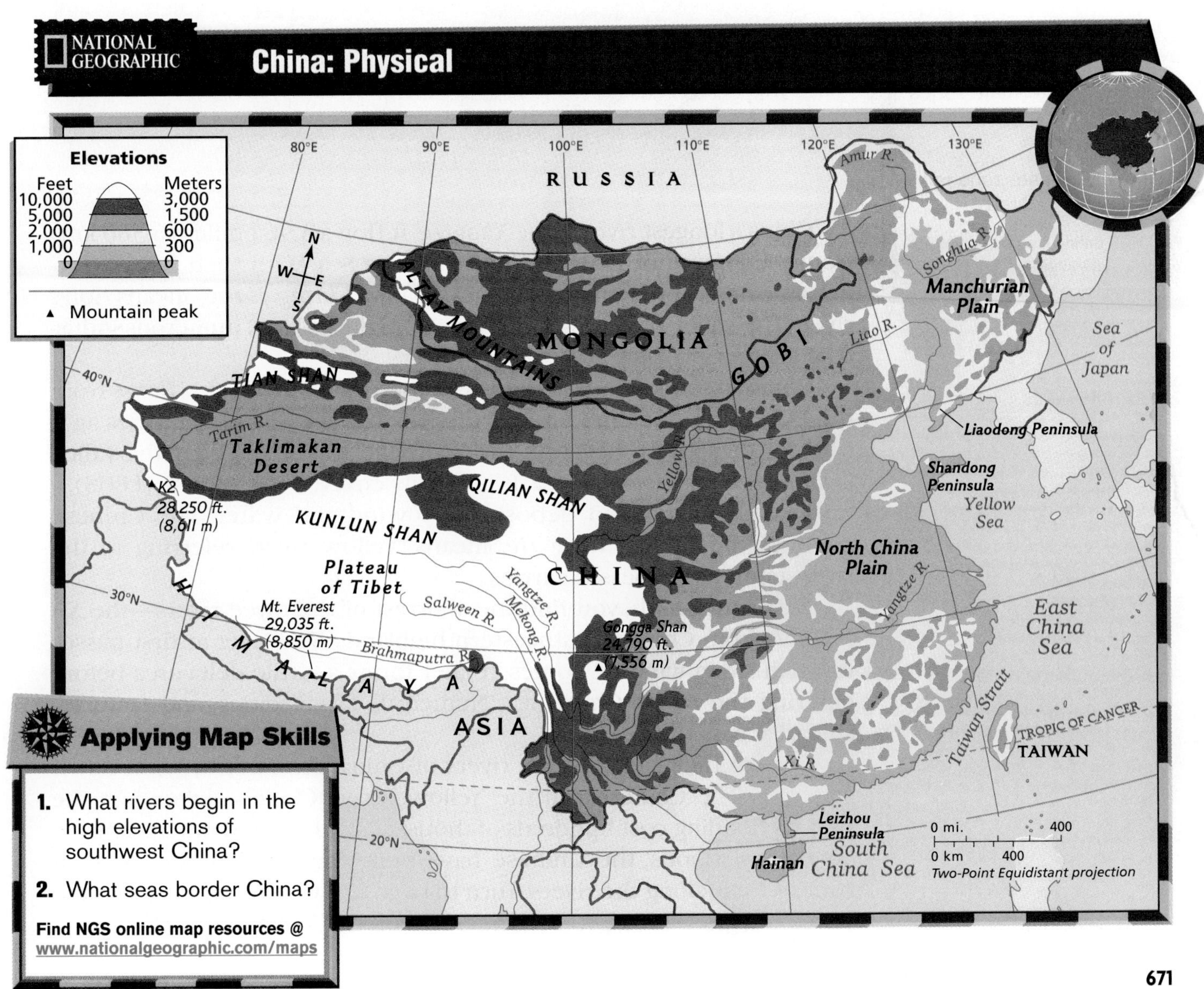

Applying Map Skills

1. What rivers begin in the high elevations of southwest China?
2. What seas border China?

Find NGS online map resources @ www.nationalgeographic.com/maps

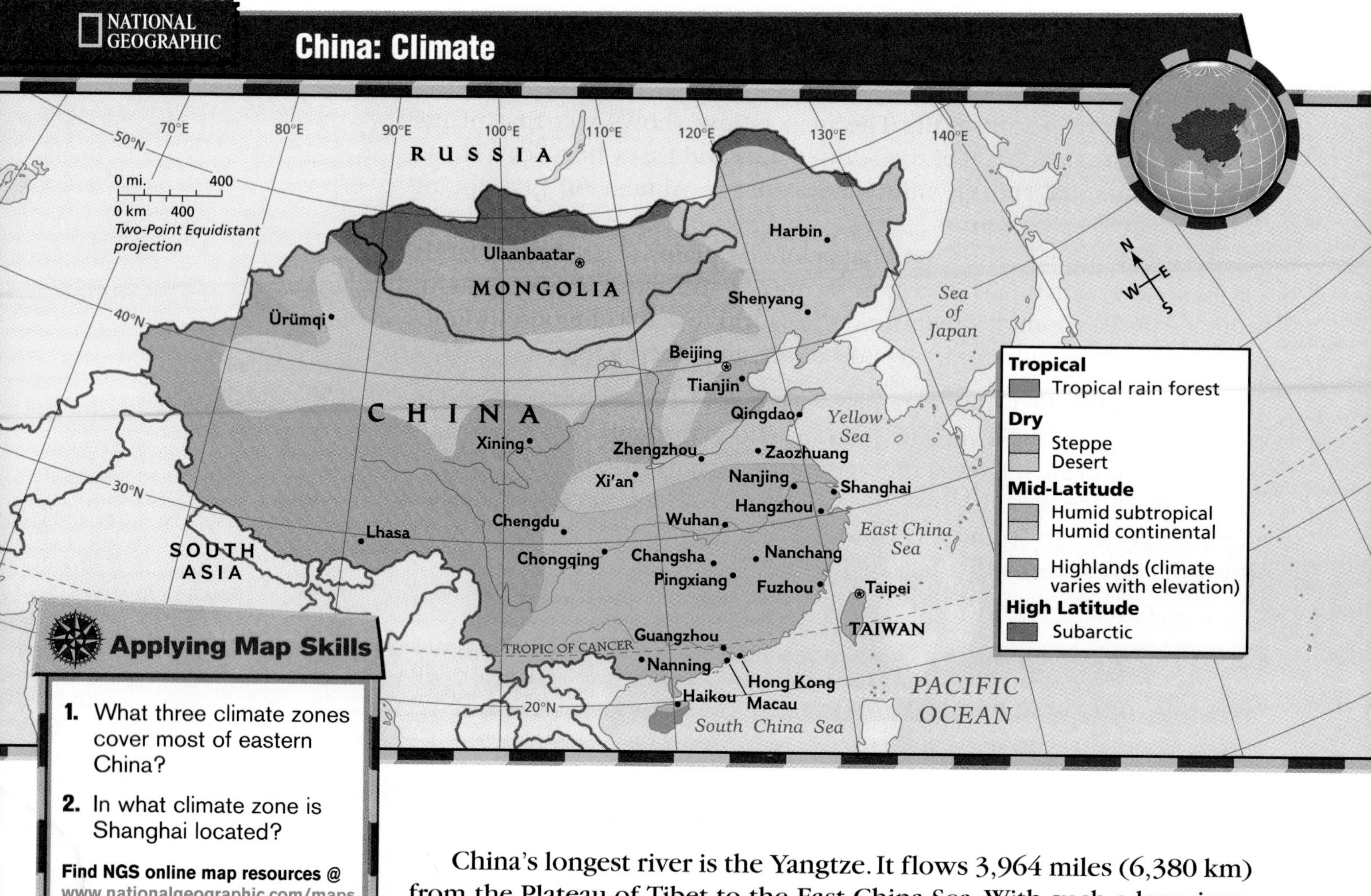

Applying Map Skills

1. What three climate zones cover most of eastern China?
2. In what climate zone is Shanghai located?

Find NGS online map resources @ www.nationalgeographic.com/maps

China's longest river is the Yangtze. It flows 3,964 miles (6,380 km) from the Plateau of Tibet to the East China Sea. With such a long journey, it is no surprise that its Chinese name, *Chang Jiang,* means "long river." The valley of the Yangtze has rich farmland and numerous industrial centers.

China's second-longest waterway, the Yellow River, also flows from the Plateau of Tibet and crosses the North China Plain. Centuries ago, Chinese civilization began in the Yellow River valley. Today the valley is an important farming area. It is thickly covered with **loess** (LEHS), a fertile, yellow-gray soil deposited by wind and water. The Chinese name of the river, *Huang He,* means "yellow river," referring to the large amounts of loess it carries.

Far to the south, you find the shortest of the three rivers—the Xi. It flows from China's southeastern highlands. The river at first passes through steep winding gorges. It later forms a fertile delta area before entering the South China Sea. Numerous farms, cities, and factories sprawl across the delta.

Despite their benefits, the rivers of China also have brought much suffering. The Chinese call the Yellow River "China's sorrow." In the past, its flooding cost hundreds of thousands of lives and much damage. To control floods, the Chinese have built dams and **dikes,** or high banks of soil, along the rivers. Turn to page 674 to learn more about the Three Gorges Dam, a project underway on the Yangtze River.

An Unsteady Land In addition to floods, people in eastern China face another danger—earthquakes. Their part of the country stretches along the Ring of Fire, a name that describes Pacific coastal areas with volcanoes and frequent earthquakes. Eastern China lies along a **fault,** or crack in the earth's crust. As a result, earthquakes in this region are common—and can be very violent. Because so many people live in eastern China, these earthquakes can bring great suffering.

✓Reading Check What are China's three major rivers?

China's Climate

Like the United States, China has many different climates. The map on page 672 shows you the seven climate zones of China. Location, elevation, and wind currents affect the type of climate found in any particular area of the country. Southeastern China has a humid subtropical climate with hot, humid summers. The northeast has a humid continental climate with cold winters. In the deserts of the northwest, summers are hot and winters are cold—but rain hardly ever falls. In the southwestern part of China, the high Plateau of Tibet has cool summers and bitterly cold winters.

Monsoons greatly affect China's climates. Cold, dry air blows from central Asia in winter. In summer the monsoons blow in from the sea, bringing warm, moist air. The summer monsoons often bring typhoons to coastal areas in the south. **Typhoons**—called hurricanes in the Atlantic Ocean—are tropical storms with strong winds and heavy rains.

✓Reading Check How many different climate zones does China have?

Assessment

Defining Terms

1. **Define** loess, dike, fault, typhoon.

Recalling Facts

2. **Place** Why is the Plateau of Tibet called the Roof of the World?
3. **Place** What are China's two large deserts?
4. **Region** What lowland region is drained by the Yangtze and Yellow Rivers?

Critical Thinking

5. **Drawing Conclusions** Why do most people live in the plains of eastern China?
6. **Analyzing Information** How are China's rivers both a blessing and a disaster?

Graphic Organizer

7. **Organizing Information** Draw a diagram like this one. In the proper places on the circle, fill in the physical features you would encounter if you traveled completely around China.

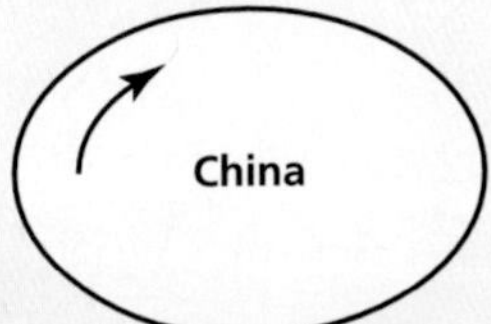

Applying Geography Skills

8. **Analyzing Maps** Look at the climate map on page 672. In what climate zone is Beijing located?

Making Connections

ART SCIENCE LITERATURE TECHNOLOGY

The Three Gorges Dam

Since 1919, Chinese officials have dreamed of building a dam across the Yangtze, the third-longest river in the world. Curving through the heart of China, the river provides an important highway for moving people and products from town to town. Yet the Yangtze is unpredictable. For thousands of years, floods have harmed the millions of people who live along its banks. Now construction is underway to build the dam.

The Dam

In 1994 the Chinese government began a 17-year-long project to build a massive dam. It will eventually be 1.5 miles (2.4 km) wide and more than 600 feet (183 m) high. The dam, called the Three Gorges Dam, will benefit China in several ways. First, it will control water flow and stop floods. Second, its system of locks will allow large ships to travel inland. This will reduce trade and transportation costs for the millions of people who live inland. Third, the dam will create electricity using water-driven engines. Engineers believe that the dam will one day create one-ninth of China's electric power.

Controversy

Even with all the proposed benefits, many people within China and elsewhere have questioned the wisdom of building the dam. When completed, the dam will create a deep reservoir nearly 400 miles (644 km) long. This reservoir will flood more than 100 towns and force nearly 2 million people to move. Many of these people must leave the farms that their families have worked for centuries. Historians point out that the reservoir will also wash away more than 1,000 important historical sites, including the homeland of the first people to settle the region about 4,000 years ago.

Environmentalists caution that the dam may create pollution and health risks. Industrial sites, once they lie underwater, may leak hazardous chemicals. Sewage from communities surrounding the dam could flow directly into the reservoir and into the Yangtze River. In the past, this problem was less serious because the fast-moving waters of the Yangtze carried waste quickly out to sea.

Making the Connection

1. How have the unpredictable waters of the Yangtze River affected the Chinese?
2. How might pollution become a more significant problem after the completion of the dam?
3. **Interpreting Points of View** List three reasons in support of constructing Three Gorges Dam and three reasons against it.

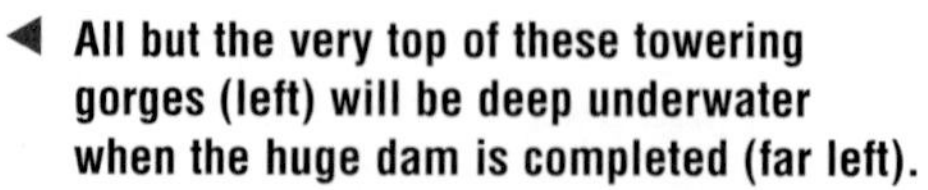

◀ **All but the very top of these towering gorges (left) will be deep underwater when the huge dam is completed (far left).**

Section 2

China's New Economy

Guide to Reading

Main Idea

China's rapidly growing economy has changed in recent years.

Terms to Know

- communist state
- invest
- consumer goods
- tungsten
- terraced field

Places to Locate

- Beijing
- Shanghai
- Hong Kong
- Macau

Reading Strategy

Draw a diagram like this one. Write two statements about the Chinese economy under the headings in each oval.

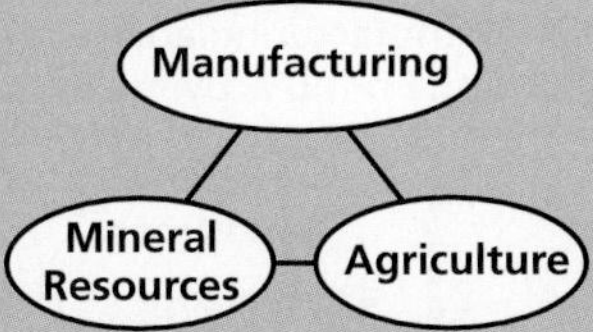

NATIONAL GEOGRAPHIC **Exploring Our World**

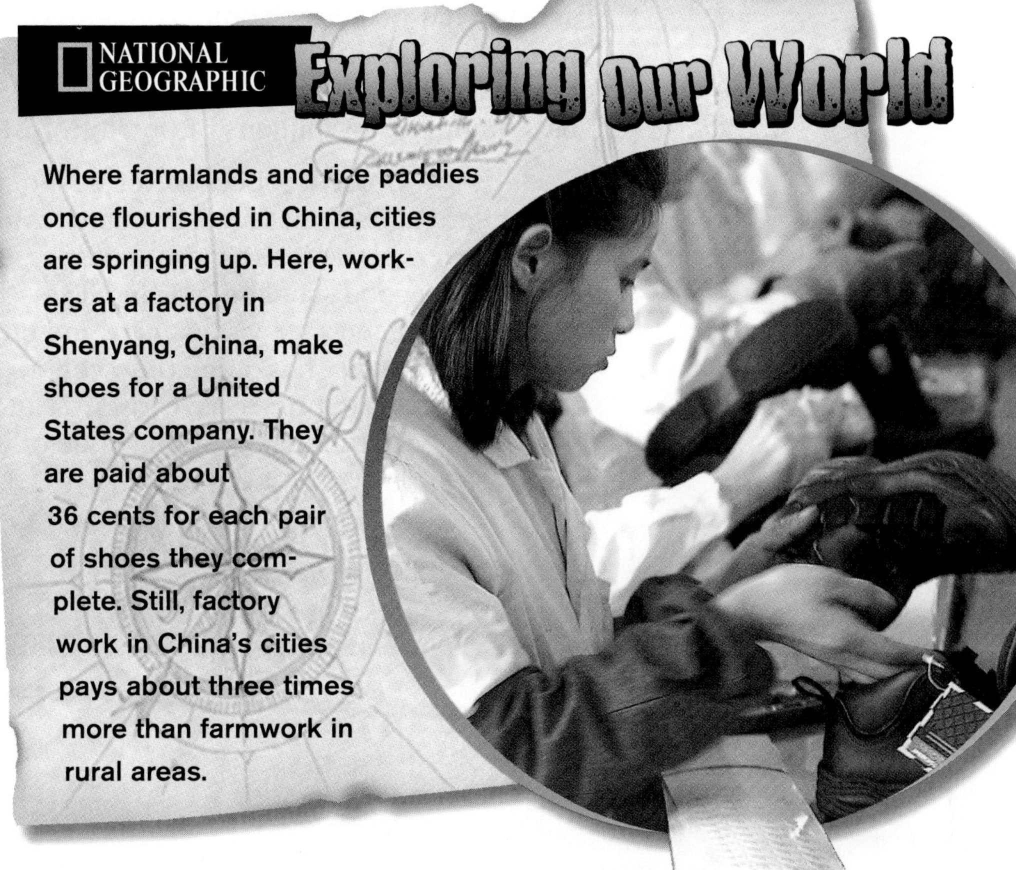

Where farmlands and rice paddies once flourished in China, cities are springing up. Here, workers at a factory in Shenyang, China, make shoes for a United States company. They are paid about 36 cents for each pair of shoes they complete. Still, factory work in China's cities pays about three times more than farmwork in rural areas.

Since 1949, China has been a **communist state,** in which the government has strong control over the economy and society as a whole. Government officials—not individuals or businesses—decide what crops are grown, what products are made, and what prices are charged. China discovered that the communist system created many problems. China fell behind other countries in technology, and manufactured goods were of poor quality.

A New Economy

In recent years, China's leaders have begun many changes to make the economy stronger. Without completely giving up communism, the government has allowed many features of the free enterprise system to take hold. The government now wants individuals to choose what jobs they want and where to start their own businesses. Workers can keep the profits they make. Farmers can grow and sell what they wish.

As a result of these and other changes, China's economy has boomed. The total value of goods and services produced in China increased four times from 1978 to 1999. Farm output also rose rapidly. Because of mountains and deserts, only 10 percent of China's land is farmed. Yet China is now a world leader in producing various agricultural products.

Foreign Trade Eager to learn about new business methods, China has asked other countries to **invest,** or put money, in Chinese businesses. Many companies in China are now jointly owned by Chinese and foreign businesspeople. Foreign companies expect two benefits from investing in China. First, they can pay Chinese workers less than they pay workers in their own countries. Second, companies in China have hundreds of millions of possible customers for their goods.

Results of Growth Because of economic growth, more of China's people are able to get jobs in manufacturing and service industries. Wages have increased, and more goods are available to buy. Some Chinese now enjoy a good standard of living. They can afford **consumer goods,** or products such as televisions, cars, and motorcycles.

Not everyone has adjusted well to the new economy. Many Chinese find that prices have risen faster than their incomes. Some Chinese have become very rich, while others remain poor.

Applying Map Skills

1. What three cities form a large manufacturing area in southern China?
2. In which regions of China do people grow wheat and not rice?

Find NGS online map resources @ www.nationalgeographic.com/maps

Leading Rice-Producing Countries

Analyzing the Graph

The most important food crop in Asia is rice.

Place **How many millions of tons of rice does China produce in a year?**

Visit gwip.glencoe.com and click on **Chapter 24—Textbook Updates.**

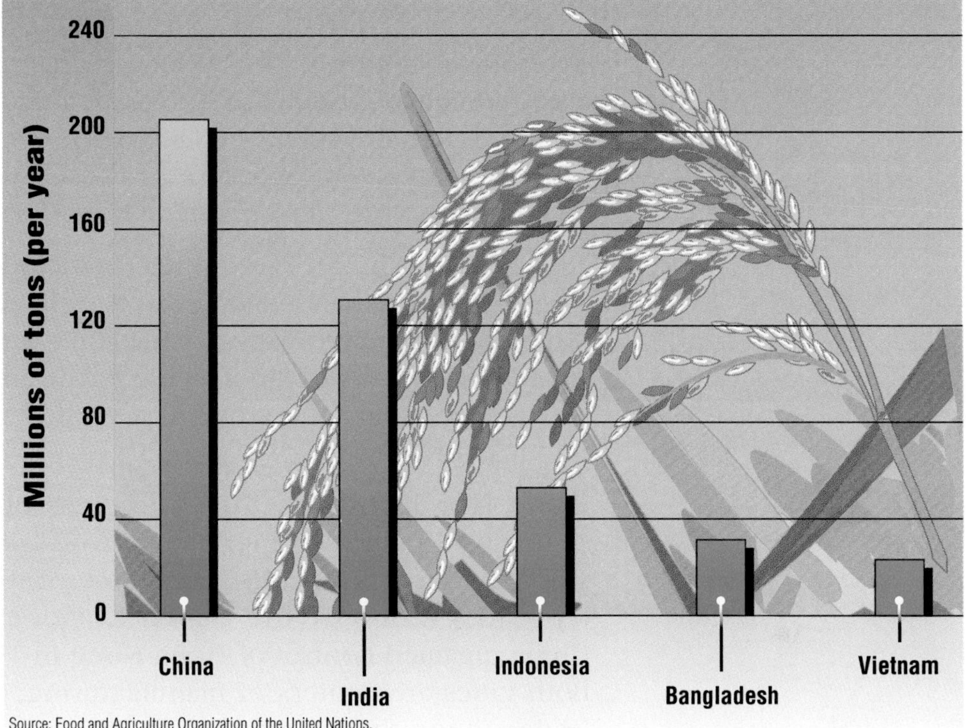

Source: Food and Agriculture Organization of the United Nations.

China's economic growth has also hurt the environment. Many factories dump poisonous chemicals into rivers. Others burn coal, which gives off smoke that pollutes the air. This pollution leads to lung disease, which causes one-fourth of all deaths in China.

Reading Check **What two benefits do foreign-owned businesses expect from operating in China?**

China's Economic Regions

The physical geography of China influences its economy. Climate zones and the availability of resources also affect economic activity. China has three economic regions: the north, south, and west.

The North The climate in the north is partly dry and often cold. As a result, farmers grow hardy crops like wheat, corn, and soybeans. The map on page 676 shows you that the north is rich in natural resources. China is a world leader in mining coal and iron ore. Other minerals include petroleum, copper, and tungsten. **Tungsten** is a metal used in electrical equipment. Trees in this region provide lumber and wood products.

Factory workers produce textiles, chemicals, electronic equipment, airplanes, and other metal goods. **Beijing** (BAY•JIHNG), China's capital and a major industrial city, is located in the north.

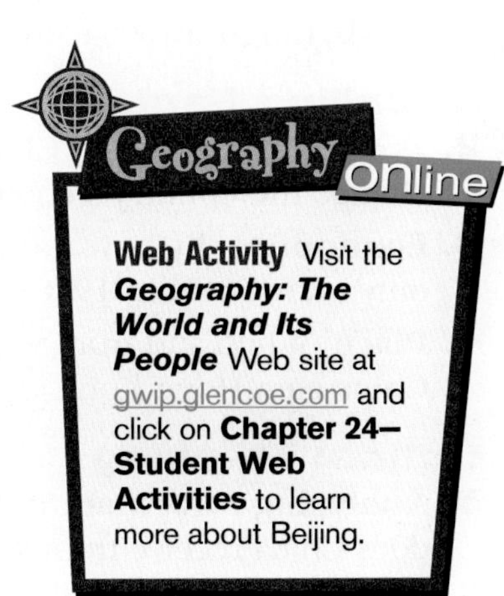

Geography Online

Web Activity Visit the ***Geography: The World and Its People*** Web site at gwip.glencoe.com and click on **Chapter 24—Student Web Activities** to learn more about Beijing.

The South The south region has fertile soil, a humid climate, and a long growing season. In hilly areas, farmers grow crops on terraced fields. A **terraced field** has strips of land cut out of a hillside like stair steps. Rice is the south's major crop. Farmers also grow tea, fruits, and vegetables and raise silkworms, which produce silk thread.

In addition to fertile soil, the south is rich in minerals such as bauxite, iron ore, and tin. The south also has many urban manufacturing areas. Some cities, such as **Shanghai,** are located on or near the coast. Others, such as Wuhan (WOO•HAHN) or Guangzhou (GWAHNG•JOH), are on rivers. Workers in these industrial cities make ships, machinery, textiles, and electrical equipment.

The West China's western region includes large areas of mountains, deserts, and grasslands. Herders graze sheep on the grasslands. The dry and cold Plateau of Tibet provides only limited grazing land for hardy animals such as yaks. In low-lying fertile areas, farmers can grow corn, wheat, and other food crops. The west is also rich in petroleum, coal, and iron ore.

Hong Kong and Macau The cities of **Hong Kong** and **Macau** (muh•KOW) are an important part of the economic changes taking place in China. Both cities were once controlled by a European country—Hong Kong by the United Kingdom, and Macau by Portugal. China regained control of Hong Kong in 1997 and of Macau in 1999. Both cities are centers of manufacturing, trade, and finance. Chinese leaders hope that the successful businesses in these cities will help spur economic growth in the rest of the country.

✓Reading Check **Which economic region has the longest growing season? Why?**

Assessment

Defining Terms

1. **Define** communist state, invest, consumer goods, tungsten, terraced field.

Recalling Facts

2. **Economics** Why did China's leaders begin to change the country's economy in recent years?
3. **Economics** By how much did China's economy increase from 1978 to 1999?
4. **Place** When and from what countries did China gain Hong Kong and Macau?

Critical Thinking

5. **Analyzing Information** What benefits does China receive from foreign investment?
6. **Summarizing Information** What are three results of China's economic growth?

Graphic Organizer

7. **Organizing Information** Draw a chart like this one. Then list the agricultural and manufactured products of China's economic regions.

Region	North	South	West
Economic Products			

Applying Geography Skills

8. **Analyzing Maps** Look at the economic activity map on page 676. Which economic region of China has the fewest manufacturing centers?

Critical Thinking Skill

Distinguishing Fact From Opinion

Distinguishing fact from opinion can help you make reasonable judgments about what others say and write. Facts can be proved by evidence such as records, documents, or historical sources. Opinions are based on people's differing values and beliefs.

Learning the Skill

The following steps will help you identify facts and opinions:

- Read or listen to the information carefully. Identify the facts. Ask: Can these statements be proved? Where would I find information to prove them?
- If a statement can be proved, it is factual. Check the sources for the facts. Often statistics sound impressive, but they may come from an unreliable source.
- Identify opinions by looking for statements of feelings or beliefs. The statements may contain words like *should, would, could, best, greatest, all, every,* or *always.*

Practicing the Skill

Read the paragraph below, then answer the questions that follow.

> Anyone who thinks the Internet is not used in China has been asleep at the mouse. China's government-owned factories and political system may seem old-fashioned. When it comes to cyberspace, however, China is moving at Net speed. Internet use is growing explosively. Two years ago, only 640,000 Chinese were using the Internet. Now more than 4 million are. International Data Corp. estimates that by 2001, the online population should hit 27 million. China will become the greatest market for computer sales in history.

Adapted from *Business Week,* August 2, 1999.

1. Identify facts. Can you prove that Chinese Internet use is increasing?
2. Note opinions. What phrases alert you that these are opinions?
3. What is the purpose of this paragraph?

Applying the Skill

Watch a television commercial. List one fact and one opinion that are stated. Does the fact seem reliable? How can you prove the fact?

GO TO Practice key skills with **Glencoe Skillbuilder Interactive Workbook, Level 1.**

◀ Chinese students attend an Internet exhibit in Beijing.

Section 3

China's People and Culture

Guide to Reading

Main Idea

The arts and ideas of ancient times still influence China today.

Terms to Know

- dynasty
- human rights
- exile
- calligraphy
- pagoda

Places to Locate

- Beijing
- Taiwan
- Tibet

Reading Strategy

Make a chart like this one. Then list two key facts in the right column for each item in the left column.

China	
History	
Government	
Urban and Rural Life	
Arts	

NATIONAL GEOGRAPHIC **Exploring Our World**

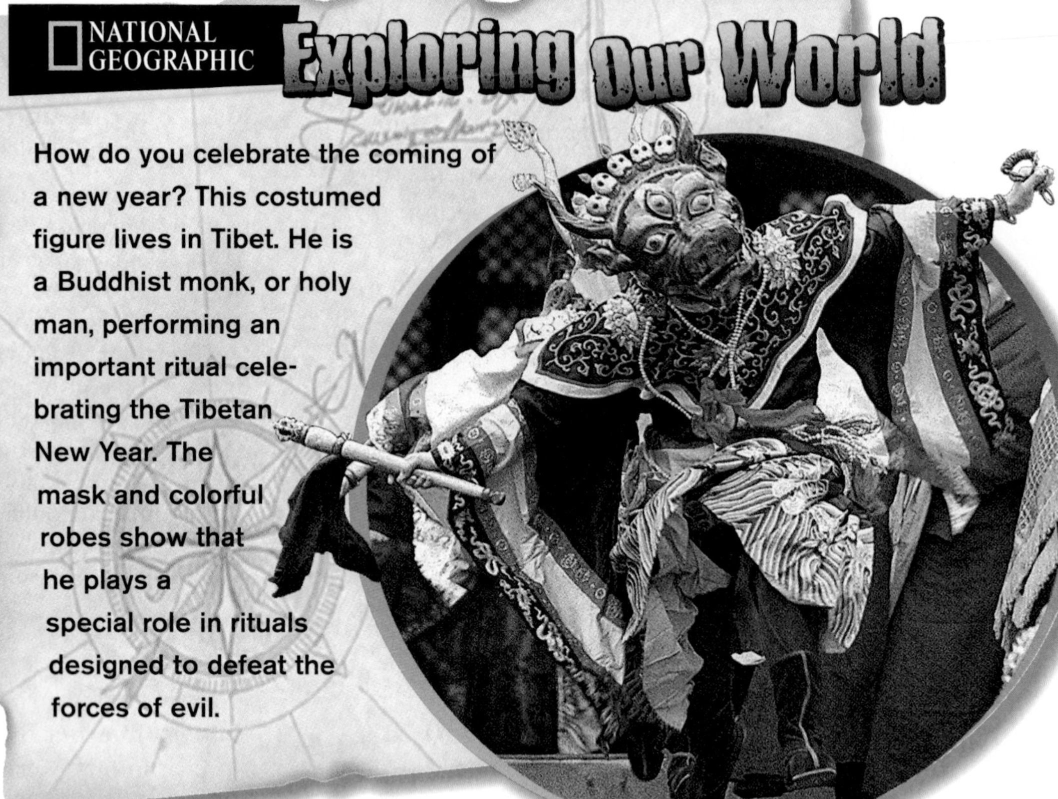

How do you celebrate the coming of a new year? This costumed figure lives in Tibet. He is a Buddhist monk, or holy man, performing an important ritual celebrating the Tibetan New Year. The mask and colorful robes show that he plays a special role in rituals designed to defeat the forces of evil.

China's population of 1.25 billion is about one-fifth of the world's people. About 92 percent of these people belong to the ethnic group called Han Chinese. They have a unique culture. The remaining 8 percent belong to 55 other ethnic groups. Most of these groups, such as the Tibetans, live in the western part of China. They have struggled to protect their traditions from Han Chinese influences.

China's History

China's civilization is more than 4,000 years old. For centuries—in fact, until the early 1900s—rulers known as emperors or empresses governed China. Many lived in the Imperial Palace, located in the heart of **Beijing.** A **dynasty,** or a line of rulers from a single family, would hold power until it was overthrown. Then a new leader would start a new dynasty. Under the dynasties, China built a highly developed culture and conquered neighboring lands.

As their civilization developed, the Chinese tried to keep out foreign invaders. In many ways, this was easy. On most of China's borders, natural barriers such as seas, mountains, and deserts already provided protection. Still, invaders threatened from the north. To defend this area, the Chinese began building the Great Wall of China about 2,200 years ago. Over the centuries, the wall was continually rebuilt and lengthened. In time, it snaked more than 4,000 miles (6,437 km) from the Yellow Sea in the east to the deserts of the west. It still stands today.

Chinese thinkers believed that learning was a key to good behavior. About 500 B.C., a thinker named Kongfuzi (KOONG•FOO•DZUH), or Confucius, taught that people should be polite, honest, brave, and wise. Children were to obey their parents, and every person was to respect the elderly and obey the country's rulers. Kongfuzi's teachings became the foundation of Chinese life. The teachings shaped China's government and society until the early 1900s.

During Kongfuzi's time, another thinker named Laozi arose. His teachings, called Daoism (DAHW•ehzm), stated that people should live simply and in harmony with nature. While Kongfuzi's ideas appealed to government leaders, Laozi's beliefs attracted artists and writers.

Beginning about A.D. 100, another religion, Buddhism, won followers among the Chinese. This faith came to China from South Asia. Buddhism taught that prayer, right thoughts, and good deeds could help people find relief from life's problems. Over time, the Chinese mixed Buddhism, Daoism, and the ideas of Kongfuzi. This mixed spiritual heritage still influences many Chinese people today.

The early Chinese were inventors as well as thinkers. Did you know that they were using paper and ink before people in other parts of the world? Other Chinese inventions included silk, the clock, the magnetic compass, printed books, gunpowder, and fireworks. For hundreds of years, China was the most advanced civilization in the world.

Communist China Foreign influences increasingly entered China during the 1700s and 1800s. Europeans especially wanted to get such fine Chinese goods as silk, tea, and pottery. The United Kingdom and other countries used military power to force China to trade.

In 1911 a Chinese uprising overthrew the last emperor. China became a republic, or a country governed by elected leaders. Disorder followed until the Nationalist political party took over. A Communist party gained power as well. After World War II, the Nationalists and the Communists fought for control of China. General Chiang Kai-shek (jee•AHNG KY•SHEHK) led the Nationalists. Mao Zedong (MOW DZUH•DOONG) led the Communists.

In 1949 the Communists won and set up the People's Republic of China under Mao Zedong. The Nationalists under Chiang Kai-shek fled to the offshore island of **Taiwan.** There they set up a rival government.

✓Reading Check **Why was the Great Wall of China built?**

Clay Warriors

One of the most fascinating archaeological finds in China was the clay army buried to guard the tomb of China's first emperor. The huge vault, covering 20 square miles (52 sq. km), was discovered in 1974. The clay warriors stand in four separate underground pits. In pit one are 6,000 life-size figures in military formation. Pit two contains 1,400 chariots and men. The third pit has an elite command force, and the fourth pit is empty, possibly abandoned before the work was completed. Each of the nearly 7,500 foot soldiers, horsemen, archers, and chariot riders were individually crafted more than 2,200 years ago.

China's Government and Society

After 1949 the Communists completely changed the mainland of China. All land and factories were taken over by the government. Farmers were organized onto large government farms, and women joined the industrial workforce. Dams and improved agricultural methods brought some economic benefits. Yet many government plans went wrong, and individual freedoms were lost. Many people were killed because they opposed communism.

After Mao Zedong died in 1976, a new Communist leader, Deng Xiaoping (DUHNG SHOW•PIHNG), decided to take a new direction. He wanted to make China a more open country. One way to do this was to give people more economic freedom. The government kept tight control over all political activities, however. It continued to deny individual freedoms and acted harshly against any Chinese who criticized its actions. In 1989 thousands of students gathered in Beijing's Tiananmen (TEE•EHN•AH•MEHN) Square. The students called for more democracy in China. The government answered by sending in tanks and troops. These forces killed thousands of protesters and arrested many more.

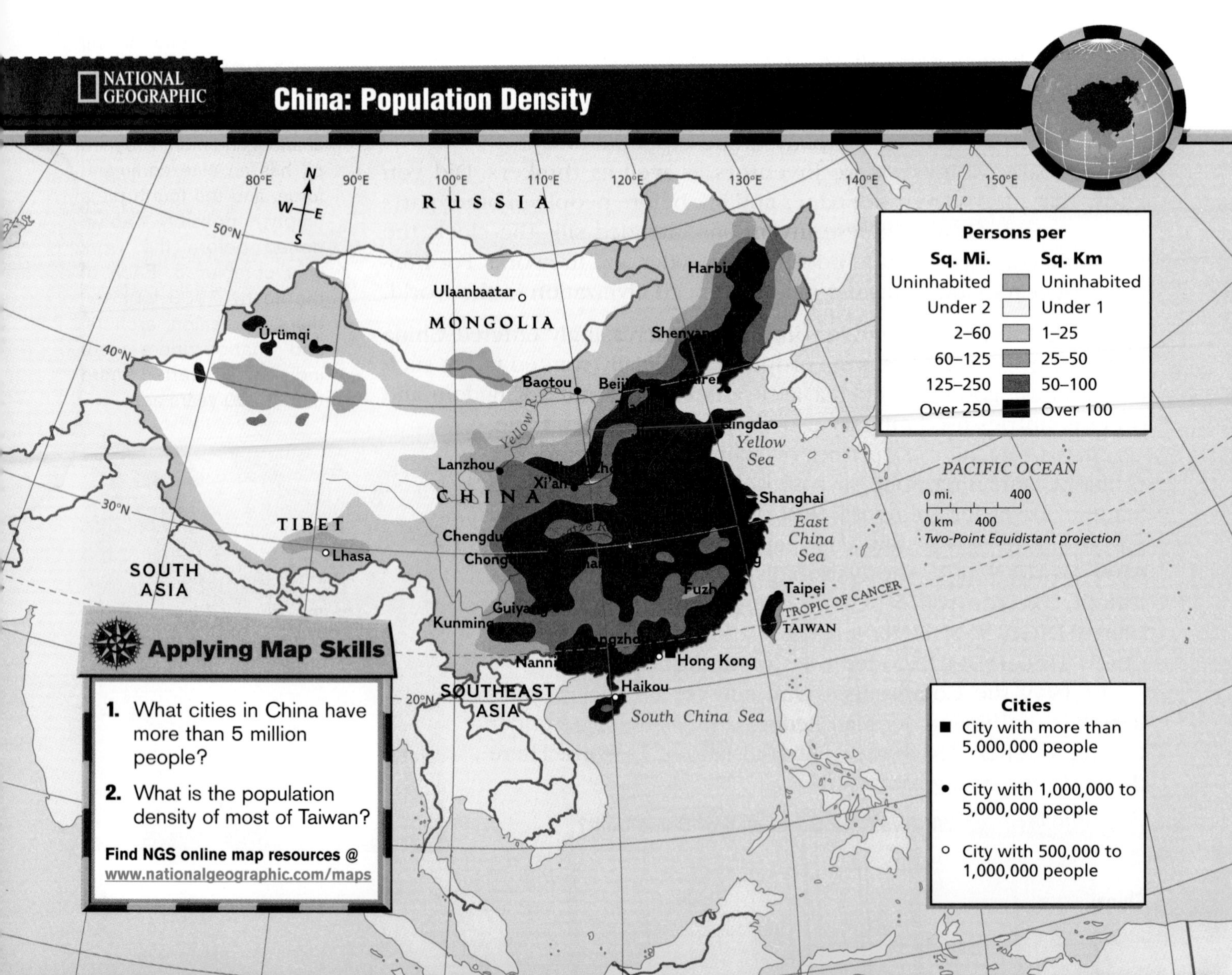

Countries around the world have protested the Chinese government's continued harsh treatment of people who criticize it. They say that Chinese leaders have no respect for **human rights**—the basic freedoms and rights, such as freedom of speech, that all people should enjoy. Because of China's actions, some people say that other countries should not trade with China.

China's leaders have also been criticized for their actions in **Tibet.** Tibet was once a separate Buddhist kingdom. China took control of the area in 1950 and crushed a rebellion there about nine years later. The Tibetan people have demanded independence since then. The Dalai Lama (DAH•LY LAH•muh), the Buddhist leader of Tibet, now lives in exile in India. Someone in **exile** is unable to live in his or her own country because of political beliefs. The Dalai Lama travels around the world trying to win support for his people.

Rural and Urban

Hundreds of thousands of people use bicycles—not cars—to get around Beijing and other cities. Still, about 70 percent of China's people live on small plots of land in rural areas.

Place **About how many people live in China's cities?**

Rural Life About 70 percent of China's people live in rural areas. The map on page 682 shows that most Chinese are crowded into the fertile river valleys of eastern China. Families work hard in their fields. They often use hand tools because mechanical equipment is too expensive.

Village life has improved in recent years. Most rural families now live in three- or four-room houses. They have enough food and some modern appliances. Many villages have community centers. People gather there to watch movies and play table tennis and basketball.

Urban Life More than 360 million Chinese people live in cities. China's cities are growing rapidly as people leave farms in the hopes of finding better-paying jobs. Living conditions in the cities are crowded, but most homes and apartments have heat, electricity, and running water. Many people now earn enough money to buy extra clothes and televisions. They also have more leisure time to attend concerts or Chinese operas, walk in parks, or visit zoos.

✓Reading Check **Why have people in other countries criticized China's government?**

China's Culture

China is famous for its traditional arts. Chinese craft workers make bronze bowls, jade jewelry, decorated silk, glazed pottery, and fine porcelain. The Chinese are also known for their painting, sculpture, and architecture.

The Chinese love of nature has influenced painting and poetry. Chinese artists paint on long panels of paper or silk. Artwork often shows scenes of mountains, rivers, and forests. Artists attempt to portray the harmony between people and nature.

Many Chinese paintings include a poem written in **calligraphy,** the art of beautiful writing. Chinese writing is different from the print you are reading right now. It uses characters that represent words or ideas instead of letters that represent sounds. There are more than 50,000 Chinese characters, but the average person recognizes only about 8,000. It takes many years to learn to write Chinese.

The Chinese developed the first porcelain centuries ago. Porcelain is made from coal dust and fine, white clay. Painted porcelain vases from early China are considered priceless today.

Most buildings in China's cities are modern. Yet traditional buildings still stand. Some have large tiled roofs with edges that curve gracefully upward. Others are Buddhist temples with many-storied towers called **pagodas.** These buildings hold large statues of the Buddha.

Foods Cooking differs greatly from region to region. In coastal areas, people enjoy fish, crab, and shrimp dishes. Central China is famous for its spicy dishes made with hot peppers. Most Chinese eat very simply. A typical Chinese meal includes vegetables with bits of meat or seafood, soup, and rice or noodles. Often the meat and vegetables are cooked quickly in a small amount of oil over very high heat. This method—called stir-frying—allows the vegetables to stay crunchy.

✓Reading Check **Why does it take many years to learn to read and write Chinese?**

Assessment

Defining Terms

1. **Define** dynasty, human rights, exile, calligraphy, pagoda.

Recalling Facts

2. **History** Who are two thinkers who influenced life in China?
3. **History** Who led the Nationalists after World War II? Who led the Communists after World War II? Who won control of China?
4. **Culture** What scenes are commonly found in Chinese paintings?

Critical Thinking

5. **Making Predictions** How would the teachings of Kongfuzi prevent rebellions in China?
6. **Summarizing Information** Why did Europeans want to force China to trade with them?

Graphic Organizer

7. **Organizing Information** Draw a time line like this one. Then list at least five dates and their events in China's history.

Applying Geography Skills

8. **Analyzing Maps** Look at the population density map on page 682. How does the population density in western China differ from that in eastern China?

China's Neighbors

Guide to Reading

Main Idea

Taiwan and Mongolia have been influenced by Chinese ways and traditions.

Terms to Know

- high-technology industry
- steppe
- nomad
- empire
- yurt

Places to Locate

- Taiwan
- Mongolia
- Taipei
- Gobi
- Ulaanbaatar

Reading Strategy

Draw a diagram like this one. Then write statements that are true of each country under their headings in the outer ovals. Where the ovals overlap, write statements that are true of both countries.

Taiwan | Mongolia

NATIONAL GEOGRAPHIC **Exploring Our World**

In the remote, harsh land of western Mongolia, a centuries-old tradition continues. Hunters train eagles to bring their kill back to the human hunter. The people say that female eagles make the best hunters. Because they weigh more than males, they can capture larger prey. Like all eagles, they have superb vision—eight times better than a human's.

Taiwan is an island close to China's mainland, and **Mongolia** borders China on the north. Throughout history, Taiwan and Mongolia have had close ties to their larger neighbor.

Taiwan

About 100 miles (161 km) off the southeastern coast of China lies the island country of Taiwan. It is slightly larger than the states of Connecticut and Massachusetts put together. Through Taiwan's center runs a ridge of steep, forested mountains. On the east, the mountains descend to a rocky coastline. On the west, they fall away to a narrow, fertile plain. This flat area is home to 90 percent of the island's people. Like southeastern China, Taiwan has a humid subtropical climate, with mild winters and hot, rainy summers.

Taiwan's Economy Taiwan has one of the world's most prosperous economies. Taiwan's wealth comes largely from high-technology industries, manufacturing, and trade with other countries. **High-technology industries** produce computers and other kinds of

Taiwan

Many electronic industries have headquarters in Taiwan.

Place **What kinds of products do high-technology factories in Taiwan produce?**

electronic equipment. Workers in Taiwan's factories make many different products, including computers, calculators, radios, televisions, and telephones. You have probably seen goods from Taiwan sold in stores in your community.

Taiwan has a growing economic influence on its Asian neighbors. Many powerful companies based in Taiwan have recently built factories in the People's Republic of China and Thailand. Despite their political differences, Taiwan and mainland China have increased their economic ties since the 1990s.

Agriculture also contributes to Taiwan's booming economy. The island's mountainous landscape limits the amount of land that can be farmed. Still, some farmers have built terraces on mountainsides to grow rice. Other major crops include sugarcane and fruits. In fact, Taiwan's farmers produce enough food not only to feed their own people but also to export.

Taiwan's History and People For centuries, Taiwan generally was part of China's empire. Then in 1895, Japan took the island after defeating China in war. The Japanese developed the economy of Taiwan but treated the people very harshly. After Japan's loss in World War II, Taiwan returned to China.

In 1949 the Nationalists under Chiang Kai-shek arrived in Taiwan from the mainland. Along with them came more than 1 million refugees fleeing Communist rule. Fearing a Communist invasion, the Nationalists kept a large army in the hope of someday retaking the mainland. They also blocked other political groups from sharing in the government.

By the early 1990s, the Nationalists felt secure enough to make changes. Local Taiwanese were allowed more opportunities in government. The one-party system ended, and Taiwan became a democracy. Taiwan still claims to be a Chinese country, but many people would like to declare Taiwan independent. China claims Taiwan as its twenty-third province and believes that it should be under China's control. China has threatened to use force against Taiwan if the island declares its independence.

About 75 percent of Taiwan's 22 million people live in urban areas. The most populous city—with 2.6 million people—is the capital, **Taipei.** This bustling center of trade and commerce has tall skyscrapers and modern stores. If you stroll through the city, however, you will see Chinese traditions. Buddhist temples, for example, still reflect traditional Chinese architecture.

✓ Reading Check **What is the capital of Taiwan?**

Mongolia

Landlocked Mongolia is a large country about the size of Alaska. Rugged mountains and high plateaus rise in the west and central regions. The bleak desert landscape of the **Gobi** spreads over the southeast. The rest of the country is covered by **steppes,** the dry treeless plains often found on the edges of a desert.

Known as the Land of the Blue Sky, Mongolia boasts more than 260 days of sunshine. Yet its climate has extremes. Rainfall is scarce, and fierce dust storms sometimes sweep across the landscape. Temperatures are very hot in the summer. In the winter, they fall below freezing at night.

For centuries, most of Mongolia's people were nomads. **Nomads** are people who move from place to place with herds of animals. Even today, many Mongolians tend sheep, goats, cattle, or camels on the country's vast steppes. Important industries in Mongolia use products from these animals. Some factories use wool to make textiles and clothing. Others use the hides of cattle to make leather and shoes. Some farmers grow wheat and other grains. Mongolia also has deposits of copper and gold.

Ulaanbaatar

Ulaanbaatar began as a Buddhist community in the early 1600s. Today it is a modern cultural and industrial center.

Place **Why is Mongolia known as the Land of the Blue Sky?**

Mongolia's History and People

Mongolia's people are famous for their skills in raising and riding horses. In the past, they also were known as fierce fighters. In the 1200s, many groups of Mongols joined together under one leader, Genghis Khan (JEHNG•guhs KAHN). He led Mongol armies on a series of conquests. The Mongols eventually carved out the largest land empire in history. An **empire** is a collection of different territories under one ruler. The Mongol Empire stretched from China all the way to eastern Europe.

During the 1300s, the Mongol Empire weakened and fell apart. China ruled the area that is now Mongolia from the 1700s to the early 1900s. In 1924 Mongolia gained independence and created a strict Communist government. The country finally became a democracy in 1990. Since then, the Mongolian economy has moved slowly from government control to a free market system.

The Race Is On!

Magnai races his older brother across the Mongolian steppes. Magnai learned to ride horses when he was three years old. "You should visit my country. It's a Mongol tradition to welcome all visitors with hot tea, cheese, fresh cream, and candies. Even in the cities, people offer their homes to visitors."

About 90 percent of Mongolia's 2.4 million people are Mongols. They speak the Mongol language. More than 60 percent of the people live in urban areas. The largest city is the capital, **Ulaanbaatar** (OO•LAHN•BAH•TAWR). Mongolians in the countryside live on farms. A few still follow the nomadic life of their ancestors. These herder-nomads live in **yurts,** large circle-shaped structures made of animal skins that can be packed up and moved from place to place.

Mongolians still enjoy the sports and foods of their nomadic ancestors. The favorite meal is boiled sheep's meat with rice, washed down with tea. The biggest event of the year is the Naadam Festival, held all over the country in mid-summer. It consists of a number of sporting events, including wrestling, archery, and horse racing.

Since before the days of the Mongol Empire, most people in Mongolia have been Buddhists. Buddhism has long influenced Mongolian art, music, and literature. Traditional music has a wide range of instruments and singing styles. In one style of Mongolian singing, male performers produce harmonic sounds from deep in the throat, releasing several notes at once.

For centuries, Buddhist temples and other holy places dotted the country. Under communism, religious worship was discouraged. Many of these historic buildings were either destroyed or left to decay. Today, people are once again able to practice their religion. They have restored or rebuilt many of their holy buildings.

✓Reading Check **What religion do most Mongolians practice?**

Section 4 Assessment

Defining Terms

1. **Define** high-technology industry, steppe, nomad, empire, yurt.

Recalling Facts

2. **Economics** What kinds of products are made in Taiwan?
3. **Government** Why has Taiwan not claimed independence from China?
4. **Place** What kinds of landscapes cover much of Mongolia?

Critical Thinking

5. **Understanding Cause and Effect** Why did many people flee to Taiwan from China in 1949?
6. **Drawing Conclusions** Why do you think Communist leaders discouraged religious worship?

Graphic Organizer

7. **Organizing Information** Draw a diagram like this one. Then write either *Taiwan* or *Mongolia* in the center oval. Write at least one fact about the country under the headings in each of the outer ovals.

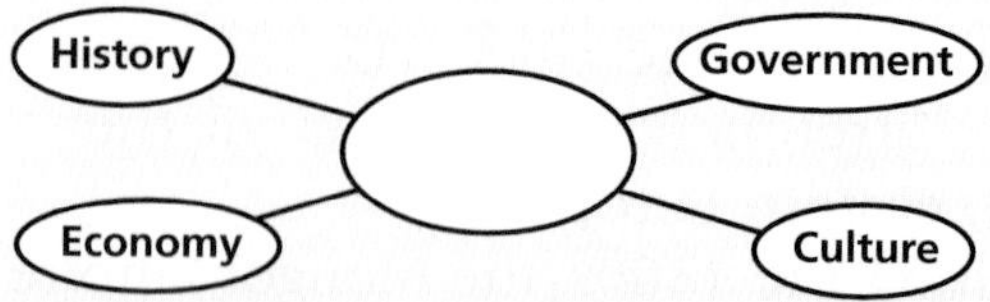

Applying Geography Skills

8. **Analyzing Maps** Look at the physical map on page 671. What mountains rise in western Mongolia? What desert is found in southern and southeastern Mongolia?

Chapter 24 Reading Review

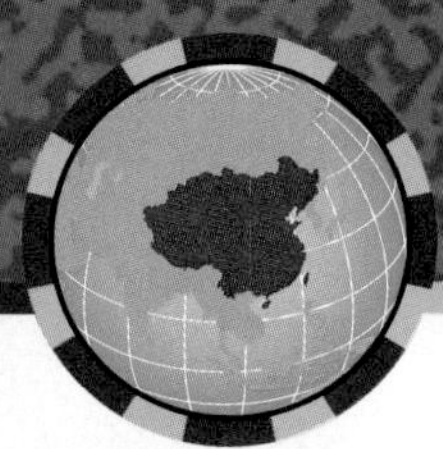

Section 1 China's Land and Climate

Terms to Know
loess
dike
fault
typhoon

Main Idea
China—the third-largest country in the world—has very diverse landforms and climates.

✓**Place** Rugged mountains and harsh deserts cover western China.

✓**Place** About 90 percent of China's people live in the lowlands of eastern China.

✓**Human/Environment Interaction** China's rivers bring fertile soil along with the danger of flooding to the eastern plains.

✓**Region** China has seven different climate zones, which depend on location, elevation, and wind patterns.

Section 2 China's New Economy

Terms to Know
communist state
invest
consumer goods
tungsten
terraced field

Main Idea
China's rapidly growing economy has changed in recent years.

✓**Economics** China's leaders have changed the economy to give the people more economic freedom. The economy has grown rapidly as a result.

✓**Economics** The northern and southern parts of eastern China are centers of farming and manufacturing. Western China has mineral resources, but the land is used mainly for herding.

Section 3 China's People and Culture

Terms to Know
dynasty
human rights
exile
calligraphy
pagoda

Main Idea
The arts and ideas of ancient times still influence China today.

✓**History** The ancient teachings of Kongfuzi, Daoism, and Buddhism still influence the people of China today.

✓**History** For thousands of years, dynasties of emperors ruled China. Today Communist leaders keep tight control over all areas of political life.

✓**Culture** China is famous for the skill of its craft workers and for its unique painting and architecture.

Section 4 China's Neighbors

Terms to Know
high-technology industry
steppe
nomad
empire
yurt

Main Idea
Taiwan and Mongolia have been influenced by Chinese ways and traditions.

✓**Location** Taiwan is an island off southeast China. The government of China does not recognize Taiwan as a separate country.

✓**Economics** Taiwan's prosperous economy has influenced other Asian economies.

✓**Place** Mongolia has rugged terrain and a harsh landscape.

✓**Culture** Some people in Mongolia still follow a traditional nomadic lifestyle, and herding remains an important economic activity.

Chapter 24

Assessment and Activities

Using Key Terms

Match the terms in Part A with their definitions in Part B.

A.

1. invest
2. dynasty
3. loess
4. high-technology industry
5. dike
6. communist state
7. terraced field
8. calligraphy
9. human rights
10. typhoon

B.

a. farming land cut out of a hillside like stair steps
b. country whose government has strong control over the economy and society
c. high banks of soil along a river to prevent flooding
d. basic freedoms of speech and movement
e. to put money into
f. the art of beautiful writing
g. storm with strong winds and heavy rains
h. fertile soil deposited by wind and water
i. line of rulers from the same family
j. businesses that produce electronic equipment

Reviewing the Main Ideas

Section 1 China's Land and Climate

11. **Place** Where do most of China's people live?
12. **Place** What three major rivers drain eastern China?

Section 2 China's New Economy

13. **Human/Environment Interaction** How has the new economy contributed to air pollution in China?
14. **Place** Why are the main grain crops in northern and southern China different?

Section 3 China's People and Culture

15. **Culture** What are the ideas of Kongfuzi? Of Laozi?
16. **Government** What kind of government does China now have?

Section 4 China's Neighbors

17. **Economics** Why is Taiwan's economy important in Asia?
18. **Place** How does Mongolia's landscape prevent much farming?
19. **Economics** How are Mongolia's main industries related to herding?

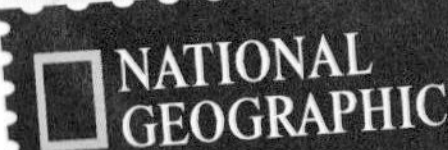

China

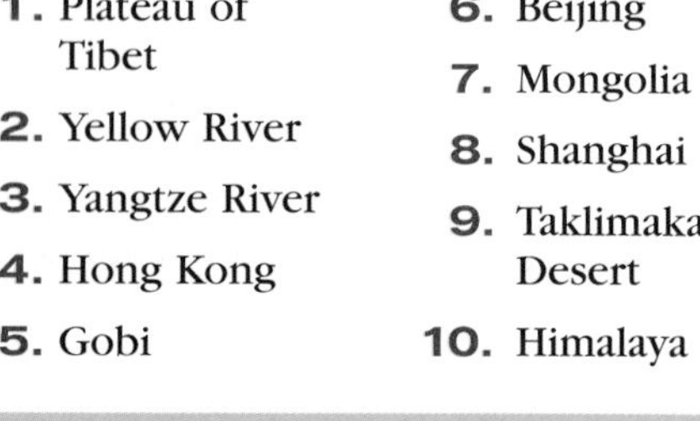

Place Location Activity

On a separate sheet of paper, match the letters on the map with the numbered places listed below.

1. Plateau of Tibet
2. Yellow River
3. Yangtze River
4. Hong Kong
5. Gobi
6. Beijing
7. Mongolia
8. Shanghai
9. Taklimakan Desert
10. Himalaya

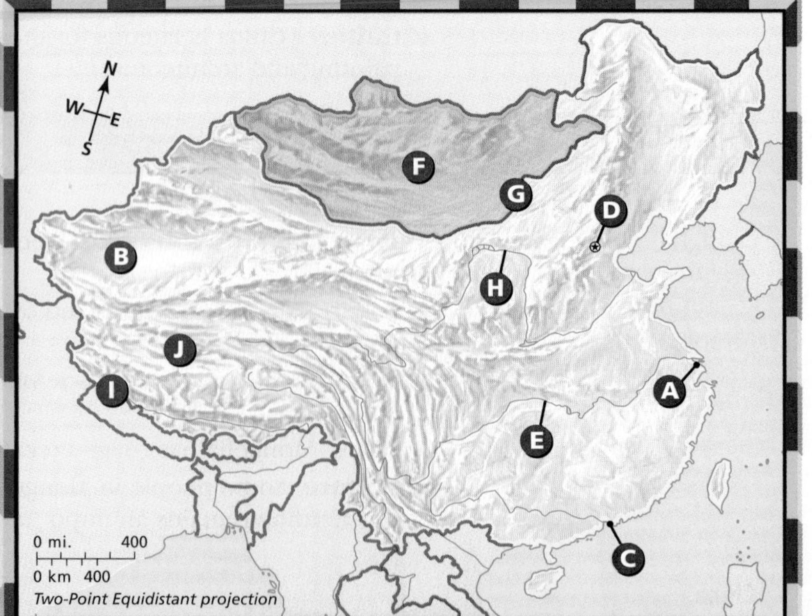

Self-Check Quiz Visit the ***Geography: The World and Its People*** Web site at gwip.glencoe.com and click on **Chapter 24—Self-Check Quizzes** to prepare for the Chapter Test.

Critical Thinking

20. **Drawing Conclusions** Why do you think China wanted to be isolated from European countries in the 1700s and 1800s?
21. **Organizing Information** Create a chart like the one below. Under each heading, write at least two facts about China.

Land & Climate	Economic Regions	History	Government	People

GeoJournal Activity

22. **Creating a Time Line** Learn more about the history of China, Mongolia, or Taiwan. Find out what important events took place, when they happened, and what effect they had on the people. Create a time line showing your findings. Include illustrations and photos.

Mental Mapping Activity

23. **Focusing on the Region** Draw a simple outline map of China and its neighbors, then label the following:

- Himalaya
- Taiwan
- Gobi
- Yangtze River
- Yellow River
- Beijing
- Ulaanbaatar
- Hong Kong

Technology Activity

24. **Developing a Multimedia Presentation** Using the Internet, research one of the arts of China. You might choose painting, architecture, literature, music, or a craft such as casting bronze or making silk. Create a museum exhibit that presents your findings. Include photographs showing examples of works from different periods in Chinese history.

Standardized Test Practice

Directions: Study the chart below, then answer the following questions.

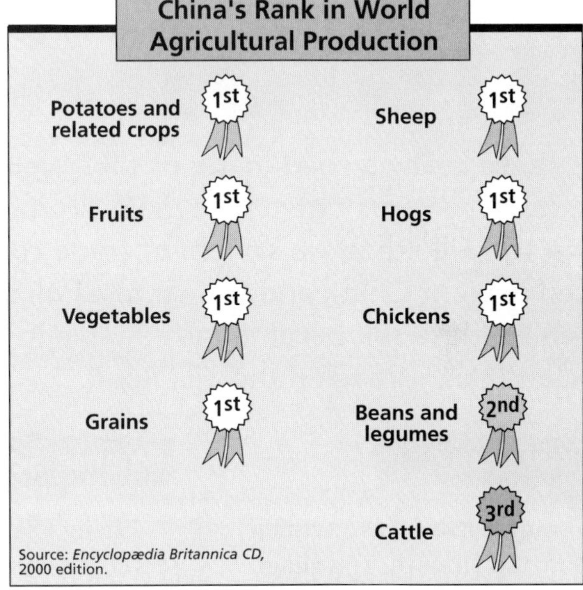

1. **In which of these categories does China NOT come in first in world production?**
   A Cattle
   B Fruits
   C Sheep
   D Vegetables
2. **All of the following are true EXCEPT**
   F China leads in growing potatoes.
   G China is the top producer of grains.
   H China raises the most hogs.
   J China is the largest producer of beans.

Test-Taking Tip: Be careful—overlooking the words NOT or EXCEPT in a question is a common error. Look for the answer choice that does NOT fit the question.

Soft and sleek, silk is a valuable textile.

The Silk Road

Was there really a road made of silk? Well, not exactly. Silk, however, was one of the main products carried along the Silk Road—a system of trade routes that linked ancient China and the empires of the West. When Chinese silk became fashionable in Rome, the precious cloth traveled the Silk Road.

A Risky Route

The road itself was anything but soft and smooth. Traveling from China, camels laden with silk and other cargo trudged through deserts, including the Taklimakan, a name meaning "go in and you won't come out." Sandstorms and intense heat made passage difficult. Farther along the route, the Pamir mountain range thrust an ice- and snow-covered barrier in the way. The road was dangerous as well. Bandits attacked often, stealing valuable goods.

Few traveled the entire 4,000-mile (6,437-km) series of routes. Instead, merchants bought goods in trading posts and oases along the way and sold them at other markets farther along, much as relay runners pass a baton.

Chinese Secret Agent

Zhang Qian, an agent on a secret mission for Chinese Emperor Wudi, may have started the silk trade. In 139 B.C. invaders swept into China, despite China's Great Wall. Zhang Qian was sent far into Central Asia to find allies to help fight the invaders. He found no allies. Instead, he brought back strong horses for the military, which he had bought with bolts of silk.

Soon the Chinese were trading silk with the Parthian Empire, now present-day Iran. It is said that Rome wanted silk after Roman soldiers spotted silk banners fluttering above Parthian troops. By the A.D. 100s, China and Rome were trading a variety of goods. From the East came such exotic items as silk, spices, and fruits. Rome paid in glass, wool, and ivory, but mostly in gold.

Ideas also traveled the Silk Road. From India, the religion of Buddhism reached China. Christianity and Islam spread eastward as well. Chinese techniques for making paper and explosives traveled west. Western methods of cloth manufacturing and better gun design went to China. The process for making silk, however, traveled nowhere until much later. The Chinese successfully guarded their secret—that silk was made from the strands of a silkworm's cocoon.

For centuries, goods and ideas traveled between East and West. In the 1300s, however, the Silk Road began to decline as sea routes proved safer than land routes. Nevertheless, even today, parts of the Silk Road are busy with trade—and tourism. In addition to camels, tour buses now travel the caravan routes.

QUESTIONS

1. How is the Silk Road "made of silk"?
2. What were some obstacles along the Silk Road?

A man and his camel travel the Silk Road in China. ▶

NATIONAL
GEOGRAPHIC
SOCIETY
Silk Road Routes
Silk Road
0 mi. 1,000
0 km 1,000
Miller projection
N
S
W
E
Velikiy
Novgorod
Moscow
Istanbul
(Constantinople)
RUSSIA
Caspian
Sea
Aral
Sea
Black Sea
Pamirs
Taklimakan
Desert
MONGOLIA
Anxi
Xi'an
CHINA
Mediterranean
Sea
Antioch
Baghdad
IRAN
Samarqand
IRAQ
INDIA
AFRICA
Arabian
Sea
Bay of
Bengal
South
China
Sea

Japan and the Koreas

To learn more about the people and places of Japan and the Koreas, view ***The World and Its People*** **Chapter 25** video.

online

Chapter Overview Visit the ***Geography: The World and Its People*** Web site at gwip.glencoe.com and click on **Chapter 25–Chapter Overviews** to preview information about Japan and the Koreas.

Japan

Guide to Reading

Main Idea

Although they have few mineral resources, Japan's people have built a prosperous country.

Terms to Know

- tsunami
- archipelago
- intensive cultivation
- clan
- shogun
- samurai
- constitutional monarchy
- megalopolis

Places to Locate

- Sea of Japan
- Hokkaido
- Honshu
- Shikoku
- Kyushu
- Mount Fuji
- Kanto Plain
- Tokyo
- Inland Sea

Reading Strategy

Make a chart like this one. In the right column, write a fact about Japan for each topic in the left column.

Japan	Fact
Land	
Economy	
History	
People	

◀ Mount Fuji overlooks Yamanashi, Japan.

NATIONAL GEOGRAPHIC **Exploring Our World**

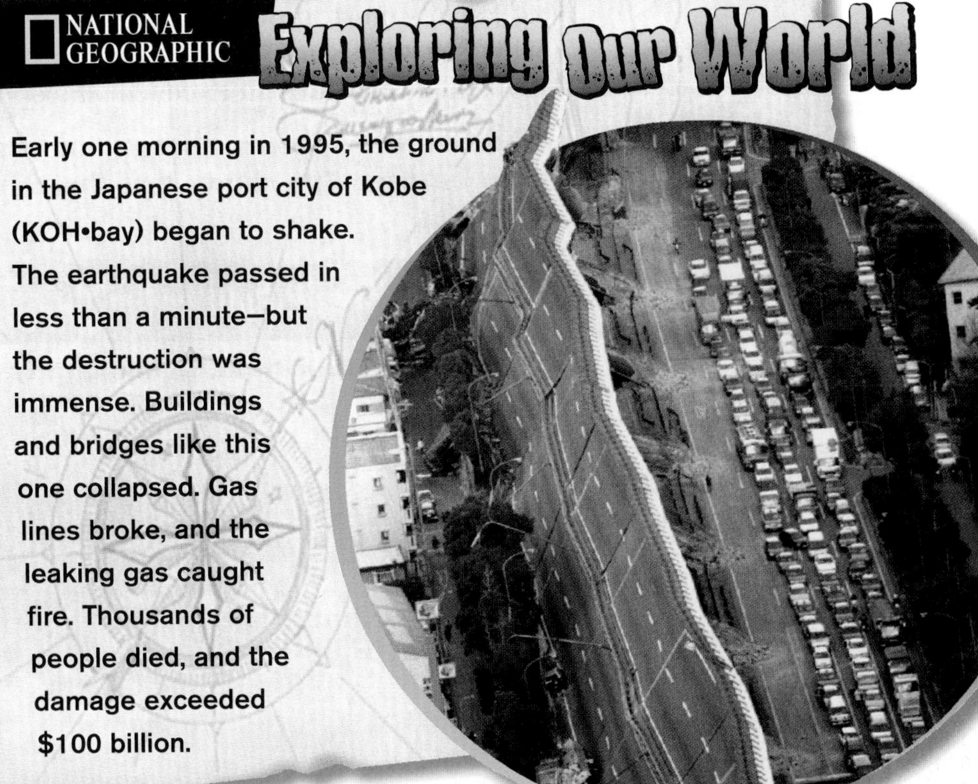

Early one morning in 1995, the ground in the Japanese port city of Kobe (KOH•bay) began to shake. The earthquake passed in less than a minute—but the destruction was immense. Buildings and bridges like this one collapsed. Gas lines broke, and the leaking gas caught fire. Thousands of people died, and the damage exceeded $100 billion.

The city of Kobe suffered an earthquake because Japan lies on the Ring of Fire. This name refers to an area surrounding the Pacific Ocean where the earth's crust often shifts. Japan experiences thousands of earthquakes a year. People in Japan also have to deal with **tsunamis** (tsu•NAH•mees). These huge sea waves caused by undersea earthquakes are very destructive along Japan's Pacific coast.

Japan's Land and Climate

Japan is an **archipelago,** or a group of islands, off the coast of eastern Asia between the **Sea of Japan** and the Pacific Ocean. Four main islands and thousands of smaller ones make up Japan's land area. The four largest islands are **Hokkaido** (hoh•KY•doh), **Honshu, Shikoku** (shee•KOH•koo), and **Kyushu** (KYOO•SHOO).

These islands are actually the peaks of mountains that rise from the floor of the Pacific Ocean. The mountains are volcanic, but many are no longer active. The most famous peak is **Mount Fuji,** Japan's highest mountain and national symbol. Rugged mountains and steep, forested hills dominate most of Japan. Narrowly squeezed between the seacoast and the mountains are plains. The **Kanto Plain** in eastern Honshu is Japan's largest plain. It holds **Tokyo,** the capital, and Yokohama, one of Asia's major port cities. You will find most of Japan's cities, farms, and industries on the coastal plains.

No part of Japan is more than 70 miles (113 km) from the sea. In bay areas along the jagged coasts lie many fine harbors and ports. One of Japan's most important seacoasts is located along the **Inland Sea.** This sea winds its way among the islands of Honshu, Shikoku, and Kyushu. It provides an excellent transportation route.

The Climate Ocean currents and winds affect Japan's climate. The map on page 706 shows that the climate differs in the north and

Applying Map Skills

1. What are Japan's four main islands?
2. What is the capital of North Korea?

Find NGS online map resources @ www.nationalgeographic.com/maps

south. Cold winds and ocean currents from the Arctic bring cold, snowy winters to Hokkaido and northern Honshu. Warm ocean currents from the Pacific give the southern part of Honshu and the southern islands a humid subtropical climate.

Reading Check **What two factors affect Japan's climate?**

Japan's Economy

Japan has few mineral resources, so it must import raw materials like iron ore, coal, and oil. However, Japan is an industrial giant known around the world for the variety and quality of its manufactured goods. Japan's modern factories use new technology and robots to make their

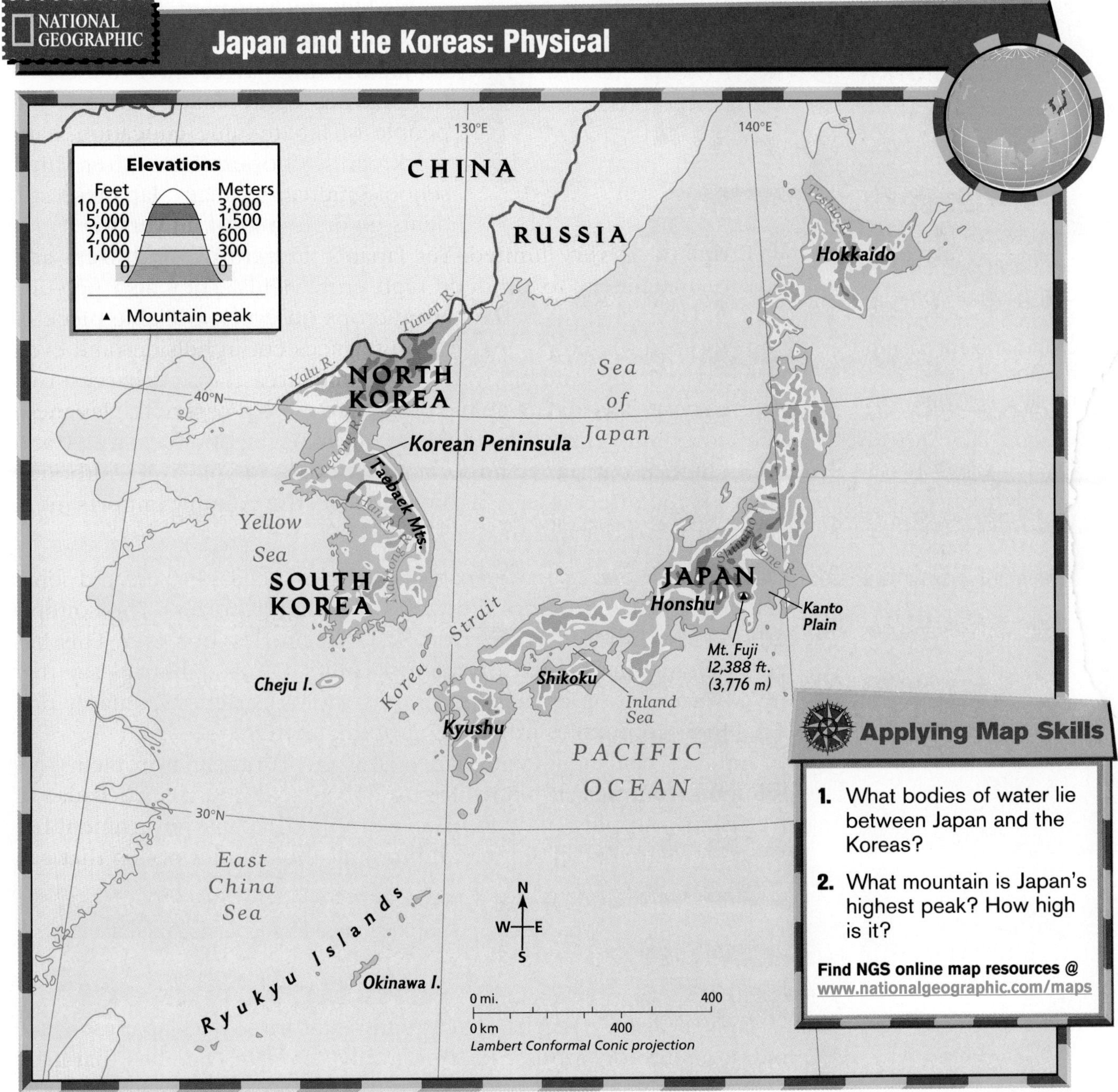

Past and Present

Past and present come together in Japan. Here, a priest of the ancient Shinto religion blesses a family's shiny new car.

Place When did Japan begin to modernize?

products quickly and carefully. These products include automobiles and other vehicles. The graph on page 16 in the **Geography Handbook** shows you that Japan leads the world in automobile production. Japan's factories also produce consumer goods like electronic equipment, watches, small appliances, and calculators. You may own a piece of electronic equipment—a television, VCR, or camera—made in Japan. Other factories produce industrial goods like steel, cement, fertilizer, plastics, and fabrics.

Japan's industries have benefited from having highly skilled workers. The people of Japan value education, hard work, and cooperation. After high school graduation, many Japanese students go on to a local university.

Farmland is very limited. Yet Japan's farmers use fertilizers and modern machinery to produce high crop yields. They also practice **intensive cultivation**—they grow crops on every available piece of land. You can see crops growing on terraces cut in hillsides and even between buildings and highways. In warmer areas, farmers harvest two or three crops a year. The chief crop is rice, a basic part of the Japanese diet. Other important crops include sugar beets, potatoes, fruits, and tea. Seafood also forms an important part of the people's diet. Although Japan's fishing fleet is large and productive, the country imports more fish than any other nation.

Economic Challenges Japan's economic success has created some challenges. Japan is one of the world's leading exporters. The country imports few finished goods from other countries, however. This has led to disagreements with trading partners. Other countries say that the government of Japan, by setting up trade restrictions, unfairly prevents their companies from selling products there.

Another challenge facing Japan is its environmental problems. Air pollution from power plants has produced acid rain. Also, because of overfishing, supplies of seafood have dropped. Japan's government has passed laws to stop pollution and to limit the amount of fish that can be caught each year.

Reading Check **What are some products made by Japanese manufacturers?**

Japan's History and Government

Japan's history reaches back many centuries. The Japanese trace their ancestry to various **clans,** or groups of related families, that lived on the islands as early as the late A.D. 400s.

The Japanese developed close ties with China on the Asian mainland. Ruled by emperors, Japan modeled its society on the Chinese way of life. The Japanese also borrowed the Chinese system of writing and accepted the Buddhist religion brought by Chinese missionaries. Today most Japanese practice Buddhism along with Shinto, Japan's own traditional religion.

In the 790s, the power of Japanese emperors began to decline. From the late 1100s to the 1860s, Japan was ruled by **shoguns,** or military leaders, and powerful land-owning warriors known as the **samurai.** Like China, Japan did not want to trade with foreign countries. In 1853 the United States government sent a fleet headed by Commodore Matthew Perry to Japan to demand trading privileges. In response to this action and other outside pressures, the Japanese started trading with other countries.

In the late 1800s, Japanese leaders began to use Western ideas to modernize the country, improve education, and set up industries. By the early 1900s, Japan was the leading military power in Asia.

In the 1930s, Japan needed more resources for its growing population. It took land in China and spread its influence to Southeast Asia. In 1941 Japanese forces attacked the American naval base at Pearl Harbor in Hawaii. This attack caused the United States to enter World War II. After four years of fighting, Japan surrendered when the United States dropped atomic bombs on two of its cities. By then, many of Japan's cities lay in ruins, and the economy had collapsed. With help from the United States, Japan became a democracy and rebuilt its economy.

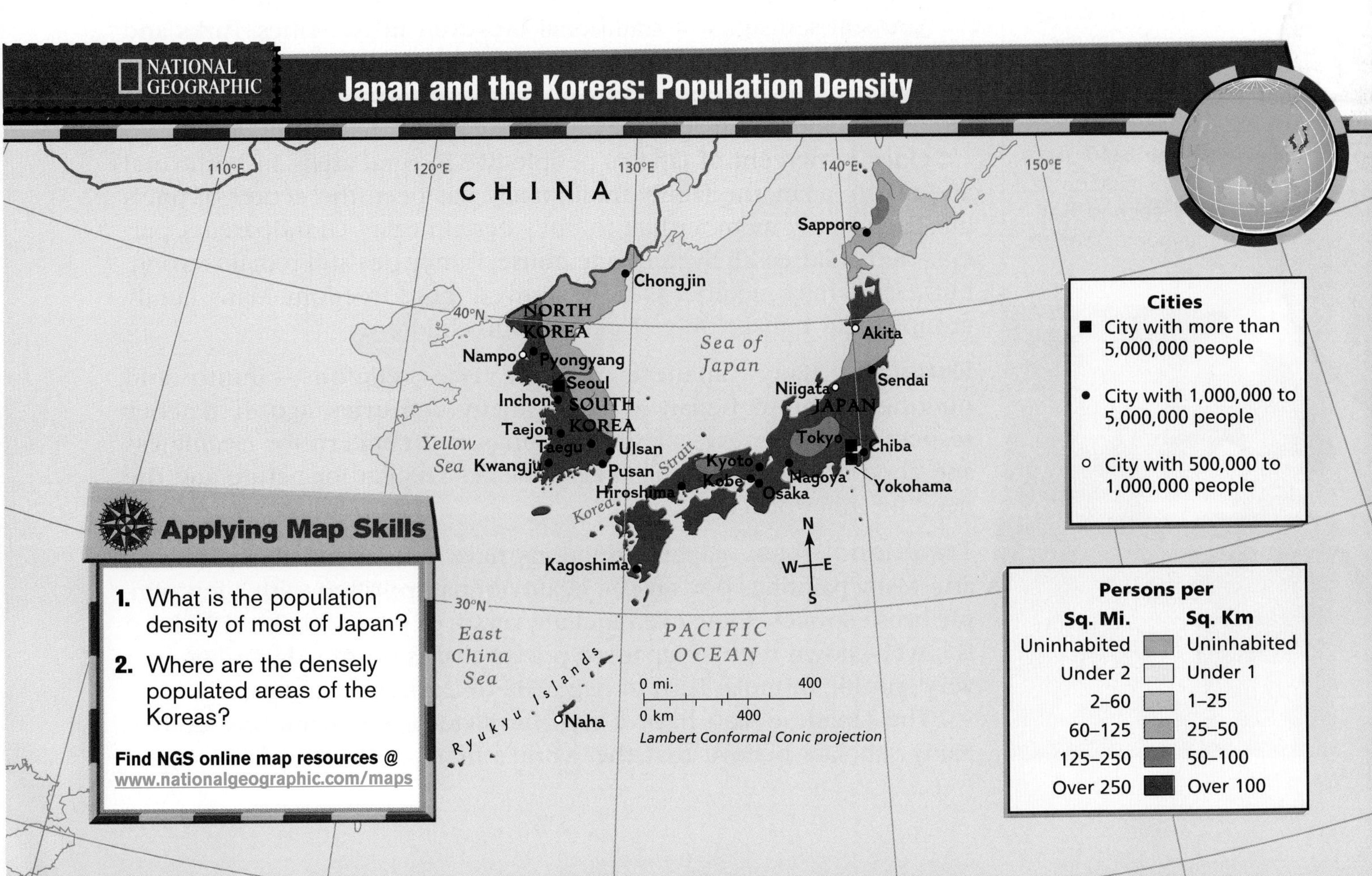

Applying Map Skills

1. What is the population density of most of Japan?
2. Where are the densely populated areas of the Koreas?

Find NGS online map resources @ www.nationalgeographic.com/maps

Japan's democracy is in the form of a **constitutional monarchy.** The emperor is the official head of state, but elected officials run the government. Voters elect representatives to the national legislature. The political party with the most members chooses a prime minister to lead the government.

Japan has great influence as a world economic power. In addition, it gives large amounts of money to poorer countries. Japan is not a military power, though. Because of the suffering that World War II caused, the Japanese have chosen to keep Japan's military small.

Reading Check **What kind of government does Japan have?**

Hard Hats to School?

Okajima Yukiko and Sataka Aya walk along ash-covered sidewalks to Kurokami Junior High School. Why are they wearing hard hats? Their city is near Japan's Mount Oyama Volcano, which has just erupted. Yukiko and Aya have grown up facing the dangers of volcanic eruptions, earthquakes, and tsunamis. "Right now we need to worry about our grades," says Yukiko. They study *sansu* (math), *rika* (science), *kokugo* (Japanese), *shakai* (social studies), *ongaku* (music), and *doutoku* (moral education). Their first class starts at 8:30 A.M., and their last class ends at 3:40 P.M. Yukiko and Aya must go to school every second Saturday of the month, too.

Japan's People and Culture

Although about the size of California, Japan has 126.7 million people—nearly one-half the population of the United States. Most of Japan's people belong to the same Japanese ethnic background. Look at the map on page 699 to see where most of Japan's people live. About three-fourths are crowded into urban areas on the coastal plains. The four large cities of Tokyo, Yokohama, Nagoya, and Osaka form a **megalopolis,** or a huge urban area made up of several large cities and communities near them.

Japan's cities have tall office buildings, busy streets, and speedy highways. Homes and apartments are small and close to one another. Many city workers crowd into subway trains to get to work. Men work long hours and arrive home very late. Women often quit their jobs to raise children and return to work when the children are grown.

You still see signs of traditional life, even in the cities. Parks and gardens give people a chance to take a break from the busy day. It is common to see a person dressed in a traditional garment called a kimono walking with another person wearing a T-shirt and jeans.

Only 22 percent of Japan's people live in rural areas. In both rural and urban Japan, the family traditionally has been the center of one's life. Each family member had to obey certain rules. Grandparents, parents, and children all lived in one house. Family ties still remain strong, but each family member is now allowed more freedom. Many family groups today consist only of parents and children.

Religion Many Japanese practice two religions—Shinto and Buddhism. Shinto began in Japan many centuries ago. It teaches respect for nature, love of simple things, and concern for cleanliness and good manners. Buddhism also teaches respect for nature and the need for inner peace.

Traditional Arts Japan's religions have influenced the country's arts. Many paintings portray the beauty of nature, often with a few simple brush strokes. Some even include verses of poetry. Haiku (HY•koo) is a well-known type of Japanese poetry that is written according to a very specific formula. Turn to page 702 to learn more about haiku.

The Japanese also have a rich heritage of literature and drama. Many scholars believe that the world's first novel came from Japan.

The novel is called *The Tale of Genji* and was written by a noblewoman about A.D. 1000. Since the 1600s, Japanese theater-goers have attended the historical plays of the Kabuki theater. In Kabuki plays, actors wearing brilliantly colored costumes perform on colorful stages.

Many of Japan's sports have their origins in the past. A popular sport is sumo, an ancient Japanese form of wrestling. Two ancient martial arts—judo and karate—also developed in this area. Today martial arts are practiced both for self-defense and for exercise.

Modern Pastimes Along with these traditional arts, the people of Japan enjoy modern pastimes. Many Japanese are enthusiastic about baseball, and the professional leagues in Japan field several teams. Despite Japan's strong emphasis on education, life is not all work for Japanese young people. They enjoy rock music, modern fashions, television, and movies. Japanese cartoon shows are popular around the world.

Baseball

A Japanese fan cheers on his team.

Place **What are some other popular pastimes in Japan?**

Reading Check **What two religions are found in Japan?**

Section 1 Assessment

Defining Terms

1. **Define** tsunami, archipelago, intensive cultivation, clan, shogun, samurai, constitutional monarchy, megalopolis.

Recalling Facts

2. **Location** Why does Japan experience earthquakes?
3. **History** Who were the samurai?
4. **Culture** How have Japan's religions influenced the country's arts?

Critical Thinking

5. **Summarizing Information** Why do the Japanese not want a large military?
6. **Synthesizing Information** What three values of the Japanese people have created good workers?

Graphic Organizer

7. **Organizing Information** Draw a diagram like this one. List Japan's economic successes in the large oval and its economic challenges in each of the smaller ovals.

Applying Geography Skills

8. **Analyzing Maps** Look at the economic activity map on page 705. What mineral resources are found in Japan?

Making Connections

ART SCIENCE LITERATURE TECHNOLOGY

Haiku

Haiku is a type of poetry that first became popular in Japan during the 1600s. A haiku is a three-line poem, usually about nature and human emotions. The traditional haiku requires 17 syllables—5 in the first line, 7 in the second line, and 5 in the third line. All of the haiku below, written by famous Japanese poets, concern the subject of New Year's Day.*

For this New Year's Day,
The sight we gaze upon shall be
Mount Fuji.
Sôkan

That is good, this too is good,—
New Year's Day
In my old age.
Rôyto

New Year's Day;
Whosoever's face we see,
It is care-free.
Shigyoku

New Year's Day:
My hovel,
The same as ever.
Issa

New Year's Day:
What luck! What luck!
A pale blue sky!
Issa

The dawn of New Year's Day;
Yesterday,
How far off!
Ichiku

▲ **This Japanese wood-block print shows two girls playing a New Year's game.**

The first dream of the year;
I kept it a secret,
And smiled to myself.
Shô-u

*The translations may have affected the number of syllables.

Making the Connection

1. How does the poet Shigyoku think most people react to New Year's Day?
2. From his poem, how can you tell that Ichiku sees the New Year as a new beginning?
3. **Making Comparisons** Compare the two poems by Issa. How does his mood change from one to the other?

Section 2

The Two Koreas

Guide to Reading

Main Idea

South Korea and North Korea share the same peninsula and history, but they have very different political and economic systems.

Terms to Know

- dynasty
- monsoon
- anthracite
- famine

Places to Locate

- Korean Peninsula
- North Korea
- South Korea
- Seoul
- Pyongyang

Reading Strategy

Create a time line like this one to record four important dates and their events in Korean history.

NATIONAL GEOGRAPHIC **Exploring Our World**

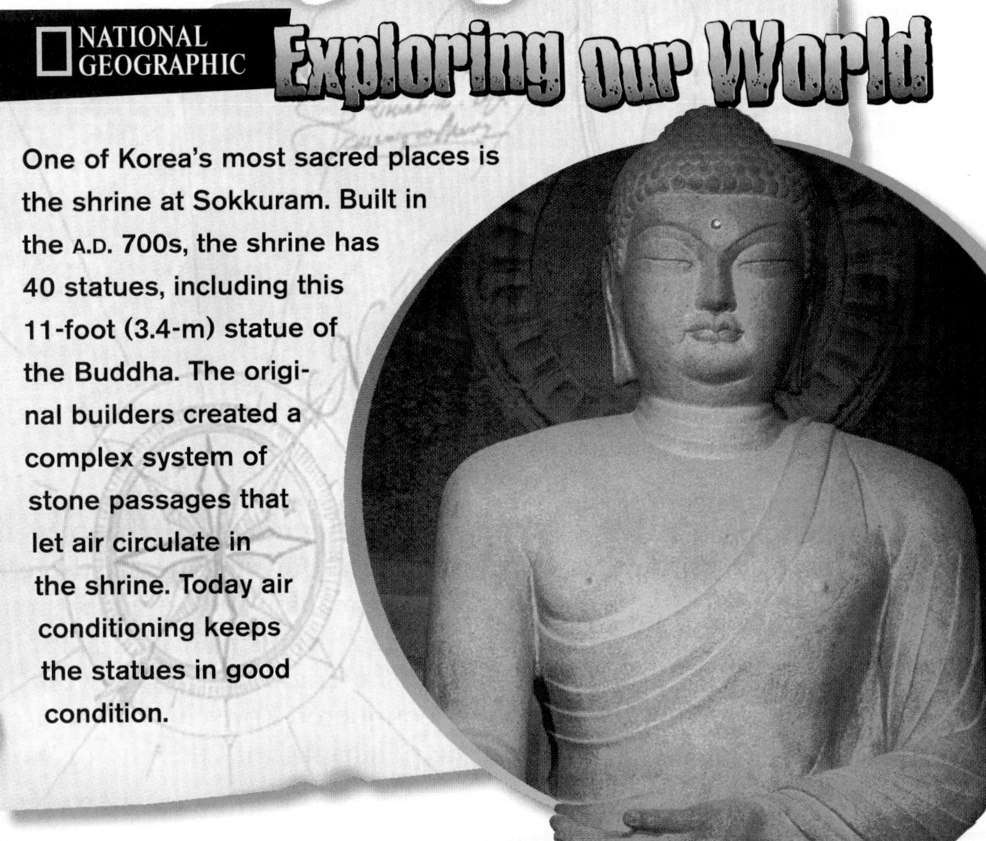

One of Korea's most sacred places is the shrine at Sokkuram. Built in the A.D. 700s, the shrine has 40 statues, including this 11-foot (3.4-m) statue of the Buddha. The original builders created a complex system of stone passages that let air circulate in the shrine. Today air conditioning keeps the statues in good condition.

The **Korean Peninsula** juts out from northern China, between the Sea of Japan and the Yellow Sea. For centuries, this piece of land held a unified country. Today the peninsula is divided into two nations—Communist **North Korea** and non-Communist **South Korea.** For nearly 50 years after World War II, the two governments were bitter enemies. Since the 1990s, they have been drawing closer together.

A Divided Country

The Koreans trace their ancestry to people who settled on the peninsula thousands of years ago. From the 100s B.C. until the early A.D. 300s, neighboring China ruled Korea. When Chinese control ended, separate Korean kingdoms arose throughout the peninsula.

From A.D. 668 to 935, a single kingdom called Silla (SIH•luh) united much of the peninsula. During this time, Korea made many cultural and scientific advances. For example, Silla rulers built one of the world's earliest astronomical observatories in the A.D. 600s.

Other **dynasties,** or ruling families, followed the Silla. In the 1400s, scholars invented a new way of writing the Korean language. This new

NATIONAL GEOGRAPHIC **On Location**

Korean Border

Nearly 50 years after the fighting stopped in Korea, troops still patrol the border between North and South Korea (above). Seoul, South Korea's modern capital (right), is only about 25 miles (40 km) from the border.

Location **Where was the line of division drawn between the two countries?**

system—called *hangul* (HAHN•GOOL)—used only 28 symbols to write words. This is far fewer than the thousands of characters needed to write Chinese, making the Korean system much easier to learn.

The Korean Peninsula was a stepping stone between Japan and mainland Asia. Trade and ideas went back and forth. In 1910 the Japanese conquered Korea and made it part of their empire. They governed the peninsula until the end of World War II in 1945.

Division and War After World War II, troops from the Communist Soviet Union took over the northern half of Korea. American troops occupied the southern half. Korea eventually divided along the 38th parallel. A Communist state arose in what came to be called North Korea. A non-Communist government controlled South Korea.

In 1950 the armies of North Korea attacked South Korea. They hoped to unite all of Korea under Communist rule. United Nations countries, led by the United States, rushed to support South Korea. China's Communist leaders eventually sent troops across the Yalu River to help North Korea. The Korean War finally ended in 1953—without a peace treaty or a victory for either side. By the 1960s, two separate countries had developed in the Korean Peninsula.

After years of bitterness, the two Koreas in the 1990s developed closer relations. In the year 2000, the leaders of North Korea and South Korea held a meeting for the first time since the division.

✓Reading Check **Why is the Korean Peninsula divided?**

South Korea

South Korea, slightly larger than Indiana, lies at the southern end of the Korean Peninsula. The forested Taebaek Mountains dominate most of central and eastern South Korea. Plains with hills and fertile river valleys spread along the southern and western coasts. Most South Koreans live in these coastal areas.

Monsoons affect South Korea's climate. A **monsoon** is the seasonal wind that blows over Asia for months at a time. During the summer, a monsoon from the south brings hot, humid weather. In the winter, a monsoon blows in from the north, bringing cold, dry weather.

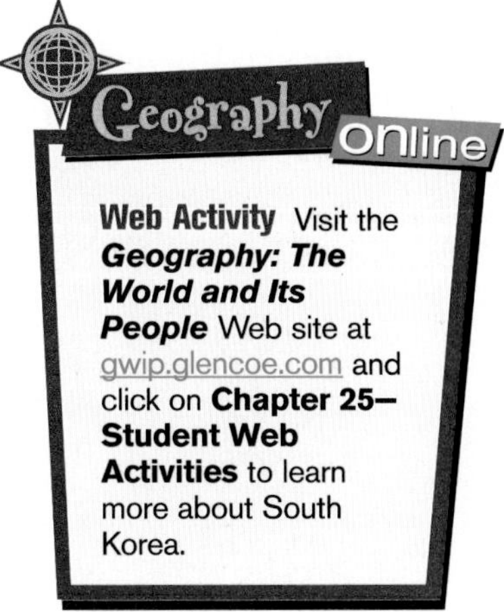

Web Activity Visit the ***Geography: The World and Its People*** Web site at gwip.glencoe.com and click on **Chapter 25—Student Web Activities** to learn more about South Korea.

Manufacturing and trade dominate South Korea's economy. High-technology and service industries have grown tremendously. The country is a leading exporter of ships, cars, textiles, computers, and electronic appliances. The map below shows you that South Korea's mineral resources include tungsten, zinc, and anthracite. **Anthracite** is a type of hard coal. In the 1990s, South Korea faced economic difficulties, but it remains one of the economic powers of Asia.

South Korean farmers own their land, although most of their farms are very small. The major crops are rice, barley, onions, potatoes, cabbage, apples, and tangerines. Rice is the country's basic food item. One of the most popular Korean dishes is kimchi, a highly spiced blend of vegetables mixed with chili, garlic, and ginger. Many farmers also raise livestock, especially chickens. Some add to their income by fishing.

South Korea's People The people of the two Koreas belong to the same Korean ethnic group. South Korea has about 46.9 million people. More than 80 percent live in cities and towns in the coastal plains. South Korea's capital of **Seoul** is the largest city.

Most city dwellers live in tall apartment buildings. Many own cars, but they also use buses, subways, and trains to travel to and from work.

NATIONAL GEOGRAPHIC

Japan and the Koreas: Economic Activity

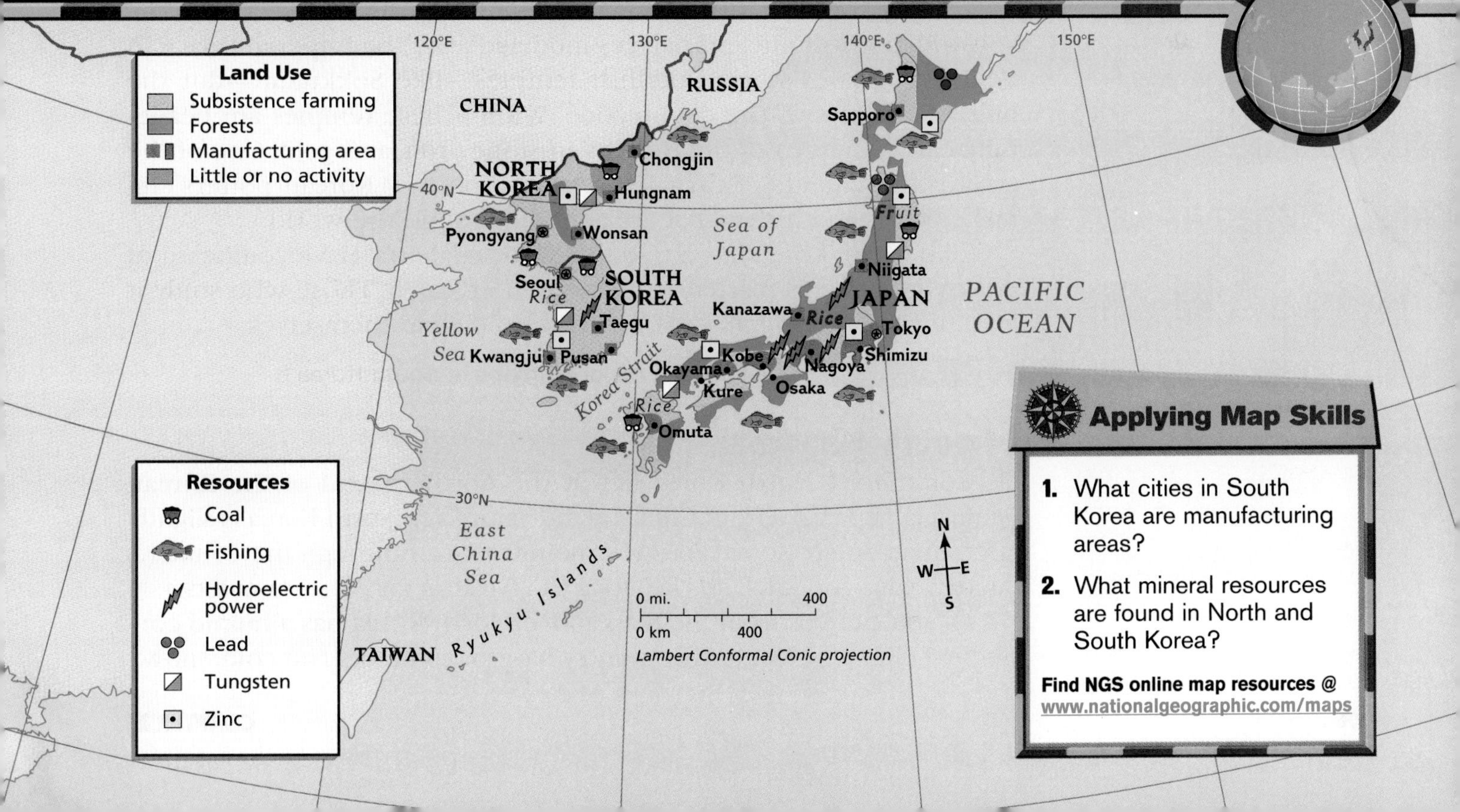

Land Use
- Subsistence farming
- Forests
- Manufacturing area
- Little or no activity

Resources
- Coal
- Fishing
- Hydroelectric power
- Lead
- Tungsten
- Zinc

120°E 130°E 140°E 150°E 40°N 30°N

CHINA, RUSSIA, NORTH KOREA, SOUTH KOREA, JAPAN, TAIWAN, Chongjin, Hungnam, Pyongyang, Wonsan, Seoul, Taegu, Kwangju, Pusan, Sapporo, Niigata, Kanazawa, Tokyo, Shimizu, Nagoya, Kobe, Osaka, Okayama, Kure, Omuta, Sea of Japan, Yellow Sea, Korea Strait, East China Sea, Ryukyu Islands, PACIFIC OCEAN, Rice, Fruit

0 mi. 400
0 km 400
Lambert Conformal Conic projection

Applying Map Skills

1. What cities in South Korea are manufacturing areas?
2. What mineral resources are found in North and South Korea?

Find NGS online map resources @ www.nationalgeographic.com/maps

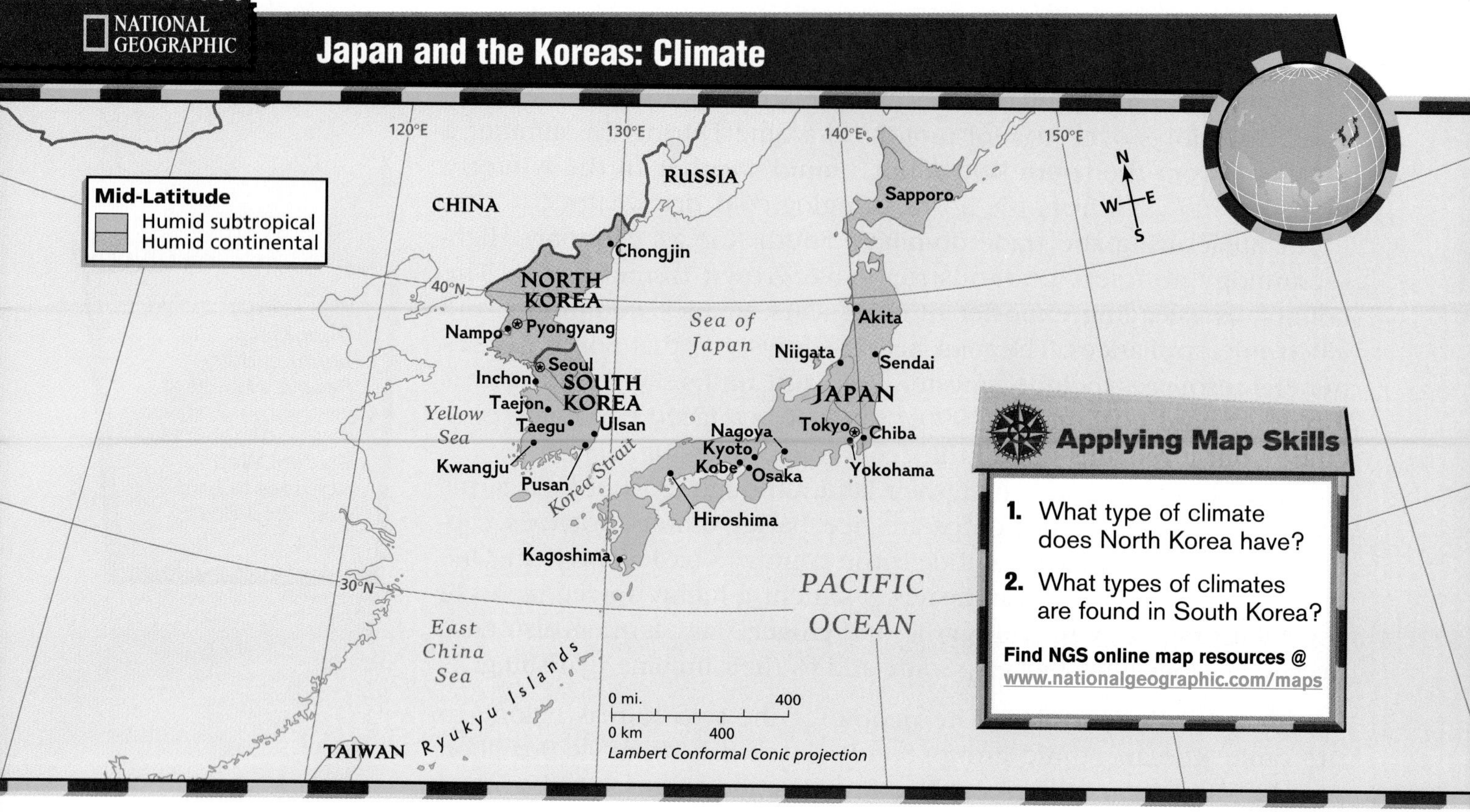

In rural areas, people live in small, one-story homes made of brick or concrete blocks. A large number of South Koreans have emigrated to the United States since the end of the Korean War.

Christianity, Buddhism, and Confucianism are South Korea's major religions. The Koreans have developed their own culture, but Chinese religion and culture influenced the traditional arts of Korea. In Seoul you will discover ancient palaces modeled after the Imperial Palace in Beijing, China. Historic Buddhist temples—like Sokkuram—dot the hills and valleys of the countryside. Within these temples are beautifully carved figures of the Buddha in stone, iron, and gold. One of the great achievements of early Koreans was pottery. Korean potters still make bowls and dishes that are admired around the world.

Like Japan, Korea has a tradition of martial arts. Have you heard of tae kwon do? This martial art originated in Korea. Those who study it learn mental discipline as well as how to defend themselves.

✓Reading Check **What are the major religions in South Korea?**

North Korea

Communist North Korea lies at the northern end of the Korean Peninsula. Separated from China by the Yalu River, North Korea is slightly larger than South Korea. Forested mountains run through the country's center. Plains and lowlands lie along the western and eastern coasts.

As you can see from the map above, North Korea has a humid continental climate. Most of the country has hot summers and cold, snowy winters. Monsoons affect the climate, but the central mountains block some of the winter monsoon. As a result, the eastern coast generally has warmer winters than the rest of the country.

The North Korean government owns and runs factories and farms. It spends much money on the military. Unlike prosperous South Korea, North Korea is economically poor. Coal and iron ore are plentiful, but industries suffer from old equipment and power shortages.

About 75 percent of North Korea's rugged landscape is forested. This leaves little land to farm, yet more than 40 percent of North Korea's people are farmers who work on large, government-run farms. These farms do not grow enough food to feed the country. A lack of fertilizer recently produced famines, or severe food shortages.

North Korea's People North Korea has about 21.4 million people. Nearly 60 percent live in urban areas along the coasts and river valleys. **Pyongyang** is the capital and largest city. Largely rebuilt since the Korean War, Pyongyang has many modern buildings and monuments to Communist leaders. Most of these monuments honor Kim Il Sung, who became North Korea's first ruler in the late 1940s. After Kim's death in 1994, his son Kim Jong Il became the ruler.

The Communist government discourages the practice of religion, although many people still hold to their traditional beliefs. The government also places the needs of the communist system over the needs of individuals and families.

Reading Check **Who controls the economy of North Korea?**

Deep Sea Diver

This Korean woman is dressed in a modern diving suit, but she is carrying on a 1,500-year-old tradition. The women of Cheju Island, off Korea's southern tip, are famous for their diving skills. At age 10, they learn to dive for shellfish and octopuses. They can go 60 feet (18 m) underwater—and hold their breath for two minutes.

Assessment

Defining Terms

1. Define dynasty, monsoon, anthracite, famine.

Recalling Facts

2. Location Where is the Korean Peninsula?
3. History When did Korea become divided?
4. Economics What products are made in South Korea?

Critical Thinking

5. Making Comparisons How does the standard of living in South Korea differ from that in North Korea?
6. Summarizing Information What country has had the greatest influence on the culture and arts of South Korea? Explain.

Graphic Organizer

7. Organizing Information Draw a diagram like this one. Write facts about each country under their headings in the outer ovals. Where the ovals overlap, write facts that are common to both countries.

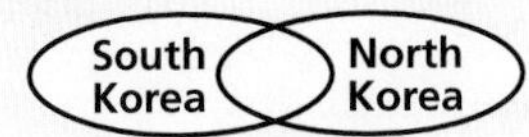

Applying Geography Skills

8. Analyzing Maps Turn to the political map on page 696. What is the capital of South Korea? Along what river is it located?

Critical Thinking Skill

Making Comparisons

When you make comparisons, you determine similarities and differences among ideas, objects, or events. By comparing maps and graphs, you can learn more about a region.

Learning the Skill

Follow these steps to make comparisons:

- Identify or decide what will be compared.
- Determine a common area or areas in which comparisons can be drawn.
- Look for similarities and differences within these areas.

Practicing the Skill

Use the map and graph below to make comparisons and answer these questions:

1. What is the title of the map? The graph?
2. How are the map and graph related?
3. Which country has the most exports and imports?
4. Does a country's size have any effect on the amount it exports? Explain.
5. What generalizations can you make about this map and graph?

Applying the Skill

Survey your classmates about an issue in the news. Summarize the opinions and write a paragraph comparing the different opinions.

GO TO Practice key skills with **Glencoe Skillbuilder Interactive Workbook, Level 1.**

NATIONAL GEOGRAPHIC

Asia's Pacific Rim

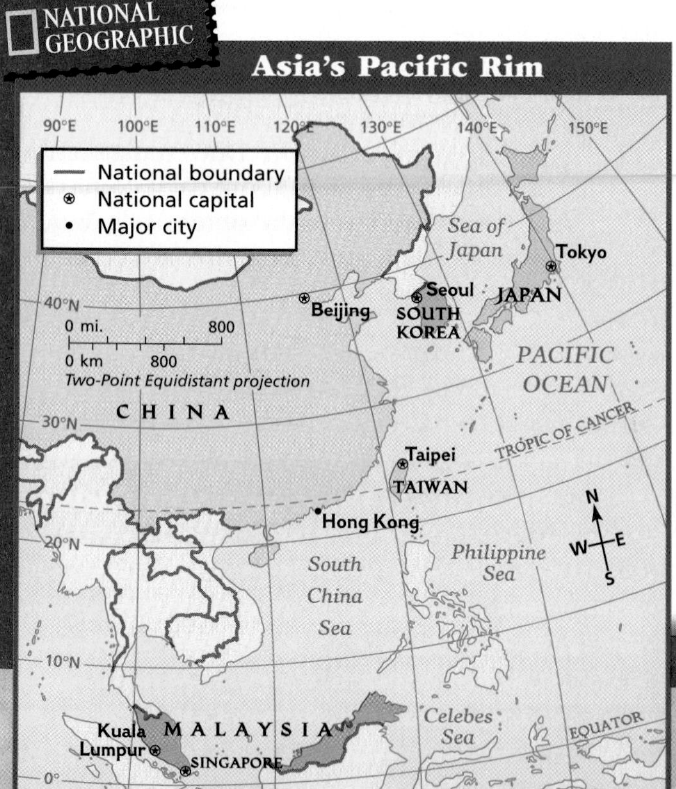

Asia's Pacific Rim: Exports/Imports

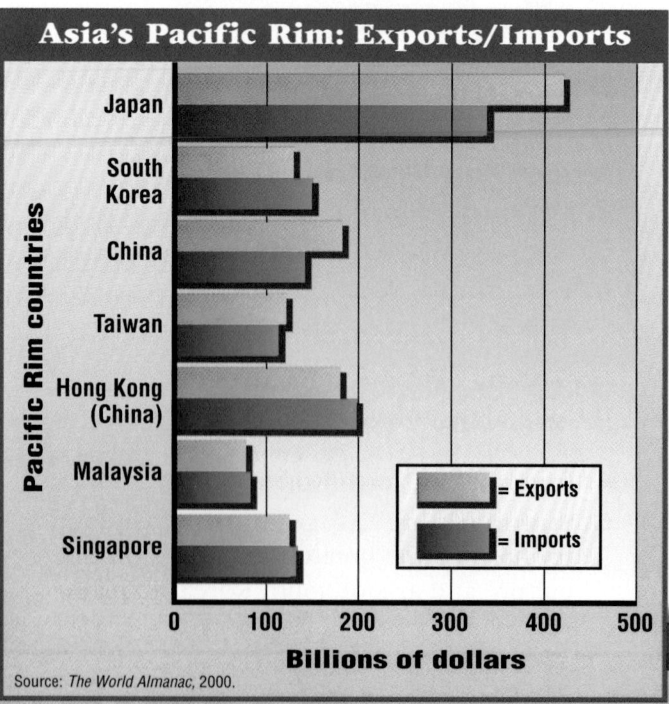

Source: *The World Almanac*, 2000.

Chapter 25 Reading Review

Section 1 Japan

Terms to Know
tsunami
archipelago
intensive cultivation
clan
shogun
samurai
constitutional monarchy
megalopolis

Main Idea

Although they have few mineral resources, Japan's people have built a prosperous country.

✓ **Location** Japan is an archipelago along the Ring of Fire in the western Pacific Ocean. Volcanoes, earthquakes, and tsunamis may strike these islands.

✓ **Place** Japan is mountainous, but its limited farmland is very productive.

✓ **Economics** Japan has few resources. Through trade, the use of advanced technology, and highly skilled workers, Japan has built a strong industrial economy.

✓ **History** The Japanese people have been strongly influenced by China and by Western countries.

✓ **Culture** Most people in Japan live in crowded cities.

✓ **Culture** Japanese religion has encouraged a love of nature and simplicity.

Section 2 The Two Koreas

Terms to Know
dynasty
monsoon
anthracite
famine

Main Idea

South Korea and North Korea share the same peninsula and history, but they have very different political and economic systems.

✓ **Location** The Korean Peninsula lies just south of northern China, and China has had a strong influence on Korean life and culture.

✓ **Government** After World War II, the peninsula became divided into two countries, with a Communist government in North Korea and a non-Communist one in South Korea.

✓ **Economics** South Korea has a strong, industrial economy.

✓ **Culture** Most South Koreans live in cities, enjoying a mix of modern and traditional life.

✓ **Government** North Korea has a Communist government that does not allow its people many freedoms and spends a great deal of money on the military.

Because of its beautiful forest-covered mountains, Korea was once known as Land of the Morning Calm. ▶

Chapter 25

Assessment and Activities

Using Key Terms

Match the terms in Part A with their definitions in Part B.

A.

1. monsoon
2. tsunami
3. intensive cultivation
4. anthracite
5. archipelago
6. dynasty
7. constitutional monarchy
8. clan
9. famine
10. megalopolis

B.

a. group of related families
b. type of hard coal
c. chain of islands
d. emperor is the official head of state, but elected officials run the government
e. seasonal wind that blows over a continent for months at a time
f. huge wave caused by an undersea earthquake
g. severe food shortage
h. huge supercity
i. ruling family
j. growing crops on every available piece of land

Reviewing the Main Ideas

Section 1 Japan

11. **Human/Environment Interaction** How do Japan's farmers achieve high crop yields?
12. **Economics** What consumer goods and industrial goods are made in Japan?
13. **History** How did Japan change in the late 1800s?
14. **Location** What four cities make up Japan's megalopolis?
15. **Culture** What are three of Japan's traditional arts?

Section 2 The Two Koreas

16. **Location** What large Asian nation lies north of the Korean Peninsula?
17. **History** Why did Korea become divided in 1945?
18. **Movement** How do summer and winter monsoons differ in Korea?
19. **Economics** What are the main economic activities in South Korea?
20. **Human/Environment Interaction** Why has North Korea suffered from famine in recent years?

Japan and the Koreas

Place Location Activity

On a separate sheet of paper, match the letters on the map with the numbered places listed below.

1. Mt. Fuji
2. Sea of Japan
3. North Korea
4. South Korea
5. Tokyo
6. Honshu
7. Yalu River
8. Seoul
9. Pyongyang
10. Hokkaido

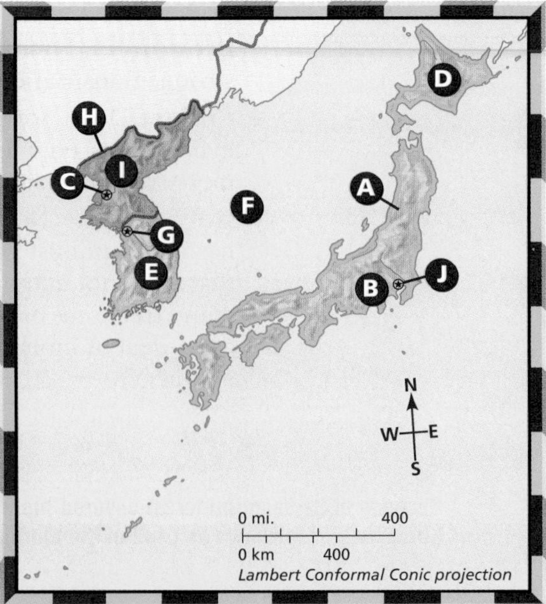

Self-Check Quiz Visit the ***Geography: The World and Its People*** Web site at gwip.glencoe.com and click on **Chapter 25—Self-Check Quizzes** to prepare for the Chapter Test.

Critical Thinking

21. **Drawing Conclusions** Why might North Korea find it difficult to change from a communist system to a non-communist system? Keep in mind the country's location.
22. **Organizing Information** Draw a chart like this one. In each column, write two main ideas about Japan, South Korea, and North Korea as they relate to the topics in the first column.

Topic	Japan	South Korea	North Korea
Land			
Economy			
History			
People			

GeoJournal Activity

23. **Writing a Poem** As you recall, a haiku is a traditional Japanese poem that requires 17 syllables—5 in the first line, 7 in the second line, and 5 in the third line. Write a haiku in which you poetically describe a scene from nature, such as a snowfall or a sunrise.

Mental Mapping Activity

24. **Focusing on the Region** Draw a map of Japan and the Koreas, then add these labels:
    - Honshu
    - North Korea
    - Korean Peninsula
    - Pacific Ocean
    - Tokyo
    - Sea of Japan

Technology Skills Activity

25. **Using the Internet** Use the Internet to research traditional Japanese culture. You might look at Japanese gardens, Buddhism, literature, or painting. Create a bulletin board display with pictures and write captions that explain what the images show.

Standardized Test Practice

Directions: Read the paragraph below, then answer the following questions.

In A.D. 1185 Japan's emperor gave political and military power to a shogun, or general. The shogun system proved to be quite strong. Even though the Mongol warrior Kublai Khan tried twice to invade Japan, he did not succeed. On the first invasion in 1274, Japanese warriors and the threat of a storm forced the Mongols to leave. On the second invasion in 1281, 150,000 Mongol warriors came by ship, but a typhoon arose and destroyed the fleet. The Japanese thought of the storm as the *kamikaze,* or "divine wind." They believed that their islands were indeed sacred.

1. In what century did shoguns gain political power in Japan?

A tenth century
B eleventh century
C twelfth century
D thirteenth century

2. In what century did the Mongol warrior Kublai Khan try to invade Japan?

F tenth century
G eleventh century
H twelfth century
J thirteenth century

Test-Taking Tip: Century names are a common source of error. Remember, in western societies, a baby's first year begins at birth and ends at age one. Therefore, if you are now 14 years old, you are in your *fifteenth* year. Using the same type of thinking, what century began in 1201?

GeoLAB ACTIVITY

Erosion: Saving the Soil

1 Background

Many Asian countries are affected by monsoons, which cause heavy rains or snow and strong winds. This type of weather can cause soil to *erode,* or wash away. When soil is blown or washed away, farmlands become less productive and crops are lost. What techniques do Asian farmers use to slow soil erosion?

2 Materials

- **4 aluminum pie pans**
- **potting soil (enough to fill each pan)**
- **water**
- **500 ml beaker or 2-cup measuring cup**
- **grass clippings or leaves**
- **pebbles (about 2 handfuls)**
- **watering can**
- **dishpan**
- **pencil**

Terraced Farming in China

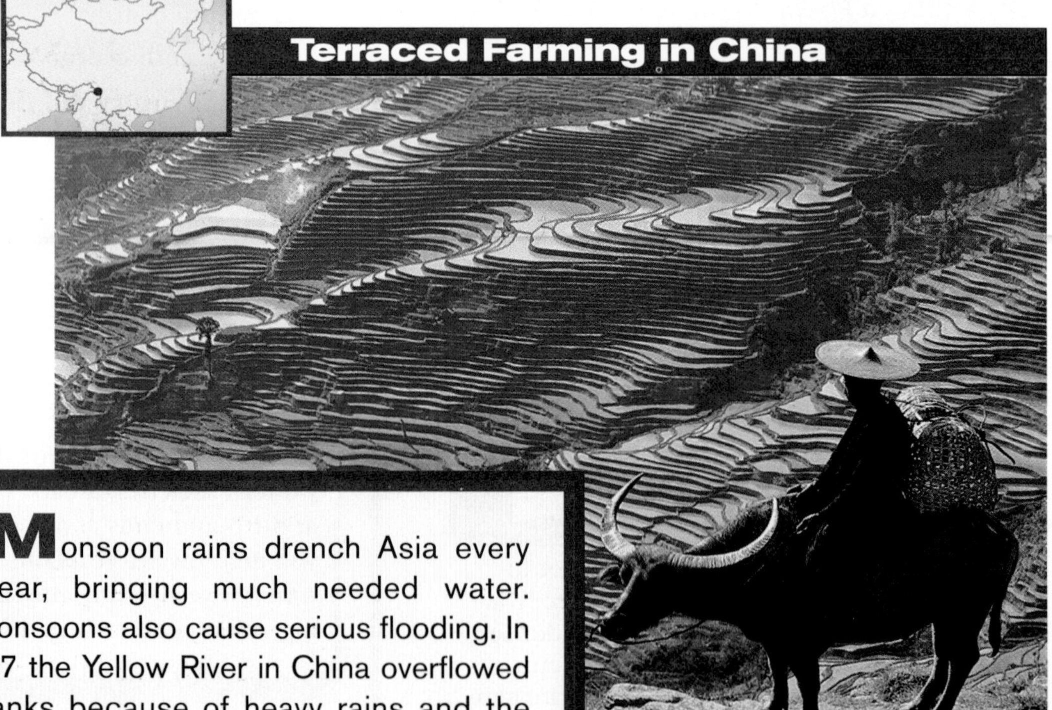

Believe It or Not!

Monsoon rains drench Asia every year, bringing much needed water. Monsoons also cause serious flooding. In 1887 the Yellow River in China overflowed its banks because of heavy rains and the spring thaw. About 1 million people died as a result—the greatest flood disaster in history.

What to Do

1. Fill each pan almost full of soil. Pat the soil until it is firm and flat. Label each pan: 1, 2, 3, and 4.
2. Pour 100 ml of water over the entire surface of each pan.
3. Prepare the pans for the experiment by doing the following:
   a. Pan 1: Use a pencil to make curved grooves across the surface of the soil. This represents contour plowing.
   b. Pan 2: Make several small walls of pebbles running in the same direction across the pan. This represents terracing.
   c. Pan 3: Lightly bury grass clippings or leaves into the soil surface. Leave some scattered across the top of the soil. This represents crop residue management.
   d. Pan 4: Leave this pan alone.
4. Add 200 ml of water to the watering can.
5. Hold Pan 1 at a small angle, with one end in the dishpan. *Slowly* pour the water from the watering can over the pan. Make sure the grooves are parallel to the dishpan so the water flows across them. Wait until all water stops running across the soil and collects in the dishpan.
6. Pour the water and soil that collects in the dishpan into the beaker. Record how much water is collected. Record your observations about how much soil washed away.
7. Repeat steps 4, 5, and 6 for each pan. Compare the results from each pan.

LAB ACTIVITY REPORT

1. Pans 1 and 2 represent two different ways of slowing soil erosion. Describe how these two techniques differ.
2. Which pan had the least soil erosion? Which had the most?
3. **Drawing Conclusions** Will any method used to stop soil erosion be 100 percent effective? Why or why not?

▲ **When pouring water over Pans 1 and 2, be sure that the grooves and pebble walls are parallel to the dishpan.**

Extending the Lab

Activity

Soil erosion can happen anywhere. Locate the steepest hill you can find on or near your school grounds. Make a sketch of the site. After a heavy rain, go back to the site. Do you see any evidence of erosion? Look for evidence such as gullies cut into the hillside, misplaced rocks, or excess soil that has washed to the bottom of the hill.

Chapter 26

Southeast Asia

The World and Its People NATIONAL GEOGRAPHIC

To learn more about the people and places of Southeast Asia, view the ***Geography: The World and Its People*** **Chapter 26** video.

Geography Online

Chapter Overview Visit the ***Geography: The World and Its People*** Web site at gwip.glencoe.com and click on **Chapter 26–Chapter Overviews** to preview information about Southeast Asia.

Section 1

Mainland Southeast Asia

Guide to Reading

Main Idea

The countries of mainland Southeast Asia rely on agriculture.

Terms to Know

- monsoon
- deforestation
- socialism
- delta

Places to Locate

- Malay Peninsula
- Myanmar
- Yangon
- Thailand
- Bangkok
- Laos
- Mekong River
- Vientiane
- Cambodia
- Phnom Penh
- Vietnam
- Hanoi

Reading Strategy

Make five charts like this one. Write a key fact about Myanmar, Thailand, Laos, Cambodia, and Vietnam in the right column for each topic listed in the left column.

Topic	Key Fact
Land	
Economy	
People	

NATIONAL GEOGRAPHIC **Exploring Our World**

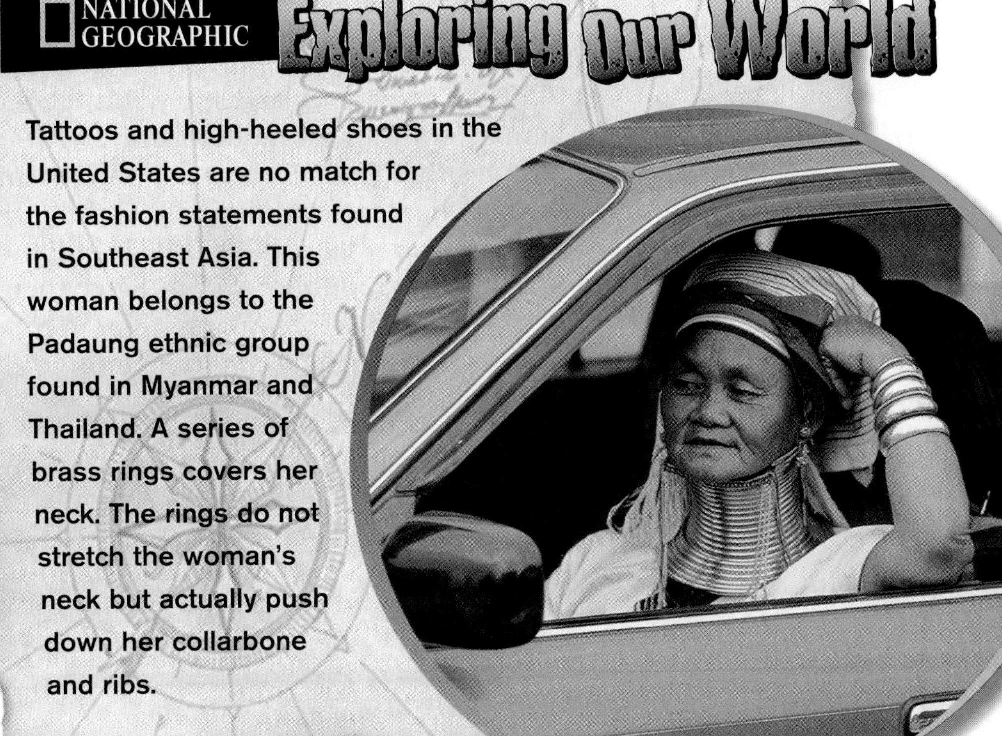

Tattoos and high-heeled shoes in the United States are no match for the fashion statements found in Southeast Asia. This woman belongs to the Padaung ethnic group found in Myanmar and Thailand. A series of brass rings covers her neck. The rings do not stretch the woman's neck but actually push down her collarbone and ribs.

South of China and east of India lies Southeast Asia. This region includes thousands of islands and a long arm of land called the **Malay Peninsula.** Several countries lie entirely on the mainland of Southeast Asia. They are Myanmar, Thailand, Laos, Cambodia, and Vietnam.

Myanmar

Myanmar, once called Burma, is about the size of Texas. Rugged, steep mountains sweep through its western and eastern borders. Two wide rivers—the Irrawaddy (IHR•ah•WAH•dee) and the Salween—flow through vast lowland plains between these mountain ranges.

Myanmar has tropical and subtropical climates influenced by **monsoons,** or seasonal winds that blow over a continent for months at a time. Wet monsoons from the Indian Ocean bring heavy rains from June to September. During the dry monsoons of the winter, winds blowing from the north bring hardly any rain at all.

◄ Petronas Towers in Kuala Lumpur, Malaysia

About two-thirds of the country's people farm. The main crops are rice, sugarcane, beans, and nuts. Some farmers work their fields with tractors, but most rely on plows drawn by water buffalo.

Factories produce and export such goods as soap, noodles, paper, textiles, and glass bottles. Myanmar also exports precious gems like rubies, sapphires, and jade. In addition, the country provides about 75 percent of the world's teakwood. Myanmar's valuable forests are decreasing because of **deforestation,** or the widespread cutting of trees.

About 75 percent of Myanmar's 48.1 million people live in rural areas. The most densely populated part of the country is the fertile Irrawaddy River valley. Many rural dwellers build their homes on poles above the ground for protection from floods and wild animals.

The capital and largest city, **Yangon** (formerly called Rangoon), is famous both for its modern university and its gold-covered Buddhist temples. Buddhism is the main religion in Myanmar. Most people are of Burman heritage, and Burmese is the main language.

Myanmar was part of British India for many years. It became an independent republic in 1948. Since then, military leaders have turned

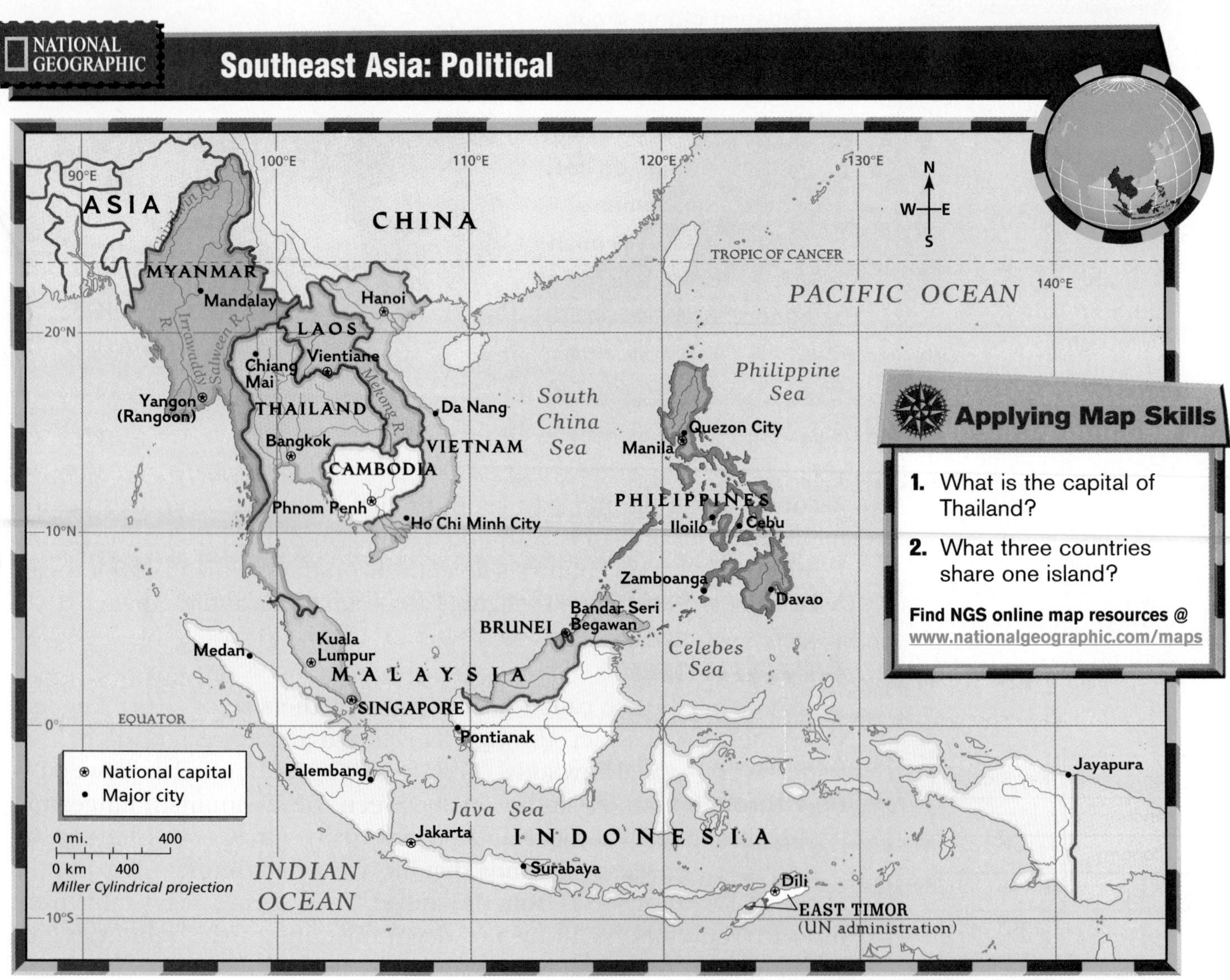

Southeast Asia: Political

Applying Map Skills

1. What is the capital of Thailand?
2. What three countries share one island?

Find NGS online map resources @ www.nationalgeographic.com/maps

Myanmar into a socialist country. **Socialism** is an economic system in which most businesses are owned and run by the government. Some people have struggled to build a democracy in Myanmar. A woman named Aung San Suu Kyi (AWNG SAN SOO CHEE) has become a leader in this struggle. In 1991 she was awarded the Nobel Peace Prize for her efforts to bring political changes without violence.

✓Reading Check **Where is Myanmar's most densely populated area?**

Thailand

The map below shows you that **Thailand** looks like a flower on a stem. The "flower" is the northern part, located on the mainland. The "stem" is a narrow strip on the Malay Peninsula. The country's main waterway—the Chao Phraya (chow PRY•uh) River—flows through a central plain. Thailand has wet summer monsoons and dry winter monsoons.

Once called Siam, *Thailand* means "land of the free." It is the only Southeast Asian country that has never been a European colony. The

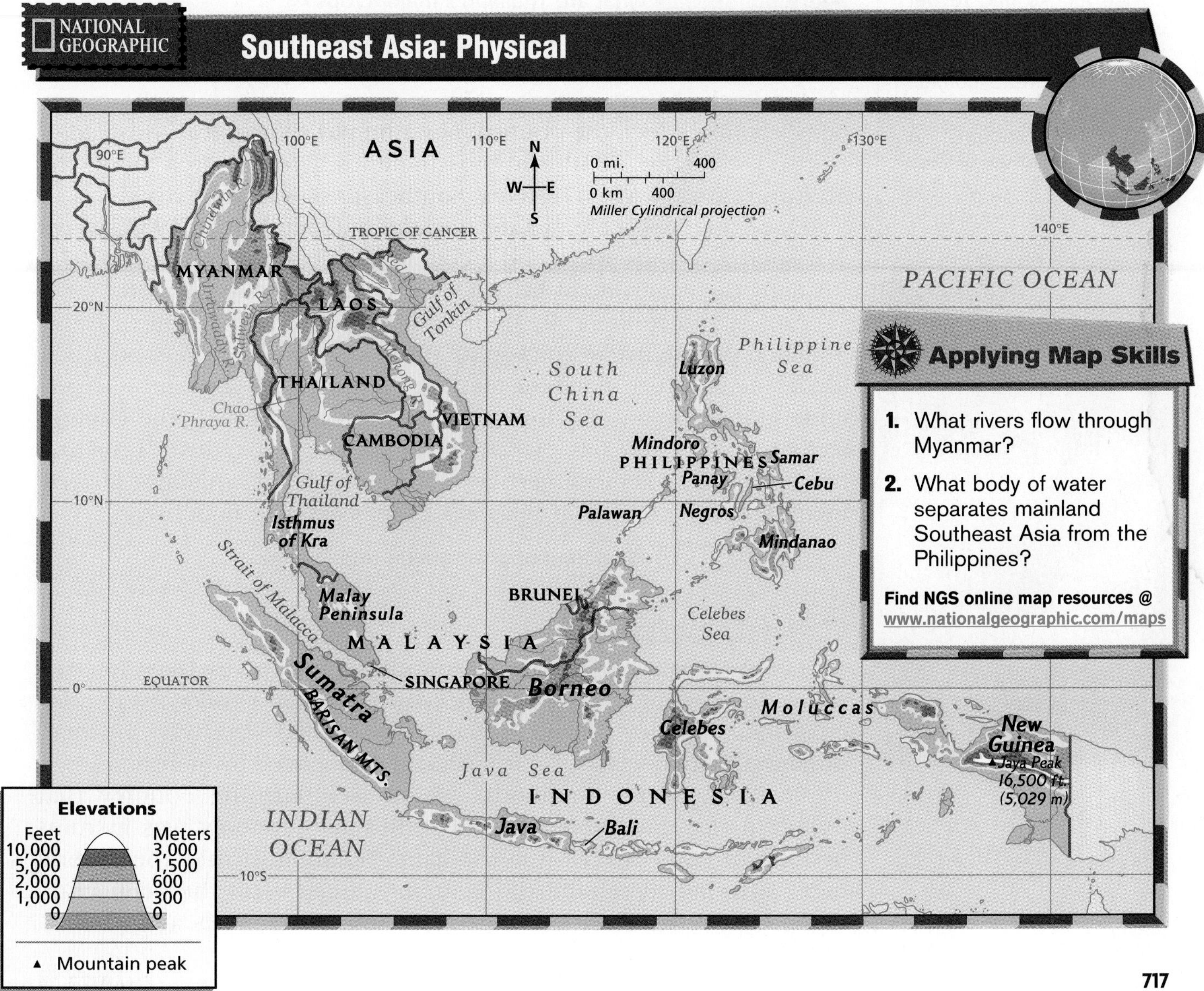

Applying Map Skills

1. What rivers flow through Myanmar?
2. What body of water separates mainland Southeast Asia from the Philippines?

Find NGS online map resources @ www.nationalgeographic.com/maps

Life as a Monk

After his grandfather died, Nattawud Daoruang became a novice Buddhist monk. "You see," he says, "Thai Buddhists believe they can get to paradise by holding onto a monk's robe. So I became a monk for a month to help my grandfather get to paradise. My family and the monks shaved my hair and eyebrows, and I had to recite the monastery rules in Pali—the language of the ancient scriptures. The novice monks had to get up at 5:00 A.M. and meditate. After that, we had free time, so we read comics and played games on the monks' Play Station™. In the afternoons, we walked around the village with the monks to get food and drink."

Thai people trace their independence as a kingdom back to the A.D. 1200s. Thailand still has a king or queen and honors its royal family.

An agricultural country, Thailand's farmers grow rice, corn, fruits, and cassava as their major crops. Large land holdings in the south provide rubber for export. Teak and other woods come from Thailand's forests. The government has taken steps to limit deforestation.

Thailand is also rich in mineral resources. It is one of the world's leading exporters of tin and gemstones. Most manufacturing is located near **Bangkok,** the capital. Workers make cement, textiles, clothing, and metal products. Tourism is an important industry as well.

Most of Thailand's 61.8 million people belong to the Thai ethnic group and practice Buddhism. Hundreds of Buddhist temples called *wats* dot the cities and countryside. Buddhist monks, or holy men, carry small bowls and walk among the people to receive food offerings.

About 80 percent of Thais live in rural villages, although thousands look for jobs in Bangkok. Here, beautiful temples and royal palaces stand next to modern skyscrapers and crowded streets. Bangkok has so many cars that daily traffic jams last for hours.

Reading Check What are Thailand's major crops?

Laos

Landlocked **Laos** is covered by mountains. Because of the mountains' cooling effect, the country has a humid subtropical—instead of tropical—climate. Southern Laos includes a fertile area along the **Mekong** (MAY•KAWNG) **River,** Southeast Asia's longest river.

Once a French colony, Laos became independent in 1953. A civil war soon tore Laos apart, and a communist state was set up in 1975. Recently, the government has opened Laos to the outside world.

Laos is an economically poor country. About 80 percent of Laos's 5 million people live in rural areas. Farmers grow rice, sweet potatoes, sugarcane, and corn along the Mekong's fertile banks. Industry is largely undeveloped because of isolation and years of civil war. The country lacks railroads and has electricity in only a few cities. **Vientiane** (vyehn•TYAHN) is the largest city and capital. The Communist government discourages religion, but most Laotians remain Buddhists.

Reading Check What kind of government rules Laos?

Cambodia

About the size of Missouri, **Cambodia** is covered by lakes, forested plains, and low mountains. The Mekong River and smaller rivers crisscross the land. They provide water, fertile soil, and waterways for transportation. Cambodia has tropical climates influenced by monsoons.

For many years Cambodia was a rich farming country that exported rice and rubber. By the 1980s, its economy was in ruins because of years of civil war and harsh Communist rule. The government is trying to rebuild the economy. Rice is still the main crop. Cambodia's few factories produce food items, chemicals, and textiles.

Most of Cambodia's 11.9 million people belong to the Khmer (kuh•MEHR) ethnic group. About 80 percent live in rural villages. The rest live in cities such as the capital, **Phnom Penh** (puh•NAWM PEHN). Buddhism is Cambodia's main religion. About 1,000 years ago, Cambodia was the center of the vast Khmer Empire, during which Hinduism was also practiced. Among the achievements of the Khmer were the magnificent temples of Angkor.

In modern times, Cambodia was under French rule, finally becoming independent in 1953. Since the 1960s, it has experienced almost constant warfare among rival political groups. A Communist government took control in the mid-1970s, and the people suffered great hardships. Many people from the cities were forced to move to rural areas and work as farmers. More than 1 million Cambodians died. Some fled to other countries as refugees. In 1993 Cambodia brought back its king, but rivalry among political groups continues.

✓Reading Check **Why is Cambodia's economy in ruins?**

Vietnam

About the size of New Mexico, **Vietnam's** long eastern coastline borders the Gulf of Tonkin, the South China Sea, and the Gulf of Thailand. In the north lies the fertile delta of the Red River. A **delta** is an area of land formed by soil deposits at the mouth of a river. In the south you find the wide, swampy delta of the Mekong River. Monsoons bring wet and dry seasons.

Farmers grow large amounts of rice, sugarcane, cassava, sweet potatoes, corn, bananas, and coffee in river deltas. Vietnam's mountain forests provide wood, and the South China Sea yields large catches of fish.

CULTURAL CLOSE-UP

Architecture

The temple of Angkor Wat in northwestern Cambodia was built during the 1100s. Dedicated to the Hindu god Vishnu, much of the temple is covered with elaborately carved characters from Hindu legends. The Khmer people designed Angkor Wat to represent the Hindu view of the universe. The moat surrounding the temple stood for the oceans. The tall central tower symbolized Mount Meru, center of the universe and home of the Hindu gods.

Looking Closer **How does the design of Angkor Wat offer information about the religious beliefs of the people who built it?**

Northern and central Vietnam are rich in coal, natural gas, and other mineral resources. Most factories lie in the south, which is a bustling commercial area. Cement, fertilizer, steel, clothing, and bicycles are manufactured. Years of warfare and strict government controls have kept Vietnam's industries from fully developing.

With 79.5 million people, Vietnam has the largest population in mainland Southeast Asia. About 80 percent live in the countryside. The largest urban area is Ho Chi Minh (HOH CHEE MIHN) City, named for the country's first Communist leader. It used to be called Saigon (sy•GAHN). Vietnam's capital, **Hanoi,** is located in the north. Most people are Buddhists and belong to the Vietnamese ethnic group. The rest are Chinese, Cambodians, and other Asian ethnic groups. Vietnamese is the major language, but Chinese and English are also spoken.

The ancestors of Vietnam's people came from China more than 2,000 years ago. From the late 1800s to the mid-1950s, Vietnam was under French rule. Vietnamese Communists drove out the French in 1954. The Communist government controlled northern Vietnam, while an American-supported government ruled the south. In the 1960s, fighting between these two groups led to the Vietnam War. During this 10-year conflict, more than 3 million Americans helped fight against the Communists. The war was costly, and the United States eventually withdrew its forces in 1973. Within two years, the Communists had captured the south. Many thousands of people fled Vietnam, settling in the United States and other countries.

In recent years, Vietnam's Communist leaders have opened the country to Western ideas, businesses, and tourists. They also have loosened government controls on the economy. In these two ways, the Communist leaders hope to raise Vietnam's standard of living.

✓Reading Check **Where are most of Vietnam's factories located?**

Assessment

Defining Terms

1. Define monsoon, deforestation, socialism, delta.

Recalling Facts

2. Economics What does Myanmar export?

3. Region How do monsoons affect climate in mainland Southeast Asia?

4. Economics What has slowed the economies of Laos and Cambodia?

Graphic Organizer

5. Organizing Information Draw a time line like this one. Then list four events and their dates in Vietnam's history.

Critical Thinking

6. Summarizing Information What makes Thailand unique among the countries of Southeast Asia?

7. Making Predictions How do Vietnam's leaders hope to improve the country's standard of living? Do you think these actions will help? Why or why not?

Applying Geography Skills

8. Analyzing Maps Look at the economic activity map on page 727. What resources are found in Thailand?

Section 2

Island Southeast Asia

Guide to Reading

Main Idea

The island countries of Southeast Asia have a variety of cultures and economic activities.

Terms to Know

- strait
- free port
- terraced field

Places to Locate

- Malaysia
- Strait of Malacca
- Kuala Lumpur
- Singapore
- Brunei
- Philippines
- Manila

Reading Strategy

Draw a chart like this one. As you read, list two facts about each country in the right column.

Country	Facts
Malaysia	
Singapore	
Brunei	
Philippines	

NATIONAL GEOGRAPHIC **Exploring Our World**

Yes, you are looking at 50,000 rubber ducks as they float down the Singapore River. Singapore, the largest port in Southeast Asia, has been described as one of the cleanest and safest cities in the world. The Great Duck Race is one way that Singapore's Red Cross Society raises money for the community.

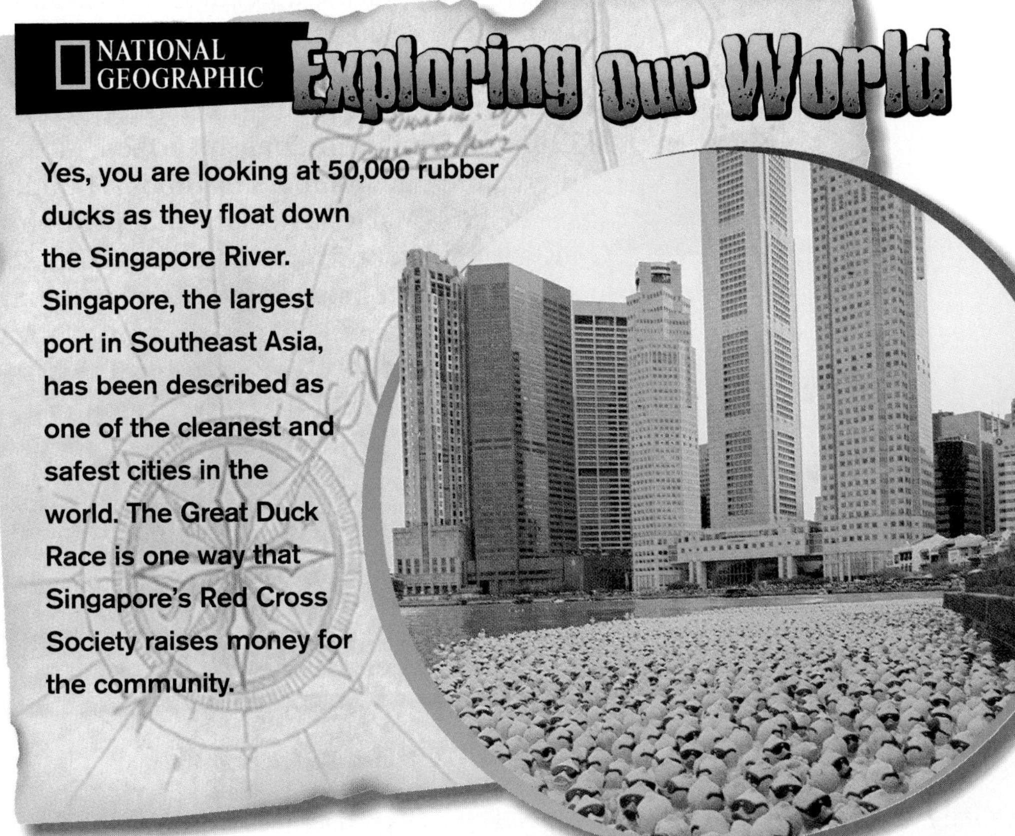

The island countries of Southeast Asia are Malaysia, Singapore, Brunei (bru•NY), and the Philippines. Indonesia also lies in this region, but it is discussed separately in Section 3.

Malaysia

Malaysia has three parts. An area known as Malaya occupies the southern end of the Malay Peninsula. The two other parts lie on the island of Borneo. They are the territories of Sarawak (suh•RAH•wahk) and Sabah (SAH•bah). Dense rain forests and rugged mountains make up their landscape. All three parts have a tropical rain forest climate.

West of Malaya lies the **Strait of Malacca.** A strait is a narrow body of water between two pieces of land. The Strait of Malacca is an important waterway for trade between the Indian Ocean and the Java Sea.

Agriculture is an important economic activity in Malaysia, but only about one-sixth of the people farm. Some work on subsistence farms and grow rice, fruits, and vegetables. Many others work on plantations. Malaysia is one of the world's leaders in exporting rubber and palm oil. Large amounts of wood are also exported.

Malaysia is rich in minerals such as tin, iron ore, copper, and bauxite. Large amounts of oil and natural gas are found in the Sabah and Sarawak regions. Factory workers make high-technology and consumer goods. Malaysia's ports are important centers of trade.

Most of Malaysia's 22.7 million people belong to the Malay ethnic group. Their ancestors came from southern China about 4,000 years ago. In the 1800s, the British—who then ruled Malaysia—brought in Chinese and South Asian workers to mine tin and to work on rubber plantations. As a result, in marketplaces today you can hear Malay, Chinese, Tamil, and English spoken. Most Malaysians are Muslims, but there are large numbers of Hindus, Buddhists, and Christians.

In 1963 Malaysia became independent and formed a constitutional monarchy. Every five years, a council of local rulers chooses a king to serve as head of state. An elected prime minister and parliament actually run the country. **Kuala Lumpur** (KWAH•luh LUM•PUR) is the capital and largest city. The Petronas Towers—the tallest buildings in the world—soar above this city. In contrast, many rural villagers live in thatched-roof homes built on posts a few feet off the ground.

✓Reading Check **Where are the three parts of Malaysia located?**

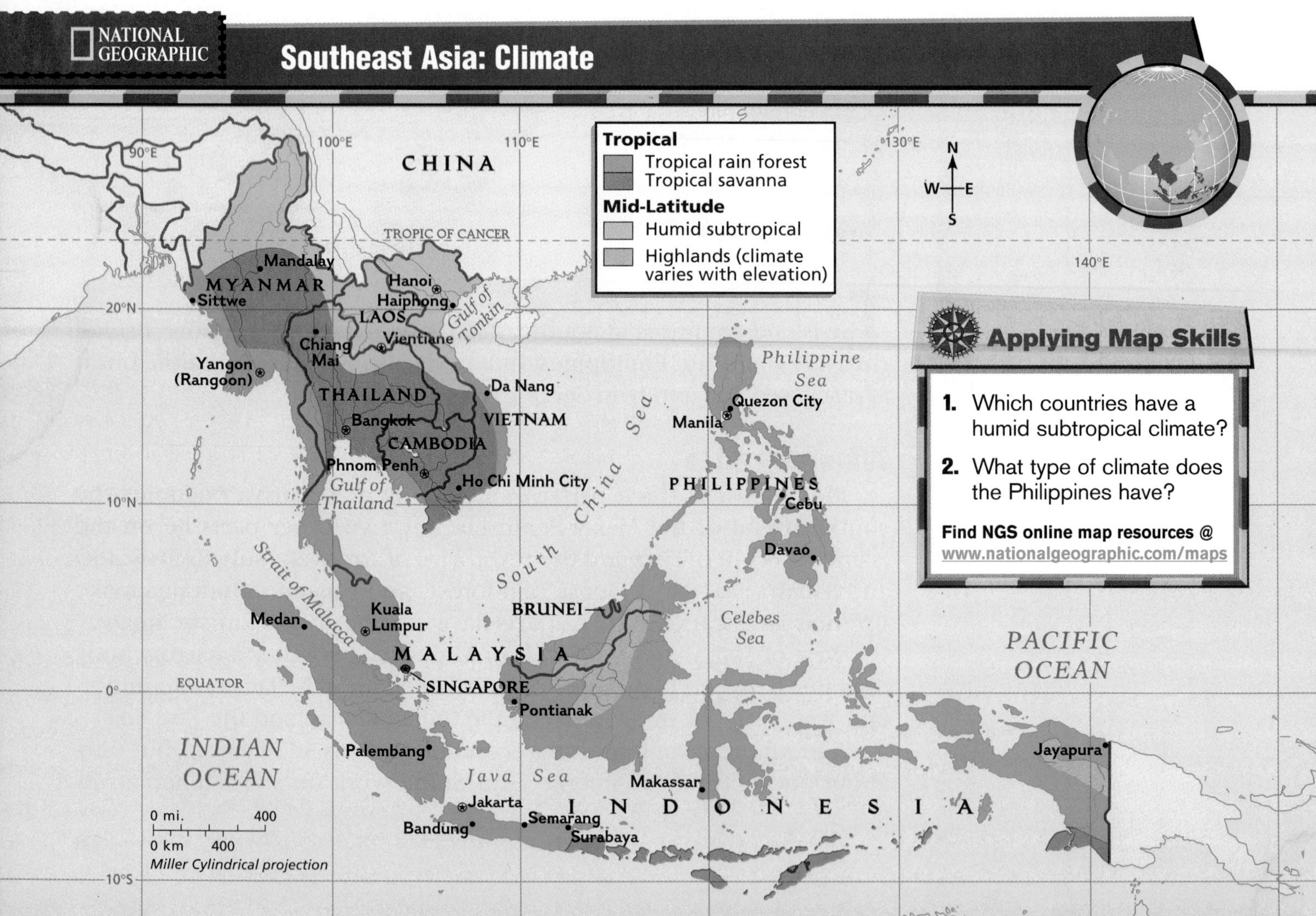

Singapore

Singapore lies off the southern tip of the Malay Peninsula. It is made up of Singapore Island and 58 smaller islands. With only 239 square miles (618 sq. km), Singapore is one of the world's smallest countries. Yet it has one of the world's most productive economies.

The city of Singapore is the capital and takes up much of Singapore Island. Once covered by rain forests, Singapore Island now has highways, factories, office buildings, and docks.

Singapore's location along a narrow sea route has resulted in an economy based mainly on trade and manufacturing. The city of Singapore has one of the world's busiest harbors. It is a **free port,** a place where goods can be loaded or unloaded, stored, and shipped again without payment of import taxes. Huge amounts of goods pass through this port. Singapore's many factories make high-tech goods, machinery, chemicals, and paper products. Because of their productive economy, the people of Singapore enjoy a high standard of living.

Founded by the British in the early 1800s, Singapore became an independent republic in 1965. Most of the country's nearly 4 million people are Chinese, but Malaysians and Indians make up about 25 percent of the population. These people practice Buddhism, Islam, Christianity, Hinduism, and traditional Chinese religions.

✓Reading Check **What is a free port?**

Brunei

On the northern coast of Borneo lies another small nation—**Brunei.** About the size of Delaware, Brunei is made up of two wedges of land that are separated by Malaysian territory. Low plains, coastal swamps, and mountains dominate the country.

Brunei has rich deposits of oil and natural gas. The export of these resources provides about half of the country's income. Brunei's citizens receive free education and medical care, and low-cost housing, fuel, and food. Today the government is investing in new industries to avoid too much reliance on fuels. All political and economic decisions are made by Brunei's ruler, or sultan, who governs with a firm hand.

Most of Brunei's 300,000 people are Malays or Chinese. Malay, Chinese, and English are the most commonly spoken languages. Islam is the leading religion. The largest urban area is the capital, Bandar Seri Begawan (BAN•dar SEHR•ee beh•GAH•wan).

✓Reading Check **Who makes economic and political decisions in Brunei?**

NATIONAL GEOGRAPHIC **On Location**

Malaysia

A Malaysian worker taps a rubber tree to get the milky liquid called latex.

Human/Environment Interaction **What other Malaysian products are grown for export?**

The Philippines

East of Vietnam in the South China Sea lie the **Philippines,** an archipelago of more than 7,000 islands. About 90 percent of the 74.7 million Filipino people live on only 11 of the islands. The largest islands are Luzon (loo•ZAWN) and Mindanao (MIHN•duh•NAH•OH).

Volcanic mountains and forests dominate the landscape. Lava from volcanoes provides fertile soil for agriculture. Farmers have built terraces on the steep slopes of the mountains. **Terraced fields** are strips of land cut out of a hillside like stair steps. The land can then hold water and be used for farming. About 40 percent of the people farm. They grow sugarcane, coconuts, and abaca—a strong fiber obtained from banana leaves.

Miners unearth coal, nickel, copper, silver, and gold. Factory workers produce high-tech goods, food products, chemicals, clothing, and shoes. **Manila,** the country's capital, is a great commercial center.

Named after King Philip II of Spain, the Philippines spent more than 300 years as a Spanish colony. As a result of the Spanish-American War, the United States controlled the islands from 1898 until World War II. In 1946 the Philippines became an independent, democratic republic.

The Philippines is the only Christian country in Southeast Asia. About 90 percent of Filipinos follow the Roman Catholic religion, brought to the islands by Spanish missionaries. The culture today blends Malay, Spanish, and American influences. American influences can be seen in the products sold along busy city streets.

Reading Check What are the two largest islands in the Philippines?

Assessment

Defining Terms

1. **Define** strait, free port, terraced field.

Recalling Facts

2. **Place** Malaysia is among the world's leading producers of what two products?
3. **Economics** On what two economic activities is Singapore's economy based?
4. **Culture** What religion do most Filipinos practice?

Critical Thinking

5. **Summarizing Information** How does Brunei's government use its fuel income?
6. **Interpreting Information** What groups influenced the culture of the Philippines?

Graphic Organizer

7. **Organizing Information** Draw a diagram like this one. In the center, list similarities of the countries listed. In the outer ovals, write two ways that the country differs from the others.

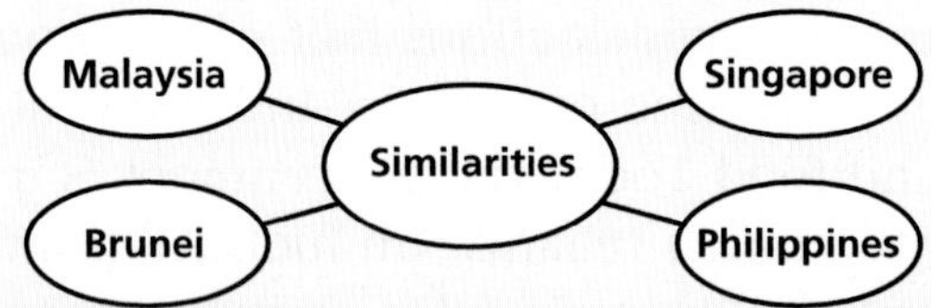

Applying Geography Skills

8. **Analyzing Maps** Look at the population density map on page 728. What cities in the Philippines have more than 1 million people?

Geography Skill

Reading a Contour Map

A trail map would show the paths you could follow if you went hiking in the mountains. How would you know if the trail follows an easy, flat route, though, or if it cuts steeply up a mountain? To find out, you need a **contour map.**

Learning the Skill

Contour maps use lines to outline the shape—or contour—of the landscape. Each contour line connects all points that are at the same elevation. This means that if you walked along one contour line, you would always be at the same height above sea level.

Where the contour lines are far apart, the land rises gradually. Where the lines are close together, the land rises steeply. For example, one contour line may be labeled 1,000 meters (3,281 ft.). Another contour line very close to the first one may be labeled 2,000 meters (6,562 ft.). This means that the land rises 1,000 meters (3,281 ft.) in just a short distance.

To read a contour map, follow these steps:

- Identify the area shown on the map.
- Read the numbers on the contour lines to determine how much the elevation increases or decreases with each line.
- Locate the highest and lowest numbers, which indicate the highest and lowest elevations.
- Notice the amount of space between the lines, which tells you whether the land is steep or flat.

Practicing the Skill

Study the contour map below, then answer the following questions.

1. What area is shown on the map?
2. What is the lowest elevation on the map?
3. What is the highest elevation on the map?
4. Where is the landscape the most flat? How can you tell?
5. How would you describe the physical geography of this island?

NATIONAL GEOGRAPHIC

Borneo: Contour Map

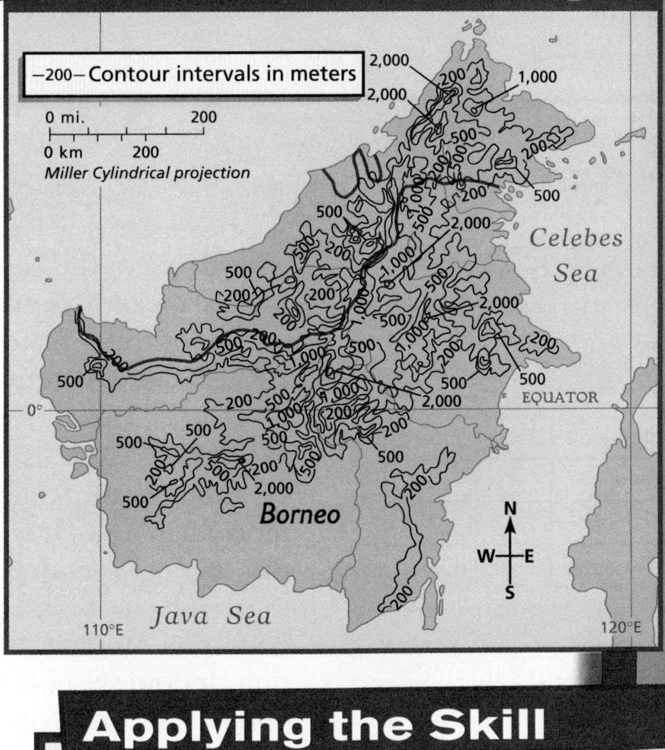

Applying the Skill

Turn to page 12 in the **Geography Handbook.** Use the contour map there to answer the five questions above.

Section 3

Indonesia

Guide to Reading

Main Idea

Indonesia has a diverse population within its many islands.

Terms to Know

- plate
- civil war
- dictatorship

Places to Locate

- Indonesia
- Sumatra
- Java
- Celebes
- Borneo
- New Guinea
- Jakarta
- Bali
- East Timor

Reading Strategy

Draw a chart like this one. Write a fact about Indonesia's land, economy, and history. Then write an effect of that fact.

Indonesia	Fact	Effect
Land		
Economy		
History		

NATIONAL GEOGRAPHIC **Exploring Our World**

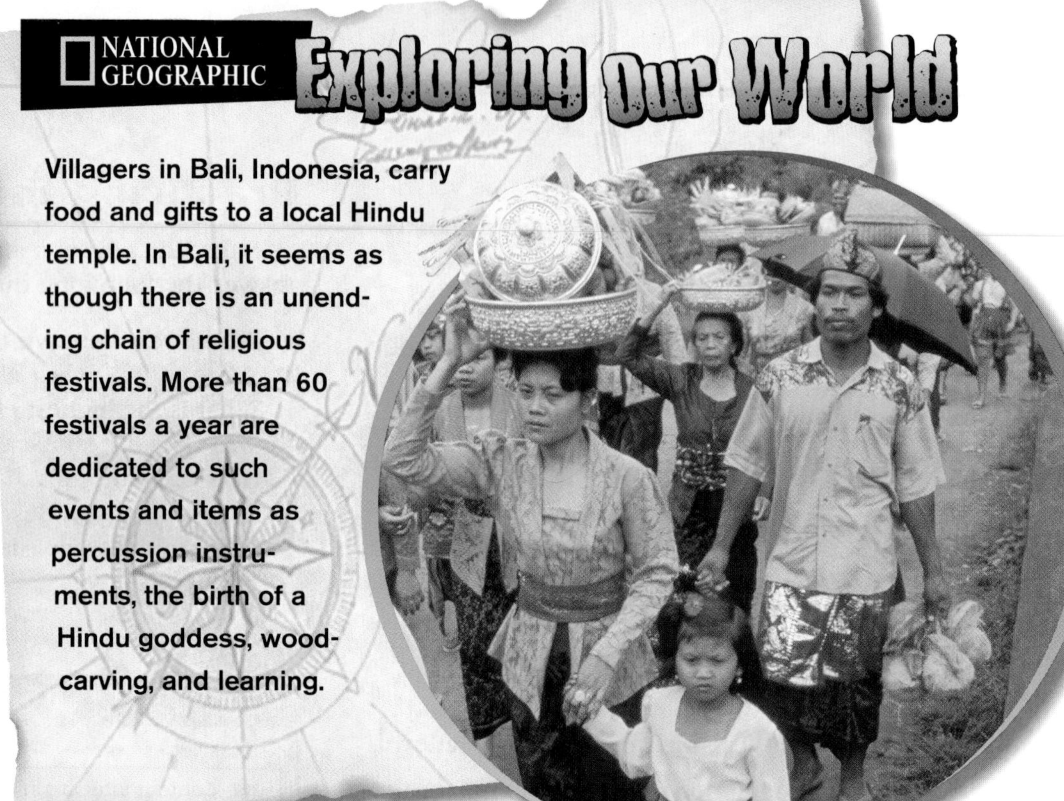

Villagers in Bali, Indonesia, carry food and gifts to a local Hindu temple. In Bali, it seems as though there is an unending chain of religious festivals. More than 60 festivals a year are dedicated to such events and items as percussion instruments, the birth of a Hindu goddess, woodcarving, and learning.

Indonesia is a large, mineral-rich country. It sprawls over an area where two of the earth's tectonic plates meet. Tectonic **plates** are the huge slabs of rock that make up the earth's crust. Indonesia's location on top of these plates causes it to experience earthquakes. The country also has 220 active volcanoes.

Indonesia's Land and Climate

Indonesia is Southeast Asia's largest country. It is an archipelago of more than 13,600 islands. The physical map on page 717 shows you the major islands of Indonesia—**Sumatra, Java,** and **Celebes** (SEH•luh•BEEZ). Indonesia also shares two large islands with other countries. Most of the island of **Borneo** belongs to Indonesia. In addition, Indonesia controls the western half of **New Guinea.** Another country—Papua New Guinea—lies on the eastern half.

Mountains rise on Indonesia's larger islands. Their rugged peaks slope down to meet coastal lowlands. The volcanoes that formed Indonesia have left a rich covering of ash that makes the soil good for farming. Because Indonesia lies on the Equator, its climate is tropical. Monsoons bring a wet season and a dry season. The tropical climate, combined with fertile soil, has allowed dense rain forests to spread.

✓Reading Check **How have volcanoes helped farming in Indonesia?**

Indonesia's Economy

Indonesia has one of the world's largest economies in regard to the amount of goods and services it produces. Agriculture provides work for nearly half of the people. Farmers grow rice, coffee, cassava, tea, coconuts, and rubber trees. Cattle and sheep are also raised.

Indonesia has large reserves of oil and natural gas. Its mines yield tin, silver, nickel, copper, bauxite, and gold. Indonesia is one of the world's leading producers of tin. Dense rain forests provide teak and other valuable woods. Some companies that own large tracts of land are cutting down the trees very quickly. The environment suffers from this deforestation. Tree roots help keep the soil in place during heavy rains. When the trees are cut down, the rich soil runs off into the sea.

Geography Online

Web Activity Visit the ***Geography: The World and Its People*** Web site at gwip.glencoe.com and click on **Chapter 26—Student Web Activities** to learn more about Indonesia.

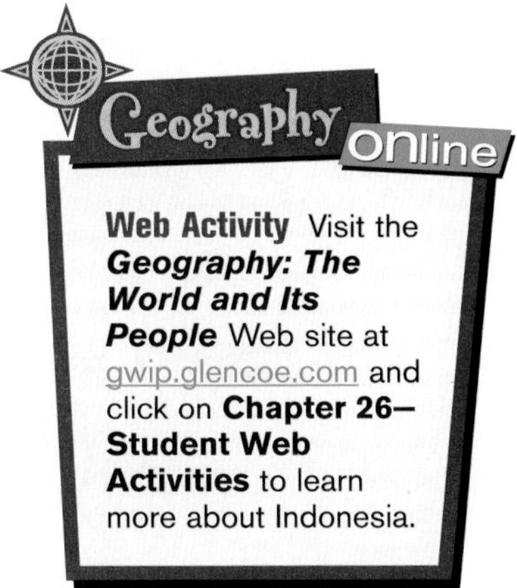

NATIONAL GEOGRAPHIC

Southeast Asia: Economic Activity

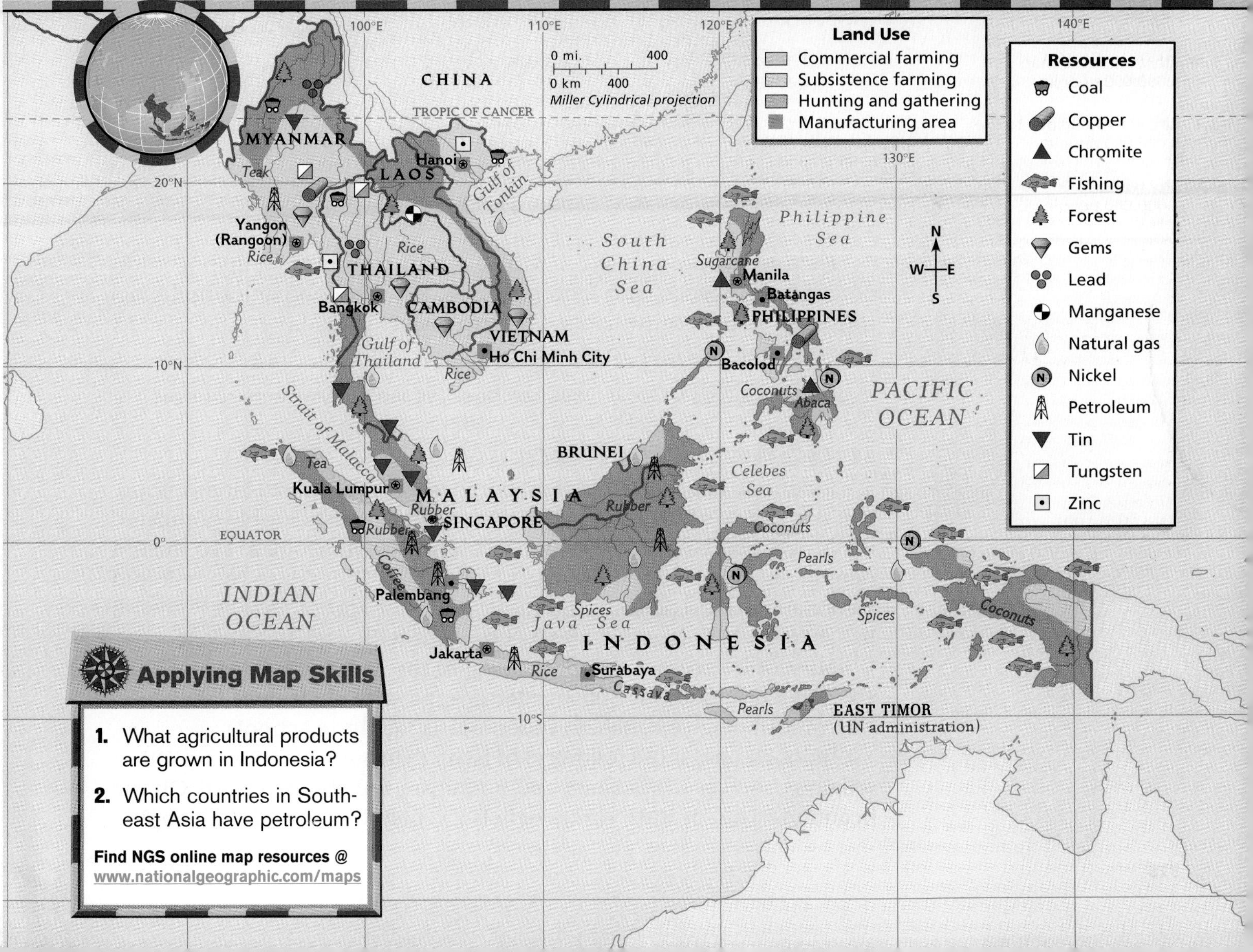

Applying Map Skills

1. What agricultural products are grown in Indonesia?
2. Which countries in Southeast Asia have petroleum?

Find NGS online map resources @ www.nationalgeographic.com/maps

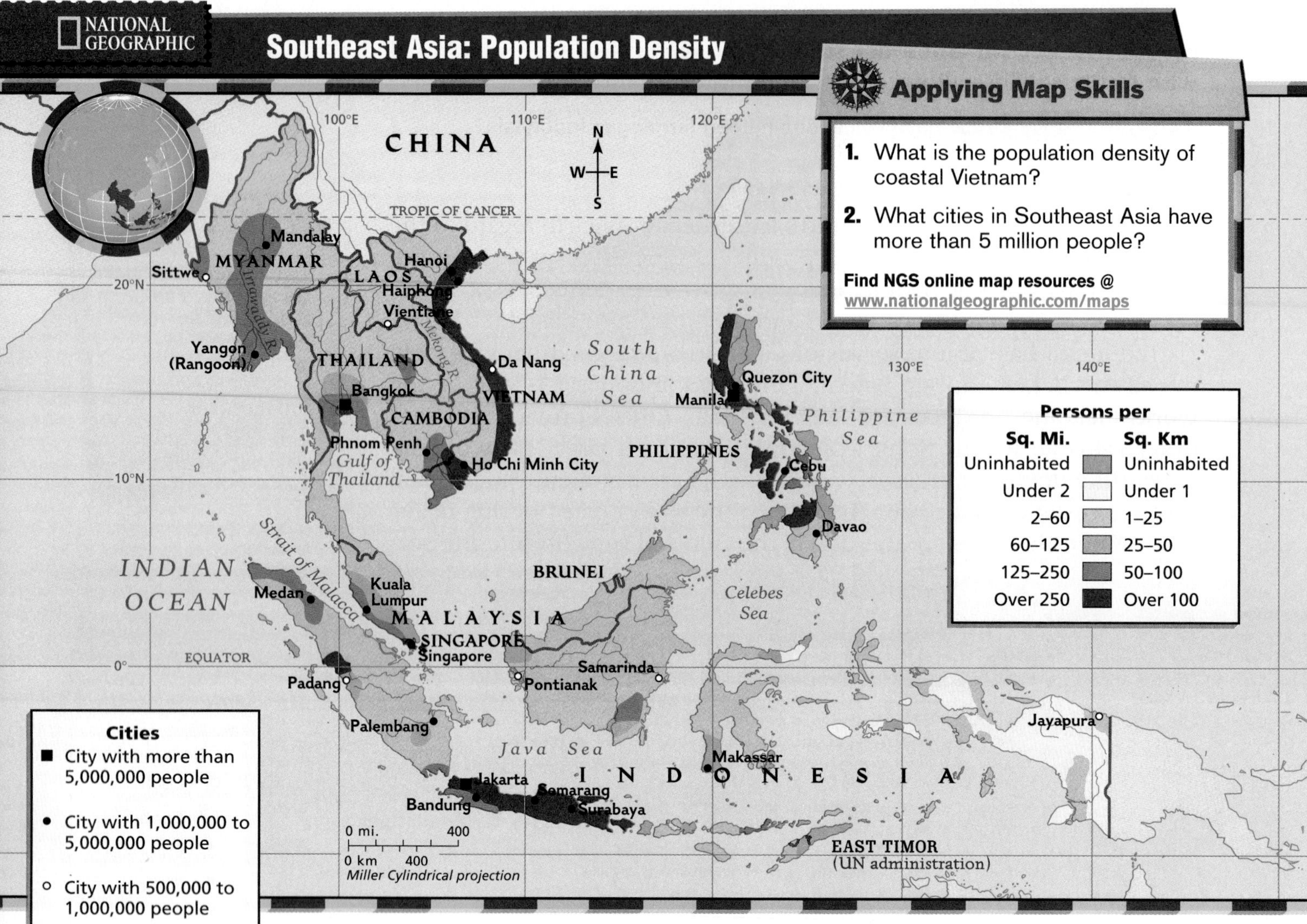

Factory workers make textiles, wood products, transportation equipment, tobacco, and food products. Foreign companies build factories on Java because labor is inexpensive. In addition, the island's location makes it easy to ship goods.

Reading Check **Of what resources does Indonesia have large reserves?**

Indonesia's People

Indonesia has about 211.8 million people—the fourth-largest population in the world. It is also one of the world's most densely populated countries. The island of Java, for example, has more than 110 million people on an area about the size of New York State. Here you will find **Jakarta** (juh•KAHR•tuh), Indonesia's capital and largest city. Jakarta has modern buildings and streets crowded with cars and bicycles.

Most of Indonesia's people belong to the Malay ethnic group. They are divided into about 300 smaller groups with their own languages. The official language, Bahasa Indonesia, is taught in schools.

Indonesia has more followers of Islam than any other country. Other religions, such as Christianity and Buddhism, are also practiced. On the beautiful island of **Bali,** Hindu beliefs are held by most of the people.

Thousands of years ago, Malays from mainland Southeast Asia settled the islands that are today Indonesia. Their descendants set up Buddhist and Hindu kingdoms. These kingdoms grew wealthy by controlling the trade that passed through the waterways between the Indian and Pacific Oceans. In the A.D. 1100s, traders from Southwest Asia brought Islam to the region. Four hundred years later, Europeans arrived to acquire the valuable spices grown here. They brought Christianity to the islands. The Dutch eventually controlled most of the islands as a colony. Independence finally came to Indonesia in 1949.

Since the 1960s, unrest and civil war have occurred on several islands. A **civil war** is a fight among different groups within a country. Most recently, the people of **East Timor,** who are largely Roman Catholic and were once ruled by Portugal, voted for independence. Indonesia has accepted the results of this election.

From the 1960s to the late 1990s, the military leader, General Suharto, ruled Indonesia. He set up a **dictatorship,** or a government under control of a single all-powerful leader. In the late 1990s, severe economic problems led to widespread unrest, and Suharto was forced to resign. Today Indonesia has a democratic government. With so many different ethnic groups, many small political parties arise. As a result, Indonesia's leaders find it difficult to form a government that is strong enough to deal with the challenges facing the country.

✓Reading Check **When did Indonesia win its independence?**

Komodo Dragon

The world's largest lizard, the Komodo dragon, is found only on a few small islands in Indonesia. Its long, forked tongue acts as a nose to "smell" nearby prey. The Komodo can grow 10 feet (3 m) long and can weigh about 300 pounds (136 kg).

Section 3 Assessment

Defining Terms

1. Define plate, civil war, dictatorship.

Recalling Facts

2. Location What five islands are the largest in Indonesia?
3. Movement Why do foreign companies want to build factories in Indonesia?
4. Government What type of government does Indonesia have today?

Critical Thinking

5. Categorizing Information List Indonesia's three main religions and who brought these religions to the islands.
6. Understanding Cause and Effect Why is it difficult for government officials to rule Indonesia?

Graphic Organizer

7. Organizing Information Draw a diagram like this one. Under the headings, list two strengths and two challenges of Indonesia.

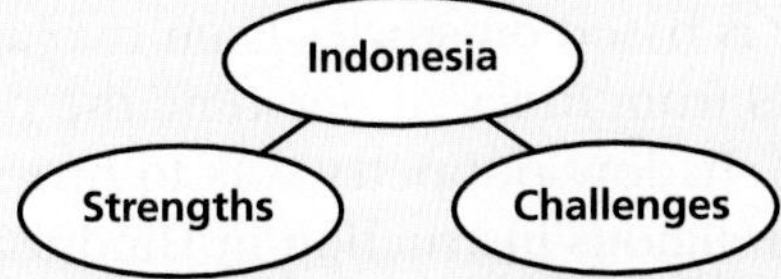

Applying Geography Skills

8. Analyzing Maps Look at the physical map on page 717. What are six bodies of water near Indonesia that make the country's location a good one for shipping goods?

Making Connections

ART SCIENCE LITERATURE TECHNOLOGY

Shadow Puppets

Late at night, long after dark has fallen on a small stage in Java, a shadow puppet show is about to begin. The glow of a lamp shines behind a wide linen screen. Puppets stand hidden from direct view. The "good" characters are on the right. The "bad" ones are placed on the left. The audience waits anxiously on the other side of the screen. Once the story begins, the performance will continue until dawn.

The Performance

Wayang kulit, the ancient Indonesian shadow puppet theater, dates back at least 1,000 years. Today there are several thousand puppeteers. This makes shadow puppets the strongest theater tradition in Southeast Asia.

Shadow puppets are flat leather puppets, many with movable limbs and mouths, that are operated by sticks. During the show, the puppets cast their shadows onto the screen. The *dalang,* or puppeteer, sits behind the screen and manipulates the figures. He brings each to life in one of the more than 200 traditional puppet stories.

The Stories

Although Islam is now the major religion of Indonesia, much of the traditional shadow puppet theater is based on stories from two ancient Hindu epics from India. At one time the principal purpose of shadow puppetry was to provide moral and religious instruction in Hinduism. Now the stories combine Hindu themes with elements of Buddhism and Islam, as well as Indonesian history and folklore. Often the performance is given in celebration of public or religious holidays or to honor a wedding or birth.

▼ The *dalang* and his orchestra

The Puppeteer

The skill of the *dalang* is critical to the show's success. The *dalang* operates all the puppets, narrates the story, provides sound effects, and directs the gong, drum, and flute orchestra that accompanies the puppet show. The puppeteer changes his voice to create a unique sound for each character. The *dalang* performs without a script or notes, adding jokes and making small changes to suit the crowd and the occasion. Because a shadow puppet show can last as long as nine hours, the *dalang* must have both a tremendous memory and great endurance.

Many *dalang*s carve their own puppets, having learned this art from earlier generations. Each figure must appear in a specific size, body build, and costume. Even the shape of the eyes tells about the figure's character and mood.

Making the Connection

1. How do shadow puppets move?
2. What kinds of stories do shadow puppet shows present?
3. **Drawing Conclusions** In what way is the *dalang* a master of many different art forms?

Chapter 26

Reading Review

Section 1 Mainland Southeast Asia

Terms to Know
monsoon
deforestation
socialism
delta

Main Idea

The countries of mainland Southeast Asia rely on agriculture.

✓ **Region** Mainland Southeast Asia includes the countries of Myanmar, Thailand, Laos, Cambodia, and Vietnam.

✓ **Place** These countries have highland areas and lowland river valleys with fertile soil. Monsoons bring heavy rains in the summer.

✓ **History** Thailand is the only country in Southeast Asia free of the influence of colonial rule.

✓ **Economics** Conflict has hurt the economies of Laos, Cambodia, and Vietnam.

Section 2 Island Southeast Asia

Terms to Know
strait
free port
terraced field

Main Idea

The island countries of Southeast Asia have a variety of cultures and economic activities.

✓ **Region** The island countries of Southeast Asia include Malaysia, Singapore, Brunei, and the Philippines.

✓ **Economics** Malaysia produces palm oil and rubber, among other goods. Its capital, Kuala Lumpur, is a commercial center.

✓ **Economics** The port of Singapore is one of the world's busiest trading centers.

✓ **Economics** Brunei has grown wealthy from oil and gas income.

✓ **Culture** The Philippines shows the influence of Malaysian, Spanish, and American culture.

Section 3 Indonesia

Terms to Know
plate
civil war
dictatorship

Main Idea

Indonesia has a diverse population within its many islands.

✓ **Place** Indonesia—the world's fourth-most populous country—is an archipelago formed by volcanoes.

✓ **Economics** Rich soil and a warm, wet climate make Indonesia good for farming.

✓ **Economics** Indonesia has rich supplies of oil, natural gas, and minerals.

✓ **Government** Leaders face the challenge of creating a nation out of a land with many different groups and political parties.

◀ People in Bangkok, Thailand, face traffic snarls and pollution that are among the worst in the world.

Chapter 26

Assessment and Activities

Using Key Terms

Match the terms in Part A with their definitions in Part B.

A.

1. free port
2. delta
3. plate
4. strait
5. deforestation
6. terraced field
7. civil war
8. socialism
9. dictatorship
10. monsoon

B.

a. land made from soil deposited at the mouth of a river
b. war fought between groups within a country
c. cutting strips of land out of a hillside
d. economic system in which the government owns many businesses
e. government under control of a single leader
f. place where shipped goods are not taxed
g. slabs of rock that make up the earth's crust
h. seasonal wind that blows over a continent for months at a time
i. the widespread cutting of trees
j. narrow body of water that runs between two land areas

Reviewing the Main Ideas

Section 1 Mainland Southeast Asia

11. **Economics** What resources are found in Thailand?
12. **History** What countries have poor economies because of recent conflict?
13. **Economics** How is Vietnam trying to improve its economy?

Section 2 Island Southeast Asia

14. **Place** What two kinds of farming are carried on in Malaysia?
15. **Economics** What economic activity is important in Singapore besides its shipping industry?
16. **Economics** What resources have made Brunei wealthy?
17. **Culture** How does religion show Spanish influence in the Philippines?

Section 3 Indonesia

18. **Economics** How do nearly half of the people of Indonesia make a living?
19. **Location** How does location make Indonesia a center of trade?
20. **Government** Why does Indonesia have many political parties?

Southeast Asia

Place Location Activity

On a separate sheet of paper, match the letters on the map with the numbered places listed below.

1. Mekong River
2. South China Sea
3. Gulf of Tonkin
4. Hanoi
5. Indonesia
6. Singapore
7. Thailand
8. Vietnam
9. Indian Ocean
10. Philippines

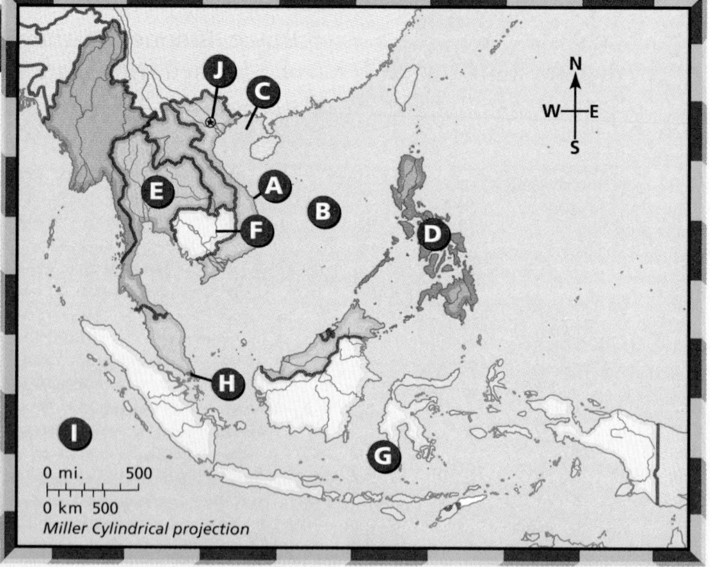

Self-Check Quiz Visit the ***Geography: The World and Its People*** Web site at gwip.glencoe.com and click on **Chapter 26—Self-Check Quizzes** to prepare for the Chapter Test.

Critical Thinking

21. **Predicting Outcomes** Experts believe that Brunei has enough oil reserves to last until 2018. What might happen to the country's economy and standard of living at that time?
22. **Organizing Information** Make a chart like this one. Under each column, write two facts about a country in Southeast Asia. Write about three countries—one from mainland Southeast Asia, one from island Southeast Asia, and Indonesia.

Country	Land	Economy	People

GeoJournal Activity

23. **Writing a Report** Learn about the culture of one of the countries in Southeast Asia. Choose one of the following topics to research: (1) the arts; (2) festivals and holidays; or (3) music and literature. Prepare a written report with illustrations or photos.

Mental Mapping Activity

24. **Focusing on the Region** Draw a map of Southeast Asia, then label the following:
    - Borneo
    - Irrawaddy River
    - Java
    - Malay Peninsula
    - Philippines
    - South China Sea
    - Strait of Malacca
    - Thailand

25. **Using the Internet** Use the Internet to learn about the foods in a Southeast Asian country. Find recipes and pictures. Prepare a display that shows a typical meal, or cook the meal yourself and share it with the class.

Standardized Test Practice

Directions: Study the graph below, then answer the questions that follow.

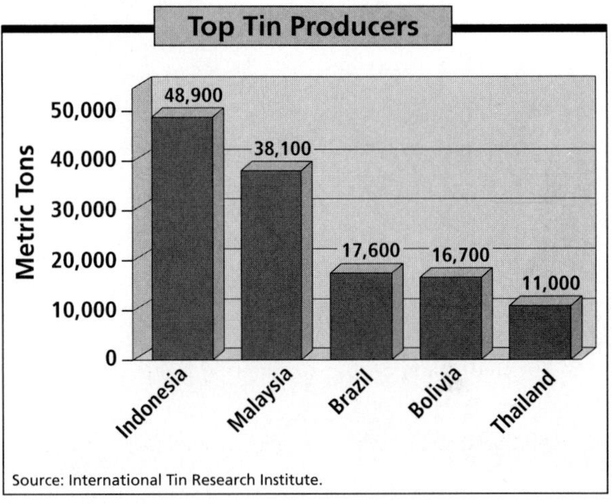

1. **About how much tin does Indonesia produce each year?**
   - A 48,900 metric tons
   - B 48,000,900 metric tons
   - C 48.9 million metric tons
   - D 48.9 billion metric tons
2. **About how much tin does Brazil produce each year?**
   - F 17,600 metric tons
   - G 17,600,000 metric tons
   - H 17.6 million metric tons
   - J 17.6 billion metric tons

Test-Taking Tip: In order to understand any type of graph, look carefully around the graph for keys that show how it is organized. On this bar graph, the numbers along the left side represent the exact number shown. You do not have to multiply by millions or billions to find the number of metric tons.

Unit 9

Fur seal on the beach, Antarctica

Boy selling fish, Samoa

Australia, Oceania, and Antarctica

Lone tree in the outback, Australia

Australia, Oceania, and Antarctica are grouped together more because of their nearness to one another than because of any similarities among their peoples. These lands lie mostly in the Southern Hemisphere. Australia is a dry continent that is home to unusual wildlife. Oceania's 25,000 tropical islands spread out across the Pacific Ocean. Frozen Antarctica encompasses the South Pole.

NGS ONLINE
www.nationalgeographic.com/education

Focus on:

Australia, Oceania, and Antarctica

LYING ALMOST ENTIRELY in the Southern Hemisphere, this region includes two continents and thousands of islands scattered across the Pacific Ocean. Covering a huge portion of the globe, the region includes landscapes ranging from polar to tropical.

The Land

Both a continent and a single country, Australia is a vast expanse of mostly flat land. The Great Dividing Range runs down the continent's eastern edge. Between this range of mountains and the Pacific Ocean lies a narrow strip of coastal land. West of the Great Dividing Range lies Australia's large—and very dry—interior. Here in the Australian "outback" are seemingly endless miles of scrubland, as well as three huge deserts.

Across the Tasman Sea from Australia lies New Zealand, made up of two main islands—North Island and South Island—and many smaller ones. Mountains and hills dominate the landscape.

North and east of New Zealand is Oceania. Its roughly 25,000 islands lie scattered across the Pacific Ocean on either side of the Equator. Some of these islands are volcanic. Others are huge formations of rock that have risen from the ocean floor. Still others are low-lying coral islands surrounded by reefs.

Antarctica, the frozen continent, covers and surrounds the South Pole. It is almost completely buried under an enormous sheet of ice.

The Climate

Australia is one of the driest continents in the world. Its eastern coast does receive rainfall from the Pacific Ocean. Mountains block this moisture from reaching inland areas, however. Much of Australia's outback has a desert climate.

No place in New Zealand is more than 80 miles (129 km) from the sea. This country has only one climate region: marine west coast. It has mild temperatures and plentiful rainfall throughout the year.

The islands of Oceania have mostly tropical climates, with warm temperatures and distinct wet and dry seasons. Rain forests cover many of the islands.

Antarctica is one of the coldest and windiest places on the earth, as well as one of the driest. It receives so little precipitation that it is considered a desert—the world's largest cold desert.

UNIT 9

Sheep grazing near Mount Egmont, New Zealand

◀ Emperor penguins examining the ice, Antarctica

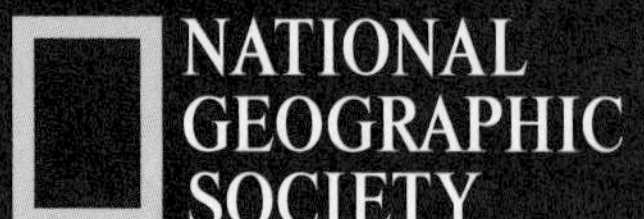

The Economy

Mines dot the Australian landscape. Its ancient rocks and soils are rich in minerals such as uranium, bauxite, iron ore, copper, nickel, and gold. Little of Australia's land is good for growing crops. Instead, vast cattle and sheep ranches—or stations, as the Australians call them—spread across much of the country. Sheep far outnumber people in New Zealand, where pastures are lush and green almost year-round. New Zealand is one of the world's leading producers of lamb and wool.

The people of Oceania depend primarily on fishing and farming. Across much of Oceania, the soil and climate are not favorable for widespread agriculture, and islanders generally raise only enough food for themselves. Yet some larger islands have rich volcanic soil. In such places, cash crops of fruits, sugar, coffee, and coconut products are grown for export.

Antarctica is believed to be rich in mineral resources. To preserve Antarctica for research and exploration, however, many nations have agreed not to mine this mineral wealth.

The People

The first settlers in this region probably came from Asia thousands of years ago. Australia's first inhabitants, the ancestors of today's Aborigines, may have arrived as long as 40,000 years ago. Not until about A.D. 1000, however, did seafaring peoples reach the farthest islands of Oceania.

The British colonized Australia and New Zealand in the 1700s and 1800s. These two countries gained their independence in the early 1900s. Many South Pacific islands were not freed from colonial rule until after World War II. Today Australia and Oceania are a blend of European, traditional Pacific, and Asian cultures.

Despite its vast size, this is the least populous of all the world's regions. It is home to only about 30 million people. More than half of these live in Australia, where they are found mostly in coastal cities such as Sydney and Melbourne. Roughly 4 million people live in New Zealand, which also has large urban populations along its coasts. Oceania is less urbanized. Antarctica has no permanent human inhabitants at all. Groups of scientists live and work on the frozen continent for brief periods to carry out their research.

Exploring the Region

1. **Which two continents lie in this region?**
2. **Why is Antarctica considered a desert?**
3. **Why is so little of Australia's land good for farming?**
4. **Where do most of the region's people live?**

◀ **Girl selling fruit, French Polynesia**

The city of Melbourne, along the southeastern coast of Australia

Australia, Oceania, and Antarctica

Physical

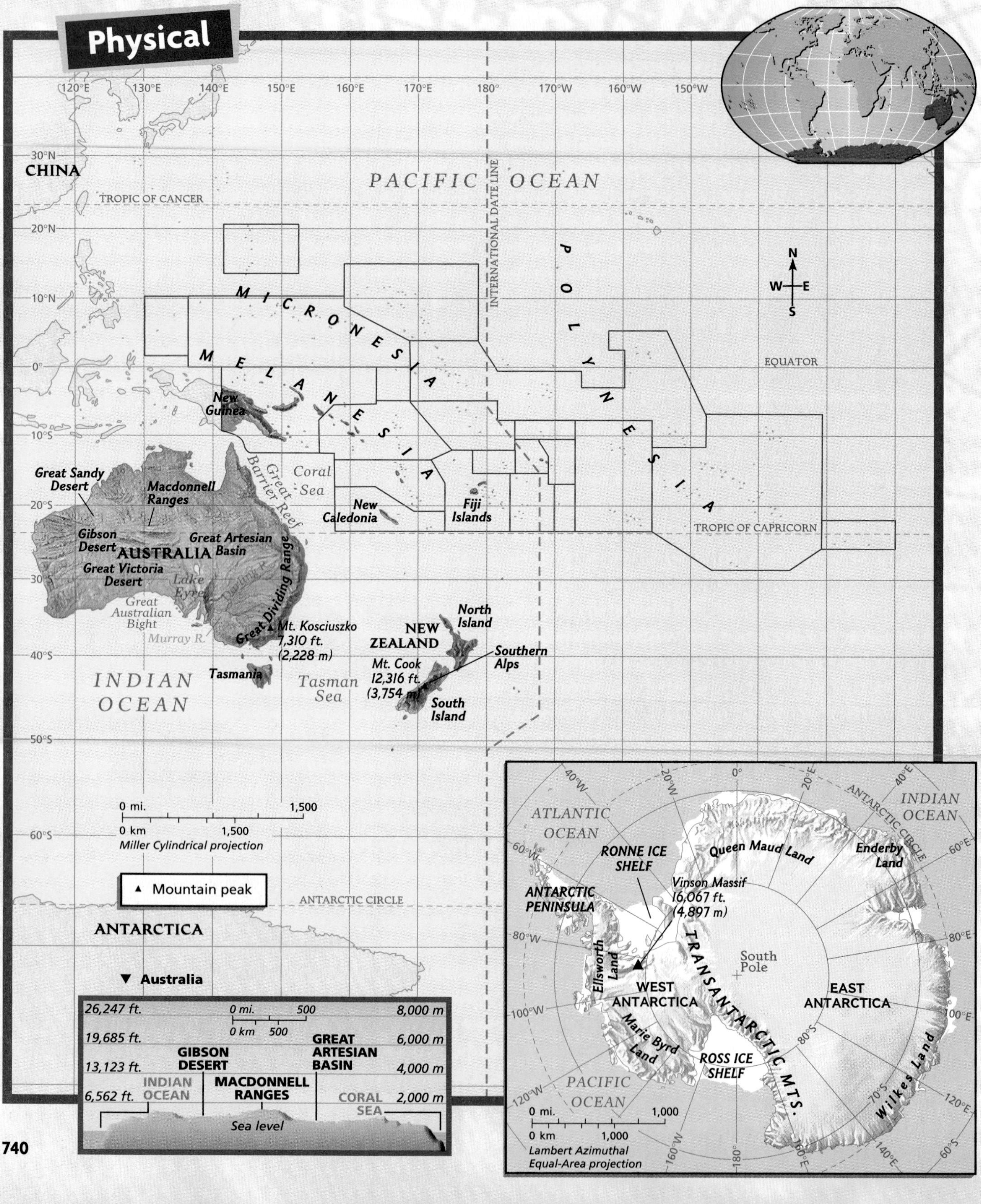

120°E 130°E 140°E 150°E 160°E 170°E 180° 170°W 160°W 150°W

30°N
CHINA
PACIFIC OCEAN
TROPIC OF CANCER
20°N
INTERNATIONAL DATE LINE
10°N
MICRONESIA
POLYNESIA
MELANESIA
0°
EQUATOR
New Guinea
10°S
Great Sandy Desert
Macdonnell Ranges
Great Barrier Reef
Coral Sea
20°S
Gibson Desert
AUSTRALIA
Great Artesian Basin
New Caledonia
Fiji Islands
TROPIC OF CAPRICORN
Great Victoria Desert
Lake Eyre
Darling R.
Great Dividing Range
30°S
Great Australian Bight
Murray R.
Mt. Kosciuszko 7,310 ft. (2,228 m)
North Island
NEW ZEALAND
Mt. Cook 12,316 ft. (3,754 m)
Southern Alps
40°S
Tasmania
Tasman Sea
South Island
INDIAN OCEAN
50°S
0 mi. 1,500
0 km 1,500
Miller Cylindrical projection
60°S
▲ Mountain peak
ANTARCTIC CIRCLE
ANTARCTICA

N
W E
S

40°W 20°W 0° 20°E 40°E
ATLANTIC OCEAN
INDIAN OCEAN
ANTARCTIC CIRCLE
60°W
RONNE ICE SHELF
Queen Maud Land
Enderby Land
60°E
Vinson Massif 16,067 ft. (4,897 m)
ANTARCTIC PENINSULA
80°W
Ellsworth Land
TRANSANTARCTIC MTS.
South Pole
80°E
WEST ANTARCTICA
EAST ANTARCTICA
100°W
100°E
Marie Byrd Land
ROSS ICE SHELF
80°S
PACIFIC OCEAN
70°S
Wilkes Land
120°W
120°E
0 mi. 1,000
0 km 1,000
Lambert Azimuthal Equal-Area projection
160°W 180° 160°E 140°E 60°S

▼ Australia

26,247 ft. 8,000 m
0 mi. 500
0 km 500
19,685 ft. 6,000 m
GIBSON DESERT
GREAT ARTESIAN BASIN
13,123 ft. 4,000 m
INDIAN OCEAN
MACDONNELL RANGES
CORAL SEA
6,562 ft. 2,000 m
Sea level

Unit 9

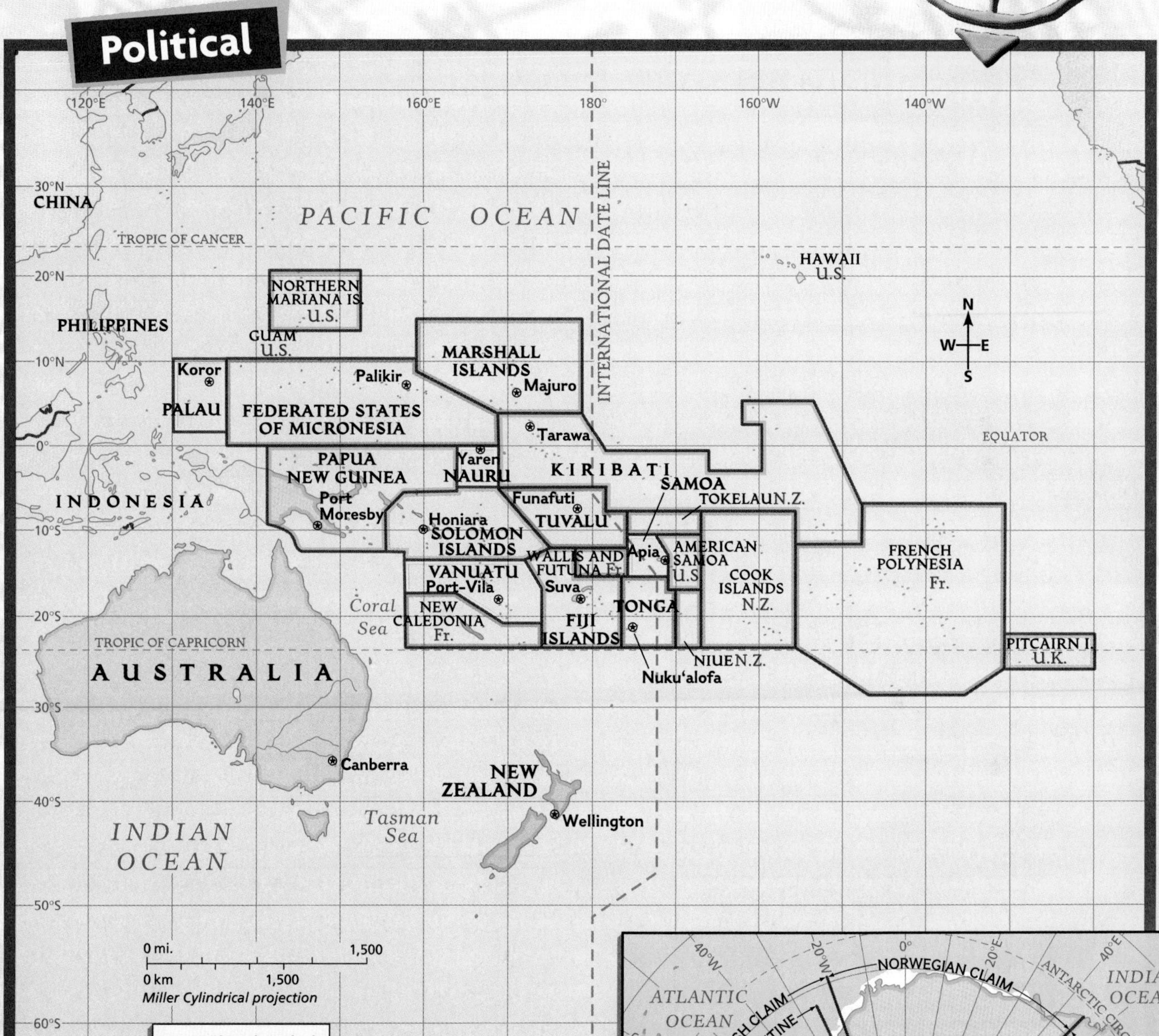

Political

120°E 140°E 160°E 180° 160°W 140°W

30°N 20°N 10°N 0° 10°S 20°S 30°S 40°S 50°S 60°S 70°S

PACIFIC OCEAN

INTERNATIONAL DATE LINE

TROPIC OF CANCER

EQUATOR

TROPIC OF CAPRICORN

ANTARCTIC CIRCLE

CHINA

PHILIPPINES

INDONESIA

NORTHERN MARIANA IS. U.S.

GUAM U.S.

HAWAII U.S.

Koror

PALAU

Palikir

FEDERATED STATES OF MICRONESIA

MARSHALL ISLANDS

Majuro

Tarawa

KIRIBATI

Yaren

NAURU

PAPUA NEW GUINEA

Port Moresby

Honiara

SOLOMON ISLANDS

Funafuti

TUVALU

SAMOA

TOKELAU N.Z.

Apia

AMERICAN SAMOA U.S.

WALLIS AND FUTUNA Fr.

VANUATU

Port-Vila

Suva

FIJI ISLANDS

TONGA

Nuku'alofa

NIUE N.Z.

COOK ISLANDS N.Z.

FRENCH POLYNESIA Fr.

PITCAIRN I. U.K.

NEW CALEDONIA Fr.

Coral Sea

AUSTRALIA

Canberra

NEW ZEALAND

Wellington

Tasman Sea

INDIAN OCEAN

ANTARCTICA

0 mi. 1,500

0 km 1,500

Miller Cylindrical projection

⊛ National capital

0° 20°E 20°W 40°W 40°E 60°W 60°E 80°W 80°E 100°W 100°E 120°W 120°E 140°W 140°E 160°W 180° 70°S 80°S

ATLANTIC OCEAN

INDIAN OCEAN

PACIFIC OCEAN

ANTARCTIC CIRCLE

NORWEGIAN CLAIM

BRITISH CLAIM

ARGENTINE CLAIM

CHILEAN CLAIM

AUSTRALIAN CLAIM

FRENCH CLAIM

NEW ZEALAND CLAIM

South Pole

ANTARCTICA

Unclaimed

0 mi. 500

0 km 500

Lambert Azimuthal Equal-Area projection

MAP STUDY

1. What body of water separates Australia from Melanesia?
2. What is the capital of New Zealand?

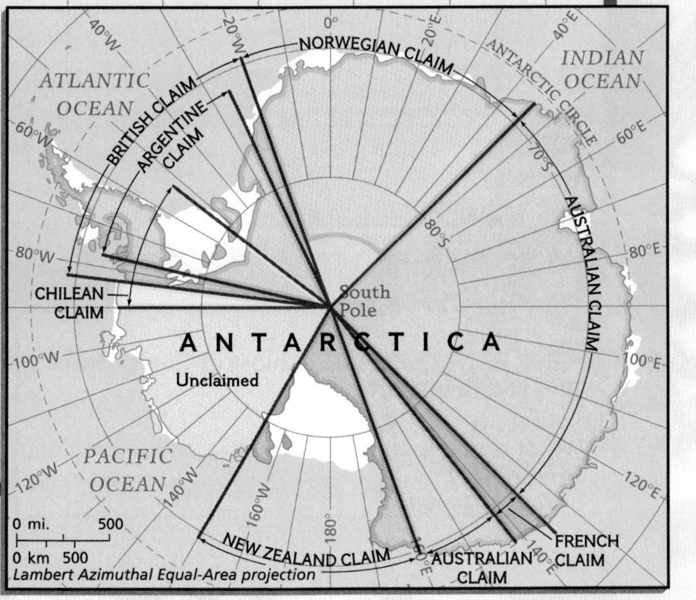

Australia, Oceania, and Antarctica

Endangered Environments

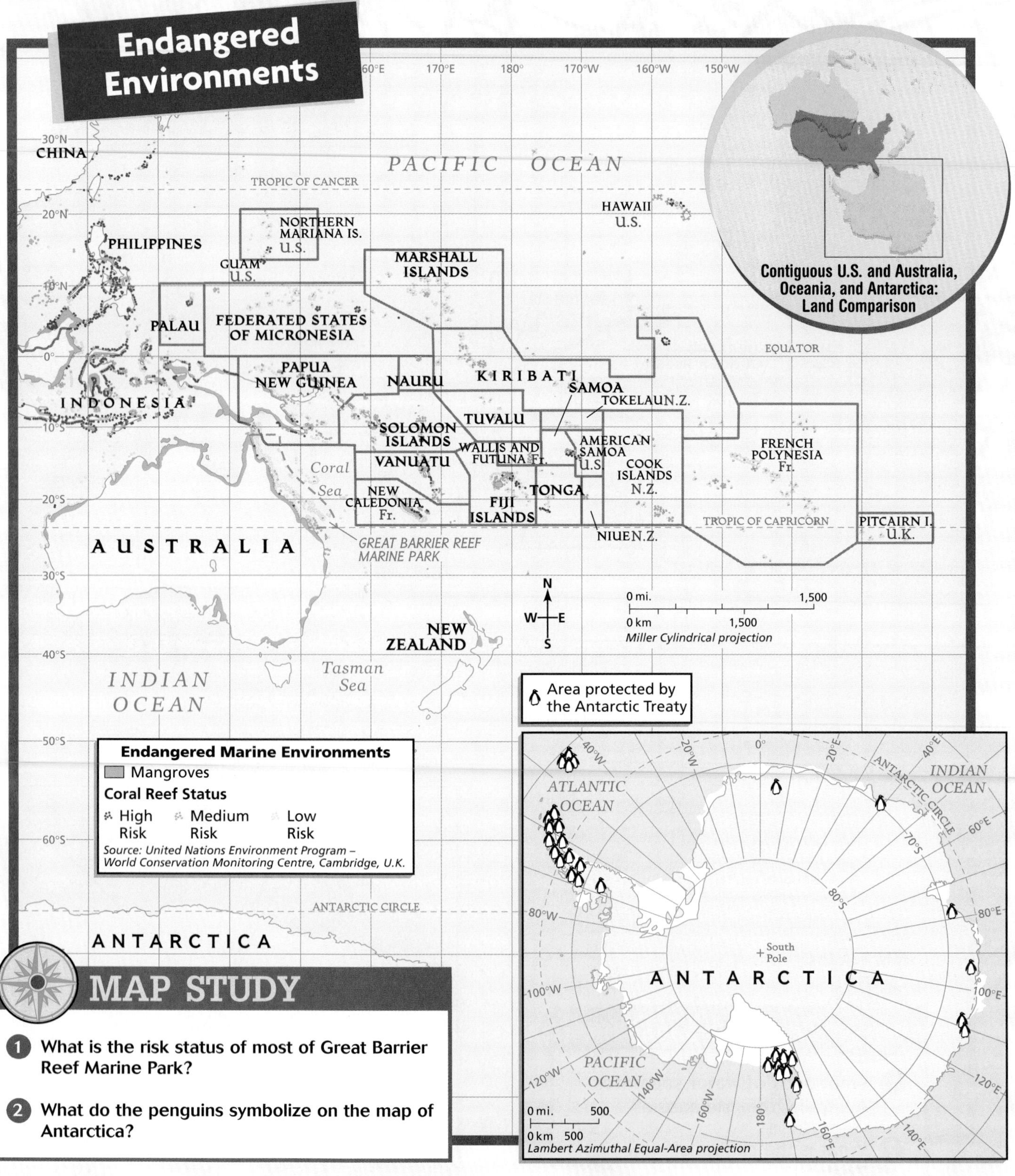

MAP STUDY

1. What is the risk status of most of Great Barrier Reef Marine Park?
2. What do the penguins symbolize on the map of Antarctica?

Geo Extremes

① HIGHEST POINT
Vinson Massif (Antarctica)
16,067 ft. (4,897 m) high

② LOWEST POINT
Bently Subglacial Trench (Antarctica)
8,366 ft. (2,550 m) below sea level

③ LONGEST RIVER
Murray-Darling (Australia)
2,310 mi. (3,718 km) long

④ LARGEST LAKE
Lake Eyre (Australia)
3,600 sq. mi. (9,324 sq. km)

⑤ LARGEST HOT DESERT
Great Victoria (Australia)
134,650 sq. mi. (348,742 sq. km)

⑥ LARGEST COLD DESERT
Antarctica
5,100,000 sq. mi. (13,209,000 sq. km)

COMPARING POPULATION: United States and Selected Countries of Australia, Oceania, and Antarctica

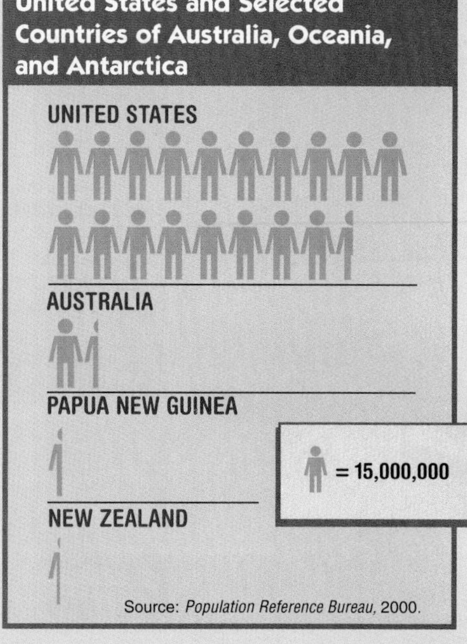

Source: *Population Reference Bureau*, 2000.

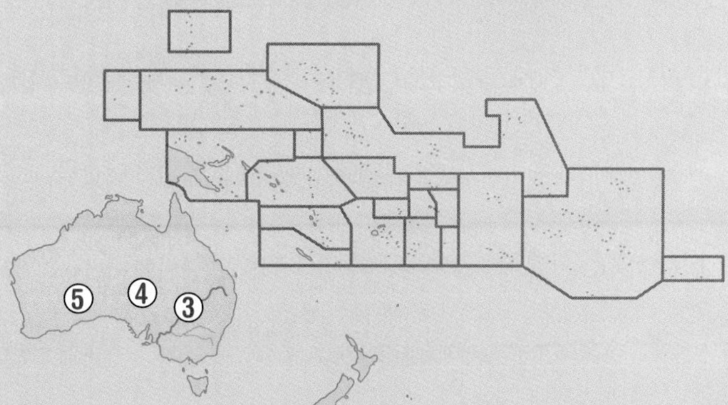

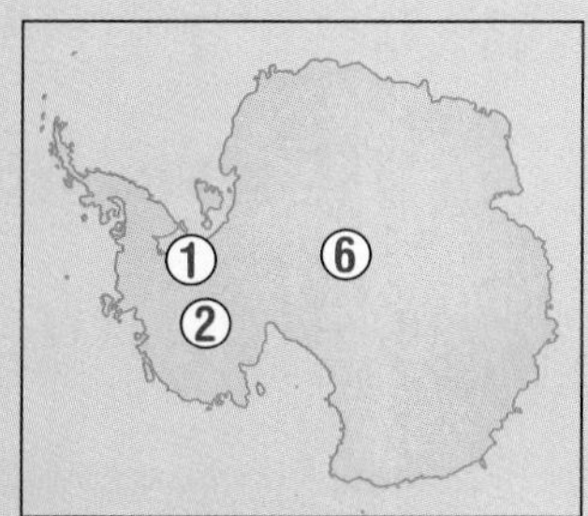

POPULATION GROWTH: Australia, 1958–2008

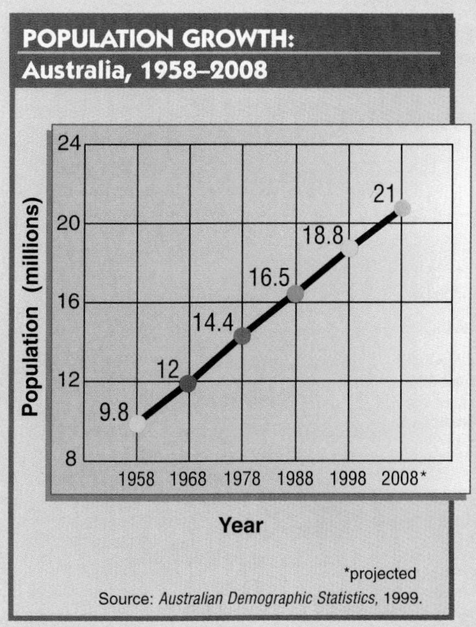

*projected
Source: *Australian Demographic Statistics*, 1999.

GRAPHIC STUDY

1. The largest cold desert in this region is also the largest desert in the *world*. What is it?
2. By how much is Australia's population expected to have grown between 1958 and 2008?

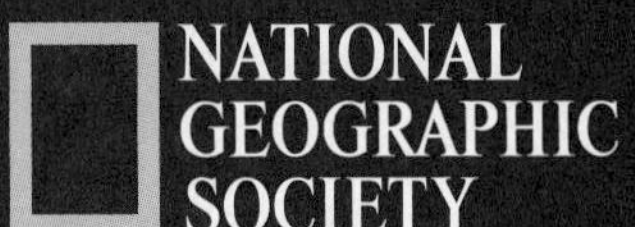

Country Profiles

AUSTRALIA

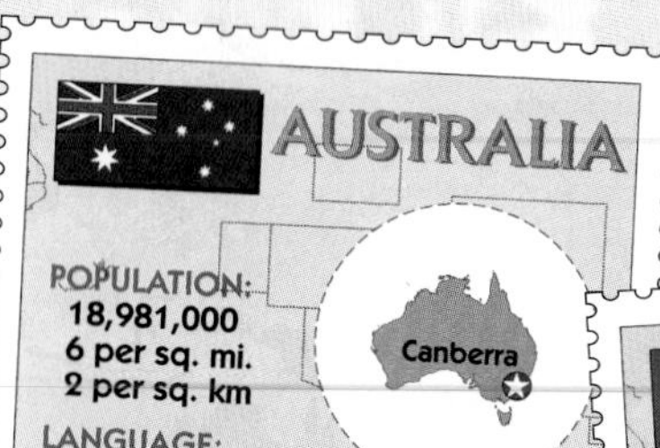

POPULATION: 18,981,000; 6 per sq. mi.; 2 per sq. km
LANGUAGE: English
MAJOR EXPORT: Coal
MAJOR IMPORT: Machinery
CAPITAL: Canberra
LANDMASS: 2,966,153 sq. mi.; 7,682,300 sq. km

FEDERATED STATES of MICRONESIA

POPULATION: 117,000; 432 per sq. mi.; 167 per sq. km
LANGUAGES: English, Local Languages
MAJOR EXPORT: Fish
MAJOR IMPORT: Foods
CAPITAL: Palikir
LANDMASS: 271 sq. mi.; 702 sq. km

FIJI ISLANDS

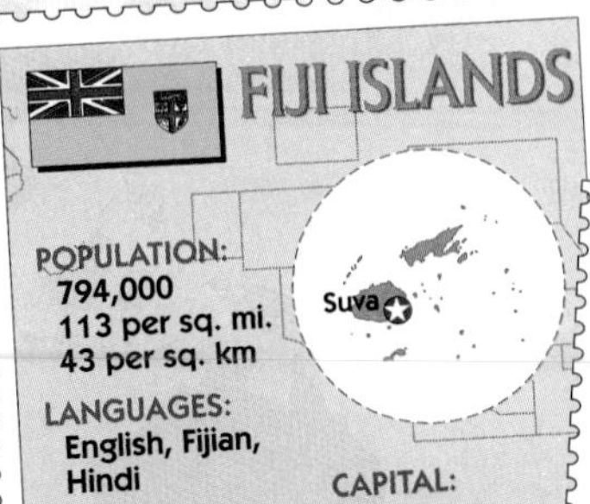

POPULATION: 794,000; 113 per sq. mi.; 43 per sq. km
LANGUAGES: English, Fijian, Hindi
MAJOR EXPORT: Sugar
MAJOR IMPORT: Machinery
CAPITAL: Suva
LANDMASS: 7,056 sq. mi.; 18,274 sq. km

KIRIBATI

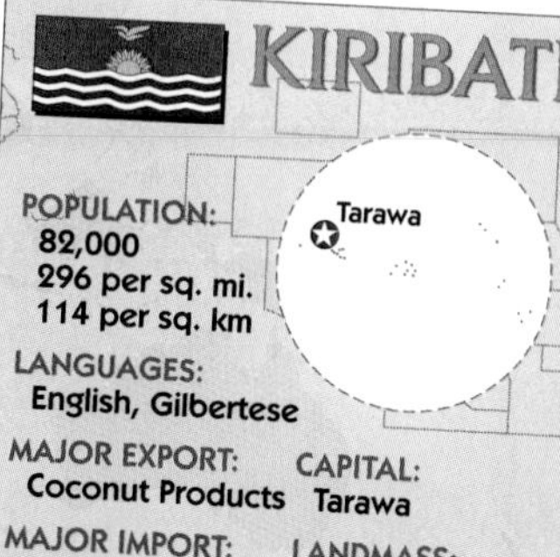

POPULATION: 82,000; 296 per sq. mi.; 114 per sq. km
LANGUAGES: English, Gilbertese
MAJOR EXPORT: Coconut Products
MAJOR IMPORT: Foods
CAPITAL: Tarawa
LANDMASS: 277 sq. mi.; 717 sq. km

MARSHALL ISLANDS

POPULATION: 62,000; 886 per sq. mi.; 343 per sq. km
LANGUAGES: English, Local Languages
MAJOR EXPORT: Coconut Products
MAJOR IMPORT: Foods
CAPITAL: Majuro
LANDMASS: 70 sq. mi.; 181 sq. km

NAURU

POPULATION: 11,000; 1,357 per sq. mi.; 524 per sq. km
LANGUAGES: Nauruan, English
MAJOR EXPORT: Phosphates
MAJOR IMPORT: Foods
CAPITAL: Yaren
LANDMASS: 8 sq. mi.; 21 sq. km

NEW ZEALAND

POPULATION: 3,817,000; 37 per sq. mi.; 14 per sq. km
LANGUAGE: English
MAJOR EXPORT: Wool
MAJOR IMPORT: Machinery
CAPITAL: Wellington
LANDMASS: 103,883 sq. mi.; 269,057 sq. km

PALAU

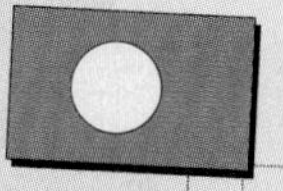

POPULATION: 19,000; 101 per sq. mi.; 35 per sq. km
LANGUAGES: English, Palauan
MAJOR EXPORT: Fish
MAJOR IMPORT: N/A
CAPITAL: Koror
LANDMASS: 188 sq. mi.; 487 sq. km

PAPUA NEW GUINEA

POPULATION: 4,669,000; 26 per sq. mi.; 10 per sq. km
LANGUAGES: English, Local Languages
MAJOR EXPORT: Gold
MAJOR IMPORT: Machinery
CAPITAL: Port Moresby
LANDMASS: 178,260 sq. mi.; 461,691 sq. km

SAMOA

POPULATION: 195,000; 178 per sq. mi.; 69 per sq. km
LANGUAGES: Samoan, English
MAJOR EXPORT: Coconut Products
MAJOR IMPORT: Foods
CAPITAL: Apia
LANDMASS: 1,093 sq. mi.; 2,831 sq. km

SOLOMON ISLANDS

POPULATION: 430,000; 39 per sq. mi.; 15 per sq. km
LANGUAGES: English, Local Languages
MAJOR EXPORT: Cocoa
MAJOR IMPORT: Machinery
CAPITAL: Honiara
LANDMASS: 10,985 sq. mi.; 28,450 sq. km

TONGA

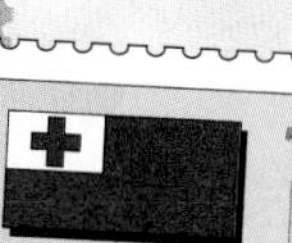

POPULATION: 109,000; 404 per sq. mi.; 156 per sq. km
LANGUAGES: Tongan, English
MAJOR EXPORT: Squash
MAJOR IMPORT: Foods
CAPITAL: Nuku'alofa
LANDMASS: 270 sq. mi.; 699 sq. km

Countries and flags not drawn to scale

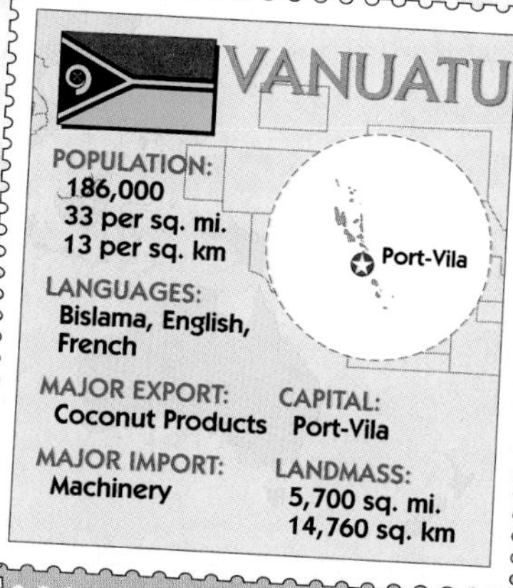

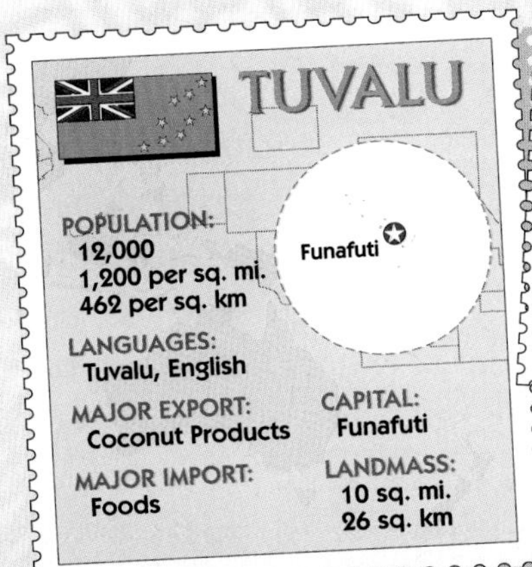

GEO BEE Questions From Buzz Bee!

The following questions are taken from National Geographic GeoBees. Use your textbook, the Internet, and other library resources to find the answers.

1. Dried coconut meat is the main export of many South Pacific islands. What is it called?
2. Ross, Amundsen, and Bellingshausen are names of seas that border which country?
3. The world's southernmost city with a metropolitan population greater than 1 million is located north of the Bass Strait. Name this city.
4. What U.S.-administered islands were named for their location about halfway between the continents of North America and Asia?
5. A 1991 international agreement prohibits mining on which continent for at least the next 50 years?
6. If you were swimming off the coast of Australia near Perth, you would be in what body of water?
7. Which continent receives the least amount of rainfall?

Chapter 27

Australia and New Zealand

The World and Its People NATIONAL GEOGRAPHIC

To learn more about the people and places of Australia and New Zealand, view ***The World and Its People*** **Chapter 27** video.

Geography Online

Chapter Overview Visit the ***Geography: The World and Its People*** Web site at gwip.glencoe.com and click on **Chapter 27–Chapter Overviews** to preview information about Australia and New Zealand.

Australia

Guide to Reading

Main Idea

Both a continent and a country, Australia has many natural resources but few people.

Terms to Know

- coral reef
- outback
- station
- marsupial
- immigrant
- boomerang
- bush

Places to Locate

- Australia
- Tasmania
- Great Barrier Reef
- Murray River
- Darling River
- Sydney
- Melbourne
- Canberra

Reading Strategy

Make a chart like this one. Then fill in two facts about Australia for each category.

Land	History
Climate	Government
Economy	People

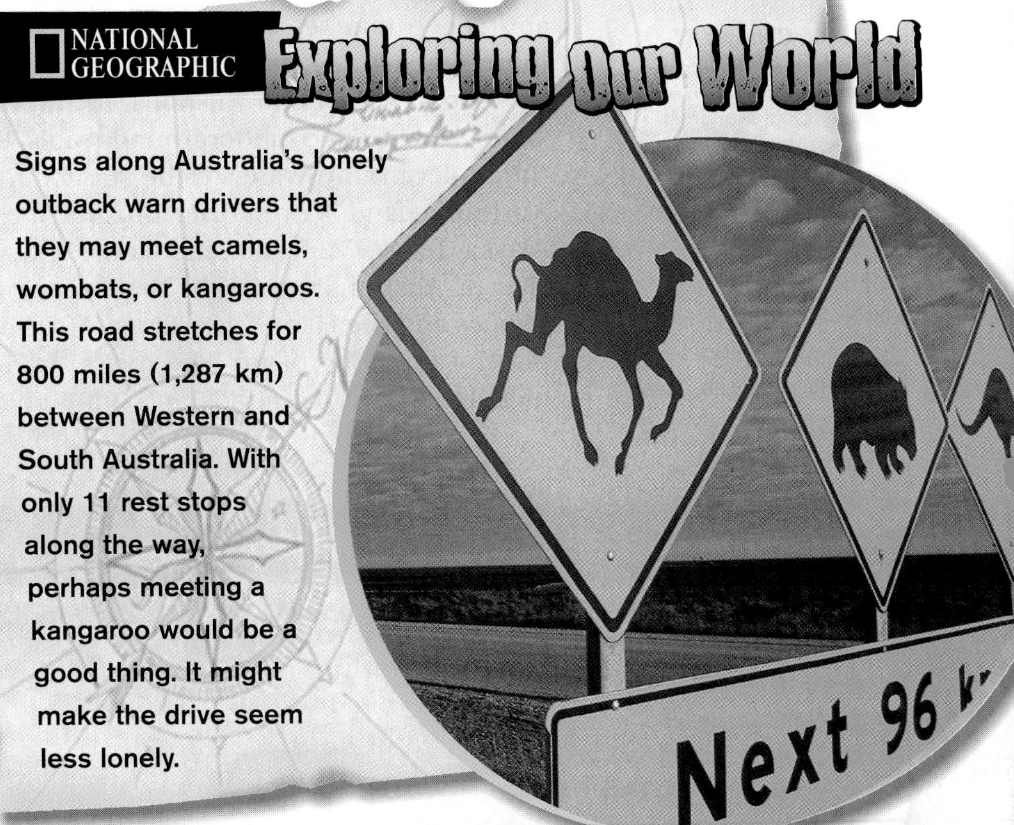

Signs along Australia's lonely outback warn drivers that they may meet camels, wombats, or kangaroos. This road stretches for 800 miles (1,287 km) between Western and South Australia. With only 11 rest stops along the way, perhaps meeting a kangaroo would be a good thing. It might make the drive seem less lonely.

Is **Australia** a country or a continent? It is both. Australia is the sixth-largest country in the world. Surrounded by water, Australia is too large to be called an island. So geographers call it a continent.

Australia's Land and Climate

Australia is sometimes referred to as the Land Down Under because it is located in the Southern Hemisphere. The Indian Ocean washes its western and southern shores. The Coral Sea, Pacific Ocean, and Tasman Sea border the eastern coast. The island of **Tasmania,** to the south, is part of Australia.

The **Great Barrier Reef** lies off Australia's northeastern coast. Coral formations have piled up for millions of years to create a colorful chain that stretches 1,250 miles (2,012 km). As you recall, a **coral reef** is a structure formed by the skeletons of small sea animals.

Plateaus and lowland plains spread across most of Australia. The longest and highest mountain range, the Great Dividing Range, runs along the eastern coast. Mt. Kosciuszko (KAH•zee•UHS•koh), the tallest mountain in Australia, measures 7,310 feet (2,228 km).

◀ Ayers Rock in central Australia

Geography Online

Web Activity Visit the ***Geography: The World and Its People*** Web site at gwip.glencoe.com and click on **Chapter 27—Student Web Activities** to learn more about the Great Barrier Reef.

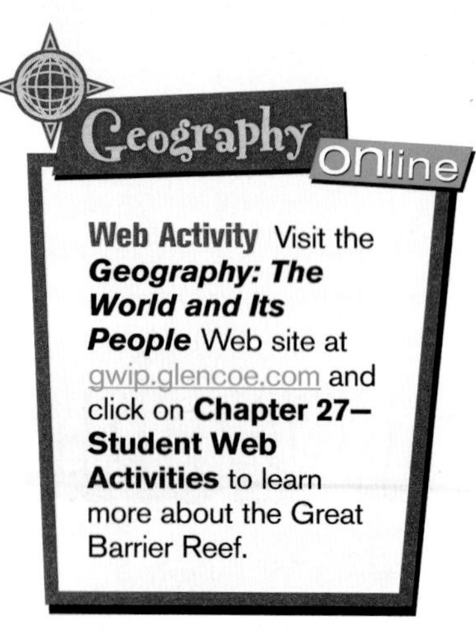

Narrow plains run along the south and southeast. These fertile flatlands hold Australia's best farmland and most of the country's people. Two major rivers, the **Murray** and the **Darling,** drain this region.

Australia's vast interior is pastureland. The people of Australia use the name outback for the inland regions of their country. Dry grasslands and mineral deposits are found here. Mining camps and cattle and sheep ranches called stations dot this region. Some stations are huge. One cattle station is almost twice as large as Delaware.

Water is scarce in Australia. In the Great Artesian Basin, however, water lies in deep, underground pools. Ranchers drill wells and bring the underground water to the surface for their cattle. Far to the west, Australia's land is even drier. Imagine a carpet of sand twice as large as Alaska, Texas, California, and New Mexico combined. That is about the size of Australia's western plateau, which includes the Macdonnell Ranges and the Hamersley Range. Most people who cross this vast, dry plateau do so by plane. The region is rich in resources such as gold, nickel, iron ore, diamonds, and uranium.

NATIONAL GEOGRAPHIC

Australia and New Zealand: Political

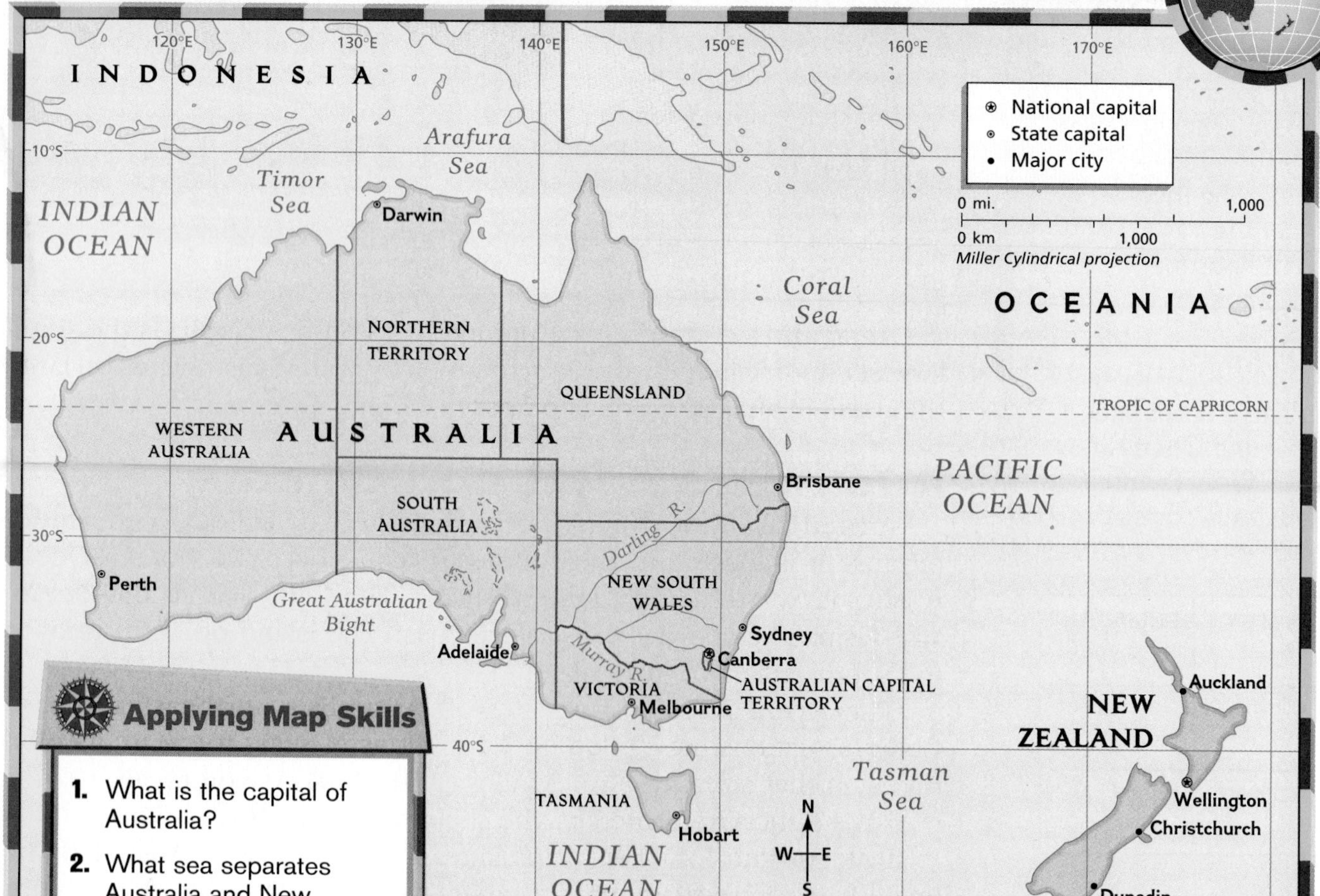

Applying Map Skills

1. What is the capital of Australia?
2. What sea separates Australia and New Zealand?

Find NGS online map resources @ www.nationalgeographic.com/maps

Desert and steppe climates are found in most of the country. Only the Great Dividing Range and Tasmania have winter temperatures that fall below freezing. Because of the country's location in the Southern Hemisphere, summer starts in December and winter starts in June.

Unusual Animals About 200 million years ago, the tectonic plate upon which Australia sits separated from the other continents. As a result, Australia's native plants and animals are not found elsewhere in the world. Two famous Australian animals are kangaroos and koalas. Both are **marsupials**, or mammals that carry their young in a pouch. Turn to page 753 to read about these and other amazing animals.

✓ Reading Check **Where do most of Australia's people live?**

Australia's Economy

Australia has a strong, prosperous economy. Australia is a treasure chest overflowing with mineral resources. These riches include iron ore, zinc, bauxite, gold, silver, opals, diamonds, and pearls. Australia also has

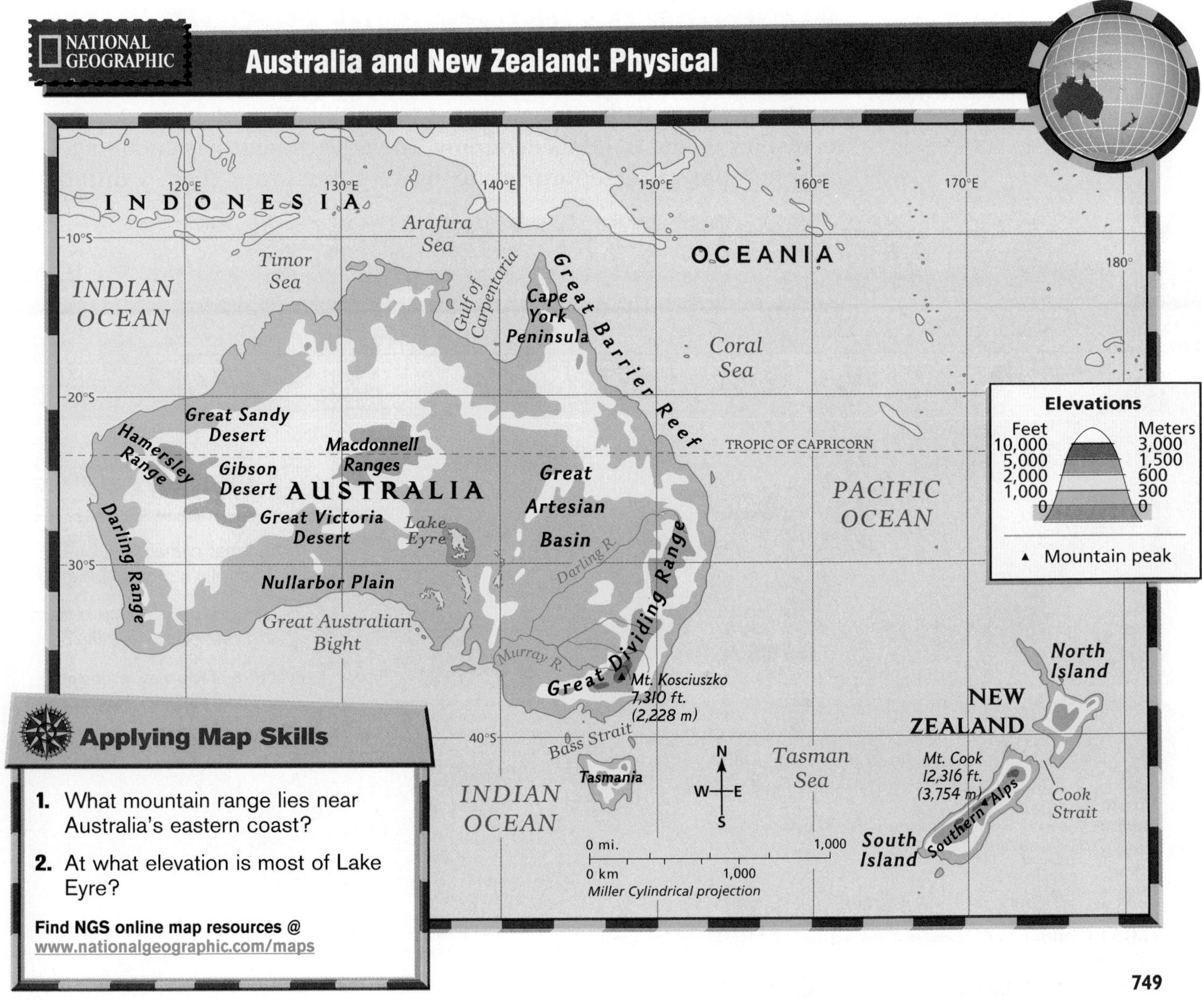

Applying Map Skills

1. What mountain range lies near Australia's eastern coast?
2. At what elevation is most of Lake Eyre?

Find NGS online map resources @ www.nationalgeographic.com/maps

energy resources, including coal, oil, and natural gas. Less than 1 percent of Australia's people work in the mining industry. Still, mineral and energy resources make up more than one-third of Australia's exports.

Australia's dry climate limits farming. With irrigation, however, farmers grow grains, sugarcane, cotton, fruits, and vegetables. Grains and sugar are exported, but most other crops are grown to feed Australia's people. The main agricultural activity is raising livestock, especially cattle and sheep. Australia is the world's top producer and exporter of wool. Ranchers also ship beef and cattle hides.

Australia's factories employ about 10 percent of the country's workers. Manufacturing, which is growing in importance, includes processed foods, transportation equipment, metals, cloth, and chemicals. High-tech industries, service industries, and tourism also play a large role in the economy. Modern ocean shipping enables Australia to export goods to very distant markets. More than half goes to Asia. The United States is also an important destination for exports.

Reading Check **What is Australia's main agricultural activity?**

Australia's History and People

Despite its huge area, Australia has few people—only 19 million. Most live in scattered areas along the coast, especially in the east and southeast. Australia has long needed more skilled workers to develop its resources and build its economy. The government has encouraged people from other countries to move here. More than 5 million

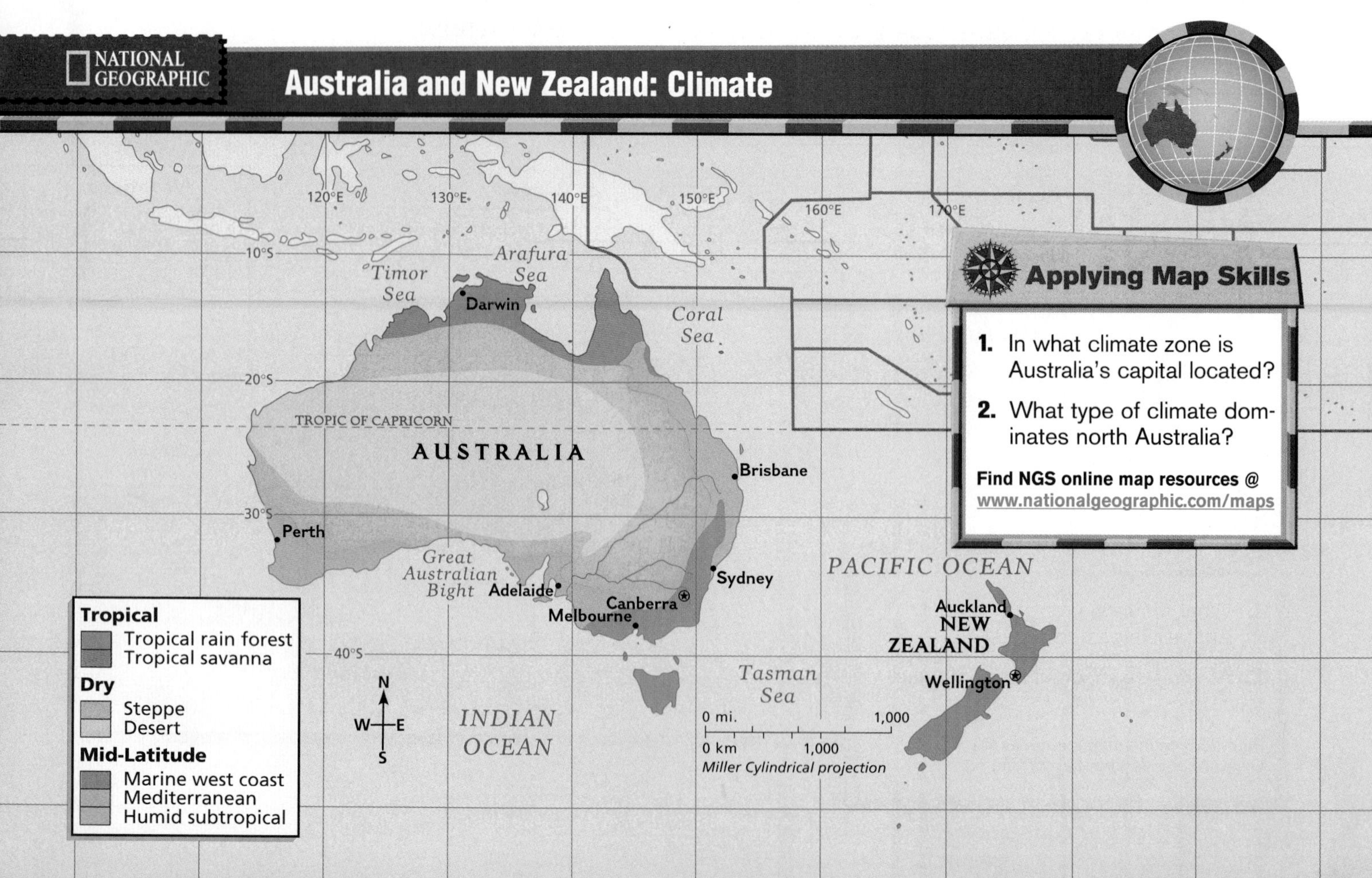

Music

The *digeridoo* is the most famous musical instrument from Australia. In its original form, it was made when a eucalyptus branch fell to the ground and was hollowed out by termites. Someone playing a *digeridoo* creates a variety of sounds by making a combination of lip, tongue, and mouth movements. Once you hear the eerie sounds, it is easy to understand why the Aborigines considered this instrument sacred and made it part of their ceremonies.

Looking Closer What other instruments are similar to the *digeridoo*?

GO TO

World Music: A Cultural Legacy
Hear music of this region on Disc 2, Track 28.

immigrants, or people who move from one country to live in another, have arrived in recent decades.

A small part of Australia's population are Aborigines (A•buh•RIHJ•neez). They are the descendants of the first immigrants who came from Asia about 30,000 to 40,000 years ago. For centuries the Aborigines moved throughout Australia gathering plants, hunting, and searching for water. They developed a unique culture. You may have heard of one of their weapons—the boomerang. This wooden tool is shaped like a bent bird's wing. The hunter throws it to stun his prey. If the boomerang misses, it curves and sails back to the hunter.

In 1770 Captain James Cook reached Australia and claimed it for Great Britain. At first the British government used Australia as a place to send prisoners. Then other British people set up colonies, especially after gold was discovered in the outback in 1851. Land was taken from the Aborigines, and many of them died of European diseases.

Today about 300,000 Aborigines live in Australia. Growing numbers of them are moving to cities to find jobs. After years of harsh treatment and isolation in the outback, the Aborigines now are demanding more opportunities. In 1967 the Australian government finally recognized the Aborigines as citizens.

The Government In 1901 the Australian British colonies united to form the independent Commonwealth of Australia. Today Australia has a British-style parliamentary democracy. A prime minister is the head of government. The political party with the most seats in the Australian parliament, or legislature, chooses the prime minister.

Like the United States, Australia has a federal system of government. This means that political power is divided between a national government

Dreamtime

Danny Ahmatt and John Meninga are Aborigines who live in Australia's Northern Territory. They live modern lives, but they also have traditional Aborigine beliefs. "We believe in *Dreamtime*," says Danny. "This means that our ancestors do not die but instead become part of nature. This is why we learn to respect our environment."

and state governments. The country has six states and two territories, the Northern Territory and the Australian Capital Territory.

Although independent, Australia for decades accepted the British king or queen as its ceremonial leader. Australians were largely of British ancestry and wanted to keep their British heritage. Since the 1960s, Australia has gradually developed its own national character. Many present-day Australians are not British but have Italian, Greek, Slavic, or Chinese backgrounds. As Australia's ties to the United Kingdom weaken, more and more Australians would like to see their country become a republic. This would mean replacing the British monarch with an Australian-born president.

City and Rural Life About 85 percent of Australia's people live in cities. **Sydney** and **Melbourne** are the largest cities. Sydney gained the world's attention as the host city for the 2000 Summer Olympic Games. **Canberra**—the national capital—has its own territory, much like Washington, D.C., in the United States. A government plan located Canberra inland to draw people into the outback.

About 15 percent of Australians live in rural areas known as the **bush.** Many rural people also live and work on the stations that dot the outback. Some farmers often have to drive several hours on unpaved roads to reach a distant rural town.

English is the major language, but "Aussies," as Australians call themselves, have unique words. For example, Australians say "G'Day," as a form of hello and cook beef on a "barbie," or barbeque grill.

Reading Check What kind of government does Australia have?

Section 1 Assessment

Defining Terms

1. **Define** coral reef, outback, station, marsupial, immigrant, boomerang, bush.

Recalling Facts

2. **Location** Why does Australia have animals not found on other continents?
3. **Economics** What are four mineral resources found in Australia?
4. **History** Who are the Aborigines?

Critical Thinking

5. **Understanding Cause and Effect** How does climate affect agriculture in Australia?
6. **Drawing Conclusions** How does life in Australia show that the country was once a colony of the United Kingdom?

Graphic Organizer

7. **Organizing Information** Make a time line like this one with at least four dates in Australia's history. Write the dates on one side of the line and the corresponding event on the opposite side.

Applying Geography Skills

8. **Analyzing Maps** Look at the economic activity map on page 755. What are the main manufacturing centers of Australia?

Making Connections

ART SCIENCE LITERATURE TECHNOLOGY

Australia's Amazing Animals

Australia is home to some fascinating and unusual animals. In fact, many of Australia's animal species are found nowhere else in the world.

Kangaroos

Ask people what comes to mind when they think of Australian animals, and they will probably say the kangaroo. Kangaroos are marsupials—mammals whose young mature inside a pouch on the mother's belly. The young kangaroo, called a joey, stays there for months, eating and growing. Australia is home to more than 50 species of kangaroo, ranging in size from the 6-foot (2-m) red kangaroo to the 9-inch (23-cm) musky rat-kangaroo. No matter what their size, all kangaroos have one thing in common—big hind feet. Kangaroos bound along at about 20 miles (32 km) per hour. In a single jump, a kangaroo can hop 10 feet (3 m) high and cover a distance of 45 feet (14 m).

Koalas

Because of their round face, big black nose, large fluffy ears, and soft fur, people sometimes call these animals koala bears. Yet they are not bears at all. The koala is a marsupial. The female's pouch opens at the bottom. Strong muscles keep the pouch shut and the young koalas, also called joeys, safe inside. The koala is a fussy eater who feeds only on leaves of eucalyptus trees. Although there are over 600 species of eucalyptus that grow in Australia, koalas eat only a few types. The leaves also provide the animals with all the moisture they need. Quiet, calm, and sleepy, koalas spend most of their time in the trees.

▲ Koala and joey

Platypus and Emu

The odd-looking platypus is one of the world's few egg-laying mammals. Sometimes called a duck-billed platypus, the animal has a soft, sensitive, skin-covered snout. The platypus is a good swimmer who lives in burrows along the streams and riverbanks of southern and eastern Australia. It uses its bill to stir the river bottom in search of food.

After the ostrich, the Australian emu is the world's second-largest bird. Although the emu cannot fly, its long legs enable it to run at speeds of up to 30 miles (48 km) per hour. Another interesting characteristic of the emu is its nesting behavior. Although the female lays the eggs, the male emu sits on them until they are ready to hatch.

◀ Kangaroo and joey

Emu ▼

Making the Connection

1. What are marsupials?
2. How far can a kangaroo hop in a single jump?
3. **Making Comparisons** Compare two different animals that live in Australia. Tell how they are alike. Tell how they are different.

Section 2

New Zealand

Guide to Reading

Main Idea

New Zealand is a small country with a growing economy based on trade.

Terms to Know

- geyser
- *manuka*
- fjord
- geothermal energy
- hydroelectric power

Places to Locate

- New Zealand
- North Island
- South Island
- Cook Strait
- Southern Alps
- Auckland
- Wellington

Reading Strategy

Make a time line like this one with at least four dates in New Zealand's history. Write the dates on one side of the line and the corresponding event on the opposite side.

NATIONAL GEOGRAPHIC **Exploring Our World**

Have you ever tasted a ripe green kiwifruit (KEE•wee•FROOT)? If so, it might have been grown on a New Zealand farm like the one shown here. After all, New Zealand is one of the world's leading producers of this tasty fruit. The kiwifruit, once known as the Chinese gooseberry, is now named for the kiwi bird—New Zealand's national symbol.

New Zealand lies in the Pacific Ocean about 1,200 miles (1,931 km) southeast of its nearest neighbor, Australia. In contrast to Australia's flat, dry land, New Zealand is mountainous and very green. Its marine west coast climate is mild and wet.

New Zealand's Land

New Zealand is about the size of Colorado. It includes two main islands—**North Island** and **South Island**—as well as many smaller islands. The **Cook Strait** separates North Island and South Island.

North Island A large plateau forms the center of North Island. Three active volcanoes and the inactive Mount Egmont are located here. You also find **geysers,** or hot springs that spout hot steam and water through a crack in the earth.

Small shrubs called ***manuka*** grow well in the plateau's fertile volcanic soil. Fertile lowlands, forested hills, and sandy beaches surround North Island's central plateau. On the plateau's slopes, sheep and cattle graze. Fruits and vegetables are grown on the coastal lowlands.

South Island The **Southern Alps** run along South Island's western coast. Snowcapped Mount Cook, the highest peak in New Zealand, soars 12,316 feet (3,754 m) here. Glaciers lie on mountain slopes above green forests and sparkling blue lakes. These glaciers once cut deep **fjords** (fee•AWRDS), or steep-sided valleys, into the mountains. The sea has filled these fjords with crystal-blue waters.

To the east of the Southern Alps stretch the Canterbury Plains. They form New Zealand's largest area of flat or nearly flat land. Farmers grow grains and ranchers raise sheep here.

Plants and Animals New Zealanders take pride in their unique wildlife. Their national symbol is a flightless bird called the kiwi. Giant kauri (KOWR•ee) trees once dominated all of North Island. About 100 years ago, European settlers cut down many of these trees, using the wood to build homes and ships. Today the government protects kauri trees. One of them is more than 2,000 years old.

✓Reading Check **Which island of New Zealand has glaciers and fjords?**

New Zealand's Economy

New Zealand has a thriving agricultural economy. Sheep are an important agricultural resource. New Zealand is the second-leading wool producer in the world. Lamb meat is another important export. Apples, barley, wheat, and corn are the main crops.

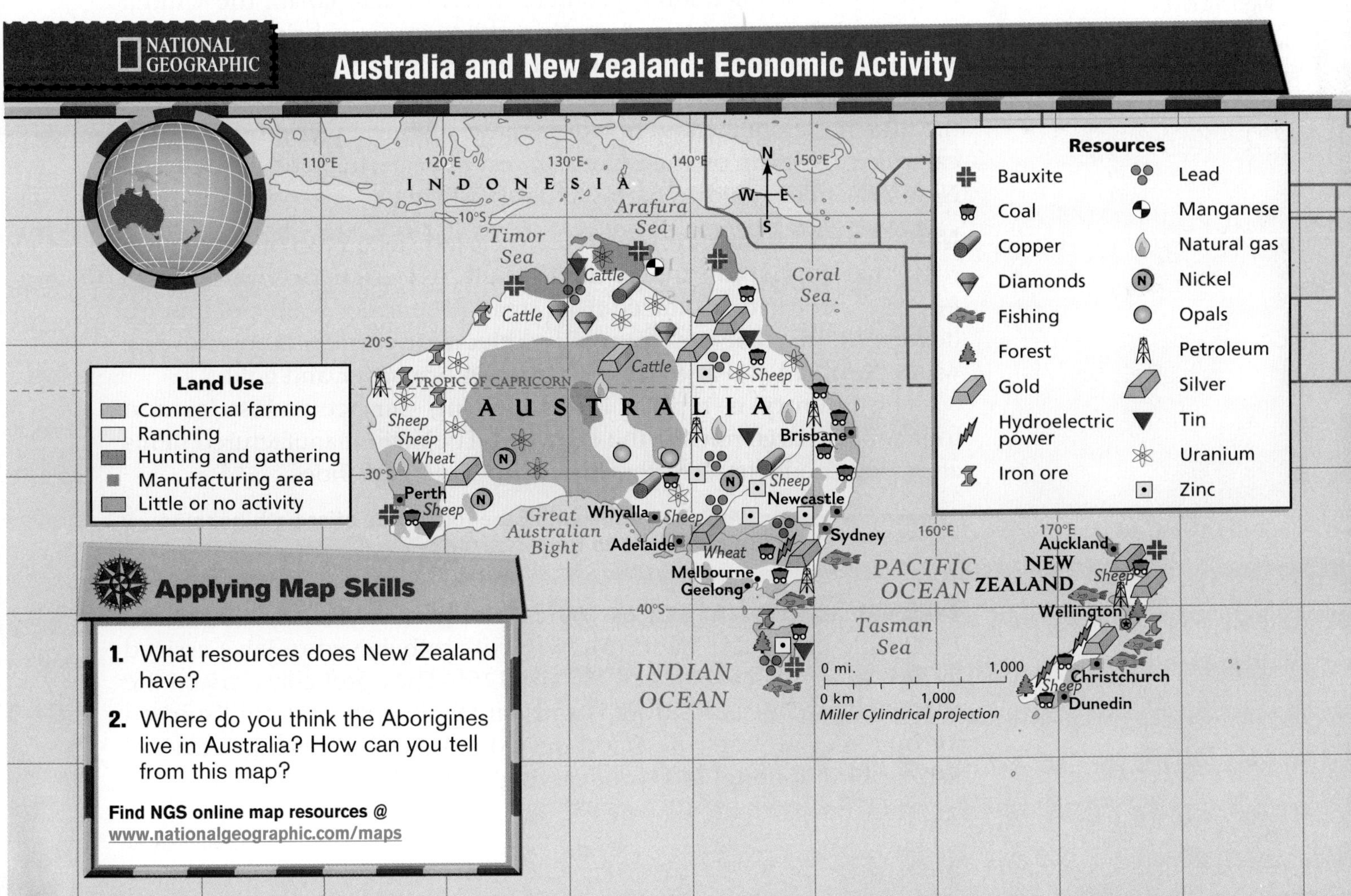

Applying Map Skills

1. What resources does New Zealand have?
2. Where do you think the Aborigines live in Australia? How can you tell from this map?

Find NGS online map resources @ www.nationalgeographic.com/maps

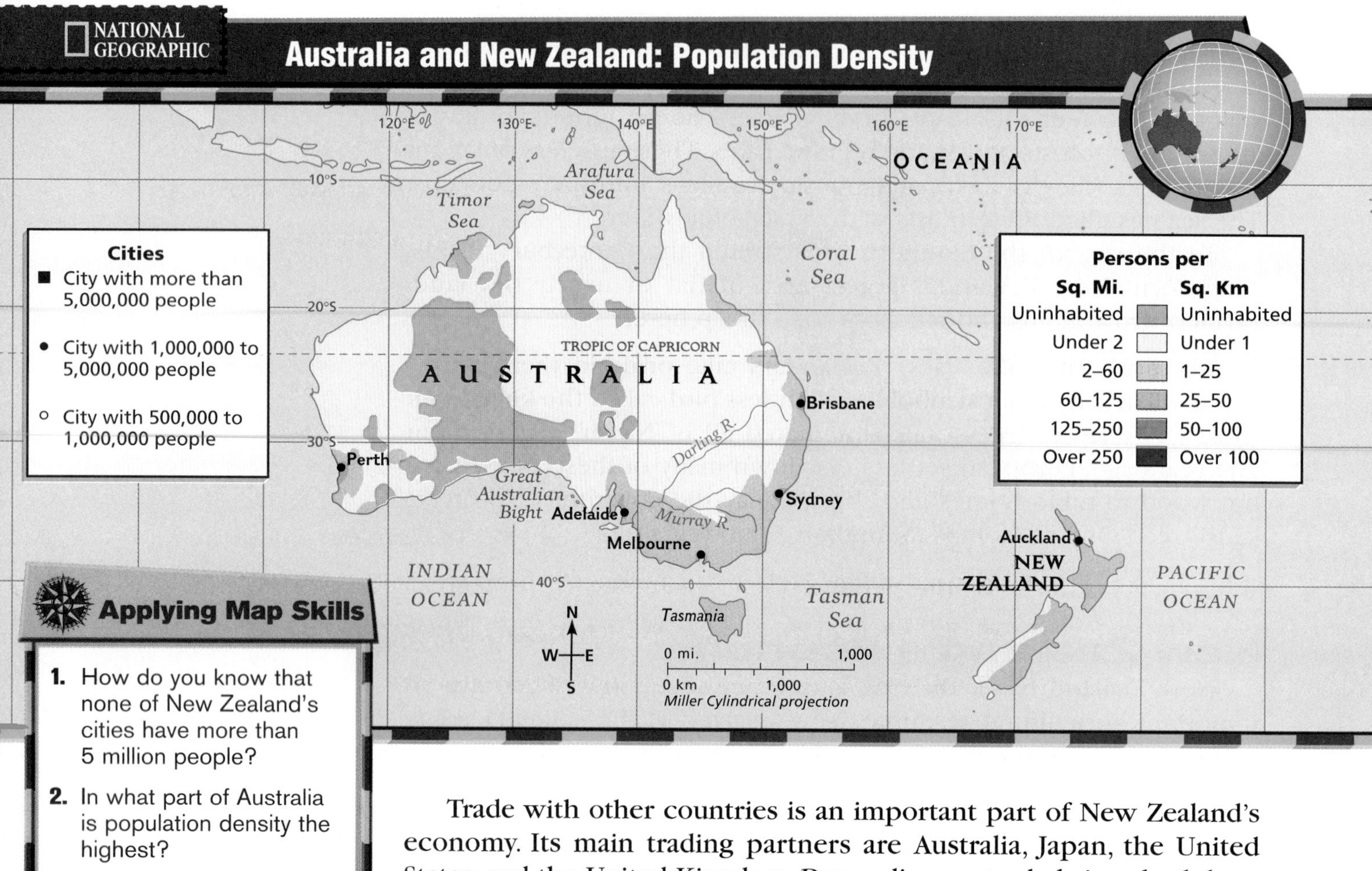

Applying Map Skills

1. How do you know that none of New Zealand's cities have more than 5 million people?
2. In what part of Australia is population density the highest?

Find NGS online map resources @ www.nationalgeographic.com/maps

Trade with other countries is an important part of New Zealand's economy. Its main trading partners are Australia, Japan, the United States, and the United Kingdom. Depending on trade brings both benefits and dangers to New Zealand. If the economies of other countries are growing quickly, demand for goods from New Zealand will rise. If the other economies slow, however, they will buy fewer products. This can cause hardship on the islands. In recent years, trade has grown, and New Zealanders enjoy a high standard of living.

Mining and Manufacturing New Zealand sits on top of the molten rock that forms volcanoes. As a result, it is rich in **geothermal energy,** electricity produced from steam. The major source of energy, however, is **hydroelectric power**—electricity generated by flowing water. New Zealand also has coal, oil, iron ore, silver, and gold.

The country is rapidly industrializing. Service industries and tourism play large roles in the economy. The main manufactured items are wood products, fertilizers, wool products, and shoes.

✓Reading Check **Why does trade with other countries offer both benefits and dangers to New Zealand?**

New Zealand's History and People

People called the Maori (MOWR•ee) are believed to have arrived in New Zealand between A.D. 950 and 1150. They probably crossed the Pacific Ocean in canoes from islands far to the northeast. Undisturbed for hundreds of years, the Maori developed skills in farming, weaving, fishing, bird hunting, and woodcarving.

The first European explorers came to the islands in the mid-1600s. Almost 200 years passed before settlers—most of them British—arrived. In 1840 British officials signed a treaty with Maori leaders. In this treaty, the Maori agreed to accept British rule in return for the right to keep their land. More British settlers eventually moved onto Maori land. War broke out in the 1860s—a war that the Maori lost.

In 1893 the colony became the first land to give women the right to vote. New Zealand was also among the first places in which the government gave help to people who were old, sick, or out of work.

New Zealand became independent in 1907. The country is a parliamentary democracy in which elected representatives choose a prime minister to head the government. Five seats in the parliament can be held only by Maoris. Today about 10 percent of New Zealand's 3.8 million people are Maori. Most of the rest are descendants of British settlers. Asians and Pacific islanders, attracted by the growing economy, have increased the diversity of New Zealand's society.

About 85 percent of the people live in urban areas. The largest cities are **Auckland,** an important port, and **Wellington,** the capital. Both are on North Island, where about 75 percent of the people live.

New Zealanders take advantage of the country's mild climate and beautiful landscapes. They enjoy camping, hiking, hunting, boating, and mountain climbing in any season. They also play cricket and rugby, sports that originated in Great Britain.

✓Reading Check **What group settled New Zealand 1,000 years ago?**

Assessment

Defining Terms

1. **Define** geyser, *manuka,* fjord, geothermal energy, hydroelectric power.

Recalling Facts

2. **Region** How do New Zealand's land and climate compare to Australia's?
3. **Economics** What two animal products are important exports for New Zealand?
4. **History** Most of New Zealand's people are descendants of settlers from what European country?

Critical Thinking

5. **Analyzing Information** Why do you think New Zealand's government guarantees the Maori a certain number of seats in the parliament?
6. **Making Predictions** With so many different peoples settling in New Zealand, how do you think the country's culture may change?

Graphic Organizer

7. **Organizing Information** Imagine that you are moving to New Zealand. Write a question you would ask for each topic in the chart below.

Physical features	Economy	Recreation
Climate	Government	Culture

Applying Geography Skills

8. **Analyzing Maps** Look at the economic activity map on page 755. Is more land in New Zealand used for farming or for ranching?

Study and Writing Skill

Outlining

Outlining may be used as a starting point for a writer. The writer begins with the rough shape of the material and gradually fills in the details in a logical manner. You may also use outlining as a method of note taking and organizing information as you read.

Learning the Skill

There are two types of outlines—formal and informal. An informal outline is similar to taking notes—you write words and phrases needed to remember main ideas. In contrast, a formal outline has a standard format. Follow these steps to formally outline information:

- Read the text to identify the main ideas. Label these with Roman numerals.
- Write subtopics under each main idea. Label these with capital letters.
- Write supporting details for each subtopic. Label these with Arabic numerals.
- Each level should have at least two entries and should be indented from the level above.
- All entries should use the same grammatical form, whether phrases or complete sentences.

▼ **A huge sheep herd pours down a ravine on North Island.**

Practicing the Skill

On a separate sheet of paper, copy the following outline for Section 2 of this chapter. Then use your textbook to fill in the missing subtopics and details.

I. New Zealand's Land
  A. North Island
    1. Central plateau surrounded by fertile lowlands
    2. Active volcanoes and geysers
  B. ____________
    1. Southern Alps on western coast
    2. ____________
  C. Plants and Animals
    1. ____________
    2. ____________
II. New Zealand's Economy
  A. Agriculture
    1. ____________
    2. ____________
  B. Trading Partners
    1. ____________
    2. ____________
    3. ____________
    4. ____________
  C. ____________
    1. ____________
    2. Wood products, fertilizers, wool products, and shoes
III. New Zealand's History and People
  A. ____________
  B. ____________

Applying the Skill

Following the guidelines above, prepare an outline for Section 1 of this chapter.

GO TO

Practice key skills with **Glencoe Skillbuilder Interactive Workbook, Level 1.**

Reading Review

Section 1 Australia

Terms to Know
coral reef
outback
station
marsupial
immigrant
boomerang
bush

Main Idea

Both a continent and a country, Australia has many natural resources but few people.

✓ **Place** The land of Australia is mostly flat and dry, with little rainfall.

✓ **Location** Because Australia has been separated from other continents for millions of years, unique plants and animals developed here.

✓ **Economics** Most of Australia's wealth comes from minerals and the products of its ranches. It is the world's leading producer and exporter of wool.

✓ **Culture** Australia has relatively few people, most of whom live along the coasts.

Sydney Opera House in Sydney, Australia ►

Section 2 New Zealand

Terms to Know
geyser
manuka
fjord
geothermal energy
hydroelectric power

Main Idea

New Zealand is a small country with a growing economy based on trade.

✓ **Place** Most people live on New Zealand's two largest islands.

✓ **Place** New Zealand has volcanic mountains, high glaciers, deep-cut fjords, fertile hills, and coastal plains. The climate is mild and wet.

✓ **Economics** New Zealand's economy is built on trade. Sheepherding is an important activity, and wool and lamb meat are major exports.

✓ **History** The people called the Maori first came to New Zealand around 1,000 years ago.

✓ **Culture** Most people live on North Island, where the country's two main cities can be found.

Chapter 27 Assessment and Activities

Using Key Terms

Match the terms in Part A with their definitions in Part B.

A.

1. boomerang
2. bush
3. station
4. geothermal energy
5. outback
6. *manuka*
7. marsupial
8. hydroelectric power
9. coral reef
10. geyser

B.

a. electricity produced from steam
b. wooden weapon that returns to the thrower
c. mammal that carries its young in a pouch
d. hot spring that shoots hot water into the air
e. rural area in Australia
f. structure formed by the skeletons of small sea animals
g. name for entire inland region of Australia
h. cattle or sheep ranch in Australia
i. electricity generated by flowing water
j. small shrub found in New Zealand

Reviewing the Main Ideas

Section 1 Australia

11. **Location** Why is Australia called the Land Down Under?
12. **Place** For what is the outback used?
13. **Economics** What does Australia lead the world in producing and exporting?
14. **History** What country colonized Australia?
15. **Culture** What percentage of people live in Australia's cities?

Section 2 New Zealand

16. **Location** On which island do most New Zealanders live?
17. **Place** What kind of climate does New Zealand have?
18. **Economics** Why can New Zealand's economy suffer if other countries have economic problems?
19. **Culture** How many New Zealanders have Maori heritage?
20. **Human/Environment Interaction** What leisure activities do New Zealanders enjoy that are made possible by the country's climate?

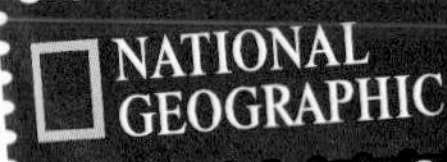

Australia and New Zealand

Place Location Activity

On a separate sheet of paper, match the letters on the map with the numbered places listed below.

1. Auckland
2. Sydney
3. Tasmania
4. Great Barrier Reef
5. Great Dividing Range
6. Southern Alps
7. Darling River
8. Wellington
9. Canberra
10. Perth

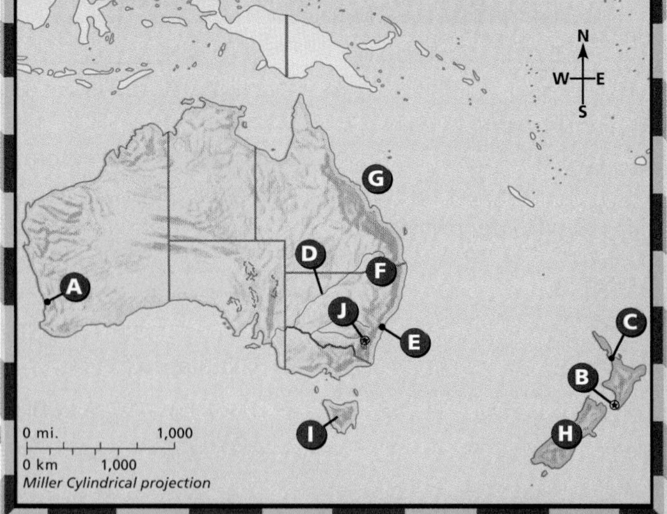

Self-Check Quiz Visit the ***Geography: The World and Its People*** Web site at gwip.glencoe.com and click on **Chapter 27—Self-Check Quizzes** to prepare for the Chapter Test.

Critical Thinking

21. **Understanding Cause and Effect** Why do most Australians and New Zealanders live in coastal areas?
22. **Organizing Information** Draw two ovals like these. In the outer ovals, write four facts about each country under their heading. Where the ovals overlap, write three facts that are true of both countries.

GeoJournal Activity

23. **Designing a Poster** Choose one of the unusual physical features found in Australia or New Zealand. You might choose the Great Barrier Reef, the Great Artesian Basin, or the geysers or glaciers of New Zealand. Research to learn more about this physical feature. Create an illustrated poster that includes a map, four photographs, and four facts about the feature.

Mental Mapping Activity

24. **Focusing on the Region** Draw a simple outline map of Australia and New Zealand, then label the following:

- North Island
- Sydney
- Melbourne
- Auckland
- Tasmania
- Tasman Sea
- Coral Sea
- Darling River
- Great Artesian Basin
- Hamersley Range

Technology Skills Activity

25. **Using the Internet** Use the Internet to find out more about one of Australia's or New Zealand's cities. Prepare a travel brochure aimed at a tourist who might visit the city. Describe the city's main attractions.

Standardized Test Practice

Directions: Study the graph below, then answer the following question.

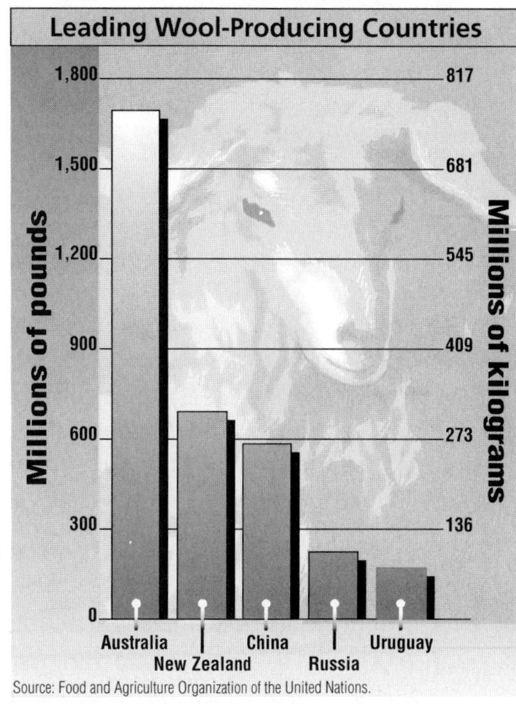

1. How much wool does Australia produce a year?

A 1,800 pounds
B 1,800,000 pounds
C about 1,700 pounds
D about 1,700,000,000 pounds

Test-Taking Tip: Remember to read the information along the sides of the graph to understand what the bars represent. In addition, eliminate answers that you know are wrong.

EYE on the Environment

OZONE
Earth's Natural Sunscreen

October 1980

October 1990

October 2000

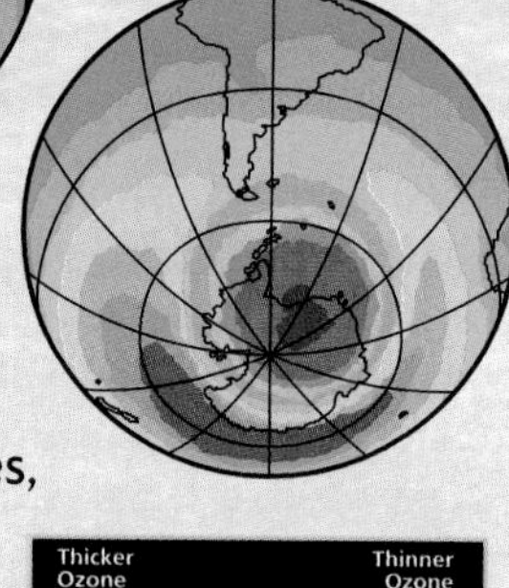

Source: Ozone Processing Team, NASA, GSFC.

The Ozone Hole If you spend lots of time outdoors, you probably know that "SPF 30" is a rating for sunscreen. The higher a sunscreen's Sun Protection Factor (SPF), the longer you can be exposed to sunlight before your skin begins to burn. Earth has a sunscreen, too. It is called ozone. Ozone is a kind of gas. A thin band of ozone high above the earth shields the planet from the sun's most harmful ultraviolet (UV) rays. The ozone layer, however, is being destroyed. The satellite images (above, right) show an expanding ozone hole above Antarctica. For several decades, the ozone layer has been in trouble.

Human-made chemicals, particularly chlorofluorocarbons (CFCs), destroy ozone and thin the ozone layer. CFCs were used for years in refrigerators, air conditioners, foam-insulated cups, aerosol sprays, and in some cleaning products.

Ozone losses of about 10 percent have occurred over Europe, Canada, and other parts of the Northern Hemisphere, too.

When ozone is destroyed, more UV rays strike the earth. Exposure to harmful rays can cause skin cancer in humans, destroy plants, and kill ocean plankton.

Reversing the Damage The good news is that ozone destruction can be reversed. Officials around the world are taking action.

In 1992 an international treaty called for a global ban of CFCs by 1996. Today there are fewer CFCs in the atmosphere.

Some scientists predict full recovery of the ozone layer by 2050.

A lifeguard in Australia prepares for a day in the sun with hat, sunglasses, and zinc cream.

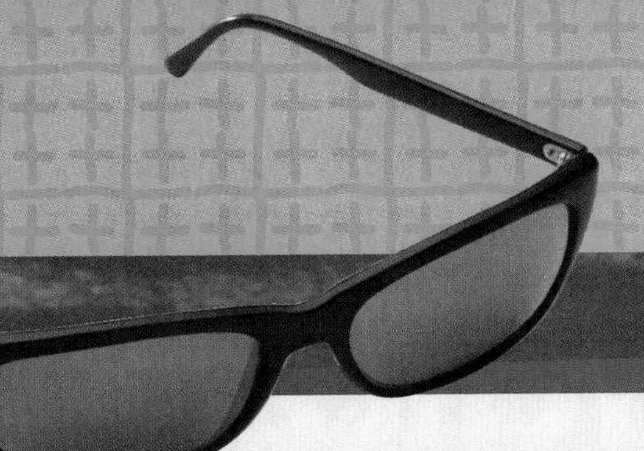

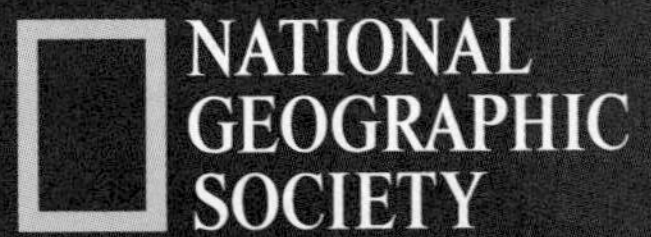

Making a Difference

Ozone Prizewinners Three scientists shared the 1995 Nobel Prize in chemistry for their research on ozone. Americans Mario Molina (photo, at right) and F. Sherwood Rowland and Dutch citizen Paul Crutzen shared the honor after describing the chemical processes by which ozone is formed and destroyed in the atmosphere. Before they explored the issue, little was known about how human-made chemicals affect ozone. The three scientists were able to show that the release of CFCs into the air damages the ozone layer. Their important research led governments around the world to ban the use of CFCs.

Mario Molina

Keeping Watch Antarctica has long been seen as a barometer of Earth's health. Scientists from all over the world live and work in research stations scattered throughout Antarctica. In 1985 scientists reported that the ozone layer over Antarctica had decreased dramatically. Since then, they have been closely watching the ozone layer, collecting data from special instruments that record ozone levels. Governments and environmental groups use this information to determine what should be done.

A scientist in Antarctica checks ozone levels.

What Can You Do?

Get Involved

Organize a "Sun Alert" campaign to warn students in younger grades about the dangers of overexposure to the sun.

Find Out More

On the Trail of the Missing Ozone, an online book, tells why we need the ozone layer and how to prevent ozone depletion. You can read it at www.epa.gov/ozone/science/missoz/index.html. Share what you learn with the class.

Use the Internet

Check current ozone levels worldwide by visiting NASA's Goddard Space Flight Center's Web site at http://jwocky.gsfc.nasa.gov

Chapter 28

Oceania and Antarctica

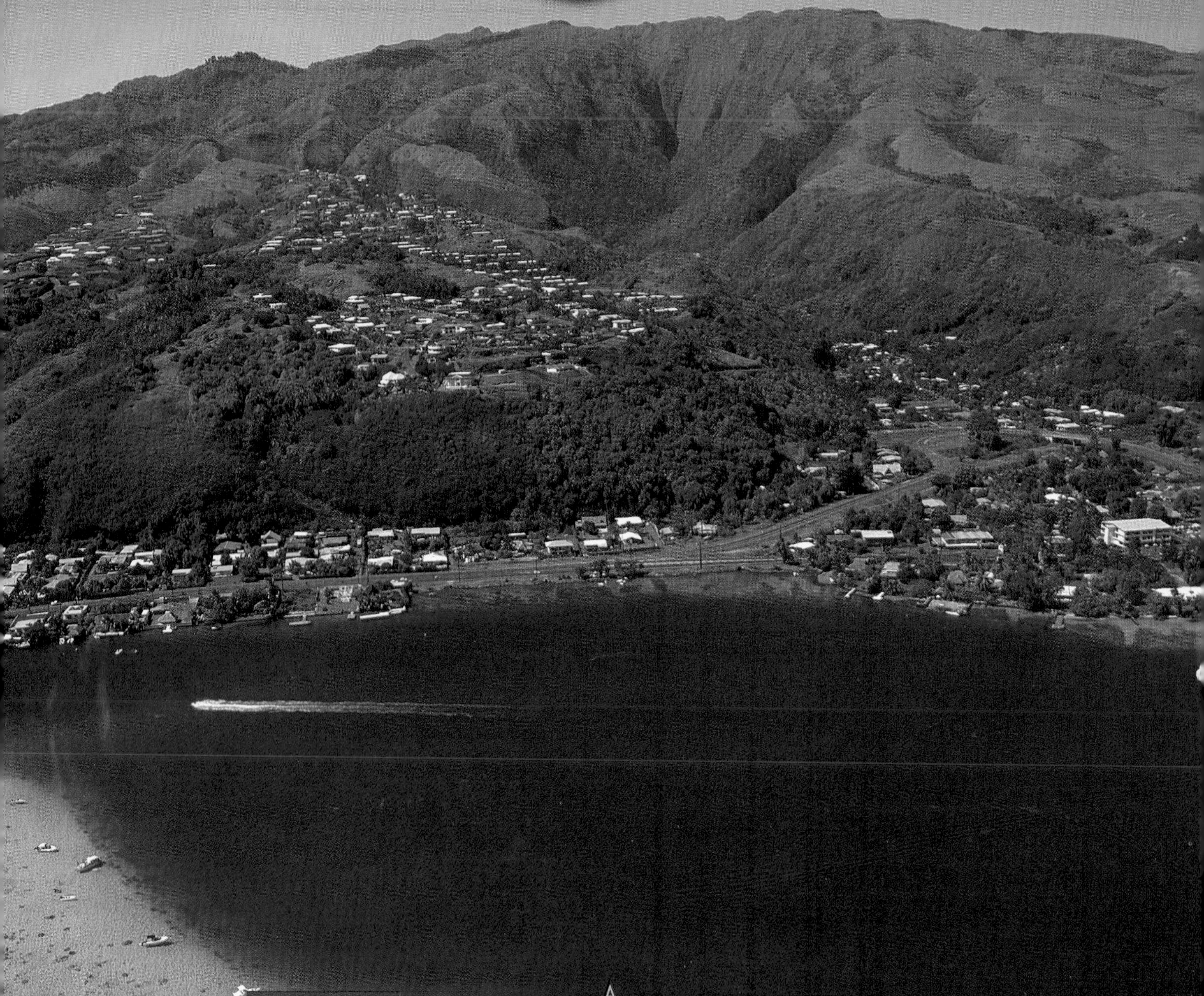

To learn more about the people and places of Oceania and Antarctica, view ***The World and Its People*** **Chapter 28** video.

Geography Online

Chapter Overview Visit the ***Geography: The World and Its People*** Web site at gwip.glencoe.com and click on **Chapter 28–Chapter Overviews** to preview information about Oceania and Antarctica.

Section 1 Oceania

Guide to Reading

Main Idea

Oceania is made up of thousands of Pacific Ocean islands organized into countries and territories.

Terms to Know

- continental island
- cacao
- copra
- pidgin language
- high island
- low island
- atoll
- typhoon
- phosphate
- trust territory

Places to Locate

- Oceania
- Melanesia
- Micronesia
- Polynesia
- Papua New Guinea

Reading Strategy

Make a chart like this one. In the right column, write two facts about each region.

Region	Facts
Melanesia	
Micronesia	
Polynesia	

◀ View of Tahiti, French Polynesia

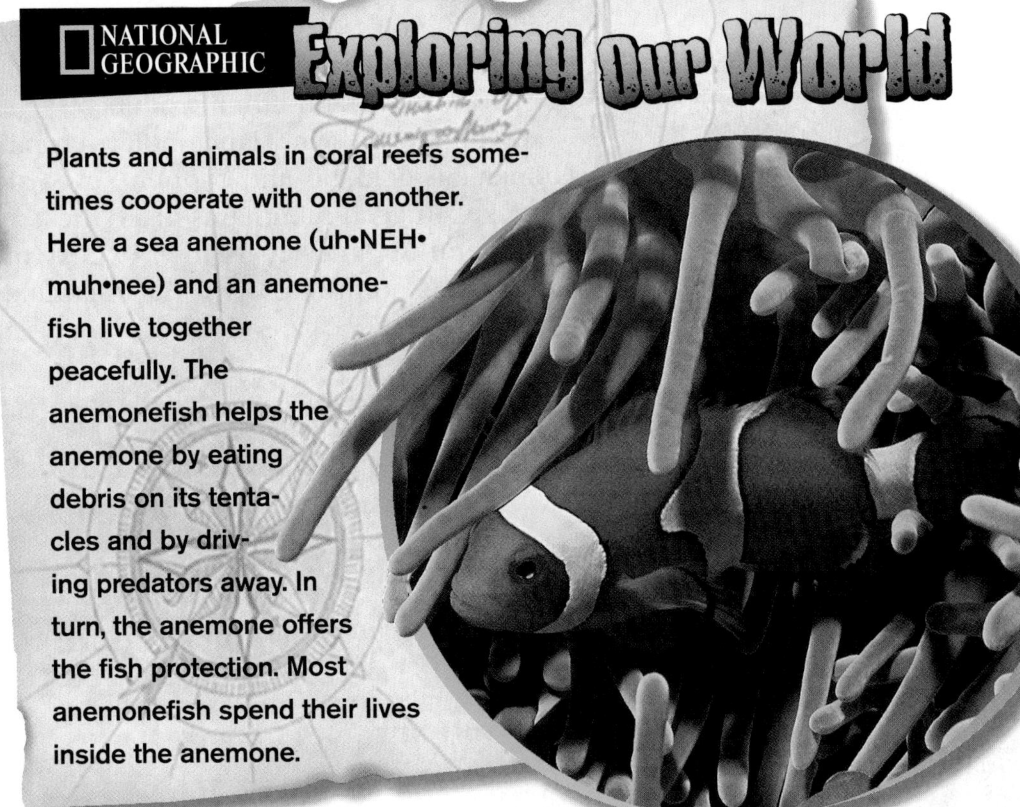

Plants and animals in coral reefs sometimes cooperate with one another. Here a sea anemone (uh•NEH•muh•nee) and an anemonefish live together peacefully. The anemonefish helps the anemone by eating debris on its tentacles and by driving predators away. In turn, the anemone offers the fish protection. Most anemonefish spend their lives inside the anemone.

Oceania is a culture region that includes about 25,000 islands in the Pacific Ocean. Geographers group Oceania into three main island regions—**Melanesia, Micronesia,** and **Polynesia.**

Melanesia

The islands of Melanesia lie just to the north and east of Australia. The largest country in size is **Papua New Guinea** (PA•pyu•wuh noo GIH•nee). It lies on the eastern half of the island of New Guinea. Slightly larger than California, the country's 4.7 million people also make it Oceania's most populous island. Southeast of Papua New Guinea are three other independent island countries: the Solomon Islands, the Fiji (FEE•jee) Islands, and Vanuatu (VAN•WAH•TOO). Near these countries is New Caledonia, a group of islands ruled by France.

Melanesia consists mostly of continental islands. A **continental island** is formed in two ways. Chunks of land may split off from a continent, or a land bridge erodes, breaking the island's connection to the continent. Rugged mountains and dense rain forests cover Melanesia's islands. Strips of fertile plains hug island coastlines. Most of Melanesia has a tropical climate. Temperatures seldom fall below 70°F (21°C) or rise above 80°F (27°C).

Most Melanesians work on subsistence farms. Papua New Guinea exports coffee, palm oil, and cacao. **Cacao** is a tropical tree whose seeds are used to make chocolate. The Solomon Islands also export palm oil and cacao. Sugarcane grown on the Fiji Islands is exported as sugar and molasses. **Copra,** or dried coconut meat, is produced on the Solomon Islands and Vanuatu. Coconut oil from copra is used to make margarine, soap, and other products.

Some Melanesian islands hold rich mineral resources. Papua New Guinea has gold, oil, and copper. New Caledonia mines large deposits of nickel. Rugged mountains make these resources difficult to reach.

Several Melanesian islands export timber and fish. Papua New Guinea has some factories that manufacture processed foods and machinery. Melanesia is also becoming a popular tourist destination.

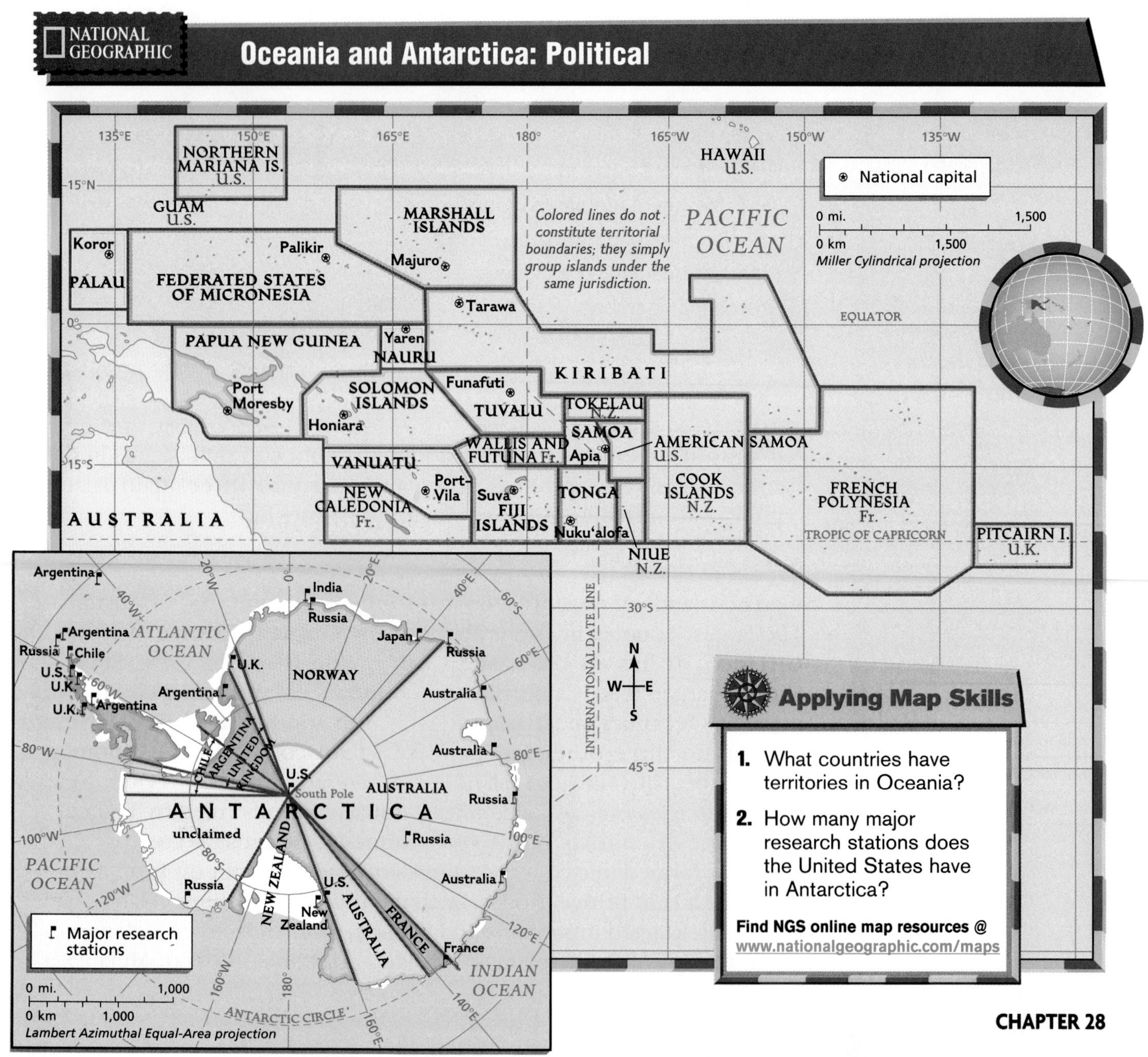

Melanesia's People Most Melanesians are originally from the Pacific islands. Exceptions include the people of New Caledonia—about one-third of whom are Europeans—and the Fiji Islands—half of whom are from South Asia. These South Asians are descendants of workers brought from British India in the late 1800s and early 1900s to work on sugarcane plantations. Today South Asians control much of the economy of the Fiji Islands. Fijians of Pacific descent own most of the land. Conflict often arises as the two different groups struggle for control of the government.

Languages and religions are diverse as well. More than 700 languages are spoken in Papua New Guinea alone. People here speak a **pidgin language** formed by combining parts of several different languages. People speak English in the Fiji Islands, while French is the main language of New Caledonia. Local traditional religions are practiced, but Christianity is widespread. The South Asian population is mostly Hindu.

Many Melanesians live in small villages in houses made of grass or other natural materials. In recent years, people have built concrete houses to protect themselves from tropical storms. Melanesians keep

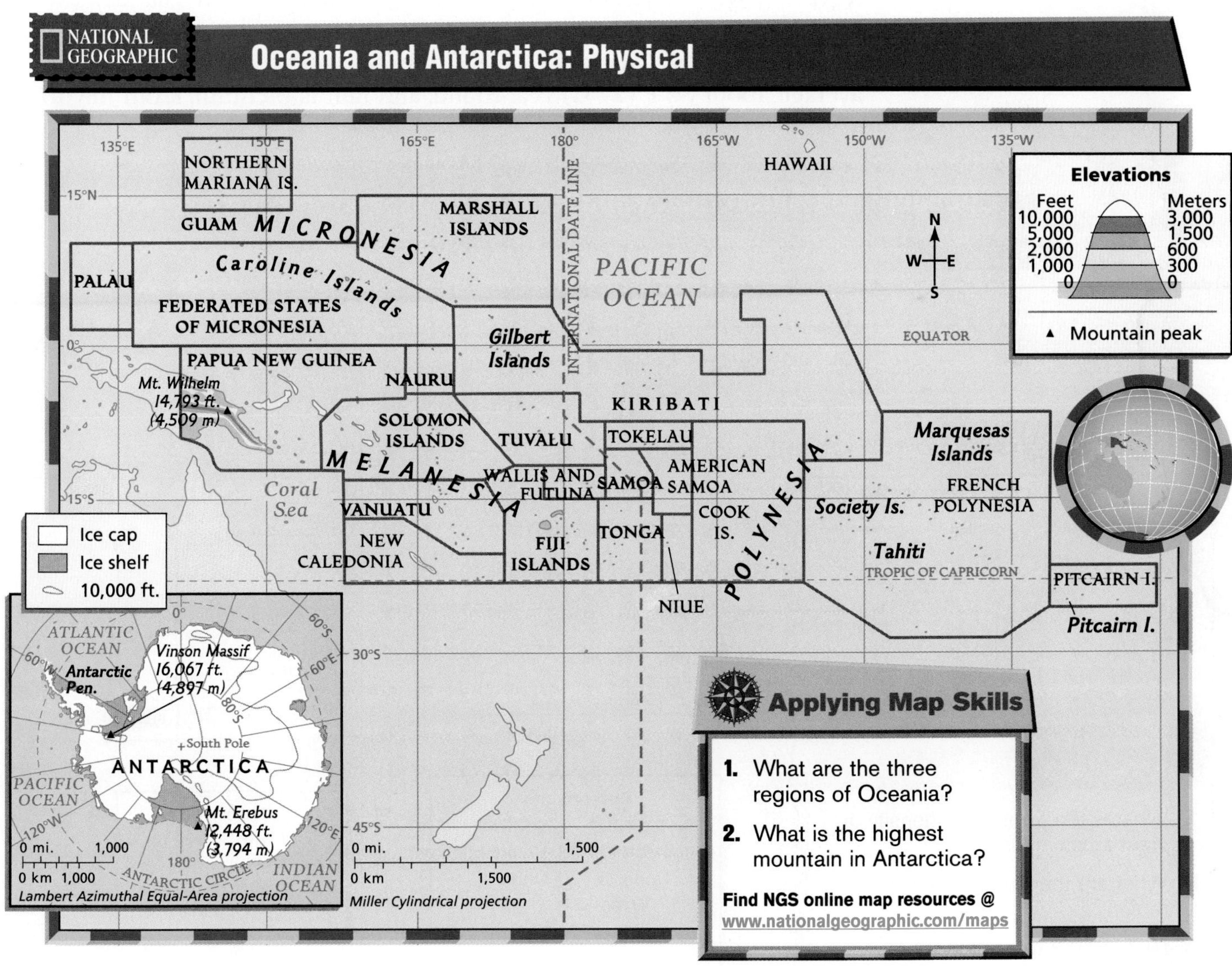

strong ties to their local group and often hold on to traditional ways. Only a small number live in cities. Port Moresby in Papua New Guinea and Suva in the Fiji Islands are the largest urban areas. Many people in these cities have jobs in business and government.

Reading Check **What is the largest country in Melanesia?**

Micronesia

The map on page 767 shows that the islands of Micronesia are scattered over a vast area of the ocean. Independent countries include the Federated States of Micronesia, the Marshall Islands, Palau (puh•LOW), Nauru (nah•OO•roo), and Kiribati (KIHR•uh•BAH•tee). The Northern Mariana Islands and Guam are territories of the United States.

Micronesia is made up of two types of islands—high islands and low islands. Volcanic activity formed the mountainous **high islands** many centuries ago. Coral, or skeletons of millions of tiny sea animals, formed the **low islands.** Most of the low islands are **atolls**—low-lying, ring-shaped islands that surround lagoons. The two types of islands have very different vegetation. The high islands have rich soil, towering waterfalls, and thick green vegetation. The low islands have maybe just a few palm trees.

Like Melanesia, Micronesia has a tropical climate. Daily temperatures average about 80°F (27°C) year-round, and rain is plentiful. From July to

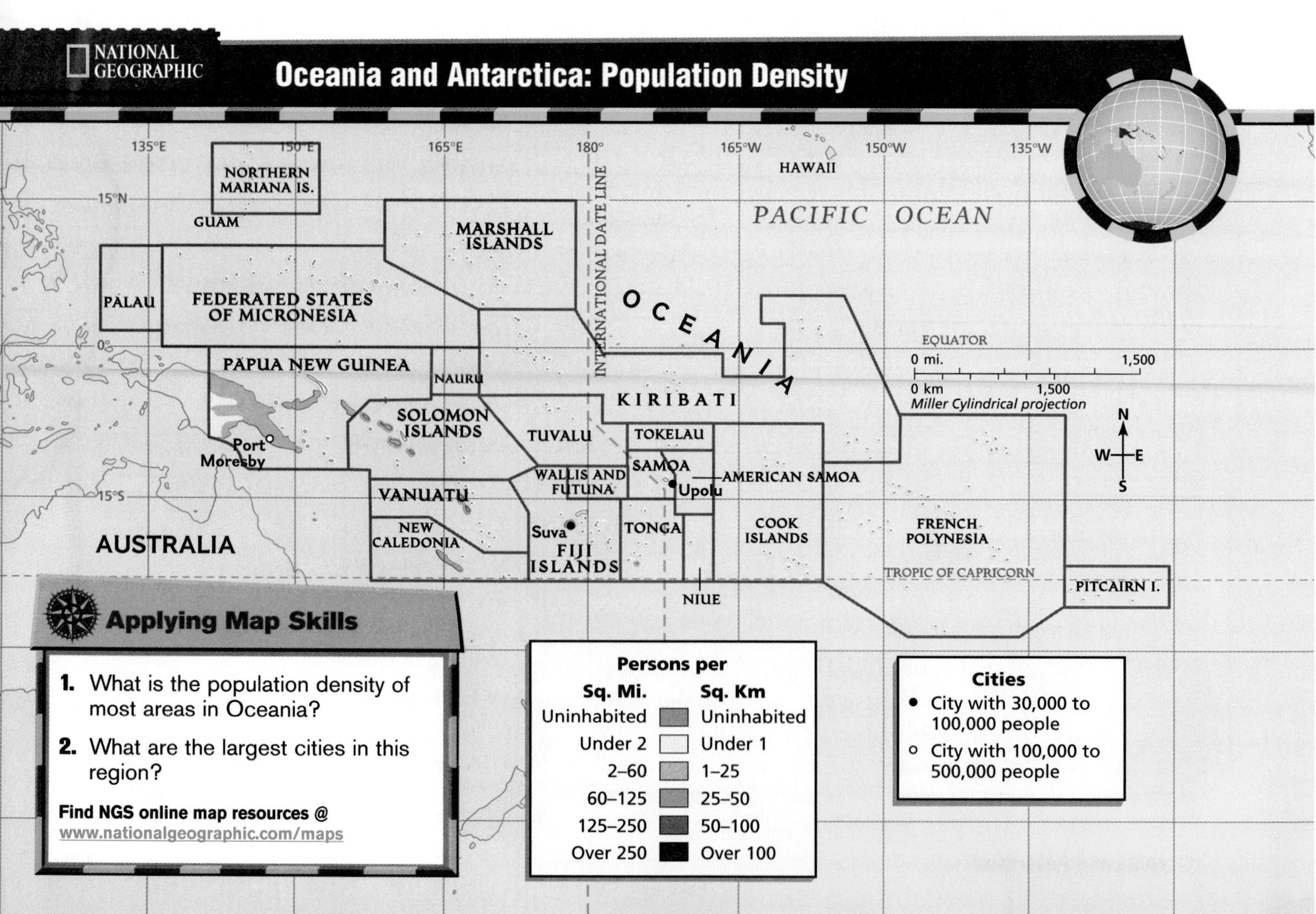

Applying Map Skills

1. What is the population density of most areas in Oceania?
2. What are the largest cities in this region?

Find NGS online map resources @ www.nationalgeographic.com/maps

October, typhoons sometimes strike the islands, causing loss of life and much destruction. A **typhoon** is another name for a hurricane, a fierce storm with winds of more than 74 miles (119 km) per hour.

On Micronesia's high islands, most people engage in subsistence farming. Farmers grow cassava, sweet potatoes, bananas, and coconuts. Some high island farmers also raise livestock. People in the low islands obtain food from the sea. On low islands, such as Palau, Guam, and the Northern Mariana Islands, recent population growth has resulted in the need to import food.

Micronesia receives financial aid from the United States, the European Union, and Australia. With this money, the Micronesians have built roads, ports, airfields, and small factories. Clothing is made on the Northern Mariana Islands. Beautiful beaches draw many tourists here, as well as to Palau, the Marshall Islands, and Guam. Several Micronesian islands have **phosphate,** a mineral salt used to make fertilizer. Phosphate supplies are now gone on Kiribati, and they have almost run out on Nauru. The Federated States of Micronesia and the Marshall Islands have phosphate but lack the money to mine this resource.

The oysters that produced these black pearls thrive in the warm waters of Oceania.

Movement **What is one of the fastest-growing industries in Polynesia?**

Micronesia's People Southeast Asians first settled Micronesia about 4,000 years ago. Explorers, traders, and missionaries from European countries came in the 1700s and early 1800s. By the early 1900s, many European countries, the United States, and Japan held colonies here.

During World War II, the United States and Japan fought a number of bloody battles on Micronesian islands. After World War II, most of Micronesia was turned over to the United States as **trust territories.** These territories were under temporary United States control. Since the 1970s, most have become independent.

Many of Micronesia's people are Pacific islanders. They speak local languages, although English is spoken on Nauru, the Marshall Islands, and throughout the rest of Micronesia. Christianity, brought by Western missionaries, is the most widely practiced religion. Micronesians generally live in villages headed by local chiefs. In recent years, many young people have left the villages to find jobs in towns.

✓ Reading Check **In what two ways were Micronesia's islands formed?**

Polynesia

Polynesia includes three independent countries—Samoa, Tonga, and Tuvalu. Other island groups are under French rule and are known as French Polynesia. Tahiti, Polynesia's largest island, is part of this French-ruled area. American Samoa, a United States territory, is also part of this region.

Most Polynesian islands are high volcanic islands, some with tall, rugged mountains. Dense rain forests cover mountain valleys and coastal plains. Some of the islands are of the low atoll type. With little soil, the only vegetation is scattered coconut palms. Because Polynesia lies in the tropics, the climate is hot and humid.

Polynesians grow crops or fish for their food. Some farmers export coconuts and tropical fruits. The main manufacturing activity is food processing. The tuna you eat for lunch may have come from American Samoa. This island supplies about one-third of the tuna brought into the United States. Tonga exports squash and vanilla.

Tourism is one of the fastest-growing industries of Polynesia. Visitors come by air or sea to the emerald-green mountains and white, palm-lined beaches. New roads, hotels, shops, and restaurants serve these tourists.

Polynesia's People Settlers came to Polynesia later than they did to the other island regions. The first to arrive were probably Melanesians or Micronesians who crossed the vast Pacific Ocean in canoes.

During the late 1800s, several European nations divided Polynesia among themselves. They built military bases on the islands and later added airfields. The islands served as excellent refueling stops for long voyages across the Pacific. Beginning in the 1960s, several Polynesian territories chose independence, while others remained territories.

About 600,000 people live in Polynesia. Most Polynesians live in rural villages and practice traditional crafts. An increasing number live in towns and cities. Papeete (PAH•pay•AY•tay), located on Tahiti, is the capital of French Polynesia and the largest city in the region.

✓Reading Check **What is the largest island in Polynesia?**

Assessment

Defining Terms

1. Define continental island, cacao, copra, pidgin language, high island, low island, atoll, typhoon, phosphate, trust territory.

Recalling Facts

2. Region What three regions make up Oceania?

3. Economics What two kinds of economic activities are most important in these regions?

4. History What groups first settled the lands of Micronesia?

Critical Thinking

5. Summarizing Information What is copra, and what is it used for?

6. Drawing Conclusions Why do many people in Melanesia speak a pidgin language?

Graphic Organizer

7. Organizing Information Make a chart like this one. List all the islands of Oceania under their specific region, then note whether they are independent countries or territories.

Melanesia	Micronesia	Polynesia	Country/Territory of ?

Applying Geography Skills

8. Analyzing Maps Look at the economic activity map on page 774. Which territory has large deposits of nickel?

Study and Writing Skill

Writing a Report

Writing skills allow you to organize your ideas in a logical manner. The writing process involves using skills you have already learned, such as taking notes, outlining, and sequencing information.

Learning the Skill

Use the following guidelines to help you apply the writing process:

- Select an interesting topic. Do preliminary research to determine whether your topic is too broad or too narrow.
- Write a general statement that explains what you want to prove, discover, or illustrate in your writing. This will be the focus of your entire paper.
- Research your topic by coming up with a list of main ideas. Prepare note cards listing facts and source information for each main idea.
- Your report should have an introduction, a body, and a conclusion summarizing and restating your findings.
- Each paragraph should express one main idea in a topic sentence. Additional sentences should support or explain the main idea by using details and facts.

An atoll in the Pacific Ocean ▼

Practicing the Skill

Read the following paragraph, then answer the questions that follow.

> Most of Micronesia's low islands are atolls—low-lying, ring-shaped islands that surround lagoons. An atoll begins as a ring of coral that forms around the edge of a volcanic island. Over time, wind and water erode the volcano, wearing it down to sea level. Eventually only the atoll remains above the surface. The calm, shallow seawater inside the atoll is called a lagoon.

1. What is the main idea of this paragraph?
2. What are the supporting sentences?
3. What might be the topic of an additional paragraph that follows this one?

Applying the Skill

Suppose you are writing a report on Oceania. Answer the following questions about the writing process.

1. How could you narrow this topic?
2. What are three main ideas?
3. Name three possible sources of information.

Section 2 Antarctica

Guide to Reading

Main Idea

Antarctica is a harsh land of rock and ice, which the world's nations have agreed to leave open to scientific study.

Terms to Know

- crevasse
- ice shelf
- iceberg
- krill
- ozone

Places to Locate

- Antarctica
- Vinson Massif
- Antarctic Peninsula
- Mount Erebus

Reading Strategy

Make a chart like the one below. Under each heading, fill in at least one fact about Antarctica.

Antarctica	
Land	Climate
Resources	People

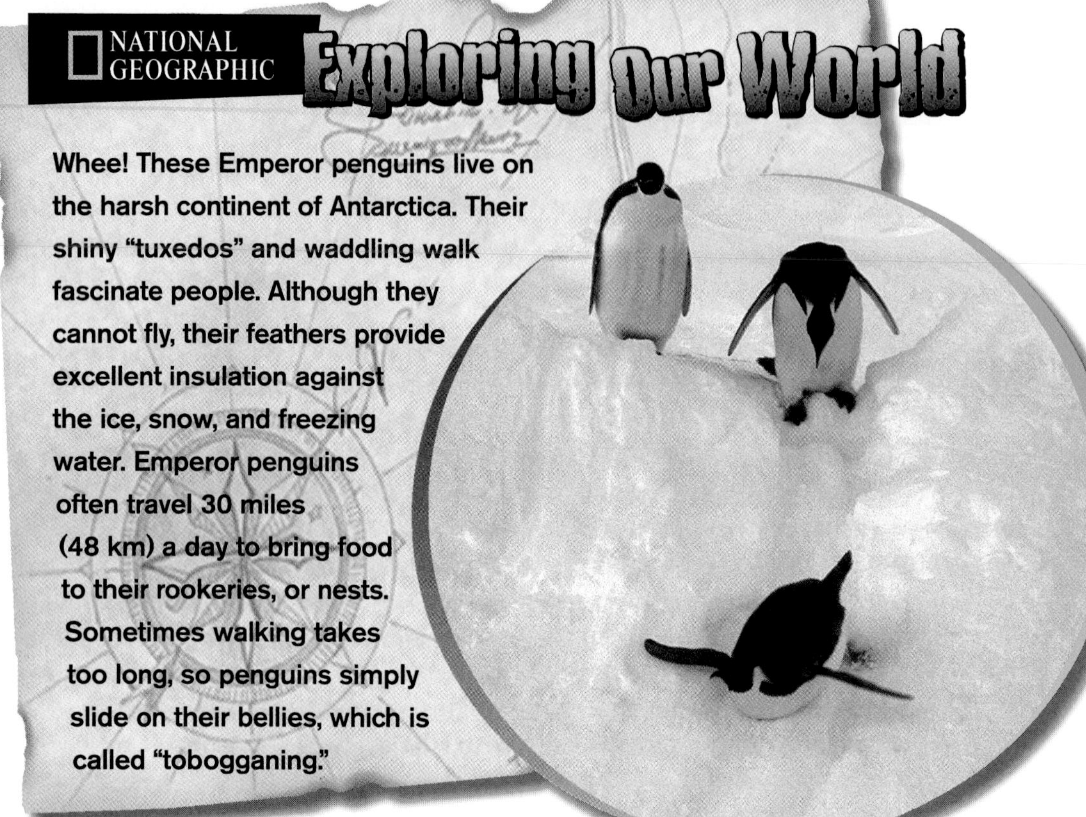

NATIONAL GEOGRAPHIC **Exploring Our World**

Whee! These Emperor penguins live on the harsh continent of Antarctica. Their shiny "tuxedos" and waddling walk fascinate people. Although they cannot fly, their feathers provide excellent insulation against the ice, snow, and freezing water. Emperor penguins often travel 30 miles (48 km) a day to bring food to their rookeries, or nests. Sometimes walking takes too long, so penguins simply slide on their bellies, which is called "tobogganing."

Antarctica sits on the southern end of the earth. Icy ocean water surrounds it. Freezing ice covers it. Cold winds blow over it. The least explored of all the continents, this frigid mysterious land is larger than either Europe or Australia.

A Unique Continent

Picture Antarctica—a rich, green land covered by forests and lush plants. Does this description match your mental image of the continent? Fossils discovered here reveal that millions of years ago, Antarctica's landscape was inhabited by dinosaurs and small mammals.

Today, however, a huge ice cap buries nearly 98 percent of Antarctica's land area. In some spots, this ice cap is 2 miles (3.2 km) thick—about the height of 10 tall skyscrapers stacked upon one another. This massive "sea" of ice holds about 70 percent of all the freshwater in the world.

The Antarctic ice cap is heavy and strong, but it also moves. In some areas, the ice cap forms **crevasses,** or cracks, that plunge more than 100 feet (30 m). At the Antarctic coast, the ice cap spreads past the land into the ocean. This layer of ice above the water is called an **ice shelf.** Huge chunks of ice sometimes break off, forming **icebergs** that float freely in the icy waters.

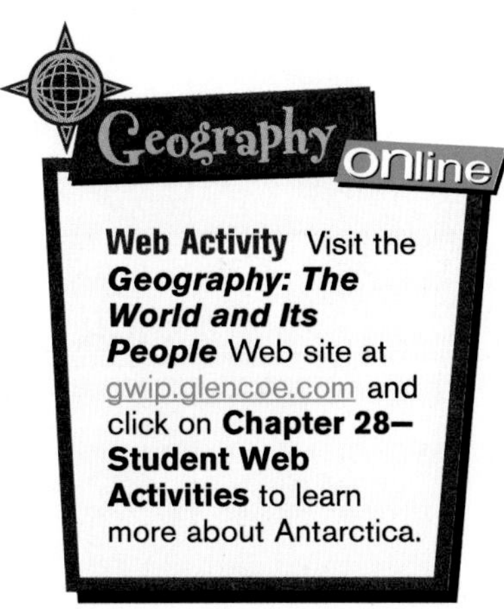

Highlands, Mountains, and Valleys Beneath the ice cap, Antarctica has highlands, valleys, and mountains—the same landforms you find on other continents. A long mountain range called the Transantarctic Mountains crosses the continent. The highest peak in Antarctica, the **Vinson Massif,** rises 16,067 feet (4,897 m). The Transantarctic Mountains sweep along the **Antarctic Peninsula,** which reaches within 600 miles (966 km) of South America's Cape Horn. East of the mountains is a high, flat plateau where you find the South Pole, the southernmost point of the earth. On an island off Antarctica's coast rises **Mount Erebus** (EHR•uh•buhs). It is Antarctica's most active volcano.

Climate Now that you have a mental picture of Antarctica's ice cap, think about this: Antarctica receives so little precipitation that it is the world's largest, coldest desert. Inland Antarctica receives no rain and hardly any new snow each year. The map below shows you that Antarctica has a polar ice cap climate. Imagine summer in a place where temperatures may fall as low as -30°F (-35°C) and climb to only

NATIONAL GEOGRAPHIC

Oceania and Antarctica: Climate

Tropical
- Tropical rain forest
- Tropical savanna

High Latitude
- Tundra
- Ice cap
- Highlands (climate varies with elevation)

Miller Cylindrical projection

Lambert Azimuthal Equal-Area projection

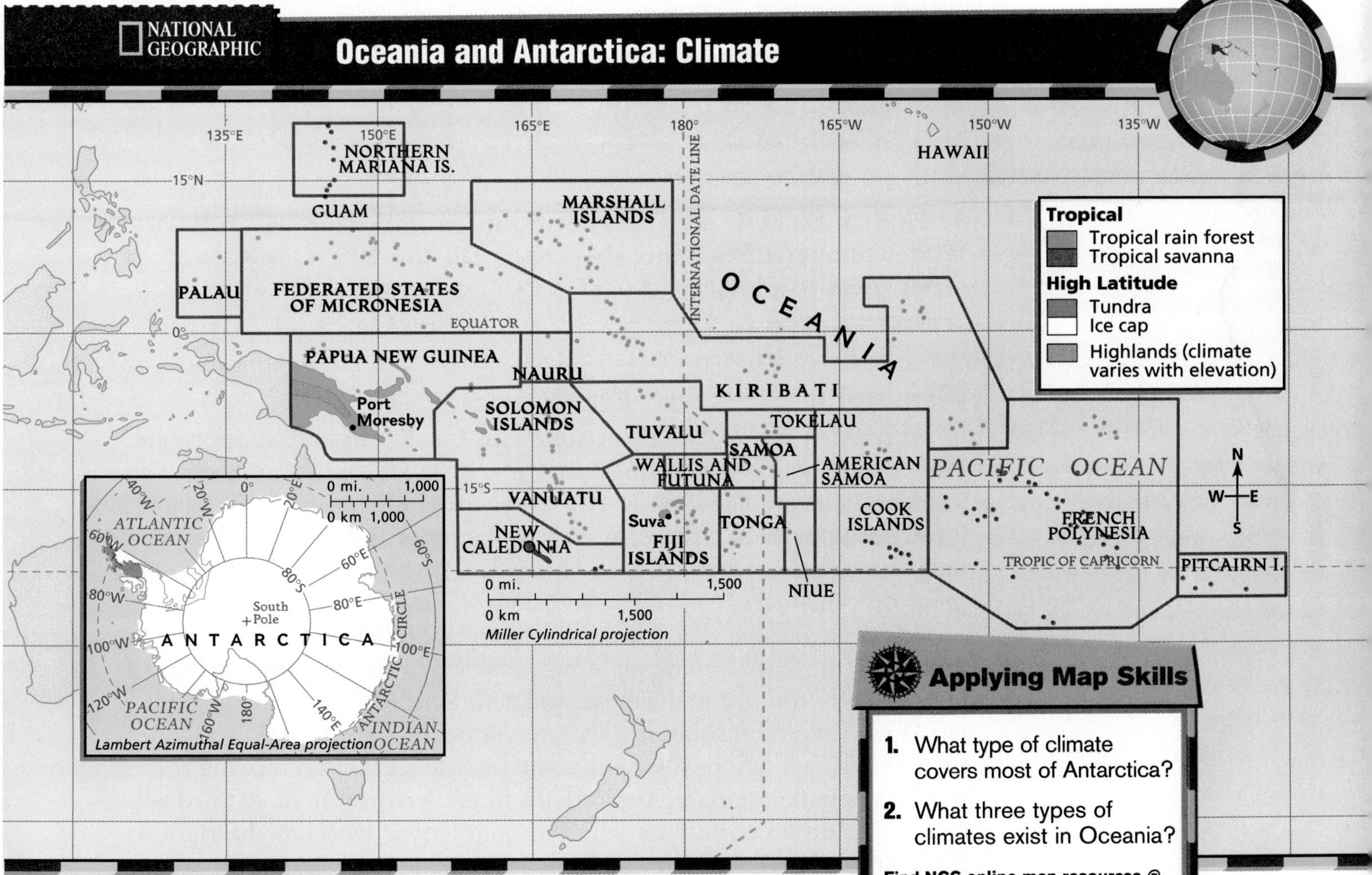

Applying Map Skills

1. What type of climate covers most of Antarctica?
2. What three types of climates exist in Oceania?

Find NGS online map resources @ www.nationalgeographic.com/maps

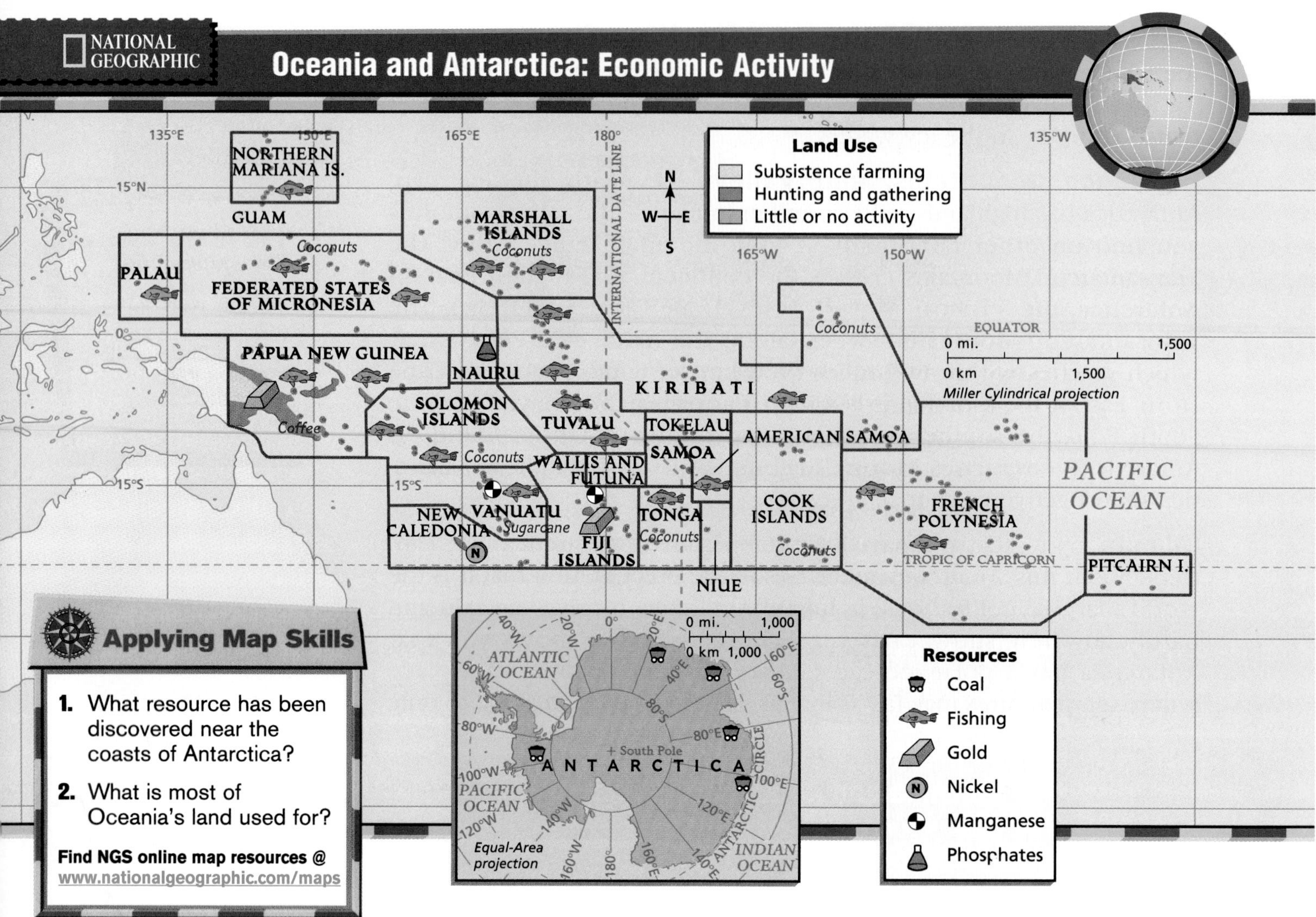

32°F (0°C). Antarctic summers last from December through February. Winter temperatures along the coasts fall to -40°F (-40°C), and in inland areas to a low of -100°F (-73°C).

Reading Check **What landforms are found under Antarctica's ice cap?**

Resources of Antarctica

Antarctica has a harsh environment, but it can still support life. Most of the plants and animals that live here are small, however. The largest inland animal is an insect that reaches only one-tenth of an inch long. Penguins, fish, whales, and many kinds of flying birds live in or near the rich seas surrounding Antarctica. Many eat a tiny, shrimplike creature called **krill.**

Scientists believe that the ice of Antarctica hides a treasure chest of minerals. They have found major deposits of coal and smaller amounts of copper, gold, iron ore, manganese, and zinc. Petroleum may lie offshore.

These mineral resources have not yet been tapped. To do so would be very difficult and costly. Also, some people feel that removing these resources would damage Antarctica's fragile environment. A third reason is that different nations would disagree over who has the right to these resources. Forty-three nations have signed the Antarctic Treaty, which prohibits any nation from taking resources from the continent. It also bans weapons testing in Antarctica.

Reading Check What is the Antarctic Treaty?

A Vast Scientific Laboratory

The Antarctic Treaty does allow for scientific research in Antarctica. Many countries have scientific research stations here, but no single nation controls the vast continent. In January—summer in Antarctica—about 10,000 scientists come to study the land, plants, animals, and ice of this frozen land. Some 1,000 hardy scientists even stay during the harsh polar winter.

Much of the research focuses on ozone. **Ozone** is a type of oxygen that forms a layer in the atmosphere. The ozone layer protects all living things on the earth from certain harmful rays of the sun. In the 1980s, scientists discovered a weakening, or "hole," in this layer above Antarctica. If such weakening continues, some scientists say, climates around the world will get warmer. By studying this layer further, they hope to learn more about possible changes.

This frozen world attracts more than just scientists, though. Each year, a few thousand tourists come to Antarctica. With such a harsh environment, however, Antarctica is the only continent in the world that has no permanent population.

Reading Check Why are scientists studying the ozone layer?

The *Endurance*

In January 1915, Ernest Shackleton and his crew in the *Endurance* became trapped in Antarctica's freezing seawater. In late October, ice crushed the wooden ship, forcing the explorers to abandon it (below). They spent five more months drifting on the ice until they reached open water and used lifeboats to get away.

Assessment

Defining Terms

1. **Define** crevasse, ice shelf, iceberg, krill, ozone.

Recalling Facts

2. **Place** What landform covers central Antarctica?
3. **Location** Where in Antarctica would you find the most living things?
4. **Human/Environment Interaction** Why do scientists come to Antarctica?

Critical Thinking

5. **Summarizing Information** Why have countries agreed not to use the resources of Antarctica?
6. **Writing Questions** Imagine that you are planning a trip to Antarctica. What questions would you ask scientists working there?

Graphic Organizer

7. **Organizing Information** Draw a chart like the one below, and then look at the political map on page 766. In your chart, list the various national claims made in Antarctica by the world's countries. Then give the number of research stations for each country.

Countries With Claims in Antarctica	Number of Research Stations

Applying Geography Skills

8. **Analyzing Maps** Look at the physical map on page 767. What is the highest point in Antarctica?

Making Connections

LITERATURE TECHNOLOGY

Antarctica's Environmental Stations

For nearly 200 years, adventurers, explorers, geographers, and scientists have been drawn to the icy wilderness of Antarctica. Scientific research is the major human activity on this remarkable continent.

Polar Science

In the 1950s, countries began to talk of preserving Antarctica as an international laboratory for scientific research. Today a formal treaty guarantees free access and research rights for scientists of many countries. Antarctica now holds more than 40 research stations.

Types of Research

Geologists, biologists, climatologists, and astronomers are some of the many scientists who come to Antarctica to study. Understanding the earth's environment is a major focus. The Antarctic ice cap contains 90 percent of the world's ice and 70 percent of its freshwater. Changes here can impact the world's oceans and climates.

Scientists in Antarctica were the first to discover the holes in the ozone layer. Such holes can expose life on the earth to too much ultraviolet radiation.

Researchers in Antarctica also study the earth's history. Locked in the continent's ice crystals and air bubbles are clues to the earth's past. Fossils show how landmasses existed before the formation of today's continents.

The harsh living conditions of Antarctica provide another subject for study. The National Aeronautics and Space Administration (NASA) sends engineers and scientists to Antarctica to learn how to survive in extreme conditions, such as those humans might someday encounter on visits to other planets.

Research station at the South Pole ▶

Life at the Edge

Living and working in Antarctica's polar wilderness demands special equipment, well-trained people, and a sizable dose of caution. Freeze-dried food, layers of warm, quick-drying clothes, insulated boots, and specially designed pyramid tents keep researchers well-fed, warm, and dry. Researchers quickly learn the importance of staying inside during whiteout conditions, when snow and fog create a total lack of visibility.

The Antarctic environment is a fragile one, and researchers take care to protect it. All trash and wastes are removed from the continent. Mining of mineral resources is banned, and laws protect native plants and animals. Such care ensures that Antarctica will continue to hold exciting discoveries for years to come.

Making the Connection

1. What do researchers study in Antarctica?
2. What discovery did researchers make about the ozone layer?
3. **Summarizing Information** What items do researchers in Antarctica use to stay warm and dry?

Chapter 28 Reading Review

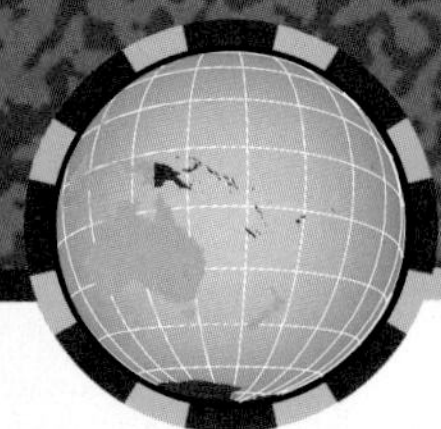

Section 1 Oceania

Terms to Know
continental island
cacao
copra
pidgin language
high island
low island
atoll
typhoon
phosphate
trust territory

Main Idea
Oceania is made up of thousands of Pacific Ocean islands organized into countries and territories.

✓ Region Oceania is a huge area of vast open ocean and about 25,000 islands.

✓ Region Geographers divide Oceania into three regions: Melanesia, Micronesia, and Polynesia.

✓ Place Continental islands were separated from the mainland by water. High islands were formed by volcanoes. Low islands were made from coral.

✓ Place Papua New Guinea, in Melanesia, is the largest and most populous country of Oceania.

✓ Economics The main economic activities are farming and tourism. Some islands have important minerals or other resources.

✓ History Most people of Oceania are descendants of people who left Southeast Asia on canoes thousands of years ago.

◀ Fijian schoolgirls buy snacks from an Indian merchant in Suva.

Section 2 Antarctica

Terms to Know
crevasse
ice shelf
iceberg
krill
ozone

Main Idea
Antarctica is a harsh land of rock and ice, which the world's nations have agreed to leave open to scientific study.

✓ Location Antarctica lies at the southern end of the earth.

✓ Place Most of the continent, which has mountain ranges and a plateau, is covered by a huge, thick ice cap.

✓ Place Most plants and animals that live in Antarctica are small. Larger animals thrive in the waters off the coast.

✓ Economics Antarctica has many minerals, but many nations have signed a treaty agreeing not to remove these resources.

✓ Culture Antarctica is a major center of scientific research but the only continent with no permanent human population.

Chapter 28 Assessment and Activities

Using Key Terms

Match the terms in Part A with their definitions in Part B.

A.

1. pidgin language
2. copra
3. trust territory
4. ice shelf
5. continental island
6. ozone
7. low island
8. iceberg
9. high island
10. krill

B.

- **a.** land once connected to a larger landmass
- **b.** tiny, shrimplike animal
- **c.** Pacific island formed by volcanic activity
- **d.** combines elements of several languages
- **e.** chunk of a glacier that floats free
- **f.** dried coconut meat
- **g.** layer of ice above water in Antarctica
- **h.** area temporarily placed under control of another nation
- **i.** Pacific island formed of coral
- **j.** layer in the atmosphere that blocks certain harmful rays of the sun

Reviewing the Main Ideas

Section 1 Oceania

11. **Location** Which region of Oceania is the farthest north?
12. **Human/Environment Interaction** Which is likely to have better farmland—a high island or a low island? Why?
13. **Place** New Caledonia is rich in what resource?
14. **Economics** What attracts tourists to Oceania?
15. **History** From where did the people who first settled Oceania originally come?

Section 2 Antarctica

16. **Place** What is significant about Mount Erebus?
17. **Location** What large marine birds feed in the seas near Antarctica?
18. **Region** What resources have been found in Antarctica?
19. **Government** What agreement bans the use of Antarctica's resources?
20. **Human/Environment Interaction** Why do scientists study the ozone layer in Antarctica?

NATIONAL GEOGRAPHIC Oceania and Antarctica

Place Location Activity

On a separate sheet of paper, match the letters on the map with the numbered places listed below.

1. Antarctic Peninsula
2. South Pole
3. Vinson Massif
4. Marshall Islands
5. Papua New Guinea
6. Fiji Islands
7. French Polynesia
8. Coral Sea
9. Solomon Islands

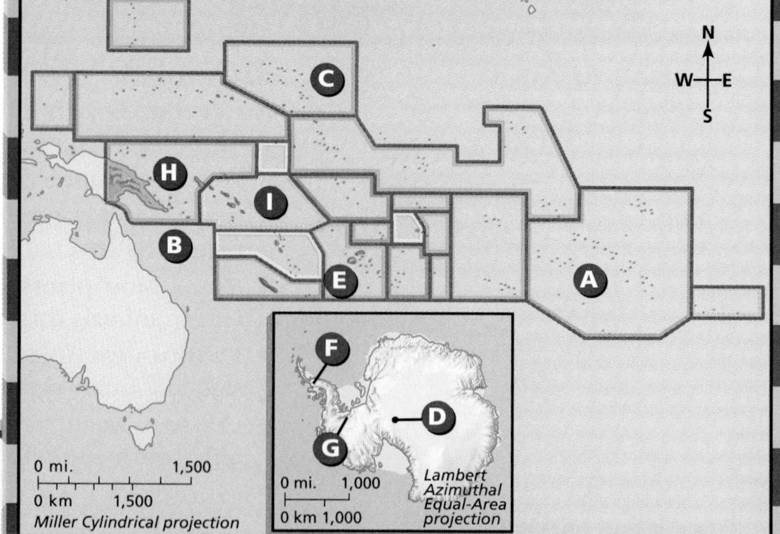

Self-Check Quiz Visit the ***Geography: The World and Its People*** Web site at gwip.glencoe.com and click on **Chapter 28—Self-Check Quizzes** to prepare for the Chapter Test.

Critical Thinking

21. **Making Generalizations** In this chapter, you read about two areas with very different climates. Write a generalization about how climate affects the way people live in each area.
22. **Organizing Information** Make a chart like this one. Under each heading, write a fact about each of the four regions you studied in this chapter: Melanesia, Micronesia, Polynesia, and Antarctica.

Region	Landforms	Climate	Economy or Resources	People

GeoJournal Activity

23. **Writing a Pamphlet** Choose one island country from Oceania. Research topics such as the land, economy, daily life, or culture. After you have completed your research, create a pamphlet about your island, encouraging tourists to visit there.

Mental Mapping Activity

24. **Focusing on the Region** Draw an outline map of Antarctica, then label the following:
    - Antarctic Circle
    - Antarctic Peninsula
    - Atlantic Ocean
    - Vinson Massif
    - Pacific Ocean
    - South Pole

Technology Skills Activity

25. **Building a Database** Research three animals of Oceania. Create a database of the information you find. Include separate fields for the following items: name of species, location, type of habitat, diet, natural predators, and population status. Then use the database to create a map showing the location of each species.

Standardized Test Practice

Directions: Read the paragraph below, then answer the following question.

Because of the clear Pacific waters, fresh fish is the primary traditional food of Oceania's people. This is especially true in the low coral islands, where there is little land suitable for farming. The rich volcanic soil of the high islands allows pineapples, coconuts, bananas, and sweet potatoes to grow. In Papua New Guinea, pork is a favorite food. Great feasts of pork, greens, and yams are social gatherings for whole villages. At these feasts, pigs are cooked for about eight hours over hot stones set in an "earth oven"—or large hole in the ground.

1. Which of the following statements best summarizes the paragraph above?

F People in the high islands are able to grow and eat pineapples, bananas, and sweet potatoes.

G In the low islands, the coral prevents much farming.

H The Pacific Ocean is the source of the fish that most people eat.

J Physical geography influences the traditional foods of Oceania's people.

Test-Taking Tip: When a question uses the word *best,* it means that more than one answer may be correct. Your job is to pick the *best* answer. This question also asks for a summary of the passage. Read through all of the answer choices before choosing the one that provides a more general restatement of the information.

Alone in a hut in 1934, Byrd fell ill from inhaling stove fumes.

"BYRD'S"-EYE VIEW: Exploring Antarctica

What sound does your breath make when it freezes? On his first expedition to Antarctica, United States Navy officer Richard E. Byrd found out. When the temperature dropped to – 64°F (– 53°C), Byrd heard what sounded like Chinese firecrackers as a slight breeze crackled across his frozen breath.

Beyond Imagination

Strange things happen in Antarctica. The sun lurks near the horizon for months and never sets. Then from mid-March to mid-September, the dark winter sets in, and the sun never rises. Antarctica is covered by thick ice and snow. Huge glaciers spill out between mountains that rim the coast, creating shelves of ice that extend out over the sea. Sometimes chunks of ice break off to form huge icebergs.

In the early 1900s, little was known about Antarctica. A few brave explorers had traveled on foot, skis, and sleds across the frozen land. Several made it to the South Pole. Much of the continent remained a mystery, however. Admiral Richard Byrd was determined to change that.

Mapping the Continent

With detailed planning, Byrd launched a major scientific expedition to Antarctica in 1928. He brought 650 tons (590 t) of supplies on his ship—everything from fur clothing and folding bathtubs to 80 sled dogs and a snowmobile! He also brought the latest technology, including radios, cameras, and three airplanes. His team of 53 professionals set up a complete village on the Ross Ice Shelf. They named it Little America.

From this base, Byrd and his crew explored the continent. On short flights from Little America, they used a mapping camera to gather data on vast areas never seen by humans. In 1929 Byrd and three companions were the first to fly over the South Pole. Such feats took great courage. Twice during flights, the engines failed. Once the pilot was able to restart them; once the plane crashed. Luckily, everyone survived. On a later expedition, huddled alone in a hut for months, Byrd almost died.

Byrd led five Antarctic expeditions and mapped nearly all of the continent. He supervised the completion of five Antarctic stations—Little America I through Little America V. His work paved the way for future researchers.

Today the United States and many other countries have scientific stations on Antarctica. From these stations, scientists record weather data, measure ozone levels, analyze ice and rock samples, and record animal behavior. Such research may answer important questions about future life on the earth.

QUESTIONS

1. What conditions did Byrd and his fellow explorers face in Antarctica?
2. Why is Byrd's work still important today?

Crunching through ice, the *U.S.S. Glacier* brings Admiral Byrd back to Antarctica in 1955. ▶

NATIONAL GEOGRAPHIC SOCIETY
GB 4
Byrd's First Flight to the South Pole
Polar Plateau
South Pole
ANTARCTICA
Byrd's 1st Flight, November 1929
ROSS ICE SHELF
Little America
Bay of Whales
Ross Sea
ANTARCTICA
Ross Ice Shelf
Area enlarged
0 mi. 200
0 km 200
Lambert Azimuthal Equal-Area projection

Appendix

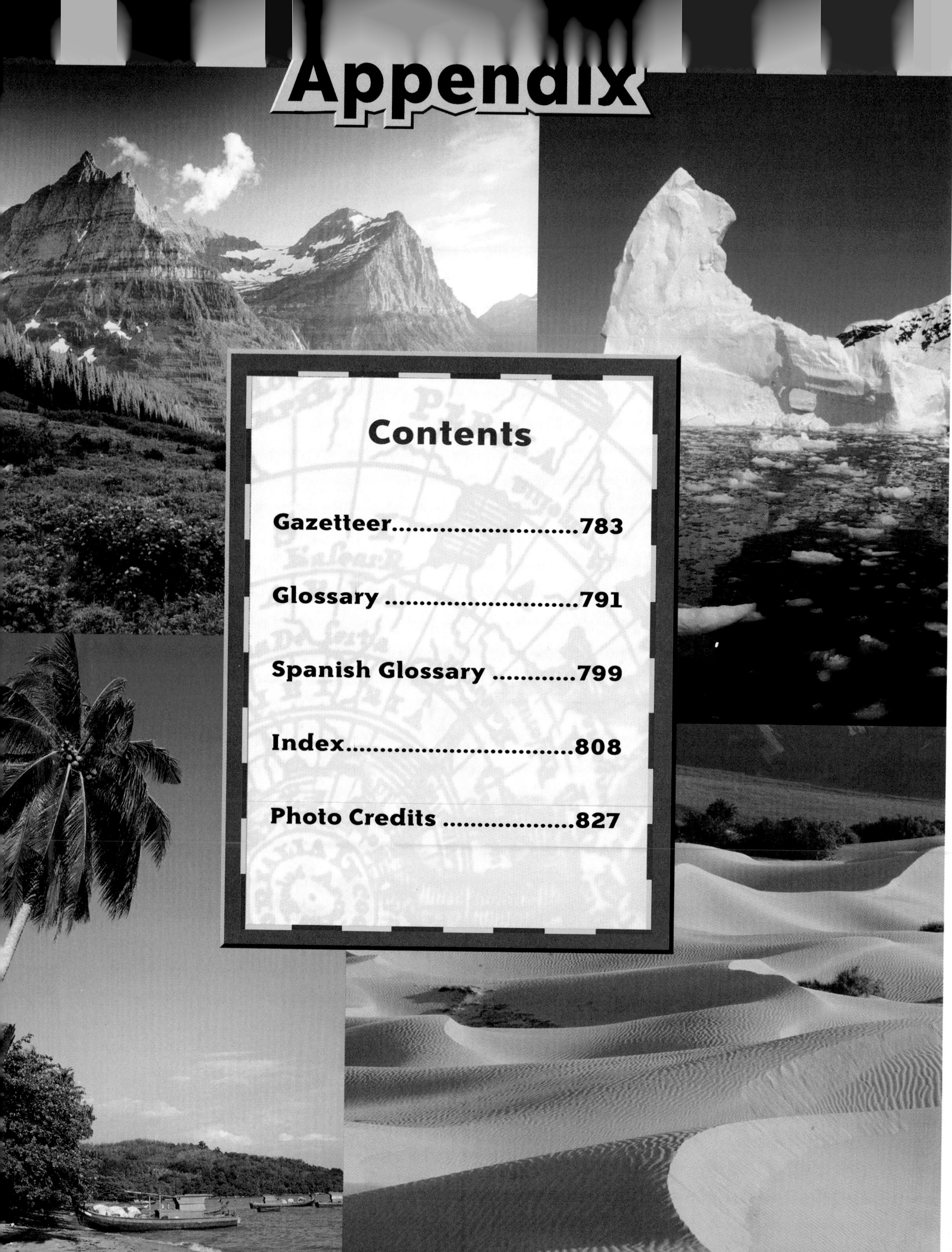

Contents

GAZETTEER

Gazetteer

A Gazetteer (GA•zuh•TIHR) is a geographic index or dictionary. It shows latitude and longitude for cities and certain other places. Latitude and longitude are shown in this way: 48°N 2°E, or 48 degrees north latitude and two degrees east longitude. This Gazetteer lists most of the world's largest independent countries, their capitals, and several important geographic features. The page numbers tell where each entry can be found on a map in this book. As an aid to pronunciation, most entries are spelled phonetically.

Abidjan [AH•bee•JAHN] Capital of Côte d'Ivoire. 5°N 4°W (p. 531)

Abu Dhabi [AH•boo DAH•bee] Capital of the United Arab Emirates. 24°N 54°E (p. 449)

Abuja [ah•BOO•jah] Capital of Nigeria. 8°N 9°E (p. 531)

Accra [ah•KRUH] Capital of Ghana. 6°N 0° longitude (p. 531)

Addis Ababa [AHD•dihs AH•bah•BAH] Capital of Ethiopia. 9°N 39°E (p. 531)

Adriatic [AY•dree•A•tihk] **Sea** Arm of the Mediterranean Sea between the Balkan Peninsula and Italy. 44°N 14°E (p. 280)

Afghanistan [af•GA•nuh•STAN] Central Asian country west of Pakistan. 33°N 63°E (p. 449)

Albania [al•BAY•nee•uh] Country on the Adriatic Sea, south of Yugoslavia. 42°N 20°E (p. 281)

Algeria [al•JIHR•ee•uh] North African country east of Morocco. 29°N 1°E (p. 449)

Algiers [al•JIHRZ] Capital of Algeria. 37°N 3°E (p. 449)

Alps [ALPS] Mountain ranges extending through central Europe. 46°N 9°E (p. 280)

Amazon [A•muh•ZAHN] **River** Largest river in the world by volume and second-largest in length. 2°S 53°W (p. 172)

Amman [a•MAHN] Capital of Jordan. 32°N 36°E (p. 449)

Amsterdam [AHM•stuhr•DAHM] Capital of the Netherlands. 52°N 5°E (p. 281)

Andes [AN•DEEZ] Mountain system extending north and south along the western side of South America. 13°S 75°W (p. 172)

Andorra [an•DAWR•uh] Small country in southern Europe between France and Spain. 43°N 2°E (p. 281)

Angola [ang•GOH•luh] Southern African country north of Namibia. 14°S 16°E (p. 531)

Ankara [AHNG•kuh•ruh] Capital of Turkey. 40°N 33°E (p. 449)

Antananarivo [AHN•tah•NAH•nah•REE•voh] Capital of Madagascar. 19°S 48°E (p. 531)

Arabian [uh•RAY•bee•uhn] **Peninsula** Large peninsula extending into the Arabian Sea. 28°N 40°E (p. 448)

Argentina [AHR•juhn•TEE•nuh] South American country east of Chile on the Atlantic Ocean. 36°S 67°W (p. 173)

Armenia [ahr•MEE•nee•uh] Southeastern European country between the Black and Caspian Seas. 40°N 45°E (p. 449)

Ashgabat [AHSH•gah•BAHT] Capital of Turkmenistan. 38°N 58°E (p. 449)

Asmara [az•MAHR•uh] Capital of Eritrea. 16°N 39°E (p. 531)

Astana Capital of Kazakhstan. 51°N 72°E (p. 449)

Asunción [ah•SOON•see•OHN] Capital of Paraguay. 25°S 58°W (p. 173)

Athens [A•thuhnz] Capital of Greece. 38°N 24°E (p. 281)

Atlas [AT•luhs] **Mountains** Mountain range on the northern edge of the Sahara. 31°N 5°W (p. 448)

Australia [aw•STRAYL•yuh] Country and continent in Southern Hemisphere. 25°S 135°W (p. 741)

Austria [AWS•tree•uh] Western European country east of Switzerland and south of Germany and the Czech Republic. 47°N 12°E (p. 281)

Azerbaijan [A•zuhr•BY•JAHN] European-Asian country on the Caspian Sea. 40°N 47°E (p. 449)

Baghdad [BAG•DAD] Capital of Iraq. 33°N 44°E (p. 449)

Bahamas [buh•HAH•muhz] Country made up of many islands between Cuba and the United States. 23°N 74°W (p. 172)

Bahrain [bah•RAYN] Country located on the Persian Gulf. 26°N 51°E (p. 449)

Baku [bah•KOO] Capital of Azerbaijan. 40°N 50°E (p. 449)

Balkan [BAWL•kuhn] **Peninsula** Peninsula in southeastern Europe. 42°N 20°E (p. 280)

Baltic [BAWL•tihk] **Sea** Sea in northern Europe that is connected to the North Sea. 55°N 17°E (p. 280)

Bamako [BAH•mah•KOH] Capital of Mali. 13°N 8°W (p. 531)

Bangkok [BANG•KAHK] Capital of Thailand. 14°N 100°E (p. 637)

Bangladesh [BAHNG•gluh•DEHSH] South Asian country bordered by India and Myanmar. 24°N 90°E (p. 637)
Bangui [BAHNG•GEE] Capital of the Central African Republic. 4°N 19°E (p. 531)
Banjul [BAHN•JOOL] Capital of Gambia. 13°N 17°W (p. 531)
Barbados [bahr•BAY•duhs] Island country between the Atlantic Ocean and the Caribbean Sea. 14°N 59°W (p. 173)
Beijing [BAY•JIHNG] Capital of China. 40°N 116°E (p. 637)
Beirut [bay•ROOT] Capital of Lebanon. 34°N 36°E (p. 449)
Belarus [BEE•luh•ROOS] Eastern European country west of Russia. 54°N 28°E (p. 281)
Belgium [BEHL•juhm] Western European country south of the Netherlands. 51°N 3°E (p. 281)
Belgrade [BEHL•GRAYD] Capital of Yugoslavia. 45°N 21°E (p. 281)
Belize [buh•LEEZ] Central American country east of Guatemala. 18°N 89°W (p. 173)
Belmopan [BEHL•moh•PAHN] Capital of Belize. 17°N 89°W (p. 173)
Benin [buh•NEEN] West African country west of Nigeria. 8°N 2°E (p. 531)
Berlin [behr•LEEN] Capital of Germany. 53°N 13°E (p. 281)
Bern [BEHRN] Capital of Switzerland. 47°N 7°E (p. 281)
Bhutan [boo•TAHN] South Asian country northeast of India. 27°N 91°E (p. 637)
Bishkek [bihsh•KEHK] Capital of Kyrgyzstan. 43°N 75°E (p. 449)
Bissau [bihs•SOW] Capital of Guinea-Bissau. 12°N 16°W (p. 531)
Black Sea Large sea between Europe and Asia. 43°N 32°E (p. 281)
Bloemfontein [BLOOM•FAHN•TAYN] Judicial capital of South Africa. 26°E 29°S (p. 531)
Bogotá [BOH•goh•TAH] Capital of Colombia. 5°N 74°W (p. 173)
Bolivia [buh•LIHV•ee•uh] Country in the central part of South America, north of Argentina. 17°S 64°W (p. 173)
Bosnia and Herzegovina [BAHZ•nee•uh HEHRT•seh•GAW•vee•nuh] Southeastern European country between Yugoslavia and Croatia. 44°N 18°E (p. 281)
Botswana [bawt•SWAH•nah] Southern African country north of the Republic of South Africa. 22°S 23°E (p. 531)
Brasília [brah•ZEEL•yuh] Capital of Brazil. 16°S 48°W (p. 173)
Bratislava [BRAH•tih•SLAH•vuh] Capital of Slovakia. 48°N 17°E (p. 281)
Brazil [bruh•ZIHL] Largest country in South America. 9°S 53°W (p. 173)
Brazzaville [BRAH•zuh•VEEL] Capital of the Congo. 4°S 15°E (p. 531)
Brunei [bru•NY] Southeast Asian country on northern coast of the island of Borneo. 5°N 114°E (p. 636)
Brussels [BRUH•suhlz] Capital of Belgium. 51°N 4°E (p. 281)
Bucharest [BOO•kuh•REHST] Capital of Romania. 44°N 26°E (p. 281)
Budapest [BOO•duh•PEHST] Capital of Hungary. 48°N 19°E (p. 281)
Buenos Aires [BWAY•nuhs AR•eez] Capital of Argentina. 34°S 58°W (p. 173)
Bujumbura [BOO•juhm•BUR•uh] Capital of Burundi. 3°S 29°E (p. 531)
Bulgaria [BUHL•GAR•ee•uh] Southeastern European country south of Romania. 42°N 24°E (p. 281)
Burkina Faso [bur•KEE•nuh FAH•soh] West African country south of Mali. 12°N 3°E (p. 531)
Burundi [bu•ROON•dee] East African country at the northern end of Lake Tanganyika. 3°S 30°E (p. 531)

Cairo [KY•ROH] Capital of Egypt. 31°N 32°E (p. 449)
Cambodia [kam•BOH•dee•uh] Southeast Asian country south of Thailand and Laos. 12°N 104°E (p. 637)
Cameroon [KA•muh•ROON] Central African country on the northeast shore of the Gulf of Guinea. 6°N 11°E (p. 531)
Canada [KA•nuh•duh] Northernmost country in North America. 50°N 100°W (p. 109)
Canberra [KAN•BEHR•uh] Capital of Australia. 35°S 149°E (p. 741)
Cape Town Legislative capital of the Republic of South Africa. 34°S 18°E (p. 531)
Cape Verde [VUHRD] Island country off the coast of western Africa in the Atlantic Ocean. 15°N 24°W (p. 531)
Caracas [kah•RAH•kahs] Capital of Venezuela. 11°N 67°W (p. 173)
Caribbean [KAR•uh•BEE•uhn] **Sea** Part of the Atlantic Ocean bordered by the West Indies, South America, and Central America. 15°N 76°W (p. 172)
Caspian [KAS•pee•uhn] **Sea** Salt lake between Europe and Asia that is the world's largest inland body of water. 40°N 52°E (p. 448)
Caucasus [KAW•kuh•suhs] **Mountains** Mountain range between the Black and Caspian Seas. 43°N 42°E (p. 448)
Central African Republic Central African country south of Chad. 8°N 21°E (p. 531)
Chad [CHAD] Country west of Sudan in the African Sahel. 18°N 19°E (p. 530)
Chile [CHEE•lay] South American country west of Argentina. 35°S 72°W (p. 173)
China [CHY•nuh] Country in eastern and central Asia, known officially as the People's Republic of China. 37°N 93°E (p. 637)
Chişinău [KEE•shee•NOW] Capital of Moldova. 47°N 29°E (p. 281)
Colombia [kuh•LUHM•bee•uh] South American country west of Venezuela. 4°N 73°W (p. 173)
Colombo [kuh•LUHM•boh] Capital of Sri Lanka. 7°N 80°E (p. 637)

Comoros [KAH•muh•ROHZ] Small island country in Indian Ocean between the island of Madagascar and the southeast African mainland. 13°S 43°E (p. 531)
Conakry [KAH•nuh•kree] Capital of Guinea. 10°N 14°W (p. 531)
Congo [KAHNG•goh] Central African country east of the Democratic Republic of the Congo. 3°S 14°E (p. 531)
Congo, Democratic Republic of the Central African country north of Zambia and Angola. 1°S 22°E (p. 531)
Copenhagen [KOH•puhn•HAY•guhn] Capital of Denmark. 56°N 12°E (p. 281)
Costa Rica [KAWS•tah REE•kah] Central American country south of Nicaragua. 11°N 85°W (p. 173)
Côte d'Ivoire [KOHT dee•VWAHR] West African country south of Mali. 8°N 7°W (p. 531)
Croatia [kroh•AY•shuh] Southeastern European country on the Adriatic Sea. 46°N 16°E (p. 281)
Cuba [KYOO•buh] Island country in the West Indies. 22°N 79°W (p. 172)
Cyprus [SY•pruhs] Island country in the eastern Mediterranean Sea, south of Turkey. 35°N 31°E (p. 281)
Czech [CHEHK] **Republic** Eastern European country north of Austria. 50°N 15°E (p. 281)

Dakar [dah•KAHR] Capital of Senegal. 15°N 17°W (p. 531)
Damascus [duh•MAS•kuhs] Capital of Syria. 34°N 36°E (p. 449)
Dar es Salaam (DAHR EHS sah•LAHM] Capital of Tanzania. 7°S 39°E (p. 531)
Denmark [DEHN•MAHRK] Northern European country between the Baltic and North Seas. 56°N 9°E (p. 281)
Dhaka [DA•kuh] Capital of Bangladesh. 24°N 90°E (p. 637)
Djibouti [jih•BOO•tee] East African country on the Gulf of Aden. 12°N 43°E (p. 531)
Doha [DOH•huh] Capital of Qatar. 25°N 51°E (p. 449)
Dominican [duh•MIH•nih•kuhn] **Republic** Country in the West Indies on the eastern part of Hispaniola. 19°N 71°W (p. 206)
Dublin [DUH•blihn] Capital of Ireland. 53°N 6°W (p. 281)
Dushanbe [doo•SHAM•buh] Capital of Tajikistan. 39°N 69°E (p. 449)

East Timor [TEE•MOHR] Previous province of Indonesia, now under UN administration. 10°S 127°E (p. 637)
Ecuador [EH•kwuh•DAWR] South American country southwest of Colombia. 0° latitude 79°W (p. 173)
Egypt [EE•jihpt] North African country on the Mediterranean Sea. 27°N 27°E (p. 449)
El Salvador [ehl SAL•vuh•DAWR] Central American country southwest of Honduras. 14°N 89°W (p. 173)
Equatorial Guinea [EE•kwuh•TOHR•ee•uhl GIH•nee] Central African country south of Cameroon. 2°N 8°E (p. 531)
Eritrea [EHR•uh•TREE•uh] East African country north of Ethiopia. 17°N 39°E (p. 531)
Estonia [eh•STOH•nee•uh] Eastern European country on the Baltic Sea. 59°N 25°E (p. 281)
Ethiopia [EE•thee•OH•pee•uh] East African country north of Somalia and Kenya. 8°N 38°E (p. 531)
Euphrates [yu•FRAY•TEEZ] **River** River in southwestern Asia that flows through Syria and Iraq and joins the Tigris River. 36°N 40°E (p. 448)

Fiji [FEE•jee] **Islands** Country comprised of an island group in the southwest Pacific Ocean. 19°S 175°E (p. 741)
Finland [FIHN•luhnd] Northern European country east of Sweden. 63°N 26°E (p. 281)
France [FRANS] Western European country south of the United Kingdom. 47°N 1°E (p. 281)
Freetown [FREE•TOWN] Capital of Sierra Leone. 9°N 13°W (p. 531)
French Guiana [gee•A•nuh] French-owned territory in northern South America. 5°N 53°W (p. 173)

Gabon [ga•BOHN] Central African country on the Atlantic Ocean. 0° latitude 12°E (p. 531)
Gaborone [GAH•boh•ROH•NAY] Capital of Botswana. 24°S 26°E (p. 531)
Gambia [GAM•bee•uh] West African country along the Gambia River. 13°N 16°W (p. 531)
Georgetown [JAWRJ•TOWN] Capital of Guyana. 8°N 58°W (p. 173)
Georgia [JAWR•juh] Asian-European country bordering the Black Sea south of Russia. 42°N 43°E (p. 449)
Germany [JUHR•muh•nee] Western European country south of Denmark, officially called the Federal Republic of Germany. 52°N 10°E (p. 281)
Ghana [GAH•nuh] West African country on the Gulf of Guinea. 8°N 2°W (p. 531)
Great Plains The continental slope extending through the United States and Canada. 45°N 104°W (p. 108)
Greece [GREES] Southern European country on the Balkan Peninsula. 39°N 22°E (p. 280)
Greenland [GREEN•luhnd] Island in northwestern Atlantic Ocean and the largest island in the world. 74°N 40°W (p. 109)
Guatemala [GWAH•tay•MAH•lah] Central American country south of Mexico. 16°N 92°W (p. 173)
Guatemala City Capital of Guatemala. 15°N 91°W (p. 173)

GAZETTEER

Guinea [GIH•nee] West African country on the Atlantic coast. 11°N 12°W (p. 531)
Guinea-Bissau [GIH•nee bih•SOW] West African country on the Atlantic coast. 12°N 20°W (p. 531)
Gulf of Mexico Gulf on part of the southern coast of North America. 25°N 94°W (p. 108)
Guyana [gy•AH•nuh] South American country between Venezuela and Suriname. 8°N 59°W (p. 173)

Haiti [HAY•tee] Country in the West Indies on the western part of Hispaniola. 19°N 72°W (p. 206)
Hanoi [ha•NOY] Capital of Vietnam. 21°N 106°E (p. 637)
Harare [hah•RAH•RAY] Capital of Zimbabwe. 18°S 31°E (p. 531)
Havana [huh•VA•nuh] Capital of Cuba. 23°N 82°W (p. 173)
Helsinki [HEHL•SIHNG•kee] Capital of Finland. 60°N 24°E (p. 281)
Himalaya [HI•muh•LAY•uh] Mountain ranges in southern Asia, bordering the Indian subcontinent on the north. 30°N 85°E (p. 636)
Honduras [hahn•DUR•uhs] Central American country on the Caribbean Sea. 15°N 88°W (p. 173)
Hong Kong [HAWNG KAWNG] Port and industrial center in southern China. 22°N 115°E (p. 637)
Hungary [HUHNG•guh•ree] Eastern European country south of Slovakia. 47°N 18°E (p. 281)

Iberian [eye•BIHR•ee•uhn] **Peninsula** Peninsula in southwest Europe, occupied by Spain and Portugal. 41°N 1°W (p. 280)
Iceland [EYES•luhnd] Island country between the North Atlantic and the Arctic Oceans, 65°N 20°W (p. 281)
India [IHN•dee•uh] South Asian country south of China and Nepal. 23°N 78°E (p. 637)
Indonesia [IHN•duh•NEE•zhuh] Southeast Asian island country known as the Republic of Indonesia. 5°S 119°E (p. 637)
Indus [IHN•duhs] **River** River in Asia that begins in Tibet and flows through Pakistan to the Arabian Sea. 27°N 68°E (p. 636)
Iran [ih•RAN] Southwest Asian country that was formerly named Persia. 31°N 54°E (p. 449)
Iraq [ih•RAHK] Southwest Asian country west of Iran. 32°N 43°E (p. 449)
Ireland [EYER•luhnd] Island west of Great Britain occupied by the Republic of Ireland and Northern Ireland. 54°N 8°W (p. 281)
Islamabad [ihs•LAH•muh•BAHD] Capital of Pakistan. 34°N 73°E (p. 637)
Israel [IHZ•ree•uhl] Southwest Asian country south of Lebanon. 33°N 34°E (p. 449)
Italy [IHT•uhl•ee] Southern European country south of Switzerland and east of France. 44°N 11°E (p. 281)

Jakarta [juh•KAHR•tuh] Capital of Indonesia. 6°S 107°E (p. 637)
Jamaica [juh•MAY•kuh] Island country in the West Indies. 18°N 78°W (p. 173)
Japan [juh•PAN] East Asian country consisting of the four large islands of Hokkaido, Honshu, Shikoku, and Kyushu, plus thousands of small islands. 37°N 134°E (p. 636)
Jerusalem [juh•ROO•suh•luhm] Capital of Israel and a holy city for Christians, Jews, and Muslims. 32°N 35°E (p. 449)
Jordan [JAWRD•uhn] Southwest Asian country south of Syria. 30°N 38°E (p. 449)

Kabul [KAH•buhl] Capital of Afghanistan. 35°N 69°E (p. 449)
Kampala [kahm•PAH•lah] Capital of Uganda. 0° latitude 32°E (p. 531)
Kathmandu [KAT•MAN•DOO] Capital of Nepal. 28°N 85°E (p. 637)
Kazakhstan [kuh•ZAHK•STAHN] Large Asian country south of Russia and bordering the Caspian Sea. 48°N 59°E (p. 449)
Kenya [KEHN•yuh] East African country south of Ethiopia. 1°N 37°E (p. 531)
Khartoum [kahr•TOOM] Capital of Sudan. 16°N 33°E (p. 531)
Kiev [KEE•ihf] Capital of Ukraine. 50°N 31°E (p. 281)
Kigali [kee•GAH•lee] Capital of Rwanda. 2°S 30°E (p. 531)
Kingston [KIHNG•stuhn] Capital of Jamaica. 18°N 77°W (p. 173)
Kinshasa [kihn•SHAH•suh] Capital of the Democratic Republic of the Congo. 4°S 15°E (p. 531)
Kuala Lumpur [KWAH•luh LUM•PUR] Capital of Malaysia. 3°N 102°E (p. 637)
Kuwait [ku•WAYT] Country on the Persian Gulf between Saudi Arabia and Iraq. 29°N 48°E (p. 449)
Kyrgyzstan [KIHR•gih•STAN] Central Asian country on China's western border. 41°N 75°E (p. 449)

Laos [LOWS] Southeast Asian country south of China and west of Vietnam. 20°N 102°E (p. 637)
La Paz [lah PAHS] Administrative capital of Bolivia, and the highest capital in the world. 17°S 68°W (p. 173)
Latvia [LAT•vee•uh] Eastern European country west of Russia on the Baltic Sea. 57°N 25°E (p. 281)

GAZETTEER

Lebanon [LEH•buh•nuhn] Country south of Syria on the Mediterranean Sea. 34°N 34°E (p. 449)
Lesotho [luh•SOH•TOH] Southern African country within the borders of the Republic of South Africa. 30°S 28°E (p. 531)
Liberia [ly•BIHR•ee•uh] West African country south of Guinea. 7°N 10°W (p. 531)
Libreville [LEE•bruh•VIHL] Capital of Gabon. 1°N 9°E (p. 531)
Libya [LIH•bee•uh] North African country west of Egypt on the Mediterranean Sea. 28°N 15°E (p. 449)
Liechtenstein [LIHKT•uhn•SHTYN] Small country in central Europe between Switzerland and Austria. 47°N 10°E (p. 281)
Lilongwe [lih•LAWNG•GWAY] Capital of Malawi. 14°S 34°E (p. 531)
Lima [LEE•mah] Capital of Peru. 12°S 77°W (p. 173)
Lisbon [LIHZ•buhn] Capital of Portugal. 39°N 9°W (p. 281)
Lithuania [LIH•thuh•WAY•nee•uh] Eastern European country northwest of Belarus on the Baltic Sea. 56°N 24°E (p. 281)
Ljubljana [lee•OO•blee•AH•nuh] Capital of Slovenia. 46°N 14°E (p. 281)
Lomé [loh•MAY] Capital of Togo. 6°N 1°E (p. 531)
London [LUHN•duhn] Capital of the United Kingdom, on the Thames River. 52°N 0° longitude (p. 281)
Luanda [lu•AHN•duh] Capital of Angola. 9°S 13°E (p. 531)
Lusaka [loo•SAH•kah] Capital of Zambia. 15°S 28°E (p. 531)
Luxembourg [LUHK•suhm•BUHRG] Small European country between France, Belgium, and Germany. 50°N 7°E (p. 281)

Macau [muh•KOW] Port in southern China. 22°N 113°E (p. 637)
Macedonia [MA•suh•DOH•nee•uh] Southeastern European country north of Greece. 42°N 22°E (p. 281). Macedonia also refers to a geographic region covering northern Greece, the country Macedonia, and part of Bulgaria.
Madagascar [MA•duh•GAS•kuhr] Island in the Indian Ocean off the southeastern coast of Africa. 18°S 43°E (p. 531)
Madrid [muh•DRIHD] Capital of Spain. 41°N 4°W (p. 281)
Malabo [mah•LAH•boh] Capital of Equatorial Guinea. 4°N 9°E (p. 531)
Malawi [mah•LAH•wee] Southern African country south of Tanzania and east of Zambia. 11°S 34°E (p. 531)
Malaysia [muh•LAY•zhuh] Southeast Asian country with land on the Malay Peninsula and on the island of Borneo. 4°N 101°E (p. 636)
Maldives [MAWL•DEEVZ] Island country southwest of India in the Indian Ocean. 5°N 42°E (p. 637)
Mali [MAH•lee] West African country east of Mauritania. 16°N 0° longitude (p. 531)
Managua [mah•NAH•gwah] Capital of Nicaragua. 12°N 86°W (p. 173)
Manila [muh•NIH•luh] Capital of the Philippines. 15°N 121°E (p. 637)
Maputo [mah•POO•toh] Capital of Mozambique. 26°S 33°E (p. 531)
Maseru [MA•zuh•ROO] Capital of Lesotho. 29°S 27°E (p. 531)
Mauritania [MAWR•uh•TAY•nee•uh] West African country north of Senegal. 20°N 14°W (p. 531)
Mauritius [maw•RIH•shuhs] Island country in the Indian Ocean east of Madagascar. 21°S 58°E (p. 531)
Mbabane [uhm•bah•BAH•nay] Capital of Swaziland. 26°S 31°E (p. 531)
Mediterranean [MEH•duh•tuh•RAY•nee•uhn] **Sea** Large inland sea surrounded by Europe, Asia, and Africa. 36°N 13°E (p. 280)
Mekong [MAY•KAWNG] **River** River in southeastern Asia that begins in Tibet and empties into the South China Sea. 18°N 104°E (p. 636)
Mexico [MEHK•sih•KOH] North American country south of the United States. 24°N 104°W (p. 173)
Mexico City Capital of Mexico. 19°N 99°W (p. 173)
Minsk [MIHNSK] Capital of Belarus. 54°N 28°E (p. 281)
Mississippi [MIH•suh•SIH•pee] **River** Large river system in the central United States that flows southward into the Gulf of Mexico. 32°N 92°W (p. 108)
Mogadishu [MOH•guh•DEE•SHOO] Capital of Somalia. 2°N 45°E (p. 531)
Moldova [mawl•DAW•vuh] Small European country between Ukraine and Romania. 48°N 28°E (p. 281)
Monaco [MAH•nuh•KOH] Small country in southern Europe on the French Mediterranean coast. 44°N 8°E (p. 281)
Mongolia [mahn•GOHL•yuh] Country in Asia between Russia and China. 46°N 100°E (p. 637)
Monrovia [muhn•ROH•vee•uh] Capital of Liberia. 6°N 11°W (p. 531)
Montevideo [MAHN•tuh•vuh•DAY•OH] Capital of Uruguay. 35°S 56°W (p. 173)
Morocco [muh•RAH•KOH] North African country on the Mediterranean Sea and the Atlantic Ocean. 32°N 7°W (p. 449)
Moscow [MAHS•KOW] Capital of Russia. 56°N 38°E (p. 401)
Mount Everest [EHV•ruhst] Highest mountain in the world, in the Himalaya between Nepal and Tibet. 28°N 87°E (p. 636)
Mozambique [MOH•zahm•BEEK] Southern African country south of Tanzania. 20°S 34°E (p. 531)
Muscat [MUHS•KAHT] Capital of Oman. 23°N 59°E (p. 449)
Myanmar [MYAHN•MAHR] Southeast Asian country south of China and India, formerly called Burma. 21°N 95°E (p. 637)

Nairobi [ny•ROH•bee] Capital of Kenya. 1°S 37°E (p. 531)

Namibia [nuh•MIH•bee•uh] Southern African country south of Angola on the Atlantic Ocean. 20°S 16°E (p. 531)
Nassau [NA•SAW] Capital of the Bahamas. 25°N 77°W (p. 173)
N'Djamena [uhn•jah•MAY•nah] Capital of Chad. 12°N 15°E (p. 531)
Nepal [NAY•PAHL] Mountain country between India and China. 29°N 83°E (p. 637)
Netherlands [NEH•thuhr•lundz] Western European country north of Belgium. 53°N 4°E (p. 281)
New Delhi [NOO DEH•lee] Capital of India. 29°N 77°E (p. 637)
New Zealand [NOO ZEE•luhnd] Major island country southeast of Australia in the South Pacific. 42°S 175°E (p. 741)
Niamey [nee•AHM•ay] Capital of Niger. 14°N 2°E (p. 531)
Nicaragua [NIH•kuh•RAH•gwuh] Central American country south of Honduras. 13°N 86°W (p. 173)
Nicosia [NIH•kuh•SEE•uh] Capital of Cyprus. 35°N 33°E (p. 281)
Niger [NY•juhr] West African country north of Nigeria. 18°N 9°E (p. 531)
Nigeria [ny•JIHR•ee•uh] West African country along the Gulf of Guinea. 9°N 7°E (p. 530)
Nile [NYL] **River** Longest river in the world, flowing north through eastern Africa. 19°N 33°E (p. 448)
North Korea [kuh•REE•uh] East Asian country in the northernmost part of the Korean Peninsula. 40°N 127°E (p. 637)
Norway [NAWR•WAY] Northern European country on the Scandinavian peninsula. 64°N 11°E (p. 280)
Nouakchott [nu•AHK•SHAHT] Capital of Mauritania. 18°N 16°W (p. 531)

Oman [oh•MAHN] Country on the Arabian Sea and the Gulf of Oman. 20°N 58°E (p. 449)
Oslo [AHZ•loh] Capital of Norway. 60°N 11°E (p. 281)
Ottawa [AH•tuh•wuh] Capital of Canada. 45°N 76°W (p. 109)
Ouagadougou [WAH•gah•DOO•goo] Capital of Burkina Faso. 12°N 2°W (p. 531)

Pakistan [PA•kih•STAN] South Asian country northwest of India on the Arabian Sea. 28°N 68°E (p. 637)
Palau [puh•LOW) Island country in the Pacific Ocean. 7°N 135°E (p. 741)
Panama [PA•nuh•MAH] Central American country on the Isthmus of Panama. 9°N 81°W (p. 173)
Panama City Capital of Panama. 9°N 79°W (p. 173)
Papua New Guinea [PA•pyu•wuh NOO GIH•nee] Island country in the Pacific Ocean north of Australia. 7°S 142°E (p. 741)
Paraguay [PAR•uh•GWY] South American country northeast of Argentina. 24°S 57°W (p. 173)
Paramaribo [PAH•rah•MAH•ree•boh] Capital of Suriname. 6°N 55°W (p. 173)
Paris [PAR•uhs] Capital of France. 49°N 2°E (p. 281)
Persian [PUHR•zhuhn] **Gulf** Arm of the Arabian Sea between Iran and Saudi Arabia. 28°N 51°E (p. 448)
Peru [puh•ROO] South American country south of Ecuador and Colombia. 10°S 75°W (p. 173)
Philippines [FIH•luh•PEENZ] Island country in the Pacific Ocean southeast of China. 14°N 125°E (p. 637)
Phnom Penh [puh•NAWM PEHN] Capital of Cambodia. 12°N 106°E (p. 637)
Poland [POH•luhnd] Eastern European country on the Baltic Sea. 52°N 18°E (p. 281)
Port-au-Prince [POHR•toh•PRIHNS] Capital of Haiti. 19°N 72°W (p. 173)
Port Moresby [MOHRZ•bee] Capital of Papua New Guinea. 10°S 147°E (p. 741)
Port-of-Spain [SPAYN] Capital of Trinidad and Tobago. 11°N 62°W (p. 173)
Porto-Novo [POHR•toh•NOH•voh] Capital of Benin. 7°N 3°E (p. 531)
Portugal [POHR•chih•guhl] Country west of Spain on the Iberian Peninsula. 39°N 8°W (p. 280)
Prague [PRAHG] Capital of the Czech Republic. 51°N 15°E (p. 281)
Pretoria [prih•TOHR•ee•uh] Executive capital of South Africa. 26°S 28°E (p. 531)
Puerto Rico [PWEHR•toh REE•koh] Island in the Caribbean Sea; U.S. Commonwealth. 19°N 67°W (p. 173)
Pyongyang [pee•AWNG•YAHNG] Capital of North Korea. 39°N 126°E (p. 637)

Qatar [KAH•tuhr] Country on the southwestern shore of the Persian Gulf. 25°N 53°E (p. 449)
Quito [KEE•toh] Capital of Ecuador. 0° latitude 79°W (p. 173)

Rabat [ruh•BAHT] Capital of Morocco. 34°N 7°W (p. 449)
Reykjavík [RAY•kyah•VEEK] Capital of Iceland. 64°N 22°W (p. 281)
Rhine [RYN] **River** River in western Europe that flows into the North Sea. 51°N 7°E (p. 280)
Riga [REE•guh] Capital of Latvia. 57°N 24°E (p. 281)
Rio Grande [REE•oh GRAND] River that forms part of the boundary between the United States and Mexico. 30°N 103°W (p. 108)
Riyadh [ree•YAHD] Capital of Saudi Arabia. 25°N 47°E (p. 449)
Rocky Mountains Mountain system in western North America. 50°N 114°W (p. 108)

GAZETTEER

Romania [ru•MAY•nee•uh] Eastern European country east of Hungary. 46°N 23°E (p. 281)
Rome [ROHM] Capital of Italy. 42°N 13°E (p. 281)
Russia [RUH•shuh] Largest country in the world, covering parts of Europe and Asia. 60°N 90°E (p. 401)
Rwanda [ruh•WAHN•duh] East African country south of Uganda. 2°S 30°E (p. 531)

Sahara [suh•HAR•uh] Desert region in northern Africa that is the largest hot desert in the world. 24°N 2°W (p. 448)
Saint Lawrence [LAWR•uhns] **River** River that flows from Lake Ontario to the Atlantic Ocean and forms part of the boundary between the United States and Canada. 48°N 70°W (p. 108)
Sanaa [sahn•AH] Capital of Yemen. 15°N 44°E (p. 449)
San José [SAHNG hoh•SAY] Capital of Costa Rica. 10°N 84°W (p. 173)
San Marino [SAN muh•REE•noh] Small European country located in the Italian peninsula. 44°N 13°E (p. 281)
San Salvador [san SAL•vuh•DAWR] Capital of El Salvador. 14°N 89°W (p. 173)
Santiago [SAN•tee•AH•goh] Capital of Chile. 33°S 71°W (p. 173)
Santo Domingo [SAN•toh duh•MIHNG•goh] Capital of the Dominican Republic. 19°N 70°W (p. 173)
Sao Tome and Principe [SOW•too•MAY PREEN•see•pee] Small island country in the Gulf of Guinea off the coast of central Africa. 1°N 7°E (p. 530)
Sarajevo [SAR•uh•YAY•voh] Capital of Bosnia and Herzegovina. 43°N 18°E (p. 281)
Saudi Arabia [SOW•dee uh•RAY•bee•uh] Country on the Arabian Peninsula. 23°N 46°E (p. 448)
Senegal [SEH•nih•GAWL] West African country on the Atlantic coast. 15°N 14°W (p. 531)
Seoul [SOHL] Capital of South Korea. 38°N 127°E (p. 637)
Seychelles [say•SHEHL] Small island country in the Indian Ocean off eastern Africa. 6°S 56°E (p. 531)
Sierra Leone [see•EHR•uh lee•OHN] West African country south of Guinea. 8°N 12°W (p. 531)
Singapore [SIHNG•uh•POHR] Southeast Asian island country near tip of Malay Peninsula. 2°N 104°E (p. 636)
Skopje [SKAW•PYAY] Capital of the country of Macedonia. 42°N 21°E (p. 281)
Slovakia [sloh•VAH•kee•uh] Eastern European country south of Poland. 49°N 19°E (p. 281)
Slovenia [sloh•VEE•nee•uh] Southeastern European country south of Austria on the Adriatic Sea. 46°N 15°E (p. 281)
Sofia [SOH•fee•uh] Capital of Bulgaria. 43°N 23°E (p. 281)
Solomon [SAH•luh•muhn] **Islands** Island country in the Pacific Ocean northeast of Australia. 7°S 160°E (p. 741)
Somalia [soh•MAH•lee•uh] East African country on the Gulf of Aden and the Indian Ocean. 3°N 45°E (p. 531)
South Africa [A•frih•kuh] Country at the southern tip of Africa, officially the Republic of South Africa. 28°S 25°E (p. 531)
South Korea [kuh•REE•uh] East Asian country on the Korean Peninsula between the Yellow Sea and the Sea of Japan. 36°N 128°E (p. 637)
Spain [SPAYN] Southern European country on the Iberian Peninsula. 40°N 4°W (p. 280)
Sri Lanka [SREE•LAHNG•kuh] Country in the Indian Ocean south of India, formerly called Ceylon. 9°N 83°E (p. 637)
Stockholm [STAHK•HOHLM] Capital of Sweden. 59°N 18°E (p. 281)
Sucre [SOO•kray] Constitutional capital of Bolivia. 19°S 65°W (p. 173)
Sudan [soo•DAN] East African country south of Egypt. 14°N 28°E (p. 531)
Suriname [SUR•uh•NAH•muh] South American country between Guyana and French Guiana. 4°N 56°W (p. 173)
Suva [SOO•vah] Capital of the Fiji Islands. 18°S 177°E (p. 741)
Swaziland [SWAH•zee•LAND] Southern African country west of Mozambique, almost entirely within the Republic of South Africa. 27°S 32°E (p. 531)
Sweden [SWEED•uhn] Northern European country on the eastern side of the Scandinavian peninsula. 60°N 14°E (p. 280)
Switzerland [SWIHT•suhr•luhnd] European country in the Alps south of Germany. 47°N 8°E (p. 280)
Syria [SIHR•ee•uh] Southwest Asian country on the east side of the Mediterranean Sea. 35°N 37°E (p. 449)

Taipei [TY•PAY] Capital of Taiwan. 25°N 122°E (p. 637)
Taiwan [TY•WAHN] Island country off the southeast coast of China, and the seat of the Chinese Nationalist government. 24°N 122°E (p. 637)
Tajikistan [tah•JIH•kih•STAN] Central Asian country east of Turkmenistan. 39°N 70°E (p. 449)
Tallinn [TA•luhn] Capital of Estonia. 59°N 25°E (p. 281)
Tanzania [TAN•zuh•NEE•uh] East African country south of Kenya. 7°S 34°E (p. 531)
Tashkent [tash•KEHNT] Capital of Uzbekistan. 41°N 69°E (p. 449)
T'bilisi [tuh•bih•LEE•see] Capital of the Republic of Georgia. 42°N 45°E (p. 449)
Tegucigalpa [tay•GOO•see•GAHL•pah] Capital of Honduras. 14°N 87°W (p. 173)
Tehran [TAY•uh•RAN] Capital of Iran. 36°N 52°E (p. 449)
Thailand [TY•LAND] Southeast Asian country east of Myanmar. 17°N 101°E (p. 637)

Thimphu [thihm•POO] Capital of Bhutan. 28°N 90°E (p. 637)
Tigris [TY•gruhs] **River** River in southeastern Turkey and Iraq that merges with the Euphrates River. 35°N 44°E (p. 448)
Tirana [tih•RAH•nuh] Capital of Albania. 42°N 20°E (p. 281)
Togo [TOH•goh] West African country between Benin and Ghana on the Gulf of Guinea. 8°N 1°E (p. 530)
Tokyo [TOH•kee•OH] Capital of Japan. 36°N 140°E (p. 637)
Trinidad and Tobago [TRIH•nuh•DAD tuh•BAY•goh] Island country near Venezuela between the Atlantic Ocean and the Caribbean Sea. 11°N 61°W (p. 173)
Tripoli [TRIH•puh•lee] Capital of Libya. 33°N 13°E (p. 449)
Tunis [TOO•nuhs] Capital of Tunisia. 37°N 10°E (p. 449)
Tunisia [too•NEE•zhuh] North African country on the Mediterranean Sea between Libya and Algeria. 35°N 10°E (p. 449)
Turkey [TUHR•kee] Country in southeastern Europe and western Asia. 39°N 32°E (p. 449)
Turkmenistan [tuhrk•MEH•nuh•STAN] Central Asian country on the Caspian Sea. 41°N 56°E (p. 449)

Uganda [yoo•GAHN•dah] East African country south of Sudan. 2°N 32°E (p. 531)
Ukraine [yoo•KRAYN] Eastern European country west of Russia on the Black Sea. 49°N 30°E (p. 281)
Ulaanbaatar [OO•LAHN•BAH•TAWR] Capital of Mongolia. 48°N 107°E (p. 637)
United Arab Emirates [EH•muh•ruhts] Country made up of seven states on the eastern side of the Arabian Peninsula. 24°N 54°E (p. 449)
United Kingdom Western European island country made up of England, Scotland, Wales, and Northern Ireland. 57°N 2°W (p. 281)
United States of America Country in North America made up of 50 states, mostly between Canada and Mexico. 38°N 110°W (p. 109)
Uruguay [YUR•uh•GWAY] South American country south of Brazil on the Atlantic Ocean. 33°S 56°W (p. 173)
Uzbekistan [UZ•BEH•kih•STAN] Central Asian country south of Kazakhstan. 42°N 60°E (p. 449)

Vanuatu [VAN•WAH•TOO] Country made up of islands in the Pacific Ocean east of Australia. 17°S 170°W (p. 741)
Vatican [VA•tih•kuhn] **City** Headquarters of the Roman Catholic Church, located in the city of Rome in Italy. 42°N 13°E (p. 281)
Venezuela [VEH•nuh•ZWAY•luh] South American country on the Caribbean Sea between Colombia and Guyana. 8°N 65°W (p. 173)
Vienna [vee•EH•nuh] Capital of Austria. 48°N 16°E (p. 281)
Vientiane [vyehn•TYAHN] Capital of Laos. 18°N 103°E (p. 637)
Vietnam [vee•EHT•NAHM] Southeast Asian country east of Laos and Cambodia. 18°N 107°E (p. 637)
Vilnius [VIL•nee•uhs] Capital of Lithuania. 55°N 25°E (p. 281)

Warsaw [WAWR•SAW] Capital of Poland. 52°N 21°E (p. 281)
Washington, D.C. Capital of the United States, in the District of Columbia. 39°N 77°W (p. 109)
Wellington [WEH•lihng•tuhn] Capital of New Zealand. 41°S 175°E (p. 741)
West Indies [IHN•deez] Islands in the Caribbean Sea between North America and South America. 19°N 79°W (p. 172)
Windhoek [VIHNT•HUK] Capital of Namibia. 22°S 17°E (p. 531)

Yamoussoukro [YAH•moo•SOO•kroh] Second capital of Côte d'Ivoire. 7°N 6°W (p. 531)
Yangon [YAHNG•GOHN] Capital of Myanmar. 17°N 96°E (p. 637)
Yangtze [YANG•SEE] **River** Principal river of China that begins in Tibet and flows into the East China Sea near Shanghai, also known as the Chang Jiang [CHAHNG jee•AHNG]. 31°N 117°E (p. 636)
Yaoundé [yown•DAY] Capital of Cameroon. 4°N 12°E (p. 531)
Yellow River River in northern and eastern China, also known as the Huang He [HWAHNG HUH]. 35°N 114°E (p. 636)
Yemen [YEH•muhn] Country south of Saudi Arabia on the Arabian Peninsula. 15°N 46°E (p. 449)
Yerevan [YEHR•uh•VAHN] Capital of Armenia. 40°N 44°E (p. 449)
Yugoslavia [YOO•goh•SLAH•vee•uh] Eastern European country south of Hungary; includes Serbia and Montenegro. 44°N 21°E (p. 281)

Zagreb [ZAH•GREHB] Capital of Croatia. 46°N 16°E (p. 281)
Zambia [ZAM•bee•uh] Southern African country north of Zimbabwe. 14°S 24°E (p. 531)
Zimbabwe [zihm•BAH•bway] Southern African country northeast of Botswana. 18°S 30°E (p. 531)

absolute location exact position of a place on the earth's surface (p. 6)
acid rain rain containing high amounts of chemical pollutants (pp. 97, 127, 154, 368)
adobe sun-dried clay bricks (p. 193)
alluvial plain area that is built up by rich fertile soil left by river floods (pp. TN9, 497)
altiplano large highland plateau (p. 260)
altitude height above sea level (pp. 184, 242, 583)
amendment change to the constitution (p. TN29)
anthracite type of hard coal (p. 705)
apartheid system of laws that separated racial and ethnic groups and limited the rights of blacks in South Africa (p. 611)
appellate court type of court that rules on a lower court's decision (p. TN33)
aquifer underground rock layer so rich in water that water actually flows through it (pp. 51, 465)
archipelago group of islands (pp. 213, 353, 695)
atoll low-lying, ring-shaped island that surrounds a lagoon (pp. 662, 768)
atmosphere layer of air surrounding the earth (p. 30)
autobahn superhighway (p. 307)
autonomy self-government (p. 593)
axis imaginary line that runs through the earth's center between the North and South poles (p. 31); *also* the horizontal (bottom) or vertical (side) line of measurement on a graph (p. 14)

bar graph graph in which vertical or horizontal bars represent quantities (p. 14)
basin low area surrounded by higher land (pp. 227, 564)
bauxite mineral used to make aluminum (pp. 215, 376, 414, 555)
bazaar marketplace (p. 462)
Bedouins nomadic desert peoples of Southwest Asia (p. 489)
bilingual referring to a country that has two official languages (pp. 158, 517)

See also the Geographic Dictionary on page 18.

birthrate number of children born each year for every 1,000 people (p. 85)
bituminous soft coal (p. TN40)
bluegrass country music with banjos and guitars (p. TN53)
blues rhythmic music sung in a mournful tone (p. TN53)
bluff steep cliff (p. TN9)
Boers name for the Dutch who were the first European settlers in South Africa (p. 610)
bog low swampy land (pp. 296, 365)
boomerang Australian weapon shaped like a bent wing that either strikes a target or curves and sails back to land on the ground near the person who threw it (p. 751)
bush rural areas of Australia (p. 752)

cabinet departments that perform duties for the executive branch (p. TN31)
cacao tropical tree whose seeds are used to make chocolate and cocoa (pp. 543, 766)
calligraphy art of beautiful writing (p. 684)
campesino Colombian farmer (p. 259)
canopy umbrella-like covering formed by the tops of trees in a rain forest (pp. 64, 208, 564)
cardinal directions basic directions on the earth: north, south, east, west (p. 11)
casbah older section of Algerian cities (p. 468)
cash crop product grown to be sold for export (pp. 258, 513)
cassava plant with roots that can be ground into flour to make bread or eaten in other ways (pp. 552, 584)
caste social class based on a person's ancestry (p. 648)
caudillo military ruler (p. 242)
channel body of water wider than a strait between two pieces of land (p. 42)
chart graphic way of presenting information clearly (p. 16)
circle graph round or pie-shaped graph showing how a whole is divided (p. 15)
city-state city and its surrounding countryside (p. 333)
civil case trial of a person or group charged with causing injury to another person or group (p. TN31)
civilizations highly developed cultures (p. 81)

civil war fight among different groups within a country (pp. 467, 490, 545)
clan group of people related to one another (pp. TN15, 517, 600, 698)
climate usual, predictable pattern of weather in an area over a long period of time (p. 54)
climograph combination bar and line graph giving information about temperature and precipitation (p. 15)
coalition government government in which two or more political parties work together to run a country (pp. 334, 649)
cold war period between the late 1940s and late 1980s when the United States and the Soviet Union competed for world influence without actually fighting each other (p. 427)
collection process in the water cycle during which streams and rivers carry water back to the oceans (p. 50)
colony overseas territory or settlement tied to a parent country (pp. 131, 156, 190, 215, 327)
commonwealth partly self-governing territory (p. 219)
communist state country whose government has strong control over the economy and society as a whole (pp. 216, 308, 367, 426, 675)
compass rose device drawn on maps to show the directions (p. 11)
compound group of houses surrounded by walls (p. 544)
condensation process in which air rises and cools, which makes the water vapor it holds change back into a liquid (p. 50)
conservation careful use of resources so they are not wasted (p. 96)
constitution plan of government (p. TN16)
constitutional monarchy government in which a king or queen is the official head of state, but elected officials run the government (pp. 293, 469, 491, 700)
consumer goods household products, clothing, and other goods people buy to use for themselves (pp. 382, 413, 676)
contiguous areas that are joined together inside a common boundary (p. 115)
continent massive land area (p. 35)
continental island island formed when chunks of land are split off from larger continents or when a piece of land that once linked an island to the mainland is eroded or covered by water (p. 765)
continental shelf plateau off each coast of a continent that lies under the ocean and stretches for several miles (p. 41)
contour line line connecting all points at the same elevation on a contour map (p. 12)
cooperative farm owned and operated by the government (p. 217)
copper belt large area of copper mines in northern Zambia (p. 618)
copra dried coconut meat, which is used to make margarine, soap, and other products (p. 776)
coral reef structure at or near the water's surface formed by the skeletons of small sea animals (pp. 119, 581, 747)
cordillera group of mountain ranges that run side by side (pp. 147, 255)
core center of the earth, formed of hot iron mixed with other metals (p. 35)
cottage industry home- or village-based industry in which family members supply their own equipment to make goods (p. 648)
crevasse deep crack in the Antarctic ice cap (p. 772)
criminal case trial of a person charged with breaking the law (p. TN31)
crop rotation varying what is planted in a field to avoid using up all the minerals in the soil (p. 97)
crust uppermost layer of the earth (p. 35)
cultural diffusion the process of spreading new knowledge and skills to other cultures (p. 81)
culture way of life of a group of people who share similar beliefs and customs (p. 77)
culture region area of the world that includes many different countries that all have cultural traits in common (p. 82)
currency form of money (p. 292)
current moving streams of water in the world's oceans, which affect the climate of land areas (p. 57)
cyclone intense storm system with heavy rain and high winds (pp. 623, 654)
czar name for emperor in Russia's past (p. 424)

death rate number of people out of every 1,000 who die in a year (p. 84)
deforestation widespread cutting of forests (pp. 97, 572, 624, 716)
delta area formed from soil deposited by a river at its mouth (pp. 42, 457, 516, 654, 719)
democracy form of government in which citizens choose the nation's leaders by voting for them (pp. 79, 131, 431)
desalinization process used to make seawater drinkable (pp. 95, 493)
desertification process by which grasslands change to desert (p. 548)
developed country country in which a great deal of manufacturing is carried out (pp. 94, 609)

developing country country that is working toward industrialization (p. 94)
devolution transfer of certain powers from the central government to regional governments (p. 293)
diagram drawing that shows steps in a process or parts of an object (p. 16)
dialect local form of a language that differs from the main language in pronunciation or the meaning of words (pp. 78, 327)
Diaspora collective name for scattered Jewish settlements around the world (p. 485)
dictator individual who takes control of a government and rules the country as he or she wishes (pp. 79, 568)
dictatorship government under the control of one all-powerful leader (pp. 465, 729)
dike high banks of soil built along rivers to control floods (p. 672)
dominion self-governing nation that accepts the British monarch as head of state (p. 157)
drought long period of extreme dryness and water shortages (pp. 56, 547, 597)
dry farming method in which the land is left unplanted every few years so that it can store moisture (p. 324)
dynasty line of rulers from the same family (pp. 680, 703)
dzong Buddhist center of prayer and study in Bhutan (p. 659)

earthquake violent and sudden movement of the earth's crust (p. 36)
economic system system that sets rules for how people decide what goods and services to produce and how they are exchanged (p. 80)
ecosystem place where the plants and animals are dependent upon one another and their surroundings for survival (p. 96)
eco-tourist person who travels to another country to view its natural wonders (pp. 209, 589)
elevation height above sea level (pp. 12, 40, 336, 517)
elevation profile cutaway diagram showing changes in elevation of land (p. 17)
El Niño combination of temperature, wind, and water effects in the Pacific Ocean that causes heavy rains in some areas and drought in others (p. 57)
embargo order that restricts or prohibits trade with another country (pp. 218, 498)
emigrate to move to another country (pp. 88, 349)
empire group of lands under one ruler (pp. 261, 687)
enclave small territory entirely surrounded by a larger territory (pp. 511, 612)
endangered species plant or animal under the threat of completely dying out (p. 594)
environment natural surroundings (p. 25)
equinox day when day and night are of equal length in both hemispheres (p. 32)
erg huge area of shifting sand dunes in the Sahara (p. 466)
erosion process of moving weathered material on the earth's surface (pp. 37, 97)
escarpment steep cliff between higher and lower land (pp. 228, 582, 608)
estancia ranch (p. 236)
ethnic cleansing forcing people from a different ethnic group to leave their homes (p. 383)
ethnic group people who share a common culture, language, or history (pp. 78, 133, 427)
evaporation process in which the sun's heat turns liquid water into water vapor (p. 49)
exclave small part of a country that is separated from the main part (p. 614)
executive branch part of governing body that enforces laws (p. TN29)
exile inability to live in one's own country because of political beliefs (p. 683)
export to trade goods to other countries (p. 92)

famine lack of food (pp. 85, 707)
fault crack in the earth's crust (pp. 37, 510, 382, 673)
favela slum area (p. 231)
federal republic government divided between national and state powers (pp. 131, 191, 309, 431)
fellahin farmers in Egypt who live in villages and work on small plots of land that they rent from landowners (p. 462)
fjord steep-sided valley cut into mountains by the action of glaciers (pp. 345, 755)
foothill low hill at the base of a mountain range (p. 261)
fossil fuel coal, oil, or natural gas (p. 127)
free enterprise system economic system in which people start and run businesses with limited government intervention (pp. 123, 430, 583)
free port place where goods can be loaded, stored, and shipped again without needing to pay any import taxes (p. 723)
free trade taking down trade barriers so that goods flow freely among countries (pp. 93, 128)

GLOSSARY

free trade zone area where people can buy goods from other countries without paying extra taxes (p. 218)

gaucho cowhand (p. 236)
geographic information systems (GIS) special software that helps geographers gather and use information about a place (pp. 10, 26)
geography the study of the earth in all its variety (p. 23)
geothermal energy electricity produced by natural underground sources of steam (pp. 356, 756)
geyser spring of water heated by molten rock inside the earth so that, from time to time, it shoots hot water into the air (pp. 356, 754)
glacier giant slow-moving sheets of ice (pp. 38, 50, 144)
Global Positioning System (GPS) group of satellites that travels around the earth, which can be used to locate exact places on the earth (p. 25)
globe spherical model of Earth (p. 4)
great circle route ship or airplane route following a great circle; the shortest distance between two points on the earth (p. 6)
greenhouse effect buildup of certain gases in the atmosphere that, like a greenhouse, hold more of the sun's warmth (p. 60)
grid system network of imaginary lines on the earth's surface, formed by the crisscrossing patterns of the lines of latitude and longitude (p. 6)
groundwater water that fills tiny cracks and holes in the rock layers below the earth's surface (p. 51)

H

habitat type of environment in which a particular animal species lives (p. 589)
hacienda large ranch (p. 190)
hajj religious journey to Makkah that Muslims are expected to make at least once during their lifetime if they are able to do so (p. 494)
harmattan dry, dusty wind that blows south from the Sahara (p. 541)
heavy industry manufactured goods such as machinery, mining equipment, and steel (pp. 350, 413)
hemisphere one-half of the globe; the Equator divides the earth into Northern and Southern Hemispheres; the Prime Meridian divides it into Eastern and Western Hemispheres (p. 5)
hieroglyphics form of writing that uses signs and symbols (pp. 189, 461)
high island Pacific island formed by volcanic activity (p. 768)
high-technology industry industry that produces computers and other kinds of electronic equipment (p. 685)
high veld flat, grass-covered plains on the interior plateau of South Africa (p. 608)
Holocaust systematic murder of more than 6 million European Jews by Adolf Hitler and his followers during World War II (pp. 308, 485)
home rule legal right to self-government (p. TN33)
human rights basic freedoms and rights that all people should enjoy (p. 683)
humid continental climate weather pattern characterized by long, cold, and snowy winters and short, hot summers (p. 66)
humid subtropical climate weather pattern characterized by hot, humid, rainy summers and short, mild winters (p. 67)
hurricane violent tropical storm with high winds and heavy rains (pp. 56, 185, 207)
hydroelectric power electricity generated by flowing water (pp. 242, 414, 565, 756)

iceberg chunk of a glacier that has broken away and floats free in the ocean (p. 773)
ice shelf layer of ice above water in Antarctica (p. 773)
immigrant person who moves to a new country to make a permanent home (pp. TN49, 132, 751)
import to buy goods from another country (p. 93)
industrialize to change an economy to rely more on manufacturing and less on farming (pp. 195, 425, 571)
inflation overall increase in the price of goods across the entire economy (p. 232)
infrastructure transportation and communication networks on which an economy depends (p. 309)
intensive cultivation growing crops on every available piece of land (p. 698)
intermediate direction any direction between the cardinal directions, such as southeast or northwest (p. 11)
invest to put money into a business (p. 676)
irrigation farming practice followed in dry areas to collect water and bring it to crops (p. 97)
Islamic republic government run by Muslim religious leaders (p. 499)

island body of land smaller than a continent and surrounded by water (p. 40)
isthmus narrow piece of land that connects two larger pieces of land (pp. 40, 205)

judicial branch part of governing body that interprets laws (p. TN31)
jute plant fiber used for making rope, burlap bags, and carpet backing (p. 647)

kibbutz settlement in Israel where the people share property and produce goods (p. 483)
krill tiny, shrimplike animal that lives in the waters off Antarctica and is the food for many other creatures (p. 774)

lagoon shallow pool of water surrounded by reefs, sandbars, or atolls (p. 662)
land bridge narrow strip of land that joins two larger landmasses (p. 181)
landfill area where trash companies dump the waste they collect (p. 127)
landform individual features of the land (p. 24)
landlocked country with no land bordering a sea or an ocean (pp. 247, 266, 375, 511)
La Niña pattern of unusual weather in the Pacific Ocean that has the opposite effects of El Niño (p. 57)
latitude location north or south of the Equator, measured by imaginary lines (parallels) numbered in degrees north or south (pp. 5, 184)
leap year year that has an extra day; occurs every fourth year (p. 31)
legislative branch part of governing body that makes laws (p. TN29)
life expectancy the number of years that an average person is expected to live (p. 431)
light industry making of such goods as clothing, shoes, furniture, and household products (p. 413)
line graph graph in which one or more lines represent changing quantities over time (p. 14)
literacy rate percentage of people who can read and write (p. 208)
llanos grassy plains (pp. 242, 256)
local wind pattern of wind caused by landforms in a particular area (p. 58)
loch narrow bay that reaches far inland (p. 290)
loess fertile, yellow-gray soil deposited by wind and water (p. 672)
longitude location east or west of the Prime Meridian, measured by imaginary lines (meridians) numbered in degrees east or west (p. 6)
low island Pacific island formed of coral and having little vegetation (p. 768)

magma hot melted rock that sometimes flows to the earth's surface in a volcanic eruption (p. 35)
mainland the major part of a country (p. 336)
mangrove tropical tree with roots that extend both above and beneath the water (p. 541)
mantle rock layer about 1,800 miles (2,897 km) thick between the core and the crust (p. 35)
manuka small shrub of New Zealand (p. 754)
map key code that explains the lines, symbols, and colors used on a map (p. 10)
maquiladora factory that assembles parts made in other countries (p. 185)
marine west coast climate weather pattern characterized by rainy and mild winters and cool summers (p. 65)
marsupial mammal that carries its young in a pouch (p. 749)
Mediterranean climate weather pattern characterized by mild, rainy winters and hot, dry summers (p. 66)
megalopolis pattern of heavy urban settlement over a large area (pp. 116, 700)
mestizo person with mixed Spanish and Native American or African background (pp. 190, 258)
migrant worker person who travels from place to place when extra help is needed to plant or harvest crops (p. 196)
migrate to move from one place to another (p. 480)
monarchy form of government in which a king or queen inherits the right to rule a country (p. 79)
monotheism belief in one God (p. 486)
monsoon seasonal wind that blows over a continent for months at a time (pp. 56, 646, 705, 715)
moor treeless, windy highland area with damp ground (pp. 290, 354)
moshav settlement in Israel where people share property but also own some private property (p. 484)
mosque place of worship for followers of Islam (pp. 384, 462, 479)

GLOSSARY

multilingual able to speak several languages (p. 316)
multinational firm that does business in several countries (p. 316)
mural wall painting (p. 189)

nationalism desire of a territory or colony to become an independent nation (p. 351)
national park area set aside to protect wilderness and wildlife and for recreation (p. 135)
nature preserve protected areas for plants and animals (pp. 378, 581)
natural resource product of the earth that people use to meet their needs (p. 90)
navigable describes a body of water wide and deep enough to allow the passage of ships (pp. 126, 260, 301, 324)
neutrality refusing to take sides in disagreements and wars between countries (p. 310)
newsprint type of paper used for printing newspapers (p. 153)
nomads people who move from place to place with herds of animals (pp. 377, 516, 687)
nonrenewable resource natural resource such as metals or minerals that cannot be replaced (p. 91)
nuclear energy power made by creating a controlled atomic reaction (p. 431)

oasis green area in a desert fed by underground water (pp. 459, 493, 518)
oil shale rock that contains oil (p. 372)
orbit path that a body in the solar system travels around the sun (p. 29)
outback inland regions of Australia (p. 748)
overgraze to allow animals to strip areas so bare that plants cannot grow back (p. 547)
ozone type of oxygen that forms a layer in the atmosphere and protects all living things on the earth from certain harmful rays of the sun (p. 775)

parliamentary democracy government in which voters elect representatives to a lawmaking body, which chooses a prime minister to head the government (pp. 157, 210, 292)
parliamentary republic see *parliamentary democracy* (p. 327)
peat wet ground with decaying plants that can be dried and used for fuel (pp. 296, 372)
peninsula piece of land with water on three sides (pp. 40, 146, 182, 408)
permafrost permanently frozen lower layers of soil in the tundra and subarctic regions (pp. 68, 410)
pesticides powerful chemicals that kill crop-destroying insects (pp. 96, 648)
phosphate mineral salt used in fertilizers (pp. 461, 555, 769)
pictograph graph in which small symbols represent quantities (p. 15)
pidgin language language formed by combining elements of several different languages (p. 767)
plain low-lying stretch of flat or gently rolling land (p. 40)
plantain kind of banana (p. 592)
plantation large farm that grows a single crop for sale (pp. 186, 207)
plateau flat land with higher elevation than a plain (pp. 40, 324)
plate huge slab of rock that makes up the earth's crust (pp. 599, 726)
plate tectonics theory that the earth's crust is not an unbroken shell but consists of plates, or huge slabs of rock, that move (p. 35)
plaza public square (p. 193)
poaching illegal hunting of protected animals (p. 581)
polder area of land reclaimed from the sea (p. 315)
pope head of the Roman Catholic Church (pp. 334, 369)
population density average number of people living in a square mile or square kilometer (p. 86)
potash type of mineral salt that is often used in fertilizers (p. 388)
prairie rolling, inland grassy area with very fertile soil (p. 146)
precipitation water that falls back to the earth as rain, snow, sleet, or hail (p. 50)
prime minister official who heads the government in a parliamentary democracy (p. 157)
privatize to transfer the ownership of factories from the government to individual citizens (p. 380)
projection in mapmaking, a way of drawing the round Earth on a flat surface (p. 7)
province regional political division similar to states (p. 143)

quota number limit on how many items of a particular product can be imported from a particular country (p. 93)

rain forest dense forest that receives high amounts of rain each year (p. 61)
rain shadow dry area on the inland side of coastal mountains (p. 59)
recycling reusing materials instead of throwing them out (p. 128)
refugee person who flees to another country to escape persecution or disaster (pp. 88, 383, 568, 595)
region area that shares common characteristics (p. 25)
relief differences in height in a landscape; how flat or rugged the surface is (p. 12)
Renaissance period of great achievement in art and learning that began in Italy in the 1300s and spread throughout Europe (p. 333)
renewable resource natural resource that cannot be used up or can fairly quickly be replaced naturally or grown again (p. 91)
republic strong national government headed by elected leaders (pp. 210, 233, 258, 303, 369, 461)
reunification bringing together the two parts of Germany under one government (p. 309)
revival religious meeting (p. TN50)
revolution one complete orbit around the sun (p. 31)
ridge narrow range of hills (p. TN8)
rural area in the countryside (pp. 134, 433)

saga long story (p. 357)
samurai powerful land-owning warriors in Japan (p. 699)
sauna wooden room heated by water sizzling on hot stones (p. 351)
savanna broad grassland in the tropics with few trees (pp. 64, 541, 563)
scale relationship between distance on a map and actual distance on the earth (p. 11)
scale bar on a map, a divided line showing the map scale, usually in miles or kilometers (p. 11)
secede to withdraw from a national government (pp. 131, 154, TN19)
secular nonreligious (pp. 467, 480)
selva tropical rain forests in Brazil (p. 228)
serf farm laborer who could be bought and sold along with the land (p. 425)
service industry business that provides services to people instead of producing goods (pp. 124, 150, 195, TN42)
shah title given to kings who ruled Iran (p. 499)
shogun military leaders in Japan (p. 699)
silt small particles of rich soil (p. 458)
sirocco hot, dry winds that blow across Italy from North Africa (p. 331)
sisal plant fiber used to make rope and twine (p. 588)
skerry rocky island (p. 349)
slash-and-burn farming method of clearing land for planting by cutting and burning forest (p. 624)
smog thick haze of fog and chemicals (p. 198)
socialism economic system in which many businesses are owned and run by the government (p. 717)
solar system Earth, eight other planets, and thousands of smaller bodies that all revolve around the sun (p. 29)
sodium nitrate chemical used in fertilizer and explosives (p. 269)
sorghum tall grass with seeds that are used as grain and to make syrup (p. 619)
spa resort that has hot mineral springs that people bathe in to regain their health (p. 378)
station cattle or sheep ranch in Australia (p. 748)
steppe partly dry grassland often found on the edges of a desert (pp. 69, 386, 406, 515, 570, 687)
strait narrow body of water between two pieces of land (pp. 42, 721)
strip mining removing coal by stripping away the overlying earth (p. TN40)
subarctic climate weather pattern characterized by severely cold and bitter winters and short, cool summers (p. 67)
subcontinent large landmass that is part of another continent but distinct from it (p. 645)
subsistence farm small plot where a farmer grows only enough food to feed his own family (pp. 186, 207, 261, 542)
suburb smaller community that surrounds a city (pp. 134, 340, 432)
summer solstice day with the most hours of sunlight and the fewest hours of darkness (p. 32)

taiga huge forests of evergreen trees that grow in subarctic regions (p. 410)
tannin substance used in processing leather (p. 236)
tariff tax added to the value of goods that are imported (p. 93)
terraced field strips of land cut out of a hillside like stair steps so the land can hold water and be used for farming (pp. 678, 724)
timberline elevation along mountains above which no trees grow (p. 70)
tornado funnel-shaped windstorm that sometimes forms during a severe thunderstorm (p. 56)
townships crowded neighborhoods outside cities in South Africa where most nonwhites live (p. 611)
trench valley in the ocean floor (p. 41)
tributary small river that flows into a larger river (pp. TN10, 653)
tropics low-latitude region between the Tropic of Cancer and the Tropic of Capricorn (p. 55)
trust territory area temporarily placed under control of another nation (p. 769)
tsetse fly insect whose bite can kill cattle or humans with a deadly disease called sleeping sickness (p. 571)
tsunami huge sea wave caused by an earthquake on the ocean floor (pp. 36, 695)
tundra vast rolling treeless plain in high latitude climates in which only the top few inches of ground thaw in summer (pp. 68, 146, 410)
tungsten metal used in electrical equipment (p. 677)
typhoon name for hurricane in Asia (pp. 56, 673, 769)

urban area in the city (pp. 134, 432)
urbanization movement to cities (p. 87)

vaquero cowhand (p. 185)
veto to disapprove a bill (p. TN30)

wadi dry riverbed filled by rainwater from rare downpours (p. 493)
water cycle process in which water moves from the oceans to the air to the ground and finally back to the oceans (p. 49)
watershed region drained by a river (p. 594)
water vapor water in the form of gas (p. 49)
weather unpredictable changes in the air that take place over a short period of time (p. 53)
weathering process that breaks surface rocks into boulders, gravel, sand, and soil (p. 37)
welfare state country that uses tax money to support people who are sick, needy, jobless, or retired (pp. 246, 349)
winter solstice day with the fewest hours of sunlight and the most hours of darkness (p. 32)

yurt large circle-shaped tent made of animal skins that can be packed up and moved from place to place (p. 688)

SPANISH GLOSSARY*

absolute location/ubicación absoluta posición exacta de un lugar en la superficie de la Tierra (pág. 6)
acid rain/lluvia ácida lluvia que contiene grandes cantidades de contaminantes químicos (págs. 97, 127, 154, 368)
adobe/adobe ladrillos secados al Sol (pág. 193)
alluvial plain/llanura aluvial área creada por el suelo fértil que se acumula después de las inundaciones causadas por los ríos (págs. TN9, 497)
altiplano/altiplano meseta grande y muy elevada; también se llama altiplanicie (pág. 260)
altitude/altitud altura sobre el nivel del mar (págs. 184, 242, 583)
amendment/enmienda cambio a la constitución (pág. TN29)
anthracite/antracita tipo de carbón mineral muy duro (pág. 705)
apartheid/apartheid sistema de leyes que separaba los grupos raciales y étnicos y limitaba los derechos de la población negra (pág. 611)
appellate court/corte de apelaciones tipo de tribunal que falla sobre las decisiones de las cortes inferiores (pág. TN33)
aquifer/manto acuífero capa de rocas subterránea en que el agua es tan abundante que corre entre las rocas (págs. 51, 465)
archipelago/archipiélago grupo de islas (págs. 213, 353, 695)
atoll/atolón isla de muy poca elevación que se forma alrededor de una laguna en la forma de un anillo (págs. 662, 768)
atmosphere/atmósfera capa de aire que rodea la Tierra (pág. 30)
autobahn/autobahn autopista muy rápida (pág. 307)
autonomy/autonomía gobernarse por sí mismo (pág. 593)
axis/eje terrestre línea imaginaria que atraviesa el centro de la Tierra entre el Polo Norte y el Polo Sur (pág. 31); también la línea vertical (del lado) u horizontal (de abajo) de una gráfica que se usa para medir (pág. 14)

bar graph/gráfica de barras gráfica en que franjas verticales u horizontales representan cantidades (pág. 14)
basin/cuenca área baja rodeada de tierras más elevadas (págs. 227, 564)
bauxite/bauxita mineral que se usa para hacer aluminio (págs. 215, 376, 414, 555)
bazaar/bazar mercado (pág. 462)
Bedouins/beduinos gente nomádica del desierto del sudoeste de Asia (pág. 489)
bilingual/bilingüe se refiere a un país que tiene dos idiomas oficiales (págs. 158, 517)
birthrate/índice de natalidad número de niños que nace cada año por cada mil personas (pág. 85)
bituminous/bituminoso tipo de carbón suave (pág. TN40)
bluegrass/bluegrass tipo de música "country" que se toca con banjos y guitarras, llamada así por la hierba azulosa de su región de origen (pág. TN53)
blues/blues música rítmica que se canta con tristeza (pág. TN53)
bluff/acantilado peñasco muy empinado (pág. TN9)
Boers/bóers los holandeses que fueron los primeros colonos en Sudáfrica (pág. 610)
bog/ciénaga tierra baja y pantanosa (págs. 296, 365)
boomerang/bumerán arma australiana con forma de ala que se lanza para que golpee un objetivo o de la vuelta y caiga a los pies de la persona que la lanzó (pág. 751)
bush/campo áreas rurales de Australia (pág. 752)

cabinet/gabinete ministerio que desempeña ciertos deberes para la rama ejecutiva (pág. TN31)
cacao/cacao árbol tropical cuyas semillas se usan para hacer chocolate y cocoa (págs. 543, 766)
calligraphy/caligrafía el arte de escribir con letra muy bella (pág. 684)
campesino/campesino agricultor (pág. 259)
canopy/bóveda techo formado por las copas de los árboles en los bosques húmedos (págs. 64, 208, 564)
cardinal directions/puntos cardinales cuatro direcciones básicas en la Tierra: norte, sur, este, oeste (pág. 11)
casbah/casbah la sección antigua de las ciudades de Argelia; también se llama *alcazaba* (pág. 468)
cash crop/cultivo comercial producto que se cultiva para exportación (págs. 258, 513)
cassava/yuca planta con raíces que se pueden convertir en harina para hacer pan o que se pueden cocinar de otras formas (págs. 552, 584)

**Véase también* el Diccionario Geográfico en la página 18.

caste/casta clase social basada en la ascendencia de una persona (pág. 648)
caudillo/caudillo gobernante militar (pág. 242)
channel/canal una masa de agua entre dos tierras que tiene más anchura que un estrecho (pág. 42)
chart/cuadro manera gráfica de presentar información con claridad (pág. 16)
circle graph/gráfica de círculo gráfica redonda que muestra como un todo es dividido (pág. 15)
city-state/ciudad estado ciudad junto con las tierras que la rodean (pág. 333)
civil case/caso civil pleito contra una persona o grupo acusado de causarle daño a otra persona o grupo (pág. TN31)
civilizations/civilizaciones culturas altamente desarrolladas (pág. 81)
civil war/guerra civil pelea entre distintos grupos dentro de un país (págs. 467, 490, 545)
clan/clan grupo de personas que están emparentadas (págs. TN15, 517, 600, 698)
climate/clima el patrón que sigue el estado del tiempo en un área durante muchos años (pág. 54)
climograph/gráfica de clima gráfica que combina barras y líneas para dar información sobre la temperatura y la precipitación (pág. 15)
coalition government/gobierno por coalición gobierno en que dos o más partidos trabajan juntos para dirigir un país (págs. 334, 649)
cold war/guerra fría período entre los fines de los 1940 y los fines de los 1980 en que los Estados Unidos y la Unión Soviética compitieron por tener influencia mundial sin pelear uno contra el otro (pág. 427)
collection/drenaje proceso durante el ciclo hidrológico en que los ríos llevan el agua de regreso a los océanos (pág. 50)
colony/colonia territorio o poblado con lazos a un país extranjero (págs. 131, 156, 190, 215, 327)
commonwealth/estado libre asociado territorio que en parte se gobierna por sí solo (pág. 219)
communist state/estado comunista país cuyo gobierno mantiene mucho control sobre la economía y la sociedad en su totalidad (págs. 216, 308, 367, 426, 675)
compass rose/rosa náutica dibujo en los mapas que muestra las direcciones; también se llama rosa de los vientos (pág. 11)
compound/complejo residencial grupo de viviendas rodeada por una muralla (pág. 544)
condensation/condensación proceso en que el aire sube y se enfría, lo cual hace que el vapor de agua que contiene se convierta de nuevo en líquido (pág. 50)
conservation/conservación uso juicioso de los recursos para no malgastarlos (pág. 96)
constitution/constitución plan para un gobierno (pág. TN16)
constitutional monarchy/monarquía constitucional gobierno en que un rey o reina es el jefe de estado oficial pero los gobernantes son elegidos (págs. 293, 469, 491, 700)
consumer goods/bienes de consumo productos para la casa, ropa y otras cosas que la gente compra para su uso personal (págs. 382, 413, 676)
contiguous/contiguas áreas adyacentes dentro de la misma frontera (pág. 115)
continent/continente masa de tierra inmensa (pág. 35)
continental island/isla continental isla formada cuando un pedazo de tierra se separa de un continente o cuando la erosión hace que el agua cubra la parte del continente que antes unía la isla a éste (pág. 765)
continental shelf/plataforma continental meseta formada por parte de un continente que se extiende por varias millas debajo del mar (pág. 41)
contour line/curva de nivel línea que conecta todos los puntos a la misma elevación en un mapa de relieve (pág. 12)
cooperative/cooperativa granja que es propiedad y es operada por el gobierno (pág. 217)
copper belt/cinturón de cobre área extensa de minas de cobre en el norte de Zambia (pág. 618)
copra/copra pulpa seca del coco que se usa para hacer margarina, jabón y otros productos (pág. 776)
coral reef/arrecife coralino estructura formada al nivel del mar o cerca de éste por los esqueletos de pequeños animales marinos (págs. 119, 581, 747)
cordillera/cordillera grupo de cadenas paralelas de montañas (págs. 147, 255)
core/núcleo centro de la Tierra, que está formado de hierro caliente y otros metales (pág. 35)
cottage industry/industria familiar industria basada en una casa o aldea en que los miembros de la familia usan sus propias herramientas para hacer productos (pág. 648)
crevasse/grieta rajadura profunda en el casquete de hielo de la Antártida (pág. 772)
criminal case/caso criminal proceso penal de una persona acusada de violar la ley (pág. TN31)
crop rotation/rotación de cultivos variar lo que se siembra en un terreno para no agotar todos los minerales que tiene el suelo (pág. 97)
crust/corteza capa de afuera de la Tierra (pág. 35)
cultural diffusion/difusión cultural el proceso de esparcir nuevos conocimientos y habilidades a otras culturas (pág. 81)
culture/cultura modo de vida de un grupo de personas que comparten creencias y costumbres similares (pág. 77)
culture region/región cultural área del mundo que incluye muchos países que tienen los mismos rasgos culturales (pág. 82)
currency/moneda tipo de dinero (pág. 292)
current/corriente movimiento de las aguas del mar que afecta el clima de las masas de tierra (pág. 57)
cyclone/ciclón tormenta violenta con vientos muy fuertes y mucha lluvia (págs. 623, 654)
czar/zar título de los antiguos emperadores rusos (pág. 424)

death rate/índice de mortalidad número de personas de cada mil que mueren en un año (pág. 84)
deforestation/deforestación la extensa destrucción de los bosques (págs. 97, 572, 624, 716)
delta/delta área formada por el suelo que deposita un río en su desembocadura (págs. 42, 457, 516, 654, 719)
democracy/democracia tipo de gobierno en que los ciudadanos seleccionan los líderes de la nación por medio del voto (págs. 79, 131, 431)
desalinization/desalinización proceso de hacer el agua de mar potable (págs. 95, 493)
desertification/desertización proceso por el cual los pastos se convierten en desiertos (pág. 548)
developed country/país desarrollado país donde hay mucha manufactura de productos (págs. 94, 609)
developing country/país en vías de desarrollo país que está industrializándose (pág. 94)
devolution/devolución transferencia de ciertos poderes del gobierno central a los gobiernos regionales (pág. 293)
diagram/diagrama dibujo que muestra los pasos en un proceso o las partes de un objeto (pág. 16)
dialect/dialecto forma local de un idioma que se diferencia del idioma normal por su pronunciación o por el sentido de algunas palabras (págs. 78, 327)
Diaspora/diáspora nombre dado a los poblados judíos alrededor del mundo (pág. 485)
dictator/dictador individuo que toma control de un país y lo gobierna como quiere (págs. 79, 568)
dictatorship/dictadura gobierno bajo el control de un líder que tiene todo el poder (págs. 465, 729)
dike/dique muros de tierra muy altos construidos a lo largo de los ríos para controlar las inundaciones (pág. 672)
dominion/dominio naciones que se gobiernan por sí solas que aceptan al monarca británico como jefe de estado (pág. 157)
drought/sequía largos períodos de sequedad y de escasez de agua (págs. 56, 547, 597)
dry farming/agricultura en seco método de cultivar en que la tierra se deja sin sembrar cada varios años para que almacene humedad (pág. 324)
dynasty/dinastía serie de gobernantes de la misma familia (págs. 680, 703)
dzong/ dzong centro budista en Bután para rezar y estudiar (pág. 659)

earthquake/terremoto movimiento violento e inesperado de la corteza de la Tierra (pág. 36)
economic system/sistema económico sistema que establece reglas que determinan cómo las personas deciden cuáles bienes y servicios van a producir y cómo los van a intercambiar (pág. 80)
ecosystem/ecosistema lugar en el cual las plantas y animales dependen unos de otros y de sus alrededores para sobrevivir (pág. 96)
eco-tourist/ecoturista persona que viaja a otro país para ver sus bellezas naturales (págs. 209, 589)
elevation/elevación altura por encima del nivel del mar (págs. 12, 40, 336, 517)
elevation profile/perfil de elevaciones diagrama que muestra los cambios en la elevación de la tierra como si se hubiera hecho un corte vertical del área (pág. 17)
El Niño/El Niño combinación de la temperatura, los vientos y los efectos del agua en el océano Pacífico que causa lluvias fuertes en algunas áreas y sequía en otras (pág. 57)
embargo/embargo orden que limita o prohibe el comercio con otro país (págs. 218, 498)
emigrate/emigrar mudarse a otro país (págs. 88, 349)
empire/imperio grupo de países bajo un gobernante (págs. 261, 687)
enclave/enclave territorio pequeño totalmente rodeado por un territorio más grande (págs. 511, 612)
endangered species/especie en vías de extinción planta o animal que está en peligro de desaparecer completamente (pág. 594)
environment/medio ambiente alrededores naturales (pág. 25)
equinox/equinoccio día en que el día y la noche tienen la misa duración en los dos hemisferios (pág. 32)
erg/ergio inmensas áreas en el Sahara en que se mueven las dunas de arena (pág. 466)
erosion/erosión proceso de mover los materiales desgastados en la superficie de la Tierra (págs. 37, 97)
escarpment/escarpa acantilado empinado entre una área baja y una alta (págs. 228, 582, 608)
***estancia*/estancia** rancho (pág. 236)
ethnic cleansing/limpieza étnica forzar a personas de un grupo étnico distinto a abandonar el lugar donde viven (pág. 383)
ethnic group/grupo étnico personas que comparten una cultura, idioma o historia en común (págs. 78, 133, 427)
evaporation/evaporación proceso mediante el cual el calor del sol convierte el agua líquida en vapor de agua (pág. 49)
exclave/territorio externo parte pequeña de un país que está separada de la parte principal (pág. 614)
executive branch/rama ejecutiva parte del gobierno que hace que se cumplan las leyes (pág. TN29)
exile/exilio tener que vivir fuera de su país nativo por causa de sus creencias políticas (pág. 683)

export/exportar comerciar y mandar bienes a otros países (pág. 92)

famine/hambruna falta de alimentos (págs. 85, 707)
fault/falla fractura en la corteza de la Tierra (págs. 37, 510, 582, 673)
favela/favela barrio pobre y deteriorado (pág. 231)
federal republic/república federal nación en que el poder está dividido entre el gobierno nacional y el de los estados (págs. 131, 191, 309, 431)
fellahin/felás granjeros en Egipto que viven en aldeas y cultivan pequeños terrenos que arriendan de un hacendado (pág. 462)
fjord/fiordo valle creado por el movimiento de glaciares en las montañas que deja laderas sumamente empinadas (págs. 345, 755)
foothill/estribaciones colinas bajas al pie de una cadena de montañas (pág. 261)
fossil fuel/combustibles fósiles carbón, petróleo o gas natural (pág. 127)
free enterprise system/sistema de libre empresa sistema económico en que la gente empieza y administra negocios con poca intervención del gobierno (págs. 123, 430, 583)
free port/puerto libre lugar donde las mercancías se pueden cargar, almacenar y embarcar de nuevo sin tener que pagar derechos de importación (pág. 723)
free trade/libre comercio eliminar las barreras al comercio para que se puedan mover productos libremente entre países (págs. 93, 128)
free trade zone/zona de cambio libre área donde la gente puede comprar bienes de otros países sin pagar impuestos adicionales (pág. 218)

gaucho/gaucho vaquero (pág. 236)
geographic information systems (GIS)/ sistemas de información geográfica (SIG) programas de computadoras especiales que ayudan a los geógrafos a obtener y usar la información geográfica sobre un lugar (págs. 10, 26)
geography/geografía el estudio de la Tierra y de toda su variedad (pág. 23)
geothermal energy/energía geotérmica electricidad producida por fuentes de vapor subterráneas naturales (págs. 356, 756)
geyser/géiser manantial de agua calentado por rocas fundidas dentro de la Tierra que, de vez en cuando, arroja agua caliente al aire (págs. 356, 754)
glacier/glaciar capa de hielo inmensa que se mueve muy lentamente (págs. 38, 50, 144)
Global Positioning System (GPS)/Sistema global de posición (GPS) grupo de satélites que le dan la vuelta a la Tierra y se usan para localizar lugares exactos en la Tierra (pág. 25)
globe/globo terráqueo modelo esférico de la Tierra (pág. 4)
great circle route/línea de rumbo ruta que sigue un círculo máximo; usada por aviones y barcos porque es la distancia más corta entre dos puntos en la Tierra (pág. 6)
greenhouse effect/efecto invernadero la acumulación de ciertos gases en la atmósfera que mantienen más del calor del Sol, como hace un invernadero (pág. 60)
grid system/sistema de coordenadas geográficas red de líneas imaginarias en la superficie de la Tierra, formada por las líneas de latitud y longitud que se cruzan (pág. 6)
groundwater/agua subterránea agua que llena las rajaduras y hoyos en las capas de roca debajo de la superficie de la Tierra (pág. 51)

habitat/hábitat tipo de ambiente en que vive una especie animal en particular (pág. 589)
hacienda/hacienda un rancho grande (pág. 190)
hajj/*hajj* viaje religioso a La Meca que todo musulmán debe hacer por lo menos una vez en la vida si puede (pág. 494)
harmattan/harmattan viento seco y lleno de polvo que sopla hacia el sur desde el Sahara (pág. 541)
heavy industry/industria pesada manufactura de productos como maquinaria, equipo de minería y acero (págs. 350, 413)
hemisphere/hemisferio una mitad del globo terráqueo; el ecuador divide la Tierra en los hemisferios norte y sur; el primer meridiano la divide en hemisferios este y oeste (pág. 5)
hieroglyphics/jeroglíficos forma de escribir que usa signos y símbolos (págs. 189, 461)
high island/isla oceánica isla del Pacífico formada por actividad volcánica (págs. 768)
high-technology industry/industria de alta tecnología industria que produce computadoras y otras clases de equipo electrónico (pág. 685)
high veld/veld pastos llanos de la meseta interior de Sudáfrica (pág. 608)
Holocaust/Holocausto la matanza sistemática de más de 6 millones de judíos europeos por Adolfo Hitler y sus seguidores durante la Segunda Guerra Mundial (págs. 308, 485)
home rule/autogobierno derecho legal a tener un gobierno propio (pág. TN33)
human rights/derechos humanos libertades y derechos básicos que todas las personas deben disfrutar (pág. 683)

humid continental climate/clima húmedo continental patrón del estado del tiempo con inviernos largos, fríos y con mucha nieve y veranos cortos y calurosos (pág. 66)
humid subtropical climate/clima húmedo subtropical patrón del estado del tiempo con veranos calurosos, húmedos y lluviosos e inviernos cortos y templados (pág. 67)
hurricane/huracán tormenta tropical violenta con vientos y lluvias fuertes (págs. 56, 185, 207)
hydroelectric power/energía hidroeléctrica electricidad generada por una corriente de agua (págs. 242, 414, 565, 756)

iceberg/iceberg pedazo de un glaciar que se ha desprendido y flota libremente en los océanos (pág. 773)
ice shelf/plataforma de hielo capa de hielo sobre el mar en la Antártida (pág. 773)
immigrant/inmigrante persona que se muda permanentemente a un país nuevo (págs. TN49, 132, 751)
import/importar comprar productos de otro país (pág. 93)
industrialize/industrializar cambiar una economía de manera que dependa más de la manufactura que de la agricultura (págs. 195, 425, 571)
inflation/inflación aumento en el precio de productos en toda la economía (pág. 232)
infrastructure/infraestructura redes de transporte y comunicación de las cuales depende una economía (pág. 309)
intensive cultivation/cultivo intensivo labrar toda la tierra posible (pág. 698)
intermediate direction/puntos intermedios cualquier dirección entre los puntos cardinales, como sudeste o noroeste (pág. 11)
invest/invertir poner dinero en un negocio (pág. 676)
irrigation/irrigación práctica agrícola en áreas secas de colectar agua y llevarla a los cultivos (pág. 97)
Islamic republic/república islámica gobierno dirigido por líderes musulmanes (pág. 499)
island/isla masa de tierra más pequeña que un continente, rodeada de agua (pág. 40)
isthmus/istmo lengua de tierra que conecta a dos masas de tierra más grandes (págs. 40, 205)

judicial branch/rama judicial parte del gobierno que interpreta las leyes (pág. TN31)
jute/yute fibras de una planta que se usan para hacer soga, sacos y el revés de alfombras (pág. 647)

kibbutz/kibutz poblado en Israel donde las personas comparten la propiedad y producen bienes (pág. 483)
krill/krill animales diminutos parecidos a los camarones que viven en las aguas alrededor de la Antártida y sirven de alimento para muchos otros animales (pág. 774)

lagoon/laguna masa de agua poco profunda rodeada por arrecifes, bancos de arena o un atolón (pág. 662)
land bridge/puente de tierra franja de tierra que une a dos masas de tierra mayores (pág. 181)
landfill/vertedero de basura lugar donde las compañías que recogen la basura botan los residuos que colectan (pág. 127)
landform/accidente geográfico característica particular de la tierra (pág. 24)
landlocked/rodeado de tierra país que no tiene tierras bordeadas por un mar u océano (págs. 247, 266, 375, 511)
La Niña/La Niña patrón infrecuente en el estado del tiempo del océano Pacífico que tiene los efectos contrarios a los de El Niño (pág. 57)
latitude/latitud posición al norte o al sur del ecuador, medida por medio de líneas imaginarias (paralelos) numeradas con grados norte o sur (págs. 5, 184)
leap year/año bisiesto año que tiene un día adicional; cada cuarto año (pág. 31)
legislative branch/rama legislativa parte del gobierno que hace las leyes (pág. TN29)
life expectancy/expectativas de vida el número de años que se espera que viva la persona promedio (pág. 431)
light industry/industria ligera fabricación de productos como muebles, ropa, zapatos y artículos para el hogar (pág. 413)
line graph/gráfica lineal gráfica en que una o varias líneas representan cambios de cantidad a través del tiempo (pág. 14)
literacy rate/índice de alfabetización porcentaje de personas que saben leer y escribir (pág. 208)
llanos/llanos planicie cubierta de hierba (págs. 242, 256)
local wind/vientos locales patrones en los vientos causados por los accidentes geográficos de un área en particular (pág. 58)
loch/rías bahías estrechas que llegan hasta muy dentro de la tierra (pág. 290)
loess/loes suelo amarillento y fértil depositado por el viento y el agua (pág. 672)

SPANISH GLOSSARY

longitude/longitud posición al este o el oeste del primer meridiano, medida por medio de líneas imaginarias (meridianos) numeradas con grados este u oeste (pág. 6)

low island/isla coralina isla del Pacífico formada por coral que tiene poca vegetación (pág. 768)

magma/magma roca caliente y fundida que a veces fluye hasta la superficie de la Tierra en erupciones volcánicas (pág. 35)

mainland/territorio continental la parte principal de un país (pág. 336)

mangrove/mangle árbol tropical con raíces que se extienden por encima y por debajo del agua (pág. 541)

mantle/manto capa de rocas de 1,800 millas (2,897 km.) de grueso entre el núcleo y la corteza (pág. 35)

manuka/manuka pequeño arbusto de Nueva Zelanda (pág. 754)

map key/leyenda explicación de las líneas, símbolos y colores usados en un mapa; también se llama clave del mapa (pág. 10)

***maquiladora/*maquiladora** fábrica donde se ensamblan piezas hechas en otros países (pág. 185)

marine west coast climate/clima húmedo marítimo patrón del estado del tiempo con inviernos lluviosos y templados y veranos frescos (pág. 65)

marsupial/marsupial mamífero que lleva a sus crías en una bolsa (pág. 749)

Mediterranean climate/clima húmedo mediterráneo patrón del estado del tiempo con inviernos lluviosos y templados y veranos calurosos y secos (pág. 66)

megalopolis/megalópolis área extensa de mucha urbanización (págs. 116, 700)

mestizo/mestizo persona cuya ascendencia incluye indios americanos o africanos y españoles (págs. 190, 258)

migrant worker/trabajador itinerante persona que viaja a distintos lugares donde hacen falta trabajadores para sembrar y cosechar cultivos (pág. 196)

migrate/migrar mudarse de un lugar a otro (pág. 480)

monarchy/monarquía tipo de gobierno en que un rey o reina hereda el derecho de gobernar un país (pág. 79)

monotheism/monoteísmo creencia en un solo Dios (pág. 486)

monsoon/monzón vientos que soplan en un continente por varios meses seguidos en ciertas estaciones del año (págs. 56, 646, 705, 715)

moor/páramo área elevada y sin árboles pero con mucho viento y tierra húmeda (págs. 290, 354)

moshav/*moshav* poblados en Israel en que la gente comparte alguna propiedad pero también tiene propiedad privada (pág. 484)

mosque/mezquita edificio de devoción islámico (págs. 384, 462, 479)

multilingual/multilingüe que puede hablar varios idiomas (pág. 316)

multinational/multinacional compañía que hace negocios en varios países (pág. 316)

mural/mural pintura hecha sobre una pared (pág. 189)

nationalism/nacionalismo deseo de un territorio o colonia de hacerse independiente (pág. 351)

national park/parque nacional área reservada para proteger la flora y la fauna y para la recreación (pág. 135)

nature preserve/santuario natural área protegida para las plantas y animales (págs. 378, 581)

natural resource/recurso natural producto de la Tierra que la gente usa para satisfacer sus necesidades (pág. 90)

navigable/navegable describe una masa de agua ancha y profunda suficiente para que los barcos puedan viajar por ella (págs. 126, 260, 301, 324)

neutrality/neutralidad negarse a ponerse a favor de uno de los adversarios en un desacuerdo o una guerra entre países (pág. 310)

newsprint/papel de periódico tipo de papel en que se imprimen los periódicos (pág. 153)

nomads/nómadas gente que se muda de un lugar a otro con sus manadas o rebaños de animales (págs. 377, 516, 687)

nonrenewable resource/recurso no renovable recurso natural, como metales o minerales, que no puede reemplazarse (pág. 91)

nuclear energy/energía nuclear energía producida por medio de una reacción atómica controlada (pág. 431)

oasis/oasis área verde en medio de un desierto a donde llegan aguas subterráneas (págs. 459, 493, 518)

oil shale/esquistos grasos rocas que contienen aceite (pág. 372)

orbit/órbita trayectoria que los cuerpos en el sistema solar siguen alrededor del Sol (pág. 29)

outback/tierra adentro el interior de Australia (pág. 748)

overgraze/pastar excesivamente cuando el ganado despoja los pastos hasta tal punto que las plantas no pueden crecer de nuevo (pág. 547)

ozone/ozono tipo de oxígeno que forma una capa en la atmósfera que protege a todas las cosas vivas de ciertos rayos del Sol que son peligrosos (pág. 775)

parliamentary democracy/democracia parlamentaria gobierno en que los votantes eligen a representantes a un cuerpo que hace las leyes y que selecciona a un primer ministro para que sea el jefe del gobierno (págs. 157, 210, 292)

parliamentary republic/república parlamentaria *véase* parliamentary democracy/democracia parlamentaria (pág. 327)

peat/turba suelo mojado con plantas en descomposición que se puede secar y usar para combustible (págs. 296, 372)

peninsula/península masa de tierra con agua alrededor de tres lados (págs. 40, 146, 182, 408)

permafrost/permafrost capa de suelo congelada en la tundra y las regiones subárticas; también se llama permagel (págs. 68, 410)

pesticides/pesticidas sustancias químicas poderosas que matan a los insectos que destruyen los cultivos (págs. 96, 648)

phosphate/fosfato sal mineral que se usa en los abonos (págs. 461, 555, 769)

pictograph/pictograma gráfica en que pequeños símbolos representan cantidades (pág. 15)

pidgin language/idioma rudimentario lenguaje formado al combinar elementos de varios idiomas distintos (pág. 767)

plain/llanura extensión de tierra plana u ondulante a elevaciones bajas (pág. 40)

plantain/plátano de cocinar tipo de banano (pág. 592)

plantation/plantación granja grande en que se siembra un solo cultivo para venderse (págs. 186, 207)

plateau/meseta planicie a elevaciones más altas que las llanuras (págs. 40, 324)

plate/placa plancha de roca inmensa que forma parte de la corteza de la tierra (págs. 599, 726)

plate tectonics/tectónica de placas teoría que dice que la corteza de la Tierra no es una envoltura enteriza, sino que está formada por placas, o planchas de roca inmensas, que se mueven (pág. 35)

plaza/plaza sitio donde se reúne el público (pág. 193)

poaching/caza furtiva cacería ilegal de animales protegidos (pág. 581)

polder/pólder área de tierra ganada del mar (pág. 315)

pope/papa líder de la Iglesia Católica Apostólica Romana (págs. 334, 369)

population density/densidad de población promedio de personas que viven en una milla cuadrada o kilómetro cuadrado (pág. 86)

potash/potasa tipo de sal mineral que a menudo se usa en los abonos (pág. 388)

prairie/pradera área de pastos ondulantes en el interior con suelo muy fértil (pág. 146)

precipitation/precipitación agua que regresa a la Tierra en la forma de lluvia, nieve, aguanieve o granizo (pág. 50)

prime minister/primer ministro líder del gobierno en una democracia parlamentaria (pág. 157)

privatize/privatizar transferir la propiedad de fábricas de las manos del gobierno a las de individuos (pág. 380)

projection/proyección una de las maneras de dibujar la Tierra redonda en una superficie plana para hacer un mapa (pág. 7)

province/provincia división política regional, parecida a un estado (pág. 143)

quota/cuota límite en la cantidad de un producto que se puede importar de un país en particular (pág. 93)

rain forest/bosque húmedo bosque denso que recibe grandes cantidades de lluvia todos los años (pág. 61)

rain shadow/sombra pluviométrica área seca en el lado interior de montañas costeras (pág. 59)

recycling/reciclaje usar materiales de nuevo en vez de botarlos (pág. 128)

refugee/refugiado persona que huye de un país a otro para evitar la persecución o un desastre (págs. 88, 383, 568, 595)

region/región área destacada por ciertas características (pág. 25)

relief/relieve las diferencias en altitud de una zona; lo plana o accidentada que es una superficie (pág. 12)

Renaissance/Renacimiento período de grandes logros en el arte y el estudio de la antigüedad que comenzó en Italia en los años 1300 y continuó por toda Europa (pág. 333)

renewable resource/recurso renovable recurso natural que no se puede gastar, que la naturaleza puede reemplazar o que se puede cultivar de nuevo (pág. 91)

republic/república gobierno nacional fuerte encabezado por líderes elegidos (págs. 210, 233, 258, 303, 369, 461)

reunification/reunificación juntar de nuevo las dos partes de Alemania bajo un mismo gobierno (pág. 309)

revival/renacimiento espiritual reunión religiosa (pág. TN50)

revolution/revolución una órbita completa alrededor del Sol (pág. 31)
ridge/cadena de colinas serie de lomas estrechas (pág. TN8)
rural/rural área en el campo (págs. 134, 433)

saga/saga historia larga (pág. 357)
samurai/samurai propietarios y guerreros poderosos del Japón (pág. 699)
sauna/sauna cuarto de madera calentado por agua que hierve sobre piedras calientes (pág. 351)
savanna/sabana pastos extensos en los trópicos con pocos árboles (págs. 64, 541, 563)
scale/escala relación entre las distancias en un mapa y las distancias verdaderas en la Tierra (pág. 11)
scale bar/barra de medir la escala en un mapa, línea con divisiones que muestra la escala del mapa, generalmente en millas o kilómetros (pág. 11)
secede/secesión separarse de un gobierno nacional (págs. 131, 154, TN19)
secular/secular no religioso (págs. 467, 480)
***selva*/selva** bosque húmedo tropical, como el de Brasil (pág. 228)
serf/siervo labrador que podía ser comprado y vendido con la tierra (pág. 425)
service industry/industria de servicio negocio que proporciona servicios a la gente en vez de producir productos (págs. 124, 150, TN42, 195)
shah/sha título de los reyes que gobernaban Irán (pág. 499)
shogun/shogun líder militar en Japón (pág. 699)
silt/cieno pequeñas partículas de suelo fértil (pág. 458)
sirocco/siroco vientos calurosos y secos que soplan a través de Italia desde el norte de África (pág. 331)
sisal/sisal fibra de una planta que se usa para hacer soga y cordel (pág. 588)
skerry/*skerry guard* isla rocosa (pág. 349)
slash-and-burn farming/agricultura por tala y quema método de limpiar la tierra para el cultivo en que se cortan y se queman los bosques (pág. 624)
smog/smog neblina espesa compuesta de niebla y sustancias químicas (pág. 198)
socialism/socialismo sistema económico en que muchos negocios son propiedad y están dirigidos por el gobierno (pág. 717)
solar system/sistema solar la Tierra, ocho planetas adicionales y miles de astros más pequeños que giran alrededor del Sol (pág. 29)
sodium nitrate/nitrato de sodio sustancia química usada en abonos y explosivos (pág. 269)
sorghum/sorgo cereal de tallo alto cuyas semillas sirven de alimento y del cual se hace un jarabe para endulzar (pág. 619)
spa/termas balneario con manantiales de agua mineral caliente en que la gente se baña para recobrar su salud (pág. 378)
station/estación rancho donde se crían ganado vacuno u ovejas en Australia (pág. 748)
steppe/estepa pastos parcialmente secos que a menudo se encuentran en los bordes de un desierto (págs. 69, 386, 406, 515, 570, 687)
strait/estrecho masa de agua delgada entre dos masas de tierra (págs. 42, 721)
strip mining/explotación a cielo abierto quitar las capas de tierra para sacar el carbón que está debajo (pág. TN40)
subarctic climate/clima subártico patrón del estado del tiempo con inviernos extremadamente fríos y veranos cortos y frescos (pág. 67)
subcontinent/subcontinente masa de tierra grande que forma parte de un continente pero se puede diferenciar de él (pág. 645)
subsistence farm/granja de subsistencia terreno pequeño en el cual un granjero cultiva sólo lo suficiente para alimentar a su propia familia (págs. 186, 207, 261, 542)
suburb/suburbio comunidad pequeña en los alrededores de una ciudad (págs. 134, 340, 432)
summer solstice/solsticio de verano día con más horas de sol y menos horas de oscuridad (pág. 32)

taiga/taiga bosques enormes de árboles de hoja perenne en regiones subárticas (pág. 410)
tannin/tanino sustancia usada en el procesamiento del cuero (pág. 236)
tariff/arancel impuesto sobre el valor de bienes importados (pág. 93)
terraced field/terrazas franjas, parecidas a escalones, que se cortan en la ladera de una colina para que el suelo aguante el agua y se pueda usar para la agricultura (págs. 678, 724)
timberline/límite de los árboles elevación por encima de la cual no crecen árboles en las montañas (pág. 70)
tornado/tornado tormenta en forma de un torbellino que a veces se forma durante una tormenta eléctrica fuerte (pág. 56)
townships/municipios barrios abarrotados de gente en las afueras de las ciudades de Sudáfrica donde viven la mayoría de las personas que no son blancas (pág. 611)
trench/fosa marina valle en el fondo del mar (pág. 41)
tributary/afluente río pequeño que desagua en un río más grande (págs. TN10, 653)
tropics/trópicos región entre el Trópico de Cáncer y el Trópico de Capricornio (pág. 55)
trust territory/territorio en fideicomiso área que está bajo el control temporario de otra nación (pág. 769)

tsetse fly/mosca tsetsé insecto cuya picada puede matar al ganado o a los seres humanos por medio de la enfermedad del sueño (pág. 571)
tsunami/tsunami ola inmensa causada por un terremoto en el fondo del mar (págs. 36, 695)
tundra/tundra inmensas planicies ondulantes y sin árboles en latitudes altas con climas en que sólo varias pulgadas del suelo de la superficie se deshielan (págs. 68, 146, 410)
tungsten/tungsteno metal usado en equipos eléctricos (pág. 677)
typhoon/tifón nombre para un huracán en Asia (págs. 56, 673, 769)

urban/urbano parte de una ciudad (págs. 134, 432)
urbanization/urbanización movimiento hacia las ciudades (pág. 87)

vaquero/vaquero pastor de ganado vacuno (pág. 185)
veto/vetar rechazar un proyecto de ley (pág. TN30)

wadi/uadi lecho de un río seco que llenan los aguaceros poco frecuentes (pág. 493)
water cycle/ciclo hidrológico proceso mediante el cual el agua se mueve de los océanos al aire, del aire a la tierra y de la tierra a los océanos una vez más (pág. 49)
watershed/cuenca fluvial región drenada por un río (pág. 594)
water vapor/vapor de agua agua en forma de gas (pág. 49)
weather/estado del tiempo cambios en la atmósfera que son difíciles de pronosticar y tienen lugar durante un período de tiempo corto (pág. 53)
weathering/desgaste proceso que rompe la superficie rocosa en peñas, grava, arena y suelo (pág. 37)
welfare state/estado de bienestar social estado que usa el dinero recaudado por los impuestos para mantener a personas que están enfermas, pobres, sin trabajo o retiradas (págs. 246, 349)
winter solstice/solsticio de invierno día con menos horas de sol y más horas de oscuridad (pág. 32)

yurt/*yurt* tienda de campaña grande y circular hecha de pieles de animales que se puede desmantelar y llevar de un lugar a otro (pág. 688)

INDEX

c=*chart* *m*=*map*
d=*diagram* *p*=*photo*
g=*graph* *ptg*=*painting*

INDEX

INDEX

INDEX

M

INDEX

INDEX

INDEX

INDEX

INDEX

INDEX

U

PHOTO CREDITS

Cover (tl)PhotoDisc, (tr)Carol Beckwith & Angela Fisher/Robert Estall Photo Agency, (c)PhotoDisc, (bl)PhotoDisc, (br)CORBIS; **iv–v** Ken Stimpson/Panoramic Images, Chicago, All Rights Reserved; **ix** Owen Franken/CORBIS; **vi–vii** PhotoDisc; **xvi; 1** PhotoDisc; **2** Craig Aurness/CORBIS, (bl)Todd Gipstein/CORBIS, (br)Craig Lovell/CORBIS; **3** (tr)Robert Caputo/AURORA, (bl)Peter Turnley/CORBIS, (br)Roger Ressmeyer/CORBIS; **20** (l)Robert Landau/CORBIS, (r)Arne Dedert/AFP; **20–21**Stone/S. Purdy Matthews; **22** Norman Kent/oi2.com; **23** NASA/National Geographic Image Collection; **24** (l)Richard T. Nowitz/National Geographic Image Collection, (r)Yann Arthus-Bertrand/CORBIS; **26** Galen Rowell/CORBIS; **29** Maria Stenzel/National Geographic Image Collection; **30** Timothy G. Laman/National Geographic Image Collection; **34** Natalie Fobes/National Geographic Image Collection; **37** Michael K. Nichols/National Geographic Image Collection; **39** David Doubilet/National Geographic Image Collection; **40** (l)Kenneth Garrett/National Geographic Image Collection, (t)Michael K. Nichols/National Geographic Image Collection; **46** AP/Wide World Photos; **47** Matt Meadows; **48** Annie Griffiths Belt/National Geographic Image Collection; **49** George Grall/National Geographic Image Collection; **52** Southampton Oceanography Centre; **53** J. Blair/National Geographic Image Collection; **54** Medford Taylor/National Geographic Image Collection; **60** (l)Bruce Dale/National Geographic Image Collection, (r)Jodi Cobb/National Geographic Image Collection; **63** Phil Schermeister/National Geographic Image Collection; **64** (l)Michael K. Nichols/National Geographic Image Collection, (r)Beverly Joubert/National Geographic Image Collection; **67** (t)Annie Griffiths Belt/National Geographic Image Collection, (l)James P. Blair/National Geographic Image Collection, (bc)Jodi Cobb/National Geographic Image Collection, (br)Raymond K. Gehman/National Geographic Image Collection; **68** (t)Natalie Fobes/National Geographic Image Collection, (c)George F. Mobley/National Geographic Image Collection, (l)Maria Stenzel/National Geographic Image Collection; **69** (l)James L. Stanfield/National Geographic Image Collection, (r)Phil Schemeister/National Geographic Image Collection; **70** Pat Jerrold, Papilio/CORBIS; **71** Bill Curtsinger/National Geographic Image Collection; **74** (l)Calvin Larsen/Photo Researchers, (r)Stone/Joseph Sohm; **74–75** Planet Earth Pictures/FPG International/PictureQuest; **75** (tl)Francois Gohier/Photo Researchers, (tr, b)©1995 Jan Sonnenmair/AURORA; **76** Steve McCurry/National Geographic Image Collection; **77** Kenneth Garrett/National Geographic Image Collection; **79** (l)Black Star/National Geographic Image Collection, (r)Steven L. Raymer/National Geographic Image Collection; **80** (l)Steve McCurry/National Geographic Image Collection, (r)Steve McCurry/National Geographic Image Collection; **84** Gerd Ludwig/National Geographic Image Collection; **87** AFP/CORBIS; **89** Bettmann/CORBIS; **90** Jim Sugar Photography/CORBIS; **91** (t)Ric Ergenbright/CORBIS, (b)Steve McCurry/National Geographic Image Collection; **93** (l)H.Edward Kim/National Geographic Image Collection, (r)George F. Mobley/National Geographic Image Collection; **95** Bryan & Cherry Alexander; **96** James P. Blair/National Geographic Image Collection; **97** Jodi Cobb/National Geographic Image Collection; **102** (l)Steve McCurry, (r)Michael Lewis; **102–103** David R. Stoecklein; **105** Susie Post, (l)Norbert Rosing; **106** Richard Nowitz/PhotoTake.NYC/Picture Quest; **107** Eugene Fisher & Barbara Brundege; **114** Owen Franken/CORBIS; **115** David Hiser/National Geographic Image Collection; **118** (l)Steven L. Raymer/National Geographic Image Collection, (r)Vincent Musl/National Geographic Image Collection; **121** Michael S. Yamashita/National Geographic Image Collection; **122** Chris Johns/National Geographic Image Collection; **123** Karen Kasmauski/Matrix; **125** Gregory Scott Doramus/Omnigraphix; **126** Annie Griffiths Belt/CORBIS; **127** Joel Satore/National Geographic Image Collection; **130** The Stock Market; **131** Ira Block/National Geographic Image Collection; **134** Mike Habermann, courtesy Music of the World; **136** CORBIS; **140** Ray Pfortner, Peter Arnold Inc.; **140–141** Michael Mathers, Peter Arnold Inc.; **141** (l)Stone/David Young-Wolff, (r)David Schmidt; **142** David A. Harvey/National Geographic Image Collection; **143** Raymond K. Gehman/National Geographic Image Collection; **146** Richard T. Nowitz/National Geographic Image Collection; **150** Anna Susan/National Geographic Image Collection; **153** David A. Harvey/National Geographic Image Collection; **155** Marie-Louise Brimberg/National Geographic Image Collection; **156** Michael Evan Sewell/Visual Pursuit; **157** Marie-Louise Brimberg/National Geographic Image Collection; **159** Paul A. Souders/CORBIS; **160** (l)Daniel J. Wiener/National Geographic Image Collection, (r)Bruce Dale/National Geographic Image Collection; **164** Giraudon/Art Resource, New York; **165** Michael S. Yamashita; **166** (l)Stone/David Levy, (r)Stone/Oliver Benn; **166–167** Kenneth Garrett/NGS; **169** Stone/Norbert Wu, Stone/William J. Hebert; **170** Sisse Brimberg; **171** Stone/Chad Ehlers; **180** Randy Faris/CORBIS; **181** Bettmann/CORBIS; **188** Tomasz Tomaszewski/National Geographic Image Collection; **190** Cotton Coulson/National Geographic Image Collection; **192** James L. Amos/National Geographic Image Collection; **193** David A. Harvey/National Geographic Image Collection; **194** Nik Wheeler/CORBIS; **195** (l)Joel Satore/National Geographic Image Collection, (r)Tomas Tomaszewski/National Geographic Image Collection; **198** Albert Moldvay/National Geographic Image Collection; **202** Nik Wheeler/CORBIS; **203** Matt Meadows; **204** SuperStock; **205** Art Wolfe; **208** (t)Jan Butchofsky-Houser/CORBIS, (b)Vincent Musl/National Geographic Image Collection; **210** Michael S. Yamashita/CORBIS; **213** Jonathan Blair/National Geographic Image Collection; **215** ©Robert A. Tyrrell; **217** (l)Tony Arruza/CORBIS, (r)Michael K. Nichols/National Geographic Image Collection; **221** George Mobley/National Geographic Image Collection; **224** (l)Artville, (r)Giraudon/Art Resource, New York; **225** Loren McIntyre; **226** PhotoDisc; **227** Alex Webb/Magnum; **232** (l)Jim Zuckerman/CORBIS, (r)Yann Arthus-Bertrand/CORBIS; **234** Jeremy Horner/CORBIS; **235** Robert van der Hilst/CORBIS; **237** Winfield I. Parks, Jr./National Geographic Image Collection; **239** Pablo Corral V/CORBIS; **240** Kit Houghton Photography/CORBIS; **241** Michael K. Nichols/National Geographic Image Collection; **242** Pablo Corral V/CORBIS; **243** Robert Caputo/Aurora & Quanta Productions; **245** Louis O. Mazzatenta/National Geographic Image Collection; **247** (l)Jack Fields/CORBIS, (r)Louis O. Mazzatenta/National Geographic Image Collection; **252** (t)Michael & Patricia Fogden, (b)William Albert Allard; **252–253** Stuart Franklin; **253** (l)Michael Doolittle, (r)Marc Van Roosmalen Bat Conservation International; **254** Owen Franken/CORBIS; **258** Richard S. Durrance/National Geographic Image Collection; **260** Frank & Helen Schreider/National Geographic Image Collection; **263** Tiziana and Gianni Baldizzone/CORBIS; **264** Johan Reinhard/National Geographic Image Collection; **265** Art Wolfe; **266** Maria Stenzel/National Geographic Image Collection; **268** (l)Richard T. Nowitz/National Geographic Image Collection, (r)James L. Stanfield/National Geographic Image Collection; **271** William A. Allard/National Geographic Image Collection; **274** (l)IFA-Bilderteam-Travel/Bruce Coleman Inc., (r)Stone/Robert Everts; **274–275** SuperStock; **277** Stone/D.C. Lowe, (l)Stone/Chris Haigh; **278** Stone/Bert Blokhuis; **279** Stone/Ron Sanford; **288** James L. Stanfield/National Geographic Image Collection; **289** London Aerial Photo Library/CORBIS; **293** Emory Kristof/National Geographic Image Collection; **295** Adam Woolfitt/CORBIS; **296** Thad Samuels Abell II/National Geographic Image Collection; **298** (l)Thad Samuels Abell II/National Geographic Image Collection, (r)Tim Thompson/CORBIS; **299** Michael St. Maur Sheil/CORBIS; **300** James L. Stanfield/National Geographic Image Collection; **301** (l)James P. Blair/National Geographic Image Collection, (r)Felix Zaska/CORBIS; **303** Ric Ergenbright/CORBIS; **306** Owen Franken/CORBIS; **308** Ric Ergenbright/CORBIS; **310** Sisse Brimberg/National Geographic Image Collection; **311** Bob Krist/CORBIS; **313** Michael John Kielty/CORBIS; **315** SuperStock; **320** AP/Wide World Photos; **321** Reuters/CORBIS; **322** Mark L. Stephenson/CORBIS; **323** ©David Cumming, Eye Ubiquitous/CORBIS; **326** (l)Medford Taylor/National Geographic Image Collection, (r)Charles O'Rear/CORBIS; **327** Adam Woolfitt/CORBIS; **330** National Geographic Image Collection; **332** (t)Richard T. Nowitz/National Geographic Image Collection, (b)Vittoriano Rastelli/CORBIS; **333** Louis O. Mazzatenta/National Geographic Image Collection; **334** Thad Samuels Abell II/National Geographic Image Collection; **335** (l)Bettmann/CORBIS, (r)Gianni Dagli Orti/CORBIS; **336** Ira Block/National Geographic Image Collection; **339** Panoramic Images; **341** James L. Stanfield/National Geographic Image Collection; **344 345** Tomasz Tomaszewski/National Geographic Image Collection; **348** (l)©Buddy May/CORBIS, (r)Richard S. Durrance/National Geographic Image Collection; **349** Bryan & Cherry Alexander; **352** Jonathan Blair/CORBIS; **353** ©Ian Yates; Eye Ubiquitous/CORBIS; **355** SuperStock; **357** Sisse Brimberg/National Geographic Image Collection; **358** SuperStock; **359** Richard T. Nowitz/CORBIS; **362** (l)Robert Winslow, (r)Stone/Johan Elzenga; **362–363** Stone/Oliver Strewe; **363** (l)Martin Bond/Science Photo Library/Photo Researchers, (r)Mike Lewis, Northamptonshire Grammar School, United Kingdom; **364** Bob Krist/CORBIS; **365** Tomasz Tomaszewski/National Geographic Image Collection; **368 369 370** James L. Stanfield/National Geographic Image Collection; **371** Priit J. Vesilind/National Geographic Image Collection; **373** Steven L. Raymer/National Geographic Image Collection; **375** James Stanfield/National Geographic Image Collection;

377 Dean Conger/CORBIS; **379** Owen Franken/CORBIS; **381** Steve Raymer/CORBIS; **382** Peter Wilson/CORBIS; **384** Catherine Karnow/CORBIS; **386** Gerd Ludwig/National Geographic Image Collection; **390** (l)Kelly-Mooney Photography/CORBIS, (r)Craig Aurness/CORBIS; **394** (l)Bruce Dale, (r)Stone/Alain Le Garsmeur; **394–395** Marc Moritsch/National Geographic Image Collection; **397** Stone/Simeone Huber, (bl)Stone/Paul Harris; **398** B. Klipinitsen, M. Moshkov, Sovfoto/Eastfoto/PictureQuest; **399** Jay Dickman; **404** Gerd Ludwig/National Geographic Image Collection; **405** Tom Brakefield/CORBIS; **408** Gerd Ludwig/National Geographic Image Collection; **410** Dmitry Shparo/National Geographic Image Collection; **411** Michael Boys/CORBIS; **412** Gerd Ludwig/National Geographic Image Collection; **414** Dennis Chamberlin/National Geographic Image Collection; **417** Wolfgang Kaehler/CORBIS; **420** (l)Bios/M. Gunther/Peter Arnold Inc., (r)Gerd Ludwig; **420–421** Peter Turnley/CORBIS; **421** Stiftung Jugend forscht e.V./Deutsche Bank AG; **422** Michael Nichols/National Geographic Image Collection; **423** Sisse Brimberg/National Geographic Image Collection; **425** Roger Tidman/CORBIS; **426** Kremlin Museums, Moscow, Russia/The Bridgeman Art Library; **427** Marc Garanger/CORBIS; **430** Dean Conger/CORBIS; **431 432** Peter Turnley/CORBIS; **434** (l)Marc Garanger/CORBIS, (r)David Turnley/CORBIS; **436** Farrell Grehan/CORBIS; **437** Steve Raymer/CORBIS; **440** Giraudon/Art Resource, New York; **441** Sovfoto/Eastfoto/PictureQuest; **442** (l)Stone/Hugh Sitton, (r)Zefa/The Stock Market; **442 443** X. Richer/Hoaqui, Photo Researchers; **445** Stone/James Strachan, (bl)David Coulson; **446** Stone; **447** Stone/Wayne Eastep; **455** Stone/Jeff Rotman; **456** Reza/National Geographic Image Collection; **457** Kenneth Garrett/National Geographic Image Collection; **461** Otto Lang/CORBIS; **463** SuperStock; **464** George Steinmetz/National Geographic Image Collection; **466 468** K.M. Westermann/CORBIS; **471** Kenneth Garrett/National Geographic Image Collection; **474** P. Boulat/Cosmos/Woodfin Camp and Associates; **475** (l)Matt Meadows, (r)Science Pictures Limited/CORBIS; **476** James L. Stanfield/National Geographic Image Collection; **477** Patrick Ward/CORBIS; **480** James L. Stanfield/National Geographic Image Collection; **481** Dean Conger/CORBIS; **482** I. Talby/Index Stock; **484** (l)Steve Kaufman/CORBIS, (r)Duby Tal/Albatross/Index Stock; **488** Dean Conger/National Geographic Image Collection; **489** Dave Bartruff/CORBIS; **490** Annie Griffiths Belt/National Geographic Image Collection; **492** James L. Stanfield/National Geographic Image Collection; **495** AP/Wide World Photos; **497** Charles & Josette Lenars/CORBIS; **499** (l)Alexandra Avakian/National Geographic Image Collection, (r)Jon Spaull/CORBIS; **504** Art & Immagini srl/CORBIS; **505** Stone/Sylvain Grandadam; **506–507** James L. Stanfield, (br)©1993 Ed Kashi; **507** (l)©1993 Ed Kashi, (r)courtesy Sandra Postel; **508** Dugald Bremner/National Geographic Image Collection; **509** Reza/National Geographic Image Collection; **514** James L. Stanfield/National Geographic Image Collection; **515** Wolfgang Kaehler; **517 519 520** Gerd Ludwig/National Geographic Image Collection; **521** Michael S. Yamashita/CORBIS; **524** (l)Stone/Hugh Sitton, (r)Stone/Jacques Jangoux; **524–525** Stone/Manoj Shah; **527** Stone/Ian Murphy, (bl)Stone/Renee Lynn; **528** Stone/Ian Murphy; **529** Stone/Will Curtis; **539** Stone/Nicholas Parfitt; **540** Wolfgang Kaehler; **541** AP/Wide World Photos; **544** (l)Robert W. Moore/National Geographic Image Collection, (r)AP/Wide World Photos; **545** ©1993 Greenpeace/Lambon; **546** (l)Davis Factor/CORBIS, (r)Bowers Museum of Cultural Art/CORBIS; **547** Steve McCurry/Magnum Photos, Inc.; **549** Carol Beckwith & Angela Fisher/Robert Estall Photo Agency; **551** Nik Wheeler/CORBIS; **552** Carol Beckwith & Angela Fisher/Robert Estall Photo Agency; **555** Robert W. Moore/National Geographic Image Collection; **557** AP/Wide World Photos; **560** Michael A. Hampshire; **561** James L. Stanfield; **562** SuperStock; **563** Robert Caputo/Aurora & Quanta Productions; **568** Michael K. Nichols/National Geographic Image Collection; **570** AP/Wide World Photos; **574** David Turnley/CORBIS; **575** AP/Wide World Photos; **578** Robert Caputo/Stock Boston; **579** Matt Meadows; **580** Sharna Balfour, Gallo Images/CORBIS; **581** Carol Beckwith & Angela Fisher/Robert Estall Photo Agency; **584** The Purcell Team/CORBIS; **585** Frank Lane Picture Agency/CORBIS; **586** Darrell Gulin/CORBIS; **587** J. Jafferji/OSF/Animals Animals; **589** Wolfgang Kaehler; **591** Robert Caputo/Aurora & Quanta Productions; **592** Art Wolfe; **594** Chinch Gryniewicz, Ecoscene/CORBIS; **596** Dave Bartruff/CORBIS; **598** AP/Wide World Photos; **604** (l)Gerry Ellis/ENP Images, (r)Jose Azel/Aurora/PictureQuest; **604–605** Michael Nichols/NGS; **605** (tl)Lisa Hoffner/Wildeye Photography, (tr)Lisa Hoffner/WildEye Photography, (b)Stone/Art Wolfe; **606–607** Wolfgang Kaehler; **610** Jack Vartoogian; **611** Nik Wheeler/CORBIS; **612** Turnley Collection/CORBIS; **614** Des & Jen Bartlett/National Geographic Image Collection; **618** Walter Edwards/National Geographic Image Collection; **619** Chris Johns/National Geographic Image Collection; **622** Chris Johns/National Geographic Image Collection; **623** Michael K. Nichols/National Geographic Image Collection; **624** AP/Wide World Photos; **630** (l)Stone/Tim Davis, (r)Stone/David Sutherland; **630–631** Waranun Chutchawan-Tipakorn; **633** Stone/Hilarie Kavanagh, (bl)Stone/Martin Puddy; **634** Stone/Paul Chesley; **635** Stone/Keren Su; **643** Stone/John Lamb; **644** Steve McCurry/National Geographic Image Collection; **645** George F. Mobley/National Geographic Image Collection; **648** Steve McCurry/National Geographic Image Collection; **649** Rudi Von Briel/PhotoEdit; **651** Brian Vikander/CORBIS; **652** Jonathan Blair/National Geographic Image Collection; **654** Brian Vikander/CORBIS; **655** Ed Kashi/National Geographic Image Collection; **657** Steve McCurry/National Geographic Image Collection; **658** Robert Caputo/National Geographic Image Collection; **663** Robert Holmes/CORBIS; **666** (l)Stone/Chris Noble, (r)Robert Weight, Ecoscene/CORBIS; **666–667** Takehide Kazami, Peter Arnold Inc.; **667** (l)Future Generations, (r)Galen Rowell/Mountain Light; **668** Stone; **669** Keren Su/CORBIS; **674–680** AFP/CORBIS; **681** The Telegraph Colour Library/FPG; **683** (t)Owen Franken/CORBIS, (b)Joseph Sohm, ChromoSohm Inc./CORBIS; **685** How-Man Wong/CORBIS; **686** Marc Garanger/CORBIS; **687** Nik Wheeler/CORBIS; **688** James L. Stanfield/National Geographic Image Collection; **692** Cary Wolinsky/Stock Boston; **693** Keren Su/CORBIS; **694** Dallas & John Heaton/CORBIS; **695** Reuters NewMedia Inc./CORBIS; **698** Karen Kasmauski/Matrix; **700** Roger Ressmeyer/CORBIS; **701** Michael S. Yamashita/CORBIS; **702** Asian Art & Archaeology, Inc./CORBIS; **703** Carmen Redondo/CORBIS; **704** (l)Nathan Benn/CORBIS, (r)Wolfgang Kaehler/CORBIS; **707** Catherine Karnow/CORBIS; **709** Neil Beer/CORBIS; **712** Yann Layma/Stone; **713** Matt Meadows; **714** AFP/CORBIS; **715 718** Paul Chesley/National Geographic Image Collection; **719** Kevin R. Morris/CORBIS; **721** AFP/CORBIS; **723** Earl & Nazima Kowall/CORBIS; **726** Roger Ressmeyer/CORBIS; **729** Wolfgang Kaehler/CORBIS; **730** David Hanson/Stone; **731** AP/Wide World Photos; **734** (l)Stone/David Madison, (r)Stone/David Hiser; **734–735** Stone/Oliver Strewe; **737** Stone/Oliver Strewe, (bl)Stone/Johnny Johnson; **738** Stone/Nicholas DeVore; **739** Stone/Glen Allison; **746** Charles & Josette Lenars/CORBIS; **747** R. Ian Productions P Lloyd/National Geographic Image Collection; **751** Penny Tweedie/CORBIS; **752** Paul A. Souders/CORBIS; **753** (tr)Australian Picture Library/CORBIS, (br)Earl & Nazima Kowall/CORBIS, (l)Charles Philip Cangialosi/CORBIS; **754 758** Kevin Fleming/CORBIS; **759** Australian Picture Library/CORBIS; **762** (r)Christine Osborne/CORBIS; **762–763** Penny Tweedie/CORBIS; **763** (tl)PhotoDisc, (tr)Bettmann/CORBIS, (b)George F. Mobley; **764** Douglas Peebles/CORBIS; **765** Hal Beral/CORBIS; **769 771** David Doublet/National Geographic Image Collection; **772** Wolfgang Kaehler/CORBIS; **775** Underwood & Underwood/CORBIS; **776** Galen Rowell/CORBIS; **777** AP/Wide World Photos; **780** Byrd Antarctic Expedition; **781** Andrew H. Brown; **782** PhotoDisc.

Focus on Tennessee

xv Doug Barnette Photography, Chattanooga,TN; **TN1** CORBIS, (l)Chase Swift/CORBIS, (r)Raymond Gehman/CORBIS; **TN2** Pat O'Hara/CORBIS; **TN3** SuperStock; **TN7** Doug Barnette Photography, Chattanooga,TN; **TN8** Donna Jett; **TN9** Richard Hamilton Smith/CORBIS; **TN10 TN12** Doug Barnette Photography, Chattanooga,TN; **TN13** AP/Wide World Photos; **TN14** Raymond Gehman/CORBIS; **TN16** Burstein Collection/CORBIS; **TN18** (t)FPG, (b)White House Historical Association; **TN19** Stock Montage/SuperStock; **TN20 TN21 TN22** Bettmann/CORBIS; **TN24** Buddy Mays/CORBIS; **TN26** Library of Congress; **TN27** Minnesota Historical Society/CORBIS; **TN28** State of Tennessee Dept of General Services; **TN29** William J. Weber; **TN31** AP/Wide World Photos; **TN36** Lawrence Migdale/Photo Researchers; **TN38** Dave G. Houser; **TN41** (l)State of Tennessee Photographic Services, (r)Raymond Gehman/CORBIS; **TN42** (l)Dave G. Houser, (r)Andre Jenny/Focus Group/PictureQuest; **TN44** Reuters NewMedia Inc./CORBIS; **TN46** Mark C. Burnett; **TN46–47** Doug Barnette Photography, Chattanooga,TN; **TN47 TN48** AP/Wide World Photos; **TN52** AFP/CORBIS; **TN53** (l)Kevin Fleming/CORBIS, (r)CORBIS; **TN54** AP/Wide World Photos.